CONTEMPORARY ISSUES IN DEVELOPMENTAL PSYCHOLOGY

CONTEMPORARY ISSUES IN DEVELOPMENTAL PSYCHOLOGY

Second Edition

Edited and with commentary by

Norman S. Endler, *York University*

Lawrence R. Boulter, *York University*

Harry Osser, *Queen's University*

Foreword by
J. McV. Hunt, *University of Illinois*

Holt, Rinehart and Winston
New York   Chicago   San Francisco   Atlanta
Dallas   Montreal   Toronto   London   Sydney

to our wives, Beatty, Lou, and Odette,
for their unfailing . . .

Library of Congress Cataloging in Publication Data

Endler, Norman Solomon, 1931–   comp.
    Contemporary issues in developmental psychology.

Bibliographies.
Includes index.
    1. Developmental psychology—Addresses, essays,
lectures.   I. Boulter, Lawrence R.   II. Osser,
Harry.   III. Title   [DNLM: 1. Psychology.   BF713
C761]
BF713.5.E5   1976   155   75–41414
ISBN 0–03–008421–0

FOREWORD

My foreword to the first edition of *Contemporary Issues in Developmental Psychology* noted that the importance of books of readings in colleges increased markedly when the GI's returned to the campuses from World War II. It was then that the reserve desks of most college libraries became frustrating bottlenecks for students seeking the classical writings in the humanities or papers in the original investigative literature of the sciences. Thereafter, because of the high birthrate and the insatiable demand of our technological culture for educated people, the numbers of students increased more rapidly than reserve-desk facilities for access to the burgeoning literature of the sciences. Consequently, the bottlenecks at these desks became even more tightly jammed. Despite the facts that the birthrate has slacked off and certain of the reasons for seeking an education have diminished since the first edition of this book of readings was published in 1968, the reserve desks of college libraries have not yet caught up. If college students are to read basic sources, therefore, they must continue to have some mode of access other than lists of readings journals on library reserve. What is still called for is a radical innovation that will provide students with just such an opportunity. Although books of readings are hardly the ultimate, radical solution to this problem of access, they constitute an exceedingly important intermediate remedy.

Important remedy that they are, books of readings have an inevitable and fundamental defect. The selection of readings is always that of the editor or editors. It is all too seldom that an editor's selection matches the wishes of the instructor of a course. The success and usefulness of a book of readings is in large part, therefore, a function of the degree to which the predilections of the editor match those of instructors in the topical domain for which the book was planned. The editors of *Contemporary Issues in Developmental Psychology* have attempted to remedy this defect by basing their choice of readings on the issues that they consider dominant at their time of choice. Insofar as their judgment of the dominance of issues reflects the actual state of affairs, their selection has an objective basis.

In their first edition, the editors of *Contemporary Issues* utilized their sense of the history of developmental psychology as a basis for choosing contributions reflecting the basic changes following World War II, both in methods of investigation and in theoretical beliefs. They achieved the "new look," as indicated by the word *contemporary* in the title, by including no articles published before 1955. It is now eight years since the choices for that first edition were made. During this near-decade, information from an unprecedented volume of research has been accumulating. Serving to modify both investigative strategy and theoretical beliefs by forcing new distinctions, these new findings have also decreased or increased the significance of certain issues, and changed the nature of others. Thus, maintaining an emphasis upon *contemporary* issues has called for a new edition. The editors have attempted to pursue this aim by again utilizing their sense of the history of the field as a basis for choosing contributions that reflect the more recent changes in methods of investigation and theoretical beliefs since the first edition was published. This continues, in my judgment, to be the first merit of their approach.

A second merit of the editors' method of reducing this mismatch of editor and instructor selection derives from their focus on the topical domains where the main investigative action is now taking place. Again, in the second edition, they have gone beyond this derivative merit by candidly and informatively pointing out in their commentaries and introductions the new developments that are not fully represented in their selections for each topic. These discussions with their bibliographies provide a framework and jumping-off place for literature other than that selected on the various chapter topics. In doing this, the editors have again produced a book whose value goes beyond that of the traditional books of readings.

A third merit of their selection consists in the fact that papers have been chosen to reflect both sides of many of the issues. Moreover, in the first of two introductory chapters of this second edition, the editors have synopsized and analyzed three theoretical positions in developmental psychology. They have described what they see as the recent changes in the emphasis within each of these three main theoretical positions. In the second chapter (of this second edition) they have again delineated the general issues of investigative strategy and theoretical emphasis, and have attempted to show how these have been modified during the past decade. In their introductions and commentaries for each subsequent chapter, they have not only made a valiant and valuable attempt to bring into focus the issues, but they have pointed out how various selections are designed to contribute toward either clarification or resolution of these issues.

Some degree of mismatch between the predilections of editors and instructors must inevitably remain despite the efforts of the editors to reduce it. On the other hand, the merits of their selection strategy continue to exist for this second edition. If their first edition was successful and if their scholarship was helpful to both instructors and to students who used the book, their continued emphasis on what is ''contemporary'' should make this second edition equally successful. It too does a highly creditable job of reflecting the present status of developmental psychology.

I can repeat for this second edition that ''students who master its selection of original papers and its editors' contributions will have gone a long way toward a mastery of contemporary developmental psychology.''

J. McVicker Hunt

Department of Psychology
University of Illinois
Champaign, Illinois
December 1975

PREFACE

A primary reason for the second edition of a book of readings entitled *Contemporary Issues in Developmental Psychology* is easy to give. While time alone does not solve or dissolve issues, progress or changes in points of view and information can. Change has been shown either by some issues becoming more differentiated (e.g., remembering being more explicitly distinguished from learning as a separate area of developmental research); by becoming less dominant (e.g., the stability of IQ); by becoming more dominant (e.g., sex differences); or by issues becoming altered in significance as a consequence of other changes (e.g., the changing status of motivation concepts, as cognitive factors receive increasing attention). Thus, an attempt must be made to justify the term "contemporary." This we have endeavored to do. At the same time we have sought to find the most recently reported research and thought relevant to contemporary issues both because it reflects current research techniques (though not necessarily better techniques) and, more importantly, because these articles best convey the current context of theories and issues that we have sought to characterize in Chapters 1 and 2, and in the introduction to Chapter 3 through 13.

As a consequence, 37 (almost 85 percent) of the 44 articles reprinted in this second edition were not in the first; of those 37, 33 (70 percent) were published since the first edition (1968), and 24 of these 33 were first published in 1970 or later. That is, 75 percent of all the present articles were published after the first edition. At the same time as this substantial change, there has been little change in our aims and our biases, which, as stated in the preface to the first edition, are:

1. To focus on the essential issues in developmental psychology;
2. To indicate the research methodology, variables, and findings, via selected examples from the developmental research literature;
3. To discuss theory relevant to developmental processes;
4. To indicate the implications and applications of theory and empirical findings in developmental psychology.

We have focused on issues, largely as a didactic device, in an effort to press the student to think about and integrate his knowledge. Results and methodology from numerous studies lose their value unless one can either integrate them into a conceptual scheme, or discover in the attempt that the scheme has flaws.

There have, of course, been some changes in the field, and they are reflected in our emphases. Chapter 1, a new chapter, provides a framework of three theoretical viewpoints having both historical and contemporary importance: environmentalist theory, cognitive theory,[1] and psychoanalytic theory. Chapter 2 (like Chapter 1 in the first edition) focuses on contemporary issues. Since the original edition, there has been greater emphasis on research and theorizing in the areas of infancy and cognition. Another change is our increased concern with person-by-situation interactions, discussed both in Chapters 2 and 12. As well, greater emphasis on development as a "life-span" process is reflected in Chapter 2 and the introduction to Chapter 3; greater concern with the biology and psychology of sex differences is reflected in the introductions to Chapters 4 and 12; and continued delineation of the importance of the phylogenetic context is provided in Chapter 2 and in the introductions to Chapters 3 through 9 and 12. These and other changes have necessitated the new Chapter 1 (Theories of Development), complete revision of the chapter on Contemporary Issues (Chapter 2), as well as new introductions and commentaries for Chapters 3 through 13. Table 1, at the end of this preface and of Chapter 2, serves the same didactic purpose that it did in the first edition—to assist the student in relating specific articles to particular issues.

We wish to thank the authors of the articles included here and the publishers for permitting us to reproduce their papers. As before, they make this book possible. Once again, J. McV. Hunt has

---

[1]In a recent personal communication J. McV. Hunt (October 29, 1975) expressed the opinion that instead of cognitive, "interactionism is a term better calculated to catch the dynamic essence of this kind of theory. The approach emphasizes a process in which past achievements of all kinds (anatomic, cognitive, epistemic, and motivational) are involved in coping with the environmental situations encountered."

agreed to write a foreword and we wish to express our thanks. Becky White Loewy and George F. Mischel read and commented on portions of the book at the request of the publishers. We are grateful for their thoughtful criticisms.

We wish to thank Beverly Brady, Ann-Sofi Hedell, and Ursula Wiggins for their excellent secretarial assistance, Louise Turnpenny for defusing a few emergencies, and especially Eva Hamilton for the splendid job she did in relieving us of a multitude of administrative responsibilities.

Toronto, Ontario   *Norman S. Endler*
Toronto, Ontario   *Lawrence R. Boulter*
Kingston, Ontario   *Harry Osser*
December 1975

Summary Table of Issues and Articles

TABLE 1
Summary Table Relating Specific Articles to Issue Areas*

CHAPTER

ISSUE AREAS	Three	Four	Five	Six	Seven	Eight	Nine	Ten	Eleven	Twelve	Thirteen
Research Strategy	1–4	5, 7	10	16	18	24				37, 39	41, 42, 44
Nature-Nurture		5–7	10			22	26	30, 33	34	37	
Phylogeny, Ontogeny, and Culture		5	11, 12	13, 16	18	23, 24	27, 28		36	38, 39	43, 44
Early Experience and Learning	1	6	8–12	13–17	18–21	22, 23	28	30, 33	34	37, 39	42
Motivation and Reinforcement			8		18–21	22			34		41, 42
Perception	3		10	15	18, 19	22–25					
Intelligence, Concept Development, and Language	4			13, 16 17			26–29	30–33	34–36		
Personality		6	8, 9, 12						34	37–40	41–44
Stability	1, 4		8					30	34	37, 38	43, 44
Person-by-Situation Interactions	4							30, 33	34–36	37	41, 42
Socialization	1	6	8, 9, 12		19	24, 25			34–36	37–39	41–44

Numbers in each cell refer to article numbers.

CONTENTS

CONTRIBUTORS

Mary Jean Bach
Nancy Bayley
Richard Q. Bell
J. W. Berry
Sidney W. Bijou
Herbert G. Birch
Roger Brown
Jerome S. Bruner
Byron A. Campbell
Stella Chess
Michael Cole
Victor H. Denenberg
David Elkind

Hans G. Furth
Robert M. Gagné
Eleanor H. Gibson
John P. Gluck
Ruth K. Goldman
Harry F. Harlow
Margaret K. Harlow
Alan Hein
Richard Held
Wayne H. Holtzman
J. McV. Hunt
Julian Jaynes
Jerome Kagan

Howard H. Kendler
Lawrence Kohlberg
R. Kramer
Eric H. Lenneberg
Michael Lewis
William T. McKinney, Jr.
N. H. Mackworth
Bruce Masterton
Edith D. Neimark
Katherine Nelson
Donald R. Peterson
Jean Piaget
David Premack

Harriet L. Rheingold
Arnold J. Sameroff
L. C. Skeen
Norman E. Spear
Stephen J. Suomi
Alexander Thomas
Benton J. Underwood
Jane van Lawick-Goodall
Joachim F. Wohlwill
E. P. Willems
Laurens D. Young
James Youniss

Chapter 1

THEORIES
OF
DEVELOPMENT

WHAT IS DEVELOPMENTAL PSYCHOLOGY?

One continuous, if somewhat subdued, debate in contemporary psychology concerns the question of whether developmental psychology exists as a distinct area of study within the main body of psychological research (Baer & Wright, 1975). One viewpoint is that psychologists representing broad interest areas (e.g., social psychology, experimental psychology, and developmental psychology) differ from each other by offering slightly varying approaches to, and perhaps different emphases on, the basic problems of general psychology. The implication is that developmental psychologists differ from others merely in their choice of subjects, electing to study immature organisms rather than mature ones. A second view, the one taken in this book, is that whereas developmental psychology does indeed focus upon the basic problems of general psychology, it offers a unique perspective on them.

The Defining Attributes

Wohlwill (1973) in commenting on the nature of developmental psychology argues that "In a very real sense it represents the whole field of psychology in microcosm, which is to be expected of a field defined not in terms of subject matter but in terms of a focus on the child and his development, encompassing every facet of behavior" (p. 13). Zigler (1963, p. 344) offers a succinct account of the core interests, problems, and tasks of developmental psychology in stating that the developmentalist directs her or his attention to the phenomenon of growth and change, and to the orderly, sequential, and lawful nature of the transformations that occur from conception to maturity. Zigler envisages the central theoretical task of developmental psychology to be the generation of principles and constructs to account for the phenomenon of change not simply as a function of time, but rather as related to the processes underlying behavioral changes. Anderson (1957, p. 32) supplies a description of some of the critical features of change. He comments that the mature organism, compared to the immature one, is able to respond to both a greater variety and a larger number of stimuli at one time. Further, the mature organism has an increased repertoire of skills, more complex response modes, and the ability to deal with features of the environment that had previously been too remote in time and space. Thus he is more capable of solving complex problems than is the immature organism. There is a consensus among developmental psychologists that their central problem is to both describe and explain changes in behavior over the course of development.

Agreement also exists regarding two other attributes of developmental psychology; these attributes have broad implications but, perhaps, rather low profile in developmental psychology textbooks.

1

1. A comprehensive psychology of development will pertain to and will be constructed in terms of all animal species. (See, e.g., Aronson, Tobach, Lehrman, & Rosenblatt, 1970; Barnett, 1973; Moltz, 1971; Schneirla, 1966.) This is not simply to say that the understanding of the development of one species will contribute to an understanding of another, and so forth seriatim through the animal kingdom. Rather, it is to say that part of one's understanding of the development of any particular species (including *homo sapiens*) will come from knowledge of how its development is *similar to*, and how it *differs from*, that of other species.

2. A full-blown psychology of development will eventually encompass the complete lifespan of species instead of merely early life or childhood. Development does not stop with the departure of parents, the onset of puberty, the production of offspring, the right to vote, or any other event short of death. The values and implications of this view are part of the salutary consequences of a series of conferences recently held at West Virginia University (see Baltes & Schaie, 1973; Goulet & Baltes, 1970; and Nesselroade & Reese, 1973).

Age and the Nature of Change

The principal problem must be to create a general theory of growth and change. The deep interest of developmental psychologists in the nature of change shows up in their attention to the age variable and to the associated processes that occur in time. Kessen (1960) has suggested that if a behavior is "related to age in an orderly and lawful way, then it can be characterized as being a developmental phenomenon. The corollary is that behavioral change is development when it follows an invariant sequence over age" (p. 36). Wohlwill (1973, p. 22) observes that in one way or another all psychologists are interested in the nature of psychological change. There are, however, differences in approach to questions of the nature of change. For example, one approach involves observing changes in specific responses in an experimentally defined set of conditions. Another approach, which Wohlwill proposes is the typical developmental one, incorporates the goal of studying many responses changing under ill-defined and probably undefinable conditions. In fact, both approaches are followed by developmentalists, and the difference in methodologies relates to differences in basic theoretical positions. Common goals among developmental psychologists do, however, exist, one being their concern to isolate the mechanisms of change and the details of their operations, so that it will eventually be possible to comprehend the structural dynamics of developmental processes.

The Utility of Developmental Studies

Baldwin (1960, p. 21), in discussing the specific role that developmental psychology can play in illuminating broad psychological problems, draws our attention to the value that may be obtained by examining differences—be they differences among species, age group within a species, or even in members of a particular age-group (i.e., individual differences). The fact that these differences are so large and obvious should add significantly to our understanding of the sources of behavior.

It is certainly the case that for a theory to provide comprehensive coverage of behavior, it must incorporate evidence, for example, on the differences between the behavior of immature and mature organisms, especially where it is clear that the mechanisms and processes that underlie such behavior are not identical. In general, explanations of the *origins* of behavior are almost certain to be quite different from explanations of the *persistence* of such behaviors. For example, Rosenblatt (1970) reviews evidence showing that while hormonal changes appear to be the major determinants of the initiation of maternal behavior in rats, continued hormonal activity is not necessary for its postparturition maintenance. Stimulation from the rat pups themselves is important in sustaining maternal care, as well, apparently, as in guiding adaptation of the maternal behavior to the rapidly changing capacities of the rat pups. It is worth noting also that learning theorists have long been cognizant of the distinction between the origin or initiation of behavior and the persistence or maintenance of behavior. Theories of learning have tended largely to be theories of behavior maintenance (Hilgard & Bower, 1975).

In addition to these and other implications for psychological theory, there is a practical source of usefulness in developmental studies. One illustration of this is that the more exact our knowledge of the growth of children becomes, the more likely will we be able to design valid means of environmental intervention; such intervention might involve suggestions for improvements in child care or, among other possibilities, restructuring of educational programs.

THEORETICAL APPROACHES TO DEVELOPMENTAL PSYCHOLOGY

There are presently no theories of development that attempt to cover all details of developmental progressions; however, there are three theoretical positions that are structured around different sets of hypotheses (Langer, 1969). Brief characterizations of each theory will be given, to be followed by a more complete account of the assumptions, goals, and research methodology that distinguish the three approaches.

Environmentalist Theory

The environmentalist position views the organism as essentially *reactive,* being inherently at rest, and becoming active only as a result of the influences of *external* stimulation. The analogical base for this model is the machine. Complex behavioral phenomena such as thinking are interpreted as being ultimately reducible to simpler phenomena (e.g., stimulus-response associations) that accumulate to define the organism's development. This represents the learning theory or behavioristic account of development.

Cognitive Theory

Cognitive theory posits an inherently *active* organism, which acts on its environment and does not simply react to it. The result is that the organism is intimately involved in the *construction* and definition of its environment. The analogy here is to a living organism composed of a number of interrelated systems of action, that is, the individual is interpreted in organic rather than mechanical terms. From this theoretical viewpoint development is seen as the outcome of a series of qualitative changes in behavior, which are discussed in terms of the acquisition of different mental operations, rather than stimulus–response bondings.

Psychoanalytic Theory

Psychoanalytic theory views the organism as *reacting* to both internal instinctual urges and external environmental forces (physical and social stimuli). This theory focuses upon description and explanations of instinctual and pathological phenomena, particularly with respect to the role of certain forms of early experience in the shaping of psychopathology in later life. Discussions of normal development are concentrated upon the analysis of the means by which arational instincts are transformed into rational processes in the course of the individual's progress through several stages of psychosexual functioning. In the more recent form of psychoanalytic theory, the role of rational processes in the individual's development is stressed, and more attention is being paid to psychosocial development than was previously the case (Erikson, 1963).

Analysis of the Environmentalist Position

White (1970) lists the assumptions of the environmentalist position: (1) The environment may be unambiguously characterized in terms of stimuli; (2) behavior may be unambiguously characterized in terms of responses; (3) a class of stimuli exists such that, if one (or more) is applied contingently and immediately following a response, the response probability is increased or decreased in some measurable fashion; such stimuli are reinforcers; (4) learning may be completely characterized in terms of various possible couplings among stimuli, responses, and reinforcers; and (5) unless there is definite evidence to the contrary, all classes of behavior may be assumed to be learned, manipulable by the environment, trainable and extinguishable (pp. 665–666).

White proposes that the central core of learning theory, as it is applied to developmental psychology, is derived from the Hull–Spence theory of learning, which includes three levels of theoretical development: (1) Two underlying assumptions are that the universal and elementary basis of all learning is the formation of an S–R bond, and that this elementary bonding process occurs as bits of the environment become attached to bits of behavior; (2) It is assumed that all the more complex kinds of problem solving are potentially decomposable into sets of interacting S–R bonds. (3) Complex behaviors have been interpreted as S–R systems without much specification of the form of the composition laws that might be predictive for them. This refers to such careful speculative extensions of learning theory as Berlyne's (1965) treatment of thinking and Kendler and Kendler's (1962) attempt to incorporate the cognitive activity of representation in an S–R mediation scheme (p. 668).

White (1970, p. 666) suggests that most work in developmental psychology carried out by researchers oriented to learning theory derives from the third level of development of the Hull–Spence analysis, which involves the attempt "to enlarge the framework of S–R analysis to encompass verbal behavior, curiosity and exploration, attention, symbolization, inference and reasoning and planning," as well as to examine social and personality processes. For example, Bandura and Walters (1963) offer strong support for the suggestion that imitation must be considered as a basic mechanism of learning. They argue that it is necessary to modify learning theory to account for the fact that individuals who have had no previous status in the child's reinforcement history can nevertheless serve as successful models of imitation. This implies that imitation can serve as a generalized basis for the transmission of behavior patterns outside a context of reinforcement and nonreinforcement. According to Bandura (1965) the child's ability to imitate provides a mechanism that allows the addition of new behaviors to his or her repertoire through the observation of other people's behavior. White (1970, p. 677), in commenting on the explanatory usefulness of the concept of imitation, suggests that it can account for a tremendous amount of children's learning. He quotes Bandura's view that imitation permits very efficient learning, particularly because it affords the child (as viewer) relatively risk-free means of learning to adapt to physically and socially dangerous situations. Without such a concept, White argues, it would be difficult to understand how it is the child learns so much in the absence of obvious reinforcers.

White (1970, p. 686) points out that although learning theory does not offer a theory of child development, it represents nevertheless a viewpoint that is generally understood. In its stress on environment, learning, reinforcement, and peripheralism, learning theory offers a distinctive choice over the cognitive position's emphasis on maturation, stages, development, and central structures as causative agents. White's reading of the experimental literature persuades him that many researchers are now much less preoccupied with the traditional variables of behaviorism, and are becoming increasingly involved with biological variables and maturation. There is also much interest in such new topics as the study of attentional, inferential, and imitative behavior, so that they are now being "pulled with the general trend of psychology toward a new cognitivism, an interest in biological variables and maturation" (p. 686).

Analysis of the Cognitive Position

Neisser (1967) offers a brief summary of the range of topics that are of central interest to cognitively oriented developmentalists: "the term 'cognition' refers to all the processes by which the sensory input is transformed, reduced, elaborated, stored, recovered and used" (p. 4).

The cognitive orientation has been significantly influenced by "biological thinking," the belief, for example, that a living organism from its very conception has some *intrinsic* properties. Harris (1957, p. 3), discussing the nature of development, states that the concept of development is fundamentally biological; that is, it has typically been associated with the organization of living structure and life processes. The essential ideas in any discussion of development include the organism as a living system, movement over time toward complexity of organization, the integration of parts and part-systems into larger units of wholes, and an end-state of organization that is maintained with some stability or self-regulation.

Piaget (1970), the principal proponent of the cognitive view, offers a view of development that is based upon the biological concept of adaptation. Piaget sees the individual acting upon his environment as well as the environment acting upon him. Central to Piaget's developmental theories are the concepts of action and interaction, which reflect a unique theoretical position. The learning theory approach to the interactions between an individual and her or his environment, for example, involve a stimulus from the environment, a response from the individual, and an internal or external consequence that is positively or negatively reinforcing. Piaget rejects this mode of analysis as essentially nonbiological and offers an interactional view of the individual's behavioral transaction with the environment. Neisser (1967, p. 7) observes that rather than being passive registrants of incoming stimulation, human beings attend to some parts of the environment and neglect others. In doing so, they actively recode and reformulate the information. What occurs between the individual and the environment is always, in Piaget's view, an *interaction* of present structures with *assimilable* aspects of the environment; a stimulus is not something that is constructed ready-made outside of the organism. In Piagetian theory, the individual constructs knowledge by actively *transforming* the incoming stimulation rather than by merely reflecting what is present in the environment. When the individual responds to some facet of the environment, then, Piaget claims, we can be sure that the person has given something of his or her own to the milieu. The dependence of a response on *both* the incoming stimulation and the individual's own inner structuring is, for Piaget, characteristic of all behavior.

Piaget's main theoretical interest, as Furth (1969, p. 9) indicates, involves the analysis of two questions: (1) What is the nature of intelligence? and (2) What is the source of knowledge? Furth suggests that Piaget's life's work is dominated by his search for answers to these theoretical questions. To shed light on such questions, Piaget is concerned with the structure of actions that, in the course of development, via the constantly changing environment and maturational processes of a physiological kind, undergo constant modification and become coordinated into more complex sequences. Unlike those who take a learning theory position, Piaget does not attempt to interpret these changes through a mechanistic-causal explanation; that is, he does not try to define through experiment the antecedent conditions in the environment and in the organism that induce particular changes. Instead, he concentrates on describing that invariant sequential ordering of the operations of thinking that constitutes the development of intelligence. At any given stage the child's cognitive processes reflect a total structure, or organization, that permits certain kinds of adaptive behavior to occur but not others. For example, at the stage of concrete operations, the child has access to those cognitive operations that permit him or her to classify, to relate, and to number. Until the next stage (formal operations) is reached, however, the child cannot theorize about or test hypothetical situations. Piaget emphasizes that the structure, or general organization of the stages, determines the nature of the learning process and the range of what the person can learn. As progress from one stage to another is achieved, the child not only evidences an increase in knowledge, but more significantly, the structure of her or his thinking is altered.

Although Piaget does not concern himself principally with a mechanistic-causal explanation of changes in behavior, he is nevertheless vitally interested in the factors that govern development. As Inhelder (1962, p. 32) argues, the genesis of the mechanisms of knowledge cannot be explained by any of the classical factors of developmental theory. It is not due solely to maturation, as we observe only the phenotypes, never genotypes. It does not result solely from learning on the basis of experience, as the capacity to learn is itself tied to development. It does not result from the social transmission of information alone as the child transforms the elements received while assimilating them. Piaget (1967) advances the hypothesis that the hereditary, physiological, maturational, and environmental factors and their interaction in the development of intelligence are not the primary causes of this development. Rather, they are themselves subordinated to the regulatory mechanism that characterizes development—the *equilibration* process. This involves the notion that development proceeds from relative disequilibrium to increasing equilibrium, so that when the individual is in disequilibrium (e.g., when a problem cannot be immediately resolved) he or she will operate to establish greater equilibrium. By such means the individual changes and thereby develops. Through such processes the child advances from the early to the later stages of intellectual development.

Some researchers have moved from the traditional learning theory position in order to explore new topics of research, thereby recasting some features of learning theory. Similarly there has been a parallel movement among cognitive psychologists that has resulted in the analysis of some experiential variables that appear to be implicated in the course of cognitive growth (e.g., Sigel, Roeper, & Hooper, 1966). Such work is necessary to explain the process of development from one stage to another, which has tended to be one of the weakest aspects of cognitive theory.

Analysis of the Psychoanalytic Position

Langer (1969) remarks that whereas the cognitive and environmentalist theories both characterize the child as essentially rational, by contrast the psychoanalytic theory sees the child as essentially affective and irrational. In this view, the child learns to gain control over his or her impulses in a very gradual manner. However, control is never complete, so that she or he is always in a state of conflict between the desire to express instinctual impulses and the necessity to conform to the externally imposed social standards of conduct. Psychoanalytic theory posits an individual who is, of necessity, always either responding to or defending against internal (instinctual) urges and external (physical and social) stimuli. It is these instinctual and environmental forces, Freudians believe, that represent the major determinants of development. The specific nature of the motivational forces that energize the individual's behavior is seen as a function of the particular stage of psychosexual development attained.

Erikson (1963) offers an argument concerning the individual's progression from one stage of psychosexual development to another in the form of an epigenetic[1] principle. This principle states that the child has instinctual energies available at birth that become invested in different body zones in a prescribed sequence and at relatively fixed times during the course of development. Whenever a body zone is instinctually energized it begins to function. For example, when the mouth is stimulated, the ensuing behavior of either sucking food or using the mouth to explore the environment becomes the predominant mode of action during this period of life, and characterizes one stage of sexual and social development. A change in the functioning of the child occurs when there

---

[1]In biology, *epigenesis* (as opposed to *preformationism*) refers to the theory that the embryo develops from the successive differentiation of structures that were originally undifferentiated. According to Gottlieb (1970), epigenesis "denotes the fact that patterns of activity and sensitivity are not immediately evident in the initial stages of embryonic development and that various behavioral capabilities of the organism become manifest only during the course of development" (p. 111). With respect to psychological development, there are two viewpoints regarding the epigenesis of behavior. *Predetermined epigenesis* assumes that behavioral sequences are predetermined by neural growth factors and differentiation (maturation), while *probabilistic epigenesis* assumes that behavioral development is not invariant, and "that the sequence or outcome of individual behavioral development is probable (with respect to norms) rather than certain" (Gottlieb, 1970, p. 123).

is a shift of instinctual energy to another body zone, an event resulting in the attainment of a new stage of psychosexual and social development.

Although life follows an epigenetic sequence according to Erikson (1963), the transition from one stage to the next is *not* due to the interaction of the preceding stage with the environment. Rather, the transitions are programmed (or predetermined) by endogenous factors (shifts in instinctual energy) in a manner analogous to the maturationally determined (fixed time-interval) critical periods (see Chapter 5). Erikson's *psychosocial stages* of development are essentially derived from Freud's (1905) *psychosexual stages*. Freud's theory is essentially *biological* and is concerned with the derivation of pleasure from specific body zones at different ages. The basic stages are the oral, anal, phallic, latent, and ultimately the genital (adult sexual gratification). In normal development the child progresses from one stage to the next; in abnormal development (fixation) problems associated with one stage persist. Largely derivative, Erikson's *psychosocial* theory is much more concerned with the social or interpersonal problems the child encounters. Progressing from one stage to the next, the child encounters various psychosocial crises (e.g., trust vs. mistrust; autonomy vs. shame, doubt; initiative vs. guilt; industry vs. inferiority; identity vs. identity diffusion; intimacy vs. isolation; generativity vs. self-absorption; and integrity vs. despair). There are therefore eight basic stages in psychosocial development, and these occur in an invariant sequential order. Resolution of problems at one stage determines how well the child can cope with problems at a later stage. In addition to focusing on social aspects, Erikson is also concerned with the effects of cultural differences on development. His major focus is on ego-identity, and he has basically reformulated Freudian psychoanalytic psychology into an ego psychology.

The principal area of developmental research and theory from the psychoanalytic perspective is the development of personality. This has led to the investigation of the role of internal conflicts and disturbing influences, particularly within the family, on the child's development. Psychoanalytic theory assumes that normal personality is based upon the individual's successful resolution of a series of major interpersonal and intrapersonal crises that occur at each stage of the individual's sexual and social development. It is hypothesized, for example, that a conflict between trust and mistrust of oneself and the environment will inevitably develop in all infants who are at the oral stage of psychosexual development. Other crises are associated with each of the later stages of development. The manner in which these crises are resolved at a particular stage determines the personality characteristics that will be expressed at that stage. In psychoanalytic theory early conflicts and the success or failure of their resolution are hypothesized to have significant effect on subsequent personality development.

THE THREE MODELS OF "MAN"

Langer (1969) in contrasting the environmental, cognitive, and psychoanalytic views of development discusses important similarities and differences in their basic assumptions, what constitutes the basic theoretical issues, how development is to be defined, and what the appropriate units of analysis and the most appropriate research methods should be. The environmentalist position asserts that the only kinds of changes that occur in development are quantitative ones, where units of experience are simply added together. The child at birth has certain reflex mechanisms available that provide the foundation for all of his or her learning. Change, in this view, comes about as the direct result of environmental actions, and can be understood by knowing the reinforcement history in each case. The experimenter's attention is directed at the child's observable behaviors, and the focus is on short-term changes in behavior. By piecing the observed elements of behavior together, it will eventually be possible to provide a complete account of development. This approach has not generated many truly developmental studies, principally because it assumes a continuity of behavioral mechanisms in going from immature to mature organisms. Not all environmentalists (e.g., Kendler & Kendler, 1962, among other neo-behaviorists) accept these assumptions about the nature of change, however.

In the cognitive view of development, change is considered to be significantly influenced by both biological and psychological factors. The child's own actions, and the knowledge that results from them, are seen to be the primary cause of development. Whereas cognitive theorists do not reject the argument that many changes may be *quantitative,* they focus their attention on the *qualitative changes.* In this view development is composed of a sequence of stages that progressively build upon each other. The individual is seen as a self-regulatory organization of functional structures that continuously renew and transform themselves through their interactions with the environment. In turn, these actions lead to the developmental reorganization (equilibration) of the individual's structures, which subserve these actions, at a new functional level or more stable stage of adaptation. Research emanating from this perspective has yielded a very rich assembly of descriptive-interpretive data on many different aspects of cognitive development, and research is beginning on the processes that underlie the child's progression through the stages of intellectual development.

Psychoanalytic theory, like cognitive theory, assumes that the child's inborn organization constitutes the initial functional and structural base of her or his development. Biologically rooted functions are the organizing forces that differentiate and relate inborn structures into increasingly complex organizations, subject to the nature of the individual's particular history of interactions with his environment. Psychoanalytic theory, again like cognitive theory, offers a stage theory but specifically of psychosexual functioning. In this view, each stage of functioning is not a transformation of an earlier stage, but rather a new stage that emerges at a given point of life and that takes precedence over the previous form of functioning. This conception is based upon the model of physiological maturation, which assumes a critical period for the emergence of a new functional structure. The implication is that the new function is potentially coded in the child's maturational sequence. At the proper time, under appropriate environmental conditions, it emerges or becomes actualized. The previous stage of functioning is, therefore, only a necessary condition for the emergence of the new stage. The discussion of other psychological processes of a less instinctual and more rational, intellectual, and social nature is less clearly and consistently dealt with in the psychoanalytic view of development. Further, contrasted to its great productivity in the realm of theory, the psychoanalytic viewpoint has produced little systematic research on developmental themes.

THE FUTURE OF THEORIES IN
DEVELOPMENTAL PSYCHOLOGY

From time to time in the history of science a model of knowledge is abandoned and a new model takes its place. Kuhn (1970) has developed an historical account of the formulation, testing, and ultimate rejection of scientific models. Kuhn uses the term "paradigm" to describe a scientific model or theory that has been accepted at some point in time. A paradigm becomes acceptable if it is more successful than its competitors in helping solve problems. Research stemming from it helps to articulate the paradigm, examine its implications, increase its precision, and reduce its ambiguities. The paradigm involves a set of expectancies that indicates what to look for, what kinds of solutions to expect, and, by implication, what to ignore. But, often because of its very precision, new and unexpected phenomena occur. Kuhn shows that there are many instances in the history of science where simple adjustment of the paradigm has not worked, and it is in these cases that the situation is ripe for a change in paradigms, a "revolution." This occurs when there is a breakdown in the normal puzzle-solving activity within the framework of a particular scientific paradigm.

There are some signs of a "new look" in developmental psychology in the shifting emphases among developmental researchers and theoreticians, for example, the growing interest in the Piagetians in learning (Etienne, 1973; Sinclair, 1973) and in the attempts by various behaviorists to deal with cognitive phenomena. Such new concerns have led White (1970) to talk about "a new cognitivism," but it is not clear whether a new paradigm is emerging in developmental psychology. If so, it may well be a blend of the behaviorist and cognitive paradigms.

References

Anderson, J. E. Dynamics of development: Systems in process. In D. B. Harris (Ed.), *The concept of development*. Minneapolis: University of Minneapolis Press, 1957, pp. 24–46.

Aronson, L. R., Tobach, E., Lehrman, D. S., & Rosenblatt, J. S. (Eds.) *Development and evolution of behavior: Essays in memory of T. C. Schneirla*. San Francisco: Freeman, 1970.

Baer, D. M. & Wright, J. C. Developmental psychology. *Annual Review of Psychology, 1975, 25,* 1–82.

Baldwin, A. L. The study of child behavior and development. In P. H. Mussen (Ed.), *Handbook of research methods in child development*. New York: Wiley, 1960, pp. 3–35.

Baltes, P. B. & Schaie, K. W. (Eds.) *Life-span developmental psychology: Personality and socialization*. New York: Academic Press, 1973.

Bandura, A. Vicarious processes: A case of no-trial learning. In L. Berkowitz (Ed.), *Advances in experimental social psychology*. Vol. 2. New York: Academic Press, 1965.

Bandura, A. & Walters, R. H. *Social learning and personality development*. New York: Holt, Rinehart and Winston, 1963.

Barnett, S. A. (Ed.) *Ethology and development*. Philadelphia: Lippincott, 1973.

Berlyne, D. E. *Structure and direction in thinking*. New York: Wiley, 1965.

Erikson, E. H. *Childhood and society*. (2d ed.) New York: Norton, 1963.

Etienne, A. S. Developmental stages and cognitive structures as determinants of what is learned. In R. A. Hinde & J. Stevenson-Hinde (Eds.), *Constraints on learning*. New York: Academic Press, 1973, pp. 371–395.

Freud, S. The psychopathology of everyday life. In A. A. Brill (Trans. and ed.), *The basic writings of Sigmund Freud*. New York: Modern Library, 1938. *(Three contributions to the theory of sex,* originally published, 1905.)

Furth, H. G. *Piaget and knowledge: Theoretical foundations*. Englewood Cliffs, N.J.: Prentice-Hall, 1969.

Gottlieb, A. Conceptions of prenatal development. In L. R. Aronson, E. Tobach, D. S. Lehrman, & J. S. Rosenblatt (Eds.), *Development and evolution of behavior*. San Francisco: Freeman, 1970, pp. 111–137.

Goulet, L. R. & Baltes, P. B. (Eds.) *Life-span developmental psychology: Research and theory*. New York: Academic Press, 1970.

Harris, D. B. Problems in formulating a scientific concept of development. In D. B. Harris (Ed.), *The concept of development*. Minneapolis: University of Minneapolis Press, 1957, pp. 3–14.

Hilgard, E. R. & Bower, G. H. *Theories of learning*. (4th ed.) Englewood Cliffs, N.J.: Prentice-Hall, 1975.

Inhelder, B. Some aspects of Piaget's genetic approach to cognition. In W. Kessen & C. Kuhlman (Eds.), Thought in the Young Child. *Monographs of the Society for Research in Child Development*, 1962, *27* (No. 2, Serial No. 83) pp. 19–34.

Kendler, H. H. & Kendler, T. S. Vertical and horizontal processes in problem solving. *Psychological Review*, 1962, *69,* 1–16.

Kessen, W. Research design in the study of developmental problems. In P. H. Mussen (Ed.), *Handbook of research methods in child development*. New York: Wiley, 1960, pp. 36–70.

Kuhn, T. S. *The structure of scientific revolutions* (2d ed.) Chicago: University of Chicago Press, 1970.

Langer, J. *Theories of development*. New York: Holt, Rinehart and Winston, 1969.

Moltz, H. (Ed.) *The ontogeny of vertebrate behavior*. New York: Academic Press, 1971.

Neisser, U. *Cognitive psychology*. New York: Appleton, 1967.

Nesselroade, J. R. & Reese, H. W. (Eds.) *Life-span developmental psychology: Methodological issues*. New York: Academic Press, 1973.

Piaget, J. *Biology and knowledge*. Chicago: University of Chicago Press, 1967.

Piaget, J. Piaget's theory. In P. H. Mussen (Ed.), *Carmichael's manual of child psychology*. (3d ed.) New York: Wiley, 1970, pp. 703–732.

Rosenblatt, J. S. Views on the onset and maintenance of maternal behavior in the rat. In L. R. Aronson, E. Tobach, D. S. Lehrman, & J. S. Rosenblatt (Eds.), *Development and evolution of behavior: Essays in memory of T. C. Schneirla*. San Francisco: Freeman, 1970.

Schneirla, T. C. Behavioral development and comparative psychology. *Quarterly Review of Biology*, 1966, *41*, 283–302.

Sigel, I. E., Roeper, A., & Hooper, F. H. A training procedure for the acquisition of Piaget's conservation of quantity. *British Journal of Educational Psychology*, 1966, *36*, 301–311.

Sinclair, H. Some remarks on the Genevan point of view on learning with special reference to language learning. In R. A. Hinde & J. Stevenson-Hinde (Eds.), *Constraints on learning*. New York: Academic Press, 1973, pp. 397–415.

White, S. The learning theory approach. In P. H. Mussen (Ed.), *Carmichael's manual of child psychology*. (3d ed.) New York: Wiley, 1970, pp. 657–701.

Wohlwill, J. F. *The study of behavioral development*. New York: Academic Press, 1973.

Zigler, E. Metatheoretical issues in developmental psychology. In M. H. Marx (Ed.), *Theories in contemporary psychology*. New York: Macmillan, 1963, pp. 341–369.

Chapter 2
CONTEMPORARY ISSUES

The three theoretical viewpoints (see Chapter 1) that are currently prominent in research and theorizing in developmental psychology—the environmentalist, the cognitive, and the psychoanalytic—share a common goal, which is to provide a comprehensive account of behavioral change. There are, however, fundamental disagreements among them on how such a plan can be realized or, in other words, where research energies should be applied. Differences exist among the three approaches with regard to how a general explanation of developmental changes may be achieved. There are differences over what meanings can be attached to the concept of development, what the critical topics of enquiry are in developmental psychology, what kinds of organisms should be investigated, and finally the kind of research program that would be appropriate for the study of change. In the following discussion of contemporary issues, the reader will notice that there is not equal representation of the three distinctive theoretical viewpoints. The basic reason for this is that each position perceives some issues as more crucial than others, and, therefore, more research has been tied to these "crucial" issues. Because much of the energy of the environmentalists has been expended on the analysis of the role of experience in development, they have not been deeply involved in research into the role of biological factors. The cognitive researchers, alternatively, have studied "intrinsic" factors—including biological factors—and have exhibited a limited attraction to an assessment of the role of learning in development. Finally, the researchers who work from a psychoanalytic perspective have pronounced their interest in the development of normal and abnormal personality. The focusing on different subsets of research issues by researchers representing the three viewpoints in developmental psychology is also reflected in the articles selected for each of the sections of this book. In some chapters there is not a single article that represents a particular viewpoint, whereas in other chapters the same viewpoint may appear to be overrepresented. This is principally a function of the topical interest and concerns of each theoretical viewpoint. . . . (See p. 29 for a summary table relating specific articles to issue areas.)

RESEARCH STRATEGY

Questions of research strategy in developmental psychology raise some general issues. They can be discussed in terms of two dimensions: (1) *subject (species) to be studied,* and (2) *methodology.*

Aside from practical considerations, a developmental psychologist's choice of *subjects* (Ss) might be determined by some combination of at least two theoretical attitudes. One involves the conviction held by many psychologists that the most likely avenue of access to an understanding of complex behavioral phenomena and complex organisms begins with the study of simpler phenomena and simpler organisms. This usually means studying the simplest known example of a phenomenon in the simplest organisms that appear to manifest it. At the same time, many psychologists are either impatient or pessimistic about this strategy and its immediate fruitfulness, preferring to study complex behavior in humans.

A second theoretical bias that may determine what subject or organism a developmental psychologist chooses to study is the extent to which a problem, or the investigator's approach to the problem, appears to gain fruitful perspective from a comparative approach. Some problem areas, and some methods of investigation, are distinctly human (such as verbal learning and the interview method respectively); in many cases, however (see Hebb & Thompson, 1968, and articles [6][1] and [7] in this volume), a comparative perspective can be particularly enlightening or promising. Then, choice of subjects will be guided by the expected phylogenetic "profile" of the phenomenon (see article [7]).

It is some combination of these two biases that appears to "earmark" much contemporary animal developmental research (Ambrose, 1968; Schneirla, 1966; see also Moltz, 1971). From this research it becomes increasingly clear that the phylogenetic context brings with it vast complexities and pitfalls along with its promise of deeper understanding. Lehrman (1974), for example, points out how very different one's conclusions might be about mate selection by birds, depending upon which species one studied. The same pitfall apparently exists regarding, for example, the social behavior, early social contacts, and many characteristics of the mothering received by different species of macaque monkeys (Kaufman, 1974; Lehrman, 1974). Some research is, of course, guided largely by nothing more complicated than interest in a particular species.

Choice of research *methodology*, the second aspect of research strategy, is a choice between two relatively distinct modes of observation: (1) naturalistic (correlational), and (2) experimental. While many sciences and problems within a science have seemed to evolve from a naturalistic to an experimental mode of observation, there is a mutual interdependence between the two. McCandless and Spiker (1956), in an influential paper, clarify and emphasize advantages of experimental research, particularly for developmental psychology. Nonetheless, Willems [3] convincingly argues the merits of an approach that appears to demand that naturalistic observation be considered the more fundamental, though he does not deny the importance of controlled observation.

Although we have indicated that a discussion of research strategy in developmental psychology involves basically the two related dimensions of subjects and methodology, there actually remains an overriding third aspect. We are referring to the investigator's choice of problem areas for research, as well as the nature of the questions asked about the content area one investigates. This raises questions requiring exceedingly more complex answers if one is to attempt answers at all. The fact of the matter almost certainly is that history is the best test of one's judgment in choosing a research area or problem. Thus, for example, even though a criterion like "breadth of implications across areas" may seem rational for evaluating the "significance" of a problem, it is not an easy criterion to apply except with hindsight. It would be fruitless, of course, to do more than briefly raise issues for which one can imagine no method of getting relevant evidence. On the other hand, the only compelling argument that might arise against an investigator's interest in particular topics would be that no method for collecting relevant evidence exists. At least, it seems clear that where beliefs exist that are dissonant with observed evidence, one presumably has a domain of importance. A paper by Webb (1961) contains a thoughtful, still relevant discussion of some criteria for choice of research area or problem.

It is also pertinent briefly to discuss research strategy in relation to the *three models of man* outlined in Chapter 1 (pp. 7–8). Associated with each model there is an emphasis on a particular method or group of functionally similar methods of inquiry. White (1970) outlines the research

---

[1]Numbers in square brackets refer to article numbers in this text.

rationale of the environmentalists and the method of inquiry that they typically use. In addition to the laboratory studies and emphasis on learning, as described by White, environmentalists also employ variants of basic experimental method, including aspects of cross-sectional, longitudinal, and correlational research. These procedures are appropriate, given that the goal of the environmentalists is to provide a fine-grained analysis of observable influences on behavior.

Those who take the cognitive view of development are particularly concerned with the "operational mechanisms of thought," and their methods of inquiry are designed to meet this need. This group has used all of the experimental techniques previously discussed, but this has typically been the case when the basic data on a particular developmental phenomenon have already been collected and interpreted. Whenever a brand new area of investigation is opened up, the typical technique used is the "clinical method." Inhelder (1962, p. 25) offers this description:

> The experimenter does not merely take account of the child's response but asks also for the child's explanation of them. And, by modifying the questions and the experimental conditions, the investigator seeks to test the genuineness and the consistency of the child's response. . . . By means of this exploratory method—one which calls for both imagination and critical sense—we believe we obtain a truer picture of the child's thought than we would by the use of standardized tests which involve the risk of missing unexpected and often essential aspects of his thought.

The psychoanalytic position focuses on the effects of antecedent conflicts on personality development. In the view of many of the proponents of this approach, its theoretical propositions can be adequately tested by asking the patient in a therapeutic situation, where conflicts are being explored, to free-associate and to talk about events that seem pertinent to the dynamics of the case. In addition, psychoanalytic propositions have also been tested through the use of the correlational technique, and in a small number of studies other experimental methods have been used.

THE NATURE–NURTURE ISSUE

One of the perennial problems in psychology has been the nature–nurture issue. Depending upon the context of the discussion it is also referred to as the heredity–environment controversy or the nativist–empiricist controversy. In the 1930s this issue was phrased in terms of whether heredity (nature) or environment (nurture) was the prime determinant of any specific behavioral phenomena. As Hebb (1953, 1972) and Anastasi (1958) point out, this is never an appropriate question about any aspect of behavior. Hebb (1953) states that some characteristic of a given behavioral event may depend on experience *given a normal heredity,* or on heredity *given a normal environment*. On logical grounds alone each is the necessary condition for the other. To ask whether heredity or environment is more important for a specific type of behavior is akin to asking whether the length or the width is more important in determining the area of a rectangle. Obviously both are essential, and consonant with this point of view most studies today are concerned with the "mechanisms" that mediate development.

The heredity–environment controversy is now largely a pseudoissue (but see *Harvard Educational Review*, 1969). However, as Anastasi and Foley (1948) indicated, historically there have been three major ways in which the heredity–environment relationship has been approached. They label these three conceptualizations: (1) isolated operations; (2) independent additive contribution; and (3) interaction. The *isolated operations* conception is that all behavior is due either to instincts or to learned habits. The *independent additive contribution* conception is that heredity and environment each make independent but joint and *additive* contributions to all behavior. If this conception were appropriate, one could presumably determine the relative contributions of heredity and environment to particular behavioral phenomena. The *interaction* conception, which is the one most prevalent today, is that all behavior is the product of interactions between hereditary and environmental factors. The nature and influence of each depends upon the contribution of the other. The questions of "which one?" and "how much?" have been replaced by the question of "how?" (Anastasi, 1958).

A remaining complication has been that definitions of heredity and environment are inevitably vague or ambiguous. Hebb (1972) has attempted to clarify this problem by codifying the factors in development. His codification, which includes six classes, serves to indicate that there are more than two factors in behavioral development. Hebb's six classes of factors include: I: genetic; II: chemical, prenatal; III: chemical, postnatal; IV: sensory, constant; V: sensory, variable; and VI: traumatic.

Factor I refers to the physiological properties of the fertilized ovum and is the hereditary variable in behavior, whereas the remaining factors constitute the environmental variables. Factors II and III are similar in principle; likewise, Factors IV and V are similar in principle. Factor IV, which is primarily the species-specific context of early learning, refers to pre- and postnatal experience that all members of a species encounter under normal conditions. Factor V, which is fundamental to later learning, refers to experiential factors that vary for different members of a species. For a more detailed exposition of these factors, the reader is referred to Hebb (1972, pp. 127–131; especially Table 1, p. 128). The important consideration is that no behavior occurs on the basis of *one* of these factors alone. Furthermore, in behavioral development, these factors interact and mutually influence one another. There is a network of reciprocal causal relationships among the various factors influencing development (see Rosenblatt, 1967, for a discussion of social-environmental factors in development).

As the reader will discover, the nature–nurture issue is at the core of developmental psychology. Virtually all other issues derive from it. Accordingly, this issue will be encountered, in some form or other, in every chapter of this book. Thus, for example, in research on early experience (see Chapter 5), where immature organisms are experimentally exposed to different environmental events, and their later behavior is examined for effects of different exposures, the question clearly arises whether these "same" early experiences would have different effects for different species, or even for genetically different members of a species.

The topic of the development of intelligence is another useful example (see Chapter 11). Vigorous disagreements persist among highly intelligent scientists (*Harvard Educational Review*, 1969) as to how properly to characterize and evaluate the roles played by heredity and environment in intelligent behavior (including, we presume, their own). Obviously, clarity still evades us, and misunderstanding continues. We know little enough about experiential factors, and even less about genetic ones; satisfactory accounts of the development of behavior in these terms are simply not yet possible. Here, as elsewhere in discussing the roles of heredity and environment in development, a caution stressed by Anastasi (1958) is instructive, as well as being a summary of the problem. Heredity does not yield behavior, intelligent or otherwise; nor for that matter, does environment. Heredity does yield what might be termed an elastic blueprint for incipient structures; given certain environmental events or event sequences, and *depending on the structure, and the earlier effects of environment upon them* (such as brain damage, learning, atrophy, and so forth), such structures can imply certain behavioral phenomena.

The nature–nurture issue also has direct relevance for the areas of learning, perception, and motivation. For learning, it takes the form of the relative influences of maturation and learning on performance (see Chapter 6). For perception it takes the form of the nativism–empiricism controversy (see Chapter 8). For motivation, the nature–nurture issue is concerned with the relative influence of organismic and experiential factors in the development of motives, as well as with the role of instinctive behavior (see Chapter 7). For example, Lorenz (1965) makes a strong argument for retaining a restricted concept of "innateness" that has clear relevance for contemporary learning, motivation, and reinforcement theories.

At this point the student might try to state possible questions raised by the nature–nurture issue for language, conceptual development (see Chapters 9 and 10), personality development, and socialization (see Chapters 12 and 13).

PHYLOGENETIC, ONTOGENETIC, AND CROSS-CULTURAL COMPARISONS

It would appear that fundamental observations relevant to the nature–nurture question could be made by studying and comparing different species. This approach would involve clear genetic differences (as, for example, between goldfish and humans) that presumably should allow examination of their role in yielding behavioral differences.

Unfortunately this comparative approach encounters a nearly insurmountable problem. The *effective* environment of any organism is largely determined by the operating characteristics and variety of its sensory systems; that is, by its capacity for detection of energy states and changes in the objective environment. Thus, at least some species are inevitably responsive to different aspects of what an adult human anthropocentrically refers to as "the environment." In other words, examining a different species can entail the need to redefine "environment."

Thus, a common referent for the term environment cannot be assumed for different species. It is worth recalling that the human, unaided by electronmicroscopes, Geiger counters, and the like, is far from being omniscient about energy changes in that special environment defined by the chemist or the physicist. This fact is at the heart of the complexity that requires an interactionist approach to the heredity–environment issue. Even so, fruitful cross-species comparisons can be made (see especially articles [5, 6, and 7]); insight into the bases of species differences in behavior, and guidance as to the form and generality of behavioral principles can be achieved. The discovery or development of behavior principles having the widest possible generality is a fundamental goal of psychology. In providing the basis for fuller understanding both of the species involved and of the nature of behavior laws, the discovery of interspecies discontinuities in behavior principles or laws (Hinde & Stevenson-Hinde, 1973) should be considered complementary to this goal.

The same questions asked about phylogenetic continuity can also usefully be raised with respect to ontogeny (see Skinner, 1966), the development of individual organisms. Thus, while the psychologist's goal is to arrive at principles of behavior that hold for all stages of development, when ontogenetic discontinuities (see p. 19) are evident, insights may be gained into developmental processes, and/or they may lead to refinement of the principles involved. This, of course, is at the heart of traditional developmental psychology and many of the papers reprinted in this volume pertain almost exclusively to ontogenetic processes (as examples see [13, 16, and 30]).

As indicated earlier, one goal of scientific psychology is the formulation of behavior principles that hold not only across species and stages of development of species but also across situations. One form of concern with situational factors is represented by research examining influences of culture on development. Thus, one might fruitfully look for cross-cultural continuities and discontinuities in behavioral phenomena as part not only of an evaluation of the generality of certain behavioral phenomena, but also of an appreciation of the culture (situation). Articles [43] and [44] exemplify cross-culturally oriented developmental research.

The discovery of phylogenetic, ontogenetic, and cross-cultural similarities and differences in development undoubtedly is basic to the discovery of fundamental laws about the development of organisms.

EARLY EXPERIENCE

In addition to asking the general questions as to whether certain behavioral principles are applicable throughout stages of development (the ontogenetic question), across species (the phylogenetic question), or across cultures (the cross-cultural question), one can ask a set of more specific questions about the effects of experience early in the life of an organism. A large theoretical and research literature has developed with respect to early experience and infancy.

Basically, three questions have been asked: (1) Do early experiences have special broad importance for an organism's later behavior, perhaps broader than is normally considered true for similar experiences by an adult organism? (2) Are different periods of early life important for different types of early experience? More specifically, for at least some early experiences of at least some species, are there "critical periods" in early life when the experiences will have their effect, or their greatest effect? (3) Is conditioning possible in newborn infants, and are the principles of adult learning applicable to infant learning?

Historically, the recent trend towards studies on early experience stems from four major sources: the writings of Freud, Hebb, Piaget, and the ethologists. Freud's (1905) theorizing has been influential in at least three research areas: (1) psychosexual development, (2) the effects of trauma, and (3) the effects of mothering. Ethologists (see Lorenz, 1937) have established imprinting as a very important early experience phenomenon, at least for some species. Hebb, in his classic book (1949), has stimulated a variety of studies in cognitive and perceptual development. Piaget (1950), who has focused on cognitive and intellectual development, does not believe that it is possible to accelerate a child's cognitive growth by experimentally manipulating the environment. Nevertheless, Piaget is not a simple nativist, but argues strongly that one important factor in the child's cognitive development is the richness of the child's interaction with his or her environment (see the discussion of Piaget, in Chapter 1, pp. 5–6).

Freud's conceptions of psychosexual development (see discussion in Chapter 1, pp. 6–7) led to a large number of studies on infant care and personality, many of which were reviewed by Orlansky (1949). (For a more recent review of research on infancy, see White, 1971.) Hunt [34] indicates that prior to World War II it was commonly believed that early experiences were important for emotional and personality development but relatively unimportant for intellectual development. However, Hunt [34] provides evidence to indicate that early experiences may be more important for intellectual than for emotional development.

In an attempt to verify Freud's trauma theory, Levine, Chevalier, and Korchin (1956) found that shocking in infancy facilitated rather than retarded avoidance learning in adulthood. Other investigators (e.g., Denenberg, 1962; Goldman, 1964; Levine, 1960; Salama & Hunt, 1964) have replicated these findings. (See the introduction to Chapter 5 for a further discussion and rationale as to why trauma may not have detrimental effects.) Brackbill (1971) has shown that continuous stimulation has a pacifying effect on infants. The evidence indicates that infantile stimulation *per se*, whether pleasant or noxious, may be associated with decreased emotionality in adulthood.

The various studies on infantile stimulation (see also Rheingold & Bayley [9] and Denenberg [11]) seriously question the psychoanalytic trauma theory, and lend credence to the general proposition that early stimulation should facilitate development (see Hebb, 1949). But the issue is much more complex, and stimulation *per se* is not always beneficial. White (1969), for example, states that although early stimulation facilitates the development of *visually directed behavior,* too much stimulation at too early an age can induce distress and crying. Unless the infant is maturationally ready, early stimulation is not necessarily beneficial. (See the introduction to Chapter 5 for a further discussion of this issue.) King (1958) had earlier suggested that a number of variables seem to be significant in this area, including: the age of the organism when the effects of the early experience are tested; the duration, amount, and quality of the infantile experience (the independent variable); the type of performance required from the organism (the dependent variable); and the interaction between the experience and the genetic background of the organism. His earlier suggestions still have considerable merit today.

A third line of extensive research stemming from Freud's theorizing involves the effects of mothering, especially maternal deprivation. Whereas the pioneer studies on maternal deprivation (Bowlby, 1952) indicated that maternal deprivation had irreversible deleterious effects, Bowlby (1971) later recanted this position and stated that the belief that institutionalized or deprived children commonly develop psychopathic or affectionless characters may be mistaken. Deprivation leads to various outcomes, "and of those who are damaged only a small minority develop those very serious disabilities which first drew attention to the pathogenic nature of the experience" (Bowlby, Ainsworth, Boston, & Rosenbluth, 1956). Most of the recent and better controlled studies indicate that it is not maternal deprivation *per se* that was at fault, but rather the more general variable of adequate "stimulation" that adequate mothering provides. Rutter (1972) suggests that the "deprivation" half of the concept may very well be misleading and the "maternal" half of the concept may be inaccurate. He suggests that, "with but few exceptions, the deleterious influences concern the care of the child or relationships with people rather than any specific defect of the mother" (Rutter, 1972, p. 119). The Rheingold and Bayley paper [9] indicates that where institutional stimulation is adequate, institutionalization *per se*, or the lack of a specific mother, need not have adverse effects. For excellent reviews of the maternal deprivation studies the reader is referred to Ainsworth (1966), Bowlby (1971), and Rutter (1972).

As indicated earlier, (p. 16) stimulation may accelerate development. However, one critical factor is the age at which infantile experiences are encountered. For example, in rats infantile stimulation *before* weaning reduces emotionality and increases open field activity in adulthood (see Denenberg & Morton, 1962), and increases the weight of the cortex (Rosenzweig, 1966). Differential effects of pre- and post-weaning stimulation are relevant to concepts of critical periods and imprinting. Hess (1972) suggests that the deprivation that occurs in most laboratory studies on imprinting may interfere with the normal development of young ducklings. He raises a number of questions, including: What is the optimal age for imprinting? How long must the imprinting last for it to have a maximum effect? Hess (1964) distinguishes between imprinting and associative learning, and emphasizes the importance of motor experience for the imprinting phenomena to occur. Moltz (1960), however, attempts to explain imprinting in terms of associative learning based on anxiety reduction. While implicitly emphasizing the importance of perceptual experience in general, he also stresses that why the perception of the familiar reduces anxiety is not explicit. (Hunt [34] suggests that early sensory or perceptual experiences may be more important than motor experiences in terms of the subsequent problem-solving ability of animals.) Bateson (1973) suggests that it is more appropriate to define imprinting (social attachment) in terms of the context within which it occurs rather than in terms of intrinsic characteristics. In discussing imprinting in birds he states that "not only are certain stages of development crucial for acquisition of preferences and habits, but those periods of sensitivity are also, in part, limited by environmental factors which can be controlled" (p. 14). Young birds are not passive during the imprinting process, Bateson continues. "They play a decidedly active part in determining the kind of stimulation they receive, both while they are preparing to learn and also during the learning process" (p. 14). He suggests that "the situation in which social attachments are formed is also striking because it provides such an obvious case of the interaction between an animal and its environment during development" (p. 13). Although imprinting is *descriptively* different from "associative learning," Bateson states that it is, at present, uncertain as to whether the underlying mechanisms are different. Bowlby (1971), as well as Hoffman and Ratner (1973) and Hoffman and Solomon (1974), has pointed to the possible relevance of imprinting for human development.

Sameroff [10] in discussing learning in infancy has suggested that conditioning in infancy is dependent on the development of both sensory and motor schemas. Although operant conditioning is possible in the infant (3 to 10 days old), classical conditioning is difficult to demonstrate. Fitzgerald and Porges (1971) and Fitzgerald and Brackbill (1971) have stated that the feasibility of conditioning infants is dependent on the maturation of the nervous system (see the introduction to Chapter 5 for a further discussion of this issue). This implies that stimulation at certain stages of development is more productive than stimulation at other stages of development.

Related to this idea of the chronological importance of stimulation is the concept of critical periods. Denenberg [11] and Caldwell (1962) suggest that the critical period hypothesis can be interpreted in two ways: (1) There is a presumably *fixed-time interval* in development beyond which stimulation has little or no effect; and (2) there are periods of *maximum susceptibility*, with the stimulus having different effects upon an organism at different ages. While Denenberg and Caldwell both favor the second interpretation, Scott (1962) favors the first. Furthermore, Denenberg proposes that emotionality is inversely related to the amount and intensity of infantile stimulation. However, as discussed earlier, White (1969) has indicated that while early stimulation may facilitate development, it is necessary to take into account the maturational level of the infant. The interaction of experiential and maturational factors is important.

Related to the issue of critical periods is the question of whether development is continuous or discontinuous; that is, does the child go through a series of stages (relatively independent of specific experiential encounters) in which each stage must be mastered before the child can proceed to the next one (see Bijou [1])? Piaget's theory of cognitive or intellectual development (see [30] and the introduction to Chapter 10) is essentially a stage theory, as are Freud's (1905) theory of psychosexual development, Kohlberg's theory of moral development (see Kohlberg, 1967, and [38]) and Erikson's (1963) theory of psychosocial development. Bijou [1] has suggested that early experience usually refers to ages rather than to stages, and to resolve this issue it is necessary to have behavioral criteria for stages rather than intellectual or theoretical propositions. Whether it is preferable to interpret behavior as reflecting the continuity of development as against the existence of stages of development is an unresolved issue.

At present, practically no one would deny the importance of early experience in development. Furthermore, most investigators are cognizant of the role of maturational factors in development. However, the exact nature of the early experience by maturation interaction is a problem that still awaits a satisfactory resolution.

LEARNING AND DEVELOPMENT

The combination of interest in developmental psychology with interest in learning again places us at the heart of the nature–nurture problem. An exhaustive catalogue of learning variables would contain considerable overlap with a detailed description (if one were possible) of what is meant by nurture. Historically, one reflection of this was in some early experimental approaches to the nature–nurture problem, which explicitly asked the question of the relative influence of maturation and learning on behavior. As the reader might guess, it is now largely considered a pseudo-issue; that is, the question is inappropriately put. Nonetheless, progress in the study of learning (see, e.g., Estes, 1970; Gibson, 1969; Mackintosh, 1974; Restle, 1975; Stevenson, 1972) continues to broaden its importance in analyzing aspects of "nurture" at the same time as it increasingly discloses the inextricably bound interaction between nature and nurture (Hinde & Stevenson-Hinde, 1973; Seligman & Hager, 1972). Regarding those aspects of nurture that clearly are distinct from learning, such as the quantity and quality of nutrition that a society happens to make generally available or how a particular season's weather conditions affect animals suckling their young, the interaction is even more compelling.

In this context it is instructive to note that Piaget (1970) distinguishes clearly between the processes of development and learning. Development has to do with *general* mechanisms of action and of thinking; it pertains to intelligence in its widest and fullest sense. Everything that can be called characteristic of human intelligence comes about chiefly through the process of development as distinct from the process of learning. Learning deals with the acquisition of *specific* skills and facts and the memorizing of *specific* information. Piaget's theory states clearly that the general development of intelligence is the basis on which any specific learning rests. Learning can only take place on condition that the child has general mechanisms to which he or she can assimilate the information contained in learning. In this sense, intelligence is the most necessary instrument of learning. A child's learning of geographical names, for example, would be quite senseless if she or he did not have a general comprehension of spatial, historical, and social relations. Learning refers, then, to increases in the content of knowledge, and development refers to structural changes in previous knowledge (i.e., reorganization of understanding).

Developmental-learning research is related to the nature–nurture issue in another, perhaps more fundamental way. Examination of the developmental research literature concerning learning and changes in learning principles as a function of development indicates the frequent use of *attained age* of the organism as the dependent variable. It is obvious though that the variable "attained age" contains a confounding of maturational and experiential effects. Indeed, a key message of earlier discussions in this chapter has been that these effects cannot, as presently conceived, be separated. It is not possible, for example, at least in our present state of knowledge, to preclude learning for any extended period by any method that will not at the same time be suspected of affecting "normal" development.

What this means is that developmental research in learning is not quite what it may appear to be. If one discovers a need for different learning principles at several particular stages of human development, that is, when there appears to be evidence of ontogenetic discontinuity, then it is reasonable to suppose that the need for different learning principles depends on the occurrence of particular experiential factors during the critical period of development. Awareness of this point is quite apparent in, for example, Kendler and Kendler's influential article (1962), particularly in their discussion of the role of language. (In addition, see the contents of Chapter 6.)

The similar question in reverse (i.e., are developmental differences, as a function of differences in experience, due to a particular maturational change during the critical time?) can to some extent be satisfied by the use of control groups not subjected to the experiential variable (see the article by Held and Hein [22]), but the analogous control procedure in the initial case is more complicated. What is required is the experimental definition of a meaningful "baseline of experience," so that any discovered deviation from it could be used to assess the roles of different, more "natural" ways of achieving various "attained ages."

This difficulty in being able to manipulate the developmental age of an organism more in keeping with the classical meaning of "independent variable" (the experimental approach), rather than within bounds similar to those of the astronomer who manipulates relative positions of heavenly bodies by choosing observation places and times appropriately (the correlational approach), is obviously not restricted to developmental studies of learning (see Wohlwill [2]). Indeed, it actually is an alternative way of stating the nature–nurture problem: Neither nature nor nurture can correctly be treated as "pure" independent variables.

MOTIVATION AND REINFORCEMENT

Motivation is a topic largely concerned with the energizing and direction of behavior, but with other aspects as well. Deprived of food for several hours, a human or a rat, when offered it, will normally proceed to eat with noticeable gusto. To explain the eating and the gusto one can choose from among several approaches. One could posit a hunger instinct, which leads "naturally" to eating by a hungry organism. This approach is almost certainly an explanatory cul-de-sac, unless at the same time the instinct and its way of influencing the organism are quite clearly defined (and related to observable phenomena), because without this definition the "explanation" is neither verifiable nor refutable, and one's understanding is not noticeably increased.

A related, though perhaps more satisfactory approach involves positing the development of some noxious state within the organism as a consequence of deprivation; eating then reduces or eliminates the noxious state. One might suppose that the animal learns simply through trial and error that a particular noxious state is alleviated by food ingestion, and another by water ingestion, and so forth, thus largely avoiding the cul-de-sac of instinct. But as Lorenz (1965) and others point out, there still remains the problem of why alleviation of a noxious state is a basis for the learning, and this seems still to require an innate mechanism, though at a level much advanced from the primitive instinct view.

Numerous views have been offered (for a detailed review see Cofer & Appley, 1964) similar to the two examples above (instinct; alleviation of a noxious state posited by the *drive reduction* theory) to deal with consummatory behavior; that is, behavior that has nutritive or other known salutary biological effects. For eating and drinking, at least, the positing of internal energizing processes that are dependent upon an organism's tissue state seems quite reasonable. Indeed, it is consistent with considerable behavioral and physiological evidence. But although the different views on motivation have lacked agreement about a detailed explanation of even consummatory behavior (see, e.g., Nisbett, 1972; Schachter & Rodin, 1973), where they have seriously diverged is in approaches to another "class" of motivated behavior; that is, behavior that occurs in the absence of recognized salutary biological effects—behavior that appears to be motivated by its immediate sensory consequences. This class includes phenomena ranging from infants' pattern preferences (e.g., see Fantz, Ordy, & Udelf, 1962) to animal and human curiosity and exploratory behavior (see Berlyne, 1960, 1972), to human "thrill seeking."

At least three approaches have been taken in dealing with this class of motivational phenomena. One approach has seemingly entered the same cul-de-sac mentioned earlier by simply positing innate drives other than hunger and thirst, such as a curiosity drive, and exploratory drive, and so on. Only slightly more successful empirically, though formally more acceptable to many, is the view that all behaviors in this class depend upon acquired secondary motives, learned and maintained on the basis of known salutary biological effects (i.e., secondary drives derived from primary drives). A common model for this approach has been avoidance learning, wherein an organism learns to "fear" a formerly neutral stimulus after it has been paired with the onset of a painful electric shock (see Herrnstein, 1969; Rescorla & Solomon, 1967).

The third approach has involved, essentially, attempts to find a unifying principle for the "difficult," second class of motivational phenomena. Attempts at this by Berlyne (1965, 1966) and by Hunt (1960, 1965) are of particular relevance for developmental psychology. They reveal clearly how this major issue in motivation theory may well be centered on the nature–nurture controversy. Most theories of motivation have placed the entire answer in nature, in the homeostatic systems that have been developed through evolution, and which are "given" more or less full-blown to each newborn species member. Berlyne, and more explicitly Hunt, have distinguished between *extrinsic motivation* (based largely on known homeostatic biological systems) and *intrinsic motivation,* which is based on the particular organism's informational (experiential) interaction with its environment.

Intrinsic motivation is concerned with self-reinforcing activities. A discrepancy between the organism's coded or stored information (based on prior experience) and the stimulus inputs of the moment activates and directs the behavior of the organism. There is presumed to be some optimal level of discrepancy: If too large, anxiety and disorganization result; if too small, boredom may occur. Berlyne (1960, 1966) believes that intrinsic motivation is influenced by many internal and external factors, but is primarily elicited by what he calls *collative variables* (novelty, surprisingness, complexity, and incongruity of stimulus patterns), all involving conflict and evoking exploratory behavior. Hunt and Berlyne both suggest the term intrinsic motivation because it is inherent or intrinsic to information processing.

This approach thus embodies an attempt to incorporate into a theory of motivation the effects of "nurture," and to avoid the constraints of a monolithic theory based on evolutionarily defined salutary biological effects. It is an attempt to give systematic recognition both to compelling observations of developmental changes in what appears to motivate organisms, particularly humans, and to a rational argument that states that the motivational significance of certain variables will depend both upon the organism's previous experience and the effects of concomitant factors. Recognition of the complexity involved here is communicated by Hunt's choice of the term *epigenesis* (1960, 1965). (See definition of epigenesis, Chapter 1, p. 6). Similar recognition and related views appear in Festinger (1957) and Helson (1964) among others. The relationship between the extrinsic and intrinsic motivational system remains to be clarified.

Recent research and theory, especially on human hunger and obesity (Nisbett, 1972; Schachter, 1971; Schachter & Rodin, 1973), have had important implications for motivational development. Nisbett's review suggests the possibility that early eating experience may have permanent effects on one's later likelihood of "obesity." Schachter's work (see also Dember, 1974; Schachter, 1971) emphasizes the importance of cognitive factors in much motivated behavior. This latter emphasis on the informational, cognitive determinants of some motivated behavior, even involving hunger, thirst, and pain, may eventually clarify in developmental terms the relation between intrinsic and extrinsic motivation, and thereby make the intrinsic–extrinsic distinction obsolete.

There is no doubt at the empirical level that one finds both phylogenetic differences and ontogenetic changes in the determinants of motivated behavior. Perhaps, by more clearly taking account of the interactions of nature and nurture, we will advance our understanding of motivation through such explicit attempts to acknowledge these effects in our theories.

Central to discussions of learning and motivation is the concept of reinforcement (Bindra, 1970). Some discussions use "reinforcement" and "reward" as interchangeable terms, but a widely accepted usage identifies reinforcers simply as stimuli whose presentation, contingent upon the occurrence of a response, changes the probability of occurrence of that response. The enduring problem, having relevance both for learning and motivation, has been the question of what makes a reinforcer a reinforcer. For pellets of food given for bar-presses by a rat, the answer has seemed straightforward. Ingestion of food leads to hunger reduction, and thus at least some reinforcers are also rewards or drive reducers. If it is assumed that all reinforcers are primary-drive–relevant, then it is frequently necessary to posit new primary drives for otherwise enigmatic reinforcers (illumination changes, novel stimuli, and such), or else to conclude that the reinforcing value of the stimulus was acquired through association with drive-relevant reinforcers. This latter, secondary reinforcement explanation has, for example, been offered to account for the reinforcing capacity of the sight, smell, and taste of food (Osgood, 1953).

The importance of reinforcement to developmental psychology lies particularly in the fact that there are phylogenetic, ontogenetic, and cultural differences in the particular events that function empirically as reinforcers. In the first case, as an obvious kind of example, while Warren and Warren (1962) find that hay and pork kidneys reinforce learning for a horse and a raccoon respectively, the reverse would undoubtedly fail, as would either hay or pork kidney with most hungry children. Similarly, while a "pat on the head" may be successful in training a dog, access to damp earth would undoubtedly be more effective when the subject was an earthworm. Similar ontogenetic and cultural differences are particularly noticeable for the human species. Young children may respond to cuddles and candy; older children to television, rock music, and peer-group membership; and adults to coffee, cigarettes, and body-rub parlors. Research and theory systematically tracing and relating these highly predictable ontogenetic changes have yet to appear (cf. Denenberg, 1971; Mason, 1971; Scott, 1967).

Piaget (1952) stresses the role of intrinsic as against extrinsic motivation for development. He points to the fact that all children—rich and poor, of low and high IQ, in developed and undeveloped societies—grow in intelligence, at least between birth and twelve years of age. This uniform growth cannot be attributed merely to external situations. It is intrinsic to the human person, as are other human characteristics. "Intrinsic" here means what biologists call "characteristic" of a species. The human child responds to situations around him or her, but these situations are not to be considered entirely external, for they correspond to the child's internal mechanisms that develop eventually into adult intelligence. Far from saying that the child is under the control of external situations, it is more correct to say that the external situations are under the control of internal human mechanisms. The child has an internal "need to know" that causes him or her to seek out and select from the objects and events in the surrounding environment. In behavioral terms, the child provides her or his own schedule of intrinsic rewards and reinforcements.

PERCEPTION:
NATIVISM AND EMPIRICISM

Researchers in perception are basically concerned with how an organism achieves an organized "awareness" of its environment. Much discussion of perception proceeds from a basic distinction drawn between *distal stimuli* (the objects and events in the environment) and *proximal stimuli* (the patterns of energy produced by objects and events on the receptors). Thus, while the visual distal stimulus might be a chair, the proximal stimulus would usually be considered to be the two-dimensional energy patterns produced on the retinae when one looks at the chair. A frequent statement of this problem has involved asking how an organism usually manages to respond appropriately with respect to distal stimuli on the basis of proximal stimuli.

There have been two general attempts to resolve this problem. One theoretical position postulates the existence of *innate*, constructive mechanisms or capacities in the organism that automatically provide what may appear to be absent in the proximal stimulus (e.g., the three-dimensionality of a chair). The innate (nativistic) capacity might be in the form of specific (undiscovered) receptors, or in fixed neural connections within a receptor, or perhaps in characteristic patterns of stimulation of known receptors. Whatever the mechanisms might be, they would *inherently* convey such perceptual properties as depth, pain, visual brightness, and so on. The second theoretical position is expressed in the hypothesis that on the basis of experience in the environment an organism learns to construct the distal stimuli out of the proximal stimuli. These two positions, each of which has several variants, constitute the nativism–empiricism controversy, which has been the historic focal point for the development of theory and research in perception. In an incisive historical paper Hochberg (1962) has traced this controversy and its impact on research in perception.

Current studies of perceptual development still revolve around the basic issues posed by the nativist–empiricist controversy, and attempt to examine the problem of how both unlearned and learned processes develop and interact in perception.

It is obligatory for researchers who want to illuminate this problem to study young organisms, and there have been many ingenious solutions to the general methodological problem that originates with the nonverbal character of the subjects (see the article by Held and Hein [22] and Bower, 1974). Both ontogenetic and phylogenetic studies have been carried out, including the classic study by Walk and Gibson (1961) on the development of depth perception in a number of different species. Gibson (1969) and Pick and Pick (1970) have reviewed the extensive literature on perceptual development. Other recent research on perceptual development that bears upon the nativism–empiricism controversy includes Gibson [23], who distinguishes two types of perceptual activity: perception of space and events in space, a property that has biological adaptive significance and was probably "built in" to the central nervous system through genetic processes; and the perception of objects, which appears to be culturally adaptive rather than biologically adaptive, so that it presumably depends upon learning processes. Berry [24] offers evidence regarding the cultural influences on perception.

Hershenson (1971) suggests that there are four major conceptual alternatives with respect to perceptual development, and therefore it may be senseless to develop a general theory of perceptual development. These conceptual alternatives are:

1. *Maturation*. This viewpoint attempts to explain perceptual development as a function of genetic and environmental factors. Infants possess "the necessary organizational blueprints for using environmental information in the development of a perceptual system—time and the appropriate environment then are all that is necessary for the predetermined organization to be manifest" (Hershenson, 1971, p. 31).

2. *Construction*. According to this viewpoint, there are basic sensory elements which are present at birth, and these are then built up into the perceptual system. "The newborn's visual behavior would be determined primarily by the sensory input; the older infant would be able to integrate such input and therefore would enjoy a more flexible relationship with his environment" (Hershenson, 1971, p. 33).

3. *Learning and Differentiation*. Perceptual learning occurs in terms of the ability to make refined discriminations. It is not clear whether the learning occurs within the perceptual system (i.e., the actual percept is changed), within the memory system, or within the response system. In terms of perceptual development, "this model would start with a system which is capable of a few global discriminations and would then be able to progressively differentiate finer and finer gradations of stimulus structure" (Hershenson, 1971, p. 34). As a function of practice, the attention span increases over space and time.

4. *Adaptation*. Adaptation, like learning, implies perceptual changes as a function of time and experience. However, what distinguishes the adaptation viewpoint from the "construction" and learning viewpoints is in terms of the nature of the changes. The *construction system* and the *learning-modified system* retain their basic structures. The *adaptation system* is a self-monitoring system, which adjusts from a baseline in terms of noted present or immediately past stimulation. Adaptation theories are concerned with "changes *from* baseline rather than changes *in* baseline" (Hershenson, 1971, p. 35). The adaptation viewpoint suggests that although the perceptual system responds to experience (changes), there is no lasting effect. Hershenson (1971) states that "the very nature of the change itself suggests that the system is not simply altering structure in the same way it had been formed" (p. 35). "Adaptation involves changes in perception that could not occur if the system had been built up over many decades of learning or of construction" (Hershenson, 1971, p. 36).

In perceptual research, it is important to be aware of physiological and evolutionary phenomena, as well as psychological phenomena. Different models can account for different aspects of perceptual development.

Not all of the current work on perceptual development has a *direct* bearing on the nativism–empiricism controversy. See, for example, Mackworth and Bruner's [25] study of the different search strategies used by adults and children on a visual task.

LANGUAGE ACQUISITION

One of the central problems discussed in the recent literature on language development concerns the role of biological factors. There are two parts to this problem—one refers to the role of physiological maturation in the ontogenesis of language, and the other relates to the question of whether language is unique to humans. Lenneberg [26] offers a series of arguments in support of the view that language acquisition is dominated by biological maturation, and that language behavior is species-specific. This view comes under attack by Premack [27], who studied the development of a surrogate language system in chimpanzees. He does not argue that chimpanzees are capable of speech; however, he maintains that the cognitive capacities displayed by these chimpanzees are similar to those that support human language. Hockett and Altmann (1968) have carried out a contrastive analysis on the communicative systems of various species, including *homo sapiens,* in order to specify the similarities and differences across the systems. Thorpe (1972) has used the set of design features that was developed by Hockett and Altmann to attempt to characterize the communicative capabilities of the chimpanzees of Premack and also Gardner and Gardner (1969). Thorpe concludes his analysis by declaring that there is only one design feature (out of sixteen) that is unique to human language—"reflectiveness," or the ability to communicate about the communicative system itself.

One of the other critical issues in the study of language development concerns the nature of infant language. Typically, researchers start to study a child's language when the infant produces words that are of recognizable adult form; such studies usually begin during the infant's second year of life. Halliday (1975), however, has investigated the language development of one child, Nigel, from 10½ months onward. Prior to 10½ months Halliday had been able to study spontaneous vocalizations that Nigel used systematically to communicate his meanings. Usually the early messages related to his immediate needs. Halliday found that with very few exceptions, Nigel's "glossogenic" utterances owed nothing to the adult language, that is, they did not depend upon imitation.

An older behavioristic account of language learning (Mowrer, 1960) posits crucial roles for imitation and reinforcement in the child's acquisition of language. The use of imitation as an explanatory concept has diminished considerably over the years, as investigators have listened to young children's speech and recorded it without bias. It has become evident, given Halliday's data on a "preverbal" child and the common observation that children produce adultlike sequences that they could not have heard (e.g., "we wented" and "the childrens are here"), that imitation cannot be used to explain all of the child's language. In a general sense imitation must have a role in language development, for the child could not acquire language unless he or she had access to samples of the language to be learned (see Ryan, 1973, for an extended discussion of imitation and language development). What is the role of reinforcement in language acquisition? It seems not to have the significant role that Mowrer suggests, for, as Brown, Cazden, and Bellugi (1969) point out, even if the child were reinforced for grammatical statements and punished for nongrammatical statements, such parent behavior only provides the child with information on the acceptability of particular sentences. The fact that the child can generate novel sentences that have not been rewarded remains unexplained. The prevalence in children's speech of sentences that are both novel and deviant with respect to adult usage cannot be explained by the traditional learning theory approach. They can, however, be parsimoniously interpreted as being derived from the child's acquisition of a rule system; in other words they illustrate the child's implicit grammatical knowledge (see Toulmin, 1974, for a discussion of the notion of "rule" in language and other social behavior).

CONCEPTUAL DEVELOPMENT
AND INTELLIGENCE

To some extent research interest in intelligence has lessened in the past few years, while research on conceptual development has been increasing. This trend in intelligence research is related to: (1) increasing recognition of the immense complexity of what is included in the broad concept of intelligence, coupled with realization of the fruitlessness of strict operational definitions of intelligence; (2) the confining preconception of inherently "fixed" intelligence; and (3) an insufficient focus upon developmental processes. The complementary trend in research on conceptual development is related to: (1) an increasing concern with *process*, that is, how conceptual ability develops; and (2) the influence of Piaget.

One issue from the area of conceptual development, which generates a considerable amount of discussion, derives from Piaget's view [30] that the stages of conceptual development are invariant (see introduction to Chapter 10 for a discussion of these stages). His interpretation of the course of development is tied to a basic assumption about the nature of the developing behavior, namely that the unfolding of the stages depends partly upon maturational processes. The fact that the stages build dependently upon one another is not necessarily inconsistent with an epigenetic interpretation of conceptual development. This point of view stresses the quality of the environment as a significant determinant of the rate with which a child proceeds to go through the Piagetian stages. Some researchers have in fact given children training on some conceptual tasks in successful attempts to accelerate their transition from one developmental stage to another (Sigel, Roeper, & Hooper, 1966; see Toulmin, 1971, for an analysis of the concept of stages).

Conceptual development also bears a fundamental relation to language capacity, although the relational details are frequently disputed. According to Bruner (1964), language is an important determinant in concept formation, for it frees the child from perceptually dominant characteristics of his environment. With the acquisition of language, the child is no longer "stimulus bound."

Piaget (1974) views thinking as a self-regulating activity that begins before language and goes far beyond language. He does not deny any role for language in the development of thought, but implies that instead of language being the precursor of thought, thought itself is ontogenetically in advance of language and is a stimulus to its development. Piaget states that language can become a proper medium for challenging thinking and for further exploration. Language cannot take on this role, however, unless the child has "formal" mechanisms of thinking; that is, when he or she can theorize about possibilities and hypothetical situations and combine and keep in mind the meaning and interrelations of several hypotheses. Furth and Youniss [31] provide some support for this Piagetian assumption, that thinking and verbal language are relatively independent. Their results suggest that deaf adolescents perform differently from nondeaf adolescents on conceptual tasks, not because of their language deficit but primarily because of their generally restricted environment (see Blank, 1974, and Nelson [29] for extended discussion of contemporary analyses of the relations between language and thinking).

There are some signs of a revival of interest in research on intelligence, which have resulted in new models of intelligence, as well as some careful analyses of the many roles of the environment in the development of intelligence (see Chapter 11 for further discussion). The picture that emerges from these studies is one of a closer interest in intellectual processes than before. There is also increasing overlap now between the newer studies of intelligence and those of conceptual development, a sensible development, as they really constitute different strategies, or approaches, to the same questions.

PERSONALITY

There are several basic issues in personality, a prime one being that of definition. Sanford (1963) has suggested that adequate personality definitions must be concerned with elements or variables denoting individual differences; their methods of organization; the ways in which they endure or change over time; and the problem of the boundaries or limits of personality. Byrne (1974) believes that personality should be concerned with the variables or dimensions of individual differences and also with situational determinants of behavior. Endler (1975) and Endler and Magnusson (1974,

1975), taking an interactionist position, postulate that personality should be primarily concerned with person–situation interactions (see Chapter 12).

In spite of the problem posed for an adequate definition of personality, one can nonetheless successfully (but not necessarily accurately) *communicate* the essence of what is meant by personality. This can be done by describing the relatively characteristic, somewhat predictable ways of behaving by which we frequently identify, recognize, or describe other people, such as, "he is shy and reserved, but friendly"; "she is pretty conceited and a bit dull, but quite bright"; "he is angry and short-tempered, but frank and dependable"; "she is anxious and frightened, but is attractive and relates well to others." (For a discussion of sex differences, see Chapter 12, pp. 556–558. People use statements like these in day-to-day social relations not only to describe and predict but also to explain behavior of *other* people. This is typically the essence of what we mean by personality in discussing other people. Jones and Nisbett (1971) have suggested that when people describe the behavior of others, they do so in terms of consistent dispositional personality constructs. When they explain their own behavior, however, they emphasize situational factors. Schneider (1973) in a paper on implicit personality theory has questioned "whether traits are the most appropriate units of person cognition and whether perceivers see traits as distributed across situations well as stimulus persons" (p. 294).

Stability in Personality and Intelligence

One basic problem in the study of personality development is that the individual's "characteristic" ways of behaving may well undergo gradual changes. The question arises whether these changes are a result of maturational, social, or cultural influences and/or are a consequence of specific changes in situational factors. The introduction and some of the papers in Chapter 12 discuss a number of recent research approaches to questions of change and stability in personality characteristics. Bloom (1964) suggests that while personality stabilizes during the first five years of life, considerable variability can still occur during early and late adolescence. Studies by Stott (1957), Engel (1959), Kagan and Moss (1960, 1962), Moss and Kagan (1961), Block (1971), Kagan and Klein (1973), and Magnusson, Dunér, and Zetterblom (1975) have been concerned with the issue of stability in personality development (see Chapter 12). Although Block (1971), analyzing the personality data from the Bayley (1955) longitudinal study, found some evidence for stability, Kagan and Moss (1962) found that dependency shows no stability over time, and Kagan and Klein (1973) suggest that the evidence for long-term stability with respect to personality is very modest indeed. In general the empirical evidence (see Mischel, 1968, 1969, 1971; and Endler, 1973, 1975) indicates that "there are both significant longitudinal personality changes over time and cross-situational differences at any particular time" (Endler, 1973, p. 288). To some extent the questions of stability and change stem from the basic nature–nurture question; that is, to what extent are different personality characteristics or dimensions genetically determined, and can the lack of stability or evidence of change be attributed to nurture?

The issue of stability has also been the focal point for considerable theory and research dealing with intelligence. Bloom (1964, p. 88), in summarizing the data on the stability of intelligence test scores, suggests that "intelligence is a developing function and that the stability of measured intelligence increases with age." He goes on to say that "a single early measure of general intelligence cannot be the basis for a long-term decision about the individual" (p. 88). In discussing intellectual development, it is essential to be aware of the environmental context within which it occurs. Bayley (1955, 1968) presents evidence of nonconstancy and cites evidence from other experiments where large changes in IQ scores have been observed. Some investigators have concluded that the lack of constancy may be due to a lack of validity of the IQ tests. This may be because IQ tests measure different functions at different ages and because we have no way of predicting an individual's environmental encounters (Hunt, 1961). If intelligence is conceptualized as a phenotype, rather than a genotype, it would be difficult to predict at age two a child's IQ at age eighteen, unless one can specify the experiences that she or he will encounter.

Consistency versus Situational Specificity

Related to the issue of stability (or continuity) versus change is the more general issue of trans-situational consistency versus situational specificity. Mischel (1968, 1969, 1971) and Endler (1973) have indicated that with respect to noncognitive personality variables and social behavior there is very little evidence for trans-situational consistency. Mischel (1968) has provided empirical evidence for behavioral *specificity* for such personality and social variables as aggression, conformity, dependency, rigidity, and other traits. There is, however, some evidence for "cognitive and intellectual cross-situation consistency and stability over time" (Endler, 1973, p. 288). Nevertheless, Hunt [34] on the basis of empirical evidence, has questioned the belief in fixed intelligence. With respect to personality variables, validity coefficients typically range from .20 to .50 with a mean of .30.

Person-by-Situation Interactions

A factor with respect to stability and consistency that has been relatively ignored until recently concerns the importance of situational factors in personality (see Endler & Hunt, 1966, 1968, 1969; Magnusson, 1971). Related to this is the relative importance of persons (traits) and situations as determinants of behavior. Endler and Hunt (1966, 1969) and Endler (1973), using the trait of anxiousness, and testing subjects that varied with respect to age, social class, geographical location, and mental health, found that neither situation nor individual differences were the major source of behavioral variance: "Individual differences contribute on the average four to five percent of the total variance and situations only about four percent for males and about eight percent for females" (Endler, 1973, p. 290). Each of the simple interactions (persons by situations, persons by modes of response, and situations by modes of response) contribute about 10 percent. For anxiousness these proportions are highly stable across samples of subjects. With respect to the trait of hostility (Endler & Hunt, 1968), while the individual differences factor accounted for about 19 percent of the variance for males and about 15 percent for females (which is higher than for the trait of anxiousness), the sum of the three simple interactions accounted for about 30 percent of the variance. Endler (1966) found that situational factors were more important than individual differences as a source of conformity variance, but that interactions were the largest determinants of behavioral variance.

The relative influences of persons and situations have been examined for a number of other personality variables, including social perception and social behavior, honesty, leadership, aggression, choice behavior, self-ratings of feelings, and talking time. (For reviews of these studies see Bowers, 1973; Endler, 1973, 1975; Endler & Magnusson, 1974, 1975; Ekehammar, 1974). Basically, the results of all these studies lead to the same conclusion: Person-by-situation interactions are more important determinants of behavior than either persons or situations *per se*.

Whether persons or situations are more important for personality development is a pseudoissue. What is important is how persons and situations interact in determining behavior. Perhaps personality research should shift its focus from traits to person-by-situation interactions as the important constructs.

Much of the research on person-by-situation interactions has *not* focused on the developmental aspects. However, Lang (1966, p. 203), comparing eight-, nine- and ten-week-old infants' reactions to visual stimuli, found that "the proportion of variance accounted for by differences between stimuli increases with age." This has possible implications for personality development. Chess,

Thomas, and Birch [37] suggest that personality development is a function of the *interaction* of constitutional temperament factors and environmental influences. Future studies in personality should focus on *how* persons and students interact in *personality development*. Personality description can be improved by describing people in terms of the kinds of responses they manifest in various situations.

SOCIALIZATION

The theoretical issues with respect to socialization can be discussed in the broader context of the nature–nurture issue (see the papers in Chapters 12 and 13). At one extreme there is the *tabula rasa* position (environmentalism), and at the other extreme there is the position of *predeterminism* (constitutional and genetic factors). However, most contemporary investigators do not adhere to either of these extreme positions, but prefer an *interactionist* viewpoint. The Freudian theory of psychosexual development, which proposes that the forces for development are primarily within the organism, with the environment providing the medium within which socialization occurs, is an example of a predetermined model. Bandura and Walters' (1963) social learning theory is an example of a model that emphasizes environmental factors.

Although many modern studies of personality development adopt a social learning position, Mischel (1973) has recently proposed a model of personality development that has an interactional focus. Mischel suggests that social-cognitive person variables develop ontogenetically, in terms of a social learning process that interacts with genetic dispositions. Subsequently, these *person* variables (social cognitive) *interact* with *situations* (social factors) in determining behavior and personality development (see Chapter 13). Another example of an interactionistic model is Piaget's theory, discussed in Chapter 1 (pp. 5–6) and in Chapter 10 (pp. 442–444).

In addition to person-by-situation interactions, many studies in the field of socialization now focus on the dynamic interaction between children and adults (and/or their peers), and are concerned with both the relationship between childrearing practices and personality and also with the effects of children's personalities on childrearing practices. Bell [41] emphasizes that not only do parents have an effect on children, but also that children have an effect on parents and influence the parents' socializing practices. Chess, Thomas, and Birch [37] make much the same point. The suggestion is that there is a dynamic interaction or transaction between parents and children. Socialization is seen as a continuous process.

Overton and Reese (1973) have made an important distinction between the reactive organism (mechanistic) model of behavior and the active organism (organismic) model of behavior. The mechanistic model is concerned with an interdependency of determinants of behavior and environmental events (see Endler, 1975, regarding interaction and personality).

Since socialization (see McCandless, 1961, 1970) is to a large extent concerned with an acculturation process, whereby the child learns the values and behaviors prescribed and proscribed by his or her particular subculture, one can to some extent regard socialization as a special case of learning. To that end, the discussion on learning and development, earlier in this chapter, is relevant here. However, as one theorist (see Maccoby, 1961) has noted, studies of socialization involve variables in addition to those found in the usual studies of learning. Furthermore, cross-cultural studies on socialization may involve additional variables. (For an excellent methodological paper on cross-cultural studies, see Holtzman [44]).

With respect to socialization one can raise the questions as to whether the principles that are relevant for our culture are also relevant for other cultures, and whether the principles that are relevant for our species are also relevant for other species. Equally important are the questions as to whether the same socialization factors are involved at different stages of development, and whether the results of early social experience are irreversible. Finally, one can raise the issue as to whether there are any basic differences between the principles of socialization and the principles of learning. The reader should keep in mind these questions and the issues related in this chapter when reading the other chapters in this book.

SUMMARY TABLE
OF ISSUES AND ARTICLES

In this second chapter we have discussed some of the pertinent contemporary issues in developmental psychology. We hope that the student, in reading the introductions, commentaries, and articles (selections) that follow, will attempt to relate what she or he reads to the various issues presented here. Table 1 was designed to assist the reader in relating specific articles to particular issues. (Hopefully, the issues presented here will raise more questions than they answer!)

TABLE 1
Summary Table Relating Specific Articles to Issue Areas*

ISSUE AREAS	CHAPTER										
	Three	Four	Five	Six	Seven	Eight	Nine	Ten	Eleven	Twelve	Thirteen
Research Strategy	1–4	5, 7	10	16	18	24				37, 39	41, 42, 44
Nature-Nurture		5–7	10			22	26	30, 33	34	37	
Phylogeny, Ontogeny, and Culture		5	11, 12	13, 16	18	23, 24	27, 28		36	38, 39	43, 44
Early Experience and Learning	1	6	8–12	13–17	18–21	22, 23	28	30, 33	34	37, 39	42
Motivation and Reinforcement			8		18–21	22			34		41, 42
Perception	3		10	15	18, 19	22–25					
Intelligence, Concept Development, and Language	4			13, 16 17			26–29	30–33	34–36		
Personality		6	8, 9, 12						34	37–40	41–44
Stability	1, 4		8					30	34	37, 38	43, 44
Person-by-Situation Interactions	4							30, 33	34–36	37	41, 42
Socialization	1	6	8, 9, 12		19	24, 25			34–36	37–39	41–44

Numbers in each cell refer to article numbers.

References[1]

Ainsworth, M. D. The effects of maternal deprivation: A review of findings and controversy in the context of research strategy. In M. D. Ainsworth *et al., Deprivation of maternal care: A reassessment of its effects.*

[1]The references included here are those cited in this chapter, with the exclusion of those articles that have been reproduced in this volume.

New York: Shocken, 1966. (Also published by Geneva: World Health Organization, 1962. Public Health Papers No. 14, pp. 97–165.)

Ambrose, J. A. The comparative approach to early child development: The data of ethology. In E. Miller (Ed.), *Foundations of child psychiatry*. Oxford: Pergamon, 1968.

Anastasi, A. Heredity, environment, and the question "How?" *Psychological Review*, 1958, *65*, 197–208.

Anastasi, A. & Foley, J. P., Jr. A proposed re-orientation in the heredity–environment controversy. *Psychological Review*, 1948, *55*, 239–249.

Bandura, A. & Walters, R. H. *Social learning and personality development*. New York: Holt, Rinehart and Winston, 1963.

Bateson, P. P. G. The imprinting of birds. In S. A. Barnett (Ed.), *Ethology and development*. Philadelphia: Lippincott, 1973, pp. 1–15.

Bayley, N. On the growth of intelligence. *American Psychologist*, 1955, *10*, 805–818.

Bayley, N. Behavioral correlates of mental growth: Birth to thirty-six years. *American Psychologist*, 1968, *23*, 1–17.

Berlyne, D. E. *Conflict, arousal and curiosity*. New York: McGraw-Hill, 1960.

Berlyne, D. E. *Structure and direction in thinking*. New York: Wiley, 1965.

Berlyne, D. E. Curiosity and exploration. *Science*, 1966, *153*, 25–33.

Berlyne, D. E. Ends and means of experimental aesthetics. *Canadian Journal of Psychology*, 1972, *26*, 303–325.

Bindra, D. The interrelated mechanisms of reinforcement and motivation, and the nature of their influence on response. In W. J. Arnold & D. Levine (Eds.), *Nebraska Symposium on Motivation: 1969*. Lincoln: University of Nebraska Press, 1970.

Blank, M. Cognitive functions of language in the preschool years. *Developmental Psychology*, 1974, *10*, 229–245.

Block, J. *Lives through time*. Berkeley, Ca.: Bancroft, 1971.

Bloom, B. S. *Stability and change in human characteristics*. New York: Wiley, 1964.

Bower, T. G. R. *Development in infancy*. San Francisco: W. H. Freeman, 1974.

Bowers, K. S. Situationism in psychology: An analysis and a critique. *Psychological Review*, 1973, *80*, 309–336.

Bowlby, J. *Maternal care and mental health*. Geneva: World Health Organization, 1952.

Bowlby, J. *Attachment and loss. Vol. I: Attachment*. Harmondsworth, Middlesex, England: Penguin Books, 1971.

Bowlby, J., Ainsworth, M. D., Boston, M., & Rosenbluth, D. The effects of mother–child separation: A follow up study. *British Journal of Medical Psychology*, 1956, *29*, 211–247.

Brackbill, Y. Cumulative effects of continuous stimulation on arousal level in infants. *Child Development*, 1971, *42*, 17–26.

Brown, R., Cazden, C., & Bellugi, V. The child's grammar from I to III. In J. P. Hill (Ed.), *Minnesota symposium on child psychology*. Vol. 2. Minneapolis: University of Minnesota Press, 1969.

Bruner, J. S. The course of cognitive growth. *American Psychologist*, 1964, *19*, 1–15.

Byrne, D. *An introduction to personality: Research theory and application*. (2d Ed.) Englewood Cliffs, N.J.: Prentice-Hall, 1974.

Caldwell, B. M. The usefulness of the critical period hypothesis in the study of filiative behavior. *Merrill-Palmer Quarterly of Behavior and Development*, 1962, *8*, 229–242.

Cofer, C. N. & Appley, M. H. *Motivation: Theory and research*. New York: Wiley, 1964.

Dember, W. N. Motivation and the cognitive revolution. *American Psychologist*, 1974, *29*, 161–168.

Denenberg, V. H. The effects of early experience. In E. S. Hafez (Ed.), *The behavior of domestic animals*. London: Balliére, 1962.

Denenberg, V. H. The mother as motivator. In W. J. Arnold & M. M. Page (Eds.), *Nebraska Symposium on Motivation: 1970*. Lincoln: University of Nebraska Press, 1971.

Denenberg, V. H. & Morton, J. R. C. Effects of pre-weaning and post-weaning manipulations upon problem solving behavior. *Journal of Comparative and Physiological Psychology,* 1962, *55,* 1096–1098.

Ekehammar, B. Interactionism in personality from a historical perspective. *Psychological Bulletin,* 1974, *81,* 1026–1048.

Endler, N. S. Conformity as a function of different reinforcement schedules. *Journal of Personality and Social Psychology,* 1966, *4,* 175–180.

Endler, N. S. The person versus the situation: A pseudo issue? A response to Alker. *Journal of Personality,* 1973, *41,* 287–303.

Endler, N. S. The case for person–situation interactions. *Canadian Psychological Review,* 1975, *16,* 12–21.

Endler, N. S. & Hunt, J. McV. Sources of behavioral variances as measured by the S-R Inventory of Anxiousness. *Psychological Bulletin,* 1966, *65,* 336–346.

Endler, N. S. & Hunt, J. McV. S-R Inventories of Hostility and comparisons of the proportions of variance from persons, responses and situations for hostility and anxiousness. *Journal of Personality and Social Psychology,* 1968, *9,* 309–315.

Endler, N. S. & Hunt, J. McV. Generalizability of contributions from sources of variance in the S-R Inventories of Anxiousness. *Journal of Personality,* 1969, *37,* 1–24.

Endler, N. S. & Magnusson, D. Interactionism, trait psychology, psychodynamics and situationism. *Reports from the Psychological Laboratories.* University of Stockholm, 1974, No. 418.

Endler, N. S. & Magnusson, D. Personality and person by situation interactions. In N. S. Endler & D. Magnusson (Eds.), *Interactional Psychology and Personality.* Washington: Hemisphere Publications (Wiley), 1975, pp. 1–25.

Engel, M. S. The stability of the self-concept in adolescence. *Journal of Abnormal and Social Psychology,* 1959, *58,* 211–215.

Estes, W. K. *Learning theory and mental development.* New York: Academic Press, 1970.

Erikson, E. H. *Childhood and society.* (2d ed.) New York: Norton, 1963.

Fantz, R. L., Ordy, J. M., & Udelf, M. S. Maturation of pattern vision in infants during the first 6 months. *Journal of Comparative and Physiological Psychology,* 1962, *55,* 907–917.

Festinger, L. *A theory of cognitive dissonance.* New York: Harper & Row, 1957.

Fitzgerald, H. E. & Brackbill, Y. Tactile conditioning of an autonomic and somatic response in young infants. *Conditioned Reflex,* 1971, *6,* 41–51.

Fitzgerald, H. E. & Porges, S. W. A decade of infant conditioning and learning research. *Merrill-Palmer Quarterly of Behavior and Development,* 1971, *17,* 71–117.

Freud, S. The psychopathology of everyday life. In A. A. Brill (Trans. & ed.), *The basic writings of Sigmund Freud.* New York: Modern Library, 1938. *(Three Contributions to the Theory of Sex,* originally published, 1905.)

Gardner, B. T. & Gardner, R. A. Teaching sign language to a chimpanzee. *Science,* 1969, *165,* 664–672.

Gibson, E. J. *Principles of perceptual learning and development.* New York: Appleton, 1969.

Goldman, J. R. The effects of handling and shocking in infancy upon adult behavior in the albino rat. *Journal of Genetic Psychology,* 1964, *104,* 301–310.

Halliday, M. *Learning how to mean.* London: Edward Arnold, 1975.

Harvard Educational Review, 1969, *39,* pp. 1, 2.

Hebb, D. O. *The organization of behavior.* New York: Wiley, 1949.

Hebb, D. O. Heredity and environment in mammalian behavior. *British Journal of Animal Behavior,* 1953, *1,* 43–47.

Hebb, D. O. *A Textbook of Psychology.* (3d ed.) Philadelphia: Saunders, 1972.

Hebb, D. O. & Thompson, W. R. The social significance of animal studies. In G. Lindzey & E. Aronson (Eds.), *The handbook of social psychology. Vol. 2. (Rev. ed.)* Reading, Mass.: Addison-Wesley, 1968, pp. 729–774.

Helson, H. *Adaptation-level theory.* New York: Harper & Row, 1964.

Herrnstein, R. J. Method and theory in the study of avoidance. *Psychological Review,* 1969, *76*, 49–69.

Hershenson, M. The development of visual perception systems. In H. Moltz (Ed.), *The ontongeny of vertebrate behavior.* New York: Academic Press, 1971, pp. 29–56.

Hess, E. H. Imprinting in birds. *Science,* 1964, *146*, 1128–1139.

Hess, E. H. Imprinting in a natural laboratory. *Scientific American,* 1972, *227*, 24–31.

Hinde, R. A. & Stevenson-Hinde, J. (Eds.) *Constraints on learning: Limitations and predispositions.* London: Academic Press, 1973.

Hochberg, J. E. Nativism and empiricism in perception. In L. Postman (Ed.), *Psychology in the making.* New York: Knopf, 1962.

Hockett, C. F. & Altmann, S. A. A note on design features. In T. A. Sebeok (Ed.), *Animal communication.* Bloomington: Indiana University Press, 1968.

Hoffman, H. S. & Ratner, A. M. A reinforcement model of imprinting: Implications for socialization in monkeys and men. *Psychological Review,* 1973, *80*, 527–544.

Hoffman, H. S. & Solomon, R. L. An opponent-process theory of motivation: III. Some affective dynamics in imprinting. *Learning and Motivation,* 1974, *5*, 149–164.

Hunt, J. McV. Experience and the development of motivation: Some reinterpretations. *Child Development,* 1960, *31*, 489–504.

Hunt, J. McV. *Intelligence and experience.* New York: Ronald, 1961.

Hunt, J. McV. Intrinsic motivation and its role in psychological development. In D. Levine (Ed.), *Nebraska Symposium on Motivation: 1965.* Lincoln: University of Nebraska Press, 1965.

Inhelder, B. Some aspects of Piaget's genetic approach to cognition. In W. Kessen & C. Kuhlman (Eds.), Thought in the young child. *Monographs of the Society for Research in Child Development,* 1962, *27* (No. 2, Serial no. 83), pp. 19–34.

Jones, E. E. & Nisbett, R. E. *The actor and observer: Divergent perceptions of the causes of behavior.* New York: General Learning, 1971.

Kagan, J. & Klein, R. E. Cross-cultural perspectives on early development. *American Psychologist,* 1973, *28*, 947–961.

Kagan, J. & Moss, H. A. The stability of passive and dependent behavior from childhood through adulthood. *Child Development,* 1960, *31*, 577–591.

Kagan, J. & Moss, H. A. *Birth to maturity: A study in psychological development.* New York: Wiley, 1962.

Kaufman, C. Mother/infant relations in monkeys and humans: A reply to Professor Hinde. In N. J. White (Ed.), *Ethology and psychiatry.* Toronto: University of Toronto Press, 1974.

Kendler, H. H. & Kendler, T. S. Vertical and horizontal processes in problem solving. *Psychological Review,* 1962, *69*, 1–16.

King, J. A. Parameters relevant to determining the effects of early experience upon adult behavior of animals. *Psychological Bulletin,* 1958, *55*, 46–58.

Kohlberg, L. Moral and religious education and the public schools: A developmental view. In T. Sizer (Ed.), *Religion and public education.* Boston: Houghton Mifflin, 1967.

Lang, A. Perceptual behavior of 8- to 10-week old human infants. *Psychonomic Science,* 1966, *24*, 203–204.

Lehrman, D. S. Can psychiatrists use ethology? In N. J. White (Ed.), *Ethology and psychiatry.* Toronto: University of Toronto Press, 1974.

Levine, S. Stimulation in infancy. *Scientific American,* 1960, *202*, 80–86.

Levine, S., Chevalier, J. A., & Korchin, S. J. The effects of early shock and handling on later avoidance learning. *Journal of Personality,* 1956, *24*, 475–493.

Lorenz, K. Z. The companion in the bird's world. *Auk,* 1937, *54*, 245–273.

Lorenz, K. Z. *Evolution and modification of behavior.* Chicago: University of Chicago Press, 1965.

Maccoby, E., E. The choice of variables in the study of socialization. *Sociometry,* 1961, *24*, 357–371.

Mackintosh, N. J. *The psychology of animal learning.* London: Academic Press, 1974.

Magnusson, D. An analysis of situational dimensions. *Perceptual and Motor Skills,* 1971, *32*, 851–967.

Magnusson, D., Dunér, A., & Zetterblom, G. *Adjustment: A longitudinal study*. Stockholm: Almqvist & Wiksell. New York: Wiley, 1975.

Mason, W. A. Motivational factors in psychosocial development. In W. J. Arnold & M. M. Page (Eds.), *Nebraska Symposium on Motivation: 1970*. Lincoln: University of Nebraska Press, 1971.

McCandless, B. R. *Children and adolescents*. New York: Holt, Rinehart and Winston, 1961.

McCandless, B. R. Socialization. In H. W. Reese & L. P. Lipsett (Eds.), *Experimental child psychology*. New York: Academic Press, 1970, pp. 571–617.

McCandless, B. R. & Spiker, C. C. Experimental research in child psychology. *Child Development*, 1956, *27*, 75–80.

Mischel, W. *Personality and assessment*. New York: Wiley, 1968.

Mischel, W. Continuity and change in personality. *American Psychologist*, 1969, *24*, 1012–1018.

Mischel, W. *Introduction to personality*. New York: Holt, Rinehart and Winston, 1971.

Mischel, W. Towards a cognitive social learning reconceptualization of personality. *Psychological Review*, 1973, *80*, 252–283.

Moltz, H. Imprinting: Empirical basis and theoretical significance. *Psychological Bulletin*, 1960, *57*, 291–314.

Moltz, H. (Ed.) *The ontogeny of vertebrate behavior*. New York: Academic Press, 1971.

Moss, H. A. & Kagan, J. Stability of achievement and recognition seeking behaviors from early childhood through adulthood. *Journal of Abnormal and Social Psychology*, 1961, *62*, 504–518.

Mowrer, D. H. *Learning theory and the symbolic processes*. New York: Wiley, 1960.

Nisbett, R. E. Hunger, obesity and the ventromedial hypothalamus. *Psychological Review*, 1972, *79*, 433–453.

Orlansky, H. Infant care and personality. *Psychological Bulletin*, 1949, *46*, 1–48.

Osgood, C. E. *Method and theory in experimental psychology*. New York: Oxford, 1953.

Overton, W. F. & Reese, H. W. Models of development: Methodological implications. In J. R. Nesselroade & H. W. Reese (Eds.), *Life-span developmental psychology: Methodological issues*. New York: Academic Press, 1973, pp. 65–86.

Piaget, J. *The psychology of intelligence*. New York: Harcourt, 1950.

Piaget, J. *The origins of intelligence in children*. New York: International Universities, 1952.

Piaget, J. Piaget's theory. In P. H. Mussen (Ed.), *Carmichael's manual of child psychology*. (3d ed.) New York: Wiley, 1970, pp. 703–732.

Piaget, J. *The child and reality: Problems of genetic psychology*. New York: Viking, 1974.

Pick, H. L., Jr. & Pick, A. D. Sensory and perceptual development. In P. H. Mussen (Ed.), *Carmichael's manual of child psychology*. (3d ed.) New York: Wiley, 1970, pp. 722–847.

Rescorla, R. A. & Solomon, R. L. Two-process learning theory: Relationships between Pavlovian conditioning and instrumental learning. *Psychological Review*, 1967, *74*, 151–182.

Restle, F. *Learning: Animal behavior and human cognition*. New York: McGraw-Hill, 1975.

Rosenblatt, J. S. Social-environmental factors affecting reproduction and offspring in infrahuman mammals. In S. A. Richardson & A. J. Guttmacher (Eds.), *Childbearing: Its social and psychological aspects*. Baltimore: Williams & Wilkins, 1967, pp. 245–301.

Rosenzweig, M. R. Environmental complexity, cerebral change and behavior. *American Psychologist*, 1966, *21*, 321–332.

Rutter, M. *Maternal deprivation reassessed*. Harmondsworth, Middlesex, England: Penguin Books, 1972.

Ryan, J. Interpretation and imitation in early language development. In R. A. Hinde & J. Stevenson-Hinde (Eds.), *Constraints on learning*. New York: Academic Press, 1973, pp. 427–443.

Salama, A. A. & Hunt, J. McV. "Fixation" in the rat as a function of infantile shocking, handling and gentling. *Journal of Genetic Psychology*, 1964, *105*, 131–162.

Sanford, N. Personality: Its place in psychology. In S. Koch (Ed.), *Psychology a study of a science. Vol. 5:*

The process areas, the person and some applied fields: Their place in psychology and science. New York: McGraw-Hill, 1963, pp. 488–592.

Schachter, S. Some extraordinary facts about obese humans and rats. *American Psychologist,* 1971, *26,* 129–144.

Schachter, S. & Rodin, J. *Obese humans and rats.* Washington, D.C.: Winston, 1973.

Schneider, D. J. Implicit personality theory: A review. *Psychological Bulletin,* 1973, *79,* 294–309.

Schneirla, T. C. Behavioral development and comparative psychology. *Quarterly Review of Biology,* 1966, *41,* 283–302.

Scott, J. P. Critical periods in behavioral development. *Science,* 1962, *138,* 949–958.

Scott, J. P. The development of social motivation. In D. Levine (Ed.), *Nebraska Symposium on Motivation: 1967.* Lincoln: University of Nebraska Press, 1967.

Seligman, M. E. P. & Hager, J. L. (Eds.) *Biological boundaries of learning.* New York: Appleton, 1972.

Sigel, I. E., Roeper, A., & Hooper, F. H. A training procedure for the acquisition of Piaget's conservation of quantity. *British Journal of Educational Psychology,* 1966, *36,* 301–311.

Skinner, B. F. The phylogeny and ontogeny of behavior. *Science,* 1966, *153,* 1205–1213.

Stevenson, H. W. *Children's learning.* New York: Appleton, 1972.

Stott, L. H. The persisting effects of early family experience upon personality development. *Merrill-Palmer Quarterly of Behavior and Development,* 1957, *3,* 145–159.

Thorpe, W. H. The comparison of vocal communication in animals and man. In R. A. Hinde (Ed.), *Non-verbal communication.* Cambridge: Cambridge University Press, 1972, pp. 27–28.

Toulmin, S. E. The concept of "stages" in psychological development. In T. Mischel (ed.), *Cognitive development and epistemology.* New York: Academic Press, 1971, pp. 25–60.

Toulmin, S. E. Rules and their relevance for understanding human behavior. In T. Mischel (Ed.), *Understanding other persons.* Oxford: Basil Blackwell, 1974, pp. 185–215.

Walk, R. D. & Gibson, E. J. A comparative and analytical study of visual depth perception. *Psychological Monographs,* 1961, *76* (Whole No. 519).

Warren, J. M. & Warren, H. B. Reversal learning by horse and raccoon. *Journal of Genetic Psychology,* 1962, *100,* 215–222.

Webb, W. B. The choice of the problem. *American Psychologist,* 1961, *16,* 223–227.

White, B. L. Child development research: An edifice without a foundation. *Merrill-Palmer Quarterly of Behavior and Development,* 1969, *15,* 49–79.

White, B. L. *Human infants: Experience and psychological development.* Englewood Cliffs, N.J.: Prentice-Hall, 1971.

White, S. The learning theory approach. In P. H. Mussen (Ed.), *Carmichael's manual of child psychology.* (3d ed.) New York: Wiley, 1970, pp. 657–701.

Chapter 3

METHOD
AND
THEORY

INTRODUCTION AND COMMENTARY

If one wishes to know the psychologists' methods in studying the development of organisms and to become informed as to the theories, aims, and biases that guide the concoction and use of these methods, surely one place to start is the writings of these psychologists. Toward that end, the reader can make a good beginning by reading Chapters 4 through 13 of this volume. However, it is more difficult to abstract from this reading valid generalizations about methods, points of view, and changes in such. These typically are not communicated in research reports, largely for the reason of limited page space in most scientific journals. Thus there is value in some separate discussion of methods and theory at the outset or perhaps, at the end of a diet of current papers on developmental psychology. It can indicate something of the context in which the other papers have developed, and/or the influence of some of the papers on change in that context (see also Nesselroade & Reese, 1973). Portions of Chapters 1 and 2 (see particularly the section on research strategy in Chapter 2, pp. 11–13), together with the comments in this introduction and the four papers reprinted in this chapter, constitute this sort of discussion.

Scientific Method and Psychology

The essence of scientific method is systematic observation made under specifiable conditions. The precision with which conditions can meaningfully be specified may usefully be considered to define a *hypothetical* dimension. Within what is commonly called scientific observation, this dimension ranges from naturalistic observation, in which an attempt is made to describe the conditions that happen to prevail at the time observations are made, to the most precise experimental observation, in which the scientist completely defines, produces, and controls the conditions under which observations are to be made.

The position(s) of psychology on this hypothetical dimension is frequently debated not only with respect to where psychology should be to achieve the goals of a science of behavior and mental life, but also with respect to where it can be if it is to be a science of important behavior. Different science areas may be located at different positions along this hypothetical dimension, and may shift toward greater precision as the science matures. Similarly, research in different areas of developmental psychology may permit different levels of precision and, in addition, may be maturing at different rates.

Methods of Developmental Psychology

Examination of the research literature of developmental psychology since about 1950 reveals a clearly increasing incidence of experimental methodology, an increase both in the quantity of research devoted to understanding development and in the ingenuity with which difficult problems are brought under experimental investigation.

At the same time, some argue, naturalistic observation, which in the past was often pursued by default when topics appeared refractory to experimental study, increasingly receives attention as a methodology necessary for full understanding of behavior. The similarity is more than superficial between some of the attitudes expressed in support of naturalistic research methods and by ethologists.

Perusal of trends in theory over that same period from about 1950 shows, particularly in the past 10 or 15 years, at least two fairly clear trends or signs of continuing change. One of these takes the form of an increasing acknowledgment of the status of humans as evolved members of an animal kingdom, but more recently a "kingdom" in which surviving species can more appropriately be considered to be related like the leaves of a complex tree than like the hierarchical rungs of a long ladder (see, e.g., Hodos & Campbell, 1969). The second trend appears to arise despite, or perhaps because of, the first—which in part emphasizes the relative uniqueness of all surviving species. Theories increasingly give status to *cognitive* factors in deriving understanding of human action. Cognitive factors are, of course, intrinsically human.

Commentaries

The articles reprinted in this section, Chapter 3, represent only some of these trends in method and theory. Regarding experimental ingenuity, nearly all other sections of this collection contain some excellent examples; articles [7, 19, and 33] explicitly draw attention to human evolutionary status or to assumptions based on it, while several articles in other sections reveal facets of the "cognitive revolution" (Dember, 1974).

Our overriding criteria for inclusion of an article in this section are that it be a paper relevant to developmental psychology and that it primarily deal with contemporary issues of method and/or theory. The trends mentioned above are variously revealed in these articles. Indeed, a fruitful activity for the student will be to read the articles especially with an eye to the many symptoms of these trends in all four articles.

In the first, Bijou [1] discusses five issues that he considers must be dealt with for developmental psychology to fulfill its promise as a fundamental and burgeoning branch of psychology. Two of the issues concern the relations (1) between general psychology and developmental psychology, and (2) between the psychology of learning and of development. Within developmental psychology Bijou sees as three remaining key issues the questions: (3) What criteria are to be used in defining developmental stages? (4) What most usefully might be meant by the longitudinal method? and (5) Is there a best approach to problems of applied developmental psychology? While Bijou conceives and discusses these issues from the point of view of, perhaps, an "immoderate" empiricist, citing Kantor (1959) and Skinner (1963) as intellectual background, most of his points are of broad significance. Furthermore, the reader will recognize some of the issues when they are raised again in subsequent articles. Thus Bijou's paper also constitutes a helpful context, especially regarding Wohlwill [2] and Willems [3].

The second paper, Wohlwill's [2], is narrower in scope and more difficult. In it is presented a major theme of Wohlwill's recent book (1973). The core of this theme is that the study of development does not (cannot) involve age or time as an independent variable, despite the fact that considerable research by developmental psychologists concerns examining this or that "as a *function* of age." One consequence of Wohlwill's point of view is that developmentalists should do research to support conclusions of the sort "under certain conditions one group grows *faster* than the other," in preference to conclusions of the sort "one group is taller than the other." This emphasis on developmental *functions* entails incorporating age into the dependent variable, letting developmental functions themselves be the dependent measures with respect to which the influence of independent variables is evaluated.

A recent reviewer (McCall, 1974, p. 674) predicted that Wohlwill's views "could provoke a renaissance in developmental research strategy." The reader can try to evaluate that prediction at the same time as he looks for similarities in some of the views expressed by Wohlwill [2] and by Bijou [1].

We have noted the increase in amount and sophistication of experimental research in developmental psychology. This, as pointed out by McCandless and Spiker (1956), is essential to the development of fruitful theory. One thing experimentation inevitably entails though is some constraint by the experimenter on conditions under which systematic observation takes place. Therefore, at least to some extent, experimentation delimits what *can* happen in the situation. Furthermore, this is but a part of the more general observer problem of the interaction between the observer and the observed. Not only is it possible that some behavioral events be unwittingly prevented by the observer's controls or actions, but also that other events may go "unobserved" due to constraints imposed by particular dependent measures. These concerns are taken up in some length in the Willems [3] paper, which is both a reasoned discussion of the meaning and merits of naturalistic observation, and a clear portrayal of ideas at the core of *ecological psychology* (see Barker, 1968).

Not only is it possible for the scientist's observation procedure itself to alter that which is being observed, but also for his or her point of view about a problem to influence, among other things, how observed behavior is conceptualized. The final paper, by Kagan [4], in this chapter bears on this problem. Kagan's discussion exemplifies the changing point of view identified with the so-called cognitive revolution. In addition, Kagan's concept of "relativism" itself appears to be a constructive constituent of that revolution, because it crystallizes effectively what has long been a concern of cognitive theorists, namely, the need to define somehow independent variables in terms of characteristics relative to the organism involved and its situation.

Finally, the reader is referred to an article by Kessen (1963), which, though not new, remains topical. From examination of a variety of research results, Kessen discusses research on infant development and endeavors to identify changing points of view about infants. Probably the key message of this article is the author's conviction that although investigators continue to have points of view and theories, their research reveals increased willingness to doubt these preconceptions.

Kessen's generalizations as to new perspectives regarding the human infant reflect, for the most part, changes from viewing the infant as a passive vessel that reacts to environmental stimulation, toward viewing her or him as an active organism that interacts with its environment. The reader will be able to relate this directly to portions of Kagan's paper [4]. Kessen's discussion also reveals something of how interactions between data and theory can lead to new, more clearly defined questions.

References

Barker, R. G. *Ecological psychology: Concepts and methods for studying the environment of human behavior.* Stanford University Press, 1968.

Dember, W. N. Motivation and the cognitive revolution. *American Psychologist,* 1974, *29,* 161–168.

Hodos, W. & Campbell, C. B. G. Scala Naturae: Why there is no theory in comparative psychology. *Psychological Review,* 1969, 76, 337–350.

Kantor, J. R. *Interbehavioral psychology.* (2d ed.) Bloomington, Ind.: Principia Press, 1959.

Kessen, W. Research in the psychological development of infants: An overview. *Merrill-Palmer Quarterly of Behavior and Development*, 1963, *9*, 83–94.

McCall, R. B. Review of *The study of behavioral development* by J. F. Wohlwill. *Science*, 1974, *184*, 673–674.

McCandless, B. R. & Spiker, C. C. Experimental research in child psychology. *Child Development*, 1956, *27*, 75–80.

Nesselroade, J. R. & Reese, H. R. (Eds.) *Life-span developmental psychology: Methodological issues.* New York: Academic Press, 1973.

Skinner, B. F. Behaviorism at fifty. *Science*, 1963, *140*, 951–958.

Wohlwill, J. F. *The study of behavioral development.* New York: Academic Press, 1973.

1. AGES, STAGES, AND THE NATURALIZATION OF HUMAN DEVELOPMENT

SIDNEY W. BIJOU

Currently, developmental psychology is expanding at a greater rate than any other branch of psychology. It is being incorporated into small departments of psychology and expanded in large ones; it is attracting first-rate graduate students; it is increasing its ranks with well-trained, eager young men and women; and it is being generously subsidized. Such acceleration will probably continue; confidence in the potentialities of a scientific study of human development is at a high peak. For one thing, the public is convinced that research in human development will ameliorate, in a substantial way, many of the pressing problems of child rearing, early education, and behavioral remediation.

How long will this favorable situation continue? It is difficult to say. However, the answer in large measure will be contingent upon the nature of what is produced. On one hand, confidence can be expected to remain high, if after a reasonable period the productions clearly advance basic knowledge of the historical-

From the *American Psychologist*, 1968, *23*, 419–427. Copyright 1968 by the American Psychological Association. Reprinted by permission of the author and the publisher.

developmental component of psychological events in the form of the concepts and principles they generate and if they establish new guidelines to applied problems in the form of demonstrated empirical relationships. On the other hand, confidence can be expected to wane, if the field continues to yield products which are peripheral to general psychological theory and offers practical solutions which turn out to be fads, gimmicks, and verbal prescriptions with only captivating face validities.

I am convinced that future productions will "live up" to the promise made, and, in many instances, surpass them, but I am not convinced that they will be achieved with reasonable dispatch. The time of initial delivery could be so extended that our supporters, professional and lay alike, would surely become discouraged. I am not saying that I expect the large augmentation of manpower and facilities to produce immediate and spectacular advancements, for I am in agreement with Leonard Ross (1966) that developmental problems are intricate; good research strategy and design come slowly with experience; data-gathering procedures in long-range studies are particularly time-consuming; and interpretations which advance theory require deliberation, discussion, and successive reformulations. My misgivings are based on the possibility of prolonged delay because of preoccupation with formulations based on tenuous assumptions and misconceptions. If this turns out to be the case, it will be a pity for all of us.

In the hope of forestalling this possibility or of accelarating its demise, I have selected for discussions five issues I believe could be the heart of much misdirected effort. I shall indicate the nature of these problems, their assumptions, and offer some reevaluations.

I realize it is folly to discuses any five issues in the time allotted. Yet I have chosen to do so because I believe that these five are equally important. It is my hope that by at least touching on all five issues, this presentation will stimulate further and broader discussion than if I had restricted myself to two or three.

Two of the issues are external—problems concerning general intersystematic relationships: (a) the relationship between general psychology and developmental psychology and (b) the relationship between the psychology of learning and the psychology of development.

The other three are internal—problems concerning relationships within developmental psychology: (a) the criteria of developmental stages, (b) the concept of the longitudinal method, and (c) the relationship between developmental psychology and applied child research.

Relationship between General Psychology and Developmental Psychology

In order to deal with the first general intersystematic issue—the relationship between general psychology and developmental psychology—I must discuss the philosophy of science inherent in a natural science approach (e.g., Kantor, 1959; Skinner, 1963) and describe what I believe general psychology is, should be, or should become. From this approach psychology is perceived as a division of the scientific enterprise which specializes in the study of the interactions between a total functioning organism and observable environmental events. Psychological events involve stimulus and response functions which evolve from the genetic endowment of the individual, the current situation, and the interactional history. This point of view has much in common with others in postulating that psychological events have these three components. However, it differs sharply with other viewpoints in the way these components are observed, conceptualized, and interrelated in the form of empirical laws. With respect to interactional history, for example, past events are conceptualized as past events. They are not transformed into hypothetical constructs.

From this point of view, developmental psychology is related to general psychology as the specialized branch concerned with the historical aspects of psychological events. One might say that developmental psychology is the study of progressive changes in interactions between a biologically changing organism (maturing and aging) and sequential changes in environmental events through a series of life periods (Bijou & Baer, 1961). Such a description of the field assumes that events and concepts of psychological development stretch in a line of successive intervals and bears on the second major concern of the field—analysis of psychological events within developmental stages.

Let me compare briefly developmental psychology, so conceived, with some of the other subdivisions of psychology. Developmental psychology is not like physiological or social psychology. These branches concentrate on a class of stimulus variables in psychological events. It is not like psychophysics or experimental psychology, since they are tied to a method of investigation. Developmental psychology is most like comparative psychology, which concentrates on similarities and differences in interactions within and between species. In fact, many, including Werner (1948), have referred to developmental psychology as a comparative psychology of individual development and have pointed out the overlapping interests of both fields. For example, both branches are interested in the development of different species under similar circumstances, and in the same species under different circumstances (cultures).

I turn now to a brief consideration of developmental psychology in light of the characteristics which constitute a strong subsystem, a strong subsystem in the sense of one which will undoubtedly survive in the future evolution of general psychology.

A substantial subsystem is concerned with problems that affect the entire discipline. Because it specializes in problems which bear on all analyses, it can contribute to the postulates of general theory. In the case of developmental psychology, the postulates relate to the nature of stages and their subdivisions, and the interaction of past and current events in the determination of behavior change.

The other characteristic of an essential subsystem is that it centers on an investigative approach. In developmental psychology, it is, of course, the longitudinal method. As we all know, the field has been greatly concerned with the nature of the longitudinal method and its role in developmental research. Such issues are still very much alive. At the 18th International Congress of Psychology Zazzo (1966) chaired a symposium entitled, "Diversity, Reality, and Fiction of the Longitudinal Method," in which, as is apparent from the title, he and the members of the panel sought to evaluate the approach. In his introductory remarks Zazzo stated: "The longitudinal approach as a universal method is an illusion which originates from this archaic belief that observation must blend with the observed reality." The concept of the longitudinal method is, indeed, one of the critical issues of developmental psychology and one which I shall discuss separately.

Relationship between the Psychology of Learning and the Psychology of Development

The second general systematic issue—the relationship between the psychology of learning and the psychology of development could perhaps have been included in the discussion of the subdivisions of psychology. But because I believe that this relationship deserves special attention, I have treated it as a separate topic. Some developmental psychologists believe that learning and development are the same and that eventually learning will account for all of psychology. Others claim that learning can deal adequately with a limited segment of development, and important problems of the field must be treated from a cognitive or psychoanalytic point of view.

The postulates of a natural science approach are at odds with both these contentions. The natural science approach insists that learning is a part of development and that the other components of developmental analysis which are not learning can also be treated adequately within this framework (Skinner, 1953, 1961). An examination of the similarities and differences between learning and development may help elaborate this thesis.

You will recall that I described development as that branch of psychology concerned with delineating lawful relationships, in progressive changes in the interactions between a physiologically changing organism and environmental events. Such changes, it was said, involve the genetic endowment of the individual, present circumstances, and historical interactions. I would like to add that "present circumstances" are analyzed as stimulus and response functions, setting events, and mediating factors (Kantor, 1959).

Now to the meaning of learning—this is difficult, not because it is a complex construct, but because it has many and varied meanings. First, let me say what learning, from a natural science point of view, is not. Learning is certainly not a causal condition. The statement that a class of behavior occurs in high frequency because of previous learning is worthless, since such a statement does not refer to specific events. We are no further ahead in an analysis of psychological events when we say, "Little Jimmy tells lies because he has learned to do so," than we are when we say, "Little Jimmy tells lies because he is 5 years old." Learning is not a hypothetical construct, conceptual or physiological; it does not, by definition, refer to observable conditions. Learning is not a change in performance, since such a definition stresses unduly the response aspect of a psychological event and is too inclusive. Learning events most certainly involve changes in behavior, but so do nonlearning events. What is left? Learning can, with good reason, refer to experiments and theory on the relationships in the strengthening and weakening of stimulus and response functions. As such, it would be a generic term which would include behavior changes under antecedent stimulus control or respondent conditioning, as well as behavior under consequent stimulus control or operant conditioning. In my opinion the science of human behavior has advanced to the point at which the term "learning" has become obsolete, except as it may be used to designate an area of psychology which specializes in an analysis, under contrived conditions, of the variables that strengthen and weaken stimulus and response functions.

On the basis of this distinction, the developmental psychologist and the learning psychologist can be discriminated from one another by the problems and the variables each studies. The developmentalist is concerned with *all* the conditions that contribute to developmental changes in behavior; the learning psychologist is concerned with the strengthening and weakening of stimulus and response functions. Zigler (1963) has suggested that the learning investigator is the one who will probably make the most significant future contributions to development. If this turns out to be the case, and I believe it will, I would contend that Zigler made an accurate prediction not because the learning investigator was well informed about learning theory, but because he was well trained in research methodology.

Criteria of Developmental Stages

So much for the two external problems of developmental psychology. I turn now to the first major internal problem—the criteria of developmental stages.

As was pointed out, one of the contributions that developmental psychology can offer psychology as a whole is a set of concepts of developmental stages that integrate readily with the general field. One could ask: "How are we progressing in this task?" Much has been written about stages, and many psychologists, as well as poets, novelists, and philosophers, have had their say as to the number of developmental stages and their general characteristics. Among psychologists, the number has ranged widely, but the criteria for each have been limited to three: (*a*) time since birth, or age; (*b*) hypothetical constructs, in combination with actual or assumed environmental events; and (*c*) empirical constructs, based on biological, physical, and social interactions. I shall review each briefly.

Time Since Birth, or Age, as a Criterion for Stages

Time since birth, or age, as the criterion for developmental stages has, of course, been most closely associated with Gesell and his coworkers. It is interesting to note, in passing, that although Gesell created many hypothetical variables (e.g., Gesell, 1954), he did not use them as criteria for establishing stages. As has been said many times over, this is not a variable but a dimension for recording events. Time as a gross indicator of physiological maturation, or of cumulative interactions with the environment, or both, does nothing to advance a functional analysis of behavior and development. In an empirically oriented cause-and-effect system physiological changes and interactions with the environment must be specified so that they can be evaluated by experimental procedures. If research demonstrates that the specific conditions do play a part in determining change in behavior, further research is required to delineate their parametric characteristics. A system of psychology using time as a causal variable can only describe interresponse relationships, can only describe behavior as a function of a conglomeration of unanalyzed conditions—biological, physical, and social. Most of us recognize this, yet now and then we find lapses in the literature. Behavior is attributed to an age or stage, and a birthday is given magical qualities. There are, for example, educational films called: "The Terrible Two's and the Trusting Three's" and "Frustrating Four's and Fascinating Five's."

Normative accounts of development can contribute to a functional analysis of development by pointing out recurring patterns of behavior and thereby suggesting experimental study of the independent variables. Many psychologists perform experiments that explore the conditions under which a phenomenon occurs.

The final point I wish to make about time is this: To say that time is inadequate as a criterion for stages does not mean that time cannot be a serviceable variable in a functional system for other purposes. However, its use requires a demonstration of a high correlation between time and some cycle—feeding, sleeping, etc. With this technique one should keep in mind that the ultimate relationship involved is between biological events and the changes in the behavior observed.

Hypothetical Constructs, in Combination with Actual or Assumed Environmental Events, as Criteria for Stages

The practice of using hypothetical constructs as criteria for stages, which is becoming increasingly prevalent, is typical of the cognitive and psychoanalytic approaches of Piaget and Erikson. Although each theorist makes different assumptions and concentrates on different aspects of development, the logic of each is the same: Behavior at a given stage is "explained" in terms of the current situation and the properties of the hypothetical constructs. The latter are innate but modifiable, within certain ranges, by experience. A serious objection to this practice is not that the theories proposed apply to only a segment of development, but that hypothetical constructs are mixed with a loosely defined set of concepts and principles because there should be something "mental" that grows and develops the way the biological components grow and develop, and the way the behavior patterns are elaborated and extended.

And after mental constructs are inserted into a system of determining conditions, research is said to be needed which separates the mental terms from the other. Thus Piaget (1966) has said:

> The comparative studies in the field of genetic psychology are indispensible for psychology in general and also for sociology, because only such studies allow us to separate the effects of biological or mental factors from those of social and cultural influences on the formation and the socialization of individuals [p. 3].

To accept hypothetical constructs as criteria for stages is to put stress on evaluating hypothetical terms and relationships. Hence we find a host of studies concerned with whether certain behaviors do, in fact, occur at a particular stage as claimed and, if so, whether their onset can be modified. Preoccupation with hypothetical "growth" variables could have adverse effects on the field of developmental psychology, first, because it discourages researchers from taking a good hard look at all the possible circumstances (not merely those claimed to be important in determining stages) which may affect behavior; second, because it deemphasizes the current need to develop, through experimental procedures, new methods of quantifying behavioral and environmental variables.

To emphasize the need to establish stages on hypothetical constructs is to misunderstand where the science of development is in its evolutionary history. I believe that the field of developmental psychology is now in transition from a behavioral-descriptive phase to a functional-analytic period. We are just beginning to see efforts devoted to the analysis of behavioral-environmental relationships and the formulations of functional laws. If this is so, there are too few serviceable empirical laws, as of now, to attempt to integrate them into more general concepts and laws by means of hypothetical terms. The speed with which we reach this advanced stage of theory building will depend, in part, on the rapidity with which we resolve some of the problems discussed here.

I cannot leave this topic without this final note. Whether we are considering the feasibility of hypothetical constructs as criteria for developmental stages or evaluating some other theoretical aspects of developmental psychology, I believe with Zigler (1963) that the field does not any longer need the grand theoretical designs proposed by Piaget, Freud, Erikson, Gesell, and Werner.

Biological, Physical, and Social Interactions as Criteria for Stages

We turn now to the third and last approach to conceptualizing developmental stages, that of basing criteria on empirically defined biological, physical, and social interactions. One example of this approach, long advocated by J. R. Kantor, in fact, as long ago as 1924, segments the stream of development into three gross periods, each with several subdivisions. The first stage—the universal stage of infancy (Bijou & Baer, 1965)—is conceived of as the period which extends from birth to the onset of functional verbal behavior. It is the period in which psychological and biological behaviors are closely related, and, in a sense, the latter imposes restrictions and limitations on the former. It is also the period of the initial elaboration of respondent and operant behaviors (Lipsitt & Kaye, 1964; Siqueland & Lipsitt, 1966) and the period of initial evolution of ecological or exploratory behavior, a form of operant behavior (Rheingold, Stanley, & Cooley, 1962). The second stage—the basic stage—extends to early childhood and is characterized as the first period free from gross biological limitations. Here interactions with particular people and things become central and prevalent, and the child has an opportunity to build up response equipment that characterizes him as a particular individual. Although the interactions acquired and maintained during this period are basic to the child's behavioral make-up, they are amenable to changes when significant environmental alterations occur (Harris, Wolf, & Baer, 1964; Kantor, 1959).

The third stage—the societal stage—is the interval from early childhood to the end of the developmental cycle. It is thought of as the interval saturated with intimate interpersonal and group conditions. Behaviors developed during this period "mark the individual as a member of a large number of cultural communities whose behavior he has evolved in shared performances with other members [Kantor, 1959, p. 168]." Included in this period are the substages of late childhood, adolescence, maturity, and advanced age.

The criteria suggested in this approach are, of course, open to successive revisions as indicated by data. Hence future research along the lines of empirically constructed stages would be expected to refine the descriptions and transitions and to point to further subdivisions. Such research would also be expected to accelerate the formulation of empirical laws with increasingly longer chains within and between developmental periods. From a systematic point of view, such statements are urgently needed.

The Concept of the Longitudinal Method of Investigation

It is obvious to all that developmental psychology has long been intimately associated with the longitudinal method. Some have argued that studies which do not use the longitudinal methods are not developmental. With the same logic, they have claimed that experimental studies can deal with the cross-sectional problems. I contend that these conceptions of the longitudinal method and developmental psychology are far too limited. Because the longitudinal method has been closely associated with the field of development from its inception, it has come to mean for many a procedure for describing sequential changes in the behavior of individuals and groups over long periods. (See, for example, Kagan's 1964 review of American longitudinal research on psychological development.) The longitudinal method can continue to refer to procedures yielding behavioral-descriptive accounts, or, hopefully, it can become a term to mean procedures for producing data on long-range interactions between a biologically changing organism and sequential environmental events. If it remains the former, the longitudinal method can have only limited use in the future work of developmental psychology; if it is modified to mean the latter, it can retain its role as the central methodology of the area. As indicated previously, I make this statement on the assumption that this field, along with others in psychology, is in the evolutionary stage of moving out of a behavioral description period and into a functional analytic phase.

To delineate functional relationships, data from many methods are required, but the emphasis must be on the experimental method. Drawing inferences about past events from reactions at the time of investigation (e.g., from responses to interviews and questionnaires) or from correlations serves only limited purposes. There is no substitute for experimental research which construct segments of history. It should be acceptable to all that the longitudinal method, like the cross-sectional method, can involve descriptive, correlational, and experimental procedures. Which procedure is used in a study depends on the objective of the study, the training and boldness of the investigator, and the situation in which the study is conducted.

Experimental longitudinal studies, like experimental cross-sectional investigations, have in the past been performed in the laboratory, field, or some combination of both. Well-known examples include Dennis' (1941) study with fraternal twins who were restricted in social stimulation and limited in motor activities during a 14-month period, Gesell and Thompson's (1929) study on the effects of training on stair climbing and cube building in twins, Watson and Rayner's (1920) study on the experimental development of reactions to aversive stimulation in a young child, McGraw's (1935) long-range study on the effects of special stimulation with fraternal twin boys, and Hilgard's (1932) group study with preschool children on the effects of academic training on achievement.

Within the past 5 years there has been a resurgence of interest in the application of the experimental method accompanied by revisions and extensions in techniques. Examples are the field studies on changes in social behavior in preschool children by Harris et al. (1964) and the laboratory studies in concept formation by Bijou (1965) and Sidman and Stoddard (1966).

A final note on the longitudinal method. In 1965 Wohlwill chaired a Society for Research in Child Development symposium entitled "Approaches to Experimental-Developmental Research in Child Psychology." Kendler, Gollin, and Bijou in the same symposium addressed themselves to the question: "How does the experimental child psychologist handle developmental changes that occur with respect to the phenomenon he is interested in?" Wohlwill concluded the discussions by saying he thought future progress in the field can profit from a two-pronged pragmatic attack.

One phase would follow closely along the lines of the strategies of Tracy Kendler and Eugene Gollin, the aim being to specify as incisively as possible the nature of the developmental processes which are operating to produce the age differences observed for some particular aspect of behavior. The second phase would carry the ball from there, designing experiments and manipulating variables whose effects are theoretically derivable from the specification of the developmental processes achieved in phase one. In order to enhance the developmental significance of such research, these effects might be measured, not simply in terms of acquisition curves, error rates or the like, but rather in terms of variables directly relating to the developmental changes, such as rate of change, asymptotic level, stability, situational generality, etc.

With this conclusion I am only in partial agreement. I believe that a one-pronged attack will suffice, a belief that is substantiated by the current work in several child laboratories.

Relationship between Developmental Psychology and the Applied Areas of Child Rearing, Education, and Remediation

The third and final internal problem in developmental psychology pertains to the relationship between developmental psychology and the applied areas of child rearing, education, and remediation. There should be nothing special about this relationship. It should be the same as that which exists between any basic and applied science—a relationship of research and development. To the question: "How well have we been doing in research and development?" the answer is uncomplicated: "Not well!"

Child developmentalists have always been responsive to practical problems. I merely echo the words of Baldwin and others when I say that in the early days of the institutes of child development great efforts were devoted to research on applied problems before there were principles to apply. In general, problems were analyzed either on a "common sense" basis or in terms of a variation of psychoanalytic theory. Recent history has shown that neither procedure has been fruitful. The common sense approach has not led to new procedures for dealing with recurrent problems, since it attempted merely to objectify the conditions that seemed to be involved and to apply statistical tests of significance. I say "attempted merely to objectify" because many of the quantifying procedures employed, such as questionnaires, structured interviews, projective techniques, and interpreted observations, produced data that were far removed from descriptions of actual interactions. In many instances, admittedly inferior quantification methods were used to study a practical problem "as it existed." Research which attempted to arrive at practical recommendations through the testing of psychoanalytic theory fared no better, not only because of the use of similar methods of measurement and research design, but because,

in addition, the concepts and principles tested were elusive.

So, as we all know, reviews by Vincent (1951), Stendler (1950), Senn (1957), and Wolfenstein (1953) indicated that recommendations presumably evolved from such studies carried the tenor of the era in which they were conducted. There was strong suspicion that the recommendations were based more on opinion than fact. Lest you think this reference applies only to research in the remote past, I recommend that you read the conclusions of 8 of the 10 chapters in Volume 1 of Hoffman and Hoffman's *Review of Child Development Research* published in 1964. For example, Caldwell's review of the effects of infant care ends with 10 conclusions. Her first, third, fifth, seventh, and ninth topic sentences, taken as samples, read as follows: (1) "The breast-bottle dilemma must remain exactly that [p. 73]." (3) "Studies concerned with oral gratification and oral activities provide little support for the hypothesis that sustained gratification leads to drive satiation [p. 80]." (5) "The relationship between parent attitudes and parent behavior is still insufficiently explored and imperfectly understood [p. 80]." (7) "The number of variables in which investigators have shown interest is small indeed [p. 81]." (9) "It is imperative that there be a general improvement of methodology in studies concerned with the effects of infant care [p. 81]."

One thing seems sure: There is not much promise in applied research which aims to determine whether treatment method A is better than treatment method B or to test the validity of some aspect of a vaguely defined personality theory. To repudiate both strategies is not to sound a retreat from applied research until we have at hand a large stock-pile of basic principles. There is an alternate constructive course: Apply known basic principles and do this in a way that the data would indicate, in a continuous manner, the effectiveness of our efforts at application.

I believe that we should approach the problems of technological research in developmental psychology with modesty and optimism. After all, the specific skills of the good mother, teacher, counselor, and therapist have preceded the developmental psychologist's application of known empirical laws. Recognizing this, we can go about the task of technological development in the hope that our efforts will catch up with the practices of the practitioners and will eventually lead to revisions in the handling of old problems and to new ways of dealing with new ones. Our optimism need not rest only in the promise of improving practical problems. Genuine technological research, especially programs with a functional-analytical orientation, will also enrich basic research.

Summary

Developmental psychology is expanding rapidly and is widely supported. Continuous growth of the field is believed to be dependent on the way the five issues discussed here will be resolved. Two of these problems concern external systematic issues.

The Relationship between General Psychology and Developmental Psychology. From a natural science orientation developmental psychology is viewed as a branch of general psychology which abstracts from general analysis that segment concerned with the influence of near and remote historical events on current interactions. It is concerned with behavior changes within stages and with the influence of interactions between stages. Since practically all psychological events have historical components, developmental psychology has much to contribute to general psychology and, in my opinion, will always remain an integral yet specialized part of the science of behavior.

The Relationship between Psychological Development and Psychology of Learning. The view that the psychology of learning and development are the same, except that the latter is concerned with changes over longer periods, is categorically rejected. Psychological development is believed to be concerned with progressive changes in interaction, the psychology of learning with changes in stimulus-response and response-stimulus relationships in contrived situations. The functional relationship between stimuli and responses plays a central role in any analysis of interaction between a biologically evolving and devolving organism and changing environmental events.

The three additional issues pertain to the following internal systematic problems:

The Problem of Criteria for Developmental Stages. This issue rests largely on what is believed to be a promising way of formulating criteria. Time and hypothetical constructs in combination with empirical constructs are rejected as criteria in favor of empirical constructs.

The Concept of the Longitudinal Method. The study of changes in organism–environment interaction over long-range periods, which is the heart of developmental psychology, should not be limited to methods that yield only descriptive accounts of behavior. Methods providing data which bear directly on cause-and-effect relationships must also be included. Research has already demonstrated its feasibility.

The Relationship between Developmental Psychology and the Applied Fields of Child-rearing, Education, and Remediation. It is reaffirmed that the relationship between the basic and applied developmental psychology should be one of research and development. For the most part, applied research in the past has not been of this sort. Rather, it has been theory testing, treatment-methods testing, and correlational analyses. Since efforts along these lines have not been fruitful, it is suggested that applied research turn toward applying currently known empirical principles generated from laboratory studies. It is argued that the functional analytic approach is particularly suited to engage in technological research because of its insistence on functional terms and principles. A genuine research and development program holds promise of demonstrating improvements in child developmental practices; it can also supply valuable ideas for basic research.

REFERENCES

Bijou, S. W. Systematic instruction in the attainment of right-left form concepts in young and retarded children. In J. G. Holland & B. F. Skinner (Eds.), *An analysis of the behavioral processes involved in self-instruction with teaching machines.* Research Report, Grant No. 7-31-0370-051.3, United States Office of Education, Department of Health, Education and Welfare, 1965.

Bijou, S. W., & Baer, D. M. *Child development: A systematic and empirical theory.* Vol. 1. New York: Appleton-Century-Crofts, 1961.

Bijou, S. W., & Baer, D. M. *Child development: The universal stage of infancy.* Vol. 2. New York: Appleton-Century-Crofts, 1965.

Dennis, W. Infant development under conditions of restricted practice and of minimum social stimulation. *Genetic Psychology Monographs,* 1941, *23*, 143–189.

Gesell, A. The ontogenesis of infant behavior. In L. Carmichael (Ed.), *Manual of child psychology.* (2nd ed.) New York: Wiley, 1954.

Gesell, A., & Thompson, H. Learning and growth in identical infant twins: An experimental study by the method of co-twin control. *Genetic Psychology Monographs,* 1929, *6*, 1–124.

Harris, F. R., Wolf, M. M., & Baer, D. M. Effects of adult social reinforcement on child behavior. *Young Children,* 1964, *20*, 8–17.

Hilgard, J. R. Learning and maturation in preschool children. *Journal of Genetic Psychology,* 1932, *41*, 40–53.

Hoffman, M. L., & Hoffman, L. W. *Review of child development research.* Vol. 1. New York: Russell Sage Foundation, 1964.

Kagan, J. American longitudinal research in psychological development. *Child Development,* 1964, *35*, 1–32.

Kantor, J. R. *Principles of psychology.* Vol. 1. Bloomington, Ind.: Principia Press, 1924.

Kantor, J. R. *Interbehavioral psychology.* (2nd ed.) Bloomington, Ind.: Principia Press, 1959.

Kendler, T., Gollin, E., & Bijou, S. W. How does the experimental psychologist handle developmental changes that occur with respect to the phenomenon he is interested in? In F. J. Wohlwill (Chm.), Approaches to experimental-developmental research in child psychology. Symposium presented at the meeting of the Society for Research in Child Development, Minneapolis, March 1965.

Lipsett, L. P., & Kaye, H. Conditioned sucking in the human newborn. *Psychonomic Science.* *1964, 1*, 29–30.

McGraw, M. B. *The growth: A study of Johnny and Jimmy.* New York: Appleton-Century, 1935.

Piaget, J. Nécessité et signification des recherches comparatives en psychologie génétique. *International Journal of Psychology,* 1966, *1*, 3–13.

Ross, L. E. Classical conditioning and discrimination learning research with the mentally retarded. *International Review of Research in Mental Retardation,* 1966, *1*, 21–54.

Rheingold, H. L., Stanley, W. C., & Cooley, J. A. Method for studying exploratory behavior in infants. *Science,* 1962, *136*, 1054–1055.

Senn, M. J. E. Fads and facts as the basis of child-care practices. *Children,* 1957, *4*, 43–47.

Sidman, M., & Stoddard, L. T. Programing perception and learning for retarded children. *International Review of Research in Mental Retardation,* 1966, *2*, 152–208.

Siqueland, E. R., & Lipsett, L. P. Conditioned head-turning in human newborns. *Journal of Experimental Child Psychology,* 1966, *3*, 356–376.

Skinner, B. F. *Science and human behavior.* New York: Macmillan, 1953.

Skinner, B. F. *Cumulative record* (Rev. ed.) New York: Appleton-Century-Crofts, 1961.

Skinner, B. F. Behaviorism at fifty. *Science,* 1963, *140*, 951–958.

Stendler, C. B. Sixty years of child rearing practices. *Journal of Pediatrics*, 1950, *36*, 122–134.

Vincent, C. E. Trends in infant care ideas. *Child Development*, 1951, *22*, 199–209.

Watson, J. F., & Rayner, R. A. Conditioned emotional reactions. *Journal of Experimental Psychology*, 1920, *3*, 1–4.

Werner, H. *Comparative psychology of mental development*. (Rev. ed.) Chicago: Follett, 1948.

Wohlwill, F. J. (Chm.) Approaches to experimental-developmental research in child psychology. Symposium presented at the meeting of the Society for Research in Child Development, Minneapolis, March 1965.

Wolfenstein, M. Trends in infant care. *American Journal of Orthopsychiatry*, 1953, *23*, 120–130.

Zazzo, R. Introductory report to the symposium on longitudinal studies. In R. Zazzo (Chm.), Diversity, reality and fiction of the longitudinal method. Symposium presented at the 18th International Congress of Psychology, Moscow, September 1966. (Études longitudinales du développement psychologique de l'enfant. *Enfant*, 1967, *2*, 131–136.)

Zigler, E. Metatheoretical issues in developmental psychology. In M. H. Marx (Ed.), *Theories in contemporary psychology*. New York: Macmillan, 1963.

2. THE AGE VARIABLE IN PSYCHOLOGICAL RESEARCH[1]

JOACHIM F. WOHLWILL

This paper examines the treatment of the age variable in the conception, design, and interpretation of developmental research. The dissatisfaction with the status of age as a concept and its use in research is attributed to the widespread tendency to consider age as an independent variable, comparable to others employed in differential research, and to study age *differences* rather than age *changes*. An alternative view is presented, which treats developmental questions as analogous to other phenomena involving changes in behavior over time. It is suggested that age be incorporated into the *dependent* variable in developmental studies, by defining the latter in terms of specified aspects or parameters of the function describing the changes which occur over age for a given behavioral variable. Implications of this view for developmental research are brought out, with particular reference to problems of description and quantitative analysis of developmental change, to the application of the experimental method in developmental research, and to the study of individual differences in the context of developmental change.

The chronological age of the individual has generally represented one of the most popular independent variables used in child development research and is included with some frequency even in research of a general experimental nature. Indeed, in spite of widespread dissatisfaction with research based on the Behavior = f (Age) paradigm, there seems little question that age, like sex, is here to stay. For the psychologist, age shares with sex the attraction of its great visibility as a dimension of individual variation in behavior, one which is

[1]This paper was written while the author was a Visiting Research Fellow at Educational Testing Service, Princeton, New Jersey, and with the aid of a Faculty Research Fellowship from the Social Science Research Council. Valuable criticisms, suggestions, and questions have been contributed by various individuals at different phases of its preparation; the author is particularly indebted to Walter Emmerich for stimulating ideas and helpful comments.

From the *Psychological Review*, 1970, *77*, 49–64. Copyright 1970 by the American Psychological Association. Reprinted by permission of the author and the publisher.

not only readily measurable but accounts for a substantial portion of variance in a variety of behavioral measures.

Considering the popularity of this variable in psychological research, there has been a notable reluctance on the part of psychologists to examine the question of scientific method, inference, and theory which arise when differences in behavior are related to age. One important exception in this regard is to be found in Kessen's (1960) thoughtful discussion of the place of statements about developmental change in psychology and of the problems of control, research design, and interpretation which such statements create. Birren (1959) has contributed a similarly valuable discussion of the role of this variable in the study of aging. Yet neither of these authors has come to grips with the particular character of the age variable as a dimension along which temporal *changes* in behavior are charted, and the implications of this fact for questions of scientific interest and research design which arise in the use of this variable.

It is the intent of this paper to suggest a reformulation of the place which the age variable occupies in behavioral research, which should meet the major criticisms that have been advanced against it and thus assuage those who have felt uneasy in its use. Once the case for such a reformulation has been presented and argued, it will be applied to an examination of selected questions of design and methodology in developmental research, to indicate something of its scope and to bring out some of the ways in which its adoption would lead to a rethinking of such issues as the place of descriptive research in developmental psychology, the appropriate forms of quantitative analysis, the conception and design of experimental studies of developmental processes, and the place of individual differences in developmental research.[2]

[2]A more comprehensive treatment of questions of methodology in developmental research, from the perspective of the role of age presented in this paper, will be found in a companion paper prepared for a recent Conference on Life-Span Developmental Psychology (Wohlwill, 1970).

Status of Age as a Variable

Dissatisfaction with research based on the paradigm, Behavior $= f$ (Age), has typically been based on the purely descriptive character of such statements, and the failure of research conforming to it to isolate the particular variables which actually determine or mediate the variation of behavior with age (cf. Bijou & Baer, 1963; Kessen, 1960). For the same reason much of developmental theorizing, built on nonexperimental research of this type, has been regarded as suspect (Zigler, 1963). Age, it is asserted, is at best a shorthand for the set of variables acting over time, most typically identified with experiential events or conditions, which are in a direct functional relationship with observed developmental changes in behavior; at worst it is merely a cloak for our ignorance in this regard.

As one way out of this predicament, some psychologists, notably those of the Skinnerian persuasion, such as Bijou and Baer (1963) and Staats and Staats (1963), have tried to circumvent the use of age altogether and to attempt to program developmental changes directly by subjecting the individual to appropriate histories of reinforcement. However successful these attempts may have been, they necessarily have dealt with narrowly delimited responses, elicited under highly specific conditions of stimulus exposure, reinforcement schedules, etc. Few outside of the Skinnerian camp would argue that this represents a viable approach to developmental problems in general. For in many areas, notably in the domain of perceptual and cognitive development, uniform changes with age occur under much too diversified a set of conditions of experience to permit the isolation of any specific factors determining these changes.

If we probe more deeply into the reasons for the uneasiness which is generally felt in using age as a main variable in psychological research, and the Skinnerians' insistence on replacing it by specifying particular determinants of developmental change, we find that they can be traced to the assimilation of the study of age differences to the model of differential research. In the usual study involving the comparison of age groups, age does indeed seem to play the role of an independent variable analogous to that of such variables as sex, IQ, socioeconomic differences, etc., which the differential psychologist has traditionally employed. This analogy is, as shall be seen, a specious one, but it accounts for the fact that the objections most commonly raised against the use of age are those which experimentalists have leveled at the differential model of research generally, that is, at those studies in which differences in behavior are related to differences in the composition or characteristics of preselected samples—objections relating to the uncertainties of causal inference, of separating out the role of the presumed independent variable from others that may be operating, etc. (Cronbach, 1957).

Yet this way of looking at the role of the age variable ignores a critical point: When an investigator compares, for instance, a group of 6-year-old and a group of 10-year-old children, he is in fact interested in studying the *changes* in behavior occurring over this age period; that is, he assumes that the 6-year-olds would come to perform as did the 10-year-olds, if he had been patient enough to wait four years to retest them. This assumption is valid, of course, only to the extent that the two age groups can be considered equivalent in respects other than age, and in particular that there are no *cohort* differences between them, that is, differences in the populations of individuals born 6 as opposed to 10 years ago. Such cohort differences would constitute a true differential variable, and the importance of teasing out their possible role in developmental studies has been persuasively argued by some psychologists (Baltes, 1968; Schaie, 1965, 1967). Yet recognition of the potentially contaminating role of cohort differences in developmental studies only serves to bring out more sharply the difference between age as a dimension of intraindividual change and such other, purely differential variables.

In order to see more clearly the implications of this emphasis on the study of behavior change, let us compare the study of age differences with that of interspecies differences.

Although ontogenetic and phylogenetic differences have on occasion been treated as analogous or closely similar, there is one major methodological difference between them. Unlike age changes, the evolutionary changes which underlie phylogenetic differences cannot be observed as they are occurring; nor can they be directly inferred from cross-sectional comparisons of the species currently in existence, since these are the product of the action of evolutionary forces which have been modifying the species within any given branch of the phylogenetic tree (cf. Simpson, 1958). It is only the developmental psychologist's inclination to opt for the cross-sectional shortcut rather than studying change directly, which has tended to obscure this important difference, and has allowed the study of developmental changes to become identified with differential types of problems.

Age as Part of the Dependent Variable in Studies of Developmental Change

Rather than treating age as an independent variable comparable to other dimensions of intraindividual variation, a very different way of conceptualizing it may be suggested, which accords to it a status equivalent to that which the time variable occupies in other fields, such as the experimental study of adaptation, learning and forgetting. Let us view age simply as a dimension along which the behavior changes which are the concern of the developmentalist are to be studied, that is, it is incorporated into the definition of the *dependent* variable of interest to him. Thus, to the extent that the investigator confines himself to charting such changes within a Behavior $= f$ (Age) paradigm, he is only *describing* a set of phenomena which are the subject of study for him. This is by no means to deprecate the role of such research—indeed, as will be argued presently, descriptive research of this kind, precisely because it deals with behavior change, occupies a far more important place than it does in other areas of behavioral investigation. Nevertheless it remains descriptive, and statements to the effect that behavior ''is a function of age'' are accordingly to be avoided, since they do not really involve functional relationship between a determining and a determined variable.

True functional relationships, for the developmental psychologist, would entail relating specified attributes of the age changes themselves to particular independent variables, whether experimentally manipulated by the investigator, or studied *in natura*. Thus, the interest might be in comparing motor development in normal and institutionalized infants, as in the work of Dennis (1960): Here the dependent variable could be defined as the age of onset of walking, or some other specified behavior which is typically subject to developmental change. Similarly, the *rate* of increase in vocabulary might be compared for twins as compared to singletons: The dependent variable would then be the rate of change in vocabulary size, or conceivably even the function describing this change in relation to age, considered in terms of specified parameters such as period of maximal growth, inflection points, asymptotal level, etc.

The first of the two examples just mentioned brings up a revealing point, namely, that in this, as in any developmental study, it is possible in principle to differentiate two individuals (or groups) either in terms of the difference in (mean) level of attainment on the behavioral dimension at a given age, or alternatively, in terms of the difference in the age at which some given level or type of behavior is attained. For instance, if we say that Individual A obtains a score X on an achievement test which exceeds Individual B's score Y by d units, an alternate way of expressing this difference is that A is accelerated relative to B, that is, it will take B some amount of time t to attain the same value X (assuming that A and B are in process of development with respect to the dimension in question).

This interchangeability between age and response magnitude on the dependent side itself represents a powerful argument for incorporating age into the definition of the dependent variable. It presupposes, however, that we are dealing with a dimension of behavior with respect to which any individual can be expected to exhibit consistent changes over the course of his development. Speaking more generally, the approach to the handling of age which is being proposed is applicable only to the extent that we are dealing with behavioral variables for which the general course of development (considered in terms of direction, form, sequence, etc.) remains invariant over a broad range of particular environmental conditions or circumstances, as well as genetic characteristics. Physical growth provides an obvious example: individuals grow taller, regardless of whether they are brought up on a diet of milk, cereal and beef, or rice and potato soup, provided they grow in a growth-sustaining environment, and possess the physiological equipment required for growth (e.g., a normally functioning pituitary gland).

Can we find similar cases in the realm of behavioral development? Most assuredly, notably in such areas as perceptual, cognitive, and linguistic development. Take, for instance, the growth of depth perception in the child, which develops apace, whether his environment is that of an urban slum or of the Kansas wheatfields, provided that he has exposure to some minimal amount of visual stimulation, and the visual apparatus and neural equipment necessary to transmit and make use of this sensory information (cf. Wohlwill, 1966, for a somewhat more extended presentation of this argument for the nonspecificity of experience). This does not mean that the particular environmental conditions may not influence the rate, terminal level, etc., of development for the variable in question; only that no specific one constitutes a *necessary* condition for the occurrence of the developmental changes. While this nonspecificity does not preclude the possibility that eventually prerequisites for development will be found of a much higher order of generality—equivalent to the role of vitamins in growth, or of patterned stimulation in perception—it makes it possible to enunciate broadly generalizable statements concerning the chracteristic form of developmental changes for a given aspect of behavior, without reference to particular determining variables.

Given, then, a variable that is developmental,

that is, for which changes with age are found which are uniform and consistent across a wide range of individuals and environmental conditions, in the sense just mentioned, it becomes profitable to approach the study of age changes in the manner which has been outlined above. More specifically, we can define the task of the developmental psychologist as one of describing these changes, of determining the structural relationships and temporal patterning of changes among sets of such variables, and of specifying functional relationships between particular situational, experiential, or organismic variables and selected parameters or attributes of these changes.

What behavioral variables qualify as developmental in this sense? Some have already been mentioned in the illustrations given, for example, speech and motor development, or space perception. Others could be cited from the field of the development of perceptual and cognitive skills, possibly curiosity and related variables, and perhaps even certain aspects of social perception and interaction, and emotional development. Variables, on the other hand, which show consistent age changes *only* for individuals subjected to specific experiences, such as swimming skill, reading or writing ability, or other responses acquired through directed teaching, differential reinforcement, or exercise would not qualify as developmental; neither would those which represent dimensions of emergent individual differences rather than of directional developmental change, such as aggressiveness, attention seeking, and the like.[3]

[3]This distinction appears so similar to that which McGraw (1946) proposed between "phylogenetic" and "ontogenetic" behaviors, that a clarification is in order, lest this discussion become falsely assimilated to the maturation-learning question. The present developmental dimensions are not conceived to be independent of environmental influences, as McGraw's phyletic skills are; only the occurrence of change—as opposed, for example, to the rate of such change, its terminal level, etc.—are considered to be independent of specific environmental conditions. Furthermore, a much broader range of behavioral variables is encompassed in the present term than in McGraw's concepts, which referred exclusively to motor development.

Time as a Dimension for the Study of Psychological Processes

The proposed treatment of the age variable would relate the study of development, that is, of age-related differences in behavior, to a variety of other phenomena of interest to psychologists which similarly involve systematic changes in behavior over time. Let us refer to just one such area: the study of perceptual adaptation. Here, too, we find time used as a dimension along which the changes in behavior of interest are charted in an essentially neutral sense, that is, without investing any causal significance in the time variable itself. Nor do we find adaptation researchers necessarily turning to other, directly manipulable variables for which time could be said to represent a mere shorthand.

For instance, in the area of dark-adaptation (cf. Bartley, 1951), research at the behavioral level has consisted of the description of the prototypical temporal function and the comparison of the slope and form of this function under different conditions of specified independent variables, such as the size and location of the retinal field, the intensity of the preceding illumination, etc. These variables can be placed into a functional relationship with the differences in the parameters of the dark-adaptation curve; they do not explain, nor were they intended to explain, the changes in response which take place over time.

If we ask what form the explanations for these changes actually take, the answer is well known in this case: we turn to an account at the level of physiological mechanisms, more specifically the cycle of breakdown and regeneration of rhodopsin. But note that such reductionist explanation does not dispense with the time dimension, which is still essential to the description of these physiological processes.

As yet, however, most response changes over time are not reducible to lower level physiological mechanisms, and in many cases no psychological mechanisms short-circuiting the time dimension can be invoked to account adequately for the changes. Cases in point would include perceptual adaptation of the "normalization" variety, as studied by Gibson (1933), and, indeed, many of the phenomena of prism adaptation recently studied. Here, to be sure, we find at least one psychological theory attempting to explain adaptation in terms of a single psychological process defined without reference to time, that is, reafferent feedback (Held & Freedman, 1963). Yet the accumulating evidence indicates that while such feedback may be a powerful determinant of amount or rate of adaptation, it is not a necessary condition for its occurrence (cf. Rock, 1966). It is of interest to note further that the prism-adaptation literature suffers from some of the same limitations as the developmental literature, in that a process assumed to be occurring over time is frequently indexed by a single quantity, the *amount* of adaptation after a certain period (usually measured indirectly, through extent of aftereffects). This has meant that the course of change of perception during the adaptation period and the parameters of the adaptation function have been neglected, to the detriment of an adequate picture of the adaptation process (e.g., Devoe, 1969; Hay & Pick, 1966).

In sum, change in response over time represents a central characteristic of diverse aspects of behavior; accordingly, in the description and functional analysis of phenomena involving such change, the time dimension is indispensable, to the extent that it is not reducible to a set of specifiable external events determining the change. The central thesis of this paper is that in the study of a variety of changes in behavior which occur during the course of the individual's development from neonate to mature adult (and possibly even beyond), age is profitably treated in these terms, that is, as a dimension essential to the investigation of the phenomena of developmental change.

Implications of the Proposed Reformulation of the Status of Age

Acceptance of the preceding argument concerning the treatment of the age variable carries with it a number of interesting impli-

cations for the conduct of research on problems of development, with particular regard to questions of methodology, design, and scientific inference. Let us focus on five of these in particular. They concern (a) the place of descriptive research, (b) the construction of viable developmental dimensions, (c) the approach to problems of quantitative analysis, (d) the meaning of the experimental method, and (e) the handling of individual differences.

The Place of Descriptive Research in Developmental Psychology

Any set of empirical data which falls into the Behavior $= f$ (Age) paradigm represents a description—typically partial—of a developmental function for a particular response. This is true regardless of the intent of an investigator to invest such data with theoretical significance for the verification or rejection of a theoretical hypothesis. Data of this type vary widely, however, in the information which can be conveyed in the description of the developmental change in question. They range from the mere finding that age represents a significant source of variance, or that there are significant differences in the incidence of given types of responses associated with age at one extreme, to a precise determination of the mathematical form of the relationship between the behavioral variable and age, with the values of the constants calculated to the nth decimal place, at the other.

In considering the place to be accorded to descriptive data of this kind, it will help to return to the earlier example of the study of dark adaptation. There would be little interest in a finding that absolute thresholds obtained after varying intervals of time following exposure to light differed significantly. Contrast this with the compelling character of the dark-adaptation curve when plotted in detail, for even a single observer, so as to exhibit the two branches of the curve. This information, while not pointing to any specific basis for adaptation, immediately presents a major finding, suggestive of a dual-process phenomenon, which an adequate account of dark adaptation needs to be able to handle.

This illustration suggests why accurate, systematic description has played such an important role in the developmental sciences—indeed, in any science dealing with systems undergoing change or motion (e.g., astronomy). The reason goes beyond the truism that it is essential to have an adequate knowledge of a phenomenon before one can set about explaining it. More to the point, the observation of such a system, precisely because it exhibits change, and thus produces variation that is measurable as it occurs over time, can provide more direct clues to the nature of the processes or mechanisms governing it than is possible in a purely static system or object. Thus in a developmental science, observation and experimentation are apt to be used in a close, coordinate interrelationship, and frequently the line between description and explanation becomes blurred.

These points are convincingly illustrated in the work on mathematical growth curves for the study of physical growth. This work runs the gamut from a purely empirical, curve-fitting approach, as favored by Sholl (1954), Waddington (1950), and others, to the derivation of growth curves from a priori mathematical models of the biological growth process (e.g., Bertalanffy, 1960; cf. also Shock, 1951). In spite of these differences in approach, all of this work is not only marked by an unselfconscious use of age as an irreducible parameter in the study of development, but relies on essentially descriptive data to provide a clear, economic specification of the essential characteristics of growth, and of differences in patterns of growth among individuals or groups. Just as in the case of dark adaptation, furthermore, such concise description of the course and characteristics of age changes has led directly to insights into the factors controlling or regulating growth, as in the study of adolescence (Tanner, 1962), and the work on effects of temporary illness on the course of growth (Tanner, 1963) to be discussed subsequently.

For a number of reasons, some obvious, others less so, we have seen little such mathematical treatment in the study of behavioral development thus far, with the notable exception of the study of the development of intelligence (e.g., Bayley, 1956; Thurstone & Ackerson, 1929). In view of the problems of scaling which arise with respect to intelligence-test data, the meaning and value of such attempts in this particular area is uncertain; however, even less precise and mathematically sophisticated modes of growth-curve analysis, such as the purely graphic approach applied to advantage by Riegel (1966) in his treatment of differential effects of aging on diverse performance variables involving linguistic habits (e.g., reading versus writing), can help us to obtain a clearer picture of the course of development along behavioral dimensions, and accordingly of the processes governing such development.

The benefits to be derived from the study of age changes at a descriptive level are not confined to the realm of quantitative changes. Questions of at least equal interest and significance arise with respect to qualitative changes, for which the analysis of developmental functions take the form of determining developmental sequences, so as to reveal the patterning of successively appearing behaviors. We need only think of the observational studies of motor development by McGraw (1943), Shirley (1931), and Gesell and his associates (cf. Gesell, 1954), or of the painstaking observations of Piaget (1952, 1954) on the development of sensorimotor schemata in infancy to appreciate the place of systematic descriptive work on the sequential appearance of behaviors in development. Piaget's sequences, to be sure, are embedded in an intricate theoretical superstructure, functioning much as a mathematical model may do in the study of growth or learning curves, the observations serving mainly to confirm the adequacy of the model, rather than to test specific hypotheses in a deductive sense. The work on the motor sequences, on the other hand, occupies a place more nearly corresponding to the empirical curve-fitting approach in the study of quantitative changes. Yet both types of research contribute importantly, and perhaps equally, to the specification of developmental process and even mechanism (cf. the laws of development formulated by Gesell, 1954, or the interpretation based on neuromuscular mechanisms which McGraw, 1946, has evolved to handle her findings of motor sequences).

There is one major difference between the qualitative and quantitative analyses of changes: In the case of the former, age ceases itself to be of importance as a continuum to which the behavioral changes are related, except for purely normative purposes; its essential role is to provide an independent criterion for ordering the responses developmentally. The main datum of interest in this type of study accordingly is the sequence of behaviors itself and the extent of its invariance across individuals. Age, or time, may nevertheless enter subsequently as a dependent variable in studying differential rates of development as a function of some condition or subject variable. For instance, the age at which a particular step in the sequence appears, or the time taken to move from Step A to Step B can be used as a measure of developmental rate.

Construction of Developmental Dimensions

A major difficulty to be faced in carrying out the analysis of developmental functions advocated in this paper is the considerable degree of dependence of behavioral measures on specifics of stimuli, situational conditions, instructions, and the like. This problem poses a challenge to developmental psychologists—that of finding measures of behaviors which distill information concerning age-related changes from the "noise" (for the developmentalist) of response variance attributable to stimuli, task conditions, etc. This is by no means as hopeless an undertaking as it may seem. For instance, in the area of the perceptual constancies, the overall picture of the developmental changes that occur is a fairly consistent one across different studies, employing different stimuli, background conditions, and even psychophysical methods (cf. Wohlwill, 1963). This suggests that a reasonably "robust"

developmental dimension can be obtained by the use of a composite measure, derived from the responses to a set of situations representative of those used in the literature.

On the other hand, where a particular variable shows a potent interaction with age—as the distance variable appears to in the constancy literature, or the complexity variable in the curiosity area—we may redefine our developmental dimension so as to incorporate this interaction. That is, rather than defining constancy in terms of amount of error at a particular distance, we can (and indeed should) define it as the extent of the regression of perceived size with distance. Similarly, in the case of curiosity, the measure used could be an index of the slope, or possibly the curvature of the function relating the response to the complexity dimension.

Speaking in a more general vein, reliance on individual measures of a variable, chosen on the basis of a restricted operational definition, leads to situation-bound measures of behavior, which are better suited to the needs of the experimentalist for detecting effects of specific conditions manipulated by him than they are to the study of developmental change. It is undoubtedly no accident that the greatest strides in the study of psychological growth have been made in the field of intelligence and related dimensions taken from the study of individual differences, which are defined in terms of a broad set of behaviors rather than isolated responses. This is not to deny the value of concise definition of behavioral dimension, nor the desirability of extending research on developmental problems to some of the variables which have been intensively studied in the laboratory of the experimentalist. But in so doing, the developmentalist will have to pay much more attention to the problems of construct validity and dimensional homogeneity (as well as reliability) than the experimentalist has been wont to do. The details of these aspects of the construction of dimensions, and the problems involved in arriving at scales for developmental assessment applicable over a large segment of the age variable, are, however, beyond the scope of this paper.

Problems of Measurement and Quantitative Analysis

Let us suppose that we have obtained measures of some adequately scaled and dimensionalized variable over a reasonably extended segment of the age continuum, for example, at five age levels between the ages of 6 and 19. The typical procedure for handling such data is to carry out an ordinary analysis of variance, which may yield a finding of a significant "effect" of age, that is, the age variable represents a significant source of variance. (Negative findings in this regard are rare, since they are not apt to be reported in print.) But is this the most adequate procedure to follow in this instance? Once we depart from the conception of age as a differential variable, and eschew interest in differences among age groups *qua* groups, aiming rather at detailed description of the age function as the first task to be tackled, a more valid approach consists in obtaining a good first approximation to the *form* of a function by means of a trend analysis.

In this connection, we may refer to Grant's (1962) argument against a hypothesis-testing approach in situations involving the testing of a model, in which the intent is not to show the influence of a particular variable, by rejecting a no-difference hypothesis, but rather to fit a set of empirical data to some theoretically derived function. Accordingly, Grant makes a plea for shifting from a hypothesis-testing strategy in such cases to a parameter-estimation strategy. The situation appears similar in our case, even if we do not start from an a priori model specifying the developmental function. A trend analysis can be construed, in effect, as a curve-fitting enterprise, where the intent is to determine, as a purely empirical fact, the general form underlying the observed function or, in our case, the variation in response with age. Obviously, the procedure covers the special case in which there may be no consistent variation with age: in this instance, neither the linear nor any higher order components would prove significant. But the main point concerns the information to be derived from the data: we are generally not interested in rejecting the

null-hypothesis of no age-related difference, but wish rather to determine the most likely form of the age function.

Apart from the specification of the form of the developmental function, through trend analysis or possibly more sophisticated curve fitting methods, the stance taken here toward the study of age changes entails a more intensive concern with the measurement of change, and methods for determining correlates of change and interrelationships among measures of change for different variables. It is clearly not possible to go into detail on these matters here (cf. the symposium on the measurement of change, Harris, 1963; also Cattell, 1963, 1966). Suffice it to call attention to the desirability of obtaining longitudinal data, in order to assess change on a per-individual basis, and to raise one further point. When dealing with the study of change, correlational approaches take on an added dimension, as it were: the teasing out of relationships among variables in process of development differs from the study of correlation at a single point in time, or even over a randomly chosen set of occasions, as in Cattell's P technique. This is true both in terms of the place of this type of correlational analysis as a tool for scientific inference, and in terms of the analytic techniques it requires. For the aim here is to determine functional relationships between changes in behavior presumed to develop in interdependence with one another.

To give a very simple example, if two behavioral variables developed in unison (Figure 2-1a), or in an identical pattern, possibly staggered in time (Figure 2-1b), the inference of a functional interdependence between them would be far more compelling than would the finding of even a substantial correlation between them at some given age level. But there are more complicated possibilities, where the evidence might be more difficult to evaluate, such as where development on some function X depends on, that is, literally awaits, the prior development to some level of another function, Y (e.g., Figure 2-1c). The analogue of this case for the development of discrete, nonquantified responses has been frequently discussed in the past under the general topic of the sequential

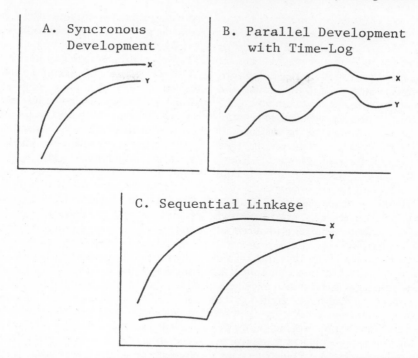

FIGURE 2–1.   Three patterns of interrelationships between variables undergoing development.

ordering of stages (cf. Flavell & Wohlwill, 1969). There is no reason to suppose that a similar pattern may not apply to continuous variables. But the question of the validity of drawing inferences as to functional interdependence remains a complex one in such cases, and the analytic tools available to study them, such as Campbell and Stanley's (1963) "cross-lagged correlation," are as yet very limited.

Meaning of the Experimental Method in the Study of Developmental Change

The determination of an age function does not qualify as an experiment. While few would disagree with this statement, it is important to be clear about the reasons behind this assertion. In the present view, it is not because age is an independent variable which is not subject to experimental manipulation, but rather because it is not an independent variable at all. The statement could be applied with equal force to studies determining the curve of adaptation for a single set of stimulus conditions, or for that matter to studies yielding a single learning curve. In these instances, time, or trials, are variables subject to experimental control; nevertheless, they do not function, in any real sense, as independent variables. (The very use of trials to criterion as a measure of learning should dispel any doubts on this score.)

An experimental study of development entails the manipulation of some particular factor or condition (or combinations thereof), in such a manner that its effects in altering the developmental function are revealed—in other words, it is this function itself which becomes the dependent variable. Relatively few instances of developmental research qualifying as experimental in this sense can be found. For it requires that the course of change on some behavioral dimension be traced over the total age period over which that variable is undergoing change, and that this be done for a control group and one or more experimental groups. Again the field of learning research provides an apt analogy: In studying the phenomenon of reminiscence, that is, of the effect of an interpolated rest period on speed of learning, we would generally not be satisfied with noting the difference between the experimental and control groups immediately following the rest period, but would want to obtain data on the total course of learning for each group (cf. Riley, 1953, 1954).

Most studies purporting to represent experimental studies of development fall short in one or another of these respects. Most typically, only a single measure of behavior is obtained, at the cessation of the duration of the experimental variable (see, for instance, the bulk of research on the effects of early experience in animals). The result is that there is no indication of the effect the variable has had on the course of the individual's development overall.

The absence of such a developmental focus, providing for follow-up testing of the behavior subsequent to the termination of the experience, is a notable shortcoming of much of the research on early experience, such as that carried out by Hebb and his associates at McGill University. Nor is the temporary as opposed to permanent character of the effects of early deprivation the only issue that we need to be concerned about. Another possibility to be considered is that an experience may have delayed effects, showing up only on behaviors which do not normally appear till some time after the termination of the experience. A case in point seems to be provided by the work of Harlow and his associates (Harlow, 1962; Seay, Alexander, & Harlow, 1964) on the effects of social isolation in infancy on later maternal and mating behavior.[4] We may also cite a study by Melzack (1954) on the effects of extended

isolation experience in dogs. Upon initial testing (shortly after the end of the isolation period), the experimental animals were markedly impaired in their ability to make adaptive avoidance responses to noxious stimuli. When retested a year later, these dogs did exhibit normal avoidance behavior; yet the control-group dogs continued to be differentiated from the experimental. They now displayed a new form of response toward the stimuli, namely aggression, which none of the isolated animals showed.

Such results, and others in which follow-up tests have been made to trace long-term effects of early experience, indicate that these effects can be properly understood only by considering them as superimposed on some assumed normal pattern of development, and assessing them by comparing the total developmental function under the normal and the special-experience conditions, that is, by letting the parameters of the developmental function serve as the dependent variable. Perhaps the most dramatic illustration of this point comes from the field of physical growth, where Tanner (1963) and his associates have made studies of the manner in which the mechanisms regulating growth (i.e., height) respond to temporary interruptions of the growth process occasioned by illness or malnutrition. As shown in the two cases illustrated in Figure 2, there is evidence for a period of accelerated growth ("catch-up" growth, as Tanner calls it), following the end of the growth-inhibition period, such that the individual attains the height he could have been expected to normally.

The point of this example is not necessarily to argue for the operation of such catch-up mechanisms in behavioral development; admittedly there is little research available that would bear on this issue. Rather, it is to point up both the importance of obtaining follow-up measures of the development of groups given deprivation or enrichment experience, as well as the complexities of design and interpretation introduced by so doing. In this connection we should note Campbell and Stanley's (1963) discussion of quasi-experimental designs; although intended primarily for the design of

---

[4]Harlow's data are ambiguous in this respect, since the experience of the groups of monkeys compared seems to have differed in unspecified ways up to the time that they reached maturity (thus the delayed effect of the isolation in infancy is in doubt); furthermore, there may well have been undetected (or unreported) differences in their behavior *before* this time.

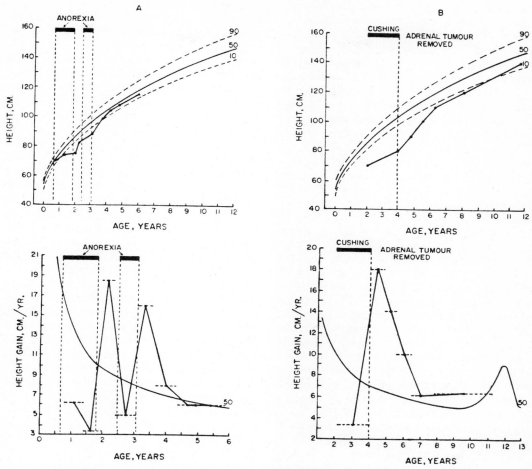

FIGURE 2-2. Two cases of "catch-up" growth, following episodes of anorexia nervosa (left) and removal of adrenal tumor (right). (Upper curves show growth in height; lower curves show height increments. Reprinted with permission from an article by A. Prader, J. M. Tanner, G. A. von Harnack, published in the *Journal of Pediatrics,*1963, Vol. 62. Copyrighted by C. V. Mosby Co., 1963.)

educational research in schools and similar field settings, it is directly applicable to the developmentalist studying the effects of some event or experience of limited duration on the course of development. Of particular relevance is Campbell and Stanley's "multiple-time series" design which entails measuring an experimental group repeatedly both before and after the experimental treatment, so that the effects of the latter can be gauged both directly,

in terms of the shift in the function occurring after the treatment, and in comparison with the overall pattern of change over the same time period displayed by a control group.

To terminate this discussion on a more positive note, let us examine the implication in the proposed analysis of the role of experience on development for the definition of the variables to be controlled or manipulated in this type of experimentation. Thus, some of the parameters which King (1958) specifies in his discussion of the design of experiments on the effects of early experience, notably age at testing and the interval between end of the experience and the test, cease to represent isolable variables once the development of the behavior is monitored over the whole portion of the age continuum over which it is measurable. The only variables of real interest remaining—apart from the type of experience and the type of behavior chosen for study—are those of age at the onset of the experience and its duration. (Admittedly, controls are required to guard against cumulative effects of one test on subsequent ones.)

Interpretation of Individual Differences in Developmental Research

Developmental theorists such as Piaget and Werner and researchers studying age differences generally have not been noted for paying systematic attention to individual differences in behavior. Conversely, differential psychologists have rarely attempted to integrate developmental changes into their work or their thinking. Exceptions to this statement could be cited: the work of Witkin and his associates (Witkin, Dyk, Faterson, Goodenough, & Karp, 1962) and, from the factor-analytic side, that of Cattell (1963, 1966), has treated questions of patterning of individual differences as a function of age, as has the body of research inspired by the differentiation hypothesis of the development of intelligence (cf. Gullford, 1967, pp. 418ff.). Tucker (1963) has, furthermore, provided a model for the handling of developmental and differential data, involving an extension of factor analysis into a three-dimensional space. Yet, with the notable exception of Emmerich's (1964, 1966) work on changes in personality structure in the preschool years, little real integration has been achieved between the focus on individual differences and on developmental changes. Emmerich (1968) has, in fact, made a sharp differentiation between what he terms the "classical developmental view," tracing changes with age, and the differential approach, which to the extent that it has dealt with questions of development, has been mainly concerned with the problem of *stability*, that is, *constancy* of individual differences across age levels.

The present reformulation of the role of the age variable suggests ways in which interindividual variation in development can be treated under both of these two approaches. First of all, at the simplest level, individuals can be differentiated in terms of the characteristics of their developmental function, instead of their standing on a given behavioral dimension at a given age. This is, in effect, what has been done in the field of physical growth at a descriptive level, in specifying channels of development, as in the Wetzel grid (Wetzel, 1947). Individual differences are thus represented as variations around some assumed prototype function, and in the ideal case can be specified in terms of the values of the constants of that function.

If this might be described as incorporating a differential dimension into the classical developmental view, as Emmerich has stated it, the converse task—that of bringing a developmental dimension into the differential approach—is a more difficult one. It would consist in tracing individual differences as they emerge during development, either with respect to nondevelopmental variables, or with respect to standardized or otherwise relativized measures of behavior. While this has been achieved at the level of cross sectional comparisons of factorial structure, the emphasis has been largely on the specification of the factors within a group, that is, of the dimensions along which characteristics of this factor space. A good illustration is provided by the research of Emmerich (1964, 1966), in which longitudinal data have been used to good advantage to separate out different types of changes in factorial patterns, some pointing to continuity, that is, constancy of the factorial definition of a given dimension, while others suggested transformations in the dimensions themselves.

Once the presence of factorially invariant individual-difference dimensions has been established over a certain age range, we can proceed to apply the rationale of developmental-function analysis in order to differentiate among individual children in terms of the pattern of change characterizing the development of the trait or attribute. More specifically, we may look at age functions for any given individual, specifying his standing on that dimension at different points in time, either in terms of standard-score measures, or possibly by recourse to factor scores on factors which have been demonstrated to be invariant over age.

One area in which analyses of this type have in fact been made is in the study of individual children's patterns of mental growth, based on patterns of changes in IQ scores. Using the longitudinal records of the Fels Research Institute study, Sontag, Baker, and Nelson (1958) have succeeded, through this kind of approach, in relating patterns in the development of intelligence to personality formation, specific events in the child's life, etc. It should prove equally feasible, as well as profitable, to undertake such analyses with respect to more purely differential dimensions such as aggressiveness or masculinity-femininity. For instance, the functional meaning of a girl's standing in late adolescence near the feminine end of the masculinity-femininity scale might be quite different, depending on whether she had consistently been highly feminine since

early childhood, as opposed to going through a pattern of increasing masculinity (i.e., tomboyishness) over the course of her childhood, with a reversal at the onset of adolescence. Data from longitudinal studies such as Kagan and Moss's (1962) lend themselves ideally to this purpose, although the authors' predominant concern with the problem of the stability of traits apparently kept them from undertaking any such individual analyses.

Finally, let us bring into focus the complementarity between the two ways of looking at the development of individual differences discussed in this section, one based on differences in the form or pattern of a prototype developmental function, considered in absolute terms, the other on differences in the pattern of change (or lack of it) in a child's standing on a differential dimension, relative to his age group. For dimensions for which individual differences are superimposed on major developmental changes in absolute standing, the two approaches are in fact formally equivalent, and the information obtained from the second is in direct correspondence with that obtained from the first. The case of the development of intelligence illustrates this situation, the difference being equivalent simply to a shift from the use of mental age to that of IQ (cf. Figure

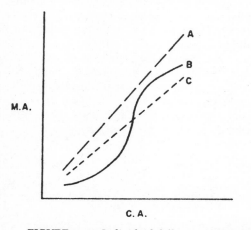 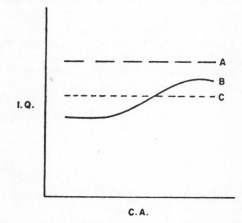

FIGURE 2–3. Individual differences in intelligence development, pictured in terms of mental age (MA) (left) and IQ (right). (A, B, and C represent three individuals, developing at different rates—A: above average; B: well below average initially, accelerating subsequently to attain average terminal level; and C: below average.)

2–3 for an illustration of this point). There is, nevertheless, an important conceptual difference between them, insofar as one couches individual differences in such developmental terms as retardation or acceleration, while the other will make reference to such expressions as normal or average, high and low, etc. (The difference is well caught in the distinction between mental retardation and mental deficiency.) This suggests further that the first approach is more appropriate for variables such as intelligence and vocabulary for which there are, indeed, major changes in level taking place with age, while the second will be more appropriate for true individual-difference scales which are basically orthogonal to the developmental dimension—notably bipolar scales in the field of personality, for variables such as aggressiveness, masculinity-femininity, etc.

Conclusion

Two points remain to be made in conclusion, one concerning the limitations on the types of analyses involving the age variable suggested in this paper, the other concerning the cost involved in applying them. First, the use of the age dimension in the manner advocated here makes sense only provided two criteria are met: (a) that substantial, reasonably situationally independent age changes occur with respect to the given behavior and (b) that the changes are not readily handled in terms of highly specific experience in the sense of the individual's reinforcement history, of practice or learning experience with a given task, or of particular events impinging on him. The rationale behind these criteria and the types of variables which may or may not conform to them have already been noted.

The second and final point to be made is that this approach places a fairly heavy burden on the developmental psychologist. First of all, it demands a mastery of requisite analytic techniques going beyond the standard armamentarium of inferential statistics acquired in the typical graduate training program. Second, it presupposes a willingness to transcend the traditional mold into which behavioral scientists are typically cast, as either experimentalists or differentialists; what is demanded, first of all, is a tolerance for and understanding of the place of painstaking descriptive analysis of behavior change, with nary a significant F or t at the end of the rainbow, and, beyond this, an ability to alternate between and effectively integrate the roles of the differentialist and experimentalist which are generally separated by a wide (and widening) gulf (cf. Cronbach, 1957). Third, and most critically, it is predicated to a considerable extent on the investigator's willingness and ability to collect longitudinal data, frequently spanning a considerable period of time. While there are certain aspects of behavioral development which may be adequately studied over a period of only two or three years (as in the case of the acquisition of Piagetian concepts, or certain aspects of language acquisition), it is typically necessary to cover a substantial segment of the period between birth and maturity. Shortcuts are sometimes possible, by combining longitudinal and cross-sectional approaches, but in general those intent on quick results, or immediate gratification, might be better advised to stay clear of developmental-analytic research of the type discussed here—or possibly to apply it to the study of faster-maturing species such as Drosophila.

REFERENCES

Baltes, P. B. Longitudinal and cross sectional sequences in the study of age and generation effects. *Human Development*, 1968, *11*, 145–171.
Bartley, S. H. The psychophysiology of vision. In S. S. Stevens (Ed.), *Handbook of experimental psychology*. New York: Wiley, 1951.
Bayley, N. Individual patterns of development. *Child Development*, 1956, *27*, 45–74.

Bertalanffy, L. V. Principles and theory of growth. In V. W. Nowinski (Ed.), *Aspects of normal and malignant growth*. Amsterdam: Elsevier, 1960.

Bijou, S., & Baer, D. M. Some methodological contributions from a functional analysis of child development. In L. P. Lipsitt & C. Spiker (Eds.), *Advances in child development and behavior*. Vol. 1. New York: Academic Press, 1930.

Birren, J. E. Principles of research on aging. In J. E. Birren (Ed.), *Handbook of aging and the individual*. Chicago: University of Chicago Press, 1959.

Campbell, D. T., & Stanley, J. C. Experimental and quasi-experimental designs for research on teaching. In N. Gage (Ed.), *Handbook of research on teaching*. Chicago: Rand-McNally, 1963.

Cattell, R. B. The structuring of change by *P* technique and incremental *R* technique. In C. W. Harris (Ed.), *Problems in measuring change*. Madison: University of Wisconsin Press, 1963.

Cattell, R. B. Patterns of change: Measurement in relation to state-dimension, trait change, ability and process concepts. In R. B. Cattell (Ed.), *Handbook of multivariate experimental psychology*. Chicago: Rand McNally, 1966.

Cronbach, L. J. The two disciplines of scientific psychology. *American Psychologist*, 1957, *12*, 671–684.

Dennis, W. Causes of retardation among institutionalized children: Iran. *Journal of Genetic Psychology*, 1960, *96*, 47–59.

Devoe, S. Age differences in the process of adaptation and of after-effects of exposure to displacing prisms for measures of object perception and body perception. Paper presented at the meeting of the Eastern Psychological Association, Philadelphia, April 1969.

Emmerich, W. Continuity and stability in early development. *Child Development*, 1964, *35*, 311–332.

Emmerich, W. Stability and change in early personality development. *Young Children*, 1966, *21*, 233–243.

Emmerich, W. Personality development and concepts of structure. *Child Development*, 1968, *39*, 671–690.

Flavell, J., & Wohlwill., J. F. Formal and functional aspects of cognitive development. In D. Elkind & J. Flavell (Eds.), *Studies in cognitive development: Essays in honor of Jean Piaget*. New York: Oxford University Press, 1969.

Gesell, A. The ontogenesis of infant behavior. In L. Carmichael (Ed.), *Manual of child psychology*. (2nd ed.) New York: Wiley, 1954.

Gibson, J. J. Adaptation, after-effect and contrast in the perception of curved lines. *Journal of Experimental Psychology*, 1933, *16*, 1–31.

Grant, D. A. Testing the null hypothesis and the strategy and tactics of investigating theoretical models. *Psychological Review*, 1962, *69*, 54–61.

Guilford, J. P. *The nature of human intelligence*. New York: McGraw-Hill, 1967.

Harlow, H. F. The heterosexual affectional system in monkeys. *American Psychologist*, 1962, *17*, 1–9.

Harris, C. W. *Problems in measuring change*. Madison: University of Wisconsin Press, 1963.

Hay, J. C., & Pick H. L., Jr. Visual and proprioceptive adaptation to optical displacement of the visual stimulus. *Journal of Experimental Psychology*, 1966, *71*, 150–158.

Held, R., & Freedman, S. J. Plasticity in human sensorimotor control. *Science*, 1963, *142*, 455–462.

Kagan, J., & Moss, H. *Birth to maturity: A study in psychological development*. New York: Wiley, 1962.

Kessen, W. Research design in the study of developmental problems. In P. Mussen (Ed.), *Handbook of research methods in child development*. New York: Wiley, 1960.

King, J. A. Parameters relevant to determining the effect of early experience upon the adult behavior of animals. *Psychological Bulletin,* 1958, *55*, 46–58.

McGraw, M. B. *The neuro-muscular maturation of the human infant.* New York: Columbia University Press, 1943. (Republished: New York: Hafner, 1963.)

McGraw, M. B. Maturation of behavior. In L. Carmichael (Ed.), *Manual of child psychology.* New York: Wiley, 1946.

Melzack, R. The genesis of emotional behavior: An experimental study of the dog. *Journal of Comparative and Physiological Psychology,* 1954, *47*, 166–168.

Piaget, J. *The origins of intelligence in children.* New York: International Universities Press, 1952.

Piaget, J. *The construction of reality in the child.* New York: Basic Books, 1954.

Prader, A., Tanner, J. M., & von Harnack, G. A. Catch-up growth following illness or starvation: An example of developmental canalization in man. *Journal of Pediatrics,* 1963, *62*, 646–659.

Riegel, K. F. Development of language: Suggestions for a verbal fallout model. *Human Development,* 1966, *9*, 97–120.

Riley, D. A. Reminiscence effects in paired-associate learning. *Journal of Experimental Psychology,* 1953, *45*, 232–238.

Riley, D. A. Further studies of reminiscence effects with variation in stimulus-response relationships. *Journal of Experimental Psychology,* 1954, *48*, 101–105.

Rock, I. *The nature of perceptual adaptation.* New York: Basic Books, 1966.

Schaie, K. W. A general model for the study of developmental problems. *Psychological Bulletin,* 1965, *64*, 92–107.

Schaie, K. W. Age changes and age differences. *Gerontologist,* 1967, *7*, 128–132.

Seay, B. M., Alexander, B. K., & Harlow, H. F. The maternal behavior of socially deprived rhesus monkeys. *Journal of Abnormal and Social Psychology,* 1964, *69*, 345–354.

Shirley, M. M. *The first two years.* Vol. 1. *Postural and locomotor development.* Minneapolis: University of Minnesota Press, 1931.

Shock, N. W. Growth curves. In S. S. Stevens (Ed.), *Handbook of experimental psychology.* New York: Wiley, 1951.

Sholl, D. A. Regularities in growth curves, including rhythms and allometry. In E. J. Boell (Ed.), *Dynamics of growth processes.* Princeton: Princeton University Press, 1954.

Simpson, G. G. The study of evolution: Methods and present status of theory. In A. Roe & G. G. Simpson (Eds.), *Behavior and evolution.* New Haven: Yale University Press, 1958.

Sontag, L. W., Baker, C. T., & Nelson, V. L. Mental growth and personality development: A longitudinal study. *Monographs of the Society for Research in Child Development,* 1958, 23 (2, Serial No. 68).

Staats, A. W., & Staats, C. K. *Complex human behavior.* New York: Holt, Rinehart & Winson, 1963.

Tanner, J. M. *Growth at adolescence.* Oxford. Blackwell, 1962.

Tanner, J. M. The regulation of human growth. *Child Development,* 1963, *34*, 817–848.

Thurstone, L. L., & Ackerson, L. The mental growth curve for the Binet tests. *Journal of Educational Psychology,* 1929, *20*, 569–583.

Tucker, L. R. Implications of factor analysis of three-way matrices for measurement of change. In C. W. Harris (Ed.), *Problems in measuring change.* Madison: University of Wisconsin Press, 1963.

Waddington, C. H. The biological foundations of measurements of growth and form. *Proceedings of the Royal Society (London),* Series B, 1950, *137*, 509–515.

Wetzel, N. C. Growth, In O. Glasser (Ed.), *Medical physics.* Chicago: Yearbook Publishers, 1947.

Witkin, H. A., Dyk, R. B., Faterson, H. F., Goodenough, D. R., & Karp, S. A. *Psychological differentiation*. New York: Wiley, 1962.

Wohlwill, J. F. The development of "over-constancy" in space perception. In L. P. Lipsitt & C. C. Spiker (Eds.), *Advances in child development and behavior*. Vol. 1. New York: Academic Press, 1963.

Wohlwill, J. F. Vers une réformulation du rôle de l'expérience dans le développement cognitif. In *Psychologie et épistémologie génétiques: Thèmes Piagetiens*. Paris: Dunod, 1966.

Wohlwill, J. F. Methodology and research strategy in the study of developmental change. In P. B. Baltes & L. R. Goulet (Eds.), *Theory and research in life-span developmental psychology*. New York: Academic Press, 1970, pp. 150–190.

Zigler, E. Metatheoretical issues in developmental psychology. In M. H. Marx (Ed.), *Theories in contemporary psychology*. (2nd ed.) New York: Macmillan, 1963.

3. TOWARD AN EXPLICIT RATIONALE FOR NATURALISTIC RESEARCH METHODS

E. P. WILLEMS

Discussions of the relative merits and usefulness of naturalistic research methods, as against explicitly arranged, controlled, manipulated laboratory methods, have a peculiar tendency to deteriorate into polemics and petulant, sarcastic argumentation, a tendency that sometimes spills over into the published literature (e.g., Epstein, 1962, pp. 269–270). It is common to hear words like "rigor" vs. "sloppiness," "control of variance" vs. "meaningfulness," "sterile" vs. "true-to-life," "rich" vs. "nit-picking," and "scientific" vs. "anecdotal." Perhaps, wading into the middle of this controversy is a useless venture, since, by and large, individual investigators will continue to use the research methods that suit their tastes, anyway. However, I believe that we have scarcely begun the business of developing strategies and methods for psychological research. The number of ways to do research is limited only by our ingenuity. Based upon this belief, I have a threefold thesis to present: (a) There are reasons for the polemical and petulant nature of methodological controversy. (b) The actual execution and practice of research can be characterized in

relatively nonpolemical and useful terms. (c) Some progress can be made toward uncovering those dimensions or issues that will constitute an explicit, public rationale for the choice of naturalistic methods in psychological research.

First, just a word on what I think are two reasons for the frequently empty disputation about naturalistic methods as against other kinds, usually experimental ones. The first reason is what is sometimes called the "tool illusion" (Baker, 1963, p. 164), or what Prof. Egon Guba once called "the law of the hammer."[1] The law of the hammer goes something like this: If you give a child a hammer, things to be pounded become the most important things around. The principle involved is that not only do we often allow methods and techniques to dictate the choice and merits of our own research problems, but we often let our own methods dictate and evaluate the merits of someone else's research problem, rather than the issues and purposes of the investigator *in*

[1]From a personal conversation.

From *Human Development*, 1967, *10*, 138–154. Copyright 1967 S. Karger, A. G., Basel, New York. Reprinted by permission of the author and the publisher.

combination with his methods and techniques. Believing in the inherent, a priori correctness and scientific efficacy of certain techniques, we prescribe and proscribe, praise and blame.

A second reason for much of the empty disputation about methods, I submit, is the very troublesome word, "natural." Too often we hear the word "natural" used in the sense of "real," and "true," as against "unreal" and "untrue," or even "unnatural," and I have used it so myself. Is the finding from a non-laboratory, field study more "true" or more "real" than the finding from a laboratory experiment? I don't know. There seems to be some agreement on what characterizes naturalistic *methods*, but little consensus and much controversy about the naturalness of *findings*. What we need is some framework to describe and characterize the actual execution of research in such a way as to allow investigators to choose methods according to their research purposes. I would hope such a framework would aid us in generating correspondence between research purposes and methods on relatively nonspeculative and nonpolemical grounds.

Description of Research Activities

A number of writers on methodology have discussed and categorized the strategies of research (e.g., Scott and Wertheimer, 1962; Underwood, 1957; Shontz, 1965; Kerlinger, 1964; Barker, 1964; 1965; Gump and Kounin, 1959–1960; Willems, 1965b; Campbell and Stanley, 1963; Sears, 1957; Webb, Campbell, Schwartz and Sechrest, 1966; Sells, 1966). From this literature there emerges the suggestion that the set of activities an investigator actually engages in while carrying out a piece of research falls somewhere in a two-dimensional descriptive space. The first, most frequently discussed, dimension describes *the degree of investigator influence upon, or manipulation of, the antecedent conditions of the behavior studied,* on the assumption that the degree of such influence or manipulation may vary from high to low, or from much to none. The second

dimension describes *the degree to which units are imposed by the investigator upon the behavior studied.* Conceiving of the two dimensions as orthogonal, with hypothetical variation from maximal to minimal on each, allows one to describe a particular set of research activities as rating somewhere from high to low on investigator manipulation of antecedent conditions, or independent variables, and also on imposition of units on the data by the investigator. Based upon this descriptive scheme, I offer two suggestions. First, in the controversies over the merits of controlled, manipulated laboratory research as against naturalistic research, what is usually called laboratory experimentation falls in the high manipulation–high imposition sector, and what is called naturalistic research falls at the low-low end. That is, the controversies usually involve the most extreme cases. Second, and perhaps more important, the descriptive space avoids arbitrary dichotomies, and suggests that degree of manipulation and imposition of units fall on continua.

There is certainly nothing sacred about this scheme I have offered, but, as a pedagogical device, it does provide an aid in discussing issues that a rationale for naturalistic methods should take into account. By way of concrete example, several years ago we conducted a study of the reasons for, or pulls toward, attending school activities reported by high school students (Willems, 1964; Willems and Willems, 1965). We selected five specific nonclass activities in several schools and tried three techniques for gathering data. In the first technique, we presented students with decks of cards, each of which contained a predetermined reason for attending, and asked the students to sort out those that were, for them, reasons for attending each of the five activities. In the second technique, the predetermined items were printed on checklists, and students were asked to check those that were, for them, reasons for attending. In the third technique, we asked the students, in standardized individual interviews, "what, if any, were for you real reasons for or pulls toward attending this activity?" and recorded their responses. Each of these three techniques yielded data on the number of reasons for attending five selected activities. When we correlated the number of such responses to the number of activities the students had actually attended, the interview data yielded the highest correlations, the card sort data the next highest, and the checklist data the lowest. In terms of the descriptive space, we had not manipulated the antecedent conditions of attendance at school activities, but we had varied the imposition upon, or restriction of, response units. And the interview method, the technique with the least restriction of the response range, yielded data with the highest predictive validity. Thus, we had a behavioral, empirical and relatively nonpolemical basis for choosing among techniques, and we ended up using one that tended toward the low-low sector of the descriptive space.

Choice of Naturalistic Methods

What, then, are some issues, or concerns, or components that should go into making up a rationale that would lead an investigator to choose methods tending toward the low manipulation–low imposition parts of the descriptive space I have discussed? The remainder of my remarks will focus on one finite, beginning set of such issues or purposes, a set which is neither necessarily independent nor exhaustive. For convenience, I shall use the term ''naturalistic'' in referring to studies and methods that tend toward the low end on either or both of the two dimensions.

Everyday Behavioral Achievement. One legitimate scientific question, a question that leads to a choice among alternative methods is, ''what kinds of actual everyday behavioral achievements do persons make?'' For example, explicitly-controlled laboratory experimentation has made great strides in untangling the theoretical issues involved in the perception of size and distance (cf. Epstein, Park and Casey, 1961). However, Brunswik pointed out (Brunswik, 1955; Postman and Tolman, 1959) that if one asks to what extent persons actually achieve veridical perception of size in their

everyday lives, something else than laboratory experimentation is called for. For Brunswik, this question of everyday functional achievement dictated a choice of methods by which he asked a subject, during her daily rounds of activity, to judge periodically the linear dimensions of objects at which she happened to be looking. The subject achieved a correlation of 0.99 between the physical size of objects and her estimates of size.

In a second example, Imai and Garner (1965) studied perceptual classification of stimuli that could be classified in various ways. When they dictated, or controlled, the attribute by which subjects were to classify, they obtained clear, lawful data on the extent to which the subjects did what they were told to do. However, only when Imai and Garner allowed subjects relatively free rein in classifying did they discover what strategies the subjects themselves chose in achieving perceptual classification.

These two examples illustrate a principle that might be included in a rationale for naturalistic methods: If the research question is what kinds of behavioral achievements persons make when left to their own resources, the methods used should come from the low manipulation–low imposition parts of the two-dimensional space for describing research activities.

Distribution of Psychology's Phenomena in Nature. Closely related to the study of the array of everyday functional achievements is another concern of any science—the distribution of its phenomena in nature. To the zoologist, the chemist, the archeologist and the geologist, this arm of science is a familiar one. However, apart from some sociological data, census tract data, mortality tables, some educational records, selective service summaries and the norms of a restricted set of psychological tests, little is known about the actual distribution of psychology's phenomena outside of the experimental laboratory. We know little about the distribution of humor, sadness, disappointment, frustration, dependency training, commitment or initiation of social contacts. While this is a time-consuming problem, it is an empirical one.

Blair Justice, a recent student in the doctoral

program at Rice University, has described his attempts to discover the distribution and intensity of potential violence among Negroes and whites in a major metropolitan area (Justice, 1966). He used two methods to obtain data that could be rated for the amount of violent involvement persons would advocate in solving racial problems. The first method was a modified participant-observation for which he solicited the aid of barbers, taxi drivers, policemen and bartenders. For the second method, which he called *natural dialogue*, he trained assistants to pose as persons waiting for medical care at a public health hospital and insert predetermined questions into conversations with others in the waiting room. The point here is that the attempt to determine the distribution of potential violence called for a choice of naturalistic methods.

A second example from a classic psychological area is pertinent here. In their study of frustration and regression, Barker, Dembo and Lewin (1943) brought children who ranged in age from two to five years to the laboratory and allowed them to play with a set of attractive toys. Later, in the same room, the children were again allowed to play, but certain attractive toys were inaccessible to them because of a wire screen barrier that had been dropped across the room, thus blocking them from the goal of the attractive toys. Under these conditions, frustration of such magnitude was induced that the children regressed, that is, the constructiveness of their play decreased markedly, and they reverted to modes of play typical of much younger children. One might well ask, however, how are frustration and regression distributed in the everyday lives of children?

Written narrative accounts describing continuous, day-long observations of at least 18 children in their everyday surroundings and routines are available at the Midwest Psychological Field Station of the University of Kansas. These records, called *specimen records* (Barker, 1963; 1964; Barker and Wright, 1955; Barker, Wright, Barker and Schoggen, 1961; Schoggen, 1964), describe the complete days of the children; their behaviors, conversations,

interactions and locations. Clifford L. Fawl (1963) used 16 of these records, representing 16 days, or over 200 h of observation of children, and analyzed them for the occurrence of goal blockage, frustration and accompanying negative affect. Fawl was surprised to find relatively few occurrences of blocked goals, and when they did occur, to find that they usually failed to produce an apparent disturbance on the part of the child. Disturbance, when it did occur was mild in intensity. In other words, in over 200 h of the everyday lives of children, there was a surprisingly infrequent occurrence of a phenomenon that has an important place in some theories of child development. Methods involving no manipulation of antecedent conditions and a content coding of behavior units inherent in a narrative record told Fawl something about the distribution of one psychology's phenomena in nature.

Arthur J. Dyck (1963), also using the specimen records, found that in the everyday lives of these children, when social contacts occurred between parents and children, parents initiated 34% of them, and that when such contacts occurred between teachers and the same children teachers initiated 73% of them. A controlled laboratory experiment, by definition and purpose, says little or nothing about such everyday distributions.

The Problem of Yield. A third issue for inclusion in a rationale for naturalistic methods is closely related to the everyday distribution of phenomena, but is important because it is often turned into a criticism of naturalistic research. The criticism often runs something like this: After all, as scientists, we are seeking general laws of behavior. Therefore, we must assure ourselves of adequate empirical yield from our studies in terms of frequency and intensity of occurrences. Many, if not all, naturalistic studies, when compared to laboratory experiments, involve a disproportionate amount of time and effort relative to data yield. *Ergo*, the optimal methods are laboratory experiments.

A demonstration of just this problem is a study reported by Gump and Kounin (1959–1960). These investigators had made extensive studies of classroom settings, seeking what effects disciplinary or control techniques had upon children other than the target child, and they wished to extend the study to other contexts, such as a public camp. They chose two camp settings for study—a cabin clean-up period and a rest period. One observer took a specimen record of the behavior of adult cabin leaders, and others took specimen records of individual campers. Over a six-week period, involving six observers, about 46 h of camper behavior were recorded. The total yield of responses by nontarget children was about one incident for every 18 pages of verbal record. Such a low frequency is an interesting finding in itself, but it fits the criticism of economy of effort and yield. How shall such a criticism be answered? In a rationale for naturalistic methods, the answer should be an empirical one, if possible, and the answer is that the economy-of-yield argument is not unidirectional; it does not apply uniquely to naturalistic studies.

A concrete example is reported by Kounin (1961), where the purpose was to study the effects of various types of control techniques by teachers upon students who ranged from low to high on commitment to the task. After carefully training their experimental teachers, the investigators arranged for a sample of adolescents to come to the university campus during the summer, for pay, to serve as experimental students. However, the investigators were completely unable to induce low commitment under this experimental arrangement; the yield for that cell of their design was zero. In intact, naturally-occurring classrooms, they were able to find students low in commitment. The problem of ratio of effort to yield is not unique to naturalistic studies.

Artificial Tying and Untying of Variables. One more in this closely related set of issues that might well enter into a rationale for naturalistic methods received most explicit treatment by Egon Brunswik. He called it "artificial tying and untying of variables" in his critiques of carefully-controlled and arranged laboratory research (Brunswik, 1955; Postman and

Tolman, 1959). Artificial tying occurs when variables are allowed or made to vary together in ways that persons never confront in their everyday lives, whereas artificial untying occurs when natural covariations of variables are eliminated through experimental control. Two studies illustrate these points and indicate another basis for choosing among methods.

In the first study (Gump and Kounin, 1959–1960), the investigators wanted again to test the effects of various kinds of control techniques by teachers upon nontarget students, this time in college classes. They arranged for student accomplices to come late to classes, and they trained teachers sometimes to try supportive, friendly reactions and sometimes threatening, punitive ones on the late arrivals. They found that punitive, as compared to supportive, reactions resulted in lowered ratings of the teachers' competence, likeability and fairness by nontarget students. On later questionnaires, however, the investigators found that most of the students were surprised that one of their college teachers would take time out to correct a student for coming late to class. In their efforts to produce an experiment, they had taken a phenomenon out of its everyday context and combined several factors in ways that were not customary for those students.

A second example is a study by Gump and Sutton-Smith (1955), who investigated the reactions of poorly-skilled boys when they were placed in more or less difficult roles in games. In the experimental game, a boy who was *It* worked in the center of a rectangular playing field and attempted to tag other players who ran to and from safe areas at each end of the rectangle. High power was given to the *It* role by having the boy who was *It* call the turns; he said when the others could run. In the low-power condition, the other players could run whenever they chose. Preselected slow runners were assigned to the two *It* conditions. The results confirmed the research hypotheses: In the low-power as opposed to the high-power *It* positions, poorly-skilled boys experienced more tagging failures, uttered more comments indicating distress and defeat, and were teased and combined against more frequently.

However, when the investigators observed what happened in gyms, camps and playgrounds, where they had not arranged and manipulated the game environment, they found that poorly-skilled boys seldom got into difficult games. If they did get involved, they avoided or were excluded from the difficult roles. The arranged experiment supported the investigators' hypotheses, but it tied or untied variables in ways that were unusual for the subjects. The naturalistic approach pointed out the ways in which the experiment failed to match the everyday event.

While this study by Gump and Sutton-Smith illustrates tying and untying of variables as a basis for choice among methods, it also demonstrates the interplay of controlled experimentation with naturalistic methods. The naturalistic methods discovered what boys actually do in games, while the experiment, by forcing poorly-skilled boys into difficult roles, suggested *why* they do what they do in games. This interplay of methods should be emphasized. For example, field workers have observed hundreds of hours devoted to social play among monkeys and apes, but it was Harlow's *experiments* that showed just how essential this activity is to the development of behavior (see Mason, 1965).

Replicability. Leaving behind the rather interrelated issues of everyday behavioral achievement, the distribution of phenomena in nature, economy and yield, and tying and untying of variables, several important issues remain to be considered in a rationale for naturalistic methods. One such issue is replicability. Naturalistic research is often criticized on the grounds that it is not replicable, and it often seems to be assumed that behavior represents a class of such unstable and complicated phenomena that unless it is constrained by experimental controls, it is not amenable to scientific study. Fortunately, replicability is not a matter for pure speculation to decide; it can be decided empirically, case by case, replication by replication.

Relatively few studies of any methodological type are explicitly replicated, but I can report on

the replication of a study using naturalistic methods (Gump and Friesen, 1964; Willems, 1964; 1965a). Paul Gump, Wallace Friesen and I studied the relation of high school size to participation by students and to what we called forces toward participation. In 1961, we studied a set of intact schools ranging in size, and their intact groups of Junior students. Gump and Friesen listed all the nonclass activities occurring in each school during the period of a semester and had Juniors indicate which ones they had attended at least once and what they had done there. These responses were rated for level or depth of participation. We then obtained data such as those described earlier on "reasons for or pulls toward attending" five activities carefully selected and matched across schools. These data were coded into categories of own forces, or attractions, and induced forces, or external pressures, toward participation. Four years later, in 1965, I replicated all these techniques on a new set of students in large and small schools. The graphical and statistical findings from the two sets of studies, four years apart, were startlingly similar. They were similar down to the comparative per cents of students reporting no participation and no external pressures toward participation.

Replication of specific *techniques* is possible for any scientific method, and replicability of *findings* is a matter to be decided on the basis of the data.

Control Groups. Replicability seems to be an empirical matter, to be decided case by case for any class of methods, but naturalistic approaches are also frequently criticized on the grounds that too seldom do they, or too seldom can they, employ proper control groups. A good example of this problem is the long controversy over the effectiveness of psychotherapy, involving Eysenck (1952); Luborsky (1954); Rosenzweig (1954); DeCharms, Levy and Wertheimer (1954); Kiesler (1966) and others. Kerlinger (1964) states the problem well when he suggests that the lack of explicit control over variables, the complexity of relations among variables and absence of random assignment of subjects to research conditions in naturalistic studies often provides "... a loophole for other variables to crawl through" (p. 363). The problems here are classic ones in the literature on methodology, and they have received careful treatment by writers such as Underwood (1957) and Campbell and Stanley (1963). The effects of passage of time, effects of variables correlated with presumed independent variables, and the equivalence of comparison groups before the occurrence of some incident whose effects are being measured are but three considerations. Appropriate control groups are serious problems for naturalistic research, but they again should be empirically solvable through a combination of ingenuity of investigators and an understanding of the function of control groups.

If a control group is a group of subjects either assigned to conditions or selected so as to yield data that will allow a choice among interpretations, the criticism can be put into perspective. One answer is to select naturally occurring, intact samples of subjects in appropriate ways, a strategy so common that I will not elaborate upon it here. However, one other possible strategy is less commonly used, at least explicitly, and does merit some treatment. This strategy involves what Shontz (1965) has called "implicit comparison groups" (p. 169). Here, the investigator capitalizes upon previous studies of his own, studies by others, or even stable generalizations in the related literature to serve the function of the control group. One example will demonstrate how this might be done.

In one of the studies I cited earlier, in which we investigated the relations between size of high school and the behavior and experience of students, we compared students in five small schools to students in one large school. Certainly, many variables operate in such a study, and it became clear that since the large school was located in an urban center while the small schools were located in small, rural towns, we would be hard pressed to defend an interpretation of our findings in terms of school size. In this case, a study by William J. Campbell (1964) came to our rescue. Campbell replicated the methods in two schools, one large and one small, which were both located in small, rural towns, and he got the same pattern of results. The importance of Campbell's findings was two-fold in our exploration into the tenability of the school-size hypothesis. In addition to eliminating rural–urban differences, the schools he compared differed less in size than ours had, and as expected on our hypothesis, there were less extreme differences on most of his measures of student behavior and experience.

Researchability of Certain Phenomena. One issue that does not require much elaboration, but which should enter into a rationale for naturalistic methods, is the fairly obvious fact that many phenomena and their correlates would not enter into a rationale for naturalistic methods, is the fairly obvious fact that many phenomena and their correlates would not enter the scientific domain at all without naturalistic methods. For ethical reasons and sometimes because of their intrinsic nature, the correlates and effects of natural disasters, physical disabilities, child rearing regimens, deaths, accidents and other classes of events are, after certain points, researchable only through naturalistic methods. And yet, if reliable data can be obtained, such phenomena should enter the science.

I should point out that researchability may clearly be a reason for using laboratory methods, or experimental methods as well. I am interested in figural aftereffects, and at present I see no reason why I could or should study them under other than carefully manipulated conditions.

Discrepant Findings and Generalization. Much of what I have said about the study of everyday behavioral achievement, the distribution of phenomena in nature, tying and untying of variables and yield is relevant to what is perhaps the most important scientific issue that a rationale for naturalistic methods should take into account. This is the problem of generalizing findings and laws to everyday life, and it has an empirical foot in the problem of discrepant findings. It is one thing to have a particular research purpose lead to a choice of naturalistic or experimental methods, but it is somehow another matter when two different approaches are used to study what is assumed to be the same phenomenon and discrepant findings are the outcome. Such discrepancies point to an important scientific function for naturalistic methods, as several examples will suggest.

S. L. Washburn reports that baboons have been studied frequently in captivity, as in zoos and primate laboratories (1963). It is common to find that when two or more baboons are confined together, one emerges as the leader. This observation is not surprising, but *how* leaders emerge in confinement is important. Washburn reports that under these conditions, the leaders emerge and maintain their leadership through physical intimidation and comparative brute power. Washburn goes on to report the results of observations of baboons in their natural habitats, and one set of findings is of special interest. Leaders also emerge in the wild, but they appear not to emerge by physical intimidation and brute power. Superior cunning, sexual expertise and attractiveness seem to be the route to leadership among baboons in the wild.

The work of Beecher on pain-relieving drugs also suggests that when the investigator's concern is to generalize to real life phenomena, naturalistic methods must enter his program of research (1956; 1959a, 1959b; 1960). Beecher's findings suggest that many controlled laboratory experiments on pain and pain-relieving drugs contribute little to the understanding of pain and analgesia as they occur in the world outside the laboratory. Compounds that seem to relieve pain in the controlled laboratory conditions often fail to do so in the wards of hospitals, while substances which, by laboratory experiment, would seem to be ineffective frequently are highly effective in the clinical situation. In other words, on the matter of pain relief, there is explicit need for naturalistic research to optimize generalization and to check laboratory findings.

In a recent investigation into decision-making procedures in groups, Hall and Williams (1966) combined variations in manipulation of antecedent conditions in a single study. They were investigating the effect of group conflict upon processes and outcomes in making group decisions, and they compared the performances of 20 established, intact groups of management trainees to 20 *ad hoc* groups, groups with no history as groups outside the laboratory. Hall and Williams explicitly set out to assess the generalizability of findings from *ad hoc* laboratory groups to established groups, and their finding was that such generalization is precarious business. The *ad hoc* groups differed from the established groups in their processes of making decisions, especially in the way they dealt with conflict.

Other examples (cf. Kavanau, 1964) of the problem of generalizing from the laboratory to everyday life could be cited, but the issues seem fairly clear. I should emphasize that the findings for Washburn's confined baboons, Beecher's laboratory subjects, and Hall and Williams' *ad hoc* groups were true, accurate and reliable *for those subjects*. However, it is also clear that the investigators would have been in error if they had made straightforward generalizations to everyday occurrences on the basis of those subjects alone. It is seductively easy to be content with results obtained in controlled laboratory experiments and to assume that caution is the only requirement for generalizing. It appears that caution is not the only requirement, and that naturalistic methods perform a uniquely-required function in the problem of generalization. Again, this is an empirical matter rather than a speculative one.

As you will have noted, I carefully picked examples that display discrepancies between the findings from controlled experiments and naturalistic studies. In no way have I done justice to those happy instances of good agreement. Just one example of such correspondence is the findings on the relation between the person's skill, or ability, and his status in the group (Sherif and Sherif, 1953; Whyte, 1943; McGrath and Altman, 1966, pp. 110–116). My point is that any program of research that includes generalization as one of its aims should purposefully include data yielded by methods that tend toward low manipulation and low imposition of units.

Marvin D. Dunnette, in a recent discussion of trends and fads in psychology (1966), says that laboratory findings:

. . . usually lead to elaborate theories or behavioral taxonomies, entirely consistent within themselves but lacking the acid test of contact with reality. . . . Psychologists who choose to partake of the advantages of the more rigorous controls possible in the psychometric or experimental laboratories must accept responsibility for assuring the day-to-day relevance of the observations they undertake [p. 346].

Conclusion

I will say three things in closing. First, as the study by Hall and Williams (1966) on group problem-solving illustrates, one of the advantages of viewing naturalism as a continuum rather than as a dichotomy is that an infinite number of ways to mix methods is made possible (cf. Jarvis, 1965; Klein, 1963). Hall and Williams systematically manipulated many antecedents of the behavior they were studying, but they explicitly and purposefully included the intact groups to study the problem of generalization.

Second, research aimed directly at the methodological problems of naturalistic methods has lagged. For example, one of the hopes and purposes of many naturalistic techniques is that they will yield data on which the distorting effects of the techniques themselves will be minimal, if not zero. Much work remains to be done in developing such methods, but some systematic empirical progress is being made. As just one instance, Purcell and Brady (1966) have reported some fascinating and suggestive findings from their program of research into the adaptation of children to electronic monitoring devices.

Finally, the execution of research is always a curious and complex product of the purposes and questions of an investigator and his choice of methods to achieve his purposes and answer his questions (Taylor *et al.*, 1959). Therefore, the evaluation of the outcomes of research should, at least in part, take into account those purposes and questions, which at times and in the best scientific interest, will lead an investigator to choose methods that tend toward naturalistic ones.

REFERENCES

Baker, R. A.: A final word from the editor. *In:* R. A. Baker (Ed.), *Psychology in the wry,* pp. 163–167 (Van Nostrand, New York, 1963).

Barker, R. G.: (Ed.) *The stream of behavior* (Appleton-Century-Crofts, New York, 1963).

Barker, R. G.: Observation of behavior: Ecological approaches. *J. Mt. Sinai Hosp. 31:* 268–284 (1964).

Barker, R. G.: Explorations in ecological psychology. *Amer. Psychol. 20:* 1–14 (1965).

Barker, R. G.; Dembo, T. and Lewin K.: Frustration and regression. *In:* R. G. Barker, J. S. Kounin and H. F. Wright (Eds.) *Child behavior and development,* pp. 441–458 (McGraw-Hill, New York, 1943).

Barker, R. G. and Wright, H. F.: *Midwest and its children* (Harper & Row, New York, 1955).

Barker, R. G.; Wright, H. F.; Barker, L. S. and Schoggen, M.: *Specimen records of American and English children* (University of Kansas Press, Lawrence, Kansas, 1961).

Beecher, H. K.: Relationship of significance of wound to pain experienced. *J. Amer. Med. Assn. 161:* 1609–1613 (1956).

Beecher, H. K.: Generalization from pain of various types and origins. *Science 130:* 267–268 (1959, a).

Beecher, H. K.: Measurement of subjective responses (Oxford, New York, 1959, b).

Beecher, H. K.: Increased stress and effectiveness of placebos and "active" drugs. *Science 132:* 91–92 (1960).

Brunswik, E.: Representative design and probabilistic theory in a functional psychology. *Psychol. Rev. 62:* 193–217 (1955).

Campbell, D. T. and Stanley, J. C.: Experimental and quasi-experimental designs for research on teaching. *In:* N. L. Gage (Ed.) *Handbook of research on teaching,* pp. 171–246 (Rand McNally, Chicago, 1963).

Campbell, W. J.: Some effects of high school consolidation. *In:* R. G. Barker and P. V. Gump. *Big school, small school,* pp. 139–153 (Stanford University Press, Stanford, Calif., 1964).

DeCharms, R.; Levy, J. and Wertheimer, M.: A note on attempted evaluations of psychotherapy. *J. Clin. Psychol. 10:* 233–235 (1954).

Dunnette, M. D.: Fads, fashions and folderol in psychology. *Amer. Psychol. 21:* 343–352 (1966).

Dyck, A. J.: The social contacts of some Midwest children with their parents and teachers. *In:* R. G. Barker (Ed.) *The stream of behavior,* pp. 78–98 (Appleton-Century-Crofts, New York, 1963).

Epstein, S.: Comments on Dr. Bandura's paper. *In:* M. R. Jones (Ed.) *Nebraska symposium on motivation,* pp. 269–272 (University of Nebraska Press, Lincoln, Neb., 1962).

Epstein, W.; Park, J. and Casey, A.: The current status of the size-distance hypotheses. *Psychol. Bull. 58:* 491–514 (1961).

Eysenck, H. J.: The effects of psychotherapy: An evaluation. *J. Cons. Psychol. 16:* 319–324 (1952).

Fawl, C. L.: Disturbances experienced by children in their natural habitats. *In:* R. G. Barker (Ed.) *The stream of behavior,* pp. 99–126 (Appleton-Century-Crofts, New York, 1963).

Gump, P. V. and Friesen, W. V.: Participation in nonclass settings. *In:* R. G. Barker and P. V. Gump, *Big school, small school,* pp. 75–93 (Stanford University Press, Stanford, Calif., 1964).

Gump, P. V. and Kounin, J. S.: Issues raised by ecological and "classical" research efforts. *Merrill-Palmer Quart. 6:* 145–152 (1959–1960).

Gump, P. V. and Sutton-Smith, B.: The "it" role in children's games. *The Group 17:* 3–8 (1955).

Hall, J. and Williams, M. S.: A comparison of decision-making performances in established and ad hoc groups. *J. Personality Soc. Psychol. 3:* 214–222 (1966).

Imai, S. and Garner, W. R.: Discriminability and preference for attributes in free and constrained classification. *J. Exp. Psychol. 69:* 596–608 (1965).

Jarvis, P. E.: T data, O data and O-T data. *Amer. Psychol. 20:* 796 (1965).

Justice, B.: An inquiry into Negro identity and potential racial violence. Unpublished doctoral dissertation (Rice University, 1966).

Kavanau, J. L.: Behavior: Confinement, adaptation and compulsory regimes in laboratory studies. *Science 143:* 490 (1964).

Kerlinger, F. N.: *Foundations of behavioral research* (Holt, Rinehart and Winston, New York, 1964).

Kiesler, D. J.: Some myths of psychotherapy research and the search for a paradigm. *Psychol. Bull. 65:* 110–136 (1966).

Klein, W.: An investigation of the spontaneous speech of children during problem solving. Unpublished doctoral dissertation (University of Rochester, 1963).

Kounin, J. S.: Dimensions of adult-child relationships in the classroom (Paper read at Topology Meeting, New York, August 1961).

Luborsky, L. A.: A note on Eysenck's article "The effects of psychotherapy: An evaluation." *Brit. J. Psychol. 45:* 129–131 (1954).

Mason, W. A.: The social development of monkeys and apes. *In:* I. De Vore (Ed.) *Primate behavior: Field studies of monkeys and apes,* pp. 514–543 (Holt, Rinehart and Winston, New York, 1965).

McGrath, J. E. and Altman, I.: *Small group research: A synthesis and critique of the field* (Holt, Rinehart and Winston, New York, 1966).

Postman, L. and Tolman, E. C.: Brunswik's probabilistic functionalism. *In:* S. Koch (Ed.) *Psychology: A study of a science.* Vol. 1, pp. 502–564 (McGraw-Hill, New York, 1959).

Purcell, K. and Brady, K.: Adaptation to the invasion of privacy: Monitoring behavior with a miniature radio transmitter. *Merrill-Palmer Quart. 12:* 242–254 (1966).

Rosenzweig, S.: A transvaluation of psychotherapy—a reply to Hans Eysenck, *J. Abnorm. Soc. Psychol. 49:* 298–304 (1954).

Schoggen, P.: Mechanical aids for making specimen records of behavior. *Child Develop. 35:* 985–988 (1964).

Scott, W. A. and Wertheimer, M.: *Introduction to psychological research* (Wiley, New York, 1962).

Sears, P. S.: Problems in the investigation of achievement and self-esteem motivation. *In:* M. R. Jones (Ed.) *Nebraska symposium on motivation,* pp. 265–339 (University of Nebraska Press, Lincoln, Neb., 1957).

Sells, S. B.: Ecology and the science of psychology. *Multivariate Behavioral Res, 1:* 131–144 (1966).

Sherif, M. and Sherif, C. W.: Groups in harmony and tension (Harper & Row, New York, 1953).

Shontz, F. C.: *Research methods in personality* (Appleton-Century-Crofts, New York, 1965).

Taylor, D. W. *et al.:* Education for research in psychology. *Amer. Psychol. 14:* 167–179 (1959).

Underwood, B. J.: *Psychological research* (Appleton-Century-Crofts, New York, 1957).

Washburn, S. L.: Phi Beta Kappa Lecture (University of Kansas, 1963).

Webb, E. J.; Campbell, D. T.; Schwartz, R. D. and Sechrest, L.: *Unobtrusive measures: Non-reactive research in the social sciences* (Rand McNally, Chicago, 1966).

Whyte, W. F.: *Street corner society: The social structure of an Italian slum* (University of Chicago Press, Chicago, 1943).

Willems, E. P.: Forces toward participation in behavior settings. *In:* R. G. Barker and P. V. Gump. *Big school, small school,* pp. 115–135 (Stanford University Press, Stanford, Calif., 1964).

Willems, E. P.: Participation in behavior settings in relation to three variables: Size of behavior settings, marginality of persons, and sensitivity to audiences. Unpublished doctoral dissertation (University of Kansas, 1965, a).

Willems, E. P.: An ecological orientation in psychology. *Merrill-Palmer Quart. 11:* 317–343 (1965, b).

Willems, E. P. and Willems, G. J.: Comparative validity of data yielded by three methods. *Merrill-Palmer Quart. 11:* 65–71 (1965).

4. ON THE NEED FOR RELATIVISM[1]

JEROME KAGAN

The psychology of the first half of this century was absolutistic, outer directed, and intolerant of ambiguity. When a college student carries this unholy trio of traits he is called authoritarian, and such has been the temperament of the behavioral sciences. But the era of authoritarian psychology may be nearing its dotage, and the decades ahead may nurture a discipline that is relativistic, oriented to internal processes, and accepting of the idea that behavior is necessarily ambiguous.

Like her elder sisters, psychology began her dialogue with nature using a vocabulary of absolutes. Stimulus, response, rejection, affection, emotion, reward, and punishment were labels for classes of phenomena that were believed to have a fixed reality. We believed we could write a definition of these constructs that would fix them permanently and allow us to know them unequivocally at any time in any place.

Less than 75 years ago biology began to drift from the constraints of an absolute view of events and processes when she acknowledged that the fate of a small slice of ectodermal tissue depended on whether it was placed near the area of the eye or the toe. Acceptance of the simple notion that whether an object moves or not depends on where you are standing is a little over a half century old in a science that has 5 centuries of formalization. With physics as the referent in time, one might expect a relativistic attitude to influence psychology by the latter

part of the twenty-third century. But philosophical upheavals in one science catalyze change in other disciplines and one can see signs of budding relativism in the intellectual foundations of the social sciences.

The basic theme of this paper turns on the need for more relativistic definitions of selected theoretical constructs. "Relativistic" refers to a definition in which context and the state of the individual are part of the defining statement. Relativism does not preclude the development of operational definitions, but makes that task more difficult. Nineteenth-century physics viewed mass as an absolute value; twentieth-century physics made the definition of mass relative to the speed of light. Similarly, some of psychology's popular constructs have to be defined in relation to the state and belief structure of the organism, rather than in terms of an invariant set of external events. Closely related to this need is the suggestion that some of the energy devoted to a search for absolute, stimulus characteristics of reinforcement be redirected to a search for the determinants of attention in the individual.

It is neither possible nor wise to assign responsibility to one person or event for major changes in conceptual posture, but Helson's recent book on adaptation-level theory (Helson, 1964), Schachter's (Schachter & Singer, 1962) hypothesis concerning the cognitive basis of affects, and Hernández-Peón's demonstration of the neurophysiological bases of selective attention (Hernández-Peón, Scherrer, & Jouvet, 1956) are contemporary stimulants for a relativistic view of psychological phenomena.

Three messages are implicit in the work of these men.

1. If a stimulus is to be regarded as an event to which a subject responds or is likely to respond then it is impossible to describe a stimulus without describing simultaneously the

[1]Preparation of this paper was supported in part by research Grant MH-8792 from the National Institute of Mental Health, United States Public Health Service. This paper is an abridged version of a lecture presented at the Educational Testing Service, Princeton, New Jersey, January 1966.

From the *American Psychologist*, 1967, 22, 131–142. Copyright 1967 by the American Psychological Association. Reprinted by permission of the author and the publisher.

expectancy, and preparation of the organism for that stimulus. Effective stimuli must be distinct from the person's original adaptation level. Contrast and distinctiveness, which are relative, are part and parcel of the definition of a stimulus.

2. The failure of one individual to respond to an event that is an effective stimulus for a second individual is not always the result of central selection after all the information is in, but can be due to various forms of peripheral inhibition. Some stimuli within inches of the face do not ever reach the interpretive cortex and, therefore, do not exist psychologically.

3. Man reacts less to the objective quality of external stimuli than he does to categorizations of those stimuli.

These new generalizations strip the phrase "physical stimulus" of much of its power and certainty, and transfer the scepter of control—in man, at least—to cognitive interpretations. *Contrast, cognitively interpreted, becomes an important key to understanding the incentives for human behavior.* Since contrast depends so intimately on context and expectancy, it must be defined relativistically.

The issue of relativism can be discussed in many contexts. Many existing constructs are already defined in terms of contextual relations. The concept of authority only has meaning if there are fiefs to rule. The role of father has no meaning without a child. The concept of noun, verb, or adjective is defined by context—by the relation of the word to other constituents. We shall consider in some detail the ways in which a relativistic orientation touches two other issues in psychology: the learning of self-descriptive statements (the hoary idea of the self-concept), and even more fundamentally, some of the mechanisms that define the learning process.

The Concept of the Self

The development and establishment of a self-concept is often framed in absolute terms. The classic form of the statement assumes that direct social reinforcements and identification models have fixed, invariant effects on the child. Praise and love from valued caretakers are assumed to lead the child to develop positive self-evaluations; whereas, criticism and rejection presumably cause self-derogatory beliefs. The presumed cause-effect sequences imply that there is a something—a definable set of behaviors—that can be labeled social rejection, and that the essence of these rejecting acts leads to invariant changes in the self-concept of the child. Let us examine the concept of rejection under higher magnification.

The concept of rejection—peer or parental—has been biased toward an absolute definition. Witness the enormous degree of commonality in conceptualization of this concept by investigators who have studied a mother's behavior with her child (Baldwin, Kalhorn, & Breese, 1945; Becker, 1964; Kagan & Moss, 1962; Schaefer, 1959; Schaefer & Bayley, 1963; Sears, Maccoby, & Levin, 1957). These investigators typically decide that harsh physical punishment and absence of social contact or physical affection are the essential indexes of an attitude called maternal rejection. It would be close to impossible for an American rater to categorize a mother as high on both harsh beating of her child and on a loving attitude. A conventionally trained psychologist observing a mother who did not talk to her child for 5 hours would probably view the mother as rejecting. This may be a high form of provincialism. Alfred Baldwin[2] reports that in the rural areas of northern Norway, where homes are 5 to 10 miles apart, and the population constant for generations, one often sees maternal behaviors which an American observer would regard as pathognomonically rejecting in an American mother. The Norwegian mother sees her 4-year-old sitting in the doorway blocking the passage to the next room. She does not ask him to move, but bends down, silently picks him up and moves him away before she passes into the next room. Our middle-class observer would be tempted to view this indifference as a sign of

[2]Personal communication.

dislike. However, most mothers in this Arctic outpost behave this way and the children do not behave the way rejected children should by our current theoretical propositions.

An uneducated Negro mother from North Carolina typically slaps her 4-year-old across the face when he does not come to the table on time. The intensity of the mother's act tempts our observer to conclude that the mother hates, or at best, does not like her child. However, during a half-hour conversation the mother says she loves her child and wants to guarantee that he does not grow up to be a bad boy or a delinquent. And she believes firmly that physical punishment is the most effective way to socialize him. Now her behavior seems to be issued in the service of affection rather than hate. Determination of whether a parent is rejecting or not cannot be answered by focusing primarily on the behaviors of the parents. Rejection is not a fixed, invariant quality of behavior qua behavior. Like pleasure, pain, or beauty, rejection is in the mind of the rejectee. It is a belief held by the child; not an action by a parent.

We must acknowledge, first, a discontinuity in the meaning of an acceptance-rejection dimension before drawing further implications. We must distinguish between the child prior to 30 or 36 months of age, before he symbolically evaluates the actions of others, and the child thereafter.

We require, first, a concept to deal with the child's belief of his value in the eyes of others. The child of 4 or 5 years is conceptually mature enough to have recognized that certain resources parents possess are difficult for the child to obtain. He views these resources as sacrifices and interprets their receipt as signs that the parents value him. The child constructs a tote board of the differential value of parental gifts—be they psychological or material. The value of the gift depends on its scarcity. A $10.00 toy from a busy executive father is not a valued resource; the same toy from a father out of work is much valued. The value depends on the child's personal weightings. This position would lead to solipsism were it not for the fact that most parents are essentially narcissistic and do not readily give the child long periods of uninterrupted companionship. Thus, most children place high premium on this act. Similarly, parents are generally reluctant to proffer unusually expensive gifts to children, and this act acquires value for most youngsters. Finally, the child learns from the public media that physical affection means positive evaluation and he is persuaded to assign premium worth to this set of acts. There is, therefore, some uniformity across children in a culture in the evaluation of parental acts. But the anchor point lies within the child, not with the particular parental behaviors.

This definition of acceptance or rejection is not appropriate during the opening years. The 1-year-old does not place differential symbolic worth on varied parental acts, and their psychological significance derives from the overt responses they elicit and strengthen. A heavy dose of vocalization and smiling to an infant is traditionally regarded as indicative of maternal affection and acceptance. This bias exists because we have accepted the myth that "affection" is the essential nutrient that produces socially adjusted children, adolescents, and adults. The bias maintains itself because we observe a positive association between degree of parental smiling and laughing to the infant and prosocial behavior in the child during the early years. The responses of smiling, laughing, and approaching people are learned in the opening months of life on the basis of standard conditioning principles. This conclusion is supported by the work of Rheingold and Gewirtz (1959) and Brackbill (1958). However, phenotypically similar behaviors in a 10- or 20-year-old may have a different set of antecedents. The argument that different definitions of rejection-acceptance must be written for the pre- and postsymbolic child gains persuasive power from the fact that there are no data indicating that degree of prosocial behavior in the child is stable from 6 months to 16 years. Indeed, the longitudinal material from the Fels Research Institute study of behavior stability (Kagan & Moss, 1962) showed no evidence of any relation between joy or anxiety in the presence of adults during the first 2–3 years of life and phenotypically similar behaviors at 6, 12, or 24 years of age. The child behaviors that are presumed, by theory, to be the consequences of low or high parental rejection do not show stability from infancy through adolescence. This may be because the childhood responses, though phenotypically similar to the adult acts, may be acquired and maintained through different experiences at different periods.

It seems reasonable to suggest, therefore, that different theoretical words are necessary for the following three classes of phenomena: (*a*) an attitude on the part of the parent, (*b*) the quality and frequency of acts of parental care and social stimulation directed toward the infant, and (*c*) a child's assessment of his value in the eyes of another. All three classes are currently viewed as of the same cloth. The latter meaning of "rejection" (i.e., a belief held by a child) is obviously relativistic for it grows out of different experiences in different children.

Self-Descriptive Labels

Let us probe further into the ideas surrounding the learning of self-evaluation statements, beyond the belief, "I am not valued." The notion of a self-concept has a long and spotted history and although it has masqueraded by many names in different theoretical costumes, its intrinsic meaning has changed only a little. A child presumably learns self-descriptive statements whose contents touch the salient attributes of the culture. The mechanisms classically invoked to explain how these attributes are learned have stressed the invariant effects of direct social reinforcement and identification. The girl who is told she is attractive, annoying, or inventive, comes to believe these appellations and to apply these qualifiers to herself. We have assumed that the laws governing the learning of self-descriptive labels resemble the learning of other verbal habits with frequency and contiguity of events being the shapers of the habit. Identification as a source of self-labels involves a different mechanism, but retains an absolutistic frame of reference. The child assumes that he shares attributes with particular models. If the model is viewed as subject to violent rages, the child concludes that he, too, shares this tendency.

Theory and data persuade us to retain some faith in these propositions. But relativistic factors also seem to sculpt the acquisition of self-descriptive labels, for the child evaluates himself on many psychological dimensions by inferring his rank order from a delineated reference group. The 10-year-old does not have absolute measuring rods to help him decide how bright, handsome, or likeable he is. He naturally and spontaneously uses his immediate peer group as the reference for these evaluations. An immediate corollary of this statement is that the child's evaluation is dependent upon the size and psychological quality of the reference group, and cannot be defined absolutely. Specifically, the larger the peer group, the less likely a child will conclude he is high in the rank order, the less likely he will decide he is unusually smart, handsome, or capable of leadership. Consider two boys with IQs of 130 and similar intellectual profiles. One lives in a small town, the other in a large city. It is likely that the former child will be the most competent in his peer group while the latter is likely to regard himself as fifth or sixth best. This difference in perceived rank order has obvious action consequences since we acknowledge that expectancies govern behavior. In sum, aspects of the self-descriptive process appear to develop in relativistic soil.

Learning and Attention

A second issue that touches relativistic definitions deals with a shift from external definitions of reinforcement—that is, reward or pleasure—to definitions that are based more directly on internal processes involving the concept of attention. Failure to understand the nature of learning is one of the major intellectual frustrations for many psychologists. The query, "What is learning?" has the same profound ring as the question, "What is a gene?" had a decade ago. Our biological colleagues have recently had a major insight while psychology is still searching. The murky question, "What is learning?" usually reduces to an attempt to discover the laws relating stimuli, pain, and pleasure, on the one hand, with habit acquisition and performance, on the other. Pain, pleasure, and reinforcement are usually defined in terms of events that are external to the organism and have an invariant flavor. Miller (1951) suggested that reinforcement was isomorphic with stimulus reduction; Leuba (1955) argued for an optimal level of stimulation, but both implied that there was a level that could be specified and measured. We should like to argue first that sources of pleasure and, therefore, of reinforcement, are often relative, and second, that the essence of learning is more dependent on attentional involvement by the learner than on specific qualities of particular external events.

The joint ideas that man is a pleasure seeker and that one can designate specific forms of stimulation as sources of pleasure are central postulates in every man's theory of behavior. Yet we find confusion when we seek a definition of pleasure. The fact that man begins life with a small core set of capacities for experience that he wishes to repeat cannot be disputed. This is a pragmatic view of pleasure and we can add a dash of phenomenology to bolster the intuitive validity of this point of view. A sweet taste and a light touch in selected places are usually pleasant. Recently, we have added an important new source of pleasure. It is better to say we have rediscovered a source of pleasure, for Herbert Spencer was a nineteenth-century progenitor of the idea that *change in stimulation* is a source of pleasure for rats, cats, monkeys, or men. But, change is short-lived, quickly digested, and transformed to monotony. Popping up in front of an infant and saying peek-a-boo is pleasant for a 3-month-old infant for about 15 minutes, for a 10-month-old infant for 3 minutes and for a 30-month-old child, a few seconds. This pleasant experience, like most events that elicit their repetition a few times before dying, is usually conceptualized as a change in stimulation. The source of the pleasure is sought in the environment. Why should change in external stimulation be

pleasant? The understanding of pleasure and reinforcement in man is difficult enough without having to worry about infrahuman considerations. Let us restrict the argument to the human. The human is a cognitive creature who is attempting to put structure or create schema for incoming stimulation. A schema is a representation of an external pattern; much as an artist's illustration is a representation of an event. A schema for a visual pattern is a partial and somewhat distorted version of what the photograph would be. Consider the usefulness of the following hypothesis:

The creation of a schema for an event is one major source of pleasure. When one can predict an event perfectly, the schema is formed. As long as prediction is not perfect the schema is not yet formed. The peek-a-boo game works for 15 minutes with a 12-week-old for it takes him that long to be able to predict the event—the "peak-a-boo." Charlesworth (1965) has demonstrated the reinforcing value of "uncertainty" in an experiment in which the peek-a-boo face appeared either in the same locus every trial, alternated between two loci, or appeared randomly in one of two loci. The children persisted in searching for the face for a much longer time under the random condition than under the other two conditions. The random presentation was reinforcing for a longer period of time, not because it possessed a more optimum level of external stimulation than the other reinforcement schedules, but because it took longer for the child to create a schema for the random presentation and the process of creating a schema is a source of pleasure.

Consider another sign of pleasure beside persistence in issuing a particular response. Display of a smile or laugh is a good index of pleasure. Indeed, Tomkins' (1962) scheme for affect demands that pleasure be experienced if these responses appear. Consider two studies that bear on the relation between pleasure and the creation of schema. In our laboratory during the last 2 years, we have seen the same infants at 4, 8, and 13 months of age and have shown them a variety of visual patterns representative of human faces and human forms. In one episode, the 4-month-old infants are shown achromatic slides of a photograph of a regular male face, a schematic outline of a male face, and two disarranged, disordered faces. The frequency of occurrence of smiling to the photograph of the regular face is over *twice* the frequency observed to the regular schematic face—although looking time is identical—and over *four times* the frequency shown to the disordered faces. In another, more realistic episode, the 4-month-old infants see a regular, flesh-colored sculptured face in three dimensions and a distorted version of that face in which the eyes, nose, and mouth are rearranged. At 4 months of age the occurrence of smiling to the regular face is over three times the frequency displayed to the distorted version, but looking time is identical. There are two interpretations of this difference (Kagan, Henker, Hen-Tov, Levine, & Lewis, 1966). One explanation argues that the mother's face has become a secondary reward; the regular face stands for pleasure because it has been associated with care and affection from the mother. As a result, it elicits more smiles. An alternative interpretation is that the smile response has become conditioned to the human face via reciprocal contact between mother and infant. A third interpretation, not necessarily exclusive of these, is that the smile can be elicited when the infant matches stimulus to schema—when he has an "aha" reaction; when he makes a cognitive discovery. The 4-month-old infant is cognitively close to establishing a relatively firm schema of a human face. When a regular representation of a face is presented to him there is a short period during which the stimulus is assimilated to the schema and then after several seconds, a smile may occur. The smile is released following the perceptual recognition of the face, and reflects the assimilation of the stimulus to the infant's schema—a small, but significant act of creation. This hypothesis is supported by the fact that the typical latency between the onset of looking at the regular face (in the 4-month-old) and the onset of smiling is about 3 to 5 seconds. The smile usually does not occur immediately but only after the infant has studied the stimulus. If one sees this phenomenon live, it is

difficult to avoid the conclusion that the smile is released following an act of perceptual recognition.

Additional data on these and other children at 8 months of age support this idea. At 8 months, frequency of smiling to both the regular and distorted faces is *reduced dramatically,* indicating that smiling does not covary with the reward value of the face. The face presumably has acquired more reward value by 8 months than it had at 4 months. However, the face is now a much firmer schema and recognition of it is immediate. There is no effortful act of recognition necessary for most infants. As a result, smiling is less likely to occur. Although smiling is much less frequent at 8 than 4 months to all faces, the frequency of smiling to the distorted face now *equals* the frequency displayed to the regular face. We interpret this to mean that the distorted face is sufficiently similar to the child's schema of a regular face that it can be recognized as such.

The pattern of occurrence of cardiac deceleration to the regular and distorted three-dimensional faces furnishes the strongest support for this argument. A cardiac deceleration of about 8 to 10 beats often accompanies attention to selected incoming visual stimuli in adults, school-age children, and infants. Moreover, the deceleration tends to be maximal when the stimuli are not overly familiar or completely novel, but are of intermediate familiarity. One hypothesis maintains that a large deceleration is most likely to occur when an act of perceptual recognition occurs, when the organism has a cognitive surprise. Let us assume that there is one trial for which this type of reaction occurs with maximal magnitude. If one examines the one stimulus presentation (out of a total of 16 trials) that produces the largest cardiac deceleration, a lawful change occurs between 4 and 8 months of age. At 4 months of age more of the infants showed their largest deceleration to the regular face (45% of the group: $n = 52$) than to the scrambled (34%), no eyes (11%), or blank faces (10%). At 8 months, the majority of the infants ($n = 52$) showed their largest deceleration to the scrambled face (50% to scrambled versus 21% to regular face).

This difference is interpreted to mean that the scrambled face now assumes a similar position on the assimilation continuum that the regular face did 16 weeks earlier.

At 13 months of age these infants are shown six three-dimensional representations of a male human form and a free form matched for area, coloration, and texture with the human form. The stimuli include a faithful representation of a regular man, that same man with his head placed between his legs, the same man with all limbs and head collaged in an unusual and scrambled pattern, the man's body with a mule's head, the mule's head on the man's body, the man's body with three identical heads, and a free form. The distribution of smiles to these stimuli is leptokurtic, with over 70% of all the smiles occurring to the animal head on the human body and the three-headed man, forms that were moderate transformations of the regular man, and stimuli that required active assimilation. The free form and the scrambled man rarely elicited smiles from these infants. These stimuli are too difficult to assimilate to the schema of a human form possessed by a 13-month-old infant. It is interesting to note that the regular human form sometimes elicited the verbal response "daddy" or a hand waving from the child. These instrumental social reactions typically did not occur to the transformations. The occurrence of cardiac deceleration to these patterns agrees with this hypothesis. At 13 months of age, the man with his head between his legs, the man with the animal head, or the three-headed man, each elicited the largest cardiac decelerations more frequently than the regular man, the scrambled man, or the free form ($p < .05$ for each comparison). Thus, large cardiac decelerations and smiles were most likely to occur to stimuli that seemed to require tiny, quiet cognitive discoveries—miniaturized versions of Archimedes' "Eureka."

It appears that the act of matching stimulus to schema when the match is close but not yet perfect is a dynamic event. Stimuli that deviate a critical amount from the child's schema for a pattern are capable of eliciting an active process of recognition, and this process behaves as if it were a source of pleasure. Stimuli that are easily assimilable or too difficult to assimilate do not elicit these reactions.

A recent study by Edward Zigler[3] adds important support to the notion that the smile indicates the pleasure of an assimilation. Children in Grades 2, 3, 4, and 5 looked at cartoons that required little or no reading. The children were asked to explain the cartoon while an observer coded the spontaneous occurrence of laughing and smiling while the children were studying the cartoons. It should come as no surprise that verbal comprehension of the cartoons increased in a linear fashion with age. But laughing and smiling increased through Grade 4 and then declined markedly among the fifth-grade children. The fifth graders understood the cartoons too well. There was no gap between stimulus and schema and no smiling. Sixteen-week-old infants and 8-year-old children smile spontaneously at events that seem to have one thing in common—the event is a partial match to an existing schema and an active process of recognitory assimilation must occur.

The fact that a moderate amount of mismatch between event and schema is one source of pleasure demands the conclusion that it is not always possible to say that a specific event will always be a source of pleasure. The organism's state and structure must be in the equation. This conclusion parallels the current interest in complexity and information uncertainty. The psychologist with an information-theory prejudice classifies a stimulus as uncertain and often assumes that he does not have to be too concerned with the attributes of the viewer. This error of the absolute resembles the nineteenth-century error in physics and biology. This is not a titillating or pedantic philosophical issue. Psychology rests on a motive-reinforcement foundation which regards pleasure and pain as pivotal ideas in the grand theory. These constructs have tended to generate absolute definitions. We have been obsessed with finding a fixed and invariant characterization of pleasure, pain, and reinforcement. Melzack & Wall (1965) point out that although the empiri-

---

[3]Unpublished paper; personal communication.

cal data do not support the notion of a fixed place in the brain that mediates pain, many scientists resist shedding this comfortable idea. Olds' (1958, 1962) discovery of brain reinforcing areas has generated excitement because many of us want to believe that pleasure has a fixed and absolute locus. The suspicious element in this discovery of pleasure spots is that there is no habituation of responses maintained by electrical stimulation to hypothalamic or septal nuclei, and minimal resistance to extinction of habits acquired via this event. Yet, every source of pleasure known to phenomenal man does satiate—for awhile or forever—and habits that lead to pleasant events do persist for a while after the pleasure is gone. These observations are troubling and additional inquiry is necessary if we are to decide whether these cells are indeed the bed where pleasure lies.

We are convinced that contiguity alone does not always lead to learning. Something must ordinarily be added to contiguity in order to produce a new bond. Psychology has chosen to call this extra added mysterious something reinforcement, much like eighteenth-century chemists chose to label their unknown substance phlogiston. If one examines the variety of external events that go by the name of reinforcement it soon becomes clear that this word is infamously inexact. A shock to an animal's paw is a reinforcement, a verbal chastisement is a reinforcement, an examiner's smile is a reinforcement, a pellet of food is a reinforcement, and a sigh indicating tension reduction after watching a killer caught in a Hitchcock movie is a reinforcement. These events have little, if any, phenotypic similarity. What then, do they have in common? For if they have nothing in common it is misleading to call them by the same name. Learning theorists have acknowledged their failure to supply an independent a priori definition of reinforcement and the definition they use is purely pragmatic. A reinforcement is anything that helps learning. And so, we ask: What has to be added to contiguity in order to obtain learning? A good candidate for the missing ingredient is the phrase "attentional involvement." Let us consider again the events called reinforcements:

a shock, food, a smile, each of these acts to attract the attention of the organism to some agent or object. They capture the organism's attention and maybe that is why they facilitate learning. Consider the idea that what makes an event reinforcing is the fact that it (a) elicits the organism's attention to the feedback from the response he has just made and to the mosaic of stimuli in the learning situation and (b) acts as an incentive for a subsequent response. The latter quality is what ties the word "reinforcement" to the concepts of motivation and need, but much learning occurs without the obvious presence of motives or needs. Ask any satiated adult to attend carefully and remember the bond syzygy-aardvark. It is likely that learning will occur in one trial. It is not unreasonable to argue that a critical component of events that have historically been called reinforcement is their ability to attract the organism's attention. They have been distinctive cues in a context; they have been events discrepant from the individual's adaptation level. If attention is acknowledged as critical in new mental acquisitions it is appropriate to ask if attention is also bedded in relativistic soil. The answer appears to be "Yes." The dramatic experiments of Hernández-Peón and his colleagues (1956) are persuasive in indicating that attention investment may not be distributed to many channels at once. One has to know the state of the organism. Knowledge of the organism's distribution of attention in a learning situation may clarify many controversial theoretical polemics that range from imprinting in chickens to emotion in college undergraduates. For example, comparative psychologists quarrel about which set of external conditions allow imprinting to occur with maximal effect. Some say the decoy should move; still others argue that the young chick should move; still others urge that the decoy be brightly colored (e.g., Bateson, 1964a, 1964b; Hess, 1959; Klopfer, 1965; Thompson & Dubanoski, 1964). The quarrel centers around the use of phenotypically different observable conditions. Perhaps all these suggestions are valid. Moving the decoy, or active following by the infant chick, or a distinctively colored decoy all maximize the organism's level of attention to the decoy. The genotypic event may remain the same across all of these manipulations.

A similar interpretation can be imposed on Held's (1965) recent hypothesis concerning the development of space and pattern perception. Held controlled the visual experience of pairs of kittens. The only exposure to light was limited to a few hours a day when one kitten was placed in a gondola and moved around by an active, free kitten in an arena whose walls were painted in vertical stripes. After 30 hours of such experience each kitten was tested. The free kitten showed appropriate visual reactions. It blinked when an object approached; it put up its paws to avoid collision when carried near to a surface; it avoided the deep side of a visual cliff. The passive passenger kitten did not show these normal reactions. Why? Held, focusing on the obvious external variable of activity versus no activity, concludes that the sensory feedback accompanying movement is necessary to develop visual-motor control. This conclusion rests on the assumption that the passive kitten sitting in the gondola was attending to the stripes on the wall as intently as the free walking kitten. This assumption may be gratuitous. If the passive kitten were staring blankly—as many human infants do—then one would not expect these animals to develop normal perceptual structures. This interpretation may not be better, but it has a different flavor than the one suggested by Held.

A final example of the central role of attention is seen in Aronfreed's (1964, 1965) recent work on the learning of self-critical comments. Aronfreed states that the learning of a self-critical comment proceeds best if the child is first punished and then hears a social agent speak the self-critical statement. He interprets this result in drive reduction language. However, suppose one asks which sequence is most likely to maximize a child's attention to the adult's comment—Punish first and then speak to the child? Or speak first and then punish? The former sequence should be more effective. The punishment is a violation of what the child expects from a strange adult and recruits the child's attention to the adult. The child is primed to listen to the self-critical commendation and thus more likely to learn it.

Distinctiveness of Cues

The above examples suggest that the organism's distribution of attention is a critical process that should guide our search for the bases of many diverse phenomena. One of the critical bases for recruitment of attention pivots on the idea of distinctiveness of the signal. Jakobson and Halle (1956) argue that the chronology of acquisition of phonemes proceeds according to a principle of distinctive elements. Distinctive elements capture the child's attention and give direction to the order of learning.

The importance of *relative distinctiveness of cues* finds an interesting illustration in the concept of affect. The concept of emotion has lived through three distinct eras in modern times. The pre-Jamesian assumed the sequence was: stimulus event—cognition—visceral response. James interchanged events two and three and said that the visceral afferent feedback occurred before the cognition. But Cannon quieted Jamesian ideas until Schachter's ingenious studies and catching explanations suggested that the individual experiences a puzzling set of visceral afferent sensations and integrates them cognitively. The language integration of visceral feelings, cognition, and context is an affect. This imaginative suggestion may be maximally valid for Western adults but perhaps minimally appropriate for children because of a developmental change in the relative distinctiveness of visceral cues.

Let us share a small set of assumptions before we proceed with the argument. Aside from pain and its surrogates, the major psychological elicitors of unpleasant visceral afferent sensations are violations of expectancies (uncertainty); anticipation of receiving or losing a desired goal; anticipation of seeing or losing a nurturant person; blocking of goal attainment; and anticipation of harm to the integrity of the body. Each of these event situations becomes conditioned to visceral afferent feedback early in life. These events—or conditioned stimuli —are salient and maximally distinctive for children and affect words are attached to the events, not primarily to the visceral afferent sensations. Thus, the 6-year-old says he is mad because mother did not let him watch television; he says he is sad because the cat died; he says he is happy because he just received a prized toy. Affect words are labels for a set of external events. With development, individuals—with the help of social institutions—learn to protect themselves against most of the unpleasant sources of visceral afferent feedback—against the apocalyptic horsemen of uncertainty, loss of nurturance, goal blocking, and bodily harm. Moreover, they erect defenses against rec- ognizing these events. They defend against recognition that they are confused, rejected, unable to attain a goal, or afraid. Thus, when events occur that are, in fact, representations of these situations, the events are not salient or distinctive and are not labeled. However, the conditioned visceral afferent sensations do occur, as they always have in the past. In the adult, the visceral afferent sensations become more distinctive or salient; whereas, for the child, the external events were salient and distinctive. The adult provides us with the situation Schachter and his colleagues have described. The adult often has visceral afferent sensations but cannot decide why he has them or what they mean. So he scans and searches the immediate past and context and decides that he is happy, sad, alienated, uncommitted, or in love. The essence of this argument is that for the child the external event is more distinctive than the visceral afferent sensations and the affect word is applied to external events. In the adult, the visceral afferent sensations are rel- atively more distinctive and the affect words are more often applied to them.

The personality differences ascribed to children in different ordinal positions are the result, in part, of differences in relative dis- tinctiveness of social agents. For the firstborn, the adult is the distinctive stimulus to whom to attend; for the second born the older sibling has

distinctive value and competes for the attention of the younger child. Only children lie alone for long periods of uninterrupted play. A parent who enters the room and speaks to the infant is necessarily a distinctive stimulus. For a fifth born whose four older siblings continually poke, fuss, and vocalize into the crib, the caretaking adult, is, of necessity, less distinc- tive and, as a result, less attention will be paid to the adult. The importance of distinctiveness with respect to adaptation level engages the heated controversy surrounding the role of stimulus enrichment with infants and young children from deprived milieux. The pouring on of visual, auditory, and tactile stimulation willy-nilly should be less effective than a single distinctive stimulus presented in a context of quiet so it will be discrepant from the infant's adaptation level. If one takes this hypothesis seriously, a palpable change in enrichment strategies is implied. The theme of this change involves a shifting from a concern with in- creasing absolute level of stimulation to focus- ing on distinctiveness of stimulation. Culturally disadvantaged children are not deprived of stimulation; they are deprived of distinctive stimulation.

The early learning of sex role standards and the dramatic concern of school children with sex differences and their own sex role identity becomes reasonable when one considers that the differences between the sexes are highly dis- tinctive. Voice, size, posture, dress, and usual locus of behavior are distinctive attributes that focus the child's attention on them.

One of the reasons why the relation between tutor and learner is important is that some tutors elicit greater attention than others. They are more distinctive. Those of us who contend that learning will be facilitated if the child is identified with or wants to identify with a tutor believe that one of the bases for the facilitation is the greater attention that is directed at a model with whom the child wishes to identify. A re- cent experiment touches on this issue.

The hypothesis can be simply stated. An individual will attend more closely to an initial stranger with whom he feels he shares attributes than to a stranger with whom he feels he does not share attributes, other things equal. The former model is more distinctive, for a typical adult ordinarily feels he does not share basic personality traits with most of the strangers that he meets. The subjects in this study were 56 Radcliffe freshmen and sophomores preselected for the following pair of traits. One group, the academics, were rated by four judges—all roommates—as being intensely involved in studies much more than they were in dating, clubs, or social activities. The second group, the social types, were rated as being much more involved in dating and social activities than they were in courses or grades. No subject was admitted into the study unless all four judges agreed that she fit one of these groups.

Each subject was seen individually by a Radcliffe senior, and told that each was participating in a study of creativity. The subject was told that Radcliffe seniors had written poems and that two of the poets were selected by the Harvard faculty as being the best candidates. The faculty could not decide which girl was the more creative and the student was going to be asked to judge the creativity of each of two poems that the girls had written. The subjects were told that creativity is independent of IQ for bright people and they were told that since the faculty knew the personality traits of the girls, the student would be given that information also. The experimenter then described one of the poets as an academic grind and the other as a social activist. Each subject listened to two different girls recite two different poems on a tape. Order of presentation and voice of the reader were counterbalanced in an appropriate design. After the two poems were read the subject was asked for a verbatim recall of each poem, asked to judge its creativity, and finally, asked which girl she felt most similar to. Incidentally, over 95% of the subjects said they felt more similar to the model that they indeed matched in reality. Results supported the original hypothesis. Recall was best when a girl listened to a communicator with whom she shared personality traits. The academic subjects recalled more of the poem when it was read by the academic model than by the social model; whereas, the social subjects recalled more of the poem when it was read by the social model than the academic model. This study indicates that an individual will pay more attention to a model who possesses similar personality attributes than to one who is not similar to the subject. Distinctiveness of tutor is enhanced by a perceived relation between learner and tutor.

Myths and superstitions are established around the kinds of experimental manipulations teachers or psychologists should perform in order to maximize the probability that learning will occur. When one focuses on the kind of manipulation—providing a model, giving a reinforcement, labeling the situation, punishing without delay—there is a strong push to establish superstitions about how behavioral change is produced. Recipes are written and adopted. If one believes, on the other hand, that a critical level of attention to incoming information is the essential variable, then one is free to mix up manipulations, to keep the recipe open, as long as one centers the subject's attention on the new material.

The most speculative prediction from this general argument is that behavioral therapy techniques will work for some symptoms—for about 20 years. A violation of an expectancy is a distinctive stimulus that attracts attention. The use of operant shaping techniques to alleviate phobias is a dramatic violation of an expectancy for both child and adult, and attention is magnetized and focused on the therapeutic agent and his paraphernalia. As a result, learning is facilitated. But each day's use of this strategy may bring its demise closer. In time, a large segment of the populace will have adapted to this event; it will be a surprise no more and its attention getting and therapeutic value will be attenuated. Much of the power of psychoanalytic techniques began to wane when the therapist's secrets became public knowledge. If therapy is accomplished by teaching new responses, and if the learning of new responses is most likely to occur when attention to the teacher is maximal, it is safe to expect that we may need a new strategy of teaching patients new tricks by about 1984.

Let us weave the threads closer in an attempt at final closure. The psychology of the first half of this century was the product of a defensively sudden rupture from philosophy to natural science. The young discipline needed roots and, like a child, attached itself to an absolute description of nature, much as a 5-year-old clings to an absolute conception of morality. We now approach the latency years and can afford to relax and learn something from developments in our sister sciences. The message implicit in the recent work in psychology, biology, and physics contains a directive to abandon absolutism in selected theoretical areas. Conceptual ideas for mental processes must be invented, and this task demands a relativistic orientation. Learning is one of the central problems in psychology, and understanding of the mechanisms of learning requires elucidation and measurement of the concept of attention. Existing data indicate that attention is under the control of distinctive stimuli, and distinctiveness depends intimately on adaptation level of subject and context, and cannot be designated in absolute terms.

These comments are not to be regarded as a plea to return to undisciplined philosophical introspection. Psychology does possess some beginning clues as to how it might begin to measure elusive, relative concepts like "attention." Autonomic variables such as cardiac and respiratory rate appear to be useful indexes, and careful studies of subtle motor discharge patterns may provide initial operational bases for this construct.

Neurophysiologists have been conceptualizing their data in terms of attention distribution for several years, and they are uncovering some unusually provocative phenomena. For example, amplitude of evoked potentials from the association areas of the cortex are beginning to be regarded as a partial index of attention. Thompson and Shaw (1965) recorded evoked potentials from the association area of the cat's cortex—the middle suprasylvian gyrus—to a click, a light, or a shock to the forepaw. After they established base level response to each of these "standard" stimuli, the investigators presented these standard stimuli when the cat was active or when novel stimuli were introduced. The novel events were a rat in a bell jar, an air jet, or a growling sound. The results were unequivocal. Any one of these novel stimuli or activity by the cat produced reduced cortical evoked responses to the click, light, or shock. The authors suggest that the "amplitude of the evoked responses are inversely proportional to attention to a particular event (p. 338)." Psychology is beginning to develop promising strategies of measurement for the murky concept of attention and should begin to focus its theorizing and burgeoning measurement technology on variables having to do with the state of the organism, not just the quality of the external stimulus. The latter events can be currently objectified with greater elegance, but the former events seem to be of more significance. Mannheim once chastised the social sciences for seeming to be obsessed with studying what they could measure without error, rather than measuring what they thought to be important with the highest precision possible. It is threatening to abandon the security of the doctrine of absolutism of the stimulus event. Such a reorientation demands new measurement procedures, novel strategies of inquiry, and a greater tolerance for ambiguity. But let us direct our inquiry to where the pot of gold seems to shimmer and not fear to venture out from cozy laboratories where well-practiced habits have persuaded us to rationalize a faith in absolute monarchy.

REFERENCES

Aronfreed, J. The origin of self criticism. *Psychological Review,* 1964, *71*, 193–218.

Aronfreed, J. Internalized behavioral suppression and the timing of social punishment. *Journal of Personality and Social Psychology*, 1965, *1*, 3–16.

Baldwin, A. L., Kalhorn, J., & Breese, F. H. Patterns of parent behavior. *Psychological Monographs*, 1945, *58* (3, Whole No. 268).

Bateson, P. P. G. Changes in chicks' responses to novel moving objects over the sensitive period for imprinting. *Animal Behavior*, 1964, *12*, 479–489. (a)

Bateson, P. P. G. Relation between conspicuousness of stimuli and their effectiveness in the imprinting situation. *Journal of Comparative and Physiological Psychology*, 1964, *58*, 407–411. (b)

Becker, W. C. Consequences of different kinds of parental discipline. In M. L. Hoffman & L. W. Hoffman (Eds.), *Review of child development research*. Vol. 1. New York: Russell Sage Foundation, 1964. Pp. 169–208.

Brackbill, Y. Extinction of the smiling response in infants as a function of reinforcement schedule. *Child Development*, 1958, *29*, 115–124.

Charlesworth, W. R. Persistence of orienting and attending behavior in young infants as a function of stimulus uncertainty. Paper read at Society for Research in Child Development, Minneapolis, March 1965.

Held, R. Plasticity in sensory motor systems. *Scientific American,* 1965, *213* (5), 84–94.

Helson, H. *Adaptation level theory: An experimental and systematic approach to behavior*. New York: Harper & Row, 1964.

Hernández-Peón, R., Scherrer, H., & Jouvet, M. Modification of electrical activity in cochlear nucleus during attention in unanesthetized cats. *Science*, 1956, *123*, 331–332.

Hess, E. H. Two conditions limiting critical age for imprinting. *Journal of Comparative and Physiological Psychology*, 1959, *52*, 515–518.

Jakobson, R., & Halle, M. *Fundamentals of language*. The Hague: Mouton, 1956.

Kagan, J., Henker, B. A., Hen-Tov, A., Levine, J., & Lewis, M. Infants' differential reactions to familiar and distorted faces. *Child Development*, 1966, *37*, 519–532.

Kagan, J., & Moss, H. A. *Birth to maturity*. New York: Wiley, 1962.

Klopfer, P. H. Imprinting: A reassessment. *Science*, 1965, *147*, 302–303.

Leuba, C. Toward some integration of learning theories: The concept of optimal stimulation. *Psychological Reports*, 1955, *1*, 27–33.

Melzack, R., & Wall, P. D. Pain mechanisms: A new theory. *Science*, 1965, *150*, 971–979.

Miller, N. E. Learnable drives and rewards. In S. S. Stevens (Ed.), *Handbook of experimental psychology*. New York: Wiley, 1951. Pp. 435–472.

Olds, J. Self stimulation of the brain. *Science,* 1958, *127*, 315–324.

Olds, J. Hypothalamic substrates of reward. *Physiological Review*, 1962, *42*, 554–604.

Rheingold, H., Gewirtz, J. L., & Ross, H. Social conditioning of vocalizations in the infant. *Journal of Comparative and Physiological Psychology*, 1959, *52*, 68–73.

Schachter, S., & Singer, J. E. Cognitive, social and physiological determinants of emotional states. *Psychological Review,* 1962, *69*, 379–399.

Schaefer, E. S. A circumflex model for maternal behavior. *Journal of Abnormal and Social Psychology*, 1959, *59*, 226–235.

Schaefer, E. S. & Bayley, N. Maternal behavior, child behavior and their intercorrelations from infancy through adolescence. *Monographs of the Society for Research in Child Development*, 1963, *28*, No. 87.

Sears, R. R., Maccoby, E. E., & Levin, H. *Patterns of child rearing*. Row Peterson, 1957.

Thompson, R. F., & Shaw, J. A. Behavioral correlates of evoked activity recorded from association areas of the cerebral cortex. *Journal of Comparative and Physiological Psychology*, 1965, *60*, 329–339.

Thompson, W. R., & Dubanoski, R. A. Imprinting and the law of effort. *Animal Behavior*, 1964, *12*, 213–218.

Tomkins, S. S. *Affect imagery consciousness*. Vol. 1: *The positive affects*. New York: Springer, 1962.

Chapter 4
BIOLOGICAL FACTORS

INTRODUCTION AND COMMENTARY

The focus of this chapter is upon a somewhat heterogeneous set of research activities. Its theme is biological factors of development, but the selection of papers included serves mainly to establish the context in which to consider these factors. Necessarily it falls short of representing all its content areas.

Interest in biological factors of development means interest in those structural features of the developing organism that are of some special relevance for understanding the organism's development. Such an interest by psychologists has taken at least three forms. It can be asked what features of the development of a particular organism can better be understood (1) by viewing the organism in its *phylogenetic context*; that is, by focusing on interspecies differences (for a recent discussion of the structure of such a context, see Hodos & Campbell, 1969; see also Razran, 1965); (2) by examining or understanding its *genetic characteristics*; that is, by focusing on interorganism (individual) differences (see, e.g., McClearn, 1964; Ehrman, Omenn, & Caspari, 1972; and Vale, 1973); and (3) by examining its *ontogenetic features* (physiological and anatomical structures): that is, by focusing on separate systems within an organism (see, e.g., Rosenzweig, 1966; and see Campbell & Spear [16]).

Phylogenetic Context

The first form of interest shown by psychologists—viewing the organism in its phylogenetic context—implies comparative or cross-species observations. For example, in considering species ranged roughly along a dimension of complexity from protozoan to *homo sapiens*, one can observe the diminishing role of reflexes and instincts in the behavior of organisms; also, generally speaking, one can notice along the same dimension the increasing dependence of newborns on parental rearing. Appreciation of this phylogenetic context can lead not only to firmer bases for evaluating a development-related phenomenon (e.g., a phenomenon's uniqueness to people, or to mammals, or to vertebrates), but it also has been the basis for the widely held conviction that the study of other species might eventually aid us to understand humans. Of course, the general possibility exists that the study of any species might aid in the understanding of any other species.

It should be noted here that the reader will encounter emphasis on this phylogenetic point of view throughout the book (see Chapter 2, p. 15). It stems from the editors' belief, which is substantiated by a fruitful and growing research literature, that a full-blown developmental psychology must be based in a phylogenetic context.

Genetic Context

Examining genetic characteristcs involves asking what features of a given organism's behavior are attributable to the genetic properties of its parents. That is, are some particular behavior potentialities genetically determined, and to what extent is the manifestation of these potentialities dependent on particular environmental factors? The familiar old issue of environment versus heredity (the so-called nature-nurture controversy; see Chapter 2, pp. 13–15), may be seen to rise again here, but it now has much more sophisticated forms (see Hebb, 1972). For example, questions now asked are: Will a given environmental treatment have the same effects on genetically different organisms of the same species? Or, what are the forms of specific interactions between genetically determined behavior potentialities and particular experiences of the developing organism?

It is probably fitting, both as an example and as a topic of much current interest, to discuss here the processes of *gender determination and differentiation*. Several excellent, recent books are available (e.g., Hutt, 1972; Money & Ehrhardt, 1972; see also Chapter 12, pp. 556–558). That the chromosomes determine the sex of human offspring is well known. Generally, if the sex chromosome pair is XX, the offspring is female; if XY, the offspring is male. Since the female parent can only contribute an X, the sex depends on whether the fertilizing sperm happens to carry an X or a Y. Beyond conception, however, sex differentiation is neither discrete nor uncomplicated, hormonal action becoming of fundamental importance.

> In the development of the human embryo, for the first six weeks after fertilization, both sexes develop in the same manner. Then the testis develops and if this fails to happen, the ovary begins to differentiate a week later. At about eight weeks the ducts begin to develop into male or female structures. At every stage male differentiation *precedes* the female, the disparity increasing with time, so that by the time sexual differentiation is complete there is a four-week discrepancy: male differentiation is completed at sixteen weeks and female at twenty weeks (Hutt, 1972, p. 44).

One of the implications of this, which is presumably one basis for the enormous complexity of adult gender differentiation, is that "In the total absence of fetal gonadal hormones, the fetus always continues to differentiate the reproductive anatomy of a female. Ovarian hormones are, according to present evidence, irrelevant at this early stage. Testicular hormones are imperative for the continuing differentiation of the reproductive structures of a male." (Money & Ehrhardt, 1972, p. 2). In addition of course, there is no doubt whatever that social-cultural factors also play a major role from birth onward (see Chapter 12, pp. 558–559).

Ontogenetic Context

Finally, one can examine developmental characteristics of particular physiological or anatomical features of a developing organism. Here one can ask for example: In what way does a particular structure or system take part in the developmental process, or, what variables of development influence the functioning of the structure or system (see, e.g., Blakemore & Cooper, 1970)? As well, one can directly study anatomical or physiological measures (e.g., body weight) over the course of developmental periods. For example, Tanner (1963, 1970) has studied, among many other things, sex differences in various growth and strength measures over broad age ranges of human males and females. One result is clear documentation of the so-called adolescent growth spurt, with which all parents are familiar, and of the strong tendency for it to begin earlier in girls than in boys.

Another set of references that partly fits here as an example (as well as in the discussion of "life-span" development in Chapter 2, pp. 1–2) is contained in a recent number of the *American*

Psychologist (Birren, 1974; Schaie, 1974; Schonfield, 1974). These articles have in common the purpose of extending developmental analysis to incorporate adulthood, middle-age and old-age. While only one explicitly deals with biological factors (Birren, 1974), all three endeavor briefly to show the practical relevance of such an analysis.

Commentaries

Although at least these three forms of concern with biological factors (phylogenetic, genetic, and ontogenetic) have always occupied the interest of developmental psychologists, current research and thought especially reflect an almost new-found, constructive awareness of the first—humans' *phylogenetic context*. Accordingly, the selections included in this chapter have been chosen to convey some of the many facets of that enormous contemporary influence.

In the first article, Harlow, Gluck, and Suomi [5] discuss a fundamental issue of comparative psychology that concerns the generalizability of research results based on different species. In particular, they examine the extent to which animal results can be helpful in understanding humans, and vice versa. Their discussion draws special attention to the latter, vice-versa situation, to make it interesting indeed—at least in Harlow's hands—for it can guide inquiry full-circle to new questions about humans. As Harlow et al. [5] point out, "Sometimes when monkey data fail to generalize to human data the answer lies in the superiority of the monkey data and the need to revise those data that are human." This also tells the plot of most of Harlow's prehensile tales of research genius, which have had and continue to have an enormous salutary influence on psychology (see, e.g., [6], [39]).

The article by Bruner [6] is long, complex, and well worth the reader's effort. It is a scholarly and insightful examination of the function served by human immaturity. By considering humans in their phylogenetic context, in the context especially of primate evolution, Bruner is led to insights and speculations that render intelligible a vast array of observations based on the development to adulthood of humans and other primates. In so doing, he provides a compelling illustration of the vitality of such an approach.

The reader may profit also from trying to detect commonalities or congruence between this and the previous paper; for example, while reading Bruner's discussion of play and the concept of "deep play," one might contemplate its applicability (generalizability?) to the relevant section near the end of Harlow et al. [5].

Finally, Bruner's suggestion that the hedgehog be considered a *specialist* might be recalled by the reader when she or he comes to the Masterton and Skeen article [7], which is next.

Masterton and Skeen report on a form of laboratory research that constitutes yet another facet of contemporary psychologists' explicit acknowledgment of the importance of the phylogenetic context as a basis for understanding humans. The research is comparative, but it is characterized by a special scheme for choosing species to study so as perhaps to shed light on the phylogeny of human intellect.

Finally, students are urged to consult a paper by Skinner (1966; or see Skinner, 1969, chap. 7), which has profound points of contact with articles [5, 6, and 7], yet at the same time is quite different in its approach.

Skinner is one of the world's best-known living psychologists, and is probably the most prominent behaviorist. In this article (1966) he endeavors, as a behaviorist, to meet with the "problem" of unlearned behavioral sequences; that is, behavior that appears primarily to have phylogenetic rather than ontogenetic determinants. In addition to providing provocative speculation and discussion concerning the role of behavior in natural selection and phylogeny, Skinner makes strong argument, in a way not unlike Bruner's [6], for studying both phylogenetic and ontogenetic factors in the development of behavior.

References

Blakemore, C. & Cooper, C. F. Development of the brain depends on the visual environment. *Nature*, 1970, *228*, 477–478.

Birren, J. E. Translations in gerontology—From lab to life: Psychophysiology and speed of response. *American Psychologist*, 1974, *29*, 808–815.

Ehrman, L., Omenn, G. S., & Caspari, E. W. (Eds.) *Genetics, environment and behavior: Implications for educational policy*. New York: Academic Press, 1972.

Hebb, D. O. *Textbook of psychology*. (3d ed.) Toronto: Saunders, 1972.

Hodos, W. & Campbell, C. B. G. Scala naturae: Why there is no theory in comparative psychology. *Psychological Review*, 1969, *76*, 337–350.

Hutt, C. *Males and females*. Middlesex: Penguin, 1972.

McClearn, G. E. Genetics and behavior development. In M. L. Hoffman & L. W. Hoffman (Eds.), *Review of child development*. Vol. 1. New York: Russell Sage Foundation, 1964, pp. 433–480.

Money, J. & Ehrhardt, A. A. *Man and woman, boy and girl*. Baltimore and London: Johns Hopkins, 1972.

Razran, G. Evolutionary psychology: Levels of learning—and perception and thinking. In B. B. Wolman (Ed.), *Scientific psychology*. New York: Basic Books, 1965, pp. 207–253.

Rosenzweig, M. R. Environmental complexity, cerebral change, and behavior. *American Psychologist*, 1966, *21*, 321–332.

Schaie, K. W. Translations in gerontology—From lab to life: Intellectual functioning. *American Psychologist*, 1974, *29*, 802–807.

Schonfield, D. Translations in gerontology—From lab to life: Utilizing information. *American Psychologist*, 1974, *29*, 796–801.

Skinner, B. F. The phylogeny and ontogeny of behavior. *Science*, 1966, *153*, 1205–1213.

Skinner, B. F. *Contingencies of reinforcement: A theoretical analysis*. New York: Appleton, 1969.

Tanner, J. M. The regulation of human growth. *Child Development*, 1963, *34*, 817–847.

Tanner, J. M. Physical growth. In P. H. Mussen (Ed.), *Carmichael's manual of child psychology*. Vol. 1. New York: Wiley, 1970.

Vale, J. R. Role of behavior genetics in psychology. *American Psychologist*, 1973, *28*, 871–882.

5. GENERALIZATION OF BEHAVIORAL DATA BETWEEN NONHUMAN AND HUMAN ANIMALS[1]

HARRY F. HARLOW, JOHN P. GLUCK, and STEPHEN J. SUOMI

The justification for generalizing nonhuman behavioral data to similar data obtained on human beings has long been questioned. It is pointless to attempt to provide a definitive answer since no definitive answer has ever existed and never will. This sounds like a thesis of ghastly gloom, but it can be said that from the depths and through the darkness that have always pervaded the problem of interspecies generalization, there have been researchers who have provided illumination and light, the reflections sometimes being scintillating and sometimes coruscant.

Most biologically trained scientists are of the opinion that generalization from nonhuman behavioral data to man is justifiable, and they differ only in the degree to which they believe this to be true. Some biological scientists are convinced that there are behavioral areas beyond the pale, whereas other scientists pale at any suggestion relative to interspecies generality. There is only one way to test the limits of interspecies generalization and that is by experimentation. Positive results could prove the existence of generality. Negative results may prove nothing other than the limitations of the method or mind of the experimenter. The sanguine position is to believe that the maximal degree of generalization has not yet been discovered. It is safe to maintain the assumption that a world of wealth related to nonhuman-human homologues is yet to be disclosed. Men

[1]Supported in part by United States Public Health Service Grant MH-11894 from the National Institute of Mental Health to the University of Wisconsin Primate Laboratory.

From the *American Psychologist*, 1972, 27, 709–716.

and methods will presumably advance rather than regress. This is, of course, an expression of faith.

Although we believe that the degree to which nonhuman animal behavior generalizes to man should be tirelessly tested, we do not believe that positive results will always be disclosed no matter how elegant the research and apparently pervasive the findings may be. At the risk of offending all and pleasing none, we take the example of Lorenz's (1952) imprinting, which we believe does not generalize to man and does not totally generalize to the greylag goose. If the maternal imprinting response of greylag goslings were really irreversible and forever persistent, no greylag goose could have ever broken away from maternal bondage, and the greylag goose as a species would have become extinct long ago.

Imprintinglike phenomena obviously exist in many species of birds and may exist in some species of mammals (Klopfer, 1971). The data are certainly not definitive. We would gladly nominate as imprinting mammals some of the ungulates—deer, elk, moose, and wild horses—whose infants must move with the mother almost from birth onward in order to survive. Imprintinglike phenomena are more apt to be found in precocial than in altricial animals. We do not believe that the imprinting phenomenon aids in the analysis of infant–mother ties in monkeys and men. It does, however, lend support to the position that infant–mother ties in an enormous range of mammals and presumably other classes are formed by a host of variables other than lactational libations.

Although the question of behavioral generalization from nonhuman to human animals has led to redundant ruminations and has been discussed for decades, the converse question has seldom appeared in print. If nonhuman animal data do not generalize to data derived from human beings, can human data be used to predict within reason the supposedly homologous behavior of nonhuman animals? Of even more practical importance, can human data and human experimental designs be used to create and achieve meaningful and important animal experiments? Most biological scientists are probably sympathetic to the possibility of this proposition and can cite countless cases where generalization from man to lower forms has been pursued successfully in the biomedical sciences. Actually, generalization from human to nonhuman animal data should be as probable and pervasive as generalization from nonhuman animals to man. However, most people feel more interest and empathy for human-oriented researches than for researches stemming from the behavioral capabilities of hoot owls and hummingbirds.

Probably because Harlow spent his effective scientific life studying monkeys, most of our researches are designed to test the maximal generality of various behaviors from man to monkeys. Occasionally when we believed that the human facts were foolish or the human theories were false, we designed experiments that would clarify, cant, or expiate error. In any and all cases we wanted to determine the replicability or relative replicability of human data by using rhesus monkeys as subjects. In addition, this research approach gave rise to satisfactory data and deductions demonstrating reasoned and rational relationships between man and lower animals. Actually, some of our researches have disclosed truths either unknown or previously unacceptable to a respectable body of human beings.

No one will question that monkeys can learn many things, some of which are intellectually complex. Whether or not monkeys can think is a problem we leave to the individual reader. Being an avowed monkey man, Harlow has struggled to demonstrate the maximal intellectual generality from man to the rhesus macaque, just as others have struggled to deny it.

Intellectual Generalization between Monkey and Man

By the late 1930s, Harlow had begun measuring the capability of monkeys to solve complex learning problems. In 1940, he spent a year at Columbia University, where he attended a seminar given by the eminent neurologist, Kurt Goldstein, who took a strong position concerning intellectual generalization from animals to men. Harlow was informed by a young, but long-time Goldstein admirer, that in order to understand Goldsteinian animal learning theory one would have to be aware of the fact that Goldstein did not believe in evolution. Goldstein believed that there were *men* and there were *animals,* not *men* and *other* animals. Men alone were capable of abstract thinking, and animals were capable only of concrete thinking (Goldstein, 1939). Without attempting to present details, Goldstein's abstract thinking had connotations similar to Köhler's insight learning, and concrete thinking had connotations like those of Thorndike's trial-and-error learning. This class of theory restricts generalization between animals and men to limited kinds of learning and denies all species, other than man, even access to abstract learning.

One particular problem which Goldstein believed could be solved only by abstract thinking was a problem designed by Weigl, a student of Goldstein's late-departed colleague, Gelb. It might be added that there were cynical and suspicious people who believed that Gelb had created almost all of Goldstein's ideas, including the concepts of concrete and abstract thinking. Some authorities even held that after Gelb's death, Goldsteinian theory suffered, drifting from the Gelb abstract level to the Goldstein concrete level. These may have been jealous people. At any rate, Goldstein had absolute faith that solution of the Weigl problem required abstract intelligence.

In the Weigl test, a human subject, child or adult, was presented with three different stimuli, one of which differed from the other two in form alone and a second that differed only in color. Thus, there might be a blue triangle, a red cross, and a red triangle. Responding to an appropriate cue, the human subject chose the object odd in color; and to a different cue, the subject chose the object odd in relation to form. Goldstein was convinced that the Weigl test was a measure of abstract thinking since it could not be solved by young children or by German soldiers who had suffered severe brain damage, particularly damage to the frontal lobes. Goldstein had great faith in the human frontal lobes, and he commonly talked with pride about the frontal lobe syndrome he had described.

Since we believed in evolution and knew that chimpanzees and monkeys had solved similar but simpler problems, we regarded Goldstein's abstract thinking pronouncements as a challenge. We cheerfully concede that the Weigl problem strained the "abstract thinking" ability of our rhesus monkeys and that the Weigl was more abstract than the simpler oddity and matching-from-sample problems which chimpanzees and monkeys had already solved. However, by providing our monkeys with distinctive differential signs on cues for differential color and form choice and by devising and utilizing a slow, stepwise training procedure, we trained the monkeys to master the Weigl problem (Young & Harlow, 1943). By Goldsteinian criteria, the monkeys had then achieved the capability of abstract thought.

We do not believe that this macaque monkey tour de force endowed the rhesus with human intelligence. It merely demonstrated that a greater degree of intellectual generality existed between man and monkey than Goldstein could concede. These data seemed so interesting to us that we were shocked and surprised to discover how many psychologists did not care. At least Goldstein cared!

Having conducted research on the degree of cortical localization of function, we are intrigued by the generalization of malfunction after damage to one cortical area to malfunction extant after damage to a different area. This statement of generalization is buttressed by a literature more lengthy than lucid. The British diagram makers of the nineteenth century believed that each and every intellectual function was localized in a specific cortical area and that there was no generalization of effect from one area to another. Subsequent neurologists, particularly Jackson (1932), Pick (1922), and Head (1920), questioned this pinpoint precision. Finally, Lashley (1929) presented his theory of equipotentiality of all cortical areas, a classic puddle-of-mud theory. Taken at face value, this theory held that all cortical areas contributed equally to all intellectual functions. Most monkey researchers have disclosed the fact that lesions in the frontal cortex and lesions in the posterior cortex are associated with different types of intellectual impairment (Blum, Chow, & Pribram, 1950; Warren & Harlow, 1952). Frontal lesions produce severe delayed memory response loss and little or no discrimination or learning set loss. Posterior lesions produce severe discrimination and learning set loss but little or no delayed response loss. Apparently intellectual loss in the frontal and posterior lobes does not generalize, as Lashley doubtless believed.

Occasional authorities have agreed with Lashley, even in the case of human lesions, as illustrated by the previously mentioned position taken by Kurt Goldstein. Although Goldstein did not believe in a generalization of significant learning from nonhuman to human animals he had vast faith in the generalization in performance produced by massive cortical lesions in diverse lobes of the brain, or so he inadvertently disclosed. For half a year Harlow listened to Goldstein, who was an inspiring teacher, talk about the behavior of the brain-injured German soldier whose exploits formed the basis for Goldstein's frontal lobe syndrome.

After convivial postseminar sessions of some months duration, Harlow questioned the master.

Dr. Goldstein, you know that the soldier whose performances you cited to illustrate your frontal lobe syndrome was shown on autopsy to have massive lesions in the thalamic and pulvinar nuclei and the striate (visual) areas of the cortex and in no other areas. How can this case with only occipital lesions be the basis for providing the data for your frontal lobe lesions syndrome?

Without hesitation, Goldstein rose with conviction and enthusiasm to reply, "Completely simple, completely simple; in man vision is so important to abstract thinking that lesions in the visual cortex give you the frontal lobe syndrome." Perhaps Goldstein was right. Generalization may be largely a matter of faith.

A fascinating field example of attempted generalization from human to nonhuman beings is found in the many attempts of humans to teach chimpanzees to speak or to otherwise master human language (Furness, 1916; Kellogg & Kellogg, 1933; and eventually Hayes, 1951). Their attempts represented a series of unmitigated, painful, perilous, and prolonged tragedies. Anyone familiar with the data would conclude that human language abilities do not generalize to anthropoid apes. Nevertheless, a parcel of orangs and chimpanzees learned to speak, providing the confused and unclear vocalization of three or possibly four sounds, none of which closely mirrored any human word, [or] can be considered speech. The Hayeses, probably in a transient triumphant tribute to surrogate parental love, produced a sound movie proving that their chimpanzee, Vicki, could speak. Any nonparent who listened to the sound effects could come to only one conclusion. Chimpanzees cannot speak, and no chimpanzee ever will speak, regardless of the training technique. Every time Vicki learned a new word she suffered severe loss in the efficient use of the previous word or words. The Hayeses were the victims of either vicarious love or Vickarious love; it makes little difference. We have already uttered the pronouncement that multiple failures to achieve interspecies generalization do not prove that it cannot exist. Perhaps in the depths of some jungle there exists one chimpanzee, one orangutan, or one gorilla capable of mastering human speech.

Do human language data generalize to chimpanzees? No, if one is concerned with vocal language. As for sign language, that may be another matter. A very important question relevant to the failure of human language development to generalize from man to chimpan-zee concerns the channel of speech selected. There are now data showing that the mouth and throat structure of simians is such that they cannot conceivably effectively evoke human language sounds. A fundamental principle in the formulation of a conditioned response is the preexistence of an appropriate unconditioned response in both species, human and subhuman. Failure to obtain generalization from men to lower animals or vice versa is often due to the lack of an appropriate unconditioned response in one or the other. This has nothing to do with the question of generalization of learning.

We would be the first to agree that human vocal language capabilities show little generalization to the champanzee, and we are glad that they do not. The chimpanzees probably feel the same way. However, a new twist to this problem of generalization of language from man to ape is the gestural approach recently achieved by the Gardners (1967). Instead of attempting to teach Washoe, their chimpanzee subject, an inappropriate vocal language, the Gardners trained Washoe in the use of sign language. Chimpanzees do not speak spontaneously, but chimpanzees gesture spontaneously. The Gardners' gifted infant chimpanzee, wondrous Washoe, rapidly mastered —with pleasure to him and profit to the Gardners—gestural language. One can almost hear Washoe say by gestures, "Look, mother, see me talk."

After living for three years in a world in which all human beings with whom he came into contact spoke and spoke only the American Sign Language, Washoe possessed a vocabulary of about 100 words (in 1971). He usually differentiated precisely between words, spoke spontaneously, and even combined the signs in proper serial order to form simple sentences. As far as we know, Washoe has not taught other chimpanzees the American Sign Language, but anything can happen.

Another nonverbal approach to the generalization of language in apes was Premack's (1970) work with Sarah, a six-year-old African-born female chimpanzee. Premack used small plastic metal-backed object "words" as the physical basis of his language, requiring his subject to place the objects in designated orders on a magnetic board. He formulated a schedule of tasks progressively increasing in difficulty, beginning with the association of specific object "words" with different types of fruits. Sarah rapidly learned to both name and request fruit. She subsequently was taught to place more than one "word" on the magnetic board to form simple "sentences"; for example, "Mary [the tester] give apple Sarah." Eventually, Sarah was able to express relationships among stimuli (e.g., same versus different) by placing the appropriate relationship-designating words on the magnetic board following the presentation of the stimulus objects.

Premack further demonstrated that his subject ascribed properties of a given stimulus to the actual word designated for that stimulus. To do so he employed an independent features analysis. On each trial of this analysis, Sarah was presented with an apple and a pair of response alternatives, one of which was related to some dimension of the apple. Alternatives included red versus green, round versus square, square with stemlike protuberances versus plain square, and plain round versus square with protuberances. After compiling Sarah's feature analysis with the actual apple present, a similar analysis was performed with the plastic word apple present instead of the apple. Premack found that Sarah ascribed the same properties to the plastic word as she did to the actual apple. He concluded that Sarah's analysis of the word was based on the object that the word represented.

The generalization of data from man to monkey or from monkey to man is doubtless well substantiated when we deal with simple learning, but there are limitations and reservations when we consider thinking and language in the erudite human form. The neocortices of monkeys, apes, and men differ, and although man may think about monkeys, monkeys probably never will think seriously about men. If, instead of problems of learning, we concern ourselves with problems of motivation, we find much more widespread generalization.

Motivational Transfer between Monkey and Man

Motivational behavior studies not only may produce more evidence of generalization from human beings to animals but also may throw new light on the theories of human behavior per se. The question of determination of the degree of transfer between complex behaviors in man and lower animals is pursued by many, either because of intellectual curiosity or some theoretical or philosophical position. No nonhuman animal can think like man, speak like man, or mold his behavior in terms of complex human cultural variables. However, many important human behaviors, particularly neonatal and infantile behaviors, occur without the intervention of thinking, recondite language, or formidable cultural variables.

Freudian theorists and behavioral theorists had long speculated about the variables binding the neonatal infant to the mother, and the leaders of both of these diverse, dichotomous camps came by different speculative routes to the same conclusion. The infant loved the mother because of repetitive association of the mother's breasts with the alleviation of the pangs of hunger. Mother love was conceived of as a learned or derived motive, conditioned upon the internal, homeostatic drive of hunger. Human data, human replication, and human need give rise to no other conclusion.

Harlow had no objection to homeostatic drives as human motives, nor secondary reinforcement as a motivational mechanism, but he had such respect for mother love that he felt it should be based at least in part on complex unlearned motives, more picturesque and less pragmatic than lactational loneliness. Furthermore, in a flash of insight it dawned on him how the real mechanics of mother love might be tested experimentally using nonhuman animals. The problem involved the degree of generalization of theories of infant love from human beings to monkeys and properly assumed that generalization existed and that it would be found by those who kept abreast with their research. Harlow believed that basic bodily contact was probably an unlearned, nativistic force that caused the child to love the mother. We tested this thesis by creating two artificial mother surrogates, one cloth covered, the other comprised of a wire-mesh body, which in final design equated all other variables (Harlow & Zimmerman, 1958). In half of the cases, the good cloth surrogate nursed from a tiny bottle on its thoracic midline and the wire did not. In the other cases, the wire mother nursed and the cloth surrogate did not. A direct test could be made of the relative importance of bodily contact in contradistinction to activities associated specifically with the breast. The infant monkeys continually clasped and clung to the cloth mother, and thus the original research showed that body texture, the skin we love to touch, was a variable of completely overwhelming importance over all activities associated with the breast, including the ingestion of milk.

These were informational studies on generalization. The data of the human theorists did not generalize to monkeys because the human theory was false. Monkey theories basically generalized to human infants because the monkey facts were true.

Having closed the doors on Anna Freud's cupboard theory of love, where infant love is associated with maternal mien and bubbling breast, we subsequently designed a family of studies (e.g., Harlow & Suomi, 1970; Harlow & Zimmerman, 1958) showing the relative importance of many variables in the formation of maternal love. All important behaviors are mediated by many variables. Body contact remained the variable of primary importance if it were skin, terrycloth, or spun nylon. Infant–mother love did not develop from satin, which is for show (Furchner & Harlow, 1969), and sandpaper and welded wire connoted not skin but sin to the neonatal animal.

In these experiments, we were able to demonstrate that activities associated with the breast, including nursing, were variables of importance secondary to good, soft bodily contact, and we believe that human breasts were put there by God for more than aesthetic purposes. Furthermore, rocking motion was a positive variable of value, and temperature was a variable with impact. Hot, or at least warm, mothers were cheerfully chosen over others, and cold mothers were adversive. An infant upon contacting an ice-cold mother designed by Suomi fled screaming in horror and never returned to the mother over a 30-day period.

In many ways these were classical experiments demonstrating that generalization from animals, even inanimate animals, to man can be better in limited ways for specific limited purposes and in limited circumstances than the generalization from men to lower animals. The researches on inanimate mothers probably generalized better to idealized real mothers than the previous research conducted on fleshy, fulsome human females themselves. Sometimes when monkey data fail to generalize to human data the answer lies in the superiority of the monkey data and the need to revise those data that are human.

Generalization of Psychopathology from Man to Nonhuman Animals

At the present time we are engaged in an epic effort to produce simulated human psychopathic states. We are plagued by the question, Do the monkey data generalize to man or not? Some authorities believe our monkey data generalize to man. Some authorities believe they do not. This might lead one to the assumption that one group of external arbitrators is right and one group is wrong. This conclusion is in error. Probably both groups are right and both groups are wrong. Cross-species generalization is seldom, if ever, complete, and the evaluation of cross-species generalization may be more an art than a science.

Some years ago we produced a syndrome of childhood depression in infant monkeys that is so much like child anaclitic depression that no thinking man has, and no thinking man ever will, question an enormous, near total generality from monkey to man. Oddly enough, the experiments were conducted in the opposite order. Human anaclitic depression was achieved by retrospective clinical data, and taking the clinical models of Spitz (1946) and Bowlby (1960), we fashioned the monkey anaclitic depression studies. The near perfect generalization which was found has since been confirmed by others on two other species of macaque monkeys and also on patas monkeys.

The etiology of the anaclitic depression was basically the same for both genera, man and macaque: maternal separation or at least the loss of a loved one. The behavioral syndrome was clearly parallel for both genera. Finally, the techniques of successful rehabilitation were for all practical purposes identical. The primary procedure was that of reinstatement of the loved object.

The simplicity in achieving de facto generalization between men and monkeys along the dimensions of anaclitic depression might suggest that behavioral generalization of any and all psychopathological patterns among primates would be simple, safe, and universally acceptable. Nothing could be further from the truth. Even adolescent reactive depression (McKinney, Harlow, & Suomi, 1972) offers uncertain generality between men and monkeys at the present time. Beyond depression, interspecies psychopathological generality is a proposition based more on faith than fact.

Degrees of Generalization

Leaving psychopathology and returning to love, we find areas where a high level of interspecific generality is obvious and others where behavioral generality is humble or hidden. Maternal love and infant love of the mother are behaviors in which the obtained data have enormous interspecies generality in most primates. Probably there is higher interspecies behavioral generality among infants than adults since maturational differentiation progressively separates different species along all dimensions. Thus, mother love and infant love for the mother are related to neonatal responses with high interspecies generality; agemate or peer love that is based on play and matures later shows less interspecific generality; father or paternal love that matures even later in life, since there are no neonatal fathers, is controlled by variables known only to God and shows low interspecies generality (Mitchell, 1969).

A criterion for making a best guess as to the degree that human data generalize to animals, and that animal data generalize to human beings, is that of anatomical similarity. Furthermore, all homologous or analogous anatomy and structures have not and should not be given equal consideration. The primary interspecies anatomical correlates for complex behaviors are those relating to the structures of the central nervous system. Thus, if we know the differential complexity of the central nervous system of two closely related or divergent species of animals and know the level of learning ability of one, we can make a reasonable prediction about the learning ability of the other, be it more complex or less complex. Frequently the degree of likelihood of behavioral generalization from one species to another can be predicted by anatomical similarities and dissimilarities. In predicting behavioral generalization, we are properly prone to seeking similarities and dissimilarities in brain structures and particularly cortical structures.

Total brain weight is a measure that has been used to predict similarities in behavioral capabilities between different species, but total brain weight is a controllable measure that is both perilous and ponderous. The elephant may never forget, but its vast cerebral mass finds problems requiring any abstract thinking to be unsolvable. Its inability to forget may stem from an absence of retroactive inhibition. The porpoise in spite of the many kind words written by porpoise friends, with its large mass of cerebral tissue is limited in its behavior to tasks that are porpoiseful but not purposeful. The porpoise's most learned lover was Lilly (1961), and it is pointless to try to gild this kind of love.

A slightly more recondite anatomical measure is wealth of fissuration rather than mass, but even this anatomical measure is correlated poorly with complex problem solution. In all probability it is more highly correlated with brain weight than with behavioral wisdom.

A highly sophisticated anatomical criterion for complex behavioral capability is that of the cytoarchitectonic structure ot the neocortex, not the mass of the brain but the delicacy of organization of the cells in or near the cortical outer fringe. This criterion works very well in seriating men, apes, monkeys, carnivores, such as dogs and cats, and ungulates including the horse and possibly the pig.

Unfortunately, the criterion of neocortical complexity and intellectual eminence comes apart at the seams when we include birds, at least certain representative birds like the pigeon. Birds have little or no cortex, and they are multiple millions of years away from a trace of any neocortex. Birds have extremely complex and differentiated striated structures, but how these came to operate in behavioral regulation as if they were neocortical neurons will remain a mystery within our life and for a longer period within the lifetimes of Aves. Yet, some of the bird-brained beasts successfully solve oddity-principle and matching-from-sample problems at a performance level equal to or beyond representative carnivores and at a level approaching that of performance of the higher primates. No one has yet tested pigeons on Weigl problems.

These data indicate that there is no single or simple anatomical measure to account for the generalization or lack of generalization between animals in relatively disparate orders. Instead of bringing order out of chaos, we have brought chaos out of orders, beaten and battered by a birdbrained beast. When correlating behavioral capabilities and cortical complexity, one need not abandon the effort to search for criteria underlying behavioral generalization.

Having agonized about the generalization or lack of generalization of behavioral performances between monkey and man and also between man and monkey, let us meditate upon a hypothetical discovery of the worst of all contingencies. Suppose we discovered that there was no generalization between behavioral performances within selected members of the primate order or within the class of mammals. Under these circumstances, would we of necessity abandon the field of comparative psychology and comparative study and devote all of our time to brooding about human uniqueness?

No, we would not. Even if behavioral data had no generalization between members of different species, similar or divergent, there might still be merit in conducting research on subhuman forms. If facts fail to generalize, one facet of facts—the research ideas behind the facts—would still generalize. Significant results obtained on lower forms have suggested, even to some individuals not enormously intellectually endowed, experiments that should be conducted on man. Many human experiments of meaning and merit would never have been created through an act described as insight, if the acts of insight had not previously been generated by observations of some proper and pious behavior of some nonhuman animal.

From the point of view of cold facts—and most facts are—it is commonly believed that some animal data generalize to man and some data do not. The only problem then is that of selecting between or among the data that generalize and those that do not. This is never an easy task since there is no completely logical or absolutely objective way to make the separation.

Perhaps the best way to struggle with the problem of behavioral generalization between different animal species is to think of it as a game, even if a dangerous game, which one pursues at his own peril. There will always be company in such endeavors. The very fact that a problem cannot be solved with certainty and is pursued with peril may come to carry a source of pleasure in its own right.

Some people wrestle with alligators as a pastime even though there is not total generality in behavior from one alligator to another. Some people play Russian roulette, trusting in total generality from one barrel to the next, particularly if the first one fails to fire. However, the behavioral acts in Russian roulette are so stereotypical that they offer little cheer or charm to the creative mind. A better illustration of the game of interspecies behavioral generalization is that of the few people who jump across the Grand Canyon for pleasure. The behavioral generality is within a single organism and not between two different organisms, but generality from leap to leap is assumed. Testing one's own generality can be an exciting and educational game even though you do not expect to always get to the other side in a single jump. But have faith, for after all there is no worthwhile activity in which there is total safety and security from a drastic letdown.

Basically the problems of generalization of behavioral data between species are simple— one cannot generalize, but one must. If the competent do not wish to generalize, the incompetent will fill the field.

REFERENCES

Blum, J. C., Chow, K. L., & Pribram, K. H. A behavioral analysis of the organization of the parieto-temporo-preoccipital cortex. *Journal of Comparative Neurology, 1950, 93*, 53–100.

Bowlby, J. Grief and mourning in infancy and early childhood. *Psychoanalytic Study of the Child, 1960, 15*, 9–52.

Furchner, C. S., & Harlow, H. F. Preference for various surrogate surfaces among infant rhesus monkeys. *Psychonomic Science, 1969, 17*, 279–280.

Furness, W. H. Observations on the mentality of chimpanzees and orang-utans. *Proceedings of the American Philosophical Society, 1916, 55*, 281–290.

Gardner, B. T., & Gardner, R. A. Teaching sign language to a chimpanzee: Methodology and preliminary results. *Psychonomic Bulletin, 1967, 1*, 36.

Gardner, B. T., & Gardner, R. A. Two-way communication with an infant chimpanzee. In A. M. Schrier & F. Stollnitz (Eds.), *Behavior of nonhuman primates*. Vol. 4. New York: Academic Press, 1971.

Goldstein, K. *The organism*. New York: American Book Company, 1939.

Harlow, H. F., & Suomi, S. J. The nature of love—simplified. *American Psychologist, 1970, 25*, 161–168.

Harlow, H. F., & Zimmerman, R. R. The development of affectional responses in infant monkeys. *Proceedings of the American Philosophical Society, 1958, 102*, 501–509.

Hayes, C. *The ape in our house*. New York: Harper, 1951.

Head, H. Discussion on aphasia. *Brain, 1920, 43*, 412–450.

Jackson, J. H. *Selected writings of J. Hughlings Jackson*. Vol. 2 (Ed. by J. Taylor). London: Hodder & Stoughton, 1932.

Kellogg, W. N., & Kellogg, L. A. *The ape and the child*. New York: McGraw-Hill, 1933.

Klopfer, P. H. Mother love: What turns it on? *American Scientist, 1971, 59*, 404–407.

Lashley, K. S. *Brain mechanisms and intelligence*. Chicago: University of Chicago Press, 1929.

Lilly, J. C. *Man and dolphin*. Garden City, N.Y.: Doubleday, 1961.

Lorenz, K. *King Solomon's ring*. London: Methuen, 1952.

McKinney, W. T., Suomi, S. J., & Harlow, H. F. Repetitive peer separations of juvenile age rhesus monkeys. *Archives of General Psychiatry,* in press.

Mitchell, G. D. Paternalistic behavior in primates. *Psychological Bulletin, 1969, 71*, 399–417.

Pick, A. Schwere Denkstörung infolge einer kombination perseveratorischer, amnestifch-aphasischer und kontaminatorischer Störungen. *Zetschrist fuer Die Gesamte Neurologie und Psychiatrie, 1922, 75*, 309–322.

Premack, D. A functional analysis of language. *Journal of the Experimental Analysis of Behavior, 1970, 14*, 107–125.

Spitz, R. A. Anaclitic depression. *Psychoanalytic Study of the Child, 1946, 2*, 313–342.

Warren, J. M., & Harlow, H. F. Discrimination learning by normal and brain operated monkeys. *Journal of Genetic Psychology, 1952, 81*, 45–52.

Young, M. L., & Harlow, H. F. Generalization by rhesus monkeys of a problem involving the Weigl principle using the oddity method. *Journal of Comparative Psychology, 1943, 36*, 201–216.

6. NATURE AND USES OF IMMATURITY[1]

JEROME S. BRUNER

To understand the nature of any species fully, we need to know more than the ways of its adults. We need to know how its young are brought from initial, infantile inadequacy to mature, species-typical functioning. Variation in the uses of immaturity tells much about how adaptation to habitat is accomplished, as well as what is likely to happen given a change in habitat. The nature and uses of immaturity are themselves subject to evolution, and their variations are subject to natural selection, much as any morphological or behavioral variant would be.

One of the major speculations about primate evolution is that it is based on the progressive selection of a distinctive pattern of immaturity. It is this pattern of progressive selection that has made possible the more flexible adaptation of our species. Too often this pattern is over-explained by noting that human immaturity is less dominated by instinct and more governed by learning.

Because our ultimate concern is with the emergence of human adaptation, our first concern must be the most distinctive feature of that adaptation. This feature is man's trait, typical of his species, of "culture using," with all of the intricate set of implications that follow. Man adapts (within limits) by changing the environment, by developing not only amplifiers and transformers for his sense organs, muscles, and

reckoning powers, as well as banks for his memory, but also by changing literally the properties of his habitat. Man, so the truism goes, lives increasingly in a man-made environment. This circumstance places special burdens on human immaturity. For one thing, adaptation to such variable conditions depends heavily on opportunities for learning, in order to achieve knowledge and skills that are not stored in the gene pool. But not all that must be mastered can be learned by direct encounter. Much must be "read out" of the culture pool, things learned and remembered over several generations: knowledge about values and history, skills as varied as an obligatory natural language or an optional mathematical one, as mute as using levers or as articulate as myth telling. Yet, though there is the gene pool, and though there exist direct experience and the culture as means for shaping immaturity, none of these directly prepares for the novelty that results when man alters his environment. That flexibility depends on something else.

Yet, it would be a mistake to leap to the conclusion that because human immaturity makes possible high flexibility in later adjustment, anything is possible for the species. Human traits were selected for their survival value over a four–five-million-year period, with a great acceleration of the selection process during the last half of that period. There were crucial, irreversible changes during that final man-making period—recession of formidable dentition, doubling of brain volume, creation of what Washburn and Howell (1960) have called a "technical-social way of life," involving tool and symbol use. Note, however, that *hominidization* consisted principally of adaptations to conditions in the Pleistocene. These preadaptations, shaped in response to earlier demands of the habitat, are part of man's evolutionary inheritance. This is not to say that close beneath the skin of man is a naked ape, that "civilization" is only a "veneer." The

[1]This article was prepared with the support of Grant MH-12623 from the National Institute of Mental Health to the Center for Cognitive Studies, Harvard University. Parts of this article were presented as the Haynes Foundation Lectures at the California Institute of Technology, and as the Compton Lectures at the Massachusetts Institute of Technology. This article was also presented as an Invited Address to the XXth International Congress of Psychology, Tokyo, August 1972.

From the *American Psychologist*, 1972, *27*, 687–708. Copyright 1972 by the American Psychological Association. Reprinted by permission of the author and the publisher.

technical-social way of life is a deep feature of the species adaptation.

But we would err if we assumed a priori that man's inheritance places no constraint on his power to adapt. Some of the preadaptations can be shown to be presently maladaptive. Man's inordinate fondness for fats and sweets no longer serves his individual survival well. And human obsession with sexuality is plainly not fitted for survival of the species now, however well it might have served to populate the upper Pliocene and the Pleistocene. But note that the species responds typically to these challenges by technical innovation rather than by morphological or behavioral change. This is not to say that man is not capable of controlling or, better, transforming behavior. Whatever its origin, the incest taboo is a phenomenally successful technique for the control of certain aspects of sexuality—although its beginning among the great apes (Van Lawick-Goodall, 1968) suggests that it may have a base that is rooted partly in the biology of propinquity, a puzzling issue. The technical innovation is contraception, which dissociates sexuality from reproduction. What we do not know, of course, is what kinds and what range of stresses are produced by successive rounds of such technical innovation. Dissociating sexuality and reproduction, for example, may produce changes in the structure of the family by redefining the sexual role of women, which in turn may alter the authority pattern affecting the child, etc. Continuous, even accelerating, change may be inherent in such adaptation. If this is so, then there is an enormous added pressure on man's uses of immaturity for instruction. We must prepare the young for unforeseeable change—a task made the more difficult if severe constraints imposed by human preadaptations to earlier conditions of life have created rigidities.

Evolution of Educability

LeGros Clark's (1963) *échelle des êtres* of the primates runs from tree shrews through the prosimian lorisformes, lemuriformes, and related forms, through the New World and Old World monkeys, through the hylobates such as the gibbon, through the great apes, through the early hominids like Australopithecus and Homo habilis and other small-brained predecessors, terminating in the modern form of Homo sapiens with his 1,300-cubic-centimeter brain. Closing the gap between great apes and modern man is, of course, a complex and uncertain undertaking, particularly where behavior is concerned, for all that remains are paleontological and archaeological fragments, and little by way of a behavior record. But there are inferences that can be made from these fragments, as well as from the evolution of primate behavior up to the great apes. Enough is known to suggest hypotheses, though no conclusions. Such an *échelle des êtres* is bound to be only a metaphor since contemporary species are only approximations to those that existed in the evolutionary tree. But it can tell us something about change in the primate order. We propose to use it where we can to make inferences, not so much about preadaptations to earlier conditions that characterize our species, but rather more to assess crucial changes that have been recurring in immaturity. My interest is in the evolution of educability.

But you will know by my credentials that I am not primarily a student of prehuman primates. I have brought the materials of primate evolution together to understand better the course of human infancy and childhood, its distinctiveness or species typicality. I propose to go back and forth, so to speak, between primate phylogeny and human ontogeny, not to establish any shallow parallel between the two, but in the hope that certain contrasts will help us see more clearly. If indeed the fish will be the last to discover water, perhaps we can help ourselves by looking at some other species.

Specifically, I should like to look at several issues whose resolution might be of particular help. The first of these has to do with the nature and evolution of social organization within a species and how this may affect the behavior of the immature. The second has to do with the structure of skill and how the evolution of primate skill almost inevitably leads to tool using. We must then pause to consider the nature of tool using and its consequences. That matter in turn leads us directly to the roles of both play and imitation in the evolution of educability. Inevitably, we shall deal with that distinctly human trait, language: what it is and how its emergence drastically alters the manner in which we induct young into the species.

My emphasis throughout is principally on the evolution of intellect—problem solving, adaptation to habitat, and the like. But it will soon be apparent that, to use the jargon (Bloom, 1956), one cannot easily separate the cognitive from the conative and the affective. I have been told that the Chinese character for *thinking* combines the character for *head* and the character for *heart*. Pity it does not also include the character for *others* as well, for then it would be appropriate to what will concern us. At the end, I try to deal with the question of what can be done better to equip the young for coping.

Any species depends, as we know from the work of the last half century (e.g., Mayr, 1963), on the development of a system of mutuality—a set of mechanisms for sharing a habitat or territory, a system of signaling that is effective against predators, dominance relations that are effective without being preempting (Chance, 1967), a system of courtship with matching mating releasers (Tinbergen, 1953), etc. There is, at the lower end of the primate line, a considerable amount of rather fixed or linear structure about such mutuality. Behavior repertoires are limited in prosimians and in monkeys, and the combinatorial richness in their behavior is not great (see Jolly, 1966), though one can make a case for their goodness of fit to habitat conditions (as Hinde, 1971, recently has). Even where there is, within a given species, an increased variety in behavior produced by enriched or more challenging environments—as in the contrast between urban and forest-dwelling rhesus monkeys (Singh, 1969) or among Japanese macaques tempted by new foods introduced in their terrain (Itani, 1958)—the difference is not toward variability or loosening of social structure, but toward the incorporation of new patterns into the species-typical social pattern. Action patterns that are altogether fixed prevail; and *play*, that special

form of violating fixity, is limited in variety, early and short lived, and irreversibly gone by adulthood—a matter to which I shall return.

There are notably fixed limits for the young of these species; and as the animal grows from infant to juvenile to adult—transitions usually marked by conspicuous changes in appearance and coat color—social induction into the group is effected rapidly, usually by the quick response of a young animal to the threat of attack by an older animal in the troop. The sharply defined estrous receptivity of the adult female almost assures that the young animal will be rejected and made virtually self-sufficient within a year. It is this sharply defined receptivity that also creates a scarcity economy in sexual access and leads to such a close link between male dominance and sexual access—perhaps the most notable source of linear, tight social structure virtually throughout the monkeys and prosimians. The comfort-contact system of mother and infant, involving not only initial nursing but also hair holding and grasping by the young for protection in flight and for sheer comfort, is obviously of great importance in prosimians, New World, and Old World monkeys. But as Dolhinow and Bishop (1970) have remarked, we must be careful about exaggerating it. Harlow's (e.g., 1959) pioneering studies do show that a macaque made solely dependent on a terry-cloth or wire-mesh mother surrogate is more backward than one dependent on a real mother. Yet, for all that, 20 minutes of play daily with peers in a play cage obliterates the difference between the three groups—another of Harlow's (Harlow & Harlow, 1962) findings. Note by way of contrast that a three-year-old chimpanzee deprived of a mother modeling the skilled act of fishing for termites seems not to be able to master the act later, even if among peers who are succeeding.

Loosening the Primate Bond

Probably the first step toward loosening the initially tight primate bond is the development of what Chance (1967) has referred to as an "attentional structure" within the group. Rather than behavior patterns leading to constant interaction and mutual release of agonistic patterns, there is instead of a deployment of attention in which the dominant animal is watched, his behavior is anticipated, and confrontation is avoided. One of the major things that induction into a tightly organized Old World monkey group means, then, is an enormous investment in attention to the requirements of the troop—mating, dominance, food foraging, etc. There is, so to speak, little attentional capacity left for anything else.

The great apes represent a crucial break away from this pattern toward a far more relaxed one, and as we shall see in a moment, the effect on the young is striking. All three of the great ape species are virtually free of predators. None of them defends a territory. None of them has a troop structure nearly as well defined and rigidly maintained as, say, the least rigid Old World species, if such a phrase makes sense. In the gorilla, the orangutan, and the chimpanzee, male dominance does not preclude copulation between a subdominant male and a female in the presence of the dominant male. It is even difficult, in fact, in the case of chimpanzee and orangutan to define a dominant male in the monkey sense (cf., e.g., Goodall, 1965; Reynolds, 1965; Schaller, 1964). Indeed the route to dominance may even involve a superior technological skill. Note the increased deference paid to a male in the Gombe Stream Reserve who had learned to produce an intimidating din by banging two discarded tin cans together (Van Lawick-Goodall, 1968). Thus, too, while estrus marks the period of maximum receptivity in which the female initiates sexual activity, her availability to a male may in fact continue even into the first two months of pregnancy (Reynolds, 1965). Doubtless the achievement of a 600–700-cubic-centimeter brain in great apes also contributes to the further evolution of cerebral control of sexual behavior of which Beach (1965) has written. The spacing of infants is over three years apart, on the average, and the bond between mother and infant, particularly in the chimpanzee, remains active for as long as five years (Van Lawick-Goodall, 1968).

One concomitant of the change is the decline in fixed patterns of induction into the group.

There is much less of what might be called training by threat from adults or actual punishment by adults of a juvenile who has violated a species-typical pattern. The prolonged infant–mother interaction includes now a much larger element of play between them, often initiated by the mother and often used to divert an infant from a frustration-arousing situation.

What appears to be happening is that, with the loosening of fixed bonds, a system of reciprocal exchange emerges, the structure of which is at first difficult to describe. In any case, the system makes it possible for chimpanzee and gorilla groups to encounter groups of conspecifics in their range without fighting; indeed, in the case of the more flexibly organized chimpanzees, such encounters may even include sexual relations between groups and an exchange of members (Reynolds, 1965; Van Lawick-Goodall, 1968). There can be little doubt that primate evolution is strongly and increasingly characterized by such reciprocal exchange. The trend probably predates the emergence of hominids. In a recent article, Trivers (1971) said,

> During the Pleistocene, and probably before, a hominid species would have met the preconditions for the evolution of reciprocal altruism: long life span, low dispersal rate; life in small, mutually dependent, stable, social groups (Lee and DeVore, 1968; Campbell, 1966); and a long period of parental care. It is very likely that dominance relations were of the relaxed, less linear form characteristic of the baboon (Hall and DeVore, 1965) [p. 45].

As Gouldner (1960) reminded us a decade ago and as new studies on remaining hunter-gatherers reassert (Lee & DeVore, 1968), there is no known human culture that is not marked by reciprocal help in times of danger and trouble, by food sharing, by communal nurturance for the young or disabled, and by the sharing of knowledge and implements for expressing skill. Lévi-Strauss (1963) posited such exchanges as the human watershed and classified them into three types: one involving the exchange of symbols and myths and knowledge; another involving the exchange of affectional and affiliative bonds, including the exchange of kin women in marriage to outside groups for political alliances, with this rare resource preserved by an incest taboo; and finally an exchange system for goods and services. The pressures in such primate groups would surely select traits consonant with reciprocity, leading to self-domestication by the selection of those capable of "fitting in." The incessant aggressiveness of the linear pattern would wane gradually.

What accompanies these changes is a marked transformation in ways of managing immaturity. The maternal buffering and protection of the young not only lengthens materially but undergoes qualitative changes. Several of these have been mentioned: a much prolonged period dominated by play; increased participation in play by adults, especially, though not exclusively, by the mother; decline in the use of punishment and threat as modes of inducting the young into the pattern of species-typical interactions. The most important, I believe, is the appearance of a pattern involving an enormous amount of observation of adult behavior by the young, with incorporation of what has been learned into a pattern of play (Dolhinow & Bishop, 1970; Hamburg, 1968; Hayes & Hayes, 1952; Köhler, 1926; Reynolds, 1965; Rumbaugh, 1970; Van Lawick-Goodall, 1968; Yerkes & Yerkes, 1929).[2] Though psychologists are chary about using the term imitation because of the difficulty of defining it, virtually all primatologists comment on the enormous increase in imitation found in chimpanzees in contrast to Old World monkeys (where there is genuine doubt whether imitation in any commonsense meaning of the term occurs at all). After its first appearance at about 17 months of age, this pattern of observing and imitating takes up much of the time of infants

and young juveniles—watching social interaction, watching the care of the young, watching copulation, watching agonistic displays, watching instrumental or tool behavior. Such observation requires free attention on the part of the young; and, indeed, the incorporation of observed behavior in play occurs most usually during the more relaxed periods in the life of the group. It was Köhler (1926), in his classic *The Mentality of Apes*, who commented initially on the intelligent rather than the mechanical or slavish nature of imitative behavior in anthropoids—how the sight of another animal solving a problem is used not to mimic but as a basis for guiding the observer's own problem solving or goal striving. He used the term "serious play" (p. 157), and the literature since the early 1920s bears him out (e.g., Dolhinow & Bishop, 1970; Hamburg, 1968). In a word, the chimpanzee adult serves not only as a buffer or protector or "shaper" for the young but as a model—though there is no indication of any intentional modeling or of behavior that is specifically "demonstrational."

To summarize briefly, the emergence of a more flexible form of social bonding in primate groups seems to be accompanied by the emergence of a new capacity for learning by observation. Such learning indeed may be necessary if not sufficient for transmission of culture. But that gets ahead of the argument still to be made; for there is still an enormous gap to be accounted for between the behavior of a grouping of great apes, however flexible, and the mode of structuring of a human society, no matter how simple it may be.

Observational Learning

There are many facets to observational learning (I cautiously continue to avoid the term *imitation*). There is ample evidence that many mammals considerably less evolved than primates can benefit from exposure to another animal carrying out a task; for example, the classic study of cats by Herbert and Harsh (1944) demonstrates improvement in escape from a puzzle box by cats who have seen other

[2]It should be noted carefully that in certain crucial ways, both mountain and lowland gorilla are exceptions to what is described here. For some interesting speculations about the lack of curiosity and imitativeness in the gorilla as related to his undemanding habitat and food supply as well as to his lack of need for cooperative efforts, see Yerkes and Yerkes (1929), Rumbaugh (1970), and particularly Reynolds (1965).

animals escape—and the more so if the cats observed were still inexpert at the task. Whether they are learning the possibility of getting out of the box, the means for doing so (by displacing a bar), or whatever, observation helps. So too with *Macaca fuscata*, the Japanese macaque, where the young animals learn to eat what the mother eats by eating what she leaves (Itani, 1958; Kawamura, 1959); or the naive, cage-reared *patas* monkey transported to a habitat and released in a natural troop, who learns from the group by following it in search of food.

But this is quite different from the sort of "serious play" to which Köhler (1926) referred. Consider an example:

> I would call the following behavior of a chimpanzee imitation of the "serious play" type. On the playground a man has painted a wooden pole in white color. After the work is done he goes away leaving behind a pot of white paint and a beautiful brush. I observe the only chimpanzee who is present, hiding my face behind my hands, as if I were not paying attention to him. The ape for a while gives much attention to me before approaching the brush and the paint because he has learned that misuse of our things may have serious consequences. But very soon, encouraged by my attitude, he takes the brush, puts it into the pot of color and paints a big stone which happens to be in the place, beautifully white. The whole time the ape behaved completely seriously. So did others when imitating the washing of laundry or the use of a borer [pp. 156–157].

I consider such behavior to be dependent on two important prerequisites, both amenable to experimental analysis:

The first is the ability to differentiate or abstract oneself from a task, to turn around on one's own performance and, so to speak, see oneself, one's own performance as differentiated from another. This involves self-recognition in which one, in some way, is able to model one's *own* performance on some selected feature of another's performance. This phenomenon in linguistics is known as *deixis:* as in learning that when I say *I*, it is not the same as when you say *I*, or that *in front* of me is not the same as *in front* of you or *in front* of the car (cf. Miller & Johnson-Laird[3]). It is a deep problem in language learning, and though it seems cumbersome and abstract in a discussion of hominid evolution, it may be amenable to demonstration. Indeed, I believe that the excellent study by Gallup (1970) indicates that there is a large gap between such Old World monkeys as the stump-tailed macaque and the chimpanzee: the latter can recognize his mirror image and guide self-directed behavior by it (e.g., inspecting by touch a spot on the forehead seen in the mirror); the former cannot. The macaque, as a matter of fact, seems able only to attack or threaten its mirror image or to ignore it. These findings are surely not proof of the emergence of deictic capacities in the ape, but they do suggest a crucial trend for guiding one's own behavior by feedback other than, so to speak, from action proper. Learning by observation is one instance of that class.

The second prerequisite for observation learning is a form of skill I now examine: *construction of an action pattern by the appropriate sequencing of a set of constituent subroutines to match a model* (Lashley, 1951). Observing the development of skilled, visually directed manipulatory activity in human infants and children, one is struck repeatedly by the extent to which such activity grows from the mastery of specific acts, the gradual perfecting of these acts into what may be called a modular form, and the combining of these into higher order, longer range sequences. Flexible skilled action may almost be conceived of as the construction of a sequence of constituent acts to achieve an objective (usually a change in the environment) while taking into account local conditions. As the Russian neurophysiologist Bernstein (1967) has put it, one can almost conceive of an initial skilled act as a motoric hypothesis concerning how to change the environment along a desired parameter. The flexibility of skill consists not only of this constructive feature but also of the rich range of "paraphrases" that are possible: for a skilled operator, there are many different ways of

[3]G. Miller & P. Johnson-Laird. Presuppositions of Language. In preparation.

skinning a cat; and the word paraphrase is not amiss, for there is in this sense something language-like about skill, the kind of substitution rules that permit the achievement of the same objective (meaning) by alternative means.

If one compares the manipulatory activity of a child (or of a young chimpanzee) and a prosimian, such as a loris, the most striking difference is precisely the extent to which manual activity of human and chimpanzee is constructed of components to meet the properties of the task. The wide range of combinations in the use of the component gestures that go into the making of the final prehension—relatively independent movement of fingers, of hand, of wrist, etc.—is striking. But as Bishop (1964) pointed out, prosimians use virtually the same grip for a variety of activities: taking hold of a branch, grooming, taking a piece of fruit, etc. My own informal observation on slow loris confirms this. The grip is adapted to the task by changing the orientation of the whole hand, by altering speed or force, etc. Napier (1962) has noted how the development of flexibility is facilitated morphologically by the evolutionary selection of phalangeal flexibility, and change in the hamate and trapezium with emergence of power and precision grips, but I part company with Napier in that it is *not* so much a change of manual morphology that separates baboon from ape from man, but the nature of the *program* that controls the use of the hands.

Imitation as "serious play"—incorporating what is observed into behavior that is not mere mimicry but is directed intelligently to an end—must of course depend on "matching to model," on constructing behavior in the manner we have just examined, and must be concerned with the kind of deictic anchoring that permits one to distinguish and relate what is analogous in my behavior and in that of another member of the species.

Effect of Tools

We must consider now the question of tools and their use, and what effect this evolutionary step may have had on the management of

immaturity. We might begin with its first emergence in chimpanzees, but before we do, it is worth considering initially a speculation by DeVore (1965) on the emergence of bipedalism and the freeing of hands. According to this speculation, and it can be nothing more, two contradictory selection pressures operated on the emerging protohominid. The first was for bipedal locomotion and easy standing, freeing the hands. The second was for a larger brain to provide the more flexible programming for the hands (as discussed above). Bipedalism, involving stronger impact on the pelvic girdle, led to selection of a smaller bony aperture of the birth canal to assure greater structural strength of the pelvis. If a bigger brained creature is to get through a smaller canal, there is required, of course, a smaller initial brain size and, therefore, greater initial immaturity (the human brain grows from approximately 335 to 1,300 cubic centimeters during development).[4] To assure the larger brain, the argument goes, there had also to be a recession in such apelike features as a heavy prognathous jaw as a base for effective dentition. Enroute, there is a critical point where the basic adaptation of the hominid must change.

So we may begin with the fact that tool using at its first appearance in apes comes before that point: it is an optional and not an obligatory adaptation. Chimpanzee survival does not depend on the use of sticks for fishing termites or on the use of crushed leaves as drinking or grooming sponges. As Jane Lancaster (1968) put it in a closely reasoned article on tool use, there is "a major change from the kind of tool use that is incidental to the life of a chimpanzee to the kind that is absolutely essential for survival of the human individual [p. 62]." Yet, in spite of the absence of "obligatory pressures," chimpanzees use tools optionally in an extraordinary variety of ways: for eating,

---

[4]For an excellent account of the changes that occur during this enlargement, making possible greater flexibility of connection and possibly better memory storage, see Altman (1967). Some of the same changes during this period of expansion also occur as a result of challenging environments (Bennett, Diamond, Krech, & Rosenzweig, 1964) and in the course of phylogeny (Altman, 1967).

drinking, self-cleaning, agonistic displays, constructing sleeping platforms, etc. Nor is it some accident of morphology: "the hands of monkeys and apes are equally suited to picking up a stick and making poking or scratching movements with it but differences in the brain make these much more likely behavior patterns for the chimpanzee [p. 61]."

I would like to make the rather unorthodox suggestion that in order for tool using to develop, it was essential to have a long period of optional, pressure-free opportunity for combinatorial activity. By its very nature, tool using (or the incorporation of objects into skilled activity) required a chance to achieve the kind of wide variation upon which selection could operate.

Dolhinow and Bishop (1970) made the point most directly. Commenting first that "many special skills and behaviors important in the life of the individual are developed and practiced in playful activity long before they are used in adult life [p.142]," they then note that play "occurs only in an atmosphere of familiarity, emotional reassurance, and lack of tension or danger [p. 142]." Schiller (1952) reported, "with no incentive the chimpanzee displayed a higher variety of handling objects than under the pressure of a lure which they attempted to obtain [p. 186]." He reported, actually, that attempting to direct play by reinforcing chimpanzees for play behavior had the effect of inhibiting play.

Functions of Play

Play appears to serve several centrally important functions. First, it is a means of minimizing the consequences of one's actions and of learning, therefore, in a less risky situation. This is particularly true of social play, where, by adopting a play face or a "galumphing gait" (Millar, 1968) or some other form of metacommunication (Dolhinow & Bishop, 1970), the young animal signals his intent to play. Now, so to speak, he can test limits with relative impunity: "There are many rules of what can and cannot be done in a troop, and most of these are learned early in life, when the

consequences of violating them are less severe than later on [Dolhinow & Bishop, 1970, p. 148]."

Second, play provides an excellent opportunity to try combinations of behavior that would, under functional pressure, never be tried.

The tendency to manipulate sticks, to lick the ends, to poke them into any available hole are responses that occur over and over again in captive chimpanzees. These responses are not necessarily organized into the efficient use of sticks to probe for objects, but they probably form the basis of complex motor patterns such as termiting [Lancaster, 1968, p. 61].

Or in Van Lawick-Goodall's (1968) account:

With the fruit, Figan devised a game of his own: lying on his back, he spins a *Strychnos* ball round and round, balancing it on his hands and kicking gently with his feet, like a circus bear. . . . Toys like this are not always at hand, but then the youngsters seem just as content to play with stones, leaves, or twigs. They may throw them, rub them over their bodies, pull leaves off stems, break and bend twigs, or poke them into holes in the ground. This form of play may be of tremendous importance in developing dexterity in manipulating objects. As the chimps grow older this skill becomes invaluable not only in routine activities such as nest-making and food-gathering, but also in the most specialized field of tool use [pp. 36–37].

And even in captivity, this same tendency to incorporate objects into manipulative patterns goes on undiminished, as one may judge from this report by Caroline Loizos (1967) of a young female chimpanzee habituating to and then "mastering in play" a tennis ball:

I bounce a tennis ball in front of the cage several times so that she hears as well as sees it and place it inside on the floor. She backs away, watching ball fixedly—approaches with pouted lips, pats it—it rolls. She backs hurriedly to the wall. Hair erection . . . J. pokes at it from a distance, arm maximally extended, watching intently; looks at

me; pokes ball and immediately sniffs
finger. . . . She dabs at ball and misses; sniffs
finger; she backs away and circles ball from a
distance of several feet, watching it intently. Sits
and watches ball . . . (pause of several
minutes) . . . walks around ball. J. walks past the
ball again even closer but quite hurriedly. She lifts
some of the woodwool in the cage to peer at the ball
from a new angle, approaches ball by sliding
forward on stomach with arms and legs tucked
underneath her, so that protruded lips are very close
to ball without actually touching it. Withdraws.
Pokes a finger towards it and sniffs
finger . . . returns to ball, again slides forward on
stomach with protruded lips without actually
connecting. Pokes with extended forefinger,
connects and it moves; she scurries backwards;
more dabs at it with forefinger and it moves again
(but not far because of the woodwool in that area of
the cage). J. dabs, ball rolls and she follows, but
jumps back in a hurry as it hits the far wall. She
rolls the ball on the spot with her finger resting on
it, then rolls it forward, watching intently the whole
time. She dabs again—arm movement now more
exaggerated, flung upwards at end of movement.
Tries to pick ball up between thumb and forefinger
very gingerly . . . fails. Rolls it towards her, sniffs
with lowered head. Picks it up and places it in front
of her—*just* touches it with lips—pushes it into
straw with right forefinger—touches it with lower
lip pushed out, pokes, flicking up hand at end of
movement, but backs away as it rolls towards her.
Bites at own thumb. Dabs at it with lips, pulls it
towards her and backs away. Examines own lip,
squinting down, where it touched ball. Picks at it
with forefinger and covers ball as it rolls (walking
on all fours, with head down to watch ball as it rolls
along at a point approximately under her belly).
Pushes with outside knuckles. Stamps on it,
dabbing at it with foot. Sits on it, rolls it with foot;
carries it gingerly with hand and puts it on shelf,
climbing up to sit beside it. It drops down—she
holds it in one hand and pats it increasingly hard
with the other. Holds it in right hand, picks at stripe
on ball with her left. Rolls it between two hands.
Rolls it between hand and shelf. Holds and pats;
bangs it on shelf. Holds and *bites*, examining ball
after each bite. Ball drops from shelf and she pats at
it on ground with right hand. Lies on her back,
balances ball on her feet, holding it there with
hands; sits up, holds ball under chin and rolls it two
or three times round back of neck and under chin. It
rolls away and she chases it immediately and brings
it back to shelf. Lies on back and holds it on feet.

Presses it against teeth with her feet and bites—all
fear appears to be gone—lies and bites at ball held
in feet, hands. Rolls it in feet, hands. Climbs to
ceiling, ball drops and she chases it at once, J.
makes playface, rolls and tumbles with ball,
around, over, under ball, bangs it; rolls it over her
own body [pp. 194–195].

Various writers (Dolhinow & Bishop, 1970;
Loizos, 1967; Van Lawick-Goodall, 1968) are
convinced that the mastery of complex tool
skills among subhuman anthropoids depends
not only on observation learning but also on
whether or not they take place in the close setting of the infant–mother interaction. Reference
was made in passing to one of the infants in the
Gombe Stream Reserve, Merlin, who lost his
mother at age three and was "taken over" by
older siblings. He mastered neither termiting
nor nest building, skills that apparently require
repeated observation.

Van Lawick-Goodall (1968) made it clear in
her detailed reporting why such repeated opportunity to observe and play is necessary;
mastery of a complex skill like termiting is a
complex process of mastering *features* of the
task—a nonmimicking approach—and then
combining the mastered features. There is, for
example, mastery of pushing a stick or grass
into an opening, though initially this will be
done without regard to appropriate rigidity of
the probe or appropriate diameter, or appropriate length. It will be played with as a part skill
once mastered—as Flint (2.8 years who had
started at play termiting) pushing a grass stalk
through the hairs of his leg. And sheer repetition will provide the familiar routinization that
permits an act to be combined with other acts to
meet the complex requirement of a stick of a
particular diameter and rigidity, pushed in a
particular way, withdrawn at a particular angle
at a certain speed, etc. A comparable set of
observations on human infants by Wood,
Bruner, and Ross[5] shows the importance of skill
to three–five-year-olds in enabling them to
benefit from demonstrations of how to put

---

[5] D. Wood, J. S. Bruner, & G. Ross. Modeling and Mastery in Construction Task. In preparation.

together an interlocking set of blocks to make a pyramid. Unless the child can master the subroutines, the demonstration of the whole task is about as helpful as a demonstration by an accomplished skier is to a beginner. As with the young chimps, so too with the young children: they take selectively from the demonstration those features of performance that are within the range of their capacity for constructing skilled acts. They are helped, but the process is slow.

One very crucial feature of tool skills in chimpanzees as in humans is the trying out of variants of the new skill in different contexts. Once Kohler's (1926) ape Sultan had "learned" to use a stick to draw in food, he tried using it very soon for poking other animals, for digging, and for dipping it through an opening in a cesspool. Once Rana had learned to climb up stacked boxes to get a suspended piece of fruit, she rapidly tried her new climbing routine on a ladder, a board, a keeper, and Köhler himself—most often forgetting the fruit in preference for the combinatory activity per se. Nor is this a response to the boredom of captivity, since the same variant exploration is to be found in the Gombe Stream animals studied by Van Lawick-Goodall (1968)—one of the most ingenious instances being the use of a twig as an olfactory probe by the juvenile female Fifi, an accomplished termiter:

> On three occasions [she] pushed a long grass stalk right into my trouser pocket, subsequently sniffing the end, when I prevented her feeling there with her hand for a banana. Each time there was in fact a banana there, and she followed me whimpering until I gave it to her [p. 206].

It is probably this "push to variation" (rather than fixation by positive reinforcement) that gives chimpanzee manipulation such widespread efficacy—such opportunism as dipping sticks into beehives for honey (Merfield & Miller, 1956), using sticks for clubbing lizards and rodents (Köhler, 1926), and using branches for striking at or throwing at big felines (Kortland & Koöij, 1963). The ecological significance of this wide potential repertory is attested to by observations of Kortland and his collaborators (Kortland, 1965; Kortland & Kooïj, 1963; Kortland & van Zon, 1969). They have reported striking differences between forest-dwelling chimpanzees from the rain forest of the Congo and Guinea and those from the Guinea savanna. An animated, dummy leopard was placed in the path of the chimpanzees. Forest apes broke and brandished branches and swung them in horizontal orbit at the dummy. The only hit was by one animal, punching the dummy in the face from in front. Savanna apes warmed up with such saber rattling, but then attacked the dummy *from the rear* with strong vertical blows with the heaviest available branch and scored violent hits— "showing both tactical cooperation between the actual assailants and vocal support by the onlookers [Kortland & van Zon, 1969, p. 12]." These authors suggest that open country prevents arboreal escape and thus poses for the animals a problem in tool manipulation that calls for great flexiblity in adapting tools to local constraints.

The play aspect of tool use (and, indeed, complex problem solving in general) is underlied by the animal's loss of interest in the goal of the act being performed and by its preoccupation with means—also a characteristic of human children (Bruner & Koslowski, in press). Consider the following episode:

> Hebb recounted how a chimpanzee he tested solved problems for banana slice incentives. On one particular day, she arranged the banana slice rewards in a row instead of eating them! Apparently, she had solved the problems for their own sake. "I was out of bananas, but I offered her another problem. . . . she solved the problem: opened the correct box and put a slice of banana into it. I took it out and then set the box again. . . . I ended up with thirty slices of banana" [Rumbaugh, 1970, p. 56].

A far cry from reinforcement in any conventional sense!

Köhler's (1926) account contains an interesting happening. He gave a handful of straw to one animal who tried to use it to draw in an out-of-reach piece of fruit. Finding the straw too flexible, the animal doubled it up, but it was too short, so he abandoned the effort. Modification is systematic, most often directed to features relevant to the task, and is combinatorial. It follows first constructions or first efforts at copying a model. But it appears first in play, not in problem solving.

Play in Relation to Tool Use

I have described these play activities at great length because I believe them to be crucial to the evolution of tool using—steps that help free the organism from the immediate requirements of his task. Play, given its concomitant freedom from reinforcement and its setting in a relatively pressureless environment, can produce the flexibility that makes tool using possible. At least two laboratory studies, one by Birch (1945) and the other by Schiller (1952), indicate the necessity of initial play with materials in order for them to be converted to instrumental ends. They both used problems involving the raking in of food with sticks of varying length—before and after an opportunity to play with sticks. Few succeeded before play. Observed during play, Birch's animals were seen to explore increasingly over three days the capacity of the sticks to lengthen an arm. When put back into the test situation, all of these animals solved the problem within half a minute. Perhaps, as Loizos (1967) has suggested, it is the very exaggeration and lack of economy of play that encourage extension of the limits.

Looked at logically, play has two crucial formal patterns: one consists of a function and its arguments; the other, an argument and the functions into which it can fit. A ball or a stick are fitted into as many acts as possible; or an act, climbing, is performed on as many objects to which it can be applied appropriately. This pattern, I would speculate, is close to one of the universal structures of language, predication, which is organized in terms of topic and comment:

> John has a hat
> John is a man

John jumps the fence, or

> Brush the hat
> Wear the hat
> Toss the hat.

It is interesting that the language play after "lights out" of the three-year-old, reported by Ruth Weir (1962) in her remarkable book *Language in the Crib,* takes precisely such a form. And I will not be the first to comment that the simultaneous appearance in man of language and tool using suggests that the two may derive from some common programming capacities of the enlarging hominid nervous system.

Another feature of play that is crucial to tool use is the feature referred to by Barsh (1972) as *dissociation*—"the ability to anticipate the potential component parts of an object" for use in a new arrangement. It is a question that occupied Köhler (1926) in terms of the ability of his animals to "dissolve visual wholes" of great visual firmness. A Russian investigator, Khroustov (1968), performed a most elegant experiment on tool using in a chimpanzee, showing to what degree these animals are capable of such dissociation. Fruit was to be extracted from a narrow tube, and sticks of appropriate diameter were provided. The animal succeeded, and knowing the capability of the species, we are not surprised. The experimenter then provided a wood plaque too wide for the job. After inspecting it, the animal broke it along the grain to obtain a stick of appropriate size. Khroustov then painted a false set of grain lines on a plaque at right angles to the true grain. The animal, using them to guide a first splintering attempt and failing, looked more closely for the true grain and used it.

To summarize once again, the great ape possesses manipulative subroutines that are practiced, perfected, and varied in play. These are then put together clumsily and selectively to meet the requirements of more extended tasks, very often in response to observing an adult in a stable and relaxed setting. The imitation observed is akin to imitation by a child of an adult speech model: the child's output is *not* a copy of the adult's; it has its own form even though it is designed to fill the same function. These initial acts are then modified in a systematic manner to fulfill further requirements of the task. The acts themselves have a self-rewarding character. They are varied systematically, almost as if in play to test the limits of a new skill. A baboon living in the same habitat as the chimpanzee is as eager to eat termites as is the latter; yet he shows none of these capacities even though he is seen to observe the chimpanzee exercising them often. He too is equipped with a good pair of hands. Note that there is an association between play and tool use, and that the natural selection of one, tools, led to the selection of the other as well, in the evolution of the hominids and man.

Adults as Models

Neither among chimpanzees nor in the infinitely more evolved society of hunter-gatherers is there much direct intervention by adults in the learning of the young. They serve principally as models and as sources of the necessary affection (Bruner, 1965). Among the primates, there is very little intentional pedagogy of any kind. Hinde (1971) recently reviewed the literature and concluded as follows:

On the whole, the mothers of nonhuman primates seem not to teach their infants. In a number of species, a mother has been seen to move a little away from her infant and then to wait while it crawled after her (e.g., Howler monkeys, Carpenter, 1934; rhesus, Hinde, Rowell & Spencer-Booth, 1964; gorilla, Schaller, 1963; chimpanzees, van Lawick-Goodall, 1968): this has the effect of encouraging the infant to walk, but can hardly be called teaching. However, it is clear that infants learn a great deal from their mothers, especially in the context of avoidance and food-getting behavior. Even avoidance of snakes differs between laboratory and wild-reared monkeys and may depend in part on parental example (Joslin, Fletcher, & Emlen, 1964). It has been shown in the laboratory that monkeys can learn to avoid situations or responses that are seen to cause pain to other individuals (Child, 1938; Hansen & Mason, 1962; Hall, 1968), and to accept

food that other individuals are seen to take (Weiskrantz & Cowey, 1963). In nature, the infant's proximity to its mother ensures that it becomes rapidly conditioned by her fear responses (e.g., Baldwin, 1969) and that its feeding behavior is influenced by her (e.g., Baldwin, 1969). In the patas monkey (Hall, 1965), Japanese macaque (*Macaca fuscata*) (Kawamura, 1959), and chimpanzee (van Lawick-Goodall, 1968), the young eat fragments that their mothers drop, as well as being especially likely to feed at the same food sources. Although by the time they are one year old, Japanese macaques are acquainted with all the types of food used by the troop, it is difficult to make them take new types of food in the laboratory. Apparently learning from the mother is normally important (Kawamura, 1959). Schaller (1963) records an infant gorilla removing food from its mother's mouth and eating it, and one case of a mother breaking off a stem for its infant to eat. Imitation, principally of the mother, is important for the development of tool-using behavior in wild-living chimpanzees (Goodall, 1964; van Lawick-Goodall, 1968); and the development of actions by imitation has also been recorded in hand-reared individuals (Hayes & Hayes, 1952; Kellogg, 1968). In the latter case, the actions may be used for social communication (Gardner & Gardner, 1969, 1971).

In squirrel monkeys, food-catching skill is learned by younger juveniles from older ones, rather than from their mothers (Baldwin, 1969). However it is by no means always the younger animals that learn food habits from older ones. Under natural conditions, young animals investigate new objects more than do older individuals, and this may lead to a transfer of feeding habits from younger to older animals. Thus, among the Japanese macaques, new foods tended to be accepted first by juveniles, and their use then diffused through the colony via their mothers and then the mothers' younger offspring and consorts (Itani, 1958). Although diffusion sometimes occurs in the opposite direction (Frisch, 1968), kinship ties are probably always important (Kawamura, 1959; Tsumori, 1967) [p. 32].

There may, however, be something like "tutor proneness" among the young—an increased eagerness to learn from adults. One study now in progress suggests how such tutor proneness may come about. Rumbaugh,

Riesen, and Wright (1972) are training chimpanzees and orangutans under the following conditions. One group receives tutoring modeling on a variety of tasks; each task is presented on each new encounter in the form of a new embodiment of the problem. A second group gets the same problems, but each time in the same form, so that this group is essentially repeating. The third group is presented the materials used by the others, but the human tutor model neither presents them as tasks nor models the solutions as in the first two instances. The tasks are mechanical puzzles, packing fitted containers within each other, searching for a hidden object, transporting an object to another part of the room, extracting candy from a container, etc. The reward is some combination of task completion and the tutor's approval. A preliminary finding of this work-in-progress is of particular interest. The apes in the more challenging first condition are the ones most likely to wait for the tutor to provide a clue before beginning on their own.

Does it then require a certain level of challenge and novelty to create tutor proneness in primates? Schaller (1964) remarked of the gorillas he observed in the Congo:

> Why was the Australopithecus, with the brain capacity of a large gorilla, the maker of stone tools, a being with a culture in the human sense, while the free-living gorilla in no way reveals the marvelous potential of its brain? I suspect that the gorilla's failure to develop further is related to the ease with which it can satisfy its needs in the forest. In its lush realm there is no selective advantage for improvement. . . . The need for tools . . . is more likely in a harsh and marginal habitat where a premium is placed on an alert mind . . . [p. 232].

And the same view was voiced by Yerkes and Yerkes (1929) in their classic work on the great apes, as well as by Vernon Reynolds (1965) who, in a penetrating article on the comparative analysis of selection pressures operating on chimpanzees and on gorilla, concluded:

> Finally, we may briefly consider the contrast in temperaments between these two anthropoid

species. Comparative behavior studies in the past often stressed this difference. Tevis (1921), for instance, wrote, "In mental characteristics there is the widest difference between the two apes that we are considering. The chimpanzee is lively, and at least when young, teachable and tameable. The gorilla, on the other hand, is gloomy and ferocious, and quite untameable" (p. 122). It is possible to suggest an explanation for this contrast between the morose, sullen, placid gorilla, and the lively, excitable chimpanzee. The difference seems to be most clearly related to the difference in social organization and foraging behavior. The herbivorous gorilla is surrounded by food: the more intensively it feeds, the slower it travels; its survival needs are easily met, and it is protected from predators by the presence of powerful males. Here there is no advantage to any form of hyper-activity except in threat displays and the charge of the big male, which is a hyper-aggressive behavior form. Chimpanzee survival, on the other hand, depends heavily on the fluidity of social groups and the ability to communicate the whereabouts of food by intense forms of activity (wild vocalizing and strong drumming). Moving rapidly about the forest, meeting up with new chimpanzees every day, vocalizing and drumming, and locating other chimpanzees by following their calls, are the basic facts of chimpanzee existence. Here an advantage may be seen in having a responsive, expressive, and adaptable temperament. Hyper-activity is the chimpanzee norm in the wild, and with it goes a volatile termperament [p. 704].

But here we encounter a seeming contradiction. The evolutionary trend we have been examining seems to have placed a major emphasis on a combination of developments: a relatively pressure-free environment with its concomitant increase in play, exploration, and observation; and at the same time, a certain challenge in the requirements of adaptation to a habitat. (Play in young gorillas and orangutans in the wild, by the way, is not nearly as elaborate as in the chimpanzee [cf. Reynolds, 1965; Rodman, 1972; Schaller, 1963; Yerkes & Yerkes, 1929], and in neither of these species is there much challenge from the habitat.)

I believe that Desmond Morris (1964) has a resolution for this apparent dilemma—that, on the one hand, a nonpressureful habitat seems crucial and, on the other, challenge is significant. He made the distinction between two modes of adaptation to habitat, *specialist* and *opportunist*—the squirrel versus the rat, certain exclusively forest-dwelling monkeys like the vervet or green versus the adaptable rhesus (cf. Hinde, 1971). Nonspecialists depend on high flexibility rather than on morphology or behavioral specialization. Aristarchus said it well and provided Isaiah Berlin (1953) with a famous book title: "The fox knows many things; the hedgehog knows one big thing."

One can only speculate that the evolution of intellectual processes in the primate stock from which man descended was in the direction of opportunism and away from specialism. It could be argued, indeed, that the original stock, as far as intellect goes, was closer to chimpanzee than to either of the contemporary pongids, though Rumbaugh (1970) believed that in certain forms of intellectual performance there are striking parallels between man and orangutan. The argument for opportunism seems in fact essential to account for the rapid fanning out of the evolved species to such a variety of habitats.

Instructional Interaction between Adults and Young

What can be said of "instruction" of the young in the protohominids and early man? Alas, nothing definite. But contemporary "simple" societies, hunter-gatherers, provide certain clues. No matter how constraining the ecological conditions, there is among such people an expansion in adult–child instructional interaction, both quantitatively and qualitatively, of a major order. Although one cannot reconstruct the Pleistocene hunter-gatherer by reference to such isolated hunter-gatherers as the contemporary !Kung Bushmen, their practices do suggest something about the magnitude of the change. !Kung adults and children play and dance together, sit together, participate in minor hunting together, join in song and storytelling together. At frequent intervals, moreover, children are the objects of intense rituals presided over by adults—minor,

as in the first haircutting, or major, as when a boy kills his first Kudu buck and undergoes the proud but painful process of scarification. Children also are playing constantly at the rituals, with the implements, tools, and weapons of the adult world. However, in tens of thousands of feet of !Kung film prepared by the Marshalls (see Bruner, 1966), one virtually never finds an instance of teaching taking place outside the situation where the behavior to be learned is relevant. Nobody teaches away from the scene, as in a school setting. Indeed, there is nothing like a school.

Often the adult seems to play the role of inducting the young into novel situations that, without the presence of a protecting and familiar adult, would be frightening—as in extended trekking, in witchcraft ceremonials, and in many other spheres where the child comes along and participates to the limit that he is able. This induction to the margin of anxiety, I believe, starts very early. A study by Sroufe and Wunsch (in press) provides a hint of just how early that may be. The study sets out to explore what makes human infants laugh. From four months (when laughing first appears in reliable and recognizable form) into the second year of life, the sufficient stimulus for laughter becomes increasingly distal—at first being principally tactile and close visual (e.g., tickle plus looming), with incongruities following later, as when the mother adopts an unusual position such as crawling on all fours. Note, however, that at all ages, the capers most likely to produce laughter when performed by the mother are the ones most likely to produce tears when performed by a stranger. The mother seems able to bring the young, so to speak, to the edge of terror. King (1966) has suggested that this feature of mothering is universal; that among birds as well as mammals, the presence of the mother reduces fear of novel stimuli and provides the assurance necessary for exploratory behavior. But it is only among humans that the adult *introduces* the novel, inducts the young into new, challenging, and frightening situations—sometimes in a highly ritualistic way, as with the *rites de passage*.

There is little question that the human young

(and the young of the primates generally) are quite ready to be lured by the novel, given even the minimum adult reassurance. "Neophilia" is what Desmond Morris (1967) calls it. Such readiness for novelty may even be attested to by a superiority, at least among the great apes and man, of the young over the old in detecting or extracting the rules and regularities in new situations. At least one laboratory study, Rumbaugh and McCormack (1967), has even found a *negative* correlation between age and the ability to master learning-set problems—tasks that have a common principle but a new embodiment on each presentation, like "pick the odd one when two are alike and one is different."[6] But note that it is in man only that adults arrange play and ritual for children that capitalize on this tendency.

It is obvious that the play and ritual in which young and adult humans are involved are saturated heavily with symbolism. Though the kind of mastery play I have been at some pains to describe in the preceding discussion is still a feature of human play, there is added to it now an extraordinary range of play forms that have as their vehicle the use of *symbols* and *conventions*—two terms that will concern us in due course. Not only are sticks, so to speak, used as arrows or spears or even as novel and unusual tools, they may be used now in a symbolic way that transcends utility—as horses, for example, when put between the legs (Vygotsky, 1967) or giant trees when propped up in the sand. The prop or "pivot" or toy (it is difficult to name the stick) is not used as a *utilitandum* (as, say, Khroustov's chimpanzee used a separated splinter to poke food out of a tube) but as a point of departure from the present perceptual situation. Though the stick must

have some feature that is horselike (it must at least be "go-between-the-leggable"), it must now also fit into an imaginary situation. It is for this reason that the great Russian psychologist Vygotsky used the term pivot: the stick is a pivot between the real and the imagined.

Once the symbolic transformation of play has occurred, two consequences follow. Play can serve as a vehicle for teaching the nature of a society's conventions, and it can also teach about the nature of convention per se. David Lewis (1969) defined a convention as an agreement about procedure, the procedure itself being trivial, but the agreement not. We drive to the right, or we exhibit a red light to port and a green to starboard. And it is evident immediately that a linguistic-cultural community depends on an easy and fluent grasp of convention on the part of its members. Symbolic play, whatever function it may serve for the individual child in working through his own problems or fulfilling his wishes at the fantasy level, has an even more crucial role in teaching that child fluency with rules and conventions.

As for pretraining in the particular system of conventions of the society, let me give an instance from an exotic culture. The reader can provide instances closer to home. This one is from Dolhinow and Bishop's (1970) review:

In New Guinea the Tangu engage in a ritual food exchange in which strict equivalence is maintained (Burridge, 1957). Equivalence is determined by mutual agreement between trading partners. The Tangu children play a game called taketak in which two lots of thirty spines of coconut palm fronds are stuck into the ground five yards apart. Individual spines within the lot are placed approximately six inches apart. The children have tops that are spun and let loose to try to touch the spines of the opponent's lot. The teams need not be equal, but the number of tops must be equal. The game proceeds as a series of bouts; within each bout, both teams must complete their turn. The game ends when, after any bout, both teams have an equivalent number of spines in and out, or, since this rarely occurs, when an end is mutually agreed upon. The object of the game is equivalence, just as in the food exchange ritual of the adults, and in both cases the outcome or equivalence is decided upon by mutual agreement. There is no winner or loser; the object is to tie [pp. 183–184].

---

[6]Rumbaugh (1970) commented in a recent review of the learning capacities of great apes: "It is frequently observed, however, that an animal that excels in learning when young remains excellent *if* frequently worked with as it grows to adulthood (at least 8 years of age) and beyond. Might it be the case that early experience in some manner determines the avenues along which intelligent behavior will be manifest. If early experiences are with formal test and learning situations, will the animal's adaptability be maximally manifest as an adult in contexts of that order" [p. 65]?

Using Symbolic Means: Language

Having gone this far into symbolic play, I now turn to language in order to be more precise about what is involved when symbolic means are used for preparing the human young for culture. Higher primate skill, as I have described it, has about it certain languagelike properties. Skilled action, like language, has paraphrases and a kind of grammar. But there is also a communicative function of language; and it is this function, in all probability, that determines many of its design features (cf. Hockett, 1960). I have emphasized the similarity between action and the structure of language in order to propose a critical hypothesis: The initial use of language is probably in support of and closely linked to action. The initial structure of language and, indeed, the universal structure of its syntax are extensions of the structure of action. Syntax is not arbitrary; its cases mirror the requirements of signaling about action and representing action: agent, action, object, location, attribution, and direction are among its cases. Whatever the language, the agent-action-object structure is the form soon realized by the young speaker. Propositions about the evolution of language are justly suspect. I offer this hypothesis not on the basis of evolutionary evidence but on developmental grounds. For what the child himself shows us is that initial development of language follows and does not lead his development of skill in action and thought. It is only *after* a distinction has been mastered in action that it appears in initial language; and when it first does so, it is referenced by paraphrase of previously learned words or phrases (cf. Slobin, 1971). Piaget (1967) put it succinctly: "language is not enough to explain thought, because the structures that characterize thought have their roots in action and in sensorimotor mechanisms that are deeper than linguistics [p. 98]."[7] And,

to use Cromer's (1968) words: "once certain cognitive abilities have developed, we find an active search . . . for new forms. Suddenly, forms (and words!) which the child has been exposed to for years become a part of his own speech [p. 219]."

At the onset of speech, then, language is virtually an outgrowth of the mastery of skilled action and perceptual discrimination. These abilities sensitize and almost drive the child to linguistic development. De Laguna (1963, orig. publ. 1927) remarked that the most likely evolutionary explanation of language lies in the human need for help, crucial to the "social-technical way of life" that is distinctly human (cf. Washburn & Howell, 1960). De Laguna went on:

> Once we deliberately ask the question: What does speech do? What objective function does it perform in human life—the answer is not far to seek. Speech is the great medium through which human cooperation is brought about. It is the means by which the diverse activities of men are coordinated and correlated with each other for the attainment of common and reciprocal ends [p. 19].

Having said that much, we must next note that with further growth, the major trend is a steadfast march *away* from the use of language as an adjunct of action or as a marker for representing the immediate experience. If in the beginning it is true (Block, p. 107, cited in de Laguna, 1963, orig. publ. 1927, pp. 89–90) that "a substantive does not denote simply an object, but all the actions with which it is in relation in the experience of the child," it is soon the case that language in the human comes increasingly to be free of the context of action. Whereas "to understand what a baby is saying, you must see what the baby is doing," nothing of the sort is true for the adult. This brings us to the famous de Laguna dictum, the implications of which will concern us for the remainder of this article:[8]

---

[7]This is not to say that once a language has been mastered to a certain level (unfortunately, not easily specifiable), it cannot then be used to signal properties of action and events that up to then had *not* been mastered by the child. It is in this sense that language can in fact be used as a medium for instruction (see Bruner, Greenfield, & Olver, 1966).

[8]For excellent accounts of the process of decontextualization in language, see Werner and Kaplan (1963) and Luria and Yudovich (1956). Both of these volumes provide rich documentation and interesting commentary on the point.

The evolution of language is characterized by a progressive freeing of speech from dependence on the perceived conditions under which it is uttered and heard, and from the behavior which accompanies it. The extreme limit of this freedom is reached in language which is written (or printed) and read. For example, it is quite indifferent to the reader of these words, under what physical conditions they have been penned or typed. This represents, we repeat, the extreme limit of the process by which language comes to be increasingly independent of the conditions of its use [p. 107].

We need not pause long on a comparison of language as it is acquired and used by man and by the chimpanzee—notably by the chimpanzee Washoe (Gardner & Gardner, 1971; Ploog & Melnechuk, 1971). For one thing, Washoe's language acquisition is not spontaneous, and she can be seen from the film record to be both reluctant and bored as a language learner. There is neither the play nor the drive of the human child, the *Funktionslust* (Bühler, 1934), that keeps the child exploring and playing with language. The young chimpanzee's grammar is tied perpetually to action. The nominatives and the attributives of early childhood speech, naming objects and attributing properties to them, are lacking and never seem to appear in Washoe. The evident delight of Matthew (Greenfield, May, & Bruner, 1972) in the use of such nominatives as "airplane," "apple," "piece," and "cow" is quite as important as the fact that these holophrases were used in a context of action. Roger Brown (1970, 1971) has commented that virtually all of the two-sign and three-sign "utterances" in Washoe's use of American sign language were either "emphasizers" of action (*Hurry open*), "specifiers" of action (*Listen dog,* at sound of barking), or indicated agents for action (*You eat, Roger Washoe tickle*). David McNeill (1972) put it concisely: Washoe's grammar can be characterized by the single proposition:

$$s \ldots p^n$$

or "statement that raises a predicated action to a higher level," a grammatical form not spontaneously present in human adult speech.[9] In a word, chimpanzee use of a taught form of human speech is strongly tied to action, beyond which it tends not to go, either spontaneously or by dint of teaching effort.

On the other hand, the development of language in humans not only moves in the direction of becoming itself free of context and accompanying action, it also frees the attention of the user from his immediate surroundings, directing attention to what is being said rather than to what is being done or seen. In the process, language becomes a powerful instrument in selectively directing attention to features of the environment represented by it.

With respect to the first of these, language processing goes on in its very nature at different levels. We process the phonological output of a speaker, interpret his syntax, hold the head words of imbedding phrases until the imbedded phrase is completed and the tail is located to match the head word, etc. At the same time, we direct attention to meanings and to references. The acts of language, argue Miller and Johnson-Laird (see Footnote 4), by their very performance free attention from control by immediate stimulation in the environment. One might even argue that the requirement of organizing what one experiences into sentence form may impose upon experience itself a certain cast—the classic arguments of Humboldt (1836) and Benjamin Lee Whorf (1956). Once language captures control of attention, the swiftness and subtlety of attention change come to match the swiftness and subtlety of linguistic maneuvering. Language permits search specifications to be set in such a fashion as to fulfill any question that may be asked. The eye-movement records collected by Yarbus (1967) provide stunning illustration of the tac-

[9]McNeill also made the cogent point that perhaps (as with Premack, 1971) chimpanzees can be taught a humanlike syntax, a not uninteresting point; but they seem not to acquire it as children do, by a process not so much of detailed learning or imitation as of spontaneous constructions of grammatical utterances most often exhibiting initial grammatical rules not present in the adult speech to which they are exposed.

tics of the language user: how, while guiding his eye movements by physical features of a picture or scene, he manages at the same time to pick up the features that answer questions he is entertaining—looking now to pick up the ages of people, now to judge their furniture, now to see what they are doing, etc.

To summarize, then, though language springs from and aids action, it quickly becomes self-contained and free of the context of action. It is a device, moreover, that frees its possessor from the immediacy of the environment, not only by preemption of attention during language use but by its capacity to direct attention toward those aspects of the environment that are singled out by language.

I have gone into this much detail regarding early language because it is a necessary preliminary to a crucial point about the management of immaturity in human culture. I have commented already on the fact that in simple, hunter-gatherer societies, there is very little formal teaching outside the sphere of action. The child is not drawn aside and told how to do it; he is shown while the action is going on, with language as an auxiliary and as a marker of action—an aid in calling attention to what is going on that is relevant. Over and beyond that, the principal use of language was probably some mix of guiding group action and giving shape to a belief system through myths and incantations, as Susanne Langer (1969) has long proposed. I rather suspect that increasing technology imposed an increasing demand on language to represent and store knowledge in a fashion to be helpful outside the immediate context of original use. L. S. B. Leakey[10] suggested that once stone instruments came to be made to match a pattern rather than by spontaneous breaking, as in fabricating an Acheulean pebble tool with a single-face edge, *models* could be fashioned and kept. He has found excellent, obsidian-grained hand axes at Olduvai that appear never to have been used; he speculates that they were "models for copy," with a religious significance as well.

[10]L. S. B. Leakey, personal communication, April 1966.

But an inert model is a poor thing; it is, in effect, an end state, something to be attained with no intervening instruction concerning means. Language does better than that, and it is interesting to see the extent to which magic becomes mixed with practice and imitation in a primitive technology. A good example is afforded by the boat building and interisland navigation of the preliterate Puluwat Islanders in the Marshalls, recently described in rich detail by Gladwin (1970) in a book entitled *East Is a Big Bird*. Theirs is a system in which East is marked by Altair at horizon elevation, distance by a commonsense speed-estimating method, with distance "logged" by noting the supposed parallax of islands at different distances over the horizon. Final homing on an island is accomplished by noting the direction of end-of-day nesting flights of boobies and frigate birds. And the lot is peppered with sundry omens given by weeds and sea turtles and the feel of things. I happen to be a navigator myself. I am impressed not only that the system works but that it is genuinely a *system;* it ties together means and ends. The framework of the system can be *told;* however, without language it would be impossible, for the ingredients of the system involve reference to the absent or invisible, to the possible, to the conditional, and even (I suspect) to the knowingly false (the white lies all navigators must tell to keep the trustful sailors trusting). There must have been hunting systems and seasonal marking systems of this sort, representable outside the setting of action, in use by very early man—probably much earlier than heretofore suspected (cf. Marshack, 1972).

Increasingly, then, language in its decontextualized form becomes among human beings the medium for passing on knowledge. And, of course, the emergence of written language—a very recent innovation from an evolutionary point of view—gives this tendency still further amplification. Once this mode of transmitting knowledge has become established, the conditions for the invention of school—a place where teaching occurs—are present. School is a very recent development in evolutionary terms, even in historical terms. I explore now some of the consequences of these developments for our mode of dealing with, informing, and shaping the immature.

From "Knowing How" to "Knowing That"

As soon as schools, pedagogues, and the storing of decontextualized information received legitimacy—and it was probably the written word that accomplished this legitimization—the emphasis shifted from *knowing how* to *knowing that*. Even growth becomes redefined in accordance with the shift—the adult "having" more knowledge, that is, "knowing about" more things. We have even come to define the needs of infancy in these terms, as "the need for experience" (rather than, as Bowlby, 1969, noted, in terms of the need for love and for predictability). Knowledge in some way becomes a central desideratum. And when, as in the United States, attention turns to the children of the underprivileged and the exploited, their difficulty is likely to be, and indeed in this case was, attributed to "cultural deprivation." Hence, an "enriched environment" was prescribed much as if the issue were avitaminosis.[11] Dewey (1916) referred early to this diagnosis as the "cold-storage" ideal of knowledge and, of course, attacked it vigorously.

But this is too simple, for in fact there is great power inherent in decontextualized knowledge—knowledge represented in a form that is relatively free from the uses to which it is to be put or to which it has been put in the past.[12] It is not too serious an oversimplification

to say that it is precisely such a process of reorganizing knowledge into formal systems that frees it of functional fixedness. By using a system of notation that redefines functional requirements in formal terms, far greater flexibility can be achieved. Rather than thinking in terms of "hammers," with all of their associated conventionalized imagery, one thinks instead in terms of force to be applied in excess of a certain level of resistance to be overcome. It is, in effect, the way of science to render the problem into this form in order to make the solving of *particular* problems mere instances of much simpler general problems and thereby to increase the range of applicability of knowledge. Why should the Puluwatan navigator struggle with such a set of complexities as I have described, when all it gets him is competence over a few hundred miles of ocean, and a shaky competence at that! He would be more accurate and more general, as well as more flexible, if he learned to take the elevation of a heavenly body, note the time, and reduce the sight to the easily solved spherical triangle of the western navigator. Such a system would serve him anywhere.

But there are two problems (at least!) in this ideal of efficient formal knowledge rather than implicit knowledge, to use Polanyi's (1958) phrase. The first grows out of the point already made about skill and its deemphasis. That deemphasis comes out of what I believe to be a misplaced confidence in the ease with which we go from *knowing that* to *knowing how*. It is not easy; it is a deep and perplexing problem. Let me call it the effectiveness problem. Just as deep is a second problem: it may well be that the message of decontextualization and formal structure is implicitly antifantasy and antiplay: Call this the engagement problem. The two together—effectiveness and engagement—bring us to the heart of the matter.

With respect to effectiveness, it is probably a reasonable hypothesis that as technology advances, the effector and the energy components of industrial activity become increasingly remote from human empathy: neither the arm nor the hand any longer give the models for energy or for artificing. Energy and the tool

[11]For a discussion of these problems in childhood as reflecting the growth of skills for surviving under hopeless conditions, see Bruner (1970), Cole and Bruner (1971), and Denenberg (1970).

[12]For a fuller discussion of the nature of thought processes employing formal and functional modes of organizing knowledge, the reader is referred to Bruner, Goodnow, and Austin (1956); Polanyi (1958); Popper (1954); Bartlett (1958); and Piaget's (1971) striking little volume on structuralism.

kit become, for planning purposes, black boxes, and the major human functions are *control* and the *organization* of work. There is a spiral. It becomes possible to talk about the conduct of work almost without reference to skill or vocation—wheat production and steel production and gross national product and energy production and balance of payments. With work and competence presented in that mode, the young become more and more remote from the nature of the effort involved in running a society. Vocation, competence, skill, a sense of place in the system—these become more and more difficult for the young to fathom—or, for that matter, for the adult. It is difficult for the child to say what he will do or what he will "be" as an adult. Effectiveness becomes elusive.

For while the new technological complexity produces an enormous increase in production processes and distribution processes, it produces no increase either in the number or in the clarity of comprehensible vocations. Production and distribution, in high technology, do not provide an operator with an opportunity to carry through from the initiation of a recognizable problem to its completion, or to see plainly how his task relates to the cycle from task initiation to task completion. Intrinsic structure and reward are removed. The result is what Norbert Wiener (1950) long ago called "work unfit for human production." The industrial revolution removed the worker from the home. Its technological elaboration made the worker's work away from home incomprehensible to the young and the uninitiated—the latter, often a worker himself. The greatest tribute to technique decontextualized from vocation, carried to an extreme where it becomes fascinating, is the *Whole Earth Catalogue*. Even the counterculture reaches a point where it is without vocations but offers only spontaneity as a contrast to overrationalized "vocationless" work.

School, separated from work which itself has grown difficult to understand, becomes its own world. As McLuhan (1964) insists, it becomes a medium and has its own message, regardless of what is taught. The message is its irrelevance to

work, to adult life. For those who wish to pursue knowledge for its own sake, this is not upsetting. But for those who do not or cannot, school provides no guide—only knowledge, the relevance of which is clear neither to students nor to teachers. These are the conditions for alienation and confusion. I would urge that when adult models become incomprehensible, they lose the power either to guide or to inspire. I do not mean to settle the question here as to whether present adult models are in fact totally relevant to the problems of those entering society now. I will, however, return to it later.

Bronfenbrenner (1970) in his book on child rearing commented on the accelerating trend toward generational separation in technical cultures. The self-sealing peer culture, the denigration of adult ideal figures, the counterculture committed to protest and romanticized ideals—these are by now familiar instruments of separation. But I believe them to be symptoms of the struggle to adjust to a social-technical order that changes at a rate faster than comprehension of it can be achieved and widely transmitted. This, you recall, is the problem with which we started: How can a system for preparing the immature for entry into the society deal with a future that is increasingly difficult to predict within a single lifetime? Many of the means for inducting the young into the social group, a heritage of the evolution of man's capacity for culture, appear to become ineffective under such conditions when such rapid change becomes the rule. Observation and imitative play, demonstration in context of skilled problem solving, induced tutor proneness, an effective teaching microcosm in the form of an extended family or a habitat group, and the concept of vocation—are all seemingly threatened. Yet, I wonder.

I do not propose to become gloomy. Surely human culture and our species are in deep trouble, not the least of which is loss of heart. But much of the trouble is real: We are degrading the biosphere, failing to cope with population, permitting technology to degrade individuality, and failing to plan. Many of the experimental and often radical efforts of the young represent, I believe, new variants of ancient, biologically rooted modes by which the young characteristically work through to maturity. And a great many of these efforts are in response to the new conditions we have been at such pains to describe—a rate of change faster than can be transmitted intergenerationally with concomitant likelihood of disastrous consequences. Let me conclude with a closer analysis of this point and, in so doing, come to what was referred to above as the problem of engagement.

Problem of Engagement

A great many of the world's schools are conventional and dull places. They do not foster much productive play and little of what Jeremy Bentham (1840), in his *Theory of Legislation*, called "deep play" and condemned as irrational and in violation of the utilitarian ideal. By deep play, Bentham meant play in which the stakes are so high that it is irrational for men to engage in it at all—a situation in which the marginal utility of what one stands to win is clearly less than the marginal disutility of what one stands to lose. Bentham proposed, good utilitarian that he was, that such play should be outlawed. But as the anthropologist Geertz (1972) commented in his close analysis of cockfighting in Bali, "despite the logical force of Bentham's analysis men do engage in such play, both passionately and often, and even in the face of law's revenge [p. 15]." Deep play is playing with fire. It is the kind of serious play that tidy and even permissive institutions for educating the young cannot live with happily, for their mandate from the society requires them to carry out their work with due regard for minimizing chagrin concerning outcomes achieved. And deep play is a poor vehicle for that.

What strikes me about the decade just past is the enormous increase in the depth of play in adolescence and, by reflection downward into lower age groups, among the young. Willingness to risk future preferment by dropping out of the system that is designed to qualify one for the future, in return for a season of communal mutuality—surely the balance of utility to disutility is not Benthamite. Such wagers are highly dangerous for the lives of the individuals involved in them. (Note that Russian roulette is the worst bargain to be had in deep play.) When one finds deep play, the inference must be that there are deep and unresolved problems in the culture. There always are, but that does not mean that one should not look carefully at what these are and what they signify for the future. There is ample reason to believe that the present forms of deep play point to a thwarted, backed-up need for defining competence, both individually and socially, to oneself and to others. Recall that in most previous cultural eras, adults provided challenge and excitement and a certain sense of muted terror for the young by induction into rituals and skills that had momentous consequences. Engagement was built into the system. One knew the steps to growing up, both ritually and in terms of skill.

If adult life ceases to be comprehensible, or begins to be less a challenge than a drag, then engagement is lost—but only for a while. I have the impression of something new emerging. What takes the place of the deposed, incomprehensible, or worn-out competence figure, the classical adult image of skill? At first, of course, protest-withdrawal figures will—the pop figures of rock and the Timothy Leary prophets who offer an intravenous version of competence via subjectivity. I believe that gradually there is emerging a new form of role bearer—the *intermediate generation*—adolescents and young adults who take over the role of acting as models. They exist visibly in context. Their skills and vocation are proclaimed, miniaturized to appropriate size, and personalized. I should like to propose that such an intermediate generation is a response to the crisis of a change rate that goes faster than we can transmit from generation to generation.

Lest we go too rapidly, consider the pointlessness of an intergeneration in a society *with* continuity. Turnbull's (1961) account of a Pygmy group in Africa serves well:

> When a hunting party goes off there are always people left in the camp—usually some of the older

men and women, some children, and perhaps one or two younger men and women. The children always have their own playground, called bopi, a few yards off from the main camp. . . .

There were always trees for the youngsters to climb, and this is one of the main sports even for those not yet old enough to walk properly. The great game is for half a dozen or more children to climb to the top of a young tree, bending it down until its top touches the ground. They then all leap off at once, and if anyone is too slow he goes flying back upward as the tree springs upright, to the jeers and laughter of his friends.

Like children everywhere, Pygmy children love to imitate their adult idols. This is the beginning of their schooling, for the adults will always encourage and help them. What else is there for them to learn except to grow into good adults? So a fond father will make a tiny bow for his son, and arrows of soft wood with blunt points. He may also give him a strip of a hunting net. A mother will delight herself and her daughter by weaving a miniature carrying basket. At an early age, boys and girls are "playing house." . . .

They will also play at hunting, the boys stretching out their little bits of net while the girls beat the ground with bunches of leaves and drive some poor tired old frog in toward the boys. . . . And one day they find that the games they have been playing are not games any longer, but the real thing, for they have become adults. Their hunting is now real hunting; their tree climbing is in earnest search of inaccessible honey; their acrobatics on the swings are repeated almost daily, in other forms, in the pursuit of elusive game, or in avoiding malicious forest buffalo. It happens so gradually that they hardly notice the change at first, for even when they are proud and famous hunters their life is still full of fun and laughter [pp. 128–129].

The transition is gradual, its excitement increased from time to time by rituals. But technological societies move away from such gradualism as they become increasingly developed. Indeed, the Protestant ethic made very early a sharp separation between what one does when young and what one does later, with the transition very sharply defined. In the western tradition there grew a puritan separation of the "works of the adult" and "the play of the babes." But it was clear to both sides what the two were about. Now "the play of the babes"

has become separate from, dissociated from, the adult community and not understood by that community any better than the young comprehend or accept the ideals of the adult community.

A place is made automatically, perhaps for the first time in our cultural tradition, for an intermediate generation, with power to model new forms of behavior. Their power comes precisely, I think, from the fact that they offer deep play, that irresistible charisma that so disturbed the tidy Jeremy Bentham. They are modeling new life styles to fit better what is perceived as the new and changing conditions, new changes that they claim to be able to see—perhaps rightly, perhaps not—more clearly than those who had adapted to something still earlier. The great question is whether the intermediate generation can reduce the uncertainty of growing up under conditions of unpredictable change, can serve as mentors as well as charismatic vendors of deep play, and as purveyors of effectiveness as well as of engagement.

I do not think that intermediate models are a transitory phenomenon. I believe that we would do well to recognize the new phenomenon and to incorporate it, even make it easier for the young adult and later juvenile to get more expert at it. Nobody can offer a blueprint on how an intermediate generation can help ready the less mature for life in an unforeseeably changing world. It is not altogether a comfortable problem either, for the way of cultural revolutions and Red Guards (both composed of intermediates) can only inspire caution. But letting the young have more of a hand in the teaching of the younger, letting them have a better sense of the dilemmas of society as a whole, all of these may be part of the way in which a new community can be helped to emerge. What may be in order is a mode of inducting the young by the use of a more communal system of education in which each takes responsibility for teaching or aiding or abetting or provoking those less able, less knowledgeable, and less provoked than he.

It was in the universities that these current matters first surfaced—a long way from the high savannas of East Africa where we began our quest for an understanding of immaturity and its uses. One becomes increasingly shaky the closer one comes to man in his contemporary technological society. I would only urge that in considering these deep issues of educability we keep our perspective broad and remember that the human race has a biological past from which we can read lessons for the culture of the present. We cannot adapt to everything, and in designing a way to the future we would do well to examine again what we are and what our limits are. Such a course does not mean opposition to change but, rather, using man's natural modes of adapting to render change both as intelligent and as stable as possible.

REFERENCES

Altman, J. Postnatal growth and differentiation of the mammalian brain, with implications for a morphological theory of memory. In G. C. Quarton, T. Melnechuk, & F. O. Schmitt (Eds.), *The neurosciences: A study program.* Vol. 1. New York: Rockefeller University Press, 1967.

Barsh, R. The evolution of tool use. Unpublished research paper, Center for Cognitive Studies, Harvard University, 1972.

Bartlett, F. C. *Thinking: An experimental and social study.* New York: Basic Books, 1958.

Beach, F. *Sex and behavior.* New York, London, & Sydney: Wiley, 1965.

Bennett, E. L., Diamond, M. C., Krech, D., & Rosenzweig, M. R. Chemical and anatomical plasticity of the brain. *Science,* 1964, *146*, 610–619.

Bentham, J. *The theory of legislation.* Boston: Weeks, Jordan, 1840.

Berlin, I. *The hedgehog and the fox.* New York: Simon & Schuster, 1953.

Bernstein, N. *The coordination and regulation of movements.* Oxford: Pergamon Press, 1967.

Birch, H. G. The relation of previous experience to insightful problem-solving. *Journal of Comparative and Physiological Psychology,* 1945, *38*, 367–383.

Bishop, A. Use of the hand in lower primates. In J. Buettner-Janusch (Ed.), *Evolutionary and genetic biology of primates.* Vol. 2. London & New York: Academic Press, 1964.

Block, S. C. Early competence in problem-solving. In K. Connolly & J. S. Bruner (Eds.), *Competence in early childhood.* (CIBA Foundation Conference) New York & London: Academic Press, 1972, in press.

Bloom, B. (Ed.) *Taxonomy of educational objectives.* New York: McKay, 1956.

Bowlby, J. *Attachment and loss.* Vol. 1. New York: Basic Books, 1969.

Bronfenbrenner, U. *Two worlds of childhood, U.S. and U.S.S.R.* New York: Russell Sage Foundation, 1970.

Brown, R. W. The first sentence of child chimpanzee. In *Psycholinguistics: Selected papers by Roger Brown.* New York: Free Press, 1970.

Brown, R. W. Are apes capable of language? *Neurosciences Research Program Bulletin,* December 1971, *9*(5).

Bruner, J. S. The growth of mind. *American Psychologist,* 1965, *20*, 1007–1017.

Bruner, J. S. *Toward a theory of instruction.* Cambridge: Harvard University Press, 1966.

Bruner, J. S. *Poverty and childhood.* Detroit: Merrill-Palmer Institute, 1970.

Bruner, J. S., Goodnow, J. J., & Austin, G. A. *A study of thinking.* New York: Wiley, 1956.

Bruner, J. S., Greenfield, P. M., & Olver, R. R. *Studies in cognitive growth.* New York: Wiley, 1966.

Bruner, J. S., & Koslowski, B. Preadaptation in initial visually guided reaching. *Perception,* 1972, *1*, in press.

Bühler, K. *Sprachtheorie.* Jena, 1934.

Chance, M. R. A. Attention structure as the basis of primate rank orders. *Man,* 1967, *2*, 503–518.

Clark, W. E. Le Gros. *The antecedents of man: An introduction to the evolution of the primates.* New York: Harper & Row, 1963.

Cole, M., & Bruner, J. S. Cultural differences and inferences about psychological processes. *American Psychologist,* 1971, *26*, 867–876.

Cromer, R. F. The development of temporal reference during the acquisition of language. Unpublished doctoral dissertation, Department of Social Relations, Harvard University, 1968.

Denenberg, V. H. (Ed.) *Education of the infant and the young child.* New York & London: Academic Press, 1970.

DeVore, I. *The primates.* New York: Time-Life Books, 1965.

Dewey, J. *Democracy and education.* New York: Macmillan, 1916.

Dolhinow, P. J., & Bishop, N. The development of motor skills and social relationships among primates through play. *Minnesota Symposium on Child Psychology,* 1970.

Gallup, G. G., Jr. Chimpanzees: Self-recognition. *Science,* 1970, *167*, 86–87.

Gardner, B. J., & Gardner, R. A. Two-way communication with an infant chimpanzee. In A. M. Schrier & F. Stollnitz (Eds.), *Behavior of nonhuman primates.* Vol. 4. New York & London: Academic Press, 1971.

Geertz, C. Deep play: Notes on the Balinese cockfight. *Daedalus,* 1972, *101*, 1–38.

Gladwin, T. *East is a big bird.* Cambridge: Harvard University Press, 1970.

Goodall, J. Chimpanzees of the Gombe Stream Reserve. In I. DeVore (Ed.), *Primate behavior: Field studies of monkeys and apes.* New York: Holt, Rinehart and Winston, 1965.

Gouldner, A. The norm of reciprocity: A preliminary statement. *American Sociological Review,* 1960, *25*, 161–178.

Greenfield, P., May, A. A., & Bruner, J. S. *Early words.* (A film) New York: Wiley, 1972.

Hall, K. R. L., & DeVore, I. Baboon social behavior. In I. DeVore (Ed.), *Primate behavior: Field studies of monkeys and apes.* New York: Holt, Rinehart and Winston, 1965.

Hamburg, D. Evolution of emotional responses: Evidence from recent research on nonhuman primates. *Science and Psychoanalysis,* 1968, *12*, 39–54.

Harlow, H. F. Love in infant monkeys. *Scientific American,* 1959, *200*, 68–74.

Harlow, H. F., & Harlow, M. K. The effect of rearing conditions on behavior. *Bulletin of the Menninger Clinic,* 1962, *26*, 213–224.

Hayes, K. J., & Hayes, C. Imitation in a home-raised chimpanzee. *Journal of Comparative and Physiological Psychology,* 1952, *45*, 450–459.

Herbert, M. J., & Harsh, C. M. Observational learning in cats. *Journal of Comparative and Physiological Psychology,* 1944, *37*, 81–95.

Hinde, R. A. Development of social behavior. In A. M. Schrier & F. Stollnitz (Eds.), *Behavior of nonhuman primates.* Vol. 3. New York & London: Academic Press, 1971.

Hockett, C. D. The origins of speech. *Scientific American,* September 1960.

Humboldt, W., von. *Ueber die Verschiedenheit des menschlichen Sprachbaues.* Berlin, 1836. (Facsimile ed., Bonn, 1960.)

Itani, J. On the acquisition and propagation of a new food habit in the natural group of the Japanese monkey at Takasakiyama. *Primates,* 1958, *1*, 84–98.

Jolly, A. *Lemur behavior: A Madagascar field study.* Chicago: University of Chicago Press, 1966.

Kawamura, S. The process of subculture propagation among Japanese macaques. *Primates,* 1959, *2*, 43–54.

Khroustov, G. F. Formation and highest frontier of the implemental activity of anthropoids. In, *Seventh International Congress of Anthropological and Ethnological Sciences,* Moscow, 1968, 503–509.

King, D. L. A review and interpretation of some aspects of the infant-mother relationship in mammals and birds. *Psychological Bulletin,* 1966, *65*, 143–155.

Köhler, W. *The mentality of apes*. New York: Harcourt, Brace, 1926.

Kortland, A. How do chimpanzees use weapons when fighting leopards? *Yearbook of the American Philosophical Society,* 1965, 327–332.

Kortland, A., & Koöij, M. Protohominid behaviour in primates. In J. Napier & N. A. Barnicot (Eds.), *The primates*. London: Symposia Zoological Society, 1963.

Kortland, A., & van Zon, J. C. J. The present state of research on the dehumanization hypothesis of African ape evolution. *Proceedings of the International Congress of Primatology,* 1969, *3*, 10–13.

Laguna, G. A., de. *Speech: Its function and development*. (Orig. publ. 1927) Bloomington, Ill.: Indiana University Press, 1963.

Lancaster, J. B. On the evolution of tool-using behavior. *American Anthropologist,* 1968, *70*, 56–66.

Langer, S. *Philosophy in a new key*. (Rev. ed.; orig. publ. 1942) Cambridge: Harvard University Press, 1969.

Lashley, K. S. The problem of serial order in behavior. In L. A. Jeffress (Ed.), *Cerebral mechanisms in behavior: The Hixon symposium*. New York: Wiley, 1951.

Lee, R. B., & DeVore, I. (Eds.) *Man the hunter*. Chicago: Aldine, 1968.

Lévi-Strauss, C. *Structural anthropology*. New York: Schoepf, Basic Books, 1963.

Lewis, D. *Convention*. Cambridge: Harvard University Press, 1969.

Loizos, C. Play behavior in higher primates: A review. In D. Morris (Ed.), *Primate ethology*. Chicago: Aldine, 1967.

Luria, A. R., & Yudovich, F. Y. *Speech and the development of mental processes in the child*. Moscow, 1956; London: Staples Press, 1959.

Marshack, H. *The roots of civilization*. New York: McGraw-Hill, 1972.

Mayr, E. *Animal species and evolution*. Cambridge: Harvard University Press, 1963.

McLuhan, M. *Understanding media*. New York: McGraw-Hill, 1964.

McNeill, D. Comments. In K. Connolly & J. S. Bruner (Eds.), *Competence in early childhood*. (CIBA Foundation Conference) New York & London: Academic Press, 1972, in press.

Merfield, F. G., & Miller, H. *Gorilla hunter*. New York: Farrar, Strauss, 1956.

Millar, S. *The psychology of play*. Baltimore, Md.: Penguin Books, 1968.

Morris, D. The response of animals to a restricted environment. *Symposium of the Zoological Society of London,* 1964, *13*, 99–118.

Morris, D. (Ed.) *Primate ethology*. London: Weidenfeld & Nickelson, 1967.

Napier, J. R. The evolution of the hand. *Scientific American,* 1962, *207*, 56–62.

Piaget, J. *Six psychological studies*. (Ed. by D. Elkind) New York: Random House, 1967.

Piaget, J. *Structuralism*. London: Routledge & Kegan Paul, 1971.

Ploog, D., & Melnechuk, T. Are apes capable of language? *Neurosciences Research Program Bulletin,* 1971, *9*, 600–700.

Polanyi, J. *Personal knowledge*. Chicago: University of Chicago Press, 1958.

Popper, K. *Nature, mind and modern science*. London: Hutchinson Press, 1954.

Premack, D. On the assessment of language competence in the chimpanzee. In A. M. Schrier & F. Stollnitz (Eds.), *Behavior of nonhuman primates*. Vol. 4. New York & London: Academic Press, 1971.

Reynolds, V. Behavioral comparisons between the chimpanzee and the mountain gorilla in the wild. *American Anthropologist,* 1965, *67*, 691–706.

Rodman, P. Observations of free-ranging orangutans in Borneo. Colloquium talk at the Center for Cognitive Studies, Harvard University, 1972.

Rumbaugh, D. M. Learning skills of anthropoids. In, *Primate behavior*. Vol. 1. New York: Academic Press, 1970.

Rumbaugh, D. M., & McCormack, C. The learning skills of primates: A comparative study of apes and monkeys. In D. Stark, R. Schneider, & H. J. Kuhn (Eds.), *Progress in primatology.* Stuttgart: Fischer, 1967.

Rumbaugh, D. M., Riesen, A. H., & Wright, S. C. Creative responsiveness to objects: A report of a pilot study with young apes. Privately distributed paper from Yerkes Laboratory of Psychobiology, Atlanta, Georgia, 1972.

Schaller, G. *Mountain gorilla.* Chicago: University of Chicago Press, 1963.

Schaller, G. *The year of the gorilla.* Chicago: University of Chicago Press, 1964.

Schiller, P. H. Innate constituents of complex responses in primates. *Psychological Review,* 1952, *59*, 177–191.

Singh, S. D. Urban monkeys. *Scientific American,* July 1969, *221*, 108–115.

Slobin, D. Cognitive prerequisites of language. In W. O. Dingwall (Ed.), *Developmental psycholinguistics: A survey of linguistic science.* College Park: University of Maryland Linguistics Program, 1971.

Sroufe, A., & Wunsch, J. P. The development of laughter in the first year of life. *Child Development,* in press.

Tinbergen, N. *The herring gull's world: A study of the social behavior of birds.* London: Collins, 1953.

Trivers, R. The evolution of reciprocal altruism. *Quarterly Review of Biology,* 1971, *46*, 35–57.

Turnbull, C. *The forest people.* New York: Simon & Schuster, 1961.

Van Lawick-Goodall, J. The behavior of free living chimpanzees in the Gombe Stream Reserve. *Animal Behavior Monographs,* 1968, *1*, 165–301.

Vygotsky, L. S. Play and its role in the mental development of the child (1933). *Soviet Psychology,* 1967, *5*, 6–18.

Washburn, S. L., & Howell, F. C. Human evolution and culture. In S. Tax (Ed.), *The evolution of man.* Chicago: University of Chicago Press, 1960.

Weir, R. H. *Language in the crib.* The Hague: Mouton, 1962.

Werner, H., & Kaplan, B. *Symbol formation.* New York: Wiley, 1963.

Whorf, B. L. *Language, thought and reality: Selected writings.* (Ed. by J. B. Carroll) Cambridge: M.I.T. Press; New York: Wiley, 1956.

Wiener, N. *The human use of human beings; cybernetics and society.* Boston: Houghton Mifflin, 1950.

Yarbus, A. L. *Eye movements and vision.* New York: Plenum Press, 1967.

Yerkes, R. M., & Yerkes, A. W. *The great apes: A study of anthropoid life.* New Haven: Yale University Press, 1929.

7. ORIGINS OF ANTHROPOID INTELLIGENCE

Prefrontal System and Delayed Alternation in Hedgehog, Tree Shrew, and Bush Baby[1]

BRUCE MASTERTON and L. C. SKEEN

Hedgehogs, tree shrews, and bush babies show measurable and consistent differences both in the size of their prefrontal system and in their ability to perform delayed alternation at long delay intervals. Further, these neurological and behavioral measures are in close correspondence with each other and with the subjects' probable recency of common ancestry with anthropoids. It is concluded that the anthropoid expansion of the prefrontal system and the capacity for delayed alternation probably had remote evolutionary origin, possibly coincident with the divergence of the anthropoid lineage from primitive placental stock in the early Paleocene.

In the century since Darwin, one of the chief goals of comparative psychology has been to demonstrate phylogenetic trends toward humanoid intelligence (James, 1890; Spencer, 1903). But despite the ingenuity and perseverance of several generations of experimental psychologists, few simple and unequivocal demonstrations of this prominent corollary of human evolution have appeared (cf. Bitterman, 1969; Harlow, Uehling, & Maslow, 1932; Warren, 1965). In retrospect, it is now evident that of the several conceptual, methodological, and technical obstacles to a persuasive demonstration, two have been particularly obtrusive.

[1]This research was supported by United States Public Health Service Grants NDS-7726, NDS-7468, and MH-11218, and National Science Foundation Grant GU-2612. L. C. Skeen is a National Science Foundation Predoctoral Fellow. The authors thank I. T. Diamond and J. A. Jane for having suggested this line of experimentation and for augmenting our histological materials with theirs. The authors also thank R. J. Ravizza and W. C. Hall for their advice on cytoarchitectonic analysis, E. Stellar for suggesting the inclusion of the interval-tracking test, S. A. Scoville and M. Robards for help in the behavioral testing, and N. Campbell for help in the allometric estimation of nuclear volumes.

From the *Journal of Comparative and Physiological Psychology*, 1972, *81*, 423–433. Copyright 1972 by the American Psychological Association. Reprinted by permission of the authors and the publisher.

The first of these obstacles was the result of a lack of information about which extant mammals are and which mammals are not the best neurological approximations to successive ancestors in mankind's ancestral lineage (Hodos & Campbell, 1969). But now, the true phylogenetic relationships of most mammals are known, at least in sufficient detail to allow their alignment along the dimension "propinquity or recency of common ancestry with mankind" (Figure 1), and to permit interpolation of successive neurological grades along mankind's line of descent (Clark, 1959; Romer, 1967; Simpson, 1945).

The second and more perplexing of the historical obstacles was, and to some extent still is, the result of a propensity for placing introspective restrictions on the definition and dimensions of intelligence regardless of their support or denial by empirical methods. This tendency can be seen by comparing the methods of classical papers (e.g., Hamilton, 1911; Hunter, 1913; Small, 1901; Thorndike, 1898). From examples such as these, it is possible to outline what might be called the traditional strategy of evolutionary psychology: First, decide what is meant by "intelligence"; second, invent an operational definition, a measurable dimension, and an appropriate test; third, align animals according to their scores on

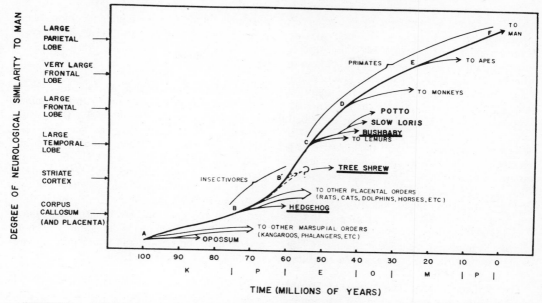

FIGURE 7–1. Phylogenetic relationships among the experimental subjects and the extinct animals in the anthropoid line of descent. (B, B′, and C represent successive ancestry of Anthropoidea whose characteristics are inferred through comparison of hedgehogs, tree shrews, and bush babies. Query designates uncertainty in ancestry of tree shrews. Modified from Masterton, Heffner, and Ravizza, 1969.)

the test. If the alignment does not parallel phyletic grade, then begin again with a new operational definition of intelligence or at least a new test.

Although there is nothing illogical about this approach, the fact must now be faced that, except for one or two possible exceptions (cf. Bitterman, 1969; Harlow et al., 1932; Warren, in press), this strategy has not yielded the expected results. One of the reasons for this lack of success might derive from the danger in generating hypotheses about how, when, and along what dimensions the humanoid variety of intelligence might have evolved without knowing the intrinsic nature and dimensions of human intelligence to begin with. Therefore, the avoidance of this obstacle requires not just an alternative strategy, but a strategy that demands no preconceptions about the nature of intelligence.

One possible alternative, explained to the first author in 1962 by I. T. Diamond and J. A. Jane, has now begun to make scattered and informal appearances (e.g., Diamond, 1967; Diamond & Hall, 1969). It is the product of a combination of neurology and psychology—much like that first envisioned at the turn of the century (cf. Elliot Smith, 1910; Herrick, 1924; James, 1890; Yerkes, 1930).

The Diamond–Jane strategy seeks first to discover trends in brain structure among animals known to have successive common ancestry with mankind—i.e., brain structure as a function of geological time—and then seeks to discover the behavioral contributions of the novel brain organization—i.e., behavior as a function of brain structure. After these steps, the final one—behavior as a function of geological time—follows from their combination. With this strategy, the question of what does and what does not qualify as intelligence is reserved until the behavioral roles of successively more humanoid brain structures are understood well enough to permit the abstraction of relatively independent psychological dimensions.

The experiment reported here is an attempt to apply the Diamond–Jane strategy to a relatively early segment of man's mammalian lineage. Representatives of ground-dwelling insectivores, arboreal insectivores, and prosimian primates were selected as subjects solely on the basis of paleontological conclusions regarding their successive common ancestry with anthropoids (Clark, 1959; Hodos & Campbell, 1969; Osman-Hill, 1953; Simpson, 1945). Hedgehogs, tree shrews, and bush babies were selected from among the currently extant representatives of these three respective grades, partly on the basis of their availability, but mostly on the basis of comparative anatomical conclusions regarding the degree of their neurological approximation to the extinct animals in mankind's ancestral lineage (Clark, 1959; Osman-Hill, 1953; Romer, 1967; Young, 1962; also see Figure 7–1).

The prefrontal system was chosen for this first evaluation because in terms of the number of synapses intervening between it and either sensory receptors or motor effectors, it is the least "sensory" and least "motor" system that is common to the neocortex of each of these animals and also to the neocortex of anthropoids. Furthermore, this same property of synaptic isolation from peripheral organs suggests a relative functional insulation of the prefrontal system from impersistent selective pressures (Hodos, 1970).

Finally, the capacity for delayed alternation was chosen as a likely behavioral indicator. This task was chosen not because of a presumed relation with intelligence, but because physiological psychology and clinical neurology have converged on the conclusion that the prefrontal system is essential for normal delayed-response performance in Anthropoidea (e.g., Warren & Akert, 1964), and because delayed alternation is one task within the class of delayed-response tasks that does not rely on good vision.

Method

There was an anatomical and a behavioral part to the experiments. The brains of normal adult specimens were studied to determine the relative amounts of tissue in their prefrontal systems. Other normal adult specimens were trained and tested on delayed-alternation tasks.

Subjects

The anatomical results are based on brain specimens selected from among the combined histological collections of I. T. Diamond's laboratory at Duke University and our own laboratory. The chief behavioral results are based on six animals: two hedgehogs (one *Hemiechinus auritus* and one *Paraechinus hindei*), two tree shrews (*Tupaia glis*), and two bush babies (*Galago senegalensis*), but a third hedgehog and bush baby were introduced later. Each of the animals was an adult wild-born male within the normal range of body weights for its species (Walker, 1964).

Anatomical Technique

Maps of the neocortex of the three grades of animals are already available (hedgehog, *Erinaceus europa*, Brodmann, 1909; tree shrew, *Tupaia minor*, Clark, 1924; bush baby, *Galago demidovii*, von Bonin, 1945). Since these maps are based solely on cytoarchitectonic distinctions in different species than those used here, anatomical analysis was focused, first, on verifying that the general cortical configuration in these species was similar to the published maps and, then, on measuring the relative size of the subcortical structures most closely connected with prefrontal cortex. Accordingly, measurements were made of the volume of nucleus medialis dorsalis (MD), the source of thalamic input to prefrontal cortex, and of nucleus caudatus, one of the chief subcortical targets of projections from prefrontal cortex (Akert, 1964; Nauta, 1964).

The animals were perfused with saline and then 10% Formalin. The brains were removed, embedded in celloidin, and sectioned at either 20, 25, or 30 μ. Every fourth serial section of the brains cut at 25 or 30 μ and every fifth serial section of the brains cut at 20 μ were stained for Nissl substance with either cresyl violet or thionin. In some series, the adjacent section was stained for myelin by the Weil technique.

Reconstructions of the nucleus medialis dorsalis and nucleus caudatus were obtained by systematic projection of the stained sections. Estimates of volume were then made by summing the areas of the serial sections and applying the appropriate corrections for magnification, section thickness, and distance between successive sections (Stephan & Andy, 1964). Since shrinkage of the tissue during celloidin embedding is certain, absolute volumes were disregarded in favor of relative volumes for which no correction for differential shrinkage was needed.

Behavioral Technique

Throughout training and testing, the animals were housed individually in a room in which the temperature and light cycle were artificially regulated. Although each animal was trained and tested during true daytime, the light cycle of the home-cage room was arranged so that the nocturnal hedgehogs and bush babies were tested during the night part of the cycle and the diurnal tree shrews were tested during the day part of the cycle.

Each animal was maintained at approximately 90% of its ad-lib body weight by small daily supplements of fresh fruit and meat. Upon entering the test apparatus for each daily session, the animals had been deprived of food for no less than 20 hr. The animals had free access to water both in the home cage and in the test apparatus.

Apparatus

The training and testing apparatus was a 36 × 17 × 18 in. plywood enclosure with a hardware-cloth floor. A partition divided the enclosure into right and left compartments; it extended from the front wall to a pressure-sensitive treadle at the rear. The treadle was a 12 × 17 in. wood platform positioned 1 in. above and horizontal to the floor. When the treadle was depressed, the delay-interval timer was activated. A 10-w. white light was located at the front end of the enclosure centered 14 in. above the floor. A speaker connected to a white-noise generator was located just below the light.

A 3 × 3 × 2 in. food cup was recessed in the front wall of each compartment. Thin horizontal light beams bisected each food cup. When either of these beams was interrupted by the animal's head or snout, a photorelay unit was activated.

Two pellet dispensers were used to discharge a .097-gm. Noyes dog pellet to the appropriate food cup following a correct response.

Stimulus, Response, and Reward Contingencies

The animals were provided with cues to indicate that they should either wait on the treadle ("delay" stimulus) or that the delay requirement had been satisfied and a response should be made ("respond" stimulus). During the delay stimulus (noise on, light off), no possible action could result in the delivery of a food pellet. The animal was required to stand on the treadle at the rear of the apparatus for a predetermined interval, after which the respond stimulus (noise off, light on) was presented. Thereafter, the first interruption of the photobeam in either goal box was counted as a response, terminated the trial, and reestablished the delay stimulus.

To be rewarded, the response had to occur to the side opposite that of the previous correct response. Following a delay, a response to the same side as the previous response constituted an error. After an error, the correct side remained unchanged for the next trial. Therefore, a succession of responses to the same side could result in a score less than 50%.

The delay and respond cues were presented simultaneously in auditory and visual modalities (white noise and white light). The intensities (54 db. SPL and −1.03 log ft. at 14 cm.) were set at levels known to be high enough for each animal to detect easily (Hall & Diamond, 1968; Masterton, Heffner, & Ravizza, 1969; Ward & Masterton, 1970), but low enough that no animal appeared to be frightened or irritated by their onset or offset.

Delay Requirements

The animals were tested at nine different delay intervals: 1, 2, 4, 8, 16, 32, 64, 128, and 256 sec. During training on the three shortest intervals, the timing clock reset whenever the animals stepped off the treadle before the delay requirement was satisfied. The animal then had to return to the treadle and wait the entire interval anew. For the longer delay intervals during training and for all delay intervals during testing, the animal had only to accumulate the total delay time on the treadle and could do so all in one waiting period or by several short waiting periods.

Procedure

Pretraining. After a minimum of 1 mo. in the laboratory, each of the animals received a cafeteria of Noyes "monkey," "dog," "rat," "cat," "fish," sucrose, dextrose, and banana food pellets in its home cage. Although sucrose was preferred for the first few days, dog pellets (Noyes, .097 gm.) proved to be preferred over the long term by every animal, and, therefore, they were used as reward throughout training and testing. For 1 wk. prior to training, each animal was stabilized at 90% of its ad-lib body weight with 5-gm. pellets, supplemented with fruit and, occasionally, with raw meat.

The animals were then put in the test chamber for two daily 1-hr. sessions. The light remained on, the noise remained off (i.e., the respond stimulus), and both food cups were filled with pellets and fruit. During the third, fourth, and fifth 1-hr. sessions, pellets were delivered every 60 sec. to alternate food cups.

In the next stage, successive approximations of alternation were rewarded with pellets from the dispensers. This procedure was continued until the animal alternated at least 50 times in 2 hr. During this phase, the white noise was turned on and its loudness gradually increased. The animal was then placed on the automated alternation schedule and gained experience with the delay and respond signals and the delay treadle (cf. Leonard, Schneider, & Gross, 1966).

Training. Each animal was trained to its asymptotic performance level at each delay interval in succession. Each daily session consisted of two warm-up trials in which both goal boxes were baited and then 50 training trials.

The criterion of asymptotic performance and, therefore, the criterion for advancing from one delay interval to the next longer delay interval was either: (a) a performance level greater than 90% for four consecutive sessions or (b) an average performance level on four consecutive sessions not exceeded by a higher average performance level in the next four sessions.

A criterion for terminating training was also adopted. This criterion was achieved when an animal's asymptotic performance at any delay interval did not exceed chance or did not remain above chance on two successive blocks of four sessions. When this criterion was met, the randomized-interval test was begun.

Randomized-Interval Test. For this test, each daily session contained 56 trials—2 warm-up trials and then 6 trials at each of the nine delay intervals. In the 54 test trials, the delay intervals were presented in random order. Several sessions were allowed for the overall performance level to stabilize and then the next seven sessions were used to collect the data reported here.

Interval-Tracking Test. The interval-tracking test was begun about 3 mo. after completion of the randomized-interval test. In this test, the delay interval was increased to the next longer delay after two successive correct responses; while after two successive incorrect responses, the delay interval was reduced to the next shorter delay. Each daily session began at the shortest delay interval (i.e., 1 sec.) and was terminated after 1 hr. Thus, the number of trials per session varied from about 50/day for the hedgehogs, which rarely reached long delay intervals, to about 20/day for the bush babies, which spent the vast majority of each session at the longest delay interval (256 sec.). The animals were allowed 16 sessions to stabilize their performance and then the next 16 sessions were used to collect the data reported here.

Results

Anatomical Results

The relative volumes of medialis dorsalis and caudate nucleus in the three animals are shown in Figure 7–2. The figure also contains loose estimates of the relative areas of prefrontal cortex as obtained from the cytoarchitectonic maps of Brodmann (1909), Clark (1924), and von Bonin (1945) and, in the case of the hedgehog, modified by our observations on *Paraechinus*. The figure shows that there is a large increase in the amount of tissue involved in the MD-prefrontal-caudate system across the three grades of animals.

It is important to note that the ordering of the three animals on the basis of their prefrontal system parallels the ordering based either on paleontology alone, on comparative anatomy

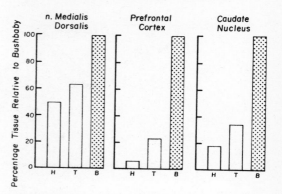

FIGURE 7–2. Amount of tissue in the prefrontal systems of hedgehog and tree shrew relative to bush baby. (Values for MD and caudate are volumes measured allometrically. Values for prefrontal cortex are areas estimated from cytoarchitectonic maps of others, modified by our own observations in the species used here.)

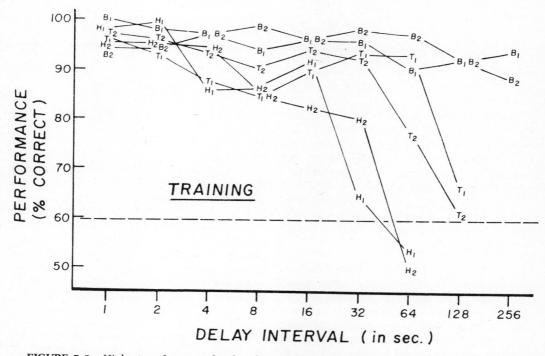

FIGURE 7–3. Highest performance levels achieved during training. (Each point represents 200 consecutive trials; chance level is 50%; dashed line is .01 significance level. Abbreviations: H—hedgehog; T—tree shrew; B—bush baby.)

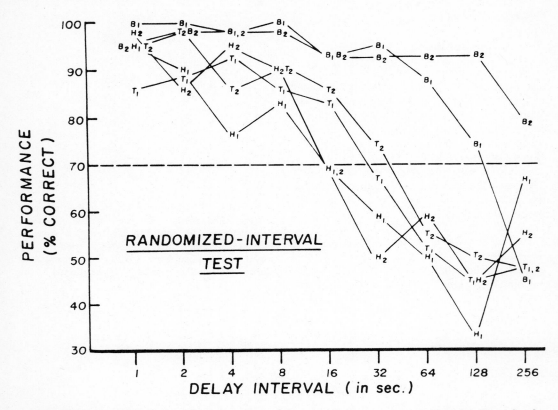

FIGURE 7–4. Performance on randomized-interval test. (Each point represents 42 trials; chance level is 50%; dashed line is .01 significance level.)

without reference to neurology, or on comparative neurology without reference to the prefrontal system (Clark, 1959; Osman-Hill, 1953). Therefore, among these three animals at least, the size of the prefrontal system is in perfect correspondence with the recency of their common ancestry with Anthropoidea.

Behavioral Results

Figure 7–3 is a summary of performance during training. The figure shows the average performance level achieved by each of the animals in the best four consecutive sessions (200 consecutive trials) on each delay interval. As the delay intervals became longer, the two bush babies performed at a higher level than the two tree shrews, and the two tree shrews performed at a higher level than the two hedgehogs. The probability that this ordering of the results might have occurred by chance alone is 2!2!2!/6! or 1/90.

Randomized-Interval Test. The results of this test are presented in Figure 7–4. If the longest delay interval at which the animal exceeded 70% (the .01 significance level) is taken as a comparative measure, we see again that the bush babies performed better than the tree shrews, and the tree shrews performed better than the hedgehogs. The probability of this ordering of performance levels is also 1/90. The absolute performance levels were lower and the magnitude of the differences among the three types of animals was greater on the randomized-interval test than during training.

Interval-Tracking Test. The results of this test are shown in Figure 7–5. Once again at long delay intervals, the bush babies performed better than the tree shrews, and the tree shrews performed better than the hedgehogs. The probability of this result occurring by chance alone is also 1/90.

Effect of Training Procedure on Test Scores. Since each animal received the randomized-interval test and the interval-tracking test only after it had been trained, it is not impossible that the test results may have been due entirely to each animal's experience during training. Therefore, an additional bush baby was introduced into the experiment. Immediately after pretraining, Bush Baby No. 3 was subjected to the interval-tracking procedure and then the randomized-interval test.

On both of these tests the third bush baby's performance level, though not quite as high as that of the other bush babies, was clearly higher than that of the hedgehogs and tree shrews (see Figure 7–6).

Relative Degree of Control Exercised by the Stimuli. During the tests, it was observed that when an animal erred at a long delay interval, it sometimes had left the delay treadle prematurely. In such an event, the animal might have alternated without first obtaining the respond signal and returned (unrewarded) to the delay treadle. If it then fulfilled the delay requirement and alternated once more, it would commit an error. Therefore, premature responses could lead to errors even though perfect spatial alternation was maintained. This possibility for "errors of impatience" arises because the apparatus provided a continuous opportunity to approach either food cup.

It was desirable, therefore, to determine whether or not there might exist a differential degree of control exercised by the delay and respond stimuli across the three varieties of animals. Accordingly, they were trained and tested on another task. This task was identical to

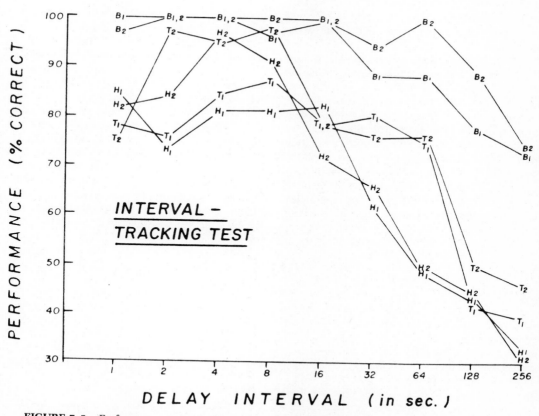

FIGURE 7–5. Performance on interval-tracking test. (Points represent a widely varying number of trials.)

the previous ones except that alternation was no longer required—responses to the right food cup were entirely ignored. Instead, the animals were rewarded only for delayed responses to the left food cup. The animal was required to wait on the treadle until the delay interval was satisfied and the respond signal replaced the delay signal. When it responded to the left food cup, reward was received, the delay signal replaced the respond signal, and the animal had to return to the treadle to wait until the next delay interval was satisfied.

Performance stabilized after only a few sessions of training and the analog of the previous randomized-interval test was then administered. Eight delay intervals (the 256-sec. delay interval was dropped) were presented seven times in random order in each of seven daily sessions. To assess the degree of control exercised by the delay and respond signals, premature responses to the left food cup and premature departures from the treadle were recorded.

The relations of these two types of errors to the errors in the previous delayed-alternation test are shown in Figure 7–7. The errors were neither consistent for individuals of one or another grade nor systematic across the grades. More important, the results of this test do *not* parallel the results of the delayed-alternation test. When these results are combined with the results on the previous delayed-alternation test, a concise description of the capacity of the more primitive grades is possible: They can delay without alternation and they can alternate without delay, but they cannot alternate with delays as well as animals of higher grades.

Discussion

The results show that there exist measurable, consistent, and parallel differences among hedgehogs, tree shrews, and bush babies in the relative amount of tissue in their prefrontal system, on the one hand, and in their capacity to perform delayed-alternation tasks, on the other. The behavioral results also show that the difference in delayed-alternation capacity is not the secondary result of a differential ability to delay or a differential ability to alternate, nor of a difference in the control exercised by the visual and auditory cues, nor of a peculiarity in the training procedure.

The joint correlation of the size of the prefrontal system and delayed-alternation capacity with the dimension "propinquity to anthropoids" suggests further that these measures changed markedly and unidirectionally during the divergence of the anthropoid lineage from the primitive placental stock. Finally, the existence of differences in the capacity for delayed alternation among animals with such remote common ancestry suggests that the evolution of this capacity began during the early Paleocene—perhaps 75 million years ago.

However, before it can be concluded that the results have anything whatever to do with a capacity eligible for inclusion under the term "intelligence," it is necessary to provide

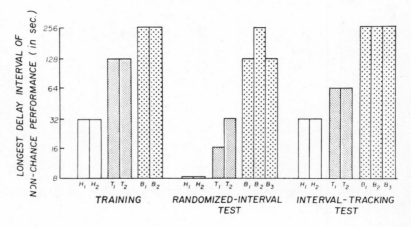

FIGURE 7–6. Longest delay interval at which delayed-alternation performance exceeded chance ($p < .01$).

evidence that the differences in the delayed-alternation test scores are probably not the direct consequence of a bias in the clearly nonintellectual requirements of the test. In the behavioral tests used here, this assurance is provided by two sets of data: first, the success of each animal in performing delayed alternation at short delay intervals; and second, the similarity between the outcomes of the randomized-interval test and the other two measures of ability.

The success of every animal at short delay intervals indicates that the conditions selected for the tests certainly do not preclude successful performance for either variety of animal. Thus, whatever the psychological limits imposed on these particular subjects by the sensory, motor, motivational, and emotional requirements, the conditions selected are adequate for high performance levels at least for some delay intervals.

Nevertheless, the differentiating results might still be a function of subtle confounds due to an interaction between delay intervals and emotional or motivational factors. This is the reason that the randomized-interval test was included. The similarity of the ordering of the species on this test with their ordering on the other measures would seem to rule out changing motivational levels within sessions and emotional interference due to the outcome of previous trials as an alternative explanation of the chief behavioral results. For such factors to provide an explanation for these data, motivational interference or emotionality would have to covary perfectly with delay intervals as well as with neurological and phyletic grade.

Still, there exists a nonnegligible possibility that genus-specific or even species-specific differences among the animals might account for the results without the necessity of referring to grade-specific differences (Warren, in press). Consequently, until the same tests are administered to more bizarre representatives of the three respective grades and a hierarchical analysis of variance applied to the results, the conclusions must be weakened accordingly.

Finally, we return to the question raised in the introduction concerning the possibility of demonstrating persistent trends in the evolution of mankind's intellectual attributes. Because the behavioral results reported here seem to fulfill the more obvious requirements for such a demonstration (Warren, in press), we are now encouraged to think that a comparative line of inquiry into the evolution of the higher mental

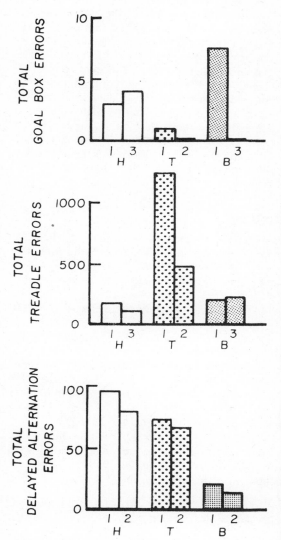

FIGURE 7–7. Total errors in delayed responding without alternation (top and middle) compared to total errors in delayed alternation (bottom) during randomized-interval tests. (Hedgehog 3 [a second Paraechinus] and Bush Baby 3 were used to replace two animals that had died [HH 2 and BB 2] [after Scoville, 1972].)

functions of man may be revitalized. The Diamond–Jane version of the inquiry upon which our optimism is based is essentially similar in reasoning to that which generated the psychological comparisons attempted in the past, but it is fundamentally different in strategy. The strategic differences that appear important to us lie in the means for selecting behavioral tests and the means for selecting the animals to be compared.

If the Diamond–Jane strategy for choosing subjects on the basis of comparative neuroanatomy and choosing behavioral measures on the basis of physiological experimentation is indeed a more productive alternative to the traditional strategy, it follows that several other evolutionary trends toward humanoid behavioral capacities should be easily demonstrable. For example, an apparently

radical increase in the size of the temporal lobe occurred during the Eocene when arboreal primates were diverging from insectivora stock. This progressive expansion of the pulvinar-inferotemporal system is still evident in a hedgehog–tree shrew–bush baby–monkey comparison. In this case, the Diamond–Jane strategy would suggest that behavioral tasks known from physiological experimentation to be sensitive to temporal lobe lesions, such as visual learning sets (e.g., Killackey, Snyder, & Diamond, 1971; Mishkin, 1966), might provide other demonstrations of systematic differences in behavioral capacity across that sequence of animals. In a similar fashion, the strategy might also exploit the differences in prosimian, simian, and pongid frontal lobes, or the differences in simian, pongid, and hominid parietal lobes.

REFERENCES

Akert, K. Comparative anatomy of the frontal cortex and thalamocortical connections. In J. M. Warren & K. Akert (Eds.), *The frontal granular cortex and behavior*. New York: McGraw-Hill, 1964.

Bitterman, M. E. Thorndike and the problem of animal intelligence. *American Psychologist,* 1969, *24*, 444–453.

Brodmann, K. *Vergleichende lokalizationslehre der Grosshirnrinde*. Leipzig: Verlag von Johann Ambrosius Barth, 1909.

Clark, W. E. Le Gros. On the brain of the tree shrew (*Tupaia minor*). *Proceedings of the Zoological Society of London,* 1924, 1053–1074. (Part IV)

Clark, W. E. Le Gros. *The antecedents of man*. Edinburgh: Edinburgh University Press, 1959. (Republished: New York: Harper & Row. 1963.)

Diamond. I. T. The sensory neocortex. In W. D. Neff (Ed.), *Contributions to sensory physiology*. Vol. 2. New York: Academic Press, 1967.

Diamond. I. T., & Hall, W. C. Evolution of neocortex. *Science,* 1969, *164*, 251–262.

Elliot Smith, G. Some problems relating to the evolution of the brain. *Lancet,* 1910, 1. (January 1)

Hall, W. C., & Diamond. I. T. Organization and function of the visual cortex in hedgehog: II. An ablation study of pattern discrimination. *Brain, Behavior and Evolution,* 1968, *1*, 215–243.

Hamilton, G. Z. A study of trial and error reactions in mammals. *Journal of Animal Behavior,* 1911, *1*, 33–66.

Harlow, H. F., Uehling, H., & Maslow, A. H. Comparative behavior of primates: I. Delayed reaction tests on primates from the lemur to the orang-outan. *Comparative Psychology,* 1932, *13*, 313–343.

Herrick, C. J. *Neurological foundations of animal behavior*. New York: Holt, 1924.

Hodos, W. Evolutionary interpretation of neural and behavioral studies of living vertebrates. In F. O. Schmitt (Ed.), *The neurosciences: Second study program*. New York: Rockefeller University Press, 1970.

Hodos, W., & Campbell, C. B. G. Scala Naturae: Why there is no theory in comparative psychology. *Psychological Review,* 1969, *76*, 337–350.

Hunter, W. S. The delayed reaction in animals and children. *Behavior Monographs,* 1913, No. 6.

James, W. *The principles of psychology.* New York: Holt, 1890. (Republished: New York: Dover, 1950.)

Killackey, H., Snyder, M., & Diamond, I. T. Function of striate and temporal cortex in the tree shrew. *Journal of Comparative and Physiological Psychology Monograph,* 1971, *74* (1, Pt. 2).

Leonard, C., Schneider, G. E., & Gross, C. G. Performance on learning set and delayed response tasks by tree shrew *(Tupaia glis). Journal of Comparative and Physiological Psychology,* 1966, *62*, 501–504.

Masterton, B., Heffner, H., & Ravizza, R. The evolution of human hearing. *Journal of the Acoustical Society of America,* 1969, *45*, 966–985.

Mishkin, M. Visual mechanisms beyond the striate cortex. In R. W. Russell (Ed.), *Frontiers in physiological psychology.* New York: Academic Press, 1966.

Nauta, W. J. H. Some efferent connections of the prefrontal cortex in the monkey. In J. M. Warren & K. Akert (Eds.), *The frontal granular cortex and behavior.* New York: McGraw-Hill. 1964.

Osman-Hill, W. C. *Primates.* Vol. 1–3. Edinburgh: Edinburgh University Press, 1953.

Romer, A. S. Major steps in vertebrate evolution. *Science,* 1967, *158*, 1629–1637.

Scoville, S. A. Visual control of behavior in primitive mammals. Unpublished master's thesis, Florida State University, 1972.

Simpson, G. G. Principles of classification and the classification of mammals. *Bulletin of the American Museum of Natural History,* 1945, *1*, 85.

Small, W. S. An experimental study of the mental processes of the rat. *American Journal of Psychology,* 1901, *12*, 206–239.

Spencer, H. *Principles of psychology.* New York: Appleton, 1903.

Stephan, H., & Andy, O. J. Quantitative comparisons of brain structures from Insectivores to Primates. *American Zoology,* 1964, *4*, 59–74.

Thorndike, E. L. Animal intelligence: An experimental study of the associative processes in animals. *Psychological Review,* 1898, *2*(4, Whole No. 8).

von Bonin, G. The cortex of galago. *Illinois Monographs in the Medical Sciences,* 1945, *5*, No. 3.

Walker, E. P. *Mammals of the world.* Vol. 1. Baltimore: Johns Hopkins University Press, 1964.

Ward, J. P., & Masterton, B. Encephalization and visual cortex in the tree shrew *(Tupaia glis). Brain, Behavior and Evolution,* 1970, *3*, 421–469.

Warren, J. M. Primate learning in comparative perspective. In A. M. Schrier, H. F. Harlow, & F. Stollnitz (Eds.), *Behavior of nonhuman primates: Modern research trends.* New York: Academic Press, 1965.

Warren, J. M. Learning: Vertebrates. In D. Dewsbury (Ed.), *Comparative psychology: A modern survey.* New York: McGraw-Hill, in press.

Warren, J. M., & Akert, K. (Eds.) *The frontal granular cortex and behavior.* New York: McGraw-Hill, 1964.

Yerkes, R. M. Robert Mearns Yerkes: Psychobiologist. In C. Murchison (Ed.), *A history of psychology in autobiography.* Vol. 2. Worcester, Mass.: Clark University Press, 1930. (Republished: New York: Russell & Russell, 1961.)

Young, J. Z. *The life of vertebrates.* (2nd ed.) New York: Oxford University Press, 1962.

Chapter 5
INFANCY, EARLY EXPERIENCE, AND CRITICAL PERIODS

INTRODUCTION AND COMMENTARY

Since the 1950s there has been a surge of experimental interest in the effects of early experience in general. Since the 1960s there has been a marked proliferation of research in the area of infancy. In fact White (1971) has suggested that if present trends continue, newborns will be used as subjects for research as frequently as the white rat or the college sophomore. Concurrent with this new specialization there has been an emphasis on: (1) early experience in humans (especially preverbal); (2) experimental studies rather than naturalistic observation; and (3) comparative studies concerned with developmental processes in different species.

This chapter is concerned with early experience in general, and specifically with infancy and with critical periods in development. Historically, the emphasis had been on predetermined development, and early experience *per se* was considered relatively unimportant (see Hunt [34]). In his theory of psychosexual development, Freud (1905) was one of the first to emphasize the importance of early experience. The *experimental* emphasis, however, probably derives from the work of the ethologists (Lorenz, 1937; Tinbergen, 1951) on imprinting and from the post–World War II work in Hebb's laboratory. Hebb (1949) and his co-workers have shown that infant animals reared in isolation and deprived of adequate stimulation do not develop normally. Brackbill (1971) has shown that continuous stimulation of infants has beneficial or pacifying effects.

Studies on the effects of early experience can focus on (1) the consequences of deprived or restricted environments. (2) the consequences of enriched environments, (3) cross-cultural comparisons, and (4) interspecies (comparative) comparisons.

Of these first two categories Hebb's studies on deprivation have dealt primarily with perceptual development, while later investigators (e.g., Ainsworth, 1966; Bowlby, 1952, 1960; Harlow, 1962) have studied the effects of stimulation on social and emotional behavior. The experiments in this field have not only demonstrated rather conclusively the importance of experience but have also suggested *how* it operates in terms of the critical-periods hypothesis.

In terms of early experience, the ethologists have influenced the research on imprinting (see Hess, 1959, 1964, 1972). Hebb (1949) has influenced the research on cognition and perception; Freud has influenced the research on psychosexual development (see Hunt, 1941; Rutter, 1971), trauma (see Levine, 1960), and on the effects of mothering (see Bowlby, 1960, 1971; Goldfarb, 1955; Harlow, 1962; Rutter, 1972, etc.). Piaget (1952) has influenced the research on an interactional theory of cognitive development (see Flavel, 1963; Furth, 1969: Hunt, 1961).

Stimulation and Enriched Environment

As indicated above, Brackbill (1971) has shown that continuous stimulation (e.g., sound, light, swaddling, temperature) has a pacifying effect on young infants. However, Levine (1960) suggests that even early *painful* stimulation may have positive effects. This latter position is at variance with the Freudian hypothesis that organisms that experience traumatic stimulation during infancy are more prone to anxiety in adulthood. Levine (1960) found that rats receiving electric shock during infancy adapt more readily than nonmanipulated rats to stressful situations in adulthood. Since then other investigators (Denenberg, 1962; Goldman, 1964; Salama & Hunt, 1964) have obtained supporting evidence for these results. The Salama and Hunt (1964) study has the merits of (1) being concerned with the effects of several *kinds* of early stimulation on the *same animals* in a number of replications, and (2) measuring varied *kinds* of adult behavior as a function of varied early experience. Their results corroborate the findings of others that both noxious and pleasant stimulation in infancy is associated with decreased emotionality as measured by defecation and urination in adulthood; that gentled and handled animals grow faster than unmolested controls; that shocked, handled, and gentled rats weigh more as adults than do unstimulated controls; and that stimulation in infancy decreases the tendency to lose weight under deprivation conditions. As indexed by error scores, variations in infantile experience produced no difference in either reward learning or shock learning. Contrary to clinical lore and the conditioning theory of fear or anxiety, infantile shock reduced rather than increased the "fixation" effects of adulthood shock (Campbell & Jaynes [20] find that *conditioned avoidance* of stimuli associated with shock in infant rats diminishes as the animals develop, unless during the period of development a few brief "reinstating" shocks are given—themselves insufficient to condition avoidance). Adaptation to strong stimulation endures but can be acquired late as well as early. Salama and Hunt (1964) suggest that varied early stimulation may serve to "inoculate" organisms against fears of strange and unfamiliar situations. With respect to humans, Hunt (1964, [34]) cites a study by Holmes (1935) with children that offers support for the position that early traumatic experiences need not have adverse effects.

In general the experimental evidence indicates that animals stimulated as infants are less emotional as adults than those who are not stimulated as infants. This is related to the general notion that early stimulation should facilitate development. Since deprivation retards development (e.g., Hebb, 1949), then enriched environment should have a remedial effect. For example Rosenzweig and Bennett (1969) have shown that young gerbils raised in an enriched environment (reared in groups in large cages with toys) subsequently perform better on learning tasks, have a greater concentration of chemicals associated with learning, and have greater brain weights than gerbils reared alone in small, bare cages. White (1969) has shown that early stimulation affects the development of *visually directed reaching* ("fisted-swiping") in human infants. Although the development of the "fisted-swiping" response is basically determined by maturational factors (e.g., by two months the infant swipes at the target but misses, but by five months his "fisted-swiping" is accurate), White speeded up the process (to three and one-half months) by enriching the environment of one-month-old infants in a state hospital. However, an enriched group of infants did not commence visual exploration of their hands until two months of age as contrasted with a control group (reared in the somewhat unstimulating hospital environment) who developed this attribute at one and one-half months of age. Since the controls had relatively little to look at they explored their hands and discovered them at an earlier age than the stimulated infants.

However, stimulation *per se* is not necessarily always beneficial. In order for development to be accelerated by stimulation a certain level of maturation must be present. In fact, White (1969) found that too much stimulation at too early an age induced crying and distress; by properly programming stimulation (e.g., starting with simple mobile objects and subsequently using more complex ones) White (1969) found distress did not occur and "fisted-swiping" occurred in *less* than three months. The interaction of maturational and experiential factors seem to be important.

Watson (1971), White (1971), Greenberg (1971), and Wachs and Cucinotta (1971) have also found that not only do enrichment procedures not always accelerate cognitive and perceptual development but occasionally they even produce retarded development. Hunt (1961, 1965) has suggested that enriched environments will facilitate development only when there is a "match" between the experiential encounters and "stored" abilities, information, and so on. That is, when the infant has acquired certain "schemata" (see Kagan [18]) he or she can then benefit from the appropriate experiential encounters. Wachs, Uzgiris, and Hunt (1971) have suggested that early overstimulation may have negative consequences akin to those produced by deprivation. However, Watson (1971) has suggested that it is not overstimulation *per se* that may be detrimental but rather *noncontingent* stimulation. (For a comprehensive review on the effects of early experience, the reader is referred to Haywood & Tapp, 1966, who focus on animal experiments, and to Haywood, 1967, who focuses on human studies.) The early experience literature testifies to the importance of the interaction of experiential and maturational factors in facilitating developmental processes.

A study by Levine and Broadhurst (1963) exemplifies the combined effects of early experience and genetic factors. They believe that the effects of early experience (and ontogenetic factors) on emotionality in adult rats are partially determined by genetic or constitutional factors (see also a study by Lindzey, Winston, and Manosevitz, 1963, which is similarly concerned with genetic influences on behavior in mice). Levine and Broadhurst hold that in addition to heredity and environment, their interaction has significant effects on adult behavior in the rat. Stress and handling, according to Levine (1960), stimulate the maturation of the central nervous system and thus enhance development. This view is similar to Hebb's (1949) theorizing that stimulation facilitates the development of cell assemblies and phase sequences (that is, closed systems in which neural firing can reverberate after the receptor inputs have ceased). Once they are developed via primary learning (stimulation, early experience) they facilitate secondary learning. They serve as mediating processes that enable the organism more readily to process subsequent sensory inputs. These notions are similar to Kagan's [18] concepts of the development of schemata, and Hunt's (1961, 1965) notions, discussed above regarding the "match" between stored or coded information and experiential encounters.

Stimulus Deprivation and Interspecies Comparisons

The above studies focused on the effects of enriched environment and alluded to the effects of deprivation. The studies to be discussed below are concerned with stimulus (including social and maternal) deprivation and on interspecies (comparative) comparisons. (For a discussion of cross-cultural studies the reader is referred to the Introduction and Commentary to Chapter 13, pp. 609–613.)

Harlow and Harlow (1962) and Harlow (1962) have suggested that social deprivation during infancy irreversibly interferes with the capacity for social adjustment in monkeys. The notion (Harlow, 1962) is that the heterosexual affectional system in monkeys evolves through a series of development stages and that there is a critical period (Harlow & Harlow, 1962) in the socialization in monkeys between the third and sixth month of life, (see the discussion on critical periods later in this introduction). (Subsequently, Harlow, Harlow, & Suomi [39] determined that it was possible to do remedial or therapeutic work with these deprived monkeys.) The Harlows suggest parallels between studies of social deprivation in monkeys and case studies of children reared in impersonal situations.

Arnold and Thoman (1966) using rats as subjects, have attempted to replicate Harlow's work on social deprivation in monkeys. They found that the maternal behavior of socially deprived rats was not basically different from nondeprived rats. This research illustrates the value of comparative studies in revealing the hazards of generalizing across species. Klopfer (1971) has examined maternal arousal and attachment in different species and suggests the value of the comparative approach in pointing to similarities and differences of operating mechanisms across different species.

The first selection in this chapter, by Young, Suomi, Harlow, and McKinney [8] examines the hypothesis that maternal separation and isolation early in life predispose rhesus monkeys to subsequent pathology. After reviewing the relevant literature on humans, which is primarily retrospective, the authors describe a prospective experiment with nonhuman primates in which they assess the hypothesis that stress in early life (separation from the mother before one year of age and confinement in a vertical chamber) predisposes rhesus monkeys to pathological reactions to separation stress later on in life. They found distinct differences between their early maternally deprived group and their normally reared group. In addition to manifesting high levels of self-biting and self-mouthing, the early maternally deprived group showed "despair-like" responses (see Bowlby, 1971) such as self-clasping, rocking, and huddling behavior. The results provide indirect evidence and support for studies with humans (e.g., Birtchnell, 1970a; 1970b) that demonstrate a relationship between the combined effects of early and late separation and pathology. Both early and later life experiences in combination influence adolescent and adult behavior in both monkeys and man.

The pioneer maternal deprivation studies Ainsworth, 1966; Bowlby, 1952, 1971: Goldfarb, 1955; Spitz, 1946) with humans indicated that institutionally reared children have more psychological problems than home-reared children. While the original interpretation of these findings was that inadequate mother-specific care was to blame, the later and better controlled studies implicate the more general variable of adequate "stimulation," which adequate mothering usually provides. The Rheingold and Bayley paper [9], one of the best examples of attempts to study early experience effects on humans, suggests that where stimulation in institutions was adequate, institutionalization *per se* or a lack of a specific mother did not have any adverse effects. The Goldman [43] paper in Chapter 13 also indicates that institutionalization *per se* does not produce adverse effects. For comprehensive discussions on the status of the maternal deprivation studies the reader is also referred to Ainsworth (1966), Bowlby (1971), and Rutter (1972).

Attachment

The maternal and social deprivation studies are relevant to social learning theory in general, and to object-relations theory specifically. The key concepts in the field of object-relations are *attachment* and *dependency*. Although both concepts are concerned with social responsiveness, they differ theoretically and methodologically (Cairns, 1972). *Attachment* refers to social processes of human infants and nonhuman animals of all ages, and *dependency* deals with "social behavior patterns in organisms that possess distinctively human capabilities (language, symbolic and conceptual mediation, capacity for long-term memory storage and precise retrieval)" (Cairns, 1972, p. 32). *Attachment* is concerned with motivated and intensely emotional relationships, and *dependency* is concerned with instrumental interpersonal behaviors. More specifically attachment refers "to the infant's tendency, during the first 24 months, to approach particular people, to be maximally receptive to being cared for by these people, and to be least afraid when with these people" (Mussen, Conger, and Kagan, 1974, p. 204). Attachment is a key concept in the early experience of the infant, because it forms the basis for social relationships in adulthood. According to Cairns (1972), the term attachment has had two separate meanings: (1) in a descriptive sense it refers to particular classes of responses that occur in dyadic relationships; and (2) in an explanatory sense it refers to a unitary process that energizes, directs, and regulates the descriptive dyadic relationships. Cairns (1972) believes that a unitary process (whether it has a genetic, evolutionary, or experiential origin) is insufficient to account for the attachment phenomenon, believing, rather, that it is due to an interaction of many factors (e.g., learning and maturation). In his paper he attempts to provide a psychobiological and social learning synthesis to the construct of attachment.

(The reader is referred to the edited volume by Gewirtz, 1972, which is exclusively devoted to the concepts of attachment and dependency.) The key substantive finding in this area is that although there is no one-to-one relationship between specific child-rearing practices and particular personality characteristics, a close emotional and affectionate relationship with an adult (not necessarily the mother) during the first few years of life is an essential ingredient for normal personality development.

Imprinting

Although Lorenz (1937) was the first to formulate the concept of imprinting (a type of social learning), Hess has been a key figure in the North American research. In an early paper, Hess (1959) discussed three aspects of the effects of early experience: (1) the persistence of early habits; (2) the profound effects of early perceptual experiences on all future learning; and (3) the phenomenon of imprinting—the notion that early social contacts determine the character of adult social behavior. In a later paper, Hess (1964) reviewed the various studies on imprinting in birds, postulating five differences between imprinting and association learning, and suggested some factors to account for differences between his results and those of other investigators. In a more recent paper, Hess (1972) provides a synthesis of results of laboratory and field techniques in the investigation of imprinting. He suggests that most laboratory imprinting experiments have involved deprivation, and that this deprivation may well have interfered with the normal development of behavior of young ducklings. Hess argues for the use of field (natural laboratory) studies in order to answer such questions as: What is the optimal age for imprinting? Which has the greater effect on behavior, first experience or the most recent experience? and How long must the imprinting experience last for it to have a maximum effect?

For a different viewpoint regarding imprinting the reader is referred to a paper by Moltz (1960); see also Hoffman and Ratner (1973). Whereas Hess distinguishes between imprinting and associative learning, Moltz believes that they are basically the same and attempts to explain imprinting in terms of associative learning based on anxiety reduction. Whereas Hess emphasizes motor experience, Moltz, as well as James (1959), and Jaynes (1958), emphasize the importance of perceptual experience for the imprinting phenomenon.

Bateson (1971, 1973) has conceptually and empirically evaluated the concept of imprinting when used with birds. He suggests that the popularization of imprinting in terms of the image of an object being "stamped instantaneously and irreversibly on the brain of the passive young bird" (1971, p. 383) is misleading in at least four ways: (1) the bird's preferences are patterned prior to imprinting; (2) young birds are *not* passive, but actively seek stimulation; (3) the learning process is gradual; and (4) the stability of imprinting is directly contingent on the length of the exposure. Descriptively, imprinting is different from associative learning, although at present it is not clear if the mechanisms underlying the two processes differ. Imprinting is important because it indicates how behavior is influenced by animal–environment interactions during development. Although the notion of the irreversibility of the imprinting process is questionable, in certain cases the consequences of imprinting are fairly stable. Bateson (1971, 1973) suggests that one should be cautious in attempting to make statements about human development on the basis of imprinting studies with animals. "Mindless generalizations based on the classical concept of imprinting can be wildly misleading and do considerable harm" (Bateson, 1971, p. 385). See Chapter 2, p. 17, for a further discussion of imprinting.

Hoffman and Ratner (1973), as well as Bowlby (1971) and Bateson (1971, 1973), have recently discussed the possible relevance of imprinting for human development. See also Sluckin (1965) for an earlier discussion of this issue.

Infancy

As indicated earlier there has been a proliferation of research on infancy since the 1960s. This has probably been influenced by a number of factors including the need to develop an adequate theory of development from infancy through adulthood; the North American discovery of Piaget; the availability of techniques for assessing infants; the greater availability of infants as experimental subjects; the influence of the early experience studies; and the limited success of remediation programs for deprived children that were usually introduced when children were four or five years old. Possibly since intervention programs with preschool children had limited success (see Jensen, 1969, and see the many critiques of Jensen by Bereiter, 1969; the Council for SPSSI, 1969; Hunt, 1969; and by Kagan, 1969; etc.) many investigators focused on infancy as the time to introduce remedial programs. However, in order to do this it was necessary to have a better understanding of infancy *per se*.

Kagan [18] in a study of attention and psychological change has suggested that conditioning *per se* is inadequate to account for the mechanisms responsible for transformations in cognitive structure and the organization of behavior. He suggests two supplementary mechanisms: the potentiation of inborn capacities (i.e., "delayed appearance of species specific behaviors after exposure to a narrow band of experience," p. 827); and the establishment of schemata. Schemata seem analogous to engrams, to phase sequences (Hebb, 1949) and Hunt's notion (1961, 1965) of the establishment of stored information (which has to be "matched" with experiential encounters), which were discussed earlier in this introduction.

A great deal of research has been recently conducted by Kagan and his associates on attention, cognitive development and the development of schemata. Very little recent experimental research has been done on infant conditionability. However, there has been a continued serious interest in the theoretical aspects of conditioning, especially during 1971. Fitzgerald and Porges (1971), and Fitzgerald and Brackbill (1971), arguing from a physiological viewpoint have suggested that the feasibility of conditioning infants is dependent on the maturation of the nervous system especially of cerebral structures. Sameroff [10] arguing from a cognitive viewpoint concludes that conditioning is dependent on the development of sensory and motor schemas. Sameroff believes that while classical conditioning in the infant (3-to-10-days-old) is difficult to demonstrate, operant conditioning is possible. Newborn infants must develop cognitive systems, on the basis of experience, for the CS and the US separately, before they can integrate these two modalities in classical conditioning. Sameroff's theory suggests a progression in cognitive structure, based on differentiation and hierarchical organization of schemas, rather than stages of development.

Critical Periods

Related to the concept of imprinting, and to the studies on infancy and early experience, is the critical period hypothesis. Scott (1962) suggests three major kinds of critical period phenomena: optimal periods for learning (intellectual development), for infantile stimulation (emotional development) and for the formation of basic social relationships (imprinting). However, both Denenberg [11] and Caldwell (1962) suggest that the critical period hypothesis has been interpreted in two different ways: (1) there is a certain limited *time interval* in development during which certain classes of stimuli are effective in producing certain profound behavioral effects; beyond this critical time period these same stimuli will have little or no effect; (2) there are periods of *maximum susceptibility* to certain classes of stimuli; the same stimulus has different effects upon an organism at different ages.

Scott (1962) who conceptualizes critical periods in the first sense (fixed time interval) has dealt primarily with socialization. He has postulated five distinct periods in the social development of dogs (neonatal, transition, socialization, juvenile and adult). Freud's (1905) notions about oral, anal and phallic psychosexual periods are in a general sense analogous to Scott's periods; and McGraw (1946) has found critical periods for optimal learning of motor skills in the human infant. As Scott points out, the critical period hypothesis is not a new one in either biology or psychology. Stockard, the embryologist, as early as 1921, was able via stimulation to induce monstrosities in fish embryos. In addition to his substantive findings, Scott's research is important methodologically in illuminating the importance of comparative research. For example, he has found that the order of the transition and socialization periods differs for dogs and humans.

Scott (1962) distinguishes two aspects of the influence of experiences during critical periods and how this affects subsequent development. There is presumably a fixed time interval, beyond which stimulation has little or no effect. In addition, a nonspecific stimulus during a critical period produces an irrevocable result. He notes that each of these effects has an analogue in embryonic development and that both growth and behavioral differentiation are based on organizing processes. Once organization occurs it inhibits further reorganization.

Denenberg [11] questions the fixed time interval concept of the critical period and suggests a different hypothesis. He favors the maximum susceptibility (sensitivity) position and states that stimulation in infancy reduces emotional reactivity of the organism; the reduction is a function of the amount of stimulus input. Denenberg presents experimental evidence to support his position.

Not only do Denenberg and Scott take different positions regarding the critical period hypothesis, but it should be noted that the former has dealt primarily with critical periods for infantile stimulation (emotional reactivity) while the latter has been mostly concerned with critical periods for socialization. Furthermore Scott has worked mostly with dogs, lambs and birds, while Denenberg has worked primarily with rats and mice. Therefore their results are not completely comparable. (See the discussion of the Arnold and Thoman research, p. 142.)

Caldwell (1962) has attempted to apply the critical period hypothesis to the study of filiative responses in humans. She distinguishes two ways of using the critical period hypothesis (similar to Denenberg's distinction) and suggests that it might be more fruitful to talk about the critical period hypothese*s*. Her paper is primarily a theoretical one and she emphasizes the importance of studying critical *events* rather than critical *time* periods. Caldwell states that in studying antecedent-consequent relationships it is important to consider ultimate (adult) as well as penultimate criteria (childhood and adolescence).

Longitudinal and Comparative Studies

The final paper in this chapter, by Van Lawick-Goodall [12], reports on some of the findings from a longitudinal study of chimpanzees at Gombe, Tanzania. Van Lawick-Goodall discusses the significance of chimpanzee research for understanding human behavior, discusses some similarities and differences between chimpanzee and human behavior, and most importantly discusses the development of the chimpanzee from infancy through adolescence and adulthood. The value of this study is that in addition to examining infancy (especially the period of infant dependence on the mother), Van Lawick-Goodall demonstrates the relationships between early experiences and subsequent behavior. Her study emphasizes the importance of longitudinal studies and comparative (inter-species) studies.

SUMMARY

The articles in this chapter not only indicate that early experiences are important, but also postulate some explanatory mechanisms. Furthermore, they emphasize that comparative studies provide us with useful leads for studying human development. These studies present evidence from a wide variety of different animals including birds, ducks, mice, rats, monkeys, chimpanzees and children.

Most of the articles in this chapter, and many in the book, are concerned with animal studies. As indicated in the introduction to Chapter 4, this stems largely from the contention that a comparative approach is necessary for an understanding of human developmental processes (see Beach, 1960; Hebb and Thompson, 1968). In addition, methodological and ethical considerations make many types of early experience studies with children unfeasible. Thus generalization from lower animals to man is always tempting, but it has its hazards (see Harlow *et al.* [5]).

In general, the research on early experience and infancy indicates that an interactionist approach (see Endler, 1975) that considers the interaction between nature and nurture is most appropriate for studying developmental processes.

References

Ainsworth, M. D. The effects of maternal deprivation: A review of findings and controversy in the context of research strategy. In M. D. Ainsworth *et al., Deprivation of maternal care: A reassessment of its effects.* New York: Shocken, 1966. (Also published by Geneva, Switzerland: World Health Organization, 1962. Public Health Papers No. 14, pp. 97–165.)

Arnold, W. J. & Thoman, E. Effects of early social deprivation on maternal behavior in the rat. Paper presented at the annual meeting of the Midwestern Psychological Association Convention in Chicago, May 7, 1966.

Bateson, P. P. G. Imprinting. In H. Moltz (Ed.), *The ontogeny of vertebrate behavior.* N.Y.: Academic Press, 1971, pp. 369–387.

Bateson, P. P. G. The imprinting of birds. In S. A. Barnett (Ed.), *Ethology and development.* Philadelphia: Lippincott, 1973, pp. 1–15.

Beach, F. A. Experimental investigations of species-specific behavior. *American Psychologist,* 1960, *15,* 1–8.

Bereiter, C. The future of individual differences. *Harvard Educational Review,* 1969, *39,* 310–318.

Birtchnell, J. Depression in relation to early and recent parent death. *British Journal of Psychiatry,* 1970, *116,* 298–306. (a)

Birtchnell, J. Early parent death and mental illness. *British Journal of Psychiatry,* 1970, *116,* 289–297. (b)

Bowlby, J. *Maternal care and mental health.* Geneva: World Health Organization, 1952.

Bowlby, J. Separation anxiety. *International Journal of Psychoanalysis,* 1960, *41,* 89–113.

Bowlby, J. *Attachment and loss. Vol. I: Attachment.* Harmondsworth, Middlesex, England: Penguin Books, 1971.

Brackbill, Y. Cumulative effects of continuous stimulation on arousal level in infants. *Child Development,* 1971, *42,* 17–26.

Cairns, R. B. Attachment and dependency: A psychobiological and social learning synthesis. In. J. Gewirtz (Ed.), *Attachment and dependency.* Washington, D.C.: Winston, 1972, pp. 29–80.

Caldwell, B. M. The usefulness of the critical period hypothesis in the study of filiative behavior. *Merrill-Palmer Quarterly of Behavior and Development,* 1962, *8,* 229–242.

Council for the Society for the Psychological Study of Social Issues. Statement by SPSSI on the current IQ controversy: Heredity versus environment. *American Psychologist,* 1969, *24,* 1039–1040.

Denenberg, V. H. The effects of early experience. In E. S. Hafez (Ed.), *The behavior of domestic animals.* London: Ballière, 1962.

Endler, N. S. The case for person-situation interactions. *Canadian Psychological Review,* 1975, *16,* 12–21.

Fitzgerald, H. E., and Brackbill, Y. Tactile conditioning of an autonomic and somatic response in young infants. *Conditioned Reflex,* 1971, *6,* 41–51.

Fitzgerald, H. E., and Porges, S. W. A decade of infant conditioning and learning research. *Merrill-Palmer Quarterly of Behavior and Development,* 1971, *17*, 71–117.

Flavell, J. H. *The developmental psychology of Jean Piaget.* New York: Van Nostrand, 1963.

Freud, S. The psychopathology of everyday life. In A. A. Brill (Trans. and ed.), *The basic writings of Sigmund Freud.* New York: Modern Library, 1938. (*Three contributions to the theory of sex,* originally published, 1905.)

Furth, H. G. *Piaget and knowledge: Theoretical foundations.* Englewood Cliffs, N.J.: Prentice-Hall, 1969.

Gewirtz, J. L. (Ed.) *Attachment and dependency.* Washington, D.C.: V. H. Winston, 1972.

Goldfarb, W. Emotional and intellectual consequences of psychologic deprivation in infancy: A re-evaluation. In P. H. Hoch & J. Zubin (Eds.), *Psychopathology of childhood.* New York: Grune & Stratton, 1955, pp. 105–119.

Goldman, J. R. The effects of handling and shocking in infancy upon adult behavior in the albino rat. *Journal of Genetic Psychology,* 1964, *104*, 301–310.

Greenberg, D. J. Accelerating visual complexity levels in the human infant. *Child Development,* 1971, *42*, 905–918.

Harlow, H. F. The heterosexual affectional system in monkeys. *American Psychologist,* 1962, *17*, 1–9.

Harlow, H. F. & Harlow, M. K. Social deprivation in monkeys. *Scientific American,* 1962, *207*(11), 137–146.

Haywood, H. C. Experiential factors in intellectual development: The concept of dynamic intelligence. In J. Zubin (Ed.), *Psychopathology of mental development.* New York: Grune & Stratton, 1967.

Haywood, H. C. & Tapp, J. C. Experience and the development of adaptive behavior. In N. R. Ellis (Ed.), *International review of research in mental retardation.* Vol. I. New York: Academic Press, 1966, pp. 109–151.

Hebb, D. O. *The organization of behavior.* New York: Wiley, 1949.

Hebb, D. O., and Thompson, W. R. The social significance of animal studies. In G. Lindzey and E. Aronson (Eds.), *The handbook of social psychology, (Rev. Ed.), Vol. 2, (No. 18).* Reading, Mass.: Addison-Wesley Co., 1968, pp. 729–774.

Hess, E. H. Imprinting. *Science,* 1959, *130*, 133–141.

Hess, E. H. Imprinting in birds. *Science,* 1964, *146*, 1128–1139.

Hess, E. H. Imprinting in a natural laboratory. *Scientific American,* 1972, *227*, 2, 24–31.

Hoffman, H. S. & Ratner, A. M. A reinforcement model of imprinting: Implications for socialization in monkeys and men. *Psychological Review,* 1973, *80*, 527–544.

Holmes, F. B. An experimental study of children's fears. In A. T. Jersild & F. B. Holmes (Eds.), *Children's fears.* New York: Teachers College *(Child Development Monograph, 20),* 1935.

Hunt, J. McV. The effects of feeding-frustration upon adult hoarding in the albino rat. *Journal of Abnormal and Social Psychology,* 1941, *36*, 338–360.

Hunt, J. McV. *Intelligence and experience.* New York: Ronald, 1961.

Hunt, J. McV. The implications of changing ideas on how children develop intellectually. *Children,* 1964, *11*, (3), 83–91.

Hunt, J. McV. Intrinsic motivation and its role in psychological development. In D. Levine (Ed.), *Nebraska Symposium on Motivation,* 1965, *13*, 189–282. (Lincoln: University of Nebraska Press.)

Hunt, J. McV. Has compensatory education failed? Has it been attempted? *Harvard Educational Review,* 1969, *39*, 278–300.

James, H. Flicker: An unconditioned stimulus for imprinting. *Canadian Journal of Psychology,* 1959, *13*, 59–67.

Jaynes, J. Imprinting: The interaction of learned and innate behavior: IV. Generalization and emergent discrimination. *Journal of Comparative and Physiological Psychology,* 1958, *51*, 238–242.

Jensen, A. R. How much can we boost I.Q. and scholastic achievement? *Harvard Educational Review,* 1969, *39*, 1–123.

Kagan, J. Inadequate evidence and illogical conclusions. *Harvard Educational Review,* 1969, *39*, 274–277.

Klopfer, P. H. Mother love: What turns it on? *American Scientist,* 1971, *59*, 404–407.

Levine, S. Stimulation in infancy. *Scientific American,* 1960, *202,* 5(80–86).

Levine, S. & Broadhurst, P. L. Genetic and ontogenetic determinants of adult behavior in the rat. *Journal of Comparative and Physiological Psychology,* 1963, *56,* 23–28.

Lindzey, G., Winston, H. D., & Manosevitz, M. Early experience, genotype, and temperament in *Mus musculus. Journal of Comparative and Physiological Psychology,* 1963, *56,* 622–629.

Lorenz, K. Z. The companion in the bird's world. *Auk,* 1937, *54*, 245–273.

McGraw, Myrtle B. Maturation of behavior. In L. Carmichael (Ed.), *Manual of child psychology.* New York: Wiley, 1946, pp. 332–369.

Moltz, H. Imprinting: Empirical basis and theoretical significance. *Psychological Bulletin,* 1960, *57*, 291–314.

Mussen, P. H., Conger, J. J., & Kagan, J. *Child development and personality.* (4th ed.) New York: Harper & Row, 1974.

Piaget, J. *The origins of intelligence in children.* New York: International Universities, 1952.

Rosenzweig, M. R. & Bennett, E. L. Effects of differential environments on brain weights and enzyme activities in gerbils, rats, and mice. *Developmental Psychobiology,* 1969, *2*, 87–95.

Rutter, M. Normal psychosexual development. *Journal of child psychology and psychiatry,* 1971, *11*, 259–283.

Rutter, M. *Maternal deprivation reassessed.* Harmondsworth, Middlesex, England: Penguin Books, 1972.

Salama, A. A. & Hunt, J. McV. "Fixation" in the rat as a function of infantile shocking, handling, and gentling. *Journal of Genetic Psychology,* 1964, *105*, 131–162.

Scott, J. P. Critical periods in behavioral development. *Science,* 1962, *138*, 949–958.

Sluckin, W. *Imprinting and early learning.* Chicago: Aldine, Atherton, 1965.

Spitz, R. A. Hospitalism: a follow-up report. In O. Fenichel *et al.* (Eds.), *The psychoanalytic study of the child, Vol. 2.* New York: International Universities Press, 1946, pp. 113–117.

Stockard, C. R. Developmental rate and structural expression: An experimental study of twins, double monsters and single deformities, and the interaction among embryonic organs during their development. *American Journal of Anatomy,* 1921, *28*, 115–277.

Tinbergen, N. *The study of instinct.* London: Oxford, 1951.

Wachs, T. D. & Cucinotta, P. The effects of enriched neonatal experiences upon later cognitive functioning. *Developmental Psychology,* 1971, *5*, 542.

Wachs, T. D., Uzgiris, I. C., & Hunt, J. McV. Cognitive development in infants of different age levels and from different environmental backgrounds: An explanatory investigation. *Merrill-Palmer Quarterly of Behavior and Development,* 1971, *17*, 283–317.

Watson, J. S. Cognitive-perceptual development in infancy: Setting for the seventies. *Merrill-Palmer Quarterly of Behavior and Development,* 1971, *17*, 139–152.

White, B. L. Child development research: An edifice without a foundation. *Merrill-Palmer Quarterly of Behavior and Development,* 1969, *15*, 49–79.

White, B. L. *Human infants: Experience and psychological development.* Englewood Cliffs, N.J.: Prentice-Hall, 1971.

8. EARLY STRESS AND LATER RESPONSE TO SEPARATION IN RHESUS MONKEYS

LAURENS D. YOUNG, STEPHEN J. SUOMI, HARRY F. HARLOW, and WILLIAM T. McKINNEY, JR.

The hypothesis that separation in early life predisposes one to later psychopathology was tested using two groups of rhesus monkeys of similar age. The experimental group had undergone the stress of early life separation and confinement in a vertical chamber. The experimental animals responded to separation and reunion with increased self-mouthing, self-clasping, huddling, and rocking. The control group responded to separation with increased locomotion and responded to reunion with increased contact clinging and proximity behaviors. The implications of these findings are discussed.

Separation experiences in early life have long been regarded in psychiatric theory and practice as traumatic events that can predispose individuals to psychopathology later in life (1, 2). In general the validity of this relationship has not been questioned (3). However, while psychiatric evidence obtained through a retrospective anamnesis may well have established the importance of separation in early life to the psychological functioning of the adult, it has also been criticized for making it appear that certain sequelae proceed inevitably from a given event (4). We know, for example, that not every individual who experiences a difficult separation in infancy eventually develops serious psychopathology. It therefore behooves investigators to regard the relationship between adult psychopathology and trauma in early life as a hypothesis and to attempt to establish experimentally whether such a relationship exists. Some have suggested that separation in early life may "leave scars" that sensitize individuals to adverse reactions to later separation (5). The experiment reported in this paper is a controlled laboratory investigation of this hypothesis in nonhuman primates.

Various efforts have been made in recent years to supplement the retrospective method in human beings with other types of studies. For example, Sethi obtained information on both childhood separations and separation experiences occurring within six months prior to the onset of depression in 116 patients (6). He found that 63 percent of the patients who scored high on a clinical inventory of depression had had a history of antecedent separation, whereas only 14 percent of those who scored low on the inventory had had such an experience. On the same inventory, 67 percent of the patients who scored high had had a separation experience before the age of 16, whereas only 37 percent of those who scored low had had such an experience. Finally, 44 percent of the patients who scored high had had *both* early and recent separation experiences, compared with 11 percent of those who scored low.

In a group of 120 hospitalized patients, Levi found significantly more incidents of separation before the age of 16 in patients who actually attempted suicide than in those who did not attempt suicide (7). The data in this study also suggested that there was a significantly higher incidence of separation experience before the age of seven in persons who actually attempted suicide than in those who only had an impulse to commit suicide.

From the *American Journal of Psychiatry*, 1973, *130*, 400–405. Copyright 1973 by the American Psychiatric Association. Reprinted by permission of the authors and the publisher.

Read in part at the 125th annual meeting of the American Psychiatric Association, Dallas, Tex., May 1–5, 1972. . . . This work was supported by Public Health Service grants MH-11894 and MH-18070 and Research Scientist Development Award MH-4753 (to Dr. McKinney) from the National Institute of Mental Health. The authors wish to express their appreciation to Elaine Moran and Robert Eising for their assistance with this project.

Hill and Price compared 1,483 depressed patients with 1,028 nondepressed patients (8). They found a significantly higher incidence of loss of father by death before the age of 15 in the depressed group. A number of additional studies have found some positive relationship between the early loss of a parent and psychiatric disturbance in later life (9–11).

Birtchnell (12), in comparing 500 hospital admissions with a matched sample of 500 persons from the surrounding community, found a higher incidence of parent death before the age of five in the patient population. He also found a higher than expected incidence of recent parent death in the hospital population (13). Birtchnell failed to find a preponderance of early or recent parent death in patients with a diagnosis of depression, although these events were significantly higher in the subpopulation with *severe* depression (14). Moreover, his statistics indicated that early and recent parent death contributed to the incidence of suicide attempts in patients, independently of a diagnosis of depression (15).

Not all studies have indicated a positive relationship between early life events and psychiatric disturbance in later life (16–18). For example, Hudgens compared 40 depressed patients with 40 closely matched controls and failed to show any differences in the incidence of stressful events in early life (19).

Other studies have indicated that the relationship between early life events and psychopathology is very complex. Paykel and associates have suggested that events of an "exit" type contribute more significantly to depression than do "entrance" events (20). A recent study by Cadoret and associates (21) comparing two groups with unipolar depression showed that, although there was no significant difference between the two groups in the actual incidence of such separation experiences as death, divorce, or separation of the parents, those patients whose onset of symptoms occurred before age 40 and who had certain other distinguishing characteristics showed a higher incidence of the *reporting* of a loss.

Many clinicians have established through intensive direct observation that dramatic behavior changes can occur in infants and young children who have undergone a major separation experience (22–24). Freud and Dann (25) studied a group of six children over a three-year period after their release from a concentration camp. Initially the children showed a high degree of attachment to each other and hostility toward the adults around them. It was only after several months that more typical child-child and child-adult behaviors began to appear. Spitz described a syndrome of "anaclitic depression" occurring in 19 of 123 children between six and 11 months of age in a foundling home (26). He postulated that this syndrome was caused by separation from the mother and could become irreversible if it was not remedied by replacement of a suitable mother or surrogate.

Bowlby characterized the human infant's response to maternal separation as occurring in three stages: "protest," "despair," and "detachment" (3). Such observations imply that loss in infancy might affect the adult individual's response to subsequent separation, but such follow-up studies are rare and give scattered results. Bowlby and associates (27) collected data on 60 children aged six to 14 hospitalized in a tuberculosis sanitarium for periods of several months and found very little indication of severe emotional impairment in adult life. Other investigators, however, on the basis of observations of institutionalized children (28, 29), have found evidence for lasting intellectual and emotional impairment that persisted into adolescence. Such studies are confounded by a complexity of variables, such as the age at separation, parent-child relationships before and after the separation, and the relative conditions of the environments (30).

In recent years some effort has been made to circumvent the difficulties involved in human clinical studies by creating animal models for human psychopathology (31–33). Nonhuman primates provide a useful model for some aspects of human behavior because of their closeness to man, their tendency to form close social bonds, the existence of a fund of knowledge about their social behavior, and the availability of suitable laboratory methods for well-controlled longitudinal studies. Early work using rhesus monkeys established the importance of the infant's tie to its mother (34). Experimental separation from the mother (35) produced a syndrome in rhesus monkeys that closely resembled the behavior of human infants described by Spitz and Bowlby. Replication of the separation experiment with other species has demonstrated a similar response to separation, with some species variation (36, 37). In the rhesus monkey, the species used in this study, the "protest" stage is characterized by frequent cooing vocalizations and increased locomotion. This stage is followed by a period of "despair," consisting of decreased locomotion and increased self-clasping, self-mouthing, and huddling. The final stage of "detachment" described in humans by Bowlby has not yet been reproduced in monkeys.

Separation from the mother before one year of age and confinement in a Harlow vertical chamber is a method that has proved effective and reliable in producing abnormal behavior in infant monkeys (38, 39). For example, monkeys 45 days of age placed in this chamber exhibit markedly abnormal behavior on removal. They are socially withdrawn, have low levels of locomotion, and exhibit high levels of self-mouthing, self-clasping, and huddling behavior.

This study attempts to assess whether such stress in early life predisposes rhesus monkeys to pathological behavior later in life when they are subjected to separation stress. Subjects who had early life separation and vertical chamber confinement were compared with subjects who had had normal laboratory rearing. The hypothesis was that these "traumatic" events early in life would predispose the subjects to more severe reactions to the stress of separation later in life.

Method

Two groups, each consisting of four rhesus monkeys almost two years of age, were used as subjects. The two groups had had different rearing experiences. The monkeys in the experimental group had been taken from their mothers at birth and housed in individual cages with cloth surrogates. They had been permitted two hours of peer experience per day throughout the first year of life. Between five months and ten months of age each subject was placed in a vertical chamber (40) for 30 days of profound environmental isolation. Following the period of internment each subject was returned to its living cage. Beginning at one year of age, the experimental subjects were housed as a group in a wire mesh cage, where they remained until the start of the present experiment. In summary, they had undergone experimental early life separation and the stress of confinement in a vertical chamber early in life.

At the start of the experiment the subjects in the control group were approximately the same age as those in the experimental group. They had been reared with their mothers for the first month of life. From one month until one year of age they had lived in a large cage complex with their mothers, with two hours of daily social interaction with each other. From one year of age until the start of the experiment they were housed together without their mothers as a group of four. Therefore they were matched with the experimental group in terms of age and peer experience after one year of age but differed regarding early life separation and vertical chamber experience.

During the present experiment each group of four monkeys was housed together in a large experimental living unit, a series of cages joined end-to-end, in which the animals could both live and be tested without being moved to a strange environment. The cage assembly is shown in Figure 8–1. The spaces between the cages permitted insertion of wire mesh partitions that divided each large unit into four smaller cages. When the wire mesh panels were removed, the open ends allowed free access through the entire length of the unit. Opaque masonite panels were placed between the two large cage assemblies to prevent visual and tactile communication between the experimental and control groups.

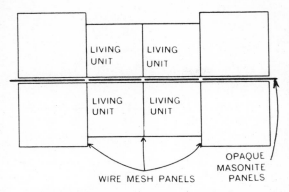

FIGURE 8–1. Cage assembly of experimental living unit.

The experiment was divided into two time periods: a four-week period of baseline observation, called the preseparation period, followed by a four-week experimental period. During the preseparation period observations were made on four days each week while the monkeys had free access to each other and to their half of the entire cage assembly.

The experimental period was further divided into separation and reunion conditions. The subjects were housed individually 23 hours per day under the separation condition and were together one hour per day under the reunion condition on the days of observation. They were housed individually all day long on the remaining days.

During the separation condition the wire panels were slid into place so that each monkey was separated from his peers. Observations were made four times per week on each of the monkeys housed in this manner. Under the reunion condition the wire mesh panels were removed so that the monkeys had free access to each other and the full cage assembly. Observations were also made on the monkeys in this condition four times per week.

Behavioral observations were made on each animal for a five-minute period each morning on four days per week during the preseparation period. Similar five-minute observations were made of each subject as it was individually housed in the morning during the separation

period and in the afternoon during the reunion condition. The five-minute observation periods were divided into 20 15-second intervals. Any of the operationally defined behavior categories that occurred during these intervals were scored as modified frequencies, that is, as the number of 15-second intervals in which a behavior occurred. The use of this scoring system has been described previously in some detail (41). Operational definitions of the behavioral categories used are given in appendix 1.

For each animal a weekly mean modified frequency score was calculated thus: the total weekly number of responses of a given subject in a given category divided by four, the number of observation periods in the week. Behavior categories that consistently had scores of zero or nearly zero were omitted from the remaining analysis. For each of the remaining categories a two-way repeated measures analysis of variance was performed for each of the three experimental conditions (preseparation, separation, and reunion). The prior rearing condition (experimental versus control) was the independent variable. Time blocks of two weeks for the preseparation condition and blocks of one week for the separation and reunion conditions were the repeated measures. The .05 level of confidence was designated as the criterion of statistical significance for each analysis. In those cases in which significance was reached or almost reached and more than two means were involved in the calculation of the mean square, a Duncan New Multiple Range test was used to compare the means with each other (42).

Results

Preseparation Condition

Four behavioral categories showed significant group effects during the preseparation condition. These were self-mouthing, locomotion, stereotyped behavior, and yielding. None of the other categories showed significant differences between the groups during this condition. The experimental group showed consistently higher levels of self-mouthing (p < .01). The control group showed higher levels of locomotion, stereotyped behavior, and yielding (p < .05).

Separation Condition

Under this condition, since the animals were alone, six social behaviors logically could not occur: yielding, contact cling, proximity, social exploration, social sex, and play. These were, therefore, excluded from the analysis of this condition. The experimental group showed significantly higher levels of self-mouthing and huddling (p < .05) during separation. The experimental group also showed higher levels of two other behaviors that did not reach significance—self-clasping and rocking. For self-mouthing the difference between the groups for the first week was significant by the Duncan test (p < .05). For rocking, the between-group differences for all four weekly means were significant by the Duncan test (p < .01). These differences are shown in graphic form in Figure 8–2.

Self-clasping, huddling, and rocking were almost never shown by the controls. On the other hand, the control group showed higher levels of locomotion (p < .05) and stereotyped behavior (p < .01) during the separation con-

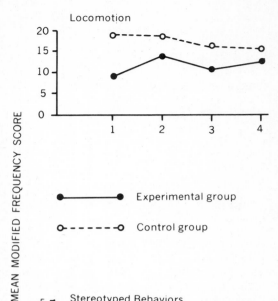

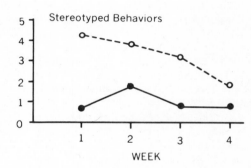

FIGURE 8–3. Locomotion and stereotyped behaviors during separation.

dition. These differences are illustrated in Figure 8–3.

Reunion Condition

There were significant group differences for the following four behaviors, with the experimental group showing higher levels during reunion: self-mouthing and locomotion (p < .01) and rocking and self-clasping (p < .05). The experimental group also displayed some huddling, which was absent among the controls. The behavior categories for reunion in which the experimental group

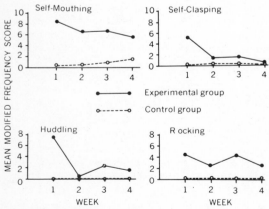

FIGURE 8–2. Self-mouthing, self-clasping, huddling, and rocking during separation.

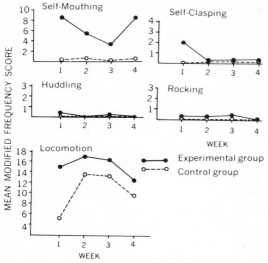

FIGURE 8–4.   Self-mouthing, self-clasping, huddling, rocking, and locomotion during reunion.

showed higher levels are illustrated in Figure 8–4. The group means for proximity and contact cling behaviors are illustrated in Figure 8–5. During reunion the control group showed significantly more contact clinging and proximity behaviors than the experimental group.

Discussion

The results of this experiment indicate that several behavioral distinctions can be made between a group of four two-year-old rhesus monkeys with a history of early life separation and vertical chamber confinement and a group of monkeys raised with their mothers and with peers. Throughout all conditions of the experiment—preseparation, separation, and reunion—a higher rate of self-mouthing behavior was observed among the experimental group than among the controls. This tendency toward self-orality has been noted before in rhesus monkeys raised without mothers from birth (43). Self-mouthing is also commonly observed in infant rhesus monkeys immediately following vertical chamber confinement (44). The observation of high rates of this behavior

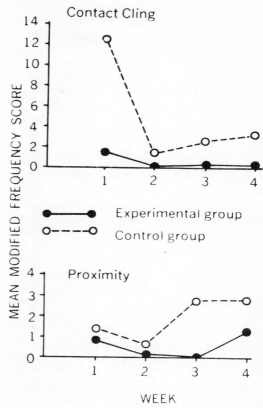

FIGURE 8–5.   Contact cling and proximity during reunion.

under varying experimental conditions in older monkeys who have had separation and chambering experiences very early in life, and the virtual absence of self-mouthing in monkeys of similar age who have not had such experiences, indicates that self-mouthing may be a stable behavioral trait related to early history.

The experimental imposition of conditions of separation and reunion revealed further behavioral differences between the two groups that appeared to be labile and dependent on the condition. Separation conditions caused the experimental animals to react with dramatic increases in self-clasping, rocking, and huddling, behaviors that were almost never seen in the control group. Such "despair-like" responses are similar to those reported in infant macaques undergoing maternal separation and vertical chamber confinement for the first time (44). The pattern resembles the stage of "despair" described by Bowlby. In some respects, therefore, our imposition of the stress of separation from peers in these older monkeys appears to have "unmasked" or at least intensified a response to stress that probably developed in very early life.

The group of monkeys raised with mothers and peers, on the other hand, showed none of the "despair-like" behaviors of the experimental group. These animals responded to separation with an increase in locomotion and stereotyped behavior. This response is similar to that observed in monkeys reared with mothers and peers who are separated for the first time at three years of age (45). The dramatic response in the control animals was observed under reunion conditions. On being allowed access to each other again after separation, the control group showed higher levels of contact clinging and proximity behavior than the experimental animals. This response has been reported previously in animals undergoing reunion after separation, and it might be regarded as a typical pattern of response to reunion for juvenile monkeys raised with mothers and peers (46). The experimental group, on the other hand, did not respond with such high levels of these "closeness" behaviors, but rather with a higher level of locomotion than the control group. It appeared that separation and chambering inhibited their capacity to respond to reunion in the usual way.

The above findings are best viewed as tentative, we hope provocative, and suggestive for further research. Additional work is necessary to extend the generality of our hypothesis. Certainly, however, the marked tendency of rhesus monkeys with a history of maternal separation and vertical chamber isolation early in life to respond to separation with behaviors remarkably like those displayed in early life is supportive of our hypothesis. It remains to be seen whether such behaviors will appear in animals with similar histories at more advanced stages in life. In future studies, more emphasis will be placed on the important effect peer groups have on the final behavioral response, and appropriate measures will be taken to control for this. Work is currently under way in our laboratory to determine to what extent other forms of separation stress will tend to recapitulate the "despair-like" behavioral responses in monkeys with a history of early life stress.

Certainly it is difficult to analogize directly to human behavior but our findings may point to fruitful areas for exploration. The remarkable similarity of the syndrome produced in older monkeys by chambering to that displayed when they were young should cause us to look for behavioral similarities in follow-up data on adults who suffered clearly traumatic manifestations as a result of separation or environmental deprivation in childhood. Few studies of this sort have been reported (30). Our data indirectly support previous studies in human subjects that show a relationship between human psychopathology and the combination of separation in early life and recent separation (6, 12–15).

It appears that early and later life experience can combine to have a powerful influence on primate behavior, in man as well as monkeys. What remains to be decided is not whether such a relationship exists but how it comes to be.

REFERENCES

1. Freud S: Mourning and melancholia (1917), in *The Complete Psychological Works*, standard ed., vol 14. Translated and edited by Strachey J. London, Hogarth Press, 1966, pp. 239–258.
2. Mack J E, Semrad E V: Classical psychoanalysis, in *Comprehensive Textbook of Psychiatry*. Edited by Freedman A M, Kaplan H I. Baltimore, Williams & Wilkins, 1967, pp. 269–319.

3. Bowlby J: Grief and mourning in infancy. *Psychoanal Study Child 15:* 9–52, 1960.
4. Bowlby J: *Attachment and Loss*. New York, International Universities Press, 1969, vol. 1, p. 8.
5. Hilgard J R, Newman M F, Fisk F: Strength of adult ego following childhood bereavement. *Am. J. Orthopsychiatry 30:* 788–798, 1960.
6. Sethi B B: Relationship of separation to depression. *Arch. Gen. Psychiatry 10:* 486–496, 1964.
7. Levi L D, Fales C H, Stein M, et al: Separation and attempted suicide. *Arch. Gen. Psychiatry 15:* 158–164, 1966.
8. Hill O W, Price J S: Childhood bereavement and adult depression. *Br. J. Psychiatry 113:* 743–751, 1967.
9. Brown F: Depression and childhood bereavement. *J. Ment. Sci. 107:* 754–777, 1961.
10. Hill O W: The association of childhood bereavement with suicidal attempt in depressive disease. *Br. J. Psychiatry 115:* 301–304, 1969.
11. Wilson I C, Alltop L B, Buffaloe W J: Parental bereavement in childhood: MMPI profiles in a depressed population. *Br. J. Psychiatry 113:* 761–764, 1967.
12. Birtchnell J: Early parent death and mental illness. *Br. J. Psychiatry 116:* 289–297, 1970.
13. Birtchnell J: Recent parent death and mental illness. *Br. J. Psychiatry 116:* 281–288, 1970.
14. Birtchnell J: Depression in relation to early and recent parent death. *Br. J. Psychiatry 116:* 298–306, 1970.
15. Birtchnell J: The relationship between attempted suicide, depression, and parent death. *Br. J. Psychiatry 116:* 307–313, 1970.
16. Pitts F V, Meyer J, Brooks M, et al: Adult psychiatric illness assessed for childhood parental loss and psychiatric illness in family members. *Am. J. Psychiatry 121* (June suppl): i–x, 1965.
17. Gregory I W: Retrospective data concerning childhood loss of a parent. *Arch. Gen. Psychiatry 15:* 362–367, 1966.
18. Beck A T: *Depression: Clinical, Experimental and Theoretical Aspects*. New York, Hoeber Medical Division, Harper & Row, 1967, pp 218–227.
19. Hudgens R W, Morrison J R, Barcha R G: Life events and the onset of primary affective disorders. *Arch. Gen. Psychiatry 16:* 134–145, 1967.
20. Paykel E S, Meyers J K, Dienelt M N, et al: Life events and depression. *Arch. Gen. Psychiatry 21:* 753–760, 1969.
21. Cadoret R J, Winokur G, Dorzab J, et al: Depressive disease: Life events and onset of illness. *Arch. Gen. Psychiatry 26:* 133–136, 1972.
22. Freud A, Burlingham D: *War and Children*. New York, International Universities Press, 1942.
23. Freud A, Burlingham D: *Infants without Families*. New York, International Universities Press, 1943.
24. Robertson J: Responses of young children to the loss of maternal care. *Nurs. Times 49:* 382–386, 1955.
25. Freud A, Dann S: An experiment in group upbringing. *Psychoanal. Study Child 6:* 127–168, 1951.
26. Spitz R: Hospitalism. *Psychoanal. Study Child 1:* 53–74, 1945.
27. Bowlby J, Ainsworth M, Boston M, et al: The effects of mother–child separation: A follow-up study. *Br. J. Med. Psychol. 29:* 211–247, 1956.
28. Goldfarb W: Emotional and intellectual consequences of psychological deprivation in infancy: A re-evaluation, in *Psychopathology of Childhood*. Edited by Hoch P, Zubin R. New York, Grune & Stratton, 1955, pp. 105–119.

29. Provence S, Lipton R C: *Infants in Institutions*. New York, International Universities Press, 1962.
30. Yarrow L J: Separation from parents during early childhood, in *Review of Child Development Research*. Edited by Hoffman M L. New York, Russell Sage Foundation, 1964, pp. 89–136.
31. McKinney W T Jr, Bunney W E Jr: Animal models of depression, I, review of evidence: Implications for research. *Arch. Gen. Psychiatry 21:* 240–248, 1969.
32. Senay E C: Toward an animal model of depression: A study of separation behavior in dogs. *J. Psychiatr. Res. 4:* 65–71, 1966.
33. Kaufman K: Mother-infant separation in monkeys: An experimental model. Read at the annual meeting of the American Association for the Advancement of Science, Chicago, Ill, Dec 26–31, 1970.
34. Harlow H F, Zimmerman R R: Affectional responses in the infant monkey. *Science 130:* 421–432, 1959.
35. Seay B, Harlow H F: Maternal separation in the rhesus monkey. *J. Nerv. Ment. Dis. 140:* 434–441, 1965.
36. Preston D G, Baker R D, Seay B: Mother-infant separation in the patas monkey. *Developmental Psychology 2:* 298–306, 1970.
37. Kaufman I C, Rosenblum L A: The reaction to separation in infant monkeys: Anaclitic depression and conversion withdrawal. *Psychosom. Med. 29:* 648–675, 1967.
38. McKinney W T Jr, Suomi S J, Harlow H F: New models of separation and depression in rhesus monkeys. Read at the annual meeting of the American Association for the Advancement of Science, Chicago, Ill, Dec 26–31, 1970.
39. Suomi, S J, Harlow H F: Apparatus conceptualization for psychopathological research in monkeys. *Behavior Research Methods and Instrumentation 1:* 1–12, 1969.
40. Harlow H F, Suomi S J, McKinney W T Jr: Experimental production of depression in monkeys. *Mainly Monkeys 1:* 6–12, 1970.
41. Suomi S J, Harlow H F, Domek C J: Effect of repetitive infant–infant separation of young monkeys. *J. Abnorm. Psychol. 76:* 161–172, 1970.
42. Duncan D B: Multiple range and multiple F tests. Biometrics *11:* 1–42, 1955.
43. Cross H A, Harlow H F: Prolonged and progressive effects of partial isolation on the behavior of macaque monkeys. *Journal of Experimental Research in Personality 1:* 39–49, 1965.
44. McKinney W T Jr, Suomi S J, Harlow H F: Depression in primates. *Am. J. Psychiatry 127:* 1313–1320, 1971.
45. McKinney W T Jr, Suomi S J, Harlow H F: Repetitive peer separations of juvenile-age rhesus monkeys. *Arch. Gen. Psychiatry 27:* 200–203, 1972.
46. McKinney W T Jr, Suomi S J, Harlow H F: Vertical chamber confinement of juvenile-age rhesus monkeys. *Arch. Gen. Psychiatry 26:* 223–228, 1972.

APPENDIX 1

Definitions of Behavioral Categories

Self-mouthing: Oral contact with any part of the body except the genital area, excluding biting.

Self-grooming: Discrete self-directed picking and/or spreading of the fur.

Self-biting: Specific, vigorous, self-directed biting.

Self-clasping: Firm manual or pedal clutching of self, excluding the genital area.

Passivity: Maintaining a static position for a minimum of three seconds with no other simultaneous behavior.

Huddling: Self-enclosed fetal-like position incorporating any or all patterns of self-clasping, self-embracing, or lowered head.

Rocking: Repetitive, nonlocomotive backward and forward movement.

Vocalization: Coo—drawn-out, dove-like cry in a variety of pitches; screech—high intensity vocalization resembling a scream.

Yielding: Oriented movement or withdrawal by an animal submitting or ceding area to another animal.

Stereotyped behavior: Identical movements maintained in a rhythmic and repetitive fashion for at least three cycles; scored independently and noninclusive of locomotion.

Locomotion: Ambulation of one or more full steps.

Environmental exploration: Any tactual or oral exploration of the physical surroundings.

Proximity: Standing within three inches of another monkey for a period of three or more seconds.

Contact cling: Maintaining gross body contact for an indefinite period of time.

9. THE LATER EFFECTS OF AN EXPERIMENTAL MODIFICATION OF MOTHERING

HARRIET L. RHEINGOLD and NANCY BAYLEY

An extensive literature in psychology attests to the effect of early experience upon later behavior. For the human infant an important determiner of early experience is maternal care. Some of the dimensions of maternal care thought to be of consequence are amounts and kinds of care, interruptions of care, the number of persons giving care, as well as their attitudes. There is not yet, however, any considerable *experimental* literature on the effects of these variables upon the later behavior of children. The present study reports an attempt to discover the presence, a year later, of a change in behavior brought about in a group of infants by an experimental modification of maternal care (5).

Sixteen children, living in an institution for approximately the first nine months of life, were the original subjects of study. From the sixth through the eighth month of life, half of them, the experimental group, were cared for

From *Child Development*, 1959, *30*, 363–372. Copyright 1959 by The Society for Research in Child Development, Inc. Reprinted by permission of the authors and the publisher.

by one person alone, the experimenter, for 7½ hours a day. They thus received more attentive care than the control subjects who were completely reared under institutional routine; and of course the number of different persons from whom they received care was markedly reduced. As a result the experimental babies became more responsive to the experimenter almost at once, while with time they became more responsive to other persons as well. They did not however do reliably better than the control subjects on the Cattell Infant Intelligence Scale or on tests of postural development and cube manipulation. At the conclusion of the study the experimental subjects returned to the full-time care of the institution. Details of the institutional care, of its experimental modification, of the tests used, and of the results may be found in the report referred to above.

One by one, all but one of both the experimental and the control subjects were placed outside the institution—in their own homes, or in adoptive or boarding homes. Approximately a year after the conclusion of the study, the children, then about 18 months of age, were seen again, in an attempt to detect the effects of the earlier treatment. Since the only clear difference between the groups at the time of the study had been an increase in social responsiveness among the experimental babies, it would be here that one would expect a difference, if any, to persist. Still, the possibility existed that differences might appear later as new functions matured. On the other hand, the subsequent, and more recent, experience of several months' duration in different life situations might reduce the chance of finding a difference.

The effects of experimental treatment were sought in two areas of behavior, the social and the intellectual. Would the experimental subjects be more socially responsive, that is, more friendly and outgoing than the control group to two examiners who visited the home? Would the experimental subjects, in addition, be more responsive to the original experimenter than to another person? If not, the variable under test is really their responsiveness to strangers. Second, would the experimental subjects now do better on a test of developmental progress?

It was planned, in addition, to use the retest data to explore the effect of type of home placement, as well as to evaluate the performance of the whole group considered as a sample of institutionalized children.

Procedure

Subjects

Fourteen of the original 16 children were located and tested; one from the experimental group and one from the control group could not be found.[1]

The mean age of the experimental group was 19.8 months (range, 17.6–22.1), of the control group, 20.1 months (range, 17.5–21.7). The experimental group had spent an average of 9.2 months in the institution before being placed in homes (range, 4.0–13.6); for the control group the mean time was 10.4 months (range, 6.5–

[1]We are grateful to Father Bernard Brogan, Director of the Catholic Home Bureau of Chicago, for his generous cooperation.

18.1). If the control subject who was still in the institution was omitted from the calculations, the average stay for the control group became 9.2 months (range, 6.5–12.2). In respect, then, to age and to duration of stay in the institution both groups were similar.

The children left the institution at different ages. Two experimental subjects left after only three weeks of treatment. One control subject left in the sixth week of the study, another in the seventh week. All the other subjects stayed at least through the eight weeks of treatment.

The home placements were varied. Three experimental and two control subjects returned to their own homes. With one exception, the own parents of these five subjects were of foreign birth and the homes were marked by poverty. Two of the experimental and four of the control subjects were in adoptive homes which, in general, were superior to the own homes in socioeconomic status. Two experimental subjects were living in boarding homes, pending a release for adoption. And one control subject, a Negro boy, remained in the institution only because a home could not be found for him. Furthermore, there was no difference between the experimental and the control groups in the intellectual stimulation provided by the homes or in the friendliness of the mothers, according to ratings made by the Experimenter and the Examiner after each visit. In type of home placement, therefore, there appeared to be no major difference. Rather, the difference between homes within each group appeared to be larger than any difference between the groups.

The Tests

Each child was seen in his own home. The homes were scattered widely through Chicago, its suburbs and neighboring cities, with one home in another state. Two persons, the original Experimenter and an Examiner, visited the homes together, with one exception: the child who lived out of the state was examined by the Experimenter alone. The Experimenter knew all the children but, of course, had been especially familiar with the experimental subjects. She served *only* as a stimulus person in the social tests. The Examiner had no previous acquaintance with any of the children and did not know which had been the experimental subjects. She also served as a stimulus person in the social tests, but it was she alone who recorded the children's responses to both the Experimenter and herself, and who administered the test of developmental progress.

The social test resembled those reported in the first study, but was made more suitable for older children. It was composed of three parts, each of which set up a rather natural situation between adult and child, with an easy transition between the parts. In the first part, the responses to the stimulus person in the first few minutes after her entrance into the home were recorded. During this time the stimulus person did not talk to or approach the child but sat at some distance from him and talked to the mother, occasionally smiling at the child. The Examiner recorded the child's responses to whichever stimulus person happened first to engage his attention, then to the other person. At an appropriate moment one of the persons smiled and spoke warmly to the child, saying, "Hi (child's name) come to me," accompanying her words by stretching out her arms in invitation. This constituted the second situation. In the third situation, the stimulus person actually approached the child, smiling, talking, and gesturing as in the second situation. After the child's responses had been recorded, the other stimulus person presented herself to the child similarly. The order of stimulus persons was determined by the convenience of the moment: whoever was closer to the child or was receiving more glances was the first stimulus person.

The child's responses were recorded on a checklist under these categories: *positive facial expression,* which included seven items of behavior ranging from "stares with expression" to "laughs"; *physical approach* with nine items ranging from "shows toy" through "makes physical contact" to "makes social overtures while in the stimulus person's lap"; *vocalizations* for which a child received a score of one for each part of the test in which he vocalized, whether he said discrete sounds, jargon, or words; *negative facial expression,* which included eight items ranging from "a fleeting sober expression" to "cries"; *physical retreat* with six items ranging from "hangs head" to "leaves room"; and *response to mother* (during the social test period) which included a series of six items, from "turns toward mother" to "stays in contact with mother."

Within each category, items of behavior were thus arranged in what seemed a reasonable progression in terms of duration or amplitude of response. Each item within a category was arbitrarily assigned a value of one. Because the items were arranged in ascending order, the score for any item was one plus the value of all other items below it in that category. The scores for the categories of positive facial expression, physical approach, and vocalizations were summed to yield a measure of *positive social responsiveness.* Similarly, the sum of both negative categories gave a measure of *negative social responsiveness.* The sum of these two measures was the measure of *total social responsiveness.* The category of "response to mother" was calculated separately and not included in the other measures.

After the social tests, the Cattell Infant Intelligence Scale (2) was administered by the Examiner, with the Experimenter *not* present. Lastly, the number of words in the child's vocabulary was calculated from his performance on the language items of the Cattell and from the mother's report.

Results

The Effect of Treatment

Table 9–1 shows that both the experimental and the control subjects responded similarly to the Experimenter and to the Examiner. The close agreement of all means, and of the ranges, is apparent in the part, as well as in the total, scores. The only difference of any size between the two stimulus persons appeared in the experimental group's response to mother. But since only one subject of the seven gave a response to the mother when the Experimenter

TABLE 9–1.
Means and Ranges of the Social Test

Subjects	EXPERIMENTER Mean	EXPERIMENTER Range	EXAMINER Mean	EXAMINER Range	COMBINED SCORE Mean
*Experimental Group**					
Total Social Responsiveness	32.1	27–39	30.9	27–38	31.6
Positive	17.4	2–30	16.0	2–37	16.7
Negative	14.7	1–37	14.7	3–29	14.7
Response to Mother	2.3	0–16	5.7	0–19	4.0
Control Group†					
Total Social Responsiveness	28.0	14–39	28.3	22–44	28.4
Positive	19.8	5–32	20.2	4–37	20.1
Negative	8.2	3–12	8.2	2–18	8.0
Response to Mother	4.5	0–11	4.8	0–10	5.4

*N is 7.
†N is 6 for responses to Experimenter and to Examiner, but 7 for Combined Score. See text for explanation.

was the stimulus person, and only three subjects of the seven, when the Examiner was the stimulus person, this difference, as all the others, was not statistically significant. From the results we conclude that the experimental subjects did not appear to remember the Experimenter.

Furthermore, since the experimental and the control groups gave similar scores to both persons, it was assumed that they were of approximately equal stimulating value. Therefore, a combined score for each subject (the average of a subject's responses to both stimulus persons) was used in the analyses which follow. This procedure made it possible to add to the control group the subject who was seen by the Experimenter alone. If every other subject responded similarly to both stimulus persons, it may be assumed that this subject would too. (It will be seen in Table 1 that the addition of this subject to the control group made the combined means slightly different from the separate means.)

The combined scores showed that the experimental subjects were more responsive to both persons than the control subjects, but the difference was not statistically significant. The part scores, further, revealed that the control group gave more positive responses, the experimental group, more negative responses.

Again, the differences were not statistically reliable. Moreover, inspection of the data revealed that the negative responses of only two of the seven experimental subjects were responsible for the difference between the groups. The findings therefore do not warrant the conclusion that the experimental subjects were either more or less responsive to the stimulus persons, positively or negatively.

Because some of the subjects made no response to their mothers during the social tests, the means for this category of behavior were not subjected to test. Only three of the seven experimental subjects and five of the control subjects made some contact with the mother during social simulation by one or the other of the stimulus persons, a difference which permits no conclusive statement of difference.

Although vocalizations had been included in the measure of positive social responsiveness (as explained above), a measure which did not differentiate the groups, they were also analyzed separately. Inspection showed that five of the seven experimental subjects vocalized to one or the other of the stimulus persons but only one of the control subjects did. The difference was significant by the Fisher exact probability test at $p = .051$ (onesided), a finding in agreement with the original study in which, at the end of the experimental treatment, the experimental subjects also vocalized more than the control subjects.

On the Cattell Infant Intelligence Scale the mean IQ for the experimental group was 97.4 (range, 82–110); for the control group it was 95.4 (range, 83–122). More attentive care given during a limited period in the first year of life therefore appeared to produce no difference in IQ on retest a year later.

The experimental subjects had a larger spoken vocabulary than the control subjects (17.9 and 13.7 words), but the difference was again not statistically significant.

The Effect of Home Placement

It early became clear that the adoptive homes were of a higher socio-economic level than the own homes, and therefore it seemed desirable to look for differences in the performance of the children in these two types of home placement. The adoptive homes were also ranked higher than the own homes by the investigators on the basis of the friendliness of the mother during the visit and of the intellectual stimulation the home seemed to offer the child.

On the social test the children in adoptive homes gave more positive responses than those in own homes; the means were 21.6 and 15.6, respectively, but the difference was not statistically significant. It should be noted, however, that one subject in a boarding home and the subject still in the institution made higher positive scores than the mean of the adoptive home group.

Similarly, the mean IQ of the children living in adoptive homes was higher (98.8) than that of those living in own homes (95.4), but the difference was not reliable. The two children living in boarding homes had IQs of 95 and 102. And, while the child still in the institution obtained an IQ of only 83, two children in own homes had lower IQs, one of 79 and one of 82, and one child in an adoptive home had an IQ of 84.

Finally, the children in adoptive homes had a larger vocabulary than the children in own homes (means were 18.6 and 13.4, respectively), although again the difference was not significant.

In summary, there was no reliable evidence that the children in adoptive homes were more socially responsive or more developmentally advanced than those in own homes.

The Group as a Whole

We may now evaluate the performance of the group as a whole ($N = 14$), representing as it does a sample of children who spent approximately nine months of the first year of life in the care of an institution and who then experienced a major change in life situation.

In general, the group was marked by a friendliness which seemed warm and genuine. Eleven of the 14 Ss not only approached the stimulus persons but also allowed themselves to be picked up and held. Only two subjects, both boys, presented a different social response: they clung to their mothers and cried when the stimulus persons approached them. No comparable data are available for children who have lived all their lives in own homes, but in preliminary testing of the social test on three such children not one approached the examiners. Instead, they looked at the examiners from behind their mothers' skirts and retreated whenever the examiners moved in their direction.

On the Cattell Infant Intelligence Scale the mean IQ of the group was 96.4. At six months of age the mean IQ for these 14 children was 93.8; at eight months it was 94.3. They continue therefore to score in the normal range. Furthermore, the mean number of words in their vocabulary was 15.5, which compares favorably with Gesell's (3) norms of 10 words at 18 months and 20 words at 21 months. Certainly, the group showed no sign of mental dullness or of language retardation.

No child, furthermore, showed the marked apathy or attention-seeking behavior believed by some to characterize the behavior of children reared in institutions. Differences there were, to be sure, between the children, but none seemed to depart markedly from the normal in temperament or personality. In fact, several of the mothers spontaneously commented upon how easy these children were to handle in comparison with their other children. They mentioned, specifically, their good eating and sleeping habits and their ability to amuse themselves.

Discussion

The discussion will take up three separate points: (a) the effect of the experimental treatment, (b) the effect of own home versus adoptive home placement, and (c) the characteristics of the whole group considered as a sample of institutionalized children.

On the basis of the changes in social behavior produced at the time of treatment, one might have expected that the experimental subjects on retest would have been more responsive to the Experimenter than to the Examiner. Instead, no reliable difference was found in their responses to either person. The Experimenter was not remembered. Further, we did not find, except in the vocalizing of the children, any evidence that the experimental subjects were more responsive than the control subjects. It seems, therefore, that the experiences provided by the more attentive mothering were not great enough to maintain the experimentally produced difference over a year's time, except in one class of behavior.

The findings give rise to several speculations. First, it is possible that the verbal behavior of young children is more sensitive to changes in the environment than are other classes of behavior. In this connection, the responsiveness of vocalizations to conditioning in the three-month-old infant has already been demonstrated (6). Second, differences between the experimental and control groups may well have existed but in some untested area of behavior. Third, the expected (or some other) differences may make their appearance in the future in some more complex behavior incorporating the experiences of treatment. Finally, serious limitations to the study were imposed by the small number of subjects and by the diversity of home placements within each group. Differences would have to be very large indeed to surmount these limitations.

That no difference was found between the experimental and control groups in developmental status is not surprising, considering that no difference was found at the end of treatment. Some of the speculations about the course of social responsiveness may apply here, too.

We turn now to a consideration of the effect of home placement. The adoptive homes in general were of a higher socioeconomic level, the mothers were more sociable, and the homes were judged to offer more intellectual stimulation. For these reasons we would have expected the children in adoptive homes to be more socially responsive and more advanced in developmental status. But significant differences were not found. Possible explanations are that the differences between the two groups of homes may have been not as great as they seemed, or that the number of cases was too small.

Lastly, the characteristics of the group as a whole may be assessed for the effects of a life experience usually thought of as deprived. All the children had been cared for in an institution for the first half of their lives, all but one had experienced a major "separation" in going from one life situation to another, and, furthermore, three children were now living in depressed socioeconomic environments, two were in boarding homes, and one was still in the institution. Yet, as a group, the children were healthy, of normal intelligence, and they appeared to be making a satisfactory adjustment. In addition, they seemed to be more friendly to strangers than children who have lived all their lives in own homes and, according to mothers' reports, were more adaptable than their other children. In no way, then, did they resemble the emotionally disturbed and mentally retarded children described in studies of the effect of institutional or hospital life or of separation from the mother.[2] They did not show apathy or the inability to form relationships or make excessive bids for attention. Even earlier, at the beginning of the study when the infants were still in the institution, they were physically robust, mentally alert, and socially responsive.

[2]Glaser and Eisenberg (4) present a recent review of studies on maternal deprivation.

It is true that in kind and duration of experience they resemble exactly no other group of children reported in the literature. There is a tendency among workers, however, to lump together studies of children who actually differ in age and experience and to generalize from them to all children who have experiences which may be similar in only one of many possible respects. It is to be hoped that as more prospective (in contrast to retrospective) studies are carried out, the dimensions of deprivation and of its effects can be clarified. Certainly, we may expect to find that the effects will depend upon the age of the child, the nature and duration of the deprivation, and the experiences prior to and subsequent to it (1). The present study of the effects of early experience, limited as it is, emphasizes the need for more precise measurement both of deprivation and of its effects.

Summary

The present study reports an attempt to discover the presence, a year later, of a change in behavior brought about in a group of infants by an experimental modification of maternal care.

Sixteen babies, living in an institution for approximately the first nine months of life, were the original subjects of study. Half of them, the experimental subjects, received more attentive care by one person, the Experimenter, from the sixth through the eighth month of life. As a result they became more socially responsive than the control group who were cared for under the usual institutional routine. They did not, however, do better upon tests of developmental progress.

Subsequently all but one of the children were placed in homes. A year later, when the children were about 19 months old, 14 of the original 16 subjects were located, and tested for their social responsiveness and developmental progress.

The results did not reveal any statistically significant differences between the experimental and the control groups except that more of the experimental subjects vocalized during the social tests. It is concluded therefore that the experience provided by the more attentive mothering, while great enough to produce a difference at the time of study, was not great enough to maintain that difference over time, except in one class of behavior. It is possible that the verbal behavior of young children is more sensitive to changes in the environment than are other classes of behavior.

No statistically significant differences in social responsiveness and developmental status were found between children living in own homes and in adoptive homes, although the adoptive homes were of higher socioeconomic status.

Finally, the group as a whole was friendly, of normal intelligence, and apparently was making a satisfactory adjustment. They did not resemble the emotionally disturbed and mentally retarded children described in studies of the effects of institutional life or of separation from the mother.

REFERENCES

1. Ainsworth, Mary D., and J. Bowlby. Research strategy in the study of mother-child separation. *Courier,* 1954, *4*, 105–131.
2. Cattell, Psyche. *The measurement of intelligence of infants and young children.* New York: Psychol. Corporation, 1940.
3. Gesell, A., and Catherine S. Amatruda. *Developmental diagnosis.* New York: Hoeber, 1941.
4. Glaser, K., and L. Eisenberg. Maternal deprivation. *Pediatrics,* 1956, *18*, 626–642.
5. Rheingold, Harriet L. The modification of social responsiveness in institutional babies. *Monogr. Soc. Res. Child Develpm.,* 1956, *21*, No. 2. (Serial No. 63)
6. Rheingold, Harriet L., J. L. Gewirtz, and Helen W. Ross. Social conditioning of vocalizations in the infant. *J. Comp. Physiol. Psychol.,* 1959, *52*, 68–73.

10. CAN CONDITIONED RESPONSES BE ESTABLISHED IN THE NEWBORN INFANT: 1971?[1]

ARNOLD J. SAMEROFF

The learning capabilities of the human newborn are evaluated. Classical conditioning is difficult to demonstrate in the newborn, while operant conditioning is possible. Two hypotheses are evaluated as explanations for difficulties in conditioning the newborn: (a) The newborn is unable to respond to stimulus change. (b) The newborn is able to respond to a general change but cannot respond to specific differences in stimulation. It is proposed that classical conditioning may involve the integration of two sensory modalities: that of the CS and that of the US. The newborn infant must first develop cognitive systems, through his experience with various stimuli, to differentiate each modality separately before he can integrate any two modalities in classical conditioning. The roles of the orienting reaction and defensive reaction are discussed.

The title of this article is taken from Dorothy Marquis who asked the same question in 1931. She answered that question in the affirmative, but recent data suggest that her conclusion may have been premature. For the purpose of exploring the issue of newborn learning in detail, the present author has divided the literature into two parts. The section on studies of infant activity focuses on the infant's ability to alter his behavior in experimental situations. The section on studies of infant reactivity deals with the newborn's ability to respond to stimulus change in his environment. In a later section the relation between the infant's ability to react to stimuli and his ability to form new associations to these stimuli is explored. The operational definition of the newborn period used in this article is the length of time that the infant remains in the hospital after birth, currently from 3 to 10 days.

[1] An earlier version of this article was presented at the Eastern Regional Meeting of the Society for Research in Child Development, Worcester, Massachusetts, 1968. This study was supported by United States Public Health Service, National Institute of Child Health and Human Development Grant No. HD-03454. The author wishes to thank Michael Davidson and James Ison for their criticisms which were helpful in sharpening some of the ideas in this article.

From *Developmental Psychology*, 1971, 5, 1–12. Copyright 1971 by the American Psychological Association. Reprinted by permission of the author and the publisher.

Studies of Activity

In Kessen's (1963) description of infants as active as well as reactive, he suggested that the child is engaged in the process of integrating his experience and thereby constructing his world, and is not atomistically accepting the contingencies of which he finds himself a part. An empirical question that would help in the definition of a theoretical position is, What are the kinds of contingencies to which the newborn can respond; that is, which experimental paradigms will be effective in showing learning, and which paradigms will not show alteration in the performance of the infant? The two major paradigms of consequence for learning studies are the classical or respondent and the instrumental or operant.

There have been many investigations in which attempts were made to show classical conditioning in newborn infants. These studies were uniformly unsuccessful or inconclusive. A prototype of this kind of study is one done by Wickens and Wickens in 1940, who elicited foot withdrawal by using an electrotactual shock as an unconditioned stimulus. In their experimental group, they paired a buzzer with the shock for 36 trials over 3 days. On the third day, they tested for conditioning by presenting the buzzer alone and got, as they had hoped, the foot withdrawal response. However, in a control group which also had 36 trials of electrotactual shock, but without a buzzer, they were also able to get a foot withdrawal response when the infants were stimulated with the buzzer. It appeared that pairing the buzzer with the shock was irrelevant to the results they obtained. They concluded from this study that if they had conditioned anything it was to a sudden change in stimulation.

Encouraged by advances in technology over the intervening decades, Crowell (in Bijou & Baer, 1965), Gullickson (in Bijou & Baer, 1965), and Marum (in Lipsitt, 1963) each did experiments in which they tried to condition foot withdrawal elicited by electrotactual shock to an auditory stimulus. These investigators were equally unsuccessful. Lipsitt and Kaye (in Lipsitt, 1963) worked with a different aversive response. They paired a tone with the presentation of acetic acid vapor to the infant's nose. The unconditioned response was withdrawal from the vapor or heightened activity. They were also unsuccessful in obtaining this response.

There is a second group of studies[2] in which conditioning effects were purportedly found, but a number of important questions were left unanswered about control groups or peculiarities in results. These studies have been criticized by a number of authors including Lipsitt (1963) and Bijou and Baer (1965). Among these are Spelt's (1948) report of fetal conditioning, Marquis's (1931) report of conditioning sucking movements to a buzzer, Marquis's (1941) later report of conditioning infants to their feeding schedules, and Lipsitt

[2]The author has classed all studies in which sucking on a nipple was the UR and anticipatory sucking without a nipple was the CR in the questionable group because of the prepotency of the sucking response in the hungry infant. Jensen (1933) has reported onset of sucking to squeezing the infant's toe or pulling his hair. More recent evidence has indicated an unconditioned sucking response to onset of auditory stimulation (Keen, 1964; Semb & Lipsitt, 1968). The potentiation of this response and the inability of the investigator to truly decide what elicited the response (Was it the infant touching his tongue to his lips or merely touching the two lips together?) when it occurs makes sucking a complex response to control in studies of classical conditioning. It is an example of what Seligman (1970) has called a prepared response.

and Kaye's (1964) recent attempt to condition sucking movements to a tone.

During the last few years a change in paradigm took place and investigators using operant techniques have been able to find positive evidence of learning abilities in the newborn. Lipsitt, Kaye, and Bosack (1966) were able to increase the infant's sucking rate to a rubber tube by reinforcing the sucking with dextrose solution. They demonstrated both extinction and retraining effects.

Sameroff (1968) was able to differentially alter two components of the sucking response. Infants had been noted to get milk out of a nipple either by expression, that is, squeezing the nipple between tongue and palate, or by suction, that is, enlarging the oral cavity and creating a vacuum which pulls the milk out of the nipple. When the expression component was reinforced, that is, squeezing the nipple, the suction component was diminished and in many cases disappeared during the training period. When the newborns had to express above certain pressure thresholds to obtain milk, they changed their performance to match the thresholds.

Siqueland (1968) was able to influence the head turning response in newborns by operant training. He succeeded in increasing the rate of head turning in two groups (one of which was put on a 2:1 fixed-ratio schedule), and to decrease head turning in a third group which was reinforced for holding the head still.

Using a modified classical conditioning paradigm, Siqueland and Lipsitt (1966) performed three experiments using Papousek's (1961) head turning method. They stroked the cheeks of newborn infants which under normal conditions elicited ipsilateral head turns about 25% of the time. In their first experiment they paired a buzzer with the stroking and, if the infant turned his head, he received an immediate dextrose solution reinforcement. In their experimental group, the rate of head turning to the tactual stimulus increased to 80%, while in a control group in which the reinforcement was given only 8–10 seconds after the tone-touch stimulation, the rate remained at 25%. However, there was no evidence that the auditory stimulus had any influence on the results, since the head turn did not occur until the stroke was performed.

In the second experiment, Siqueland and Lipsitt investigated differentiation of two auditory stimuli, a buzzer and a tone. The positive stimulus was paired with a tactual stimulus eliciting head turning to one side, while on alternate trials the negative stimulus was paired with tactual stimulation eliciting head turning to the other side. After training by reinforcing the response to the positive stimulus with dextrose solution, they were able to show an increase of head turning to the stroke on the positive side as opposed to no increase of head turning to the stroke on the negative side. Again, however, there was no evidence that the auditory stimuli played any role in the learning since the infants responded only to the differential stroking of the cheek to one side or the other.

In the third experiment, the same authors showed some evidence for differentiation of the auditory stimuli. They used the same buzzer and tone as positive and negative stimuli, presented alternately as in the previous experiment; but, this time both were paired with a tactual perioral stimulus eliciting head turning on only one side. When the positive stimulus sounded, the tactual stimulus was applied and if a head turn occurred the infant was reinforced with dextrose solution. When the negative stimulus sounded, the infant was stroked on the same side, but a head turn did not result in reinforcement. In this situation, the infant increased his responding to the tactual stimulus following the positive auditory stimulus while the stroke associated with the negative stimulus did not increase in effectiveness in eliciting head turns. These results are interesting, both from the point of view of having a differentiation of response associated with the two auditory stimuli, and the failure to demonstrate the infant's ability to be classically conditioned. The auditory signal still did not elicit the head turning response anticipatorily; it was only after the tactual stimulus was presented that the head turn was elicited.

What differentiates those studies in which investigators were able to show learning effects in newborns from those where there was less success? Is there any generalization that can be made which will help to understand the behavior of these newborns better? One clear difference is between the classical and operant conditioning paradigms. The unsuccessful studies have typically been attempts at classical conditioning, attempts to relate a previously neutral stimulus to an unconditioned stimulus and response.

On the other hand, the unsuccessful experiments either have not been in the classical conditioning paradigm or have not yielded classical results. In all cases, a previous relationship has already existed between the stimulus and response in question. No previously neutral stimuli have been associated. The results of the various training procedures have been to strengthen or alter what Kessen (1967) has described as *organized patterns of behavior* in the newborn. In the Lipsitt, Kaye, and Bosack (1966) study, an already existing low sucking rate to an oral stimulus was enhanced. In the Sameroff (1968) study, already existing expression and suction components of the sucking response were modified. In Siqueland's (1968) operant conditioning of head turning, an already existing organized component of the rooting-sucking-feeding complex was modified; and in Siqueland and Lipsitt's (1966) three experiments, an already existing relation between tactual perioral stimulation and head turning was enhanced.

If classical conditioning has not been demonstrated in the newborn, when can it be said to have been reliably shown? Polikanina (1961) paired a tone CS with ammonia vapor as an US eliciting motoric avoidance as a response. She found a conditioned response to the tone in 50% of the trials after 3–5 weeks. Papousek (1967) worked with the head turning response. He paired a bell CS with stroking the infant's cheek and found stable conditioned responses after an average of 3 weeks (i.e., the bell alone regularly elicited the head turn). Thus, it seems that some time during the first few weeks of life something changes so that the same classical conditioning which was not demonstrated in the first week of life in the work of Lipsitt and Kaye (in Lipsitt, 1963) and Siqueland and Lipsitt (1966) became possible during the third week of life, as seen in the work of Polikanina (1961) and Papousek (1967).

A *caveat* must be included here about considering the Polikanina (1961) or Papousek (1967) studies as evidence for successful classical conditioning. The Polikanina study included no controls for pseudo-conditioning. As a result, her findings may be identical in origin to those of Wickens and Wickens (1940). The Papousek head turning paradigm that was also used in the Siqueland and Lipsitt (1966) studies is not true classical conditioning. The milk reinforcement as a consequence of the head turning made the procedure a mixed model during training, and an operant after criterion was reached. Morgan and Morgan (1944), also without controls, claimed no eyeblink conditioning was possible before 45 days of life. Janos (1965) presented the best case for conditional eyeblink, but he got it only after 86 days. He was also able to show differentiation of response to two auditory cues.

The failure to classically condition newborns requires that an attempt be made at some theoretical explanation of the data. A starting point for such an explanation will be an analysis of the task. Since the problem seems to be related to the establishment of an association to a previously neutral stimulus, a first requirement for the subject in the classical conditioning paradigm is that he be able to perceive this neutral stimulus. A starting hypothesis can be that the newborn is unable to detect changes in his environment. To test this hypothesis, a series of studies related to the infant's abilities to respond to stimulus change is reviewed in the next section.

Studies of Reactivity

The focus of studies in this class is on the infant's response to stimulation and the changes in this response as the stimulation is either varied or repeated. For example, studies of perception using habituation or eye orientation fall into this class. The main concern, however, is

with a group of responses which the Russians, especially Sokolov (1963), have called the orienting reaction.

The function of the orienting reaction is to prepare the organism to deal with novel stimulation (Lynn, 1966). Lynn (1966), following Sokolov (1963), lists five classes of responses in the orienting reaction. They include (*a*) increases in the sensitivity of the sense organs, (*b*) motor orientation of the sense organs toward the source of stimulation, (*c*) changes in general skeletal musculature, (*d*) desynchronization of the EEG with accompanying lowered amplitude and increased frequency, and (*e*) a number of autonomic responses consisting of GSR, vasoconstriction in the limbs and vasodilation in the head, decrease in respiratory frequency with increase in amplitude, and heart-rate deceleration. In the last decade, several studies have produced evidence for the existence of various components of the orienting reaction in the newborn. They are listed below following Lynn's (1966) categorization.

1.   Increase in the Sensitivity of the Sense Organs. Stechler, Bradford, and Levy (1966) stimulated newborn infants with an air puff to the abdomen in two conditions while measuring the GSR. In the first condition, the infants were awake with eyes open and fixated on a patterned visual stimulus. In the second condition the infants were awake with eyes open but not fixated on any apparent stimulus. The electrodermal response was much stronger in the fixated condition as compared with the unfixated condition. The existence of the orienting reaction can be inferred from the lower sensory thresholds for GSR elicitation in the fixating group.

2.   Motor Orientation of Sense Organs. Motor orientation of head and/or eyes to visual stimuli has been found by Fantz (1963), Hershenson (1964), Wolff (1966), and Salapatek and Kessen (1966). Eye orientation to auditory stimulation has been reported by Wolff (1966) and Turkewitz, Moreau, and Birch (1966). The rooting reflex is an orientation of the head to perioral tactual stimulation.

3. Changes in General Skeletal Musculature. Motor quieting and cessation of ongoing activity to novel stimuli have been found by Papousek (1967) and Bronschtein and Petrowa (1952).

4. Desynchronization of the EEG. Generalized EEG responses have been reported by Dreyfuss-Brissac and Blanc (1956) and Ellingson (1967) to indicate that the newborn can react to novel stimuli with a change to the low amplitude, fast activity which has been described as part of the orienting reaction.

5. Autonomic Responses. Sokolov (1963) used the vasomotor responses as one of his prime indicators for the orienting reaction. However, as yet, vasomotor responses have not been investigated in the newborn, so little can be said about them. More work has been done with other autonomic responses. Until recently there was some question as to whether the GSR could be found in newborns. However, Crowell, Davis, Chun, and Spellacy (1965) and Stechler, Bradford, and Levy (1966) in a study cited above, both found the GSR by careful experimental preparation. Respiration has not received much attention as an orienting reaction component. Sameroff (1970) has found respiratory slowing to auditory stimulation in some conditions. Steinschneider (1968) reported that white noise stimuli between 55 and 100 decibels increased respiratory rate. However, if only the first respiratory cycle following stimulus change was considered, the low intensity stimuli, 55 and 70 decibels, resulted in respiratory deceleration. The different direction of response to the low intensity stimuli might be interpreted as an orienting reaction component.

The one response that seems to be quite different from what was expected in an orienting reaction is the heart-rate response. Authors working with newborns have consistently shown heart-rate acceleration to novel stimuli. The heart-rate-decelerative response to stimulation does exist in the 4-month-old infant (Kagan & Lewis, 1965). Lipton, Steinschneider, and Richmond (1966) found some

heart-rate deceleration before acceleration in infants 2½ months of age, and Lewis, Bartels, and Goldberg (1966) also found initial deceleration before acceleration in a third of their awake subjects between the ages of 2 and 8 weeks. Schulman (1968), in a recent study, was able to find consistent deceleration in awake 1-week-olds, further lowering the age boundary. In newborns, Schachter, Williams, Khachaturian, Tobin, and Druger (1968) found a triphasic response to auditory clicks, the first phase being a short deceleration.

From this survey of the newborn orienting reaction literature, it can be seen that the field has moved in the last 10 years from little or no knowledge to an almost complete outline of newborn reactivity. Apparently, the one component of the orienting reaction about which there is some serious question is the heart-rate response. Is the heart-rate-decelerative component of the orienting reaction undeveloped, or can some other explanation be put forth as to why acceleration seems to be the predominate heart-rate response in the newborn? One hypothesis is related to the significance of the heart-rate-accelerative response. Graham and Clifton (1966) have shown that the heart-rate-accelerative response is a part of the adult's reaction to many stimulus situations. It has a role in a reaction to stimulation different from the orienting reaction, the defensive reaction.

According to Sokolov (1963) the defensive reaction differs from the orienting reaction in that rather than increase in the sensitivity of the sensory systems, there is a decrease and a reaction away from the source of stimulation. The defensive reaction avoids the stimulus source, whereas the orienting reaction approaches the source of stimulation. Perhaps the heart-rate acceleration to stimulation found in newborn infants is part of the defensive reaction rather than a sign of an immature orienting reaction.

A question which immediately arises is, What kind of stimulation gives rise to one reaction over another? Sokolov (1963) defined the defensive reaction as occurring when stimulation increases above a certain limit and threatens the integrity of the body, that is, becomes painful. However, in the case of the newborn there are stimuli which are not painful, but which elicit defensive reactions (Kessen & Mandler, 1961). Loud noises or loss of support evoke obvious defensive reactions in the form of startles or Moro reflexes. Less obvious defensive reactions, expressed only autonomically, can occur to any intense stimulus.

It may be that there are two kinds of defensive reactions, a quantitative one and a qualitative one. The quantitative defensive reaction would be the response to the high intensity stimuli which Sokolov (1963) discussed. The qualitative defensive reaction would be to stimuli for which there is no cognitive or neuronal model. Given the limited experience of the newborn, it would be expected that there would not be a model for most of the stimuli he encounters. Therefore, it can be expected that the newborn's initial reaction to most novel stimulation is defensive and that for an orienting reaction to occur there must first be a habituation of this defensive reaction. Bartoshuk (1962), Bridger (1961), and Graham, Clifton, and Hatton (1968) have shown habituation of the accelerative heart-rate response and startle response to auditory stimulation. Sameroff (1970) found a change in direction of respiratory response to auditory stimuli from acceleration in 1-day-old infants to deceleration in 4-day-olds.

Studies of orientation to visual stimulation in which defensive reactions have not been found might be thought to contradict this position. However, no study has been performed on the just born newborn, so that it can be hypothesized that the defensive reaction to general low intensity visual stimuli has already been habituated by the time the first experiments were performed, possibly *in utero*. Studies using low-intensity stimuli are different from studies where loud sounds or bright lights, which would seem to be novel for the newborn, lead to clear defensive reactions. The point could be confirmed if heart-rate response to the kinds of low-level visual stimuli that elicit orientation behavior in the newborn were to be studied. A finding of heart-rate deceleration would further support the existence of the full orienting reaction in the newborn.

Another hypothesis explaining the change from accelerative heart-rate responses in the newborn to decelerative responses in the 3-month-old has been proposed by Graham and Jackson (1970). They suggested the difference in findings might be a function of the state of the infant during the experimental sessions, that newborns are typically examined while they are asleep or drowsy, and 3-month-olds are examined while they are awake. The ability of Schulman (1968) and Lewis, Bartels, and Goldberg (1966) to find the decelerative response only in waking infants support the Graham and Jackson (1970) hypothesis.

The significance of the preceding discussion as to whether or not the orienting reaction exists in the newborn is in the light it throws on the infant's ability to respond to changes in his environment, especially novel ones. Sokolov (1963) maintained that preceding conditioning, there must be an initial orienting reaction to the conditional stimulus. Therefore, if the orienting reaction is incomplete in the newborn, there can be no conditioning until it matures.

For learning to occur, the infant must react to new contingencies in his environment. If he is unable to respond to new situations, it is unlikely that he can show changes in his behavior related to these new situations. That the orienting reaction seems to be present in the newborn, boosts the infant one rung up the ladder.

The second rung on the ladder is related to the distinction between a "neutral" stimulus and a "new" stimulus. Classical conditioning is defined as the association of a previously neutral CS with the nonneutral US. An additional problem in newborn conditioning is that a neutral stimulus is also a new stimulus. How many newborns have had previous experience with electric shock or acetic acid vapors or even bells and buzzers? Since, from the studies described in this section, it seems that the newborn can respond to general changes in stimulation, the first hypothesis related to his inability to be classically conditioned seems disconfirmed. The next hypothesis to explain his inability could be that the newborn is unable to respond differentially to the specific stimuli that have been used in studies of early classical conditioning. To elaborate this hypothesis, one must move away from the empirical base of the preceding two sections and explore some theoretical positions in the next section.

Cognitive Schemas

Until now stimuli and responses have been discussed only as observables. The attempt to explain all of behavior on the basis of observables has been a goal of radical behaviorists for a number of decades. A high point in this attempt was Skinner's (1957) explanation of language behavior. However, Skinner's work was judged by Chomsky (1959) to be inadequate for linguistic analysis. Learning theorists of a less fundamentalist bent have dealt with the issue of nonobservables in the explanation of complex human behavior (Kendler, 1963) by inferring covert analogies of overt S-R processes. The use of covert mediation to reinforce the reductionism in the S-R approach to behavior has not resolved the inability of a nonhierarchical model to explain complex thought processes (Scheerer, 1954). Piaget (1960) also believed that the associationist position was inadequate to explain the complexities of logical behavior and language. Instead, Piaget formulated a theory in which the same cognitive *functions* were used to explain both the complex symbolic behavior of the adult and the simple sensory-motor behavior of the infant, while at the same time the cognitive structural elements associated with the two age periods were quite different. The addition that Piaget makes to behaviorism is to fill in the black box with a cognitive organization composed of structural elements called *schemas*. The schema is a cognitive structure which is adapted through the organism's interaction with the environment. The general function of adaptation is composed of two subfunctions: assimilation, the incorporation of a stimulus into a previously organized schema; and accommodation, the process by which a schema alters itself in order to incorporate new

inputs. Focusing on the active internal organization that accompanies the adaptation process, Piaget (1960) is able to trace the development from innate sensory-motor schemas to the formal logical operations of the adult human. What for many may seem to be an unnecessary complication in theory for understanding simple behaviors is for Piaget an excellent application of Occam's razor. Piaget has extended accepted principles of biology which function in the development of chemical and physical systems to the sphere of psychology. Intelligent behavior from a Piagetian viewpoint can be regarded as a more complexly organized *adaptive* system of the human animal in keeping with his parallel more complexly organized biological system. However, the functions of assimilation, accommodation, and their organization need not be different for the two systems.

Initially the infant comes into the world with a set of built-in reflex schemas. These schemas may have been previously tuned or adapted *in utero* to an optimal input, but almost immediately begin adapting to new inputs. For example, the sucking schema seems optimally fitted to the tactual input of the nipple, but is readily adapted to sucking on a finger, tube, tongue, blanket, or anything else that stimulates the lips. Experiments such as Lipsitt and Kaye (1964), Lipsitt, Kaye, and Bosack (1966), and Sameroff (1968) have shown that the sucking schema is sensitive to many input contingencies and can be readily altered by manipulating variables directly related to food getting. It is through the adaptation of these already existing reflex schemas that any demonstration of learning has been possible in the newborn.

It is when one departs from these built-in schemas that difficulties arise. In the typical classical conditioning problem, there is an attempt to relate two previously unrelated stimuli in different sensory modalities. For adults, both the CS and the US already are part of various schematic hierarchies. In the typical newborn study, only the US is part of the schema, for example, tactual stimulation leading to head turning. The "newness" of the CS for the infant also means that it is unrelated to any of his activity schemas other than through the possibility of generalizing assimilation. As a consequence, there is no place for the CS in the infant's cognitive structure.

The failure of classical conditioning attempts can occur for two possible reasons. The first is that the infant cannot coordinate two separate schemas in the newborn period; the second is that an independent schema for the CS must first exist before a coordination can be made between the US-UR and CS schemas. Both reasons are probably true in the context of the development of the entire schematic structure. Werner (1957) made the point in his orthogenetic principle that development proceeds through both differentiation *and* hierarchic integration. There is a simultaneous process of differentiation in the sensory systems as various stimuli are related to different activities of the organism, and at the same time these various activities are integrated at higher levels.

The relations to be established in experimental classical conditioning situations might be placed midway in the developmental sequence between (*a*) the differentiation of innate schemas and (*b*) the subsequent integration of these schema systems. In an experiment, an attempt is made to coordinate schemas artificially that are not coordinated in the organism's real world. For control purposes, the experimental association is made between elements different from those which arise in the organism's normal environment. As a result of this controlled reliable relationship, the organism might be able to make coordinations which would only appear at a later stage in the more erratic real world.

To return to the initial problem, how would it be possible to obtain classical conditioning in the infant? The answer cannot be found by generalizing from a procedure used with adult dogs. There is no compelling reason to differentiate between the adult dog or rat and the older prelinguistic child. Both can have perceptually differentiated the world, and can have established differentiated modalities of perception.

In contrast, the newborn rat, dog, or infant has not yet achieved this differentiation. It is not even clear that the infant initially differentiates inputs from the auditory, visual, or tactual systems other than at the level of the perceiving organ, the reflex schema. The sensory system in the mouth seems to be highly developed (Jensen, 1932; Sameroff, 1968). The same cannot be said for the visual system, as recent studies by Salapatek (1968) and Salapatek and Kessen (1966) have indicated; nor for the auditory system (Stubbs, 1934). Before a specific auditory input can be related to other response schemas, the auditory schema must itself become differentiated. An interactionist position is called for, since it does not seem appropriate to call a perceptual system immature if its maturity depends on an interaction with the environment. If conditioning is to occur in the classical sense that a specific previously neutral stimulus will now elicit a response, the organism must first be able to differentiate that stimulus from the other stimuli in its environment. For Piaget (1952), the only possibility of recognizing an input is through the subject's response to it, through what has been called motor recognition or recognitory assimilation. Until the response to one specific stimulus is adequately differentiated from responses to other specific stimuli in the auditory schematic hierarchy, there can be no connection of these to other schemas.

For example, it may be that in the typical conditioning study the modality of the CS and the modality of the US are distant on some dimension, thus making their schematic coordination difficult. Using a CS and US in modalities that are less different might lead to more successful results. Ignoring the differentiation problem for the present, the earliest and most stable conditioning should occur if the sensory modalities of the CS and US are identical. There is evidence that this is, indeed, the case. Kasatkin (1948), on the basis of Russian research, ranks the sensory modalities of CSs on the basis of the age at which they can first be used in successful conditioning. Earliest on the list are changes of body position which involve proprioceptive as well as vestibular stimulation. Neurologically, the interrelations between proprioceptive receptors and motor centers are very close, from the gamma efferent fibers through the cerebellum and into cortical areas.

Brackbill, Lintz, and Fitzgerald (1968; Abrahamson, Brackbill, Carpenter, & Fitzgerald, in press) made a more general point in differentiating the conditioning of autonomic versus somatic responses. Rather than accepting a developmental progression from one to the other in conditionability, they have demonstrated in the first months of life that they could obtain an autonomic CR to an autonomic CS (temporal conditioning of the pupillary response) and somatic CR to a sensory CS (tactual stimulus associated with eyeblink), but could not cross-condition between the somatic and autonomic systems, that is, obtain an eyeblink to temporal conditioning or a pupillary response to a tactual stimulus.

Schema Differentiation

There is no reason to believe that the response systems associated with perception are any more differentiated at birth than the response systems associated with motor activity. Researchers from Gesell and Amatruda (1945) to White, Castle, and Held (1964) have spelled out the development from global responses to specific, directed motor functioning in coordination with other response systems. Recent research indicates the same can be said for the perceptual systems.

The case is clearer for the differentiation of stimuli leading to sucking behavior, but a parallel case can be made for audition. Initially, there is an innate global response to suck on anything sensed by the mouth that does not elicit a defensive reaction, such as a hot nipple. Differentiation occurs through accommodation of the response to the specific object sucked upon, and is evidenced by the increase in coordination and stability of sucking in the first days of life found by Halverson (1944), Kron, Stein, and Goddard (1963), and Sameroff (1967). However, the infant does not act differently on the basis of this differentiation of response. He will suck on a dry nipple for 20 minutes even though he is hungry (Sameroff, 1967).

This situation changes after a few weeks. The 3-week-old infant will begin to reject a nonnutritive nipple when hungry (Piaget, 1952). The differentiation between sucking alone and the complex of sucking, warm feeling in the mouth, and swallowing, now makes a difference in the infant's behavior. There is an integration of new elements into the set of schemas which permits differentiations to be made in the infant's response to his environment.

An analogous case can be made for auditory stimuli. The initial differentiation of auditory inputs found in Siqueland and Lipsitt's (1966) third experiment could not be integrated at that stage with other response schemas. It was only after a period of differentiation and stabilization of the auditory schema that it could be coordinated with other behaviors, as was evidenced by Papousek's (1967) success in obtaining head turning to the tone alone without mediating oral stimulation after 3 weeks of age.

Papousek's (1967) research is a case study of the infant's changing ability to respond to auditory stimuli. When number of trials to a conditioning criterion was compared for groups of newborns, 3-month-old infants, and 5-month-old infants, the data showed an inverse correlation with age: 177, 42, and 28 trials, respectively. The longer experience that the older infants had in responding to differential auditory stimuli in their natural environment was reflected in their faster conditioning in the experimental situation. An alternate hypothesis is that the infants had somehow matured neurologically, thus making faster conditioning possible. However, a maturation hypothesis is weakened by Papousek's extinction data. The three age groups extinguished their responses in almost identical numbers of trials: 27, 25, and 27, respectively. The extinction data indicate that the neurological mechanisms are not radically different in the three age groups, so that the differential ability to be conditioned must lie in the differential development of the cognitive organization.

More recently, Papousek (1969) has found further related effects in attempts to condition infants to differentiate head turning responses. A bell signal indicated that a head turn to one side would be reinforced; a buzzer indicated that a head turn in the opposite direction would be reinforced. In Papoušek's (1967) original work, differentiation training began when the newborn group was an average of 44 days old, because it followed three other procedures—conditioning, extinction, and reconditioning. In the later study, Papoušek (1969) investigated the ability of younger infants to learn the differentiation. In one group, he began training at an average age of 31 days when the infants had completed only one previous procedure—conditioning of a head turn to the left. In another group, he began differentiation training with newborns, completely eliminating any previous procedures. The results were surprising in that, while the group that began differentiation at 44 days took 224 trials, reaching criterion at an average age of 72 days, the group that began at 31 days took 278 trials and reached criterion at an average of 71 days of age. Thus, the younger subjects were unable to capitalize on their earlier start.

To support a maturation hypothesis, the newborn group should also have reached criterion at around 72 days of age. However, they provided surprising results. They required an average of 814 trials, and were 128 days old when the differentiation criterion was reached, almost double the age of the other two groups. It thus seems that not only must the auditory schemas become differentiated before conditioning can take place, but also that the infant's experience must be paced or an input overload of the schema can occur with consequent retardation in its development.

Summary

Rather than hypothesize stages of development in the newborn period, the proposed theory has a progression in cognitive structure based on differentiation and hierarchic integration of schemas. On the activity side, the newborn initially can respond with prenatally organized cognitive schemas, which can assimilate, that is, are adapted either genetically or *in utero* to include specific stimuli. Development is through the increasing differentiation and enlargement of the activity schemas by accommodation to a growing number of stimuli. The initial limited range of stimuli to which the reflex was sensitive is expanded as a function of feedback from the infant's experience with differential effects of his responding.

On the reactivity side, suprathreshold novel stimuli, that is, those which are not assimilated by the innate reflex schemas, elicit a defensive reaction. Repeated exposure to novel stimuli builds up the infant's schema repertoire. As the repertoire grows, the likelihood of encountering a stimulus for which there is no differentiated schema declines, reducing the chances for eliciting the qualitative defensive reaction. Subsequently, the response to the novel stimulus will be an orienting reaction. The activity-reactivity dichotomy is more than a division between those stimuli that can be assimilated to existing schemas and those that cannot, because it also includes the dynamic experiential aspect of the qualitative defensive reaction and orienting reaction in the adaptation process. Eventually, sufficient plasticity is achieved within the cognitive framework. Separate schema systems can then be coordinated making possible the association necessary for classical conditioning in the experimental situation.

To conclude, the evidence strongly indicates that before classical conditioning can occur there must be a differentiation of the schema systems related to both the US and CS. For distance receptors, this development seems to take about 3 weeks, after which the infant begins to be able to coordinate his differentiated perceptual response systems with other sensory-motor schemas such as sucking or head turning.

REFERENCES

Abrahamson, D., Brackbill, Y., Carpenter, R., & Fitzgerald, H. E. Interaction of stimulus and response in infant conditioning. In H. E. Fitzgerald & Y. Brackbill (Eds.), *Design and method in infant research*. Chicago: University of Chicago Press, in press.

Bartoshuk, A. K. Response decrement with repeated elicitation of human neonatal cardiac acceleration to sound. *Journal of Comparative and Physiological Psychology*, 1962, *55*, 9–13.

Brackbill, Y., Lintz, L. M., & Fitzgerald, H. E. Differences in the autonomic and somatic conditioning of infants. *Psychosomatic Medicine*, 1968, *30*, 193–201.

Bijou, S. W., & Baer, D. M. *Child development. II: University stage of infancy*. New York: Appleton-Century-Crofts, 1965.

Bridger, W. H. Sensory habituation and discrimination in the human neonate. *American Journal of Psychiatry*, 1961, *117*, 991–996.

Bronschtein, A. I., & Petrowa, J. P. Die Erforschung des akustischen Analysators bei Neugeborenen und Kinder im frühen Säuglingsalter. *Pawlow-Zeitschrift für höhere Nerventätigkeit*, 1952, *2*, 441–455.

Chomsky, N. Review of B. F. Skinner's *Verbal behavior*. *Language*, 1959, *35*, 26–58.

Crowell, D. H., David, C. M., Chun, B. J., & Spellacy, F. J. Galvanic skin reflex in newborn humans. *Science*, 1965, *148*, 1108–1111.

Dreyfuss-Brissac, C., & Blanc, C. Electro-encephalogramme et maturation cerébrale. *Encephale*, 1956, *3*, 205–245.

Ellingson, R. J. The study of brain electrical activity in infants. In L. P. Lipsitt & C. C. Spiker (Eds.), *Advances in child development and behavior*. Vol. 3. New York: Academic Press, 1967.

Fantz, R. L. Pattern vision in newborn infants. *Science*, 1963, *140*, 296–297.

Gesell, A. L., & Amatruda, C. S. *The embryology of behavior: The beginnings of the human mind*. New York: Harper, 1945.

Graham, F. K., & Clifton, R. K. Heartrate change as a component of the orienting response. *Psychological Bulletin*, 1966, *65*, 305–320.

Graham, F. K., Clifton, R. K., & Hatton, H. M. Habituation of the heartrate response to repeated auditory stimulation during the first five days of life. *Child Development*, 1968, *39*, 35–52.

Graham, F. K., & Jackson, J. C. Arousal systems and infant heart rate responses. In H. W. Reese & L. P. Lipsitt (Eds.), *Advances in child development and behavior*. Vol. 5. New York: Academic Press, 1970.

Halverson, H. M. Mechanisms of early infant feeding. *Journal of Genetic Psychology*, 1944, *64*, 185–223.

Hershenson, M. Visual discrimination in the human newborn. *Journal of Comparative and Physiological Psychology*, 1964, *58*, 270–276.

Janos, O. *Vekove a individualni rozdily ve vyssi nervove cinnosti kojenco*. [Age and individual differences in the higher nervous activity of the infant] Prague: Statni Zdravotnicke Nakladatelstvi, 1965.

Jensen, K. Differential reactions to taste and temperature stimuli in newborn infants. *Genetic Psychology Monographs*, 1932, *12*, 361–479.

Kagan, J., & Lewis, A. Studies of attention in the human infant. *Merrill-Palmer Quarterly*, 1965, *11*, 95–128.

Kasatkin, N. I. *Rannie uslovnye reflexsy v ontogeneze cheloveka*. [Early conditioned reflexes in human ontogenesis] Moscow: Izdatelstvo Akademiye Medistvo Nauk SSR, 1948.

Keen, R. Effects of auditory stimulation on sucking behavior in the human neonate. *Journal of Experimental Child Psychology*, 1964, *1*, 348–354.

Kendler, T. S. Development of mediating responses in children. *Monographs of the Society for Research in Child Development*, 1963, *28* (28, Serial No. 86).

Kessen, W. Research in the psychological development of infants: An overview. *Merrill-Palmer Quarterly of Behavior and Development*, 1963, *9*, 83–94.

Kessen, W. Sucking and looking: Two organized congenital patterns of behavior in the human newborn. In H. W. Stevenson, E. H. Hess, & H. L. Rheingold (Eds.), *Early behavior*. New York: Wiley, 1967.

Kessen, W., & Mandler, G. Anxiety, pain, and the inhibition of distress. *Psychological Review*, 1961, *68*, 396–404.

Kron, R. E., Stein, M., & Goddard, K. E. A method of measuring sucking behavior of newborn infants. *Psychosomatic Medicine*, 1963, *25*, 181–191.

Lewis, M., Bartels, B., & Goldberg, S. State as a determinant of infants' heartrate response to stimulation. *Science*, 1966, *155*, 486–488.

Lipsitt, L. P. Learning in the first year of life. In L. P. Lipsitt & C. C. Spiker (Eds.), *Advances in child development and behavior*. Vol. 1. New York: Academic Press, 1963.

Lipsitt, L. P., & Kaye, H. Conditioned sucking in the human newborn. *Psychonomic Science*, 1964, *1*, 29–30.

Lipsitt, L. P., Kaye, H., & Bosack, T. N. Enhancement of neonatal sucking through reinforcement. *Journal of Experimental Child Psychology*, 1966, *4*, 163–168.

Lipton, E. L., Steinschneider, A., & Richmond, J. B. Autonomic function in the neonate: VII. Maturational changes in cardiac control. *Child Development*, 1966, *37*, 1–16.

Lynn, R. *Attention, arousal and the orientation reaction*. Oxford: Pergamon, 1966.

Marquis, D. P. Can conditioned reflexes be established in the newborn infant? *Journal of Genetic Psychology*, 1931, *39*, 479–492.

Marquis, D. P. Learning in the neonate: The modification of behavior under three feeding schedules. *Journal of Experimental Psychology*, 1941, *29*, 263–282.

Morgan, J. J. B., & Morgan, S. S. Infant learning as a developmental index. *Journal of Genetic Psychology*, 1944, *65*, 281–289.

Papousek, H. Conditioned head rotation reflexes in infants in the first months of life. *Acta Paediatrica*, 1961, *50*, 565–576.

Papousek, H. Experimental studies of appetitional behavior in human newborns and infants. In H. W. Stevenson, E. H. Hess, & H. L. Rheingold (Eds.), *Early behavior*. New York: Wiley, 1967.

Papousek, H. Elaborations of conditioned headturning. Paper presented at the meeting of the XIX International Congress of Psychology, London, 1969.

Piaget, J. *The origins of intelligence in children*. New York: International Universities Press, 1952.

Piaget, J. *Psychology of intelligence*. New York: Littlefield, Adams, 1960.

Polikanina, R. I. The relation between autonomic and somatic components in the development of the conditioned reflex in premature infants. *Pavlvo Journal of Higher Nervous Activity*, 1961, *11*, 51–58.

Salapatek, P. Visual scanning of geometric figures by the human newborn. *Journal of Comparative and Physiological Psychology*, 1968, *66*, 247–248.

Salapatek, P., & Kessen, W. Visual scanning of triangles in the human newborn. *Journal of Experimental Child Psychology*, 1966, *3*, 155–167.

Sameroff, A. J. Nonnutritive sucking in newborns under visual and auditory stimulation. *Child Development*, 1967, *38*, 443–452.

Sameroff, A. J. The components of sucking in the human newborn. *Journal of Experimental Child Psychology*, 1968, *6*, 607–623.

Sameroff, A. J. Respiration and sucking as components of the orienting reaction in newborns. *Psychophysiology*, 1970, *7*, 213–222.

Schachter, J., Williams, T. A., Khachaturian, Z., Tobin, M., & Druger, R. The multiphasic heart rate response to auditory clicks in neonates. Paper presented at the meeting of the Society for Psychophysiological Research, Washington, D. C., 1968.

Scheerer, M. Cognitive theory. In G. Lindzey (Ed.), *Handbook of social psychology*. Vol. 1. Cambridge, Mass.: Addison-Wesley, 1954.

Schulman, C. A. Effects of auditory stimulus on heartrate in high-risk and low-risk premature infants as a function of state. Paper presented at the meeting of the Eastern Psychological Association, Washington, D. C., April 1968.

Seligman, M. E. P. On the generality of the laws of learning. *Psychological Review*, 1970, *77*, 406–418.

Semb, G., & Lipsitt, L. P. The effects of acoustic stimulation on cessation and initiation of nonnutritive sucking in neonates. *Journal of Experimental Child Psychology*, 1968, *6*, 585–597.

Siqueland, E. R. Reinforcement patterns and extinction in human newborns. *Journal of Experimental Child Psychology*, 1968, *6*, 431–442.

Siqueland, E. R., & Lipsitt, L. P. Conditioned head-turning behavior in newborns. *Journal of Experimental Child Psychology*, 1966, *3*, 356–376.

Skinner, B. F. *Verbal behavior*. New York: Appleton, 1957.

Sokolov, Ye. N. *Perception and the conditioned reflex*. New York: Macmillan, 1963.

Spelt, D. K. The conditioning of the human fetus in utero. *Journal of Experimental Psychology*, 1948, *38*, 338–346.

Stechler, G., Bradford, S., & Levy, H. Attention in the newborn: Effect on motility and skin potential. *Science*, 1966, *151*, 1246–1248.

Steinschneider, A. Sound intensity and respiratory responses in the neonate. *Psychosomatic Medicine*, 1968, *30*, 534–541.

Stubbs, E. M. The effect of the factor of duration, intensity, and pitch of sound stimuli on the responses of newborn infants. *University of Iowa Studies in Child Welfare*, 1934, *9*(4), 75–135.

Turkewitz, G., Moreau, T., & Birch, H. G. Head position and receptor organization in the human neonate. *Journal of Experimental Child Psychology*, 1966, *4*, 169–177.

Werner, H. The concept of development from a comparative and organismic view. In D. B. Harris (Ed.), *The concept of development*. Minneapolis: University of Minnesota Press, 1957.

White, B. L., Castle, P., & Held, R. Observations on the development of visually-directed reaching. *Child Development*, 1964, *35*, 349–364.

Wickens, D. D., & Wickens, C. A study of conditioning in the neonate. *Journal of Experimental Psychology*, 1940, *25*, 94–102.

Wolff, P. H. The causes, controls, and organization of behavior in the neonate. *Psychological Issues*, 1966, *5*(1, Whole No. 17).

11. CRITICAL PERIODS, STIMULUS INPUT, AND EMOTIONAL REACTIVITY

A Theory of Infantile Stimulation[1]

VICTOR H. DENENBERG[2]

Experiments, using rats and mice, do not support the critical period hypothesis that there are certain limited time periods in infancy during which a particular class of stimuli will have profound effects upon subsequent behavior. Where findings are consistent with the hypothesis, further research has shown that the "critical period" is a complex function of amount of infantile stimulation. The central hypothesis of this paper is that amount of stimulus input in infancy acts to reduce emotional reactivity in a monotonic fashion. From this it follows that an inverted U function should be obtained between amount of infantile stimulation and adult performance for tasks involving some form of noxious element and which are of "moderate" difficulty. For tasks which are "easy" or "difficult," the relationships between performance in adulthood and infantile stimulation should be monotonic, though opposite in slope. Data supporting this theory are discussed.

This paper has two purposes. The first is to question certain aspects of the critical period hypothesis (Scott, 1958, 1962 [14]). The second, more important, purpose is to develop a somewhat different hypothesis: that stimulation in infancy reduces the organism's emotional reactivity; this reduction is a monotonic function of amount of stimulus input. In turn, this hypothesized change in emotional reactivity offers a useful mechanism by which one can explain a number of disparate and seemingly unrelated changes in adult performance.

The data to be considered, and the generalizations therefrom, come specifically from research with rats and mice which have received various forms of stimulation between birth and weaning. For more general reviews of

[1] Much of the research described in this paper was supported, in part, by Grant M-1753 from the National Institute of Mental Health, National Institutes of Health, United States Public Health Service, and by several grants from the Purdue Research Foundation.

[2] It is a pleasure to acknowledge the contributions of Mark W. Stephens, whose incisive comments, both conceptual and editorial, have significantly improved this paper.

From *Psychological Review*, 1964, *71*, 335–351. Copyright 1964 by the American Psychological Association. Reprinted by permission of the author and the publisher.

early experience research and the critical period hypothesis see Denenberg (1962b) and Scott (1962).

Critical Periods

Recently Scott (1962) has suggested that there are three major kinds of critical period phenomena: one for the formation of basic social relationships, a second concerned with optimal periods for learning, and a third involving infantile stimulation. This discussion is concerned only with the last of these.

There are at least two different ways in which the critical period hypothesis has been interpreted. One is that the same physical stimulation at different ages has different effects upon S; this says, simply, that S's age is an important parameter and can scarcely be questioned. The second interpretation is that there are certain *limited* time periods in development during which a particular class of stimuli will have particularly profound effects and that the same stimulation before or after this interval will have little, if any, effect upon the developing organism. This approach stems directly from the embryological meaning of critical periods, and it is in this context that Scott (1958, 1962; Scott

& Marston, 1950; Williams & Scott, 1953) has developed and described the critical period hypothesis. The term, critical period, when used in this paper, will refer to this second interpretation.

Operationally, a test of the critical period hypothesis requires several experimental groups which receive the same stimulation at different ages and a control group which does not receive the stimulation at all. If some of the experimental groups do not differ from the control while others do, this may be construed as evidence supporting the critical period hypothesis. (On the other hand, any significant differences among the experimental groups are support for the first meaning of the hypothesis.)

Although it is obvious that the age at which S is stimulated in an important parameter, when one carefully examines experiments investigating critical periods in infancy in rats and mice, there is little evidence supporting the hypothesis that stimulation must occur only during certain delimited time intervals to affect the organism's subsequent behavior. Interestingly, the only unequivocal demonstrations of critical periods are to be found in papers which used physiological, rather than behavioral, endpoints (Bell, Reisner, & Linn, 1961; Levine & Lewis, 1959a).

The general conclusion noted above might not be apparent from a casual inspection of the literature. There are several studies which, if taken in isolation, appear to support the hypothesis. For example, two early experiments on critical periods (Denenberg, 1958, 1960) seemed to support the concept. In the first study mice initially conditioned between 20 and 40 days of age had essentially the same reconditioning scores at 50 days, and all these scores were significantly higher than either a 50-day control group or a group which was initially conditioned at 16 days. These data suggested a critical period around 20 days of age such that conditioning experience prior to that date did not affect subsequent reconditioning performance; experience after that date appeared to have the same effect upon reconditioning, regardless of the original age of conditioning or the actual amount of conditioning. A subsequent study with older Ss (Denenberg, 1960)

established that it was indeed the age of the animals rather than the time interval between conditioning and reconditioning which mediated the effects.[3]

However, another study with the mouse, though not directly comparable to the two above, disclosed some complexities concerning critical period phenomena which cast doubt on the degree of generality of the hypothesis. Denenberg and Bell (1960) studied avoidance learning in adulthood as a joint function of age of infantile stimulation (i.e., critical periods), intensity of stimulation in infancy, and intensity of electric shock during adult performance. These latter two parameters had been held constant in prior research. Analyses of the learning data revealed that critical periods were not significant as a main effect; but the Periods × Adult Shock and the Periods × Adult Shock × Infantile Stimulation interactions were significant. The disturbing thing was that the age variable (i.e., critical periods) was dependent upon the particular level of stimulation used in the adult learning task. By the selection of certain combinations of infantile stimulation levels and adult shock levels one could "prove" that stimulation during certain "critical periods" could facilitate, have no effect, or interfere with avoidance learning in adulthood. The phenomena, then, appear to be far more complex than previously recognized in the generalizations afforded by the critical period hypothesis.

These data suggest that any single "critical period" is, at least in part, dependent upon the parameter of stimulus intensity. Thus, Denenberg's prior studies (1958, 1960) should be looked upon with caution since different shock levels may have yielded very different findings.

Critical period research with the rat has generally used the procedure called *handling* rather than shock. This consists of removing the

[3] A number of investigators have also shown, with the rat, that stimulation in infancy has different consequences as compared to equivalent stimulation in adulthood. (These include handling in infancy and early adulthood, Levine, 1956; raising rats in groups of 6 or 12 during infancy or adulthood, Seitz, 1954; subjecting rats to handling and auditory stimulation in infancy and adulthood, Spence & Maher, 1962a; and temporarily blinding or deafening rats in infancy or later life, Wolf, 1943.)

pups from the home cage, and placing the young into containers (e.g., cans containing wood shavings, small wooden compartments, grid-floored boxes). The pups are left there for a short duration (generally 2 to 3 minutes though some *E*s have used intervals of 8 minutes or longer) and are then returned to the home cage. This is generally done once a day for different prescribed periods.

In a series of experiments Denenberg and Karas (1960, 1961) found that rats handled for the first 10 days of life were superior with respect to body weight, avoidance learning, and survival capability to ones handled during the second 10 days. In general, both 10-day groups were superior to *S*s which had been handled for 20 days in infancy.

These data suggested that it might be possible to handle *S*s for fewer than 10 days and possibly isolate specific critical periods related to different dependent variables. Therefore Denenberg (1962a) handled different groups of rats for 3- or 5-day intervals at different ages during the first 10 days of life. Measures of body weight, avoidance learning behavior, and survival time, with one exception, did *not* support the critical period hypothesis. The exception was that *S*s handled for the first 5 days of life were not significantly better than controls in avoidance learning while *S*s handled on Days 6–10 were superior to controls and equal to *S*s handled on Days 1–10.

Though the avoidance learning findings are compatible with the critical period hypothesis, another possibility, based upon the Denenberg and Bell mouse study, is that the failure to modify avoidance learning by handling during the first 5 days was because the stimulation induced by handling was not sufficiently intense to affect *S*. Denenberg and Kline (1964) tested this hypothesis by giving different groups of rats electric shock (0.2 milliampere) on Days 1–5, 1–3, 3–5, 2, or 4. The shocked groups (with the exception of the group shocked only on Day 2) were significantly better in avoidance learning than a nondisturbed control group.

In conclusion, experimental research with the mouse and rat investigating stimulation between birth and weaning has established that the critical period hypothesis is not sufficient to

account for the findings. In instances where the data are consistent with the hypothesis further study has found that the "critical period" is a complex function of the parameter of stimulus intensity. Research to date indicates that, for the rat and mouse at least, there may be as many "critical periods" as there are combinations of independent variable parameters and dependent variable measures (Denenberg, 1962a). Meyers (1962) and Lindholm (1962) have recently arrived at a similar conclusion.

Then should the term "critical periods" be abandoned when discussing the effects of infantile stimulation? Not at the present time, certainly. The concept has had, and will continue to have, great heuristic value. However, conclusions concerning critical periods must be limited to the particular experimental operations involved until enough empirical evidence has been obtained to indicate the limits of generalization. In terms of current research strategy it appears more reasonable to study the functional relationships among various classes of independent and dependent variables between birth and weaning than to design experiments which try to isolate critical periods during this crucial stage of development.

Theory of Infantile Stimulation and Adult Performance

One approach to the problem of understanding the effects of stimulation in infancy is by means of the critical period hypothesis. A different approach is to examine the diverse research findings to see if any common factor can be discerned. Such an examination of the literature leads to the conclusion that stimulation administered between birth and weaning brings about a reduction in "emotional reactivity." Furthermore, the greater the stimulation in infancy, the less emotional *S* will be in adulthood. The central hypothesis of this paper is that *emotional reactivity is reduced as a monotonic function of amount of stimulus input in infancy*.

Before discussing this hypothesis in detail, and showing some of its consequences, it is first necessary to define "emotional reactivity" and show that this intervening variable is modified by stimulation in infancy. This will be done by showing, on the stimulus side, that different methods of stimulating S in infancy have similar consequences in adulthood; and, on the response side, by showing that different operational measures of emotional reactivity yield internally consistent results (Miller, 1959). The two most common methods of stimulating Ss in infancy have been handling and shocking. Emotional reactivity has been measured by procedures as divergent as open-field testing, consummatory behavior, behavior in a learning situation, and behavior when given an opportunity to emerge from the home cage.

Handling and Emotional Reactivity

Open-Field Behavior. In two experiments Denenberg and Morton (1962a) found that rats handled daily between birth and weaning were significantly more active and had a significantly smaller defecation rate than nonhandled controls. Similar findings were obtained by Denenberg and Whimbey (1963). Rats handled for the first 10 or 20 days of life were found to be significantly more active and to defecate significantly less than nonhandled controls (Denenberg, Morton, Kline, & Grota, 1962). In a study relating infantile stimulation to age of testing Denenberg and Smith (1963) handled or shocked rats during the second 10 days of life and tested independent groups at 50, 100, 150, or 200 days of age. Both groups which received stimulation in infancy were significantly more active than the controls and had a significantly lower defecation percentage. The open-field test was also used by Schaefer (1963), but his index of emotionality was the amount of time spent crouching during the 2 minutes after presentation of a sharp click. Handled Ss crouched significantly less than nonhandled controls.

Consummatory Behavior. Levine (1957, 1958) handled, shocked, or did not disturb rats between birth and weaning. When adult, the Ss were deprived of water for 18 hours and then given the opportunity to drink. Levine (1957),

hypothesized that since deprivation constitutes a novel internal stimulus complex for nonhandled Ss, the novelty should result in greater emotional disturbance and produce reduced water consumption following a period of deprivation [p. 609].

In both experiments handled and shocked Ss consumed significantly more water than nondisturbed controls. In a similar type of experiment Spence and Maher (1962a) also found that handled Ss consumed significantly more water than controls.

Emergence-from-Cage Behavior. Hunt and Otis (1963) exposed their experimental rats to a variety of stimulus conditions in infancy, including handling. In their first two experiments their measure of emotionality was a "timidity" test. The home cage of an S which had been deprived of food and water for 22 hours was placed on an open alley upon which were placed pellets of food. Handled Ss were found to emerge significantly further into the runway than nondisturbed controls. In their third experiment they recorded S's behavior when E opened the cage door to attach a plastic milk cup to it, scoring S with respect to the degree of "boldness" manifested. Subjects not disturbed in infancy were found to be significantly more timid than those receiving stimulation in infancy.

Behavior in a Learning Situation. Several indexes of emotional behavior were recorded by Levine (1956) while testing handled and nonhandled Ss for avoidance learning. These were defecation and activity during habituation trials, percentage of Ss freezing after the first shock trial, and the number of trials on which Ss showed freezing behavior. On all four measures nonhandled controls were found to be significantly more emotional than Ss handled in infancy.

Electric Shock and Emotional Reactivity

Open-Field Behavior. Subjects receiving 0.25 milliampere of current for 3 minutes daily on Days 11–20 were significantly more active and defecated significantly less than nondisturbed controls when tested at 50, 100, 150, or 200 days of age (Denenberg & Smith, 1963). Rats given 3 minutes of either 0.5 milliampere or 0.8 milliampere shock on Day 4 of life were significantly more active than Ss receiving the same stimulation on Day 2; the latter group did not differ from nondisturbed controls (Kline & Denenberg, unpublished). The effect of electric shock is measurable at weaning as well. Rats given 30 seconds of 0.2 milliampere current on Days 1 and 2 of life were significantly less emotional than nondisturbed controls at the time of weaning as measured by time to emerge into the open field and activity in the field (Denenberg, Carlson, & Stephens, 1962).

Consummatory Behavior. Rat pups were given 3 minutes of electrical stimulation (variable current from 0.10 milliampere to 0.37 milliampere, disregarding S's resistance) from Day 1 through Day 20. These Ss consumed significantly more water in adulthood than nondisturbed controls; the findings were replicated in a second experiment (Levine, 1957, 1958). A similar finding was obtained by Lindholm (1962) who shocked rats for the first 10 days, the second 10 days, the first 20 days of life, and did not disturb a control group. No specified shock level was used; instead, the shock was set high enough to make the Ss move and squeal in the apparatus. The intensity of the shock was increased as S matured. When adult, the Ss were deprived of water for 24 hours and then given an opportunity to drink. The Ss shocked in infancy took significantly less time to initiate drinking and consumed significantly more water than the nondisturbed group. A subsequent analysis determined that the differences in consummatory behavior could all be attributed to the latency to approach the water tubes.

Stimulus Input and Emotional Reactivity: The Monotonicity Hypothesis

The data summarized above are sufficient to justify the conclusion that stimulation in infancy will result in a reduction in emotional reactivity in adulthood. It remains to be demonstrated that a monotonic relationship obtains between amount of stimulus input in infancy and emotional reactivity. Two experiments have explicitly tested this hypothesis (Denenberg, Carlson, & Stephens, 1962; Denenberg & Smith, 1963). In addition, there are three other experiments in the literature which offer support for the hypothesis (Levine, 1957, 1958; Lindholm, 1962).

Amount of stimulus input was varied by Denenberg and his co-workers by handling rats for 0 (control), 10, or 20 days in infancy. In adult open-field testing the controls had the highest defecation rate while the group handled for 20 days had the lowest rate; all differences were significant. In the second study (Denenberg & Smith, 1963) one group of rats received 3 minutes of shock daily from Day 11 through Day 20, a second group was placed on the unelectrified grid (handled group), and a third group was not disturbed. Figure 11–1 shows the percentage of Ss in each group defecating before and after adult avoidance learning training. The greater the stimulus input in infancy, the smaller (significantly) was the percentage of defecators in adulthood. Furthermore, the shocked Ss were the only ones whose defecation percentage was significantly reduced following avoidance learning training.

Levine (1957, 1958) compared water consumption following 18 hours of thirst for Ss which had been shocked, handled, or not

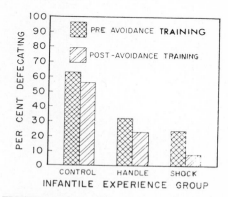

FIGURE 11–1. Percentage of rats defecating before and after avoidance learning as a function of stimulation (from Denenberg & Smith, 1963).

disturbed in infancy. In both experiments the shocked *S*s consumed the most water, followed by the handled group, with the controls consuming the least. The difference between shocked and handled *S*s approached significance in the first study ($p < .10$) and was significant in the second study; nonhandled controls consumed significantly less than either experimental group in both studies.

In the Lindholm (1962) experiment rats were shocked for the first 10 days of life, the second 10 days, or the first 20 days, while a control group was not disturbed (his postweaning experimental group is not pertinent to this discussion). Consummatory behavior following 24 hours of thirst found that the controls had the greatest latency and consumed the least amount of water, followed by the two 10-day groups, with the 20-day group having the shortest latency and ingesting the greatest amount of water.

To summarize: Stimulus input in infancy has been varied by number of days of handling (0, 10, 20) (Denenberg *et al.*, 1962), number of days of shock (0, 10, 20) (Lindholm, 1962), and form of stimulation (nondisturbed controls, handled, shocked) (Denenberg & Smith, 1963; Levine, 1957, 1958). Emotional reactivity has been measured by open-field behavior and consummatory behavior. In each instance the greater the amount of stimulus input in infancy

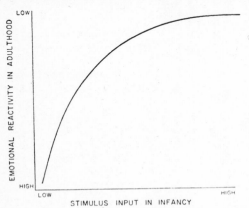

FIGURE   11–2. Theoretical   curve   relating stimulus input in infancy to emotionality in adulthood.

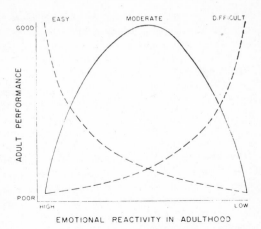

FIGURE 11–3. Theoretical relationship between performance in adulthood and emotionality level for tasks of varying degrees of difficulty.

the less was the level of *S*'s emotional reactivity in adulthood. Figure 11–2 presents an idealized curve showing this theoretical relationship. The negatively accelerated form of the curve is suggested by the findings of the five experiments cited above. In each instance the greatest change in behavior occurred between the control group and the group receiving the intermediate amount of stimulation.

Relationship between Emotional Reactivity and Adult Performance

When one examines the dependent variables used in studies of infantile stimulation, it is apparent that many of them contain some form of noxious element (avoidance learning, underwater swimming, thirst, starvation). Obviously, then, *S*'s emotionality or level of arousal will have a significant effect upon his performance in such tasks. It is reasonable to expect that there will be an optimal level of emotionality for efficient performance. As one moves away from this optimal level, performance should drop off, thus resulting in an inverted ∪ function (cf. Hebb, 1955).

However, another parameter is needed. The Yerkes-Dodson Law (Broadhurst, 1957) posits that the optimal level of motivation for a task decreases as task difficulty increases. Assuming that the more emotional S is more motivated, it follows that highly emotional Ss should have the best performance when the level of task difficulty is quite low while the least emotional Ss should be the best performers when the task is very difficult (Broadhurst, 1957; Karas & Denenberg, 1961). In both of these instances the relationship between performance and emotionality should be monotonic, though opposite in slope. It is only when a task is of "moderate" difficulty that one should expect to obtain the nonmonotonic inverted ∪ function. Figure 11–3 presents the theoretical relationship between adult performance and S's emotionality for tasks of different levels of difficulty.[4]

Some Relationships between Stimulus Input in Infancy and Adult Performance

A number of experiments have been carried out, the results of which are consistent with the predictions made by the theory depicted in Figures 11–2 and 11–3. For example, Karas and Denenberg (1961) explicitly tested the theory by assuming that the greater the number of days of handling in infancy, the greater the reduction in emotional reactivity in adulthood. In addition, they assumed that "spaced" handling would result in greater emotional reduction than "massed" handling. Experimental rats were space or mass handled for 10 or 20 days while controls were not disturbed. The criterion task was an underwater discrimination Y maze similar to the one used by Broadhurst (1957) who had shown that maze performance was related to S's level of emotionality. The discrimination task was an "easy" one (86.6 percent correct choices, highly comparable to Broadhurst's value of 86.4 percent errorless trials on his "easy" task), thus leading to the deduction that the most emotional Ss should exhibit the best performance with a monotonic

decline in performance as emotional reactivity decreased (see Figure 11–3). Analysis of the swimming time scores found that the rank order of the five groups was as predicted, thus confirming the hypotheses.

Several studies have found an inverted ∪ relationship between amount of stimulation in infancy and later performance. In the experiments by Denenberg (1962a) and Denenberg and Karas (1960, 1961) rat pups were handled for 0 (controls), 3, 5, 10, or 20 days in infancy. One can average the data for the 3-day, 5-day, and 10-day groups (irrespective of age of stimulation), add in the findings of the control and 20-day groups, and plot the functional relationship between number of days of handling in infancy and later performance. The averaging procedure acts to partially balance out the age of stimulation. One can, in other words, disregard "critical periods" between birth and weaning and examine amount of stimulation within that period. Such an analysis is shown in Figure 11–4 for 21- and 69-day body weight, avoidance learning, and survival time (Denenberg, 1962a). The general function of these data may be described by an inverted ∪ curve. Both too much and too little handling led to less than optimal performance. The optimal amount of handling varied with different dependent variables.

This same general function was obtained when electric shock was used to stimulate Ss in infancy. Rats were shocked on the second or fourth day of life using 0.2 milliampere, 0.5 milliampere, or 0.8 milliampere electricity; one group of controls was handled, another not disturbed (Denenberg & Kline, 1964; Kline & Denenberg, 1964). The Ss were given avoidance learning training between 60 and 69 days of age. Figure 11–5 presents the relationship between intensity of stimulation in infancy and adult learning. The inverted ∪ function is clearly present.

Evidence that this inverted ∪ function has some degree of interspecies generality is seen in Figures 11–6 and 11–7, which show the performance of mice. Figure 11–6 summarizes an experiment by Denenberg (1959) in which Ss were given classical buzzer-shock conditioning

---

[4]Still another parameter which may be relevant is rate of development. Denenberg and Karas (1959), in comparing the effects of handling upon the rat and mouse, point out that the mouse is a more rapidly developing organism and they suggest the hypothesis that the more rapid an organism's development, the greater the effect of infantile experience.

at 25 days under 0.2 milliampere, 0.5 milliampere, or 0.8 milliampere shock. At 50 days they were taken to an extinction criterion, split into thirds, and reconditioned under 0.2, 0.5, or 0.8 milliampere shock. The adult reconditioning data are plotted as a function of shock level at 25 days. The inverted ∪ function adequately describes all three curves.

Bell and Denenberg (1963) gave mice 0.1 milliampere, 0.3 milliampere, or 0.5 mil-

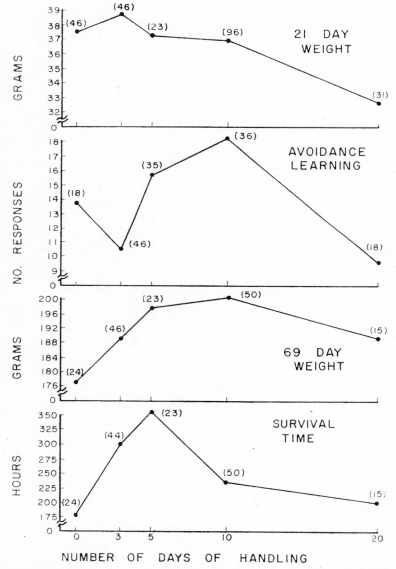

FIGURE 11–4. 21-day body weight, avoidance learning, 69-day body weight, and survival time in rats as a function of number of days of handling in infancy. (Numbers in parentheses indicate the N per point, from Denenberg, 1962a.)

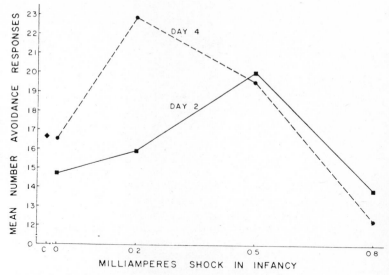

FIGURE 11–5. Number of avoidance learning responses in rats as a function of infantile shock intensity on Day 2 or Day 4 (from Kline & Denenberg, 1964).

liampere shock in infancy, handled other groups (0.0 milliampere) and did not disturb still others. Adult avoidance learning performance, plotted in Figure 11–7, again reveals the inverted U function.

The relationship between stimulus input in infancy and adult performance aids in interpreting other data. For example, Levine, Chevalier, and Korchin (1956) found that rats handled for the first 20 days of life performed best in an adult avoidance learning task, followed by *S*s which had been handled and

shocked, with nonhandled controls the poorest learners. These data exhibit a rough inverted U function with the group receiving the intermediate amount of stimulation exhibiting the best performance.

The theory depicted in Figures 11–2 and 11–3 leads to the prediction that *S*s with the greatest amount of stimulus input in infancy should have the best performance when the task is quite difficult. There are, as yet, no data relevant to this prediction.

It should be possible to generalize the

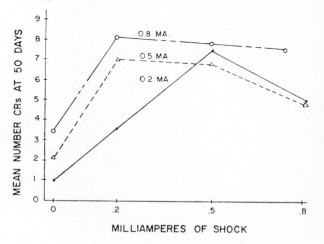

FIGURE 11–6. 50-day conditioning scores in mice for three shock levels as a function of infantile shock intensity (from Denenberg, 1959).

FIGURE 11-7. Number of avoidance responses in mice as a function of stimulation in infancy. (C: nonstimulated controls; O: handled, nonshocked;) 0.1, 0.3, 0.5: milliamperes of shock, from Bell & Denenberg, 1963.)

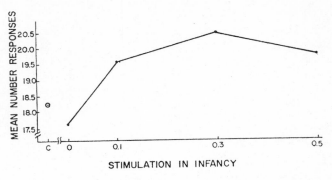

STIMULATION IN INFANCY

parameter of "task difficulty" beyond the usual learning context. For example, the inverted U curves for body weight and survival time in Figure 11-4 were obtained after Ss had undergone avoidance learning training. For Ss which did *not* receive avoidance training, the controls lived longest, followed by Ss handled for 10 days, with the 20-day group dying earliest. In other words, those data parallel the "easy" curve in Figure 11-3 while the results of the groups which had avoidance training follow along the curve of the "moderate" group. Since avoidance learning has been shown to be a stressor (Brady, Porter, Conrad, & Mason, 1958; Denenberg & Karas, 1961), this suggests the hypothesis that stress experience, prior to a terminal stress, may act in a manner similar to the task difficulty parameter. This leads to the interesting prediction that Ss subjected to a severe, but nonlethal stress, would be best able to survive a subsequent lethal stress, if they had received a considerable amount of stimulation in infancy.

It is pertinent to ask here about the relationship between stimulation in infancy and performance on a task which minimizes the emotional component. One would expect little or no relationship between infantile stimulation and later behavior. This is exactly what Denenberg and Morton (1962b) found in a series of three experiments. Handling in infancy did not have any effect upon problem-solving behavior as measured by the Hebb-Williams maze test. The authors concluded that,

These findings suggest that preweaning stimulation such as shock and handling affects emotional

processes but does not have any direct effect upon perceptual or problem-solving behavior [p. 1098].

Schaefer (1963) has obtained similar results.

Similarly, Spence and Maher (1962b) suggested that the obtained differences in learning performance between Ss stimulated in infancy and controls may be a function of emotional rather than learning factors. Their experiment on this point, while equivocal, does offer some support for this position.

Comparisons with Bovard's Theory

Though Bovard's (1958) theory is concerned with the effects of handling upon viability, there are certain points of agreement and disagreement to be noted between his position and the one presented here. The major point of disagreement is that Bovard combines the results of preweaning and postweaning handling (the term "gentling" has been commonly used to describe the procedure of manually manipulating rodents postweaning), while this theory has been limited to preweaning stimulation. There are logical and empirical reasons for making such a distinction. The postweaning rat is a very different organism, behaviorally and biologically, from the preweaning animal, and it is not logical to assume that stimulation administered to the immature, recently born rat has the same consequences as the same stimulation administered to a weanling. The experiments cited in Footnote 3 offer general support for this conclusion. Clear evidence that handling and electric shock after weaning do not affect rats in the same manner as handling and shock before weaning can be found in the monograph by Brookshire, Littman, and Stewart (1961).

A paper directly relevant to this issue is the one by Levine and Otis (1958). They either handled or gentled rats before or after weaning; a control group was not disturbed. Pre-weaning handling or gentling had the same effect of significantly increasing body weight and survival rate while postweaning handling or gentling had no significant effect, compared to the control group. In addition to showing that preweaning stimulation has different consequences from postweaning stimulation, the Levine and Otis (1958) paper failed to substantiate Weininger's (1953, 1956) results which Bovard used as part of the empirical base for his theory. Ader (1959) and J. H. Scott (1955) have also failed to replicate Weininger's findings. Even the Hammett (1922) reference cited by Bovard is not supportive of his position, since the experimental data reported in that paper were not concerned with the effects of gentling rats. Hammett does refer back to his 1921 paper, and it is that portion of Hammett's paper which Bovard refers to in his reference to Hammett. Several other researchers have also cited the Hammett (1921) paper when discussing the positive effects of postweaning gentling. This is most interesting, since Hammett presents absolutely no data supporting such a conclusion. Hammett (1921) carried out five experiments concerning the effects of parathyroidectomy or thyroidectomy upon survival. The first three studies do not permit a valid evaluation of the effects of gentling because of lack of appropriate controls (though the experiments were valid for Hammett's purposes). The fourth and fifth experiments (see Hammett, 1921, p. 201) can be used to evaluate the effects of gentling since Hammett shifted the rats at weaning from one colony room to the other, thus balancing environmental conditions for the two different stocks of animals. The only significant effect in the fourth experiment was that the two colony stocks differed in genetic makeup; gentling failed to have any effect. And the fifth experiment contradicts this: all rats, regardless of genetic stock or whether or not they were gentled, survived the parathyroidectomy operation. One can only conclude that those who have cited Hammett's work as proof that gentling enhances survival ability have allowed their fertile imagination to inhibit their reading comprehension. All these experiments suggest that the postweaning handling (or gentling) phenomenon is rather tenuous with respect to modification of the rat's physiology.

There is some degree of agreement between Bovard's theory and the present one concerning preweaning stimulation. In so far as behavioral indices of emotional reactivity correlate with what Bovard (1958) calls stress, then the two theories are in agreement that "early [preweaning] handling raises the threshold for response to stress [p. 259]." Bovard, however, does not believe that handling is stressful while Levine (1956) and Denenberg (1959) have taken the opposite position. Bovard believes that "early stress lowers resistance to later stress [p. 260]." Since electric shock—a stimulus typically considered to be stressful—and handling have similar functional properties *vis à vis* emotional reactivity, the Levine and Denenberg position appears to be on firmer ground. Further evidence that stressful stimulation in infancy can have beneficial results, rather than the deleterious results predicted by Bovard, is discussed in the next section.

Discussion

The hypothesis that emotionality decreases as a monotonic function of stimulus input may not appear reasonable at first glance because of our knowledge of conditioned fears, traumatic experiences in childhood, etc. It must be emphasized that this hypothesis is based upon, and is restricted to, data obtained on rodents which have been stimulated prior to weaning. Weaning has been used as a criterion point, not because of any clinical implications concerning mother-young separation, but because all of S's senses are functioning by this time and because it is only after weaning that there is any evidence of long-term retention of a learned fear response (Campbell & Campbell, 1962; Denenberg, 1958, 1959; Lindholm, 1962).

Furthermore, the consequences of handling or electric shock after weaning have been shown to be very different from their effects prior to weaning (Brookshire, Littman, & Stewart, 1961).

Scott (1962) has made a similar suggestion and has indicated that the transition point may occur at about 16 days of age, when the eyes open. Up to that age the critical factor mediating infantile stimulation is hypothesized by Scott to be the adrenal cortical stress mechanism while the psychological process of reduction of fear through familiarity is presumed to predominate between 17 days when the eyes open and 30 days.

The traditional assumption that traumatic experiences in infancy must inevitably have deleterious effects in later life is clearly not consonant with many of the studies cited above. Several other experiments, in fact, may also be noted which contradict this classical assumption. Baron, Brookshire, and Littman (1957) found that rats given 1.25 milliamperes of electric current continuously for 3 minutes on Days 20 and 21 were better escape and avoidance learners in adulthood than controls. Infant rats either placed on a laboratory shaker which oscillated 180 times per minute or shocked with 0.1 milliampere electricity were found to exhibit earlier maturation of the adrenal ascorbic acid depletion response to stress (Levine & Lewis, 1959b). Using the same dependent variable Schaefer, Weingarten, and Towne (1962) showed that placing rat pups into a refrigerator at 7° to 10° Centigrade also resulted in earlier maturation of the adrenal responses. Finally, Werboff and Havlena (1963) induced febrile convulsions in 3-day old rats by means of microwave diathermy. The Ss so treated weighed significantly more at weaning and were significantly more resistant to audio-genic seizures.

Certain parallels may be noted between this theory and the arousal or activation theories of Hebb (1955), Duffy (1957), and Malmo (1959). All the theories are concerned with the intensity dimension of stimulation or arousal, and the inverted ∪ function relating the intensity dimension to performance is common to all. The theory proposed here contributes to general arousal theory in two ways. First, intensity of infantile stimulation is specifically implicated as a major parameter affecting later differences in "chronic" or general level of arousal. Brookshire et al. (1961) have isolated what may be a similar phenomenon with the postweaning rat. They suggest that their "pure shock" residual factor of shock trauma may act to modify S's arousal level. The second contribution is a methodological one: the techniques used in infantile stimulation are also procedures for experimentally generating individual differences in chronic arousal level. This opens up a new avenue of attack for those interested in individual differences in arousal level.

Though the proposed theory does account for a considerable number of experimental findings, contrary data are to be noted. For example, Spence and Maher (1962a) subjected rats to intense auditory stimulation between birth and weaning, handled a second group but did not give them auditory stimulation, moved the cages of a third group, and did not disturb a fourth group. Using water consumption as their index of emotionality no differences were found among the experimental groups though the stimulated Ss consumed significantly more water than the undisturbed controls. No reason can be suggested to account for the failure to find a monotonic relationship between stimulus intensity in infancy and consummatory behavior.

Finally, this theory is not meant to be a substitute for the critical period hypothesis. In fact, the functional relationships are most clearly seen when Ss are stimulated at different ages (but for the same number of days) and the data averaged so that age of stimulation is equated. Ultimately, any general theory of infantile stimulation will have to account for both age of stimulation and stimulus input and will have to relate these to the psychology and biochemistry of ontogeny (Levine, 1962).

REFERENCES

Ader, R. The effects of early experience on subsequent emotionality and resistance to stress. *Psychol. Monogr.*, 1959, *73*, 2 (Whole No. 472).

Baron, A., K. H. Brookshire, and R. A. Littman. Effects of infantile and adult shock-trauma upon learning in the adult white rat. *J. Comp. Physiol. Psychol.*, 1957, *50*, 530–534.

Bell, R. W., and V. H. Denenberg. The interrelationships of shock and critical periods in infancy as they affect adult learning and activity. *Anim. Behav.*, 1963, *11*, 21–27.

Bell, R. W., G. Reisner, and T. Linn. Recovery from electroconvulsive shock as a function of infantile stimulation. *Science*, 1961, *133*, 1428.

Bovard, E. W. The effects of early handling on viability of the albino rat. *Psychol. Rev.*, 1958, *65*, 257–271.

Brady, J. V., R. W. Porter, D. G. Conrad, and J. W. Mason. Avoidance behavior and the development of gastroduodenal ulcers. *J. exp. Anal. Behav.*, 1958, *1*, 69–73.

Broadhurst, P. L. Emotionality and the Yerkes-Dodson law. *J. exp. Psychol.*, 1957, *54*, 345–352.

Brookshire, K. H., R. A. Littman, and C. N. Stewart. Residue of shock-trauma in the white rat: A three-factor theory. *Psychol. Monogr.*, 1961, *75* (10), (Whole No. 514).

Campbell, B. A., and E. H. Campbell. Retention and extinction of learned fear in infant and adult rats. *J. Comp. Physiol. Psychol.*, 1962, *55*, 1–8.

Denenberg, V. H. Effects of age and early experience upon conditioning in the C57BL/10 mouse. *J. Psychol.*, 1958, *46*, 211–226.

Denenberg, V. H. The interactive effects of infantile and adult shock levels upon learning. *Psychol. Rep.*, 1959, *5*, 357–364.

Denenberg, V. H. A test of the critical period hypothesis and a further study of the relationship between age and conditioning in the C57BL/10 mouse. *J. Genet. Psychol.*, 1960, *97*, 379–384.

Denenberg, V. H. An attempt to isolate critical periods of development in the rat. *J. Comp. Physiol. Psychol.*, 1962, *55*, 813–815. (a)

Denenberg, V. H. The effects of early experience. In E. S. E. Hafez (Ed.), *The behaviour of domestic animals*. London, Baillière, 1962, pp. 109–138. (b)

Denenberg, V. H., and R. W. Bell. Critical periods for the effects of infantile experience on adult learning. *Science*, 1960, *131*, 227–228.

Denenberg, V. H., P. V. Carlson, and M. W. Stephens. Effects of infantile shock upon emotionality at weaning. *J. Comp. Physiol. Psychol.*, 1962, *55*, 819–820.

Denenberg, V. H., and G. G. Karas. Effects of differential handling upon weight gain and mortality in the rat and mouse. *Science*, 1959, *130*, 629–630.

Denenberg, V. H., and G. G. Karas. Interactive effects of age and duration of infantile experience on adult learning. *Psychol. Rep.*, 1960, *7*, 313–322.

Denenberg, V. H., and G. G. Karas. Interactive effects of age and adult experiences upon weight gain and mortality in the rat. *J. Comp. Physiol. Psychol.*, 1961, *54*, 685–689.

Denenberg, V. H., and N. J. Kline. Stimulus intensity *vs.* critical periods: A test of two hypotheses concerning infantile stimulation. *Canad. J. Psychol.*, 1964, *18*, 1–5.

Denenberg, V. H., and J. R. C. Morton. Effects of environmental complexity and social groupings upon modification of emotional behavior. *J. Comp. Physiol. Psychol.*, 1962, *55*, 242–246. (a)

Denenberg, V. H., and J. R. C. Morton. Effects of preweaning and postweaning manipulations upon problem-solving behavior. *J. Comp. Physiol. Psychol.*, 1962, *55*, 1096–1098. (b)

Denenberg, V. H., J. R. C. Morton, N. J. Kline, and L. J. Grota. Effects of duration of infantile stimulation upon emotionality. *Canad. J. Psychol.*, 1962, *16*, 72–76.

Denenberg, V. H., and S. A. Smith. Effects of infantile stimulation and age upon behavior. *J. Comp. Physiol. Psychol.*, 1963, *56*, 307–312.

Denenberg, V. H., and A. E. Whimbey. Infantile stimulation and animal husbandry: A methodological study. *J. comp. physiol. Psychol.*, 1963, *56*, 877–878.

Duffy, E. The psychological significance of the concept of "arousal" or "activation." *Psychol. Bull.*, 1957, *64*, 265–275.

Hammett, F. S. Studies of the thyroid apparatus. I. The stability of the nervous system as a factor in the resistance of the albino rat to the loss of the parathyroid secretion. *Amer. J. Physiol.*, 1921, *56*, 196–204.

Hammett, F. S. Studies of the thyroid apparatus. V. The significance of the comparative mortality rates of parathyroidectomized wild Norway rats and excitable and non-excitable albino rats. *Endocrinology*, 1922, *6*, 221–229.

Hebb, D. O. Drives and the C.N.S. (conceptual nervous system). *Psychol. Rev.*, 1955, *62*, 243–254.

Hunt, H. F., and L. S. Otis. Early "experience" and its effects on later behavioral processes in rats: I. Initial experiments. *Trans. N.Y. Acad. Sci.*, 1963, *25*, 858–870.

Karas, G. G., and V. H. Denenberg. The effects of duration and distribution of infantile experience on adult learning. *J. Comp. Physiol. Psychol.*, 1961, *54*, 170–174.

Kline, N. J., and V. H. Denenberg. Qualitative and quantitative dimensions of infantile stimulation. Unpublished manuscript, Purdue University, Department of Psychology, 1964. (Ditto)

Levine, S. A further study of infantile handling and adult avoidance learning. *J. Pers.*, 1956, *25*, 70–80.

Levine, S. Infantile experience and consummatory behavior in adulthood. *J. Comp. Physiol. Psychol.*, 1957, *50*, 609–612.

Levine, S. Noxious stimulation in infant and adult rats and consummatory behavior. *J. Comp. Physiol. Psychol.*, 1958, *51*, 230–233.

Levine, S. The psychophysiological effects of early stimulation. In E. Bliss (Ed.), *Roots of behavior*. New York: Hoeber, 1962.

Levine, S., J. A. Chevalier, and S. J. Korchin. The effects of early shock and handling on later avoidance learning. *J. Pers.*, 1956, *24*, 475–493.

Levine, S., and G. W. Lewis. Critical periods and the effects of infantile experience on maturation of stress response. *Science*, 1959, *129*, 42–43. (a)

Levine, S., and G. W. Lewis. The relative importance of experimenter contact in an effect produced by extra-stimulation in infancy. *J. Comp. Physiol. Psychol.*, 1959, *52*, 368–369. (b)

Levine, S., and L. S. Otis. The effects of handling before and after weaning on the resistance of albino rats to later deprivation. *Canad. J. Psychol.*, 1958, *12*, 103–108.

Lindholm, B. W. Critical periods and the effects of early shock on later emotional behavior in the white rat. *J. Comp. Physiol. Psychol.*, 1962, *55*, 597–599.

Malmo, R. B. Activation: A neuropsychological dimension. *Psychol. Rev.*, 1959, *66*, 367–386.

Meyers, W. J. Critical period for the facilitation of exploratory behavior by infantile experience. *J. Comp. Physiol. Psychol.*, 1962, *55*, 1099–1101.

Miller, N. E. Liberalization of basic S-R concepts: Extensions to conflict behavior, motivation and social learning. In S. Koch (Ed.), *Psychology, a study of a science*. Vol. 2. New York: McGraw-Hill, 1959, pp. 196–292.

Schaefer, T., Jr. Early "experience" and its effects on later behavioral processes in rats: II. A critical factor in the early handling phenomenon. *Trans. N. Y. Acad. Sci.*, 1963, *25*, 871–889.

Schaefer, T., F. S. Weingarten, and J. C. Towne. Temperature change: The basic variable in the early handling phenomenon? *Science*, 162, *135*, 41–42.

Scott, J. H. Some effects at maturity of gentling, ignoring, or shocking rats during infancy. *J. Abnorm. Soc. Psychol.*, 1955, *51*, 412–414.

Scott, J. P. Critical periods in the development of social behavior in puppies. *Psychosom. Med.*, 1958, *20*, 42–54.

Scott, J. P. Critical periods in behavioral development. *Science,* 1962, *138*, 949–958.

Scott, J. P., and M. V. Marston. Critical periods affecting the development of normal and maladjustive social behavior in puppies. *J. Genet. Psychol.,* 1950, *77*, 25–60.

Seitz, P. F. D. The effects of infantile experiences upon adult behavior in animal subjects: I. Effects of litter size during infancy upon adult behavior in the rat. *Amer. J. Psychiat.,* 1954, *110,* 916–927.

Spence, J. T., and B. A. Maher. Handling and noxious stimulation of the albino rat: I. Effects on subsequent emotionality. *J. Comp. Physiol. Psychol.,* 1962, *55*, 247–251. (a)

Spence, J. T., and B. A. Maher. Handling and noxious stimulation of the albino rat: II. Effects on subsequent performance in a learning situation. *J. Comp. Physiol. Psychol.,* 1962, *55*, 252–255. (b)

Weininger, O. Mortality of albino rats under stress as a function of early handling. *Canad. J. Psychol.,* 1953, *7*, 111–114.

Weininger, O. The effects of early experience on behavior and growth characteristics. *J. Comp. Physiol. Psychol.,* 1956, *49*, 1–9.

Werboff, J., and J. Havlena. Febrile convulsions in infant rats, and later behavior. *Science,* 1963, *142*, 684–685.

Williams, E., and J. P. Scott. The development of social behavior patterns in the mouse, in relation to natural periods. *Behaviour,* Leiden, 1953, *6*, 35–64.

Wolf, A. The dynamics of the selective inhibition of specific functions in neurosis: A preliminary report. *Psychosom. Med.,* 1943, *5*, 27–38.

12. THE BEHAVIOR OF CHIMPANZEES IN THEIR NATURAL HABITAT*

JANE VAN LAWICK-GOODALL

In 1960, at the instigation of the late Dr. L. S. B. Leakey, I began a longitudinal study of free-living chimpanzees (*Pan troglodytes schweinfurthi*) in the Gombe National Park, Tanzania, East Africa. This park comprises a narrow stretch of rugged, mountainous country running for some ten miles along the eastern shores of Lake Tanganyika and inland three miles or less to the tops of the peaks of the rift escarpment. The rift is intersected by many steep-sided valleys, which support permanent streams. In the valleys, riverine gallery forest is found; between the valleys the slopes are often more open, supporting deciduous woodland. Many of the higher ridges and peaks are covered only with grass. The area supports a population of between 100 and 150 chimpanzees.

This chimpanzee population is divided into communities of individuals who recognize and may interact with each other. Within such a community, which may include up to 50 or so individuals, chimpanzees mostly move about in small temporary associations, the membership of which is constantly changing as individuals or groups of individuals split off to move about alone or to join other associations. These groups

*This is an edited version of the Adolf Meyer Lecture, read at the 125th annual meeting of the American Psychiatric Association, Dallas, Tex., May 1–5, 1972.

From *The American Journal of Psychiatry*, 1973, *130*, 1–12. Copyright 1973, the American Psychiatric Association. Reprinted by permission of the author and the publisher.

may be all males, they may be females and youngsters, or they may be combinations of different age-sex classes. Chimpanzees, especially males, often move about quite on their own.

Some individuals in the community meet only when attractions, such as a local abundance of food or a female in oestrus, happen to draw them together; others meet more often; and some show strong bonds of mutual attraction and associate very frequently—traveling, grooming, feeding, and resting together. A mother and her dependent offspring is the one association that may remain stable over a period of years, though such a family unit frequently moves about with other associations.

In the wild, chimpanzees probably always live in male-dominated societies. Individuals of a community who frequently associate show a fairly well-defined dominance hierarchy, while among chimpanzees who meet only seldom the relative social status may be less clear-cut. As yet there is little information on relationships between individuals of different communities, but we do know that at least some chimpanzees may penetrate the home range of a neighboring community and peacefully travel, feed, or mate with its members.

Chimpanzees are promiscuous in that a female, during oestrus, may be mated by many males and no stable pair-bonds are formed. However, young females in particular may move with the same adult male (sometimes possibly copulating exclusively with him) during successive periods of oestrus (1).

Chimpanzees are omnivorous, feeding mainly on a variety of plant materials, especially fruits, but also consuming many insects, occasional bird's eggs or fledglings, and sometimes actively hunting and killing medium-sized mammals.

These apes follow no set route, day after day, in their search for food. Within a fairly large home range (which may be 20 square miles or more) they are nomadic, sleeping close to where dusk finds them. They typically move on the ground when traveling, although they do spend a good deal of time in the trees both during feeding and at night. They construct quite elaborate nests for sleeping: each individual typically makes a new nest every night, except for youngsters of up to five or six years (sometimes older), who share one with their mothers.

In the wild, a female chimpanzee does not give birth until she is at least 12 or 13 years old, and she has only one infant every four or five years. Life expectancy in the wild is not yet known but is probably between 40 and 50 years. The longevity record for a captive chimpanzee is about 47 years.

From 1963 onward, observations of social interactions between the different individuals of the nomadic community were considerably facilitated by the establishment of an artificial feeding area where bananas were offered to chimpanzees passing by. This attraction of the chimpanzees to a specific area has enabled detailed longitudinal records on the behavior of approximately 70 different individuals of both sexes and all ages. Since 1965, a growing team of investigators has been contributing to the understanding of the behavior of the Gombe Stream chimpanzees. Hugo van Lawick has built up a unique documentary film and still-photograph record of their behavior.

The need for a study extending over a great many years is due not only to the fact that the chimpanzee has a long life expectancy, or that there is a fairly high mortality rate (due mainly to disease and injury), but also to the fact that these apes are highly individualistic, differing markedly from one another in behavior as well as appearance. Thus a great many individuals must be studied in depth, through as much of their life cycles as possible, before one can make meaningful generalized statements about chimpanzee behavior. The understanding of individual differences is, in fact, one of the principal aspects of our research.

Significance of Chimpanzee Research for Understanding Human Behavior

The chimpanzee is man's closest living relative. Recent biochemical research has already revealed striking similarities in, for example, the number and form of the chromosomes, the blood proteins, immune responses, and DNA (2, 3). Neuroanatomical research has shown that the structure and circuitry of the chimpanzee brain is closer to that of the human brain than is that of any other living primate. Behavioral research, in the field and in the laboratory, has highlighted remarkable similarities in this sphere also. Taken together, these findings suggest that, at some point in the distant past, man and chimpanzee shared a common ancestor. If this is true, we may assume that characteristics shared by modern man and modern chimpanzee were present in our stone-age ancestors.

Field studies provide information on the ways in which the structure and behavior of the species in question are adapted to its environment. Thus, since the chimpanzee is man's closest relative, and since he lives in an environment similar to that in which early man is thought to have emerged, an understanding of his behavior may well shed new light on the behavior of early man. This is of utmost significance to those concerned with human evolution—those who are trying to understand how and why man has become what he is today. As Hamburg (4) has pointed out, some aspects of our behavior today—for example, our tendency toward violent action—seem unsuitable for the world in which we now live. Such tendencies, however, were undoubtedly shaped, over millions of years, to ensure the survival of our ancestors in a very different kind of world—a world that was in all probability far more like the world of the chimpanzee. We desperately need a greater understanding of aggression in man, and an appreciation of its evolutionary history and significance would be quite helpful.

Laboratory studies of the chimpanzee, under controlled conditions, can be very meaningful in understanding some aspects of human behavior. This ape is the best experimental model for those investigating human mental disorders. It is possible, for instance, to create in a chimpanzee a condition resembling human psychosis or one closely similar to some human depressions (5). But in order to work in a meaningful way toward a cure for the depressed or psychotic chimpanzee subject, it is essential to have access to a wealth of background knowledge concerning the normal behavior of the species and the conditions under which abnormal behavior is likely to develop.

Finally, increasing scrutiny of chimpanzee behavior is likely to pinpoint crucial areas in need of careful study in human subjects. Compared with human society, chimpanzee society involves extremely simple cultural traditions. The individual chimpanzee expresses his underlying motivations in a relatively straightforward way, with little masking of his responses. Thus it will be possible to tease out the biological roots of certain aspects of chimpanzee behavior despite its complexity; it may then be rewarding to reexamine the behavior in question in man to see whether similar factors may be involved.

Some Significant Long-Term Findings at Gombe

I should first like to outline some of the interesting findings that our longitudinal study is revealing, particularly those relating to the different stages of the life cycle in wild chimpanzees.

Period of Infant and Juvenile Dependence on the Mother

One of the striking findings to emerge from the study at Gombe is the length of the period of infant and juvenile dependence on the mother. The infant relies completely on his mother for food, transport, and protection until he is at least six months old. He may then take his first unsteady steps and begin to ingest minute amounts of solid food. However, riding on the mother continues to be his normal method of getting from place to place until, sometime in the fourth year, he begins to make increasingly longer journeys under his own steam. Milk continues to be his major source of nourishment for at least two years and possibly longer.

Youngsters are not finally weaned until their fifth or sixth year in most instances. The youngest to be weaned, to date, was four and a half years old; one, about six and a half years old at the time of this writing, is still not finally weaned. Juveniles may continue to sleep in a nest with their mothers after being weaned. Usually they start sleeping in their own nests during their sixth or seventh year; this often coincides with the birth of a younger sibling.

During the final stages of weaning, a young chimpanzee may go through a period of apparent depression during which he frequently reverts to earlier forms of infantile behavior such as clinging to his mother during travel and maintaining much closer contact with her than previously. His frequency of play is likely to decrease at such a time, and he may appear listless and apathetic.

These symptoms were especially pronounced in one youngster, Flint, the son of a very aged female, Flo. Flint was weaned early, at four and a half years, toward the end of his mother's pregnancy. He went through a period of depression, as outlined above, during which he constantly solicited social grooming from Flo and, when she rejected any of his other demands (e.g., wanting a share of her food), was likely to fly into wild tantrums, screaming and hitting the ground—even, on occasion, attacking his mother. When the new infant was born Flint recovered somewhat: he stopped riding Flo's back, pestered her less, and in general seemed more lively (though he did continue to push into his mother's nest each night with his infant sister). A few months later, however, he once more became lethargic, once more demanded constant grooming, and reverted to riding his mother's back even though the new infant was clinging beneath. These symptoms showed no signs of abating until, when she was about six months old, Flint's sibling died. After this Flint became much more active, but he has remained abnormally dependent on his old mother and is still, at the age of eight years and three months, sleeping in her nest. He has traveled about without Flo for more than an hour or so only on very rare occasions.

Similar symptoms of depression have appeared in other five- and six-year-olds for a few months immediately following the birth of a sibling, when they therefore no longer have first claim on the caretaking responses of the mother. In some cases this appears to be offset by the intrinsic fascination of the new baby for the juvenile sibling (6).

The significance, for the youngster, of the affectionate bond with his mother was illustrated dramatically when three individuals, all between three and four years old, lost their mothers. Two of these were "adopted" by elder siblings with whom they traveled and slept at night. But in spite of this, and in spite of the fact that they seemed well integrated into the chimpanzee society, both became increasingly listless and both showed declining frequency of play during the first few months. Subsequently the behavior of one of them, Merlin, became increasingly abnormal and he developed a number of unusual patterns and stereotypes of the kind associated with early social deprivation in the laboratory chimpanzee (7). These included rocking back and forth, hanging upside down and motionless for minutes on end, and pulling out his hairs individually during self-grooming. In addition he showed more submission and aggression and spent more time in social grooming than is normal for youngsters of his age. In some social responses and in some tool-using techniques, Merlin's behavior appeared to show some regression (6). He finally died of a paralytic disease but was so emaciated by then that it was almost certain that he would have died anyway . . .

The second orphan, Beattle, was adopted by an older and more experienced female than Merlin's sister. Beattle not only traveled and slept with her sister but was also permitted to ride about on her guardian's back, a luxury denied to Merlin, who was probably too heavy for his sister. Beattle's condition gradually improved and, about a year after her mother's death, her behavior was comparable with that of other youngsters her age. We might speculate that the added social security she derived from close physical contact with an experienced, almost-adult female who knew how to behave in moments of social excitement helped to minimize the psychological shock caused by her mother's death. We cannot, however, draw any firm conclusions from so inadequate a sample.

The third three-year-old had no elder sibling and after her mother's death wandered about for the most part quite alone. She quickly became lethargic, stopped playing almost entirely, and two months after her mother's death stopped visiting the feeding area. She was not seen again and was finally presumed dead.

During its sixth or seventh year a juvenile is increasingly likely to become accidentally separated from its mother. Initially this usually results in obvious distress on the part of the child (and sometimes on the part of the mother, too). The lost youngster starts to whimper and then scream as it scans the countryside in all directions, often from the top of a tall tree. Perhaps it is only after a series of such accidental separations that the juvenile itself finally initiates a brief bout of independent travel. The young male may start to move about in groups without his mother during his seventh or eighth year, but he does not normally spend more than a few days at a time away from her until his ninth or tenth year. The female may remain almost constantly with her mother for even longer.

The long period of dependency on the mother may be considered adaptive in the chimpanzee, as in man, in relation to social learning. In simpler forms of life, much behavior is almost entirely genetically coded, although at all levels individual experience undoubtedly plays some role in the development of behavior. But as the mammalian brain becomes increasingly complex, culminating in the brain of higher primates and of man himself, social learning plays a vastly more crucial role. The adult chimpanzee lives in a complex society: he must learn to recognize 30 or more individuals in order to react appropriately when he meets them. In addition to appreciating the status of each of these individuals in relation to his own, he must also know how the presence or absence of a high-ranking associate may affect his own or his companions' ranking in the hierarchy in a given group. Chimpanzees have an elaborate system of communication with each other, and their behavioral repertoire also includes such complex patterns as cooperative hunting and tool using. Learning undoubtedly plays a major role in the development of a youngster, and the years when he associates closely with his mother are undoubtedly to his advantage: he can rely on her to react appropriately to individuals of high or low rank, to assist him in times of stress, and to lead him to appropriate food sources. Initially, when the mother cares for his every need, the infant can direct most of his energy into exploring his physical and social environment, and even when he becomes a juvenile and must to some extent fend for himself, he can still spend much time, under the benign leadership of his mother, in gradually acquiring the skills and competences that will fit him for adult life.

It has been shown experimentally that nonhuman primates are able to learn through direct observation of the behavior of others (8, 9), and the wild chimpanzee infant certainly has much opportunity for learning of this sort. An infant often watches intently while his mother, or another older individual, is engaged in tool using, nest making, feeding, and a whole variety of social behaviors. Subsequently he may be seen to imitate the actions he has observed— either immediately, as when he picks up a grass tool just discarded by his model and endeavors to use it in a similar manner, or a short while later, as when a youngster watches an adult male performing a charging display and, when things are calm again, repeats some of the display movements himself, often in a seemingly playful context. Behaviors of this sort may be practiced time and time again. Thus, while a gradual maturation of locomotor and manipulative patterns undoubtedly plays a vital role in the development of many of the complex activities of the adult chimpanzee, it is almost certain that learning, through both trial and error and direct observation of models, is also a very significant factor (10).

Affectionate Bonds in the Chimpanzee Family

When we refer to a family in chimpanzee society, we mean a mother and her offspring of different ages, together with her daughters' offspring. There is no "father" as such. The male, after playing his role in the conception of an infant, has no further part in the raising of an offspring since, as I already mentioned, no permanent pair bonds develop between male and female chimpanzees. Our study has revealed, however, that the affectionate bonds between mothers and their offspring and between siblings are sometimes strong and long-lasting.

As we have seen, the young male associates very closely with his mother until he is nine or ten years of age. Moreover, all five of the males we observed whose mothers were alive during their adolescence continued to associate with them frequently during that period. We have now been able to make detailed observations on the relationships between three old females and their socially mature sons—that is, males more than 15 or 16 years of age. One of these females had two such sons, the others one each. All these young males associated quite frequently with their mothers, and during such times social grooming between mother and son was frequent. Moreover, on a few occasions mothers were observed to hurry to the assistance of adult as well as adolescent sons; similarly, sons occasionally assisted their mothers. Sade (11) has reported similar lasting bonds between mothers and sons in the rhesus monkey population on Cayo Santiago.

Of interest is the fact that we have not yet observed a sexually mature male try to mate with his mother. Our sample size is too small for conclusions to be drawn about this, since it involves only one mother with two adult sons and another with one. However, in one instance the mother, during four days of oestrus, was mated by every other mature male in her group with the exception of her two adult sons, who were also in the group. Some inhibition of mother-son mating has been observed in two other longitudinal studies of primate societies, Japanese monkeys (12) and rhesus macaques (13).

Females tend to remain closely associated with their mothers for even longer than males but to date we have been able to follow the development of a relationship between a mother and her daughter into the latter's adulthood in only one case; in other cases either the mother or the daughter died before the daughter became adult.

Of the five mother-daughter pairs we have been able to follow through the juvenile and at least the early adolescent period, two mothers showed affectionate and protective behavior toward their daughters similar to that described for the mother-son relationship. However, the other three mothers were far less tolerant of their female offspring than of their sons, and all three daughters showed fear of their mothers in some contexts, especially in feeding situations. Nishida and Kawanaka (14) describe two adolescent females who initially associated frequently with their mothers but who, when they became sexually receptive, began to travel about independently of their mothers for much of the time.

In the case where we have been able to document the relationship with a mother and her daughter from the latter's infancy to social maturity (the old female Flo and her daughter Fifi), the bond between the two has always been of a very relaxed and tolerant nature. In 1971 Fifi had her first infant (our major hallmark for social maturity in a female), so that for the first time we now have the opportunity to study the development of bonds between grandmother and grandson and between nephew and uncle in wild chimpanzees . . . Fifi still associates frequently with her mother and youngest brother, Flint, and the relationship between these individuals is presently being carefully studied by M. Hankey.

The extension of the affectionate bond between a mother and her offspring beyond weaning means that when the mother has a new infant this youngest member of the family is likely to have a great deal of contact with his older sibling, who will usually still be semidependent on the mother. He will also have (though to a lesser extent) contact with older independent siblings during those times when they associate with the mother. Thus, as Sade (11) has pointed out, the parent-offspring relationship may ramify into other relationships of potential importance.

We have already seen that an orphaned infant may be adopted by an older sibling; this was the case even when the caretaker (of an infant of 14 months) was a juvenile *male*. This orphan was too young to survive without her mother's milk, but if we examine the three cases in which the orphans were between three and four years old we find that one of those adopted by a sister survived to become a normal youngster; the second, although he eventually died, nevertheless lived for 18 months after the death of his mother. The third, with no elder sibling, disappeared and almost certainly died within three months.

Observations on two pairs of brothers suggest that long-term bonds, similar to those observed between a mother and her son, may typically be formed between brothers. Similar close bonds are found in rhesus monkey brothers (11).

To date we have been able to study the relationship between only one pair of chimpanzee sisters, the eldest of whom is close to social maturity and the other approaching adolescence. These two associate with their mother almost all the time, and the bond between all three is very close.

Other than juvenile-infant pairs, we have been able to document in detail the relationships between brothers and sisters in only three families, and these data suggest that the bonds between siblings of different sex tend to become weaker as the individuals mature. Mating does occasionally occur between brothers and sisters, but it is extremely rare. One young female (Fifi) repeatedly ran off screaming when she was first approached by her two brothers in a sexual context, although she was quick to respond to the courtship displays of other males. Eventually both brothers did achieve sexual intercourse with their sister, but thereafter they were observed to copulate with her only a few times during the two years prior to her pregnancy. One other young female was observed to be mated by her elder brother only a few times during 12 or more periods of oestrus; another adolescent female, who has been sexually receptive for over a year, has not yet been observed mating with her elder brother.

Adolescence

Adolescence is another area about which our longitudinal observations are yielding interesting information.[1] This period of the life cycle is considered by some to be solely culturally determined and therefore unique to man. However, chimpanzees (as well as most other nonhuman primates) show both physiological and behavioral changes around puberty and during the following few years; this makes it appropriate to distinguish a period of adolescence. It commences just prior to puberty (approximately eight years of age) and ends when the individual reaches social maturity (about 12 or 13 years of age in the female and some two years later in the male).

The female, as we have seen, tends to associate with her mother for an even longer period of time than the male. Since a mother is

[1] Anne Pusey, a graduate student at Stanford University, is currently making a detailed study of adolescence.

quite likely to be nursing an infant during her daughter's adolescence (and even if she is not, she will certainly associate with other females and infants from time to time), it is unnecessary for the adolescent female to leave her family group in order to gain experience concerning her future role as a mother. Some adolescent females are fascinated by small infants and spend much time playing with, grooming, or carrying them. A female with this "maternal" approach is likely to become very preoccupied with her own infant sibling. Other females seem less interested, particularly for a while after the onset of regular sexual cycling.

The female sexual cycle is characterized by menstrual bleeding and periodic swelling and deturgescence of the anogenital region. The increase in genital swelling coincides with a very marked increase of attraction and receptivity to males. The average length of the cycle is about 34 days. Maximum genital swelling averages six to seven days; menstruation occurs between six and 12 days from the start of detumescence. These swellings first appear as a very slight turgidity of the clitoris in a seven- or eight-year-old female and, with each successive month, gradually get larger. Some five to ten months prior to menarche (between eight and a half and ten years of age for captive chimpanzees, according to Asdell [15] and Riopelle [16]) the adolescent female develops a much larger swelling and suddenly becomes sexually attractive to adult males.

Females show a great deal of individual variation in their initial responses to the sexual advances of mature males. Since courtship typically comprises many gestures that occur also in aggressive contexts, some females are extremely fearful initially and may try to escape, screaming, when a male approaches for copulation. Other females seem to take sexual approaches as a matter of course.

For several months prior to her first period of receptivity, one adolescent female (Fifi) frequently remained very close to older females who showed genital swellings, apparently in order to be on hand when they were mated. She would then either jump on the back of the other female and press her own genital area as close to the male's penis as she could or else go round behind him, turn her back on him, and press her genital area against his rump during copulation. As might be expected, she was quick to respond to the slightest courtship gesture when she herself became receptive for the first time.

In many groups of nonhuman primates, exchange of genes between groups occurs when males from neighboring ranges change groups. This is well documented for rhesus monkeys (13, 17), Japanese monkeys (12), and baboons (18), and it almost certainly occurs in gorillas (19, 20). Some male chimpanzees at Gombe have sometimes been absent from the feeding area for up to two months; during such times they may have visited neighboring communities and possibly mated with their females. If that were so, however, one would expect males from neighboring communities to occasionally mingle with individuals of our habituated group, but there is no evidence that this has occurred.

Transfer of females from one group to another is known to occur occasionally among baboons (18) and among gorillas (19). Among chimpanzees, however, there is much evidence that females, principally adolescent females, play a major role in widening the gene pool. At Gombe there are a number of records of adolescent females temporarily leaving their home communities during periods of oestrus and mixing and mating with males of neighboring communities (1). In at least two cases, young "stranger" females have gradually become integrated into our community of habituated chimpanzees, although to date no habituated adolescent female has permanently left our area. Nishida and Kawanaka (14) have now recorded 39 cases of females transferring from one community to another during oestrus; the majority of these females were adolescent.

It is especially interesting to note that it is the

adolescent female herself who appears to initiate the change in range; she does not normally seem to be forced to leave her home area by threatening behavior on the part of males. In our own species, it is very often the women who leave their natal groups and move to live with their new husbands in villages—or even countries—that may be quite strange to the women concerned.

Adolescence often seems to be a stressful period for the male chimpanzee. He has a growth spurt after which he tends to become more aggressive, particularly toward females. By the time he is about ten years old he is able to dominate many females who a few years earlier were themselves able to subdue him with ease. At the same time he must learn to behave with increasing caution to avoid arousing the aggression of the mature males, some of whom are quick to threaten him for behavior they tolerated when he was a mere juvenile. Nevertheless, despite the fact that he may become increasingly fearful of these older males, he often seems to deliberately choose to associate with them. Many of his first journeyings without his mother are made with adult males.

When he is with older males the adolescent tends to occupy a peripheral position in the group. He desists from sexual activity with a popular female—or at least waits for a quiet moment when the big males are resting peacefully. He sits a few yards away from a group of males who are grooming each other but usually does not dare to join them. He often feeds at a slight distance from his superiors. Yet he can often be observed watching the older males very intently.

After associating for a while with his superiors, and particularly if he has been the victim of their aggression, the adolescent male moves away from them and either travels about for a while on his own or returns to his mother if she is still alive. Indeed, his relationship with his mother may well be one of the most stabilizing factors at this time of social change

for, despite his larger size and more aggressive behavior to females in general, his behavior toward her remains remarkably constant.

At some period during his adolescence, the young male may engage in a number of status conflicts if there is another male of similar age and social rank as himself with whom he associates quite frequently. These conflicts mainly involve bluff, but may sometimes lead to physical attacks. The charging display appears to have special significance in this context. This is a typically male performance that occurs in a variety of situations, principally when a male arrives at a new food source, when he meets up with other chimps after a separation, or when he is frustrated in the attainment of some goal (when, for instance, he is inhibited from feeding or mating due to the proximity of a superior male). During the display he runs slowly or very fast, on all fours or upright, with hair bristling; he may drag or throw branches, hurl rocks, sway branches, leap through the trees, or (in the case of two individuals) beat his chest like a gorilla. This display enables the performer to look larger, more powerful, and more dangerous than he may really be; it appears to be a useful technique in the acquisition of a higher social status. The more frequent and the more impressive the display, the more rapidly the adolescent may rise in the hierarchy. Since such a display only seldom involves a physical attack on a rival it is adaptive in that it enables a chimpanzee to acquire status without any great risk of injury to himself.

During the final years of adolescence the male gradually begins to threaten and occasionally attack the lower-ranking males of the adult male hierarchy. When he is able to subdue even one of them consistently he can be considered part of their hierarchy and thus socially mature.

Dominance

The past ten years of research at Gombe have brought to light some interesting facts concerning dominance, particularly with regard to those qualities which enable a chimpanzee to acquire the alpha position in his community. In 1963 Goliath, a powerful and aggressive male in his prime (perhaps about 25 years of age) was the alpha male. He had a spectacular charging display during which he covered the ground very fast indeed, dragging and occasionally hurling branches. Early in 1964, however, Goliath was displaced from his top-ranking position in the community by an older and much less robust male, Mike. Mike apparently accomplished this by means of bluff and, without doubt, superior intelligence.

In 1963 Mike was among the lowest-ranking of all the adult males, frequently threatened or even attacked by most of the others. Then he began to incorporate empty four-gallon kerosene cans into his charging displays. Other males had occasionally seized hold of such a can (from my camp area) during a display, but it seemed that only Mike was able to profit from the experience and deliberately use cans to enhance his performance. He soon learned to keep up to three cans ahead of him as he ran, very fast, hitting or kicking them along as he went. He made a great deal of noise: other males as well as females and youngsters rushed out of his way.

After charging past a group of males a few times and scattering them, Mike then sat with his hair erect; the other males, previously his superiors, approached him with gestures of submission or appeasement, crouching before him, touching, kissing, or grooming him. Mike rose to become alpha male of his community in about four months without engaging in any actual attacks on other males that we observed. He maintained that position even when we took the cans away (for we too disliked the noise) for the following six years.

Mike, in his turn, was relieved of his top-ranking position by a younger, very large, and extremely aggressive male, Humphrey. For about a year previously Mike, who was getting old, had appeared uneasy in his alpha position

and was being ignored during displays by some of the younger males. Only one fight was observed between Mike and his successor, although other incidents may have occurred prior to this. Unlike Goliath, who had maintained a very high-ranking position for several years after losing his alpha rank, Mike dropped rapidly to a low position in the hierarchy. This was possibly due to the fact that at the time of the takeover, he was very much older than Goliath had been (21).

In chimpanzee society dominance is something of a conundrum. The usual interpretation of the phenomenon is that it enables a high-ranking individual to have prior access to desirable foods, females, or resting places. Competition over these resources is rare in chimpanzee society, at least at Gombe. Possibly a high-ranking position is desirable because, once an individual has attained it, he need no longer fear threat or attack from too many other chimpanzees of higher rank. Whatever the underlying motivation or ultimate reward, however, many chimpanzees do seem preoccupied with raising their social status, while others are less concerned and tend to keep out of the way during times of social excitement.

The story of Mike's rise to alpha male provides an excellent example of the way in which chimpanzees typically rely on threat or bluff rather than actual physical violence in their interactions with each other. Fights do occur, but they are generally brief; even when they appear vicious, they seldom result in observable physical injury. Moreover, after a fight the victim ordinarily approaches the aggressor showing postures and gestures that have been labeled submissive or appeasing and in response to which the aggressor usually reaches out to touch or pat or kiss the subordinate. This reassurance behavior serves to calm the agitated victim and helps to ensure generally relaxed and peaceful relationships among those individuals who frequently associate in the community (22).

Similarities in Chimpanzee and Human Behavior

I have outlined various aspects of the life cycle of wild chimpanzees that it has been possible to document because of the long-term nature of our study. As knowledge is gradually accumulated about a variety of different monkey and ape species, it is possible to trace certain evolutionary trends of increasing complexity, culminating in man. Some of the data I have discussed so far clearly illustrate the high position of the chimpanzee on this evolutionary ladder. If, for instance, we take a primitive New World monkey, the marmoset, we find that infants are weaned at six months and attain sexual maturity at 14 months. The gestation period is 140 days, and estimated longevity in captivity about ten years (23). If we next take the rhesus monkey we find that weaning takes place any time between six months and a year, or sometimes a little later. The monkey is reproductively mature at about four years of age, though it does not acquire full size until about ten years. The average gestation period is 164 days and the life expectancy in captivity about 30 years (23). Now we come to the chimpanzee, where the youngster is not weaned until he is about five years old and is dependent on his mother for another three or four years, where reproductive maturity is not reached until seven to eight years in the male and (in the wild) about 11 or 12 years in the female. Moreover, the male does not become socially mature for some five or six years after puberty and is unlikely to be reproductively effective in his society until he is at least 12 years old and probably older. The longevity record is almost 50 years in captivity. In all these characteristics the chimpanzee can be seen to be very close indeed to man.

I should now like to discuss some of the behavior patterns of chimpanzees that strikingly resemble some patterns in man.

Cooperative Hunting and Food Sharing

As mentioned earlier, chimpanzees are omnivorous. They quite frequently hunt fairly large prey animals such as the young of bushpig, bushbuck, and baboons, and young or adult monkeys of various species. Sometimes the capture of prey is a very individual and opportunistic event: one chimpanzee happens upon a suitable victim, seizes and kills it, and begins to feed. On other occasions, however, male chimpanzees may hunt in a group and show behavior that can clearly be labeled as cooperation. For instance, one chimpanzee may cautiously creep up a tree toward a potential victim, such as a young baboon that has become slightly separated from its troop, while other male chimpanzees stand around the base of this tree and also near trees that might act as escape routes for the quarry. Not until the victim becomes aware of danger and tries to make a break will the chimpanzees on the ground leave their positions and converge on the fleeing baboon.

Meat is a delicacy for chimpanzees, and normally a great deal of excited calling accompanies the successful capture of prey. This attracts the attention of any other chimpanzees in the vicinity and they typically converge upon the hunters and cluster around, either watching intently or actually begging from the chimpanzees who have acquired shares of the carcass. When begging, a chimpanzee may hold his hand to the mouth of an eating individual in the hope that he will be given the remains of the mouthful . . . or he may hold out his hand toward the other, palm up, in the typical begging gesture of man.

Often begging behavior is rewarded. This is significant since food sharing among adults has not been recorded in any other nonhuman primate in the wild. After chewing for a while on a mouthful of meat and leaves (leaves are almost always eaten with meat) a chimpanzee will nearly always allow a begging individual to take it. Sometimes he will permit others to chew on the carcass at the same time as himself, or let them detach pieces for themselves. Occasionally he will actually tear off a piece himself and hand it to the one who is begging (6, 24, 25).

Tool Using and Tool Making

With respect to his tool-using behavior, the chimpanzee comes considerably closer to man than does any other living primate. Tool using in animals has always fascinated people because, for many years, man was typically referred to as *the* tool-using animal. A variety of animals (including invertebrates) do use objects as tools if we define tool using as "the use of an external object as a functional extension of mouth or beak, hand or claw, in the attainment of an immediate goal" (10). It should be emphasized, however, that tool-using ability in itself does not necessarily indicate any special kind of intelligence. The Galapagos woodpecker finch uses a cactus spine to probe insects from crevices in the bark. This is fascinating behavior, but it does not make this bird more intelligent than the ordinary woodpecker, which uses its long beak and tongue for the same purpose. The Galapagos finch employs a behavioral adaptation, the woodpecker a morphological one.

The point at which tool using in a nonhuman animal acquires significance, when viewed in relation to the evolution of tool use in man, is when a species or an individual within that species can adapt its ability to manipulate objects to a wide variety of purposes and, in particular, when it can use an object spontaneously to solve a completely novel problem. The chimpanzee has shown itself capable of using a wide variety of objects for a wide variety of purposes, both in the wild and in captivity. Moreover, if an object is not suitable for the specific purpose for which it is to be used, the chimpanzee will modify it accordingly, so that he may be said to show at least the beginnings of tool-making behavior.

Our research at Gombe has shown that one community of chimpanzees uses four different kinds of objects—grasses, sticks, leaves, and rocks—in a wide variety of different contexts. Sticks are used to plunge into ant or bee nests during feeding and occasionally as levers to enlarge the opening of such a nest. Sticks were used by chimpanzees to try and force open banana boxes at our feeding area. They may also be used during aggressive displays to intimidate other chimpanzees, baboons, or humans. One infant "clubbed" an insect on the ground. Grass stems are used when the chimpanzees are feeding on termites; they are also used as "investigation probes" to touch objects that the chimpanzees cannot reach with their hands or of which they are afraid. The end of the grass is then sniffed. Sticks and grasses may be trimmed to size and made more suitable in any of the above contexts. Leaves are used to wipe dirt off the body, and also as a "sponge" to sop up water in a hollow in a tree trunk when the chimp cannot reach the fluid with his lips. Here again the object is modified; before dipping the leaves into the water the chimpanzee crumples them by briefly chewing them. This makes his sponge considerably more absorbent and effective. Rocks are used as missiles during aggressive incidents and may be thrown forcefully and with good aim. One infant pounded an insect on the ground with a rock that he held in his hand. Once a chimpanzee used a twig to pick his nose; another individual used one to pick at something in her teeth.

There is not space here to detail the tool-using performances of laboratory- and home-raised chimpanzees, although some of them are very impressive. However, man is still the only primate to "make tools to a regular and set pattern" (26), and he is the only creature who relies on tools for his very survival (27).

Nonverbal Communication Patterns

Perhaps it is in the repertoire of postures and gestures which form the nonverbal communication system that some of the most striking behavioral similarities between man and chimpanzee are found. Chimpanzees may bow, kiss, hold hands, touch and pat each other, embrace, tickle one another with their fingers, bite, punch, kick, scratch each other, and pull out one another's hair. Not only do many of these movements look remarkably like many of the expressive postures and gestures of our own species, but the contexts likely to elicit the behaviors may be strikingly similar in the chimpanzee and man.

When an adult chimpanzee is frightened he may reach out to touch or even embrace another who happens to be nearby; this physical contact often has a calming effect on the gesturer. If both individuals were frightened, then both may be reassured. Similar contact-seeking behavior occurs commonly in man in stressful situations.

When two or more chimpanzees become suddenly excited—if, for instance, they suddenly come across a large amount of a favored food—they often exhibit intense contact-seeking behavior, embracing, kissing, holding hands, and patting each other, all while screaming loudly. Eventually they calm down sufficiently to start feeding. This behavior may be similar to that shown by a human child who, when told of a special treat, may fling his arms around the bearer of good news. When peace was declared in London after World War II, the streets were full of people embracing, clasping hands, kissing, laughing, and crying.

After a young chimpanzee has been threatened or attacked, his need for reassuring physical contact with the aggressor is sometimes well illustrated. As he approaches the adult, still screaming, his behavior is tense; his limbs are flexed so that he is close to the ground and his movements are often jerky. As he gets close to the aggressor he may actually turn and move away for a few steps, but then he turns back again as his desire for contact apparently overcomes his desire to flee. When he finally reaches his superior he adopts a submissive posture, crouched close to the ground, still screaming and with his teeth and gums exposed in a wide grin of fear. In response the other chimpanzee will usually reach out and touch or gently pat the youngster, sometimes continuing for almost a minute until the subordinate quiets

and gradually relaxes. Here again we find a similar pattern in man. In most societies people who have been quarreling will "make up" by means of physical contact, whether this be the cuddling and petting of a child or marital partner, or a more formal clasping of hands or brief pat on the back.

At this point I should like to emphasize that while the form of reassurance behavior looks very similar in man and chimpanzee—not only with respect to the gestures themselves and the context in which they may occur, but also in the relaxing effect of the physical contact on the submissive individual—the motivations underlying the behavior are probably quite different in man and chimpanzee. This is a fascinating and complex subject that I hope to discuss in detail elsewhere.

When two chimpanzees meet after a separation they may show gestures and postures that strikingly resemble some forms of human greeting. In such a context chimpanzees may bow, kiss, touch, or pat one another, hold hands, or embrace. A male may chuck a female or an infant under the chin. In chimpanzee society, reunion after separation often involves behaviors that serve to reestablish or emphasize the relative social status of the individuals concerned; originally, greeting behavior in man undoubtedly served a similar function. Indeed, this is still the case on some formal occasions, though human greeting behavior has for the most part become ritualized in our different cultures.

There are also similarities in the aggressive behaviors of man and chimpanzee. A quick upward jerk or a waving of the arm serves as a threat in both species, as may a level stare directed unwaveringly at a subordinate. A chimpanzee may adopt an upright posture when threatening and wave his arms above his head as he advances on the object that has elicited his aggression. He may throw objects overarm or underhand toward his victim. He may brandish a stick or make deliberate clubbing movements. Attacking chimpanzees may bite, hit, and kick their opponents. Female chimpanzees in particular sometimes scratch at and occasionally pull out handfuls of hair from their victims' heads.

The Uniqueness of the Human Primate

It will have become apparent that even while I have been stressing the similarities between man and his closest living relative, many points of difference have been touched on. In fact, the longer I study chimpanzees and the more amazed I become at the extent of the behavioral similarities in the chimpanzee and man, the more I stand in awe of the gigantic evolutionary stride that our own species has taken in the last few million years. Let me very briefly enumerate a few of the characteristics that make man unique among the primates and that are highlighted by an understanding of the chimpanzee.

The chimpanzee has a wide range of calls. Each call is fairly reliably associated with some specific emotion—a scream usually signifies fear, a bark aggression, and so on. This means that the chimpanzee is able to communicate reasonably specific information about his feelings and his environment through the use of calls alone. But his repertoire of grunts and hoots cannot be compared with human language. Moreover, recent research into the speech centers of the human brain suggests that our language did not even originate from this type of primitive vocal communication.

The chimpanzee cannot convey information about the past and the future; he cannot pass on, through his vocabulary of calls, experiences of his own that might benefit his group or his species as a whole. It is true that recent work in teaching chimpanzees to communicate by means of sign language (28, 29) and with plastic word symbols (30) has shown convincingly that the chimpanzee is capable of a greater sophistication of mental process than most people were formerly prepared to accept, such as the ability to appreciate abstract concepts. But the chimpanzee intellect is dwarfed by that

of a species that can produce a Plato, an Einstein, a Beethoven.

When the chimpanzee Washoe, trained in sign language, was shown herself in a mirror for the first time and was asked, in sign language, "What is it?" she signed back, "Me, Washoe." This suggests that the chimpanzee may show the beginnings of self-awareness. But man not only is conscious of himself as an individual being, he also questions the reason for his existence, he searches for clues as to how he came to be the way he is, he strives to understand his own behavior and the world and the universe in which he finds himself.

The chimpanzee, especially as a young adult, does show what might be considered the beginning of an affectionate heterosexual pair bonding: a male and a female may wander off together during the female's period of oestrus and sometimes for longer. At such times they may stay on their own, away from others of their kind (1). But this kind of relationship cannot be compared in any way with the tenderness and passion, the understanding and compassion, the exaltation and peace, that mark human heterosexual love in its highest form.

It is of interest that man has also leapt ahead of the chimpanzee in what we might call negative as well as positive intellectual evolution. Man can use language to the advantage of himself, his group, his species. With words he can inspire others to acts of goodness and self-sacrifice. He can also use words to incite his fellowmen to deeds of evil and destruction. Despite his awareness of himself and of the individual existence of his fellowmen, and despite his understanding of the world he lives in, he can destroy not only human and animal life but the very environment that, as he alone among living creatures is capable of appreciating, enables him to live. Man, with his tremendous capacity to love, has a capacity to hate far transcending the worst of the squabbles that may break out between chimpanzees. Two neighboring communities of chimpanzees may occasionally indulge in displays of power as individuals hurl rocks and wave branches or even briefly attack one another. But they show nothing even remotely comparable to the horror of human warfare.

Today we are all aware of the tremendous need for a better understanding of our own species, yet only too often the scientist, searching for the biological basis of some human pattern of behavior, is confounded because intellect and culture have conspired to confuse the picture. We cannot afford to neglect any approach that might give us a better understanding of even a few aspects of man's evolution, his biology, his social behavior. And I believe the study of the chimpanzee is important in this respect.

And so we are continuing our intensive study at the Gombe Stream Research Center, where postdoctoral, graduate, and undergraduate students from the universities of Dar-es-Salaam, Stanford, Cambridge, and others are working as a team in our efforts to understand chimpanzee behavior more completely. Dr. David A. Hamburg is setting up a new facility at Stanford—"Gombe West"—where chimpanzees will be studied in groups in large outdoor compounds. Here we shall investigate problems that cannot be tackled in the field but that we know from our experience are relevant to the understanding of the behavior of the species. An initial area of inquiry will be the problems of adolescence; methods and goals will be closely linked not only with the research at the Gombe Stream but also with ongoing studies of human behavior. We hope that some problems arising in research with human subjects may be solved through work with the chimpanzees; in turn, work with chimpanzees may pinpoint areas of behavior that merit careful investigation in human subjects.

The study of the chimpanzee, with all his complexity of behavior and his close evolutionary relationship to man, is exciting and worthwhile in itself. If our research can help, even in the smallest way, in the better understanding of man, then our work will be even more rewarding.

Acknowledgments

I should like to express gratitude to Tanzania's president, Mwalimu Julius Nyerere, to the prime minister, and to the many other government officials who have encouraged and assisted us in our work. The research was initially financed by the Wilkie Foundation and subsequently by the National Geographic Society, the Science Research Council, and the Wenner Gren Foundation for Anthropological Research; I should like to thank all these organizations. At present the work is financed by the Grant Foundation and I am particularly grateful to Dr. Douglas Bond, the president, and Mr. Philip Sapir, the director.

I could not have carried out the work in the field without the help of my husband, Baron Hugo van Lawick; I should like to thank him and also the many students and Tanzanian field assistants and helpers who have helped us collect an ever-increasing volume of information on chimpanzee behavior. I should also like to express my gratitude to the late Dr. L. S. B. Leakey, who gave me the opportunity to begin this research.

The Gombe Stream Research Center is now formally affiliated with Stanford University, thanks to the efforts of Dr. David A. Hamburg, and I should like to take this opportunity to express my deep gratitude to him for all that he has done in the past to stimulate our research at Gombe and for the exciting new research opportunities that his farsighted efforts are now providing at "Gombe West" at Stanford.

REFERENCES

1. McGinnis P: Sexual behavior of wild chimpanzees (in preparation).
2. Sarich VM, Wilson AC: Quantitative immunochemistry and the evolution of primate albumins: micro-complement fixation. *Science 154:* 1563–1566, 1966.

3. Sarich VM, Wilson AC: Immunological time scale for hominid evolution. *Science 158:* 1200–1202, 1967.
4. Hamburg DA: The relevance of recent evolutionary changes to human stress biology, in *Social Life of Early Man.* Edited by Washburn S. Chicago, Aldine, 1963, pp. 278–288.
5. Hamburg DA: *Psychiatry as a Behavioral Science.* New Jersey, Prentice-Hall, 1971.
6. van Lawick-Goodall J: The behavior of free-living chimpanzees in the Gombe Stream area. *Animal Behavior Monograph 1*(3):161–311, 1968.
7. Davenport RK, Menzel EW: Stereotyped behavior of the infant chimpanzee. *Arch. Gen. Psychiatry 88:*99–104, 1963.
8. Darby CL, Riopelle AJ: Observational learning in the rhesus monkey. *J. Comp. Physiol. Psychol. 52:*94–98, 1959.
9. Hayes KJ, Hayes C: Imitation in a home-raised chimpanzee. *J. Comp. Physiol. Psychol. 45:*450–459, 1952.
10. van Lawick-Goodall J: Tool-using in primates and other vertebrates, in *Advances in the Study of Behavior.* Edited by Lehrman DS, Hinde RA, Shaw E. New York, Academic Press, 1970, pp. 195–249.
11. Sade DS: Some aspects of parent-offspring and sibling relations in a group of rhesus monkeys, with a discussion of grooming. *Am. J. Phys. Anthropol. 23:*1–18, 1965.
12. Imanishi K: The origin of the human family: A primatological approach, in *Japanese Monkeys.* Edited by Altmann S. Edmonton, Canada, University of Alberta and Yerkes Regional Primate Center, 1965 (processed).
13. Sade DS: Inhibition of son-mother mating among free-ranging rhesus monkeys, in *Science and Psychoanalysis,* vol 12, Animal and Human. Edited by Masserman JH. New York, Grune & Stratton, 1968, pp. 18–38.
14. Nishida T, Kawanaka K: Inter-unit-group relationships among wild chimpanzees of the Mahali Mountains. Kyoto University, *African Studies 7:*131–169, 1972.
15. Asdell SA: *Patterns of Mammalian Reproduction.* New York, Comstock, 1946.
16. Riopelle AJ: Growth and behavioral changes in chimpanzees. *J. Morphol. Anthropol. 53:*53–61, 1963.
17. Boelkins RC, Wilson AP: Intergroup social dynamics of the Cayo Santiago rhesus (*Mucaca mulatta*) with special reference to changes in group membership by males (in press).
18. Ransom TW: Ecology and social behavior of baboons in the Gombe National Park. Department of Psychology, University of California, Berkeley, 1971 (unpublished doctoral dissertation).
19. Schaller GB: *The Mountain Gorilla: Ecology and Behavior.* Chicago, University of Chicago Press, 1963.
20. Fossey D: Personal communication, Feb 24, 1972.
21. Bygott JD: Aggressive behavior of male chimpanzees in a natural habitat (in preparation).
22. van Lawick-Goodall J: Some aspects of aggressive behavior in a group of free-living chimpanzees. *Int. Soc. Sci. J. 23*(1):89–97, 1971.
23. Napier JR, Napier PH: *A Handbook of Living Primates.* New York, Academic Press, 1967.
24. van Lawick-Goodall J: *In the Shadow of Man.* Boston, Houghton-Mifflin, 1971.
25. Teleki G: *Predatory Behavior in a Group of Wild Chimpanzees.* Lewisburg, Pa., Bucknell University Press (in press).
26. Oakley KP: *Man the Tool-Maker,* 4th ed. London, British Museum, 1958.
27. Tobias PV: Australopithecus, Homo habilis, tool-using and tool-making. *South African Archaeology Bulletin 20*(part 4):167–192, 1965.

28. Gardner RA, Gardner BT: Teaching sign language to a chimpanzee. *Science 165:*664–672, 1969.
29. Gardner BT, Gardner RA: Two-way communication with an infant chimpanzee, in *Behavior of Non-Human Primates,* vol 4. Edited by Schrier AM, Stollnitz F. New York, Academic Press, 1971, pp. 117–184.
30. Premack D: Language in chimpanzee? *Science 172:*808–822, 1971.

Chapter 6

LEARNING AND MEMORY

INTRODUCTION AND COMMENTARY

Interest in learning by psychologists means interest in behavioral changes that are attributable primarily to practice or experience in some situation; it means interest in the process of acquisition and modification of behavior potentiality that can be shown to be largely a function of practice or experience variables. Thus the concept of learning is a constituent—a major constituent—of the larger "nurture." If one recognizes that "nurture" and "nature" as behavior determiners are interdependent concepts, neither one being definable nor measurable independent of the other, then one also recognizes the considerable scope of learning as a factor in behavior. This scope is only slightly diminished when one restricts one's examination to learning as it relates to development. In most areas of developmental research learning enters as an important consideration. Accordingly, some of the articles in most other chapters of this book specifically deal with learning in some fashion.

However, in a developmental, phylogenetic context one can examine the learning process for at least two distinguishable reasons. (1) *Focusing upon developmental processes* one can ask about behavioral phenomena at some stage(s) of development, "What special role, if any, does learning play in the development of these behaviors, and therefore, what conditions for learning have existed to account for their development?" For example, one might study the development of aggression in children by endeavoring to demonstrate what conditions have existed for the learning of aggressive behavior (Bandura & Walters, 1963). (2) *Focusing upon learning processes* one can ask about principles derived from specific learning experiments, "To what extent or in what form do these principles hold throughout stages of human development from birth (or even earlier) to adulthood?" Similarly, one can ask whether the study of different species leads to different learning principles.

A possible consequence of the focus on learning processes is that learning principles may differ phylogenetically (see, e.g., Hinde & Stevenson-Hinde, 1973; Seligman & Hager, 1972) and/or ontogenetically (see, e.g., Kendler & Kendler, 1968). A possible consequence of the focus on developmental processes is that learning may be found to play a primary role in the development of some classes of behavior, but be only indirectly involved in the development of others.

The relation between the concepts of learning and *memory* is clear (see article [14] by Gagné) and has long been acknowledged. If a person reads a short poem through once and then immediately is asked to recite it "by heart" (!), whether one is observing how much the person remembers or how much he or she learned, seems largely a matter of point of view or emphasis.

211

Nonetheless, until about 1960 experiments emphasizing learning vastly outnumbered those on memory, as did theoretical essays as well. It is only in the past ten to fifteen years that significant empirical and theoretical advances, especially regarding human memory, have evoked the interest in memory that its relation to learning warrants. In a recent review monograph short-term memory and long-term memory are considered now to be part of "the set of concepts and assumptions drawn from contemporary theories of learning" (Estes, 1970, p. 8). Psychologists have begun to learn about memory (or, rather, to remember learning less!).

Learning Processes

Elsewhere in this volume most learning-related articles are more or less identifiable with the focus on developmental processes, and therefore that focus is not represented in this chapter. At least to a greater degree, the articles on learning included in this chapter emphasize *learning processes,* and the question of phylogenetic or ontogenetic changes in learning principles.

The paper by Harlow [13] is probably his clearest exposition in a single paper of a series of techniques and results that have profoundly influenced the direction and methodology not only of the flourishing developmental and comparative study of primate learning (Schrier, Harlow, & Stollnitz, 1965), but also of human and other animal learning. By means of several ingenious experimental techniques, Harlow has examined learning capacity in the rhesus monkey from the first few days after birth to about 50 months of age. It will be noted that Harlow has endeavored to define, at least intuitively, a dimension of learning complexity, and his emphasis has been on the maturation of capacity for increasingly complex learning within a particular species.

The next paper in this chapter, by Gagné [14], also concerns learning as a process in development. Gagné outlines the idea of *cumulative* learning as an approach to understanding the development of human intellect. In so doing, he not only shows how his conception of the cumulative consequences of learning might be a fruitful way to conceptualize intellectual growth, but he also provides instructive comparative discussion of alternative views, notably Piaget's (see Chapter 1, pp. 5–6, and Chapter 10, pp. 442–443, of this volume). The reader might also profit from comparing Gagné with Bijou [1] in terms of their concepts of "learning."

The reader will benefit also from reading a recent paper by Goulet (1968) that examines research on children's verbal learning. His review accomplishes at least two significant results: (1) The survey of experiments conveys what is now known about a variety of topics relevant to children's verbal learning, as well as revealing a number of important development-related questions yet to be properly asked and answered; and (2) the methodological discussion throughout the article serves well to emphasize in specific terms a topic of other papers in this volume; namely, the nature of *developmental* research in comparison to research that simply studies behavior "as a function of age."

The Gibson paper [15], like previous articles in this chapter, concentrates on the learning process, though in a particular way. Its focus is somewhat sharper in that it is on the relatively discrete learning problem, or skill, of reading and its ontogeny. In this it is a departure from traditional verbal learning research (Goulet, 1968) and is important for this reason. Furthermore, it is important as an impressive demonstration both of the relevance of the perceptual learning analysis employed and of the fruitful questions raised by this analysis.

Ontogeny of Memory

The final two articles [16 and 17] in this chapter have been chosen to convey some issues, ideas, and methods that one encounters in the relatively newly flourishing research in the ontogeny of memory.

The first of these, by Campbell and Spear [16], is a landmark paper, certain to be catalyst and springboard for a wealth of fruitful research and thought on the ontogeny (and phylogeny) of memory. It warrants very careful reading. The authors begin by documenting a seeming paradox: Early life experiences have enduring, far-reaching effects on humans (and many other animals as well), and yet memory for early life experiences is relatively poor, in humans justifying the term "infantile amnesia." After carefully discussing various ways of understanding development-related changes in remembering, they briefly outline possible resolutions of the "paradox." The concept of *reinstatement* (see articles [20 and 21], and the introduction to Chapter 7, p. 282) is offered as one such resolution.

The second article on the ontogeny of memory, by Bach and Underwood [17], is an excellent example of specific research methods, results, and interpretation bearing on the development of memory (as well, perhaps, as on reading, as discussed by Gibson [15]). Their verbal retention test enabled recall errors to be distinguished as either associative, acoustic (similar sound), or neutral. The authors discuss their finding that second graders made more acoustic errors, while sixth graders made more associative errors. While one aspect of these experiments is simply a study of verbal recall errors "as a function of age" (see the introduction to Chapter 3 and Wohlwill's paper [2]), the research also obviously constitutes an invaluable step toward understanding the development of human memory.

References

Bandura, A. Walters, R. H. Social learning and personality development. New York: Holt, Rinehart and Winston, 1963.

Estes, W. K. *Learning theory and mental development*. New York: Academic Press, 1970.

Goulet, L. R. Verbal learning in children: Implications for developmental research. *Psychological Bulletin*, 1968, *69*, 359–376.

Hinde, R. A. & Stevenson-Hinde, J. (Eds.) *Constraints on learning*. New York: Academic Press, 1973.

Kendler, H. H. & Kendler, T. S. Mediation and conceptual behavior. In *The psychology of learning and motivation*, vol. 2, 1968. K. W. Spence & J. T. Spence (Eds.), New York: Academic Press, 1968, pp. 197–244.

Schrier, A. M., Harlow, H. F., & Stollnitz, F. (Eds.) *Behavior of nonhuman primates*. Vols. 1 & 2. New York: Academic Press, 1965.

Seligman, M. E. P. & Hager, J. L. (Eds.) *Biological boundaries of learning*. New York: Appleton, 1972.

13. THE DEVELOPMENT OF LEARNING IN THE RHESUS MONKEY*

HARRY F. HARLOW

During the last five years we have conducted an integrated series of researches tracing and analyzing the learning capabilities of rhesus monkeys from birth to intellectual maturity. Control over the monkey's environment has been achieved by separating the infants from their mothers at birth and raising them independently, using techniques and methods adapted from those described by van Wagenen (12).

There are many characteristics that commend the rhesus monkey as a subject for investigation of the development of learning. At birth, or a few days later, this animal attains adequate control over its head, trunk, arm, and leg movements, permitting objective recording of precise responses on tests of learning. The rhesus monkey has broad learning abilities, and even the neonatal monkey rapidly learns problems appropriate to its maturational status. As it grows older, this monkey can master a relatively unlimited range of problems suitable for measuring intellectual maturation. Although the rhesus monkey matures more rapidly than the human being, the time allotted for assessing its developing learning capabilities is measured in terms of years—not days, weeks, or months, as is true with most subprimate forms. During this time a high degree of control can be maintained over all experimental variables, particularly those relating to the animal's learning experiences. Thus, we can assess for all learning problems the relative importance of nativistic and experiential variables, determine

*A Sigma Xi-RESA National Lecture, 1958–59.

Reprinted from *American Scientist,* 1959, *47,* 459–479, the journal of Sigma Xi, The Scientific Research Society of North America. Reprinted by permission of the author and the publisher.

the age at which problems of any level of difficulty can first be solved, and measure the effects of introducing such learning problems to animals before or after this critical period appears. Furthermore, the monkey may be used with impunity as a subject for discovering the effects of cerebral damage or insult, whether produced by mechanical intervention or by biochemical lesions.

The only other creature whose intellectual maturation has been studied with any degree of adequacy is the human child, and the data from this species attest to the fact that learning capability increases with age, particularly in the range and difficulty of learned tasks which can be mastered. Beyond this fact, the human child has provided us with astonishingly little basic information on the nature or development of learning. Obviously, there are good and sufficient reasons for any and all such deficiencies. There are limits beyond which it is impossible or unjustifiable to use the child as an experimental subject. The education of groups of children cannot be hampered or delayed for purposes of experimental control over either environment or antecedent learning history. Unusual motivational conditions involving either deprivation or overstimulation are undesirable. Neurophysiological or biochemical studies involving or threatening physical injury are unthinkable.

Even aside from these cultural limitations, the human child has certain characteristics that render him a relatively limited subject for the experimental analysis of the maturation of learning capability. At birth, his neuromuscular systems are so undeveloped that he is incapable of effecting the precise head, arm, hand, trunk, leg, and foot movements essential for objective measurement. By the time these motor functions have adequately matured, many psychological developmental-processes, including those involving learning, have appeared and been elaborated, but their history and nature have been obscured or lost in a maze of confounded variables.

By the time the normal child has matured physically, he is engaging each day in such a fantastic wealth of multiple learning activities that precise, independent control over any single learning process presents a task beyond objective realism. The multiple, interactive transfer processes going on overwhelm description, and their independent experimental evaluation cannot be achieved. Even if it were proper to cage human children willfully, which it assuredly is not, this very act would in all probability render the children abnormal and untestable and again leave us with an insuperable problem.

It might appear that all these difficulties could be overcome best by studying the development of learning abilities in infraprimate organisms rather than monkeys. Unfortunately, the few researches which have been completed indicate that this is not true. Animals below the primate order are intellectually limited compared with monkeys, so that they learn the same problems more slowly and are incapable of solving many problems that are relatively easily mastered by monkeys. Horses and rats, and even cats and dogs, can solve only a limited repertoire of learning tasks, and they learn so slowly on all but the simplest of these that they pass from infancy to maturity before their intellectual measurement can be completed. Even so, we possess scattered information within this area. We know that cats perform more adequately on the Hamilton perseverance test than do kittens and that the same relationship holds for dogs compared with puppies (2, 3). It has been demonstrated that mature and aged rats are no more proficient on a multiple-T maze than young rats (11), and that conditioned responses cannot be established in dogs before 18–21 days of age [1]; but such data will never give us insight into the fundamental laws of learning or maturation of learning.

Neonatal and Early Infantile Learning: The First Sixty Days

Because learning and the development of learning are continuous, orderly processes, classifying learning into temporal intervals is an arbitrary procedure. However, a criterion that may be taken for separating early learning from later learning is the underlying motive or incentive. Solid foods are precluded as incentives for monkey learning prior to 40–60 days of age, forcing the experimenter to depend upon such rewards as liquid nutrients, shock avoidance, exploration, and home cage conditions. It is recognized that these same rewards may be used to motivate older primates on learning tasks, but for them the convenient incentive of solid food becomes available. Another arbitrary criterion that may be taken for choosing this temporal period lies in the fact that fear of strange, new situations—including test situations—only appears toward the end of this period.

Conditioned Responses. The earliest unequivocal learned responses which we obtained from the rhesus monkey were conditioned responses in a situation in which an auditory stimulus was paired with electric shock. The standard procedure was to adapt the neonatal monkeys during the first two days of life by placing them for ten minutes a day in the apparatus, which consisted of a cubic Plexiglas stabilimeter with a grid floor, enclosed in a sound-deadened cabinet with a one-way-vision screen on the front (see Figure 13–1). Conditioning trials were initiated on the third day, the tone and shock intervals being mechanically fixed at two seconds and one second, respectively, and administered either separately or paired. The animals were divided into three groups and were given daily trials as follows: five experimental subjects (T-S group) were given eight paired tone-shock trials and two test trials; four pseudoconditioning controls (P-C group) were given eight shock trials and two test trials in which tone only was presented; and four stimulus-sensitization controls (T-O group) received ten tone trials but never received shock

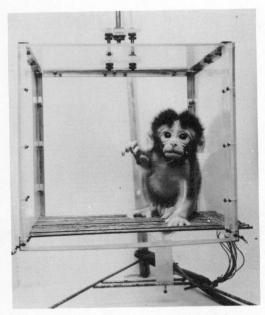

FIGURE 13–1.   Neonatal monkey in stabilimeter.

from the grid floor. Conditioned and unconditioned responses were measured in terms of both the continuous, objective activity records taken from an Esterline-Angus recorder and the check-list records made by two independent human observers.

The learning data presented in Figure 13–2 show early and progressive learning. The differences between the frequency of conditioned responses by the five experimental subjects and the four subjects in each of the control groups were significant, even though clear-cut evidence of pseudoconditioning was found in one of the P-C animals. It will be noted that the observers recorded a higher frequency of conditioned responses than could be identified from the stabilimeter record. The observational data indicate that these tone-shock conditioned responses were learned by three subjects on the second test day and that unequivocal conditioning took place in four of the five subjects. The observational data also show that the form of the conditioned response changes with training, starting as a diffuse response and gradually becoming more precise.

As training progressed, most subjects responded to the conditioned stimulus by standing erect, sometimes on one foot.

Limited tests failed to demonstrate any generalization of the conditioned response to the experimenter or to auditory stimuli presented outside the test situation. Retention tests made fifteen days after the completion of the original training revealed very considerable learning loss, ranging among individual subjects from no definite indication of retention, to conditioned responses on about half the test trials.

Straight-Runway Performance. An apparently simple learned response, which has been frequently used by psychologists in studying rat learning, is the straight runway. We produced such an apparatus by simply using the monkey's living cage as the runway and introducing a nursing booth at one end prior to each feeding period. At the time of testing, the subject was taken to the far end of the home cage, faced toward the nursing booth, released, and allowed thirty seconds to enter the booth. The number of daily trials was determined by number of feeding sessions, twelve a day during the first two weeks, and ten a day subsequently.

The subjects were divided into three groups: For the light-conditioned animals (L-C group) the nursing booth was suffused with flashing

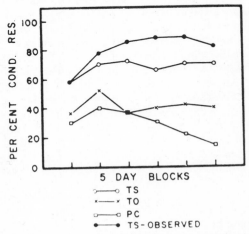

FIGURE 13–2.   Conditioned response to tone.

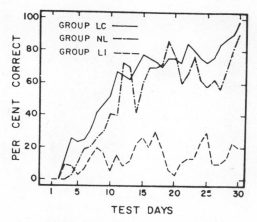

FIGURE 13–3.   Straight-runway performance.

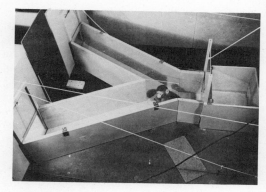

FIGURE 13–4.   Infant monkey Y-maze.

green light during each of the training trials; for the no-light monkeys (N-L group) there were no conditioning cues other than those afforded by the test situation and the act of orientation; for the light-extinguished subjects (L-I group) the nursing booth was suffused with green light, but this light was immediately extinguished when the monkey entered the booth and simultaneously there began a five-minute delay period before feeding.

The data presented in Figure 13–3 offer evidence of rapid and progressive improvement in performance. Many of the failures during the first ten days resulted from locomotor limitations or from the disturbing effects of reorientation and restraint by the experimenter. It is clear, however, that learning occurred early in life and that the cue of green light added little or nothing to the cues provided by the presence of the experimenter and postural orientation. The L-I group, which did not receive food upon approach to the nursing booth, was significantly inferior to the other two groups, and it is possible that the green light became a cue for absence or delay of feeding.

Spatial Discrimination.   Two groups of ten monkeys each were tested on a spatial discrimination problem requiring choice of the right or left alley of the Y-maze illustrated in Figure 13–4. One group of subjects began training at fifteen days of age (group 15), after

four days of adaptation, and the other group started maze learning at forty-five days of age (group 45). Two trials were given each day, a correct trial being rewarded by entrance into the home cage, a highly effective incentive for the infant monkey, whereas an incorrect response, defined as entrance into the incorrect antechamber, was punished by a one-minute delay before rerunning. A rerun technique was used throughout this test, i.e., whenever the monkey made an error, it was returned to the starting position and run again until it made the correct choice and reached the home cage. Spatial discrimination learning was continued for twenty-five days; on the twenty-sixth day the position of the correct goal box was reversed and the same training schedule of two trials per day continued.

The percentage of correct initial responses made by group 15 on days 1, 2, 5, 10, and 15

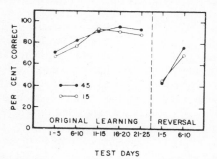

FIGURE 13–5.   Per cent correct response on Y-maze.

are 45, 60, 75, 75, and 95, respectively. Comparable percentages for group 45 are 80, 55, 65, 85, and 100. Despite the high percentage of correct responses made by group 45 on day 1, the two learning curves, as illustrated in Figure 13–5, are very similar. Excluding a single member in each group that failed to adapt to the test situation and never met the criterion of 18 correct responses in 20 consecutive trials, the mean number of trials to this criterion, excluding the criterional trials, was 8.5 for group 15 and 6.2 for group 45.

The percentage of correct responses dropped below chance for both groups of monkeys during the first five reversal trials, and trial 1 was especially characterized by multiple, persistent, erroneous choices. During all these trials the animals made many violent emotional responses as indicated by balking, vocalization, and autonomic responses, including blushing, urination, and defecation. Even so, all but one subject in group 15 attained the criterion of 18 correct responses in 20 consecutive trials, and the mean number of trials to learn, not including the criterional trials, was 19.2 for group 15 and 11.9 for group 45.

Although the performance of the older group was superior to that of the younger, particularly on the reversal problem, the differences were not statistically significant. Certainly the 15-day-old macaques solved this spatial learning task with facility, and their performance leaves little to be gained through additional maturation.

Object Discrimination. Two groups of four newborn monkeys were trained on a black-white discrimination, i.e., a nonspatial or object discrimination, by teaching them to select and climb up a black or white ramp for the reward of a full meal delivered through a nursing bottle. An incorrect choice was punished by a three-minute delay in feeding. As can be seen in Figure 13–6, not only the ramp, but the entire half of the test situation was black or white, as the case might be, and the positions of these half-cages were reversed on fifty per cent of the trials. The number of test trials was stabilized at nine per day after the first few days of life.

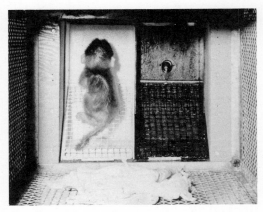

FIGURE   13–6. Black-white   discrimination apparatus.

Learning by the neonatal macaques in this test situation proved to be almost unbelievably rapid, even allowing for the fact that a maximally efficient stimulus display was provided by the totally black and totally white halves of the test chamber. As can be seen in Figure 13–7, the group of infants trained from birth on the object-discrimination problem attained the criterion of ninety per cent correct responses on two consecutive days beginning at nine days of age. This was a total of less than 100 trials, many of which were failed through physical inability to climb the ramp. A second group, run as a maturational control, was rewarded for climbing up either of two gray ramps for the first ten days. On day 11 the black and white

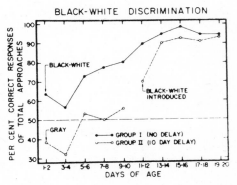

FIGURE   13–7. Black-white   discrimination learning.

ramps were substituted, and these monkeys solved the black-white discrimination problem, the first formal learning problem they had ever faced, by the second test day, averaging less than thirteen trials to achieve the criterion.

After the black-white discrimination problem was solved, the infants were tested on discrimination reversal, i.e., the color of ramp previously correct was now made incorrect, and the color of the ramp previously incorrect became correct. The results were very similar to those obtained in the spatial discrimination problem. The infants made a great many errors when the problem was first reversed and showed very severe emotional disturbances. This was particularly true when the reversal went from white correct to black, since infant monkeys strongly prefer white to black.

We have also a considerable body of data showing that the infant monkey can solve form discriminations and color discriminations as well as the black-white brightness-discrimination problem. It is not possible in these other situations, particularly in the case of form discrimination, to attain the maximally efficient stimulus display previously described. For this reason—and a control study suggests that it is for this reason alone—the number of trials required to learn increases and the age at which learning can be demonstrated also advances. Even so, it has been possible to obtain discrimination between a triangle and a circle by the 20- to 30-day-old monkey after less than 200 training trials.

Infant Learning: The First Year

The most surprising finding relating to neonatal learning was the very early age at which simple learning tasks could be mastered. Indeed, learning of both the simple conditioned response and the straight runway appeared as early as the animal was capable of expressing it through the maturation of adequate skeletal motor responses. Thus, we can in no way exclude the possibility that the monkey at normal term, or even before normal term, is capable of forming simple associations.

Equally surprising is the fact that performance may reach or approach maximal facility within a brief period of time. The five-day-old monkey forms conditioned reflexes between tone and shock as rapidly as the year-old or the adult monkey. The baby macaque solves the simple straight-alley problem as soon as it can walk, and there is neither reason nor leeway for the adult to do appreciably better. Although we do not know the minimal age for solution of the Y-maze, it is obviously under fifteen days. Such data as we have on this problem indicate that the span between age of initial solution and the age of maximally efficient solution is brief. One object discrimination, the differentiation between the total-black and total-white field, shows characteristics similar to the learning already described. The developmental period for solution lies between six and ten days of age, and a near maximal learning capability evolves rapidly. However, it would be a serious mistake to assume that any sharply defined critical periods characterize the development of more complex forms of learning or problem solving.

Object Discrimination Learning. Although the 11-day-old monkey can solve a total-black *versus* total-white discrimination problem in less than thirteen trials, the 20- to 30-day-old monkey may require from 150 to 200 trials to solve a triangle-circle discrimination problem when the stimuli are relatively small and placed some distance apart. It is a fact that, even though the capability of solving this more conventional type of object-discrimination problem exists at twenty days, object-discrimination learning capability has by no means attained full maturity at this time.

The development of complete object-discrimination capacity was measured by testing five different age groups of naive rhesus monkeys on a single discrimination problem. Discrimination training was begun when the animals were 60, 90, 120, 150, or 366 days of age, and, in all cases, training was preceded by at least fifteen days of adaptation to the apparatus and to the eating of solid food. There were eight subjects in group 366 (as defined by

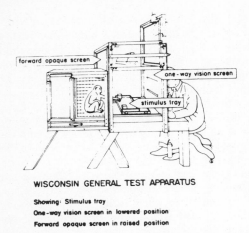

FIGURE 13–8. Wisconsin General Test Apparatus.

age), ten in group 60, and fifteen in each of the other groups. A Wisconsin General Test Apparatus, illustrated in Figure 13–8, was used throughout the test sessions. A single pair of three-dimensional stimuli differing in multiple attributes such as color, form, size, and material was presented on a two-foodwell test tray of the Klüver type. The animals were given twenty-five trials a day, five days a week, for four weeks, a total of 500 trials. A noncorrection method was always used.

Figure 13–9 presents the number of trials taken by the five different groups of monkeys, and performance by a 30-day-old group on a triangle-circle discrimination is plotted on the far left. Whether or not one includes this group, it is apparent that the ability of infant monkeys to solve the object-discrimination problem increases with age as a negatively accelerated function and approaches or attains an asymptote at 120 to 150 days.

Detailed analyses have given us considerable insight into the processes involved in the maturation of this learning function. Regardless of age, the monkeys' initial responsiveness to the problem is not random or haphazard. Instead, almost all the subjects approached the problem in some systematic manner. About twenty per cent of the monkeys chose the correct object from the beginning and stayed with

their choice, making no errors! Another twenty per cent showed a strong preference for the incorrect stimulus and made many errors. Initial preference for the left side and for the right side was about equally frequent, and consistent alternation-patterns also appeared. The older, and presumably brighter, monkeys rapidly learned to abandon any incorrect response tendency. The younger, and presumably less intelligent, monkeys persisted longer with the inadequate response tendencies, and very frequently shifted from one incorrect response tendency to another before finally solving the problem. Systematic responsiveness of this type was first described by Krechevsky (8) for rats and was given the name of "hypotheses." Although this term has unfortunate connotations, it was the rule and not the exception that our monkey subjects went from one "hypothesis" to another until solution, with either no random trials or occasionally a few random trials intervening. The total number of incorrect, systematic, response tendencies be-

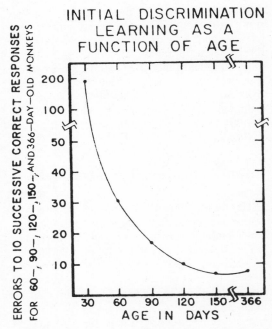

FIGURE 13–9. Initial discrimination learning as a function of age.

fore problem solution was negatively correlated with age.

These data on the maturation of discrimination learning capability clearly demonstrate that there is no single day of age nor narrow age-band at which object-discrimination learning abruptly matures. If the ''critical period'' hypothesis is to be entertained, one must think of two different critical periods, a period at approximately twenty days of age, when such problems can be solved if a relatively unlimited amount of training is provided, and a period at approximately 150 days of age, when a full adult level of ability has developed.

Delayed Response. The delayed-response problem has challenged and intrigued psychologists ever since it was initially presented by Hunter (6). In this problem the animal is first shown a food reward, which is then concealed within, or under, one of two identical containers during the delay period. The problem was originally believed to measure some high-level ideational ability or ''representative factor''—a capacity that presumably transcended simple trial-and-error learning. Additional interest in the problem arose from the discovery by Jacobsen (7) that the ability to solve delayed-response problems was abolished or drastically impaired by bilateral frontal lobectomy in monkeys.

Scores of researches have been conducted on delayed-response problems. Almost all known laboratory species have been tested and all conceivable parameters investigated. In so far as the delayed response is difficult, it appears to be less a function of period of delay or duration of memory than an intrinsic difficulty in responding attentively to an implicit or demonstrated reward. However, in spite of the importance of the problem and the vast literature which has accumulated, there has been no previous major attempt to trace its ontogenetic development in subhuman animals.

Ten subjects in each of four groups, a 60-, 90-, 120-, and 150-day group, were tested on so-called zero-second and five-second delayed responses (the actual delay period is approximately two seconds longer) at the same time

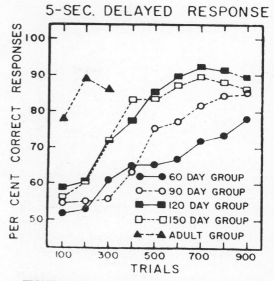

FIGURE 13–10. Delayed-response learning as a function of age.

they began their discrimination learning. A block of ten trials at each delay interval was presented five days a week for eighteen weeks, a total of ninety test days. These 900 trials at each delay interval constituted the test program for Series I, which was followed by Series II during which time delay intervals of 5, 10, 20, and 40 seconds were introduced in counterbalanced order for twelve test weeks of five days each at the rate of eight trials a day for each condition.

The results for the four infant groups on the five-second delayed responses and the performance of a group of adults with extensive previous test experience on many different problems are presented in Figure 13–10. The four infant groups show increasing ability to solve delayed responses both as a function of experience and as a function of age. The performance of all infant groups is inferior to the adult group, but differences in part learning experiences preclude any direct comparison.

The performance of the four infant groups of monkeys on the five-second delayed responses for trials 1–100, 201–300, 401–500, 601–700, and 801–900 is plotted in Figure 13–11. Be-

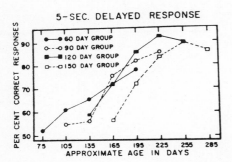

5-SEC. DELAYED RESPONSE

FIGURE 13–11. Delayed-response performance of different maturational groups with age held constant.

cause performance during trials 1–100 is poor regardless of group, it is apparent that a certain minimum experience is required to master the delayed-response task. At the same time, the increasingly steep slopes of the learning curves make it apparent that efficiency of delayed-response learning and performance is in large part a function of age. The group data suggest that, after extensive training as provided in this study, seventy per cent correct responses may be attained by 150 days of age, eighty per cent by 200 days, and ninety per cent by 250 days.

The performance at the 40-second delay interval by all monkeys tested in Series II is presented in Figure 13–12. The performances of the three older groups and the two younger groups are similar, and there are no significant differences between the adult group and the two older infant groups. Similar results were ob-

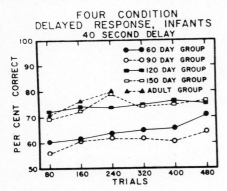

FIGURE 13–12. Delayed-response generalization to 40-second interval.

tained on the 5-, 10-, and 20-second delay intervals of the Series II tests except for the fact that the differences between the younger and older groups diminished progressively with decreasing delay intervals.

Very marked individual differences were disclosed during delayed-response testing, a finding which typifies this task regardless of species or age. Some monkeys, as well as some other animals, fail to adapt to the requirements of the test. Inspection of individual records reveals that the capability of solving this problem first appears at about 125 to 135 days of age and that essentially faultless performance may appear by 200 to 250 days in perhaps half the infant monkey subjects. Thus, some monkeys at this age may possess an adult capability, and these data are in keeping with the results obtained in the Series II tests. Recently, we have completed a study on a 30-month-old group of five monkeys on zero- and five-second delayed responses, and their learning rates and terminal performance are at adult levels. Thus, it appears that we have definitive data on the maturation and acquisition of delayed-response performance by rhesus monkeys.

It is obvious that the capability of solving the delayed-response problem matures at a later date than the capacity of solving the object-discrimination problem. This is true regardless of the criterion taken, whether it is the age at which the task can be solved after a relatively unlimited number of trials or the age at which a full adult level of mastery is attained. At the same time, it should be emphasized that this capacity does develop when the monkey is still an infant, long before many complex problems can be efficiently attacked and mastered. Thus, there is no reason to believe that the delayed response is a special measure of intelligence or of any particular or unusual intellectual function.

Object Discrimination Learning Set. The present writer, in 1949, demonstrated that adolescent or adult monkeys trained on a long series of six-trial discrimination problems showed progressive improvement from problem to problem. As successive blocks of problems

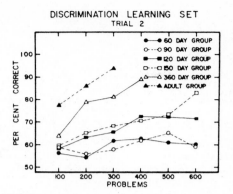

FIGURE 13–13. Learning set formation as a function of age.

were run, the form of the learning curve changed from positively accelerated, to linear, to negatively accelerated; finally, there appeared to be two separate curves or functions, i.e., performance changed from chance on trial 1 to perfection or near perfection on and after trial 2. From trial 1 to 2 the curve is precipitate and from trial 2 onward it is flat. This phenomenon, called "learning set formation" or "interproblem learning," has proved to be a useful tool in comparative, physiological, and theoretical psychology. To obtain evidence concerning the maturational factors involved, the performance of various age groups of monkeys was measured on this task.

The same five infant groups previously tested on a single object-discrimination problem served as subjects for learning-set training. Upon completion of the original discrimination problem they were tested on four discrimination problems a day five days a week, each problem six trials in length. Group 366 was trained on 400 problems and the other monkeys on 600 problems. The individual test-trial procedures were identical to those employed in regular object-discrimination learning, but a new pair of stimuli was introduced for each new problem.

The trial 2 performance of the five groups of infant monkeys is plotted in Figure 13–13, and data from mature monkeys tested in previous experiments are also given. The two younger groups fail to respond consistently above a sixty

per cent level even though they were approximately ten and eleven months of age at the conclusion of training. The two older groups show progressive, even though extremely slow, improvement in their trial 2 performances, with groups 120 and 150 finally attaining a seventy and eighty per cent level of correct responding. These data are in general accord with those obtained from an earlier, preliminary experiment and indicate that the year-old monkey is capable of forming discrimination learning sets even though it has by no means attained an adult level of proficiency.

In Figure 13–14 the trial 2 learning-set performance for the various groups is plotted in terms of age of completion of consecutive 100-problem blocks, and these data suggest that the capacity of the two younger groups to form discrimination learning sets may have been impaired by their early, intensive learning-set training, initiated before they possessed any effective learning-set capability. Certainly, their performance from 260 days onward is inferior to that of the earlier groups with less experience but matched for age. The problem which these data illustrate has received little attention among experimental psychologists. There is a tendency to think of learning or training as intrinsically good and necessarily valuable to the organism. It is entirely possible, however, that training can either be helpful or harmful, depending upon the nature of the training and the organism's stage of development.

Because of the fundamental similarities

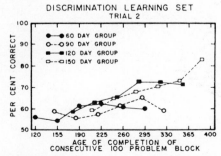

FIGURE 13–14. Learning set plotted for age of completion of consecutive 100 problem blocks.

existing between the learning of an individual problem and the learning of a series of problems of the same kind, it is a striking discovery that a great maturational gulf exists between efficient individual-problem learning and efficient learning-set formation. Information bearing on this problem has been obtained through detailed analyses by the author. The author's error-factor analysis technique (5) reveals that, with decreasing age, there is an increasing tendency to make stimulus-preservation errors, i.e., if the initially chosen object is incorrect, the monkey has great difficulty in shifting to the correct object. Furthermore, with decreasing age there is an increasing tendency to make differential-cue errors, i.e., difficulty in inhibiting, on any particular trial, the ambiguous reinforcement of the position of the stimulus which is concurrent with the reinforcement of the object *per se*.

In all probability, individual-problem learning involves elimination of the same error factors or the utilization of the same hypotheses or strategies as does learning-set formation. However, as we have already seen, the young rhesus monkey's ability to suppress these error factors in individual-problem learning does not guarantee in any way whatsoever a capacity to transfer this information to the interproblem learning-set task. The learning of the infant is

specific and fails to generalize from problem to problem, or, in Goldstein's terms, the infant possesses only the capacity for concrete thinking. Failure by the infant monkey to master learning-set problems is not surprising inasmuch as infraprimate animals, such as the rat and the cat, possess the most circumscribed capabilities for these interproblem learnings, and it is doubtful if the pigeon possesses any such ability at all. Indeed, discrimination learning-set formation taxes the prowess of the human imbecile and apparently exceeds the capacity of the human idiot.

Most of the findings which we have reported for the maturation of learning in the rhesus monkey had been predicted, but this was not true in the case of the string tests. Two of the theoretically simple patterns, the parallel strings and the two crossed strings, are illustrated in Figure 13–15. We had assumed that the infant monkey would solve the parallel pattern with few or no errors, but, as can be seen in Figure 13–16, this assumption did not accord with fact. The infant monkeys made many errors, learned slowly, and in many cases failed to reach a level of perfect responsiveness after prolonged training. The data on the relatively simple two-crossed-strings pattern (Figure 13–17) show that the six-month-old rhesus monkey is just beginning to reach the age at which this prob-

FIGURE 13–15. Infant monkeys shown responding incorrectly to both the parallel pattern and the two crossed-string pattern. A correct response involves pulling the string with the food attached.

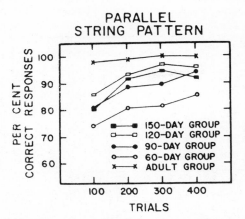

FIGURE 13–16. Parallel string pattern performance as a function of age.

lem can be mastered. Unfortunately, our data on patterned-strings learning are incomplete, but it is obvious that this capacity is a function which is maturing during the second half of the first year of life and probably for a considerable period of time henceforward. In retrospect, we realized that the relatively late maturation of string-test learning was in keeping with known

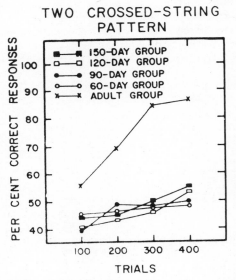

FIGURE 13–17. Two cross-string pattern performance as a function of age.

facts. The crossed-strings pattern has never been solved by any infraprimate animal, and this task cannot be resolved by the human infant (9, 10) until the second or third year of life.

The Development of Terminal Learning Ability

At the present time we have completed a series of experiments which clearly demonstrate that the capability of solving problems of increasing complexity develops in rhesus monkeys in a progressive and orderly manner throughout the first year of life. Furthermore, when we compare the performances of the year-old monkey and the adult monkey, it becomes obvious that maturation is far from complete at the end of the first year. Although our data on early development are more complete than our data on terminal learning capacities, we have already obtained a considerable body of information on middle and late learning growth.

Hamilton Perseverance Test. Just as we were surprised by the delayed appearance of the capability of mastering the patterned-strings tests, so were we surprised by the delay before performance on the Hamilton perseverance test attains maximal efficiency.

Three groups of monkeys were initially tested at 12, 30, and 50 months of age, respectively. The groups comprised six, five, and seven monkeys, and all were tested twenty trials a day for thirty days. On the perseverance problem the animal is faced with a series of four boxes having spring-loaded lids which close as soon as they are released. Only one box contains food, and the rewarded box is changed in a random manner from trial to trial with the provision that the same box is never rewarded twice in succession. In the present experiment the subjects were allowed only four responses per trial, whether or not the reward was obtained, and an error was defined as any additional response to an unrewarded box after the initial lifting of the lid during a trial. Infraprimate animals make many errors of this kind, but as can be seen in Figure 13–18, the mature

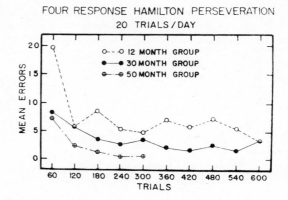

FOUR RESPONSE HAMILTON PERSEVERATION
20 TRIALS/DAY

FIGURE 13–18. Mean number of errors per 60-trial block on Hamilton perseverance test.

monkey makes few such errors and learns rather rapidly to eliminate these. We were surprised by the inefficient performance of the year-old monkey and unprepared to discover that maximally efficient performance was not attained by the 30-month-old monkeys.

The mature monkey finds a simple plan for attacking the perseverance problem. Typically, it chooses the extreme left or right box and works systematically toward the other end. If it adopts some more complex strategy, as responding by some such order as box 4–2–3–1, it will repeat this same order on successive trials.

Since the animal's procedural approach to the perseveration problem appeared to be an important variable, measures were taken of changes in the animal's order of responding from trial to trial, and these were defined as response-sequence changes. The data of Figure 13–19 show that the 50-month-old monkeys adopt the invariant type of behavior described above but that this is not true for either the 12- or 30-month-old groups. If a subject adopts an invariant response pattern, the problem is by definition simple; failure to adopt such a pattern can greatly complicate the task. In view of this fact it is not surprising that the 30-month-old subjects made so many errors; rather, it is surprising that they made so few—their error scores represent a triumph of memory over inadequate planning.

Relatively little research on the Hamilton perseverance method has been conducted by psychologists in spite of the fact that the origi-

FOUR RESPONSE HAMILTON PERSEVERATION
20 TRIALS/DAY

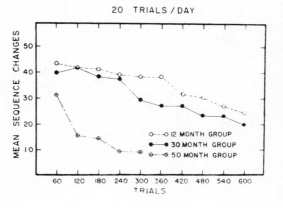

FIGURE 13–19. Mean number of sequence changes per 60-trial block on Hamilton perseverance test.

nal studies resulted in an effective ordering of Hamilton's wide range of subjects in terms of their position within the phyletic series. Furthermore, the limited ontogenetic material gave proper ordering of animal performance: kittens, puppies, and children were inferior to cats, dogs, and human adults. Above and beyond these facts, the perseverance data give support to the proposition that the rhesus monkey does not attain full intellectual status until the fourth or fifth year of life.

Oddity Test. Probably the most efficient tests that have been developed for measuring the maximal intellectual capability of the subhuman primates are the multiple-sign tests, whose solution is dependent upon appropriate responses to multiple, simultaneously presented cues. One of the simplest of these tests is that of oddity. Each oddity problem utilizes two identical pairs of stimuli, the ''A'' and the ''B'' stimuli. On any trial, three of the stimuli are presented simultaneously, as is shown in Figure 13–20, and the odd or different stimulus is correct and rewarded.

We have now completed a series of experiments using the two-position oddity problem, in which the correct stimulus is either in the right or left position, never in the center. In Figure 13–21 are presented data from a group of ten monkeys tested on 256 problems at 20 months of age and again at 36 months of age.

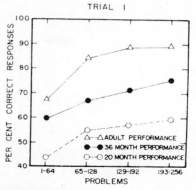

FIGURE 13–21. Performance on oddity problems as a function of age.

Comparable data for a group of six adult rhesus monkeys are also graphed. These data indicate increasingly efficient performance as a function of age. The performance differences at each of the three age levels are statistically significant, and there is every reason to believe that intellectual maturation as measured by this test is incomplete at three years.

Additional oddity learning data obtained by the same training techniques are presented in Figure 13–22. Again a group of ten monkeys was trained on oddity, first at 12 months of age and subsequently at 36 months of age. At 30 months of age, however, this group was divided into two groups of five monkeys each, one group being trained on a series of 480 six-trial discrimination problems and the other, 2400 delayed-response trials. The differences between the two groups on the oddity problems are statistically significant, with every indication of negative transfer from the learning-set to the oddity training. This is consistent with the fact that a single stimulus is uniformly correct on every discrimination problem but reverses frequently during the trials of each oddity problem. The transfer from delayed response to oddity may have been positive, since performance of the 36-month-old group with delayed-response training is superior to the comparable 36-month-old group whose performance is included in Figure 13–21. But, in

FIGURE 13–20. Correct response to oddity problem.

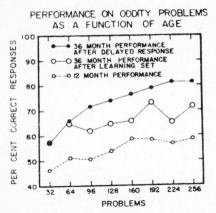

PERFORMANCE ON ODDITY PROBLEMS
AS A FUNCTION OF AGE

● 36 MONTH PERFORMANCE
  AFTER DELAYED RESPONSE
○—○ 36 MONTH PERFORMANCE
  AFTER LEARNING SET
○----○ 12 MONTH PERFORMANCE

FIGURE 13–22. Performance on oddity problems as a function of age and past experience.

neither case does a 36-month-old group attain an adult performance level.

For the neonatal and infant rhesus monkey each learning task is specific unto itself, and the animal's intellectual repertoire is composed of multiple, separate, and isolated learned experiences. With increasing age, problem isolation changes to problem generalization, and this fundamental reorganization of the monkey's intellectual world apparently begins in its second year of life. From here on, we can no longer specify the monkey's learning ability for any problem merely in terms of maturational age and individual differences. The variable of kind and amount of prior experience must now be given proper value. This is the characteristic of monkey learning, and, in fact, learning by all higher primates as they come of intellectual age.

Monkeys do not attain full oddity performance at three years of age, and oddity learning is by no means the most complicated learning task that the adult rhesus monkey can solve. Oddity-nonoddity learning, in which the subject is required to choose either the odd or the nonodd stimulus, depending upon the color of the test tray presented on a particular trial, can be solved relatively routinely by the adult monkey. Considerably more complex learning problems have been mastered by highly trained rhesus subjects. We are in no position to determine the monkey's age of intellectual maturity, but four or five years of age is a reasonable estimate.

Summary and Interpretation

Half a decade is entirely too brief a period to establish a definitive program on the maturation of learning ability in the rhesus monkey, particularly in the later age ranges. However, within this period of time we have developed the techniques and conducted tests which demonstrate that such a program is entirely feasible. The monkey is capable of solving simple learning problems during the first few days of life and its capability of solving ever increasingly complex problems matures progressively, probably for four to five years.

Early in life, new learning abilities appear rather suddenly within the space of a few days, but, from late infancy onward, the appearance of new learning powers is characterized by developmental stages during which particular performances progressively improve. There is a time at which increasingly difficult problems can first be solved, and a considerably delayed period before they can be solved with full adult efficiency.

The monkey possesses learning capacities far in excess of those of any other infrahuman primate, abilities probably comparable to those of low-level human imbeciles. The monkey's learning capabilities can give us little or no information concerning human language, and only incomplete information relating to thinking. These are the generalizable limits of learning research on rhesus monkeys, but they still leave us with an animal having vast research potentialities. There is a wealth of learning problems which the monkey can master, and at present the field is incompletely explored. The maturation of any learning function can be traced and the nature and mechanisms underlying interproblem and intertask transfer can be assessed. There exist great research potentialities in analyzing the fundamental similarities and differences among simple and complex learnings within a single species. The monkey is the subject ideally suited for studies involving neurological, biochemical, and pharmacological correlates of behavior. To date, such studies have been limited to adult monkeys, or monkeys of unspecified age, but such limited researches are no longer a necessity. We now know that rhesus monkeys can be raised under completely controlled conditions throughout a large part, and probably all, of their life span, and we may expect that the research of the future will correlate the neurophysiological variables, not with the behavior of the static monkey, but with the behavior of the monkey in terms of ontogenetic development.

REFERENCES

1. Fuller, J. F., Easler, C. A., and Banks, E. M. Formation of conditioned avoidance responses in young puppies. *Am. J. Physiol., 160,* 462–466 (1950).
2. Hamilton, G. V. A study in trial and error reactions in animals. *J. Anim. Behavior, 1,* 33–66 (1911).
3. Hamilton, G. V. A study of perseverance reactions in primates and rodents. *Behav. Monogr., 3,* No. 2, 1–63 (1916).
4. Harlow, H. F. The formation of learning sets. *Psychol. Rev., 56,* 51–65 (1949).
5. Harlow, H. F. Analysis of discrimination learning by monkeys. *J. Exp. Psychol., 40,* 26–39 (1950).
6. Hunter, W. F. The delayed reaction in animals and children. *Behav. Monogr. 2,* 21–30 (1913).
7. Jacobsen, C. F. An experimental analysis of the frontal association areas in primates. *Arch. Nerv. Ment. Dis., 82,* 1–14 (1935).
8. Krechevsky, I. "Hypothesis" vs. "chance" in the pre-solution period in sensory discrimination learning. *Univ. Calif. Publ. Psychol., 6,* 27–44 (1932).
9. Matheson, E. A study of problem solving behavior in pre-school children. *Child Develpm., 2,* No. 4, 242–262 (1931).
10. Richardson, H. M. The growth of adaptive behaviour in infants. *Genet. Psychol. Monogr., 12,* 195–357 (1932).
11. Stone, C. P. The age factor in animal learning: II. Rats on a multiple light discrimination box and a difficult image. *Genet. Psychol. Monogr., 6,* No. 2, 125–202 (1929).
12. van Wagenen, G. The monkey. In *The care and breeding of laboratory animals,* E. J. Farris (Ed.), pp. 1–42. New York: Wiley, 1950.

14. CONTRIBUTIONS OF LEARNING TO HUMAN DEVELOPMENT[1]

ROBERT M. GAGNÉ

Models of human intellectual development are critically considered. Two well-known models, often contrasted, are growth-readiness, associated with the writings of Hall and Gesell, and cognitive adaptation, developed by Piaget and used extensively by other investigators. A 3rd model, cumulative learning, is given an exposition in this article. Applications of this model are discussed, including an analysis of the conservation of liquid volume as a learned capability of young children. Implications of the cumulative learning model for transfer of learning are also described.

One of the most prominent characteristics of human behavior is the quality of change. Among those who use the methods of science to account for human behavior are many whose interest centers upon the phenomena of behavioral change, and more specifically, on change in behavior capabilities. Sometimes, changes in behavior capabilities are studied with respect to relatively specific forms of behavior, usually over relatively limited periods of time—hours, days, or weeks. In such instances, the investigator names the processes he studies *learning* and *memory*. Another major class of phenomena of capability change comprises general classes of behavior observed over longer periods of time—months and years. The latter set of events is usually attributed to a process called *development*.

The reality of these two kinds of capability change is obvious in everyday experience, and requires no special experimentation to verify. The capabilities of the young child, for example, change before our eyes every day, as he learns new names for things, new motor skills, new facts. In addition, his more general capabilities develop, over the months, as he becomes able to express his wants by means of word phrases, and later to communicate in terms of entire sentences and even longer sequences of ideas, both in oral and printed form. From these common observations one can distinguish in at least an approximate sense between the specific short-term change called learning, and the more general and long-term change called development.

To distinguish learning and development is surely a practically useful thing, for many purposes. At the same time, the two kinds of processes must be related to each other in some way. The accumulation of new names for things that the child learns is quite evidently related to the capability he develops for formulating longer and more complex sentences. The specific printed letters he learns to discriminate are obviously related to the development of his skill in reading. The question is, how? What is the nature of the relation between the change called learning, on the one hand, and the change called development, on the other?

Over a period of many years, several different answers have been proposed for this question of the relation between learning and development. Investigators in this field have in general been concerned with accumulating evidence which they interpret as being consonant or dissonant with certain theories, or models. Usually the model they have in mind is fairly clear, even though it may not be explicitly represented in their writings.

[1] This article is a slightly modified version of the Address of the Vice President, Section I (Psychology), American Association for the Advancement of Science, Annual Meeting of the Association, Washington, D. C., December 1966.

Models of Human Behavioral Development

It is my purpose here to consider what certain of these models are, and what their implications are for continuing research on human learning and development. Specifically, I am interested in contrasting certain features of models which appear to be of commanding interest in present-day research. I hope by this means to clarify some issues, so that they may, perhaps, be subjected to experimental testing in a manner that will allow us to sharpen and strengthen our inferences about the nature of human behavioral development.

It is inevitable that the theme of genetically determined growth, or maturation, as opposed to influences of the environment, will run through any discussion of the nature of behavioral development. Everyone will agree, surely, that development is the result of an interaction of growth and learning. There are enormous practical consequences associated with this issue—for example, in designing education for the young. If growth is the dominant theme, educational events are designed to wait until the child is ready for learning. In contrast, if learning is a dominant emphasis, the years are to be filled with systematically planned events of learning, and there is virtually no waiting except for the time required to bring about such changes.

It will be clear enough that my own views emphasize the influence of learning, rather than growth, on human behavioral development. But this is not because I deny the importance of growth. Rather it is because I wish to come to grips with the problem of what specific contributions learning can make to development, and by inference, what kinds of learned capabilities enter into the process of development. I want particularly to contrast a model of development which attempts to account specifically for learning effects with certain other models that do not do so. When I describe this model, you will perhaps agree that it can be conveyed briefly by means of the statement: Within limitations imposed by growth, *behavioral development results from the cumulative effects of learning.*

To set the stage for a model of this sort, it seems desirable first to mention two other models that are more or less in current use, and which have been in existence for some time. The first of these may be called the *growth-readiness model,* which has been associated in previous times with such theorists as G. Stanley Hall (1907) and Arnold Gesell (1928), among others. Briefly, it states that certain organized patterns of growth must occur before learning can effectively contribute to development. Major evidence for this theory comes primarily from studies of the development of physical and motor functions in young children. A prototype study in this field (Gesell & Thompson, 1929) involved special training in stair-climbing for one of a pair of identical twins at the age of 46 weeks, no special training for the other twin. At 53 weeks, the untrained twin did not climb as well as the trained twin. But after 2 weeks of training, one-third as much as the total given to the trained twin, she actually surpassed the trained twin in performance. What this and many similar studies are usually interpreted to mean is that training for a motor performance might as well wait, in fact had better wait, until the child is maturationally "ready," before beginning the specific regime of training leading to the desired proficiency. The findings are consistent with this model. Other writers have pointed out that giving the untrained twin no special training doesn't mean that the child is learning nothing during this period. Unfortunately, the study is not therefore a truly critical one for testing predictions from the theory. Actually, it must be said that much other evidence bearing upon this model suffers from this kind of defect.

A second model of considerable importance, particularly because it has attracted much attention, is that of Piaget. Although the interaction of the child with his environment is given a specific role in this theory, it is well to recognize that it is in some fundamental sense a theory which assigns only a contributory importance to the factor of learning (Flavell, 1963,

p. 46; Sonstroem, 1966, p. 214). The model may be summarized, briefly and therefore not without some injustice, in the following statements:

1.   Intellectual development is a matter of progressive internalization of the forms of logic. The sequence of development manifests itself at first through motor action, later through concrete mediation of ideas, and still later through complete symbolic representation.

2.   Progress in development is affected by the interaction of the child with his environment. New experiences are *assimilated* into existing cognitive structures, and newly acquired structures in turn make possible *accommodation* to the demands imposed by the environment. The total process, as Flavell (1963, p. 47) points out, may be considered one of *cognitive adaptation*.

This theory has been accompanied by a great mass of observational evidence, gathered over a period of many years, by Piaget and his colleagues in Geneva. They have observed children's performance of a variety of tasks, including those having to do with number, quantity, time, movement, velocity, spatial and geometrical relations, the operations of chance, and reasoning, among others. Generally speaking, the method has been to present the child with a concrete situation, say, two arrays of beads differing in spatial arrangement, and to ask probing questions in the attempt to determine the nature of the child's understanding of the situation. The behavior of the same child may then be tested again at a later age; or his behavior may be compared with that of older children on the same task.

There have been a number of confirming studies of Piaget's findings carried out by several investigators in various countries of the world (Dodwell, 1961; Elkind, 1961; Lovell, 1961; Peel, 1959). More important for present purposes, however, are the several studies which have attempted to induce particular kinds of intellectual development by means of specific instruction (or learning). Many of these are described by Flavell (1963, p. 370 ff.), and need not be reviewed here. One prototype

investigation, by Wohlwill and Lowe (1962), took the following form: Kindergarten children were tested on a task dealing with "conservation of number," requiring them to recognize that the rearrangement of a set of objects in space does not alter their number. Three different groups of the children were given three different varieties of training, each designed to provide them with a mediational way of arriving at conservation of number. A fourth group served as a control, and was given no training. The results were that no effects could be shown of any of the kinds of training. The group improved their performance somewhat, but the experimental groups gained no more than the control group. Other experiments by Smedslund (1961a, 1961b, 1961c, 1961d, 1961e) lead to much the same conclusion.

Another example is provided by a recent experiment reported by Roeper and Sigel (1966), this time concerned with the tasks of conservation of quantity, using standard situations described by Piaget and Inhelder (1964) for conservation of substance, liquid substance, weight, and volume. In this case the trained groups of 5-year-old children were given fairly extensive general training in classifying, in reversibility, in seriation, three mental operations identified by Piaget as involved in the development of ideas of conservation in children. To summarize individual results very briefly, it was found that some trained children *did* improve on some tasks, but not on all of them. In contrast, the untrained control children showed no improvement. But the effectiveness of training was by no means general—one child might achieve a success in conservation of weight, but not in conservation of volume.

There have been quite a number of experiments using conservation-type tasks, and I have only mentioned here what seem to me a couple of representative examples. Generally speaking, the results seem to be summarizable as follows. Tasks which require young children to respond to situations reflecting conservation of substance, volume, weight, and number do not appear to be readily modifiable by means of instruction and training which is aimed rather directly at overcoming the typical deficiencies exhibited by children. Where such training has been shown to have some effect, it is usually a very specific one, tied closely to the situation presented in training, and not highly generalizable. On the whole, any impartial review of these studies would doubtless be forced to conclude that they do not contradict Piaget's notions of cognitive adaptation, and in fact appear to lend some support to the importance of maturational factors in development.

It is my belief that there is an alternative theory of intellectual development to which many students of child behavior would subscribe. In particular, it is one which would be favored by those whose scientific interest centers upon the process of learning. Naturally enough, it is one which emphasizes learning as a major causal factor in development, rather than as a factor merely involved in adaptation, as is true in Piaget's theory; or rather than a strictly incidental factor, as in the theory of maturational readiness. It is easy enough to identify the philosophical roots of such a theory in American psychology. Perhaps the proponents who most readily come to mind are John B. Watson (1924) and B. F. Skinner (1953), both of whom have given great weight to the importance of environmental forces, of learning, in the determination of development.

But philosophy is not enough. As Kessen (1965, p. 271) points out, for some reason not entirely clear, those theorists who have generally emphasized the influences of environment, as opposed to growth, have also generally espoused a rather radical type of associationism. Thus, they have maintained not only that learning is a primary determinant of intellectual development, but also that what is learned takes the form of simple "connections" or "associations." To account for how a child progresses from a stage in which he fails to equate the volume of a liquid poured from one container into a taller narrower container, to a stage in which he succeeds in judging these volumes equal, seems to me quite impossible to accomplish on the basis of learned "connections." At the least, it must be said that there is no model which really does this. Furthermore,

the experiments which have tried to bring about such a change, largely on the basis of "associationistic" kinds of training, have not succeeded in doing so.

In contrast to a weak and virtually empty "associationistic" model, it is not surprising that a theory like Piaget's has considerable appeal to students of development. It tells us that there are complex intellectual operations, which proceed generally from stages of motor interaction through progressive internal representation to symbolic thought. As an alternative, we may choose a theory like Bruner's (1965), which conceives the developmental sequence to be one in which the child represents the world first enactively (through direct motor action), then ikonically (through images), and finally symbolically. These are models with a great deal of substance to them, beside which the bare idea of acquiring "associations" appears highly inadequate to account for the observed complexities of behavior.

The Cumulative Learning Model

The point of view I wish to describe here states that learning contributes to the intellectual development of the human being because it is *cumulative* in its effects. The child progresses from one point to the next in his development, not because he acquires one or a dozen new associations, but because he learns an ordered set of capabilities which build upon each other in progressive fashion through the processes of differentiation, recall, and transfer of learning. Investigators of learning know these three processes well in their simplest and purest forms, and spend much time studying them. But the cumulative effects that result from discrimination, retention, and transfer over a period of time within the nervous system of a given individual, have not been much studied. Accordingly, if there is a theory of *cumulative learning*, it is rudimentary at present.

If one cannot, as I believe, put together a model of cumulative learning whose elements are associations, what will these entities be? What is it that is learned, in such a way that it can function as a building block in cumulative learning? Elsewhere (Gagné, 1965) I have outlined what I believe to be the answer to this question, by defining a set of learned capabilities which are distinguishable from each other, first, as classes of human performance, and second, by their requirements of different conditions for their acquisition. These are summarized in Figure 14–1.

The basic notion is that much of what is learned by adults and by children takes the form of complex rules. An example of such a rule is, "Stimulation of a neural fiber changes the electrical potential of the outer surface of the neural membrane relative to its inner surface." I need to emphasize that "rule" refers to what might be called the "meaning" of such a statement, and not to its verbal utterance. These ideas are learned by individuals who have already learned, and can recall, certain simpler rules; in this instance, for example, one of these simpler rules would be a definition of electrical potential. Simple rules, in their turn, are learned when other capabilities, usually called concepts, have been previously learned. Again, in this instance, one can identify the presence of concepts like "stimulation," "fiber," "electric," "surface," and "membrane," among

others. In their turn, the learning of concepts depends upon the availability of certain discriminations; for, example, the idea of surface has been based in part on prior learning of discriminations of extent, direction, and texture of a variety of actual objects. In the human being, multiple discriminations usually require prior learning of chains, particularly those which include verbal mediators. And finally, these chains are put together from even simpler learned capabilities which have traditionally been called "associations" or "S-R connections."

The identification of what is learned, therefore, results in the notion that all these kinds of capabilities are learned, and that each of them is acquired under somewhat different external conditions. By hypothesis, each of them is also learned under different *internal* conditions, the most important of these being what the individual already has available in his memory. It is clear that associations, although they occupy a very basic position in this scheme, are not learned very frequently by adults, or even by 10-year-olds. Mainly, this is because they have already been learned a long time ago. In contrast, what the 10-year-old learns with great frequency are rules and concepts. The crucial theoretical statement is that the learning of such things as rules and concepts depends upon the recallability of previously learned discriminations, chains, and connections.

Examples of Cumulative Learning

Some verification of the idea of cumulative learning has come from studies of mathematics learning, an example of which is Gagné, Mayor, Garstens, and Paradise (1962). Seventh-grade students acquired a progressively more complex set of rules in order to learn the ultimate performances of adding integers, and also of demonstrating in a logical fashion how the addition of integers could be derived from number properties. The results of this study showed that, with few exceptions, learners who

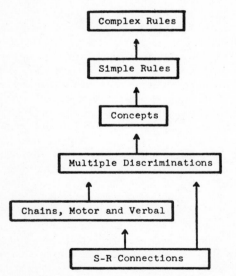

FIGURE 14–1. A general sequence for cumulative learning.

were able to learn the capabilities higher in the hierarchy also knew how to do the tasks reflected by the simpler rules lower in the hierarchy. Those who had not learned to accomplish a lower-level task generally could not acquire a higher-level capability to which it was related.

These results illustrate the effects of cumulative learning. They do so, however, in a very restricted manner, since they deal with a development period of only 2 weeks. Another form of restriction arises from the fact that only rules were being learned in this study, rather than all of the varieties of learned capabilities, such as concepts, discriminations, chains, and connections. In another place (Gagné, 1965, p. 181) I have attempted to spell out in an approximate manner a more complete developmental sequence, applicable to a younger age, pertaining to the final task of ordering numbers. In this case it is proposed that rules pertaining to the forming of number sets depend upon concepts such as joining, adding, and separation; that these in turn are dependent upon simpler capabilities like multiple discriminations in distinguishing numerals; while these depend upon such verbal chains as naming numerals and giving their sequence. Following this developmental sequence to even earlier kinds of learning, it is recognized that children learn to draw the numerals themselves, and that at an even earlier stage they learn the simplest kinds of connections such as orally saying the names of numerals and marking with a pencil.

It should be quite clear that this cumulative learning sequence is only a suggested, possible one, and not one which has received verification, as was true of the previous example. I doubt that it is at all complete. It attempts to show that it is possible to conceive that all of the various forms of learned capabilities are involved in a cumulative sense in the first-grade task of ordering numbers—not only the specific rules that are directly connected with the task, but also a particular set of concepts, discriminations, chains, and connections which have been previously learned. Normally, such prior learning has taken place over a period of several years, of course. And this means that it

would be quite difficult to establish and verify a cumulative learning sequence of this sort in its totality. If such verification is to be obtained, it must be done portion by portion.

A Cumulative Learning Sequence in Conservation

Can a cumulative learning sequence be described for a task like the conservation of liquid, as studied by Piaget (cf. Piaget & Inhelder, 1964)? Suppose we consider as a task the matching of volumes of liquids in rectangular containers like those shown in Figure 14-2. When the liquid in A is poured into Container B, many children (at some particular age levels) say that the taller Container B has more liquid. Similarly, in the second line of the figure, children of particular ages have been found to say that the volume in the shallower Container B, exhibiting a larger surface area, is the greater.

What is it these children need to have learned, in order to respond correctly to such situations as these? From the standpoint of the cumulative learning model, they need to have learned a great many things, as illustrated in Figure 14-3.

First of all, you may want to note that "conservation of liquid" is not a behaviorally defined task; accordingly I have attempted to state one that is, namely, "judging equalities and inequalities of volumes of liquids in rec-

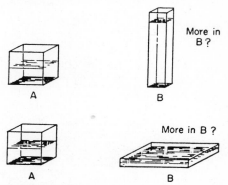

FIGURE 14-2. Two tasks of "conservation of liquid" of the sort used by Piaget and other investigators.

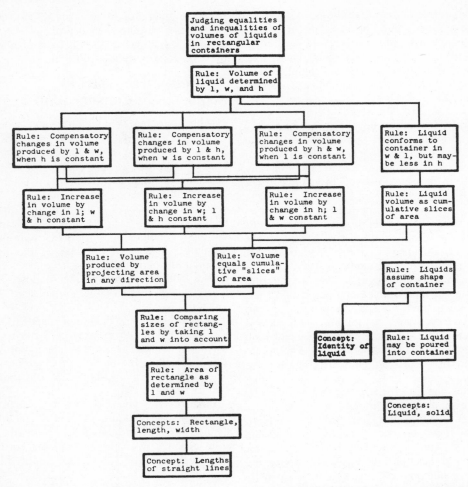

FIGURE 14–3.   A cumulative learning sequence pertaining to the development of nonmetric judgments of liquid volume.

tangular containers." However, such behavior is considered to be rule-based, and could be restated in that form.

"Nonmetric" is also a word requiring comment. What this diagram attempts to describe is a cumulative learning sequence (in other words, a developmental sequence), that obtains approximate volume matchings without the use of numbers, multiplication, or a quantitative rule. I believe such a learning sequence can occur, and perhaps sometimes does occur, in children uninstructed in mathematical concepts of volume. Choosing this particular

sequence, then, has the advantage of application to children who are more like those on whom Piaget and others have tried the task. But let it be clear that it is by no means the *only* learning route to the performance of this task. There must be at least several such sequences, and obviously, one of them is that which *does* approach the final performance through the multiplication of measured quantities.

The first subordinate learning that the child needs to have learned is the rule that volume of a liquid (in rectangular containers) is determined by length, width, and height. A change in any of these will change volume. This means that the child knows that any perceived change in any of these dimensions means a different volume. Going down one step in the learnings required, we find three rules about compensatory changes in two dimensions when another dimension remains constant. That is, if the height of a liquid remains the same in two different containers one can have the same volume if a change in width is compensated by a change in length. Similarly for the other instances of compensatory change.

Now, in order for a child to learn these compensatory rules, the model says, he must have previously learned three other rules, relating to change in only one dimension at a time. For example, if length is increased while width and height remain constant, volume increases. Again, similarly for the other single dimensions. These rules in turn presuppose the learning of still other rules. One is that volume of a container is produced by accumulating "slices" of the same shape and area; and a second is that volume can be projected from area in any direction, particularly, up, to the front or back, and to the right or left. Finally, one can work down to considerably simpler rules, such as those of comparing areas of rectangles by compensatory action of length and width; and the dependence of area upon the dimensions of length and width. If one traces the development sequence still farther, he comes to the even simpler learned entities, concepts, including rectangle, length, width, and an even simpler one, the concept of length of a straight line.

Just to complete the picture, the model includes another branch which has to do with liquids in containers, rather than with the containers themselves, and which deals on simpler levels with rules about liquids and the concept of a liquid itself. This branch is necessary because at the level of more complex rules, the child must distinguish between the volume of the liquid and the volume of the container. Of particular interest also is the concept of liquid identity, the recognition by the child that a given liquid poured into another container is still the same liquid. Such a concept may fairly be called a "logical" one, as Piaget

does. Bruner (1966) presents evidence tending to show that identity of this primitive sort occurs very early in the child's development, although its communication through verbal questions and answers may be subject to ambiguities.

Having traced through the "stages" in learning which the model depicts, let me summarize its characteristics as a whole, and some of their implications.

1. First, it should be pointed out that this model, or any other derived in this manner, represents the hypothesis-forming part of a scientific effort, not the verification part. This specific model has not been verified, although it would seem possible to do so. In the process of verification, it is entirely possible that some gaps would be discovered, and this would not be upsetting to the general notion of cumulative learning.

2. According to this way of looking at development, a child has to learn a number of subordinate capabilities before he will be able to learn to judge equalities of volume in rectangular containers. Investigators who have tried to train this final task have often approached the job by teaching one or two, or perhaps a few, of these subordinate capabilities, but not all of them in a sequential manner. Alternatively, they may have given direct practice on the final task. According to the model, the incompleteness of the learning programs employed accounts for the lack of success in having children achieve the final task.

3. In contrast to other developmental models, some of them seemingly based on Piaget's, the cumulative learning model proposes that what is lacking in children who cannot match liquid volumes is not simply logical processes such as "conservation," "reversibility," or "seriation," but concrete knowledge of containers, volumes, areas, lengths, widths, heights, and liquids.

Generalization and Transfer

There is still another important characteristic of a cumulative learning model remaining to be dealt with. This is the fact that any learned capability, at any stage of a learning sequence, may operate to mediate other learning which was not deliberately taught. Generalization or transfer to new tasks, and even to quite unanticipated ones, is an inevitable bonus of learning. Thus the child who has been specifically instructed via the learning sequence shown in the previous figure has actually acquired a much greater learning potential than is represented by the depicted sequence itself.

Suppose, for example, we were to try to get a child who had already learned this sequence to learn another requiring the matching of volumes in cylindrical containers. Could he learn this second task immediately? Probably not, because he hasn't yet learned enough about cylinders, volumes of cylinders, and areas of circles. But if we look for useful knowledge that he *has* acquired, we find such things as the rule about liquids assuming the shapes of their containers, and the one about volumes being generated by cumulative "slices" of areas. The fact that these have been previously learned means that they do not have to be learned all over again with respect to cylinders, but simply recalled. Thus a cumulative learning sequence for volumes of liquids in cylinders could start at a higher "stage" or "level" than did the original learning sequence for rectangular containers. Cumulative learning thus assumes a built-in capacity for transfer. Transfer occurs because of the occurrence of specific identical (or highly similar) elements within developmental sequences. Of course, "elements" here means rules, concepts, or any of the other learned capabilities I have described.

It will be noted that the final tasks of the developmental sequences I have described are very specific. They are performances like "matching volumes in rectangular containers." Does the existence of transfer imply that if enough of these specific tasks are learned, the child will thereby attain a highly general principle which might be called *substance conservation?* The answer to this question is "no." The model implies that an additional hierarchy of higher-order principles would have to be acquired before the individual might be said to have a principle of substance conservation. Transferability among a collection of

such specific principles will not, by itself, produce a capability which could be called the principle of substance conservation, or the principle of conservation.

What *is* possible with a collection of specific principles regarding conservation, together with the transfer of learning they imply, is illustrated in Figure 14–4.

Suppose the learner, making use of transfer of learning where available, has acquired all four of the specific conservation principles shown in the bottom row—dealing with conservation of number, conservation of liquid volumes in both rectangular and cylindrical containers, and conservation of solid volumes. Others could be added, such as conservation of weight, but these will do for present purposes. The property of learning transfer makes possible the ready acquisition of still more complex principles, such as the example given here—judging the volumes of liquids in irregularly shaped containers. It is easy to see that by *combining* the principles applicable to volume of rectangular containers, and others applicable to cylindrical containers, a learner could easily acquire a capability of estimating volumes of irregularly shaped containers. Other kinds of combinations of previously acquired knowledge are surely possible. As I have pointed out, this is the kind of generalizing capability made possible by the existence of learning transfer.

In contrast to this new entity in the developmental sequence, an external observer may, if he wishes, look at the *collection* of what the individual has learned about conservation, and decide he will call this collection the principle of conservation. An external observer is perfectly capable of doing this, and he may have legitimate reasons for doing so. But what he achieves by so doing is still an abstraction which exists in his mind, and not in the mind of the learner. If the external observer assumes that because he can make this classification of such an entity as a principle of conservation, the same entity must therefore exist as a part of the learner's capabilities, he is very likely making a serious mistake. The learner has only the specific principles he has learned, along with their potentialities for transfer.

I believe that many of the principles men-

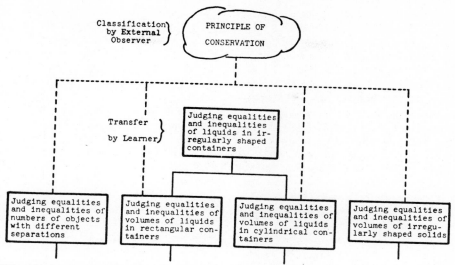

FIGURE 14–4. The contrast between a principle acquired by the learner through transfer from previously learned principles, and a "principle of conservation" used as a classificatory aid by an external observer.

tioned by Piaget, including such things as reversibility, seriation, and the groupings of logical operations, are abstractions of this sort. They are useful descriptions of intellectual processes, and they are obviously in Piaget's mind. But they are not in the child's mind.

Another example of how such abstractions may be useful for planning instructional sequences, but not as integral components of intellectual development, may be seen in exercises in science for elementary school children, titled *Science—A Process Approach,* developed by the Commission on Science Education of the American Association for the Advancement of Science (1965). One of the processes these exercises intend that young school children learn is called Observation. But it would be incorrect to think that the designers of this material believe that something like the Principle of Observation is to be directly taught to children as an intellectual entity. Observation in this case is an abstraction, which exists in the minds of the designers, but not in the minds of children. What the children *do* learn is a rather comprehensive collection of specific capabilities, which enable them to identify several fundamental properties of the world of objects—tastes, odors, sounds, the solid-liquid

distinction, color, size, shape, texture, as well as changes in these. Each is a fairly specific capability, applying to a class of properties only one step removed in abstraction from the objects themselves. At the same time, transfer of learning makes it possible for the child to build upon these things he has learned, and to learn to identify objects or changes in them in a manner which requires the use of several senses at once.

These instructional materials make it clear that the specific capabilities of observation are considered to have transfer value to other kinds of things which are learned later on—to classifying and measuring and predicting and inferring, as well as to other activities involved in scientific experimentation. Transfer of these specific capabilities takes place in many ways and in many directions. But the processes themselves are not acquired as a part of the child's mental constitution. They are merely external names for a collection of capabilities, as well as for the developmental sequences on which these are built.

Returning to the general theme, it should be clear that the various kinds of capabilities that children learn cumulatively, despite their relative specificity, provide a totality of transferable knowledge that is rich in potentialities for further learning. New combinations are possible at any time between principles acquired, let us say, in a context of containers of water, on the one hand, and in the very different context of exchanges of money, on the other. Furthermore, it is recognized that such generalizations can readily occur when the individual himself initiates the intellectual activity; the new learning does not have to be guided by external instruction. The process of cumulative learning can involve and be contributed to by the operations of inductive and deductive thinking. The cumulative learning model obviously does not provide a theory of thinking; but it suggests the elements with which such a theory might deal.

Summary

What I have attempted to describe is a model of human intellectual development based upon the notion of cumulative learning, which contrasts in a number of respects with developmental theories whose central theme is maturational readiness, as well as with those (of which the best known is Piaget's) of cognitive adaptation. It is a model which proposes that new learning depends primarily upon the combining of previously acquired and recalled learned entities, as well as upon their potentialities for transfer of learning.

As for the entities which are learned, the model assumes that complex principles are formed from combinations of simpler principles, which are formed by combining concepts, which require prior learning of discriminations, and which in turn are acquired on the basis of previously learned chains and connections. The "stage" in which any individual learner finds himself with respect to the learning of any given new capability can be specified by describing (a) the relevant capabilities he now has; and (b) any of a number of hierarchies of capabilities he must acquire in order to make possible the ultimate combination of subordinate entities which will achieve the to-be-learned task. In an oversimplified way, it may be said that the stage of intellectual development depends upon what the learner knows already and how much he has

yet to learn in order to achieve some particular goal. Stages of development are not related to age, except in the sense that learning takes time. They are not related to logical structures, except in the sense that the combining of prior capabilities into new ones carries its own inherent logic.

The entities which are acquired in a cumulative learning sequence are relatively specific. They are specific enough so that one must specify them by naming the class of properties of external objects or events to which they will apply. At the same time, they possess great potential for generalization, through combination with other learned entities by means of a little understood, but nevertheless dependable, mechanism of learning transfer.

This kind of generalization through learning transfer is internal to the learner, and thus constitutes a genuine and measurable aspect of the learner's intellectual capability. Another kind of generalization is not necessarily a part of the learner. This is the classification an external observer may make of a collection of learned capabilities. While the observer naturally has the capability of making such a generalization (and often does so), the learner may not have such a capability. Thus, an external observer may classify a collection of learner capabilities as "the conservation principle," or "the principle of reversibility." Such abstractions have a number of uses in describing intellectual capabilities. Because they are so described, however, does not mean that the learner possesses them, in the same sense that the external observer does.

Intellectual development may be conceived as the building of increasingly complex and interacting structures of learned capabilities. The entities which are learned build upon each other in a cumulative fashion, and transfer of learning occurs among them. The structures of capability so developed can interact with each other in patterns of great complexity, and thus generate an ever-increasing intellectual competence. Each structure may also build upon itself through self-initiated thinking activity. There is no magic key to this structure—it is simply developed piece by piece. The magic is in learning and memory and transfer.

REFERENCES

Bruner, J. S. The growth of mind. *American Psychologist,* 1965, *20*, 1007–1017.

Bruner, J. S. On the conservation of liquids. In J. S. Bruner, et al., *Studies in cognitive growth: A collaboration at the Center for Cognitive Studies.* New York: Wiley, 1966.

Commission on Science Education. *Science—A process approach,* 3rd experimental edition, Parts 1–7. Washington: American Association for the Advancement of Science, 1965.

Dodwell, P. C. Children's understanding of number and related concepts. *Canadian Journal of Psychology,* 1961, *15*, 29–36.

Elkind, D. Children's discovery of the conservation of mass, weight, and volume: Piaget replication study II. *Journal of Genetic Psychology,* 1961, *98*, 219–227.

Flavell, J. H. *The developmental psychology of Jean Piaget.* Princeton: Van Nostrand, 1963.

Gagné, R. M. *The conditions of learning.* New York: Holt, Rinehart and Winston, 1965.

Gagné, R. M., Mayor, J. R., Garstens, H. L., & Paradise, N. E. Factors in acquiring knowledge of a mathematical task. *Psychological Monographs,* 1962, *76*(7, Whole No. 526).

Gesell, A. *Infancy and human growth.* New York: Macmillan, 1928.

Gesell, A., & Thompson, H. Learning and growth in identical twin infants. *Genetic Psychology Monographs,* 1929, *6*, 1–124.

Hall, G. S. *Aspects of child life and education.* New York: Appleton, 1921.

Kessen, W. *The child.* New York: Wiley, 1965.

Lovell, K. *The growth of basic mathematical and scientific concepts in children.* New York: Philosophical Library, 1961.

Peel, E. A. Experimental examination of some of Piaget's schemata concerning children's perception and thinking, and a discussion of their educational significance. *British Journal of Educational Psychology,* 1959, *29*, 89–103.

Piaget, J., & Inhelder, B. *The early growth of logic in the child.* New York: Harper & Row, 1964.

Roeper, A., & Sigel, I. Finding the clue to children's thought processes. *Young Children,* 1966, *21*, 335–349.

Skinner, B. F. *Science and human behavior.* New York: Macmillan, 1953.

Smedslund, J. The acquisition of conservation of substance and weight in children. I. Introduction. *Scandinavian Journal of Psychology,* 1961, *2*, 11–20. (a)

Smedslund, J. The acquisition of conservation of substance and weight in children. II. External reinforcement of conservation of weight and of the operations of addition and subtraction. *Scandinavian Journal of Psychology,* 1961, *2*, 71–84. (b)

Smedslund, J. The acquisition of conservation of substance and weight in children. III. Extinction of conservation of weight acquired ''normally'' and by means of empirical controls on a balance scale. *Scandinavian Journal of Psychology,* 1961, *2*, 85–87. (c)

Smedslund, J. The acquisition of conservation of substance and weight in children. IV. An attempt at extinction of the visual components of the weight concept. *Scandinavian Journal of Psychology,* 1961, *2*, 153–155. (d)

Smedslund, J. The acquisition of conservation of substance and weight in children. V. Practice in conflict situations without external reinforcement. *Scandinavian Journal of Psychology,* 1961, *2*, 156–160. (e)

Sonstroem, A. M. On the conservation of solids. In J. S. Bruner, et al., *Studies in cognitive growth.* New York: Wiley, 1966.

Watson, J. B. *Psychology from the standpoint of a behaviorist.* Philadelphia: Lippincott, 1924.

Wohlwill, J. F. & Lowe, R. C. An experimental analysis of the development of the conservation of number. *Child Development,* 1962, *33*, 153–167.

15. THE ONTOGENY OF READING

ELEANOR J. GIBSON

Despite decades of concern on the part of educators, parents, and proponents of home-spun wisdom, we seem to know little more about how to teach reading than our great grandparents did. In fact we do not even know why it has to be taught. Why doesn't it just grow, like language? No one teaches a child to speak. We do not know much about how a child acquires speech either, but in recent years studies of the developmental process have been very instructive. I think the reason for this is that we have begun to look at the process as a piece of natural history, somewhat as the ethologist looks at behavior. Observation followed by a careful analysis may be the essential preliminary to a good theory. Perhaps we have not really tried it with reading.

I would like to consider, as a start, the natural history of the origins of reading skill, before it is "taught" in a formal sense. Where does its developmental history begin?

I think we could agree that it has twin beginnings. One is its linguistic origin—it is a special form of speech; and one is its origin in writing—making marks on a piece of paper. The origin of reading in speech is obvious. Long before the child goes to school he has learned to segment a sequential stream of acoustic information; to divide it into valid units of structure; to discriminate these units by means of an economical set of distinctive features; to assign symbolic meanings to units of an appropriate size; to infer the rules that structure the units in permissible ways; and even to recombine units in these rulelike ways so as to produce original messages. Surely this massive achievement must transfer in some way to the perception of written speech, which is also processed sequentially. It, too, must be

From the *American Psychologist*, 1970, *25*, 136–143. Copyright 1970 by the American Psychological Association. Reprinted by permission of the author and the publisher.

segmented, discriminated, assigned symbolic meaning, and its combination rules mastered. That there is a carry-over is clear from a comparison of hearing children with deaf children, who must do without this head start.

I am going to leave the early history of speech to people more expert than I and begin with the early history of writing behavior. It starts, in James Gibson's opinion, with what he calls the "fundamental graphic act." It consists of producing visible traces on a piece of paper or some other surface such as rock or sand. The traces left on rock surfaces by prehistoric men are the earliest known attempt at graphic communication; pictorial, to be sure, not symbolic, but the evolution of writing seems to have been a gradual transition from pictures to symbols. Pictures have a projective relationship to what they stand for, while symbols bear a coded relationship to their surrogates. In infants, the earliest graphic act is not even a picture, only a scribble, but the child's scribbling is remarkable for one thing—his intense interest in the visible marks that he is making. It seems to me comparable to babbling, in the early stages of speech acquisition, and the motivation for both may well be built-in and arise spontaneously when opportunity is afforded.

As early as 12 months, according to the Cattell Infant Intelligence Tests (Cattell, 1960), a child given a paper and pencil will make marks on the paper. At 14 months, he will make a definite scribble, that is, a progressive, continuous tracing. The tester simply says, "Tommy write." If necessary, after a few minutes he gives a demonstration. By 18 months, the average child needs no demonstration, but scribbles spontaneously. At 27 months, he can draw a line as distinct from a scribble. At 30 months, he can draw a line as distinct from a circular stroke.

It has often been held that scribbling yields satisfaction simply as a motor activity—as "arm gymnastics," a mere exercise of kinesthesis. Gibson and Yonas (1968) compared this with the alternative hypothesis that what motivates the child is the resulting new source of visual stimulation. They compared the scribbling behavior of children given a stylus that did not leave a trace with that when the stylus left marks on a surface. The children ranged in age from 15 to 38 months and were observed at home in a playlike situation. Each child had a session with both tools, which were identical except for the marking potential of one. Elimination of the trace significantly reduced scribbling activity. Mean time of voluntary scribbling was 72 seconds with the tracing tool as against 21 seconds with the nontracing tool. Some of the children stopped immediately on discovering that the nontracing tool "didn't work." One 16-month-old child had no previous experience with tracing tools. When given the marking stylus, she waved it and struck the paper until a fortuitous mark resulted, after which she began to scribble with great interest and increasing control. These children were not only interested in making scribbles, but the older subjects were also eager for the experimenter to look at them and demanded that she do so. What the child can see in practicing the graphic act are variable properties of lines, such as curve–straight, vertical–horizontal, long–short, and features of graphic structure, such as intersection, closure, symmetry, and continuation.

How does the child come to distinguish the important variables of graphic information? I have thought for some time that letters, like the phonemic information that they code to, are discriminable and convey information by virtue of their distinctive features; and that letters share a set of distinctive features that characterizes them as writing, contrasted with pictures and scribbling. How early does a child begin to recognize "writing" as such? Must he learn to identify and name the letters first? At Cornell University, Linda Lavine is studying preschool children's responses to simple line drawings, geometric figures, letters, numbers, words printed in upper and lower case, cursive writing, scribbling, artificial letters, and characters from strange scripts. The drawings, characters,

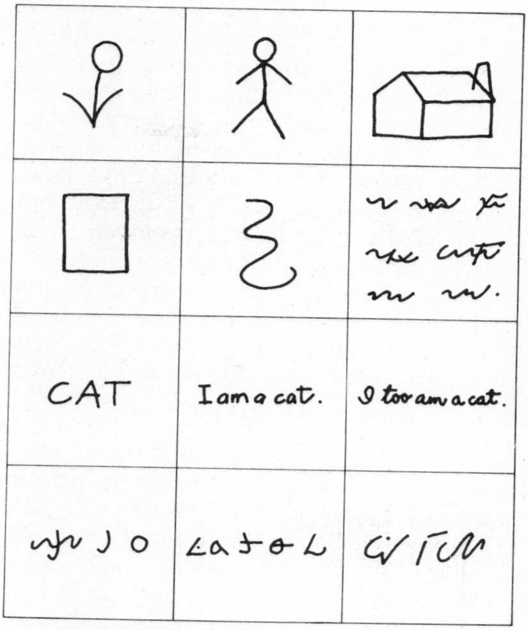

FIGURE 15–1. Redrawn samples of material presented to preschool children for differentiation as "writing."

and scribbles were inscribed on 4 × 6 inch cards, inked in lines of approximately equal thickness. A few characters (Roman capitals and some pseudoletters) were a little heavier. Size varied as it might in everyday printing or writing. Figure 15–1 shows samples of the material. The children were merely told, "I'm going to show you some things, and I want you to tell me what they are."

Children of three and four from the Cornell Nursery School served as the first subjects. All the three-year-old children showed that they could separate the pictures from the writing, the numbers, and the scribbles. The children of four could not only do this, they could separate the scribbles from the writing. However, in a cooperative nursery school, few of the four-year-olds could distinguish scribbling from writing. Children in seven different kindergartens were tested. They varied markedly; but in the school with the highest socioeconomic status, 75% distinguished scribbling from cursive writing, although they could not write yet. They identified all the printed characters correctly as letters, although in many cases none or only a few could be named. They also frequently called the artificial letters and the samples of other script (e.g., Hebrew script) writing. This is particularly interesting, because it substantiates the idea that there is something categorical in the structure of writing that distinguishes it from random marks on paper and from pictures even when none or only a few individual characters can be identified. We intend to find out, in future experiments, what the visual information (the graphic composition) is that permits this early classification of a set.

The distinctive features of *individual* letters—those features by which they differ from one another so that a unique pattern characterizes each one—have been investigated in a number of experiments by my students and myself. Gibson, Osser, Schiff, and Smith (1963) obtained a confusion matrix for the 26 Roman capitals based on the errors of 90 four-year-old children. We compared the errors with a list (intuitively derived) of 12 features including verticality, horizontality, diagonality, curvature, openness or closure, intersection, etc. The straight–curve and diagonality distinctions also emerged from a multidimensional analysis performed for us by Warren Torgerson. More recently, Gibson, Schapiro, and Yonas (1968) have obtained confusion matrices for two sets of nine Roman capitals and for a set of nine artificial graphemes. In this experiment, the subjects made a same–different judgment. The data included both errors and latencies. Forty-eight adults and 60 seven-year-old children took part in the experiments.

The results seem to me to confirm the hypothesis that letters are distinguished from one another by way of distinctive features that are shared to greater and lesser degrees by different pairs of letters, but that yield a unique pattern for every member of the set. Mean latencies for pairs of *different* letters varied very significantly, by more than 100 milliseconds at extremes of the range. Latencies and errors were highly correlated, and the degree of confusability for given pairs ranked the same in

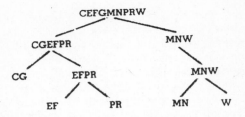

FIGURE 15–2.   Tree structure resulting from a hierarchical cluster analysis of latency data for discriminating pairs of letters by adult subjects.

a replication of the experiment. The artificial grapheme pairs also had a significant spread of latencies. The mean latency for discriminating artificial graphemes was nearly identical with that for letters. This may indicate that although the artificial graphemes were unfamiliar and had no names, we were successful in building into them the same set of distinctive features that characterizes letters as a set.

Each of the matrices was subjected to Johnson's (1967) hierarchical cluster analysis to find out what underlies the structure of the matrix. This should tell us what features are used by the observer when he must decide whether a given pair is the same or different. The analysis looks progressively (in steps) for the most compact and isolable clusters, then for the next most compact and so on until it winds up with loose clusters and finally the whole set. The results can be turned upside down and diagrammed in a tree structure. Figure 15–2 shows the tree resulting from an analysis of 48 adult subjects' latency data for nine characters paired in all combinations. The first split separates the letters with diagonality from all the others. On the left branch, the "round" letters, C and G, next split off from the others. At the third branch, the square right-angular letters, E and F, split off from letters differentiated from them by curvature. The error data for these letters with the same subjects reveal an identical structure.

Now consider the hierarchical structure for 60 seven-year-old children in Figure 15–3. It is similar, but not quite the same. The first split is a clean curve-straight one. On the second branch, the round letters are split off from the P

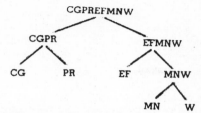

FIGURE 15–3. Tree structure resulting from a hierarchical cluster analysis of latency data for discriminating pairs of letters by seven-year-old children.

and R. The square letters next split off from those with diagonality. This is very neat, and it suggests to me that children at this stage may be doing straightforward sequential processing of features, while adults have progressed to a more Gestalt-like processing picking up higher orders of structure given by redundancy and tied relations. This is speculative, but it would be a most adaptive kind of development, achieving the highest level of differentiation with the greatest economy.

Differentiating letters, however fundamental, is still a very low-order aspect of reading skill. The heart of the matter is surely the process of decoding the written symbols to speech. We should know a great deal about how the writing-to-speech code is learned. I am afraid that we do not, but we do know that it is not a simple matter of paired-associate learning, either of a letter to a sound, or of a written word to a spoken one. Since writing is alphabetic, why doesn't a child just pair each letter with a corresponding phoneme and decode the letters one at a time? For one thing he cannot, because the letter-to-sound correspondence in English orthography is not a one-to-one matching of each letter to a sound element. For another, as research at the Haskins Laboratory has shown us (Liberman, Cooper, Shankweiler, & Studdert-Kennedy, 1967), phonemes are not recognized by the hearer as invariant over a speech segment smaller than a syllable, so such a method would be impossible even with "regular" orthography. The presumed "elements" carry information about their context (and vice versa) as well as about

themselves. This is true not only of speech but of written language as well.

Furthermore, a skilled reader does not read letter by letter. Cattell (1885) showed long ago that a word, if not too long or unfamiliar, can be read with as short an exposure time as a single letter. (For a five-letter word like START, for instance, one millisecond is enough if contrast is good.) This finding led many educators after Cattell to conclude that reading should be taught by the so-called "whole word" method. But difficulties arose here, too. Many children taught this way could not recognize new words. They did not analyze component relationships within words (Bowden, 1911). Research from our own laboratory (Bishop, 1964), and from others (Jeffrey & Samuels, 1967) has shown that knowledge of component relationships within the word is necessary for transfer.

I think the solution to this apparent dilemma is to aim our research at discovering the *unit-forming principles* in reading activity. What are the rules, the constraints, the structure for creating units? Only if we know this will we know how to teach so as to optimize perception of the most economical units for reading.

There are many possibilities. The white spaces between words might seem to afford an obvious basis for segmentation into words, at least. Carry-over from principles of unit formation in speech, as I mentioned earlier, is another possibility, and suggests at least three levels of rules: regular correspondence between clusters of graphemes and phonemes (often referred to as "pronounceability" of a string of letters); morphological rules; and grammatical syntax. There also may be *orthographic rules,* that is, spelling patterns that give structure without regard to the speech they decode to. We have begun investigating all these possibilities, and I would like to mention briefly some of the experiments.

Consider first the white spaces between words. We know that nearly all kindergarten children toward the end of their fifth year can recognize letters as letters even when they cannot identify individual ones. Can they recognize words as words before formal instruction has begun? At Cornell, Lorelei Brush and Nancy Tither asked children to point out words in various samples of print. The children were about six years old, just finishing kindergarten. Nearly half of these children could not point out words correctly, even after a demonstration. They sometimes ignored the spaces between words and sometimes chose letters as word units. It is not obvious, therefore, that the word is automatically a unit for a child. Even if it were, simple segmentation of this sort would not provide the rules for which we are looking.

I have been especially attracted to the idea that there is a carry-over to reading of unit-forming principles in speech. Clusters of phonemes do map with considerable regularity to clusters of letters. Certain combinations of sounds may begin a word, for instance, and also are spelled congruently in a consistent way in this position. These might be called pronounceable combinations, and it could be that pronounceability forms units for the skilled reader. There might be articulatory or acoustical encoding of what is read, so that the unit is formed on a kind of analysis-by-synthesis principle. Early in my research on reading, I investigated this possibility, that is, that pronounceability of letter strings facilitates reading them because of the correspondence with component clusters of letters. Gibson, Pick, Osser, and Hammond (1962) did tachistoscopic experiments with two kinds of letter strings, one that we called pronounceable and one that we called unpronounceable. The pronounceable ones began and ended with consonant clusters permissible in English speech that also map regularly to spelling in those positions. The medial vowel clusters were also regular in their context. An example would be the nonsense word GLURCK. The unpronounceable control words were made by exchanging the initial and final consonant clusters so that the word was no longer a permissible sequence of sounds or letters in English, for example, CKURGL. The pronounceable combinations were read with far greater accuracy with short exposures than were the unpronounceable ones.

Although I replicated this finding many times, I came to have misgivings about its interpretation. Several people suggested to me that the pronounceable words merely had higher sequential probability of the letters, calculated by summed bigram or trigram frequency. Was the correspondence with heard speech really important? I decided to run the experiment with deaf subjects. If it were the pronounceability of the letter strings that facilitated their reading, we should find an interaction with ability to hear and speak them. With the cooperation of the students and faculty at Gallaudet College, this hypothesis was tested (Gibson, Shurcliff, & Yonas, 1970, in press). There was no interaction. The deaf subjects profited just as much in reading so-called pronounceable combinations as hearing subjects did. The term "pronounceable" now seems misleading to me. I believe the difference between the two types of words can be accounted for by rules of orthography, that is, spelling patterns. I do not mean simply statistical structure, like transitional probability, but real rules such as what consonant combinations can begin a word.[1] There is a kind of grammar for letter sequences that generates permissible combinations. This grammar may be analogous to that devised artificially by Miller (1958) for his experiment on memory for redundant strings of letters, but it is natural to the writing system. At Cornell, Richard Rosinski and Kirk Wheeler have found that most children can differentiate permissible from nonpermissible combinations of letters during the third grade.

Morphological usage is another possible cause of units, either carried over from speech or found in orthography. Berko (1958) found that morphological transforms, such as the past tense, had been learned so as to transfer to new words or nonsense words spoken to a child of four years. Should not this be true for reading, too? If endings that mark tenses or verb forms carry over as units to reading, we might expect

[1]The results of this study were subjected to a multiple regression analysis in which several summed frequency counts (all that we could find) were tested as predictors. All turned out to be remarkably unsuccessful.

that a child could read a longer word, with a short exposure, when part of its letters are accounted for by such an ending. A four-letter word is about as long as a third grader can read with a brief exposure. But if we expand the word by adding an *ed* or *ing* does this vocally well-known transformation create a larger unit that is easily detected? Lynne Guinet and I have been trying such an experiment with third- and fifth-grade children.

Table 15–1 shows samples of the words we used. There were three kinds of stem words: real words, pronounceable pseudowords and unpronounceable ones, both anagrams of the real words. There were three kinds of verb transformations added to the words; an *s* to form the third person present, an *ed* to form a past tense, and an *ing* to form a progressive. We used stems of varied length (three to six letters). No child was shown more than one form of a stem word. The main findings are very clear. The third graders make many more errors than the fifth graders, for any kind of word. Real words are read with fewer errors than pseudowords, and pronounceable pseudowords with many fewer errors than unpronounceable ones. The longer the word, the more the errors. But would this be true if the length were increased by a regular ending? To our disappointment we found very little evidence that this method of increasing length increased span of perception. The evidence was in this direction for the pronounceable pseudowords, but not for the other two types. We cannot say that there

was automatic carry-over of such a structural principle from speech.

There was evidence, however, that the ending itself gains status as a structural unit. Errors in responding to the transformed words did not occur very frequently in the endings, as compared with nontransformed words of equal length. But when there was an error in the ending, there was a significant tendency for it to be a substitution of another regular ending, for instance, *ing* for *ed*. This substitution of an ending happened more often for the transformed words than for the nontransformed ones, and the tendency was more marked for fifth than for third graders. It is as if the subject detected the ending first as a marker or feature added to the stem word, and only then identified it specifically.

Because I have become convinced that rulelike information in orthography structures units for reading, I want to know how these rules or spelling patterns are learned. Two hypotheses that seemed most reasonable to me were first that there is abstraction of an invariant pattern over many variable contexts; and second that a learning set develops for finding regular patterns in orthography. A training procedure was designed therefore to provide opportunities of both sorts. Gibson, Farber, and Shepela (1967) constructed a large number of "problems" that required the subject to sort positive from negative instances, like a simple concept-learning experiment. All the problems had four positive instances, each of which

TABLE 15–1
Words and Morphological Transformations Presented for Tachistoscopic Identification to Third- and Fifth-Grade Subjects

ITEM	THIRD PERSON		PAST TENSE		PROGRESSIVE	
	Stem word	Transformed word	Stem word	Transformed word	Stem word	Transformed word
Real word	RAIN	RAINS	START	STARTED	LISTEN	LISTENING
Pseudoword (pronounceable)	NAIR	NAIRS	TRAST	TRASTED	TENSIL	TENSILING
Pseudoword (unpronounceable)	NRAI	NRAIS	TRSTA	RTSTAED	TSLENI	TSLENING

TABLE 15–2
Distinctive Clusters in Invariant Positions and Variable Contexts, All Varied across Problems

SO*NG*	TE*A*M	*CH*OP
RI*NG*	RE*A*D	*CH*IN
BA*NG*	S*EA*L	*CH*AT
HU*NG*	L*EA*N	*CH*UM

contained a cluster of two letters in an invariant position—initial, medial, or final. The other letters always varied. Table 15–2 shows sets of the positive instances from three of the problems. The negative instances for each problem were words containing various similarities to the positive ones in order to control for sorting on the basis of a single letter or some other superficial similarity.

The child was given one problem at a time. On the first trial, the experimenter laid two cards, one bearing a single positive instance and one a single negative instance, before him, and said, "This is mail for you, and this other [negative instance] is for someone else. You sort the mail and put all yours here [indicating positive card] and everyone else's here." The child then was given a randomly arranged deck of negative and positive instances to sort. The experimenter corrected him when he was wrong. He sorted for one problem four times, and then went on to another whether he had succeeded in a perfect sort or not, following a procedure much like that of a discrimination learning-set experiment.

We first tried this training procedure on kindergarten children and first graders, running them on six problems a day for five consecutive days. This task was extremely hard for the kindergarten children. Only 1 out of 12 developed an indubitable learning set. This child could sort all the new problems correctly on the first sort by the fifth day. The task was somewhat easier for first-grade children; about half of a first-grade sample showed evidence of developing a learning set to abstract common patterns of orthography.

We wondered whether these subjects had really attained a set to search for invariant structure over a series of items, or whether more specific habits already had been learned in first grade that helped on this task. My student, Arlene Amidon, and I therefore tried an experiment comparing success on the spelling pattern problems with success on analogous problems in which the elements were color chips instead of letters.

Subjects for this experiment were first-grade and third-grade children, some run first with colors and some run first with letters. For the first-grade children, color and letter patterns were equally (and very) difficult. If success occurred on the color problem, however, it transferred to the spelling patterns. For third graders, the letter patterns were picked up much more easily than the color patterns, and color problems were far more likely to be solved if they followed solution of letter problems than if they were given first.

We concluded from this that a set to look for structure can be developed and can transfer to new problems, and that the ability to detect structure in letter patterns improves with age and schooling. It seems that this is more than specific learning, since it transferred to color patterns. The third graders, I think, had learned mostly to search actively for invariant spelling patterns. Following a task in which a child found them, he could pursue an analogous search for color patterns. Finding structure, I think, is rewarding, and when these children had found it, they repeated their successful strategy.

How could we assist the first graders toward success in finding the structure, so as to facilitate transfer to new cases? Lowenstein (1969) compared three procedures in a new experiment with first graders. One group was given no special hints or help, as in the preceding experiments. One group was given specific help. When a problem was first presented, the experimenter said, "You will be able to find your own mail, because all the cards will have these two letters on them." The pair of common letters was pointed out. This was repeated for each problem. A third group was told, "You will be able to find your own mail because your cards will have the same two letters on them." But they were never told which letters. After two days of practice, all the subjects had a posttest set of problems without any further instructions.

The group given specific help made very few errors during training, even on the first day. The group given no help made many, although some improvement occurred. The group given the general hint made many more errors to begin with than the children given specific help (a mean of 6 errors), but they improved steadily and on the posttest had a median of 0 errors; whereas errors rose on the posttest to a median of 5.5 for the group that had received specific help. This was more than five times as many as they had made on Day 1. Although 70% of the subjects in the "specific" group made no errors on Day 2, only 20% made no errors on Day 3, the posttest. But in the group given the general instruction to look for an invariant letter pattern, 40% made no errors on Day 2, and 60% made none on Day 3.

Response latencies confirmed these results. The specific group showed no change from Day 1 to Day 3, whereas the group given the general hint showed a steady and significant decrease in latency over the three days.

We conclude then that first-grade children can easily sort words on the basis of presence or absence of two specific letters that have been pointed out to them. But it is not this ability as such that leads to detecting common spelling patterns across items. I think there must be a search for an invariant pattern and discovery of such structure for transfer of this kind of abstraction to new problems. Subjects given no special instructions or hints may eventually accomplish this on their own—20% of the subjects in the control group made no errors on Day 3 (the same percentage as the "specific" help group on Day 3). But it is clearly better to have attention directed to search for invariant features in the stimulus array, and finding them is reinforcing; it leads to repetition of the successful strategy and thus to consistently accelerated performance.

This is the point that I wish to emphasize in concluding. Motivation and reinforcement for cognitive learning such as speech and reading are internal. Reinforcement is not reduction of a drive, but reduction of uncertainty, specifically the discovery of structure that reduces the information processing and increases cognitive economy. This is perceptual learning, not just remembering something.

I realize that my evidence for this conclusion is as yet rather slender, and therefore I am aiming my research efforts at obtaining better evidence and further clarification of the process. A current experiment is aimed at promoting discovery of semantic structure and consequent transfer of the strategy to a new problem. But that is another story, since we have only begun the experiments. I feel confident enough to predict, however, that the search for invariants and the discovery of structure are basic forces in cognitive motivation. If this proves true, methods of teaching that would promote efficient strategies of perceptual search and detection of invariant order should be a first concern in instructional programs.

REFERENCES

Berko, J. The child's learning of English morphology. *Word,* 1958, *14*, 150–177.

Bishop, C. H. Transfer effects of word and letter training in reading. *Journal of Verbal Learning and Verbal Behavior,* 1964, *3*, 215–221.

Bowden, J. H. Learning to read. *Elementary School Teacher,* 1911, *12*, 21–33.

Cattell, J. M. Ueber die Zeit der Erkennung und Benennung von Schriftzeichen Bildern und Farben. *Philosophische Studien,* 1885, *2*, 635–650.

Cattell, P. *The measurement of intelligence of infants and young children.* (Rev. ed.) New York: Psychological Corporation, 1960.

Gibson, E. J., Farber, J., & Shepela, S. Test of a learning set procedure for the abstraction of spelling patterns. *Project Literacy Reports,* 1967, No. 8, Cornell University, Ithaca, New York.

Gibson, E. J., Osser, H., Schiff, W., & Smith, J. An analysis of critical features of letters, tested by a confusion matrix. In *A basic research program on reading* (Cornell University and United States Office of Education Cooperative Research Project No. 639). Ithaca, N. Y.: Cornell University, 1963.

Gibson, E. J., Pick, A., Osser, H., & Hammond, M. The role of grapheme-phoneme correspondence in the perception of words. *American Journal of Psychology,* 1962, *75*, 554–570.

Gibson, E. J., Schapiro, F., & Yonas, A. Confusion matrices for graphic patterns obtained with a latency measure. In *The analysis of reading skill: A program of basic and applied research* (Cornell University and United States Office of Education, Final Report, Project No. 5-1213). Ithaca, N. Y.: Cornell University, 1968.

Gibson, E. J., Shurcliff, A., & Yonas, A. Utilization of spelling patterns by deaf and hearing subjects. In H. Levin & J. P. Williams (Eds.), *Basic studies on reading.* New York: Harper & Row, 1970, in press.

Gibson, J. J., & Yonas, P. M. A new theory of scribbling and drawing in children. In *The analysis of reading skill: A program of basic and applied research* (Cornell University and United States Office of Education, Final Report, Project No. 5-1213). Ithaca, N. Y.: Cornell University, 1968.

Jeffrey, W. E., & Samuels, S. J. Effect of reading training on initial learning and transfer. *Journal of Verbal Learning and Verbal Behavior,* 1967, *6*, 354–358.

Johnson, S. C. Hierarchical clustering schemes. *Psychometrika,* 1967, *32*, 241–254.

Liberman, A. M., Cooper, F. S., Shankweiler, D. P., & Studdert-Kennedy, M. Perception of the speech code. *Psychological Review,* 1967, *74*, 431–461.

Lowenstein, A. M. Effects of instructions on the abstraction of spelling patterns. Unpublished master's thesis, Cornell University, 1969.

Miller, G. A. Free recall of redundant strings of letters. *Journal of Experimental Psychology,* 1958, *56*, 484–491.

16. ONTOGENY OF MEMORY[1]

BYRON A. CAMPBELL and NORMAN E. SPEAR

Over the past half century a substantial number of studies have demonstrated that capacity for long-term memory increases during development. This paper presents a brief review of those findings and then examines a variety of mechanisms, both behavioral and neurological, which might account for the increase in memory during ontogenesis.

This paper is addressed to one of the major paradoxes in psychology today. On the one hand, there is a tremendous wealth of literature documenting both the permanence and pervasiveness of experiences occurring during the early stages of development in both animals and man. Adult social behaviors (Harlow & Harlow, 1962), resistance to stressor agents (Levine & Mullins, 1968), birdsongs (Hinde, 1969), sexual behavior (Harlow, 1962), and many other adult behaviors have all been shown to be critically dependent on events occurring early in life. Yet on the other hand, it is apparent from our own experience, from extensive research of childhood memories in adults (Dudycha & Dudycha, 1941; Schachtel, 1947), and from recent research on animals (Campbell, 1967) that memories of specific events occurring

[1]This work was supported in part by National Institutes of Health Grants MH01562 and MH08501 to Byron A. Campbell and in part by National Institutes of Health Grants MH12064, MH18619, and MH47359 to Norman E. Spear.

From the *Psychological Review,* 1972, *79*, 215–236. Copyright 1972 by the American Psychological Association. Reprinted by permission of the authors and the publisher.

early in life are typically more fragile than memories of similar events experienced in adulthood.

Because of the strong implications for human personality, a great deal more attention has been paid in recent years to critical periods of development than to the phenomenon of poorer memory in infancy. Nonetheless, we believe that this is a phenomenon of major significance and one that deserves much more attention. As a first step, it is necessary to distinguish between memory of a past experience and other lasting effects of that experience.

Memory, in the view of most psychologists, is a loosely defined concept that describes the ability of animal and human subjects to recall or relearn more rapidly previously practiced behaviors. As concepts, learning and retention have defied precise definition, and it is well beyond the scope of the present review to attempt to improve on that state of affairs. Nonetheless, it is evident that much of what is influenced by early experience is mediated by changes in neural, endocrine, autonomic, and other structures; changes that can in no way be considered learned although they may drastically alter subsequent capacity to learn. Total light deprivation in infancy, for example, produces retinal degeneration (Riesen, 1961), and deprivation of patterned light alters the adult neurophysiological response to certain visual stimuli (Wiesel & Hubel, 1965). Similarly exposure to early stress permanently changes adrenal reactivity (Levine & Mullins, 1968), and rearing animals in enriched environments appears to alter brain size and neurochemical activity (Rosenzweig, Krech, Bennett, & Diamond, 1968).

In a like fashion, there are critical periods in development where exposure to members of the same species is necessary for the individual to acquire many species-specific behaviors. These critical interactions appear to be genetically preprogrammed so that normal development occurs only if the appropriate stimuli are present at predetermined times. While these experiences may permanently alter underlying neural or physiological structures, there is no evidence that the organism necessarily "remembers" the specific stimuli to which it was exposed. In

man, a child may develop normally under the care of one parent for the first few years of life, but have no specific recollection of that parent if separated from it and subsequently reared in another family setting. Yet the parental care given during those first few years is critical for normal development. The ability to recall a specific event is often independent of the effects of that experience.

It is the premise of this paper that learning and retention represent discrete psychological phenomena which can be investigated developmentally independent of other lasting effects of early experience, effects which we believe are mediated by processes other than simple retention of learned material. Moreover this paper will focus on phenomena which are customarily studied under the heading "long-term retention," with particular attention paid to changes in retention taking place over days, weeks, or even months. In addition, an effort will be made to distinguish between developmental differences in retention due to strength of original learning versus developmental differences in retention due to differences in retention processes per se; the present paper is addressed primarily to the latter.

I: Development of Long-term Memory

Ontogenesis of Long-Term Memory in Man

In man, the rapid forgetting of information acquired during early childhood is often described as infantile amnesia (Schachtel, 1947). When adolescents, young adults, or the aged are asked to recall the events of their childhood it is universally evident that little of the first three to five years of life is subject to conscious retrieval (cf. Dudycha & Dudycha, 1941; Schachtel, 1947; Waldfogel, 1948, for comprehensive reviews). Most individuals are completely amnestic for that period being unable to recall even a single event occurring prior to three years of age and some have no childhood memories prior to age nine (Saul, Snyder, & Sheppard, 1956). The number of events that can be recalled for any one year also increases sharply with age (Waldfogel, 1948). Even then there is considerable question as to the nature of these early memories, since the most vivid memories of early childhood are those that are frequently recalled or rehearsed. For most young adults, recall of early childhood usually begins to achieve some clarity by the late preschool or early school years with the conciseness of memory continuing to increase through the primary school years (Waldfogel, 1948). The majority of research on infantile amnesia took place prior to 1940 during which time numerous theories were put forth to explain the phenomenon. Allport (1937, p. 161) summarized the four major theories of that time as follows: (a) Infant experiences are not verbalized and, therefore, cannot be held as concepts in consciousness; (b) the areas of the cortex involved in conscious memory are not myelinized and, therefore, are unable to hold "traces" of experience; (c) the apperceptive context of early life is so different from that of adulthood that events occurring in it cannot be recalled; (d) when the infant encounters the "reality principle" he represses into the unconscious all memories of his self-indulgent life up to that date. It goes without saying that none of these explanations has been empirically established; instead the entire phenomenon of infantile amnesia appears to have been repressed by the scientific community rather than investigated systematically. One goal of the present paper is to reawaken interest in this important phenomenon.

Unfortunately infantile amnesia has not been the target of many well-controlled experimental studies. Levy (1960) in a study performed for other reasons, found that memory of innoculation increased from birth to 18 months of age. Before six months, infants showed no memory of previous injection experience; after that, retention increased gradually with age. These data offer some experimental support for the phenomenon of infantile amnesia, although they give no indication as to whether the rapid forgetting of infancy is due to poorer original learning or to a deficiency in the retention process per se. In general the phenomenon of

infantile amnesia is in dramatic contrast to the extent and quality of learning that takes place during those years. Preschool children acquire a vast array of complex behaviors and show striking memory for preschool and home incidents over short intervals. Yet years later they are completely amnesic not only for specific incidents but for the entire environment as well.

The absence of careful experiments studying long-term forgetting by children compared to adults is no mystery. Practical barriers in such experiments are considerable, some of which have been noted in reviews by Keppel (1964) and Goulet (1968). The most immediate difficulties concern the task: Material to be learned must not be so simple as to be immediately overlearned by all adults but not so difficult as to be impossible or frustrating to learn by younger subjects. For example, words or numbers cannot be used with most preschoolers because they simply cannot read them.

Once a task is selected, the next step is to devise means for controlling the degree of original learning prior to initiating the retention interval. As Keppel (1964) and Goulet (1968) have noted, the failure to achieve this has made nearly all potentially relevant experiments conducted prior to 1960 of little value in analyzing changes in retention during development. Appropriate procedures have been devised for verbal learning (Underwood, 1964), but their application in experiments with children is time consuming and expensive in practice (e.g., Amster, Keppel, & Meyer, 1970).

In recent years an increasing number of well-controlled experiments on age and retention of verbal learning have appeared, but they have been directed more toward implications of interference theory than the development of memory itself. Thus, these studies have included either young subjects who are too old (e.g., Walen, 1970) or retention intervals that are too short (Bach & Underwood, 1970) to provide experimental evidence relevant to our concern with infantile amnesia.

Certain of the methodological problems encountered in studying the development of long-term memory with human subjects can be overcome when animals are used as subjects, a circumstance common to many areas of psychology and biology. Campbell (1967) has described some recent advances in methodology which permit clearer interpretation of the deficit in long-term retention found in young rats compared to adults. We turn now to a brief review of these experiments.

Ontogenesis of Long-Term Memory in Infraprimate Mammals

During the first half of this century there were numerous ontogenetic studies of learning as part of an effort to understand and define animal intelligence, but little attention was focused on long-term retention despite the then current interest in early childhood memory. The first major parametric ontogenetic investigation of long-term memory was reported by Campbell and Campbell (1962). In this study 18-, 23-, 38-, 54-, and 100-day-old rats were conditioned to fear a distinctive compartment of a double compartment shuttle box, and then tested for retention of fear 0, 7, 21, or 42 days after original training. Retention, as measured by avoidance of the fear side, increased dramatically with age. Eighteen-day-old rats showed nearly 100% avoidance of the fear side when tested immediately after training, but only chance avoidance at the 21- and 42-day retention intervals. In contrast, 54- and 100-day-old subjects showed little or no forgetting at any retention interval. In a second experiment, retention of conditioned punishment was investigated over 0-, 21-, and 42-day intervals in rats which were 23 and 100 days of age when conditioned. Again, juveniles were clearly inferior to adults.

Similar finding have obtained with active avoidance (e.g., Kirby, 1963), escape (e.g., Smith, 1968), and appetitive discrimination (Campbell, Jaynes, & Misanin, 1968) tasks. Kirby trained 25-, 50-, and 100-day-old rats on a simple runway avoidance problem. The age groups did not differ during acquisition or extinction, but 25-day-old subjects showed inferior retention in relearning tests 25 and 50 days following original learning. Smith found no significant differences during acquisition of a

T-maze escape task, yet performance of 25-day-old rats was substantially poorer following a 75-day retention interval than those of their adult counterparts who showed almost no forgetting. Campbell et al. trained young and adult rats to approximately equal performance levels on a discriminated operant task (lever press for food). Juveniles showed considerably poorer retention than adults of both the discrimination and the basic instrumental response in tests (extinction) 38, 75, and 150 days after original training.

Crockett and Noble (1963) and Thompson, Koenigsberg, and Tennison (1965) have failed to find age differences in retention. In the Crockett and Noble experiment, relearning of a light-motivated escape response was comparable in rats 21 and 90 days of age after a 60-day retention interval. Unfortunately control groups without prior acquisition experience were not included, making it difficult to interpret the results. Thompson et al. trained 25- and 100-day-old rats in avoidance shuttle boxes scaled to the physical size of the animals. No differences in retention were obtained when the physical size of the apparatus was increased proportionately at the time of relearning, but no young subjects were trained and tested in the same size apparatus. According to the generalization decrement hypothesis (cf. pp. 222–224), greater forgetting would have occurred under this condition.

More recently, Schulenburg, Riccio, and Stikes (1971) and Feigley and Spear (1970) have shown in several experiments that retention of passive-avoidance responding also increases with age. Similarly, Campbell, Lytle, and White[2] have systematically compared acquisition and retention of escape and passive avoidance responding in preweanling and weanling (15–35-day-old) rats. In these extensive experiments, rate of forgetting was inversely proportional to age, with the 15-day-old subjects showing extremely rapid forgetting.

[2]B. A. Campbell, L. D. Lytle, and B. C. White. Species differences in ontogeny of memory: Support for neural maturation as a determinant of forgetting. Submitted to the *Journal of Comparative and Physiological Psychology,* 1972.

Strength of Original Learning versus Differences in Retention and Retrieval Mechanisms as Determinants of the Rapid Forgetting in Infancy

Taken together, the above studies demonstrate unequivocally that rate of forgetting is more rapid in infancy than adulthood. But what is not clear is whether the rapid forgetting of infancy is due to differences in strength of original learning or to ontogenetic differences in the storage and/or retrieval mechanisms of retention. Any of these could underlie the observed differences in long-term retention.

There are, however, a number of features of the preceding studies which suggest that the rapid forgetting of infancy represents a deficit in retention and is not simply the result of poorer original learning. One critical question is whether young rats forget more rapidly than adults when degree of original learning is equal to or greater than that of the adult. Several different techniques have been used to assess and equate degree of original learning in ontogenetic studies of memory in animals. They are as follows.

Rate of Acquisition. Concerning the problem of assessing retention effects unconfounded by learning differences, Underwood (e.g., 1964) has noted that final degree of learning will usually be lower following slower rates of attaining a common criterion of performance. However, it is usually assumed (although there are exceptions) that strength of original learning is the same for all groups attaining a common criterion of performance prior to a retention test if rates of attaining that criterion are the same. Several developmental studies appear to meet these conditions. As noted earlier, the studies of Kirby (1963), of Feigley and Spear (1970; active avoidance), and of Smith (1968; T-maze escape) found no systematic differences in either the rate or asymptotic level of learning, yet forgetting was significantly greater in the younger subjects. Similarly in the Campbell et al. (1972) study, rate of forgetting in the T-maze escape experiment was more rapid in 20-day-old rats than in the 25- and 35-day-olds even though rate of acquisition was at least as

rapid in the younger age group. In the passive-avoidance experiment by Campbell et al., there were no apparent differences in the number of trials to criterion between the 16-and 25-day-old animals, yet the 16-day-old subjects forgot significantly faster. In addition there are a number of instances where the retention of older subjects is superior even though rate of learning was significantly slower or poorer in those groups (e.g., the 100-day-old subjects in the Kirby experiment and the 35-day-old subjects in the Campbell et al. study [see Footnote 3]). Thus when degree of original learning is assessed by rate and asymptotic level of learning, retention of equally learned responses remains typically poorer in young rats.

Resistance to Extinction. Another widely used measure of response strength is resistance to extinction. By this measure, strength of original learning was the same across ages in the Campbell and Campbell (1962) and Kirby (1963) experiments. As noted before, forgetting was more rapid in the younger subjects.

Effect of Overtraining. Another approach is to deliberately overtrain young subjects, by administering either more intense shocks or longer durations of shock. Using this procedure, Schulenburg et al. (1971) found that lengthening shock duration from one to five seconds increased long-term memory in 15- and 21-day-old rats on a passive-avoidance task, but that these young subjects were still markedly inferior to adult subjects receiving only one second of shock. Using a similar approach, Feigley and Spear (1970) varied intensity of shock during acquisition of a passive-avoidance response. Weanling subjects showed inferior retention at all shock levels when compared to adults.

Relearning. Another indication that strength of original learning is comparable across ages in the preceding experiments stems from the finding that the number of trials required to relearn the criterion response does not differ at short retention intervals. Klein and Spear (1969), for example, compared weanling and adult rats on the relearning of an avoidance response .08, 1.0, 4.0, or 24 hours after original learning and found identical retention functions ("Kamin Effects") for both groups. Long-term retention of avoidance responding is, as noted earlier, much poorer in weanlings than adults. This and the above findings demonstrate that at least some responses can be learned and stored for short intervals with the same fidelity in young and adult animals and suggest that other processes specific to the early stages of development act to produce the poor long-term memory characteristic of infancy. This is not to imply that all responses are acquired equally at all ages nor that much of what is subsumed under the phenomena of infantile amnesia in man is not the result of weaker original learning. We do, however, wish to emphasize that forgetting of responses acquired in infancy is more rapid than those acquired in adulthood, and that this rapid forgetting is not necessarily due to poorer original learning.

In this context, the aim of the present paper is to examine some of the processes most likely to underlie the ontogenesis of long-term memory. In our view, two broad classes of variables are potential determinants of the poorer memory found in infancy. First there are a number of interference and information-processing mechanisms which may change with age. These include retroactive and proactive interference, stimulus generalization decrement, stimulus differentiation, and related processes, all of which might act to impair long-term memory more in the early stages of development. Second, there are a variety of structural and chemical changes in the central nervous system occurring during this period which may determine the changing memory capacity of the developing animal. These variables are not necessarily independent, since maturation of the central nervous system may alter the shape of the primary stimulus generalization gradient, susceptibility to interference, etc. Nevertheless, our goal is to examine the relative importance of these two classes of variables as determinants of poorer memory in infancy.

As will soon become apparent, there is little evidence to support either view. Hence the major purpose of the present paper is not to deduce which of the many possible mechanisms underlies the rapid forgetting of infancy. Instead the purpose is to describe in some detail a variety of processes that may underlie this change. These possibilities stem directly from present knowledge of behavioral processes and neurological development. Our prime hope in writing this paper is to stimulate research on what we consider a major problem of unusual current importance.

II: Developmental Changes in Interference and Information-Processing Mechanisms

Retroactive and Proactive Interference as Determinants of Poorer Memory in Infancy

Until the late 1950s, it was generally agreed that retroactive interference was the major source of forgetting (e.g., McGeoch & Irion, 1952). But in 1957, Underwood demonstrated that forgetting in the laboratory was directly proportional to the number of previous lists learned, a finding which ultimately led many investigators to conclude that proactive interference was the major source of forgetting, both in the laboratory and in normal life (e.g., Underwood & Postman, 1960). This emphasis also stimulated a search for extraexperimental sources of interference, particularly within the context of language. While the results of this research are not unambiguous, it is generally accepted that extraexperimental experiences can contribute substantially to the proactive interference pool (e.g., Postman, 1971).

In the context of developmental psychology, the question is a simple but unanswered one: What are the relative contributions of retroactive and proactive interference to the basic phenomenon of poorer memory in infancy? According to the simplest model of proactive interference, older animals should forget more rapidly because they have lived longer with a correspondingly higher probability of having acquired previously learned habits which might

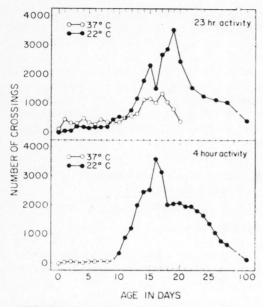

FIGURE 16–1. Spontaneous activity of rats in stabilimeter cages during postnatal development. (Each point in the upper panel represents a different group of six to eight animals tested for 23 hours, while the data in the lower panel represent a single group of animals tested for four hours each day.) (Reprinted from an article by W. H. Moorcroft, L. D. Lytle, and B. A. Campbell published in the *Journal of Comparative and Physiological Psychology,* 1971, Vol. 75. Copyrighted by the American Psychological Association, 1971.)

interfere with retention of more recently learned material. But as the data cited above indicate, this prediction is contrary to fact.

Retroactive interference, in contrast, remains a somewhat more viable candidate as the basis for the rapid forgetting of infancy. This would be particularly true if the total amount learned at any developmental stage were proportional to the animal's overall level of behavioral activity. Figure 16–1 illustrates how exploratory behavior, as measured by a four-hour exposure to a simple stabilimeter cage scaled to the size of the rat, changes during development (from Moorcroft, Lytle, & Campbell, 1971). As can be seen, little activity occurs prior to 10 days of age, but between 10 and 15 days of age activity leaps to a level 3–4 times that of the 10-day-old and

nearly 10 times that of the adult rat. Hyperreactivity to novel stimuli and generally high levels of exploratory and play activity also rise and then decline in the normal home cage environment during these same ages (Bolles & Woods, 1964). The decrease in overall activity levels parallels, from 15 days of age to adulthood, the development of long-term memory. While it is not typical to assume a correlation between activity level and learning, it is not an unreasonable possibility. One could easily argue that the young animal is learning a great deal about the spatial-perceptual-social characteristics of the environment as it moves about; the more it approaches and withdraws from stimuli in different directions and under varying conditions, the more it learns. In contrast, the older animal, inactive and maintained in a familiar environment, learns less than its weanling counterpart. Given this analysis, which is obviously not dependent on gross levels of motor activity although supported by those findings, it follows that retroactive interference from learning occurring during the retention interval is likely to be higher in young than adult animals.

On the other hand, the implicit assumption stemming from the data presented in the previous section is that long-term memory increases monotonically between birth and maturity. Thus the low level of activity prior to 10 days of age makes retroactive extraexperimental interference an unlikely basis for the presumably rapid rate of forgetting during this period. However, no developmental retention studies have been reported showing age-related differences in retention unconfounded by learning differences among rats younger than 15 days. Separation of learning and retention factors among such neonates probably will prove most difficult, if possible at all. What might stem from this pattern of behavioral development is a two-factor theory of forgetting during ontogenesis. During the early stages of development, long-term forgetting may be due primarily to immaturity of the central nervous system, accompanied by closely linked deficits in short-term memory and learning rate; later in development interference-type processes together with the consequences of central nervous system growth (see Section III) may play a greater role in determining rate of long-term forgetting.

It is also impossible to distinguish between retroactive and proactive interference on the basis of these data. First, proactive interference is known to be more effective when acquired immediately prior to original learning (Spear, 1971; Underwood & Freund, 1968). In the present instance, rate of forgetting appears to be correlated with the amount of exploratory activity elicited just before original learning as well as the amount of interpolated activity. Second, proactive interference produces less interference when prior learning is acquired through spaced learning over long periods of time or, more generally, when the interfering and critical materials are easily differentiated (Underwood & Ekstrand, 1966). In the present instance it seems not implausible to assume that extraexperimental proactive interference is minimized for the adult by the extensive familiarity subjects acquire with proximal environmental stimuli during the course of development. To the extent that the rapid forgetting typical of early developmental stages is due to interference processes, it seems difficult if not impossible to assess the relative contributions of proactive and retroactive interference to this process. In all likelihood, both contribute substantially to memory decrements over time, with their relative weights being determined by the specific experimental or situational circumstances. Moreover, as Deese and Hulse (1967) point out, the theoretical distinction between retroactive and proactive interference is greatly diminished when long retention intervals are used.

Maturation of Species-Specific Behavior

During the normal course of development, many drastic changes take place in the animals' behavior repertoire. Some are learned, some are contingent upon changes in physical capability, some are preprogrammed in unknown ways such that they emerge at a particular stage when the proper stimulus appears, and still others are hormonally dependent. Male preweanling rats respond to the dam by rooting and sucking; at sexual maturity the same rat responds to the same female by copulating. Similarly, pain produces withdrawal and flight in the young animal and attack in the adult (Hutchinson, Ulrich, & Azrin, 1965), and unfamiliar environments may elicit more fear or general arousal in older animals (Candland & Campbell, 1962; Sluckin, 1965). These age-related modifications of behavior could act to either permanently or temporarily interfere with the performance of a previously learned response as an animal develops. As a hypothetical example, we suspect it would be possible to train an immature female ring dove to peck at a ring dove egg in a nest for food reinforcement, and that the dove would show good retention of the response over long time periods. But if the bird was brought into broodiness by parturition or other means, it seems quite likely that the bird would now respond to the eggs by brooding rather than pecking, resulting in a measured loss in retention of the pecking response. If this dominance of unlearned behavior over learned behavior did develop, it would then be of further interest to see if the learned behavior reappeared when the hormonal or other conditions controlling the unlearned behavior were removed.

In short, there must be many situations in which an emerging unlearned response takes precedence over a previously learned response to that stimulus. The extent of this interference is undoubtedly proportional to the animal's repertoire of unlearned behaviors and is thus unlikely to be a major source of forgetting in man.

Maturational Changes in Information-Processing Mechanisms

As a corollary to the above observation that emerging of species-specific behaviors may interfere with previously learned responses, it seems reasonable to consider the possibility that changes in mode or style of information processing may also interfere with the retrieval of previously learned material. In higher mammals such as man, enormous changes take place in the way in which sensory information is encoded and responded to. The most obvious changes occur in the use of language. To a preverbal child, a book is simply another object in its environment; later the object is verbally labeled as "book"; still later it is responded to by reading either overtly or covertly the title; and finally the title evokes a variety of emotional or evaluative responses ranging from interest to aversion. Underwood (1969, p. 571) has suggested other instances in which attributes forming critical components of childhood memories may not correspond to those forming comparable memories in the adult, and at least one subsequent experiment has yielded confirming evidence (Bach & Underwood, 1970). Failure to retrieve memories acquired prior to maturity might be one consequence of this shift in mode of information processing. Similarly modes of problem solving appear to change developmentally in man from overt stimulus–response solutions to covert mediated solutions utilizing a complex of previously acquired behaviors (Kendler & Kendler, 1962).

Findings and observations such as these again raise the question as to the effect of such changes on memory. Is memory for a task learned at an early stage of development less accessible because stimulus information of that type is now processed in a different fashion? This is an intriguing possibility because the greatest changes in information processing appear to take place in preschool and early school years, exactly those periods for which typical adults have the poorest recall (cf. Inhelder, 1969). To date there have been few empirical investigations on the effects of changes in mode of information processing, but we believe it to be a promising area for research even though the methodological difficulties are formidable.

Differentiation

During the course of development, all mammals must pass through a stage in which they actively learn the stimulus characteristics of their environment. The motivation and reinforcement for this learning are obscure and are the source of continuing discussion, but whether motivated by curiosity, fear, or primary or derived motives and incentives, it is irrelevant to the observation that such learning does take place. Even the lowly laboratory rat, housed in stimulus-impoverished environment, learns the characteristics of his home cage environments (Candland & Campbell, 1962). The implications of this observation for our analysis of developmental changes in memory are substantial; if an animal does not differentiate between the home cage environment and the test environment, criterion responses acquired in the latter will either be enhanced or extinguished in the home environment depending on the similarity of stimulus–response contingencies in the two environments.

Stimulus Generalization

By definition, stimulus events are never reproduced completely; consequently, performance on each successive trial in a learning task, regardless of intertrial interval, is determined by the perceived similarity of the ongoing trial to previous trials and the strength of the acquired response. In well-trained adult animals, presumably little stimulus generalization decrement occurs from trial to trial even over long retention intervals, but in young animals, the possibility exists that growth-induced changes in body and physiological makeup substantially alter the perception of the test environment resulting in a performance decrement. A description of some of the growth-induced changes which might act to impair performance of habits acquired early in development follows.

Changes in Perception of the Conditioned Stimulus. By far the most commonly considered source of age-induced stimulus generalization decrement is the change in perceived size of the environment that is thought to occur as the animal matures. From this it follows that to a young rat, a maze may look like a great cavern from which escape requires a massive effort, but on retest after a retention interval, the same apparatus may appear much different because the visual angles from which the apparatus is viewed have changed or because the size of the apparatus, relative to the animal's body size, is now much smaller. Similarly the child's view of the world changes from one which is populated by giants and distinguished by spots of gum underneath tabletops, to the adult view of the world as we know it. This hypothesis is so intuitively appealing that some psychologists have considered this the major mechanism underlying forgetting in infancy. Perkins (1965), for example, states in reference to Campbell and Campbell's (1962) report showing poorer retention of fear in infancy that "the stimulus situation to which fear was learned may be so altered by stimulus changes resulting from growth that there is nearly complete generalization decrement resulting from maturation induced changes [pp. 46–47]." Additional evidence for this view stems from the observation that handwriting characteristics of the early school years reappear when adult humans are asked to write their names slowly, and that long-forgotten memories are sometimes recalled when phrases typical of childhood such as "No, I won't" are shouted in the uncontrolled fashion of childhood (Tomkins, 1963, p. 334).

Maturational Changes in Perception of Unconditioned Stimuli. When relearning is used as a measure of retention, the possibility exists that the unconditioned stimulus will be perceived as either qualitatively or quantitatively different. For example, a specified intensity of shock may produce intense pain in young rats and only mild stimulation in adult rats resulting in a performance decrement. Research on this particular question is ambiguous. Campbell (1967), using a matched-impedance shock source, found no differences in aversion thresholds across a wide range of ages in either rats or guinea pigs, but Paré (1969) has recently reported that young rats are much more sensitive to constant current dc shock than adults. Similarly Klein and Spear

(1969) have obtained data suggesting that sensitivity to electric shock changes between 15 and 25 days of age, and Campbell (1967) observed that the tetanization thresholds were lower for young animals. This factor probably does not seriously affect the data showing poorer retention by infants than adults, however. Feigley and Spear (1970) have shown that the extent to which weanlings (21–25 days old) show greater retention deficit than adults does not differ over wide variations in shock intensity for both active- and passive-avoidance tasks. Furthermore, the magnitude of the retention deficit was not influenced by shock intensity for either weanlings or adults.

It is also difficult to equate amount of reinforcement in appetitive studies across ages. Obviously the typical 45-milligram Noyes pellet constitutes a greater proportion of the young animal's nutritive requirements than the adult animal's, and the difficulties in scaling the size of the pellet during retesting constitute major methodological questions (cf. Campbell, 1967; Campbell & Jaynes, 1968). Whether changes in absolute pellet size or changes in pellet size relative to body size produce generalization decrement has not been investigated.

Experimental Tests of the Generalization Decrement Hypothesis. To date there have been few experimental tests of the generalization decrement hypothesis, and the results are thus far ambiguous. In the first direct test, Thompson et al. (1965) trained 25-, 50-, and 100-day-old rats in shuttle boxes scaled to the size of the rat, and then retested them in the largest of the three boxes after retention intervals of 0, 50, or 100 days. Using this procedure, no differences in long-term retention were found as a function of the age at time of training, a result which they interpreted as showing that the rapid rate of forgetting typically found in young rats is the result of generalization decrement. Unfortunately the design of the experiment is incomplete in first failing to demonstrate rapid forgetting in young rats with test apparatuses of the same size, and then in not demonstrating that adult animals show a generalization decrement when apparatus size is changed in the retention test. In addition, rate of acquisition varied significantly across age groups, further complicating interpretation of the results.

In a more recent test of the generalization decrement hypothesis, Feigley and Spear (1970) trained young rats in an avoidance box appropriate for adults or in a smaller apparatus roughly scaled to the weanling body size. After a 28-day retention interval they were tested in the larger box; thus, rats trained in the smaller box were tested in an apparatus which increased in volume by a magnitude roughly proportional to the rats' own increase in body size. No differences in this long-term retention were found, thus contradicting the conclusions of Thompson et al. With both boxes, Feigley and Spear found retention of the young rats to be significantly poorer after 28 days than adult rats trained and retested in the same-size apparatus.

Stimulus Generalization Gradients as a Function of Age. A question closely related to the above issue of whether or not young animals show growth-induced generalization decrements during the retention interval concerns the nature of the primary stimulus generalization gradient itself. Many theorists (e.g., Prokasy & Hall, 1963) have contended that the primary stimulus generalization gradient reflects the animals' failure to discriminate the original training stimulus from the test stimulus. From this reasoning it follows that young animals with little prior stimulus experience should show flatter generalization gradients than adults. Unfortunately, it is not clear at this time whether generalization gradients in infancy are typically flatter, steeper, or the same as in adulthood, since there is conflicting evidence to support each view (Frieman, Rohrbaugh, & Riccio, 1969; Peterson, 1962; Rudolf, Honig, & Gerry, 1969). In the present context, flatter generalization gradients in infancy may leave the younger animal more susceptible to extraexperimental interference or facilitation, while steeper generalization gradients in infancy may maximize decrements in response strength produced by maturation-induced changes in perception.

III. Neurological Correlates of Memory Development

In addition to above described behavioral changes taking place during development that might be related to the poorer memory of infancy, there are an equal or greater number of changes in the central nervous system which might also influence memory. The purpose of this section is to review some of those changes and to speculate on the manner in which they might produce the observed ontogenetic differences in memory. Before proceeding to this discussion, it is necessary to reiterate the distinction between the processes of learning and memory, since learning capacity may mature at one rate and retention capability at another. In the data reviewed earlier, there were numerous instances in which young animals acquired new material at the same rate as adult animals but then showed much more rapid loss of those responses over long time periods. Within the field of human memory, for example, it is well established that certain variables (meaningfulness, intralist similarity, intertrial interval) may have quite different effects on learning rate and retention (cf. Keppel, 1964; Spear, 1970; Underwood, 1966), thus providing further precedent for instances of functional independence between learning and retention.

The ontogenetic distinction between learning and retention recalls the concept of encephalization as Yerkes (1912) applied it to a study of retention in the earthworm. In a classic experiment, Yerkes trained earthworms to avoid shock and approach moist earth in a T-maze. At criterion, the caudal section was severed from the head ganglion and then retested periodically in the maze. Surprisingly, the caudal section appeared to retain the response until a new head ganglion regenerated. Yerkes interpreted this as showing that memory could be stored in the worms' primitive ladder nervous network, but that regeneration of the head ganglion (encephalization) somehow dominated or disrupted the memory trace resulting in loss of the habit. Unfortunately this experiment has never been successfully replicated, and it now seems likely that Yerkes' original finding was an artifact (Ratner, 1967).

Nonetheless, the concept of encephalization-induced memory loss is one which may have considerable relevance to the high rates of forgetting observed in young mammals born with immature central nervous systems. In the simplest sense, it seems quite possible that continued neurological development following the acquisition of a learned response could act to either disrupt the memory-storage mechanism(s) or to block retrieval of previously learned materials. Surprisingly, there has been little or no speculation about either of these possibilities during the past several decades or more, a period during which there has been an astronomical increase in the amount known about the central nervous system and its development.

Myelinization

Prior to the 1950s, functional development of the central nervous system was most commonly linked to myelinization. Flechsig (1896) was the first to observe that myelin was either absent or grossly deficient in neonatal mammals, a finding which led him to postulate that myelinization preceded function. In man, for example, he believed that the ability to form associations did not appear until two to three months postnatally, the time at which myelin is first observed in the cortical association areas. Elaborating on this reasoning, many early psychologists attributed the phenomenon of infantile amnesia to incomplete myelinization (Allport, 1937, p. 161). In fact, there is a striking correlation between the development of long-term memory in both rat and man and myelinization.

In mammals, myelinization proceeds in a roughly caudocranial order. Myelin first appears in the spinal cord, then in the medulla, pons, and midbrain, and finally in the telencephalon. The cerebral cortex also myelinates sequentially starting at the projection centers and ending at the association centers (Jacobson, 1963).

In the rat, the first evidence of myelin appears

in the ventral spinal roots at about 2 days postnatally, and it is not until the rat is about 10 days old that myelin begins to appear in the cerebrum. Within the telencephalon, thalamic fibers begin to myelinate between 10 and 12 days and are not fully myelinated until 40–50 days postnatally. In the cortex, myelinization does not begin in many regions until 21 days and is not complete until the rat is approximately 60 days of age (Jacobson, 1963) with the period of most rapid deposition occurring between 30 and 40 days (Bass, Netsky, & Young, 1969).

The major effect of myelin in nervous tissue is to increase speed of nerve conduction. The thicker the myelin sheath, the more rapid the speed of transmission. Consequently the changes in speed of neural conduction that occur developmentally are nothing short of remarkable. Figure 16–2 illustrates the increase in conduction velocity that occurs in the corticospinal tract of the kitten. Comparable changes occur in other brain regions and in other mammals, such as the rat and man, which show comparable changes in myelinization (Grafstein, 1964; O'Brien, 1970).

A related characteristic of the young organism is the relative fatigability of its central nervous system. With repetitive stimulation, the refractory period of cortical responses increases and the amplitude decreases relative to the adult

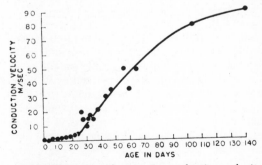

FIGURE 16–2. Changes in conduction velocity in the kitten cortico-spinal tract during ontogenesis. (Reprinted with permission from an article by D. P. Purpura, R. J. Shofer, E. M. Housepian, and C. R. Nobach published in *Progress in brain research*, Vol. 4. Copyrighted by Elsevier Publishing Co., 1964.)

pattern of responding. As a result of these factors, the central nervous system of the young animal is only able to receive and treat a relatively small amount of information per unit of time (Scherrer, 1968, p. 488).

How might these changes affect memory? Clearly deposition of myelin in axon sheaths is not a primary memory storage mechanism, nor is it likely that changes in the refractory period directly influence memory, yet these changes may interfere with retrieval of learned material by a simple principle analogous to primary stimulus generalization.

If the central nervous system can process only limited amounts of information early in development, then the amount of information encoded in a stimulus sequence preceding the elicitation of a criterion response is necessarily less in infancy than adulthood. Consequently, when an animal is tested for retention after a period during which neurological growth has occurred, the amount of information processed per unit time in the test environment would be greater than it was during original learning. This change could conceivably result in a generalization decrement leading to poorer performance. Similarly changes in speed of transmission per se could produce a generalization decrement. Proprioceptive feedback, for example, is more rapid in the adult than young rat.

Cell Differentiation

Another dimension of central nervous system growth that may influence learning and memory is the maturation of cell structure. In immature mammals, the pyramidal cells of the cortex, for example, are small, densely packed, and the dendritic structure incompletely elaborated (Eayrs & Goodhead, 1959; Purpura et al., 1964). As maturation proceeds, the dendritic structure becomes more and more complex until the cell acquires its adult characteristics. The time course of this growth sequence in the rat has been illustrated by Eayrs and Goodhead (1959) and is reproduced in Figure 16–3.

Using a Golgi stain and a light microscope technique, Eayrs and Goodhead also estimated the growth of axodendritic junctions by count-

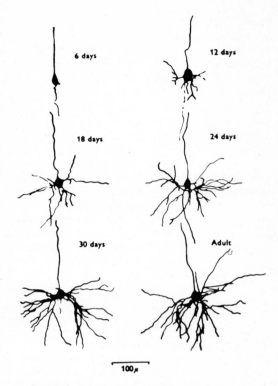

FIGURE 16–3. Characteristic changes in appearance of pyramidal cells in the rat from six days of age to maturity. (Reprinted with permission from an article by J. T. Eayrs and B. Goodhead in the *Journal of Anatomy*, 1959, Vol. 93. Copyrighted by Cambridge University Press, 1959.)

ing the number of times dendrites of a given cell appeared to make contact with axons. Their findings are summarized in the left panel of Figure 16–4. More recently, Aghajanian and Bloom (1967) counted the number of synaptic junctions in the molecular layer of the rat's parietal cortex at different stages of development using electron microscopy. Their results are reproduced in the right panel of Figure 16–4. In both cases it is evident that the majority of synaptic junctions are formed between 10 and 30 days of age, and it is just in this age range where the rat shows the greatest increase in long-term memory.

There are at least two ways in which number of synaptic connections may determine the poorer memory of the rat early in development. First it may be that memory is simply pro-

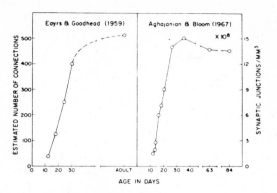

FIGURE 16–4. Estimated number of synaptic junctions in the rat cerebral cortex during postnatal maturation. (Reprinted and adapted with permission from articles by the following authors: J. T. Eayrs and B. Goodhead in the *Journal of Anatomy*, 1959, Vol. 93. Copyrighted by Cambridge University Press, 1959; and G. K. Aghajanian and F. E. Bloom in *Brain Research*, 1967, Vol. 6. Copyrighted by Elsevier Publishing Co., 1967.)

portional to the number of synaptic junctions functioning at the time of original learning. Long-term memory may depend on redundancy. Second is the possibility that the increase in number of synaptic junctions following learning somehow impedes access to the previously learned response. Because of the vast increase in synaptic connections, sensory information necessary to elicit the learned response would almost surely be processed in different ways at different stages of development, thereby altering retrieval pathways. In short, it is quite possible that memories acquired early in development are stored with the same fidelity as adult memories, but that access to them is impeded by further central nervous system development. It is tantalizing to speculate that the reason early childhood memories return during senescence is because the most recently formed parts of the central nervous system are the first to atrophy (Paulson & Gottlieb, 1968).

In a more general sense, forgetting in infancy may parallel the disappearance of reflexive behaviors during ontogenesis. It is well established that the Babinski, rooting, and grasping reflexes, as well as many others, are inhibited by the functional maturation of higher brain centers, and that many of these reflexes reap-

pear following cortical insult or arteriosclerosis. Thus the reflexes of infancy are always present in the central nervous system but inaccessible (not elicitable) for most of the typical mammals' life span. Because of the many parallels between reflexive and learned behaviors, it would not be at all surprising if some portion of what is learned in infancy is permanently stored but rendered inaccessible by further central nervous system development.

Development of Electrical Activity

Ever since Berger (cf. Brazier, 1961) succeeded in recording the electrical (electroencephalogram [EEG]) activity of the cortex, scientists have been attempting to identify components of this activity that might be associated with learning. To date this effort, while successful in many ways, has not identified the specific aspects of EEG activity that are critically associated with learning. Moreover, the extensive findings showing that memory persists following temporary disruption or cessation of EEG activity have led most investigators to abandon the notion that memory was stored in ongoing central nervous system electrical activity. Instead, most investigators now appear to believe that EEG activity is the manifestation of neurochemical activity at the synapse and that memory is encoded by morphological changes (e.g., chemical changes, neural growth, or changes in nucleic acid structure) either in the cell body or in the synaptic structure.

As a result, EEG activity can probably be best considered as a composite index of all brain components which influence nervous transmission. As such, the EEG becomes a useful index of maturational development of brain function. For the rat, there are a few signs of electrical activity in the cortex at birth. Action potentials are absent, although they can be elicited in subcortical structures, and there are few signs of spontaneous electrical activity. On Day 6, a primitive EEG pattern appears, but the major changes in the spectrum of EEG activity occur between 15 and 28 days of age. This progression of development is beautifully summarized in Figure 16–5 taken from Deza

DEVELOPMENT OF CORTEX

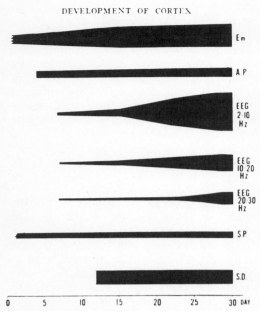

FIGURE 16–5. Ontogenesis of electrical activity in the rat brain. (The width of the horizontal bars indicates progressive changes in either amplitude or frequency of brain electrical activity. The various measures are as follows: membrane potential [Em], action potential discharge [AP], cortical EEG activity [EEG], cortical steady potential [SP], and spreading depression [SD]. (Reprinted with permission from an article by L. Deza and E. Eidelberg in *Experimental Neurology*, 1967, Vol. 17. Copyrighted by Academic Press, 1967.)

and Eidleberg (1967). Thus, as with many of the previous indexes of neurological maturation, there is a striking correlation between maturation of cortical electrical activity and the development of memory.

Neural Transmitters

Of the known neural transmitters, acetylcholine is the most likely to be directly involved in the memory storage and retrieval process. Rosenzweig, Bennett, Diamond, Wu, Slagle, and Saffram (1969) have shown that enriched early experience, with the increased opportunities for learning that accompanies it, leads to an increase in both brain size and concentration of acetylcholinesterase, the enzyme which degrades acetylcholine. More directly relevant to memory and retrieval are the numerous studies showing that anticholinergic drugs such as scopolamine produce amnesia and/or dissociation (Berger & Stein, 1969a, 1969b). Conversely, anticholinesterases have been reported to enhance memory in some circumstances and impair it under others (Deutsch & Deutsch, 1966). The status and interpretation of this research remains very much in doubt, however, and there is as yet no consensus on the role that acetylcholine plays in the memory process. Among the other known central nervous system transmitters—norepinephrine, dopamine, and serotonin—none have been found to affect the memory process directly, although they may act to

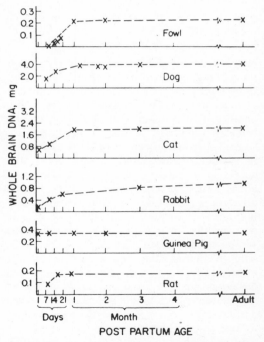

FIGURE 16–6. Changes in total brain DNA content of several representative species during postnatal growth. (Reprinted with permission from an article by P. Mandell, H. Rein, Harth-Edel, and R. Mardell in *Comparative Neurochemistry.* Copyrighted by Pergamon Press, 1964.)

influence memory storage and retrieval by altering levels of arousal or emotional state (Seiden & Peterson, 1968; Stein & Berger, 1969).

Developmentally there is a remarkable similarity in the ontogeny of the major neural transmitters. All develop in a caudalrostral direction (Friede, 1966; Robinson, 1968), and all show the greatest increase in concentration between 10 and 30 days of age, with more gradual increases continuing until the rat is 50–100 days old (for review see Friede, 1966; Himwich, 1970). Within the monoamine group, serotonin is the first to reach adult levels of concentration, norepinephrine second, and dopamine the last. Acetylcholinesterase, which is probably correlated with concentration of acetylcholine, also continues to increase until the rat is approximately 100 days of age (Friede, 1966).

This pattern of neural transmitter development parallels the development of memory, but again it is difficult to assign any special significance to the correlation between the two processes.

Deoxyribonucleic Acid, Ribonucleic Acid, Protein Synthesis, and Metabolic Rate

In recent years, numerous attempts have been made to implicate deoxyribonucleic acid (DNA), ribonucleic acid (RNA), protein synthesis, and metabolic rate in the brain to the memory storage and retrieval processes. While the status of these theories is unclear, a brief review of how these characteristics change during development in relation to the ontogenesis of learning and memory is in order.

Brain DNA and RNA both continue to increase postnatally in most mammals. Figure 16–6 shows the time course of these changes in several representative species. Increases occur in the dog, cat, rabbit, and rat; but no increase is seen in the guinea pig which is born with a mature central nervous system after a long gestation period. In the rat, both RNA and DNA attain their maxima about 14 days postpartum,

well before long-term memory reaches adult levels, indicating that there is no simple relationship between total quantities of these brain constituents and memory. With respect to total DNA, an index of the number of cells in the brain, this is not surprising, since the mere presence of a cell body does not indicate that it has reached functional maturity. As noted earlier, dendritic arborization and the formation of synaptic clefts continue to develop long after the cell body is formed. In addition, the brain cells that are formed postnatally consist almost entirely of primitive microneurons, cells that are unlikely to be critical to learning and memory (Altman, 1970).

From these data, it also appears that total brain RNA is unrelated to the increase in long-term memory that occurs in the rat after 14 days postpartum. This is not to say that DNA or RNA are not essential substrates of the memory process, as they undoubtedly are (Booth, 1967), but to indicate that total quantities of these substances in the brain are simply not predictive of long-term memory.

In recent years, more attention has been paid to the overall role of protein synthesis in memory storage than to RNA and DNA. Numerous studies have shown that inhibition of protein synthesis by antibiotics such as puromycin and acetoxycycloheximide act to impair memory consolidation (Agranoff, 1970; Barondes, 1970; Flexner, Flexner, & Roberts, 1967). While there are many difficulties in interpreting these findings, there is a strong possibility that some aspect of protein synthesis is critical to memory. Unfortunately, the present synthesis inhibitors are ubiquitous in that they inhibit the formation of all proteins. This makes it virtually impossible to examine the relation between rate of protein synthesis and the development of long-term memory, since growth of the brain is predominantly dependent on synthesis of new proteins. When and if the proteins critical to memory storage are identified, then it may be possible to relate concentrations of those proteins to the development of long-term memory. At present, what is known is that the total amount of protein in the brain increases extremely rapidly beginning at age 10 in the rat and reaches an asymptote about 30 days of age (Agrawal & Himwich, 1970).

Another dimension of brain function that has been occasionally implicated in long-term retention is that of metabolic rate. Here the assumption is that the memory trace (or access to that trace) is gradually eroded over time by the turnover of cell body constituents, and that alteration in metabolic rate either accelerates or retards forgetting by speeding or slowing the turnover process. To date, the several experimental tests of this hypothesis are at variance with each other, and it is not yet clear whether brain metabolism is in anyway related to forgetting (Gleitman & Rozin, 1971). When this concept is considered in the developmental context, it first appears as though there might be a relationship between metabolic rate and forgetting, since it is well known that basal metabolic rate is much higher in childhood than adulthood (Keele & Neil, 1965). Brain metabolism, however, is not linked to body metabolism. In fact, it shows quite a different developmental pattern. Instead of decreasing during development, brain metabolism increases rapidly in the early postnatal stages to a maximum and then maintains that level into adulthood with only a slight decline as aging occurs. Thus the rapid rate of forgetting in infancy is not determined by a period of heightened brain metabolism.

The foregoing analysis of ontogenetic differences in memory can also be related to the decay theory of forgetting, now undergoing something of a resurgence in popularity (e.g., Gleitman, 1971; McGaugh & Dawson, 1971). That theory simply states that over time the memory trace, as represented in the central nervous system, diminishes in strength. In this context a major aim of Section III was to identify some of the central nervous system's mechanisms which might account for the rapid decay of memory in the neonate. Perhaps the identification of critical variables will be easier in those preparations where memory is declining most rapidly.

What is more important, however, is the fact that the effects many of these changes have on memory can now be investigated. For example, demyelinating agents (Bubis & Luse, 1964) and dietary deficiencies (Dobbing, 1964) can be used to alter concentration or rate of myelin deposition, central nervous system poisons such as 6 hydroxydopamine (Ungerstedt, 1968) can be used to destroy catecholaminergic synaptic clefts at different stages of development, various drugs can be used to block or enhance synaptic transmission, and higher brain centers can be temporarily paralyzed by topical application of potassium chloride.

Similarly, if more obviously, the effects of various environmental conditions on memory such as interpolated environmental complexity, body size relative to the environment, hormonally induced changes in species-specific behaviors, and many others are subject relatively easily to experimental study.

IV: Resolution of the Paradox

There are at least two possible resolutions to the paradoxical combination of poorer retention by immature mammals and the critical importance of early experience for adult behavior. One possibility, as noted in the introduction, is that key early experiences may permanently alter structure and function of the autonomic, endocrine, and central nervous systems.

Another possible resolution of this paradox is through mechanisms which act to maintain memories that are normally forgotten. The requirements of such a mechanism are that it be unavailable to the animal under controlled laboratory conditions, but at least potentially available to the animal in its natural environment. "Reinstatement" (Campbell & Jaynes, 1966) is such a mechanism. Campbell and Jaynes found that retention by immature rats was greatly facilitated if they were reexposed to the conditions of original training at points distributed throughout the retention interval. However, such reexposures by themselves were only a fractional portion of the experience necessary for original learning. Animals given only this "reexposure" training gave no evidence of learning.

The purpose in introducing the term "reinstatement" was to reemphasize the importance of such a phenomenon, rather than for innovation. In fact a similar mechanism for conserving memory was proposed long ago by Sechenov (1863). In discussing factors responsible for weakening of the memory trace, Sechenov noted the apparently poorer memory of immature humans: "Indeed, what objects does the child remember? It remembers only those which are often before its eyes; the infant soon forgets even its mother should she die" (p. 70). Then he describes how a reinstatementlike mechanism might act to conserve retention in the adult:

An adult, upon meeting another person even for a short time, receives from him a multitude of diverse sensations; the facial expression of the person, his features, pose, gait, manner of speaking, sound of voice, the subject of conversation, etc.—all remain in the memory for a more or less considerable time, depending on the strength of the impression; in the end, however, the traces of the impression begin to weaken. But one day another person is met, who along with other sensations induces one closely resembling the sensation produced by the first person. The latter sensation is revived in the memory, and becomes refreshed to a degree that it seems to be experienced anew. If these conditions are repeated from time to time, the traces remain (p. 70).

Sechenov then suggests that one reason for the poorer retention by children may result from the lesser opportunity for those experiences which conserve memory: "In the child, however, these conditions, even if they are present, are incomparably less pronounced" (p. 71).

Operationally, reinstatement is defined as better performance on a retention test by animals which have been briefly reexposed to the conditions of original learning during the retention interval in comparison with performance by animals receiving no such reexposure. Two critical assumptions underlie the significance of this phenomenon. First, it is assumed that the reinstatement conditions are in themselves insufficient to establish learning. The second critical aspect of the reinstatement trials is their distribution throughout the retention interval— presumably if they were simply added as

overtraining trials at the time of original learning, the benefit to retention would be a good deal less than is found with more even distribution throughout the retention interval. Both of these suppositions have been confirmed empirically, the first by Campbell and Jaynes (1966, 1969), Shubat and Whitehouse (1968), and Silvestri, Rohrbaugh, and Riccio (1970), and the second by Greenfield and Riccio (in press).

The generality of reinstatement has become increasingly apparent. Studies with the rat have established that reinstatement is effective in maintaining retention of "fear conditioning" (e.g., Silvestri et al., 1970), discrimination learning (Campbell & Jaynes, 1969), and in grade school children using a matching task (Hoving, Coates, Bertucci, & Riccio, 1972). In the latter experiment, children first learned to associate pairs of pictures, then eight weeks later they were asked to match pictures from a pool in accord with the original pairings. Children in the "reinstatement" condition were presented a story during the retention interval which included pairs of pictures matched as they had been during original learning. Eight weeks after learning, children given the reinstatement treatment required only about two-thirds as many trials to relearn the correct pairings as children not given this reinstatement treatment and about one-third as many trials as children given only the reinstatement treatment but not original learning.

Other variables which have been shown to influence the magnitude of the reinstatement effect are the duration of each reinstatement trial and its content. Effects of these variables, though not uninteresting, are nevertheless straightforward and predictable. For example, Campbell and Jaynes (1969) trained weanling rats on a brightness discrimination, then measured their retention 10 weeks after original learning. Five groups of rats differed in their duration of exposure when reintroduced to this same task once each week during the retention interval: Either 0, 7.5, 15, 30, or 60 minutes of additional practice on the original brightness-discrimination task constituted the weekly reinstatement experience. Although 60 minutes of practice per week was nearly sufficient to eliminate the performance differences between rats given and those not given original learning, results of the other conditions permitted the conclusion of better retention the longer the duration of each reinstatement session.

Questions concerning which specific features of the reinstatement experience are critical for improving retention may also be relevant to the question, "What is forgotten?" Some cataloging of effective memory attributes probably is necessary for understanding animal memory (cf. Spear, 1971), and if certain elements of a conditioning trial are found to be both necessary and sufficient for reinstatement, these elements are in turn implicated as critical memory attributes. For example, Silvestri et al. (1970) found effective reinstatement of fear conditioning even though only the conditioned stimulus (without the unconditioned stimulus) was presented on each reinstatement trial. Silvestri et al. noted that the short duration of the conditioned-stimulus-only reinstatement trials was probably responsible for the occurrence of reinstatement instead of extinction, an assumption they then verified empirically. They also found that without the conditioned stimulus neither presentation of a "new" aversive stimulus nor the original unconditioned stimulus during reinstatement trials was sufficient to improve retention. Thus reinstatement of the conditioned stimulus dimension is probably more important than reinstatement of the unconditioned stimulus for maintenance of the target memory.

The fear-conditioning procedure used by Silvestri et al. involved alternate placement in the black and white compartments of a two-compartment box. The rat received footshocks in the black compartment but not in the white. Placement for an equivalent period into both compartments also constituted the reinstatement procedures which were effective even without the presence of shock in either compartment. Suppose the animals had been placed in only one of the compartments for reinstatement. Would reexposure to the presumably aversive compartment yield a different degree of re-instatement than reexposure to the previously more "safe" compartment? Greenfield (1969) conducted an appropriate experiment within this context and found reinstatement to be more effective when animals were placed only in the compartment in which they were previously shocked than if they were placed in the previously "safe" compartment. Of course, such a design does not permit identification of which memory attributes were forgotten independent of which were acquired originally. However, parallel results have been obtained in a reinstatement experiment by B. A. Campbell (in preparation) employing a brightness discrimination task. Campbell found reinstatement more effective when animals were exposed only to the nonreinforced stimulus during the retention interval than when animals were exposed only to the reinforced stimulus. Thus, in both experiments, the stimulus most effective in reinstatement was the stimulus associated with inhibition of responding. Whether this is due to more rapid forgetting of memory attributes associated with inhibition or to the fact that inhibition was more critical than excitation for original learning has yet to be determined.

V: Implications for the Ontogeny of Human Memory

The relevance of animal studies to human memory and cognitive processes has been subject to increasingly critical examination over the past decade. In the present instance, the same caution should be observed; there are obviously vast differences in the qualitative aspects of behavioral development between rats and man. Man, for example, has an enormously greater capacity to encode and store complex information, and much of what is subsumed under the rubic "infantile amnesia" refers to the absence of memory for complex events and experiences that are easily recalled if learned in adulthood. Needless to say, we cannot equate the rapid forgetting of specific tasks such as passive-avoidance responding in rats with infantile amnesia in man. Moreover, there are substantial differences in rate of forgetting for different tasks in the rat. Some, like the passive-avoidance task, decline extremely rapidly, while others are forgotten much more slowly. Whether this reflects differences in strength of original learning, the relative susceptibility of inhibitory versus active responses to forgetting, or that some responses are more "natural" than others and therefore less likely to be forgotten is as yet unknown. But even if the basis for these differential rates of forgetting were known for the rat, it would still be an open question as to whether those same mechanisms operated in man.

On the other hand, there are a great many similarities between the ontogenesis of behavior and nervous system function in man and rat. Both are born with immature central nervous systems, are virtually helpless at birth, and are completely dependent on parental care. Similarly, both pass through periods of intense play and social interactions culminating in adult sexual behavior, and in both species complex social dominance hierarchies emerge during development.

Sequentially, the overall pattern of brain development is remarkably similar in rat and man. In both species, for example, the spinal motor roots are the first to myelinate and the cortical association areas the last. The time sequence is, of course, vastly different. At birth the human central nervous system is somewhat more advanced than that of the rat. In man, the spinal motor roots are fully myelinated at birth whereas myelinization does not begin in that area in the rat until two days postnatally. Similarly some brain stem and cerebellar structures show considerable myelinization at birth in man where no such development is evident in the rat. On the other hand, there is no sign of myelin in forebrain structures such as the thalamus, striatum, fornix, or cortex in either species. In man, the cortical association areas show traces of myelin at three months postnatally, but the rate of deposition is extremely slow, continuing past the tenth year postnatally and possibly into the third or fourth decade. Myelinization of the thalamic radiations begins about the same time but is completed by the eighth to ninth year. Other forebrain areas commence myelinization at about the same time, but deposition is much more rapid and nearly complete at 12 months of age (Yakovlev & Lecours, 1967). However by weight the amount of myelinization present in the frontal lobes is only 40% of the adult level at 10 months of age (O'Brien, 1970) indicating the extent to which myelin deposition continues in that area after the first year of life.

Other indexes of brain function confirm this general pattern of development. At birth, spontaneous EEG activity can be recorded in the human infant, although much of that activity is believed to be subcortical in origin (Ellingson, 1967). The pattern of EEG activity changes drastically during the first three postnatal years and then more gradually during the subsequent years into adolescence (Scheibel & Scheibel, 1964). Similarly, speed of nerve conduction continues to increase during development and fatigability decreases just as it does in the rat.

In summary, changes in central nervous system structure and function comparable to those occurring in the rat during the first months of life appear in man during the first years of life. For both species, these changes parallel the emergence of long-term memory as judged by improved retention of instrumental tasks in the rat and the disappearance of infantile amnesia in man. But whether central nervous system development is critical for the emergence of long-term memory is still an open question, since the sequence of behavioral development and the continuing acquisition of new responses could also account for the poor memory of infancy in both rat and man. The aim of this paper has been to review and analyze some of these changes in the hope it would stimulate research on the relative contribution of neurological and behavioral variables to the development of long-term memory. To the extent that future research on infrahuman animals points to either neurological or behavioral variables as critical for the emergence of long-term memory, the greater the necessity for examining those processes in man.

REFERENCES

Aghajanian, G. K., & Bloom, F. E. The formation of synaptic junctions in developing rat brain: A quantitative electron microscopic study. *Brain Research*, 1967, *6*, 716–727.

Agranoff, B. W. Recent studies on the stages of memory formation in the goldfish. In W. L. Byrne (Ed.), *Molecular approaches to learning and memory*. New York: Academic Press, 1970.

Agrawal, H. C., & Himwich, W. A. Amino acids, proteins and monoamines of the developing brain. In W. A. Himwich (Ed.), *Developmental neurobiology*. Springfield, Ill.: Charles C Thomas, 1970.

Altman, J. Postnatal neurogenesis and the problem of neural plasticity. In W. A. Himwich (Ed.), *Developmental neurobiology*. Springfield, Ill.: Charles C Thomas, 1970.

Allport, G. W. *Personality: A psychological interpretation*. New York: Holt, 1937.

Amster, H., Keppel, G., & Meyer, A. Learning and retention of letter pairs as a function of association strength. *American Journal of Psychology*, 1970, *83*, 22–39.

Bach, M. J., & Underwood, B. J. Developmental changes in memory attributes. *Journal of Educational Psychology*, 1970, *61*, 292–296.

Barondes, S. H. Some critical variables in studies of the effect of inhibitors of protein syntheses on memory. In W. L. Byrne (Ed.), *Molecular approaches to learning and memory*. New York: Academic Press, 1970.

Bass, N. H., Netsky, M. G., & Young, E. Microchemical studies of postnatal development in rat cerebrum: I. Migration and differentiation of cells. *Neurology*, 1969, *19*, 258–268.

Berger, B. D., & Stein, L. An analysis of learning deficits produced by scopolamine. *Psychopharmacologia*, 1969, *14*, 271–283. (a)

Berger, B. D., & Stein, L. Asymmetrical dissociation of learning between scopolamine and Wy 4036, a new benzodiazapine tranquilizer. *Psychopharmacologia*, 1969, *14*, 351–358. (b)

Bolles, R. C., & Woods, P. J. The ontogeny of behavior in the albino rat. *Animal Behavior*, 1964, *12*, 427–441.

Booth, D. A. Vertebrate brain ribonucleic acids and memory retention. *Psychological Bulletin*, 1967, *68*, 149–177.

Brazier, M. A. B. *A history of the electrical activity of the brain: The first half century*. New York: Macmillan, 1961.

Bubis, J. J., & Luse, S. A. An electron microscopic study of experimental encephalomyelites in the rat. *American Journal of Pathology*, 1964, *44*, 299–307.

Campbell, B. A. Developmental studies of learning and motivation in infraprimate mammals. In H. W. Stevenson, E. H. Hess, & H. L. Rheingold (Eds.), *Early behavior: Comparative and developmental approaches*. New York: Wiley, 1967.

Campbell, B. A., & Campbell, E. H. Retention and extinction of learned fear in infant and adult rats. *Journal of Comparative and Physiological Psychology*, 1962, *55*, 1–8.

Campbell, B. A., & Jaynes, J. Reinstatement. *Psychological Review*, 1966, *73*, 478–480.

Campbell, B. A., & Jaynes, J. Effect of duration of reinstatement on retention of a visual discrimination learned in infancy. *Developmental Psychology*, 1969, *1*, 71–74.

Campbell, B. A., Jaynes, J. R., & Misanin, J. Retention of a light-dark discrimination in rats of different ages. *Journal of Comparative and Physiological Psychology*, 1968, *66*, 467–472.

Candland, D. K., & Campbell, B. A. Development of fear as measured by behavior in the open field. *Journal of Comparative and Physiological Psychology*, 1962, *5*, 593–596.

Crockett, W. H., & Noble, M. E. Age of learning, severity of negative reinforcement, and retention of learned responses. *Journal of Genetic Psychology*, 1963, *103*, 105–112.

Deese, J., & Hulse, S. H. *The psychology of learning*. (3rd ed.) New York: McGraw-Hill, 1967.

Deutsch, J. A., & Deutsch, D. *Physiological psychology*. Homewood, Ill.: Dorsey Press, 1966.

Deza, L., & Eidleberg, E. Development of cortical electrical activity in the rat. *Experimental Neurology*, 1967, *17*, 425–438.

Dobbing, J. The influence of early malnutrition on the development and myelination of the brain. *Proceedings of the Royal Society of Biology*, 1964, *159*, 503–509.

Dudycha, G. J., & Dudycha, M. M. Childhood memories: A review of the literature. *Psychological Bulletin*, 1941, *38*, 668–682.

Eayrs, J. T., & Goodhead, B. Postnatal development of the cerebral cortex in the rat. *Journal of Anatomy*, 1959, *93*, 385–401.

Ellingson, R. J. The study of brain electrical activity of infants. In L. P. Lipsitt & C. C. Spiker (Eds.), *Advances in child development and behavior*. New York: Academic Press, 1967.

Feigley, D. A., & Spear, N. E. Effect of age and punishment condition on long-term retention by the rat of active- and passive-avoidance learning. *Journal of Comparative and Physiological Psychology*, 1970, *73*, 515–526.

Flechsig, P. *Gehrirn & Seele*, Leipzeig, 1896.

Flexner, L. B., Flexner, J. B., & Roberts, R. B. Memory in mice analyzed with antibiotics. *Science*, 1967, *155*, 1377–1383.

Friede, R. L. *Topographic brain chemistry*. New York: Academic Press, 1966.

Frieman, J. P., Rohrbaugh, M., & Riccio, D. C. Age differences in the control of acquired fear by tone. *Canadian Journal of Psychology*, 1969, *23*, 237–244.

Gleitman, H. Forgetting of long-term memories in animals. In W. K. Honig & P. H. R. James (Eds.), *Animal memory*. New York: Academic Press, 1971.

Gleitman, H., & Rozin, P. Learning and memory. *Fish Physiology*, 1971, *6*, 196–278.

Goulet, L. R. Verbal learning in children: Implications for developmental research. *Psychological Bulletin*, 1968, *69*, 359–376.

Grafstein, B. Postnatal development of the corpus collosum in the cat. In P. Kellaway & I. Peterson (Eds.), *Neurological and electroencephalographic correlative studies in infancy*. New York: Grune & Stratton, 1964.

Greenfield, H., & Riccio, D. C. Conditioned reinstatement in rats: Effect of exposure distribution and cue. *Psychological Reports*, 1972, in press.

Harlow, H. F. The heterosexual system in monkeys. *American Psychologist*, 1962, *17*, 1–9.

Harlow, H. F., & Harlow, M. K. Social deprivation in monkeys. *Scientific American*, 1962, *207*, 136–146.

Himwich, W. A. *Developmental neurobiology*. Springfield, Ill.: Charles C Thomas, 1970.

Hinde, R. A. *Bird vocalizations in relation to current problems in biology and psychology*. New York: Cambridge University Press, 1969.

Hoving, K. L., Coates, L., Bertucci, M., & Riccio, D. C. Reinstatement of effects in children. *Developmental Psychology*, 1972, in press.

Hutchinson, R. R., Ulrich, R. E., & Azrin, N. H. Effects of age and related factors on the pain-aggression reaction. *Journal of Comparative and Physiological Psychology*, 1965, *59*, 365–369.

Inhelder, B. Memory and intelligence in the child. In D. Elkind & J. H. Flavell (Eds.), *Studies in cognitive development*. Oxford: Oxford University Press, 1969.

Jacobson, S. Sequence of myelinization in the brain of the albino rat. A. Cerebral cortex, thalamus and related structures. *Journal of Comparative Neurology*, 1963, *121*, 5–29.

Keele, C. A., & Neil, E. *Samson Wright's applied physiology*. (11th ed.) Oxford: Oxford University Press, 1965.

Kendler, H. H., & Kendler, T. S. Vertical and horizontal processes in problem solving. *Psychological Review*, 1962, *69*, 1–16.

Keppel, G. Verbal learning in children. *Psychological Bulletin*, 1964, *61*, 63–80.

Kirby, R. H. Acquisition, extinction, and retention of an avoidance response in rats as a function of age. *Journal of Comparative and Physiological Psychology*, 1963, *56*, 158–162.

Klein, S. B., & Spear, N. E. Influence of age in short-term retention of active avoidance learning in rats. *Journal of Comparative and Physiological Psychology*, 1969, *69*, 583–589.

Levine, S., & Mullins, R. F., Jr. Hormones in infancy. In G. Newton & S. Levine (Eds.), *Early experience and behavior*. Springfield, Ill.: Charles C Thomas, 1968.

Levy, D. M. The infant's earliest memory of inoculation: A contribution to public health procedures. *Journal of Genetic Psychology*, 1960, *96*, 3–46.

Mandel, P., Rein, H., Harth-Edel, S., & Mardell, R. Distribution and metabolism of ribonucleic acid in the vertebrate central nervous system. In D. Richter (Ed.), *Comparative neurochemistry*. New York: Pergamon Press 1964.

McGaugh, J. L., & Dawson, R. G. Modification of memory storage processes. In W. K. Honig & P. H. R. James (Eds.), *Animal memory*. New York: Academic Press, 1971.

McGeoch, J. A., & Irion, A. L. *The psychology of human learning*. (2nd ed.) New York: Longmans, Green, 1952.

Moorcroft, W. H., Lytle, L. D., & Campbell, B. A. Ontogeny of starvation-induced behavioral arousal in the rat. *Journal of Comparative and Physiological Psychology*, 1971, *75*, 59–67.

O'Brien, J. S. Lipids and myelination. In W. A. Himwich (Ed.), *Developmental neurobiology*. Springfield, Ill.: Charles C Thomas, 1970.

Paré, W. P. Age, sex, and strain differences in the aversive threshold to grid shock in the rat. *Journal of Comparative and Physiological Psychology*, 1969, *69*, 214–218.

Paulson, G., & Gottlieb, G. Development reflexes: The reappearance of foetal and neonatal reflexes in aged patients. *Brain Research*, 1968, *91*, 37–52.

Perkins, C. C., Jr. A conceptual scheme for studies for stimulus generalization. In D. I. Mostofsky (Ed.), *Stimulus generalization*. Stanford: Stanford University Press, 1965.

Peterson, N. Effect of monochromatic rearing on the control of responding by wavelength. *Science*, 1962, *136*, 774–775.

Postman, L. Transfer, interference and forgetting. In J. W. Kling & L. A. Riggs (Eds.), *Woodworth and Schlossberg's experimental psychology*. (3rd ed.) New York: Holt, Rinehart and Winston, 1971.

Prokasy, W. F., & Hall, J. F. Primary stimulus generalization. *Psychological Review*, 1963, *70*, 310–322.

Purpura, D. P., Shofer, R. J., Housepian, E. M., & Noback, C. R. Comparative ontogenesis of structure-formation relationships in cerebral and cerebellar cortex. In D. P. Purpura & J. P. Schade (Eds.), *Progress in brain research*. Vol. 4. *Growth and maturation of the brain*. Amsterdam: Elsevier, 1964.

Ratner, S. C. Annelids and learning: A critical review. In W. C. Corning & S. C. Ratner (Eds.), *Chemistry of learning*. New York: Plenum Press, 1967.

Riesen, A. H. Stimulation as a requirement for growth and function in behavioral development. In D. W. Fiske & S. R. Maddi, (Eds.), *Functions of varied experience*. Homewood, Ill.: Dorsey Press, 1961.

Robinson, N. Histochemistry of rat brainstem monoamine oxidase during maturation. *Journal of Neurochemistry*, 1968, *15*, 1151–1158.

Rosenzweig, M. R., Bennett. E. L., Diamond, M. C., Wu, S., Slagle, R. W., & Saffram, E. Influence of environmental complexity and visual stimulation on development of occipital cortex in rats. *Brain Research*, 1969, *14*, 427–445.

Rozensweig, M. R., Krech, D., Bennett, E. L., & Diamond, M. C. Modifying brain chemistry and anatomy by enrichment or impoverishment of experience. In G. Newton & S. Levine (Eds.), *Early experience and behavior*. Springfield, Ill.: Charles C Thomas, 1968.

Rudolf, R. L., Honig, W. K., & Gerry, J. E. Effects of monochromatic rearing on the acquisition of stimulus control. *Journal of Comparative and Physiological Psychology,* 1969, *67,* 50–57.

Saul, L. J., Snyder, T. R., & Sheppard, E. On earliest memories. *Psychoanalytic Quarterly,* 1956, *25,* 228–237.

Schachtel, E. G. On memory and childhood amnesia. *Psychiatry,* 1947, *10,* 1–26.

Scheibel, M. E., & Scheibel, A. B. Some neural substrates of postnatal development. In M. L. Hoffman & L. W. Hoffman (Eds.), *Review of child development research.* New York: Russell Sage Foundation, 1964.

Scherrer, J. Electrophysiological aspects of cortical development. In E. A. Asraytan (Ed.), *Progress in brain research.* Amsterdam: Elsevier, 1967.

Schulenburg, C. J., Riccio, D. C., & Stikes, E. R. Acquisition and retention of a passive-avoidance response as a function of age in rats. *Journal of Comparative and Physiological Psychology,* 1971, *74,* 75–83.

Sechenov, I. M. *Reflexes of the brain.* Cambridge: M.I.T. Press, 1965. (Originally published, 1863.)

Seiden, L. S., & Peterson, D. D. Blockage of l-dopa reversal of reserpine-induced conditioned avoidance response suppression by disulfiram. *Journal of Pharmacology and Experimental Therapeutics,* 1968, *163,* 84–90.

Shubat, E. E., & Whitehouse, J. M. Reinstatement: An attempt at replication. *Psychonomic Science,* 1968, *12,* 215–216.

Silvestri, R., Rohrbaugh, M. J., & Riccio, D. C. Conditions influencing the retention of learned fear in young rats. *Developmental Psychology,* 1970, *2,* 389–395.

Sluckin, W. *Imprinting and early learning.* Chicago: Aldine, 1965.

Smith, N. Effects of interpolated learning on the retention of an escape response in rats as a function of age. *Journal of Comparative and Physiological Psychology,* 1968, *65,* 422–426.

Spear, N. E. Verbal learning and retention. In M. R. D'Amato, *Experimental psychology: Psychophysics, methodology and learning.* New York: McGraw-Hill, 1970.

Spear, N. E. Forgetting as retrieval failure. In W. K. Honig & H. James (Eds.), *Animal memory.* New York: Academic Press, 1971.

Stein, L., & Berger, B. D. Paradoxical fear-increasing effects of tranquilizers: Evidence of repression of memory in the rat. *Science,* 1969, *166,* 253–256.

Thompson, R. W., Koenigsberg, L. A., & Tennison, J. C. Effects of age on learning and retention of an avoidance response in rats. *Journal of Comparative and Physiological Psychology,* 1965, *60,* 457–459.

Tomkins, S. S. *Affect, imagery, consciousness.* Vol. 2. *The negative affects.* New York: Springer, 1963.

Underwood, B. J. Interference and forgetting. *Psychological Review,* 1957, *64,* 49–60.

Underwood, B. J. Degree of learning and the measurement of forgetting. *Journal of Verbal Learning and Verbal Behavior,* 1964, *3,* 112–129.

Underwood, B. J. *Experimental psychology.* (2nd ed.) New York: Appleton-Century-Crofts, 1966.

Underwood, B. J. Attributes of memory. *Psychological Review,* 1969, *76,* 559–573.

Underwood, B. J., & Ekstrand, B. R. An analysis of some shortcomings in the interference in forgetting. *Psychological Review,* 1966, *73,* 540–549.

Underwood, B. J., & Freund, J. S. Effect of temporal separation of two tasks on proactive inhibition. *Journal of Experimental Psychology,* 1968, *78,* 50–54.

Underwood, B. J., & Postman, L. Extraexperimental sources of interference in forgetting. *Psychological Review,* 1960, *60,* 457–459.

Ungerstedt, U. 6-Hydroxydopamine induced degeneration of central monoamine neurons. *European Journal of Pharmacology,* 1968, *5,* 107–110.

Waldfogel, S. The frequency and affective character of childhood memories. *Psychological Monographs*, 1948, *62*(4, Whole No. 291).

Walen, S. R. Recall in children and adults. *Journal of Verbal Learning and Verbal Behavior*, 1970, *9*, 94–98.

Wiesel, T. N., & Hubel, D. H. Comparison of the effects of unilateral and bilateral eye closure on cortical unit response in kittens. *Journal of Physiology*, 1965, *28*, 1029–1041.

Yakovlev, P. I., & Lecours. A. The myelogenetic cycles of regional maturation of the brain. In A. Minkowski (Ed.), *Regional development of the brain in early life*. Philadelphia: Davis, 1967.

Yerkes, R. M. The intelligence of earthworms. *Journal of Animal Behavior*, 1912, *2*, 332–352.

17. DEVELOPMENTAL CHANGES IN MEMORY ATTRIBUTES

MARY JEAN BACH and BENTON J. UNDERWOOD[1]

Two experiments investigated attribute dominance in memory for words of second- and sixth-grade subjects. The attributes studied were the acoustic and the associative; dominance was inferred from the nature of errors on a recognition task. Both experiments showed dominance of the acoustic attribute for second-grade subjects and dominance of the associative attribute for sixth-grade subjects. The evidence also indicated that the acoustic attribute was forgotten more rapidly than the associative attribute.

The memory for a word may be conceptualized as consisting of a collection of attributes (Underwood, 1969). These attributes represent different types of encoded information and they serve to discriminate one memory from another as well as to serve as retrieval cues. In the present study the interest is in two attributes, namely, the acoustic attribute and the verbal-associative attribute. The acoustic attribute of the memory for a word is its sound patterning when pronounced. The verbal-associative attribute of a word consists of one or more other words which may be elicited by it. It is assumed that at the time of learning these two attributes may become a part of the memory for

[1] The authors wish to thank Earl Hartman, Principal, South Park School, and Harry Brown, Principal, Wilmot Elementary School, both of Deerfield, Illinois, and their cooperative teachers for making the students available for this study.

From the *Journal of Educational Psychology*, 1970, *61*, 292–296. Copyright 1970 by the American Psychological Association. Reprinted by permission of the authors and the publisher.

a word. Other attributes may also be involved but the present study is not analytical with regard to them.

The central purpose of the present study was to determine if developmental changes occur in the dominance of the two attributes under consideration. Available evidence leads to the expectation that such changes should occur. With college students, the recognition memory for common words is dominated by the verbal-associative attribute, the acoustic attribute playing at best a very minor role (Underwood & Freund, 1968). On the other hand, memory for consonants (where associative attributes would be minimal) appears to be dominated by the acoustic attribute (e.g., Wickelgren, 1965). As new words are acquired by a young child, the verbal-associative attributes to these words should be minimal in number and they should also lack stability. A new word to a young child should, in a manner of speaking, be comparable to a relatively meaningless consonant sound to an adult. It seems possible, therefore, that the acoustic attribute may be dominant in the young child even for the memory for a word that is called a common word by an adult. As the child grows older and receives more and more educational experiences, it is to be anticipated that the associative attributes will become more and more dominant in the memory for words.

A procedure previously used to detect differences in attribute dominance in recognition memory for adults (Underwood & Freund, 1968) was adapted for use with children. The subject was presented 40 words, one at a time, for learning. For recognition the subject was given a multiple-choice test for each of the 40 words. Four alternatives were available for each word, namely, the correct word, an associate of the correct word, a word that was acoustically similar to the correct word, and a fourth word which was neutral in that it had neither associative nor acoustic relationships to the correct word. To illustrate: one word presented to the subject for learning was BAD. On the multiple-choice test the subject was required to choose from among the four words, BAD, GOOD, BAG, and DOT. It was anticipated that age differences in the dominance of the attributes of memory could be detected by differences in the types of errors made on the recognition test.

The developmental variable was represented by two grade levels, namely, the second grade and the sixth grade. Since there is suggestive evidence (Baddeley & Dale, 1966) that differential rates of forgetting may occur for different attributes, two retention intervals, 0 and 48 hours, were used. Thus, with two grade levels and two retention intervals, four different groups were required. Finally, the experiment was replicated, two different schools being used. The results for these two experiments will be reported separately.

Method

Materials

The 40 words presented for learning and the additional words used on the recognition test are shown in Table 17–1. The 160 words were selected from the readers of the subjects in the

TABLE 17–1
Words Used on the Recognition Test

CORRECT	ASSOCIATE	NEUTRAL	ACOUSTIC
cat	dog	put	sat
bad	good	dot	bag
boy	girl	cap	toy
lamp	light	deep	lamb
hard	soft	keep	card
hop	jump	ask	top
sell	buy	ice	tell
game	party	air	name
wood	tree	baby	would
round	sun	color	sound
better	more	rope	letter
clean	neat	road	seen
new	old	cry	who
ride	car	pipe	hide
chair	table	part	bear
pail	sand	front	nail
bird	cage	pencil	heard
burn	fire	ruler	turn
snow	sled	cake	show
shoe	foot	push	blue
give	take	add	live
bed	sleep	once	said
cow	milk	sign	how
day	night	corn	say
high	low	city	lie
glad	happy	box	had
book	story	kind	took
chief	police	dress	leaf
just	about	again	must
fast	slow	farm	past
cent	penny	town	sent
drink	water	gate	think
race	run	been	face
smile	laugh	soon	while
leg	arm	fun	beg
strong	kite	open	bring
boat	sea	tiny	goat
room	house	time	broom
talk	speak	horn	walk
far	near	wish	jar

second grade whose reading word population consisted of a total of 537 words (McKee, Harrison, McCowen, Lehr, & Durr, 1966). The word-association tables and other information from Entwisle (1966) were used in choosing the associated words for the recognition test. The words chosen to have acoustic similarity to the correct words resulted from the experimenter's judgments and this also determined the choice of the neutral words.

Procedure

The subjects were run individually in an isolated room on the premises of each school. Each word was printed in lower case letters on a sheet of paper, and each was presented for 5 seconds on the single learning trial. As each word was presented, both the experimenter and subject pronounced it. The subject was fully informed as to the task, being told that he was to try and remember each word so that he could later pick it out from among other words. On the recognition test the subject was shown the four words on a single sheet, 18 × 24 inches, with a word in each quarter section, and was asked to choose the word he had been shown earlier. The test was unpaced but the subject was forced to make a choice for each set of four words. The order of the four words in each set was determined randomly. A single random order of the 40 words was used on the learning trial. Ten of the 20 words occurring during the first half of the learning trial appeared during the first 20 words tested for recognition, and 10 occurred during the last 20. Therefore, 10 of the 20 words occurring during the last 20 words presented for learning occurred during the first half of testing, and 10 occurred during the last half of testing. Within these restrictions, positions were random.

Subjects

In Experiment I there were 27 subjects in each of the four groups, while in Experiment II there were 30 subjects in each group. In Experiment I the subjects from the second grade and those from the sixth grade came from the same school; this was also true for Experiment II but the school differed from that used for Experiment I. Within each grade, within each experiment, the subjects were assigned to the 0- and 48-hour retention conditions on a random basis.

Results

The restrictions on the nature of the conclusions which can be drawn from the results must be clear at the outset. It is not known that

acoustic similarity and associative similarity, as represented by the words on the multiple-choice task, are equivalent in level or degree of similarity to the correct response. Therefore, to say that one of these attributes dominates at a given grade level can only have meaning with reference to these particular materials. The hypothesis under consideration states that there will be changes in the relative frequency with which the different types of errors occur at the two grade levels. Thus, the hypothesis predicts an interaction between error type and grade and is irrelevant to any differences in the absolute level of error frequency for the two types.

The mean numbers of errors of each type for all conditions are presented in Table 17–2. Some general characteristics of the data will be pointed out first, following which the interaction effects will be examined. It may first be noted that the error frequency is somewhat higher in Experiment II than in Experiment I. This presumably reflects a difference in the populations sampled. Second, in both experiments recognition performance was better

TABLE 17–2
Mean Recognition Errors as a Function of Type, Grade, Interval, and Experiment

INTERVAL (hrs.)	TYPE			TOTAL
	Associative	Acoustic	Neutral	
Experiment I				
Second grade				
0	4.37	4.96	2.30	11.63
48	7.15	6.30	4.67	18.11
Sixth grade				
0	7.41	5.19	3.33	15.93
48	8.81	5.44	4.93	19.19
Experiment II				
Second grade				
0	4.77	5.90	2.47	13.13
48	8.83	7.70	5.03	21.57
Sixth grade				
0	7.07	5.40	2.57	15.03
48	9.57	6.40	5.50	21.47

for the second-grade subjects than for the sixth-grade subjects. In Experiment I this difference between grades was statistically significant ($F = 6.87$, $df = 1/104$, $p < .05$), while in Experiment II the difference did not approach significance ($F = 1.29$). Nevertheless, the fact remains that the recognition performance of second-grade subjects was as good as, or better than, that of sixth-grade subjects. The third fact of general interest is that under all conditions when the subject makes an error he is far more likely to choose an acoustic or associative distractor than the neutral distractor. This indicates that an associative attribute or an acoustic attribute, or both, were frequently a part of the memory for the word. Finally, the evidence is clear in showing forgetting over 48 hours.

Interaction of Error Type and Grade

The mean errors for all conditions on immediate recognition are plotted for each experiment in Figure 17–1. The results for both experiments are very similar, namely, second-grade subjects produce a somewhat greater frequency of acoustic than associative errors, and for sixth-grade subjects the relationship is reversed. The interaction term is highly sig-

nificant in both experiments; in Experiment I, $F = 8.48$, $df = 2/205$, $p < .01$; in Experiment II, $F = 7.63$, $df = 2/232$, $p < .01$. This finding indicates that there are developmental changes in the dominance of attributes in the memory for words.

Retention-Interval Effects

A careful examination of Table 17–2 suggests that forgetting is more rapid for second-grade subjects than for sixth-grade subjects. This is true in spite of the fact that the initial level of performance (0 hours) was somewhat higher for the second-grade subjects than for the sixth-grade subjects. In neither experiment taken separately is the grade difference in rate of forgetting significant statistically, but border-line statistical significance is achieved if the results for both experiments are combined, $F = 3.91$, $df = 1/224$, $p < .05$. For reasons which will become apparent later, this differential rate of forgetting might be expected.

The triple interaction of Grade × Retention Interval × Error Type was far from significant ($Fs = .10$ and 1.24 for Experiments I and II, respectively). Therefore, in examining the

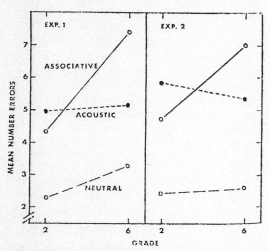

FIGURE 17–1. Frequency of errors by types as a function of grade and experiment.

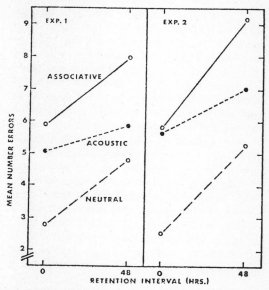

FIGURE 17–2. Frequency of errors by types as a function of retention interval and experiment.

influence of the retention interval on error types, the results for the two grades have been combined and are shown in Figure 17–2. Statistically, the interaction term is significant for Experiment II, $F = 4.93$, $df = 2/232$, $p < .01$, but not for Experiment I ($F = 2.40$). Combining both experiments produces a highly significant interaction term ($F = 7.24$). Thus, while there is some ambiguity, the evidence in Figure 17–2 suggests that with the passage of time acoustic errors increase in frequency less rapidly than either associative or neutral errors, with the latter two types increasing at about the same rate as the retention interval increases. In terms of percentage of total errors, there is an absolute decrease in acoustic errors over time.

Discussion

Both experiments have shown with high reliability that acoustic errors are more frequent than associative errors for second-grade subjects, while for sixth-grade subjects the reverse is true. This finding is interpreted as indicating that the memory for a word for younger subjects is more likely to be dominated by the acoustic attribute than is the memory for a word by the older subjects. To say that one attribute dominates another may be interpreted in two basic ways. First, it could mean that only one attribute becomes a part of the memory, the other not becoming a part. Were this true across all words for a given subject, however, the correlations between frequency of acoustic errors and frequency of associative errors should be high and negative. Although the correlations were not reported, it can be stated that such relationships were not present in the data. This is not definitive, however; a given subject may encode some words on one attribute only, and other words only on a different attribute. Thus, second-grade subjects may simply encode more of their words acoustically than do sixth-grade subjects. The second meaning which may be given to the statement that one attribute dominates another would assume that both attributes (and others not considered here) become a part of the memory but that subjects differ as a function of age in their preference for, or confidence in, one attribute over the other. Clearly, techniques are available which would allow a decision concerning these two alternative ways of viewing the differences in attribute dominance as a function of age. For example, if both attributes are a part of the memory for a word, a forced choice between the two remaining wrong alternatives following an initial error (acoustic or associative) should not result in equal frequencies for the two alternatives.

Relative to associative and neutral errors, the acoustic errors increased less rapidly over the 48-hour retention interval. This was true for both second-grade and sixth-grade subjects. This trend was not strong, but it occurred in both experiments and for the combined data was highly significant statistically. This may be interpreted as more rapid forgetting of the acoustic attribute than the associative attribute. Of course, other alternatives could be invoked, for example, differential change in the subject's confidence in the reliability of a particular attribute. However, the notion of differential forgetting has some appeal. Although of questionable statistical significance, the data indicated that over time the superior performance of the second-grade subjects over the sixth-grade subjects diminished. If the acoustic attribute dominates the immediate memory of the second-grade subjects, and if this attribute is forgotten more rapidly than the associative attribute, the second-grade subjects after 48 hours have less information (or, less preferred information) than do the sixth-grade subjects. But, even assuming differential forgetting, the question must arise as to the responsible mechanism. It is possible to speculate concerning differences in interpolated interference for the two classes of attributes, but at this point it would be only speculation. Nevertheless, that differential forgetting may have occurred is quite in line with the conclusions of other investigators (Baddeley & Dale, 1966).

REFERENCES

Baddeley, A. D., & Dale, H. C. A. The effect of semantic similarity on retroactive interference in long- and short-term memory. *Journal of Verbal Learning and Verbal Behavior,* 1966, *5*, 417–420.

Entwisle, D. R. *Word associations of young children.* Baltimore: Johns Hopkins Press, 1966.

McKee, P., Harrison, M. L., McCowen, A., Lehr, E., & Durr, W. K. *Jack and Janet; Up and away; Come along.* Boston: Houghton Mifflin, 1966.

Underwood, B. J. Attributes of memory. *Psychological Review,* 1969, *76*, 559–573.

Underwood, B. J., & Freund, J. S. Errors in recognition learning and retention. *Journal of Experimental Psychology,* 1968, *78*, 55–63.

Wickelgren, W. A. Acoustic similarity and intrusion errors in short-term memory. *Journal of Experimental Psychology,* 1965, *70*, 102–108.

Chapter 7

MOTIVATION
AND
ATTENTION

INTRODUCTION AND COMMENTARY

The Concept of Motivation

Stagner (1961), a well-known psychologist, has stated that "psychologists generally agree that the task of motivation theory is to explain the energizing of activity" (p. 49). Regardless of this apparent agreement, and having taken more than a decade for it to mature, understanding what psychologists mean by motivation remains difficult for at least two reasons.

1. Despite the exceedingly rich vocabulary of motivation in the common language, motivation theorists have for various reasons tended to focus on relatively narrow ranges of phenomena, and usually on some monolithic principle, as bases for theories of motivation. For example, a traditional and influential view in psychological research and theory has been based on the belief that organisms' homeostatic reactions to biological needs are the wellspring of all motivated behavior (see Cofer & Appley, 1964, chap. 7 for a history of this position). Other psychologists, having looked to behavior for a criterion by which to identify motivational variables, have focused on facilitation or *invigoration* of behavior, independent of any necessary relation to a recognized biological need state. (Both Brown, 1961, and Cofer & Appley, 1964, provide a thorough discussion of this view). Still others have insisted that an affective (emotional, pleasant–unpleasant, positive–negative, etc.) dimension be made the core of motivational theory (see McClelland, Atkinson, Clark and Lowell, 1953; and Young, 1961).

What results from this multiplicity of somewhat selective views of motivation (only a few of which have been mentioned here) is an exceedingly complex, if not inscrutable array of motivation research and theory. (See, e.g., Bindra, 1974, and Solomon & Corbit, 1974, as current theoretical views that also convey this complexity.)

2. The second reason for difficulty in understanding psychologists' conceptions of motivation is intimately related to the first. It stems from the fact that motivation, as conceived by most, is not directly observable, but is *inferred* from behavior and from antecedent manipulations of the environment or the organisms' state. Indeed, frequently it has been inferred by a process of elimination; that is, when changes in behavior have not been attributable to other factors such as learning, perception, or situational variables.

Obviously, this sort of inference has the attendant danger of over-inclusion. It is compellingly easy to "think motivation" and thence to attribute to some motivational wellspring every piece of behavior one observes. What this can yield is an unwieldy concept, the meaning of which has deceptively inclusive value at the common language level, and no value at the level of scientific discourse.

The Ontogeny of Motivation

The special question of the *development* of motivation has seldom arisen from some of the theoretical conceptualizations. Where the focus has been upon biological need states, motivation has usually been considered an organismic "given." Study of learned, secondary motivation based upon primary need states had been the only explicit developmental orientation, but more recent experiments examining influences of early experience (see Chapter 5) constitute an important departure from this tendency. The early ethologists' view, with its heavy reliance on "innate" mechanisms, offers similar treatment of motivation in terms of "givens." It does, however, include explicit emphasis on evolutionary development. Some concern with development has arisen from affect (emotion-based) theories. McClelland et al. (1953), for example, assume that experience is necessary for any motivational development. Also, concerning what seem to be "naturally" pleasant and unpleasant stimuli (the "sweetness" of sugar, e.g.) the question has arisen whether they represent structural, "sensory biases" (see Lorenz, 1965, on innateness) or are, in fact, learned phenomena based perhaps on satisfaction of need states. Young (1966) assumes that "innate neural mechanisms" play a basic role, but he also emphasizes the development of "acquired dispositions" based on these innate mechanisms.

A seminal paper by Hunt (1960) constitutes the beginning of a major attempt to place motivation in a developmental context. He draws heavily on the writings of Hebb (e.g., Hebb, 1946, 1949, 1955), research on early experience (see Chapter 5), as well as on the work of Piaget (see Chapter 10). Hunt (1960) emerges with the integrating concept of "intrinsic motivation"; that is, motivation based on informational interaction of an active, "expectant" organism with its environment. He develops this view more fully and convincingly in a subsequent, lengthy paper (Hunt, 1965), and the critically interested student whose appetite has been whetted should consult that paper as a more complete basis for evaluation of this approach. Here, Hunt is no longer satisfied with the notion of "spontaneous" activity, which was given some status in the earlier paper; in its place he develops the idea of "incongruity" as an instigator of activity. However, in that earlier paper he clearly lays the groundwork for his later views. His emphasis on stimulus (informational) properties of many motivational phenomena is noteworthy as an attempt to move away from a monolithic, biological energy conception.

Cognitive Factors

Hunt's approach also constitutes one early facet of a so-called cognitive revolution (Dember, 1974) as it has been manifest in motivational psychology. Perhaps the most influential other facet of this trend has been the compelling research by Schachter and his colleagues (see, e.g., Schachter, 1971) revealing the considerable plasticity of human reactions to numerous traditionally motivational variables as a function of a person's "expectation," or other cognitive predisposition, regarding the motivational variables. While this research bears strongly on an ontogeny of motivation, specific pertinent research has apparently not yet been done.

Attention

A third facet of this trend is the increasing prominence of "attention" as a descriptive and often explanatory concept (see, e.g., Jeffrey, 1968). As a descriptive term it arises from the distinction between the "nominal" and "effective" stimuli in any situation; attention refers to the controlling relation in which certain stimuli are behaviorally effective, while others, though also present in the situation, are not, or are less so. Thus, in terms of research on human development, an infant's visual attention (looking) might be evoked by some drawings in an array more than by others. If, for example, familiarity is found to be a determining factor, and if one can treat such visual attention as preference behavior (Irwin, 1971), its probable cognitive *and* motivational significance is hard to miss.

Kagan's article [18] describes and discusses part of a growing body of research fitting this form. He summarizes several experiments with infants in which different measures of "attention" (see also Jeffrey, 1968) were used to assess relations between attentional indicants either of preference or arousal, and familiarity. Kagan shows how the research enables one to distinguish three development-related classes of relations: (1) attention evoked simply by physical change in stimulation; (2) attention influenced by changes away from familiar patterns of stimulation; and (3) attention serving the child's "interpreting" of unusual but familiar patterns. The theory Kagan applies is a very recognizable offspring of the point of view espoused by Hunt (1960).

The research by Lewis [19] also fits this context. Considering the face as an example of a developing schema for infants, it focuses on infant reactions to human faces. The report not only provides a careful analysis in terms of different infant response measures (fixation, smiling, vocalizing, fret/crying) of reactions to various facelike displays "as a function of age," but it also further inculcates the conceptual relation between motivation and attention.

Reinstatement

The final two articles included in this chapter are about a unique research paradigm and concept developed by Campbell and Jaynes [20, 21]. The concept "reinstatement" refers to that frequency of recurrence of an event, or "reminders" of the event, during development that is sufficient to maintain some related behavior but is not sufficient to initiate the behavior. The first demonstration [20] that such a frequency can be found involved weanling rats given considerable shock exposure in a distinctive compartment. Subsequently, one shock each week was sufficient to maintain an aversive reaction to the shock compartment over 28 days, though the three "reinstating" shocks themselves produced no detectable aversion in control rats.

The reinstatement paradigm suggests one important bridge between research on early experience (see Chapter 5, pp. 140–147), in which learning details have not been emphasized, and more traditional learning analysis of responsiveness to noxious stimuli: The experiment suggests a very plausible mechanism for the lasting effects of at least some early experience (see also Campbell & Spear [16]).

That reinstatement does not only pertain to noxious experiences is shown in [21], where Campbell and Jaynes extend it to discrimination learning involving food reward, and in [16], where Campbell and Spear discuss reinstatement as a factor in the ontogeny of memory. Finally, preliminary evidence is available showing that reinstatement can also be defined for children's experiences (Hoving & Choi, 1972; Hoving, Coates, Bertucci, & Riccio, 1972). In these experiments children (six to eight years) were given paired-associate training on common object names and tested for relearning after eight weeks. Four weeks after original learning some of the children had been given some form of reinstatement of the paired objects. Relearning tests not only confirmed a reinstatement effect, but also indicated that the response items were a necessary component of the reinstating treatment.

References

Bindra, D. A motivational view of learning, performance and behavior modification. *Psychological Review,* 1974, *81*, 199–213.

Brown, J. S. *The motivation of behavior*. New York: McGraw-Hill, 1961.

Cofer, C. N., & Appley, M. A. *Motivation: Theory and Research*. New York: Wiley, 1964.

Dember, W. N. Motivation and the cognitive revolution. *American Psychologist,* 1974, *29*, 161–168.

Hebb, D. O. On the nature of fear. *Psychological Review,* 1946, *53*, 259–276.

Hebb, D. O. *The organization of behavior.* New York: Wiley, 1949.

Hebb, D. O. Drives and the C.N.S. (Conceptual nervous system). *Psychological Review,* 1955, *62*, 243–254.

Hoving, K. L. & Choi, K. Some necessary conditions for producing reinstatement effects in children. *Developmental Psychology,* 1972, *7*, 214–217.

Hoving, K. L., Coates, L., Bertucci, M., & Riccio, D. C. Reinstatement effects in children. *Developmental Psychology,* 1972, *6*, 426–429.

Hunt, J. McV. Experience and the development of motivation: Some reinterpretations. *Child Development,* 1960, *31*, 489–504.

Hunt, J. McV. Intrinsic motivation and its role in psychological development. In D. Levine (Ed.), *Nebraska Symposium on Motivation: 1965.* Lincoln: University of Nebraska Press, 1965, pp. 189–282.

Irwin, F. W. *Intentional behavior and motivation: A cognitive theory.* Philadelphia: Lippincott, 1971.

Jeffrey, W. E. The orienting reflex and attention in cognitive development. *Psychological Review,* 1968, *75*, 323–334.

Lorenz, K. *Evolution and modification of behavior.* Chicago: University of Chicago Press, 1965.

McClelland, D. C., Atkinson, J. W., Clark, R. A., & Lowell, E. L. *The achievement motive.* New York: Appleton, 1953.

Schachter, S. *Emotion, obesity and crime.* New York: Academic Press, 1971.

Solomon, R. L. & Corbit, J. D. An opponent-process theory of motivation: I. Temporal dynamics of affect. *Psychological Review,* 1974, *81*, 119–145.

Stagner, R. Homeostasis, need reduction, and motivation. *Merrill-Palmer Quarterly,* 1961, *7*, 49–68.

Young, P. T. *Motivation and Emotion.* (2d ed.) New York: Wiley, 1961.

Young, P. T. Hedonic organization and regulation of behavior. *Psychological Review,* 1966, *73*, 59–86.

18.   ATTENTION AND PSYCHOLOGICAL CHANGE IN THE YOUNG CHILD

JEROME KAGAN

One of the great unanswered psychological questions concerns the mechanisms responsible for the transformations in organization of behavior and cognitive structure that define growth and differentiation. Until recently most of these changes were viewed as the product of learning. The child was presumably born unmarked, and the imposing hand of experience taught him the structures that defined him. Hence, many behavioral scientists agreed that learning was the central mystery to unravel, and conditioning was the fundamental mechanism

From *Science,* 1970, *170*, 826–832. Copyright 1970 by the American Association for the Advancement of Science. Reprinted by permission of the author and the publisher.

of learning. There is a growing consensus, however, that conditioning may be too limited a process to explain the breadth and variety of change characteristic of behavioral and psychological structures. What was once a unitary problem has become a set of more manageable and theoretically sounder themes.

Category of Change

It is always desirable to categorize phenomena according to the hypothetical processes that produced them. But since psychology has not discovered these primary mechanisms, it is often limited to descriptive classifications. One category includes alterations in the probability that a stimulus will evoke a given response, which is a brief operational definition of conditioning. Half a century of research on the acquisition of conditioned responses has generated several significant principles, some with developmental implications. It is generally true, for example, that the acquisition of a conditioned response proceeds faster as the child matures (1). Although the explanation of this fact is still not settled, it is assumed that, with age, the child becomes more selectively attentive and better able to differentiate the relevant signal from background noise. Thus a newborn requires about 32 trials before he will turn his head to a conditioned auditory stimulus in order to obtain milk; a 3-month-old requires about nine trials (2, 3).

A second category of change refers to the delayed appearance of species-specific behaviors after exposure to a narrow band of experience. A bird's ability to produce the song of its species (4) or a child's competence with the language of his community (5) requires only the processing of particular auditory events, with no overt response necessary at the time of initial exposure. The environment allows an inherited capacity to become manifest. Close analysis indicates that the development of these and related behaviors does not seem to conform to conditioning principles, especially to the assumption that the new response must occur in temporal contiguity with the conditioned stimulus. This class of phenomena suggests, incidentally, the value of differentiating between the acquisition of a disposition to action and the establishment of and successive changes in cognitive structures not tied directly to behavior. This distinction between behavioral performance and cognitive competence is exemplified by the difference between a child's learning to play marbles and his ability to recognize the faces of the children with whom he plays.

A third category of change, and the one to which this essay is primarily devoted, involves the initial establishment and subsequent alteration of representations of experience, called schemata (singular: schema). A schema is a representation of experience that preserves the temporal and spatial relations of the original event, without being necessarily isomorphic with that event. It is similar in meaning to the older term "engram." Like the engram, the construct of schema was invented to explain the organism's capacity to recognize an event encountered in the past. Although the process of recognition is not clearly understood, the neurophysiologist's suggestion that a cortical neuronal model is matched to current experience captures the essential flavor of the concept (6). It is important to differentiate between the notion of schema as a representation of a sensory event and the hypothetical process that represents the organism's potential action toward an object. Piaget (7) does not make this differentiation as sharply as we do, for his concept of sensory-motor scheme includes the internal representation of the object as well as the organized action toward it.

There is some evidence that some form of primitive representation of experience can be established prior to or soon after birth. Grier, Counter, and Shearer (8) incubated eggs of White Rock chickens (Gallus gallus) from 12 to 18 days under conditions of quiet or patterned sound. Within 6 hours after hatching, each chick was tested for responsiveness to two auditory stimuli, the 200-hertz tone presented prenatally and a novel 2000-hertz sound. The control chicks moved equivalent distances toward both sounds; the experimental chicks moved significantly closer to the 200-hertz sound than to the novel one. Similarly, infant laughing gulls (Larus atricilla) 6 to 13 days old seem able to form representations of their parents' calls, for they orient toward and approach the calls of their own parents but orient away from the calls of other adult gulls (9).

A central assumption surrounding early schema formation states that the first schemata represent invariant stimulus patterns that are part of a larger context characterized by high rate of change (movement, contour contrast, and acoustic shifts). Hence a schema for the human face should develop early, for the face is characterized by an invariant arrangement of eyes, nose, and mouth within a frame that moves and emits intermittent, variable sounds. Experimental observations of young infants suggest that the face is one of the earliest representations to be acquired. Since the establishment of a schema is so dependent upon the selectivity of the infant's attention, understanding of developmental priorities in schema formation should be facilitated by appreciation of the principles governing the distribution of attention. These principles will be considered in the sections that follow.

Contrast, Movement, and Change

Ontogenetically, the earliest determinant of duration of orientation to a visual event is probably inherent in the structure of the central nervous system. The infant naturally attends to events that possess a high rate of change in their physical characteristics. Stimuli that move, have many discrete elements, or possess contour contrast are most likely to attract and hold a newborn's attention. Hence, a 2-day-old infant is more attentive to a moving or intermittent light than to a continuous light source; to a solid black figure on a white background than to a stimulus that is homogeneously gray (10, 11). The newborn's visual search behavior seems to be guided by the following rules (12):

If he is alert and if light is not too bright, his eyes open up.

If his eyes are open but no light is seen, he searches.

If he sees light but no edges, he keeps searching.

If he sees contour edges, he holds and crosses them.

The preference for the study of contour is monitored, however, by the area of the stimulus field, and there seems to be an optimum amount of contour that maintains attention at a maximum. Four-month-old infants exposed to meaningless achromatic designs with variable contour length were most attentive to those with moderately long contours (13). Karmel (14) has reported that, among young infants, duration of attention to meaningless achromatic figures is a curvilinear function of the square root of the absolute amount of black-white border in the figure.

The behavioral addiction to contour and movement is in accord with neurophysiological information on ganglion potentials in vertebrate retinas. Some cells respond to movement; others, to onset of illumination, to offset, or to both. Objects with contour edges should function better as onset stimuli than do solid patterns, because the change in stimulation created by a sharp edge elicits specialized firing patterns that may facilitate sustained attention (15).

There is some controversy over the question of whether contour or complexity exerts primary control over attention in the early months, where complexity is defined in terms of either redundancy or variety or number of elements in the figure and where contour is defined in terms of the total amount of border contained in the arrangement of figures on a background. Existing data support the more salient role of contour over complexity. McCall and Kagan (13) found no direct relation, in 4-month-olds, between fixation time and number of angles in a set of achromatic meaningless designs. Rather, there was an approximate inverted-U relation between attention and total length of contour in the figure. Similarly, fixation time in 5-month-old infants was independent of degree of asymmetry and irregularity in the arrangement of nine squares; however, when these indices of complexity were held constant but area and amount of contour were varied, fixation times were a function of contour (16). Finally, the average evoked cortical potentials of infants to checkerboard and random matrix patterns were independent of redundancy of pattern, but they displayed an inverted-U relation with density of contour edge (17).

Although indices of attention to auditory events are considerably more ambiguous than those used for vision, it appears that stimuli that have a high rate of change, such as intermittent sounds, produce more quieting and, by inference, more focused attention than continuous sounds (18). Nature has apparently equipped the newborn with an initial bias in the processing of experience. He does not, as the 19th-century empiricists believed, have to learn what he should examine. The preferential orientation to change is clearly adaptive, for the locus of change is likely to contain the most information about the presence of his mother or of danger.

Discrepancy from Schema

The initial disposition to attend to events with a high rate of change soon competes with a new determinant based largely on experience. The child's attentional encounters with events result, inevitably, in a schema. Somewhere during the second month, duration of attention comes under the influence of the relation between a class of events and the infant's schema for that class. One form of this relation, called the discrepancy principle, states that stimuli moderately discrepant from the schema elicit longer orientations than do either minimally discrepant (that is, familiar) events or novel events that bear no relation to the schema. The relation between attention and magnitude of discrepancy is assumed to be curvilinear (an inverted U). Although an orientation reflex can be produced by any change in quality or intensity of stimulation, duration of sustained attention is constrained by the degree of discrepancy between the event and the relevant schema. Consider some empirical support for the discrepancy principle.

One-week-old infants show equivalent fixations to an achromatic representation of human faces (see Figure 18–1) and a meaningless achromatic design, for contour is assumed to be the major determinant of atten-

tion at this early age. Even the 8-week-old shows equivalent fixations to a three-dimensional representation of a face and an abstract three-dimensional form (19). But a 4-month-old shows markedly longer attention to the regular achromatic face than to the design (13), presumably because he has acquired a schema for a human face and the laboratory representation is moderately discrepant from that schema. If the representation of the face is too discrepant, as when the facial components are rearranged (see Figure 18–1), fixation times are reduced (20, 21).

Fixation times to photographic representations of faces drop by over 50 percent after 6 months and are equivalent to both regular and irregular faces during the last half of the first year (20, 21). This developmental pattern is in accord with the discrepancy principle. During the opening few weeks of life, before the infant has established a schema for a human face, photographs of either regular or irregular faces are so discrepant from the infant's schema that they elicit equivalent epochs of attention. As the schema for a human face becomes well established, between 2 and 4 months, the photograph of a strange face becomes optimally discrepant from that schema. During the latter half of the first year, the face schema becomes so well established that photographs of regular or irregular faces, though discriminable, are easily assimilated and elicit short and equivalent fixations.

A second source of support for the discrepancy principle comes from research designs in which familiarity and discrepancy are ma-

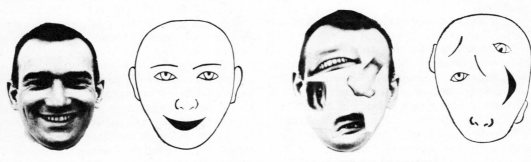

FIGURE 18–1.   Achromatic representations of four facelike stimuli shown to infants.

nipulated through repeated presentation of an originally meaningless stimulus, followed by a transformation of the standard. Fixation times are typically longer to the transformation than to the last few presentations of the habituated standard (22). For example, 4-month-old infants were shown three objects in a triangular arrangement for five repeated trials. On the sixth trial, infants saw a transformation of the standard in which one, two, or three of the original objects were replaced with new ones. Most infants displayed longer fixations to the transformation than to the preceding standard. When the analysis was restricted to the 42 infants who displayed either rapid habituation or short fixations to the last four presentations of the standard trials 2 through 5), an increasing monotonic relation emerged between amount of change in the standard (one, two, or three elements replaced) and increase in fixation from the last standard to the transformation (23).

Although fixation time cannot be used as an index of sustained attention to auditory stimuli, magnitude of cardiac deceleration, which covaries with motor quieting, provides a partial index of focused attention. Melson and McCall (24) repeated the same eight-note ascending scale for eight trials to 5-month-old girls; this repetition was followed by transformations, in which the same eight notes were rearranged. The magnitude of cardiac deceleration was larger to the discrepant scale than to the preceding standard. The curvilinear form of the discrepancy principle finds support in an experiment in which 5½-month-old male infants were shown a simple stimulus consisting of five green, three-dimensional elements arranged vertically on a white background (far left in Figure 18–2). The order of stimulus presentation was SSSSSSSSTSSTSSTS, in which S was the standard and T was one of three transformations of differing discrepancy from the standard. Each infant was shown only one of the three transformations in Figure 18–2. The magnitude of cardiac deceleration was larger to the moderate transformation of the standard (oblique arrangement of the five elements in Figure 18–2, second from left) than to the two more serious transformations (22). This finding is partially congruent with an earlier study on younger infants that used the same stimuli but established the schema over a 4-week period. The girls, but not the boys, displayed larger decelerations to the transformations than to the standard (25).

The most persuasive confirmation of the curvilinear relation between attention and discrepancy was revealed in an experiment in which firstborn, 4-month-old infants were shown a three-dimensional stimulus composed of three geometric forms of different shape and hue for 12 half-minute presentations (26). Each infant was then randomly assigned to one of seven groups. Six of these groups were exposed to a stimulus at home that was of varying discrepancy from the standard viewed in the laboratory. The seventh was not exposed to any experimental stimulus. The mother showed the stimulus to the infant, in the form of a mobile above his crib, 30 minutes a day for 21 days. The seven experimental groups are summarized in Figure 18–3.

Three weeks later each subject returned to the laboratory and saw exactly the same stimulus he

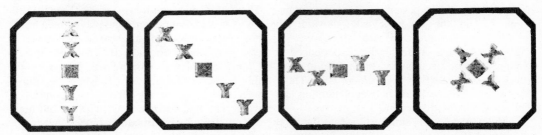

FIGURE 18–2. Standard (far left) and three transformations shown to infants in study of reaction to discrepancy.

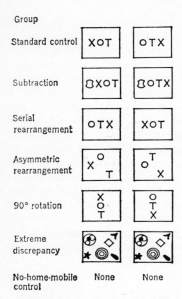

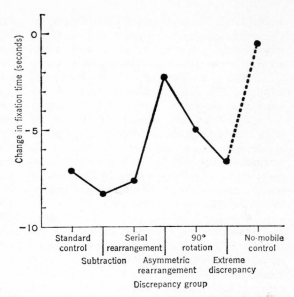

FIGURE 18–3. Summary of the home mobile conditions of the seven experimental groups. The drawings illustrate in schematic form the stimulus to which each child was exposed at home. **FIGURE 18–4.** (right). Change in mean total fixation time across the two test sessions for each of the seven experimental groups.

viewed initially at the age of 4 months. The major dependent variable was the *change in fixation time* between the first and second test sessions. Figure 18–4 illustrates these change scores for total fixation time across the first six trials of each session.

The infants who saw no mobile at home showed no change in fixation time across the 3 weeks, which indicates that the laboratory stimulus was as attractive on the second visit as it had been on the first. The infants who had an opportunity to develop a schema for the asymmetric and vertical rotation mobiles and, therefore, could experience a moderate discrepancy on the second visit, showed the smallest drop in attention across the 3 weeks. By contrast, the infants who experienced a minor or major discrepancy showed the greatest drop in interest ($F = 5.29$, $P < .05$). There was a curvilinear relation between attention and stimulus-schema discrepancy.

The incidence of smiling to familiar and discrepant stimuli also supports the discrepancy principle. It is assumed that the infant is likely

to smile as he assimilates an initially discrepant event (7). Hence, very familiar and totally novel stimuli should elicit minimum smiling, whereas moderately discrepant events should elicit maximum smiling. The smile to a human face or a pictorial representation of a face during the first 7 months is most frequent at 4 months of age among infants from varied cultural settings (27). It is assumed that, prior to 4 months, the human face is too discrepant to be assimilated, and after this time it is minimally discrepant and easily assimilated. The smile of assimilation is not restricted to human faces. Three different auditory stimuli (bronze bell, toy piano, and nursery rhyme played by a music box) were presented to 13-week-old infants in two trial blocks on each of 2 successive days (28). Frequency of smiling was lowest on the first block of trials on day 1, when the sounds were novel, and on the second block on day 2, when they had become very familiar, but highest on the two intermediate blocks, when the infant presumably was able to assimilate them after some effort.

A final illustration of the display of the smile as a sign of assimilation comes from a study in progress in which 60 children, 5½ to 11½ months old, watched a hand slowly move an orange rod clockwise in an arc until it contacted a set of three differently colored light bulbs. As the rod touched one of the lights, all three turned on. This 11-second sequence was repeated eight or ten times (depending upon the age of the child) during which most children remained very attentive. Each child then saw only one of four transformations for five successive trials: (i) the bulbs did not light when the rod touched them, (ii) the hand did not appear, (iii) the rod did not move, or (iv) no hand appeared and no bulbs lit, but the rod moved. After the fifth presentation, the original sequence was repeated three more times. The proportion of infants who smiled was largest on the sixth repetition of the standard and on the third presentation of the transformation. Figure 18–5 illustrates the pattern of smiling to this episode for one 7½-month-old girl who displayed maximum smiling on trials 4 and 5 of the initial familiarization series and trials 3, 4, and 5 of the transformation series, during which the hand did not appear. Thus both duration of fixation and probability of smiling seem to be curvilinearly related to degree of discrepancy between an event and the child's schema for that event. Moreover, the child seems to become most excited by moderately discrepant events that are perceived as transformations of those that produced the original schema. If the infant does not regard a new event as related to a schema, he is much less excited by it. To illustrate, 72 infants, 9½ and 11½ months old, were exposed to one of two different transformations after six repeated presentations of a 2-inch (5-cm) wooden orange cube. The infants exposed to the novel event saw a yellow, rippled, plastic cylinder differing from the standard in color, size, texture, and shape. The infants exposed to the moderate transformation saw a 1-inch (2.54-cm) wooden orange cube, in which only size was altered. Almost half (43 percent) of the females in the moderate group displayed an obvious increase in vocalization when the smaller cube appeared, suggesting they were excited by this transformation. By contrast, only one female exposed to the novel yellow form showed increased vocalization, and most showed no change at all ($P < .05$). There was no comparable difference for boys.

The onset of a special reaction to discrepancy at about 2 months may reflect the fact that structures in the central nervous system have matured enough to permit long-term representation or retrieval of such representations. It is probably not a coincidence that a broad band of physiological and behavioral phenomena also occur at this time. The latency of the visual evoked potential begins to approach adult form, growth of occipital neurons levels off, alpha rhythm becomes recognizable (29), the Moro reflex begins to disappear,

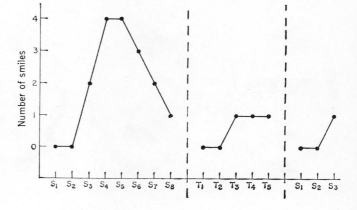

FIGURE 18–5. Frequency of smiling to the light episode for a 7½-month-old girl (S, standard presentation; T, transformation).

habituation to repeated presentations of a visual event becomes a reliable phenomenon (30), and three-dimensional representations of objects elicit longer fixations than two-dimensional ones (11).

Activation of Hypotheses

Two empirical facts require the invention of a third process that influences attention and, subsequently, produces change in cognitive structures. The relation between age and fixation time to masklike representations of a human face (see Figure 18–6) decreases dramatically across the period from 4 to 12 months, but it increases, just as dramatically, from 12 to 36 months (21). If discrepancy from schema exerted primary control over attention, increased fixation times after 1 year should not have occurred, for the masks should have become less discrepant with maturity. Furthermore, educational level of the infant's family was independent of fixation time prior to 1 year but was positively correlated with fixation time (correlation coefficient of 0.4) after 1 year (21). These data suggest the potential usefulness of positing the emergence of a new cognitive structure toward the end of the first year. This structure, called a *hypothesis,* is the child's interpretation of a discrepant event accomplished by mentally transforming it to a form he is familiar with, where the "familiar form" is the schema. The cognitive structure used in the transformation is the hypothesis. To recognize that a particular sequence of sounds is

human speech rather than a series of clarinet tones requires a schema for the quality of the human voice. Interpretation of the meaning of the speech, on the other hand, requires the activation of hypotheses which, in this example, are linguistic rules. The critical difference between a schema and a hypothesis is analogous to the difference between the processes of recognition and interpretation and bears some relation to Piaget's complementary notions of assimilation and accommodation (7).

It is assumed that the activation of hypotheses to explain discrepant events is accompanied by sustained attention. The more extensive the repertoire of hypotheses, the longer the child can work at interpretation and the more prolonged is his attention. The interaction between discrepancy and the activation of hypotheses is illustrated in the pattern of fixation times of 2-year-olds to four related stimuli: a doll-like representation of a male figure; the same figure with the head placed between the legs; the same figure with the head, arms, and legs rearranged in an asymmetric pattern; and an amorphous free form of the same color, size, and texture as the other three. Duration of fixation was significantly longer to the two moderately discrepant forms (8.5 seconds) than to the regular figure (7 seconds) or to the free form (5.5 seconds) (21).

In sum, events that possess a high rate of change, that are discrepant from established schemata, and that activate hypotheses in the service of interpretation elicit the longest epochs of attention. These events are most

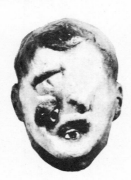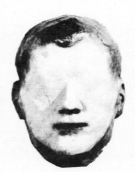

FIGURE 18–6. Facelike masks shown to infants from 4 to 36 months of age.

likely to produce changes in cognitive structures, for the attempt to assimilate a transformation of a familiar event inevitably leads to alterations in the original schema.

Summary

This article began by suggesting that different processes are likely to mediate alterations in behavior and cognitive structure and that conditioning principles do not seem sufficient to explain all the classes of change. Although the acquisition of conditioned responses, the potentiation of inborn capacities, and the establishment of schemata probably implicate different processes, all three involve selective attention to sensory events, whether these events function as conditioned stimuli, releasers of innate response dispositions, or the bases for mental representations. Hence, better understanding of the forces that control selectivity and duration of attention should provide insights into the nature of psychological growth, especially the lawful alterations in cognitive structure that seem to occur continually as a function of the child's encounter with discrepant events. The heart of this article was devoted to this theme. It was argued that events that possessed a high rate of change in their physical characteristics, that were moderately discrepant from established schemata, and that activated hypotheses in the service of assimilation had the greatest power to recruit and maintain attention in the young child.

Unfortunately, quantification of the fragile process of attention is still inelegant, for an infant displays a small set of relatively simple reactions to an interesting event. The infant can look at it, vocalize, be quiet, thrash, smile, or display changes in heart rate, respiration, or pattern of electrocortical discharge. Each of these variables reflects a different aspect of the attention process. Fixation time provides the clearest view and seems controlled by movement, contour, discrepancy, and the activation of hypotheses. Smiling seems to reflect the state that follows effortful assimilation. Cardiac deceleration occasionally accompanies attention to discrepant events, but not always, and vocalization can index, among other things, the excitement generated by a stimulus that engages a schema. It is important to realize, however, that a specific magnitude for any of these responses serves many different forces. The future mapping of these magnitudes on a set of determinants will require a delicate orchestration of rigorous method, ingenious theory, and a keen sensitivity to nature's subtle messages.

REFERENCES AND NOTES

1. L. P. Lipsitt, in *Advances in Child Development and Behavior,* L. P. Lipsitt and C. C. Spiker, Eds. (Academic Press, New York, 1963), p. 147.

2. H. Papousek, in *Early Behavior,* H. W. Stevenson, E. H. Hess, H. L. Rheingold, Eds. (Wiley, New York, 1967), p. 249.

3. Infants over 3 months old who had learned the conditioned response continued to turn their head to the auditory stimulus even though they were completely satiated for milk and did not drink. This phenomenon replicates similar observations with pigeons and rats who, after having acquired a conditioned response to obtain food, continued to respond even though ample food was available without any effort [see B. Carder and K. Berkowitz, *Science 167,* 1273 (1970); A. J. Neuringer, *ibid. 166,* 399 (1969)]. One interpretation of this phenomenon assumes that when an organism is alerted or aroused, for whatever reason, he issues those responses that are prepotent in that context. This view is congruent with the demonstration that intracranial stimulation of the hypothalamus elicits behaviors appropriate to the immediate situation [E. S. Valenstein, V. C. Cox, J. W. Kakolewski, *Psychol. Rev. 77,* 16

(1970)]. If food is available, the rat eats; if water, he drinks; if wood chips, he gnaws. Intracranial stimulation, like transfer from the home to the experimental chamber, alerts the animal, and prepotent behavior is activated.

4.   F. Nottebohm, *Science 167*, 950 (1970).
5.   R. W. Brown and U. Bellugi, *Harvard Educ. Rev. 34*, 135 (1964).
6.   H. W. Magoun, in *On the Biology of Learning*, K. H. Pribram, Ed. (Harcourt, Brace & World, New York, 1969), p. 171.
7.   J. Piaget, *The Origins of Intelligence in Children* (International Universities Press, New York, 1952).
8.   J. B. Grier, S. A. Counter, W. M. Shearer, *Science 155*, 1692 (1967).
9.   C. G. Beer, *ibid. 166*, 1030 (1969).
10. P. Salapetek and W. Kessen, *J. Exp. Child Psychol. 3*, 113 (1966); R. L. Fantz and S. Nevis, *Merrill-Palmer Quart. 13*, 77 (1967); M. M. Haith, *J. Exp. Child Psychol. 3*, 235 (1966).
11. R. L. Fantz, in *Perceptual Development in Children*, A. H. Kidd and J. L. Rivoire, Eds. (International Universities Press, New York, 1966), p. 143.
12. M. M. Haith, paper presented at the regional meeting of the Society for Research in Child Development, Clark University, Worcester, Massachusetts, March 1968.
13. R. B. McCall and J. Kagan, *Child Develop. 38*, 939 (1967).
14. B. Z. Karmel, *J. Comp. Physiol. Psychol. 69*, 649 (1969).
15. S. W. Kuffler, *Cold Spring Harbor Symp. Quant. Biol. 17*, 281 (1952); *J. Physiol. London 16*, 37 (1953).
16. R. B. McCall and W. H. Melson, *Develop. Psychol.*, in press.
17. B. Z. Karmel, C. T. White, W. T. Cleaves, K. J. Steinsiek, paper presented at the meeting of the Eastern Psychological Association, Atlantic City, New Jersey, April 1970.
18. R. B. Eisenberg, E. J. Griffin, D. B. Coursin, M. A. Hunter, *J. Speech Hear. Res. 7*, 245 (1964); Y. Brackbill, G. Adams, D. H. Crowell, M. C. Gray, *J. Exp. Child Psychol. 3*, 176 (1966).
19. G. C. Carpenter, paper presented at the Merrill-Palmer Infancy Conference, Detroit, Michigan, February 1969.
20. R. A. Haaf and R. Q. Bell, *Child Develop. 38*, 893 (1967); M. Lewis, *Develop. Psychol. 1*, 75 (1969).
21. J. Kagan, *Change and Continuity in Infancy* (Wiley, New York, in press).
22. R. B. McCall and W. H. Melson, *Psychonom. Sci. 17*, 317 (1969).
23. R. B. McCall and J. Kagan, *Develop. Psychol. 2*, 90 (1970).
24. W. H. Melson and R. B. McCall, *Child Develop.*, in press.
25. R. B. McCall and J. Kagan, *J. Exp. Child Psychol. 5*, 381 (1967).
26. C. Super, J. Kagan, F. Morrison, M. Haith, J. Weiffenbach, unpublished manuscript.
27. J. L. Gewirtz, in *Determinants of Infant Behaviour*, B. M. Foss, Ed. (Methuen, London, 1965), vol. *3*, p. 205.
28. P. R. Zelazo and J. M. Chandler, unpublished manuscript.
29. R. J. Ellingson, in *Advances in Child Development and Behavior*, L. P. Lipsitt and C. C. Spiker, Eds. (Academic Press, New York, 1963), p. 53.
30. C. Dreyfus-Brisac, D. Samson, C. Blanc, N. Monod, *Etud. Neo-natales 7*, 143 (1958).
31. This work was supported by grants from the National Institute of Child Health and Human Development (HD 4299) and the Carnegie Corporation of New York. I thank Robert McCall, Marshall Haith, and Philip Zelazo for comments on the manuscript.

19. INFANTS' RESPONSES TO FACIAL STIMULI DURING THE FIRST YEAR OF LIFE[1]

MICHAEL LEWIS

Four photographic facial stimuli varying in realism were presented to approximately 120 infants within the first year of life in order to observe any developmental changes in attention to facial patterns as a function of schema development. Fixation time, smiling, vocalization, and fret/cry behaviors were observed in order to determine the differential effectiveness of these stimuli in eliciting these responses. The fixation data varied over the first year with realistic patterns eliciting more attention in the first half year. Differences in smiling and vocalization to these patterns remained invariant over age and indicated that realistic faces elicited more smiling and vocalization than distorted faces. Finally, large sex differences were apparent. The difference between these response measures suggest that classes of responses elicited by the same stimuli may be under the service of more than one motive. It was suggested that attention was affected by schema development while smiling and vocalizing were affected by such processes as innate releasing mechanisms or social learning.

Research on the response to human faces proceeds from a variety of experimental objectives. There are those investigators who are interested in the infant's response to the face as a measure of social interaction (Ambrose, 1961; Gewirtz, 1965). Others wish to determine what aspects of the face are attractive to the infant and how much of the facial pattern need be present to elicit responses such as smiling or attention (Spitz & Wolf, 1946; Watson, 1966). Still another interest in human faces deals with the general exploration of schemata development using the face as a developing schema (Kagan, Henker, Hen-Tov, Levine, & Lewis, 1966; Lewis, 1965).

What is it about a facial pattern that elicits

interest? Spitz and Wolf (1946) in their early work have demonstrated that a particular kind of array is necessary in order to elicit one kind of social response, that is, the smile. They found that an oval having two dark areas for "eyes" elicited a smiling response in the infant. Moreover, Watson (1966) showed that for infants from 8 to 26 weeks of age facial orientation is another important consideration. In several papers (Fantz, 1965; Kagan & Lewis, 1965; Lewis, Meyers, Kagan, & Grossberg, 1963) facial stimuli were shown to elicit more fixation than stimuli such as bull's-eye, checkerboard, stripes, solid colors, and other patterns. However, Fantz (1965) was able to show that when the facial features were scrambled, the resulting array elicited as much fixation as did the nondistorted face.

Kagan and Lewis (1965) showed that photographs of faces elicited more fixation than a facelike stimulus such as the face of a panda bear, while Lewis, Kagan, and Kalafat (1966) showed that a photograph of a male face elicited more fixation than a line drawing of a face when presented to 6-month-old infants. However, when these stimuli were shown to the same

[1]This experiment was conducted at Fels Research Institute and supported, in part, by Grants HD–00868, FR–00222, and FR–05537 from the National Institute of Mental Health, United States Public Health Service. Appreciation for data analysis is given to Lynn Godfrey, Judy Lovett, Betty Bartels, Susan Goldberg, Cornelia Dodd, and Helen Campbell.

From *Developmental Psychology*, 1969, *1*, 75–86. Copyright 1969 by the American Psychological Association. Reprinted by permission of the author and the publisher.

subjects at 13 months, the line drawing elicited more fixation than did the photograph.

Investigation of developmental changes in response to facial stimuli over the first year is rare. Most of the existing studies are concerned only with the development of the smiling response. Moreover, the work on the smiling response and its change over age has dealt primarily with live human faces, either male or female, and not with pictures of faces or facelike stimuli. Thus, the purpose of the present study was to investigate the developmental trends in the interest value of faces and facelike stimuli over the first year of life.

Working from the notion of schema development (Kagan, 1967; Kagan et al., 1966; Lewis, 1965; Lewis, Goldberg, & Rausch, 1967), it was hypothesized that the attentional value of facial stimuli would change over the first year. The most realistic face would elicit more interest in the earlier months before complete schema acquisition and the least realistic (most distorted face) would elicit interest in the later months after the schema was well developed.

Method

Subjects

In order to observe age differences in response to facial stimuli, children from four different age groups were studied. To avoid the effects of repeated presentation, a cross-sectional design was used. One hundred and twenty subjects were tested. The sample included 15 boys and 15 girls at each of four age levels: 12 weeks of age ($\pm$ 4 days), 24 weeks of age ($\pm$ 7 days), 36 weeks of age ($\pm$ 7 days), and 57 weeks of age ($\pm$ 9 days). These infants were obtained by advertizing in the local newspapers. They were all Caucasian and appeared to have no neurological defects.

Apparatus

The seating arrangement varied for each age group. The youngest subjects were placed in a slightly reclining chair, while the oldest sub-jects sat in a baby feeder or high chair. The mother sat to the side and rear of the subject. Both infant and mother were completely enclosed and, except for several observation windows, were surrounded by a uniform gray area. Immediately in front of the subject and approximately 18 inches from his head was a gray screen on which the stimuli were presented by rear-screen projection.

Procedure

After the subject was placed in the appropriate position, four different face stimuli were presented in random order to each subject. Since Kagan and Lewis found little difference between a female and male face, variations of a male face were used. The stimuli, shown in Figure 19–1, were: (a) regular face—a photograph of a male, (b) cyclops face—a photograph of a one-eyed face, (c) schematic face—a line drawing of a face with all the features in their normal positions, and (d) scrambled face—a line drawing with all the features misplaced. Three of these stimuli a, b, and c have been used by others (Haaf & Bell, 1967; Kagan, 1967; Kagan et al., 1966), and have been ordered in terms of realism with the regular face being the most realistic, followed by the schematic and then the scrambled face. The introduction of the cyclops was to determine the interest value of a distorted photograph and, in terms of realism, would fall between regular and scrambled faces on the continuum of realism. It might be noted that it is possible to order these stimuli on other dimensions such as complexity, that is, number of stimulus elements and black-white contrast. Each of the four stimuli was presented three times in random order for 12 seconds. There was a 12-second intertrial interval during which the screen was relatively dark. The order of presentation was as follows: schematic, scrambled, cyclops, regular, schematic, regular, scrambled, cyclops, scrambled, cyclops, schematic, regular. If the subject became sleepy or upset during the presentation, the episode was terminated and resumed when the subject was again in an alert state.

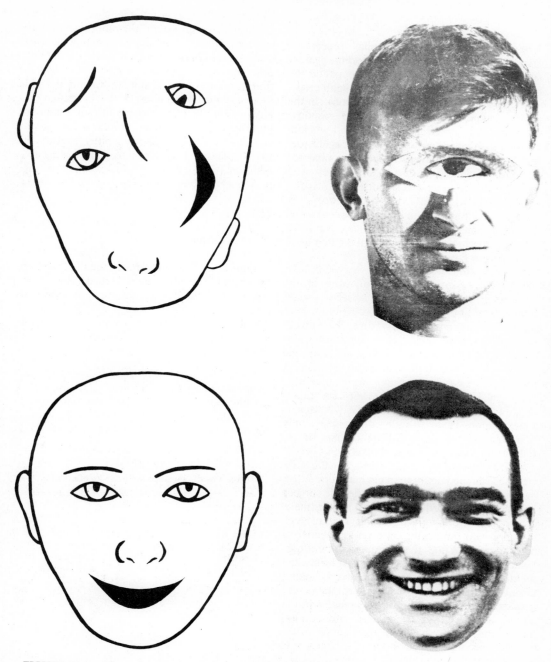

FIGURE 19–1.   These four facial arrays were used as stimuli: scrambled (top left), cyclops (top right), schematic (bottom left), and regular (bottom right).

Measures

Work with young infants has repeatedly demonstrated that a variety of response measures are necessary in order to understand the meaning of the infants' behavior (Kagan et al., 1966; Lewis, 1967; Lewis et al., 1966). In the present experiment a variety of response measures were used. Fixation time was obtained in order to see which stimuli were preferred. Smiling and vocalization were obtained to compare the results for live faces with photographs of faces and distortions (Gewirtz, 1965; Watson, 1966). Finally, fret/cry behaviors were observed in order to see if stranger anxiety, often occurring within the second half of the first year, would be exhibited when these stimuli were presented.

Fixation time was recorded by two independent observers who were unaware of the stimulus being presented. The observers were hidden behind the enclosure and were not visible to the infant. The first time the subject oriented his head and eyes toward the array, each observer depressed a key marking the duration of that fixation on an event recorder. A variety of fixation measures were obtained. However, since Kagan et al. (1966) and Lewis et al. (1966) have shown that first fixation is more responsive to stimulus differences, only first fixation was scored. The interscorer reliability for first fixation (FF) was .90.

Smiling, vocalizing, and fret-cry were also recorded independently on an event recorder by two observers, regardless of whether the subject was oriented toward the array. That is, these behaviors were obtained during picture presentation and during the base periods between presentation. While the amounts of smiling, vocalizing, and fret/cry were small during the picture presentation, they were even smaller during the base period. In general, there was one and one-half to eight times as much smiling and vocalizing during the stimulus presentation than during the base period. This same difference between base and stimulus periods was found for the fixation data.

For the purpose of this paper, only those behaviors emitted during or immediately after a fixation will be used in the analysis. It was found that for smile, vocalization, and fret/cry, approximately 93% of these behaviors occurred during fixation, 2% were emitted after, and 5% prior to fixation. The 5% emitted prior to fixation were not included since it was not possible to determine what elicited the particular behavior. The interscorer reliability for amount of time was .93 for smiling, .87 for vocalization, and .84 for fret/cry. The reliability coefficients for all measures were obtained by having two additional observers record behavior approximately 30% of the experimental sessions.

Results

Fixation Data

Figure 19–2 presents the FF data for each age group and for each stimulus. Observation of the data suggests significant sex, age, and stimulus effects.

Table 19–1 presents the results of an analysis of variance which indicates significant age, sex, stimulus, and Age × Stimulus effects.

Sex Effects. It is clear from Figure 19–2 and from the analysis of variance that boys look significantly longer at the stimuli than do girls ($F = 9.68$, $df = 1/112$, $p < .01$). Moreover, this was significant at 3 months ($t = 2.51$,

TABLE 19–1
Analysis of Variance for First Fixation Time

SOURCE	SS	df	ms	F
Between subjects	23,042.00	119	193.63	6.17*
Age (A)	3,022.12	3	1007.37	9.68*
Sex (B)	1,579.59	1	1579.59	.34
A × B	165.99	3	55.33	
Error$_b$	18,274.30	112	163.16	
Within subjects	9,819.27	360	27.28	4.46*
Stimulus (C)	341.47	3	113.82	3.16*
A × C	726.35	9	80.71	.71
B × C	54.37	3	18.12	.54
A × B × C	123.20	9	13.69	
Error$_w$	8,573.88	336	25.52	
Total	32,861.27	479		

*$p < .01$.

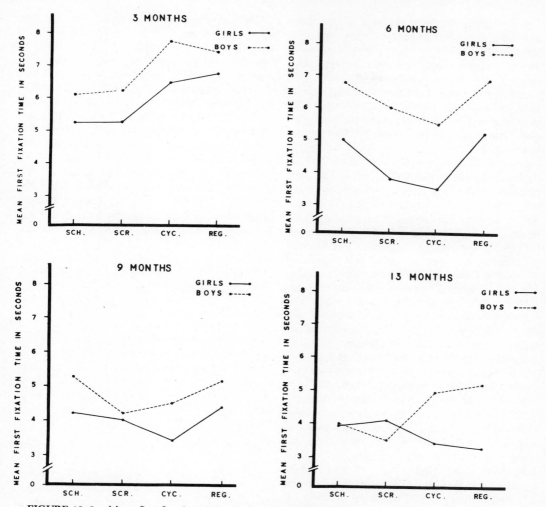

FIGURE 19–2. Mean first fixation time as a function of stimulus and sex for each age level.

$p < .05$),[2] 6 months ($t = 2.83, p < .02$), and 9 months ($t = 2.49, p < .05$), but was not significant at 13 months.

Age Effects. There was a perfect ordering between age and length of time looking at the stimuli (6.73, 5.48, 5.12, and 4.46 mean seconds for the 3-, 6-, and 9- and 13-month-old subjects, respectively). The data reflect the decreased interest that facial stimuli had for these subjects with increased age ($F = 6.17$,

[2]All tests are two-tailed unless otherwise stated.

$df = 3/112$, $p < .01$). Age differences were determined by obtaining the critical difference between means for the .01 level which was .58 seconds. Between-group differences indicate the 3-month data were significantly different from each of the other age groups, while the 13-month data were significantly different from the 6- and 9-month data. There were no significant 6- and 9-month differences.

Stimulus Effects. The main effect of stimulus differences was significant ($F = 4.46$, $df = 3/$

336, $p < .01$). The order of stimulus preference over all ages is regular, schematic, cyclops, and scrambled faces (5.50, 5.07, 4.90, and 4.78 mean seconds fixation, respectively). Significant differences between means (.58 seconds, $p < .01$) were found such that regular face was different from cyclops and scrambled with the biggest differences between regular and scrambled, the two ends of the realism continuum.

Age × Stimulus Effects. The stimulus differences are related to age. In order to determine the nature of this interaction, critical difference between means test was used (1.25 seconds, $p < .01$). Figure 19–2 indicates that as infants became older, they showed less stimulus differentiation. That is, there are significant stimulus differences at 3 and 6 months of age, but none at 9 and 13 months. This was reflected in the monotonically decreasing mean differences over the four age levels. Since perceptual ability would not be expected to deteriorate, one would hypothesize that with increasing age the stimuli elicit equal attention.

Observation of stimulus differences at each age level indicates several puzzling results. At 3 months, regular and cyclops, the two photographs, elicit significantly more fixation than schematic and scrambled faces, the two line drawings. At 6 and 9 months, schematic and regular were looked at longer than cyclops and scrambled faces. That is, faces with all their features were preferred to faces with missing or distorted features. While the same was true for the 9-month-olds, the differences were not significant, nor were there any significant stimulus differences at 13 months.

Thus, stimulus differences as well as stimulus differentiation were a function of age. Because of the minimum stimulus differentiation at the older ages, differences in developmental trends in stimulus interest are not obvious. By a simple transformation, the fixation trends over age become more easily observable. For each age level and sex, the mean time the subject fixated on each stimulus was compared to the sum of the fixation time for all four stimuli, and a percentage fixation time score was obtained.

The stimuli, ordered previously on realism, were regular—most realistic, scrambled—least realistic, and cyclops and schematic—intermediate. The percentage data indicate that regular, the most realistic facial stimuli, elicits decreasing interest vis-à-vis the other stimuli over the first year (.28, .29, .26, .25 for the 3-, 6-, 9-, and 13-month-olds, respectively), scrambled, the least realistic indicates an increase in interest over age (.22, .23. .24, and .26). The intermediate stimuli show the least change (.26, .24, .25, and .26). A chi-square test was performed using the number of subjects showing greater fixation time for regular than scrambled faces at 3 and 13 months. Combining sexes, the chi-square frequency distribution (20, 11, 9, 20) was significant ($\chi^2 = 5.46$, $df = 1$, $p < .04$). Thus, interest in the least realistic face accompanied distinterest in the most realistic face.

Smiling Data

The data on smiling are presented in Table 19–2. The small amounts of time smiling (less than 2 seconds out of 12) reflect both the short duration of a smile and the few infants who smiled at the stimuli at each age. Because of this, nonparametric statistics are used throughout this section (see Siegel, 1956).

Age Effects. The mean amount of time smiling across stimuli and sex for 3-, 6-, 9-, and 13-month-olds was .30, .13, .61, and .66 seconds for the 3-, 6-, 9-, and 13-month-olds, respectively. A Kruskal-Wallis one-way analysis of variance was performed with sex combined. The results indicate a significant age effect ($H = 12.48$, $df = 3$, $p < .01$) with significantly more smiling in the second half than the first half year. This held for each of the four stimuli.

Stimulus Differences. The data from Table 19–2 indicate that stimulus differences remained consistent over the four age levels. The mean time smiling across age was .67, .55, .30, and .19 seconds for regular, schematic, cyclops, and scrambled faces. A Friedman two-way analysis of variance was performed and indicated a significant stimulus effect ($\chi^2 = 11.34$,

TABLE 19–2
Mean Time Smiling in Seconds by Stimulus, Age, and Sex

AGE AND SEX	SCHEMATIC		SCRAMBLED		CYCLOPS		REGULAR		TOTAL
	No.[a]	$\bar{x}$[b]	No.	$\bar{x}$	No.	$\bar{x}$	No.	$\bar{x}$	$\bar{x}$
3 months									
Boys	4	0.30	3	0.07	2	0.06	3	0.21	0.16
Girls	5	0.67	3	0.60	3	0.20	7	1.38	0.71
6 months									
Boys	3	0.46	2	0.05	1	0.02	4	0.47	0.25
Girls	3	0.21	2	0.06	3	0.20	4	0.42	0.22
9 months									
Boys	8	0.64	6	0.26	5	0.18	5	0.78	0.47
Girls	9	2.08	5	0.82	6	0.62	9	1.94	1.36
13 months									
Boys	8	1.00	6	1.02	8	0.63	8	1.51	1.04
Girls	8	1.29	6	0.73	6	0.42	6	1.43	0.97

[a]*Number of subjects who showed smiling regardless of the length of time of the smile.*
[b]*Mean amount of smiling over all trials for all subjects whether they smiled or not.*

$df = 3, p < .01$). Individual sign tests revealed that regular and schematic faces elicited significantly more smiling than cyclops and scrambled faces ($p < .03$ or better).

Unlike the fixation data, stimulus differences as a function of age are invariant and appear to indicate that regardless of fixation changes, smiling, at least in the first year, is elicited most by a class of facial patterns having all features in their normal position.

Sex Effects. While girls tended to smile more than boys, a Mann-Whitney U test revealed no significant differences in amount of smiling. However, the data do suggest sex differences in terms of differential smiling between stimuli which parallels the fixation data. Friedman two-way analysis of variance over age for each sex reveal significant differences in smiling between stimuli for girls ($\chi^2 = 31.86, df = 3, p < .001$), but not for boys ($\chi_r^2 = 5.75$). Finally, a difference score between the sum of schematic plus regular faces versus cyclops plus scrambled faces was obtained for each sex. Boys' difference scores were compared to girls' by a Mann-Whitney U test which revealed significant sex differences in smiling. Girls showed more differentiation than boys ($Z = 2.59, p < .01$).

Vocalization Data

Table 19–3 presents the vocalization data. As with the smiling data, there was relatively little vocalization for these stimuli at these age levels. Because of the large number of zero scores, nonparametric analyses were again appropriate.

Age Effects. The mean vocalization scores across age are .59, .60, 1.38, 1.39 seconds for the 3-, 6-, 9-, and 13-month-old age groups and indicates a monotonic increase in vocalization over age. A Kruskal-Wallis one-way analysis of variance reveals a significant age effect ($H = 14.83, df = 3, p < .01$).

Stimulus Effects. The data indicate that the mean number of seconds vocalizing was 1.16, .86, .98, .97 for regular, schematic, cyclops, and scrambled faces, respectively. A Friedman two-way analysis of variance results in a significant main effect for stimulus differences ($\chi_r^2 = 8.19, df = 3, p < .05$). A sign test was

TABLE 19–3
Mean Time Vocalizing in Seconds by Stimulus, Age, and Sex

AGE AND SEX	SCHEMATIC		SCRAMBLED		CYCLOPS		REGULAR		TOTAL
	No.[a]	$\bar{x}$[b]	No.	$\bar{x}$	No.	$\bar{x}$	No.	$\bar{x}$	$\bar{x}$
3 months									
Boys	7	0.48	8	0.66	12	0.67	9	0.64	0.61
Girls	6	0.88	8	0.77	9	1.01	10	1.43	1.02
6 months									
Boys	4	0.38	8	1.04	7	0.79	8	0.78	0.75
Girls	9	1.18	7	0.97	8	1.40	11	1.56	1.28
9 months									
Boys	10	0.78	9	0.83	10	0.80	9	0.78	0.80
Girls	13	2.03	12	2.34	14	2.05	14	2.60	2.26
13 months									
Boys	8	0.97	10	1.14	13	1.46	11	1.65	1.31
Girls	7	1.15	7	1.28	7	0.74	10	2.25	1.36

[a]*Number of subjects who showed vocalizing regardless of the length of time on the vocalization.*
[b]*Mean amount of vocalizing over all trials for all subjects whether they vocalized or not.*

performed combining age and comparing vocalization to regular to each of the other three facial stimuli. The results indicated a significant difference at less than the .01 level for each comparison.

Sex Effects. Girls showed more vocalization at each age level than boys and except for scrambled at 6 months and cyclops at a year, girls vocalized more than boys to each stimulus. Combining age and stimuli resulted in a significant sex difference (Mann-Whitney U test, $Z = 2.45$, $p < .02$). Finally, girls showed a significant stimulus differentiation ($\chi_r^2 = 12.53$, $df = 3$, $p < .01$), while boys did not. This lack of differentiation for boys is consistent with the smiling and fixation data.

Fret/Cry Data

Fret/cry behavioral data were included in the present study in order to determine whether any of the present photographic stimuli would elicit consistently fearful or unpleasant responses especially since stranger anxiety should occur somewhere within the second half of the first year. Nonparametric statistics were again used due to the lack of a normal distribution.

Age Effects. The data in Table 19–4 revealed that the mean amount of crying over age was .87, .35, .36, .08 mean seconds for the 3-, 6-, 9-, and 13-month-old subjects. A Kruskal-Wallis one-way analysis of variance indicated significant effect ($H = 22.57$, $df = 3$, $p < .008$) such that the mean amount of crying decreased over age. Individual Mann-Whitney U tests revealed significant age differences between groups ($p < .01$ or better) except for the 6–9 comparison.

Stimulus and Sex Effects. There were no significant stimulus effects ($\chi_r^2 = 5.01$, $df = 3$) nor any sex effects ($Z = .98$).

Behavioral Correlations

Table 19–5 presents the rank-order correlations between measures considered for each age level with stimuli combined. A rank of 1 was given to that subject who smiled most, who vocalized most, or exhibited the most fret/cry.

The data reveal that for girls, smiling was positively correlated with vocalization and was significantly correlated for 6- and 13-month-old subjects. Further, smiling was negatively correlated with fret/cry, this being significant at

TABLE 19–4
Mean Time Fret/Cry in Seconds by Stimulus, Age, and Sex

AGE AND SEX	SCHEMATIC		SCRAMBLED		CYCLOPS		REGULAR		TOTAL
	No.[a]	$\bar{x}$[b]	No.	$\bar{x}$	No.	$\bar{x}$	No.	$\bar{x}$	$\bar{x}$
3 months									
Boys	11	0.71	11	1.89	11	1.91	12	2.00	1.63
Girls	9	0.63	8	0.37	9	0.91	9	0.94	0.71
6 months									
Boys	5	0.77	4	0.51	5	0.71	8	0.95	0.74
Girls	8	0.28	6	0.19	8	0.63	9	0.37	0.37
9 months									
Boys	6	0.24	4	0.41	6	0.71	8	0.30	0.42
Girls	8	0.47	7	0.53	4	0.03	5	0.51	0.38
13 months									
Boys	3	0.04	3	0.14	4	0.14	2	0.11	0.10
Girls	4	0.00	2	0.00	2	0.03	4	0.09	0.03

[a]*Number of subjects who showed fret/cry regardless of the length of time of the fret/cry.*
[b]*Mean amount of fret/cry over all trials for all subjects whether they fretted/cried or not.*

3 months. Finally, while vocalization was positively correlated with fret/cry, the correlation was very low and not significant. The boys' data, in general, parallel that of the girls' and indicate a positive correlation between smiling and vocalization which was significant at 9 and 13 months. There were no other consistent relations for the boys.

Discussion

Age differences indicate that while the facial stimulus elicited significantly less fixation as a function of age, these same stimuli elicited significantly greater vocalization and smiling. The increase in vocalization and smiling (but not the differential expression) and decrease in fret/cry behaviors, however, are probably a function of the general increase or decrease in the base amount of these response repertoires as a function of age. The decrease in fixation time reflects the general inability of photographic facial stimuli to continue to elicit consistent attention over the first year of life. The little existing evidence suggests that three-dimensional faces as well as live faces show this same age pattern (Kagan, 1967; Laroche & Tcheng, 1963).

TABLE 19–5
Behavioral Correlations with Stimuli Combined for Each Age and Sex

BEHAVIOR	SMILE	VOCALIZING	FRET/CRY
		3 months	
Smile	—	.22	−.53*
Vocalizing	.07	—	.15
Fret/Cry	−.16	−.21	—
		6 months	
Smile	—	.48*	−.40
Vocalizing	.17	—	.25
Fret/Cry	.33	.36	—
		9 months	
Smile	—	.12	−.06
Vocalizing	.50*	—	.13
Fret/Cry	−.11	.21	—
		12 months	
Smile	—	.64**	−.10
Vocalizing	.62**	—	.14
Fret/Cry	.23	−.13	—

Note.–Boys' data to the bottom and left; girls' data to the top and right.

*$p < .05$, one-tailed.
**$p < .01$, one-tailed.

Sex differences were observed for each measure with the exception of fret/cry. These differences were reflected either in the different amounts of response such as total amount of time looking or vocalizing or in the differential expression of the response as a function of the stimulus. Thus, while boys looked longer than girls, girls showed greater stimulus differentiation. In the vocalization and smiling data, however, girls both exhibited more of the response as well as greater differential expression. These differences have now been demonstrated in several samples of infants within the first year for several types of visual and auditory stimuli (Kagan & Lewis, 1965; Lewis et al., 1966), tactile stimuli (Bell & Costello, 1964), as well as in play behavior (Goldberg & Lewis, 1969), and strongly suggest early sex differences in response to stimulation. The implication of these early differences is that either differential learning experiences must influence perceptual cognitive development at extremely early ages (in the present case, prior to the twelfth week of life) or that these differences must be innate and related to sexually distinct response repertoires. The nature of these differences requires further investigation; however, it is clear (*a*) that investigators using infants as subjects should not pool their data across sex, and (*b*) the use of both sexes is necessary in order to make any statement about infant behavior.

Stimulus differences without considering any age interaction indicate surprising consistency across all four response measures. Regular face elicited the most fixation, smiling, vocalization, and fret/cry, while scrambled face elicited the least (except for vocalization which was next to least). Schematic and cyclops faces, in general, fell between these two extremes and tended to confirm the continuum generated by these stimuli.

The fixation data, especially the interaction between age and stimulus preference, are not easily interpreted although it is clear that stimulus interest in terms of fixation time varies over age. This is especially true for the first 6 months of life. It is equally clear from the data

that, in general, facial stimuli seem to lose their ability to hold the infant's attention over the four age levels. While the explanation of these facts is difficult to explain, there is a growing theoretical body of literature which might account for these results.

Recently, investigators (Kagan, 1967; Kagan et al., 1966; Lewis, 1965) have hypothesized on the development of schema in the infant. A schema was defined as a relatively persistent organized classification of information, a model which the organism uses in arranging information. At any given point in his development, an infant has schemata at different points of development which, with time, will codify and then alter toward or be rejected for new schemata. When the input from the environment or experiment matches a recently or nearly formed schema, the infant will spend long periods of time looking at that input. After the schema is well developed, the infant will lose interest in stimuli which match it. Thus, if a stimulus array partially violates an existing schema, the violation will elicit attention. However, if the violation is so radical that the infant cannot perceive his schema within it, he will not spend time looking at the stimulus (Berlyne, 1960; Fiske & Maddi, 1961; Piaget, 1954; Sokolov, 1963). Applying the present data to this theoretical framework, it might be argued that in the early months, before a face schema is sufficiently formed, regular face, closest to the emergent schema would elicit the most attention while scrambled face, a major violation, would elicit the least. Once the face schema is well developed, distortions of that schema should elicit more attentive behavior. The percentage-of-time-looking data tend to support this view. While this explanation is limited in that at no time was the fixation time for scrambled significantly greater than regular face and complexity and black-white contrast were not completely controlled—they were between scrambled and schematic and between cyclops and regular—the explanation by the use of schema development does tend to order the data. However, until the stimuli are matched for such stimulus dimensions of black-white contrast, contour, size, complexity, etc., no definite statement can be made about schema development or matching of internal expectations with external events. The difficulty involved in such stimulus matching argues for alternative approaches to the study of schema development. Lewis et al. (1967) and Lewis and Goldberg (1969) have suggested the orienting response (OR) paradigm as an alternative method for this investigation.

The smiling response was of particular interest because it has been investigated extensively using live stimuli. The results indicate that smiling increased over age except for a decrease at 6 months of age. This same trough at 6 months using live faces instead of the photographs used in this study have been found by others (Gewirtz, 1965; Laroche & Tcheng, 1963; Watson, 1966). The increased smiling in the second half of the first year is consistent with the Laroche and Tcheng data but not with those of Gewirtz. The use of photographs instead of live faces or three-dimensional models results in no greater differences than are found between investigations using live faces.

The vocalization data are in some ways similar to the smiling data as reflected in the relatively high correlations between the two measures. Moreover, both the amount of smiling and vocalization increases with age. While there were minimum stimulus differences, regular face tended to elicit more vocalization than any of the other stimuli.

The stimulus differences in smiling (and to some extent in vocalizing) remained invariant over all age levels and thus do not show an Age × Stimulus interaction as observed for the fixation data. The smiling data indicate that facial patterns having all features in their "normal" position is the important variable in eliciting a smiling response for any age level. This suggests that behavior elicited by a single set of stimuli may involve a variety of motives and, therefore, involve different response systems.

It is clear that smiling and vocalizing can serve a multitude of needs or motives. Lewis and Goldberg (1969) have demonstrated that smiling was produced by violating children's expectations and this has also been found by Charlesworth (1966). However, Kagan et al. (1966) argued that stimuli which match emerging schema would elicit smiling and vocalization. Moreover, Spitz's work would lead one to believe that realistic facial stimuli, regardless of schema development would elicit more smiling. His work strongly suggests that faces, particularly ones with eyes, may act as an innate releasing mechanism (Tinbergen, 1951) for the smiling response, especially in the opening months of life. A final alternative for differential smiling rests on Gewirtz's work dealing with secondary reinforcement and smiling. That smiling and vocalization were invariant over age while fixation differences varied argues against the notion that these responses are elicited solely by schema development. That faces may serve as innate releasers is intriguing in light of the work with socially deprived and nonsocially deprived infants. These studies indicate that, at least for the first 8 to 12 weeks, smiling and vocalization are relatively independent of the environment, that is, influenced by learning (Gewirtz, 1965; Lenneberg, Rebelsky, & Nichols, 1965; Provence, 1965). These findings lend support to a notion of initial innate releasers for these responses, after which environmental reinforcers become increasingly important.

Finally, it is important to note that smiling differences between stimuli often reveal the ability to discriminate where fixation data do not. For example, at 3 months, there were no differences between regular-cyclops and scrambled-schematic faces in fixation time, but there were significant smiling differences. Moreover, while there were no stimulus differences in fixation at 9 and 13 months, there were significant stimulus differences in smiling. These results again point out the need for multiple-response measures in measuring infant perceptual behavior.

One of the major reasons for observing fret/cry behavior was to determine the relationship of the advent of stranger anxiety and the presentation of these four stimuli. While there were some indications of stimulus differences, especially at 3 months of age, there were no fret/cry stimulus differences in the latter half of the year when stranger anxiety would be expected to be present. The present data gave no indication of a fear response. A recent paper by Morgan and Ricciuti (1965) indicates that fearful responses are elicited by strangers not so much by their presence as by their approach to the infant. In that a live face has to be presented, the presentation (moving over the infant) might constitute an approach, whereas the appearance of a picture at a certain locus might not. Moreover, the subject might be able to discriminate between something living and a two-dimensional picture or inanimate object. In

any event, the four stimuli failed to elicit any consistent or observable fear responses. However, observation of many of the subjects in the present study indicate that the approach of an unknown person (male experimenter) was able to elicit an anxiety response even though the stimuli themselves failed to do so.

In summary, the various measures of attention showed two patterns. Fixation time seemed to vary as a function of schema development with realistic faces eliciting more attention in the earlier months than nonrealistic patterns. Smiling and vocalization, however, remained invariant with patterns having all facial features in their normal position eliciting consistently more response.

REFERENCES

Ambrose, J. A. The development of the smiling response in early infancy. In B. M. Foss (Ed.), *Determinants of infant behavior*. Vol. I. London: Methuen, 1961.

Bell, R. Q., & Costello, N. S. Three tests for sex differences in tactile sensitivity in the newborn. *Biologia Neonatorum*, 1964, 7, 335–347.

Berlyne, D. E. *Conflict, arousal and curiosity*. New York: McGraw-Hill, 1960.

Charlesworth, W. Persistence of orienting and attending behavior in infants as a function of stimulus-locus uncertainty. *Child Development*, 1966, 37, 473–492.

Fantz, R. L. Visual perception from birth as shown by pattern selectivity. *Annals of the New York Academy of Sciences*, 1965, 118, 793–814.

Fiske, D. W., & Maddi, S. R. *Functions of varied experience*. Homewood, Ill.: Dorsey, 1961.

Gewirtz, J. L. The course of infant smiling in four childrearing environments. In B. M. Foss (Ed.), *Determinants of infant behavior*. Vol. III. New York: Wiley, 1965.

Goldberg, S., & Lewis M. Play behavior in the year-old infant: Early sex differences. *Child Development*, in press.

Haaf, R. A., & Bell, R. Q. A facial dimension in visual discrimination by human infants. *Child Development*, 1967, 38, 893–899.

Kagan, J. On the need for relativism. *American Psychologist*, 1967, 22, 131–142.

Kagan, J., Henker, B., Hen-Tov, A., Levine, J., & Lewis, M. Infants' differential reactions to familiar and distorted faces. *Child Development*, 1966, 37, 519–532.

Kagan, J., & Lewis, M. Studies of attention in the human infant. *Merrill-Palmer Quarterly*, 1965, 11, 95–127.

Laroche, J. L., & Tcheng, F. *Le Sourire du Nourrisson*. Louvain: Publications Universitaire, 1963.

Lenneberg, E. H., Rebelsky, F. G., & Nichols, I. A. The vocalizations of infants born to deaf and to hearing parents. *Human Development*, 1965, 8, 23–37.

Lewis, M. Exploratory studies in the development of a face schema. Paper presented at the symposium on "The Origins of Social Behavior," American Psychological Association Meeting, Chicago, 1965.

Lewis, M. The meaning of a response or why researchers in infant behavior should be oriental metaphysicians. *Merrill-Palmer Quarterly*, 1967, 13, 7–18.

Lewis, M., & Goldberg, S. The acquisition and violation of expectancy: An experimental paradigm. *Journal of Experimental Child Psychology,* 1969, *7,* 70–80.

Lewis, M., Goldberg, S., & Rausch, M. Attention distribution as a function of novelty and familiarity. *Psychonomic Science,* 1967, *7,* 227–228.

Lewis, M., Kagan, J., & Kalafat, J. Patterns of fixation in infants. *Child Development,* 1966, *37,* 332–341.

Lewis, M., Meyers, W., Kagan, J., & Grossberg, R. Attention to visual patterns in infants. *American Psychologist,* 1963, *18,* 357. (Abstract)

Morgan, G. A., & Ricciuti, H. N. Infants' responses to strangers during the first year. Unpublished paper based on an unpublished doctoral dissertation, Cornell University, 1965.

Piaget, J. *The construction of reality in the child.* New York: Basic Books, 1954.

Provence, S. Disturbed personality development in infancy: A comparison of two inadequately nurtured infants. *Merrill-Palmer Quarterly,* 1965, *2,* 149–170.

Siegel, S. *Nonparametric statistics for the behavioral sciences.* New York: McGraw-Hill, 1956.

Sokolov, Y. N. *Perception and the conditioned reflex.* (Trans. by S. W. Wardenfield) New York: Macmillan, 1963.

Spitz, R. A. The smiling response: A contribution to the ontogenesis of social relations. *Genetic Psychology Monographs,* 1946, *34,* 57–125.

Tinbergen, U. *The study of instinct.* Oxford: University Press, 1951.

Watson, J. S. Perception of object orientation in infants. *Merrill-Palmer Quarterly,* 1966, *12,* 73–94.

20.   REINSTATEMENT[1]

BYRON A. CAMPBELL and JULIAN JAYNES

Reinstatement is defined as periodic partial repetition of an experience such that it maintains the effects of that experience through time. This principle is demonstrated in a developmental study on the effects of early fear in rats, and is then discussed in relation to clinical and developmental theory.

In most of the phyla from arthropods to man early experience exerts a multiplicity of effects on adult behavior (Beach & Jaynes, 1954; Scott, 1962). Sometimes such effects are the simple persistence in adult behavior of habits formed early in life. In other instances it may be that early experience influences later behavior by structuring the individual's perceptual or response capacities. And in still others, there is a critical period of development during which some aspect of behavior, on which later behaviors depend, is learned and molded for life.

In this paper we suggest yet another mechanism. Although obvious and disarmingly simple, it yet seems to the authors of such neglected importance as to warrant this note and the coining of a term for it. By *reinstatement* we denote a small amount of partial practice or repetition of an experience over the developmental period which is enough to maintain an early learned response at a high level, but is not enough to produce any effect in animals which have not had the early experience. The

[1]This research was supported in part by Public Health Service Grant M-1562 from the National Institutes of Mental Health and by National Science Foundation Grant GB 2814.

following experiment is meant as a demonstration of this phenomenon in a commonly studied instance of learning.

Method

The subjects were 30 albino rats of the Wistar strain born and raised in the Princeton colony. They were divided into three groups of 10 each, with an equal number of males and females in each. The apparatus used was one commonly used in fear experiments (Campbell & Campbell, 1961). It consisted of two compartments separated by a door, a black one with a grid floor, and a white compartment with a solid metal floor. Shock could be administered to the grid of the black compartment. To two of the three groups an early fear-arousing experience was given in the black compartment. This consisted of placing the rat just after weaning, when approximately 25 days old, on the grid side of the apparatus with the door fixed so that the rat could not escape, then giving the rat 15 2-second 170-volt shocks on a 20-second variable interval schedule, taking approximately 5 minutes, then removing the animal and placing him on the nonshock side for 5 minutes, and then repeating this entire procedure once. Thus each animal received a total of 30 shocks. At the end of this period the rat was removed and placed in a home cage. A third control group was run through this procedure without any shock being administered to the grid. During the next month a total of three shocks—the reinstatements—were given to one of the early experience groups and to the control group. These shocks were administered 7, 14, and 21 days after the original training session. The procedure was to administer, at some random number of seconds up to a minute after the animal was placed on the grid side of the apparatus, a single 2-second shock of the same intensity as before. The rat was then placed in the white compartment for an identical period of time and then returned to its home cage. On alternate weeks the animal was placed first on the nonshock side of the cage and then on the

shock side, with half of the animals being placed on the shock side for the first reinstatement procedure and half on the safe side. Otherwise this procedure was precisely the same as the training procedure except that only 1 instead of 30 shocks was administered. The second pretrained group was given the same procedure except that no shock was administered. One week after the third reinstatement procedure, when the animals were 53 days of age, they were all tested for the effects of their early experience. This was done by placing them individually in the black compartment (where all of them had been shocked at one time or another) with the door removed so that the animal could run freely into the white compartment. The time spent in the white compartment over the ensuing hour was then recorded.

Results and Discussion

The results were unequivocal. As seen in Figure 20–1, the group that had received the early fearful experience followed by three 2-second shocks administered at weekly intervals, spent an increasing percentage of its time in the white compartment during the

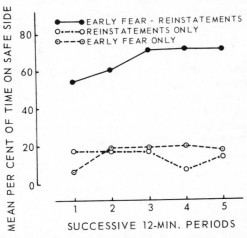

FIGURE 20–1. The effect of reinstatement of early fear on later behavior.

1-hour test period, thus showing the effects of the early fearful experience with the black compartment. In contrast, the group that had had a similar early experience just after weaning, but no reinstatement of it in the intervening month, failed to show any significant fear of the black compartment, spending on the average all but about 10 minutes of the hour on that side. Similarly the group which had not had any early traumatic experience, but had received the three brief shocks over the month, failed to acquire any significant fear of the black compartment. The difference between the first group and the other two groups is, as it appears on the graph, highly reliable statistically ($p < .01$, Mann-Whitney $\cup$ test).

There is nothing dramatically surprising about this finding. It is indeed what anyone thinking carefully about learning and practice would expect, namely, that there is some small amount of practice over certain time intervals which could maintain a previously learned response and yet not be enough to train naïve animals to perform that response. The possibility that this mechanism of reinstatement has wide and important applicability in the ontogeny of behavior in many vertebrate species seems beyond question.

In theoretical analyses of human growth and development traumatic events in infancy and childhood have long occupied a central, if controversial, role. In Freud's early analyses, traumatic events in childhood were considered a major cause of adult behavior disorders. With time, this view was gradually modified such that White writing in 1956 summed up current opinion by stating:

Undoubtedly it is true that some adult neuroses have their origin in violently frightening events. . . . The theory has long since been abandoned, however, that all neuroses, or even a majority of neuroses, take their start from traumatic events [1956, p. 238].

The early trauma theory has inconsistencies with certain facts of memory and learning as well. First, on a mere phenomenological level, we know that memory becomes more and more dim the further back into our childhood we try to remember. Second, in rats, the earlier in life that a fearful experience is given the animal, the more likely it is to be forgotten in adulthood (Campbell & Campbell, 1962). Third, in chickens, the earlier in the critical period that the chick is imprinted, the more likely it is to be forgotten when the animal reaches the juvenile stages (Jaynes, 1957). This evidence seems to indicate that the organism is constantly forgetting, time or neurological maturation or perhaps other processes constantly changing the mnemonic traces of events and feelings. And all the evidence suggests that the earlier the experience has occurred, the more profound and the faster the forgetting.

In this context reinstatement is proposed as a major mechanism by which the effects of early experiences can be perpetuated and incorporated into adult personality. Following an early experience, either pleasant or unpleasant, three developments may occur. First, the experience may be gradually forgotten as described above. Second, it may be remembered and persist indefinitely if it is occasionally reinstated. The language-based cultures of human societies are particularly rich in methods of such reinstatement, including ones so simple as occasionally reminding a child of a previous event or feeling. Even the child may occasionally reinstate the experience himself under the prompting of his ethical value system. A third possibility is the active repression of the experience, and we suggest here that the repression itself—as well as the experience—may undergo either forgetting or maintenance by reinstatement in exactly the same way. Again, the language-based cultures of man contain many reinstatement-of-repression mechanisms such as parental conversational taboos, etc., which determine what repressions are maintained into adult life. In a general sense, we propose that any learned response, whether acquired in infancy or adulthood, conscious or unconscious, instrumental or autonomic, joyful or traumatic, can be maintained at a high level by an occasional reinstatement.

Moreover, reinstatement as a principle has considerable adaptive significance, particularly in the learning of fear. Young organisms, at least after a short initial period of apparent fearlessness in some species, become highly vulnerable to the acquisition of fears. These fears have, of course, great survival value in keeping the young organism away from danger.

But if they all persisted and could not be forgotten, they would imprison the animal in his own prior experience, making adult adaptive behavior impossible. It is thus essential to adult activity that most early experiences be forgotten, and that only those experiences which are periodically reinstated by a particular habitat or culture be retained.

REFERENCES

Beach, F. A., & Jaynes, J. Effects of early experience upon the behavior of animals. *Psychological Bulletin,* 1954, *51*, 239–263.

Campbell, B. A., & Campbell, E. H. Retention and extinction of learned fear in infant and adult rats. *Journal of Comparative and Physiological Psychology,* 1962, *55*, 1–8.

Jaynes, J. Imprinting: The interaction of learned and innate behavior: II. The critical period. *Journal of Comparative and Physiological Psychology,* 1957, *50*, 6–7.

Scott, J. P. Critical periods in behavioral development. *Science,* 1962, *138*, 949–958.

White, R. W. *The Abnormal Personality.* (2nd ed.) New York: The Ronald Press, 1956.

21. EFFECT OF DURATION OF REINSTATEMENT ON RETENTION OF A VISUAL DISCRIMINATION LEARNED IN INFANCY[1]

BYRON A. CAMPBELL and JULIAN JAYNES

Weanling rats were trained on a light-dark discrimination and then given one reinstatement per week for 10 weeks. They were then tested for retention of the original discrimination. Five different durations of reinstatement were used: 0, 7.5, 15, 30, and 60 minutes. The longer the weekly reinstatement, the better the retention of the discrimination when tested either by relearning or resistance to extinction.

There has been a curious paradox in the traditional views about psychological development. Early experience is felt to be a

[1]This research was supported in part by Public Health Service Grant MH-01562 from the National Institute of Mental Health and in part by National Science Foundation Grant GB 5626.

From *Developmental Psychology*, 1969, *1*, 71–74. Copyright 1969 by the American Psychological Association. Reprinted by permission of the authors and the publisher.

strong influence on adult behavior, and yet many types of early acquired behaviors are quickly forgotten in laboratory conditions (Campbell, 1967). To partially resolve this paradox, the authors have introduced the concept of reinstatement (Campbell & Jaynes, 1966). Reinstatement is defined as periodic partial repetition of an experience, such that it maintains the effects of that experience through time. While there is nothing dramatically new about this concept, the authors feel that reinstatement has a spectrum of applicability and an importance in developmental theory which warrants its introduction as a new term.

Particularly in the ontogenetic development of fear, reinstatement has considerable adaptive significance. The young of most higher vertebrates, after an initial period of fearlessness, acquire fearful responses of potential survival value with readiness (Jaynes, 1958; Schaffer & Emerson, 1964). But in order that these fears do not later imprison the animal in his own early experience, it is more evolutionarily adaptive if most of them are forgotten, and only those fears which are periodically reinstated by a particular habitat or culture are retained. It was from considerations along this line that the authors demonstrated reinstatement first in an aversive situation. Rats that had experienced an early traumatic shock experience had forgotten it a month later unless they were given one brief reinstatement of the experience each week over the developmental period (Campbell & Jaynes, 1966).

Of equal if not greater importance is the applicability of reinstatement to the results of appetitive learning. The present study is a demonstration of reinstatement in the retention of a visual discrimination learned in infancy and a study of the effects of varying its duration.

Method

Subjects

The subjects were 160 21–25-day-old female rats of the Wistar strain purchased from Perfection Breeders, Douglassville, Pennsylvania. The rats were housed in group cages for 2–3 days prior to the experimental treatment, then housed individually in small cages during retention interval.

Apparatus

The apparatus consisted of eight standard operant conditioning units, housed in individually sound-insulated chambers. Each unit was $8 \times 9 \times 7\frac{1}{2}$ inches and contained a $2 \times \frac{3}{4}$ inch bar which projected $2\frac{1}{4}$ inches from the wall above the grid floor. Depression of a lever (approximately 15-gram force required) delivered the food pellet to a food cup situated 1 inch to the left of the lever. Water was available at all times. The discrimination stimulus was a $7\frac{1}{2}$-watt white light, located $3\frac{1}{2}$ inches above the bar. A dim house light located over the cage produced an illumination level of approximately .1 footcandle when the discrimination light was off.

Design

The basic plan of this experiment was to train animals on a simple light-dark discrimination for 4 successive days, then give each animal one reinstatement session per week for 10 successive weeks, with different groups receiving different durations of reinstatement. On the week following the tenth week of reinstatement training, half of the animals were tested for retention by relearning and the other half by extinction. These effects of reinstatement training on retention of the original discrimination were compared against control groups which received no original training but did receive equal amounts of reinstatement training.

Discrimination Training

The discrimination training consisted of 4 days in the lever boxes and was the same procedurally for all groups. The animals were placed in the boxes at 4 P.M. each day and left in the boxes overnight until 10 A.M. the next morning. During this time they had ad libitum access to food via the lever-pressing response. Water was available ad libitum. At 4 P.M. on the first day, the rat was weighed and placed in the lever box. At 10 A.M. on the following day the animal was removed from the box, and placed in an individual cage without access to either food or water. The animal remained in the individual cage until 4 P.M. when he was weighed and placed in the lever box. The procedure was repeated for 4 successive days. Control animals were removed from their home cages for the same period of time each day and left in restraining cages from 10 A.M. to 4 P.M. daily without food and water just as the experimental animals were for this same period of time. Throughout training, the light above the bar was on for 2 minutes and off for 2 minutes, the animal being rewarded only during the light-off or dark period. During this 2-minute positive interval, bar presses were reinforced on a 15-second variable-interval schedule, such that an animal could receive a maximum of eight pellets during a single positive period. Reinforcement consisted of a 20-milligram J. P. Noyes pellet. Number of responses during the positive and negative periods were recorded every 4 hours on electromagnetic counters.

Reinstatement Training

Following the 4 days of discrimination training the animals were assigned randomly to one of five reinstatement training conditions: 0, 7.5, 15, 30, or 60 minutes of reinstatement training per week. At the same time, comparable groups of control animals who had received no original discrimination training were assigned to the same reinstatement training conditions. The reinstatement procedure was carried out once weekly for each group and the day of the week on which the reinstatement procedure took place was systematically counterbalanced for all groups so that some animals received their reinstatement training in the early portion of the week and some in the latter. The reinstatement procedure consisted of placing the animal in the lever box for the specified reinstatement time, for example, 7.5, 15, 30, or 60 minutes with the same schedule of reinforcement conditions present as in original training. The group receiving zero reinstatement training was removed from the home cage once each week, placed in the restraining cage for approximately 10 minutes, and then returned to the home cage. The above reinstatement procedure was carried

out for 10 successive weeks. Number of bar presses during the positive and negative periods were recorded for each reinstatement.

Retention Test

During the week following the 10 reinstatement training sessions half of the animals were given a 24-hour extinction test and half were given a 24-hour relearning test. The extinction test consisted of placing the animals in the lever boxes with all conditions identical to those of original training and reinstatement training, with the exception that the lever press was never followed by reinforcement. The retraining test consisted of placing the animals in the lever boxes with all conditions identical to those of original and reinstatement training, including the delivery of reinforcement on a 15-second variable interval schedule. Bar presses during both the positive and negative stimulus periods were recorded every 20 minutes of the first 4 hours and every 4 hours of the extinction session thereafter for both the extinction and retraining tests.

Results

Reinstatement Training

Figure 21–1 shows the percentage of correct responding during acquisition and the 10 days of reinstatement training for the 7.5-minute, 15-minute, 30-minute, and 60-minute reinstatement groups. The previously trained experimental groups receiving only 7.5 and 15 minutes of reinstatement each week gradually declined in percentage of correct responding over the 10 reinstatement sessions, whereas animals in the longer 30- and 60-minute sessions gradually increased in percentage of correct responding during the same time. The control animals, which had not been previously trained, showed little systemic improvement above chance level (50%) with either 7.5, 15,

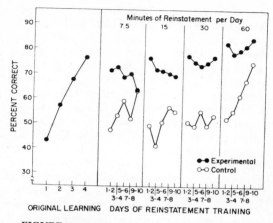

FIGURE 21-1. Percentage of responses to the positive stimulus during acquisition and reinstatement.

Relearning Test

Figure 21-2 shows percentage of correct responding during the first 2 hours of the relearning test in which animals were reinforced on the original training schedule for responding during the light-off (positive) period. Here it is evident that the longer the reinstatement per week, the higher the percentage of correct responding during the relearning test. Animals who had received no reinstatement training showed little or no retention of the discrimination when their performance is compared to the original discrimination training. In contrast, those animals who received 7.5, 15, or 30 minutes of reinstatement training each week following the 4 days of original discrimination training performed substantially and significantly better than control animals who received only the 10 weeks of reinstatement training. The control group receiving 60 minutes of reinstatement training per week, however, showed substantial discrimination learning, but their scores were still inferior to the corresponding experimental group ($p < .05$). Data for the subsequent 22 hours of

or 30 minutes of weekly reinstatement training. None of the improvements shown by these groups were statistically significant. (The highest F was 2.06, $df = 4/60$, $p > .05$ for the 7.5-minute group.) The 60-minute group, however, showed a significant and steady increase in percentage of correct responding over the 10 reinstatement periods ($F = 22.6$, $df = 4/60$, $p < .001$).

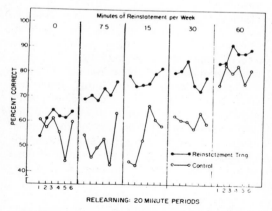

FIGURE 21-2. Percentage of responses to the positive stimulus during successive 20-minute periods of the first 2 hours of the relearning test as a function of duration of reinstatement.

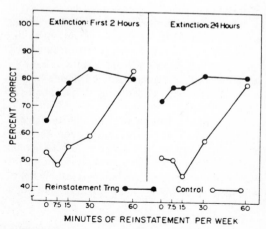

FIGURE 21-3. Percentage of responses to the positive stimulus during the first 4 hours and the total 24 hours of the extinction test as a function of duration of reinstatement.

the relearning test are not shown since differences between the group were gradually obscured by further learning and satiation.

Extinction Test

Figure 21–3 shows percentage of correct responding during the first 2 hours of the extinction test (left panel) and for the entire 24-hour period. The results fully agree with those of the other animals who were tested by relearning. In the experimental group that had had early training, the longer the weekly reinstatement, the better the discrimination was evidenced in extinction. In the control groups, the extinction scores revealed no appreciable learning had taken place during the 7.5-, 15-, or 30-minute reinstatements, while the rats undergoing the 60 minutes per week had learned the discrimination.

Discussion

The present study demonstrates that an appetitive habit which would ordinarily be forgotten can be maintained by additional amounts of training—reinstatements—that are too small or too brief in duration to establish the habit *de novo*. As might be expected, retention of the habit was greater the longer the duration of reinstatement. Reinstatement is thus a concept which is applicable to appetitive training as well as to aversive conditioning (Campbell & Jaynes, 1966).

The authors would like to clarify several confusions which have arisen since the first paper on this subject. First, the authors would like to reiterate that the concept is not in the nature of a discovery so much as a refocusing of scientific attention in such a way as to provide a paradigm for future experimentation. Second, reinstatement is to be differentiated from the concept of simple rehearsal as genus is to species. In the context of human learning studies, rehearsal is usually considered a voluntary and often unwanted response of reviewing a previously learned task without external cues or rewards. This is a kind of reinstatement, which, since it is self-initiated, might be called auto-reinstatement. Finally, the authors do not mean, of course, that the animal has to be returned to the identical treatment; the principle of stimulus generalization applies here as with any other form of learned behavior. Moreover, as was pointed out earlier, many types of events or experiences can be reinstated through verbal mediation. This is particularly true in the parent-child relationship where the parent frequently resorts to recreating former experiences and reinstating the pleasures or unhappinesses associated with the occasion.

One further question of importance that arises from this research is whether or not reinforcement is a necessary part of the reinstatement procedure. Two possibilities exist. One is a simple associationistic point of view which holds that repetition of any part of an experience tends to reinstate the whole area without reinforcement. The other is that reinstatement is not effective unless the original response is followed by primary (or possibly secondary) reinforcement. On close examination these two alternatives may not be so divergent since it is obvious that repeatedly exposing an animal to an environment in which a response had been previously reinforced would lead to extinction of that response, and a new "association" would develop. On the other hand *short* brief exposures to the original learning situation may serve to maintain the perceptual relevance of various environmental stimuli thereby maintain the original response.

REFERENCES

Campbell, B. A. Developmental studies of learning and motivation in infra-primate mammals. In H. W. Stevenson (Ed.), *Early behavior: Comparative and developmental approaches*. New York: Wiley, 1967.

Campbell, B. A., & Jaynes, J. Reinstatement. *Psychological Review*, 1966, *73*, 478–480.

Jaynes, J. Imprinting: The interaction of learned and innate behavior. III. Practice effects on performance, retention, and fear. *Journal of Comparative and Physiological Psychology*, 1958, *51*, 234–257.

Schaffer, H. R., & Emerson, P. E. The development of social attachments in infancy. *Monographs of the Society for Research in Child Development*, 1964, *29*(3, Whole No. 94).

Chapter 8

PERCEPTION

INTRODUCTION AND COMMENTARY

The type and range of recent studies in the development of perception have been critically reviewed by Pick and Pick (1970). They argue that the resurgence of interest in perceptual development over the past twenty years derives from the failure of classical learning theory to handle the problems of the nature of the stimulus input, Piaget's study of children's spatial conceptions, as well as the prominence given by Hebb and the ethologists to the role of early experience and sensory stimulation in ontogenesis. This chapter will cover some aspects of the development of visual functioning, as this has been the focus of the major part of studies in perceptual development. Pick and Pick (1970) provide an analysis of research in other areas of perceptual processing.

Nativism–Empiricism: A Basic View

The question of whether spatial abilities are completely the result of learning or innately determined has dominated the study of visual perception from its inception, and still remains a challenging issue. Historically, there have been two major positions on this question (often characterized as the nativist–empiricist controversy). The nativist position is that we perceive an already organized world at birth as we are born with the appropriate neural connections. The empiricist view is that we *learn* to perceive the world, and that knowledge is derived from experience rather than being predetermined by genetic factors.

The argument that visual perception is learned has been vigorously discussed since Berkeley wrote *An Essay towards a New Theory of Vision* in 1709. At the heart of Berkeley's thesis is his view that the retinal image is an inadequate determinant of perception. The point is that whereas the retinal image is two-dimensional, humans, among many species, have access to three-dimensional perception. There are other problems in viewing the information displayed in the retinal image as an explanation of perceptual experience. For example, the retinal stimulation provided by an external object changes as a function of the distance of the object, its illumination, and so on, yet the object is seen as essentially unchanging.

The proposition that perceptual organization is either entirely genetically predetermined or is entirely learned does not find many contemporary adherents. The basic question in research and theorizing concerns the *interactions* of inborn and experiential variables in the development of a perceptual system. Hebb (1949), who has been a major theoretical influence on studies in perceptual development, proposes that whereas there is an innate mechanism that allows for the separation of figure and ground in perception, this merely provides a foundation for perceptual development. His view is that the immature organism constructs his or her world through the interaction of the innate figure–ground mechanism, eye-movements, and learning.

Hershenson (1971) believes that it may be unrealistic to think in terms of a general theory of perceptual development, because different models may account for different aspects of perceptual development. According to Hershenson there are four major conceptual schemes that have been proposed as explanatory mechanisms of perceptual development: (1) maturation; (2) construction; (3) learning and differentiation; and (4) adaptation. See Chapter 2, pp. 22–23, for a discussion of these conceptual schemes. Hershenson's classification cuts across the nativist–empiricist controversy by emphasizing physiological, evolutionary, and psychological phenomena in perceptual development.

Nativism–Empiricism: Research and Methods

One means of exploring the question of the role of learning in the development of visual spatial abilities is to study subjects who have had little opportunity for learning. This general approach has led to various kinds of perceptual investigations. One line of research involves the examination of the perceptual capabilities of neonatal infants. Techniques have been developed that accommodate to the restricted capabilities of the newborn, including such indicators of perceptual sensitivity as sucking, ocular orientation, conditioned responses, and heartrate (Kessen, Haith, and Salapatek, 1970). Experimental evidence indicates that the young infant is at least able to process information at a low level of organization. Wertheimer (1961), for example, has found that in some degree the discrimination of the direction of the source of sound is innate. He tested an infant three minutes after birth by presenting him with click noises and discovered that the infant's eyes moved generally in the direction of the sound source. Fantz (1963) offers some evidence that infants are capable of even more complex perceptual operations in that they can discriminate between different visual patterns. Salapatek and Kessen (1966) provide a more fine-grained analysis of infant vision, studying elementary pattern recognition by examining neonatal responses to a triangle. The investigators demonstrated convincingly that infants scan forms in a nonrandom way, which strongly suggests that the infant's visual world already has some order to it.

Bower (1966, see also 1973) used an operant conditioning procedure to study the visual capacities of infants of fifty to sixty days of age. He discovered that at this age infants respond to the shape of an object and can, in addition, recognize it in new orientations. This means that the young infant already possesses a well-formed notion of *shape constancy;* that is, the infant is not responding to retinal shape but is instead capable of computing the invariances in a shape that has been transformed one or more times.

Epstein (1964) has described experiments relevant to the *genesis* of visual space perception, and discusses three categories of experiments. The first category includes studies in which organisms have been deprived of visual stimulation until the time of testing. The experiment by Held and Hein [22] is of this kind. The second category consists of studies in which naive, newborn organisms are tested soon after birth. The classic study by Walk and Gibson (1961) investigating depth perception in many different species is of this sort. The third category includes studies in which the experimenter raises animals from birth under specific conditions. An example of this type is Hess's (1950) study in which groups of ducks were raised under different conditions of illumination.

Haber and Hershenson (1973, chap. 15) and Bronson (1974) provide reviews of recent research into the infant's perceptual apparatus, with Bronson offering an intriguing account of the possible relations between neurological and behavioral development in infancy. The conclusion one can draw from this research is that at birth the infant has available a well-coordinated and functional visual system that quickly becomes modified by experience, as well as by maturational changes.

A second approach to the nativist–empiricist controversy has been to use a *deprivation* technique in order to assess the influence of certain types of experience in determining the functioning of perceptual mechanisms. In one such study, Hubel and Wiesel (1963) found that whereas connections between the eye and the brain for slope detection are present at birth, visual deprivation can lead to a disruption of these connections. In other words, postnatal stimulation is an essential condition for the continued full functioning of the innate perceptual (i.e., eye–brain) connections. In a related study, Hirsch and Spinelli (1970) examined the question of whether highly specific visual stimulation will produce equally highly specific eye–brain connections. These researchers put masks on kittens so that they saw black vertical lines through one eye, and black horizontal lines through the other. The kittens were presented with a stimulus dot that moved either horizontally or vertically. Electrophysiological recordings revealed elongated receptive fields that were oriented either horizontally or vertically depending upon the type of stimulation received by the eye. This is in sharp contrast to the fact that normal cats show only random arrangements in their receptive fields. Thus it was demonstrated that original neural connections can be *modified* as a function of the nature of the stimulation impinging upon the eyes. In another deprivation experiment Held and Hein [22] tested the hypothesis that a special kind of environmental contact (i.e., self-produced movement with its concurrent visual feedback) is necessary for the development of visually guided behavior. The experimental results showed that the kittens who were permitted to locomote performed significantly better on tests of visually guided behavior than the kittens who were transported. The Hubel and Wiesel (1963), Hirsch and Spinelli (1970), and Held and Hein [22] studies indicate the complex interaction of innate and experiential factors in the development of perception. It appears that the neural mechanisms that mediate perception demand certain environmental conditions for their optimal growth.

Although there is considerable agreement among contemporary researchers that learning has a significant role in perceptual development, it is conceivable that learning or experience may not have an identical role in all types of perceptual development and at all stages of development. Gibson [23] argues along these lines in discussing two general types of perceptual activity: the perception of space and events in space that has biologically adaptive significance; and the perception of objects and permanent items, which is much more dependent on long-term learning, and refers to culturally adaptive behavior. Gibson (1969) offers a theory of perceptual learning that describes development as involving increases in five discrimination. Perceptual learning then is concerned with *differentiation*, which refers to the processes by which the individual detects those relevant features of part of the environment in order to achieve optimal adaptation. Another aspect of the question of the role of experience in development is expressed in research on cultural factors in long-term perceptual development. There are examples in the literature of differences in the formulation of perceptual categories and in making perceptual judgments (see Lloyd, 1972). Berry [24] provides some evidence of some perceptual activities that are significantly shaped by cultural forces.

Perception and Cognition

One current emphasis in research on perceptual development is on the essential unity of human cognition. (See the discussion on language and thinking in the introduction to Chapter 9, p. 370). Many studies involve the exploration of relationships between the development of perceptual and other cognitive skills and strategies. Mackworth and Bruner [25] demonstrate that visual search patterns are linked up with a variety of cognitive operations, including attention, memory, and the utilization of available mental schemata. (See also Appel et al., 1972, for a discussion of some of the relationships between perception and memory.)

References

Appel, L. F., Cooper, R. G., McCarrell, N., Simms-Knight, J., Yussen, S. R., & Flavell, J. H. The development of the distinction between perceiving and memorizing. *Child Development*, 1972, *43*, 1365–1381.

Bower, T. Slant perception and shape constancy in infants. *Science,* 1966, *151*, 832–834.

Bower, T. *Development in infancy.* San Francisco: W. H. Freeman, 1973.

Bronson, G. The postnatal growth of visual capacity. *Child Development,* 1974, *45*, 873–890.

Epstein, W. Experimental investigations of the genesis of visual space perception. *Psychological Bulletin,* 1964, *61*, 115–128.

Fantz, R. L. Pattern vision in newborn infants. *Science,* 1963, *140*, 296–297.

Gibson, E. J. *Principles of perceptual learning and development.* New York: Appleton, 1969.

Haber, R. N. & Hershenson, M. *The psychology of visual space perception.* New York: Holt, Rinehart and Winston, 1973, pp. 353–370.

Hebb, D. O. *The organization of behavior.* New York: Wiley, 1949.

Hershenson, M. The development of visual perception systems. In H. Moltz (Ed.), *The ontogeny of vertebrate behavior.* New York: Academic Press, 1971, pp. 29–56.

Hess, E. H. Development of the chick's responses to light and shade cues of depth. *Journal of Comparative and Physiological Psychology,* 1950, *43*, 112–122.

Hirsch, H. V. B. & Spinelli, D. N. Visual experience modifies distribution of horizontally and vertically oriented reception fields in cats. *Science,* 1970, *168*, 869–871.

Hubel, D. H. & Wiesel, T. N. Receptive fields of cells in striate cortex of very young, visually inexperienced kittens. *Journal of Neurophysiology,* 1963, *26*, 994–1002.

Kessen, W., Haith, M. M., & Salapatek, P. H. Infancy. In P. H. Mussen (Ed.), *Carmichael's handbook of child psychology.* New York: Wiley, 1970, pp. 287–445.

Lloyd, B. B. *Perception and cognition: A cross-cultural perspective.* Baltimore: Penguin, 1972.

Pick, H. L., Jr. & Pick, A. D. Sensory and perceptual development. In P. H. Mussen (Ed.), *Carmichael's handbook of child psychology.* New York: Wiley, 1970, pp. 773–847.

Salapatek, P. & Kessen, W. Visual scanning of triangles by the human newborn. *Journal of Experimental Child Psychology.* 1966, *3*, 155–167.

Walk, R. D. & Gibson, J. A comparative and analytical study of visual depth perception. *Psychological Monographs,* 1961, *75*, 15 (Whole No. 519).

Wertheimer, M. Psychomotor coordination of auditory and visual space at birth. *Science,* 1961, *134*, 1962.

22. MOVEMENT-PRODUCED STIMULATION IN THE DEVELOPMENT OF VISUALLY GUIDED BEHAVIOR[1]

RICHARD HELD and ALAN HEIN

Full and exact adaptation to sensory rearrangement in adult human Ss requires movement-produced sensory feedback. Riesen's work suggested that this factor also operates in the development of higher mammals but he proposed that sensory-sensory associations are the prerequisite. To test these alternatives, visual stimulation of the active member (A) of each of 10 pairs of neonatal kittens was allowed to vary with its locomotor movements while equivalent stimulation of the second member (P) resulted from passive motion. Subsequent tests of visually guided paw placement, discrimination on a visual cliff, and the blink response were normal for A but failing in P. When other alternative explanations are excluded, this result extends the conclusions of studies of adult rearrangement to neonatal development.

Hebb's writing (1949) has stirred interest in the effects of exposure to the environment on the development of spatial perception and coordination. The main experimental attack on the problem has used the technique of rearing animals in restricted environments (deprivation) from the time of birth or shortly thereafter. An alternative approach consists in experimentally analyzing the conditions for modifying certain sensorimotor coordinations in adults on the assumption that they are similarly plastic during the entire exposure-history of the organism (Hein & Held, 1962; Held, 1955, 1961). If this supposition is true, the analysis carried out on adults must also define the kind of contact with the environment required for development. Use of the rearrangement technique for studying plasticity in adult human Ss has yielded results which suggest its complementarity to the procedures of neonatal deprivation (Held & Bossom, 1961). This experiment demonstrates the convergence of the two approaches.

In the human adult, change in stimulation

dependent upon the natural movements of S has been shown essential to the achievement of full and exact compensation for sensory rearrangements (Hein & Held, 1958; Held, 1955; Held & Bossom, 1961; Mikaelian & Held, in press). A suggestive parallel between these findings and those of deprivation studies comes from two experiments on kittens reared under different conditions of deprivation. In one experiment Ss were allowed visual experience in an illuminated and patterned environment only while they were restrained in holders which prevented them from freely moving about (Riesen & Aarons, 1959). When subsequently tested they showed deficiencies in visually guided behavior compared with their normally reared litter mates. Related deficits followed rearing in a second experiment in which Ss were allowed to move about freely in light but with diffusing hoods over their eyes (Riesen, 1961c). The exposure factor lacking under both conditions was the variation in visual stimulation produced by the full range of S's movement in normal circumstances; a result consistent with our findings.

Riesen has suggested that his deprived Ss showed deficits because they lacked sufficient opportunity for developing sensory-sensory associations in the manner proposed by Hebb

[1]This research was supported by a grant from the National Science Foundation.

From *Journal of Comparative and Physiological Psychology*, 1963, 56, 872–876. Copyright 1963 by the American Psychological Association and reprinted by permission of the authors and the publisher.

(Riesen, 1961c)—even the patterned surroundings viewed by the holder-restrained Ss may not have provided sufficient variation in visual stimulation for forming the necessary associations. This interpretation agrees with ours in asserting that the variation in visual stimulation accompanying movement is essential for the development of certain coordinations but it omits our qualification that this variation can be effective only when it is concurrent with and systematically dependent upon self-produced movements. (Hein & Held, 1962; Held, 1961). The alternative to our interpretation asserts that changes in stimulation irrespective of their relation to self-produced movements are sufficient. To decide between these two alternatives, we reared different sets of kittens from birth under the two implied conditions of exposure and subsequently compared their development. Under one condition stimulation varied as a result of S's own locomotion whereas under the other it was equivalently varied by transporting Ss through an equivalent range of motion while they were restrained from locomoting.

Method

Subjects

Ten pairs of kittens were used; each pair from a different litter.

Exposure Apparatus and Procedure

The exposure apparatus diagramed in Figure 22–1 was designated to equate the visual stimulation received by each member of a pair of Ss. Stimulation varied with the locomotor movements of the active S (A in Figure 22–1) but varied with equivalent motion of the passive S (P). To attain this equivalence, the gross motions of A were mechanically transferred to P. These movements were restricted to rotations around three axes. The radial symmetry of the visible environment made variations in visual stimulation, contingent upon these movements, equal over time for the two Ss.

The P was placed in the gondola and held there by a neckyoke and body clamp. The lever from which the gondola was suspended was

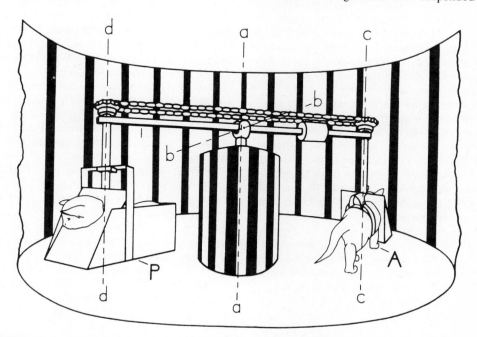

FIGURE 22–1. Apparatus for equating motion and consequent visual feedback for an actively moving (A) and a passively moved (P) S.

then balanced by appropriate placement of a counter-weight. When attached to the opposite end of the lever by a second neckyoke and body-clamp, A was free to move itself in both directions around the three axes of rotation a-a, b-b, and c-c while pulling P through the equivalent movements around a-a, b-b, and d-d by means of the mechanical linkages to the gondola. The distance between c-c and d-d was 36 in. The range of motions normally performed by Ss was somewhat reduced by the experimental apparatus. Use of ball bearings and aluminum in the construction of the apparatus reduced friction and inertia insofar as possible. The importance of these restraints is mitigated, we believe, by previous findings in rearrangement studies which indicate that similar restraints, and constant changes in the inertia over-come by muscular movement, do not affect the adaptation process (Held & Hein, 1958; Held & Schlank, 1959). Head motion was not restricted for either A or P. This restriction seemed unnecessary since Riesen and Aarons (1959) have shown that kittens reared from birth with variations in visual stimulation consequent upon free head motions, but otherwise restricted, failed to learn a simple spatial discrimination. Because of its constraints, P could not locomote. However, its limbs were free to move and to slide along the smooth floor of the gondola. According to our observations these movements frequently occurred.

The apparatus was surrounded by a galvanized iron cylinder that was 24 in. high with a diameter of 48 in. The lever support mechanism was enclosed within a second cylinder that was 11 in. high with a diameter of 12 in. The smaller cylinder served to obscure each S's view of its mate. Patterning was provided by vertically oriented 1 in. wide stripes of black and white masking tape separated by 1 in. of bare metal. Additional texture was provided by the rough side of a piece of masonite which served as the floor. The floor was uniform throughout thus providing equivalent visual stimulation for the two Ss. Sight of the paws and other body parts was excluded by appropriate extensions of the neck stocks.

Testing Apparatus and Procedure

We used tests of visually guided behavior that minimized S's gross movements in the visible environment in order not to confound the conditions of testing with those of exposure, a confusion which past investigators have generally disregarded. For this purpose responses to stimuli were used that require no conditioning with repetition of movements but which are nonetheless contingent upon a capacity to make visual-spatial discriminations. Following the leads of earlier work, we have used three such tests:

1. Visually-guided paw placement (Riesen, 1961c). S's body was held in E's hands so that its head and forelegs were free. It was slowly carried forward and downward towards the edge of a table or some other horizontal surface. A normally-reared S shows visually-mediated anticipation of contact by extending its paws as it approaches the edge.

2. Avoidance of a visual cliff (Walk & Gibson, 1961). The visual cliff consists essentially of a narrow platform supported by vertical sides that drop a few inches to a large plate of glass. The S placed on the platform can descend to the glass on either one of two sides. Its view on the "deep" side is through the glass to a patterned surface 30 in. below. On the other side it views a similarly patterned surface attached to the underside of the glass. In our apparatus, both surfaces were illuminated from below and hence the clean glass surface was practically invisible. For the vertical sides of the platform, we substituted planes inclined 35° from the vertical.

3. Blink to an approaching object (Riesen, 1958). The S was held in a standing position in a neckyoke and body clamp with a large sheet of Plexiglas positioned directly in front of its face. The E moved his hand quickly toward S, stopping just short of contact with the Plexiglas.

Several additional tests were performed to check the status of peripheral receptor and response mechanisms. These included observations of pupillary reflex to light, the tactual placing response, and visual pursuit of a moving object. The S, held in a standing position in a neckyoke and body clamp, was light-adapted in the normally illuminated laboratory prior to observation of the pupillary reflex. Change in pupillary size was then noted when a light beam from a penlight was moved across the eye from outer to inner canthus. To determine the presence of the tactual paw-placing response S was supported as in the visual paw-placing test. It was then carried to the edge of a table where the dorsa of its front paws were brought into contact with the vertical edge of the table. Observations of experimental Ss were compared with those of normals which, in response to this stimulus, place the paws on the horizontal surface of the table. Visual pursuit was elicited by E's hand moving slowly across S's visual field.

General Procedure

The 10 pairs of Ss were divided into two Groups, X and Y, whose members were reared with minor differences. Each of the eight pairs of Group X was reared in darkness from birth until member A attained the minimal size and coordinational capacity to move itself and its mate in the apparatus. This age varied between 8 and 12 weeks. They then began exposure in the apparatus for 3 hr. daily. The two pairs of Group Y received 3 hr. daily exposure, beginning at 2 and ending at 10 weeks of age to the patterned interior of the laboratory while restrained in holders that allowed some head movement but prevented locomotion. They then began exposure in the apparatus for 3 hr. daily. When not exposed, all Ss were kept in lightless cages together with their mothers and litter mates. We had found in pilot studies that Ss reared in this fashion did not show the freezing, agitation, or fear responses reported to follow social isolation by Melzack (1962) and Riesen (1961a).

Six repetitions of the paw-placement test were performed after each daily exposure period for all Ss. On the first day that one S of each pair in Group X displayed visual paw placing, both were tested on the visual cliff. They were retested on the following day. For

TABLE 22–1
Ratio of Descents to Shallow and Deep Sides of Visual Cliff

PAIR NUM-BER	AGE IN WEEKS[a]	EXPOSURE IN APPARATUS (IN HR.)		RATIO OF DESCENTS SHALLOW/ DEEP	
		A	P	A	P
1X	8	33	33	12/0	6/6
2X	8	33	33	12/0	4/8
3X	8	30	30	12/0	7/5
4X	9	63	63	12/0	6/6
5X	10	33	33	12/0	7/5
6X	10	21	21	12/0	7/5
7X	12	9	9	12/0	5/7
8X	12	15	15	12/0	8/4
1Y	10	30	126	12/0	6/6
2Y	10	33	126	12/0	8/4

[a]*At the beginning of exposure in the experimental apparatus.*

each test and retest S was required to descend from the central platform six times. Immediately following trials on the visual cliff on the second day, member P of each pair was put in a continuously illuminated room for 48 hr. Retesting of visual placing and renewed trials on the visual cliff followed this unrestricted exposure. The testing procedure differed slightly for pairs of Group Y. On the first day that A displayed visual paw placing, it was tested on the visual cliff and retested on the following day. However, its mate (P) was not placed on the cliff at this time; instead, the passive exposure procedure was continued for 3 hr. daily for a total of 126 hr. The paw placing and visual cliff tests were then administered to P.

Results

The principal results of this experiment are summarized in Table 22–1. The amount of time required for the development of a visually-guided paw-placement in the members of each pair of litter mates is indicated in the column under the heading Exposure in Apparatus. After those periods of exposure required by A, every P mate failed to display the response. Observations suggest a tendency for the placing response to develop in the livelier of the active Ss with fewer hours of exposure than required by the quieter ones. The blink response to an approaching hand developed concurrently with the placing response. Pupillary reflex to light, tactual placing response, and visual pursuit were each noted on first elicitation, just prior to the initial exposure in the apparatus.

On the day that the visually-guided placing response was shown by A, he was tested on the modified visual cliff. All As behaved like normally reared Ss which had been observed previously in a pilot experiment. As shown by the totals of Table 22–1, each A descended to the shallow side of the cliff on every trial of the first day and repeated this performance on the trials of the following day. The P members of Group X were tested on the cliff on the same days as their actively exposed litter mates. They showed no evidence of discriminating the shallow from the deep side. Observations of the P members of Group Y on the cliff, after their prolonged passive exposure, gave similar results and they also failed to perform visual paw-placement. Following the 48 hr. period of freedom in an illuminated room, the P members of Group X were retested. They then displayed normal visually-guided paw-placement and performed all descents to the shallow side of the visual cliff.

Discussion

The results are consistent with our thesis that self-produced movement with its concurrent visual feedback is necessary for the development of visually-guided behavior. Equivalent, and even greatly increased, variation in visual stimulation produced by other means is not sufficient. However, before concluding that our thesis is valid we must consider other alternative explanations of the deficits in the behavioral development of neonates following deprivation. These alternatives assert that loss of function does not reflect deficiencies in a

process of the central nervous system that depends upon exposure for its development. Instead, the capacity to perform is allegedly present but prevented from operating by either peripheral blockage or other suppressive effects of the special rearing conditions. Such negative effects fall into two categories: (a) anatomical or physiological deterioration and (b) behavioral inhibition.

Included under anatomical or physiological deterioration said to result from deprivation, are the findings of atrophy in peripheral parts of the visual nervous system, a literature reviewed by Riesen (1961b); the assumption that maturation of the retina is prevented (Walk & Gibson, 1961); and the suggestion that general debility results from lack of use of various organs (Hess, 1962). In the present experiment, the relevance of peripheral atrophy is contra-indicated by the presence of pupillary and pursuit reflexes and the rapid recovery of function of the passive Ss once given their freedom. Debility specific to the motor systems of these Ss can be ruled out on the grounds that their tactual placing responses and other motor activities were indistinguishable from those of normals. In addition, differential losses in the periphery or differential debility could hardly be expected to result from those differences between active and passive exposures which occurred in the experimental apparatus.

Inhibition of performance attributable to the effects of shock, fright, or overactivation upon exposure to the novel and increased stimulation that follows release from the deprived state has been suggested by Sutherland (1959) and Melzack (1962). Sutherland has also suggested that habits developed during deprivation may compete with and inhibit the normal response. However, both our active and passive Ss were raised under very similar conditions insofar as restriction was concerned and under the rather mild conditions of deprivation of this experiment we did not observe any signs of shock, excitement, or fright. Moreover, the passive Ss were not observed performing responses that might have competed with the expected response.

These findings provide convincing evidence for a developmental process, in at least one higher mammal, which requires for its operation stimulus variation concurrent with and systematically dependent upon self-produced movement. This conclusion neither denies nor affirms that other processes, such as maturation, occur concomitantly. The results demonstrate the complementarity of studies of adult rearrangement and neonatal deprivation.

REFERENCES

Hebb, D. O. *The organization of behavior.* New York: Wiley, 1949.

Hein, A., and R. Held. Minimal conditions essential for complete re-learning of hand-eye coordination with prismatic distortion of vision. Paper read at Eastern Psychological Association. Philadelphia, 1958.

Hein, A., and R. Held. A neural model for labile sensorimotor coordinations. In E. E. Bernard and M. R. Kare (Eds.), *Biological prototypes and synthetic systems.* Vol. 1. New York: Plenum Press, 1962, pp. 71–74.

Held, R. Shifts in binaural localization after prolonged exposures to atypical combinations of stimuli. *Amer. J. Psychol.,* 1955, *68*, 526–548.

Held, R. Exposure-history as a factor in maintaining stability of perception and coordination. *J. Nerv. Ment. Dis.,* 1961, *132*, 26–32.

Held, R., and J. Bossom. Neonatal deprivation and adult rearrangement: Complementary techniques for analyzing plastic sensory-motor coordinations. *J. Comp. Physiol. Psychol.,* 1961, *54*, 33–37.

Held, R., and A. Hein. Adaptation of disarranged hand-eye coordination contingent upon reafferent stimulation. *Percept. Mot. Skills,* 1958, *8*, 87–90.

Held, R., and M. Schlank. Adaptation to optically increased distance of the hand from the eye by re-afferent stimulation. *Amer. J. Psychol.,* 1959, *72*, 603–605.

Hess, E. H. Ethology: an approach toward the complete analysis of behavior. In R. Brown, E. Galanter, E. H. Hess, and G. Mandler (Eds.), *New directions in psychology.* New York: Holt, Rinehart and Winston, 1962, pp. 159–266.

Melzack, R. Effects of early perceptual restriction on simple visual discrimination. *Science,* 1962, *137*, 978–979.

Mikaelian, H., and R. Held. Two types of adaptation to an optically-rotated visual field. *Amer. J. Psychol.,* in press.

Riesen, A. H. Plasticity of behavior: Psychological aspects. In H. F. Harlow and C. N. Woolsey (Eds.), *Biological and biochemical bases of behavior.* Madison: Univer. Wisconsin Press, 1958, pp. 425–450.

Riesen, A. H. Excessive arousal effects of stimulation after early sensory deprivation. In P. Solomon, P. E. Kubzansky, P. H. Leiderman, J. H. Mendelson, R. H. Trumbull, and D. Wexler (Eds.), *Sensory deprivation.* Cambridge: Harvard Univer. Press, 1961, pp. 34–40. (a)

Riesen, A. H. Stimulation as a requirement for growth and function in behavioral development. In D. W. Fiske and S. R. Maddi (Eds.), *Functions of varied experience.* Homewood, Ill.: Dorsey, 1961, pp. 57–80. (b)

Riesen, A. H. Studying perceptual development using the technique of sensory deprivation. *J. Nerv. Ment. Dis.,* 1961, *132*, 21–25. (c)

Riesen, A. H., and L. Aarons. Visual movement and intensity discrimination in cats after early deprivation. of pattern vision. *J. Comp. Physiol. Psychol.,* 1959, *52*, 142–149.

Sutherland, N. S. Stimulus analyzing mechanisms. In *Mechanization of thought processes: National physical laboratory symposium No. 10,* Vol. 2. London: Her Majesty's Stationery Office, 1959, pp. 575–609.

Walk, R. D., and E. J. Gibson. A comparative and analytical study of visual depth perception. *Psychol. Monogr.,* 1961, *75*, 15 (Whole No. 519).

23. THE DEVELOPMENT OF PERCEPTION AS AN ADAPTIVE PROCESS

ELEANOR J. GIBSON[1]

Since the time of Darwin and the acceptance of the doctrine of evolution of species, psychologists have contemplated the phylogenetic development of behavior as a mark of adaptation to an animal's environment. In the late nineteenth century, the comparative psychologist's eagerness to fit behavior into the evolutionary scheme took some amusing, and by hindsight, naive trends. G. J. Romanes, one of the best of the so-called "anecdotalists," spoke for them when he said, "I hold that if the doctrine of Organic Evolution is accepted, it carries with it, as a necessary corollary, the doctrine of Mental Evolution, at all events as far as the brute creation is concerned" (1895, p. 8). In two volumes called *Mental Evolution in Animals* and *Mental Evolution in Man* he prepared a tree and a chart which served, he thought, to represent the "leading features of psychogenesis throughout the animal kingdom" and also the "principal stages of Mental Evolution in Man."

The chart lists, under "products of intellectual development," a number of faculties which are ranked from lowest to highest—from protoplasmic movements to morality. Then, in a column titled the "psychological scale," there is listed in correlation with the faculties the animal order where each faculty presumably first makes its appearance. "Memory" comes in with the echinoderms, "association by contiguity" with molluscs, "association by similarity" with fish, "recognition of persons" with reptiles and cephalopods, "recognition of pictures, understanding of words, and dreaming" with birds, and "morality" with anthropoid apes and the dog. Along with this, in a third column, is "psychogenesis in man," and we find the order of appearance of the faculties recapitulated; association by contiguity at 7 weeks, association by similarity at 10 weeks, recognition of persons at 4 months, recognition of pictures and words at 8 months, and so on.

Evidence for this order was based almost entirely on anecdote and informal observation. As comparative psychology developed an experimental method, the work of Romanes and his generation was derided and banished as a shameful page in the history of a new science. Yet the adaptiveness of behavior and evolutionary continuity were never quite forgotten. One no longer looked for faculties but for "laws" of behavior. Hull's theory of learning, which converted half the psychological world, stressed the biological adaptiveness of the conditioned reflex and the principle of reinforcement, which operated by reducing biological drives or need conditions, thereby strengthening behaviors useful to the organism (Hull 1943). The continuity was there too, because it was presumed that one could investigate these mechanisms in the rat and apply the findings to man.

Seeking to understand man's behavior by experimenting with the rat has fallen off in

[1]Eleanor Jack Gibson, whose article was a Spring 1969 Sigma Xi National Lecture, is Professor of Psychology at Cornell, and President of the Eastern Psychological Association. She is a Smith graduate with a Ph.D. from Yale (1938), and the wife of psychologist James J. Gibson. Her research is at present concerned with problems of perceptual development and especially the processing of graphic information. Her *Principles of Perceptual Learning and Development* (Appleton-Century, 1969) won the Century Award. Address: Department of Psychology, Cornell University, Ithaca, N.Y. 14850.

From the *American Scientist*, 1970, *58*, 98–107, the journal of Sigma Xi, The Scientific Research Society of North America, Inc. Reprinted by permission of the author and the publisher.

fashion, in its turn, but the ethologists have revived the biological tradition begun by Darwin and furthered by Romanes in a new and more sophisticated spirit of naturalism. Behavior that is specific to the species has become of interest and is studied in relation to the ecology of the species, thus revealing its adaptiveness.

In this abbreviated sketch of the influence of evolutionary concepts on psychology, where does perception come in? Do only executive behaviors like spinning webs, building nests, running through mazes, or pressing bars have adaptive value? Or is there a phylogenesis of perception and a parallel development in the individual? Is there perceptual learning which is adaptive? Or must learning be only on the response side, as behaviorists believed?

Karl Lashley was one of the first to raise these questions and to point out the role of perception in species-specific behavior and in evolution. In the "Experimental Analysis of Instinctive Behavior" (Lashley 1938) he stressed the importance of studying the innate components of "sensory organization," as well as the motor aspects of behavior. The essential first step, he said, was "analysis of the properties of the stimulus situation which are really effective in arousing the behavior." Understanding of the motor activities "hinges on these perceptual problems." Much of his work, from the early naturalistic studies of terms to later studies of stimulus equivalence in the rat, was directed at this problem. He never forgot the importance of evolution for understanding an animal's behavior. In "Persistent Problems in the Evolution of Mind" (1949), he told us that "the limits of capacity of each order of animals are set by the kinds of relations among objects that it can perceive. The development of the individual is a slow maturation of such capacities" (p. 460). "It is not the fact of learning but what is learned that differentiates animals in the evolutionary scale. The learning of higher animals involves a perception of relations which is beyond the capacity of the lower" (p. 458).

The latter statement he illustrated by comparing the behavior of a spider monkey and a chimpanzee in a matching problem. The monkey was required to choose a red or a green square, according as a red or a green square was given as a model. When the squares were placed as in row *a* in Figure 23–1, the monkey never improved above chance in 1000 trials. But when there was *contact* between the model and the test square, as in rows *b*, *d*, *e*, and *g*, he quickly achieved errorless choice. He saw the model, Lashley thought, as a pointer or a signal but did not perceive the relation of similarity. The chimpanzee, on the other hand, grasped it quickly.

Background of the Theory

To tell you how I see perceptual development as a mark of adaptiveness, I must explain first what I think perception is and what perceptual learning is. Then I will distinguish two modes of perceiving and illustrate with experiments what we know about their development in phylogeny and in the individual.

Perception is extracting information from stimulation (Gibson 1966). Stimulation emanates from the objects and surfaces and events in the world around us and it *carries information about* them; though different from them, it *specifies* them. If we were to consider stimulation only as individual rays of light or vibrations in the air, this specification would not be intelligible, because information about objects and layout of the world around us lies in relations, like edges between things; it is not punctate, but structured over space and time. Not only is there information about things in stimulation; there is rich information, far more, potentially, than we utilize.

Let me give an example. Some animals especially bats and dolphins, locate food and find their way around by means of echolocation. The dolphin emits clicking sounds at varying rates from one per second to bursts of 500 or more. These clicks are thought to be used for food-finding and navigation. To quote a dolphin expert, "The click trains, or sonar, search the seascape in front of a dolphin in much the same way that the cone of light from a miner's headlamp shows his way through a mine. In the

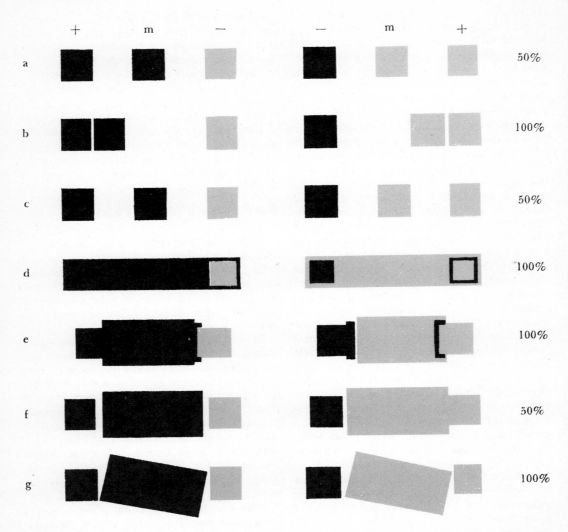

FIGURE 23–1. Arrangements of red and green squares presented to a spider monkey and a chimpanzee in a matching task. The percentages at the right represent the final level of accuracy attained in each situation (from Lashley 1949; reproduced by permission of the *Quarterly Review of Biology*).

presence of reflected light, we see where we look. In the presence of reflected sound, or the echoes of their own clicks, dolphins hear where they point their beam of sound. The click-echoes returned from the environment before the moving dolphin are information-bearing. The echoes contain information about the size, shape, location, movement if any, and texture of the living and nonliving things in the water" (McVay 1967, p. 8). It has in fact been demonstrated that dolphins can differentiate in this way objects of different sizes and shape and even different metallic substances, and can swim an obstacle course without collision. Three points emerge from this: one, that potential stimulus information about features of the environment is vast; second, that the information accurately specifies the layout of the world and the objects in it; and third, that perception is an active process, a search for the relevant information that specifies the path an animal needs to travel, the obstacles to be avoided, the mate or the food to be approached.

So perception, functionally speaking, is extracting information about the world from stimulation, a highly adaptive process since the animal must somehow discover where to go, what to seize, and what to avoid. What kind of world is there to perceive? We can describe it in several ways. I choose a classification that refers to properties of the environment. These include properties of the *spatial layout* (surfaces, edges, drop-offs); properties of *events* (motion, occlusion, appearance, disappearance, and reappearance); and properties of *objects* that make them distinguishable and identifiable. For man at least we can include another class; man-made symbols—*coded items* that stand for objects and events, such as speech and writing.

Animals perceive the surfaces and objects and events in their surroundings by way of stimulation which specifies them. But they seldom do this perfectly, and the potential information in stimulation is vastly greater than that which becomes effective. To understand how potential information becomes effective we need the concepts of *perceptual development* and *perceptual learning*. As the higher-order invariants and structure that uniquely specify objects and events are progressively extracted from the total stimulus flux, so does perception become more differentiated and more specific to those things. This is a process which goes on in the evolution of species and also, I think, in the development of the individual.

How do animals *learn* to perceive the permanent distinguishable properties of the world in the changing flux of stimulation? Not, I believe, by association, but by a process of extracting the invariant information from the variable flux. I think several processes are involved, all attentional ones. (See Gibson 1969 for a detailed statement of the theory of perceptual learning.) One is perceptual abstraction, akin to what James called ''dissociation by varying concomitants'' (note the dissociation as opposed to association; something is being pulled *out* from context, instead of being added *on*). Another is filtering of the irrelevant, an attenuation in the perceiving of random, varying, noninformative aspects of stimulation. A third is active, exploratory search. The dolphin beaming his clicking sounds is an example of the latter.

Another example is active touch (Gibson 1962). When a blindfolded subject is handed an unfamiliar object and asked to learn to identify it so as to be able to match it visually to one of a larger set of similar objects, what does he do? He runs his fingers round its contours searching for distinguishing features, and presses it with different finger combinations to determine its proportions. The stimulation to which he exposes himself is constantly varying and, from the point of view of individual receptors, never the same. Yet he picks up from this variable flux of tactual-kinaesthetic stimulation constant structural properties like curves, edges, and indentations which are translatable into visual properties.

With respect to the search process in perceptual learning, a very important question is what terminates the search and thus selects what is learned. For many years no one questioned the proposition that external reinforcement (e.g. food or shock) is the selective principle for learning things like bar-pressing or choosing one arm of a maze rather than another. But is a distinctive feature selected as relevant because it wins a reward or avoids punishment? Is this the way that higher-order structural relations are detected? Although this might happen in a teaching situation, I do not think it is the true principle of perceptual learning. So much of it goes on very early in life and is necessarily self-regulated. No experimenter is on hand to deliver reinforcement; probably not even a parent could provide it deliberately, since he seldom has any way of knowing just what the child is perceiving.

I think the reinforcement is internal—the *reduction of uncertainty*. Stimulation is not only full of potential information; there is too much of it. There is a limit to what can be processed, and variable, random, irrelevant stimulation leads only to perception of confusion—what someone has referred to as cognitive clutter as opposed to cognitive order. But distinctive features, invariants, and higher-order structure serve the function of reducing uncertainty, taking order and continuity out of chaos and flux. The search for invariants, both low-level contrastive features and high-level order, is the task of perception, while detection of them at once reduces uncertainty and is reinforcing.

Perceptual Development in Species and Individuals

With this brief background of theory, I propose to return to my first question. Is there perceptual development, in the animal series and in the individual, and is it adaptive? Are there trends in what is responded to, as Lashley suggested? In order to give some specific answers, I shall compare two modes of perceiving and give evidence, in both cases, of species differences and of development within the life span.

The two modes are perception of *space and events in space* and the perception of *objects and permanent items*, like written letters, that can be approached and examined closely. I have chosen to contrast these because there is reason to think that in their phylogenetic development there is a considerable difference between them. Localizing oneself in the spatial layout or monitoring events going on in the space around one seem to develop earlier and to be neurologically more primitive than fine-grain identification of objects and outline figures such as letters.

This difference is akin to a distinction within visual perception drawn in a recent paper by Trevarthen (1968), who speaks of "two mechanisms of vision." One of these he calls "ambient vision." It has to do with orientations of the head, postural adjustments, and locomotion in relationship to spatial configurations of contours, surfaces, events, and objects. The other he calls "focal vision." It is

applied to one space and a specific kind of object; it serves to examine and identify.

"Ambient vision in primates," says Trevarthen, "resembles the vision of primitive active vertebrates. . . . At any instant, an extensive portion of the behavioral space around the body is mapped by this ambient visual mode; in primates, somewhat more than a frontal hemisphere is apprehended. With large rotations of the head or whole body, an animal may quickly scan all of the space close to his body and thus obtain a visual impression of the large features in it. The visual mechanism is strongly stimulated by parallax changes caused by translation of the eye, and the receptor mechanism is particularly sensitive to the velocities of displacement of continuities in the light pattern on the retina" (p. 328).

"In contrast with this vision of ambient space, focal vision, enormously developed in diurnal primates, is applied to obtain detailed vision." Its scope at any given instant is restricted, but it is extended over time by sampling movements of the eyes. An area of interest may thus be brought to full attention and "analyzed as if carried close in by a zoom lens" (p. 329).

Focal vision in primates appears to be primarily a function of the cortex. Even in rodents a comparable, though less pronounced, distinction may exist. Schneider (1967) working with hamsters found that ablation of the visual cortex left the animal with only a minimal ability to tell *what* he was seeing, but left nearly intact his ability to find *where* it was. He was unable to discriminate and identify objects, but could localize them in space. Ablation of the superior colliculus produced the opposite effect; the hamster knew what he was seeing but behaved as if he didn't know where it was.

I shall say no more about this neurological distinction, since I have made no contribution to it, but it supports the point I intend to make; that discrimination of events in space is primitive, both phylogenetically and ontogenetically, while development progresses toward differentiation of form in objects and two-dimensional projections. In other words, fine-grain identification of objects or patterns is the later achievement; its development continues over a long time; learning plays a prominent role in it as compared with perceiving the spatial layout and events; and we can expect to find more striking phylogenetic differences.

Perception of Space

Consider, first, development of the perception of space and of events in space. Is there phylogenetic continuity here within the vertebrate phylum? Indeed there is. The similarities between species are far greater than their differences in this respect. We can adduce evidence for this in three important cases— perception of imminent collision (called ''looming''); perception of depth-downward; and perceived constancy of the sizes of things.

Looming can be defined as accelerated magnification of the form of an approaching object. It is an optical event over time. It specifies a future collision (Schiff, Caviness, and Gibson, 1962). If a vehicle or even a small object such as a baseball is perceived as coming directly toward him by a human adult, he ducks or dodges out of the way. Is the perception of imminent collision together with its avoidance instinctive? If so, in what species, and how early? Schiff (1965) constructed an artificial looming situation in which nothing actually approached the animal observer but there was abstract optical information for something approaching.

In Schiff's experiments, a shadow was projected by a shadow-casting device on a large translucent screen in front of the animal. The screen was large enough to fill a wide visual angle. The projected shadow could be made to undergo continuously accelerated magnification until it filled the screen or, on the other hand, continuously decelerating minification. Magnification resulted in a visual impression of an object approaching at a uniform speed. Minification gave a visual impression of an object receding into the distance. The projected silhouette could be varied in form, so as to compare, for instance, jagged contours with smooth ones, or silhouettes of meaningful objects with meaningless ones. Subjects studied included fiddler crabs, frogs, chicks, kittens, monkeys and humans.

The crabs responded to magnification (but not to minification) by running backwards, flinching, or flattening out. Frogs jumped away from the ghostly approaching object. Chicks responded more often to magnification than minification by running, crouching, and hopping. Kittens (28 days old) tended to respond to magnification with struggle and head movements, but the kittens were restrained in holders and well-differentiated avoidance behavior did not show up clearly. Rhesus monkeys (including infants five to eight months of age) were observed in the situation under four conditions (magnification, minification, lightening of the screen, and darkening of the screen). Both young and adult animals withdrew rapidly in response to the approach display, leaping to the rear of the cage. Alarm cries frequently accompanied retreat in the younger animals. The receding display brought responses which might be described as curiosity, but never retreat. The lightening and darkening of the screen had no effect, and this served as a control, that is, a change of mere stimulation as compared with change of magnification.

The adaptiveness of the responses to optical magnification is illustrated by the turtle. Hayes and Saiff (1967) investigated what they termed the "visual alarm reaction" in the turtle. A looming shadow on a screen was used, as in Schiff's experiments. The turtles responded to magnification by withdrawing the head into the shell.

What about a human subject? Schiff measured the galvanic skin reflex in adult human subjects in the looming situation. There was decrease of skin resistance in the majority of subjects for magnification but not for minification. Human infants, Burton White found (1969), began to blink at a rapidly approaching object (with air currents controlled) at about three weeks of age. The reliability of the response increased for another 10 or 12 weeks. Perhaps sensitivity to visual approach of a missile takes this long to mature or be learned in the human infant; but perhaps another indicator response would show that it is picked up even earlier. Some observers claim that attempted head withdrawal to visual looming occurs as early as two weeks in human infants.

Does it matter what shape or object characteristics the expanding silhouette has? Schiff tried objects of different shapes as shadow-casters, but he did not find that silhouettes of these objects had a differential influence on avoidance behavior, as long as there was accelerated magnification of the shadow. It was

the event of looming as such, not an identifiable object, that controlled the avoidant behavior. The functional usefulness of this lack of specificity is obvious; quick avoidance of a fast approaching object is often necessary for avoidance of collision, while fine-grain identification of the object hardly matters.

Now let me give you some phylogenetic comparisons for avoidance of a falling-off place, that is, a drop-off of the ground. Depth downwards is specified in the light to the animal's eye. Does this information by itself cause the animal to avoid it? Some years ago,

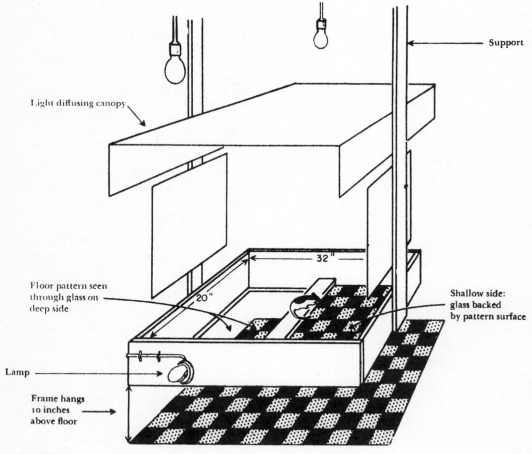

FIGURE 23–2. Drawing of a visual cliff (from Walk and Gibson 1961; copyright by American Psychological Association and reproduced by permission).

Dr. Richard Walk and I constructed an apparatus for answering this question (Gibson and Walk 1960). We called it a "visual cliff." "Cliff," because there was a simulated drop-off downward, and "visual" because we attempted to eliminate all other information for the drop-off. Figure 23–2 shows an apparatus constructed for testing small animals, such as a rat or a chick. The animal is placed on a center board. A checker-board floor extends out from the center board on one side, an inch or two below it. A similar floor is 10 inches or more below on the other side. A sheet of glass extends from the center board, above the floor, an inch or two below the board, so that tactual information for the cliff is eliminated, and air currents and echoes equated.

What is the visual information? Figure 23–3 shows the difference in the density of optical texture from the two checkered surfaces in the light projected to the animal's eye. For some animals binocular parallax might yield differential information about the two sides. The best information, our experiments suggested, was the motion perspective produced by the animal's own movements—especially head movements—as the cliff edge is observed in comparison to the shallow edge. Differences in texture density were eliminated and a monocular animal was used to make this obervation.

Many animal species have been tested on the visual cliff: rodents, birds, turtles, cats (including lions, tigers, and snow leopards), sheep and goats, dogs, and of course primates (Walk and Gibson 1961; Routtenberg and Glickman 1964). All these species, save flying ones or swimming ones, avoided the cliff edge of the apparatus and chose the safe, shallow edge on the basis of visual information alone. Texture must be present on the ground under the animal, however, for a safe surface of support to be perceived. The animal will not walk out upon a homogeneous, untextured surface—he demands "optical support" as well as felt support. This surely has value for survival.

Avoidance of a drop-off and dependence upon optical support must be developmentally primitive. This conclusion is suggested not only by the continuity of the behavior within the vertebrate phylum, but also by ablation experiments and ontogenetic data. When the striate cortex of the cat is removed (Meyer 1963) pattern vision in the sense of identifica-

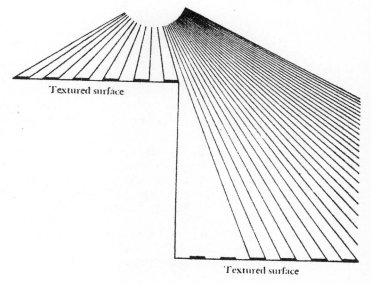

FIGURE 23–3. Cross section of a visual cliff. The diagram shows the pattern of light projected to the subject's eye from a textured surface at a shallow depth below his station point on a center runway and from an identical surface farther below (from Walk and Gibson 1961; copyright by American Psychological Assoc. and reproduced by permission).

Textured surface

Textured surface

tion goes, but a cat will still avoid a cliff, if he can move freely.

Ontogenetically, Walk and I found that cliff avoidance develops very early and, in some species, without any opportunity for learning. Precocial animals such as chicks and goats avoid a cliff a few hours after birth, as soon as they can be tested. Rats reared in the dark avoid a cliff as soon as they are brought out, with no opportunity for preliminary visual experience. Primates cannot be tested at birth, but human infants avoid a cliff as early as they can crawl. Monkeys, like human infants, are carried by their mothers in early infancy. But monkeys placed on the untextured glass without optical support at three days of age (Rosenblum and Cross 1963) showed indications of emotional disturbance (crouching, vocalization, self-clasping, and rocking), whereas there was no disturbance when they were placed on the glass with a texture just below it.

We may conclude that perception of a safe surface in contrast to a drop-off appears early in evolution and early in life, and that little learning may be required for its appearance. It is modified by biased circumstances, such as prolonged dark rearing, but terrestrial animals do not generally have to be taught this useful adaptation.

Now consider my third case: perceived constancy of the sizes of things. Information for size constancy is given normally by motion; motion of the object toward or away from a stationary observer, or movement of the observer toward the object. Since information for constant size—the rule relating size and distance—is given in motion, it should belong with my "primitive" mode of perceiving. Let us see if it does, if there is continuity over species and early development without any marked dependence on learning with external reinforcement.

As for continuity among animal species, size constancy has been demonstrated in the chimpanzee, by Köhler (1915); in the monkey by Klüver (1933) and by Locke (1937); in the cat by Gunter (1951) and by Freeman (1968); in the weanling rat (Heller 1968); in the duckling (Pastore 1958); and in fish (Herter 1953). It is

no surprise to the thoughtful biologist that animals other than man exhibit size constancy. How indeed could they locomote or seize things accurately if the apparent sizes of things around them were constantly shrinking or expanding as distance changed with the target's movement or the observer's position?

Is learning involved in perceiving things as constant in size? It might well be, since the conditions for extracting the invariant depend on motion of an object or of the observer in relation to it. The mother's face approaches the baby as she bends to pick it up; the baby moves his hand toward and away from his eyes and moves them together and apart, for hours at a time. These are guaranteed opportunities for presenting him with appropriately structured stimulation. But such learning would have to take place very early, for Bower (1966) has found evidence of size constancy as young as two months in the human infant. He used the method of operant conditioning, the response being a leftward turning of the head. The infant was trained to respond thus to a 30-cm. white cube placed one meter from his eyes. The reinforcement for the head-turning response was an experimenter popping up and "peek-a-booing" at the infant and then disappearing again (an ingenious and, it turns out, remarkably effective reinforcement. The infant learns to do something to *get a perception*). After training, three new stimuli were introduced for generalization tests. These were the 30-cm. cube placed 3 meters away; a 90-cm. cube placed 1 meter away; and the 90-cm. cube placed 3 meters away (see Figure 23–4). These and the original training situation were presented in a counter-balanced order.

The conditioned stimulus situation would be expected to elicit the most head-turnings, and the one appearing to the infant most like it, the next most. If the infant has size constancy, one would expect the cube identical with the training one to evoke the next most responses, even when it is farther away (test stimulus 1). If size constancy hasn't been attained, one might expect the cube projecting the same-sized retinal image (test stimulus 3) to elicit most response. The infants, in practice, responded to

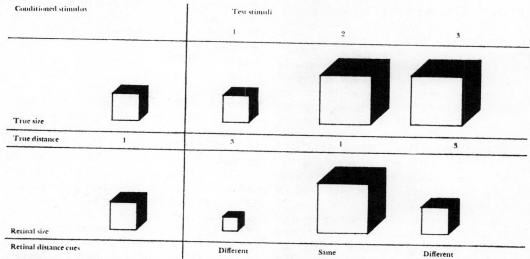

FIGURE 23–4. Schematic representation of cubes of different sizes placed at different distances in Bower's investigation of size constancy in infants (from "The visual world of infants" by T. G. R. Bower. Copyright © 1966 by Scientific American, Inc. All rights reserved.)

test stimulus 1 next most often after the training situation, evidence that they perceived the cube in its true, objective size. Next most often came the larger cube placed at the same distance as the training cube; and last of all, the larger cube placed at 3 meters where it projected the identical-sized retinal image.

Does this result mean that *no* learning is involved in the development of size constancy? Definitely not, since even eight weeks gives a lot of opportunity for visual experience. But it means that any learning could not have involved association with specific motor acts, such as reaching a certain distance or walking so many paces. But perceived motion of an object could provide an opportunity for discovery of the rule relating projective size of object to nearness of the object. Dark-reared rats (Heller 1968) did not exhibit size constancy when first brought into the light, despite normal performance on the visual cliff. Some visual experiences with objects moving in space may be necessary, therefore, for size constancy to develop, but it does so very early. Later changes, appearing when judgmental methods are used (Piaget 1961), probably indicate development of a more

analytical attitude toward perceiving objects rather than the mere localizing of things in their true sizes.

Perception of Objects

Now, let me turn to my other class of perceptions—the fine-grain identification of objects, and the use of coded stimuli to substitute for them. Is there continuity over species and early appearance as there is with the spatial perceptions?

There is continuity, yes, but in this instance there is a good case for a striking evolutionary change, and also for a long course of perceptual learning in the individual. The human child must learn the distinctive features of the objects, representations, and symbolic items that human life requires him to differentiate.

What about the *phylogeny* of object identification? Certainly animals identify some objects at quite an early age. The herring gull chick identifies by a spot of red the beak of its parent hovering over it. This information is referred to by the ethologists as an "innate releaser." Releasers seem in many cases to be very simple unlearned signals for the discharging of a fixed unlearned pattern of responses, like the chemical signal that releases attack behavior in some species of snake. A mere trace of the chemical in a box will bring the attack. Sometimes the effective stimulus pattern is more complex, as is the visual pattern that constitutes "owlness" and releases mobbing behavior in the chaffinch, or the quite complex and informative song patterns of many birds, but the role of learning is still minimal in these cases.

Do we have studies of learned object identification in any animals but primates? Of course, the studies of imprinting in precocial animals come to mind. Certain properties of an object like high brightness contrast and motion release in the newborn animal a following response, and following the moving object serves, presumably, to "impress" its features on the "mind" of the subject so that he will later discriminate it from other objects and approach it rather than others. Here, in a manner insuring that the precocial animal will take to his parent or at least to his species, is a very immediate kind of learning that seems to contain the rudiments of perceptual learning. It is not a matter of association of stimulus and response; the response is ready to go at once and, besides, recognition can be measured by other responses than following. There is no external reinforcement; the mother can butt an infant goat away and he will follow her just the same. What is learned is typical of perceptual learning: an increased specificity of response to visual and auditory stimulation characteristic of the releasing object. To what extent there is increased differentiation we really don't know, for early imprinting is quickly followed by opportunities for learning to discriminate feature-contrasts that insure more precise differentiation.

We can study this latter process most easily in the young human animal, so I shall trace some of the steps in his learning to differentiate complex objects in his environment. Does he begin, like the precocial animal, with innate attention to high-contrast visual stimulation and to motion? Some people think so and like to compare the turning of the eyes or head toward a voice or a shiny moving thing to imprinting. One of the first and most prominent objects in an infant's world is the face of his caretaker. Studies of development of recognition of a human face tell us much (Gibson 1969, Ch. 16). At first, it appears to be motion of the head (like a nod) that is compelling, but very shortly the eyes emerge as a prominent feature—the dominant feature for a discriminative response. They are bright, and they move. After a time, the facial contour, the contours of brow and nose around the eyes, and later the mouth (especially in motion) differentiate as critical features. But not until nearly four months must these features be present in an invariant and "face-like" relation for the recognition response to occur. At four months, a "realistic" face is smiled at more. Not until six months are individual faces differentiated, and not until much later still are facial expressions. We know little as yet about how this learning goes on, but it is perceptual learning; there is increasing differentiation of more and more specific stimulus information. Motor responses play little or no role, nor does reinforcement.

"Learning-to-learn" about objects was demonstrated in a long-term experiment with infants 6 to 12 months old by Ling (1941). She presented infants with a pair of solid wooden objects, differently shaped. Both were colored bright yellow and were of a graspable size. They were presented to the infant on a board within reaching distance. One was fastened tightly to the board. The other was removable and was furthermore sweet to taste, having been dipped in a saccharine solution. The infant learned over a period of days to reach at once for the shape that was sweetened. Then five series of problems were presented to him. The first series had four problems: circle vs. cross, circle vs. triangle, circle vs. square, and circle vs. oval. After successive mastery of these, the child progressed to a series in which one of the forms was rotated; then a series in which sizes were transformed; a fourth, in which the number of "wrong" blocks was increased; and a fifth, in which the positive and negative shapes were reversed. There was evidence of more and more rapid learning as the series continued, as well as transfer of discriminations with rotation and change of size. What were the babies learning that transferred? Distinctive features of the shapes they were comparing, to be sure, but something more general too, Ling thought. They learned search strategies of systematic observation and comparison, "attention to form differences, rather than improvement in form discrimination *per se*." Compared with control babies of the same age, they made a more immediate and minute examination of the stimulus patterns and inhibited extraneous bodily movement.

Now I want to finish with the top-level achievement of fine-grain identification—the identification of written symbols. Only man does this and only a well-grown, well-tutored man at that. Monkeys can indeed learn to discriminate a pair of fairly small line drawings from one another, but they are much slower at this task and make many more errors than human children of four or five (Hicks and Hunton 1964; Hunton and Hicks 1965). Both phylogenetically and ontogenetically, this is the peak of perceptual achievement. Here we find that education is most essential. How is one letter discriminated from another? I think by learning the distinctive features for the set of letters. There is evidence to show that this is the way letters really are discriminated, that there is a set of distinctive features, not idiosyncratic to an individual perceiver or to a given graphic character but characterizing the set and permitting each letter to be distinguished by its unique pattern of features within the set.

The set of letters, in this case, must be differentiated as a set from other outline drawings or similar things. Linda Lavine, at Cornell, found that this is done quite early. Children from three to five were shown a systematically chosen sample of graphic items: handwritten Roman letters, numerals, lower-case letters, cursive handwriting, artificial letters, scribbles, and simple line drawings of objects—a flower, a stick man, a child's attempt at drawing a house or a face, and so on. The children were asked to "tell me which of these are writing." Most children of three and four could separate

the drawings of objects from the rest, but not the scribbling. Most children of five could differentiate the numbers and letters, whatever type or case, from both scribbling and pictures although they could seldom identify individual numbers or letters. Habits of observing differences between small objects, like those shown by Ling's babies, probably carry over from object perception to the perception of line drawings, and the set of graphic symbols is somehow differentiated from other marks on paper before individual items can be identified.

To discover what features are actually noted in comparing letters and identifying them, we performed a number of discrimination experiments using both children and adults (Gibson, Schapiro, and Yonas 1968). These experiments, which simply required the subject to decide whether a pair of letters was the same or different, allowed us to construct a "confusion matrix" for a set of letters. The time taken to judge same or different and the errors were entered in matrices to show which pairs were most often confused and which least. Then the matrices were analyzed to find what proximities or clusters underlie the structure of the matrix. This tells us what features are being used by the observer when he must decide whether a given pair is the same or different.

The method of analysis was a hierarchical cluster analysis (Johnson 1967). It looks progressively (in steps) for the most compact and isolable clusters, then for the next most compact, and so on till one winds up with loose clusters and finally the whole set. The results can be turned upside down and diagrammed in a tree structure. Figure 23–5 shows on the left the tree resulting from an analysis of 48 adult subjects' latency data for 9 letters. The first split separates the "sharp" letters with diagonality from all the others. On the left branch, the "round" letters, C and G, next split off from the others. At the next branch, the square right-angular letters E and F split off from letters differentiated from them by curvature. The error data for these letters with the same subjects reveal an identical structure.

On the right of Figure 23–5 is the hierarchical structure for 60 seven-year-old children, with

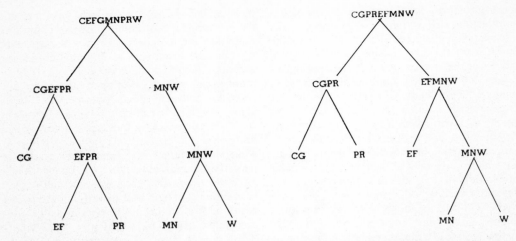

FIGURE 23–5. Tree structure yielded by confusions in making same-different judgments. The structure on the left was obtained with adult subjects; that on the right with seven-year-old children.

the same letters. It is similar to the adults' but not quite the same. The first split is a simple curve-straight one. On the second branch, the round letters are split off from the P and R. The square letters are now split off from those with diagonality. This is very neat, and it suggests to me that children at this stage are doing straightforward sequential processing of features, while adults have progressed to a more Gestalt-like processing, picking up higher orders of structure given by redundancy and tied relations. This is speculative, but it would be a highly adaptive kind of development, achieving the highest level of differentiation with the greatest economy of processing.

Conclusion

Is the development of perception an adaptive process? It is as much so as the development of locomotion. Nature seems to have insured first the means of detecting the information needed for getting around and avoiding such dangers as obstacles, pitfalls, and missiles. Discrimination of objects by simple signs based on single physical characteristics of high vividness is primitive too. But fine-grain differentiation of multidimensional complex sets of objects is high in the evolutionary scheme and in development, a process where adaptation is achieved only through education.

REFERENCES

Bower, T. G. R. 1966. The visual world of infants. *Scient. Amer. 215:*80–92.

Freeman, R. B. 1968. Perspective determinants of visual size-constancy in binocular and monocular cats. *Amer. J. Psychol. 81:*67–73.

Gibson, E. J., and R. D. Walk. 1960. The "visual cliff." *Scient. Amer. 202:*64–71.

Gibson, E. J., F. Schapiro, and A. Yonas. 1968. Confusion matrices for graphic patterns obtained with a latency measure. Pp. 76–96 in Final report, Project No. 5-1213, Contract No. OE6-10-156, Cornell University and the U.S. Office of Education.

Gibson, J. J. 1962. Observations on active touch. *Psychol. Rev. 69:*477–91.

Gibson, J. J. 1966. *The senses considered as perceptual systems.* Boston: Houghton-Mifflin.

Gunter, R. 1951. Visual size constancy in the cat. *Brit. J. Psychol. 42:*288–93.

Hayes, W. N., and E. I. Saiff. 1967. Visual alarm reactions in turtles. *Anim. Behav. 15:102*–06.

Heller, D. P. 1968. Absence of size constancy in visually deprived rats. *J. Comp. Physiol. Psychol. 65:*336–39.

Herter, K. 1953. *Die Fischdressuere und ihre sinnes physiologischen Grundlagen.* Berlin: Akademie-Verlag.

Hicks, L. H., and V. D. Hunton. 1964. The relative dominance of form and orientation in discrimination learning by monkeys and children. *Psychon. Sci. 1:*411–12.

Hull, C. L. 1943. *Principles of behavior.* New York: Appleton.

Hunton, V. D., and L. H. Hicks. 1965. Discrimination of figural orientation by monkeys and children. *Percept. Mot. Skills 21:*55 –59.

Johnson, S. C. 1967. Hierarchical clustering schemes. *Psychometrika 32:*241–54.

Klüver, H. 1933. *Behavior mechanisms in monkeys.* Chicago: Univ. Chicago Press.

Köhler, W. 1915. Untersuchungen am Schimpansen und am Haushuhn. *Abh. preuss. Akad. Wiss.* (phys.-math.) No. 3, 1–70.

Lashley, K. S. 1938. Experimental analysis of instinctive behavior. *Psychol. Rev. 45:*445–71.

Lashley, K. S. 1949. Persistent problems in the evolution of mind. *Quart. Rev. Biol. 24:*28–42.

Ling, B. C. 1941. Form discrimination as a learning cue in infants. *Comp. Psychol. Monogr. 17,* Whole No. 86.

McVay, S. 1967. How hears the dolphin? *Princeton Alumni Weekly,* October, pp. 6–9.

Meyer, P. M. 1963. Analysis of visual behavior in cats with extensive neocortical ablations. *J. Comp. Physiol. Psychol. 56:*397–401.

Pastore, N. 1958. Form perception and size constancy in the duckling. *J. Psychol. 45:*259–61.

Piaget, J. 1961. *Les mécanismes perceptifs.* Paris: Presses Universitaires de France.

Romanes, G. J. 1893. *Mental evolution in man.* New York: D. Appleton.

Romanes, G. J. 1895. *Mental evolution in animals.* New York: D. Appleton.

Rosenblum, L. A., and H. A. Cross. 1963. Performance of neonatal monkeys on the visual cliff situation. *Amer. J. Psychol. 76:*318–20.

Routtenberg, A., and S. E. Glickman. 1964. Visual cliff behavior in undomesticated rodents, land and aquatic turtles, and cats (panthera). *J. Comp. Physiol. Psychol. 58:*143–46.

Schiff, W. 1965. The perception of impending collision: A study of visually directed avoidant behavior. *Psychol. Monogr. 79,* Whole No. 604.

Schiff, W., J. A. Caviness, and J. J. Gibson. 1962. Persistent fear responses in rhesus monkeys to the optical stimulus of "looming." *Science 136:*982–83.

Schneider, G. E. 1967. Contrasting visuomotor functions of tectum and cortex in the Golden Hamster. *Psychol. Forsch. 31:*52–62.

Trevarthen, C. B. 1968. Two mechanisms of vision in primates. *Psychol. Forsch. 31:*299–337.

Walk, R. D., and E. J. Gibson. 1961. A comparative and analytical study of visual depth perception. *Psychol. Monogr. 75,* No. 15.

White, B. L. In press, 1969. Child development research: An edifice without a foundation. *Merrill-Palmer Quarterly.*

24. ECOLOGICAL AND CULTURAL FACTORS IN SPATIAL PERCEPTUAL DEVELOPMENT*

J. W. BERRY

Abstract. A model was proposed in which spatial perceptual development was considered as a function of ecology, and as a function of mediating variables (cultural, socialization, nutritional, and genetic) which were themselves viewed as functionally adapted to ecology. Data on visual discrimination and spatial skill development were reported for eight subsistence-level samples, and were considered to support the proposed model. Some interactions among the variables, and age and sex differences in the data were discussed.

It is once again a legitimate enterprise for behavioural scientists to investigate the possible role of ecology in shaping human behaviour. Long gone is the environmental determinism which was so easily discarded; workers in both psychology and anthropology have returned now to an ecological perspective, taking care, however, to detail their enquiry and to avoid facile generalizations. For psychology, Brunswik (Hammond, 1966), Barker (1965, 1968) and Wohlwill (1966, 1970), and for anthropology, Steward (1955), Helm (1962), Rappaport (1967) and Vayda (1969) have all attempted to comprehend the nature of ecological-behavioural interactions.

In its weakest form the approach merely

*Paper delivered at a Symposium on Cross-Cultural Research held by the Centre for the Study of Human Abilities, Memorial University, St. John's, Newfoundland, October 29 and 30th, 1970.

The paper is an empirical and theoretical extension of work originally published in 1966, and includes data and ideas stemming from recent field work in Australia and New Guinea. A further extension is being made in the form of a monograph, exploring more fully than is possible here the interaction in the data and their theoretical implications.

The research was made possible by grants from the Canada Council, the Government of Quebec, University Research Committees of the University of Sydney and of Queen's University, and by the Australian Research Grants committee.

From the *Canadian Journal of Behavioural Science*, 1971, *3*, 324–336. Copyright 1971 by the Canadian Psychological Association. Reprinted by permission of the author and the publisher.

asserts that behavioural and ecological variables interact in some systematic way (cf. Vayda & Rappaport, 1968), and in its strongest, (not currently espoused) it would assert some ecological determination of behaviour. In its moderate forms, it asserts the ecological limitation of behavioural development (e.g. Meggars, 1954), the ecological source of the probability of behaviour (e.g. Brunswik, op. cit.) or the behavioural adaptation to ecological pressures; it is this latter version which will be explored in this paper.

For psychologists the role of ecological factors is basic to our science (e.g. in Stimulus-Response theory); however, we have usually explored these ecological-behavioural interactions from a molecular point of view. The molar approach, which characterises the present study, examines not only the fleeting ecology (the Stimulus) but also the long-term impact on the development of the organism of the persistent and surrounding ecology, more usually termed the physical environment.

The model in Figure 24–1 exemplifies this molar approach. The overriding arrow indicates the conventional stimulus impinging on the individual, as well as the culturally unmediated expectancies based on previous interactions with the environment. The underriding arrow illustrates the potential transformation that the organism can make on his physical surrounds, either through the conventional Response or through group activity such as Technology. The intermediate bonds indicate four of the numer-

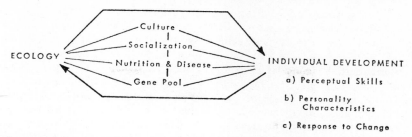

FIGURE 24-1. Model relating Individual development to Ecological and other variables.

ous possible mediating factors present in all mankind:

(i) *Culture*: within this model, culture is viewed as a group's adaptation to recurrent ecological pressures (cf. Vayda, 1969) and as a contributor to the direction of development of individual human beings. It is also considered to act as a mediator (filter) of the ecology for individuals. In this study particular attention will be paid to language and technology.

(ii) *Socialization,* although technically a part of culture, is singled out for special attention because of its dominant role in shaping human behaviour, and because of its known adaptive relationship (in subsistence-level societies) to ecological variables (Barry, Child, & Bacon, 1959). Both techniques of socialization and its content will be considered in this study.

(iii) & (iv) *Nutrition, Disease and Gene pool* are included in the model because of their generally-accepted role in mediating ecology and individual development. Aspects of nutrition and disease considered most important include protein availability and parasites (Cravioto, 1968), while the Gene Pool is held to be adaptive to the ecological pressures, and in turn a contributor to group and individual differences.

This model is unabashedly *functional,* emphasizing as it must *interactions* rather than *causal sequences.* It of course shares the accepted deficiencies of all functional analyses (Collins, 1965), but gains as a relatively powerful heuristic device for exploring ecological, cultural and behavioural interactions.

It is not possible in a single paper to explore all the possible varieties of individual development; to illustrate the model then, one aspect only has been chosen—visual spatial skill development. Other data are also available on selected value and personality attributes, and on predisposition to acculturative stress, but these will be reported elsewhere.

The Argument

Originally (Berry, 1966) the argument was that the "ecological demands" placed on a group of people, plus their cultural adaptation to this ecology ("cultural aids") would lead to the development of certain perceptual skills. Specifically, it was argued, persons who inhabit ecologies where hunting was the mode of sustenance should develop perceptual discrimination and spatial skills adapted to the ecological demands of hunting:

"1. He must first of all in order to hunt effectively develop the ability to isolate slight variation in visual stimulation from a relatively featureless array; he must learn to be aware of minute detail.

2. Secondly, in order to navigate effectively in this environment he must learn to organize these small details into a spatial awareness, an awareness of his present location in relation to objects around him." (Berry, 1966, p. 212) Further it was argued that "cultural aids" such as language coding, arts and crafts, and socialization would be adapted to these ecological demands, and assist in the development of the requisite skills.

The strategy was to test for differences between two cultural groups (Temne and Eskimo) which were greatly ecologically discrepant, the Eskimo experiencing to a large degree the demands of a hunting ecology while the Temne did so not at all. Visual Discrimination and Spatial test results were so divergent (all differences were significant beyond the .01 level) that an overall relationship was difficult to comprehend; were the data on the same dimension at all? Further, considerations of "functional equivalence" (Berry, 1969a) led to the doubting of the usefulness of the original strategy, where ecological divergence was so great. Hence the present strategy is to seek out and rank a number of samples from cultural groups on the ecology dimension, and to examine the nature of the relationship between the ecological and behavioural (perceptual) variables.

The original procedure of analysing the cultural aids as adaptive to the ecology and mediating perceptual skill development has been retained. For language aids, it is argued that the presence of "geometrical spatial" terms would assist in transmitting spatial and orienting concepts and information, and that their presence in a language would be consistent with the spatial demands placed on that group by their ecology (cf. Whorfian Hypothesis). For arts and crafts aids, it is argued that their use would assist the early learning of spatial manipulations and the discrimination of detail, and the development of these techniques would be consistent with the ecological demands.

For socialization, the argument is necessarily more complex, since a somewhat arbitrary distinction is made between *content* and *technique* (although it will be argued later that they are functionally related).

With regard to the *content* of the socialization process, Barry, Child, and Bacon (1959) have shown that there is a significant tendency for child rearing practices to relate to a specific economic variable: the degree to which food is accumulated at the subsistence-level. In detail, they were able to demonstrate that in high food accumulation societies (agricultural and pastoral), there was a strong tendency to emphasize responsibility and obedience during socialization, while in low food accumulation societies (hunting and gathering), achievement, self-reliance and independence were emphasized. Their rationale centred on the functional adaptation of child rearing practices in order to mold adults with personality characteristics best suited to their particular economic pursuits. Despite criticism (Whiting, 1968) of this study, Barry (1969) was able to confirm these relationships while meeting the criticisms.

With regard to the *technique* of socialization, Witkin and his co-workers (1962) have been able to demonstrate consistent relationships between methods of child rearing and "cognitive style." Generally, techniques employed to achieve mother-child separation and to control aggressive behavior are related to the "psychological differentiation" attained by a growing child. Specifically, for our perceptual concerns, "field-independence" has been shown to stem from the encouragement of responsibility and self assertion and by parental stimulation of the child's curiosity and interests, and is characterized by an "analytic" approach to a perceptual field. At the opposite pole, "field-dependence" stems from a stress on conformity, from arbitrary or impulsive discipline, and from the use of irrational threats to control aggression, and is characterized by a "global" approach to a perceptual field.

Within a functional model, one would expect to find content and technique related to the socialization goals of a particular cultural group. That is to say, one would not expect to discover a society in which independence and self-reliance are conveyed as goals by a harsh, restrictive method of socialization. Nor, conversely, would one expect to discover societies in which conformity is taught by a method characterized by a stimulation of the child's own interests and of his curiosity. This functional expectation is open to empirical check and will be examined for each society in this study.

With respect to the role of genetic factors, no data have been collected in this study. Since it is proposed however that cultural and genetic factors are functionally adapted to ecological demands, no opposition is envisaged between these two variables in their mediation of perceptual development. That is to say, for the purposes of the model, it is not necessary to assess the relative operation of these two variables, although for broader purposes one might wish to do so. The focus upon socio-cultural variables (to the exclusion of the genetic) in this study reflects the lack of competence, but not necessarily the bias, of the investigator. Sample characteristics pertaining to the nutrition and disease variables were observed within the communities, although no individual data were taken. Generally data on the adequacy of nutrition (especially of protein) and on the presence of disease (especially of eye problems and parasitic infections) are used to predict performance on tests of perceptual development.

The argument may now be summarized: hunting peoples are expected to possess good visual discrimination and spatial skill, and their cultures are expected to be supportive of the development of these skills through the presence of a high number of "geometrical spatial" concepts, a highly developed and generally shared arts and crafts production, and socialization practices whose content emphasizes independence and self reliance, and whose techniques are supportive and encouraging of separate development. Implicit in this argument is the expectation that as hunting diminishes in importance across samples ranked in terms of this ecology dimension, the discrimination and spatial skills will diminish, as will each of the three cultural aids.

Method

To assess this argument, eight samples of subsistence-level peoples were studied; four were termed "traditional", living as close to traditional ways as could be found, while four were termed "transitional", comprising samples undergoing Westernization. In general the two kinds of samples were employed to assess the impact of acculturation; in two of the four areas (Sierra Leone & Baffin Island), the traditional and transitional samples were of the same culture, allowing a further assessment— that of persistence of psychological and cultural characteristics beyond the subsistence-level. Table 24–1 indicates the area, culture, and numbers in each of the eight samples. Two groups of Scots were also administered the tests in order that the battery data might be related to scores from better-known Western samples.

The data were collected in communities considered to be representative of their societies, and in each community, samples were drawn so that males and females were approximately equally represented. The age range 10 to 70 years was also sampled, with approximately equal proportions in age ranges: 10–15, 16–20, 21–30, 31–40, and over 40. These two sampling aims were set so that sex and age differences could be adequately examined. In all communities, interpreter/assistants were employed to assist in the sampling, interviewing and testing. This was carried out largely in the traditional language, in an attempt to establish and maintain adequate communication.

In addition to the main dependent variables (tests of discrimination and spatial skills) individual data were collected on severity of socialization, years of education (if any), religion, language, near and far visual acuity and colour blindness; other dependent variables in the same battery have been reported on previously (Berry, 1967, 1968, 1969b). Community data were also gathered to assess degree of

TABLE 24–1
Sample Locations

AREA AND CULTURE	RURAL/TRADITIONAL	n	URBAN/TRANSITIONAL	n	TOTAL n
Sierra Leone (Temne)	Mayola	90	Port Loko	32	122
New Guinea (Indigene)	Telefomin	40	Hanuabada	30	70
Australia (Aborigine)	Santa Teresa	30	Yarrabah	30	60
Baffin Island (Eskimo)	Pond Inlet	91	Frobisher Bay	31	122
Scotland	Inverkeilor	62	Edinburgh	60	122
Total n		313		183	496

Westernization (to ensure correct Traditional vs Transitional placement), ecology (to ensure correct placement on the ecology dimension), typical socialization (as a check on self reported experiences), arts and crafts, linguistic distinctions made about "geometrical-spatial" concepts, and typical diet and disease (to assess the other mediating variables). Analyses of these individual and group data are too detailed to report here, and are being prepared as part of a monograph (Berry nd). In general, the contextual (both individual and group gathered) data are internally consistent and are supportive of the proposed model. That is to say community observations support the individual reports with respect to socialization. Further, all mediating variables vary consistently with the ecological setting; rank orderings of these variables for the four samples within the Traditional and Transitional community groups are identical with the rank ordering on the ecological dimension (degree of food accumulation and its concomitant, the presence of hunting).

The major dependent variables were a tachistoscopic test of visual discrimination ability and three tests of spatial skill. The discrimination test consisted of a series of cards with india-ink figures on them, each with increasingly large gaps (from 1 mm to 15 mm) placed randomly in their sides. The smallest gap detected and drawn on paper was taken as the measure of discrimination ability, and the score is expressed in millimetres of gap detected. For all Ss, tests were conducted in a portable tachistoscope (mercury-cadmium battery operated, with a camera shutter set at 20 milliseconds) and the target was 25 cm from the eyes. Since visual acuity (tested by the Landolt Rings) did not differ across samples, ability to detect these random gaps was taken as a measure of discrimination ability, similar to that demanded in a hunting ecology.

The three tests of spatial skills were Kohs Blocks (Original 17 design series), a short form (6 items) of the Embedded Figures Test (Witkin 1950); and the Ravens Matrices (Series A, Ab, B; Raven, 1956). Although all these tests undoubtedly have characteristics other than spatial, it is contended that these are largely spatial in nature. In the case of Kohs Blocks, time limits were extended 30 seconds for each design 1 to 10, while the Matrices were untimed.

Results

Discrimination Skill results are presented in Figure 24–2, while Spatial scores are given in Figures 24–3, 24–4, and 24–5. A low score on

TABLE 24–2
Sex Differences in Three Tests of Spatial Ability

Traditional	N	Kohs mean	Eft mean	Matrices mean
Mayola				
males	45	8.8	55.5	13.7
females	45	3.9	0	11.4
$p <$		.01	.01	.01
Telefomin				
males	20	11.9	56.4	15.7
females	20	7.1	0	13.7
$p <$		.05	.01	NS
Santa Teresa				
males	20	41.8	595.6	22.3
females	10	35.9	575.8	25.0
$p <$		NS	NS	NS
Pont Inlet				
males	46	76.8	720.0	27.0
females	45	80.6	754.1	26.6
$p <$		NS	NS	NS
Inverkeilor				
males	27	91.7	756.0	29.7
females	35	89.1	738.7	29.4
$p <$		NS	NS	NS
Port Loko				
males	20	17.9	228.8	14.1
females	12	11.8	15.6	13.6
$p <$		NS	.01	NS
Yarrabah				
males	15	48.6	718.2	26.4
females	15	53.5	529.7	23.0
$p <$		NS	NS	NS
Hanuabada				
males	18	62.2	661.9	24.8
females	12	63.3	716.1	28.1
$p <$		NS	NS	NS
Frobisher Bay				
males	16	92.8	794.0	29.1
females	15	86.9	797.7	28.7
$p <$		NS	NS	NS
Edinburgh				
males	31	98.4	881.4	31.8
females	29	82.6	745.1	29.9
$p <$		.05	.01	NS

the discrimination test indicates that a small gap (expressed in millimetres) could be detected, while a high score indicates that only larger gaps were noticed. For the three spatial tests, a high score indicates high spatial skill. In each table Traditional sample scores are given on the left, while the Transitional scores are on the right. The ranking on the ecology dimension is of course standard throughout the four tables with Mayola and Pond Inlet designating the high and low food accumulating extremes within the Traditional samples, and Port Loko

and Frobisher Bay in the same respective positions within the Transitional samples. Telefomin (New Guinea) and Santa Teresa (Arunta Aboriginal) are high-medium and low-medium respectively in the former samples, while Yarrabah (coastal Aborigine) and Hanuabada (coastal New Guinea) are high-medium and low-medium respectively for the latter samples. Note that the Traditional and Transitional Aborigine and New Guinea samples reverse their positions on the ecology dimension, there being little ecological con-

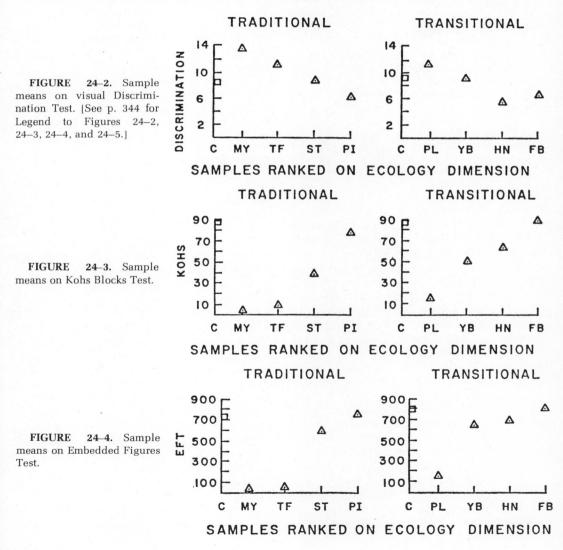

FIGURE 24–2. Sample means on visual Discrimination Test. [See p. 344 for Legend to Figures 24–2, 24–3, 24–4, and 24–5.]

FIGURE 24–3. Sample means on Kohs Blocks Test.

FIGURE 24–4. Sample means on Embedded Figures Test.

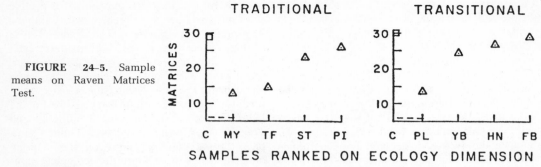

FIGURE 24-5. Sample means on Raven Matrices Test.

SAMPLES RANKED ON ECOLOGY DIMENSION

Legend

	Traditional
MY	Mayola
TF	Telefomin
ST	Santa Teresa
PI	Pond Inlet
C	Comparison (Inverkeilor)

	Traditional
PL	Port Loko
YB	Yarrabah
HN	Hanuabada
FB	Frobisher Bay
C	Comparison (Edinburgh)

tinuity between central and coastal peoples in these two culture areas. In each Figure the scores of the comparison (Scottish) samples appear adjacent to the y-axis.

Sex differences, especially in spatial ability, have received previous attention (Berry, 1966; MacArthur, 1967). Table 24–2 provides mean scores for each sex and level of significance for three tests of spatial skill. It is apparent that, contrary to usual findings stemming from Western or Industrialized samples, there is no general superiority of males in tests of spatial ability in these data. The most that may be said is that a pattern of superiority emerges either where male-female role separations are strong (as in urban-industrial society) or where there is no high development in these skills generally, as among the Temne and Telefomin peoples.

Age trends were also previously examined for the Temne and Eskimo data (Berry, 1966, p. 226–227) and may be further explored here. It was considered that where ecological demands for these skills is low, relatively flat de-

velopmental curves (from ages 10 to 70) would appear for the three spatial tests. This expectation (which had previously been expressed by Ferguson, 1954, p. 107) is borne out in both Temne and Telefomin samples; they have relatively little growth of these skills with age, past a basic ability to produce a numerical score on these tests. For the other samples, however, the usual inverted U curve appears across this age range.

Discussion

The original strategy was to test for the significance of differences between the ecological extremes within the traditional and transitional groups (Temne and Eskimo); in all tests (t tests for discrimination and spatial ability) the Eskimo scored significantly higher at the .01 level (Berry, 1966, p. 216, 220). The present approach to the data is merely to note firstly that these extremes are significantly different, and secondly that when samples which are ecologically intermediate are included, the pattern of the data displays only a single error in the rank ordering of the dependent variables (Hanuabada and Frobisher Bay on discrimination ability). Such a patterning of data is taken to confirm, without statistical appraisal, the general expectation that across a grading of food accumulation and hunting, peoples will attain the levels of visual discrimination and spatial ability appropriate to the ecological demands.

Comment upon specific characteristics of each graph must await specific analyses of the contextual data; however the single error in ranking should receive some attention now. The major predicted determinant of discrimination ability lies in the hunting demands typically placed on persons; however transitional groups typically perform slightly better on this test than traditional peoples (even though hunting activity usually is diminished), and this may be attributable to the effects of Western education, especially literacy. Given the much higher average education of the Hanuabadans in relation to the Frobisher Bay Eskimo (7.3 vs 3.0 years), the reversal in the rank ordering is not so surprising.

To what extent do these data support the proposed model? As noted . . . mediating variables of socialization, arts and crafts and language are considered to be related to the ecological dimension in the predicted rank orderings. This conclusion has resulted from field observation and from ethnographic or linguistic reports, and are supported, in the case of socialization, by self reporting from subjects in the various samples. That is, the Temne and Telefomin respondents report (and are reported in the literature as having) harsh techniques of socialization, emphasizing conformity and reliance upon the group; at the other extreme the Eskimo and Arunta have decidedly lenient and individually supportive socialization, while the other samples are rank ordered as they are on the ecological dimension. Further, within each sample, both individual and group data on socialization content and technique betray no gross inconsistencies between these two aspects of the socialization process. In each sample observed and reported content (including aims) of child rearing are consistent with the techniques employed. For arts and crafts practices, Eskimo and Arunta peoples generally are well-known internationally for exhibiting skill in artistic design and execution, while Temne and Telefomin output is of relatively poor quality and tends to be produced by only a few specialists among these peoples. Finally, the possession of geometrical-spatial terms in the languages of these samples is rank ordered consistently with the ecological dimension. It is

therefore considered that these mediating variables are adapted to the ecological demands made upon these groups, and are available to the appropriate extent for the nurturing of the discrimination and spatial skills demanded by the group's ecology.

Although no data have been collected on disease, nutrition or gene pool, the functionally adaptive nature of protein nutrients may be illustrated. We know that a sufficient level of protein is necessary for perceptual/cognitive development (Cravioto, 1968; Dawson, 1966, 1967), and from our hypothesis, we expect that there is a stronger requirement for perceptual development among some peoples than among others. Specifically, we would expect from the model that to hunt effectively, sufficient proteins should be available; and we note, that within the ecological dimension as proposed, it is precisely the hunters who get the protein. In a sense then those who need the protein most to exist in a particular ecology have it available through hunting (Eskimo and Arunta), while those who need it least have lesser amounts available through reliance on rice or cassava farming (Temne and Telefomin).

With respect to the dependent variables, visual discrimination and spatial skills, it is apparent from the data that the visual skills are developed to a degree predictable from an analysis of the ecological demands facing the group, and the cultural aids developed by them. Further it is apparent that there are relationships between the ecological and psychological variables which are more than dichotomized ones; they appear to covary in a systematic way (cf. weak version of ecological-behavioural interaction) and can be demonstrated to be adaptive to the ecological demands placed on the group (cf. moderate version of ecological-behavioural interaction). Finally the psychological underpinnings of technological development, often isolated as spatial ability, are shown to develop in relation to an ecology, which by way of technological change is open to change itself.

REFERENCES

Barker, R. G. Explorations in ecological psychology. *American Psychologist*, 1965, *20*, 1–14.
Barker, R. G. *Ecological Psychology*. Stanford: Stanford University Press, 1968.

Barry, H. Cross-cultural research with matched pairs of societies. *Journal of Social Psychology*, 1969, *79*, 25–33.

Barry, H., Child, I., & Bacon, M. Relation of child training to subsistence economy. *American Anthropologist*, 1959, *61*, 51–63.

Berry, J. W. Temne and Eskimo perceptual skills. *International Journal of Psychology*, 1966, *1*, 207–229.

Berry, J. W. Independence and conformity in subsistence-level societies. *Journal of Personality and Social Psychology*, 1967, *7*, 415–418.

Berry, J. W. Ecology, perceptual development and the Muller-Lyer illusion. *British Journal of Psychology*, 1968, *59*, 205–210.

Berry, J. W. On cross-cultural comparability. *International Journal of Psychology*, 1969, *4*, 119–128. (*a*)

Berry, J. W. Ecology and socialization as factors in figural assimilation and the resolution of binocular rivalry. *International Journal of Psychology*, 1969, *4*, 271–280. (*b*)

Berry, J. W. Ecology, Culture and Perceptual Development. Monograph in preparation, n.d.

Collins, P. Functional analyses, in Leeds, A. and Vayda, P. (Eds.), *Man, Culture and Animals*. Washington, D.C.: American Association for the Advancement of Science, 1965.

Cravioto, J. Nutritional deficiencies and mental performance in childhood, in Glass, D. (Ed.), *Environmental Influences*. New York: Rockefeller University Press, 1968.

Dawson, J. L. M. Kwashiorkor, gynaecomastia and femininization processes. *Journal of Tropical Medicine and Hygiene*, 1966, *69*, 175–179.

Dawson, J. L. M. Cultural and physiological influences upon spatial-perceptual processes in West Africa, pts. 1 & 2. *International Journal of Psychology*, 1967, *2*, 115–128; 171–185.

Ferguson, G. On learning and human ability. *Canadian Journal of Psychology*, 1954, *8*, 95–112.

Hammond, K. R. (Ed.) *The Psychology of Egon Brunswik*. New York: Holt, Rinehart and Winston, 1966.

Helm, J. The ecological approach in anthropology. *American Journal of Sociology*, 1962, *67*, 630–639.

MacArthur, R. S. Sex differences in field-dependence for the Eskimo: Replication of Berry's findings. *International Journal of Psychology*, 1967, *2*, 139–140.

Meggars, B. J. Environmental limitations on the development of culture. *American Anthropologist*, 1954, *56*, 801–824.

Rappaport, R. A. *Pigs for the Ancestors*. New Haven: Yale University, 1967.

Raven, J. C. *Coloured Progressive Matrices Sets A, Ab, B*. London: H. K. Lewis, 1956.

Steward, J. H. *Theory of Culture Change*. Urbana: University of Illinois Press, 1955.

Vayda, P. (Ed.) *Environment and Cultural Behaviour*. Garden City: Natural History Press, 1969.

Vayda, P. and Rappaport, R. A. Ecology, cultural and non cultural. Chapter 18 in Clifton, J. (Ed.) *Introduction to Cultural Anthropology*. Boston: Houghton Mifflin, 1968.

Whiting, J. W. M. Methods and problems in cross-cultural research, in Lindzey, G. & Aronson, E. (Eds.), *Handbook of Social Psychology* (2nd ed., Vol. 2), Reading: Addison-Wesley, 1968.

Witkin, H. A. Individual differences in ease of perception of embedded figures. *Journal of Personality*, 1950, *19*, 1–15.

Witkin, H. A., et al. *Psychological Differentiation*. New York: Wiley, 1962.

Wohlwill, J. F. The physical environment: A problem for a psychology of stimulation. *Journal of Social Issues*, 1966, *22*, 29–38.

Wohlwill, J. F. The emerging discipline of environmental psychology, *American Psychologist*, 1970, *25*, 303–312.

25. HOW ADULTS AND CHILDREN SEARCH AND RECOGNIZE PICTURES

N. H. MACKWORTH and J. S. BRUNER

Abstract. The eye fixations of 20 young adults and 20 children, aged six, were recorded while they were recognizing or inspecting a series of displays. The test photographs presented three levels of definition for one particular scene: very blurred, blurred, or sharp. Each picture was presented for two 10-second trials. Either the very blurred or the sharp picture was given first to a particular S. The eye tracks were therefore recorded either during attempts at visual comprehension or during casual inspection. The position and sequence of the fixations of each S were recorded individually on a Polaroid copy of the original display. Eight different analysis procedures were used to study the eye tracks and all showed reliable differences between adults and children. With the sharp pictures, children lacked adequate coverage of the display; their eye tracks averaged only two-thirds the length of the adult tracks, mostly because children had twice as many very small eye movements. Adults were more skillful at visually selecting the informative areas within out-of-focus pictures; this skill calls for a delicate balance between central and peripheral vision. Children were less consistent than adults in regard to the areas they visually selected from the out-of-focus displays. Only adults attempted to relate important areas of such displays by long leaping movements of the eyes. The direction of these long movements altered when S already knew the nature of the display. Adult fixation times increased by 40% when Ss had to comprehend the out-of-focus displays rather than merely inspect them. In the second part of the paper, theoretical interpretations are provided.

Sight is the dominant sense in humans, and its effectiveness depends upon eye movements, which centralize significant features of the visual stimulus upon the fovea. The aims of the present study were to determine the nature of the visual selection during the process of trying to identify pictures, and how it changes with age. To slow down the recognition process so that it could be examined, the clarity of some of the pictures was reduced by defocusing. Bruner and Potter [1964] used this technique when recording verbal reports from children and adults; they showed pictures which were initially very blurred, and were slowly brought into focus. Young children shifted their comments from one feature to another in a picture with little connection, but older Ss showed an increasing attempt to relate and classify the data [see also Potter, in Bruner,

Olver and Greenfield, 1966]. The verbal reports obtained in these studies obviously required some prior degree of perceptual identification.

An earlier stage of this process of identifying a blurred picture can be studied by determining eye-fixations, while the Ss are looking at the pictures. Ss might, for example, be expected to spend more time on areas which they considered potentially informative, but not recognizable. When, as in reading, the required order is from left to right, it is relatively simple to record eye movements. The analysis of pictorial material is, however, complicated by the fact that each S has his own idiosyncratic pattern of search for features that might yield meaning. In the free situation that we employed, several different aspects of the search process had to be measured to analyze this serial acquisition of visual data during attempted recognition. In this sense, our study was also methodological in objective.

Four specific questions gave form to this investigation: (1) Does the degree of blurring

From *Human Development*, 1970, *13*, 149–177. Printed by permission of S. Karger A. G., Basel/New York and the authors.

affect the way a picture is searched? (2) Does it make a difference if the S knows the meaning of a blurred picture beforehand? (3) Are there differences in visual search between children and adults? (4) How should the records of visual patterns of behavior be measured to assess the main features of visual information-processing?

Method

Eye movements were recorded by the Mackworth Stand Camera. The seated S leaned slightly forward against a forehead rest, biting on his individual dental wax impression mould supported on a bite-bar. A beam of light was reflected off the left eye and superimposed optically on a Polaroid photograph of the scene picture. The eye-marker record indicated the temporal order of the eye fixations. The accuracy of location of the eye-marker was such that the gaze position could be recorded to the nearest square inch on an 8 × 10 inch picture. This meant an accuracy of plus or minus half an inch from the actual position. Since the stimulus scene was viewed from a distance of 28 inches, the eye-marker was placed to within plus or minus one degree of visual angle from the correct position of the scene [Mackworth, 1967].

The displays were color prints selected from the series used by Bruner and Potter [1964], [see also Potter, in Bruner, Olver and Greenfield, 1966]. The main experiment consisted of two sequences of pictures given to undergraduates and 6-year-old children in the first grade. Each of four groups consisted of ten subjects. Ten undergraduates and ten children received the *Recognition Series*. They were shown a very blurred picture of a fire hydrant for 10 sec and then asked to guess what it was. Two seconds later they were shown the same picture for a further 10 sec. This was followed by two 10-second exposures of a less blurred version of the same scene. Finally, they were given two 10-second exposures of the same scene sharply focused. Another ten undergraduates and another ten children received the *Inspection Series*. They saw the sharply focused

picture first, followed by the blurred and then the very blurred ones, again with two 10-second exposures of each display. These Ss were simply asked to look at each picture. Comparable studies have been carried out on adults with twelve additional pictures [Mackworth, Millikan and Morandi, in preparation], and roughly similar results have been obtained.

Results

Which of the myriad possible indices of eye-movements could provide useful answers to our questions? Eight different measures stood up to a detailed study. We shall consider each in turn. In the *Recognition Series,* all Ss identified the picture correctly during the initial presentation of the blurred picture.

1. Mean Fixation Times

The mean visual fixation time for each S in a 10-second exposure was obtained by dividing 9 sec by the number of fixations made by that S. (Ten percent of the total time of 10 seconds was deducted to allow for movements between fixations.) The results are shown in table 25–1. Analysis of variance of the total number of fixations made by each S during a 10-second presentation of the hydrant pictures showed significant effects of presentation series and

TABLE 25–1
Mean Visual Fixation Times (msec)

TRIALS	VERY BLURRED	BLURRED	SHARP	MEANS
Recognition series				
Adults	449[1]	398	367	405
Children	413[1]	401	416	410
Means	431	399	392	407
Inspection series				
Adults	322	294	330[1]	316
Children	371	304	335[1]	337
Means	346	299	333	326

[1]*Display shown first in series.*

amount of blurring, (p < 0.01). The mean duration of fixations was nearly 100 msec longer when the Ss had to comprehend the nature of out-of-focus displays than when they were fully aware of the identity of these blurred pictures. The fixations also tended to be longer when the Ss were looking at very blurred displays (p < 0.01). There was also an age effect which was less pronounced (p < 0.05). The grand mean of the fixations of the children was longer than that of the adults. There were no significant interactions. However, in the *Recognition Series* the children's mean fixation times were shorter than those of the adults for the very blurred picture.

2. Clustering of Group Fixations

The main interest of the experiment focused on the *spatial patterns* made by the fixations on the displays. Fixation density was a first approach to such pattern analysis. It was estimated both for each *group of Ss* and for each *individual*. Initially our concern was with the group data. We refer to this measure as the clustering of group fixations, which indicated the popularity of specific areas within the pictures. The greater the consensus in the group, the higher was the concentration on these popular areas in the pictures. The pictures were divided for analysis into ten columns and eight rows, so that each grid square was a square inch, subtending about 2 degrees at the fovea. The total number of fixations (for the ten Ss in a group) falling on each square of a picture in a particular trial was determined and then converted into percentages of the total number of fixations made by that group in that trial. Since there were 80 squares in each picture, any square receiving 1.25% or more of the total fixations for the group attracted more than the mean number of fixations that would have resulted from a random search. Thus 5% represented a definite concentration of the "group gaze" upon a particular square. Therefore, all squares receiving more than 5% of pooled fixations were identified, and the actual percentages of fixations in these high-density squares were summed. The results are shown in table 25–2.

TABLE 25–2
Percentage of Group Fixations in High-Density Areas (More than 5% per Square Inch)

TRILS	VERY BLURRED 1	2	BLURRED 1	2	SHARP 1	2	MEANS
Recognition series							
Adults	45[1]	48	34	19	0	0	24
Children	13[1]	29	25	19	20	19	21
Means	34		24		10		
Inspection series							
Adults	38	26	31	12	24[1]	16	21
Children	6	30	17	15	29[1]	14	18
Means	25		18		21		

[1]*Display presented first.*

There was a marked consensus of the *adult* gaze for the very blurred, unrecognized pictures, which continues when the picture was shown for a second trial. Table 25–2 also suggests that the very blurred picture in the *Recognition Series* was not handled in a consensual fashion by the *children* on its first presentation, but that on the second presentation there was a marked increase in the popularity of certain fixation areas. This was also true for the children in the *Inspection Series*. In the *Recognition Series*, once the picture came into sharp focus, adult Ss were more idiosyncratic than children. However, this was not the case in the *Inspection Series*, because the initial presentation of the sharp picture produced about the same concentration of gaze on popular areas among adults and children alike. Adults, in a word, will be more conventional in their visual search especially with the very blurred displays. But in the children such conventionality is limited to clearly focused displays or displays that have been well worked over.

3. Individual Fixation Densities

Individual fixation densities for each S were determined in much the same way as the group data, except that any square inch was regarded

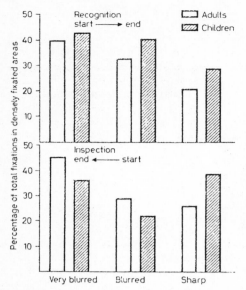

FIGURE 25–1. Percentage of total fixations in densely fixated areas for very blurred, blurred, and in-focus pictures, in recognition and inspection conditions.

as a high density area if it received more than 10% of the total fixations made during a 10-second inspection by one S. This 10% level represented about three fixations, because each S made approximately 30 fixations in a trial. Note, therefore, that most of the 80 squares were not directly fixated at all by a particular S, especially as some squares were glanced at more than once. Analysis of variance was carried out on the total percentage of fixations *per* S that fell within these "high density areas." There was a highly significant effect of blurring (p <0.001, F = 9.4, df 2/72), and significant interactions between age and blurring (p <0.05, F = 3.3, df 2/72), and also between series and blurring (p <0.05, F = 4.7, df 2/72). Figure 25–1 illustrates these effects.

Adults and children in the *Recognition Series* now showed the same reaction—greater concentration of gaze when looking at the initial blurred picture, gradually dispersing as the picture came into focus. The adults showed a more marked effect; their gaze was twice as concentrated on the very blurred pictures. In the *Inspection Series,* however, there was a dif-

ference. With the children, there was as much concentration of gaze on the sharp picture as on the very blurred one, whereas the adults again showed a marked increase in visual concentration as the picture became defocused.

4. Rated Search Scores

Two further indices are concerned with effectiveness of search. Effective search was considered to be a composite of (1) *concentration of gaze upon highly informative areas* plus (2) *a wide coverage of the display* in order not to miss important details. This necessary combination of (1) *a high rated search score* plus (2) *a long eye track* in the time allowed were conflicting requirements which did not come equally easily to adults and to children. Nor was there much similarity between the evidence from *Recognition* and *Inspection Series.* This was to be expected since this reverse order very markedly altered the amount of information processed by the Ss at the start of any given trial.

The Rated Search score was based upon the Informativeness Index, calculated for each square inch of the stimulus pictures. The Informativeness Index was obtained in a separate experiment [Mackworth and Morandi, 1967; Pollack and Spence, 1968; Mackworth, Millikan and Morandi, in preparation]. Each picture was cut up into the 80 squares already described; a new group of Harvard students was presented with these squares one at a time and asked to rate each square on its informativeness, with regard to the set of squares in front of them. The Ss did not know what the total picture signified. A ten-point rating scale from "Highly Informative" to "Completely Uninformative" was used. A highly informative square (rated "9") would always be completely recognizable on a second occasion. A completely uninformative square (rated "0") would never be recognizable again on a second viewing. ("Recognizable" meant that the S believed he could pick it out again on a second trial.)

The Rated Search Score was determined for the present eye movement study by assigning a numerical value to each fixation in each eye track according to the informativeness rating given by these previous subjective estimates to that square in which the fixation fell. The sum of these values over the 10-second period was the Rated Search Score for the given S who had made that particular eye track. If he had looked more often at highly rated squares, his Rated Search Score would be higher than that of a S who let his eyes wander more widely over areas that had been rated very low for informativeness. Such areas have subsequently been shown to be, in fact, hard to recognize [Mackworth, Millikan and Morandi, in preparation].

Table 25–3 shows mean Rated Search Scores for each group. Analysis of variance on individual data revealed significant effects of series (p <0.01, F = 12.0, df 1/36), age (p <0.05, F = 6.8, df 1/36), blurring (p <0.01, F = 27.5, df 2/72), and Trials (p <0.05, F = 6.7, df 2/36). The adults showed a higher Rated Search Score than the children for ten out of the twelve trials. This age difference was especially marked when the very blurred pictures were being inspected for comprehension; that is, when they were presented first in the *Recognition Series*. Then five of the ten children each scored lower than 100 on this Rated Search measure, whereas only one of the ten adults gave such a low Rated Search reading. The frequency distributions of the Rated Search Scores from individual attempts at particular pictures did not obviously depart from normality. The range of the actual readings was

TABLE 25–3
Mean Rated Search Scores per Eye Track

TRIALS	VERY BLURRED 1	2	BLURRED 1	2	SHARP 1	2	MEANS
Recognition series							
Adults	122	118	153	132	160	154	140
Children	101	91	134	120	142	113	117
Means	110	104	143	121	151	133	
Inspection series							
Adults	148	143	168	163	169	171	160
Children	122	121	153	168	171	140	146
Means	135	131	160	165	170	155	

TABLE 25–4
Mean Rated Search Scores per Fixation

TRIALS	VERY BLURRED 1	2	BLURRED 1	2	SHARP 1	2	MEANS
Recognition series							
Adults	6.2	5.8	7.0[1]	5.5	6.4	6.4	6.2
Children	4.5	4.2	6.0[1]	5.4	5.8	5.8	5.3
Means	5.3		6.0		6.1		
Inspection series							
Adults	5.5	5.2	5.5	5.2	6.4[1]	5.8	5.6
Children	4.4	4.6	5.3	5.5	6.9[1]	5.8	5.4
Means	4.9		5.4		6.2		

[1]*Presentation on which nature of picture was recognized.*

fairly large, but individual scores were seldom greater than 220 or less than 100. Note that the possible range of scores was from 0 (since some picture areas had "0" informativeness) to a possible maximum of about 360 (some areas had "9" on the informativeness scale, and an occasional S made as many as 40 fixations during the 10-second test: 9 × 40 = 360).

Table 25–3 shows that the out-of-focus pictures had lower Rated Search Scores than the sharply focused ones. But there was a possible artifact here that must be considered. Children showed longer and therefore fewer fixations in a 10-second period. Similarly, the blurred pictures produced longer and therefore fewer fixations per trial. We may ask whether there is any real difference in the informativeness of areas visited by adults or children in pictures of different clarity—or whether this apparent difference merely reflects the rate at which the displays were fixated. We may compute any effect of age or display on Rated Search Scores corrected for fixation rates, by converting Rated Search Scores into *Informativeness per Fixation*. This score is presented in table 25–6. Again, for the *Recognition Series*, adults showed more skill in picking informative areas than did the children. In effect, the adults "zeroed into" these informative areas from the start, even with the very blurred pictures. Children, on the other hand, showed a markedly lower information extraction from the very

TABLE 25–5
Group Mean Readings for Track Length (Inches per 10 Sec Trials)

TRIALS	VERY BLURRED 1	2	BLURRED 1	2	SHARP 1	2	MEANS
Recognition series							
Adults	46	38	47	48	60	54	49
Children	43	42	45	42	45	40	43
Means	42		46		50		
Inspection series							
Adults	44	49	51	60	46	61	52
Children	55	48	47	55	41	40	48
Means	49		53		47		

blurred or not yet recognized picture. In the *Inspection Series* the matter is less clear; in the main, the difference between adults and children disappears, which is not surprising, given that they both have equally clear information about the identity of the picture from the start. Yet, even in this series the children still showed a marked deficit, compared with adults, in staying with the informative areas when the picture was very blurred. This is either a matter of variability in the absence of clear visual

TABLE 25–6
Frequency Distribution of Length of Eye Movements (Percentages) and Length of Eye Movement (Degrees/Half-Inches): Recognition and Inspection Series

	STEPS UP TO 3 INCHES 0–1	1–2	2–3	3–4	4–5	5–6	LEAPS OVER 3 INCHES 7–8	9–10	11–12	13–14	15–17
Adults											
Very blurred	17	18	19	14	9	6	7	5	3	0	0
Blurred	14	20	16	14	9	8	8	4	4	2	1
Sharp	11	19	15	16	9	6	10	5	4	1	1
Children											
Very blurred	23	19	11	11	8	6	9	6	3	2	1
Blurred	21	19	13	10	8	8	10	5	3	1	0
Sharp	24	17	16	11	7	6	9	5	3	1	0

constraints, or of an ignoring of adult visual convention.

Table 25–6 becomes more meaningful when one realizes that it shows a range in the mean Rated Scores per fixation from 4.2 to 7.0. This range of nearly three points was three times the range in the mean estimated informativeness of the displays themselves. (The Very Blurred averaged 3.1; the Blurred, 3.4; and the Sharp rose only to 4.1.) We suggest that this range in Rated Search Scores per fixation indicated a considerable (visual) feature selection effect due to aiming the gaze, since by visual choice alone the adults effectively doubled the informativeness of the areas they selected compared to those available for scrutiny. Similarly, the Rated Search Scores per fixation were, of course, all higher than the informativeness means for the displays, but such Rated Search Scores were always highest for the trials on which the Ss first understood the picture.

5. Track Lengths

The second component of effective search was the length of the eye track, a further means of estimating the efficiency with which the whole picture was being searched. An S who concentrated upon the main object in the picture might receive a high Rated Search Score, but have a short track length. Track length assesses the amount of the picture covered and is the total distance moved by an individual gaze during a 10-second trial. It is simply the sum of the lengths in inches of all distinct eye-movements greater than half a degree (quarter of an inch). Track length is known to agree fairly closely with other measures of display coverage such as the proportion of grid cells entered [Luborsky, Blinder and Schimek, 1965].

The total range of eye-track lengths varied greatly, from about 20 to 85 in with a normal distribution, as recorded during the 10-second exposures of the sharp display. Figure 25–2 shows three sample eye tracks, each lasting 10 sec. Figure 25–2a was a particularly wide-stepping adult with a 66-inch track, which shows repeated attempts to link the two parts of the picture together. Such wide leaps of the gaze will be discussed later. Figure 25–2b represents a child who was all tangled up in the middle of the hydrant; he directly inspected only five of the available 80 square inches. Figure 25–2c shows a child who concentrated on the hydrant also, but moved along the edge in tiny steps. Such children would appear to make

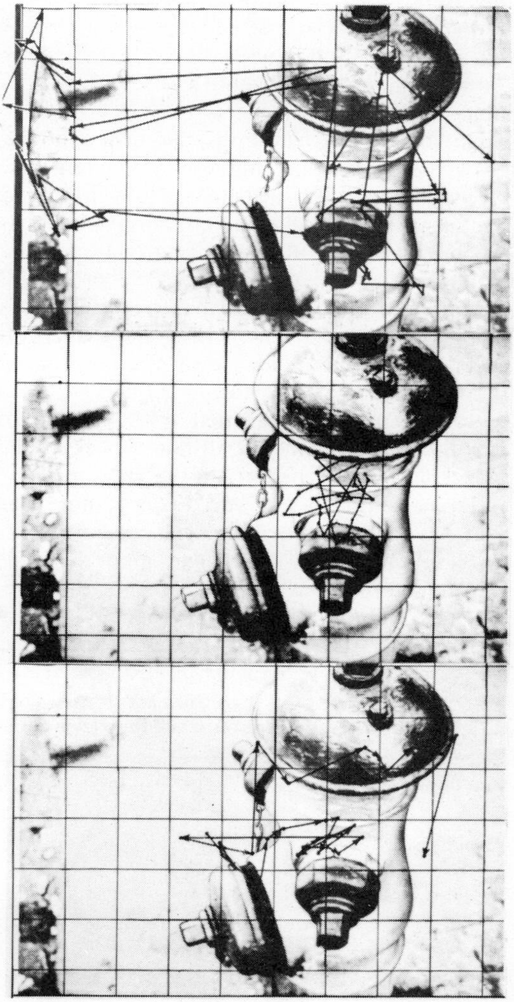

Figure 25–2. Three individual eye-track records: *a* long eye-track (66 inches) from adult; *b* extremely short eye-track (14 inches) from 6-year-old; *c* a first-grader's preoccupation with detail (27 inches).

little use of peripheral vision, in contrast to many adults.

Adults had longer eye tracks than children, in ten out of the twelve trials, as shown in table 25–5. This general age comparison showed a statistically reliable difference (p <0.05) on a two-tailed test as calculated by the Wilcoxon matched-pairs signed rank test [Siegel, 1956]. The difference in track length due to age was especially marked with the sharp pictures where adults averaged 55 in and children only 41 in. For the very blurred displays, both age groups gave virtually the same track lengths, adults 44 in and children 47 in, a nonsignificant difference.

The correlation between track length and Rated Search Scores was also examined. It was found that there was a significant correlation both for children (r = 0.27, p <0.01) and for adults (r = 0.50, p <0.001). Thus the correlation coefficient between these two measures of search efficiency was nearly twice as great for the adults as for the children—a finding which again suggests that the children were less conventional than adults in their looking patterns.

6. Lengths of Eye Movements

The interfixation distance measurements were divided into two kinds of active eye movements: (1) short *steps* involved a movement from one object to the next, both such items being covered by central vision during the first fixation; and (2) *leaps* involved a movement so long that the two areas successively fixated by foveal vision were quite separate. In other words, the leap was considered as an expression of a movement towards a target chosen in peripheral vision during the previous fixation. For the purposes of this analysis, steps were defined as movements up to 3 in across the pictures, and leaps were defined as movements over 3 in. Thus leaps represented movements greater than 6 degrees of visual angle. (The display material was sufficiently lacking in visual details to justify the assumption that central vision was subtending such a wide area, especially as we wished to make quite sure that leaps really were linking visually separate patches of display.)

The children had considerably more of the very short steps of ¼–½ in (table 25–6). Since the eye marker measured ¼ inch in diameter, in terms of the size of the original display, movements less than this were not distinguishable, nor was it likely that such minute movements of less than ½ degrees represented true voluntary eye movements [Gaarder, 1968]. With the sharply focused displays, children made 24% of all their eye movements as little steps of half an inch or less in length, but these very short steps formed only 11% of all adult fixations. This large difference was statistically significant (p <0.0001). Similarly, with the blurred pictures 21% of all movements were these very small steps with the children, but only 14% with the adults (p <0.01). With the very blurred pictures, the trend was the same but the difference was somewhat smaller, although still reliably different; 23% for children and 17% for adults (p <0.05).

One reason for these differences due to age is that the children may have lacked some precision in the aiming accuracy of their oculomotor system. This defect may have produced more fine adjusting movements after the initial main leap towards an important visual feature. Another possible reason for these age differences might be the lower visual acuity of children than adults [Weymouth, 1963]. Indeed visual acuity may have partly determined the length of eye movements even in adults, since 22% of adult eye movements were leaps when the display was sharp, but only 16% with the very blurred display (p <0.05). But no such change was found with the children, the nonsignificant trend being in the opposite direction—19% with the sharp and 21% with the very blurred display.

The most likely interpretation of all is related to the comment by Woodworth [1938] that the distance between visual fixations is not so much a matter of the width of clear vision as it is of the difficulty of the presentation; it is well known that small visual steps are characteristic of children when reading [Vernon, 1958]. It is therefore possible that the increased number of

very small steps made by the children was partly due to their greater difficulty in processing the visual data. Mackworth [1967] gave an example of fixations crowding together during the comprehension of a difficult word. The useful field of view is the area around the fixation point from which information is being temporarily stored and then processed during a visual task. Mackworth [1965] has shown that the useful field of view is reduced from the normal perimeter-sized field when the rate of visual information processing is increased by crowding more stimuli onto the visual display area.

Obviously the nature of the task and the display will alter the length of eye movements. In our studies, for instance, adults averaged only about one-third of their eye movements as less than one inch in length. Our pictures were well lit without glare at 85 millilamberts or 70 footlamberts and the displays were being scanned either for recognition or casual inspection. But the incidence of eye movements of one inch or less may rise to about 50% when adults are making a detailed visual search for small objects against a difficult background [Mackworth and Hiebert, in preparation]. The difference in the incidence of leaps of more than 3 in was even more striking. The present studies on adults showed about one-quarter of the movements were as long as 3 inches or more, whereas, adults making this detailed visual

TABLE 25–7

Percentage of Successive Eye Movements that Were Leaps (over 3 inches): Recognition and Inspection Series

	1–4	5–8	9–12	13–16
Adults display				
Very blurred	8.3	15.4	21.7	22.7
Blurred	10.8	20.8	20.8	19.2
Sharp	15.8	22.8	24.2	23.4
Means	11.6	19.7	22.2	21.8
Children display				
Very blurred	18.7	23.7	19.4	27.5
Blurred	13.1	20.6	24.4	20.6
Sharp	16.2	21.9	22.5	19.4
Means	15.3	22.1	22.1	22.5

search (with the same lighting conditions) will have only 5% leaps in their scanning pattern.

The cognitive analysis of the picture also affects the size of the eye movements. The leap movements are shown in table 25–7, as trends against time. Here the first 16 eye movements in each presentation have been analyzed in successive groups of four. Note that there was a marked increase in leaps after the first four eye movements. These data suggest that initially, for about a second, S s "felt" their way around the picture with small steps, so that each field of view overlapped the previous one. Once they had established the relative position of the various objects in the picture, they then swung boldly from one informative area to another, in order to form cognitive relations between these widely separated visual details.

The differences between the first and second sets of four eye movements was significant (p <0.01 both for adults and for children). When considering the separate displays, the children showed more than twice as many leaps at the beginning of the very blurred display as did the adults. Comparing the first eight eye movements for the two age groups, the mean difference of 9.4% was again significant (p <0.01). The children were perhaps swinging wildly around before they had established the informative areas they should be interrelating.

7. Direction of Eye Movements

Assessing the direction of eye movements is peculiarly difficult in a task where there are few directional constraints unlike reading. We are principally interested in the direction of leaps rather than steps, since the latter are mainly determined by some sort of proximity rule. Among the leaps, moreover, we want to assess those that are being directed to preferred areas rather than to areas rarely visited. Accordingly, the following plan was adopted. Only eye movements greater than 3 in (6 degrees) were analyzed, and we took only those among them that terminated in a square that had received 2% or more of the S's leaps. This double-filtering technique eliminated all the small steps and also one-third of the leaps.

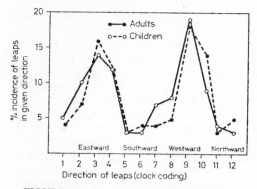

FIGURE 25–3. A record of the direction of leaps indicating a horizontal tendency for long leaps by adults and children.

With this analysis, there were more than four times as many horizontal leaps as vertical leaps across all the displays. Figure 25–3 makes it clear that this was true for both age groups. The display (figure 25–2) consisted of two quite separate clusters of detail, the central hydrant and the assorted debris strung out along the sidewalk towards the far left of the picture. At first interpretation, the numerous horizontal leaps seemed to be merely attempts to connect these two isolated areas of interest. But other quite different scenes also give charts identical to figure 25–2. Since the 6-year-old children showed exactly the same trend as the adults, the phenomenon would seem most unlikely to be related to reading habits. (We assume that Harvard undergraduates have read a good deal more than our 6-year-olds!) The predominance of horizontal leaps is more likely to have been due to a very general characteristic of the visual field; its E–W axis is rather wider than its N–S axis [Chaikin, Corbin and Volkman, 1962]. Certainly, behavioral evidence supports this interpretation since moving objects can be perceived twice as far out in the horizontal periphery as they can in the vertical dimension [McColgin, 1960]. Finally, Brandt [1945] also found that there were twice as many horizontal eye movements as there were vertical ones with a wide range of different pictures.

A psychological factor was detected in our data on leap direction. The adult S s modified the general direction of their leaps before the picture was recognized; the children did not. A quarter (26%) of the leaps given by the adults were vertical when the very blurred picture was presented first, in the *Recognition Series*, almost all of these being along the hydrant area. When the same picture was presented last, in the *Inspection Series*, only 3% of the leaps were vertical. This difference was established at the p <0.001 level for a two-tailed test of differences between percentages. The comprehension requirement therefore greatly affected the visual linkages attempted by adults. They realized that the elements of the vertical hydrant were an important feature in the display, even though they did not establish its nature until later.

But the children showed no such differential effect due to the order of presentation of the very blurred pictures. The data showed 10% of the children's leaps were vertical when they were looking at the very blurred picture at the beginning of the *Recognition Series*, and 12% when they were looking at this same picture at the end of the Inspection Series, a difference which was not statistically significant.

8. Repeat Index

A detailed study of the effects of presenting the picture a second time was made by means of the Repeat Index of consistency of search. Those squares looked at during both trials by an individual were identified; then all the fixations falling on these squares during the second trial

were counted. The number so obtained was divided by the total number of squares entered during the first trial to give the Repeat Index. For example, suppose an individual looked at 20 squares during the initial trial, and 10 of these same squares were inspected during the second trial, seven of them being looked at once and three being looked at twice (3×2) during the second trial, then the Repeat Index would be $(7 + 6)/20 = 0.65$. Thus, the more squares the subject looked at in the first trial, the lower would be the Index, but the more of these he picked up again in the second trial, the higher would be the Index. Note that the Repeat Index can exceed 1.0 because each multiple entry during the *second* trial affects the result, e.g., 20 squares visited on the first trial, of which 10 are revisited once (10), four twice (8), and three thrice (9), yielding the value 27/20 or 1.35.

On the group means, adults always showed a higher consistency than children, with an overall mean of 0.87 for adults, and 0.67 for children (table 25–8). Adults also showed an increasing consistency with defocusing of the pictures, presumably because there were fewer informative areas to structure the visual patterns in different ways. Children, however, did not show this trend. In fact, their Repeat Index was lower for the very blurred picture when it was shown last in the sequence, than it was for the sharp picture shown first in the same Inspection sequence. It has already been shown that children varied more from person to person than adults, and this further evidence demonstrated that children also varied more within themselves from one trial to the next.

Specific Discussion

Consider first the four specific questions with which we started our task:

Question 1. Does the Degree of Blurring Affect the Way a Picture is Searched?

Comparing the means for the different levels of blurring, it was found that the fixations were longest and the gaze most concentrated with the very blurred pictures (tables 25–1 and 25–2; and figure 25–1).

TABLE 25–8
Group Means for Repeat Index of Consistency

	VERY BLURRED	BLURRED	SHARP	MEANS
Recognition series				
Adults	1.00	0.71	0.67	0.79
Children	0.74	0.49	0.62	0.62
Means	0.87	0.60	0.65	
Inspection series				
Adults	1.06	0.87	0.88	0.94
Children	0.65	0.70	0.76	0.70
Means	0.85	0.78	0.82	

Question 2. Does it Make a Difference if S Knows the Meaning of a Blurred Picture Beforehand?

The effect of the attempt to comprehend a picture on the nature of the visual search can be illustrated by the following statements:

a) Fixation times were considerably longer when comprehension was needed rather than inspection alone. For example, fixation times were longer by about 40% or increased by 127 msec when the adults were trying to grasp the meaning of the very blurred picture, than when they were idly scanning it at the end of the *Inspection Series* (table 25–1).

b) Informative areas were fixated more often during the first of the two 10-second exposures with each picture. This result was particularly clear during the successful search trial, in which the picture was recognized. In the second or repeat exposure with the same picture, the less informative areas were looked at, and the *S*s scanned more widely. Again this effect was more noticeable after the picture was recognized (table 25–4).

c) Leaps were fewer during the first second of a presentation when the adults were determining the theme of a picture because they concentrated on the main details. Leaps then appeared more often, indicating attempts to relate visually quite different regions, in order to see the picture as a whole. The children did not show this early concentration (table 25–7).

d) The *direction of the leaps* changed when the meaning was comprehended. Horizontal scanning was most common with the clearly focused pictures (figure 25–3). When the display was very blurred, the adults showed vertical leaps related to the vertical arrangement of the picture, *before* they had grasped the meaning of the picture. But other adults, who *already knew the meaning* of the very blurred picture before they saw it, gave no such effect. With children, the attempts at comprehension of the very blurred picture did *not* affect the direction of their leaps.

Question 3. Are there Differences in Visual Search between Children and Adults?

All eight measures emphasized differences between these two age groups.

a) Fixation times were slightly longer for the children (table 25–1).

b) Group agreement on visual concentration was much less marked in the young *S*s, especially on the first presentation of a very blurred display, even if they already knew its meaning (table 25–2).

c) Individual visual concentration measures show that the children did indeed concentrate their gaze with the very blurred displays and when they saw the sharp pictures first of all (figure 25–1). But there was, however, little agreement between children on the areas they chose for such detailed concentration. With children, therefore, it is essential to have *individual records of visual concentration*. But with adults, the *group visual concentration* measures give a reasonable understanding of what most individuals are doing.

d) Rated Search Scores show that the children concentrated less upon the informative areas. This held up in various displays, whether or not the *S*s were trying to understand the picture. This age effect was specially marked when very blurred pictures were being studied for comprehension. This age effect may be due to the greater variability in children or to the fact that adults have developed certain visual conventions (table 25–3). The age effect on informativeness of visual search (per eye track in 10 sec) was still present even when we removed the influence of the slower searching by the children. That is, *the Rated Search Score per fixation* still showed these advantages in favor of the adults. The concentration upon informative areas during comprehension, especially on the first display, was even more marked when this average score per fixation was examined. Indeed the highest Rated Search Scores per fixation were observed in the 10 sec while the *S*s were grasping the meaning of the pictures. Children and adults both showed this effect (table 25–4).

e) Track lengths were shorter for the children. This difference was especially noticeable with the sharply focused displays where the children's tracks for the given 10 sec averaged only two-thirds of the length achieved by the adults (table 25–5 and figure 25–2).

f) Lengths of eye movement show that the

children had twice as many very short visual steps of half an inch or less (one degree or less), when the Ss were looking at the sharp pictures (table 25–6). On the other hand, the children had more than twice as many leaps during the first second of the very blurred displays—when the adults were more cautiously feeling their way (table 25–7).

g) Direction of leaps. The children's failure (unlike the adults) to develop any vertical leaps between important features of the display during the presentation has already been mentioned above.

h) Repeat index of consistency. Consistency of search could be measured because all the pictures were always presented twice. Adults tended to return to the same areas as before, although they were less consistent with the sharp pictures starting the Inspection Sequence. On the average, children were less consistent than adults; during the second trial children were less likely to return to the same areas that they had already inspected during the first trial. Such erratic behavior was especially common in the out-of-focus pictures, presumably because here the children were less able to anchor their gaze to the highly informative regions (table 25–8).

i) Contour effects. The outlines of the objects in the sharp displays did *not* draw many fixations from the adults [see also, Mackworth and Morandi, 1967]. We also found that neither bright nor dark elements of a picture attracted the attention of the adult observers unless these elements gave useful information. Some children did, however, tend to concentrate upon the outlines of the well-focused hydrant; in addition, with the very blurred pictures, only the children often ended their long leaping movements on the edges of the large patches of color, especially when these had a high brightness contrast with the background (figure 25–1).

Question 4. How Should the Records of Visual Patterns of Behavior be Measured to Assess the Main Features of Visual Information Processing?

A wide variety of measures is needed to

examine in detail the hypothesis one is testing. There is no such thing as *the* measure that characterizes eye movements. A variety served us in good stead. We have found eight metrics to be reliable, and all of these have given results of interest. Yarbus [1967] has emphasized the individual differences in visual patterns and we agree with his point of view. Nevertheless, there remains the possibility of grouping together the recordings from several individuals looking at the same display, at least with adults.

General Discussion

1. Development of Perceptual Skills

Developmental trends in the ability to direct attention are only beginning to be understood. It has become evident, for example, that the child is able from the start to analyze many features of his environment. Fantz's findings [1958, 1961] indicate to what degree discrimination between different displays is possible. He found that babies one month old could choose to look at black stripes ⅛th inch across and that infants below six months of age spent more time looking at a cartoon face than at a featureless oval displayed simultaneously. Many studies have confirmed this early work. For instance, Hershenson [1967], Mundy-Castle and Anglin [1969], Salapatek and Kessen [1966], and Salapatek [1968] point out that the child can discriminate between simple object and background virtually from birth. Gibson [1969] would insist that all development can be described as increasingly fine and veridical discrimination. This starts so early that Mackworth and Otto [1970] have now shown that the visual orienting response and its habituation take place just as rapidly in 2- to 3-year-old children as in those aged 6 to 7. "Cerebral programs" developed very early in life are adequate for the successful intake and learning of simple visual information, provided that little systematic research or interpretation of the stimuli are entailed.

What happens in the course of growth to the search patterns of children as indicated by their eye movements? There is one property in the eye movements of the young that particularly bears inspection as a basis for analyzing growth. It is the relation between "steps" and "leaps." We noted that the young had difficulty in combining the two in an effective search strategy that could both "dig out" fine features by close and long inspection, and at the same time scan broadly to test peripheral items for possible relevance to the integrated or constructed perceptual field. This lack of coordination between analysis and synthesis is the issue that has been discussed many times by Piaget under the heading of the schema [Piaget, 1961; Flavell and Wohlwill, 1969]. To some extent this is the issue of the study by Vurpillot [1968]. She used a eye camera developed by Mackworth [1968], and found that in a task involving comparison of two figures, young children did not scan enough features to make a proper determination before coming to a decision. Older children were more apt to compare the requisite number of features in this task. In a similar study, those children who were rated selective on the Kagan scale of Impulsivity-Selectiveness showed the greatest number of comparisons [Drake, 1967].

In a deeper sense, this difference in eye movement lengths relates to the old question as to whether children are "global" or "fragmented" in their perceptual organization [e.g., Werner, 1935; Gibson and Olum, 1960]. On the basis of these data, they seem to be *both,* but successively and not simultaneously. The task of working the center and the periphery in a common scanning program seems to be beyond their ability in the deployment of their visual inspection mechanism.

Possibly the very small eye-tracks of some normal young children looking at these pictures might also be related to a small useful field of view. Mackworth and Hiebert [in preparation] consider how fast visual search uses much smaller visual fields, presumably to prevent the visual system from becoming overloaded. The effective visual fields narrowed down during a visual search task from more than 6 degrees at a leisurely pace to 1 or 2 degrees during fast search. Luria, Pravdina-Vinarskaya and Yarbus

[1963, 1964] have reported on a brain-lesioned patient who could see only one object at a time. He could not move back and forth between two aiming points only 5 or 6 degrees apart, although he could follow a continuously moving stimulus. Young children might suffer from a similar overload with its consequent tunnel vision. Having arrived at a "good place" on which to rest the gaze, they seem to feel "disinclined" to leap into the unknown areas of the sharp pictures. Atkin [1969] has recently shown that a velocity for ocular pursuit of a moving target is often selectively initiated by data from the periphery of the retina *before* the adult S could possibly have used the input from the fovea arriving on the moving stimulus. Such mechanisms may well take years to develop.

Other brain lesion research, (Trevarthen, 1965) on split-brain monkeys, has led to an important distinction between central seeing to identify, and peripheral seeing to locate. Such emphasis on a dual system and upon a "constructionist" view of cognitive functioning emphasizes the significance of the distinction between the functional center and the functional periphery in vision [Held, 1967; Ingles, 1967; Trevarthen, 1968]. In effect, to use the terminology of Trevarthen [1968], there is a foveal system, that deals principally with identification of objects, and a more diffuse system that is involved in locating, searching and generally monitoring the whole field. When one is focally attending, the task is usually identification. The peripheral monitoring process not only helps keep objects generally located, but also examines their candidacy for closer inspection. This has to be a well-used and effective procedure to prevent confusion from too many details. In our studies, only about 25% of the 80 square inches were fixated by one or more of the 30 fixations made during a 10-second spell [see also Yarbus, 1967]. As Neisser [1966] points out, the successive play of focal attention very likely is central to the construction of a visual field out of sampled portions of it. We do not yet know in detail the relative role of "leaps" and "steps" in this process of construction, but we believe they play a crucial part. Further studies of this interrelationship between peripheral and central seeing would be most valuable if children were compared with adults in various kinds of task which allowed analysis by eye movement studies of the schemata, strategies, programs or plans that the *S* was trying to utilize to achieve success.

2. Linking Program and Picture

A further issue that needs considering has to do with the conditions necessary for a strategy of search to emerge. Visual search must develop from a state in which the gaze is controlled by the nature of the stimulus and its intrinsic features to one in which it is, in the words of Yarbus [1967], an instrument of thought. The key to this development is programmatic selectivity. We use "programmatic," because what is involved is a serially ordered search, including many movements of the eyes and/or head, all governed by a program for "constructing" a perceptual world. This point of view is by now familiar in many theoretical accounts [Bartlett, 1932, 1958; Craik, 1943; Bruner, 1957a, 1957b; Pribram, 1960; Miller, Galanter and Pribram, 1960; Mackworth, 1965b]. A great deal of this kind of programmatic search is based on the construction and use of models memorizing redundant features of stimulation.

We know from the work of Luria, Karpov, and Yarbus [1966] as well as from Tyler [1969a] that patients with frontal lobe tumors cannot utilize established mental models to guide the normal selective visual search of a display. This breakdown in the visual selectivity of the gaze arises from an absence of a model of the stimulus data, which leads to a lack of a mismatch input to guide the search. This is especially found in ambiguous scenes (without any special verbal instruction to the patient) when the perceived object is evoking a number of possible alternatives from which the *S* must choose by comparing each vaguely perceived object with various singly emerging hypotheses. No longer can the normal perceptual activity proceed as an active investigatory and orienting process. The *S* therefore cannot integrate the separate visual cues to compare the resulting visual hypotheses with the object he is perceiving. All displays will be scanned in about the same vague way and after the initial exploration, frontal patients will look at quite limited parts of the picture for long periods. Sometimes the frontal deficiency in scanning can be emphasized by specific verbal instructions. Typically, a normal *S* will show highly predictable and differentiated patterns of search in response to such different questions as "Tell me the ages of the people in the picture," or "Are they poor or rich?" With extensive lesions to the frontal lobe, there is no such differentiation.

Tyler [1969b] has found a similar strikingly defective stimulus exploration in some aphasic patients. Even with simple pictures there was almost a total absence of normal scanning in cases with severe receptive aphasia; these were patients oblivious of their excessive use of words and neologisms, who had great difficulty in understanding speech or writing. Tyler indicates that they were suffering from a severe disturbance of visual perceptual thinking, which cannot be explained by concepts limited to verbalization. Other aphasic patients with motor disorders of speech had some minor limitations of scanning very like the frontal cases. For example, they cut short their explorations of a complex picture after 5 sec or so. But patients with only defects in naming common objects had completely normal scanning patterns. Speech disorders usually classified as due to either sensory, motor or naming defects were therefore all found to give different visual scanning behavior and these differences may help to elucidate the reasons for their malady.

It is interesting that our children's data also showed a lack of eye-track differentiation by informative areas in the display. In the absence of the supporting visual framework of a clear picture, the children seemed not to be able to "work" the highly informative areas of the display in search of constraints, as we know also from the work of Potter and of Mosher [see Bruner, Olver and Greenfield, 1966]. Furthermore, even when given good visual support, they could not deploy their gaze between particulars and the general ambient pattern into which these particulars must be placed.

An inkling concerning the earliest development of such selective strategies is provided by a recent study by Mundy-Castle and Anglin [1969]. They worked with infants between 10 days and 3 months of age. Their stimuli were two highly decorated balls, separated by about 15 degrees of visual arc. One ball descends into a window on the left; remains for 6 sec and disappears, then after 3.5 sec another appears on the right for 6 sec, the cycle then repeating itself. The infant is in a sitting position in a "Harvard chair" [Bruner, 1969]. The first recognition response of the youngest infants is to watch the general area of the two windows (where the balls appear) more than other areas around the room. Shortly after, there follows a "locked on" looking phase. The infant looks fixedly at one ball while it is on view, and when it disappears, shifts his gaze to the other window. Eventually the infants may shift a moment before the ball disappears, clearly showing a more subtle anticipation. A third phase begins to appear around 60 days of age, which is crucial to our discussion. Now the baby looks at the ball that is on display, but from time to time he gazes at the other window, with a quick movement and a rapid return to the ball on display. He is responding *both* to the single object on display *and* to the two loci where objects can appear. Now he has learned to respond to both the immediate stimulus and to its context.

Yet we know that there is a long period ahead in which the child is unable to use this rudimentary strategy on more complex displays and on ones which by virtue of interference or "noise" are ambiguous. This long development is only now coming under investigation.

3. Psychological Models and Visual Choice

The present work can be regarded as a study of the relation between perception and the properties of the stimulus picture. For example, the Rated Search Score per fixation is a measure which provides a way in which the interaction between display and S can be taken into account and quantified. This metric depends on both the estimated content of the figure and the selective search by the individual. Green and Courtis [1966] have written an elegant obituary for information theory, as applied to perception. The fatal fact here is that an S viewing a picture draws on his past experience as well as on the immediate sense data. The perceiver is searching for the "perceptual hypothesis" that will best organize the raw sensory data. The kind of hypotheses he entertains and where he looks within the display for relevant cues must depend on the task presented to him *and* on his past experience.

The pattern of looking, therefore, partly depends on the mental schemata that the organism has established. Yarbus [1967] notes, for instance, that the problem facing the S at the moment of perception often determines the search behavior just as much as the display itself. The most dramatic quantitative demonstration, so far, of the relation between the line-of-sight and internal psychological models is found in the work of Tikhomirov and Poznyanskaya [1966]. They showed that when a chess master is looking at a chess problem, he visually examines the most probable moves by his opponent, thereby revealing many changes in his own mental program, each lasting only a few seconds. Many successive visual search patterns are therefore elicited, but there is only one simple external stimulus pattern interacting with a host of cerebral programs.

While the direction of the gaze may usually give indications of the direction of attention, looking is not the same as perceiving. The sensory input is but one set of threads in the whole rich fabric of thought. The brain itself must supply and weave the strands running in the other direction. Without these perceptual strands, based on previous experience, there would be no perception at all.

Zinchenko, Chzhi-Tsin and Tarakanov [1963] have noted that in perception the initial familiarization stage is isolation of the informative areas, and the second step is the investigation of these areas. This second step of *recognition* includes the comparison between the external stimulus pattern and various internal mental images. Pribram [1967] has suggested that the initial *familiarization* stage, which involves the formation of a mental model, is mediated by the amygdala, as a reinforce-register mechanism—while the further stage of *recognition* is mediated by the hippocampus, a match-mismatch mechanism relating the mental model to external events.

Zinchenko *et al.* [1963] believe that after the familiarization stage, a considerable portion of the information contained in the object becomes redundant and is not normally employed in recognition. Comparison of a few key characteristics with the model previously formed suffices for recognition [Zinchenko *et al.*, 1963, p. 10]. There is now also good quantitative fixation-time evidence for this suggestion in the study by Gould [1967] on adults matching a sample dot pattern to a series of surrounding dot patterns. Familiarization with the sample pattern took much longer than did the subsequent recognition of the same pattern: 480 sec for familiarization and 360 sec for recognition. Contrary to what one might expect, from a consideration of the views of Sternberg [1967], Ss must have been making a point-to-point comparison between the memorized internal pattern and the various patterns on display; this comparison being terminated by the detection of at least one difference. For example, mismatching patterns were rejected even faster than matching patterns, especially if the mismatching patterns differed greatly from the memorized standard, as regards the number of dots in the pattern.

Gould's [1967] adult Ss never looked back at the standard, and normal 6-year-olds seldom do after they have memorized a simple geometric figure. As shown by Grandstaff, Mackworth and de la Pena [in preparation], children attending an aphasia clinic have much more difficulty in storing such figures, and therefore have to refresh their memories more often by looking back at the sample. In contrast to normal children, aphasic children also show marked delays in orienting and habituating to a novel color among a set of very simple geometric symbols. Perhaps even larger differences

may be found by using the representational displays of the type used in this report, since representational displays test the selective strategies and the use of hypotheses to locate the important areas, rather than simple information transmission and storage.

4. Pictorial Versus Verbal Development

A puzzle that we have already mentioned and partly resolved, is the question of "global" as opposed to "detailed" perception in childhood. A second concerns the fact that there was so small a difference between the duration of the fixations of adults and children when they were looking at these pictures. Zinchenko, Chzhi-Tsin and Tarakanov [1963] found that, for children between 3 and 6 years old, the number of eye movements increased with age during an initial *familiarization* with an unfamiliar simple figure. But the same picture, once it was familiar, produced fewer eye movements in the older than in the younger children. This would suggest increasing efficiency in information processing in the older children: inspect when in doubt, desist when the object is placed and recognized.

It appears from our data on mean fixation times that by the sixth year the processing speed found when pictures are being examined has almost reached the maximum level of development. Six-year-olds and adults show almost the same mean fixation times when they are looking at sharp pictures (375 m/sec for children and 348 m/sec for adults), a result confirmed by many other experiments on the viewing of shapes, pictures or photographs. For example, the adult pictorial times are identical with those quoted by Buswell [1935], Enoch and Fry [1957], White and Ford [1960], and Zusne and Michel [1964] and the children's times closely resemble the results of Zinchenko *et al.* [1963].

On the other hand, there are considerable differences in fixation times between adults and children when they are *reading*. First-grade children show fixation times of about 546 m/sec; this is obviously much longer than children's fixation times for pictures. Reading fixations shorten steadily as the children grow older and more skilled; eventually, adults show mean fixation times of only about 250 m/sec for the reading of print [Buswell, 1922, 1935]. Indeed, by the time they are adults, people are moving their eyes more rapidly across print than across pictures.

Thus, children are smarter with pictures than words, whereas adults are smarter with words than pictures. Why then does pictorial processing begin to lag so far behind reading during the school and college years? There would seem to be at least four possible reasons: (a) First grade children are much more familiar with pictorial images than with the written word [Gibson, 1965; Bruner, Oliver and Greenfield, 1966]. (b) Adults have a greatly increased familiarity with words but have little extra familiarity with pictures; this pictorial illiteracy has been greatly deplored by Arnheim [1965]. (c) Slow progress in learning may arise from the fact that the repertoire of visual images may be much greater than that for the average verbal material because reading is usually concerned with only a few thousand words [French, Carter and Koenig, 1930]. The number of pictorial items is too large to obtain an estimate of it. (d) Pictorial learning may also be much harder because pictures may have to be stored as double-entry items, both as words and images. Because the visual input changes every moment, it is probable that naming pictorial material greatly helps recognition, but such verbal recoding may require an irreducible minimum of time [Hellyer, 1963]. The difficulty for adults in achieving faster pictorial processing is revealed by the finding that 30 highly trained art students (all of whom had 4 to 5 years of experience) had developed mean fixation times of 287 m/sec, which were only 40 m/sec shorter than a group of artistically naive adults looking at the same pictures [Buswell, 1935].

Conclusions

1. During a 10-second exposure of an 8 × 10 inch picture, the viewer directly fixates only about one-quarter of the 80 square inches in the area shown. He, therefore, has to compromise between looking foveally at important areas and covering as much as possible of the whole scene.

2. New ways have been devised to measure the relative amounts of these two conflicting requirements. These yardsticks take into consideration both the need to fixate the informative areas, as measured by the Rated Search Score per fixation, and also the general coverage of the scene, as measured by the Length of the Eye Track, in inches, during the 10-second trial.

3. Adults showed considerable skill in selecting important visual features by altering their line of sight. From out-of-focus pictures, they chose those areas which averaged a reading on the informativeness scale which was twice as high as the mean for the whole picture.

4. The cognitive aspects of this visual selection were clear throughout the experiments. For instance, the highest Rated Search Scores per fixation were recorded while Ss were grasping the meaning of the picture. Furthermore, the average Rated Search Score per fixation fell off whenever a trial was repeated, as if Ss began with the important regions and then worked further afield the second time around.

5. Children could not place their gaze so skillfully. This result was most clearly demonstrated whenever they were trying to identify out-of-focus pictures. The children were, however, able to find the important details in the sharp pictures. But in these sharp pictures, they became so hooked by the details that their eye tracks now averaged only two-thirds the length of those made by the adults. Apparently some of the 6-year-old children lacked an effective program for visual search, which would have enabled them to achieve the parallel processing seen in healthy adults. These children could not examine details centrally and *simultaneously* monitor their peripheral fields for stimuli which might be candidates for closer inspection. This inability to use central and peripheral vision together affected much of the children's behavior. For instance, they usually showed about twice as many very small visual

steps as the adults. They also occasionally tracked around definite contours in the sharp pictures, a visual affinity for sharp edges which was seldom seen in adults.

6. Because the children were so distracted by details they were also most erratic in their viewing of out-of-focus displays. Their Repeat Index scores of consistency indicated that they were less likely than adults to return to the regions that they had examined initially. The adults were less consistent with sharp pictures than they were with the blurred ones, because focusing the image displayed a wider selection of areas which were highly informative.

7. During the first second of viewing the very blurred pictures, the children recorded twice as many long leaping eye movements as did the adults. Perhaps only the adults were searching their memory for relevant material. Later in the viewing period, the adults increased their long leaping eye movements with all displays. Such leaps between important areas were not seen in children at all, *nor* when adults were merely inspecting a known display.

8. Marked cognitive effects were also noted in the visual fixation times, which became quite prolonged for both adults and children when Ss were trying to identify a very blurred image. Adult times increased by about 40% over the reading for the same display when adults were merely inspecting the very blurred image with whose nature they were familiar. Children showed a similar but less marked increase in fixation times.

9. Children had slightly longer fixation times compared with adults when both groups were looking at simple well-focused pictures—a result in marked contrast to the very much longer differences in fixation times normally found between 6-year-old children and adults in the reading situation. This discrepancy between viewing and reading could have arisen because most formal education concentrates upon reading, with but little attention to perceptual factors—and also because even a 6-year-old has a fairly large repertoire of pictorial shapes. Since fixation times are reduced by previous experience with the display, they can be used to assess how far people have progressed towards memorizing a visual pattern. Other writers have shown how recognition involves the matching of inner model and outer pattern; any imperfection in this mental model should slow down the process of recognition and therefore lengthen visual fixations.

10. After many attempts, we could not find any definite sequence as regards the order in which the various areas within the picture were being inspected. This suggested that Ss "look now and think later"—a cycle which was constantly repeated during the search for meaning.

11. The analysis of eye tracks does not need to be restricted to qualitative studies, especially as it is now possible to relate the fixations to the picture content.

12. Our eight ways of studying visual choice can help to elucidate the development of "cerebral programs" in children by analyzing the development of their perceptual skills. The use of out-of-focus representational pictures as stimulus material is one way to emphasize the role of selective viewing as the essential strategy for recognition. The cerebro-visual system can succeed only if it can find the dominant visual features that trigger and match the internal patterns of experience.

Acknowledgement

It is a pleasure to acknowledge the advice and help received from Professor Karl Pribram. In addition, we thank both Teri Kros and Leslie Pearson for the testing and analysis. Thanks are also due to Jane F. Mackworth for her comments on the draft versions of the manuscript.

The research reported herein was supported through the Cooperative Research Program of the Office of Education, US Department of Health, Education, and Welfare, Contract No. OE-4-10-136, Project No. E-020, to Harvard University, Center for Cognitive Studies and in part by the National Aeronautic and Space Administration Research Grant NsG718 to the Harvard University Guggenheim Center for Aerospace Health and Safety. Further support was also received at Stanford from the National Institute of Mental Health Grant No. MH 12970.

REFERENCES

Arnheim, R.: Visual thinking. In Kepes, *Education of vision,* Vol. 1, pp. 1–15 (Braziller, New York, 1965).

Atkin, A.: Shifting fixation to another pursuit target: Selective and anticipatory control of ocular pursuit initiation. *Exp. Neurol.,* 1969, *23:* 157–173.

Bartlett, F. C.: Remembering (Cambridge University Press, London, 1932).

Bartlett, F. C.: Thinking (Allen and Unwin, London, 1958).

Brandt, H. F.: The psychology of seeing (Philosophical Library, New York, 1945).

Bruner, J. S.: On perceptual readiness. *Psychol. Rev. 64:* 123–152 (1957a).

Bruner, J. S.: On going beyond the information given. In *Contemporary approaches to cognition,* pp. 41–69 (Harvard University Press, Cambridge, 1957b).

Bruner, J. S.: *Processes of cognitive growth: Infancy* (Clark University Press with Barre Publishers, Worcester, Mass., 1968).

Bruner, J. S.: Eye, hand and mind; in Elkind and Flavell, *Studies in cognitive development: Essays in honor of Jean Piaget,* pp. 223–236 (Oxford University Press, New York, 1969).

Bruner, J. S., Olver, R. R., and Greenfield, P. M.: *Studies in cognitive growth* (John Wiley and Sons, New York, 1966).

Bruner, J. S. and Potter, M. C.: Interference in visual recognition. *Science 144:* 424–425 (1964).

Buswell, G. T.: Fundamental reading habits: A study of their development. *Educational Monograph,* 1922 (Supplement 21).

Buswell, G. T.: How people look at pictures: A study of the psychology of perception in art (The University of Chicago Press, Chicago, 1935).

Chaikin, J. D., Corbin, H. H., and Volkman, J.: Mapping a field of short-time visual search. *Science 138:* 1327–1328 (1962).

Craik, K. J. W.: *The nature of explanation* (Cambridge University Press, London, 1943).

Drake, D. M.: Perceptual correlates of impulsive and reflective behavior. Doctoral dissertation, Harvard University (Harvard Graduate School of Education, Cambridge, Mass., 1968).

Enoch, J. M. and Fry, G. A.: Personal communication (1957).

Fantz, R. L.: Pattern vision in young infants. *Psychol. Rec. 8:* 43–47 (1958).

Fantz, R. L.: The origin of form perception. *Sci. Amer. 204:* 66–72 (1961).

Fantz, R. L.: Ontogeny of perception; in Schrier, Harlow and Stollnitz, *Behavior of non-human primates,* vol. II, pp. 365–403 (Academic Press, New York, 1965).

Flavell, J. H. and Wohlwill, J. F.: Formal and functional aspects of cognitive development; in Elkind and Flavell, *Studies in cognitive development: Essays in honor of Jean Piaget,* pp. 67–120 (Oxford University Press, New York, 1969).

French, N. R.; Carter, C. W., and Koenig, W.: The words and sounds of telephone conversations. *Bell System Techn. J. 9:* 290–324 (1930).

Gaarder, K.: Interpretative study of evoked responses elicited by gross saccadic eye movements. *Percept. Motor Skills 27:* 683–703 (1968).

Gibson, E. J.: Learning to read. *Science 148:* 1066–1072 (1965).

Gibson, E. J.: Principles of perceptual learning and development (Appleton-Century-Crofts, New York, 1969).

Gibson, E. J. and Olum, V.: Experimental methods of studying perception in children; in Mussen, Handbook of research methods in child development, pp. 311–373 (John Wiley & Sons, New York, 1960).

Gould, J. D.: Pattern recognition and eye-movement parameters. *Percept. Psychophys. 2:* 399–407 (1967).

Grandstaff, N. W.; Mackworth, N. H., and de la Pena, A.: Matching of symbols by normal and aphasic children: A line of sight study (in preparation).

Green, R. T. and Courtis, M. C.: Information theory and figure perception: The metaphor that failed. *Acta Psychol. 25:* 12–36 (1966).

Held, R.: Dissociation of visual functions of deprivation and re-arrangement. *Psychol. Forsch. 31:* 338–348 (1967).

Hellyer, S.: Stimulus-response coding and amount of information as determinants of reaction time. *J. Exp. Psychol. 65:* 521–522 (1963).

Hershenson, M.: Development of the perception of form. *Psychol. Bull 67:* 326–336 (1967).

Ingle, D.: Two visual mechanism underlying the behavior of fish. Symposium on locating and identifying: Two modes of visual processing. *Psychol. Forsch, 31:* 44–51 (1967).

Luria, A. R.; Karpov, A., and Yarbus, A. L.: Disturbances of active visual perception with lesions of the frontal lobes. *Cortex 2:* 202–212 (1966).

Luria, A. R.; Pravdina-Vinarskaya, E. N., and Yarbus, A. L.: Disorders of ocular movement in a case of simultanagnosia. *Brain 86:* 219–228 (1963).

Luria, A. R.; Pravdina-Vinarskaya, E. N., and Yarbus, A. L.: Eye movement mechanisms in normal and pathological vision. *Soviet Psychol. Psychiat. 2:* 28–39 (1964).

Mackworth, N. H.: Visual noise causes tunnel vision. *Psychonom. Science 3:* 67–68 (1965a).

Mackworth, N. H.: Originality. *Amer. Psychologist 20:* 51–66 (1965b).

Mackworth, N. H.: A stand camera for line-of-sight recording. *Percept. Psychophys. 2:* 119–127 (1967).

Mackworth, N. H.: The wide-angle reflection eye camera for visual choice and pupil size. *Percept. Psychophys. 3:* 32–34 (1968).

Mackworth, N. H.; Grandstaff, N. W., and de la Pena, A.: Orienting and habituation in normal and aphasic children: A line-of-sight study (in preparation).

Mackworth, N. H. and Hiebert, J.: Fast visual scanning needs small fields and long fixations (in preparation).

Mackworth, N. H.; Millikan, J., and Morandi, A. J.: Active visual choices in viewing (in preparation).

Mackworth, N. H. and Morandi, A. J.: The gaze selects informative details within pictures. *Percept. Psychophys. 2:* 547–552 (1967).

Mackworth, N. H. and Otto, D. A.: Habituation of the visual orienting response in young children. *Percept. Psychophys. 7:* 173–178 (1970).

McColgin, F. H.: Movement thresholds in peripheral vision. *J. Opt. Soc. Amer. 50:* 774–779 (1960).

Miller, G. A.; Galanter, E. H., and Pribram, K. H.: Plans and the structure of behavior (Holt and Co., New York, 1960).

Mundy-Castle, A. C. and Anglin, J.: Research reported in Bruner, Early skill acquisition as problem solving. Paper presented at XIX International Congress of Psychology, London, 1969.

Neisser, U.: Cognitive psychology (Appleton-Century-Crofts, New York, 1967).

Pavlov, I.: Conditioned reflexes (Oxford University Press, London, 1927).

Piaget, J.: The origins of intelligence in children, 2nd ed. (International University Press, New York, 1952).

Pollack, I., and Spence, D.: Subjective pictorial information and visual search. *Percept. and Psychophys. 3:* 41–44 (1968).

Pribram, K. H.: A review of theory in physiological psychology, in *Annu. Rev. Psychol.,* Palo Alto, Cal., Annual Reviews Inc., 1960, pp. 1–40.

Pribram, K. H.: The limbic systems, efferent control of neural inhibition and behavior; in Adey and Tokizane, Progress in brain research, pp. 318–336 (Elsevier Publishing Company, Amsterdam, 1967).

Riggs, L. A.: Visual acuity; in Graham, *Vision and Visual Perception,* pp. 321–349 (John Wiley and Sons, New York, 1965).

Salapatek, P. A.: Visual scanning of geometric figures by the human newborn. *J. Comp. Physiol. Psychol. 66:* 247–258 (1968).

Salapatek, P. A. and Kessen, W.: Visual scanning of triangles by the human newborn. *J. of Exp. Child Psycho. 3:* 155–167 (1966).

Siegel, S.: Nonparametric statistics for the behavioral sciences (McGraw-Hill, New York, 1956).

Sternberg, S.: Two operations in character recognition: Some evidence from reaction-time measurements. *Percept. Psychophys. 2:* 45–53 (1967).

Tikhomirov, O. K. and Poznyanskaya, E. D.: An investigation of visual search as a means of analyzing heuristics. *Soviet Psychol. 2:* 2–15 (1966–1967).

Trevarthen, C. B.: Functional interactions between the cerebral hemispheres of the split-brain monkey; in Ettlinger, Functions of the corpus callosum, pp. 24–41 (Little, Brown and Company, Boston, 1965).

Trevarthen, C. B.: Two mechanisms of vision in primates. *Psychol. Forsch. 31:* 229–337 (1968).

Tyler, H. R.: Defective stimulus exploration in aphasic patients. *Neurology 19:* 105–112 (1969a).

Tyler, H. R.: Disorders of visual scanning with frontal lobe lesions; in Locke, *Modern Neurology: Papers in Tribute to Derek Denny-Brown,* pp. 381–393 (Little, Brown and Company, Boston, 1969b).

Vurpillot, E.: The development of scanning strategies and their relation to visual differentiation. *J. of Exp. Child Psychol. 6:* 632–650 (1968).

Werner, H.: The concept of development from a comparative and organismic point of view; in Harris, *The Concept of Development,* pp. 125–148 (University of Minnesota Press, Minneapolis, Minn., 1957).

Weymouth, F. W.: Visual acuity in children; in Hirsch and Wick, *Vision of Children: An Optometric Symposium,* pp. 119–149 (Chilton Book Company, New York, 1963).

White, D. T. and Ford, A.: Eye movements during simulated radar search. *J. Opt. Soc. Amer. 50:* 909–913 (1960).

Woodworth, R. S.: Experimental psychology, 1st ed. (Holt and Company, New York, 1938).

Vernon, M. D.: *Backwardness in Reading: A Study of its Nature and Origin* (Cambridge University Press, New York, 1958).

Yarbus, A. L.: Eye movements and vision (Plenum Press, New York, 1967).

Zinchenko, V. P.; Chzhi-Tsin, V., and Tarakanov, V. V.: The formation and development of perceptual activity. *Soviet Psychol. Psychiat. 1:* 3–12 (1963).

Zusne, L. and Michel, K. M.: Nonrepresentational shapes and eye movements. *Percept. Motor Skills 18:* 11–20 (1964).

Chapter 9

LANGUAGE DEVELOPMENT

INTRODUCTION AND COMMENTARY

Comparative Analysis of Language

The uniqueness of humans in the animal kingdom has been attributable in part, to the fact that they normally acquire in the first few years after birth the phonological, the morphological, the syntactic, and the semantic components of language as well as learning how to use language appropriately. This is not to say that nonhuman species do not have intricate communication systems; in fact, Hockett and Altmann (1968) have argued that for each species, at every level of the phylogenetic scale up to *homo sapiens,* the associated communication system shows a closer and closer approximation to human language. They explore what they consider to be several crucial differences between the communicative systems of humans and animals. Among the features that they claim is unique to human language is *duality of patterning.* This refers to the fact that human speech is organized on the basis of a small number of phonemes (consonants, vowels, plus certain stress and intonational phenomena), which are combined and permuted to generate words, which themselves can be organized into syntactic sequences. Hockett and Altmann link duality of patterning to *productivity*—supposedly another unique feature of human language—the ability to create novel messages. Other distinctive features of the human linguistic code are thought to be *displacement,* the ability to talk about things remote in space and time; *prevarication,* the ability to lie; *learnability,* the capacity for speakers of one language to learn another one; and finally *reflectiveness,* the ability to communicate about the communication system itself. Thorpe (1972) argues that many species below the level of humans have access to one or more of these features, the single significant exception being that of *reflectiveness,* which does appear to be unique to humans. (It is interesting to consider other parallels to this: People can think about thinking, or, in more general terms, we have knowledge of our knowledge. See Gleitman, Gleitman, and Shipley, 1972, for a study of the development of linguistic knowledge.)

Lenneberg [26] states the case for a biological predisposition for the development of a language that is anchored in the operating characteristics of the human brain. He argues several points: Language behavior is found in every human culture; the onset of language is age-correlated; the same acquisition strategy is employed by every language learner; and language behavior may be specifically impaired by circumscribed brain lesions, while leaving other skills relatively intact. Comparative studies of the organizational properties of a large number of languages indicate the existence of *language universals;* that is, all of the languages so far investigated exhibit a high degree of formal similarity to each other. Such evidence leads Lenneberg to conclude that *any* behavior with such characteristics must have a highly specific biological foundation.

In his discussion of language-definitional universals, Slobin (1973) says that all human beings share the same general definition of the form and functions of language:

> Everywhere language consists of utterances performing a universal set of communicative functions (such as asserting, denying, requesting, ordering, and so forth), expressing a universal set of underlying semantic relations, and using a universal set of formal means (such as combinable units of meaning, made up of combinable units of sound, etc). Furthermore, language—everywhere—is grammatical, in the sense that the meaning of a message is not fully determined by any combination of the meaning of its elements (p. 179).

Other kinds of evidence that human beings are preprogrammed for language come from a theoretical interpretation of child language data collected cross-culturally that suggests that every child brings the same set of operating principles to the task of language learning (Slobin, 1973; see also Bever, 1970, for a discussion of how the child derives meaning from the speech he hears), and from research which demonstrates that preverbal human infants are, at a very young age, sensitive to some linguistic (phonemic) categories in the language they are to acquire (Eimas et al., 1971). The view that only human beings have the cognitive capacities to develop language behavior has come under sharp attack in recent studies of the development of symbolic systems in chimpanzees (e.g., Premack [27] and Gardner & Gardner, 1969). It is not yet clear either the extent to which these chimpanzees evidence the full range of cognitive capacities of humans, or what level of development they have achieved (see Brown, 1973, for a discussion of "linguistic apes").

The Development of Language in Children

Research in child language can be subdivided historically into two periods. The first period—up to the 1950s—was characterized by studies that were normative-descriptive and uninfluenced by linguistic theory; the second, beginning in the 1960s, during which the approach to the study of child language was radically altered through the primary stimulus provided by Chomsky's transformational-generative grammar (Chomsky, 1957; see also Chomsky, 1965). The importance of Chomsky's ideas to the psychological study of language is that he demonstrated that language development could not be interpreted as representing the acquisition of lists of words and sentences, but instead must be viewed as reflecting the availability of rule systems. In Brown's [28] account of what we presently know of the child's acquisition of language, he points out that Chomsky's work in linguistics led to the posing of new questions and to studies designed to reveal the *knowledge* that underlies the child's *linguistic creativity;* that is, his or her ability to both produce and understand novel speech. As Brown signifies, the major research goal was to write a "pivot" grammar that accounted for all of a child's syntactic knowledge. Although these attempts were never satisfactorily realized, what clearly emerged from them was evidence that the child's sentences were systematically organized right from the beginning. However, one serious weakness of the pivot grammar approach was its overemphasis on syntactic features and its neglect of the meanings that the speaker intended to communicate.

Recent research (Bloom, 1970; Bowerman, 1973; Schlesinger, 1971) indicates that the pivot grammar approach *underestimates* the child's linguistic knowledge. For example, Bloom (1970) obtained descriptions of the situations in which the child's speech occurred to discover that sentences in the child's speech which were structurally identical were, nevertheless, encoding different grammatical or functional meanings. She has found, for example, that noun–noun combinations in the earliest sentences express at least five different kinds of underlying relational meanings, for example, conjunction (boot, umbrella), attribution (party, hat), possession (Daddy, hat), subjective–locative (sweater, chair), and subject–object (Mommy, book). Current research on the child's semantic intentions includes work with both verbal and preverbal children; see, for example, the studies of the young child's semantic resources by McNamara (1972), Clark (1973), and Halliday (1975). Psycholinguistic interest in the child's semantic knowledge parallels a change in emphasis in linguistic research and theorizing, as some linguists (e.g., Fillmore, 1968, and Chafe, 1970) have moved away from a syntactically based to a semantically based grammar. Chafe's (1970) work consists, in part, of an account of the many different semantic roles that can be played by a noun, or a noun phrase, in various linguistic contexts. Brown (1973) presumes, quite properly, that the child has to acquire such knowledge and also that it would be profitable to uncover how the child does this.

Language and Thinking

Associated with the development of interest in the child's semantic system, there is a growing concern over the mutual relationship between the development of language and thinking. The traditional view of the relationships between language and thinking has been that language structures thought. The extreme form of this argument is characterized as the Whorfian hypothesis (or linguistic determinism), which suggests that the speaker's language restricts both the way one views the world and the way one thinks (Carroll, 1956; see also Jenkins, 1969, for a review of these arguments). Whereas until the last few years psychological accounts of child language were principally influenced by linguistic theory, the development of language is now interpreted in terms of cognitive theory, particularly by the Piagetian theory of intellectual development (see Chapter 10). This means that the child's language development is examined in the context of his or her general cognitive development. As in the case of perceptual development (see Chapter 8) researchers in child language are beginning to acknowledge the interdependencies among the varied types of cognitive skills and processes. Slobin (1973) has suggested that the pacesetter in linguistic growth is the child's *cognitive* growth. Sinclair (1970) offers a similar proposal in arguing that young children acquire only those linguistic structures that encode conceptual relations *already* evolved as part of their cognitive development. The view that language is acquired as a representation of logically prior conceptual learning derives from Piaget (1967) and is generally shared by current researchers in child language. For example, Brown (1973) traces early language learning to its roots in sensorimotor intelligence, and Nelson [29] offers a model to account for the child's initial translation of nonlinguistic meanings into words. By contrast, Blank (1974) examines the possible influences of language in affecting cognitive functioning, and also provides a critique of the methodology used to elucidate the role of language in cognition.

Socialization: Social Rules and Language

In addition to the child's acquisition of the structural rules of language, he or she must also learn other sets of rules concerning, for example, the social and cognitive uses of language. The child needs to know how to use language to structure experience, as well as when speech or silence is indicated, and what style of speech is appropriate. Bernstein (1971) has developed a sociolinguistic interpretation of socialization that assumes that the child learns within the family both the formal rules of his or her language and those rules that define its social and cognitive uses. In his theory Bernstein explores the ways in which different socialization practices influence language usage in children. Bernstein and Henderson (1969) have offered an indirect test of the Bernstein theory by examining the values attached to language as a teaching instrument in mothers of lower-and middle-class background (see also Glucksberg, Krauss, & Higgins; and Ervin-Tripp, 1973, for further discussion of sociolinguistic themes).

References

Bernstein, B. *Class, codes and control. Vol. 1: Theoretical studies towards a sociology of language.* London: Routledge, 1971.

Bernstein, B. & Henderson, D. Social class differences in the relevance of language to socialization. *Sociology,* 1969, *3*, 1–20.

Bever, T. G. The cognitive basis for linguistic structures. In J. R. Hayes (Ed.), *Cognition and the development of language.* New York: Wiley, 1970, pp. 279–352.

Blank, M. Cognitive functions of language in the preschool years. *Developmental Psychology,* 1974, *10*, 229–245.

Bloom, L. *Language development: Form and function in emerging grammars.* Cambridge: M.I.T. Press, 1970.

Bowerman, M. *Early syntactic development.* Cambridge: Cambridge University Press, 1973.

Brown, R. *A first language: The early stages.* Cambridge: Harvard University Press, 1973.

Carroll, J. S. (Ed.) *Language, thought and reality: Selected works of Benjamin Lee Whorf.* Cambridge: M.I.T. Press, 1956.

Chafe, W. L. *Meaning and structure of language.* Chicago: University of Chicago Press, 1970.

Chomsky, N. *Syntactic structures.* The Hague: Mouton, 1957.

Chomsky, N. *Aspects of the theory of syntax.* Cambridge: M.I.T. Press, 1965.

Clark, E. V. What's in a word? On the child's acquisition of semantics in his first language. In T. E. Moore (Ed.), *Cognitive development and the acquisition of language.* New York: Academic Press, 1973.

Eimas, P. D., Siqueland, E. R., Juscyk, P., & Vigorito, J. Speech perception in infants. *Science,* 1971, 303–306.

Ervin-Tripp, S. *Language acquisition and communicative choice.* Palo Alto, Ca.: Stanford University Press, 1973.

Fillmore, C. J. The case for case. In E. Bach & R. T. Harms (Eds.), *Universals in linguistic theory.* New York: Holt, Rinehart and Winston, 1968, pp. 1–87.

Gardner, B. T. & Gardner, R. A. Teaching sign language to a chimpanzee. *Science,* 1969, *165*, 664–672.

Gleitman, L. R., Gleitman, H., & Shipley, E. F. The emergence of the child as grammarian. *Cognition,* 1972, *1–3*, 137–164.

Glucksberg, S., Krauss, R. M., & Higgins, E. T. The development of referential communication skills. In F. D. Horowitz (Ed.), *Review of child development research,* Vol. IV. New York: Russell Sage Foundation, 1975.

Halliday, M. Learning how to mean. *Explorations in the development of language.* London: Edward Arnold, 1975.

Hockett, C. F. & Altmann, S. A. A note on design features. In T. A. Sebeok (Ed.), *Animal communication.* Bloomington: Indiana University Press, 1968.

Jankins, J. J. Language and thought. In J. F. Voss (Ed.), *Approaches to thought.* Columbus: Merrill, 1969, pp. 211–237.

McNamara, J. Cognitive base of language learning in infants. *Psychological Review,* 1972, *79*, 1–13.

Piaget, J. *Six psychological studies.* New York: Random House, 1967.

Schlesinger, I. M. Production of utterances and language acquisition. In D. I. Slobin (Ed.), *The ontogenesis of grammar.* New York: Academic Press, 1971, pp. 63–101.

Sinclair, H. The transition from sensorimotor behavior to symbolic activity. *Interchange,* 1970, *1*, 119–126.

Slobin, D. I. Cognitive prerequisites for the development of grammar. In C. A. Ferguson & D. I. Slobin (Eds.) *Studies of child language development.* New York: Holt, Rinehart and Winston, 1973.

Thorpe, W. H. The comparison of vocal communication in animals and men. In R. A. Hinde (Ed.), *Non-verbal communication.* Cambridge: Cambridge University Press, 1972, pp. 27–47.

26. ON EXPLAINING LANGUAGE

ERIC H. LENNEBERG

Many explanations have been offered for many aspects of language; there is little agreement, however, on how to explain various problems or even on what there is to be explained. Of course, explanations differ with the personal inclinations and interests of the investigator. My interests are in man as a biological species, and I believe that the study of language is relevant to these interests because language has the following six characteristics. (i) It is a form of behavior present in all cultures of the world. (ii) In all cultures its onset is age correlated. (iii) There is only one acquisition strategy—it is the same for all babies everywhere in the world. (iv) It is based intrinsically upon the same formal operating characteristics whatever its outward form (*1*). (v) Throughout man's recorded history these operating characteristics have been constant. (vi) It is a form of behavior that may be impaired specifically by circumscribed brain lesions which may leave other mental and motor skills relatively unaffected.

Any form of human behavior that has all of these six characteristics may likewise be assumed to have a rather specific biological foundation. This, of course, does not mean that language cannot be studied from different points of view; it can, for example, be investigated for its cultural or social variations, its capacity to reflect individual differences, or its applications. The purpose of this article, however, is to discuss the aspects of language to which biological concepts are applied most appropriately (*2*). Further, my concern is with the development of language in children—not with its origin in the species.

From *Science*, 1969, *164*, 635–643. Copyright 1969 by the American Association for the Advancement of Science. Reprinted by permission of the author and publisher.

Predictability of Language Development

A little boy starts washing his hands before dinner no sooner than when his parents decide that training in cleanliness should begin. However, children begin to speak no sooner and no later than when they reach a given stage of physical maturation (Table 26–1). There are individual variations in development, particularly with respect to age correlation. It is interesting that language development correlates better with motor development than it does with chronological age. If we take these two variables (motor and language development) and make ordinal scales out of the stages shown in Table 26–1 and then use them for a correlation matrix, the result is a remarkably small degree of scatter. Since motor development is one of the most important indices of maturation, it is not unreasonable to propose that language development, too, is related to physical growth and development. This impression is further corroborated by examination of retarded children. Here the age correlation is very poor, whereas the correlation between motor and language development continues to be high (*3*). Nevertheless, there is evidence that the statistical relation between motor and language development is not due to any immediate, causal relation; peripheral motor disabilities can occur that do not delay language acquisition.

Just as it is possible to correlate the variable language development with the variables chronological age or motor development, it is possible to relate it to the physical indications of brain maturation, such as the gross weight of the brain, neurodensity in the cerebral cortex, or the changing weight proportions of given substances in either gray or white matter. On

TABLE 26–1
Correlation of motor and language development

AGE (YEARS)	MOTOR MILESTONES	LANGUAGE MILESTONES
0.5	Sits using hands for support; unilateral reaching	Cooing sounds change to babbling by introduction of consonantal sounds
1	Stands; walks when held by one hand	Syllabic reduplication; signs of understanding some words; applies some sounds regularly to signify persons or objects, that is, the first words
1.5	Prehension and release fully developed; gait propulsive; creeps downstairs backward	Repertoire of 3 to 50 words not joined in phrases; trains of sounds and intonation patterns resembling discourse; good progress in understanding
2	Runs (with falls); walks stairs with one foot forward only	More than 50 words; two-word phrases most common; more interest in verbal communication; no more babbling
2.5	Jumps with both feet; stands on one foot for 1 second; builds tower of six cubes	Every day new words; utterances of three and more words; seems to understand almost everything said to him; still many grammatical deviations
3	Tiptoes 3 yards (2.7 meters); walks stairs with alternating feet; jumps 0.9 meter	Vocabulary of some 1000 words; about 80 percent intelligibility; grammar of utterances close approximation to colloquial adult; syntactic mistakes fewer in variety, systematic, predictable
4.5	Jumps over rope; hops on one foot; walks on line	Language well established; grammatical anomalies restricted either to unusual constructions or to the more literate aspects of discourse

almost all counts, language begins when such maturational indices have attained at least 65 percent of their mature values. (Inversely, language acquisition becomes more difficult when the physical maturation of the brain is complete.) These correlations do not prove causal connections, although they suggest some interesting questions for further research.

Effect of Certain Variations in Social Environment

In most of the studies on this topic the language development of children in orphanages or socially deprived households has been compared with that of children in so-called normal, middle-class environments. Statistically significant differences are usually reported, which is sometimes taken as a demonstration that language development is contingent on specific language training. That certain aspects of the environment are absolutely essential for language development is undeniable, but it is important to distinguish between what the children actually do, and what they can do.

There is nothing particularly surprising or revealing in the demonstration that language deficits occur in children who hear no language, very little language, or only the discourse of uneducated persons. But what interests us is the underlying capacity for language. This is not a spurious question; for instance, some children have the capacity for language but do not use it, either because of peripheral handicaps such as congenital deafness or because of psychiatric disturbances such as childhood schizophrenia; other children may not speak because they do not have a sufficient capacity for language, on account of certain severely retarding diseases.

There is a simple technique for ascertaining the degree of development of the capacity for speech and language. Instead of assessing it by means of an inventory of the vocabulary, the grammatical complexity of the utterances, the clarity of pronunciation, and the like, and computing a score derived from several subtests of this kind, it is preferable to describe the children's ability in terms of a few broad and general developmental stages, such as those shown in Table 26–1. Tests which are essentially inventories of vocabulary and syntactic constructions are likely to reflect simply the deficiencies of the environment; they obscure the child's potentialities and capabilities.

I have used the schema described to compare the speech development of children in many different societies, some of them much more primitive than our own. In none of these studies could I find evidence of variation in developmental rate, despite the enormous differences in social environment.

I have also had an opportunity to study the effect of a dramatically different speech environment upon the development of vocalizations during the first 3 months of life (4). It is very common in our culture for congenitally deaf individuals to marry one another, creating households in which all vocal sounds are decidedly different from those normally heard and in which the sounds of babies cannot be attended to directly. Six deaf mothers and ten hearing mothers were asked, during their last month of pregnancy, to participate in our study. The babies were visited at home when they were no more than 10 days old and were seen biweekly thereafter for at least 3 months. Each visit consisted of 3 hours of observation and 24

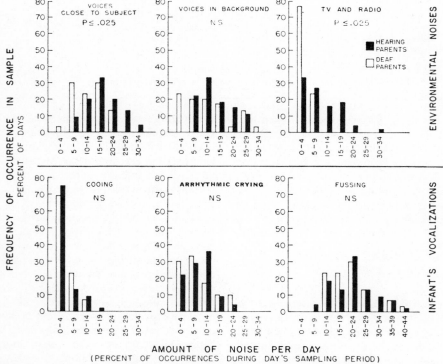

FIGURE 26–1.   Frequency distributions of various noises. The basic counting unit is individual recording days.

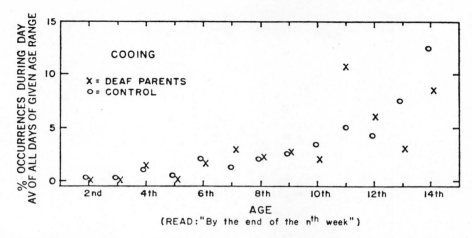

FIGURE 26–2. Each baby's day was divided into 6-minute periods; the presence or absence of cooing was noted for each period; this yielded a percentage for each baby's day; days of all babies were ordered by their ages, and the average was taken for all days of identical age. Nonaveraged data were published in (4).

hours of mechanical recording of all sounds made and heard by the baby. Data were analyzed quantitatively and qualitatively. Figure 26–1 shows that although the environment was quantitatively quite different in the experimental and the control groups, the frequency distributions of various baby noises did not differ significantly; as seen in Figure 26–2, the developmental histories of cooing noises are also remarkably alike in the two groups. Figure 26–3 demonstrates that the babies of deaf parents tend to fuss an equal amount, even though the hearing parents are much more likely to come to the child when it fusses. Thus the earliest development of human sounds appears to be relatively independent of the amount, nature, or timing of the sounds made by parents.

I have observed this type of child-rearing through later stages, as well. The hearing children of deaf parents eventually learn two languages and sound systems: those of their deaf parents and those of the rest of the community. In some instances, communication between children and parents is predominantly by gestures. In no case have I found any adverse effects upon the language development of standard English in these children. Although the mothers made sounds different from the children's, and although the children's vocalizations had no significant effect upon attaining what they wanted during early infancy, language in these children invariably began at the usual time and went through the same stages as is normally encountered.

Also of interest may be the following observations on fairly retarded children growing up in state institutions that are badly understaffed. During the day the children play in large, bare rooms, attended by only one person, often an older retardate who herself lacks a perfect command of language. The children's only entertainment is provided by a large television set, playing all day at full strength. Although most of these retarded children have only primitive beginnings of language, there are always some among them who manage, even under these extremely deprived circumstances, to pick up an amazing degree of language skill. Apparently they learn language partly through the television programs, whose level is often quite adequate for them!

From these instances we see that language capacity follows its own natural history. The child can avail himself of this capacity if the environment provides a minimum of stimulation and opportunity. His engagement in language activity can be limited by his environmental circumstances, but the underlying

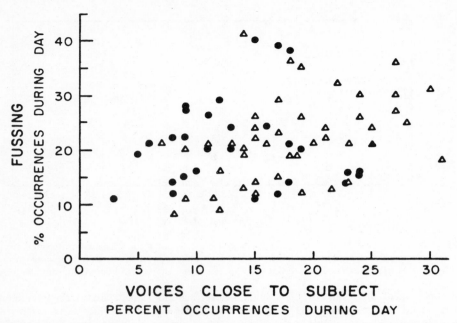

FIGURE 26–3. Relation between the amount of parents' noises heard by the baby and the amount of fussing noises made by the baby. Each symbol is one baby's day; (solid circles) deaf parents; (triangles) hearing parents.

capacity is not easily arrested. Impoverished environments are not conducive to good language development, but good language development is not contingent on specific training measures (5); a wide variety of rather haphazard factors seems to be sufficient.

Effect of Variations in Genetic Background

Man is an unsatisfactory subject for the study of genetic influences; we cannot do breeding experiments on him and can use only statistical controls. Practically any evidence adduced is susceptible to a variety of interpretations. Nevertheless, there are indications that inheritance is at least partially responsible for deviations in verbal skills, as in the familial occurrence of a deficit termed congenital language disability (2, chapter 6). Studies, with complete pedigrees, have been published on the occurrence and distribution of stuttering, of hyperfluencies, of voice qualities, and of many other

traits, which constitute supporting though not conclusive evidence that inheritance plays a role in language acquisition. In addition to such family studies, much research has been carried out on twins. Particularly notable are the studies of Luchsinger, who reported on the concordance of developmental histories and of many aspects of speech and language. Zygosity was established in these cases by serology (Figure 26–4). Developmental data of this kind are, in my opinion, of greater relevance to our speculations on genetic background than are pedigrees.

The nonbiologist frequently and mistakenly thinks of genes as being directly responsible for one property or another; this leads him to the fallacy, especially when behavior is concerned, of dichotomizing everything as being dependent on either genes or environment. Genes act merely on intracellular biochemical processes, although these processes have indirect effects on events in the individual's developmental history. Many alterations in structure and function indirectly attributable to genes are more im-

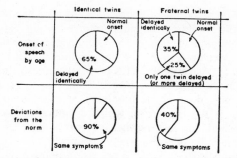

FIGURE 26–4. The onset of speech and its subsequent development tend to be more uniform among identical twins than fraternal twins.

mediately the consequence of alterations in the schedule of developmental events. Therefore, the studies on twins are important in that they show that homozygotes reach milestones in language development at the same age, in contrast to heterozygotes, in whom divergences are relatively common. It is also interesting that the nature of the deviations—the symptoms, if you wish—are, in the vast majority, identical in homozygotes but not in heterozygotes.

Such evidence indicates that man's biological heritage endows him with sensitivities and propensities that lead to language development in children, who are spoken to (in contrast to chimpanzee infants, who do not automatically develop language—either receptive or productive—under identical treatment). The endowment has a genetic foundation, but this is not to say that there are "genes for language," or that the environment is of no importance.

Attempts To Modify Language Development

Let us now consider children who have the capacity for language acquisition but fail to develop it for lack of exposure. This is the case with the congenitally deaf, who are allowed to grow up without either language or speech until school age, when suddenly language is brought to them in very unnatural ways. Before this time they may have half a dozen words they can utter, read, write, or finger-spell, but I have known of no profoundly deaf child (in New England, where my investigations were conducted) with whom one could communicate by use of the English language before school age.

When deaf children enter an oralist school, lipreading and speech become the major preoccupation of training. However, in most children these activities remain poor for many more years, and in some, throughout life. Their knowledge of language comes through learning to read and write. However, teachers in the oral tradition restrict expression in the graphic medium on the hypothesis that it interferes with lipreading and speech skills. Thus, exposure to language (i) comes much later in these children's lives than is normal, (ii) is dramatically reduced in quantity, (iii) is presented through a different medium and sensory modality, and (iv) is taught to the children rather as a second language is taught, instead of through the simple immersion into a sea of language that most children experience. The deaf children are immediately required to use grammatically correct sentences, and every mistake is discussed and explained to them.

The results of this procedure are interesting but not very encouraging from the educational point of view. During the early years of schooling, the children's spontaneous writings have a very unusual pattern; there is little evidence that the teachers' instruction in "how to compose correct sentences" is of any avail. Yet, careful analysis of their compositions shows that some subtleties of English syntax that are usually not part of the grammar taught in the school do make their appearance, sometimes quite early. There can be no question that the children do not simply imitate what they see; some of the teachings fall by the wayside, whereas a number of aspects of language are automatically absorbed from the written material given to the children.

There are other instances in which efforts are made to change a child's language skills by special training, as in the mildly retarded, for example. Many parents believe that their retarded child would function quite normally if somebody could just teach him to speak. At Children's Hospital in Boston I undertook a pilot study in which a speech therapist saw a small number of children with Downe's syndrome (mongolism) for several hours each week, in an effort to speed up language development. Later, two graduate students in linguistics investigated the children's phonetic skills and tried to assess the capacities of each child for clearer enunciation. Throughout these attempts, it was found that if a child had a small repertoire of single words, it was always possible to teach him yet another word, but if he was not joining these words spontaneously into phrases, there was nothing that could be done to induce him to do so. The articulatory skills were somewhat different. It was often possible to make a child who had always had slurred speech say a specific word more clearly. However, the moment the child returned to spontaneous utterances, he would fall back to the style that was usual for him. The most interesting results were obtained when the retarded children were required simply to repeat well-formed sentences. A child who had not developed to a stage in which he used certain grammatical rules spontaneously, who was still missing the syntactic foundations and prerequisites, could not be taught to repeat a sentence that was formed by such higher rules. This was true even in sentences of very few words. Similar observations have since been made on normal children (6), with uniformly similar results; normal children, too, can repeat correctly only that which is formed by rules they have already mastered. This is the best indication that language does not come about by simple imitation, but that the child abstracts regularities or relations from the language he hears, which he then applies to building up language for himself as an apparatus of principles.

What Sets the Pace of Language Development?

There is a widespread belief that the development of language is dependent on the motor skills of the articulating organs. Some psychologists believe that species other than man fail to develop language only because of anatomical differences in their oral structures. However, we have evidence that this is not so.

It is important that we are clear about the essential nature of language. Since my interests are in language capacities, I am concerned with the development of the child's knowledge of how language works. This is not the same as the acquisition of "the first word." The best test for the presence and development of this knowledge is the manner in which discourse is understood. In most instances, it is true that there is a relation between speech and understanding, but this relation is not a necessary one (7).

By understanding, I mean something quite specific. In the realm of phonology, understanding involves a process that roughly corresponds to the linguists' phonematization (in contrast, for example, to a "pictographic" understanding: phonematization results in seeing similarities between speech sounds, whereas pictographic understanding would treat a word as an indivisible sound pattern). In the realm of semantics, understanding involves seeing the basis on which objects are categorized, thus enabling a child to name an object correctly that he has never seen before. (The child does not start out with a hypothesis that "table" is the proper name of a unique object or that it refers to all things that have four appendages.) In the realm of grammar, understanding involves the extraction of relations between word classes; an example is the understanding of predication. By application of these tests, it can be shown empirically that Aunt Pauline's favorite lapdog does not have a little language knowledge, but, in fact, fails the test of understanding on all counts.

A survey of children with a variety of handicaps shows that their grasp of how language works is intimately related to their general cognitive growth, which, in turn, is partly dependent on physical maturation and partly on opportunities to interact with a stimulus-rich environment. In many retarding diseases, for example, language development is predicted best by the rate of advancement in mental age (using tests of nonverbal intelligence). In an investigation of congenitally blind children (8), we are again finding that major milestones for language development are highly correlated with physical development. A naive conception of language development as an accumulation of associations between visual and auditory patterns would be hard put to explain this.

Brain Correlates

In adults, language functions take place predominantly in the left hemisphere. A number of cortical fields have been related to specific aspects of language. The details are still somewhat controversial and need not concern us here. It is certain, however, that precentral areas of the frontal lobe are principally involved in the production of language, whereas the postcentral parietal and superior temporal fields are involved in sensory functions. These cortical specializations are not present at birth, but become only gradually established during childhood, in a process very similar to that of embryological history; there is evidence of differentiation and regulation of function. In the adult, traumata causing large leftsided central cortical lesions carry a highly predictable prognosis; in 70 percent of all cases, aphasia occurs, and in about half of these, the condition is irreversible (I am basing these figures on our experience with penetrating head injuries incurred in war).

Comparable traumatic lesions in childhood have quite different consequences, the prognosis being directly related to the age at which the insult is incurred. Lesions of the left hemisphere in children under age 2 are no more injurious to future language development than are lesions of the right hemisphere. Children whose brain is traumatized after the onset of language but before the age of 4 usually have transient aphasias; language is quickly reestablished, however, if the right hemisphere remains intact. Often these children regain language by going through stages of language development similar to those of the 2-year-old, but they traverse each stage at greater speed. Lesions incurred before the very early teens also carry an excellent prognosis, permanent residues of symptoms being extremely rare.

The prognosis becomes rapidly worse for lesions that occur after this period; the young men who become casualties of war have symptoms virtually identical with those of stroke patients of advanced age. Experience with the surgical removal of an entire cerebral hemisphere closely parallels this picture. The basis for prognosticating operative success is, again, the age at which the disease has been contracted for which the operation is performed.

If a disturbance in the left hemisphere occurs early enough in life, the right hemisphere remains competent for language throughout life. Apparently this process is comparable to regulation, as we know it from morphogenesis. If the disease occurs after a certain critical period of life, namely, the early teens, this regulative capacity is lost and language is interfered with permanently. Thus the time at which the hemispherectomy is performed is less important than the time of the lesion.

Critical Age for Language Acquisition

The most reasonable interpretation of this picture of recovery from aphasia in childhood is not that there is vicarious functioning, or taking over, by the right hemisphere because of need, but rather that language functions are not yet confined to the left hemisphere during early life. Apparently both hemispheres are involved at the beginning, and a specialization takes place later (which is the characteristic of differentiation), resulting in a kind of left-right polarization of functions. Therefore, the recovery from aphasia during preteen years may partly be regarded as a reinstatment of activities that had never been lost. There is evidence that children at this age are capable of developing language in the same natural way as do very young children. Not only do symptoms subside, but active language development continues to occur. Similarly, we see that healthy children have a quite different propensity for acquiring foreign languages before the early teens than after the late teens, the period in between being transitional. For the young adult, second-language learning is an academic exercise, and there is a vast variety in degree of proficiency. It rapidly becomes more and more difficult to overcome the accent and interfering influences of the mother tongue.

Neurological material strongly suggests that something happens in the brain during the early teens that changes the propensity for language acquisition. We do not know the factors involved, but it is interesting that the critical period coincides with the time at which the human brain attains its final state of maturity in terms of structure, function, and biochemistry (electroencephalographic patterns slightly lag behind, but become stabilized by about 16 years). Apparently the maturation of the brain marks the end of regulation and locks certain functions into place.

There is further evidence that corroborates the notion of a critical period for primary language acquisition, most importantly, the developmental histories of retarded children. It is dangerous to make sweeping generalizations about all retarded children, because so much depends on the specific disease that causes the retardation. But if we concentrate on diseases in which the pathological condition is essentially stationary, such as microcephaly vera or mongolism, it is possible to make farly general predictions about language development. If the child's mental developmental age is 2 when he is 4 years old (that is, his I.Q. is 50), one may safely predict that some small progress will be made in language development. He will slowly move through the usual stages of infant language, although the rate of development will gradually slow down. In virtually all of these cases, language development comes to a complete standstill in the early teens, so that these individuals are arrested in primitive stages of language development that are perpetuated for the rest of their lives. Training and motivation are of little help.

Development in the congenitally deaf is also revealing. When they first enter school, their language acquisition is usually quite spectacular, considering the enormous odds against them. However, children who by their early teens have still not mastered all of the principles that underlie the production of sentences appear to encounter almost unsurmountable difficulties in perfecting verbal skills.

There is also evidence of the converse. Children who suddenly lose their hearing (usually a consequence of meningitis) show very different degrees of language skill, depending on whether the disease strikes before the onset of language or after. If it occurs before they are 18 months old, such children encounter difficulties with language development that are very much the same as those encountered by the congenitally deaf. Children who lose their hearing after they have acquired language, however, at age 3 to 4, have a different prospect. Their speech deteriorates rapidly; usually within weeks they stop using language, and so far it has proved impossible to maintain the skill by educational procedures [although new techniques developed in England and described by Fry (9) give promise of great improvement]. Many such children then live without language for a relatively long time, often 2 to 3 years, and when they enter the schools for the deaf, must be trained in the same way that other deaf children are trained. However, training is much more successful, and their language habits stand out dramatically against those of their less fortunate colleagues. There appears to be a direct relation between the length of time during which a child has been exposed to language and the proficiency seen at the time of retraining.

Biological Approach: Defining Language Further

Some investigators propose that language is an artifact—a tool that man has shaped for himself to serve a purpose. This assumption induces the view that language consists of many individual traits, each independent of the other. However, the panorama of observations presented above suggests a biological predisposition for the development of language that is anchored in the operating characteristics of the human brain (10). Man's cognitive apparatus apparently becomes a language receiver and transmitter, provided the growing organism is exposed to minimum and haphazard environmental events.

However, this assumption leads to a view different from that suggested by the artifact assumption. Instead of thinking of language as a collection of separate and mutually independent traits, one comes to see it as a profoundly integrated activity. Language is to be understood as an operation rather than a static product of the mind. Its modus operandi reflects that of human cognition, because language is an intimate part of cognition. Thus the biological view denies that language is the cause of cognition, or even its effect, since language is not an object (like a tool) that exists apart from a living human brain.

As biologists, we are interested in the operating principles of language because we hope that this will give us some clues about the operating principles of the human brain. We know there is just one species *Homo sapiens*, and it is therefore reasonable to assume that individuals who speak Turkish, English, or Basque (or who spoke Sanskrit some millennia ago) all have (or had) the same kind of brain, that is, a computer with the same operating principles and the same sensorium. Therefore, in a biological investigation one must try to disregard the differences between the languages of the world and to discover the general principles of operation that are common to all of them. This is not an easy matter; in fact, there are social scientists who doubt the existence of language universals. As students of language we cannot fail to be impressed with the enormous differences among languages. Yet every normal child learns the language to which he is exposed. Perhaps we are simply claiming that common denominators must exist; can we prove their existence? If we discovered a totally isolated tribe with a language unknown to any outsider, how could we find out whether this language is generated by a computer that has the same biological characteristics as do our brains, and how could we prove that it shares the universal features of all languages?

As a start, we could exchange children between our two cultures to discover whether the same language developmental history would occur in those exchanged. Our data would be gross developmental stages, correlated with the emergence of motor milestones. A bioassay of this kind (already performed many times, always with positive results) gives only part of the answer.

In theory, one may also adduce more rigorous proof of similarity among languages. The conception of language universals is difficult to grasp intuitively, because we find it so hard to translate from one language to another and because the grammars appear, on the surface, to be so different. But it is entirely possible that underneath the structural difference that makes it so difficult for the adult speaker to learn a second language (particularly one that is not a cognate of his own) there are significant formal identities.

Virtually every aspect of language is the expression of relations. This is true of phonology (as stressed by Roman Jakobson and his school), semantics, and syntax. For instance, in all languages of the world words label a set of relational principles instead of being labels of specific objects. Knowing a word is never a simple association between an object and an acoustic pattern, but the successful operation of those principles, or application of those rules, that lead to using the word "table" or "house" for objects never before encountered. The language universal in this instance is not the type of object that comes to have a word, nor the particular relations involved; the universal is the generality that words stand for relations instead of being unique names for one object.

Further, no language has ever been described that does not have a second order of relational principles, namely, principles in which relations are being related, that is, syntax in which relations between words are being specified. Once again, the universal is not a particular relation that occurs in all languages (though there are several such relations) but that all languages have relations of relations.

Mathematics may be used as a highly abstract form of description, not of scattered facts but of the dynamic interrelations—the operating principles—found in nature. Chomsky and his students have done this. Their aim has been to develop algorithms for specific languages, primarily English, that make explicit the series of computations that may account for the structure of sentences. The fact that these attempts have only been partially successful is irrelevant to the argument here. (Since every native speaker of English *can* tell a well-formed sentence from an ill-formed one, it is evident that some principles must exist; the question is merely whether the Chomskyites have discovered the correct ones.) The development of algorithms is only one province of mathematics, and in the eyes of many mathematicians a relatively limited one. There is a more exciting prospect; once we know something about the basic relational operating principles underlying a few languages, it should be possible to characterize formally the abstract system *language* as a whole. If our assumption of the existence of basic, structural language universals is correct, one ought to be able to adduce rigorous proof for the existence of homeomorphisms between any natural languages, that is, any of the systems characterized formally. If a category calculus were developed for this sort of thing, there would be one level of generality on which a common denominator could be found; this may be done trivially (for instance by using the product of all systems). However, our present knowledge of the relations, and the relations of relations, found in the languages so far investigated in depth encourages us to expect a significant solution.

Environment and Maturation

Everything in life, including behavior and language, is interaction of the individual with its milieu. But the milieu is not constant. The organism itself helps to shape it (this is true of cells and organs as much as of animals and man). Thus, the organism and its environment is a dynamic system and, phylogenetically, developed as such.

The development of language in the child may be elucidated by applying to it the conceptual framework of developmental biology. Maturation may be characterized as a sequence of states. At each state, the growing organism is capable of accepting some specific input; this it

breaks down and resynthesizes in such a way that it makes itself develop into a new state. This new state makes the organism sensitive to new and different types of input, whose acceptance transforms it to yet a further state, which opens the way to still different input, and so on. This is called epigenesis. It is the story of embryological development observable in the formation of the body, as well as in certain aspects of behavior.

At various epigenetic states, the organism may be susceptible to more than one sort of input—it may be susceptible to two or more distinct kinds or even to an infinite variety of inputs, as long as they are within determined limits—and the developmental history varies with the nature of the input accepted. In other words, the organism, during development, comes to crossroads; if condition A is present, it goes one way; if condition B is present, it goes another. We speak of states here, but this is, of course, an abstraction. Every stage of maturation is unstable. It is prone to change into specific directions, but requires a trigger from the environment.

When language acquisition in the child is studied from the point of view of developmental biology, one makes an effort to describe developmental stages together with their tendencies for change and the conditions that bring about that change. I believe that the schema of physical maturation is applicable to the study of language development because children appear to be sensitive to successively different aspects of the language environment. The child first reacts only to intonation patterns. With continued exposure to these patterns as they occur in a given language, mechanisms develop that allow him to process the patterns, and in most instances to reproduce them (although the latter is not a necessary condition for further development). This changes him so that he reaches a new state, a new potential for language development. Now he becomes aware of certain articulatory aspects, can process them and possibly also reproduce them, and so on. A similar sequence of acceptance, synthesis, and state of new acceptance can be demonstrated on the level of semantics and syntax.

That the embryological concepts of differentiation, as well as of determination and regulation, are applicable to the brain processes associated with language development is best illustrated by the material discussed above under the headings "brain correlates" and "critical age for language acquisition." Furthermore, the correlation between language development and other maturational indices suggests that there are anatomical and physiological processes whose maturation sets the pace for both cognitive and language development; it is to these maturational processes that the concept differentiation refers. We often transfer the meaning of the word to the verbal behavior itself, which is not unreasonable, although, strictly speaking, it is the physical correlates only that differentiate.

Pseudo-Homologies and Naive "Evolutionizing"

The relation between species is established on the basis of structural, physiological, biochemical, and often behavioral correspondences, called homologies. The identification of homologies frequently poses heuristic problems. Common sense may be very misleading in this matter. Unless there is cogent evidence that the correspondences noted are due to a common phylogenetic origin, one must entertain the possibility that resemblances are spurious (though perhaps due to convergence). In other words, not all criteria are equally reliable for the discovery of true homologies. The criteria must pass the following two tests if they are to reveal common biological origins. (i) They must be applicable to traits that have a demonstrable (or at least conceivable) genetic basis; and (ii) the traits to which they apply must not have a sporadic and seemingly random distribution over the taxa of the entire animal kingdom. Homologies cannot be established by relying on similarity that rests on superficial inspection (a whale is not a fish); on logical rather than biological aspects (animals that move at 14 miles per hour are not necessarily related to one another); and on anthropocentric imputation of motives (a squirrel's hoarding of nuts may have nothing in common with man's provisions for his future).

Comparisons of language with animal communication that purport to throw light on the problem of its phylogenetic origins infringe on every one of these guidelines. Attempts to write generative grammars for the language of the bees in order to discover in what respect that language is similar to and different from man's language fail to pass test (i). Syntax does not have a genetic basis any more than does arithmetic or algebra; these are calculi used to describe relations. It may be that the activities or circumstances to which the calculi are applied are in some way related to genetically determined capacities. However, merely the fact that the calculus may or may not be applied obviously does not settle that issue.

The common practice of searching the entire animal kingdom for communication behavior that resembles man's in one aspect or another fails test (ii). The fact that some bird species and perhaps two or three cetaceans can make noises that sound like words, that some insects use discrete signals when they communicate, or that recombination of signals has been observed to occur in communication systems of a dozen totally unrelated species are not signs of a common phylogeny or genetically based relationship to language. Furthermore, the similarities noted between human language and animal communication all rest on superficial intuition. The resemblances that exist between human language and the language of the bees and the birds are spurious. The comparative criteria are usually logical (12) instead of biological; and the very idea that there must be a common denominator underlying all communication systems of animals and man is based on an anthropocentric imputation.

Everything in biology has a history, and so every communication system is the result of evolution. But traits or skills do not have an evolutionary history of their own, that is, a history that is independent of the history of the species. Contemporary species are discontinuous groups (except for those in the process of branching) with discontinuous communication behavior. Therefore, historical continuity need not lead to continuity between contemporary communication systems, many of which (including man's) constitute unique developments.

Another recent practice is to give speculative accounts of just how, why, and when human language developed. This is a somewhat futile undertaking. The knowledge that we have gained about the mechanisms of evolution does not enable us to give specific accounts of every event of the past. Paleontological evidence points to the nature of its fauna, flora, and climate. The precursors of modern man have left for us their bones, teeth, and primitive tools. None of these bears any necessary or assured relation to any type of communication system. Most speculations on the nature of the most primitive sounds, on the first discovery of their usefulness, on the reasons for the hypertrophy of the brain, or the consequences of a narrow pelvis are in vain. We can no longer reconstruct what the selection pressures were or in what order they came, because we know too little that is securely established by hard evidence about the ecological and social conditions of fossil man. Moreover, we do not even know what the targets of actual selection were. This is particularly troublesome because every genetic alteration brings about several changes at once, some of which must be quite incidental to the selective process.

Species Specificities and Cognitive Specialization

In the 19th century it was demonstrated that man is not in a category apart from that of animals. Today it seems to be necessary to defend the view (before many psychologists) that man is not identical with all other animals—in fact, that every animal species is unique, and that most of the commonalities that exist are, at best, homologies. It is frequently claimed that the principles of behavioral function are identical—in all vertebrates, for example—and that the differences between species are differences of magnitude, rather than quality. At other times, it is assumed that

cognitive functions are alike in two species except that one of the two may have additionally acquired a capacity for a specific activity. I find fault with both views.

Since behavioral capacities (I prefer the term cognition) are the product of brain function, my point can well be illustrated by considering some aspects of brain evolution. Every mammalian species has an anatomically distinct brain. Homologies are common, but innovations can also be demonstrated. When man's brain is compared with the brain of other primates, extensive correspondences can be found, but there are major problems when it comes to the identification of homologies. Dramatic differences exist not only in size but also in details of the developmental histories; together with differences in cerebrocortical histology, topography, and extent, there are differences in subcortical fiber-connections, as pointed out by Geschwind (13) most recently and by others before him. The problem is, what do we make of the innovations? Is it possible that each innovation (usually an innovation is not a clear-cut anatomical entity) is like an independent component that is simply added to the components common to all the more old-fashioned brains? And if so, is it likely that the new component is simply adding a routine to the computational facilities already available? Both presumptions are naive. A brain is an integrated organ, and cognition results from the integrated operation of all its tissues and suborgans. Man's brain is not a chimpanzee's brain plus added "association facilities." Its functions have undergone reintegration at the same pace as its evolutionary developments.

The identical argument applies to cognitive functions. Cognition is not made up of isolated processes such as perception, storing, and retrieval. Animals do not all have an identical memory mechanism except that some have a larger storage capacity. As the structure of most proteins, the morphology of most cells, and the gross anatomy of most animals show certain species specificities (as do details of behavioral repertoires), so we may expect that cognition, too, in all of its aspects, has its species specificities. My assumption, therefore, is that man's cognition is not essentially that of every other primate with merely the addition of the capacity for language; instead, I propose that his entire cognitive function, of which his capacity for language is an integral part, is species-specific. I repeat once more that I make this assumption not because I think man is in a category all of his own, but because every animal species must be assumed to have cognitive specificities.

Conclusion

The human brain is a biochemical machine; it computes the relations expressed in sentences and their components. It has a print-out consisting of acoustic patterns that are capable of similar relational computation by machines of the same constitution using the same program. Linguists, biologists, and psychologists have all discussed certain aspects of the machine.

Linguists, particularly those developing generative grammar, aim at a formal description of the machine's behavior; they search mathematics for a calculus to describe it adequately. Different calculations are matched against the behavior to test their descriptive adequacy. This is an empirical procedure. The raw data are the way a speaker of a language understands collections of words or the relationships he sees. A totally adequate calculus has not yet been discovered. Once available, it will merely describe, in formal terms, the process of relational interpretation in the realm of verbal behavior. It will describe a set of operations; however, it will not make any claims of isomorphism between the formal operations and the biological operations they describe.

Biologists try to understand the nature, growth, and function of the machine (the human brain) itself. They make little inroads here and there, and generally play catch-as-catch-can; everything about the machine interests them (including the descriptions furnished by linguists).

Traditionally, learning theory has been involved neither in a specific description of this particular machine's behavior nor in its physical constitution. Its concern has been with the use of the machine: What makes it go? Can one make it operate more or less often? What purposes does it serve?

Answers provided by each of these inquiries into language are not intrinsically antagonistic, as has often been claimed. It is only certain overgeneralizations that come into conflict. This is especially so when claims are made that any one of these approaches provides answers to all the questions that matter.

REFERENCES AND NOTES

1.   E. H. Lenneberg, in *The Structure of Language, Readings in the Philosophy of Language*. J. A. Fodor and J. J. Katz, Eds. (Prentice-Hall, Englewood Cliffs, N.J., 1964).
2.   For complete treatment, see E. H. Lenneberg, *Biological Foundations of Language* (Wiley, New York, 1967).
3.   E. H. Lenneberg, I. A. Nichols, E. F. Rosenberger, in *Disorders of Communication*, D. Rioch, Ed. (Research Publications of Association for Research in Nervous and Mental Disorders, New York, 1964), vol. 42.
4.   E. H. Lenneberg, F. G. Rebelsky, I. A. Nichols, *Hum. Develop.* 8, 23 (1965).
5.   R. Brown, C. Cazden, U. Bellugi, in *The 1967 Minnesota Symposium on Child Psychology*, J. P. Hill, Ed. (Univ. of Minnesota Press, Minneapolis, in press).
6.   D. Slobin, personal communication.
7.   E. H. Lenneberg, *J. Abnorm. Soc. Psychol.* 65, 419 (1962).
8.   ———, S. Fraiberg, N. Stein, research in progress.
9.   D. B. Fry, in *The Genesis of Language: A Psycholinguistic Approach*, F. Smith and G. A. Miller, Eds. (MIT Press, Cambridge, 1966).

10. For details, see E. H. Lenneberg, *Perception and Language,* in preparation.
11. N. Chomsky, "The formal nature of language" (in 2, appendix A).
12. See, for instance, C. F. Hockett, in *Animal Communication,* W. E. Lanyon and W. N. Tavelga, Eds. (American Institute of Biological Sciences, Washington, D.C., 1960); and in *Sci. Amer. 203,* 89 (1960).
13. N. Geschwind, *Brain 88,* 237, 585 (1965).
14. I thank H. Levin and M. Seligman for comments and criticisms.

27. LANGUAGE IN CHIMPANZEE?

DAVID PREMACK

Can apes be taught language? Although this question is of biological import, it may ultimately be more important to the fundamental question, What is language? The ape, when properly trained, emerges as the unclear middle case: Neither wholly comparable to man (the clear positive case) nor to parrot (the clear negative), the "talking" ape puts the question of language to its first severe test (*1*).

The approach I have taken to the twofold question of what language is and whether an ape can be taught it can be expressed in terms of two parallel lists. The first is a list of exemplars, things an organism must be able to do in order to give evidence of language. The second is a corresponding list of instructions for training the organism so that it may be taught the exemplars in question.

The exemplars I am dealing with here concern selected aspects of: (i) words; (ii) sentences; (iii) questions; (iv) metalinguistics (using language to teach language); (v) class concepts such as *color, shape,* and *size;* (vi) the copula; (vii) the quantifiers all, none, one, and several; and (viii) the logical connective if-then. This list is in no sense exhaustive, nor are the items on it of comparable logical order. They are simply topics that were chosen to illustrate the present approach.

Each word of the language used with the chimp is a piece of plastic, backed with metal, that adheres to a magnetized slate (Figure

From *Science,* 1971, *172,* 808–822. Copyright 1971 by the American Association for the Advancement of Science. Reprinted by permission of the author and the publisher.

27–1). Sentences are written on the vertical. The two sentences shown in Fig. 27–1 can be paraphrased in English as, "No Sarah take honey-cracker" and "Sarah take jambread," respectively (*2*). Since the language is written rather than spoken or gestured, words and sentences are permanent. The permanence of the sentence makes it possible to study language without a memory problem. In addition, because the experimenter makes the words, while the chimp merely uses them, the difficulty of any task can be modulated by controlling the number and kind of words available to the chimp at any given time (*3*). There are no phonemes in the language; we have deliberately made the basic unit the word (*4, 5*).

Mapping a Social Exchange

The first step in introducing a naive subject to words is to establish a social exchange between subject and trainer. A feeding routine provided an effective transaction with Sarah, an African-born, female chimpanzee about 6 years old when the study began. The trainer began by placing a piece of fruit on the table between Sarah and himself and looking on in a friendly manner while she took it and ate it. After the transaction was well established, the trainer placed a piece of colored plastic from the language system alongside the piece of fruit. The fruit was then placed out of reach, while the plastic chip was easily within reach. Sarah was induced to make a prescribed response with the language element (in this case, to place it on the

FIGURE 27–1. The physical basis of the language is pieces of plastic that vary in color, size, and shape. Each piece is a word, and each is backed with metal so that it will adhere to magnetized slate. Sentences are written on the vertical.

language board), after which she was given the fruit. The chimp was almost immediately proficient in this act. Causing objects to adhere to a vertical surface was something she did easily, in contrast, for example, to producing human sound.

The rest of the training consisted of making simultaneous changes in some aspect of the transaction and in some aspect of the language system, in order to establish a correspondence between them. We started with the fruits that were offered. When the fruit was a banana, the plastic chip was of one kind; when an apple, of a different kind; when an orange, of still a third kind. On each trial the chimp's task was the same—to place on the board the piece of plastic that was beside the fruit. The chimp was then given the fruit.

Two kinds of tests showed whether or not Sarah had formed an association between elements of the object class and the corresponding elements of the language class. In the first kind, the chimp was given two words and only one piece of fruit. This was done to determine whether she could match the word with the fruit. However, she could know more than such a choice trial would indicate. For example, if she were less interested in the fruit that was offered than in the fruit that was not offered, she could use the "wrong" word as a request for the fruit that she preferred. This possibility was detected by obtaining independent preference orderings on the fruits and on the words.

On one occasion, for example, Sarah chose between all possible pairs of the five different fruits on which she had been trained up to that time; on another occasion, she chose between all possible pairs of the corresponding words. The agreement between her preferences among the words and among the fruits averaged better than 80 percent. In addition, most of her errors occurred on choice trials involving nonpreferred fruit. It was therefore reasonable to conclude that she knew what word went with what fruit, even though her choice sometimes suggested the contrary.

The next perceptual class was mapped in the same fashion. Each change in donor (the person giving the fruit) was accompanied by a change in the second language element. For example, when Mary was present and the fruit was apple, Sarah had to write, "Mary apple" in order to receive the apple; with Randy present, "Randy apple"; and so on. Associations for members of the donor class were tested in the same way that elements of the object class were: when one trainer was present with two or more donor words, the subject matched the word to the trainer. A preference ordering could also have been determined for donors and their names, but it did not prove necessary. She did not appear to attempt to influence donors, perhaps because, typically, only one donor was present in a session, whereas many foods were present.

In addition to being required to place two pieces of plastic on the board, Sarah was required to observe a proper order. "Mary apple" was acceptable but "apple Mary" was not, since the target sentence was "Mary give apple Sarah." The correct order of the words was required from the beginning so that no incorrect orders had to be unlearned. We also observed an antiregression rule. Once Sarah had reached a two-word stage, we rejected one-word fragments, just as we rejected two-word fragments when she had reached a three-word stage, and so on.

The fruit and the donor were easily mapped; the other two classes in this example presented some practical difficulties. For example, the attempt to map the recipient ran into a predictable problem: Sarah was reluctant to produce response sequences calling for a recipient other than herself. Similarly, the attempt to map the operator by varying the action upon the fruit, sometimes cutting it or inserting it in a pail, encountered the same problem. Some of the outcomes were so nonpreferred that, once she had associated the language element with the outcome, she would not form the sentence. However, these were strictly practical problems, and we usually dealt with them by arranging appropriate contingencies. For instance, when Sarah wrote, "Mary give apple Gussie," thereby denying herself the apple, she was given a tidbit she preferred.

In summary, while many variations are yet to be explored, the basic procedure for introducing words to a naive organism was straightforward. A transaction was established between the subject and the trainer. Then a decision was made as to the salient perceptual classes into which the transaction should be divided, a decision which proved to be remarkably easy (5). Each class was then rotated through a series of values such as: apple, banana; Mary, Randy; give, insert; Sarah, Jim; the other classes being held constant. As the value of the perceptual class was changed, a corresponding change was made in the language element; and as each new class was mapped, the language requirement was increased.

Same-Different and the Interrogative

To call two bananas "same" and a banana and an apple "different," neither object need be named. In this sense, same-different has no linguistic prerequisites. It can be contrasted with, for example, "name of" (which is a relation between an item and its name) or the still more demanding if-then (which is a relation between sentences). In addition to being an appropriate starting point, same-different offers possibly the simplest of all contexts in which to introduce the question. Since the question can be of great service in the teaching of further language, it can hardly be introduced too early.

Before attempting to teach Sarah the words "same" and "different," we used a match-to-sample procedure to determine whether or not she was capable of the perceptual judgments that underlie the linguistic distinction. We gave Sarah two cups and a spoon and taught her to put the two cups together; we also gave her two spoons and a cup and taught her to put the two spoons together. Subsequently, we gave her a large assortment of other objects, always in sets of threes, and found that she was capable of matching all the like pairs, not just those on which she had been trained.

If the acquisition of language is the mapping of existing knowledge, as is often suggested (6), then teaching same-different should be easy. We placed two cups before Sarah, gave her a piece of plastic meaning "same," and required her to place it between them. Next, she was given a cup and a spoon and was required to place between them a piece of plastic meaning "different." We tested her associations by requiring her to choose between "same" and "different." Sarah was presented, as before, with either two cups or with a cup and a spoon. This time she was given both the words "same" and "different" and was required to choose between them. She made 4 errors in 26 trials, none on the first 5 trials. Next, she was given extensive transfer tests, which showed that she could apply the words to items not used in training. In principle, Sarah could go about the cage picking up pairs of objects and labeling them "same" or "different." Relations of this kind that she had been capable of recognizing before, she could now label as such. This, rather than any new concept, is what the language training contributed.

In the exercises above, the chimp was already being asked the question, "What is the relation between the two objects—are they the same or different?" However, Sarah was asked this question without an explicit interrogative marker. The only markers she had so far were the implicit one of the space between the objects, into which she was to insert her answer, and the fact that a trial did not end until she had completed the construction by adding the third item.

The question could be made explicit by any of the three standard linguistic devices: inflection, word order, or an interrogative particle. We chose the latter as the simplest, both in the sense of involving the least change for the subject and of being the most compatible with the present physical system. So we simply added an interrogative marker to the schema she was already receiving. For example where we had previously written:

A   A

"same"   "different"

we henceforth wrote:

A   ?   A

"same"   "different"

The variation in mechanical devices that languages use to identify a question obscures the basically simple nature of the question. Any completable construction is a potential question. It becomes a question once it suffers one or more missing elements. That is the structural view. From the psychological point of view, we must add that a question arises when a speaker finds himself unable to complete certain constructions and has at hand a listener whom he regards as a probable source of missing elements. If this analysis is correct, then the

ontogenetically earliest context in which to introduce the question—and with great didactic benefit to all subsequent language training—is that offered by the simplest possible completable constructions. Same-different is such a construction, since it can be introduced as a relation between unnamed objects and thus has no linguistic prerequisites.

Since questions rely on missing elements, with a two-term relation such as same-different, two question forms can be generated directly: one by removing the predicate ("same" or "different"), another by removing one, or even both, of the objects instancing the predicate (A or B). A third form can be generated indirectly by appending the interrogative marker, which itself stands for the missing element or elements, to the head of the construction and then requiring that it be replaced by a further element—specifically either "yes" or "no." Examples of all three questions are shown in Figures 27–2 and 27–3.

An example of two versions of a *wh* question is shown in the upper panel of Figure 27–2. These questions can be paraphrased as, "X is what to X?" and "X is what to Y?" The alternatives are "same" or "different," and Sarah's task was to replace the interrogative marker with the appropriate word.

Two versions of a second type of *wh* question are shown in the lower panel of Figure 27–2; they can be paraphrased as, "X is the same as what?" and "X is different from what?" Now the alternatives are no longer the words "same" or "different," but the objects themselves. Sarah's task remained the same: that is, to replace the interrogative particle with the proper object and thereby complete the construction.

The Yes-No Question

The yes-no question, the third form that can be generated in this context, is shown in four versions in Figure 27–3. They can be paraphrased as (i) "Is X the same as X?"; (ii) "Is X different from X?"; (iii) "Is X different from Y?"; and (iv) "Is X the same as Y?" These questions were formed not by removing any

What is A to A?   same/different

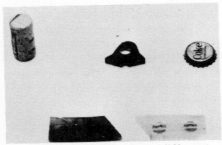

What is A to B?   same/different

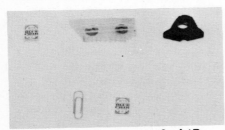

What is A the same as?   A/B

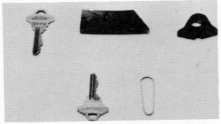

What is A not the same as?   A/B

FIGURE 27-2. Four *wh* questions, with English paraphrases.

item from the sentence, but by adding the interrogative marker to the head of the sentence. Three linguistic items were involved in ques-

tions of this form: "yes," "no," and the interrogative marker itself. Of the three, Sarah was already familiar with two—the interrogative marker, introduced in the *wh* forms, and "no," the negative particle that was taught her earlier as an injunction against carrying out the action called for by a sentence. An example of the kinds of pairs of sentences used to teach her the negative particle is shown in Figure 27-1. The training consisted simply of arresting the chimp's hand whenever she reached for an item referred to in a sentence containing a negative particle. The training was quickly effective. We have considered other ways of introducing negation, but injunction against action seems as basic as any (7).

Sarah was given explicit training on the first two forms of the yes-no question shown in Figure 27-3. She was then tested without prior training on the other two forms. This was designed to find out whether she could transfer from one form to the other. Training started with the question, "? X same X" (Are X and X the same?), where X represents any of the several objects used in the original matching-to-sample. The only alternative given her was "Yes," the one word in the yes-no construction that was unknown to her. She displaced the interrogative marker, thus forming the sentence, "Yes, X same X." Next she was given the question, "? X different X" (Are X and X different?). Her one alternative was the word "no." She used it to displace the interrogative marker and form the sentence, "No, X different X." She was given seven trials on each of the two forms.

At step two, she was given the same questions, with both the words "yes" and "no," and was required to choose between them. She made 2 errors in 15 trials, 1 on the first 5 trials. Rather than being given the usual transfer test, with new items substituted for training items, she was tested on the other two forms of the yes-no question. The four forms of the yes-no question were intermingled, and Sarah was asked them in more or less random order. Her alternatives were "yes" and "no," as before, and the objects substituted for X and Y were those used in training.

On the questions in Figure 27-3, she made

Is A the same as A?   yes/no

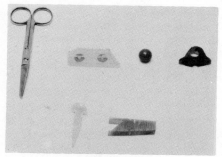

Is A the same as B?   yes/no

Is A not the same as B?   yes/no

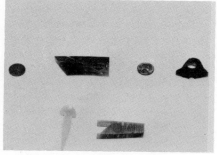

Is A not the same as A?   yes/no

the following number of errors per total number of trials: 6 out of 33; 11 out of 43; 2 out of 27; and 11 out of 51. Errors were concentrated in the forms in which the word "different" appeared. She made 25 errors in 94 trials on "different" questions, only 8 errors in 60 trials on "same" questions. Her error distributions were otherwise about equal. She made approximately the same number of errors on the two forms introduced in the transfer test as on the two old forms (new: 13 out of 78; old: 20 out of 76), and about the same number on questions requiring yes-no answers (yes: 17 out of 78; no: 16 out of 70).

The data suggest that Sarah learned the "different" question simply as a correlation between "different" and "no": that is, write "no" whenever "different" is present. This simple rule failed, however, when the second form of the question was introduced in the transfer test. There, "different" questions required both "yes" and "no" answers, as did "same" questions. This explains why, after making virtually no errors on the "different" question in the original training, she went on to make numerous errors on this same question when the second version was introduced. Interestingly, although Sarah could just as easily have written "yes" whenever "same" appeared, she apparently did not learn the "same" question in this manner. The introduction of the second form of the "same" question did not occasion a large number of errors: she learned these questions at her usual level of proficiency. Still, the data do not necessarily reflect an inherent difficulty in the yes-no question. They may reflect an unsound training program that allowed an inadequate rule to develop.

How general or abstract was Sarah's conception of "missing item"? Was it specific to the same-different construction, or would she be able to use the interrogative marker as a general particle in any known construction? The evidence favored the latter. This is fortunate,

FIGURE 27–3. Four yes-no questions, with English paraphrases. "Different" would be a more suitable paraphrase than "not same," since a negative particle was not used.

since the ability to define elements of language abstractly is necessary to a creative system of language (8).

Metalinguistics

In contrast to same-different, which can be a relation between unnamed objects, "name of" requires that one of the two terms in the relation be a linguistic one: for example, "X name of Y," where X is the name and Y is the object named. This concept, like the interrogative, has special value for teaching further language and should therefore be introduced early in training.

We placed before Sarah the word "apple" and, at a small distance from it, an actual apple. We then required her to place between them the piece of plastic that meant "name of." On the next trial, we presented the word "banana," an actual banana, and "name of." The procedure was exactly like the one we used to teach same-different.

After five trials on each of the two positive instances, Sarah was given five trials on each of the two negative instances. The same materials and the same procedure were used in all trials. We gave her the word "apple" and the object banana on some trials, and the word "banana" and the object apple on other trials. In both cases, we required her to place between the word and the object the piece of plastic meaning "not name of." "Not name of" was formed as a single unit by attaching the negative particle to the name for the positive case (Figure 27–4).

Choice trials in which Sarah was given the same materials but was required to choose between "name of" and "not name of" served to establish that she had formed the appropriate associations. In addition, she was tested by being asked questions. For example, she was asked, "? 'banana' name of apple" (Is "banana" the name of the object apple?). The alternatives given her were "yes" and "no." She answered this question correctly, as she did 15 of the 18 comparable questions with the *wh* form (Figure 27–2) and other versions of the yes-no form (Figure 27–3).

The standard training paradigm, consisting of two positive and two negative instances of the

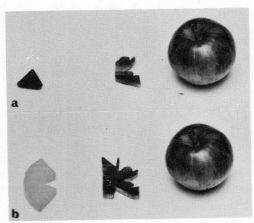

FIGURE 27–4. Examples of the relations "X is the name of Y" and "X is not the name of Y." Note that the name of the negative relation amounts to the negative particle built on to the name for the positive relation (see Figure 27–1 for the free form of the negative particle).

concept, was followed by a transfer test. The transfer test simply replaced the training items with new items and repeated the choice trials and questions. Sarah was asked, for example, "? name of dish" (What is the name of the object dish?). The alternatives given her were "dish," "pail," "apple," and "raisin"— words that had been introduced in the original mapping of the social transaction. She answered correctly about 80 percent of the questions on both the choice and the transfer tests. Her performance indicated that she could apply "name of" to instances other than the ones used in training.

Having introduced "name of," we went on to use it to generate new instances of itself. For example, figs interested Sarah but, like many of the foods she enjoyed, they had not yet been named. We placed before her a fig and a piece of plastic meaning "fig." We then placed the word "name of" between them. Next we placed a second piece of plastic slightly apart from the fig and put the word "not name of" between them. Had Sarah attended to the lesson? In order to answer this question, we resorted to the interrogative, giving her both the *wh* and yes-no forms of the question. She was asked, in effect, "What is the relation between the piece of plastic and the fig?'' The alternatives were ''name of'' and ''not name of.'' We also asked her, in effect, ''Is this piece of plastic the name of fig?'' In this case, the alternatives were ''yes'' and ''no.'' Her generally correct answers permitted us to move to the last step, which required her to use the appropriate word in a sentence.

The materials set before Sarah were a fig and a number of words: ''fig,'' the piece of plastic she had been told was not the name of fig, the names of two other fruits, ''give,'' ''Sarah,'' and ''Mary.'' Sarah was given the fig when she produced the sentence, ''Mary give fig Sarah,'' which she did correctly on eight of the first ten trials. She was equally proficient when the same procedure was applied to Cracker Jack, peach, and other items. Notice that the negative trials—in which she is told that X is not the name of Y—serve to rule out the possibility that the name is conferred simply by the physical contiguity between the language element and the object. Both when it is asserted that X is the name of Y and when it is denied, the spatiotemporal relation between the language element and the subject are identical. Yet only in the case of assertion does the subject go on to use the language element as the name of the designated referent.

At a much later stage of training, it was possible to introduce new words in a far less formal way. The trainer simply held up together a piece of plastic and an object and called attention to the pair. Sarah used the piece of plastic as the name of the object with which it was paired no less effectively than names introduced by the formal procedure. This suggests that she recognized the plastic and nonplastic objects as members of classes that took the relation ''name of'' with respect to one another. This is reasonable, since the plastic was always the name of the other item, never vice versa, and ''name of'' was the only relation members of the two classes took with respect to each other. The presumptive instructions of the implicit naming procedure could have been made ambiguous if either two pieces of plastic or two objects were held up together. Then it would have been unclear which was to be the name of which, whether they were synonyms, or

whether some predicate other than ''name of'' was intended. We did not give Sarah such tests, since they might have confused her.

Class Concepts: Color, Shape, Size

''Name of'' could not have been introduced until at least some items had been named. Similarly, the class concepts *color, shape,* and *size* could not be introduced until names of individual members of each class had first been established. We introduced *color* as the relation between individual colors and the objects that instanced them: for example, ''Red color of apple.'' The names of individual colors were therefore the linguistic prerequisites for the general concept *color.*

Of three possible methods of introducing the names of colors, and of properties in general, I will discuss only the one we found to be highly effective. The procedure is based upon the use of a set of objects having nothing in common except the property to be named. For example, in teaching the names for ''red'' and ''yellow,'' we used a set of red and a set of yellow objects that, in both cases, were completely dissimilar except for the common property of color. The red set consisted of a ball, toy car, Life Saver, and three comparable items; the yellow set, of a block, crayon, flower, and three comparable items. None of the items in either set was named, although we have no evidence that this is a necessary condition for teaching collective names.

We placed before Sarah one of the red objects; the words ''give,'' ''Mary,'' and ''Sarah''; and the piece of plastic that meant ''red.'' Only the latter was unfamiliar to her. Moreover, she had often used the other words to form the sentence, ''Mary give Sarah _____.'' The only word now available to her for completing the sentence was ''red.'' In addition, at this stage of training (only one unfamiliar word) she was always required to use all the words given her. With this convergence of factors, it is not too surprising that she formed the sentence, ''Mary give Sarah red,'' whereupon the red object was handed to her. (It is the outcome that is important here, not the method: if the present method had failed, another one would have been substituted.)

On the next trial, the same conditions obtained, except that Sarah was given a yellow object and the word "yellow." This time she produced, "Mary give Sarah yellow," and was handed the yellow object. Trials of this kind were repeated until the six objects in each set had all been used at least once. She was then advanced to choice trials, where the procedure remained the same except for being required to choose between "red" and "yellow." If a red object were present on a given trial, she was required to produce one sentence; if a yellow object were present, a different sentence. She was correct on eight of the first ten trials and was advanced to the transfer test. In this case, the transfer test included not only new red and yellow objects, but also objects that were indistinguishable except for their color, such as small cards painted red or yellow. She had her customary success on both phases of the transfer test. Exactly the same procedure was used to teach her the words "round" and "square," and later the words "large" and "small" (9).

Property Names Introduce Class Names

Having established "red" and "yellow," "round" and "square," and "large" and "small" (two instances of each of the three main class concepts), we introduced the class concepts *color, shape,* and *size*. In each case, the class concept was introduced as the relation between a property and an item instancing that property. As shown in Figure 27–5, the items instancing the properties were sometimes actual objects and sometimes names of objects. (The occasional use of objects was forced upon us by limitations in Sarah's vocabulary.) The fact that we could teach Sarah a property by the name of an object no less than by the actual object was, of course, highly encouraging; it was the first unqualified suggestion that the pieces of plastic had the referential function of words.

In teaching class names, we took advantage of the interrogative, which by now was a well-

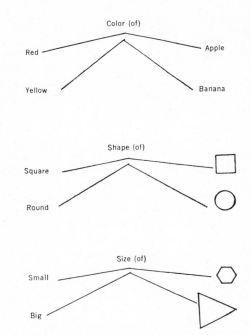

FIGURE 27–5. The cases used to teach the relations "color of," "shape of," and "size of." Words were used in the first case, objects in the other two.

established form for Sarah. "Red ? apple" (What is the relation between red and apple?) was the first question we asked her. We followed this with the same question concerning "yellow" and "banana." On both trials, the only word available to her was "color of." She substituted this word for the interrogative marker, thereby forming the sentences, "Red color of apple" and "Yellow color of banana." The next set of trials comprised questions concerning negative instances of the same concepts. The only word available to her on these trials was "not color of" (see Figure 27–4 for an analogy in the case of "name of" and "not name of"). Substituting it for the interrogative particle, Sarah produced "Yellow not color of apple" and "Red not color of banana" (10).

The same questions were repeated in step two. Both the words "color of" and "not color of" were available, and she was required to choose between them. She was correct on eight of the first ten trials and was advanced to the transfer tests. There she was required to choose between the same alternatives, but now with items not used in training. For example, she was asked, "red ? cherry," and was required to fill in either "color of" or "not color of." It was not possible at this stage to test the transfer of the general concept *color* to individual colors other than red and yellow, for these were the only color names she had been taught. In addition, there were few red or yellow objects that had been named at this time; therefore most of the transfer tests were carried out with objects rather than their names. For example, she was asked, "? red color of feather" (Is red the color of the feather?"), where the feather was an actual one, and her alternatives were "yes" and "no." Sentences composed of a mixture of words and objects were written on a work shelf rather than on the magnetic board, since many of the objects that appeared in these sentences would not adhere to the board. We called such strings "hybrid sentences" and used them whenever limitations in vocabulary made them convenient. A language in which words are no less material than the things they map not only makes it easy to form hybrid strings, but also bridges the chasm that some philosophers interpose between words and things.

Because *color* was the first class concept taught Sarah, the only relevant alternatives we could ask her to choose between at first were "color of" and "not color of." In the early stages, therefore, we could only ask her whether, in effect, red was or was not the color of apple. But after the class concepts, *shape* and *size,* were introduced, we could require her to choose among various concepts and their negations. Ultimately we asked her whether, for, example, "red" was the color, shape, size, or name of the object apple. Her performance was not impaired by the increased alternatives.

Productive Use of Class Concepts

The productivity that was illustrated earlier, in the generating of new names with the concept "name of," can also be shown with the class concepts *color, shape,* and *size.* Productivity, the ability of a concept to generate new instances of itself, is a characteristic of many concepts that express relation, when at least one term in the relation is represented linguistically. Apparently, a class can be introduced on the basis of as few as two values—for example, "red" and "yellow" as the inductive basis for *color.* Afterwards, the class concept can be used to generate new instances of itself indefinitely. For instance, we introduced the color names "brown" and "green" with the sentences, "Brown color of chocolate" and "Green color of grape," where "brown" and "green" were the only words unknown to Sarah. She was asked, "? color of chocolate," and was given "brown" as the only alternative. She replaced the interrogative marker with the only alternative available to her and formed the sentence, "Brown color of chocolate." She did the same with "green." This points up the fact that in a system such as ours, where the subject uses words but cannot make them, one can be certain that, if the subject will work at all, she will form the appropriate sentence from the first opportunity.

To determine whether Sarah could understand "brown" in a sentence structurally different from the training sentence, we gave her the instruction, "Sarah take brown," and at the same time confronted her with four colored wooden disks, only one of which was brown. We followed this with the more complex, "Sarah insert brown (in) red dish," where a red and a green dish were present with the four wooden disks. In both cases, she operated upon the brown disk in the correct manner, thereby showing that her comprehension of the word was not limited by syntactic context. The same point is made by other tests which show the reverse. After learning to use a property name as a noun ("Mary give Sarah red"), she can then understand the word when it is used as a modifier ["Insert apple (in) red dish"]. Although these are early tests rather than final ones, we have yet to find any evidence that Sarah's understanding of a word is restricted to the syntactic context in which it was originally learned (*11*).

General Functions: Sentence

The subject may produce properly ordered strings of words, yet not be forming a sentence. A sentence differs from a string of words in that it has an internal organization. The organization can be represented by a tree diagram or the application of parentheses, both of which will show the relations between any one word in the sentence and all the others.

One of the simplest relations requiring syntax is the symmetrical two-term relation that can be found in geometrical prepositions. For example, "red on green and green on red." One form of the relation has no edge over the other, unlike, for example, "fly on horse," which is notably more probable than the reverse. The interchangeability in the first case makes it impossible to distinguish physically between the class of items that can take one position in the relation and the class of items that can take the other position. The position of an item in the relation can be determined only by the order of its corresponding word in the sentence or by inflectional differences.

We used four color words that Sarah knew—"red," "green," "blue," and "yellow"—to train her in the preposition "on." Small cards, painted one of the four colors, but indistinguishable otherwise, were used as the objects. One of the two cards was placed on top of the other, the top card offset a bit so that the bottom one could be seen. We trained her in the comprehension mode, requiring her to respond to the trainer's sentences. We then tested her ability to produce the same sentences herself. The training proceeded in three steps, the first restricting her to one pair of colors, the second dealing with her ability to generalize to the other colors, and the last examining her transfer from comprehension to production.

In the first step of the training, the red card was placed on the table before the subject. The trainer wrote on the board, "Green on red," handed Sarah the green card, and then induced her to place it on the one that was already there. Next, the opposite sentence, "Red on green," was presented, with the green card down and the red card handed to Sarah as the one to be placed on top. Subsequently, she was given both cards and was presented first with one form of the sentence and then with the other. Once she was proficient at producing the card arrangement called for by the sentence, she was given sentences using all four color words. She performed as well on the ten new cases as she had on the two training cases.

The last step concerned Sarah's ability to produce sentences appropriate to the trainer's behavior rather than to behave in ways appropriate to the trainer's sentences. On each trial she was given three words—two color words and "on." She was required to place them on the board in a way that corresponded to, or described, the trainer's placement of the cards. Thus, if the trainer put the blue card on the green one, Sarah, who held the words "green," "blue," and "on," was required to write, "Blue on green." She was correct on eight of the first ten trials (*12*).

Compound Sentence

Consider the sentence, "Sarah insert banana pail apple dish." In English, the sentence instructs Sarah to put the banana in the pail and the apple in the dish. The procedure used to teach Sarah to respond correctly to this sentence was based on three steps, all in the comprehension mode. First, she was trained on each of the four simple sentences which make up the compound sentence: "Sarah insert banana pail"; "Sarah insert apple pail"; "Sarah insert banana dish"; and "Sarah insert apple dish." The trainer wrote each sentence, one at a time, on the board; at the same time, he offered Sarah a choice of fruit and containers and required her to place the designated fruit in the designated container.

Next, Sarah was given all possible pairs of the sentence, side by side, in the manner of a paragraph. For example:

Sarah	Sarah
insert	insert
banana	apple
dish	pail

Since no change was made in the composition of the individual sentences, this step was intended merely to accustom her to carrying out two acts of insertion, as is required by the compound sentence.

In the final step, all possible pairs of sentences were again combined, this time one immediately above the other. This conjunction of two simple sentences was gradually converted into one compound sentence. The procedure generated sentences of the following kind:

(i)	(ii)	(iii)
Sarah	Sarah	Sarah
insert	insert	insert
banana	banana	banana
pail	pail	pail
Sarah	insert	apple
insert	apple	dish
apple	dish	
dish		

Neither the deletion of the second use of "Sarah" nor the subsequent deletion of the second use of "insert" disrupted her performance. Sarah performed correctly 75 to 80 percent of the time (her customary level during this phase of the project), and continued to do so when the changes were made. Nor was her performance impaired in the transfer tests, which included substitutions for both the verbs and the nouns.

The Copula: Learned as Nonsense Syllable

The concepts of subset or class member, both of which are among the several meanings of "is" ("Red is a color," "Apple is a fruit"), could probably be taught most efficiently by a method analogous to the one we used to teach the names of properties. Using a set of items that had only one common property, we had required her to request each of them by writing the same sentence: for instance, "Give red." This same approach could be adapted to the present concept by temporarily removing the names of the individual fruits and then requiring her to request the items by a class name. For example, where she had previously written, "Give apple," "Give banana," and so on,

remove the individual names and require her to request the same set of items by writing, "Give fruit." This would serve to teach the class word "fruit." Repeating the same procedure with "chocolate," "caramel," and "gumdrop" would serve to teach another class word, "candy." Then "is" could be introduced as follows: "Apple, banana is fruit"; "Chocolate, caramel is candy"; "Apple, banana is not candy"; and "Chocolate, caramel is not fruit." These training sentences provide the standard two positive and two negative instances of the concept. More important, they provide strings in which the only unknown is the new predicate itself; both of the arguments, the names of the class members and the names of the classes, are established words.

In fact, we taught Sarah "is" in quite a different way, one that proved to be inefficient. This is interesting because of the suggestion it contains as to what makes a method inefficient. We gave Sarah the question, "red ? color" (What is the relation between red and color?). The only alternative given her was the word "is," which she used to replace the interrogative marker, thereby forming the sentence, "Red is color." We repeated the procedure with "round ? shape." Sarah formed the sentence, "Round is shape" in the same fashion. After being given the usual five trials on each of the two positive instances, she was given the same number of trials on each of two negative instances. She was asked, "red ? shape" (What is the relation between red and shape?) as well as "round ? color" (What is the relation between round and color?). In both instances, the alternative given her was "is not" ("is" and the negative particle). She displaced the interrogative marker, thereby forming "Round is not color" and "Red is not shape."

At step two, she was asked the same questions, was given both the words "is" and "is not," and was required to choose between them. She made 10 errors on the first 22 trials. All of the errors were caused by her failure to use the negative form, resulting in such answers as "Round is color" and "Red is shape." Following this unprecedented failure at step two, she was returned to step one, given five trials on each of the "is not" cases, and advanced again to step two. This time she made 14 errors, 11 of them on "is not." She was returned to step one, given only two trials on each of the negative cases, and retested on step two trials. On this third and final test she made no errors in 18 trials.

On the transfer test, she was asked all of the previous questions, with the words "yellow" and "triangular" substituted for the training words "red" and "round," and was required to choose between "is" and "is not," as before. For example, she was asked, "yellow ? shape." She answered correctly, replacing the interrogative marker with "is not" and forming the sentence, "Yellow is not shape." She made only 3 errors on 26 trials, none on the first 5 trials. Thus, even though "is" was acquired with many errors, it was successfully transferred to nontraining items.

What exactly did "is" mean to Sarah? Unfortunately, we cannot say, because we did not teach her any other concepts with which to contrast "is." Concepts might be said to come in clusters. Only by teaching at least two members of a cluster is it possible to say what either one means. This is not a new point, but a methodological stricture that we adhered to in nearly all previous cases: (i) from the beginning, no class was given only one member—in mapping the original social transaction, "apple" was contrasted with "banana," "orange," and so forth; (ii) we taught not one property class, but "color," "shape," and "size," and for the same purpose; (iii) the logical connectives are an unfinished cluster—the meaning of if-then will remain in doubt until she passes tests on "and" and "or" (13). These cases differ somewhat from "is," however, in that what constitutes contrasting alternatives is intuitively clear. It is less clear what constitutes the semantic neighbors of "is." If, when asked the relation between apple and fruit, Sarah wrote, "apple is fruit" rather than, say, "Apple color of fruit," we would not regard this correct reply as especially informative. That is to say, "is" and "color of" do not belong to the same cluster.

Moreover, the subject's successful performance on a transfer test cannot substitute for its ability to discriminate between neighboring concepts. Sarah passed the transfer test on "is" by writing, for example, "Yellow is not shape," and "Yellow is color," where "yellow" was a nontraining item. This established that, on her own, she assigned to "yellow" and "color" the same relation that she was taught to assign to "red" and "color." But, unfortunately, it does not tell us what that relation was. That information can come only from the subject's ability to discriminate a word from close alternatives.

Pluralization

Pluralization, in keeping with the rest of the system, was introduced in the form of a separate particle rather than as an inflectional change. Since we found it mechanically awkward to pluralize both noun and verb, we arbitrarily restricted pluralization to the verb. For example, we wrote, "Red, green is pl color," but not "Red, green is pl color pl," where "pl" after a word is the plural marker. Since this prohibits our studying noun-verb agreement, the restriction is temporary. Ultimately we will pluralize both grammatical classes, though not necessarily with the same particle.

· The first sentence given Sarah in her training with the plural was "red, yellow is ? color," which largely defies translation into English. The only alternative given her was the plural marker "pl," with which she displaced the interrogative marker to form the sentence, "Red, yellow is pl color" (Red and yellow are colors). Next she was given the comparable sentence with respect to shapes: namely, "round, square is ? shape," which is no more translatable than its counterpart in colors. Again she displaced the interrogative marker with the only alternative given her, thereby forming the sentence, "Round, square is pl shape," in effect, round and square are shapes.

The two negative instances given her were "red, yellow is not ? shape" and "round, square is not ? color." She displaced the interrogative marker with the only alternative given her, making the sentences, "Red, yellow is not pl shape" and "Round, square is not pl color" (Red and yellow are not shapes; Round and square are not colors). The training departed from the standard procedure in that she was given the same alternative, "pl," on both positive and negative trials. This was done because the negative particle is appended to the verb rather than to the plural marker: that is, "is + pl" equals "are," and "is not + pl" equals "are not." We rejected, as making little sense, the alternative of appending the negative marker to "pl"; that is, "pl not."

The trials at step two were modified to accommodate the fact that the negative particle was not appended to the new word, as it usually was. We put two interrogative markers in the sentence, indicating a need for two words, and offered three alternatives rather than the usual two. For example, Sarah was asked, "red, yellow ? ? color," and was given the alternatives "is," "is not," and "pl." She displaced the two interrogative markers with the particles "is" and "pl" in the proper order—"Red, yellow is pl color." She was equally successful in displacing the two interrogative markers in the sentence, "round, square ? ? color" with "is not" and "pl," forming the sentence, "Round, square is not pl color." The use of two interrogative markers may have been an unnecessary crutch. After only five trials, we reverted to the use of a single interrogative marker for both words, and she made no errors in 15 such trials. We viewed her successful replacement of one interrogative marker with the appropriate two words as a step toward the eventual achievement of answering questions not with a word, but with a complete sentence (14).

The many errors Sarah made in learning the copula are in contrast to the relatively few errors she made in learning most other concepts. Pluralization and the question, for example, map well-defined states of affairs, which is, I think, the main reason they were learned easily. The interrogative marker visually represents the missing item or items in well-learned constructions. Referents are equally clear in the case of the plural marker. In analytic sentences such as "Red, yellow is pl color," "pl" is called for when there are two or more items in the subject (15). In synthetic sentences such as "Apple, orange is pl big," "pl" has a double

cue—the linguistic one noted above and a nonlinguistic one. The nonlinguistic cue is the state of affairs mapped by the sentence, in this case large apple and a large orange.

In teaching a two-term predicate such as "is," where the predicate is itself the unknown, both arguments of the predicate must be properly instanced. They were, it would seem, when she was taught the property classes. In teaching "color of" as the relation between "red" and "apple," both "red," as a kind of property, and "apple," as an object instancing that property, had been established by prior training. But in teaching "is" as the relation between "red" and "color," "color" was not properly instanced. Strictly speaking, we had no word for "color," only a word for "color of," having neglected earlier to teach her a genitive particle. Rather than take the time to map the concept "of," such that *color* could then have been taught as a class, I tried to substitute the available "color of." The many errors she made and the drill that was necessary to instill the word "is" suggest that this was a mistake. The pattern of her learning in this case is reminiscent of paired-associate learning, where the subject is required to learn an *arbitrary* association between words or nonsense syllables. If the training method is proper, the predicate will not occur as an arbitrary associate of two words. Instead, it will be the name of a conceptual relation that is instanced by these words. (The new word will be arbitrary in either case, but there will be a relation that is named in one case and not in the other.) I think we may expect different learning patterns in the two cases, drill and numerous errors being far more likely in the one than the other.

Object Classes

The three object classes we taught Sarah were "fruit," "breadstuff," and "candy," in that order. We started her with the question, "banana is ?" and gave her only one alternative, the word "fruit." She displaced the interrogative marker to form the sentence, "Banana is fruit." Next we gave her the same question with respect to cracker and breadstuff, a class invented for the occasion. The usual five trials on each of the two positive instances were followed by an equal number of trials on two negative instances. She was given the question, "banana is not ?" and the word "breadstuff," with which she displaced the interrogative marker. By a corresponding procedure, she was also led to produce the sentence, "Cracker is not fruit."

On trials at step two she was given the same questions, but was required to choose between the words "fruit" and "breadstuff." She made 1 error in 15 trials, none on the first 5 trials. On the transfer tests, the same questions were repeated in the presence of the same alternatives, but with the words "bread," "cookie," "grape," and "peach" substituted for the training words "banana" and "cracker." She made 7 errors in 46 trials, 1 on the first 5 trials.

But what meaning would failure have had in this case? Having been taught that banana is a fruit, suppose Sarah chose not to call peach or grape a fruit. In what sense could she be considered to be in error? In the present exercises, she was not asked yes-no questions, which would have required her to decide whether or not peach, for example, was a fruit. Instead, she was merely asked *wh* questions, which required her to decide only whether a peach was more like a fruit or a breadstuff. Nevertheless, errors are difficult to interpret in the case of object classes. An item cannot partly be and partly not be a color, or a shape, or a size. Yet every object class is subject to this ambiguity. A stone that barks or a dog that never moves—are they animate or inanimate? That is to say, intermediate items can always be proposed in the case of object classes (for example, banana bread in the case of fruit and breadstuff). Notice, however, that there are no intermediate items for colors and shapes, shapes and sizes, sizes and colors. One may waver in deciding whether to call black and white colors, but whatever one decides on that point, he will have no tendency to classify either as a shape or a size.

Because object classes are the victims of intermediate cases, whereas property classes are not, we assigned a higher priority to property classes, used them to map class membership, and then tried to use the mapping to set up object classes. Though logically defensible perhaps, it was tutorially inefficient, and the procedure described at the outset of this section seems clearly preferable.

Quantifiers: All, None, One, Several

"All" and "none" were the first quantifiers taught Sarah, followed by "one" and "several." Two sets of five crackers each were used in the training. All the crackers in one set were round; in the other, square. The square set was placed before Sarah and she was given the question, "? crackers is pl square" (What or how many crackers are square?). The only word given her was "all," so she used it to displace the interrogative marker. The resulting sentence was "All crackers is pl square" (All crackers are square). We repeated the procedure with the set of round crackers and the word "none." She displaced the interrogative marker and formed the sentence, "None crackers is pl square."

In the case of all-none, we arbitrarily elected to pluralize both forms: "All is pl round" and "None is pl round." The same questions were repeated, with Sarah choosing between "all" and "none." She quit after only eight trials, which was not uncommon; but she made three errors in the eight trials, which was uncommon. She was given 20 more choice trials of the same kind on the next lesson. She made 12 errors, 6 on "none" and 6 on "all."

The lessons were modified by adding a third set of crackers (all triangular) and two further questions. The original and modified lessons are diagrammed in Figure 27–6. The top portion of the figure shows the original form of the lesson, and the bottom portion, the revised form. A sense of the task confronting Sarah can be gained by covering up all the material in each lesson except for one question and one set of crackers. Notice that in the first lesson only one question was asked—it was simply asked in the presence of two different sets of crackers. In the revised lesson, however, three different

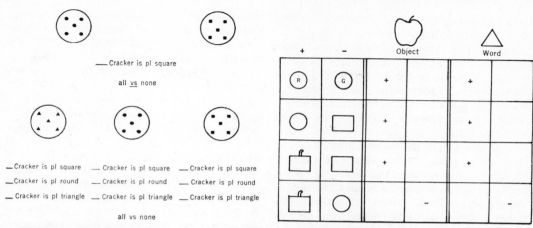

FIGURE 27–6 (left). Exercises used to teach all-none, with the original, unsuccessful version above, and the modified, successful version below. **Figure 27–7** (right). Features analyses of the object, apple, and the word, "apple."

questions were asked, each one in the presence of three different sets of crackers. Her alternatives on both lessons were the same: namely, "all" and "none." On the revised lesson she made 4 errors in 15 trials; the errors were divided almost evenly among the possibilities. Sarah's 74 percent correct is still below criterion, but it is an improvement over the preceding lessons.

The original lesson in all-none was atypical in that it provided Sarah with less information than the standard lesson does. Sarah is given two pieces of positive and two pieces of negative information in the standard lesson. However, in the first version of the present lesson, Sarah was given only half the usual information. Only one sentence was associated with each set: "All crackers are square" with the square set; and "None of the crackers is square" with the round set. Usually, "All crackers are round" would have been associated with the round set, and "None of the crackers is round" with the square set. The revised lesson, in which three sentences were associated with each set, provided the missing information. Two sets of crackers would have been sufficient to convey the standard amount of information, but we added a third set for emphasis. In doing so, we may actually have provided too much information.

What is the optimal amount of information for teaching the various concepts? We have relied heavily on two positive and two negative instances of each concept, and the present failure suggests that they may actually be necessary. But it will be some time before we really know. Systematic changes in training procedures, of a kind needed to answer such questions, have been deferred. At this stage, we have concentrated on teaching as many exemplars of language as possible and have not changed training programs unless forced to do so by failure.

A number of set arrangements are possible in teaching the distinction between "one" and "several." In the approach we used, there was no overlap between the sets. Six sets were used to teach "one," and six different sets to teach "several." All sets consisted of five crackers of two different shapes. The sets used to teach "one" contained one cracker of a different shape from the other four. The sets used to teach "several" contained two or three crackers of one shape, and the remainder (up to five) of a different shape. "Several" could thus mean either two or three crackers of the same shape. This condition was fulfilled for each shape by four sets. For instance, "Several crackers are round" could be applied to the following four sets: two round and three square, two round and three triangular, three round and two square, three round and two triangular.

Each of the 12 training sets was placed before her and she was asked a question appropriate to it. For example, in the presence of the set containing only one square cracker, she was asked the question, "? cracker is square" (What or how many crackers are square?). The only alternative given her was "one," with which she replaced the interrogative marker to form the sentence, "One cracker is square." On other occasions, a set containing two round and three square crackers was placed before her and she was asked the question, "? cracker is pl square" (What or how many crackers are square?). Since the only alternative given her was "several," she made the sentence, "Several cracker is pl square."

On trials at step two, she was presented with the same sets and questions as on step one, but she was now given both "one" and "several" and was required to choose between them. She made only one error on the first ten trials. The one-several distinction may be simpler than the all-none distinction, not merely because it was taught later, but also because "one" and "several" correspond with the absence and presence, respectively, of the plural marker. Thus, we say, "One is round" but "Several is pl round."

Because her terminal performance on all-none was substandard (74 percent correct), she was given a review on this distinction. We used ten questions from the revised lesson, with the same three sets shown in Figure 27–4; she was correct on eight of the ten trials. Then the sets from the all-none and one-several exercises were combined for the first time. She was asked the same questions as before, but was required to choose among all four alternatives—"all," "none," "one," and "several." She was correct on eight of the first ten trials.

The transfer test presented a special problem. The sets used to instance the quantifiers differed from one another solely in terms of shapes. This is a narrower inductive base than we had used with previous words. Moreover, all the *shape* words Sarah knew had been used in training. Thus, we had either to teach her new *shape* words or to conduct the transfer test with a class

concept other than the one used in training. Could she transfer the quantifiers not only to nontraining items, but also to items that differed in properties other than shape?

The class concepts used in the transfer test were *color* and, to a lesser extent, *size*. Sets differing in color were prepared by dyeing pieces of apple red or green, and by leaving the yellow or green peel on slices of ripe or unripe banana. Sets based on size were composed of pieces of bread of two different sizes. Of the 18 sets used in the training of the four quantifiers, 10 were duplicated with either color or size values substituted for the original shape values. For example, color sets consisted of: five red pieces of apple, one red and four green pieces, two red and three green pieces; five yellow pieces of banana, one yellow and four green pieces, and so on. Seven of the sets were based on color and three on size. She was asked the same questions as before, though now they were framed in terms of color and size rather than shape; and she was given all four quantifiers to choose from. For example, in the presence of a set consisting of three green and two pieces of red apple, she was asked, "? apple is pl green" (What or how many apples are green?). She answered correctly by replacing the interrogative marker with "several," thereby forming the sentence, "Several apple is pl green." She was correct on nine of the first ten trials. If she had failed this test, we might then have sought to devise training procedures conducive to cross-dimensional transfer. But she succeeded, and that on the basis of a training program that would seem to make a minimal contribution to cross-dimensional transfer. The success must be attributed to Sarah, not to the training program. Indeed, if an organism were deficient in matters of transfer, it is by no means clear what one would do to overcome the deficiency, though it would be of great interest to try.

A last test concerned Sarah's ability to use the quantifiers in sentences of a grammatical structure different from those used in training. The training sentences had all been descriptive or declarative: All (one, none, several) cracker (apple, banana) is (pl) round (square, red, big, and so on). In the test, the quantifiers occurred in imperative sentences. A dish and a large number of both crackers and candies were arrayed before her. She was told, "Sarah insert all the crackers in the dish," and she was allowed to keep whatever she put into the dish. The routine was familiar to her, as was the use of the imperative sentence; the only new element was the application of quantifiers to imperative sentences.

She responded correctly to the first five instructions: (i) "Sarah insert one cracker dish," (ii) "Sarah insert some cracker dish," (iii) "Sarah insert one candy dish," (iv) "Sarah insert all candy dish," and (v) "Sarah insert several candy dish." On the next two instructions, when told to insert "none" cracker and "several" cracker, she obeyed insofar as the crackers were concerned, but supplemented the instructions a little with candy, inserting one piece in the first case and all in the second. The trainer decided to allow the performances to pass on the grounds that (i) the action on the candy was not specifically interdicted and (ii) the explicit instructions dealing with crackers were, in fact, carried out. The trainer gave one more instruction, "Sarah insert one candy dish." At this point Sarah took all the candy, and the lesson was terminated. The first five instructions, and even the next two to some extent, point to the same conclusion: Sarah's grasp of the quantifiers was not limited by a syntactic factor; she understood them in sentences of a grammatical form different from those used in training.

Logical Connective: If-Then

With concepts such as same-different, it is possible to perform a few simple tests, before any language training is started, to determine whether or not the subject is capable of making the perceptual judgments upon which the concept depends. Thus we either (i) find knowledge to be present, (ii) attempt to devise a means of instilling it if it is not, or (iii) give up the idea of mapping it with words. Unfortunately, this procedure is based on the assumption that one can both state and assess the perceptual judgment underlying the linguistic distinction. Consider if-then, the conditional

relation, as exemplified by the simple instruction, "If Mary take red then Sarah take green." What tests will reveal beforehand whether or not it is sensible to attempt to teach Sarah to map the relation with words?

Failing to answer that question, we applied a contingency training procedure to Sarah. We exposed her to differential reinforcement, a standard procedure for training animals, in which the subject is rewarded for doing one thing but not for doing another. If a subject cannot be influenced by such experience, it seems unlikely that it could be taught to recognize if-then relations. On the other hand, the fact that a subject's behavior can be influenced by such procedures is no guarantee that the subject can recognize relations of this kind and learn to label them as such (16). We began by allowing Sarah to choose freely between a piece of apple and a piece of banana, simply to confirm that she still had no particular preference. Next, she was given a piece of chocolate when she chose apple, but not when she chose banana. She soon ceased to choose banana, since it was not followed by chocolate, which she preferred to both fruits.

The particular contingency used with Sarah was carefully chosen—all of the words used to describe it were familiar to her, except those concerning the conditional relation itself. For example, the following sentences would accurately describe the contingency training she received: (i) "If Sarah take apple then Mary give Sarah chocolate" and (ii) "If Sarah take banana then Mary no give Sarah chocolate." Notice that "if" and "then" are the only unfamiliar words. In addition, the sentences that are combined to form the conditional sentences are familiar. Thus we have progressed from same-different, where the known terms were nonlinguistic items (actual cups and spoons); through "name of," where one of the known terms was a word; to the present point, where the known terms are sentences. Sentences (i) and (ii) above are, thus, strict training procedures in that they require the introduction of only one new term.

In English, the conditional relation is marked by discontinuous constituents (if-then). This poses an interesting problem, but not one that we need grapple with at this time. Therefore, we marked the conditional with a single particle, as in symbolic logic: "Sarah take apple ⊃ Mary give Sarah chocolate." We began the language training by giving Sarah the question, "Sarah take apple ? Mary give Sarah chocolate" (What is the relation between Sarah's taking apple and Mary's giving chocolate?). She used her one alternative, the conditional particle, to displace the interrogative marker and form the sentence, "Sarah take apple ⊃ Mary give Sarah chocolate." She was then given a piece of apple, followed by a piece of chocolate, both of which she ate. Next she was given the question, "Sarah take banana ? Mary no give Sarah chocolate" (What is the relation between Sarah's taking banana and Mary's not giving chocolate?). Again her only alternative was the conditional particle, which she used to form the sentence, "Sarah take banana ⊃ Mary no give Sarah chocolate." This time she was given a piece of banana (which she sometimes ate), but it was not followed by a piece of chocolate. We gave Sarah five trials on each of the two questions. Then we moved to a series of trials in which we gave her one of two pairs of sentences: (i) "Sarah take apple ⊃ Mary give Sarah chocolate" and "Sarah take banana ⊃ Mary no give Sarah chocolate"; or (ii) "Sarah take apple ⊃ Mary no give Sarah chocolate" and "Sarah take banana ⊃ Mary give Sarah chocolate."

The first pair states that the choice of apple, but not the choice of banana, will lead to chocolate; in the second pair, the statement is reversed. Pieces of both banana and apple were set before her on each trial, and she was considered to have responded correctly whenever her choice of fruit led to her being given chocolate. She made over 20 errors, accompanied by emotional outbursts, based on the persistent choice of apple. She then abandoned this approach, only to alternate between the two fruits for about 14 trials. Finally, she took into account the sentences and consistently chose the fruit that led to the chocolate.

Although it took Sarah longer to learn the conditional relation than most of the other concepts, once she had learned it she gave her customary performance on the transfer tests. Extensive changes were made in both the antecedents and the consequents. She was given such pairs of sentences as "Mary take red ⊃ Sarah take apple" and "Mary take green ⊃ Sarah take banana," which required her to observe what object Mary chose, match Mary's action with the antecedent in the appropriate sentence, and then carry out the appropriate consequent. Sentences such as "Red is on green ⊃ Sarah take apple" and "Green is on red ⊃ Sarah take banana" involved a change of verb in the antecendent. She responded at the same level, approximately 80 percent correct, on both the transfer tests and the final training tests.

Perhaps the complexity of the conditional relation was responsible for her difficulty in understanding the relation. Indeed, how shall we assess the complexity of a concept except through the subject's performance in learning it? But this assumes that the training for all cases is equally effective, which is doubtful. In the prelanguage phase, we had taught her that the choice of apple was always correct. This was a serious error, for it probably gave her little incentive to pay attention to the instructions, except to consistently choose apple. Training in the prelanguage phase should have included at least two correct alternatives. She would not then have entered the language training phase with a fixed response disposition, but would have had to pay attention to the instructions in order to learn which of the two positive items was correct on a given trial (17).

Conjunction: And

It proved possible to obtain an idea of her capacity for understanding the concept of conjunction in advance of introducing a particle for "and." Instead of trying to teach Sarah conjunction-like behavior in a prelanguage phase, we set the stage in such a way as to invite her to engage in such behavior on her own. She essentially took the invitation.

Rather than giving her, in the presence of a single kind of fruit, a set of words from which she could compose, for example, the sentence,

"Mary give Sarah apple," we gave her essentially the same set of words, but in the presence of two, and later three, different kinds of fruit. At first, she requested each piece of fruit with a separate sentence. After about eight such invitations, she wrote, "Mary give Sarah apple banana"; still later, "Mary give Sarah apple banana orange," naming all three of the fruits before her. This is already conjunction, it can be argued, even though there is not a particle for "and." Her adding one word to another eliminated the redundant elements that would have been present if the same request had been made with separate sentences. The actual introduction of "and" consisted simply of making the particle available to her and requiring her to use it (*13*).

Symbolization: When Is a Piece of Plastic a Word?

When does a piece of plastic cease to be a piece of plastic and become a word? We might answer, When it is used as a word: that is, when it occurs along with other words of appropriate grammatical class in sentences and when it occurs as the answer or part of the answer to questions. For example, we consider a small piece of blue plastic to be the word for apple because (i) it is used when, for example, the subject requests apple and (ii) it is used by the subject to answer, "What is the name of apple?" We might add that the piece of plastic is a word when the properties ascribed to it by the subject are not those of the plastic itself, but those of the object it designates.

We can determine whether this condition obtains by using the matching-to-sample procedures again—this time to obtain independent analyses of the features of both the word and its referent. An analysis of the features of the apple was made by giving Sarah a series of trials. On each trial she was given the apple and a pair of alternatives and was required to indicate which of the alternatives she considered to be more like the apple. The alternatives were red versus green; round versus square; square with stemlike protuberance versus plain square; and plain round versus square

with protuberances (see Figure 27–7). The alternatives could be words or objects instancing the properties named by the words. That is, the subject could be required to decide whether the apple was more like the words "red" versus "green" or more like a red patch versus a green patch. Our use of the latter approach was dictated by Sarah's limited vocabulary.

After obtaining a features analysis of the apple, we repeated the test exactly with the word "apple" (a piece of blue plastic). The subject assigned the same properties to the plastic that she had earlier assigned to the apple (Figure 27–7). The properties she assigned to the word "apple" show that her analysis of the word was based not on the physical form of the blue piece of plastic, but on the object that the plastic represents.

Strictly speaking, we do not know the necessary and sufficient conditions for this effect, or even the specific point in training when the effect first becomes demonstrable. There are several intermediate possibilities, but consider the two major alternatives: (i) in the course of acquiring language, the organism learns how to symbolize; (ii) symbolization is an integral property of perhaps all learning and makes language possible. What form would symbolization take in lower organisms if the latter were true? A pigeon exposed to the fact that a vertical line preceded food A, and a horizontal line food B, would ascribe to the vertical line whatever features it ascribed to food A, and to the horizontal line whatever features it ascribed to food B. A nonlaboratory example may make the point still clearer. A dog noses a leash in a hallway. Is a walk into the house or out of it? into the fields or into town? with birds or without? squirrel scent or not? and so forth. When asked these questions of the walk, in one case, and of the leash, in the other, the dog's answers should be the same. We do not know if this is so, but can find out simply by adapting the procedures we used with the chimpanzee to the other species.

Assumption (ii) above seems the more reasonable, since it does not require the further assumption that it is possible to teach an organism that does not symbolize in the first place to symbolize. Of course it may be possible, but I do not see how, any more than I can see how to teach an organism that does not transfer to do so. Symbolization and transfer both lie at the heart of language learning. I suspect they have in common the fact that neither is instilled by the present training procedures, but is a capacity of the organism that is utilized by the training.

Clever Gretel?

Was Sarah responding to the plastic language or to nonlinguistic cues arising from the trainer's face or body? In principle, this could be tested by eliminating the nonlinguistic cues. Trainers could wear dark glasses, or, after presenting Sarah with a question, station themselves behind an opaque screen, or simply look away from her. But these measures were practically useless. When the trainer put several questions on Sarah's board and then walked away, leaving her to answer them, Sarah worked erratically or quit altogether, in somewhat the way a conversation falters when one person ceases to pay attention to the other. Social contact may be Sarah's primary motivation. In any case, she did not work under these circumstances.

It was necessary to approach the problem of nonlinguistic cues from the opposite direction. Rather than use a trainer who was competent in the language but who divested himself of normal social behavior, we used a trainer who engaged in normal social behavior but who was not competent in the language. Sarah was adapted to a new trainer who had not been taught the language. Then this "dumb" trainer gave her a series of simple tests involving familiar materials. (Familiar materials were used since the question was whether or not she could respond to old words when the cues were solely linguistic.)

On the production side, she was required to request the object that was present on a trial by writing the simple sentence, "Give Sarah X," where X was either a nut, candy, or one of three fruits. She was given a set of eight words to choose from on these trials: for example, "smoke, eat, give, green, Sarah, Debbie, candy, banana." Also on the production side, she was asked a series of *wh* questions such as "red ? apple." Her alternatives were "color of, size, shape, name, if-then." The only irrelevant word was if-then; all the other words were correct at some time in some sentence.

On the comprehension side, she was given the instruction, "Sarah take blue" (or "yellow" or "green") in the presence of one of the three colored cards. She was also given simple conditional instructions such as "Jon insert yellow ⊃ Sarah take cracker." (Jon, the "dumb" trainer, was identified simply by hanging his name around his neck, which is how all personal names, including Sarah's, were taught in the beginning.) Additional tests, all roughly of this order of complexity, were included in the battery.

The tests were conducted by coding the words with numbers and using a two-way communication system between the "dumb" trainer inside the test area, and a second trainer outside. On a representative production trial, the "dumb" trainer consulted his code sheet (which consisted of a parallel list of numbers and colored pictures of the words), gave Sarah the words called for, and then placed before her the piece of fruit indicated on the trial. After she had arranged her choice of words in a column on the board, he translated her sentence into a sequence of numbers that he read over the microphone to the trainer outside. Depending on whether or not the spoken sequence agreed with the one on the outside trainer's list, the inside trainer heard "yes" or "no" through his headphones, and then either did or did not give Sarah the piece of fruit, along with a bit of praise.

On the first and second production tests described above, Sarah made 6 errors on the first 20 trials and 3 errors on the first 10 trials, respectively. Although this was below her usual performance level, especially for such simple materials, it was well above chance. (She performed at the 70 percent level on both exercises; chance would be approximately 13 percent and 20 percent, respectively, if order were not considered, and still less if it were.) On the first and second comprehension tests described above, she made 4 errors on the first 15 trials and 3 errors on the first 10 trials, respectively. Again, the performance level was above chance, but below her usual level (*18*).

More surprising than the decrement in her accuracy was a deterioration in the form of her behavior. The most striking aspect of this deterioration was a regression to an earlier form of sentence production that was once her dominant form. Early in training she had not produced sentences in their final order: she put correct words on the board in incorrect orders and then made one or two changes before settling on a final order. Although she had abandoned this mode of sentence production at least 10 months earlier, she reverted to it with the "dumb" trainer. In addition, the verticality of her sentences suffered. Ordinarily, words were placed more or less below one another, but with the "dumb" trainer she failed to maintain this orderliness. The sprawling sentence was another characteristic of her early behavior.

Changes of this kind are often ascribed to emotional factors. This is a possibility, even though she was adapted to the new trainer, for the conditions of adaptation differed from those of testing. In addition, she was cut off from her usual trainers. Whatever the proper interpretation of these morphological changes, they accompanied a performance level which, though poorer than usual, was nonetheless substantially above chance. Sarah "talked" to a trainer who did not know the language. She was less accurate in "talking" with him than with trainers who knew the language, but accurate enough to infirm the hypothesis that her performance was based mainly on nonlinguistic cues.

Training Procedure

The basic operation in the training procedure was one-to-one substitution. Each new word or particle was introduced at a marked location as the only unknown in a string of known elements. At one extreme, the known elements were actual objects, as when same-different was taught; and at the other extreme, sentences, as when if-then was taught. All the strings produced by the act of completion naturally were admissible strings in the language.

One-to-one substitution may be the simplest of all training procedures. When the subject's task is that of completing an admissible string, one-to-one substitution eliminates all of the following possible sources of difficulty: (i) which words to use and how many, (ii) where to put the words in the string, and (iii) which operations to use—simply addition, or rearrangement and deletion as well. The other operations—rearrangement, many-to-one substitution, deletion, and so forth—will occur in the broader use of the language. They may either be taught as such or, as was more nearly the case with Sarah, observed to occur spontaneously (*19*), but they do not seem appropriate to the initial training. There we want the fewest possible operations that are compatible with learning. What constitutes optimal training procedures? Strictly speaking, we do not know, but must find out. Without this information, failure can only be ambiguous. It could indicate an incapacity of the species, or merely that the training was improper. Only when we know what constitutes proper training can we be certain who failed—teacher or "pupil."

REFERENCES AND NOTES

1. Because man is the only creature with natural language, we tend to assign a definitional weight to every aspect of human language. Yet it is equally reasonable to suppose that only certain features are critical, while others are secondary and should not be given definitional weight. The distinction I would like to draw is between language as a general system and the particular form this system takes in its use by man. See R. A. Gardner and B. T. Gardner for another attempt to teach language to chimpanzee [*Science 165*, 664 (1969)].

2. A literal translation of the sentences in Fig. 1 would be "No Sarah honey-cracker take" and "Sarah jam-bread take." In the beginning, Sarah was taught with the verb in the terminal position, as shown in Fig. 1, but this rule was violated so often by her English-speaking trainers that we had to accept the normal English verb position: for example, "Sarah take jam cracker." The two forms are now generally used interchangeably. However, with the one trainer who has insisted on the terminal verb position, Sarah uses the terminal position; with all other trainers she uses both forms.

3. Notice that in this system, unlike the human one, production need not lag behind comprehension. The subject does not make, but merely uses, the words; and it can do so from the beginning, without having to undergo elaborate motor learning. Thus, the earliest training can occur in the production mode as well as in the comprehension mode. This can be an advantage in training young subjects, since the control of their attention is more certain when they are required to respond rather than merely to observe.

4. Elsewhere we have described an early phonemic system that may be suitable for the chimp [D. Premack and A. Schwartz, in *Genesis of Language,* F. Smith and G. A. Miller, Eds. (M.I.T. Press, Cambridge, Mass., 1966), pp. 295–335] and an intermediate system of words with an implicit phonemic structure that can be made explicit whenever the experimenter wishes (5).

5. D. Premack, in *Behavior of Non-human Primates,* A. Schrier and F. Stollnitz, Eds. (Academic Press, New York, in press), vol. 4.

6. L. S. Vygotsky, *Thought and Language.* E. Hanfmann and G. Vakar, Ed. and trans. (M.I.T. Press, Cambridge, Mass., and Wiley, New York, 1962).

7. When the negative particle is introduced in an injunctive fashion, as in the present case, perhaps it should be used to negate a concept before it is used in the yes-no question. Sarah was taught to combine "no" and "same" (when the word "different" was not available to her) as, for example, "A no same B." But this training in a declarative rather than an imperative use of the negative particle followed the yes-no question.

8. N. Chomsky, *Aspects of the Theory of Syntax* (M.I.T. Press, Cambridge, Mass., 1966).

9. Of two procedures that might be used to teach property names, one has failed and the other has not yet been tried. We first tried to teach "red" and "yellow" by dyeing two like pieces of apple red and yellow, respectively, and then requiring Sarah to write, "Give red" or "Give yellow." We also tried to teach her "round" and "square" by offering her two cookies that were identical except for shape and requiring her to write, "Give round" or "Give square." (The two cases differ in that apple was then a named object, whereas cookie was not.) Both failed for reasons that we can only speculate about (5). Notice that this method differs from the one described in the text only in the use of two objects that are identical except for the properties to be named, rather than sets of objects that are entirely dissimilar except for the property to be named. The method we have yet to try is simply to introduce the property name as a modifier of an already named object: for example, "Give red apple."

10. The negative of a concept was formed by appending the negative particle to the name of the concept. This was so until relatively late in the project, when we discarded the composite form. But even during early stages of the project, the composite form was only a training device. Once Sarah had passed the transfer test, the negative particle was detached from the name and she was required to negate the concept herself. For example, when she was asked during training, "red ? banana," she was given the single particle "not color of." But when she was asked the same question after having passed the transfer test, she was given the separate particles "not" and "color of" and was required to choose between them or to use both. If she used both, then she had to use them in the proper order. In brief, the appended negative was a training device, discarded during early stages once the transfer test had been passed, and eliminated altogether in later stages of the project.

11. A control is lacking in the present test. It is not sufficient that only one of the four disks be brown: at least some of the other disks must have additional properties that are equally characteristic of chocolate. Suppose that in Sarah's experience chocolate was not only always brown, but always triangular. In this case, one of the disks should be triangular. When given the instruction, "Take brown," her taking the brown rather than the triangular disk would show that she was responding specifically to the color brown. This is but one of several controls which hindsight has recognized the need for, but which the now uncooperative, sexually mature subject has made it difficult to apply.

12. The order of the elements in the sentence and the order of the things referred to by the sentence are the same in the case of "on"—a consequence of the vertical sentence. However, Sarah has since been taught "in front of" by the same procedure used to teach "on," showing that her use of word order does not depend on an isomorphism of this kind.

13. Although we have taught Sarah both "and" and "if-then" and are training her in "or" (A or B, but not both), we have not yet been able to complete tests that would specifically require her to contrast these particles. Until we do, we cannot know what the connectives really mean to her. The tests themselves are not difficult to arrange, but inducing her to take them is another matter. Performing correctly on the following set of instructions would indicate an ability to distinguish one connective from another. "Sarah take: A and B, B and A, A or B, B or A, if A then B, if B then A." Notice that, for the test to discriminate between the conjunction and the conditional, Sarah must not impose an order rule of her own. She must respond in the same way to "A and B" as she does to "B and A."

14. At this stage, Sarah did not ask questions, she only answered them. Moreover, her answers did not consist of sentences composed from scratch. Rather, she inserted into the trainer's questions words which, when appropriate, transformed an interrogative sentence into either a declarative or an imperative one. The trainer's questions were kept on the board before Sarah, not to avoid possible memory problems, but to allow her to answer in this extremely simple form. However, in introducing the question in this way, we neither limit answers to one word, nor rule out answers consisting of sentences composed from scratch. In principle, we can attain sentences composed from scratch in three steps: (i) Teach the subject not to answer the trainer's question, but to copy it and then to insert her answer into the copy; (ii) Take interrogative markers away from the subject so that her copy will be blank where the trainer's question has an interrogative marker, and require her to insert her answer into the blank; and (iii) Erase the trainer's question before allowing the subject to answer.

15. The assumption that Sarah pluralizes when there are two or more items in the subject suggests an important test we have yet to make. This assumption leads us to predict that she will write, "Apple, banana is pl fruit" as well as "Red, yellow is pl color," but that she will *not* write, "Red apple is pl round," for, although "red apple" is two words, it does not refer to two items.

16. Several researchers have used a so-called conditional discrimination problem, in which the subject is required to respond differentially, depending on, typically, a contextual cue. Both chimps and monkeys have solved such problems [H. W. Nissen, *J. Psychol. 36*, 271 (1953); H. F. Harlow, *Psychol. Rev. 56*, 51 (1949); A. J. Riopelle and E. L. Copeland, *J. Exp. Psychol. 48*, 143 (1954)]. Although this type of problem can be made very complex, it seems doubtful that it is any more appropriately described in terms of the conditional relation than is simple reward and punishment. And simple reward and punishment are effective in modifying the behavior of nonprimates. The question of interest is this: If an organism can be modified by a procedure that is reasonably described in terms of the conditional relation, does it follow that the organism can be taught to label the relation? An affirmative answer would make rats and pigeons eligible for such learning; a negative answer would require an account of what must be present, in addition to simple modifiability, to make such learning possible.

17.   The conclusion that the procedure was improper need not have been reached in hindsight. The standard training program consists of two positive and two negative instances of the concept, followed by choice trials in which the original material is repeated in the presence of both alternatives—words in production trials and nonlinguistic items in comprehension trials. The actual training did not conform to this format: there were neither two positive nor two negative instances. We are attempting to devise a standard training procedure that, whether it is necessary or not, will be sufficient to teach most language exemplars. But occasionally we stray from our own program. It is embarrassing, on the one hand, to discover that we have strayed; but it is often comforting on the other, for the deviations are typically accompanied by poor learning performances.

18.   At the end of the test series, the ''dumb'' trainer was tested for language comprehension. Although he was ignorant to begin with, he was exposed during testing to conditions that made learning possible. The tests showed that, although he learned certain things correctly, he also mislearned many other things, and that, on balance, his knowledge could not account for Sarah's performance. First, the data reported here came from the first session of each kind, when the trainer was least likely to have learned anything. Second, there was no conformity between Sarah's errors and those of the trainer. Most of the trainer's errors were systematic—words that he had mislearned, whereas none of Sarah's errors were of this kind.

19.   D. Premack, in *Cognitive Processes of Nonhuman Primates,* L. E. Jarrard, Ed. (Academic Press, New York, in press).

20.   Parts of this article were reprinted from D. Premack, *J. Exp. Anal. Behav. 14,* 107 (1970), copyright 1970 by the Society for the Experimental Analysis of Behavior, Inc., by permission. M. Morgan, J. Olson, R. Funk, D. Peterson, J. Scott, and A. Premack were the research assistants for this study. The research was supported by grant MH-15616 from the National Institutes of Health.

28. DEVELOPMENT OF THE FIRST LANGUAGE IN THE HUMAN SPECIES[1]

ROGER BROWN

The fact that one dare set down the above title, with considerable exaggeration but not perhaps with more than is pardonable, reflects the most interesting development in the study of child speech in the past few years. All over the world the first sentences of small children are being as painstakingly taped, transcribed, and analyzed as if they were the last sayings of great sages. Which is a surprising fate for the likes of ''That doggie,'' ''No more milk,'' and ''Hit ball.'' Reports already made, in progress, or projected for the near future sample development in children not only from many parts of the United States, England, Scotland, France, and Germany, but also development in children learning Luo (central East Africa),

[1]The first five years of Brown's work were supported by Public Health Service Grant MH-7088 from the National Institute of Mental Health, and the second five years by Grant HD-02908 from the National Institute of Child Health and Development. The author is deeply grateful for the generosity of this support and the intelligent flexibility with which both grants have been administered.

This article was delivered as a Distinguished Scientific Contribution Award Address at the annual meeting of the American Psychological Association, Honolulu, September 1972.

From the *American Psychologist*, 1973, *28*, 97–106. Copyright by the American Psychological Association. Reprinted by permission of the author and the publisher.

Samoan, Finnish, Hebrew, Japanese, Korean, Serbo-Croatian, Swedish, Turkish, Cakchiquel (Mayan-Guatemala), Tzeltal (Mayan-Mexico), American Sign Language in the case of a deaf child, and many other languages. The count you make of the number of studies now available for comparative analysis depends on how much you require in terms of standardized procedure, the full report of data, explicit criteria of acquisition, and so on. Brown (in press), whose methods demand a good deal, finds he can use some 33 reports of 12 languages. Slobin (1971), less interested in proving a small number of generalizations than in setting down a large number of interesting hypotheses suggested by what is known, finds he can use many more studies of some 30 languages from 10 different language families. Of course, this is still only about a 1% sample of the world's languages, but in a field like psycholinguistics, in which "universals" sometimes have been postulated on the basis of one or two languages, 30 languages represent a notable empirical advance. The credit for inspiring this extensive field work on language development belongs chiefly to Slobin at Berkeley, whose vision of a universal developmental sequence has inspired research workers everywhere. The quite surprising degree to which results to date support this vision has sustained the researcher when he gets a bit tired of writing down Luo, Samoan, or Finnish equivalents of "That doggie" and "No more milk."

It has, of course, taken some years to accumulate data on a wide variety of languages and even now, as we shall see, the variety is limited largely to just the first period of sentence construction (what is called Stage I). However, the study of first-language development in the preschool years began to be appreciated as a central topic in psycholinguistics in the early 1960s. The initial impetus came fairly directly from Chomsky's (1957) *Syntactic Structures* and, really, from one particular emphasis in that book and in transformational, generative grammar generally. The emphasis is, to put it simply, that in acquiring a first language, one cannot possibly be said simply to acquire a repertoire of sentences, however large that repertoire is imagined to be, but must instead be said to acquire a rule system that makes it possible to generate a literally infinite variety of sentences, most of them never heard from anyone else. It is not a rare thing for a person to compose a new sentence that is understood within his community; rather, it is really a very ordinary linguistic event. Of course, *Syntactic Structures* was not the first book to picture first-language learning as a largely creative process; it may be doubted if any serious linguist has ever thought otherwise. It was the central role Chomsky gave to creativity that made the difference, plus, of course, the fact that he was able to put into explicit, unified notation a certain number of the basic rules of English.

In saying that a child acquires construction rules, one cannot of course mean that he acquires them in any explicit form; the preschool child cannot tell you any linguistic rules at all. And the chances are that his parents cannot tell you very many either, and they obviously do not attempt to teach the mother tongue by the formulation of rules of sentence construction. One must suppose that what happens is that the preschool child is able to extract from the speech he hears a set of construction rules, many of them exceedingly abstract, which neither he nor his parents know in explicit form. This is saying more than that the child generalizes or forms analogies insofar as the generalizations he manifests conform closely to rules that have been made explicit in linguistic science.

That something of the sort described goes on has always been obvious to everyone for languages like Finnish or Russian which have elaborate rules of word formation, or morphology, rules that seem to cause children to make very numerous systematic errors of a kind that parents and casual observers notice. In English, morphology is fairly simple, and errors that parents notice are correspondingly less common. Nevertheless they do exist, and it is precisely in these errors that one glimpses from time to time that largely hidden but presumably general process. Most American children learning English use the form *hisself* rather than *himself* when they are about four years old. How do they come by it? It actually has been in the language since Middle English and is still in use among some adults, though called, for no good reason, a "substandard" form. It can be shown, however, that children use it when they have never heard it from anyone else, and so presumably they make it up or construct it. Why do they invent something that is, from the standard adult point of view, a mistake? To answer that we must recall the set of words most similar to the reflexive pronoun *himself*. They are such other reflexive pronouns as *myself, yourself,* and *herself*. But all of these others, we see, are constructed by combining the possessive pronoun, *my, your,* or *her* with *self*. The masculine possessive pronoun is *his* and, if the English language were consistent at this point, the reflexive would be *hisself*. As it happens, standard English is not consistent at this point but is, rather, irregular, as all languages are at some points, and the preferred form is *himself*. Children, by inventing *hisself* and often insisting on it for quite a period, "iron out" or correct the irregularity of the language. And, incidentally, they reveal to us the fact that what they are learning are general rules of construction—not just the words and phrases they hear.

Close examination of the speech of children learning English shows that it is often replete with errors of syntax or sentence construction as well as morphology (e.g., "Where Daddy went"). But for some reason, errors of word formation are noticed regularly by parents, whereas they are commonly quite unconscious of errors of syntax. And so it happens that even casual observers of languages with a well-developed morphology are aware of the creative construction process, whereas casual observers of English find it possible seriously to believe that language learning is simply a process of memorizing what has been heard.

The extraction of a finite structure with an infinite generative potential which furthermore is accomplished in large part, though not completely, by the beginning of the school years (see Chomsky, 1969, for certain exceptions and no doubt there are others), all without explicit tuition, was not something any learning theory was prepared to explain, though some were prepared to "handle" it, whatever

"handle" means. And so it appeared that first-language acquisition was a major challenge to psychology.

While the first studies of language acquisition were inspired by transformational linguistics, nevertheless, they really were not approved of by the transformational linguists. This was because the studies took the child's spontaneous speech performance, taped and transcribed at home on some regular schedule, for their basic data, and undertook to follow the changes in these data with age. At about the same time in the early 1960s, three studies of, roughly, this sort were begun independently: Martin Braine's (1963) in Maryland, Roger Brown's (Brown & Bellugi, 1964) at Harvard with his associates Ursula Bellugi (now Bellugi-Klima) and Colin Fraser (Brown & Fraser, 1963), and Susan Ervin (now Ervin-Tripp) with Wick Miller (Miller & Ervin, 1964) at Berkeley. The attempt to discover constructional knowledge from "mere performance" seemed quite hopeless to the MIT linguists (e.g., Chomsky, 1964; Lees, 1964). It was at the opposite extreme from the linguist's own method, which was to present candidate-sentences to his own intuition for judgment as grammatical or not. In cases of extreme uncertainty, I suppose he may also have stepped next door to ask the opinion of a colleague.

In retrospect, I think they were partly right and partly wrong about our early methods. They were absolutely right in thinking that no sample of spontaneous speech, however large, would alone enable one to write a fully determinate set of construction rules. I learned that fact over a period of years in which I made the attempt 15 times, for three children at five points of development. There were always, and are always, many things the corpus alone cannot settle. The linguists were wrong, I think, in two ways. First, in supposing that because one cannot learn everything about a child's construction knowledge, one cannot learn anything. One can, in fact, learn quite a lot, and one of the discoveries of the past decade is the variety of ways in which spontaneous running discourse can be "milked" for knowledge of linguistic structure; a great deal of the best evidence lies not simply in the child's own sentences but in the exchanges with others on the level of discourse. I do not think that transformational linguists should have "pronounced" on all of this with such discouraging confidence since they had never, in fact, tried. The other way in which I think the linguists were wrong was in their gross exaggeration of the degree to which spontaneous speech is ungrammatical, a kind of hodgepodge of false starts, incomplete sentences, and so on. Except for talk at learned conferences, even adult speech, allowing for some simple rules of editing and ellipses, seems to be mostly quite grammatical (Labov, 1970). For children and for the speech of parents to children this is even more obviously the case.

The first empirical studies of the 1960s gave rise to various descriptive characterizations, of which "telegraphic speech" (Brown & Fraser, 1963) and "Pivot Grammar" (Braine, 1963) are the best known. These did not lead anywhere very interesting, but they were unchallenged long enough to get into most introductory psychology textbooks where they probably will survive for a few years even though their numerous inadequacies are now well established. Bloom (1970), Schlesinger (1971), and Bowerman (1970) made the most telling criticisms both theoretical and empirical, and Brown (in press) has put the whole, now overwhelmingly negative, case together. It seems to be clear enough to workers in this field that telegraphic speech and Pivot Grammar are false leads that we need not even bother to describe.

However, along with their attacks, especially on Pivot Grammar, Bloom (1970) and Schlesinger (1971) made a positive contribution that has turned out to be the second major impetus to the field. For reasons which must seem very strange to the outsider not immersed in the linguistics of the 1960s, the first analyses of child sentences in this period were in terms of pure syntax, in abstraction from semantics, with no real attention paid to what the children might intend to communicate. Lois Bloom added to her transcriptions of child speech a systematic running account of the nonlinguistic context. And in these contexts she found evidence that

the child intends to express certain meanings with even his earliest sentences, meanings that go beyond the simple naming in succession of various aspects of a complex situation, and that actually assert the existence of, or request the creation of, particular relations.

The justification for attributing relational semantic intentions to very small children comprises a complex and not fully satisfying argument. At its strongest, it involves the following sort of experimental procedure. With toys that the child can name available to him he is, on one occasion, asked to "Make the truck hit the car," and on another occasion "Make the car hit the truck." Both sentences involve the same objects and action, but the contrast of word order in English indicates which object is to be in the role of agent (hitter) and which in the role of object (the thing hit). If the child acts out the two events in ways appropriate to the contrasting word orders, he may be said to understand the differences in the semantic relations involved. Similar kinds of contrasts can be set up for possessives ("Show me the Mommy's baby" versus "Show me the baby's Mommy") and prepositions ("Put the pencil on the matches" versus "Put the matches on the pencil"). The evidence to date, of which there is a fairly considerable amount collected in America and Britain (Bever, Mehler, & Valian, in press; de Villiers & de Villiers, in press; Fraser, Bellugi, & Brown, 1963; Lovell & Dixon, 1965), indicates that, by late Stage I, children learning English can do these things correctly (experiments on the prepositions are still in a trial stage). By late Stage I, children learning English also are often producing what the nonlinguistic context suggests are intended as relations of possession, location, and agent-action-object. For noncontrastive word orders in English and for languages that do not utilize contrastive word order in these ways, the evidence for relational intentions is essentially the nonlinguistic context. Which context is also, of course, what parents use as an aid to figuring out what their children mean when they speak.

It is, I think, worth a paragraph of digression to point out that another experimental method, a method of judgment and correction of word sequence and so a method nearer that of the transformational linguist himself, yields a quite different outcome. Peter and Jill de Villiers (1972) asked children to observe a dragon puppet who sometimes spoke correctly with respect to word order (e.g., "Drive your car") and sometimes incorrectly (e.g., "Cup the fill"). A second dragon puppet responded to the first when the first spoke correctly by saying "right" and repeating the sentence. When the first puppet spoke incorrectly, the second, tutorial puppet, said "wrong," and corrected the sentence (e.g., "Fill the cup"). After observing a number of such sequences, the child was invited to play the role of the tutorial puppet, and new sentences, correct and incorrect, were supplied. In effect, this is a complicated way of asking the child to make judgments of syntactic well-formedness, supplying corrections as necessary. The instruction is not given easily in words, but by role-playing examples de Villiers and de Villiers found they could get the idea across. While there are many interesting results in their study, the most important is that the children did not make correct word-order judgments 50% of the time until after what we call Stage V, and only the most advanced child successfully corrected wrong orders over half the time. This small but important study suggests that construction rules do not emerge all at once on the levels of spontaneous use, discriminating response, and judgment. The last of these, the linguist's favorite, is, after all, not simply a pipeline to competence but a metalinguistic performance of considerable complexity.

In spite of the fact that the justification for attributing semantic intentions of a relational nature to the child when he first begins composing sentences is not fully satisfactory, the practice, often called the method of "rich interpretation," by contrast with the "lean" behavioral interpretation that preceded it, is by now well justified simply because it has helped expose remarkable developmental universals that formerly had gone unremarked. There are now I think three reasonably well-established developmental series in which constructions and the meanings they express appear in a nearly invariant order.

The first of these, and still the only one to have been shown to have validity for many different languages, concerns Stage I. Stage I has been defined rather arbitrarily as the period when the average length of the child's utterances in morphemes (mean length of utterance of MLU) first rises above 1.0—in short, the time when combinations of words or morphemes first occur at all—until the MLU is 2.0, at which time utterances occasionally will attain as great a length as 7 morphemes. The most obvious superficial fact about child sentences is that they grow longer as the child grows older. Leaning on this fact, modern investigators have devised a set of standard rules for calculating MLU, rules partially well motivated and partially arbitrary. Whether the rules are exactly the right ones, and it is already clear that they are not, is almost immaterial because their only function is a temporary one: to render children in one study and in different studies initially comparable in terms of some index superior to chronological age, and this MLU does. It has been shown (Brown, in press) that while individual children vary enormously in rate of linguistic development, and so in what they know at a given chronological age, their constructional and semantic knowledge is fairly uniform at a given MLU. It is common, in the literature, to identify five stages, with those above Stage I defined by increments of .50 to the MLU.

By definition, then, Stage I children in any language are going to be producing sentences of from 1 to 7 morphemes long with the average steadily increasing across Stage I. What is not true by definition, but is true in fact for all of the languages so far studied, is that the constructions in Stage I are limited semantically to a single rather small set of relations and, furthermore, the complications that occur in the course of the Stage are also everywhere the same. Finally, in Stage I, the only syntactic or expressive devices employed are the combinations of the semantically related forms under one sentence contour and, where relevant in the model language, correct word order. It is important to recognize that there are many other things that *could* happen in Stage I, many ways of increasing *MLU* besides those actually used in Stage I. In Stage I, *MLU* goes up because simple two-term relations begin to be combined into three-term and four-term relations of the same type but occurring on one sentence. In later stages, *MLU*, always sensitive to increases of knowledge, rises in value for quite different reasons; for instance, originally missing obligatory function forms like inflections begin to be supplied, later on the embedding of two or more simple sentences begins, and eventually the coordination of simple sentences.

What are the semantic relations that seem universally to be the subject matter of Stage I speech? In brief, it may be said that they are either relations or propositions concerning the sensory-motor world, and seem to represent the linguistic expression of the sensory-motor intelligence which the work of the great developmental psychologist, Jean Piaget, has described as the principal acquisition of the first 18 months of life. The Stage I relations also correspond very closely with the set of "cases" which Charles Fillmore (1968) has postulated as the universal semantic deep structures of language. This is surprising since Fillmore did not set out to say anything at all about child speech but simply to provide a universal framework for adult grammar.

In actual fact, there is no absolutely fixed list of Stage I relations. A short list of 11 will account for about 75% of Stage I utterances in almost all language samples collected. A longer list of about 18 will come close to accounting for 100%. What are some of the relations? There is, in the first place, a closed semantic set having to do with reference. These include the nominative (e.g., "That ball"), expressions of recurrence (e.g., "More ball"), and expressions of disappearance or nonexistence (e.g., "All gone ball"). Then there is the possessive (e.g., "Daddy chair"), two sorts of locative (e.g., "Book table" and "Go store") and the attributive (e.g., "Big house"). Finally, there are two-term relations comprising portions of a major sort of declarative sentence: agent-action (e.g., "Daddy hit"); action-object (e.g., "Hit

ball"); and, surprisingly from the point of view of the adult language, agent-object (e.g., "Daddy ball"). Less frequent relations which do not appear in all samples but which one would want to add to a longer list include: experiencer-state (e.g., "I hear"); datives of indirect object (e.g., "Give Mommy"); comitatives (e.g., "Walk Mommy"); instrumentals (e.g., "Sweep broom"); and just a few others. From all of these constructions, it may be noticed that in English, and in all languages, "obligatory" functional morphemes like inflections, case endings, articles, and prepositions are missing in Stage I. This is, of course, the observation that gave rise to the still roughly accurate descriptive term *telegraphic speech*. The function forms are thought to be absent because of some combination of such variables as their slight phonetic substance and minimal stress, their varying but generally considerable grammatical complexity, and the subtlety of the semantic modulations they express (number, time, aspect, specificity of reference, exact spatial relations, etc.).

Stage I speech seems to be almost perfectly restricted to these two-term relations, expressed, at the least, by subordination to a single sentence contour and often by appropriate word order, until the *MLU* is about 1.50. From here on, complications which lengthen the utterance begin, but they are, remarkably enough, complications of just the same two types in all languages studied so far. The first type involves three-term relations, like agent-action-object; agent-action-locative; and action-object-locative which, in effect, combine sequentially two of the simple relations found before an *MLU* of 1.50 without repeating the term that would appear twice if the two-term relations simply were strung together. In other words, something like agent-action-object (e.g., "Adam hit ball") is made up *as if* the relations agent-action ("Adam hit") and action-object ("Hit ball") had been strung together in sequence with one redundant occurrence of the action ("hit") deleted.

The second type of complication involves the retention of the basic line of the two-term relation with one term, always a noun-phrase, "expanding" as a relation in its own right. Thus, there is development from such forms as "Sit chair" (action-locative) to "Sit Daddy chair" which is an action-locative, such that the locative itself is expanded as a possessive. The forms expanded in this kind of construction are, in all languages so far studied, the same three types: expressions of attribution, possession, and recurrence. Near the very end of Stage I, there are further complications into four-term relations of exactly the same two types described. All of this, of course, gives a very "biological" impression, almost as if semantic cells of a finite set of types were dividing and combining and then redividing and recombining in ways common to the species.

The remaining two best established invariances of order in acquisition have not been studied in a variety of languages but only for American children and, in one case, only for the three unacquainted children in Brown's longitudinal study—the children called, in the literature, Adam, Eve, and Sarah. The full results appear in Stage II of Brown (in press) and in Brown and Hanlon (1970). Stage II in Brown (in press) focuses on 14 functional morphemes including the English noun and verb inflections, the copula *be*, the progressive auxiliary *be*, the prepositions *in* and *on*, and the articles *a* and *the*. For just these forms in English it is possible to define a criterion that is considerably superior to the simple occurrence-or-not used in Stage I and to the semiarbitrary frequency levels used in the remaining sequence to be described. In very many sentence contexts, one or another of the 14 morphemes can be said to be "obligatory" from the point of view of the adult language. Thus in a nomination sentence accompanied by pointing, such as "That book," an article is obligatory; in a sentence like "Here two book," a plural inflection on the noun is obligatory; in "I running," the auxiliary *am* inflected for person, number, and tense is obligatory. It is possible to treat each such sentence frame as a kind of test item in which the obligatory form either appears or is omitted. Brown defined as his criterion of acquisition, presence in 90% of obligatory contexts in six consecutive sampling hours.

There are in the detailed report many surprising and suggestive outcomes. For instance, "acquisition" of these forms turns out never to be a sudden all-or-none affair such as categorical linguistic rules might suggest it should be. It is rather a matter of a slowly increasing probability of presence, varying in rate from morpheme to morpheme, but extending in some cases over several years. The most striking single outcome is that for these three children, with spontaneous speech scored in the fashion described, the order of acquisition of the morphemes approaches invariance, with rank-order correlations between pairs of children all at about .86. This does not say that acquisition of a morpheme is invariant with respect to chronological age: the variation of rate of development even among three children is tremendous. But the order, that is, which construction follows which, is almost constant, and Brown (in press) shows that it is not predicted by morpheme frequency in adult speech, but is well predicted by relative semantic and grammatical complexity. Of course, in languages other than English, the same universal sequence cannot possibly be found because grammatical and semantic differences are too great to yield commensurable data, as they are not with the fundamental relations or cases of Stage I. However, if the 14 particular morphemes are reconceived as particular conjunctions of perceptual salience and degrees of grammatical and semantic complexity, we may find laws of succession which have crosslinguistic validity (see Slobin, 1971).

Until the spring of 1972, Brown was the only researcher who had coded data in terms of presence in, or absence from, obligatory contexts, but then Jill and Peter de Villiers (in press) did the job on a fairly large scale. They made a cross-sectional study from speech samples of 21 English-speaking American children aged between 16 and 40 months. The de Villiers scored the 14 morphemes Brown scored; they used his coding rules to identify obligatory contexts and calculated the children's individual *MLU* values according to his rules.

Two different criteria of morpheme acquisition were used in the analyses of data. Both constitute well-rationalized adaptations to a cross-sectional study of the 90% correct criterion used in Brown's longitudinal study; we will refer to the two orders here simply as 1 and 2. To compare with the de Villiers' two orders there is a single rank order (3) for the three children, Adam, Eve, and Sarah, which was obtained by averaging the orders of the three children.

There are then three rank orders for the same 14 morphemes scored in the same way and using closely similar criteria of acquisition. The degree of invariance is, even to one who expected a substantial similarity, amazing. The rank-order correlations are: between 1 and 2, .84; between 2 and 3, .78; between 1 and 3, .87. These relations are only very slightly below those among Adam, Eve, and Sarah themselves. Thanks to the de Villiers, it has been made clear that we have a developmental phenomenon of substantial generality.

There are numerous other interesting outcomes in the de Villiers' study. The rank-order correlation between age and Order 2 is .68, while that between *MLU* and the same order is .92, very close to perfect. So *MLU* is a better predictor than age in their study, as in ours of morpheme acquisition. In fact, with age partialed out, using a Kendall partial correlation procedure, the original figure of .92 is only reduced to .85, suggesting that age adds little or nothing to the predictive power of *MLU*.

The third sequence, demonstrated only for English by Brown and Hanlon (1970), takes advantage of the fact that what are called tag questions are in English very complex grammatically, though semantically they are rather simple. In many other languages tags are invariant in form (e.g., *n'est-ce pas*, French; *nicht wahr*, German), and so are grammatically simple; but in English, the form of the tag, and there are hundreds of forms, varies in a completely determinate way with the structure of the declarative sentence to which it is appended and for which it asks confirmation. Thus:

"John will be late, won't he?"
"Mary can't drive, can she?"

And so on. The little question at the end is short enough, as far as superficial length is concerned, to be produced by the end of Stage I. We know, furthermore, that the semantic of the tag, a request for confirmation, lies within the competence of the Stage I child since he occasionally produces such invariant and simple equivalents as "right?" or "huh?" Nevertheless, Brown and Hanlon (1970) have shown that the production of a full range of well-formed tags is not to be found until after Stage V, sometimes several years after. Until that time, there are, typically, no well-formed tags at all. What accounts for the long delay? Brown and Hanlon present evidence that it is the complexity of the grammatical knowledge that tags entail.

Consider such a declarative sentence as "His wife can drive." How might one develop from this the tag "can't she?" It is, in the first place, necessary to make a pronoun of the subject. The subject is *his wife*, and so the pronoun must be feminine, third person, and since it is a subject, the nominative case—in fact, *she*. Another step is to make the tag negative. In English this is done by adding *not* or the contraction *n't* to the auxiliary verb *can;* hence *can't*. Another step is to make the tag interrogative, since it is a question, and in English that is done by a permutation of order—placing the auxiliary verb ahead of the subject. Still another step is to delete all of the predicate of the base sentence, except the first member of the auxiliary, and that at last yields *can't she?* as a derivative of *His wife can drive*. While this description reads a little bit like a program simulating the process by which tags actually are produced by human beings, it is not intended as anything of the sort. The point is simply that there seems to be no way at all by which a human could produce the right tag for each declarative without *somehow* utilizing all of the grammatical knowledge described, just how no one knows. But memorization is excluded completely by the fact that, while tags themselves are numerous but not infinitely so, the problem is to fit the one right tag to each declarative, and declaratives are infinitely numerous.

In English all of the single constructions, and also all of the pairs, which entail the knowledge involved in tag creation, themselves exist as independent sentences in their own right, for example, interrogatives, negatives, ellipses, negative-ellipses, and so on. One can, therefore, make an ordering of constructions in terms of complexity of grammatical knowledge (in precise fact, only a partial ordering) and ask whether more complex forms are always preceded in child speech by less complex forms. This is what Brown and Hanlon (1970) did for Adam, Eve, and Sarah, and the result was resoundingly affirmative. In this study, then, we have evidence that grammatical complexity as such, when it can be disentangled, as it often cannot, from semantic complexity, is itself a determinant of order of acquisition.

Of course, the question about the mother tongue that we should really like answered is, How is it possible to learn a first language at all? On that question, which ultimately motivates the whole research enterprise, I have nothing to offer that is not negative. But perhaps it is worth while making these negatives explicit since they are still widely supposed to be affirmatives, and indeed to provide a large part of the answer to the question. What I have to say is not primarily addressed to the question, How does the child come to talk at all? since there seem to be fairly obvious utilities in saying a few words in order to express more exactly what he wants, does not want, wonders about, or wishes to share with others. The more exact question on which we have a little information that serves only to make the question more puzzling is, How does the child come to *improve* upon his language, moving steadily in the direction of the adult model? It probably seems surprising that there should be any mystery about the forces impelling improvement, since it is just this aspect of the process that most people imagine that they understand. Surely the improvement is a response to selective social pressures of various kinds; ill-formed or incomplete utterances must be less effective than well-formed and complete utterances in accomplishing the child's intent; parents probably approve of well-formed utterances and disapprove or correct the ill-formed. These ideas sound sensible and may be correct, but the still-scant evidence available does not support them.

At the end of Stage I, the child's constructions are characterized by, in addition to the things we have mentioned, a seemingly lawless oscillating omission of every sort of major constituent including sometimes subjects, objects, verbs, locatives, and so on. The important point about these oscillating omissions is that they seldom seem to impede communication; the other person, usually the mother, being in the same situation and familiar with the child's stock of knowledge, usually understands, so far as one can judge, even the incomplete utterance. Brown (in press) has suggested the Stage I child's speech is well adapted to his purpose, but that, as a speaker, he is very *narrowly* adapted. We may suppose that in speaking to strangers or of new experiences he will have to learn to express obligatory constituents if he wants to get his message across. And that may be the answer: The social pressures to communicate may chiefly operate outside the usual sampling situation, which is that of the child at home with family members.

In Stage II, Brown (in press) found that all of the 14 grammatical morphemes were at first missing, then occasionally present in obligatory contexts, and after varying and often long periods of time, always present in such contexts. What makes the probability of supplying the requisite morpheme rise with time? It is surprisingly difficult to find cases in which omission results in incomprehension or misunderstanding. With respect to the definite and nondefinite articles, it even looks as if listeners almost never really need them, and yet child speakers learn to operate with the exceedingly intricate rules governing their usage. Adult Japanese, speaking English as a second language, do not seem to learn how to operate with the articles as we might expect they would if listeners needed them. Perhaps it is the case that the child automatically does this kind of learning but that adults do not. Second-language learning may be responsive to familiar sorts of learning variables, and first-language learning may not. The two, often thought to be similar processes, may be profoundly and ineradicably different.

Consider the Stage I child's invariably uninflected generic verbs. In Stage II, American parents regularly gloss these verbs in one of four ways: as imperatives, past tense forms, present progressives, or imminent-intentional futures. It is an interesting fact, of course, that these are just the four modulations of the verb that the child then goes on, first, to learn to express. For years we have thought it possible that glosses or expansions of this type might be a major force impelling the child to improve his speech. However, all the evidence available, both naturalistic and experimental (it is summarized in Brown, Cazden, & Bellugi, 1969), offers no support at all for this notion. Cazden (1965), for instance, carried out an experiment testing for the effect on young children's speech of deliberately interpolated "expansions" (the supplying of obligatory functional morphemes), introduced for a period on every preschool day for three months. She obtained no significant effect whatever. It is possible, I think, that such an experiment done now, with the information Stage II makes available, and expanding only by providing morphemes of a complexity for which the child was "ready," rather than as in Cazden's original experiment expanding in all possible ways, would show an effect. But no such experiment has been done, and so no impelling effect of expansion has been demonstrated.

Suppose we look at the facts of the parental glossing of Stage I generic verbs not, as we have done above, as a possible tutorial device but rather, as Slobin (1971) has done, as evidence that the children already intended the meanings their parents attributed to them. In short, think of the parental glosses as veridical readings of the child's thought. From this point of view, the child has been understood correctly, even though his utterances are incomplete. In that case there is no selection pressure. Why does he learn to say more if what he already knows how to say works quite well?

To these observations of the seeming efficacy of the child's incomplete utterances, at least at home with the family, we should add the results of a study reported in Brown and Hanlon (1970). Here it was not primarily a question of the omission of obligatory forms but of the contrast between ill-formed primitive constructions and well-formed mature versions. For certain constructions, yes-no questions, tag questions, negatives, and wh-questions, Brown and Hanlon (1970) identified periods when Adam, Eve, and Sarah were producing both primitive and mature versions, sometimes the one, sometimes the other. The question was, Did the mature version communicate more successfully than the primitive version? They first identified all instances of primitive and mature versions, and then coded the adult responses for comprehending follow-up, calling comprehending responses "sequiturs" and uncomprehending or irrelevant responses "nonsequiturs." They found no evidence whatever of a difference in communicative efficacy, and so once again, no selection pressure. Why, one asks oneself, should the child learn the complex apparatus of tag questions when "right?" or "huh?" seems to do just the same job? Again one notes that adults learning English as a second language often do not learn tag questions, and the possibility again comes to mind that children operate on language in a way that adults do not.

Brown and Hanlon (1970) have done one other study that bears on the search for selection pressures. Once again it was syntactic wellformedness versus ill-formedness that was in question rather than completeness or incompleteness. This time Brown and Hanlon started with two kinds of adult responses to child utterances: "approval," directed at an antecedent child utterance, and "disapproval," directed at such an antecedent. The question then was, Did the two sets of antecedents differ in syntactic correctness? Approving and disapproving responses are, certainly, very reasonable candidates for the respective roles, "positive reinforcer" and "punishment." Of course, they do not necessarily qualify as such because reinforcers and punishments are defined by their effects on performance (Skinner, 1953); they have no necessary, independent, nonfunctional properties. Still, of course, they often are put forward as plausible determinants of performance and are thought, generally, to function as such. In order differentially to affect the child's syntax, approval and disapproval must, at a minimum, be governed selectively by correct and incorrect syntax. If they should be so governed, further data still would be needed to show that they affect performance. If they are not so governed, they cannot be a selective force working for correct speech. And Brown and Hanlon found that they are not. In general, the parents seemed to pay no attention to bad syntax nor did they even seem to be aware of it. They approved or disapproved an utterance usually on the grounds of the truth value of the proposition which the parents supposed the child intended to assert. This is a surprising outcome to most middle-class parents, since they are generally under the impression that they do correct the child's speech. From inquiry and observation I find that what parents generally correct is pronunciation, "naughty" words, and regularized irregular allomorphs like *digged* or *goed*. These facts of the child's speech seem to penetrate parental awareness. But syntax—the child saying, for instance, "Why the dog won't eat?" instead of "why won't the dog eat?"—seems to be set right automatically in the parent's mind, with the mistake never registering as such.

In sum, then, we presently do not have evidence that there are selective social pressures of any kind operating on children to impel them to bring their speech into line with adult mod-els. It is, however, entirely possible that such pressures do operate in situations unlike the situations we have sampled, for instance, away from home or with strangers. A radically different possibility is that children work out rules for the speech they hear, passing from levels of lesser to greater complexity, simply because the human species is programmed at a certain period in its life to operate in this fashion on linguistic input. Linguistic input would be defined by the universal properties of language. And the period of progressive rule extraction would correspond to Lenneberg's (1967 and elsewhere) proposed "critical period." It may be chiefly adults who learn a new, a second, language in terms of selective social pressures. Comparision of the kinds of errors made by adult second-language learners of English with the kinds made by child first-language learners of English should be enlightening.

If automatic internal programs of structure extraction provide the generally correct sort of answer to how a first language is learned, then, of course, our inquiries into external communication pressures simply are misguided. They look for the answer in the wrong place. That, of course, does not mean that we are anywhere close to having the right answer. It only remains to specify the kinds of programs that would produce the result regularly obtained.

REFERENCES

Bever, T. G., Mehler, J. R., & Valian, V. V. Linguistic capacity of very young children. In T. G. Bever & W. Weksel (Eds.), *The acquisition of structure*. New York: Holt, Rinehart and Winston, in press.

Bloom, L. *Language development: Form and function in emerging grammars*. Cambridge: M.I.T. Press, 1970.

Bowerman, M. Learning to talk: A cross-linguistic study of early syntactic development with special reference to Finnish. Unpublished doctoral dissertation, Harvard University, 1970.

Braine, M. D. S. The ontogeny of English phrase structure: The first phase. *Language,* 1963, *39,* 1–14.

Brown, R. *A first language; The early stages*. Cambridge: Harvard University Press, in press.

Brown, R., & Bellugi, U. Three processes in the acquisition of syntax. *Harvard Educational Review,* 1964, *34,* 133–151.

Brown, R., Cazden, C., & Bellugi, U. The child's grammar from I to III. In J. P. Hill (Ed.), *Minnesota symposium on child psychology*. Vol. 2. Minneapolis: University of Minnesota Press, 1969.

Brown, R., & Fraser, C. The acquisition of syntax. In C. N. Cofer & B. S. Musgrave (Eds.), *Verbal behavior and learning: Problems and processes.* New York: McGraw-Hill, 1963.

Brown, R., & Hanlon, C. Derivational complexity and order of acquisition in child speech. In J. R. Hayes (Eds.), *Cognition and the development of language.* New York: Wiley, 1970.

Cazden, C. B. Environmental assistance to the child's acquisition of grammar. Unpublished doctoral dissertation, Harvard University, 1965.

Chomsky, C. *The acquisition of syntax in children from 5 to 10.* Cambridge: M.I.T. Press, 1969.

Chomsky, N. *Syntactic structures.* The Hague: Mouton, 1957.

Chomsky, N. Formal discussion of Wick Miller and Susan Ervin. The development of grammar in child language. In U. Bellugi & R. Brown (Eds.), The acquisition of language. *Monographs of the Society for Research in Child Development,* 1964, *29*(1), 35–40.

de Villiers, J. G., & de Villiers, P. A. A cross-sectional study of the development of grammatical morphemes in child speech. *Journal of Psycholinguistic Research,* 1973, in press.

de Villiers, J. G., & de Villiers, P. A. Development of the use of order in comprehension. *Journal of Psycholinguistic Research,* 1973, in press.

de Villiers, P. A., & de Villiers, J. G. Early judgments of semantic and syntactic acceptability by children. *Journal of Psycholinguistic Research,* 1972, *1*, 299–310.

Fillmore, C. J. The case for case. In E. Bach & R. T. Harms (Eds.), *Universals in linguistic theory.* New York: Holt, Rinehart and Winston, 1968.

Fraser, C., Bellugi, U., & Brown, R. Control of grammar in imitation, comprehension, and production. *Journal of Verbal Learning and Verbal Behavior,* 1963, *2*, 121–135.

Labov, W. The study of language in its social context. *Studium Generale,* 1970, *23*, 30–87.

Lees, R. Formal discussion of Roger Brown and Colin Fraser. The acquisition of syntax. And of Roger Brown, Colin Fraser, and Ursula Bellugi. Explorations in grammar evaluation. In U. Bellugi & R. Brown (Eds.), The acquisition of language. *Monographs of the Society for Research in Child Development,* 1964, *29*(1), 92–98.

Lenneberg, E. H. *Biological foundations of language,* New York: Wiley, 1967.

Lovell, K., & Dixon, E. M. The growth of grammar in imitation, comprehension, and production. *Journal of Child Psychology and Psychiatry,* 1965, *5*, 1–9.

Miller, W., & Ervin, S. The development of grammar in child language. In U. Bellugi & R. Brown (Eds.), The acquisition of language. *Monographs of the Society for Research in Child Development,* 1964, *29*(1), 9–34.

Schlesinger, I. M. Production of utterances and language acquisition. In D. I. Slobin (Ed.), *The ontogenesis of grammar.* New York: Academic Press, 1971.

Skinner, P. F. *Science and human behavior.* New York: Macmillan, 1953.

Slobin, D. I. Developmental psycholinguistics. In W. Dingwall (Ed.), *A survey of linguistic science.* College Park: Linguistics Program, University of Maryland, 1971.

29. CONCEPT, WORD, AND SENTENCE
Interrelations in Acquisition and Development[1]

KATHERINE NELSON

A conceptual model is proposed to account for the child's initial translation of meanings into words. The model is discussed in terms of the characteristics of word acquisition and of the relation between first words and first sentences. While concept formation theory, semantic feature theory, and Piagetian theory are each alone inadequate to account for this process, each makes a necessary contribution to an adequate solution. The resulting model rests upon the assumption that the young child translates the dynamic functional relations of objects into conceptual "core" meanings to which identificational features of concept instances are attached. It differentiates between the meaning of a concept and its referents and relates these to concept generation and concept identification, respectively. Some wider implications of the model for acquiring concepts and general semantic categories and for constructing sentences are briefly considered.

What is the relation between the young child's acquisition of conceptual knowledge, learning of words, and production of first sentences? Recent advances in psycholinguistics focusing on semantics and semantic development have made this a highly relevant question, but the answer to it is obscured both by inappropriate psychological models of concept learning and by an inadequate understanding of the young child's cognitive structures and processes. It is not surprising therefore that most of the theorizing about child language acquisition has been done from the viewpoint of the language structure—syntactic (e.g., Brown, 1973; McNeill, 1970), semantic (e.g., Bowerman, 1973; Greenfield, Smith, & Laufer, 1974), or lexical (Clark, 1973)—rather than from the perspective of the child's cognitive structures.[2]

Moreover, attempts to fit semantic theories to the language acquisition process have thus far failed to solve some basic and very general problems, for example: How is semantic information acquired and organized by the child? How are the basic categories of semantic roles (e.g., agent, action, object) generated? How does the child's prelinguistic knowledge of the world get translated into both specific lexical terms and general categories of semantic relations? What does the young child bring to language learning that makes such translation possible? Without answers to these questions a complete and coherent theory of the acquisition of language is not possible.

The aim of this article is to provide a description of the child's formation of concepts, learning of words that fit those concepts, and construction of concept-relating statements. To do this, a psychological model of conceptual structure will be proposed that can be related to the emerging linguistic structure. This is one primary advantage of the model. A second is that it can account for very primitive concepts, such as those possessed by the one-year-old child, as well as for more sophisticated con-

[1]Preparation of this article was supported by a grant from the Carnegie Corporation of New York. It was prepared in part at the University of Sussex where facilities were generously made available to me by the social psychology faculty. The evolution of these ideas owes a great deal to the discussions of the Category Group at Yale, 1972. I am particularly indebted to William Kessen, Jane Platt, and Leslie Rescorla of that group for continuing discussions and critical suggestions and to Leslie Rescorla for use of examples from pilot data.

From the *Psychological Review*, 1974, *81*, 267–285. Copyright 1974 by the American Psychological Association. Reprinted by permission of the author and the publisher.

[2]Most exceptions to this generalization (e.g., Bloom, 1973; Edwards, 1974) have relied primarily upon Piaget's model of sensorimotor development, but, as discussed in more detail below, this model was not designed to explain the acquisition of language and in fact resists such application (Sinclair-deZwart, 1973). A more direct precursor of the present effort is MacNamara (1972).

cepts. A new approach of this type is necessary because current and traditional models of concept formation are not designed to solve the problem at issue: How does the child match words to his concepts? They are, rather, designed to answer a different question: How does the child form a concept to fit the word? For this reason, attempts to fit these models to the word-learning process have not been successful in accounting for the data. Instead, the assumptions underlying them have led to the tendency to pose the basic question backwards and to suppose that the child learns meaning from his encounters with the language rather than from encounters with the physical and social world. Although most developmental psychologists and psycholinguists would probably not state the problem in this reversed form, the reversal and its assumptions nevertheless pervade much discussion and theorizing about the subject.

This article has four parts. First, a consideration of the facts to be explained and some definitions of terms to be used will be presented. Second, alternative theories of concept formation and theories of language acquisition related to them will be considered. Next, a model of the functional core concept will be presented, and in the final section this model will be elaborated in terms of its relation to the development of language.

Preliminaries: Characteristics of Early Words and Concepts

While the most recent research on language acquisition has focused on the acquisition of grammatical structure, the process of learning to talk is a continuous one that has no clear starting point. Normal children babble and can discriminate phonemes and intonation patterns early in infancy (Eimas, Siqueland, Juscyk & Vigorito, 1971; Kaplan & Kaplan, 1970; Lenneberg, 1967), and most infants begin to respond differentially to some parental speech between 8 and 10 months of age. By 15 months a child is likely to have produced 10 different words (although all may not be in the currently active vocabulary) and at 19 months will have

learned to say 50 or more (Nelson, 1973b). At about this same time, the average child in our culture begins to conjoin 2 or more words into constructions which express certain basic semantic relations (Brown, 1973). Thus, the sequence from first reliable response to the speech of others to first produced sentence occupies about one year in the life of the average child. (There is nothing inevitable about this timetable or about the appearance of the "milestones" themselves; see Nelson, 1973b, for many exceptions. This sequence can be thought of, however, as a modal pattern; it has in fact been termed universal by some, e.g., Lenneberg, 1967).

The speech forms that children first begin to use may be purely expressive, such as games ("peekaboo"), greetings ("hi"), and many other ritually useful forms such as "boom," "go away," and "stop it" which serve to regulate relations between people but do not have stable identifiable referents. The speech forms that are of concern in this article, however, are those that are referential in the sense that they name people, objects, actions, attributes, and relations. Children learn expressive as well as referential forms from the beginning of speech acquisition, and some children appear to specialize in one type rather than another (Nelson, 1973b). A different type of analysis from that set forth here will be necessary to account for the learning of expressive terms, however.

Of the words first learned by young children between 9 and 24 months, the following observations are of greatest importance:

1. There is a small set of words that are learned at the outset by a large number of children. These consist largely of names for food, people, animals, and things that move or change in some way (Nelson, 1973b). The one outstanding general characteristic of the early words is their reference to objects and events that are perceived in dynamic relationships: that is, actions, sounds, transformations—in short, variation of all kinds. This characteristic dynamic base results from principles utilized by the child rather than being adult imposed. Such a conclusion is supported by the obvious fact

that the child selects from among those words spoken to him by adults those that he will use (Leopold, 1948; Nelson, 1973b).

2. In addition, it has been widely observed by students of child language that when a word that expresses his meaning is not available, the young child from the very beginning of language acquisition will frequently invent one (e.g., Leopold, 1948; Werner & Kaplan, 1964). Such productions must reflect the child's preexisting conceptual organization which does not always quite match that of the language community.

3. Once acquired, a word is usually generalized to other "similar" things (Leopold, 1949; Lewis, 1951; Nelson, 1973a, 1973b). Similarity may be based on many different dimensions, of which the static perceptual dimension of shape or form is only one; others include function, action, or affect. Piaget (1962), Leopold (1948), and Werner and Kaplan (1964) among others have provided extensive examples of this early propensity for generalization, and Clark (1973) has recently analyzed some of the overextensions of word meanings found in early language diary studies. Bloom (1973) has suggested that there are stages of generalization reflecting the use of different cognitive principles at different ages, but the evidence for this hypothesis is, at present, slight. Furthermore, the child's meanings may also be underextended or simple "different from" adult meanings. "Overextension" oversimplifies the generalization phenomenon.

In summary, the above properties of early word learning express the following general principles of concept–word relations: (a) selectivity from a larger set of parent words on the basis of the dynamic properties and relations of the referents, (b) generation or the production of concepts to which the child will attach his own word if none is available, and (c) generalization of word use to new concept instances along as yet not understood dimensions of similarity. A theory that attempts to explain the acquisition of words and meanings must therefore take these principles into account. In addition, an adequate theory must

reflect the constraints of the year-old child's information processing capabilities in terms of his capacity for attention, memory, inference, knowledge, and strategy. Much remains to be learned about these constraints, and what is known cannot be reviewed in detail here. For some different perspectives on the problems and issues involved, the reader is referred to Bower (1974), Kagan (1971), Kessen (1971), Kessen, Haith, and Salapatek, (1970), and Piaget (1954).

At this point, some terminological distinctions must be made explicit. It is first important to distinguish between perceptual input that is easily specified in terms of simple features or additive combinations of features, such as "red triangles"; and relational, configurational, or intermodal input that is resistant to simple dimensionalizing, such as "running barking dog." A second important distinction contained in these examples is that between *static* and *dynamic* information. The world of the young child is composed largely of *complex dynamic* events, and this characteristic is therefore basic to an understanding of the natural concepts of children. When theories of concept formation built on combinations of simple static cues are applied to this problem, it has usually been assumed that the child first extracts such cues from the complex dynamic perceptual array and then recombines them. Alternatively, the label "cue" or "feature" has been applied to the information actually used by young children no matter what the level of its complexity actually is. Although both alternatives have been used, neither has been made explicit, and neither sheds much light on the problem of how the child actually operates on and utilizes complex dynamic perceptual events to form a concept. This problem in turn is compounded by the relative neglect of the study of the perception of events or of spatial and temporal sequences (cf. Gibson, 1969).

Conceptual and *concept* here refer to cognitive organizations of information about objects and events encountered in the world. It is assumed that the organization or structure of a concept can change with experience and development and that the organization of relations between concepts may also change. Concepts serve the individual by increasing predictability in a way that is supplementary to that of perceptual models (e.g., Sokolov, 1963). That is, many more things are known about a new object that may be identified as an instance of an already formed concept than the set of perceptual attributes that served to identify it. This fact—that the concept goes beyond the bounds of a generalized perceptual model—is the basis for positing a conceptual level independently of perceptual and semantic knowledge. Concepts may of course vary in abstraction or generality; increasing conceptual organization and the formation of more elaborated concepts are assumed to be products of development. These developments will be considered at a later point. It is important to note here, however, that while semantic knowledge must ultimately conform to the language, conceptual knowledge need not. The interconnections between the two may change with development. In particular, the child may initially acquire semantic structures to fit concepts (as described below), but at a later point, the acquisition of semantic knowledge—and conceptual knowledge—may become, to a large extent, language dependent (cf. Vygotsky's, 1962, distinction between spontaneous concepts and scientific concepts). The level of conceptual and semantic development that is to be discussed in this article is a very early one, before the child has access to knowledge through language; thus the problem is how to fit conceptual knowledge *to* the language in the first place. The solution, however, has implications that go beyond the initial problem.

Theories of Concept Formation and Language Learning

Abstraction Theory

The traditional psychological theory of concept formation is based on the abstraction of common elements (or attributes), a notion formulated in essentially modern terms in 1690 by Locke (1924). Bolton (1972) has put this view succinctly:

Substituting "concept" for "idea," [Locke's] view asserts that it is by a process of abstraction that concepts are formed; we observe a number of particular objects and abstract (literally, draw away) from them those features that are common to several of them. Concepts are formed when objects are classified. From Locke's account, it is evident that there are two aspects to this process. Not only must we notice similarities to form a general idea, but we must also set aside particular differences, which are not relevant to the concept in question. The former corresponds to what we now call generalization, the latter to discrimination [p. 100].

There have been many damaging assessments of the abstraction theory in both its ancient and modern forms. Cassirer's (1953) critique is most relevant to the present problem:

The concepts of the manifold species and genera are supposed to arise for us by the gradual predominance of the similarities of things over their differences, i.e., the similarities alone by virtue of their many appearances, imprint themselves upon the mind, while the individual differences, which change from case to case, fail to attain like fixity and permanence. The similarity of things, however, can manifestly only be effective and fruitful, if it is understood and judged *as such* . . . The psychology of abstraction first of all has to postulate that perceptions can be ordered for logical consideration into "series of similars." Without a process of arranging in series, without running through the different instances, the consciousness of their generic connection—and consequently of the abstract object—could never arise. This transition from member to member, however, manifestly presupposes a *principle* according to which it takes place, and by which the form of dependence between each member and the succeeding one, is determined [pp. 14–15].

Later,

The concept, however, is not deduced thereby, but presupposed; for when we ascribe to a manifold an order and connection of elements, we have already presupposed the concept, if not in its complete form, yet in its fundamental function [p. 17].

A basic objection to the abstraction theory then is that it presupposes what it is meant to explain: namely, the principle by which common elements are abstracted *as* common and thereby the definition of the concept itself. A second critical point is that what we mean by concepts ordinarily implies principled organization, not solely the association of diverse elements with an arbitrary response, and the theory of abstraction cannot account for this organization. The proposed definition of the concept as "a common response to dissimilar stimuli" (Kendler & Kendler, 1962) solves the first problem but not the second. These points have been recently reviewed and discussed at length by Arnheim (1969), Bolton (1972), Olson (1970), Pikas (1966), Rosch (1973), Saltz (1971), and Bransford.[3]

Application of the abstraction theory to the acquisition of a first language is straightforward. The child hears the word "dog" paired with an example of dog and associates the two. Again, he hears "dog" in conjunction with another instance of dog, and, after many instances of this kind, he abstracts a concept of *dog* consisting of the set of attributes which all of the instances of dog have in common.[4] As this concept is associated with the word "dog" the child becomes able to use the word appropriately in the presence of new instances of *dog*. When this model of concept learning is enriched by the addition of active hypothesis testing on the part of the child, so that he produces the word in the presence of doubtful new instances and awaits confirmation that he has used the word correctly, it conforms to the description given by Brown (1956, 1958) of the Original Word Game.

However, this theory fails as a model of the child's word learning in terms of the characteristics outlined previously. Concept selection

and generation by the child is not accounted for; only identification of concept instances specified by the parent is. Further, the abstraction process in itself is one that places an extreme load on the information-processing capacity of the child. It is difficult to account for the enormous number of natural language concepts that the child acquires in the course of early childhood (for example, the 7,500 word vocabulary of the school-entering child) with such a time-consuming mechanism—both the constraints of limited time during childhood and limited short-term memory and processing capacity of the child dictate against it.

This is well illustrated by laboratory studies with young children carried out within the abstraction paradigm (e.g., Kendler, 1963; Kendler & Kendler, 1962), which have shown the young child to be a slow and inflexible "concept former" compared to older children and adults. This is true despite the fact that in the usual laboratory paradigm the problems encountered appear superficially to be less severe because of the artificial conditions imposed—that is, the concept domain is well defined, it is limited, and its components (e.g., colors and forms) are well specified and learned prior to the experimental session. Further, the child is informed that his task is to identify that component or combination of components that the experimenter has selected. He makes a guess and receives feedback from the experimenter, usually on every trial, as to whether or not he is correct. These conditions are not comparable in any particular to those met in the child's natural word-learning situation, where the referent concept domain is undefined, the the number of possible concepts is unlimited, the components are unspecified, and the feedback is unreliable. Paradoxically, while laboratory studies carried out under such apparently more favorable conditions, have shown the young child to be a relatively deficient concept former, the child under the apparently more difficult conditions of natural language learning is found to be a highly competent concept former. This fact alone would indicate that the abstraction model is inadequate by itself to a solution of the language problem. Some more powerful model is needed.

[3]J. D. Bransford. "The Problem of Conceptual Abstraction: Implications for Theories of Learning and Memory." Unpublished manuscript, 1970. (Available from J. D. Bransford, Department of Psychology, Vanderbilt University, Nashville, Tennessee 37203.)

[4]Throughout this article, language terms will be put into quotation marks (e.g., "dog"), while the referent concept appears in italics (e.g., *dog*).

Semantic Feature Theory

A recent account of the acquisition of word meaning derived from a structural model based on semantic features resembles in certain crucial respects the abstraction theory of concept formation. The common assumption of all semantic feature models is that meanings of lexical items (i.e., words) can be specified in terms of a set of elementary components, although there is, as yet, no general agreement as to how to identify or order these sets. Bierwisch (1970) claims, however:

> . . . that all semantic structures might finally be reduced to components representing the basic dispositions of the cognitive and perceptual structure of the human organism. According to this hypothesis, semantic features cannot be different from language to language, but are rather part of the general human capacity for language. . . . Hence what is learned during the process of language acquisition, is not the semantic components, but rather their particular combinations in special concepts, and the assignment of phonemic forms and morphological properties to these concepts [pp. 181–182].

Building on this notion of "semantic primitives," Clark (1973) has constructed a theory of semantic feature acquisition and applied it to the acquisition of first words. Clark proposes that the child initially attaches words to only one or two *features* of the word's referents and gradually adds to the set of features in accordance with adult usage, thus acquiring the appropriate "fixed set" of features that define the adult meaning. In this way she accounts for the child's early overextensions of words. Crucial to this account is the notion of "feature." At the level of first words, semantic features, according to Clark, appear to be identical to perceptual attributes (including perceptual complexes and dynamic relations), for example, [four-legged], [large], and [runs], which in turn are derived from innate perceptual categories of processing information (e.g., shape, size, and movement). At a later point, however, features are more abstract, for example, [time], [simultaneous], and [prior] in the meaning structures of the words "before" and "after." At the same time it is claimed that the child proceeds from more general to more specific in the addition of features.

This version of semantic feature theory endows the child with a set of primitive perceptual categories and a strategy for organizing the world in terms of the language: Attach "features" (derived from the categories) one at a time, from more general to more "specific," to words in accordance with the perceptual attributes of apparent referents. This appears to be no more or no less than a revised version of the abstraction of critical attributes plus hypothesis testing, and a rather conservative version at that. Its connection to abstract *semantic* (as opposed to perceptual or conceptual) features is obscure, however. [Four-legged] certainly represents a different level of linguistic abstraction from semantic features such as [simultaneous] or [prior]. Further, there is no independent specification of a primitive or general order of features which would enable one to apply this account meaningfully. Perceptual features as used here seem to include both static complexes and dynamic relations, and it is unclear what a general perceptual feature might be.

Whether or not one accepts the view that semantic features are initially synonymous with perceptual attributes and relations, what is overlooked here is the child's own independent organization of these elements, that is, of the existence of a cognitive level intermediate between perception and language. As Clark (1973) states, "As soon as he has attached some feature (s) of meaning to [the word] it simply has that meaning for him [p. 72]." Thus percepts are transferred directly to semantics, and meaning structure is derived from the language. The theory can then account for the identification of referents in the same way that abstraction theory can, but it cannot account for conceptual meaning independent of lexical items. The evidence for this version of semantic feature theory is weak, resting precariously on the reanalysis of diverse diary study data. Analysis of vocabulary data from longitudinal studies (Bloom, 1973; Nelson, 1973b) does not provide support for it, and further research is needed following individual children in the acquisition of specific semantic domains in order to shed light on the issues raised by it.

The theories just considered are all concerned with how people identify the commonalities among things in order to group together a set of things, resulting in a concept. These theories are therefore concerned with discerning the invariability from the variability that exists *between* things. The theories to be discussed next are primarily concerned with variability and invariability *within* things and the relations of things. (This useful distinction was made by Elkind, 1969.) They are not concerned therefore with invariant common attributes but with individual function and identity.

Piagetian Theory

Much attention has been given recently to the application of the Piagetian theory of sensorimotor development to the explanation of the structure of child language (Bloom, 1973; Brown, 1973; Edwards, 1974). These efforts are built upon the parallel between Piaget's description of the establishment of basic categories of thought during the sensorimotor period (roughly birth to 18 months) and the basic semantic relations expressed in early sentences. For example, the cognitive categories of agent, object, causation, space, and time are shown by Piaget to develop through the child's interactions with the environment. Similarly, a small set of basic semantic roles such as agent, object, action, and location has been identified in the child's first sentences. This striking similarity appears to provide a key to the relation between thought and language as well as an explanatory principle for the sequence of language development.

However, as Sinclair-deZwart (1973) notes, "to take Piaget as a handbook for developmental psycholinguistics is not a simple task. . . . A direct transposition of his theory of cognitive development is impossible [p. 25]." In the present case the concern is with the relation between *particular* concepts and *general* structures, and here the Piagetian account has provided little help. In the same paper, Sinclair-deZwart (who is the primary psy-

cholinguistic interpreter of Piagetian thought) notes in regard to development during the preoperational period (between two and six years):

> . . . knowledge of objects, their properties, and their behavior develops—moving toward more and more specificity . . . the development of logic and that of knowledge of the physical world are contrastive and complementary: A logical structure is more powerful when it becomes more general and less linked to a particular content, whereas understanding of object properties is more powerful when it becomes more specific and differentiated. We are tempted to think that syntactic structures and lexicon follow similar opposite and complementary directions, with here, too, a close link between the two so that new acquisitions in either lead to new acquisitions in the other [p. 14].

It is the forging of the initial link between these two that is being studied here, but unfortunately, as Sinclair-deZwart points out, Piagetian theory does not provide the essential tools.

In Piagetian theory the concept of permanent objects develops through the child's exercise of his sensorimotor schemes; the first notions of objects are tied to the child's own actions, as well as to the spatial and temporal locations of the object. Thus the object is embedded in a set of schemes; it is not identified in isolation but within a system of possible relationships. The child's sensorimotor schemes are analogous on the level of action organizations to cognitive organizations or concepts. Thus it is possible to claim in a similar way that at this point the concept does not exist outside the relationships into which it can enter but is rather defined in their terms.[5]

For Piaget, there is a functional relationship between the sensorimotor scheme and the preconcept characteristic of the preoperational child, and, finally, the true concept which is

[5]Sensorimotor schemes, according to Piaget, exist on a different, not yet internalized, level from either preconcepts or true concepts. In the present account, however, it is assumed that information from action schemata is organized cognitively. This provides another difficulty in the way of direct translation.

established only in the operational period. The latter have fixed socially determined definitions (Piaget, 1962) and are subject to the rules of logical class structures. It can be objected, however, that natural language concepts rarely have well-defined boundaries and inclusion rules and are therefore much closer to the "preconcept" of Piaget's preoperational child: fluid, open, and prototypical. (The recent model of "focal" concepts proposed by Rosch, 1973, shares these characteristics, which she claims are descriptive of many natural language concepts.) Although Piaget (1962) has devoted considerable thought to the characteristics of preconcepts and their reflection in the language of the young child, there is as yet no link established between the specific action scheme or the preconcept and the general categories of thought that develop in infancy. Logical structures appear to develop and exist independently of specific content just as syntactic structures seem to develop independently of lexical content in current theories. But, as Sinclair-deZwart pointed out, one must influence the other, and this seems especially true early in development.

Nevertheless, Piaget's sensorimotor schemes provide an important principle of similarity for the young child to operate with: Those things are similar that can be acted upon in the same way. With some modification, this can serve as the foundation stone for a complete model of the child's early concepts and can help to illuminate both his word learning and sentence construction.

Relational Concept Theory

The principle of similarity through action found in Piaget's sensorimotor schemes has an important conterpart in Cassirer's (1953) relational theory of concepts, which proposes that the essence of a concept is function rather than substance. According to this theory, a concept is defined in terms of logical relationships (or logical acts) rather than in terms of common elements. Thus concept acquisition involves the attempt to comprehend the exemplars of the concept within a function or relational rule rather than through the specification of a set of critical attributes.

Cassirer not only emphasizes essential function at the expense of the structural similarity of things but also makes an important related distinction between what the concept *means* and how it can be *identified*, which is consistent with the distinction to be set forth in this article. For example, Cassirer (1953) states:

> By the side of what the content *is* in its material, sensuous structure, there appears what it *means* in the system of knowledge; and thus, its meaning develops out of the various logical "acts" which can be attached to the content [p. 25].

And,

> The content of the concept cannot be dissolved into the elements of its extension, because the two do not lie on the same plane but belong in principle to different dimensions. The meaning of the *law* that connects the individual members is not to be exhausted by the enumeration of any number of instances of the law; for such enumeration lacks the generating principle that enables us to connect the individual members into a functional whole [p. 25].

Bransford (see Footnote 3) based a model of language processing on the Cassirer theory, distinguishing four classes of concepts and relating them explicitly to linguistic categories: (*a*) possible objects (nouns), (*b*) possible properties of objects (adjectives), (*c*) possible transformations that objects undergo (verbs), and (*d*) possible properties of transformations (adverbs). He proposed that the psychological meaning of a concept is a function of the types of relations into which it can enter with other concepts. This meaning is extracted initially from the "propositions" (or "logical acts") in which it appears. Bransford maintained that these propositions could be either symbolic (i.e., linguistic) or preceptual. Dynamic events were said to be perceptual propositions *analogous* to linguistic propositions, and these events were said initially to define the meanings of objects and classes of objects for young children. The original principles of concept formation were thus dynamic and functional rather than static. Although there were clearly analogies of perception, thought, and language contained in this theory, the connections are not spelled out.

It is noteworthy, however, that this linguistic application of Cassirer's theory has defined the development of sentential relationships, just as the linguistic application of Piagetian theory has been the definition of sentential relationships based on semantic roles. This is in contrast to the natural application of abstraction theory to semantic feature representation in the lexicon. This observation supports the notion that these are important separate but related aspects of language as well as of thought. They are, in fact, distinguished in semantics as system and structure (Leech, 1969; cf. Perfetti, 1972).

On the concept level, these two potentially separable aspects can be specified as (a) distinguishing entities (objects, events, abstractions) on the basis of a set of currently useful roles or relationships[6] and (b) finding the stable characteristics of the set of entities grouped according to this principle and setting up an attribute hierarchy according to which new instances of the concept can be identified independently of knowledge about their participation in the defining relations. The first of these aspects is equivalent to Piaget's action schemes and Cassirer's logical relationships. Neither of these theorists, however, provides adequately for the second step. For example, at some point, the infant must cease to be dependent upon recognition through application of a sensorimotor scheme and come to recognize objects on the basis of their properties. According to Piaget, this development takes place during the fifth and sixth stages of sensorimotor development, but relatively little attention has been given to it by him. Cassirer also neglected this step, not only because it had received undue attention in other theories but also because he was concerned primarily with mathematical concepts to which it is largely irrelevant. In

short, what is needed is a conjoining of the relational and abstraction theories.

It is suggested, in addition, that the structural distinction outlined above between functional meaning and identifying attributes is related to the process distinction between concept generation and concept identification. Psychological theories have not generally distinguished between these processes, and thus identifying attributes have been taken as the basic components of the concept and the means by which new concepts are derived, given meaning, and related to other concepts through a hierarchy of classes. However, on the basis of his own research on concept formation in adults, Deese (1967) pointed out this duality: "The feature representation [of a concept] . . . is secondary to the grouping [of instances], and, in fact, is often invented solely for the purpose of justifying the more basic cognitive operation [p. 645]." In summary, the proposal of this article is that the more basic cognitive operation is that of the scheme and the functional concept, while traditional abstraction theory and semantic feature theory describe the secondary process of feature representation. The implications of these suggestions will be explored below.

Functional Core Concepts

Consider three essential levels in the concept formation process:

1. Concepts,
2. Instances,
3. Attributes.

From top to bottom, these proceed from whole to part. Only the instances at Level 2, however, appear in the child's world as perceptual wholes. Both concepts and attributes are cognitive constructions, one the product of synthesis and the other the product of analysis. Every theory must suppose that the child (like the adult) engages in both of these constructional activities, thereby reducing the environmental variability with which he must contend. The function of the concept is to produce fewer wholes (by combining instances) than would otherwise be present for analysis. Abstraction

---

[6]What are useful rules at any given time depends inevitably on what cognitive distinctions have already been set up as well as on what the state of the world is like.

theories assume that the analysis comes first; that invariant attributes are abstracted and combined into definitional sets as instances and their attributes are accreted. Semantic feature theory proposes in addition that the child builds up this concept gradually by progressively more differentiated analysis from a single feature to a complex set of features.

However, analysis is not the *prerequisite* to the synthesis of concepts. Rather, a dual process is found to be at work—first categorizing according to some principle and then identifying common attributes. But if categorizing does not depend upon analysis, what is its basis? By going back to the instances at Level 2 above (the original wholes) and considering them in the context of their relations to other instances and concepts, the solution is apparent. Whole elements (which may or may not have *individual* identity) take on definitions as concepts in terms of the synthesis of their functional or dynamic *relations*. Subsequently, other whole elements that enter into the same set of relations can be granted concept status within this previously defined concept. Analysis of parts of the whole is unnecessary to this initial concept formation process. At the outset, analysis is also unnecessary to identification of new instances of the concept, which takes place on the basis of the similarity of relations into which the concept instance enters. It is subsequent to the concept formation itself and for different purposes—primarily for the identification of instances outside of their definitional contexts—that analysis of the concept instances takes place, and common identifying attributes of the concept are found. Thus synthesis of the functional relationships of an individual whole is the essence of the concept formation process.

Development of Functional Core Concepts

It is both simpler and more illuminating to view the proposed structure of concepts in a developing rather than in a fully developed form. For this purpose, let us examine the hypothetical development of the concept of *ball*

for the infant of about 12 months of age. In doing this, the following four component processes must be kept in mind:

1. Identification of an individual whole. It is assumed that objects are distinguished as such, not as images or two-dimensional "pictures" or as collections of one or more salient features. The child's early perceptual and motor exploration of objects in space suffices to ensure that this minimal assumption is true of the year-old child (cf. Bower, 1974; Piaget, 1954). Not every object that is perceived as an individual whole will be conceptualized in the sense outlined below, however. Trees, for example, may be perceived as objects on the basis of figure-ground relationships but lack the functional importance that would lead to the formation of a relational concept. Identifying perceptual attributes are necessarily distinguished in recognizing an object as the same object over time. However, there is no reason to assume that an object must be identifiable as persisting through time (i.e., object permanence) or to be distinguishable from other similar objects in order for it to be conceptualized. Indeed, conceptualizing a single object in its various transformations through time and space may involve the same processes as conceptualizing a set of objects.

2. Identification of important relationships of objects and assigning individuals on the basis of their functional relations to a synthesized cognitive "chunk" or concept. As noted, this process need not imply the prior establishment of individual identity (i.e., *bee* is conceptualized as validly as *doggie* although individuals may not be distinguished in the first group while they are in the second). For similar reasons, conceptualizing does not require more than one member; a single object in its relations may be conceptualized as readily as (perhaps more readily than) a collection of objects.

3. Identification of new concept instances by noting the salient stable ("invariant") characteristics of members included in the concept on functional grounds and forming a hierarchy of identificational attributes therefrom.

4. Attaching a name to the concept so formed.

The order in which these processes are listed implies a usual temporal or sequential order for initial concept formation and naming. Subsequently, naming may come to play a part in drawing a child's attention to single objects, relationships, and instances that share common attributes, causing him to look for an underlying relation that will form the basis for a concept. This process, however, is usual only after an initial period of applying names to instances of concepts that have been generated in the sequence given above.

The development of a new concept begins, then, when the child focuses his attention upon a new, not previously conceptualized object, in this example, a ball, which acts as a center for his interaction with another person—here, his mother. Out of this interaction emerge the following actions and relationships:

$$
\mathrm{BALL_1} \begin{cases} \text{In living room, porch} \\ \text{Mother throws, picks} \\ \quad \text{up, holds} \\ \text{I throw, pick up, hold} \\ \text{Rolls, bounces} \\ \text{On floor, under} \\ \quad \text{couch.} \ldots \end{cases}
$$

Here the instance BALL₁ maps into a concept consisting of relations to self, to other people, to places, and actions and the effects of actions over time. The specific actions and relations change depending upon the context of the interaction. A chief characteristic is that they are variable over time; the only constant in this series is the ball itself. However, the ball never exists for the child outside of one of these relations. Therefore, in order to form a concept of the ball or the "idea of ballness" rather than *ball* as many different objects in different relationships, the child must synthesize over time the various relations into which the ball enters. This functional synthesis is the core of the child's concept. Note especially at this point:

1. The concept develops on the basis of the experience of a single instance; it does not depend upon comparing instances and finding similarities. (There is no boundary to a single instance; concept development begins with the first focal experience with the object.)

2. The concept emerges directly from the child's interaction with the world; it does not depend upon cueing through words.

3. The concept depends upon a prior notion of the boundaries of objects, events, and their relationships. The ball is not confused with self, floor, mother, or playpen, nor is it seen as an unbounded collection of attributes; identity as whole object has already been conferred upon it. This point is important, because, although it is maintained that the concept is defined contextually, the context is articulated from the beginning. Concept *ball* never exists as a vague undifferentiated situational whole.

Once functional synthesis has taken place with regard to an object, other objects may acquire status within the same functional synthesis or concept. For example,

$$
\mathrm{BALL_2} \begin{cases} \text{On playground} \\ \text{Boy throws, catches} \\ \text{Rolls, bounces} \\ \text{Over ground, under} \\ \quad \text{fence.} \ldots \end{cases}
$$

Certain functions here are the same as those for BALL₁: throwing, rolling and bouncing; although the relations of location and actor are different. Boy stands in the same relation to the functions of *ball* as do *Mother* and *I*. Applying labels to these relationships yields the following scheme:

$$
\mathrm{BALL_{1,2}} \begin{cases} \text{Location of activity:} \\ \quad \text{living room, porch,} \\ \quad \text{playground} \\ \text{Actor: Mother, I, boy} \\ \text{Action: throw, pick} \\ \quad \text{up, hold, catch} \\ \text{Movement of ball:} \\ \quad \text{roll, bounce} \\ \text{Location of object: on} \\ \quad \text{floor, under couch,} \\ \quad \text{under fence.} \ldots \end{cases}
$$

Some relations will eventually be identified as irrelevant to the defining functional core, for example, location of activity. The child must learn, therefore, which relations are concept *defining* and which are not. For some concepts the child may retain relations that the adult regards as superfluous; for example, bedtime may not be acceptable as bedtime unless Mother puts him to bed.

The proposal here, then, is that from the child's interactions with people and objects, specific concepts emerge, each of which is composed of a functional core synthesized from the various relationships and acts into which each concept enters. Initially, all of the relational information that is salient to the child may be retained, including information about possible actors and locations. Later, this specific information may be replaced with more general and abstract specifications (e.g., human, location suitable for play), while only the specific defining functions of each particular concept (e.g., rolls, bounces) are retained in the core. The inclusion of this relational information in the functional core of the child's first concepts furnishes a mechanism by which these concepts may be translated into statements about possible relationships; that is, a mechanism for forming sentences. When a number of such concepts have been formed, they can provide the foundation for generalizing relationships such as agent, object, location, and so on (see discussion below).

Given such a functional concept, the child can identify new instances of the concept by noting that the relationships into which they enter are identical to an already available construct. Thus, BALL₂ is responded to verbally or behaviorally as *ball* because it shares crucial identifying actions and relationships with BALL₁. What these crucial core functions will be may vary from child to child and concept to concept, depending upon individual experience, but there will also be uniformities among children reflecting the constraints of the appearances and uses of objects in the world.

In order to recognize new instances of his functional concept outside the context of its core actions and relationships, however, the child must depend upon additional identifying information. He needs to be able to pick out a ball from other objects even when it is not in action. In order to do this, he needs to *analyze* the whole (object) into its relevant parts (attributes). It is assumed that this process begins to take place any time a concept is formed. Thus, although it is secondary, it is not discontinuous with the primary formation process. For this purpose, the child may pick out one or two salient static perceptual attributes and rely upon them, for example, roundness in the following case:

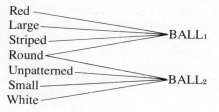

Initially, when the concept consists of only one member, a number of object-identifying attributes that will prove to be irrelevant may be stored with the concept. Adding new members enables the child to drop irrelevant (that is, variant) attributes from this set.

The use of a single identificational feature such as roundness for identifying concept members does not imply that other attributes are not attended to. Color, for example, is a highly salient dimension for young children, although it is rarely useful for the purpose of identifying concept members, and is, in fact, seldom used for category generalization by young children (Clark, 1973). However, color is extremely relevant and useful in enabling the child to distinguish *between* instances of the same category, that is, for establishing the identity of single objects. Thus the invariant perceptual attributes of objects will be used by the child both to distinguish members of one concept from another and to distinguish among the concept members themselves. Different features will typically be used for these somewhat different functions.

At this point then, the concept contains functional-relational information as well as perceptual-descriptive information. An additional variable that may come to be attached to the structure of some of the child's concepts is the name of the objects (or some other word that is used by others in the situation). The names of some such concepts may come to be used by the child himself, while others may only be recognized when used by other people, and other concepts may have no names attached to them. Because the child's concepts are built up through his interactions with people and things, many different factors will determine whether or not concepts acquire names. For example, the child may direct his attention to situations ignored by the parents; he may form concepts based on relations salient to him which are not coded by the adult language; or his parents may fail to name in appropriate ways those concepts which both share. *Thus, while it can be stated that naming is dependent upon the existence of concepts, the existence of concepts need not lead directly and easily to naming them.*

It is important to think of the child's concepts as being from the outset abstract wholes, neither words nor images, although capable of being represented in either form. The concept is a dynamic set of functions and relationships. The object, word, or image is its static representation. Naming may begin when the child recognizes that a word used by others is used consistently in the context of instances of one of his concepts. It could be that he is specifically tuned to look for such relationships.

The account thus far is in accord with the facts of language learning set forth in the first section of this article, including the principles of selectivity on the basis of dynamic relationships and the generalization of word usage to new instances. It is also in accord with what is known of the development of cognitive structures in infancy, for example, Piaget's account (1954), although much remains to be discovered about the specific cognitive constraints and structures of the prelanguage and beginning language periods. In addition, there is preliminary experimental evidence in favor of the hypothesis that the child forms a concept on the basis of function and generalizes it on the basis of invariant form (Nelson, 1973a). Children between 12 and 15 months of age were asked to choose "the ball" from a set of 10 objects each of which differed from a standard ball in either its form or its function as determined by adult ratings. For example, a sphere that was mounted in a rigid stand and could be rotated but could not be thrown or bounced was held to be like in form, while a cylinder that could be both rolled and bounced was held to be like in function. Children's initial choices (i.e., identification of new instances) reflected both form and function, but after experience with the objects, choices shifted to those reflecting primarily function (i.e., those that were in accord with the functional definition of the concept). Further experiments exploring attention to and encoding of these and other dimensions are currently being conducted with younger subjects (8 to 12 months of age).

Unfortunately, most of the language diary studies (such as those analyzed by Clark, 1973, and Ingram, 1971) do not permit the kind of analysis needed to determine the basis for original word meanings and their possible shifts over time. Nevertheless, Clark's analysis of referential shifts and generalizations disclosed many that were based on movement or sound, which are among those that enter into functional meanings. And, as emphasized previously, the outstanding characteristic of children's first words is their basis in dynamic or functional relations; that is, they refer to things that move or change in some way or that child can act upon. "Dog," "cat," "car," and "ball" are the most common "thing" words among the first 10 words produced by young children (Nelson, 1973b). Of the clothing items found in early vocabularies, two thirds are shoes and other footwear, and these are typically the items that the child acts on. It is furthermore noteworthy that early vocabularies do not include items that are just "there," that the child sees but does not interact with and that do not themselves move, for example, furniture. It appears then that object-specific variation is a more important basis for the formation of concepts than is the relation of the child to static objects. It seems likely from these considerations that the relations at the functional core of the child's first concepts will be actions and the results of actions, whether these are caused by the child himself or by others, animate or inanimate. This fundamental function center may emerge from the perceptual salience of movement or variation, from the importance of the child's active involvement with objects, or possibly from some inherent cognitive processing disposition. The important point is that the child is never in a position of having to construct relationships among static objects; he lives in, interacts with, and utilizes information from a world of dynamic relations from the outset.

Development of Language from the Functional Core

The description outlined in the previous section assumed that initially not only this functional variation but all of the relational information associated with the concept was an integral part of its core. Thus, when instances of these first concepts came to be named, it would be expected that they would be named only in the context of one of the definitionally specified actions and relationships. The word, the object, the action, and the relations to other objects would all be used in a totality that included the child as definer and integral member. This, in fact, appears to describe accurately what is usually termed the holophrastic stage, which lasts for varying lengths of time for different children during the second year. The term "holophrastic" designates the idea of sentential relations incorporated into single words. The proposition here, however, is that the word refers to the object in one of a set of relations that defines the concept. The concept contains all of the known relational information; the word that is attached to it then may refer to the whole concept while naming the object in one of its defining relations as an instance of that concept. Presumably, the name will not be used independently of these relations at this point; early object word use would be expected to be restricted to a definable set of relations for each concept. This hypothesis remains to be investigated.

In order to move beyond the point where object words refer to instances within a set of functional relationships, the child must detach the functional object concept from the totality of its relationships so that the functional core retains only the object-specific functions plus abstract markers for other relations into which it can enter. Thus the concept of *ball* considered earlier would become

$$\text{BALL} \begin{cases} Core = rolls,\ bounces \\ \text{Location} = L_i \\ \text{Actors} = X_j \\ \text{Action} = A_k \\ \text{Location (object)} = P_l \end{cases}$$

where L_i = place for play, X_j = human, A_k = set of actions that can be performed on small rigid objects, and P_l = indefinite number of spaces contained within the boundaries of L_i. Each of these possible relations would be specified by a list of possible entries. These abstract specifications, however, are also shared with other object concepts where they serve similar functions. When the differentiation of the functional core from other relational specifications has taken place, the child becomes able both to name the concept independently of its involvement in a defining relationship (for example, as represented in a picture or in a new location) and to express the concept and the relations independently, thereby making it possible to form relational statements, that is, two-word (or longer) utterances.

In addition, as instances have been added, a set of identifying attributes has been abstracted and stored with the concept. Other relationships may also have been added, such as possessor. Then the total picture of the concept becomes

$$\text{BALL} \begin{cases} \text{Functional core relationships: rolls, bounces} \\ \text{Noncore implicit relationships: actor } (X_j), \text{ action } (A_k), \text{ location } (P_l, L_i) \\ \text{Optional relationships: possessor } (O_m) \dots \\ \text{Descriptive features: shape (round } \dots), \text{ rigidity (} \dots), \text{ texture (} \dots), \text{ size (} \dots), \text{ color (} \dots) \\ \text{Names: "ball," "baseball" } \dots \end{cases}$$

This structure describes also an identificational hierarchy which may be used to assign any new object to the concept *ball*. In identifying new instances of the concept, information about it is most reliable from top to bottom of the relational structure. Descriptive features may also be stored in hierarchical fashion, with most reliable at the left to least reliable for concept assignment at the right. The functional core may be considered to be determining, while all the other information is probabilistic. Thus, the minimal statement "X is a ball" implies the functional core but no more. Additional statements may be derived by the child from the noncore relations and descriptive features. That is, the child may name one of the noncore relations such as actor in combination with the concept name, thus specifying which optional relation is involved, for example, "Daddy ball," "throw ball," "ball chair." He is unlikely to say either "ball roll" or "ball red" (much less "ball round"). The first would be redundant: Ball specifies roll. The second is apparently sometimes useful (if a particular ball is wanted) but uninteresting information. Children in the early stages of talking do often comment on changes in the state of objects (e.g., "open," "hurt," "broken," "all gone") but not on their invariant attributes.

It is hypothesized that, because the relations of actor upon, actions upon, location, and possession are in general not object concept specific, their presence in many different object concepts will lead to the cognitive organization of their recurring functional relationships. That is, the actor category will take on the values of all possible actors in available concepts. Therefore, when concepts can be detached by the child from their nondefining functional relationships, it will become possible for the child to recombine his known concepts and make new statements. For example, he will be able to say "I throw hat" as well as "Daddy throw ball."

This observation brings to light the heretofore avoided questions of the interrelations between concepts as well as the status of non-object concepts (e.g., actors, actions, properties, and locations). It has been convenient to begin with the concept of an object both because such concepts have been studied so extensively and because they constitute such an important portion of the child's early word referents. Many early words that are clearly referential are, however, not referent to objects but to people, animals, and actions. One of the latter whose reference has been traced by a colleague recently is "up," which appeared among the first five words used by a year-old child and was generalized to all vertical movement of the child himself or of objects (e.g., being picked up) on the first day of its use. One must suppose that there is a core representation of this action concept which could be specified as something like Vertical Movement. This representation might also include actors (child, mother, etc.), objects, and places. On the other hand, it seems more probable that in the case of such early action or relational concepts only the movement itself is conceptualized, and the concept contains no other specific information. It is a relation indifferent to particular elements. (This is apparently in accord with Bloom's, 1973, idea that early words refer to general relations of objects.) Thus the child would use the word to name and identify a function, but the actors and objects involved in the function would neither be part of the concept nor would they be separately named—they would act as part of the ground for this conceptual figure.

Concepts referring to actors (people and animals, and perhaps vehicles and other objects perceived as capable of independent movement), however, must contain some of the same kind of relational information as those of objects. Most children do acquire a number of names for particular people in addition to "Mommy" and "Daddy" during the early word-learning period, as well as some general people ("baby," "girl") and animal ("doggie," "kitty," and many others) terms. Such named actors vary in terms of the number of functions they perform and relationships they enter into from the point of view of the young child. *Mommy* and *Daddy* may have potentially very extensive and general noncore functions while at the other extreme *duck* may be restricted to quacking or swimming, and even a particular person (e.g., *the mailman*) may be restricted to a single function or relation to the child. Thus, actor concepts may range from the very general, like the most general action concepts (*Mommy* is "mommy" no matter what she does or where she does it), to the highly specified, like specific object concepts.

Thus far we have seen that object concepts, as well as actor and action concepts, have been built up, and some have received names that refer to the object in one of its possible relations. It is apparent that labeling objects *independently* of their functional relationships (e.g., "X is a ball") is a significant advance over naming them in the context of their actions and relationships. It requires not only the acquisition of a set of static identifiers but also the differentiation of the functional core into its general and specific parts. Unfortunately, there are few available data specifying the context of the use of very early words, so that this implication is not verifiable at present. Many researchers, however, have noted that children very frequently show a marked acceleration of labeling objects and learning names for new objects just prior to producing two-word sentences (e.g., Halliday, in press; Nelson, 1973b). Such a correlation is implied by the course of development sketched here, in that labeling and combining are both manifestations of an emerging ability to detach the concept from its original relationships and put it into relation with independently defined concepts.

This new ability to recombine known concepts with previously unrelated concepts implies a significant cognitive reorganization and accompanying increase in cognitive flexibility on par with the advance that takes place later on in the shift from concrete to formal operations.

What emerges then must be a kind of network of concepts defining the possible relations among actor, action, and object concepts. In the semantics of sentence construction the obligatory arguments of verbs have been emphasized in the theory of case grammars, although not all of them must be expressed in the surface form of a particular sentence formed with a given verb. Verbs may be thus central to the sentence-formation process (cf. Chafe, 1970; Healy & Miller, 1970, 1971; Schank, 1972) because they entail the fewest specific *conceptual* implications.

This would be true according to the principle implied above that whatever information is specifically implied by the concept will not be expressed in the language. Because verbs (or actions) are relations without specific elements, these elements must be specified in the sentence or implied by prior sentences or the situation. At the conceptual level, however, some actions and things acted upon are specified for actors while actions and some actors are specified for objects. These core specifications need not be expressed in linguistic expressions. Optional actions or functions may need to be expressed, however, for clarification. Thus we cannot invariably specify what information needs to be added to actor and object concepts in the same way that we can with action concepts (verbs) *because* they are less general.

The specification of relations, both obligatory (core) and optional, constitutes the lexical meaning of a word; thus lexical meanings predict possible sentences into which words can enter. Lexical reference, on the other hand, is defined by the instances to which the word can be extended.

On the basis of these considerations we can make some predictions about early sentences.

1. Core relationships will be expressed only if the function is apparently missing, for example, the child may protest the lack of Mommy's putting him to bed, or request that the ball be rolled to him, or ask if the doggie will go "bowwow." During the time that the child is *building up* a concept, he may also comment on one of its core functions, for example, "open" in reference to a box or plastic bottle or "all gone" in reference to an empty cup. Such comments become less prominent as the child consolidates these basic concepts.[7] When the conceptual structure is more advanced, however, and has been differentiated so that sentences may be constructed, the functional core, which is implicit in the concept itself, will not usually form part of the child's sentence.

2. Optional relationships (that is, actors and actions upon, locations and possessors in the case of the BALL concept) will enter the child's early sentences. The less central to the concept core, the more probable the use in a sentence. For example, the optional possessives ("Mommy sock," "Daddy hat") are found in many early sentences. On the other hand, actor–action sentences are less common than actor–object and action–object-acted-upon sentences. The result of action is rarely encoded in a sentence. (The force of this can be appreciated by trying to find a word for what it is that cars do—they *are driven* and are *ridden in,* but they *go* or they *move* hardly expresses the dynamic character that is observed by the child who stands at the window watching cars go by. This movement is so implicit in the concept of *car* that it is never expressed except in relation to the driver—e.g., "drive slow.")

3. Identifying attribute terms will be used not to name concept instances but to distinguish among concept instances, that is, to name particulars. For this purpose, terms that are most useful for distinguishing among concept instances (such as color and size) will appear in early sentences rather than attribute terms most useful for identifying concept membership (e.g., shape or internal features). The latter terms will be subsumed within the concept name. Thus children will say "The red block"

and "The big truck" but will not say "The square block" or "The wheeled wagon."

These predictions are consonant with observations in the literature, but need to be specifically studied in terms of the development of both concepts and speech. Some supporting evidence in regard to the child's use of modifiers is already available (see Footnote 7).

What factors might facilitate the reorganization from relationally bound concepts to the formation of general functional categories? Increasing numbers of people, action, and object concepts may be expected to lead to the recognition of redundancies that lead to general abstract categories. In addition, it is quite probable that increasing use—and interpretation of the use by others—of words for concepts may in itself lead to recognition of their independence of *specific* relationships and therefore to reorganization and recombination in the language. In this way, parental use of language, the child's own prelinguistic cognitive structures, and his functional use of early words may all come to influence his progress toward linguistic competence (cf. Nelson, 1973b).

Concluding Observations

The purpose of this discussion has been to formulate a conception of the concept formation process that describes the cognitive achievement of the preverbal child in such a way that it can be related to the known facts of the acquisition of vocabulary and of the beginnings of syntax. In doing this, a general view of the structure of natural language concepts has been put forward that is potentially applicable to a number of related problems. Space limitations prevent the consideration of these problems here and the present article is, therefore, confined to the proposition that the view advanced is consistent with the facts of language acquisition as they are presently known, while it has been shown that other possible models offer only incomplete explanations of these facts.

From the fundamental distinctions developed here, however, the more general proposal is advanced that all concepts can be conceived in terms of a core meaning to which is attached a

[7]K. Nelson, Some Attributes of Adjectives Used by Young Children." Manuscript in preparation.

set of identifying, referential features. Normally, the core meaning will be functional; that is, it will reflect a set of relationships or, in Cassirer's terms, "logical acts." In the case of thing concepts, identifying features will be perceptual attributes; in other cases they may be contextual, situational, or abstract attributes. In the limiting case of mathematical concepts there need be no independent referential set at all— the function in itself sufficiently identifies its members. In any case, identification of new instances depends upon the analysis of concept members to determine what these patterns may be, and this process is dependent upon the prior process of concept formation.

The functional meaning is designated the *core* in that it is indifferent to the set of critical identifying features attached to it. The identifying features may change whenever a new instance is found that fits the core definition and is not adequately identified by the current set of critical attributes. The referential features are always probable; the functional meaning is determining. Thus, a hierarchy of attributes is generated from the determining functional features, the presence of all of which are sufficient to positively identify an instance as a member of Concept X through those identifying features which are only correlated with the usual occurrence of X. Which features will be isolated for utilization at any given time will depend upon the context of the occurrence of the instance and upon the degree of analysis that the concept has been subjected to in the course of its cognitive history. Such a concept structure provides a set of principles for concept formation independent of the identification of the similarities of members. It also has implications for the establishment of (hierarchical) semantic structures and relationships and for concept development during childhood, which cannot be explored here.

As applied to the language-learning child, this model emphasizes that an object is first identified as having important functional relations; that these relate the object to self and other people through a set of acts; and that perceptual analysis is derivative of the functional concept, not a priori essential to it. It is important to bear in mind that this process is not proposed as a stage theory of development. Although language development may depend on the acquisition and elaboration of concepts, as shown above, there is no "functional stage" or "attributive stage." Rather, all concept acquisition is assumed to involve both of these processes, whether the concepts are formed in infancy or in adulthood. Similarly, although it is maintained that the young child begins with dynamic relations and derives static identifiers, it is possible, of course, at a later time to teach a child a new concept through a verbal rule expressing its "critical attributes" or simply by pointing at exemplars. Unless the child (or adult) identifies the essential functional core of the concept, however, and not just its descriptive features, he is likely to be badly misled about the true meaning of the word concept to be learned. Thus in the course of development there will emerge words without an adequate conceptual base as well as concepts without words. It is hypothesized, however, that the child, as well as the adult, will always search for the functional core when learning a new word. This question, like the others raised above, remains one for future exploration.

REFERENCES

Arnheim, R. *Visual thinking*. London: Faber & Faber, 1969.

Bierwisch, M. Semantics. In J. Lyons (Ed.)., *New horizons in linguistics*. Baltimore, Md.: Penguin Books, 1970.

Bloom, L. M. *One word at a time*. The Hague: Mouton, 1973.

Bolton, N. *The psychology of thinking*. London: Methuen, 1972.

Bourne, L. E. *Human conceptual behavior*. Boston: Allyn & Bacon, 1966.

Bower, T. G. R. *Aspects of development in infancy*. San Francisco: W. H. Freeman, 1974.

Bowerman, M. *Early syntactic development*. Cambridge, England: University Press, 1973.

Brown, R. Language and categories (Appendix). In J. S. Bruner, J. J. Goodnow, & G. A. Austin, *A study of thinking*. New York: Wiley, 1956.

Brown, R. *Words and things*. New York: Free Press of Glencoe, 1958.

Brown, R. *A first language: The early stages*. Cambridge, Mass.: Harvard University Press, 1973.

Cassirer, E. *Structure and function and Einstein's theory of relativity*. (Trans. by W. C. Swaby & M. C. Swaby). New York: Dover Publications, 1953. (Originally published, Chicago: Open Court Publications, 1923.)

Chafe, W. L. *Meaning and structure of language*. Chicago: University of Chicago Press, 1970.

Clark, E. V. What's in a word? On the child's acquisition of semantics in his first language. In T. E. Moore (Ed.), *Cognitive development and the acquisition of language*. New York: Academic Press, 1973.

Deese, J. Meaning and the change of meaning. *American Psychologist*, 1967, *22*, 641–651.

Edwards, D. Sensory-motor intelligence and semantic relations in early child grammar. *Cognition*, 1974, in press.

Eimas, P. D., Siqueland, E. R., Juscyk, P., & Vigorito, J. Speech perception in infants. *Science*, 1971, *171*, 303–306.

Elkind, D. Conservation and concept formation. In D. Elkind & J. H. Flavell (Eds.), *Studies in cognitive development*. New York: Oxford University Press, 1969.

Gibson, E. J. *Principles of perceptual learning and development*. New York: Appleton-Century-Crofts, 1969.

Greenfield, P. M., Smith, J. H., & Laufer, B. *Communication and the beginnings of language: The development of semantic structure in one-word speech and beyond*. New York: Academic Press, 1974, in press.

Halliday, M. Learning how to mean. In E. & E. Lenneberg (Eds.), *Foundations of language development: A multidisciplinary approach*. In press.

Healy, A. F., & Miller, G. A. The verb as a main determinant of sentence meaning. *Psychonomic Science*, 1970, *20*, 372.

Healy, A. F., & Miller, G. A. The relative contribution of nouns and verbs to sentence acceptability and comprehensibility, *Psychonomic Science*, 1971, *24*, 94–96.

Ingram, D. Transitivity in child language. *Language*, 1971, *47*, 888–910.

Kagan, J. *Change and continuity in infancy*. New York: Wiley, 1971.

Kaplan, E. L., & Kaplan, G. A. Is there any such thing as a pre-linguistic child? In J. Eliot (Ed.), *Human development and cognitive process*. New York: Holt, Rinehart and Winston, 1970.

Kendler, H. H., & Kendler, T. S. Vertical and horizontal processes in problem solving. *Psychological Review*, 1962, *62*, 1–16.

Kendler, T. S. Development of mediating responses in children. In J. C. Wright & J. Kagan (Eds.), Basic cognitive processes in children, *Monographs of the Society for Research in Child Development*, 1963, *28* (2, Serial No. 86), 33–52.

Kessen, W. Early cognitive development: Hot or cold? In T. Mischel (Ed.), *Cognitive development and epistemology*. New York: Academic Press, 1971.

Kessen, W., Haith, M., & Salapatek, P. Human infancy: A bibliography and guide. In P. Mussen (Ed.), *Carmichael's manual of child psychology*. (Vol. 1.) New York: Wiley, 1970.

Leech, G. N. *Towards a semantic description of English*. Bloomington: Indiana University Press, 1969.

Lenneberg, E. H. *Biological foundations of language*. New York: Wiley, 1967.

Leopold, W. F. Semantic learning in infant language. *Word*, 1948, *4*, 179.

Leopold, W. K. *Speech development of a bilingual child*. (Vol. 3) Evanston: Northwestern University Press, 1949.

Lewis, M. M. *Infant speech* (2nd ed.) London: Kegan Paul, 1951.

Locke, J. *Essay on the human understanding* (abridged ed.). Oxford, England: Clarendon Press, 1924.

MacNamara, J. Cognitive basis of language learning in infants. *Psychological Review,* 1972, *79*, 1–13.

McNeill, D. *The acquisition of language*. New York: Harper & Row, 1970.

Nelson, K. Some evidence for the cognitive primacy of categorization and its functional basis. *Merrill-Palmer Quarterly of Behavior and Development*, 1973, *19*, 21–39. (a)

Nelson, K. Structure and strategy in learning to talk. *Monograph of the Society for Research in Child Development*, 1973, *38*, (1–2, Serial No. 149). (b)

Olson, D. *Cognitive development: The child's acquisition of diagonality*. New York: Academic Press, 1970.

Perfetti, C. A. Psychosemantics: Some cognitive aspects of structural meaning. *Psychological Bulletin*, 1972, *78*, 241–259.

Piaget, J. *The construction of reality in the child*. (Trans. by M. Cook) New York: Basic Books, 1954.

Piaget, J. *Play, dreams and imitation*. (Trans. by C. Gattegno & F. M. Hodgson) New York: Norton, 1962.

Pikas, A. *Abstraction and concept formation*. Cambridge: Harvard University Press, 1966.

Rosch, E. H. On the internal structure of perceptual and semantic categories. In T. E. Moore (Ed.), *Cognitive development and the acquisition of language*. New York: Academic Press, 1973.

Saltz, E. *The cognitive basis of human learning*. Homeward, Ill.: Dorsey, 1971.

Schank, R. C. Conceptual dependency: A theory of natural language understanding. *Cognitive Psychology*, 1972, *3*, 552–631.

Sinclair-deZwart, H. Language acquisition and cognitive development. In T. E. Moore (Ed.), *Cognitive development and the acquisition of language*. New York: Academic Press, 1973.

Sokolov, Y. N. *Perception and the conditioned reflex*. (Trans. by S. W. Waydenfeld) New York: Macmillan, 1963.

Vygotsky, L. S. *Thought and language*. (Trans. by E. Hanfmann & G. Vakar) Cambridge: M.I.T. Press, 1962.

Werner, H., & Kaplan, B. *Symbol formation*. New York: Wiley, 1964.

Chapter 10
CONCEPTUAL DEVELOPMENT

INTRODUCTION AND COMMENTARY

There has been a rapid growth of interest in the study of conceptual development, particularly since the 1950s. This phenomenon relates almost entirely to the stimulation provided by the empirical research and the theorizing of the Swiss psychologist Jean Piaget, who for a period of nearly fifty years has been concerned with describing and explaining the course of human conceptual growth.

In order to understand the complexities involved in studying the child's development of concepts, consider the enormous range of concepts in the adult's repertoire, such as "red," "science," "large," "triangularity," "soft," "energy," "chair," "intelligence," "ugliness," "matter," and "life." The list could properly include many thousands of different concepts. The central problem for the developmental psychologist is to demonstrate how the child acquires the concepts available to the adult.

A concept is an economical way of dealing with the environment. Typically we do not have to recapitulate all our past encounters with human beings in order to identify a human being. Once the concept "human being" has been acquired, it is almost impossible to forget. Another way of viewing the functional properties of a concept is to consider the behavior of a person toward a really novel object. He or she inspects it very carefully with as many senses as possible, and the inspection procedure may be very prolonged. If objects were not categorized (i.e., by forming concepts), every slightly novel object (or virtually every object) would have to be responded to in the painstaking fashion referred to above. This would mean that a new response would have to be affixed to every stimulus in the environment. If this were the case, over a lifetime very little significant learning could be accomplished. A concept, then, can be briefly defined as the imposition of a particular system of regularity on nature. It functions to reduce the complexity of the environment.

Cognitive Approach: Piaget

There are essentially two broad approaches taken to the contemporary study of conceptual development, the first by *cognitive psychologists* (Piaget and the information-processing theorists) and the second by the *neobehaviorists*. The Piagetian view of conceptual development is outlined in the first selection (Piaget [30]). One of the basic problems in biology is to explain how structures evolve so that organisms can adapt to their environments. This biological question has been posed by Piaget in his analysis of the nature of conceptual development, and he concludes that intellectual structures (e.g., concepts) develop in the individual in order to support adjustment to the demands of the environment. The individual's adaptation is achieved by the two complementary processes of assimilation and accommodation. Assimilation refers to the psychological process by which the individual modifies the environment to his or her needs, and accommodation is the process by which the individual has to adapt behavior to the environment.

Whenever the child is faced with a problem, he or she is, in Piagetian terms, in a state of "disequilibrium" (i.e., not adapted to the environment). When disequilibrium occurs, the dual processes of accommodation and assimilation are focused upon the specific problem. If it is resolved, equilibrium is not only restored, but it is reestablished at a higher level than before. The individual now is better adapted to the environment than previously. Over time, children gradually become capable of dealing with broader and broader ranges of problems as they acquire more and more complex strategies of processing environmental information.

In examining the child's development of such real concepts as "number," "time," and "space," Piaget has observed that the adaptive modes of immature versus mature human beings are qualitatively different (Piaget, 1947, 1952, 1954, 1956; Inhelder & Piaget, 1958; see also Flavell, 1963, and Ginsburg & Opper, 1969, for excellent summaries and interpretations of Piagetian research and theory). On the basis of studies of what he considers to be the laws under which knowledge develops and changes, Piaget has formulated a "stage" theory of conceptual development in which each stage reflects the direction and course of mental development. As the child passes from one stage of development to another, information-processing strategies that were developed in earlier stages become integrated with strategies developed at later stages.

In Piagetian theory the order of succession of the stages of development is constant; the age of attainment of a particular stage, however, will vary among individual children as a function of many growth and experiential factors. Several variables that Piaget (1966) deems significant are: (1) *biological factors*, encompassing the maturation of the nervous system and the appearance not only of sequential stages but also age-specific development; (2) *equilibration factors*, relating to autoregulation and involved with the sequential processing that results from the interaction of the individual and his environment; (3) *socialization factors,* which break down further into (a) those general to human societies, and (b) those characteristics of the educational and cultural features of particular societies. Clearly, Piaget cannot be characterized as a nativist. Consider, for example, these remarks:

"The explanation of cognitive behavior by means of innate ideas is, in general, a facile and rather easy solution, which accordingly has always been criticized by empiricists. However, after the excesses of explanation by learning alone, a return to nativism is to be expected but with the attendant rule of lapsing into its traditional faults; that is nativism cannot explain the details of the (primarily biological) mechanisms that are at work" (Piaget, 1968, p. 978). In fact, he argues strongly that a highly significant factor in the child's cognitive development is the richness of his or her interactions with the environment. As conceptual development occurs, Piaget views the child as progressing through three major stages—sensorimotor, preoperational, and operational—which, in turn, are further broken down into a number of substages. This schema can be outlined as follows:

1. Sensorimotor stage (birth to two years)
2. Preoperation stage
   a. Preconceptual thought (two to four years)
   b. Intuitive thought (four to seven years)
3. Operational stage
   a. Concrete-operational thought (seven to eleven years)
   b. Formal-operational thought (eleven to sixteen years)

Contemporary researchers into Piaget's theory have devoted a considerable amount of attention to the concrete-operational stage, presumably for the very good reason that concepts such as conservation, seriation, and inclusion, all of which are crucial in logical thinking, are developed during this period. Conservation refers to the fact that, despite certain alterations in the perceivable features of an object, the object has not been essentially changed. For very young children, pouring a pint of milk from a bottle into a shallow pan often leads them to judge that there is less milk in the pan than there was in the bottle. This concept of conservation, in particular, has been the target of study of a very large number of investigations—somewhat to Piaget's consternation, in fact, even though it is one of the basic themes around which he has organized much of his research and thinking about conceptual development.

There have been numerous attempts to accelerate the development of logical thinking in children, the majority of which have been designed to induce "conservation" responses in nonconserving children. In one study, Gelman (1969) proposed that successful conservation behavior involves the development of attentional and discriminational skills. She was thus able to formulate training procedures to enhance these skills in her nonconserving subjects. The training scheme was quite effective in that it appeared to facilitate the development of the target responses, which were principally the mastery of a selection of length and number conservations tasks. Halford (1972) has argued, however, that even where a training procedure has been successful it may not reflect accurately the process by which conservation develops spontaneously. According to Piaget (1967) development derives from the child's relatively independent constructions and reconstructions, rather than by the passive absorption of external information. (See the discussion in Chapter 1 of the distinction Piaget draws between learning and development.) As Halford points out, Piaget does not offer precise details on the nature and development of these constructions, so that, conceivably, studies such as Gelman's—which originate in learning theory—will illuminate these problems of Piagetian theory.

Language and Conceptual Processes

A major theme in current research on the development of concepts concerns the relationships between language and conceptual processes. Bruner (1964) focuses attention on the developmental aspects of this broad topic. Interested in the problem of the child's integration of the information obtained through environmental encounters, he suggests that as the child develops he or she changes his or her mode of *representing* the environment. This occurs until finally the child employs a *symbolic* mode in which language is used to reorder experience as well as to represent it. To Bruner language is the great emancipator in the child's cognitive life, for it frees her or him from the perceptually dominating characteristics of the environment. In Bruner's interpretation of the language and thinking controversy, language is not only necessary for thought but, eventually in the developmental process, strongly determines its shape and texture. Bruner supports his general argument with evidence from his studies of children's conservation behavior.

Furth and Youniss [31] present a viewpoint on the role of language in thought that is sharply different from Bruner's. Unlike Bruner they suggest that the development of language and the development of thought are relatively independent of one another. In a review of their imaginative experiments where deaf and nondeaf subjects were tested for various logical skills, Furth and Youniss conclude that their studies indicate that language has only a somewhat indirect facilitatory effect on the development of concrete operations. It can, however, have a direct facilitatory effect on certain formal operations. The major thrust of their argument is that language is *never* a sufficient or necessary condition of operatory functioning. (See Blank, 1974, Cromer, 1974, and Piaget, 1967, for discussions of the role of language in cognition.)

Cognitive Approach: Information Processing

Perhaps the second most influential cognitive theoretical approach to conceptual behavior, next to that of Piagetian psychology, is information processing theory. This approach, exemplified in the work of Newell, Simon, and Shaw (1958), Hunt (1962), and Reitman (1965) analyzes conceptual behavior into its various processes such as the reception, classification, storage, and retrieval of information for hypothesis generation and testing purposes. An example of developmental research conceived within an information-processing paradigm can be observed in Neimark [32], who studies the ontogenesis of the child's ability to analyze and solve experimental problems and the role of memory factors in such tasks. Neimark argues that her particular experimental strategy provides data on the nature of the kinds of information processing that underlie the behavior of children at different cognitive developmental stages described by Piaget.

Behavioristic Approach: Harlow

Researchers who have worked in the mainstream of North American behavioristic psychology have not evidenced much curiosity about the *development* of conceptual behavior. This lack of interest is traceable, in part, to the common behaviorist assumption that the governing laws are the same for *all* behaviors and *all* organisms, whether the behaviors are simple or complex or whether the organisms are high or low in the phylogenetic scale. This position does not lead naturally to a concern for developmental processes. In fact, research on conceptual behavior from the behaviorist viewpoint has not been as prolific as research on the development of learning. Not every behaviorist, however, has chosen to avoid research on conceptual development; in fact, Harlow [13] and Kendler and Kendler (1970) among other neobehaviorists, have made very important contributions in this area. Two assumptions shared by neobehaviorist researchers are that discrimination is significantly involved in concept formation and that it functions by directing attention to the relevant features of a stimulus as well as by permitting the neglect of irrelevant features. A further assumption is that reinforcement is the agent by which discriminative responses develop.

The neobehaviorist Harlow [13] has made an important contribution to the study of conceptual processes through his work in a special type of learning that he calls "learning set"—the discrimination process that involves the elimination of both responses and response tendencies that are inappropriate to a particular learning situation. For Harlow, discrimination plays an essential role in learning set, itself a process underlying concept formation.

Harlow employs several ingenious techniques in his research. One such procedure presents his experimental subject (typically a rhesus monkey) with an extended series of discrimination problems. During the course of the testing the monkeys eventually work their way through several hundred such discrimination problems.

The results of such experiments demonstrate that although each discrimination task is different, the monkeys do not have to start afresh in each successive problem—in fact, they improve their performance on successive tasks. Harlow interprets these results as supportive evidence that a learning-how-to-learn ability develops when subjects work their way through a series of similar problems, or, in other words, develop a learning set. It is clear that learning set is a special case of transfer of training, where the transfer is between numerous problems drawn from one class of problems.

Concept formation, according to Harlow, is basically a process of broad stimulus generalization achieved by extensive training on a wide range of problems within one class (i.e., concept formation derives from the process of learning-set formation). Gelman (1969) has adapted the discrimination learning-set procedure in order to facilitate the acquisition of various conservation skills in young children who, prior to the "attentional" training, had not conserved. Her results indicate some success; however, see Halford's comments on the meaning of this and other training studies (Halford, 1972, pp. 186–187).

Behavioristic Approach: Kendler and Kendler

Other psychologists who work within the neobehaviorist tradition have also adapted basic S–R theory so that they may integrate certain complex behaviors such as concept formation into their theories. An example of such adaptation is present in the work of Kendler and Kendler (e.g., T. Kendler & Kendler, 1970.) For their learning model they utilize a mediation model. An earlier behaviorist model, Thorndike's single-unit S–R model, viewed learning simply as the change in the strength of an association bond between an external stimulus and an observable response. The model was a single-unit one because it required no assumptions to be made about events that might intervene between the stimulus and the response. The mediation model, by contrast, postulates that the stimulus and the response are terminal points in a more complicated chain of events. The external stimulus (S), according to this view, evokes an implicit response (r) that embodies the discrimination of the stimulus by the learner. The occurrence of the implicit response (r) changes the incoming stimulation by providing an implicit stimulus (s) to which the overt response (R) becomes associated. The mediating response is significant in that it *produces* the stimuli for further responses. Therefore, the formula that designates the single-unit model is S–R. The mediation model, however, is described by the sequence S–r–s–R.

H. Kendler and Kendler (1962) argue that conceptual behavior can be understood only if mediation processes are revealed through experiments. In their research, Kendler and Kendler have used the reversal-learning technique, which is a variation in the learning-set experiment. The reversal-learning technique relates fundamentally to the transfer from an initial discrimination to a subsequent one (i.e., the subject must learn to do the opposite of what he or she previously did). This technique has been used in a program of research that was designed to elucidate the role of mediation processes in concept formation (T. Kendler, 1963).

In one experiment, an attempt was made to obtain information on the role of verbalization in a mediation experiment (H. Kendler & Kendler, 1962). Children of four and seven years of age were presented with a variation of the reversal-shift problem. In an initial task they learned to discriminate between a pair of stimuli that differed simultaneously in size and brightness. During the time spent learning the discrimination, one-third of each age group was encouraged to verbalize the relevant dimension, another third to verbalize the irrelevant dimension, and the remaining children not encouraged to verbalize at all.

The results showed that for both age groups, the effects of relevant verbalization were superior to those of irrelevant verbalization in aiding the child to deal with the reversal-shift problem. The four-year-olds' performance on the reversal-shift task was facilitated by their learning relevant verbalization and hindered if they learned the irrelevant verbal labels. The effects, however, were small. Among the seven-year-olds, those in the relevant-verbalization group performed quite similarly to those in the nonverbalization group. Irrelevant labels on the other hand yielded gross interference, such that the seven-year-olds in this group performed slightly worse than the four-year-old children in the nonverbalization group. Other results favored the older children; for example, those in the relevant-verbalization and nonverbalization groups performed better than the younger children in the relevant-verbalization group.

One interpretation of these findings is that the older group made more use of verbalizations than the younger group, so that providing them with relevant mediating responses did not ensure that they would be used. The importance of this point is expressed by Kendler and Kendler when they suggest that the development of mediational processes is closely related to the development of the ability to associate words with actions.

Kendler [33] reviews many of the studies that the Kendler and Kendler research group has carried out on the role of mediational processes in the development of conceptual behavior. Making a valiant attempt to close the gap between the cognitive and behavioristic explanations of complex behaviors, he argues that neither explanation can account for the behavior of organisms at *every* stage of their development. He suggests that a behavioristic account fits the facts of early development and that a cognitive account is more suitable for later development. For a summary of developmental trends over a wide range of behaviors that is consonant with this view, see White (1970).

References

Blank, Marion. Cognitive functions of language in the preschool years. *Developmental Psychology*, 1974, *10*, 229–245.

Bruner, J. S. The course of cognitive growth. *American Psychologist*, 1964, *19*, 1–15.

Cromer, R. The development of language and cognition: The cognition hypothesis. In B. Foss (Ed.), *New perspectives in child development*. Baltimore: Penguin Books, 1974, pp. 184–252.

Flavell, J. H. *The developmental psychology of Jean Piaget*. Princeton: Van Nostrand, 1963.

Gelman, R. Conservation acquisition: A problem in learning to attend to relevant attributes. *Journal of Experimental Child Psychology*, 1969, *7*, 167–187.

Ginsburg, H. & Opper, S. *Piaget's theory of intellectual development: An introduction*. Englewood Cliffs, N. J.: Prentice-Hall, 1969.

Halford, G. S. The impact of Piaget on psychology in the seventies. In P. C. Dodwell (Ed.), *New horizons in psychology 2*. Baltimore: Penguin Books, 1972, pp. 171–196.

Hunt, E. B. *Concept learning: An information processing problem*. New York: Wiley, 1962.

Inhelder, B. & Piaget, J. *The growth of logical thinking*. New York: Basic Books, 1958.

Kendler, H. H. & Kendler, T. S. Vertical and horizontal processes in problem solving. *Psychological Review*, 1962, *69*, 1–16.

Kendler, T. S. Development of mediating responses in children. In J. C. Wright & J. Kagan (Eds.), Basic cognitive processes in children. *Monographs of the Society for Research in Child Development*, 1963, *28* (Serial No. 86), 33–48.

Kendler, T. S. & Kendler, H. H. An ontogeny of optional shift behavior. *Child Development*, 1970, *41*, 1–27.

Newell, A., Simon, H. A., & Shaw, J. C. Elements of a theory of human problem solving. *Psychological Review*, 1958, *65*, 151–166.

Piaget, J. *The psychology of intelligence*. London: Routledge, 1947.

Piaget, J. *The child's conception of number*. New York: Humanities Press, 1952.

Piaget, J. *The construction of reality in the child*. New York: Basic Books, 1954.

Piaget, J. *The origins of intelligence in the child*. New York: International Universities, 1956.

Piaget, J. Nécessité et signification des récherches comparatives en psychologie génétique. *International Journal of Psychology*, 1966, *1*, 3–13.

Piaget, J. Language and thought from the genetic viewpoint. In D. Elkind (Ed.), *Psychological studies*. New York: Random House, 1967.

Piaget, J. Quantification, conservation and nativism: Quantitative evaluations of children aged two to three years are examined. *Science*, 1968, *162*, 976–981.

Reitman, W. R. *Cognition and thought*. New York: Wiley, 1965.

White, S. H. Some general outlines of the matrix of developmental changes between five and seven years. *Bulletin of the Orton Society*, 1970, *20*, 41–57.

30. THE STAGES OF THE INTELLECTUAL DEVELOPMENT OF THE CHILD*

JEAN PIAGET

A consideration of the stages of the development of intelligence should be preceded by asking the question, What is intelligence? Unfortunately, we find ourselves confronted by a great number of definitions. For Claparède, intelligence is an adaptation to new situations. When a situation is new, when there are no reflexes, when there are no habits to rely on, then the subject is obliged to search for something new. That is to say, Claparède defines intelligence as groping, as feeling one's way, trial-and-error behavior. We find this trial-and-error behavior in all levels of intelligence, even at the superior level, in the form of hypothesis testing. As far as I am concerned, this definition is too vague, because trial and error occurs in the formation of habits, and also in the earliest established reflexes: when a newborn baby learns to suck.

Karl Bühler defines intelligence as an act of immediate comprehension; that is to say, an insight. Bühler's definition is also very precise, but it seems to me too narrow. I know that when a mathematician solves a problem, he ends by having an insight, but up to that moment he feels, or gropes for, his way; and to say that the trial-and-error behavior is not intelligent and that intelligence starts only when he finds the solution to the problem, seems a very narrow definition. I would, therefore, propose to define intelligence not by a static criterion, as in previous definitions, but by the direction that intelligence follows in its evolution, and then I would define intelligence as a form of equilibration, or forms of equilibration, toward which all cognitive functions lead.

*This paper is based on three lectures presented to the Menninger School of Psychiatry, March 6, 13, & 22, 1961.

From the *Bulletin of the Menninger Clinic*, 1962, *26*, 120–128. Copyright 1962 by the Menninger Foundation. Reprinted by permission of the author and the publisher.

But I must first define equilibration. Equilibration in my vocabulary is not an exact and automatic balance, as it would be in Gestalt theory; I define equilibration principally as a compensation for an external disturbance.

When there is an external disturbance, the subject succeeds in compensating for this by an activity. The maximum equilibration is thus the maximum of the activity, and not a state of rest. It is a mobile equilibrium, and not an immobile one. So equilibrium is defined as compensation; compensation is the annulling of a transformation by an inverse transformation. The compensation which intervenes in equilibration implies the fundamental idea of reversibility, and this reversibility is precisely what characterizes the operations of the intelligence. An operation is an internalized action, but it is also a reversible action. But an operation is never isolated; it is always subordinated to other operations; it is part of a more inclusive structure. Consequently, we define intelligence in terms of operations, coordination of operations.

Take, for example, an operation like addition: Addition is a material action, the action of reuniting. On the other hand, it is a reversible action, because addition may be compensated by subtraction. Yet addition leads to a structure of a whole. In the case of numbers, it will be the structure that the mathematicians call a "group." In the case of addition of classes which intervene in the logical structure it will be a more simple structure that we will call a grouping, and so on.

Consequently, the study of the stages of intelligence is first a study of the formation of operational structures. I shall define every stage by a structure of a whole, with the possibility of its integration into succeeding stages, just as it was prepared by preceding stages. Thus, I shall distinguish four great stages, or four great periods, in the development of intelligence: first, the sensori-motor period before the appearance of language; second, the period from about two to seven years of age, the preoperational period which precedes real operations; third, the period from seven to 12 years of age, a period of concrete operations (which refer to concrete objects); and finally after 12 years of age, the period of formal operations, or positional operations.

Sensori-Motor Stage

Before language develops, there is behavior that we can call intelligent. For example, when a baby of 12 months or more wants an object which is too far from him, but which rests on a carpet or blanket, and he pulls it to get to the object, this behavior is an act of intelligence. The child uses an intermediary, a means to get to his goal. Also, getting to an object by means of pulling a string when the object is tied to the string, or when the child uses a stick to get the object, are acts of intelligence. They demonstrate in the sensori-motor period a certain number of stages, which go from simple reflexes, from the formation of the first habits, up to the coordination of means and goals.

Remarkable in this sensori-motor stage of intelligence is that there are already structures. Sensori-motor intelligence rests mainly on actions, on movements and perceptions without language, but these actions are coordinated in a relatively stable way. They are coordinated under what we may call schemata of action. These schemata can be generalized in actions and are applicable to new situations. For example, pulling a carpet to bring an object within reach constitutes a schema which can be generalized to other situations when another object rests on a support. In other words, a schema supposes an incorporation of new situations into the previous schemata, a sort of continuous assimilation of new objects or new situations to the actions already schematized. For example, I presented to one of my children an object completely new to him—a box of cigarettes, which is not a usual toy for a baby. The child took the object, looked at it, put it in

his mouth, shook it, then took it with one hand and hit it with the other hand, then rubbed it on the edge of the crib, then shook it again, and gave the impression of trying to see if there were noise. This behavior is a way of exploring the object, of trying to understand it by assimilating it to schemata already known. The child behaves in this situation as he will later in Binet's famous vocabulary test, when he defines by usage, saying, for instance, that a spoon is for eating, and so on.

But in the presence of a new object, even without knowing how to talk, the child knows how to assimilate, to incorporate this new object into each of his already developed schemata which function as practical concepts. Here is a structuring of intelligence. Most important in this structuring is the base, the point of departure of all subsequent operational constructions. At the sensori-motor level, the child constructs the schema of the permanent object.

The knowledge of the permanent object starts at this point. The child is not convinced at the beginning that when an object disappears from view, he can find it again. One can verify by tests that object permanence is not yet developed at this stage. But there is there the beginning of a subsequent fundamental idea which starts being constructed at the sensori-motor level. This is also true of the construction of the ideas of space, of time, of causality. What is being done at the sensori-motor level concerning all the foregoing ideas will constitute the substructure of the subsequent, fully achieved ideas of permanent objects, of space, of time, of causality.

In the formation of these substructures at the sensori-motor level, it is very interesting to note the beginning of a *reversibility*, not in thought, since there is not yet representation in thought, but in action itself. For example, the formation of the conception of space at the sensori-motor stage leads to an amazing decentration if one compares the conception of space at the first weeks of the development with that at one and one-half to two years of age. In the beginning there is not one space which contains all the objects, including the child's body itself; there is a multitude of spaces which are not coordinated: there are the buccal space, the tactilokinesthetic space, the visual and auditory spaces; each is separate and each is centered essentially on the body of the subject and on actions. After a few months, however, after a kind of Copernican evolution, there is a total reversal, a decentration such that space becomes homogenous, a one-and-only space that envelops the others. Then space becomes a container that envelops all objects, including the body itself; and after that, space is mainly coordinated in a structure, a coordination of positions and displacements, and these constitute what the geometricians call a "group"; that is to say, precisely a reversible system. One may move from A to B, and may come back from B to A; there is the possibility of returning, of reversibility. There is also the possibility of making detours and combinations which give a clue to what the subsequent operations will be when thought will supersede the action itself.

Pre-Operational Stage

From one and one-half to two years of age, a fundamental transformation in the evolution of intelligence takes place in the appearance of symbolic functions. Every action of intelligence consists in manipulating significations (or meanings) and whenever (or wherever) there is significations, there are on the one hand the "significants" and on the other the "significates." This is true in the sensori-motor level, but the only significants that intervene there are perceptual signs or signals (as in conditioning) which are undifferentiated in regard to the significate; for example, a perceptual cue, like distance, which will be a cue for the size of the distant object, or the apparent size of an object, which will be the cue for the distance of the object. There, perhaps, both indices are different aspects of the same reality, but they are not yet differentiated significants. At the age of one and one-half to two years a new class of significants arises, and these significants are differentiated in regard to their significates. These differentiations can be called symbolic function. The appearance of symbols in a children's game is an example of the ap-

pearance of new significants. At the sensori-motor level the games are nothing but exercises; now they become symbolic play, a play of fiction; these games consist in representing something by means of something else. Another example is the beginning of delayed imitation, an imitation that takes place not in the presence of the original object but in its absence, and which consequently constitutes a kind of symbolization or mental image.

At the same time that symbols appear, the child acquires language; that is to say, there is the acquisition of another phase of differentiated significants, verbal signals, or collective signals. This symbolic function then brings great flexibility into the field of intelligence. Intelligence up to this point refers to the immediate space which surrounds the child and to the present perceptual situation; thanks to language, and to the symbolic functions, it becomes possible to invoke objects which are not present perceptually, to reconstruct the past, or to make projects, plans for the future, to think of objects not present but very distant in space—in short, to span spatio-temporal distances much greater than before.

But this new stage, the stage of representation of thought which is superimposed on the sensori-motor stage, is not a simple extension of what was referred to at the previous level. Before being able to prolong, one must in fact reconstruct, because behavior in words is a different thing from representing something in thought. When a child knows how to move around in his house or garden by following the different successive cues around him, it does not mean that he is capable of representing or reproducing the total configuration of his house or his garden. To be able to represent, to reproduce something, one must be capable of reconstructing this group of displacements, but at a new level, that of the representation of the thought.

I recently made an amusing test with Nel Szeminska. We took children of four to five years of age who went to school by themselves and came back home by themselves, and asked them if they could trace the way to school and back for us, not in design, which would be too difficult, but like a construction game, with concrete objects. We found that they were not capable of representation; there was a kind of motor-memory, but it was not yet a representation of a whole—the group of displacements had not yet been reconstructed on the plan of the representation of thought. In other words, the operations were not yet formed. There are representations which are internalized actions, but actions still centered on the body itself, on the activity itself. These representations do not allow the objective combinations, the decentrated combinations that the operations would. The actions are centered on the body. I used to call this egocentrism; but it is better thought of as lack of reversibility of action.

At this level, the most certain sign of the absence of operations which appear at the next stage is the absence of the knowledge of conservation. In fact, an operation refers to the transformation of reality. The transformation is not of the whole, however; something constant is always untransformed. If you pour a liquid from one glass to another there is transformation; the liquid changes form, but its liquid property stays constant. So at the pre-operational level, it is significant from the point of view of the operations of intelligence that the child has not yet a knowledge of conservation. For example, in the case of liquid, when the child pours it from one bottle to the other, he thinks that the quantity of the liquid has changed. When the level of the liquid changes, the child thinks the quantity has changed—there is more or less in the second glass than in the first. And if you ask the child where the larger quantity came from, he does not answer this question. What is important for the child is that perceptually it is not the same thing any more. We find this absence of conservation in all object properties, in the length, surface, quantity, and weight of things.

This absence of conservation indicates essentially that at this stage the child reasons from the configuration. Confronted with a transformation, he does not reason from the transformation itself; he starts from the initial configuration, then sees the final configuration, compares the two but forgets the transforma-

tion, because he does not know how to reason about it. At this stage the child is still reasoning on the basis of what he sees because there is no conservation. He is able to master this problem only when the operations are formed and these operations, which we have already sensed at the sensori-motor level, are not formed until around seven to eight years of age. At that age the elementary problems of conservation are solved, because the child reasons on the basis of the transformation per se, and this requires a manipulation of the operation. The ability to pass from one stage to the other and be able to come back to the point of departure, to manipulate the reversible operations, which appears around seven to eight years of age, is limited when compared with the operations of the superior level only in the sense that they are concrete. That is to say, the child can manipulate the operations only when he manipulates the object concretely.

Stage of Concrete Operations

The first operations of the manipulation of objects, the concrete operations, deal with logical classes and with logical relations, or the number. But these operations do not deal yet with propositions, or hypotheses which do not appear until the last stage.

Let me exemplify these concrete operations: the simplest operation is concerned with classifying objects according to their similarity and their difference. This is accomplished by including the subclasses within large and more general classes, a process that implies inclusion. This classification, which seems very simple at first, is not acquired until around seven to eight years of age. Before that, at the pre-operational level, we do not find logical inclusion. For example, if you show a child at the pre-operational level a bouquet of flowers of which one half is daisies and the other half other flowers and you ask him if in this bouquet there are more flowers or more daisies, you are confronted with this answer, which seems extraordinary until it is analyzed: The child cannot tell you whether there are more flowers than daisies; either he reasons on the basis of the whole or of the part. He cannot understand that the part is complementary to the rest, and he says there are more daisies than flowers, or as many daisies as flowers, without understanding this inclusion of the subclass, the daisies in the class of flowers. It is only around seven to eight years of age that a child is capable of solving a problem of inclusion.

Another system of operation that appears around seven to eight years of age is the operation of serializing; that is, to arrange objects according to their size, or their progressive weight. It is also a structure of the whole like the classification which rests on concrete operations, since it consists of manipulating concrete objects. At this level there is also the construction of numbers, which is, too, a synthesis of classification and seriation. In numbers, as in classes, we have inclusion, and also a serial order, as in serializing. These elementary operations constitute structures of whole. There is no class without classification; there is no symmetric relation without serialization; there is not a number independent of the series of numbers. But the structures of these wholes are simple structures, groupings in the case of classes and relations, which are already groups in the case of numbers, but very elementary structures compared to subsequent structures.

Stage of Formal Operations

The last stage of development of intelligence is the stage of formal operations or propositional operations. At about eleven to twelve years of age we see great progress; the child becomes capable of reasoning not only on the basis of objects, but also on the basis of hypotheses, or of propositions.

An example which neatly shows the difference between reasoning on the basis of propositions and reasoning on the basis of concrete objects comes from Burt's tests. Burt asked children of different ages to compare the colors of the hair of three girls: Edith is fairer than Susan, Edith is darker than Lilly; who is the darkest of the three? In this question there is

seriation, not of concrete objects, but of verbal statements which supposes a more complicated mental manipulation. This problem is rarely solved before the age of 12.

Here a new class of operations appears which is superimposed on the operations of logical class and number, and these operations are the propositional operations. Here, compared to the previous stage, are fundamental changes. It is not simply that these operations refer to language, and then to operations with concrete objects, but that these operations have much richer structures.

The first novelty is a combinative structure; like mathematical structures, it is a structure of a system which is superimposed on the structure of simple classifications or seriations which are not themselves systems, because they do not involve a combinative system. A combinative system permits the grouping in flexible combinations of each element of the system with any other element of that system. The logic of propositions supposes such a combinative system. If children of different ages are shown a number of colored disks and asked to combine each color with each other two by two, or three by three, we find these combinative operations are not accessible to the child at the stage of concrete operations. The child is capable of some combination, but not of all the possible combinations. After the age of 12, the child can find a method to make all the possible combinations. At the same time he acquires both the logic of mathematics and the logic of propositions, which also supposes a method of combining.

A second novelty in the operations of propositions is the appearance of a structure which constitutes a group of four transformations. Hitherto there were two reversibilities: reversibility by inversion, which consists of annulling, or canceling; and reversibility which we call reciprocity, leading not to cancellation, but to another combination. Reciprocity is what we find in the field of a relation. If A equals B, by reciprocity B equals A. If A is smaller than B, by reciprocity B is larger than A. At the level of propositional operations a new system envelops these two forms of reversibility. Here the structure combines inversion and reversibility in one single but larger and more complicated structure. It allows the acquisition of a series of fundamental operational schemata for the development of intelligence, which schemata are not possible before the constitution of this structure.

It is around the age of 12 that the child, for example, starts to understand in mathematics the knowledge of proportions, and becomes capable of reasoning by using two systems of reference at the same time. For example, if you advance the position of a board and a car mov-ing in opposite directions, in order to understand the movement of the board in relation to the movement of the car and to other movement, you need a system of four transformations. The same is true in regard to proportions, to problems in mathematics or physics, or to other logical problems.

The four principal stages of the development of intelligence of the child progress from one stage to the other by the construction of new operational structures, and these structures constitute the fundamental instrument of the intelligence of the adult.

31. FORMAL OPERATIONS AND LANGUAGE
A Comparison of Deaf and Hearing Adolescents[1]

HANS G. FURTH and JAMES YOUNISS

Introduction

Traditionally psychologists have viewed the acquisition and eventual internalization of the natural language as the key to the emergence of intellectual operations. The critical role of the linguistic system in thinking has become axiomatic. Indeed most current theories, whether based on information processing models or social reinforcement are incomplete without positing a linguistic system with which the user is thoroughly familiar. Our experimental findings of the past ten years with respect to intellectual development of deaf persons (Furth, 1964, 1971) seriously call into question this traditional linguistic orientation. Many of our results have shown intellectual normality in children who could not adequately comprehend nor express the natural system of language in oral or written form. With these data in hand, it became clear that most psychological theories of thinking were inapplicable to the special case of deafness and hence lacked generality if not, in fact, in adequate basis.

In distinction from these, Piaget's theory seemed to provide a proper perspective in which to view deafness and its usual concomitant of linguistic deficiency. Piaget's position stands in clear contrast to others, especially with regard to the role attributed to language on the development of thinking. His theory can dispense with language to the extent that it or any other symbolic system is not conceived as integral to thinking structures. The conception of "thinking without language" (Furth, 1966) appears to many as a philosophical *tour de force* and in fact, Piaget's theory does imply a philosophical revolution. An appreciation of this novel insight comes from Piaget's distinction between operative and figurative aspects of thinking. Any perceptual or symbolic functioning can be

[1]This investigation was supported in part by Grant No. 14-P-55084 from the US Social and Rehabilitation Services and Grant No. 02026 from the US National Institute of Child Health and Human Development.

From the *International Journal of Psychology,* 1971, pt. 1, *6*, 49–64. By permission of the International Union of Psychological Science and Cunod Editeur, Paris and the author.

viewed primarily under one or the other of these inseparable aspects, depending on one's choice and purpose. The figurative aspect focuses on the static, momentarily given "configuration" of an external event or an internal symbolic medium. The operative aspect of thinking, on the other hand, refers to the mental action or "operation" towards a given input. For instance, operative functioning assimilates a sensory cue or a symbolic medium into an adaptive response sequence or into a meaningful mental structure. Operativity and assimilation are Piaget's key terms for the essential aspect in every form of understanding, meaningful knowing and perceiving, and adaptative action. Operation and its adjective operatory are less inclusive terms than operativity and denote the developmentally later forms of operative functioning, in particular, the concrete operations of middle childhood and the formal operations of adolescence.

The present paper focuses on formal operatory thinking and represents our ongoing project to assess the functioning of deaf persons beyond the stages of concrete operations (Furth and Youniss, 1969). Concrete operations rely on perceptually present or representable situations, and can dispense with symbols altogether. In formal operatory functioning (Inhelder and Piaget, 1955), however, a symbolic medium is regularly present as the figurative aspect of that functioning. Without having to attribute to symbols a basic explanatory role, Piaget is bound to view the relation of symbolic to operative functioning as being much closer in formal than in concrete operations. Hence, the serious problem arises whether deaf adolescents are limited in formal operatory functioning even though in concrete operations they were not. We compared deaf persons to hearing language users of two types—one, a typical middle class suburban sample who employ language in academically and socially sophisticated ways and the other, a rural sample who, although thoroughly familiar with language, use it in more restricted ways. In earlier work this methodology has proved to be effective since it allows evaluation of language within its proper social context. The following pages after a short review of some prior work on concrete operations present a partial report of an investigation on thinking in deaf adolescents. Performance for three formal operatory tasks, Symbol Logic, Probability, and Combinations is described. This is followed by a more detailed description of three typical deaf adolescents and a final theoretical section which attempts to clarify a position on language within Piaget's general development theory.

Concrete Operations and Deaf Children

In line with the above rationale for studying deaf children, we designed a number of studies to measure the growth of concrete operatory intelligence and the possible influence of linguistic deficiency. Generally we have observed that deaf perform like hearing children during this phase of development. At times they required additional instructions or repeated exposure to problems; essentially they demonstrated the same growth patterns of operatory skills as linguistically sophisticated subjects.

Two studies on visual imagery (Robertson and Youniss, 1969; Youniss and Robertson, 1970) illustrate this point. Four tasks patterned after Piaget and Inhelder (1966) were used: Horizontality of Liquid, Shadow Projection, Visual Perspective, and Rotation of Square. Results for hearing and deaf subjects of ages 8–9 and 11–12 are summarized in Table 31–1 in terms of successful anticipations of images. The reader is referred to the two published papers for procedural details and full results.

Table 31–1 illustrates the following major points. (1) Hearing and deaf subjects at the same age levels performed alike in terms of percentages of success. (2) For both groups of subjects performance varied systematically as a function of figurative input: those transformations on which hearing children had difficulty were the same as those which proved difficult for deaf subjects. (3) Deaf subjects began to achieve operatory success, that is, they consistently subordinated figurative variations to stable operative structures at the same age as their hearing counterparts.

From data of this type we conclude that

TABLE 31–1
Percentages of Correct Answers on the Second Presentation of Four Imagery Problems for Deaf (D) and Hearing (H) Children at Two Age Levels

| SUBJECTS | N | HORIZONTALITY | | SHADOW PROJECTION | |
		Vert.-Horiz.	Diagonal	Vertical	Horizontal
D 8–9	16	88	61	85	67
H 8–9	16	98	55	97	66
D 11–12	16	100	86	89	78
H 11–12	16	100	85	95	85

| | | PERSPECTIVE | | | | | | | |
SUBJECTS	N	135° L	90° L	45° L	0°	45° R	90° R	135° R	180° R
D 8–9	24	21	33	88	100	83	50	38	46
H 8–9	24	46	54	100	100	75	79	58	58
D 11–12	24	75	58	100	100	88	75	75	75
H 11–12	24	67	63	100	100	75	96	83	88

| | | ROTATION OF SQUARE | | | | | | | |
SUBJECTS	N	45°	90°	135°	180°	225°	270°	315°	360°
D 8–9	24	83	75	67	88	17	92	33	58
H 8–9	24	88	88	75	67	13	79	21	54
D 11–12	24	96	96	96	88	29	100	63	75
H 11–12	24	96	92	83	92	33	96	58	79

concrete operatory intelligence cannot have its primary origin in a social language. Deaf children come to apply self-consistent operations to physical objects or events in the same way and at the same time as children immersed in a societal language. Operativity, up to this late concrete operatory stage, derives mainly from the child's own physical actions, and in this respect deaf children are not deficient.

Formal Operations in Deaf Adolescents

Subjects

Deaf Subjects. From a residential school 40 students were selected. They were profoundly deaf from earliest childhood with no other known neurological or physical disease, of at least average measured intelligence and a chronological age of not less than 14 years.

One-half of the sample consisted of students who were considered to be academically quite poor: their level of knowing language (as measured on reading tests) was below grade 3.5. The reading scores of the other half ranged from grade 4.0 to 7.2.

Can this sample of deaf adolescents, ranging in age from 14 to 20 years, be considered typical? No definite answer to this question can be given, perhaps for the one major reason that deaf people do not constitute one homogeneous group. On the other hand, all of these youngsters grew up without being able to assimilate during their early years the linguistic system of the environment. Moreover, they did not have the opportunity to acquire informally the adult deaf person's language of signs. They were exposed to formal language teaching, beginning around age five, and reached a certain level of competence which can be considered marginal for the better students and less than marginal for the other half of the sample. In sum, the better readers of the sample were better than average deaf students; but even their mastery of English language was poor compared to an ordinary hearing population. The poorer readers represented a more typical sample of deaf persons. In their case it would be unreasonable to claim even marginal linguistic competence: they knew a number of words, a small number of stock phrases, but they did not know the English language according to any reasonable criterion. Since this kind of linguistic deficiency is unknown in any other population, some examples of linguistic performance will be presented in a later section. It is understood that we are here referring not to the skill of articulated speech or lipreading but to the knowing of a language; consequently reading seems to be a fair measure of the extent to which a deaf person knows language.

Hearing Subjects. As one type of control subjects, 40 students in a rural high school were selected. They all attended 10th grade and had a chronological age around 16–17 years, corresponding to the mean age of the deaf sample. They were sampled on the basis of normal health and at least average measured intelligence. One-half was above, the other half was below average scholastic achievement. These youngsters came from homes that could be considered educationally less motivating than the typical middle class homes. The majority of fathers were engaged in semi-skilled or unskilled occupations. In addition to this rural sample another control group of 40 middle class hearing youngsters from a suburban region was used on some tasks. They were comparable in age and class placement to the rural control group.

Symbol Logic

One principal task to which the deaf and the rural hearing sample was exposed, dealt with logical expressions. We devised a symbol-picture task which required practically no verbal knowledge but nevertheless provided a means through which to observe operatory functioning.

Briefly, the task made use of symbols, followed by the picture of an object and an arrow ($\rightarrow$) or a cross arrow ($-\!/\!\rightarrow$) in between. The symbols were letters that referred to classes; *e.g.*, H referred to the class House, T to the class Tree, B to Blue, Y to Yellow. Moreover, a bar above the alphabet symbol referred to Negation, so that $\bar{H}$ referred to a class of things other than House, and $\bar{B}$ to a color other than Blue. The classes of Things and Colors were symbolically connected by symbols for conjunction ($\cdot$) or disjunction (v). By means of the symbols the following six positive concept types were generated: $H \cdot B$ (Both House and Blue, *i.e.*, Blue House); $\bar{H} \cdot B$ (Both something not a House and Blue, *e.g.*, Blue Tree); $\bar{H} \cdot \bar{B}$ (Both something not a House and not Blue, *e.g.*, Yellow Tree). Corresponding to these three conjunctive concepts, there were three disjunctive concepts: H v B (Either a House or Blue or both, *e.g.*, Yellow House); $\bar{H}$ v B (*e.g.*, Yellow Tree, which satisfies $\bar{H}$); $\bar{H}$ v $\bar{B}$ (*e.g.*, Yellow House, which satisfies $\bar{B}$). Finally, there were two negated connectives; $H \bar{} B$ ("Not Blue-House") and $\overline{H \text{ v } B}$ ("Neither House nor Blue nor Blue-House"). These eight concept types were systematically matched against four instance types that corresponded (T) or did not correspond (F) to the symbolized classes. For instance, in relation to the symbols $\bar{H}$ v B, the picture of a blue house is a FT instance, yellow house is an FF instance, a yellow tree is a TF instance and a blue tree a TT instance. With regard to the FT instance, a house is a false (F) instance of $\bar{H}$, while the blue color is a true (T) instance of B. A specific symbol pattern and an instance type were put on the blackboard; the problem consisted of making the logical judgment of correct ($\rightarrow$) or incorrect ($-\!/\!\rightarrow$) between symbol and picture. As an illustration, given the picture of a "blue house," the concept $H \cdot B$ requires $\rightarrow$, $H \cdot \bar{B}$ $-\!/\!\rightarrow$, $\bar{T} \cdot \bar{B}$ $-\!/\!\rightarrow$, T v B $\rightarrow$, $\bar{H}$ v B $\rightarrow$, $\bar{T}$ v $\bar{B}$ $\rightarrow$, $T \bar{} B$ $\rightarrow$, T v B $-\!/\!\rightarrow$.

Training on this symbol-picture logic consisted of daily classroom sessions of about 35 minutes. The teacher put a problem on the blackboard that required some completion or modification. For instance, "$\bar{H}$ v B $\rightarrow$" was put on the board and students in turn were called to the board to draw a picture to the right of the arrow that would complete the symbol-picture sequence. Corrections were provided. Note that a variety of pictures could be drawn that satisfied the logical sequence, *e.g.*, "a blue house," "a yellow tree," "a blue tree," "but not "a yellow house."

In a previous study (Furth, Youniss and Ross, 1970) we described four developmental stages in mastering this task. In stage I, children had difficulty with coordinating the negation of a symbol ($^-$) and the pictured presence or absence of a class: "$\bar{H} \rightarrow$ a tree" was hard, whereas the equivalent "H—/$\rightarrow$ a tree" was easy, because in the difficult case a pictorial *absence* of the house went with a *correct* judgment, but in the easy case the same absence went with an *incorrect* judgment. A second stage showed mastery of this particular difficulty and an equivalent performance across the positive concept types for TT and FF instances, but difficulty with the discordant TF and FT instances. This stage was followed by stage III in which success was observed on all instances of the six positive concept types including TF and FT instances; however, the negated concepts, $H \cdot B$ and $H \vee B$, were poorly understood. Success on these negated concepts constituted thus stage IV and completed the developmental sequence. We found that after some training, 52% of students at age 12 reached stage III but only a small fraction level IV; on the other hand, 79% of children between ages 6 and 9 did not perform beyond stage I. On the basis of these findings and supporting theoretical considerations we argued that stage III performance corresponded to the full establishment of concrete operatory mastery of classes whereas stage IV indicated formal operatory functioning.

In the present investigation we asked the question whether deaf adolescents after five weeks of training would reach level IV on our Symbol Logic task and thus give evidence of formal operations. Table 31–2 summarizes the results on the final logic test that had two items for each of four instance types so that there were eight problems for each of the eight concept

TABLE 31–2
Number of Subjects at Various Developmental Stages on Final Test of Symbol-Picture Logic

Subjects		Final stage			
		I	II	III	IV
Deaf	High achievers	3	4	5	8
	Low achievers	10	4	3	3
	Total	13	8	8	11
Hearing	High achievers	—	—	7	13
	Low achievers	3	6	3	8
	Total	3	6	10	21

types. On the 48 positive problems with conjunction or disjunction we used criterion scores as in Furth, *et al.* (1970): a score of 42 or better was criterion of stage III, a score of 34 to 41 was criterion of stage II and performance below that was referred to as stage I. In addition, for those subjects who fulfilled criterion of stage III, a score of 13 or more on the 16 items of *negated* conjunction or disjunction was considered criterion for stage IV. Table 31–3 summarizes the initial stage of those subjects who finally reached stages III or IV. The initial test, identical in form to the final test, was given after one week's training. Three deaf subjects from the final test were not present at the initial test.

Leaving other considerations for later, from a global viewpoint one can point to a clear overall deficit of the deaf versus the hearing sample. On the final test the number of deaf subjects reaching stage IV was significantly smaller than the

TABLE 31–3
Initial Stage of Subjects Who Reached Stages IV or III on Final Test in Symbol-Picture Logic

	N At final test	Initial stage			
		I	II	III	IV
Deaf	10 at stage IV	2	6	1	1
	6 at stage III	3	3	—	—
Hearing	21 at stage IV	—	2	15	4
	10 at stage III	—	2	8	—

number of hearing subjects and in turn, the number of deaf subjects performing at stage I was significantly larger than the number of hearing subjects. Significant differences were also found in the initial test: most hearing were at stage III and most deaf stages II and I. This result corresponds to previous observations (Furth and Youniss, 1965; Youniss and Furth, 1967) and clarifies the relation of social-linguistic environment to performance on Symbol Logic. However, from an individual viewpoint, the data give positive evidence that three deaf adolescents whose language achievement was low (paragraph meaning score of grade 2.8 to 3.2) reached stage IV on the logic test. Two of these adolescents who performed at stage I on the initial logic test manifested after a few weeks's training a mature capacity to deal with formal logical structures—in striking contrast to having failed on linguistic structures after more than twelve years intensive training. Moreover, the eight deaf high achievers who reached stage IV had reading scores in the two highest cases of grades 6.5 and 7.2, respectively. Among hearing subjects at stage IV only three of the 21 students had a reading score as low as these two highest scores of deaf students. In other words, all deaf adolescents had less facility with language than any of the hearing students excepting two cases, but performed equally well on a formal logical symbol task.

Probability

To measure probability concepts we borrowed a task from our colleague Ross (1966) in which a subject was given balls of two colors which he then had to draw out of a box in series one-by-one. Starting with the given numbers of each color he had to predict which color he would pull out of the box and while seeing the actual results, had to continue to predict and pull until the box was empty. Thus, there was the general requirement of continuously predicting the color that would most likely be drawn from the box under these conditions: odds changed with each draw and the actual results did not consistently reinforce correct predictions.

Each subject was given 15 starting situations consisting of the following initial odds: 2:2, 3:3, 4:4, once, and 2:1, 3:2, 4:2, 4:3, 5:3, and 5:4, twice. In all, a subject made 94 predictions and draws. Each time he drew out a ball, of course, the odds difference between the two colors changed; thus, over the 94 situations a subject faced varying odds. While with uneven odds the results of his draws were more frequently in accord with the rule of probability, they could in each single case turn out differently, except when there was only one color left.

The procedure can be illustrated by a starting situation of 3 green and 2 yellow balls. The subject put these 5 balls into the box; the experimenter then shook the box and the subject was told to reach in and, before drawing, to make his prediction. He should, of course, predict "green"—if he did so, a correct judgment was scored. If he in fact pulled a green ball, there would be 2 green and 2 yellow balls left in the box. Thus, his next prediction with even odds could be equally "green" or "yellow." Suppose he again pulled a green ball, there would now be 1 green and 2 yellow balls remaining. His next prediction should be "yellow"; however, suppose he pulled the green ball. Now there would be two yellow balls remaining. Both remaining predictions then should be yellow.

It can be seen that this procedure has three specific requirements: (1) The subject must comprehend the probabilistic nature of the problem. (2) He must on the one hand keep a record of the actual draws, but on the other hand ignore results of drawing out the less likely colors. (3) He must recalculate odds after each draw.

Table 31–4 presents results in terms of frequencies of pass-fail relations according to different odds for the 40 deaf, 40 rural hearing, and the 40 suburban adolescents. The top part of the table compares all situations in which odds favoring one color were > .71 and all situations in which they were < .67, but > .50. To be given a pass, subjects had to make better than 80% correct predictions across all trials with similar odds; anything less was a failure. Three important results were evident. First,

TABLE 31–4
Frequencies of Pass-Fail Relations on Probability as a Function of Odds or Ball Numbers for Subject Groups of High and Low Achievement

ODDS		DEAF			HEARING RURAL			HEARING SUBURBAN		
		High	Low	Both	High	Low	Both	High	Low	Both
(.71)	(.67)									
+	+	10	8	18	10	9	19	16	7	23
+	−	8	10	18	6	7	13	4	9	13
−	+	0	0	0	1	2	3	0	1	1
−	−	2	2	4	3	2	5	0	3	3
(4:2)	(2:1)									
+	+	11	4	15	12	7	19	17	9	26
+	−	7	6	13	5	8	13	0	5	5
−	+	1	4	5	0	0	0	0	1	1
−	−	1	6	7	3	5	8	3	5	8
(5:3)	(4:3)									
+	+	6	9	15	8	7	15	14	6	20
+	−	7	5	12	6	5	11	3	5	8
−	+	4	2	6	1	3	4	1	5	6
−	−	3	4	7	5	5	10	2	4	6

comparable proportions of deaf and hearing subjects passed both odds situations—18 deaf, 19 rural hearing, and 23 suburban subjects passed both kinds of odds situations. Second, for those subjects who were successful in only one of the two situations ($N = 48$) the overwhelming majority ($N = 44$) passed the situation when odds differences were large and failed when they were small. In other words, as odds differences approached .50, some subjects were unable to maintain a probabilistic outlook, even though they gave evidence that they had some grasp of probability in the $> .71$ situations. Third, in all the subject groups high achieving subjects performed better than their low achieving counterparts.

The middle and bottom portions of the Table expand these findings by showing pass-fail patterns for pairs of comparable odds situations. For instance, the pair 2:4 and 1:2 had identical odds, .33:.67. In 2:4, however, there were *two* more balls of one color than the other, while in 1:2 there was only *one* more. Logically these were identical situations with regard to prediction, but they differed on the nonprobabilistic factor or absolute numbers. Generally, more suburban than rural hearing or deaf adolescents were equally successful with either situation of the pair. Further, of the 37 subjects who passed only one of these odds situations, 31 passed 2:4 but failed 1:2. Similarly, in the bottom part of Table 31–4, of 47 subjects who passed only one of the odds pairs, 39 passed 3:5 but failed 3:4.

In sum, about one-half of all the subjects manifested some formal comprehension of probabilistic concepts, *i.e.,* they maintained a high level of successful prediction as odds differences continued to vary. The majority of the remaining subjects had some grasp of probability, which apparently was not on a formal level. Probability performance was contingent upon the sheer number of balls weighted in favor of one versus the other color, as is evident when one considered odds generally ($> .71$ *vs* $< .67$) or when specific situations were analyzed (2:4 *vs* 1:2 and 3:5 *vs* 3:4).

It is tempting to argue that the less successful subjects not only relied on the figurative feature of numerical differences but, apparently, confounded probabilistic more and less with numerical more and less. With advanced age, however, these two factors become separated and operatory control subordinated the figurative factor. That is to say, no matter how much more numerous one color was than the other, the principle of probability was applied consistently. Importantly, according to our analyses, deaf and rural hearing adolescents reached this point in the same way at about the same time.

Combinations

Combinatorial thinking is one of the chief characteristics of the formal operatory stage. Following Piaget's example, two tasks were therefore designed to observe combinatorial behavior of our deaf adolescents in comparison with the same two hearing controls used with Probability. On the first combination task, Numbers, subjects had to lay out all possible permutations of pairs of ordered material starting with numbers 1 and 2, to which were added successively numbers 3 to 6. The second task, Colors, was presented following Numbers and required laying out all the possible permutations of triplets for unordered chips of three colors.

For Numbers, little cards with the written numbers 1 and 2 were prepared and spread out on a table. A subject was encouraged to make pairs; he was shown the pair 1-2 and asked for "another, different one." When the subject, often with the experimenter's help, had correctly made the other pairs—1-1, 2-1, 2-2 —cards with the number 3 were added and he was instructed to do as before, namely to make as many different pairs as possible. From this point on, as soon as he had made one pair, it was removed from his view. This removal was aimed at making the task depend more on operative memory and less on perceptual guessing. Subjects were encouraged to complete the task if fewer than the nine possible pairs were made; moreover, when they had finished, they were asked how many pairs they had made and required to answer from memory since the pairs were removed during the performance. Cards with the number 4 were now added, a subject had first to predict the number of possible pairs, then make permutations of pairs based on 1, 2, 3, 4 and again recall how many pairs he had actually made after indicating that he had finished. Next, cards

with the number 5 were added and a subject's prediction of the number of possible pairs was noted; then he made as many pairs as he could, and, as before, each pair was noted by the experimenter and removed from the subject's view. As a final trial, the subject was handed a piece of paper and pencil and asked to write down pairs of numbers, based on the six numbers 1 to 6. Before proceeding with this request, he wrote down the number of pairs he thought he would be able to make.

This task was most instructive from the viewpoint of operative structure. With many deaf adolescents one could observe how the combinatorial structure took shape during the experiment. Since earlier trials included corrections of redundant or absent choices, a subject could proceed on the following trials with a better and more consistent strategy than before. At times he started with one strategy, only to change it midway and thereby fail to complete all permutations. Some individual examples of performance are presented in the next section.

For purposes of quantification, a subject's performance of the last trial—writing down of all permutations of pairs based on the first six numbers—was scored in terms of strategy, production and prediction. In terms of strategy a score of 7 indicates use of the following perfect system of anchoring: 1-1, 1-2, 1-3 . . . 2-1, 2-2 . . . 5-1 . . . 5-6, 6-6; a score of 6 was given to that system when the doubletons 1-1, 2-2 . . . 6-6 were put ahead of the rest of the pairs; a score of 5 was given to forward and reverse anchoring: doubletons followed by 1-2, 1-3, 1-4, 1-5, 1-6; 2-1, 3-1 . . . 6-1; 2-3, 2-4 . . . 2-6; 3-2, 4-2 . . .; a score of 4 consisted of a complete system of anchoring with pair reversals: 1-2, 2-1, 1-3, 3-1 . . . 2-3, 3-2, 2-4, etc.; a score of 3 was one-half of system 6 : 1-2, 1-3 . . . 1-6, 2-3 . . . 2-6, 3-4 . . ., that is no pairs were made in the reverse directions; a score of 2 included some efforts at pairing 1-2, 2-1, 2-3, 3-2, but not consistently following through as in strategy 4; finally, a score of 1 indicated a random performance.

In terms of production, a score of 4 was given for a complete writing of 36 pairs, a score of 3

TABLE 31–5

Percentages of Subjects Obtaining Different Scores in Terms of Strategy, Production, and Prediction on Two Combinatorial Tasks

SCORE	NUMBERS			COLORS		
	Deaf	Hearing		Deaf[1]	Hearing	
		Rural	Suburban		Rural	Suburban
Strategy						
7	43	28	30	3	—	10
6	18	23	25	18	20	30
5	5	18	5	18	28	28
4	10	20	28	23	23	8
3	13	8	5	12	18	12
2	5	5	8	18	2	5
1	8	—	—	9	10	8
Production						
4	65	78	65	32	40	68
3	18	8	25	41	58	30
2	18	15	10	18	—	—
1	—	—	—	9	3	3
Prediction						
3	33	53	58	6	3	10
2	43	25	23	26	3	12
1	25	23	20	68	95	78

[1]$N = 34$ for the deaf subjects on this task; $N = 40$ for all other samples.

for the same with four omissions or redundancies, a score of 2 for more than 18 pairs, and a score of 1 for fewer. In terms of prediction, a score of 3 indicates the correct number 36, a score of 2 some other number between 30 and 40, and a score of 1 any other number.

Table 31–5 summarizes the data of the deaf and the two hearing samples with the following notable results. A larger percentage of hearing subjects (38% and 33%) used strategies 4 and 5 than did deaf subjects (15%); in turn, more deaf subjects used strategy 7 (43% *vs* 28% and 30%). In terms of production there was no difference, whereas in prediction the hearing excelled the deaf sample (53% and 58% *vs* 33% with a perfect score of 3).

Table 31–5 also lists the comparative results on the color chips task, consisting of three colors, white (W), red (R), and blue (B). In this task, subjects were instructed to make all possible triplets. Because it dealt with unordered material this task was considerably more

difficult than Numbers, although all triplets were left in full view. A scoring system comparable to Numbers but with greater leniency was devised, so that strategy scores 7-4 indicated potentially successful systems with some overall order, even if not completed. A score of 7 was assigned for a combinatorial strategy in which subjects grouped triplets beginning with one color, *e.g.*, WWW, WWB, WWR, WBW, WBR . . . and maintained a systematic ordering of triplets within each subgroup. A score of 6 was given to other types of subgrouping with systematic ordering. A score of 5 referred to subgroupings similar to 7 or 6 but with only partial ordering within subgroups. A score of 4 was assigned to an overall grouping that showed no ordering within subgroups. A score of 3 corresponded to an inadequate grouping. A score of 2 was given for pairing and a score of 1 for a random production of triplets (individual subjects in the next section illustrate strategy scores of 6 and 5).

A production score of 4 was given if at least 20 triplets were produced in substantially complete sequence, *i.e.*, four or fewer triplets out of order; a score of 3 indicated the same number of triplets but with more than four triplets out of order. Scores of 2 or 1 were given to production of less than 20 triplets, 2 being a substantially complete, 1 an incomplete sequence. A prediction of 27 was rated as 3, another number between 20–30 was rated as 2, and anything else obtained a prediction score of 1. On this Color task the deaf sample was similar to the rural hearing and only the surbuban hearing sample with a production score of 4 was better (68%) than the other two groups (32% and 40%).

In sum, on two combinatorial tasks linguistically deficient deaf adolescents used similar strategies, produced similar results and predicted number of combinations like hearing adolescents. One difference was that a considerable number of hearing subjects were able to perform successfully with strategy 4 or 5 as if they were less in need than deaf adolescents of a systematic strategy in order to perform well. Other small differences were that more hearing subjects predicted the correct number of permutations on Numbers, and the suburban hearing sample produced more triplet permutations on Colors than did the deaf group. However, in general the comparability between the hearing and deaf groups was quite striking.

It should be added that deaf subjects on the initial Number task, as was pointed out, frequently started from a very low level of performance and with a few trials and corrections were observed to discover a logical system with which they were heretofore unfamiliar. Such discovery was much less frequent with hearing samples who in any case have been exposed to much more mathematical training.

Three Individual Subjects

Subject F.G. was a 19-year-old male, deaf from birth with a present severe hearing loss of 95 db. in the better ear. On *Symbol Logic* he achieved stage IV success, or only one error in

64 problems. With *Numbers* he was successful in dealing with three and four numbers, but through a system of partial grouping. With four numbers he began by giving all doubletons (11, 22, etc.), then gave 12, 13, 14, 21, 31, 41 following a reversal strategy (scored 5) which many of the hearing but hardly any of the deaf subjects used successfully. This subgrouping was followed with five numbers and produced an inadequate result with many pairs missing. He was not able to predict how many pairs he would have with five or six numbers.

On the combinatorial task with three *Colors* he obtained a strategy score of 5. He began with tripletons, WWW, BBB, RRR, then switched to patterns of one of each color, WRB, RWB, BRW, BWR . . . , then doubletons, WWB, WWR, RRB . . . , finally doubletons separated by another color, WRW, WBW, RWR . . . He made 19 of the 27 possible triplets and predicted he would make 48. In sum, his performance was indicative of an attempt to be systematic but open to the influence of each preceding production; in this way he was only partially systematic within his groupings. As new combinations were made these partially determined which combinations would come next. On *Probability* he made only four errors out of 73 judgments with uneven odds. Two of these errors were due to memory and occurred in predicting the color of the last ball in the box. He was consistently correct on the critical comparisons 2:1 *vs* 2:4 and 3:3 *vs* 3:5.

This student who gave evidence of formal operatory thinking in Symbol Logic and Probability achieved a paragraph meaning score equivalent of grade 4.3. He was considered of average academic calibre among his fellow pupils and was enrolled in the field of woodworking. Neither he nor his teachers considered him going on to further schooling. This expectation was based on his rather low achievement in the English language. It was easy to confirm that he had failed to master English. On our own test with simple written sentences he showed minimal comprehension. For instance, to the sentence, "What part of a plant cannot be seen?" he wrote, "Grass" and to the sentence, "How does a newborn baby spend most of his time?" he wrote, "New Year's Day," or for "What causes the moon to shine?" he wrote, "Night." All of these answers seem to indicate that English was for him a paired association concoction-plant-grass, baby-time-New Year's Day, and moon-night.

This very weak grounding in English contrasts sharply with other data available on this student. For instance, we observed him playing basketball in an official game where he demonstrated excelled bodily coordination and above average teamwork. In the Symbol Logic training sessions he proved to be a serious worker who paid little heed to his classmates but attended carefully to the teacher. However, he never asked questions publicly and when corrected for mistakes, studiously reworked his lessons. Finally in terms of social background, he came from an intact family of middle income; his parents and four brothers were hearing. He entered school at CA 5 and in fourteen school years attended three different schools for the deaf. According to the WISC performance scale IQ he was in the normal range.

Subject B.M. was a male of CA 18 who according to the Stanford Achievement test was reading at grade 2.8. In *Symbol Logic* he made only eight errors out of 64 items, three of which occurred with the negated connectives—thus he achieved stage IV. With *Numbers* he was consistently systematic in producing all possible pairs in an obviously ordered plan. He could not, however, predict how many pairs he would make. On *Colors* he began with WWW and proceeded with permutations containing two W's, *e.g.,* WWX, XWW, WXW . . . then he proceeded similarly with RRR and BBB. Moreover, within each color subgroup he maintained a systematic order of triplets and therefore received a strategy score of 6. He failed to produce all 27 combinations, however, and was unable to predict how many he would make. His poorest performance was on *Probability* with 19 erroneous predictions in 71 uneven odds cases. Fourteen of these errors

occurred when odds were less than .67-.33. He was clearly influenced by the frequency factor, making six errors in 13 attempts with odds 1:2 versus only one error in six attempts with odds 2:4.

As noted he was reading at a grade 2 level and expectedly his answers to our sentences manifested this weakness. To the *moon* question he answered with associate "Night." To the question, "How many sides does a cube have?" he answered, "Two sides" and to the question "What is the name of the month that follows Christmas?" he, as did most deaf adolescents wrote, "December."

B.M. was deaf from birth and currently showed a db. loss of 98. His middle income family is intact with one brother and two sisters one of whom is also deaf. His WISC performance IQ was 100 and his academic record for the past years showed little progress in the linguistic realm—grade equivalents for word meaning = 3.5, for word study skills = 2.7, for total language = 3.7. In mathematics, however, he was much better with computation = grade 8.6 and arithmetic concepts = grade 6.5. Socially, he is a well liked student and president of his class. His teachers call him a serious student and during the Symbol Logic sessions he was persistent and motivated. He, as opposed to F.G., attempted to speak in class even though his speech was not understandable. The school does not expect him to continue academically and his regular classes are preparing him for the printer's trade.

Subject J.M. was an 18-year-old male and is of special interest in a number of respects. He achieved only stage III in *Symbol Logic* with four errors on the negated connectives. Over all 64 test items he made just these four errors. When the training sessions began, he was in the infirmary with pneumonia and missed exactly two-thirds of the training sessions. On his own he asked the teacher and fellow students for past lessons and rapidly caught up with the class. Thus, his logic performance while not as excellent as F.G.'s, is quite outstanding. With *Numbers* he achieved the highest possible scores for systematic planning. He correctly predicted he would make 36 combinations with six numbers and when performing consistently followed his plan. With *Colors* his performances dropped off slightly. He used systematic groupings—*e.g.,* tripletons, doubletons, doubletons separated, etc.—but failed to complete each grouping systematically and received a strategy score of 5. On *Probability* he made but two errors in 65 situations of uneven odds. This almost perfect performance is interesting for the additional fact that 40 of his 65 predictions occurred with odds <.67.

He is not considered academically oriented and takes his vocational course in shoe repair. He is called an "easy-going" classmate and is the heavyweight wrestler on the school team. His family background is difficult to reconstruct. He comes from an economically poor background, his father is unknown, and he has lived with various guardians. His reading grade level is 3.7, with word meaning of 2.9 and word study skills of 1.8. His responses to our sentence test were mixed. He answered the *baby* question with the word "one" and to the question *moon* with "night." He answered, "Are there more deaf people in Pennsylvania or in Philadelphia?" with "Yes." On the other hand, he answered the *plant* question correctly with "*root*" and a few other questions precisely and correctly. His other academic skills were also low; on the Stanford Achievement mathematics test he obtained computation = grade 5.9 and concepts = grade 4.3.

In summary, these three adolescent boys, profoundly deaf from birth, clearly manifest severely limited mastery of English—a school subject to which they were exposed for at least twelve years—but at the same time show better than average success on measures of formal operatory thinking. Each showed, in addition, a healthy, presently functioning, social life within the school; not knowing they were deaf, one would judge them to be typical older adolescents in appearance and demeanor. More importantly, all three demonstrated a definite capacity to learn in our training sessions with Symbol Logic. In contrast, schooling seems to have had minimal effects on their progress in the English language, either oral or written.

General Discussion

The presence of concrete operations among healthy adults in all societies has never been called into question. Nor would anyone seriously assert that a deaf adult person in spite of severe linguistic deficiency would be lacking in concrete operations. The reasons for the ubiquitousness of these operations—with varying rates of emergence—are without doubt the essential communality found in the human organism with its developmental potential and in the physical and social environment. The case of formal operations, however, is different and the question of their presence in all normal adults can be legitimately raised. On this point Piaget has made a few cautious statements in which he refers to the special interest and professional activity of an individual. He sees no contradiction in observing individuals of any age who function quite logically in the limited area of their speciality, but are quite retarded and on a very inferior level in those fields that are outside their speciality (Piaget, 1970). Thus, formal operations appear to require for their development more specialized occasions within the environment than is the case with concrete operations. This is understandable since the "objects" of formal operations are within the realm of symbolic functioning. Exposure to a logical symbolic environment is, of course, less general and more subject to individual circumstances than is exposure to the concrete physical and social world. Further, as the verbal language of society is apparently the most common and important symbol system it would not be unreasonable to assume that language is a prerequisite for formal operations and that deaf persons severely deficient in linguistic knowledge would not reach the formal operatory stage.

Before discussing the general implications of our reported findings on this question, it is imperative to establish that the procedures used actually involved formal operations. Symbol Logic and Combinations explicity used formal operatory thinking. Thus, the difference between mastering a negated class (*e.g.,* $\overline{H}$) and a negated logical connective (*e.g.,* $\overline{\cdot}$) seems to be the characteristic difference between concrete and formal operations and a person who masters this distinction functions on a formal operatory level. In Probability, the evidence is not equally compelling, but the combination of memory and recalculation of odds argues strongly in favor of considering success on the task as formal operatory functioning.

Consideration must also be given to our use of training and correction on various tasks. Did our procedure merely teach adolescents a certain strategy or mode of responding? This possibility was ruled out by procedural controls. A second question arises, whether the formal operations observed at five weeks were entirely absent initially? The most convincing response to this question comes from a careful look at what happened during training: many subjects on Symbol Logic did not reach the criterion of mastery after five weeks while others did. It appears that a training procedure is at best a favorable occasion for the manifestation of an operatory mechanism. Both in Symbol Logic and in Combinations, we observed that for many subjects our investigation provided such a favorable environmental occasion. But our procedure made sure that there was no way in which a subject could mechanically learn the performance and succeed on all the changing trials. In other words, operations are not simply figurative items of information which one person transmits to another, but they are operative mechanisms of general understanding that come with gradual development in interaction with particular environmental factors.

Two general points concerning formal operatory functioning follow from our data. First, in every subject sample there were numerous cases of success on one task accompanied by failure on other formal operatory tasks. This finding suggests that for most people the stage of formal operations should not be likened to an overall, across-the-board accomplishment but rather to a potential that requires personal interest and environmental occasions. The second point is related to this phenomenon and deals with the particular effect of language. The results on the three tasks demonstrated rather large differences between subject groups on Symbol Logic, but only small differences on Probability or Combinations. Yet

there were successes on Logic in the low achieving deaf group, just as there were failures on Combinations in the suburban hearing group. How could one explain the differences observed in Logic and the lack of differences on the other tasks?

It is reasonable to put more weight on Logic than on other tasks as manifesting the operatory potential of a subject for the simple reason that extended training preceded the final test. According to the suggested criterion 28% of deaf subjects showed formal operatory success compared to 53% of the rural hearing sample. From evidence not reported here, we know that the percentage from a suburban hearing sample would be considerably higher (around 75%) than for the rural sample. These observations support a view that sees in a special environment, including its verbal aspect, a powerful factor in motivating individuals toward selective formal operatory functioning without, however, making language the determining cause underlying these operations. This view stresses three points for further clarification concerning 1) a special environment as conductive to selective formal operations, 2) language as part of that environment, 3) language as underlying the operations.

With regard to points 1 and 2, it is striking that the suburban in comparison to the rural environment did not substantially facilitate formal operatory functioning on Combinations or Probability. It is likely that the way language is used at the suburban home and at school affords more direct opportunity for developing skill in logical symbol use than in combinatorial or probabilistic thinking. However, it would be overly simplifying matters to single out language as the main difference between the two hearing samples. Of course, one can employ the word "language" in the sense of "linguistic use" and interpret verbal behavior as a reflection of more global environmental forces that include the social, vocational and cultural aspirations and values of the environment. What we are trying to stress here is the non-trivial difference between knowing a language and using a language. Failure to observe this distinction weighs down any efforts at clarifying the role of language in behavior (Furth, 1970b).

The rural sample, in contrast to the deaf sample, certainly knew language and its different language use—in contrast to the suburban sample—was due to a multitude of social factors that were reflected in, rather than being caused by, the use of language.

With regard to point 3, the evidence of the deaf sample, as documented especially in the individual examples, is compelling in that verbal language is not a prerequisite for formal operatory functioning, not even for Symbol Logic, and hence cannot be regarded as an underlying causal determinant. This statement does not deny that linguistic use can be a faciliting environmental occasion in logical symbol use. In that sense the greater accomplishment of the rural hearing over the deaf sample can be assumed to be due to the lack of symbolic use in the deaf sample. Linguistic use and particularly reading afforded training in the use of symbols for the hearing groups, the same medium in which our Symbol Logic task was expressed. In this connection the relative lack of linguistic influence on Probability and Combinations is interesting. Apart from formal training in school mathematics, the daily use of language or reading rarely focuses on these operations. It would be fully in accord with Piaget's operatory theory to assume that in an environment that stresses these particular skills, more adolescents would be found applying formal operatory functioning to this area than was the case in our investigation. In fact, even though the two combinatorial tasks required basically the same operations, hardly one among all the 120 adolescents did anywhere near as well on Colors as on Numbers. This was a clear case of not applying an already demonstrated operation in another situation that gave less figurative support to the operative functioning.

Two final remarks are in order. Our study indicated the facilitating effect of linguistic *use* on certain formal operations that were expressed in a symbolic medium, but not on other formal operations. From experimental evidence as well as for theoretical reasons we would deny an analogous facilitating effect of linguistic use to concrete operatory functioning. Deaf youngsters in the concrete operatory period function at least as well as hearing youngsters from an educationally low-motivating environment; the occasional superiority of children from an educated environment is reasonably attributed to the greater motivation to foster general thinking rather than simply to language. Moreover—and here we turn to theoretical reasons—for the functioning of concrete operatory structures physical events not verbal propositions are primary objects of thinking (Furth, 1970a). Language is more closely related to formal than to concrete operations in that it provides a figurative medium for symbolic statements. Symbolic propositions are the proper object for thinking that has reached the formal operatory stage. In other words, whereas language is never a sufficient or necessary condition of operatory functioning, the evidence from our work with linguistically deficient persons indicates that it may have, at best, an indirect facilitating effect for concrete operations, but can have a direct facilitating effect on certain formal operations precisely because of the close relation between formal operations and symbolic functioning.

A final question can be asked about the many subjects in both the deaf and the hearing rural sample who did not reach a formal operatory criterion in any of the three areas investigated. Do those deaf subjects with poor linguistic skills and those hearing subjects with poor linguistic skills and those hearing subjects in a rural setting who have not shown formal operatory structures ever develop them? This question obviously relates back to the generality of formal operatory functioning as discussed earlier where the emergence of formal structures was seen to be partly dependent on interest and environmental occasions. Our speculation is that they would be able to manifest formal operatory thinking once they are seriously engaged in some speciality. It seems consonant with Piaget's theory to hold that the mere absence of a conventional language or of an educational stimulating environment is not sufficient to terminate prematurely the normal operative development that is species-specific to humans.

REFERENCES

Furth, H. G. Research with the deaf. Implications for language and cognition. *Psychological Bulletin,* 1964, *62*, 145–164.

Furth, H. G. *Thinking without language. Psychological implications of deafness.* New York: Free Press, 1966.

Furth, H. G. *Piaget for teachers.* Englewood Cliffs, N.J.: Prentice-Hall, 1970a.

Furth, H. G. On language and knowing in Piaget's developmental theory. *Human Development,* 1970b (in press).

Furth, H. G. Linguistic deficiency and thinking. Research with deaf subjects 1964–1969. *Psychological Bulletin,* 1971 (in press).

Furth, H. G. & Youniss, J. The influence of language and experience on discovery and use of logical symbols. *British Journal of Psychology,* 1965, *56*, 381–390.

Furth, H. G. & Youniss, J. Thinking in deaf adolescents. Language and formal operations. *Journal of Communication Disorders,* 1969, *2*, 195–202.

Furth, H. G., Youniss, J. & Ross, B. M. Children's utilization of logical symbols. An interpretation of conceptual behavior based on Piagetian theory. *Developmental Psychology,* 1970, *3*, 36–57.

Inhelder, B. & Piaget, J. *De la logique de l'enfant à la logique de l'adolescent.* Paris: PUF, 1955.

Piaget, J. *Seminar notes.* Washington, D.C.: Catholic University, June, 1970 (mimeograph).

Piaget, J. & Inhelder, B. *L'image mentale chez l'enfant.* Paris: PUF, 1966.

Robertson, A. & Youniss, J. Anticipatory visual imagery in deaf and hearing children. *Child Development,* 1969, *40*, 123–135.

Ross, B. M. Probability concepts in deaf and hearing children. *Child Development,* 1966, *37*, 917–928.

Youniss, J. & Furth, H. G. The role of language and experience on the use of logical symbols. *British Journal of Psychology,* 1967, *58*, 435–443.

Youniss, J. & Robertson, A. Projective visual imagery as a function of age and deafness. *Child Development,* 1970, *41*, 215–234.

32. AN INFORMATION PROCESSING APPROACH TO COGNITIVE DEVELOPMENT*†

EDITH D. NEIMARK

Abstract. Developmental data from three experiments are reported in support of the assumptions that (a) there are two classes of preliminary transformations performed upon information at the early stages of thought: analyzing and memorializing; that (b) each transformation class has a characteristic ontogeny that (c) underlies the broader pattern of development of intelligence. Since most current developmental research may be characterized as concerned with the development of analytic transformations, some speculations on the additional role of memorializing transformations are proposed.

Introduction

It was just a little over 20 years ago that information theory was first introduced; the computer explosion followed shortly thereafter. Today, information analyses and computer analogues are so widely accepted that in some areas one is hard put to find an active investigator who doesn't think in those terms. Certainly, in the area that is once again known as cognition, the major theories[15,22,24] treat thinking as a process of information transformation. However, for all that information theory and computer terms are now so freely used among us psychologists, we have not been as precise as we could be about establishing the empirical coordinates to psychological phenomena of our borrowed concepts. For example, what exactly does "information" mean? I don't think there is a precise all-purpose answer to that question for psychologists. Rather, I think there are specific answers for specific contexts. Three factors, as a minimum, must be taken into account: the

particular stage of the activity to which one is referring, the kind of activity in question, and the age of the subject.

With respect to the first factor, the simplest diagram of information transmission starts with an input that goes to an encoder and thence to a channel, which may have a perpendicular appendage labeled "noise," to a decoder and output; this simple flow scheme may be elaborated with all sorts of subroutines and loops. Nevertheless, it is always the case that we start with something as input and end with something, generally a modified something, as output. The initial something, the final something, and all the intermediate somethings are information. Chopping a dynamic process into discrete segments is, of course, an arbitrary and artificial business, but if we are to talk meaningfully about thought as transformation of information, it must be possible, at the very least, to distinguish pretransform from post-transform states of information.

To the extent that it is possible to make this distinction, my major interest in this paper will be with information close to the input stage of the transformation process. With respect to the second factor, activity, immediate experience may constitute the input information for perceptual activity; when dealing with thought, however, even at the input stage, information has already undergone some transformation relative to, for example, input information for perception. The preliminary transformations, it

*This paper was presented at a meeting of the Section of Psychology on January 18, 1971.

†This work was supported in part by grant HD 01725–06 from the Institute of Child Health and Human Development.

seems to me, are of two general kinds, which occur more or less in sequence. The first kind of transformation is essentially *analytic;* it has to do with focusing on properties and relaions in the task situation, and it therefore implies selective attention. The second kind of transformation might be characterized as *memorializing*, an ungainly term to refer to procedures for coding material into memory storage to be retrieved for later utilization.

Back to the third factor in defining information, age; my message in this paper is that each of the preliminary transformation activities just described (i.e., analyzing and memorializing) has an ontogeny that I believe is characteristic of all human beings and proceeds in an invariant sequence. This begins to sound very like Piaget's genetic epistemology—and it is. The stages I shall describe closely parallel the Piagetian stages; in fact, I think these changes in the nature of preliminary transformation of information underly the cognitive developmental stages described by Piaget. The experiments described in this paper do not provide very convincing support for this speculation because, in fact, the experiments led to the hypothesis rather than vice versa. Most of the work from my laboratory has been concerned with the development of analytic transformations; but since research on attention is so popular and available among developmental psychologists,[11,26] and I have discussed it in detail elsewhere,[20] I'll race through it to memorializing, about which there is much less evidence. Slim as the evidence is, its implications are profound. We tend to assume that whatever is attended to will by virtue of that fact be remembered, but there is a large body of evidence[23] demonstrating the inefficiency of incidental learning relative to intentional learning. Intentional learning requires specific skills that are developed over a long period of time.[6]

Before we go on to some representative experiments, a few words on the subjects. We do not trace development back to time t_0; the youngest subjects are first-graders or nursery-school children. Since my major interest has been in the transition from concrete to formal operations thinking, children in grades 3 or 4 to 6 or 8 are included in all work along with an adult group (the ubiquitous college sophomore).

The Development of Analytic Transformations

Diagnostic Problem Solving

Much of our work has employed a problem-solving task the basic ingredients of which are illustrated in Figure 32–1. There is an answer sheet containing n unique patterns of k binary elements (black and white circles); in Figure 32–1 there are four four-circle patterns. One of these patterns is concealed in a problem board with a movable shutter over each element. The subject's task is to identify the concealed pattern by opening as few shutters as possible. After opening a shutter, S writes the letter identifying its position on the appropriate line of his answer sheet and across the face of all patterns, thereby eliminated as possible answers (as pattern 4 in Figure 32–1 is eliminated by opening shutter B). When he has the answer he writes the number of the remaining pattern on the appropriate place and removes the problem from the board to verify his answer. After a practice series to familiarize him with the mechanics, the subject does a series of problems with eight patterns of eight elements. Four of the elements are black (or white) on only one of the patterns and white (or black) on the remaining seven. By uncovering such an element, the subject could get the solution with his first shutter opening if the pattern with the unique state is the answer (and it never is), but will still have seven alternatives if it is not. Shutter openings of this sort are gambles with an expected informational outcome of 0.5436 bits as a first move. The remaining four elements are black on four of the patterns and white on the other four; they yield one bit of information regardless of the outcome, and all problems may be solved in a series of three such shutter openings.

One measure of S's solution procedure for each problem is a "strategy score," obtained by

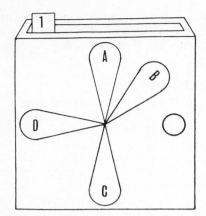
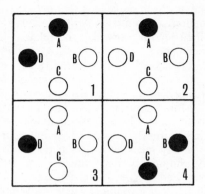

FIGURE 32–1. Schematic of a problem board with four shutters and an answer array containing four patterns. Shutter B has been opened, revealing a white circle beneath; thus, patterns 1, 2, or 3 might be the answer, but pattern 4 could not be. In this instance, gambling is not rewarded.

summing the expected informational outcome of each of a series of shutter openings and dividing by the number of shutters opened. The maximum possible strategy score is unity; lower values result from gambles and/or noninformative shutter openings (e.g., opening shutter C after having opened B). Figure 32–2 summarizes data on strategy score as a function of mental age for six groups of schoolchildren tested at several times throughout the year over a period of two or three years. The smooth curve through the scattered points shows earlier cross-sectional data for 13 groups of high- and normal-I.Q. children aged 9–14 years.[18] Both the longitudinal and the cross-sectional data indicate a shift with age from a chance score toward an optimal one. This improvement is the result of a qualitative change.

A better measure of the qualitative changes in performance with age is provided by a rating of S's own description of how he goes about solving the problem. A rating of 0 is assigned for no

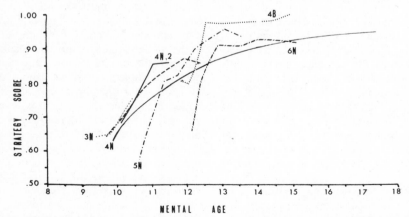

FIGURE 32–2. Longitudinal changes in strategy score over repeated testing for six groups of subjects initially tested in grades 3–6. N refers to children of normal I.Q., B to children with I.Q. > 120. The curve through the points is from an earlier cross-sectional study[18] in which independent groups were tested only once.

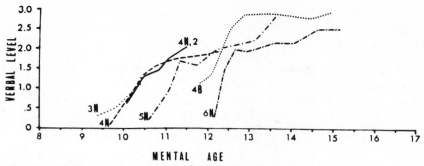

FIGURE 32–3. Longitudinal changes in the rating of S's description of his problem solving plan. Data are for the same children as in Figure 32–2.

procedure or a "magical" one (choosing lucky letters, etc.); 1 is assigned for a rule for the last move only (compare the two remaining patterns to find the circle that differentiates them). A 2 rating indicates a rule for the last move plus another rule for one additional move: an extension of the last-move rule to the preceding choice or a first-move rule (don't gamble). The 3 rating is assigned to a single fully generalized rule for all shutter openings: Halve the remaining alternatives. Figure 32–3 presents rating-scale data for the longitudinal groups. Again there is a shift with age from unplanned, random shutter opening among the younger children through application of limited local principles to induction of a general principle on the part of teen-agers. As might be expected from the similarity of Figures 32–2 and 32–3, there is a very high correlation between S's strategy score and the rating of his strategy description (in 10 or so computations for different groups,[19] r = .83–.89). This correlation confirms the observational impression that the child is quite conscious of what he is doing and can describe it accurately under appropriate questioning.

The analytic transformation of information in this task is quite complex. At first the child attends only to the consequences of his act of shutter opening, but he cannot anticipate them. In order to anticipate he must compare symbolically across patterns with respect to individual elements. The number of possible comparisons is large, and the potential information is unwieldy without some chunking

mechanism, such as a general principle for distinguishing classes of equivalent elements (e.g. safe moves and gambles). A good organizing principle also serves a memorializing function, but more of this later. Analysis at this level of abstraction corresponds to formal-operations thinking and is not evidenced much before a mental age of 11 or 12. The next task is considerably simpler.

Spontaneous Imposition of Order

In this experiment[20] the subject is given nine 1½-inch wooden cubes strewn unsystematically on a table top and asked to place them in a 3 × 3 grid inked, more or less neatly, on a white stocking cardboard. These cubes, on permanent loan from Joachim Wohlwill, have a unique picture on each face. One face contains a yellow crescent, and the crescent faces vary from block to block with respect to both number and size. Another face depicts a kite, and the kites vary in color and number. The remaining faces and their modes of variation are truck (size and color), clothing (type and color), tool (type and size), and container (type and number). The pictures are painted in colored enamel. We presented this task to groups of 20 individuals each at a number of age levels from nursery school to college and recorded several aspects of their behavior: time to placing of the first block and time to completion of the array; two ratings of organization of the completed array; and a rating of S's description of the procedure he employed in selecting block faces for the array. After *S* had completed his first array, we jumbled the blocks back onto the table and asked him to do it again with different block faces from those he had used the first time. At the end of this trial we pointed out to him existing similarities and regularities in his array before spilling the blocks back onto the table and asking *S* to make yet another arrangement, this time a systematic one.

Once again there are marked age-related qualitative differences in performance. The nursery-school children spend very little time examining the blocks (the nature of whose differing faces have already been identified in initial instructions). They tend to place the blocks quickly, with some attention to getting them inside the lines of the grid, and there is little order to their arrays. Their justification for the array, if there is one, is "I like it that way." By "order" I refer to similarity of adjacent blocks in each row or column. There are two separate ratings of order: *external order* is rated by assigning a score of 1 to each row and each column all of whose entries share membership in the same major class (e.g. kites, moons, etc.); for *internal order* a score of 1 is given for each row and column whose entries are variants of the same mode of variation within a major class (e.g. blue kites varying in number, one kite varying in color, etc.). The maximum possible rating on each scale is 6. Group mean rating as a function of age on each trial separately is shown for external and internal ordering at the bottom of Figure 32–4. Order increases with age, and there is a suggestion that ordering with respect to major class variation precedes ordering with respect to within-class variation in mode. Under the specific instructions for systematic ordering of trial 3, all groups do improve significantly, but amount of improvement seems to be limited by earlier performance. Even with urging, the youngest

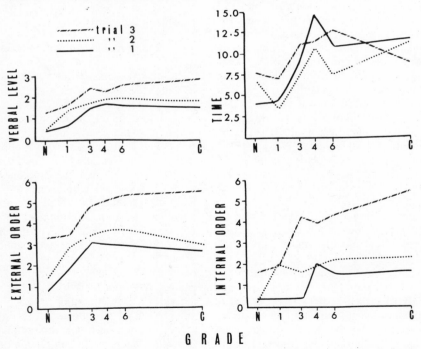

FIGURE 32–4. Performance measures for six grade levels of 23 Ss each for two spontaneous sorting trials and one instructed trial. Verbal level in upper left; latency in upper right; external and internal ordering in lower left and right, respectively.

children seem incapable of maximum ordering. They are more likely to note major class variation than within-class variation, and they tend to order in rows or columns but not both simultaneously. Older subjects, on the other hand, are increasingly able to deal with a number of properties, at the same time.

Additional information on how S's go about this task is shown in the top half of Figure 32–4. The right half shows time spent examining the blocks, and presumably planning their arrangement, prior to actual placement. It increases with age and then declines (probably because of greater familiarity and facility in categorization) for college students. The left half shows data on the rating of S's description of his plan for block arrangement on each trial. Once again, we used a 4-point rating scale quite comparable to the one employed for the problem-solving task: 0 for no plan, 1 for a limited local ordering (e.g. of adjacent pairs) or a thematic ordering, 2 for an ordering (external or internal) applied to one or more rows *or* columns, and 3 for a 3×3 ordering encompassing rows and columns.

In this experiment we see the development of analysis into properties and classification with respect to them. These are concrete operations *par excellence*, and they have been intensively studied by a number of investigators.[10] In this instance, however, except on trial 3, there was no instruction to attend to properties or to classify with respect to them; rather, subjects increasingly tend to do so spontaneously. I take this evidence as justification for my earlier assertion that preliminary analytic transformations tend to be more or less immediate and automatic, at least among older children and adults. Finally, it may be noted that the need for memorializing transformations is minimal in this task, since the material is always present.

Development of Memorializing Transformations

In view of the huge numbers of psychologists who have devoted a large part of their lifetimes to committing assorted matter to memory, and in view of the thousands of students whose study activity has been directed or coerced by them, it is amazing that there is almost no systematic evidence available on how people go about memorizing material when left to their own devices. This devastating state of affairs may be partly attributable to our being blinded by smug acceptance of existing theories. It is also partly attributable to our having been so thoroughly catechized in experimental methodology that it is against our religion ever to leave a subject to his own devices. In order to exert control over every possible variable, we present material one item at a time, carefully controlling exposure duration, varying order, and so on, with the result that we create an artificial new situation in which S is practically forced to learn by rote repetition, as Ebbinghaus or Underwood says he does. To see what S does when left to his own devices, we repeated, with minor variations[21] an elegant experiment by Moely and colleagues.[16]

Twenty-four simple line drawings of common objects (six of animals, six of vehicles, six of items of clothing, and six of articles of furniture) were arranged in a fixed, randomized array before S for a three-minute interval, during which he was to attempt to learn them in any way he wished. He was told that he could move the pictures about, take notes, or do anything that might help him. The E took careful notes on S's behavior during this time. At the end of three minutes the pictures were collected and S recalled them from memory. Groups of 20 subjects each (in grades 1, 3–6, and college) were tested individually for up to three study-test intervals. The number of items correctly recalled as a function of age on three successive trials is summarized in Figure 32–5. To no one's surprise, once again we find smooth, negatively accelerated growth functions; and, once again, these functions are the result not of older children's doing the same thing more speedily and efficiently, but of qualitative differences in approach to the task. One indication of the nature of these differences is shown in Figure 32–6, which summarizes mean duration of recall (i.e., the time from onset of recall to completion of 24 items or until S gives

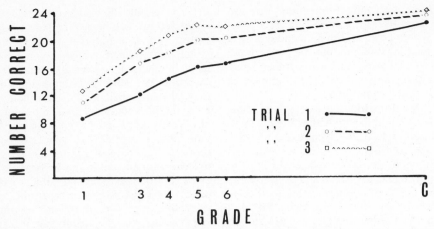

FIGURE 32–5. Group mean number of items correctly recalled as a function of grade level on three successive recall trials. Maximum possible is 24.

up) at each age level. This is a nonmonotonic function quite similar in form to the comparable time function obtained in the study of spontaneous imposition of order (Figure 32–4), and it probably reflects the operation of the same developmental factors.

Figure 32–7 gives our old friend, the rating of S's task strategy, on a 4-point scale. In this instance the rating is with respect to S's order-

ing of the 24 pictures during the three-minute study interval, and it parallels the rating scales of Figures 32–3 and 32–4: 0 for no rearrangement or aimless shifting of the pictures, 1 for forming of partial or nonexhaustive categories, 2 for four exhaustive categories with respect to major classes, 3 for an exhaustive classification with within-category organization (generally alphabetic, e.g. bear, camel, cow,

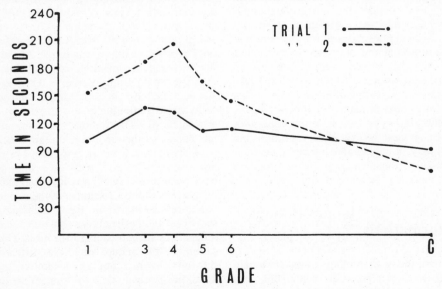

FIGURE 32–6. Duration of recall on two successive trials as a function of grade level.

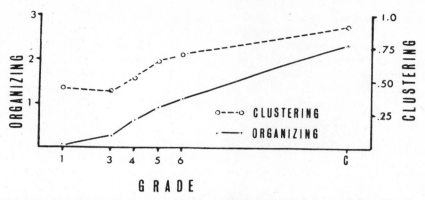

FIGURE 32–7. Clustering in free recall and rating of deliberate organizing of list material as a function of grade level.

etc., but in some cases associative pairs, e.g. sock-shoe or sink-stove). A three-level organization satisfies the requirements of a complete algorithm for recall: it encompasses all the material to be learned, and it provides an ordering for readout so that *S* knows, at a given point, what has been recalled and what remains to be reported. With the exception of one fifth-grade girl, only adults have been found to employ a three-level procedure, and about half of them do so on the very first trial (although study strategy changes very little over trials). Sorting into exhaustive categories, level 2, is employed by grade-school children, generally augmented by rehearsal of items. Among first-graders, on the other hand, level-2 categorizing is attained by only one *S* (on a later trial). The upper curve in Figure 32–7 presents the traditional Bousefield measure of clustering in free recall. Comparison of the two curves suggests, as does observation of *S*'s behavior, that clustering at the time of recall antedates organization for reading into storage (which is measured by organization rating).

What is most startling, and most difficult to convey through objective measures, is the behavior of some of the youngest children. Many of them, after surveying the pictures for less than the allotted three minutes, announce that they are ready for testing. Later, on recall, they seem genuinely surprised at how few items have been retained. Not that they have any idea of the number of items to be learned or the number they have recalled; counting or keeping track of recall appears a good deal later. One gets the impression that the young child confuses recognition with recall or, perhaps, perception with memorization (Flavell[27] reports the same impression). Although some six-year-olds do rehearse actively, they do not organize the material in any way; others appear to assume that one has only to look at the pictures in order to "get them inside the head," to be reported back later. They seem unaware of the fact that memorizing requires extra effort and the use of special techniques. Such children are, in short, unaware of intentional learning; for them, all learning is incidental learning. Among older children this is no longer true. They rehearse, they organize material, they engage in self-testing in an effort to store material, mostly through repetition, and they are amazingly good at it. On the other hand, sophisticated adults, such as college students, who are responsible for storage and retrieval of ever-greater volumes of information, seem eventually to find the techniques of rehearsal too tiring and inefficient for their purposes. Out of necessity they have been forced to invent means to evade rote memorization and invent problem-solving-like heuristics for chunking information into larger and better-organized units. So practiced do they become in the use of organizing mnemonics that by the time they reach middle-age they are almost incapable of storing information that cannot be organized into storage but must be learned by rote. At least, that is how I rationalize my own recent inability to remember proper names, by saying that I have refused to store them in the first place.

Do We Need Two Classes of Information Transformation?

Let's return now to the starting assumptions. I asserted that cognitive development can be described in terms of the operation of two very general and pervasive classes of preliminary information transformation—analysis and memorializing—and that procedures relevant to each class (or component subroutines for those who are really hooked on computer analogies) are evolved with age and age-related experience. Some of these age-related changes in transformation activity have been briefly described. There is so much more compelling developmental evidence already available (mostly from Piaget and his associates) that at this point I don't see how any one can deny the existence of qualitative developmental changes. But is there any direct evidence for the existence of two separate classes of information transformations? To be honest, I don't know of any. I can, however, suggest how a memorializing transformation would clarify interpretation of a lot of existing evidence gathered to answer totally different questions, and I can cite one experiment whose results are highly suggestive.

For a better idea of the potential role of memorializing transformations in promoting cognitive development, let's consider some tasks not specifically concerned with memory at all. Most research on the development of concrete operations has employed either free sorting into categories or a conservation task. Changes from a preoperational to a concrete-operations level of performance on these tasks have generally been explained by invoking some sort of attentional mechanism (e.g. failure to attend to the relevant property or attention to only one of two simultaneously varying prop-

erties) or an analytic mechanism (e.g. for combining information about simultaneous variation of several properties). One could, however, assert that a memorializing transformation is required as well. For example, most studies of sorting into categories[2,10,25] report an initial, rather disorganized, stage of "graphic collections" in which the child of four or five aligns similar objects so that adjacent ones share a common property but there is a shift in properties (e.g. yellow square, yellow circle, blue circle). One interpretation of these categorizations is that the child started sorting with respect to a property but that along the way he forgot the property—or, even, the instructions—and shifted to another. This is about what one would expect from a child who is unaware that it is necessary to store property information for use in guiding and anticipating subsequent action. Similarly, in the conventional conservation task, a preoperational child shown two rows each of n identically-spaced objects will agree that there is the same number of objects in each row. But, when the objects in the second row are spread out relative to the first row, he will say there are more objects in the second. Or, given two identical balls of clay, the preoperational child will say, after one of them has been flattened, that there is now more (or less) clay in the pancake than in the ball. This amazing behavior is generally explained by assuming that immediate perceptual aspects of the altered task are overwhelmingly potent relative to logical aspects (or that the child is dealing with only one of two varying properties). But logical considerations need never arise for a child who has not carried over stored information about the prior state in the first place. For him, only relatively incomparable properties are immediately available to evaluate the transformed member: e.g. if he does not remember that the water in the tall skinny glass was just poured from the short fat glass he can't be expected to retrieve the information that it's the same water when asked later which glass has more to drink? If there weren't a difference, why would you ask? Moreover, even the most successful of the many experimental attempts to produce conservation in preoperational children by training on attention to properties[8] failed to produce conservation in all subjects even after extensive training.‡ Perhaps the training was inadequate for the failures, or perhaps they were in fact attending correctly but failing to store the information and use it to judge the transformed pairs.

Second, consider the widely reported general finding of a large time lag between successful performance on a recognition test and successful performance on a test requiring reproduction.[1,7,14] Form discrimination, for example, has been trained as early as 18 months[13] and form boards are an early item on many intelligence tests, but accurate drawing of simple forms, like squares or triangles, is not attained much before age five! In this case, attention to distinguishing form properties is necessary for correct performance on any test of form discrimination. It is also sufficient for a recognition test, but it is insufficient for a production test. Accurate reproduction requires, in addition, that one has stored information about defining properties and their relations for later retrieval to direct production.

To my mind, the most compelling evidence on the existence of memorializing transformations, separate from and in addition to analytic ones, comes from an experiment by Eimas.[5] Earlier, Eimas[4] and Ingalls and Dickerson,[9] in comparaing concept attainment among a number of age groups run under the Levine[12] blank-trials procedure, had found that younger children are nonoptimal information processers and that efficiency of information utilization increases with age. In this experiment, Eimas ran an experimental group (actually, several of them, but the other manipulations had no effect whatsoever) for which the pair of stimuli presented on the last informed trial, together with an indication of which was the correct choice, were present throughout the series of blank trials (choice required but no information given). When the necessity for remembering results of the last outcome trial is removed in this way, six-year-olds, and even five-year-olds, turn out to be just as efficient in attaining the correct concept as college students. This finding suggests, to me, that young children can attend to properties and formulate hypotheses with respect to them; their difficulty stems from failure to store property information from earlier trials for use on later ones.

And so, I admit that the case for a class of memorializing transformations as separate and distinct from analytic ones is largely circumstantial, but I hope that more compelling direct evidence will be forthcoming and that I have planted a bee in your bonnet to help me look for it.

‡Most procedures employed in training research reflect the rat heritage of the learning tradition in that *S* is given a series of discrimination trials with information following response. To the author's knowledge, no one has tried the direct approach of simply telling the child what to look at or what to do. In one instance where this was done[3] the effect was immediate and dramatic.

Acknowledgments

The author is grateful to Nan Slotnick, Suzanne Martorano, Deborah Weisman, and Thomas Ulrich for their assistance in collection and analysis of the data reported.

REFERENCES

1. Birch, H. & A. Lefford. 1967. Visual differentiation, intersensory integration, and voluntary motor control. Society for Research in Child Development Monographs *32* (whole No. 110).
2. Bruner, J. S., R. S. Olver, & P. M. Greenfield. 1966. Studies in cognitive growth. John Wiley. New York, N.Y.
3. Eimas, P. D. 1967. Optional shift behavior in children as a function of overtraining, irrelevant stimuli, and age. Journal of Experimental Child Psychology. *5*: 332–340.
4. Eimas, P. D. 1969. A developmental study of hypothesis behavior and focusing. Journal of Experimental Child Psychology, *8*: 160–172.

5. Eimas, P. D. Effects of memory aids on hypothesis behavior and focusing in young children and adults. Journal of Experimental Child Psychology. In Press.
6. Flavell, J. H. 1970. Developmental studies of mediated memory. *In* H. W. Reese & L. P. Lipsitt (Eds.), Advances in Child Development and Behavior, Vol. 5, Academic Press. New York, N.Y.
7. Fraser, C., U. Bellugi, & R. Brown. 1963. Control of grammar in imitation, comprehension, and production. Journal of Verbal Learning and Verbal Behavior *2*: 121–135.
8. Gelman, R. 1969. Conservation acquisition: a problem of learning to attend to relevant attributes. Journal of Experimental Child Psychology, *7*: 167–187.
9. Ingalls, R. P. & D. J. Dickerson. 1969. Development of hypothesis behavior in human concept identification. Developmental Psychology, *1*: 707–716.
10. Inhelder, B. & J. Piaget. 1964. The Early Growth of Logic in the Child. Harper & Row, New York, N.Y.
11. Kagan, J. & M. Lewis. 1965. Studies of attention in the human infant. Merrill-Palmer Quarterly, *11*: 95–127.
12. Levine, M. 1966. Hypothesis behavior in humans during discrimination learning. Journal of Experimental Psychology, *71*: 331–338.
13. Ling, B. C. 1941. Form discrimination as a learning cue in infants. Comparative Psychology Monographs, *17*: (Whole No. 86).
14. Maccoby, E. E. & H. L. Bee, 1965. Some speculations concerning the lag between perceiving and performing. Child Development, *36*: 367–377.
15. Miller, G. A., E. Galanter & K. H. Pribram. 1960. Plans and the Structure of Behavior. Holt, Rinehart & Winston, New York, N.Y.
16. Moely, B. M., F. A. Olson, T. G. Halwes & J. H. Flavell. 1969. Production deficiency in young children's clustered recall. Developmental Psychology, *1*: 26–34.
17. Neimark, E. D. 1970. Model for a thinking machine: an information-processing framework for the study of cognitive development. Merrill-Palmer Quarterly, *16*: 345–368.
18. Neimark, E. D. & N. Lewis. 1967. The development of logical problem-solving strategies. Child Development, *38*: 107–117.
19. Neimark, E. D. & N. Lewis. 1968. Development of logical problem-solving: a one-year retest. Child Development, *39*: 527–536.
20. Neimark, E. D. & N. S. Slotnick. 1970. Spontaneous imposition of organization: a developmental study. Paper read at Eastern Psychologic Association meeting. Atlantic City, N.J.
21. Neimark, E. D., N. S. Slotnick & T. E. Ulrich. Development of memorization strategies. Developmental Psychology. (In press)
22. Neisser, U. 1966. Cognitive Psychology. Appleton-Century-Croft. New York, N.Y.
23. Postman, L. 1964. Short-term memory and incidental learning. *In* A. W. Melton (Ed.) Categories of Human Learning. Academic Press. New York, N.Y. 146–194.
24. Reitman, W. R. 1965. Cognition and Thought: an information-processing approach. Wiley, 1965. New York, N.Y.
25. Vygotsky, L. S. 1962. Thought and Language. M.I.T. Press. Cambridge, Mass.
26. Zeaman, D. & B. J. House. 1963. The role of attention in retardate discrimination learning. *In* H. R. Ellis (Ed.) Handbook of Mental Deficiency. McGraw-Hill. New York, N.Y.
27. Flavell, J. H. Personal communication.

33. ENVIRONMENTAL AND COGNITIVE CONTROL OF BEHAVIOR[1]

HOWARD H. KENDLER

Interpretations of behavior that emphasize environmental or cognitive control have been at odds with each other throughout the history of psychology. This conflict has resisted any methodological or empirical resolution because no single or simple issue has been at stake. Instead, through the years, the issues have multiplied, the problems have become confused, and the controversy has become institutionalized. Today a discussion concerning environmental and cognitive control of behavior could revolve about such issues as stimulus-response (S-R) connections versus cognitions, associations versus organization, habits versus cognitive structures, deductive explanation versus intuitive understanding, S-R versus phenomenological language, acquired versus innate ideas, learning versus perceptual models of behavior, phenomenology versus behaviorism, rationalism versus empiricism, and science versus humanism. All of these issues have gotten mixed up in the controversy that centers about environmental and cognitive control of behavior.

My intention is not to seek to clarify the entire problem by isolating individual issues and identifying historical pressures that created them. Even if such an effort were successful, problems would still remain. A purely methodological analysis will fail to come to grips with the empirical components of the controversy. And it is my belief that the ulti-

mate resolution of the controversy within the psychological community will depend on relevant empirical information although, as already implied, epistemological clarification is required.

In line with this last point, it is worth stating, even in the absence of detailed justification, that the host of problems that seem at present inextricably intertwined in the general controversy of the environmental and cognitive control of behavior do not represent logically integrated sets of methodological commitments and theoretical premises. Instead, they are a group of autonomous assumptions that have become enmeshed for a variety of historical reasons.

Problem

Taken at face value, the controversy between environmental and cognitive control of behavior can be reduced to the search for the causal origin of behavior. Environmental control means that one can trace the causal chain of a behavioral act directly back to some environmental event. Cognitive control, in contrast, suggests that the cause of a response is the manner in which the organism interprets available information. Even more simply, the controversy can be reduced to the relative importance of external and internal factors in the control of behavior.

Now admittedly, this simplistic interpretation fails to reflect all aspects of the enduring conflict between environmentally oriented S-R conceptions and cognitive interpretations of behavior. But if the conflict has become encumbered with too many unrelated issues, to make sense of the controversy some problems have to be isolated and discussed separately.

[1]Presidential Address presented at the meeting of the Western Psychological Association, San Francisco, California, April 22, 1971. The preparation of this paper was supported by National Science Foundation Grant GB-19323.

If the environmental versus cognitive control of behavior is considered within the framework of external and internal causes of behavior, then it seems that the issue becomes less polemical and more manageable, especially if two pseudo-problems are eliminated at the very beginning. The issue is not whether behavior can occur independently of intervening internal processes. Obviously we behave with our bodies, and to deny the importance of the brain and the rest of the nervous system as well as other physiological structures is an absurdity. Neither is the issue of external and internal control one of whether the organism takes a passive or active role in his own behavior in the sense that he functions either as a mechanical robot, or as a free spirit. Such a distinction reflects more the confusing heritage of the philosophical problem of free will than a meaningful psychological comparison. If we accept a psychological determinism then we cannot conclude that some forms of behavior are more determined than others.

External and internal control of behavior can, however, be meaningfully equated with the passive and active distinction when it refers to the sequence of theoretical events that determine observable behavior. External control of behavior is represented by a theory in which behavior is tied directly to certain physical characteristics of the environment so that behavioral output parallels stimulus input. Internal control is exemplified by a formulation in which the input segment of an environmental-behavioral relationship is insufficient for predicting behavior. Although this characterization of the external-internal distinction really represents and points on a dimension rather than mutually exclusive categories, the distinction nevertheless has relevance to theoretical representations in psychology. Many sensory phenomena can be interpreted by models that emphasize stimulus control, while cognitive-control models tend to be more appropriate for intellectual functioning. But exclusively correlating the external-internal control distinction to different subject-matter areas would be both oversimplified and misleading. A case in point is that of discrimination learning.

Environmental and Cognitive Control of Discrimination-Shift Behavior

A classical example of a stimulus-control model of behavior is the long-lived discrimination learning theory of Spence (1936). Its fundamental structure is simple: stimuli, defined physically, become directly associated to reinforced responses. For example, in a black-white discrimination, the choice of the correct black alley when it is on the right side increases the separate tendencies to approach both black and the cues of the right alley. A choice of the incorrect white alley when it is on the right decreases the separate tendencies to approach both white and the right cues. The black-white discrimination is learned when the net tendency to approach the black-right or black-left compound is greater than the net tendency to approach the competing white-left or white-right compound.

The Spence (1936) model can be characterized as being both a *nonselective* and *nontransformational* system. Environmental stimulation is neither culled nor converted before becoming associated with the response. In the case of our example of a nonspatial brightness discrimination, the subject neither selectively responds to white and black stimuli while ignoring the right and left cues nor does he transform the cues into some abstract representation such as "brightness" and "position" cues.

The Spence model of the animal discrimination learning was not universally adopted. Actually it arose in opposition to the Lashley-Krechevsky model (Krechevsky, 1932; Lashley, 1929) which postulated that the input segment of discrimination learning behavior of animals operated selectively. When choosing a *black-right* stimulus compound, with black correct, the subject learns only about that cue to which he is attending. If he hypothesizes that right is correct, he learns nothing about the black cue. Figure 33–1 schematically represents the essential difference between a selective and nonselective assumption as it applies to the case of a choice of a black-right stimulus compound.

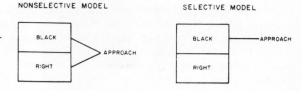

FIGURE 33–1. Comparison between nonselective and selective assumptions.

In the case of the nonselective model, both cues, black and right, become associated with the instrumental approach response, but in the case of the selective model, the association is determined by the hypothesis the subject is entertaining, which is black in this diagram.

The Lashley-Krechevsky conception anticipated several related models (Lawrence, 1949; Lovejoy, 1968; Mackintosh, 1965; Sutherland, 1959; Trabasso & Bower, 1968) which postulated that some attentional process selected out some of the incoming information. Such an assumption possesses a core of ambiguity because the term *attention* lends itself to several possible interpretations. In common language, as well as in psychological theory, attention can refer either to motivational or perceptual processes or can serve to characterize an aspect of phenomenal experience. Within the context of selective theories of animal discrimination learning, attention tended to be equated with perceptual processes, while the motivational facets of alertness and interest were ignored.

Limiting the meaning of attention to perceptual processes does not, however, eliminate all sources of ambiguity. If attention, as a perceptual process, is conceptualized as the selective focusing on certain stimulus components, while simultaneously ignoring others, then two different mechanisms can be invoked to describe such a process. Consider Figure 33–2 which represents a two-choice discrimination task involving two dimensions, *brightness* and *shape*, each possessing two values, *black* and *white*, and *circle* and *triangle*. When brightness is relevant, with black positive, one method by which a rat can attend to the relevant stimuli is to orient his receptors to the centers of the figures instead of scanning the periphery, as he would if shape were relevant.

Both Spence (1952) and Wyckoff (1952) postulated an observing response that operated simply as an instrumental act that oriented an organism's receptors toward those cues that were correlated with reinforcement. Ehrenfreund (1948) had demonstrated the significance of observing responses in discrimination learning tasks when he showed that learning to discriminate could be markedly influenced by an animal's receptor-orienting acts. It is important to note that an observing response mechanism is in no way inconsistent with Spence's nonselective and nontransformational model. It merely assumes that two single-unit S-R associations can occur successively, that is, be chained together.

Focusing on a particular segment of the environment can presumably be accomplished

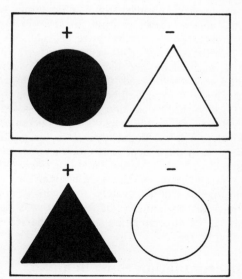

FIGURE 33–2. A two-choice discrimination task involving two dimensions.

by a mechanism that does not entail any receptor-orienting act. Such a device is *selective attention* that either gates in relevant information or filters out irrelevant information. The popularity of the concept of *selective attention*, however, is not matched by the clarity of its meaning, as is witnessed by the recent appraisal of Kristofferson (1971), a specialist in attention. "Modern theories of selective attention sit on a sea of mud, unpredictably slithering back and forth, firmly contacting nothing of that which forms their foundation by continuing to remain visible because of their insubstantiality [p. 20]." In spite of this harsh evaluation, numerous lines of evidence (e.g., Triesman & Geffen, 1967) suggest the empirical base of this phenomenon cannot be ignored. Despite its ambiguity, an apparent indigenous failing in psychological theory, selective attention should be considered as a possible mechanism in an analysis of discrimination learning, but it should not be confused with receptor orientation.

A selective attention mechanism is obviously at odds with Spence's (1936) nonselective model. Not surprisingly, they do generate conflicting predictions about discrimination learning. It is both interesting and disturbing to note, however, that in spite of the obvious difference between the selective and nonselective assumption, after 40 years of experimentation and debate, the theoretical controversy still remains unresolved. One reason is that the issue has expanded well beyond the confines of the empirical question initially posed. Psychologists, in their passionate pursuit of global principles, frequently ignore the possibility that a theoretical assumption can possess limited generality. A crucial question is whether the nonselective, nontransformational single-unit model can adequately represent certain behavioral phenomena for which it was designed, the discrimination learning behavior of the white rat.

Discrimination-Shift Behavior

The discrimination-shift behavior of the white rat serves as a reference point in our analysis of the differences between environ-

mental and cognitive control of behavior. Spence's (1936) nonselective model generates the prediction that a reversal shift should be slower than an extradimensional shift, both transfer designs being illustrated in Figure 33–3. In spite of the persistent and valiant efforts by both Tracy Kendler and myself to educate all psychologists about the importance of reversal and extradimensional shifts, some of them, certainly no more than a vast majority, still remain uninformed. Because experimental results of studies that compare reversal and extradimensional shifts play a central role in this analysis of environmental and cognitive control of behavior, it becomes essential that these experimental operations become clear. Figure 33–3 provides a simple example involving two successive discrimination tasks. In the first task, the subject is confronted with a choice between two stimulus compounds that vary on two dimensions, brightness and shape. In the initial discrimination, black is the correct stimulus while white is the incorrect one. After the first discrimination is learned, a shift in reinforcement contingencies occurs with the same set of stimuli. In a *reversal shift,* the response contingencies are reversed; the previously incorrect stimulus, white, is now correct, while the previously correct stimulus, black, is now incorrect. In an extradimensional shift, the reinforcement contingencies are shifted to the previously irrelevant form dimension.

Let us now examine the implications of the nonselective model for these two kinds of shifts. According to the nonselective model during the initial discrimination, the positive stimulus, black, is reinforced consistently, while the irrelevant cues, circle and triangle, are reinforced intermittently. As a result, at the end of the initial training, as revealed in Figure 33–4, the difference between the habit to approach black and the two irrelevant cues, circle and triangle, is less than the difference to approach black and the incorrect cue, white. Because of this, more training would be required to execute a reversal shift, from black to white, than an extradimensional shift, from black to one of the previously irrelevant cues, for example, circle.

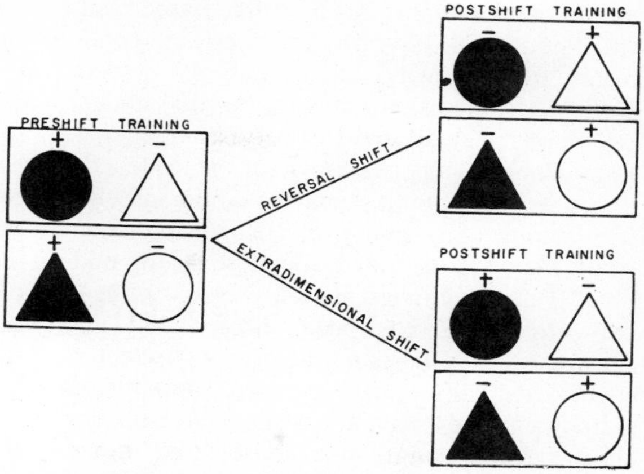

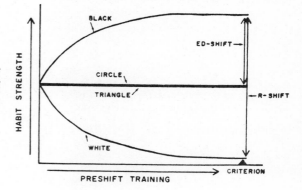

FIGURE 33–3. A comparison between reversal and extradimensional shifts.

Figure 33–4 is a highly idealized representation of the implications of the single-unit nonselective model that a reversal shift should be slower than an extradimensional shift. Wolford and Bower (1969) when simulating Spence's (1936) model noted that in some special cases, contrary to what has just been said, the model predicted a faster reversal than an extradimensional shift. In their simulation, however, the reversal and extradimensional shifts were not compared in counterbalanced designs, that is, in designs in which the four stimuli, black, white, circle, and triangle, are correct for an equal number of subjects. When the implications of Spence's model are simulated for a counterbalanced design (Kendler, Hirschberg, & Wolford, 1971), a reversal shift is found always to be slower than an extradimensional shift, a deduction consistent with the idealized representation in Figure 33–4.

And when the problem is put to empirical test, we find typically that, consistent with the nonselective model, infrahuman organisms such as chickens, rats, and monkeys, when confronted with a discrimination-shift problem for the first time, find it easier to execute an extradimensional than a reversal shift when no overlearning is given (Brookshire, Warren, & Ball, 1961; Kelleher, 1956; Mackintosh, 1962; Tighe, 1964).

Although the superiority of an extradimensional over a reversal shift is consistent with the nonselective assumption, the common observation that animals frequently exhibit a preference for one of two simultaneously presented dimensions seems to be at odds with it. For example, brightness is more salient for rats than is shape. Does not such a preference in itself indicate that some input process is operating selectively? Not necessarily! Di-

FIGURE 33–4. Schematic representation of difference between competing habits at end of preshift training. (Abbreviations: ED = extradimensional, R = reversal.)

mensional dominance, as Kendler, Basden, and Bruckner (1970) have shown, does not need to result from "selectively attending" to one particular dimension. It can be due to the psychophysical differences between the cues. For example, when compared to shape, the dimension of brightness may be dominant when its cues are black and white but not dominant when they are each a different shade of mid-gray. This assumption, based on psychophysical differences, has been incorporated into Spence's (1936) single-unit, nonselective model, and has received empirical support from a study with rats (Kendler et al., 1970). In sum, the modified, single-unit nonselective model can account for dimensional dominance without resorting to any selective attention mechanisms.

Ontogenetic Changes in Reversal-Shift Behavior

Not surprisingly, the single-unit nonselective model of discrimination-shift behavior is restricted to certain boundary conditions. Although the model applies to the behavior of rats, it is inappropriate for the behavior of human adults. College students find a reversal shift much easier to execute than an extradimensional shift (Buss, 1953, 1956; Harrow & Friedman, 1958; Kendler & D'Amato, 1955).

Discrepant results such as these often encourage one of two theoretical maneuvers: to develop some theoretical gimmick that enables the same model to explain the conflicting results or to acknowledge an emergent character in human behavior that distinguishes it from that of lower animals. A third alternative is to allow for the possibility that some of the characteristics of the single-unit model have relevance for the behavior of the college student, but additional mechanisms are also required.

A simple descriptive S-R mediational model was offered to explain the reversal behavior of college students. This model can be represented by the S-r-s-R schema (see Figure 33–5) which indicates that the external stimulus, a black circle, for example, is transformed into a hypothetical implicit response, designated by the lower-case r in the enclosed rectangle, which in turn produces a hypothetical implicit cue, s, which controls overt behavior. Thus, in the single-unit functioning, stimulus control resides primarily in the external stimulus, whereas in mediational functioning, stimulus control is exerted mainly by the implicit cue produced by the mediational response. When this simple model was proposed (Kendler & Kendler, 1962; Kendler & Vineberg, 1954), the suggestion was offered that when college students learned a discrimination between pairs of stimuli that differ on two orthogonal visual dimensions, for example, brightness and shape, they made an implicit response that represented the relevant stimuli. Because this mediational response and the cue it produced could be used during a reversal shift, but had to be abandoned for an extradimensional shift, a reversal shift was expected to be faster.

To place this model in the proper perspective, three characteristics should be noted. First, the mediational model was created in the context of supplementing the original single-unit discrimination learning theory so that in combination they could account for comparative and

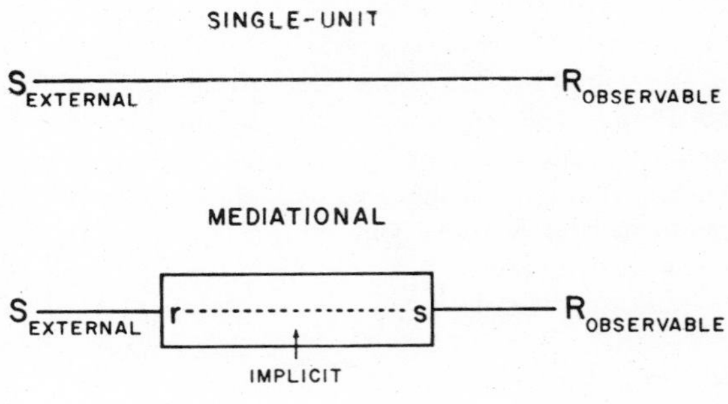

SINGLE-UNIT

FIGURE 33–5. Schematic representation of single-unit and mediational S-R mechanisms.

MEDIATIONAL

developmental differences in discrimination-shift behavior. The commitment to explain both the discrimination learning behavior of animals and men placed a special burden on the coordinated S-R theory that is usually not shared by other formulations that seek only to interpret human cognitive development. This burden, however, was not adopted in a quixotic fashion. Instead, the benefits anticipated were that when the behavior of lower animals is compared and contrasted with humans, the properties of each would become more discernible and the relationship between them clearer.

The second important attribute of the mediational model was that it was conceived more in terms of instrumental value than of deductive capacity. Without denying the ultimate necessity for formulating a mathematical model of human discrimination-shift behavior, the mediational model was initially proposed to provide a structure to guide further research and within which to interpret results. The precise characteristics of the mediational response and the cue it produced were left open-ended, not to provide sufficient ambiguity to defend it against empirical attack but, instead, in frank recognition of the different alternatives to which the mediational mechanism could be coordinated—words, images, motoric sets, etc.

The third attribute of the mediational model is that it could be characterized as *cognitive*. When a neobehaviorist (Kendler & Spence, 1971), such as myself, uses the term cognitive, he can be accused of jumping on a popular bandwagon or abandoning his behavioristic methodological orientation. Both accusations are denied. The use of the term cognitive in the title of this article, as well as to describe the mediational model, is done to further meaningful communication in the psychological community which has been victimized by seductive fads and false dichotomies. The terms cognitive and mediation are presumed to share a common meaning when applied to the reversal behavior of college students. According to the mediational model, external stimulation (S) is translated into an implicit cue (s) that controls behavior. In essence, the implicit cue (s)

represents the external environment (S). By representation is meant the substitution of one set of cues for another. In the language of cognitive psychology, this translation can be considered a case of information processing.

Is it legitimate for an S-R model to invoke a representational process? Invoking such a process is actually an extension of previous theoretical efforts. The phenomenon of classical conditioning and the theoretical construct of the fractional anticipatory goal response (r_g), both of which play central roles in the S-R formulations of neobehaviorists, are examples of representation, however primitive, in the sense that functional properties of one stimulus are shifted to that of another. It would also appear consistent for a formulation that identifies responses as primary theoretical and empirical variables to postulate response mechanisms, such as representation, capable of abstracting and transferring functional properties from one to another set of stimuli.

Equating mediation with cognition may irritate some who are convinced that any such attempt at reconciliation will of necessity do violence to the concept of cognition. If true, the difficulty stems more from the varied meanings of cognition than from an attempt at accommodation. In an effort to clarify the meaning of S-R associationism (Kendler, 1965), I distinguished among four of its major components: (*a*) a technical language; (*b*) a methodological orientation; (*c*) a pretheoretical model, that is, an informal conception that operates as an analogy; and (*d*) a group of independent theories. This classification can also be applied to cognitive psychology although its more diversified historical background, as compared to S-R psychology, would produce a wider range of positions in each category. Whereas S-R psychology has been dominated by the experimental study of learning, cognitive psychology has emerged from different, and sometimes, antagonistic traditions of perception, phenomenology, and computer simulation. In my estimation, contemporary cognitive psychology suffers from many internal stresses and strains, one being the functional role of phenomenal experience: should it serve as a possible source of theoretical notions, an exact blueprint for the construction of a theory of behavior, or as the primary dependent variable to be explained or described? My concern, however, is not to prescribe to cognitive psychologists what they should do, although if asked I could offer some suggestions. I only wish to protest against prejudgments that insist that an S-R theory, in principle, cannot ever account for behavior that is commonly characterized as being cognitive. Such an argument is tantamount to an intellectual lynching, a form of debate that is distasteful, especially to its victims. S-R models are not closed systems as some of their critics would like to believe. They have potentiality for growth as they have frequently exhibited when challenged by new sets of data.

Now that the bare skeleton of the mediational model has been described and some of its epistemological characteristics noted, we can return to the empirical problem posed by the discrepancy between the discrimination-shift behavior of lower animals and college students. One obvious question is the course of the transition that takes place between single-unit (environmental) and mediational (cognitive) control of discrimination-shift behavior. The most direct answer would come from developmental studies that cover a wide age range. Figure 33–6 reports the results of three such studies from our laboratory. Studies 1 (Kendler, Kendler, & Learnard, 1962) and 2 (Kendler & Kendler, 1970) measured the tendencies of individual subjects to respond in a reversal or

extradimensional manner in a discrimination learning task involving conventional geometric patterns that differed on two orthogonal dimensions. As can be noted for the rat, located on the left side of the figure, a preference was exhibited for an extradimensional shift (ED), but the developmental relationship for children from 3 to 10 years of age was one of an increasing tendency to prefer a reversal (R) to an extradimensional shift. Study 2 used a wider age range as well as a greater variety of stimuli and, as can be seen, a similar relationship prevailed, an increasing tendency to prefer a reversal to an extradimensional shift. A simple summary statement of these two sets of findings is that the single-unit model accounts for infrahuman behavior while the younger a child is, the more likely he is to behave according to the single-unit theory. The older he is, the more likely his performance will be consonant with the mediational model.

Study 3 (Kendler, Kendler, & Marken, 1969) was designed to distinguish between two different mediational mechanisms, selective attention or conceptual transformation. As already noted, selective attention is presumed to operate by gating in certain cues or by filtering out others. Conceptual transformation, in contrast, refers to an encoding process in which environmental stimuli are converted into a hierarchical form of representation. Whereas selective attention operates to emphasize certain cues, conceptual transformation creates cues which, strictly speaking, are not in the environment. To be specific, black and white

FIGURE 33–6. Results of three developmental studies of reversal behavior. (Abbreviations: ED = extradimensional shift, R = reversal.)

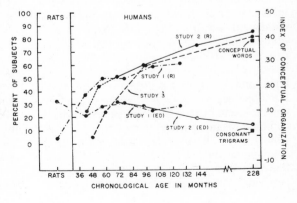

patterns, or circles and triangles, are distinct events. The transformation (r) of these separate stimulus patterns (S) into symbolic events (s) representative of the concept of brightness and shape is neither demanded by the laws of physics nor the principles of psychology. In short, the issues between selective attention and conceptual transformation are whether the crucial mechanism is perceptual or conceptual and whether the process is emphasis or transformation.

To determine whether the ontogenetic changes observed in the first two studies result primarily from selective attention or conceptual transformation is a difficult task because no simple set of experimental operations can distinguish between them. One strategy adopted was to eliminate attentional processes, either receptor-orienting or selective attention, so that only encoding reactions could serve as the basis for rapid reversals. Pictures of conceptual instances (e.g., apple, banana; shirt, pants) were substituted for two-dimensional geometrical patterns. Hence the subjects were prevented from correctly sorting the stimuli by attending to any specifically located segment of the stimulus displays because the pictures of each set (e.g., fruit, clothing) did not share simple physical properties such as shape or brightness. If under such conditions a developmental change in the ease of executing a reversal shift was obtained comparable to that exhibited in Studies 1 and 2, then one could exclude the possibility that attentional processes, either receptor-orienting or selective, were responsible. The results of Study 3, which are expressed in a derived measure of conceptual organization, located on the right ordinate, are consistent with the conceptual transformation hypothesis. With increasing age, a reversal shift in comparison to a nonreversal shift becomes easier to execute. The conceptual transformation interpretation is also supported by two other findings reported in Figure 33–6, indicated by two isolated squares near the right ordinate. With conceptually linked words, college students behave as they do when required to sort conceptually linked pictures; reversal shifts are executed relatively rapidly. When sorting

unrelated consonant trigrams (nonsense syllables), their behavior is similar to 4-year-olds when confronted with conceptually linked pictures; reversal shifts are executed relatively slowly (Kendler, Kendler, & Sanders, 1967). These data, as well as others (Kendler & Watson, 1969) that used words as stimuli and thereby excluded selective perceptual processes, also suggest that the ability to *conceptualize* two sets of stimuli determines the speed with which they can be reversed. These results from studies using pictures and words also indicate that the orderly increase in the tendency to reverse should not be misinterpreted to imply that such changes are exclusively a function of developmental level; the nature of the discrimination problem is also a significant variable.

Mediational Process

A strategic error that has been repeatedly committed in the history of psychology is to assume that certain experimental paradigms such as classical and operant conditioning, perceptual grouping tasks, and others too numerous to mention, reflect in pristine clarity fundamental psychological principles. A more realistic appraisal is that all of these basic experimental paradigms, and others as well, entail numerous interacting component processes that can be separated only by the joint efforts of further experimental refinements and theoretical speculations. Discrimination-shift experiments of the sort that have been described are no exception to this methodological generalization. Although the role of single-unit associations and mediated conceptual transformations has been emphasized in the reported comparative and ontogenetic differences, no suggestion is offered that other processes are completely excluded. The operating assumptions, however, are that single-unit and mediational conceptual processes are the dominant factors and that the discrimination-shift experimental paradigm is particularly well suited to reveal information about developmental changes in conceptual behavior.

Conceptual Development

To understand these developmental changes, it first becomes necessary to distinguish between conceptual behavior and conceptual processes. Conceptual behavior can be defined simply by the operations that are used in concept-formation and concept-identification experiments. For our purposes we can summarize the various experimental procedures by operationally defining conceptual behavior as a common response to dissimilar stimuli. By accepting such a definition we merely agree about a primary characteristic of conceptual behavior but in no way imply that conceptual behavior must result always from the same basic processes. A case in point are two studies that were designed to improve the reversal-shift performance of preschool children. In both experiments, the effectiveness of two training techniques, verbal labeling and cue training, was compared in a reversal-shift study involving two sets of geometrical patterns, such as curvilinear and rectilinear lines. The verbal-labeling subjects were required to articulate distinctive verbal labels to the instances of each conceptual category. The cue-training subjects were trained to match each line, before sorting it, with one of two critical cues, an acute angle, or a curved line. Both training procedures, when compared to a control condition, facilitated reversal performance, but verbal labeling proved to be more effective than cue training (Kendler, Glasman, & Ward, in press). The superiority of the verbal labeling is easy to interpret within the mediational model; the labeling encouraged symbolic responses (r's) that represented the instances from each category and provided cues (s's) to guide their choice behavior.

When interviewed after the experiment, the verbal-labeling subjects expectedly proved superior to both the cue-training and control subjects in labeling the two sets of lines. However, when it came to identifying the critical cues for the curvilinear and rectilinear lines, the verbal-labeling group equaled the performance of the cue-training subjects, both significantly outperforming the control subjects.

Thus, it would seem that verbal labeling helped the preschool children perceptually identify the critical cues, but cue training did not increase the tendency for these children to label the stimuli. In this experiment, the conclusion can be drawn that verbal labeling had a dual function: to encourage both labeling and cue identification. In other words, the label functioned not simply as an additional cue, as has been suggested by Miller and Dollard (1941), but instead as a unified response that represented the common property shared by a set of stimuli.

Some insights into the course of conceptual development are provided by the unpublished results of a similar study by James Ward, a graduate student at the University of California, Santa Barbara.[2] He compared the effects of verbal labeling and cue training with two tests of transfer: the previously employed reversal shift and an inductive test of transfer in which the subjects were required to sort new instances from the two categories previously discriminated. Labeling, as in the previous experiment, resulted in more rapid reversals, but cue training produced superior performance in the inductive test. If verbal labeling encouraged conceptual behavior, why did it not produce superior performance on the inductive test of transfer?

Our distinction between single-unit and mediational mechanisms suggests a possible answer. Perhaps in Ward's study the superiority of the cue-training group in the inductive test resulted from such single-unit mechanisms as primary stimulus generalization and appropriate receptor-orienting reactions. These subjects learned to recognize and look for the critical stimulus element and thereby aided their inductive test behavior. In contrast, in reversal learning, the verbal-labeling group behaved in a mediated manner by forming hierarchical conceptual categories of a very narrow range, being essentially limited to the instances sorted during preshift training.

Consistent with this latter interpretation is

[2]Unpublished study entitled "Verbal and Perceptual Processes in Mediating Behavior," 1970.

Saltz's cognitive-semantic space model of conceptual development which postulates that developmental changes are characterized by an increase in the range of instances that can be incorporated within a single concept. This point can be illustrated by reference to his study (Saltz & Sigel, 1967) in which the subjects judged whether a pair of pictures of kindergarten children were pictures of the same child or not. Sometimes the photographs were of different boys, other times they were of the same boy. The photographs varied only in terms of their facial expression or slightly different head positions. The results indicated that the younger the subject, the greater was his tendency to perceive photographs of the same boy as representing *different* children; that is, the younger the subject, the more narrow was his concept of the persons represented in the photograph. Agreeing with these findings are studies of object-sorting behavior in which children are instructed to sort as they see fit an array of heterogeneous objects. The younger the child, the greater are the number of categories he uses (Annett, 1959). As he matures, the number of categories decreases with a consequent increase in the number of instances in each.

The conceptual enlargement hypothesis, the tendency for children to develop broader concepts as they mature, would appear at first glance to be in opposition to the commonly held belief that very young children have large overgeneralized concepts, as is the case when a small child mistakenly identifies other men as "daddy." In line with this position could be cited the results of a perceptual learning study (Gibson & Gibson, 1955) which found that young children initially form diffuse concepts that, with increasing age, become differentiated into more compact categories.

The apparent conflict between an enlargement and differentiation interpretation of conceptual development can be resolved by postulating that ontogenetic changes bring into operation different behavioral mechanisms. Initially, conceptual behavior is based on single-unit mechanisms that result in overgeneralized categories. When mediational control first takes hold, narrow concepts are formed that later tend to expand. And one can further speculate that later, when more sophisticated language systems take over, an individual enters a new stage of conceptual development in which broad concepts, such as animal, can be differentiated into finer subcategories, mammals, birds, and fish. Quite obviously, perceived within this interpretative framework, the search for one global developmental principle that governs conceptual behavior is bound to fail.

Transition between Single-Unit and Mediational Control

If conceptual development is characterized by successive levels of functioning, then it becomes necessary to specify the principles that govern the transition between levels. No doubt these principles will prove to be more complex than we can now possibly imagine, but the immediate question is to determine whether these transitional problems can be clarified by experimental analyses. Two recent studies suggest an affirmative answer.

The first study was concerned with the question of whether the transition from single-unit to mediational control is sudden and complete or whether it occurs gradually, with some mediational components operating before others. To be more specific, does the first segment (S-r) of the mediational schema, the association between the external stimuli and the symbolic response, exhibit a different developmental course than does the second segment (s-R), the association between the symbolic cue and the choice response?

Observations of preschool children, when sorting two sets of conceptually related pictures, such as animals and fruits, suggest that the transition from single-unit to mediational control often occurs gradually. Frequently they fail to represent the instances by their conceptual names, even though later questioning indicates definitely that terms such as animals and fruits are within their repertoire and that they are capable of using them appropriately. The failure to use available representational responses, that is, the inability of the pictures

(S) to elicit the implicit representational responses (r), can be characterized, as Flavell, Beach, and Chinsky (1966) have done, as a *production deficiency*. The child is deficient in producing labels that are within his repertoire. Another kind of *mediational deficiency* (Reese, 1962) is a *control deficiency,* which can be illustrated by a child emitting the correct representational response, such as "black is right," but continuing to choose white stimuli. That is, control deficiency refers to failure of a potential mediator, once produced, to control behavior.

These two kinds of mediational deficiency, production and control, have been shown by Tracy Kendler (1971) to be correlated with developmental changes. The evidence to support this conclusion comes from a mediated transfer study in which the subjects ranged from kindergartners to college students. As can be seen from Figure 33–7, there is more production deficiency than control deficiency from kindergartners up. Moreover, control deficiency declines rapidly after the kindergarten level and becomes practically negligible by the fourth grade. Production deficiency stays about the same level from the kindergarten to the fourth-grade level and then declines later, but not as completely as does control deficiency. In short, verbal control of behavior occurs sooner and more completely than behavioral control of words.

Another question that can be raised about the transition between single-unit and mediational control is how the mediational representational response (r) gets triggered. What are the factors responsible for its occurrence?

Some light is thrown on this problem by a study (Kendler & Ward, 1971) in which two groups of kindergartners were required to execute a reversal shift with two sets of conceptually related pictures (e.g., animals versus vehicles). For one group, the standard experimental procedure was used in that each picture was presented singly, and immediately following the correct choice the picture was removed from view. For the other group, the pictures were presented in a cumulative fashion. After being sorted correctly, the picture remained in view so that the subject could inspect it while responding to subsequent pictures. Cumulative stimulus presentation produced faster reversal shifts than did single presentation. The major locus of beneficial effects of cumulative presentation occurred during preshift training. During this time, cumulative presentation presumably encouraged the formation of a symbolic representational response that facilitated mediational control. One possible interpretation is that during preshift training some sort of summative mechanism operates: as the number of previous sortings available for inspection increases, the probability increases that the subject will use a common representa-

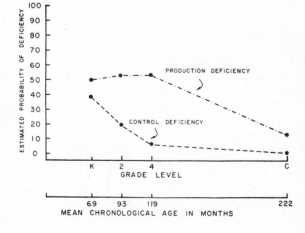

FIGURE 33–7. Developmental changes in production and control deficiencies.

tion for the instances of each sorting category. In other words, the closer in time separate instances of a common conceptual category can be viewed, the greater is the probability that an appropriate representational response will be emitted, a hypothesis that is consistent with Underwood's (1952) assumption that "for new relationships to be acquired the pertinent responses to stimuli must be contiguous [p. 219]." Evidence consistent with this proposition comes from a study (Cofer, Bruce, & Reicher, 1966) in which clustering in free recall was augmented by presenting words of a common conceptual category in blocks (i.e., successively) as compared to random presentation.

One might argue that this emphasis on contiguity applies only to concept identification but not to the actual formation of concepts. If we realize, however, that concepts based on symbolic representation are not formed full blown, but instead expand from an origin of a simple label, then contiguity can play a causal role in concept formation. Contiguous presentations of instances serve to enlarge the scope of a concept.

Concluding Remarks

A few concluding comments are now in order. The conflict between environmentally based S-R conceptions and cognitive interpretations of behavior represents, in many ways, false dichotomies. When this controversy is considered within the boundaries of discrimination-shift behavior, we note that a single-unit S-R model can be coordinated to the behavior of animals and young children, while a mediational model, involving symbolic representation and possessing characteristics of cognitive formulations, applies to the functioning of older children and adults. In short, single-unit and cognitive control models supplement each other when viewed either within a comparative or a human developmental framework.

I do not wish to leave you with the impression that the dual-process S-R developmental formulation represents an isolated attempt to interpret developmental changes in intellectual functioning. It shares characteristics with Pavlov's (1955) first- and second-signal systems, Piaget's (1952) sensorimotor versus thought processes distinction, Hebb's (1966) division between sense-dominated and mediated processes, and even with Freud's distinction between primary and secondary processes. The coordinated S-R formulation, however, differs from these approaches in that it is based primarily upon a systematic and detailed analysis of a single, well-controlled experimental paradigm, discrimination learning. The fact that it shares general conclusions with these other formulations while emerging from a different empirical base gives us some confidence that we are moving in the right direction.

REFERENCES

Annett, M. The classification of instances of four common class concepts by children and adults. *British Journal of Educational Psychology, 1959, 29*, 223–236.

Brookshire, K. H., Warren, J. M., & Ball, G. G. Reversal and transfer learning following overtraining in rat and chicken. *Journal of Comparative and Physiological Psychology, 1961, 54*, 98–102.

Buss, A. H. Rigidity as a function of reversal and nonreversal shift in the learning of successive discrimination. *Journal of Experimental Psychology, 1953, 45*, 75–81.

Buss, A. H. Reversal and nonreversal shifts in concept formation with partial reinforcement eliminated. *Journal of Experimental Psychology, 1956, 52*, 162–166.

Cofer, C. N., Bruce, D. R., & Reicher, G. M. Clustering in free recall as a function of certain methodological variations. *Journal of Experimental Psychology, 1966, 71*, 858–866.

Ehrenfreund, D. An experimental test of the continuity theory of discrimination learning with pattern vision. *Journal of Comparative and Physiological Psychology*, 1948, *41*, 408–422.

Flavell, J. H., Beach, D. H., & Chinsky, J. M. Spontaneous verbal rehearsal in a memory task as a function of age. *Child Development*, 1966, *37*, 283–299.

Gibson, J. J., & Gibson, E. J. Perceptual learning: Differentiation or enrichment? *Psychological Review*, 1955, *62*, 32–41.

Harrow, M., & Friedman, G. B. Comparing reversal and nonreversal shifts in concept formation with partial reinforcement controlled. *Journal of Experimental Psychology*, 1958, *55*, 592–597.

Hebb, D. O. *The textbook of psychology*. (2nd ed.) Philadelphia: Saunders, 1966.

Kelleher, R. T. Discrimination learning as a function of reversal and nonreversal shifts. *Journal of Experimental Psychology*, 1956, *51*, 379–384.

Kendler, H. H. Motivation and behavior. *Nebraska Symposium on Motivation*, 1965, *13*, 1–23.

Kendler, H. H., & D'Amato, M. F. A comparison of reversal shifts and nonreversal shifts in human concept formation behavior. *Journal of Experimental Psychology*, 1955, *49*, 165–174.

Kendler, H. H., Glasman, L., & Ward, J. Verbal-labelling and cue-training in reversal shift behavior. *Journal of Experimental Child Psychology*, in press.

Kendler, H. H., Hirschberg, M. A., & Wolford, G. Spence's prediction about reversal-shift behavior. *Psychological Review*, 1971, *78*, 354.

Kendler, H. H., & Kendler, T. S. Vertical and horizontal processes in problem-solving. *Psychological Review*, 1962, *69*, 1–16.

Kendler, H. H., Kendler, T. S., & Marken, R. S. Developmental analysis of reversal and half-reversal shifts. *Developmental Psychology*, 1969, *1*, 318–326.

Kendler, H. H., Kendler, T. S., & Sanders, J. Reversal and partial reversal shifts with verbal material. *Journal of Verbal Learning and Verbal Behavior*, 1967, *6*, 117–127.

Kendler, H. H., & Spence, J. T. Tenets of neobehaviorism. In H. H. Kendler & J. T. Spence (Eds.), *Essays in neobehaviorism: A memorial volume to Kenneth W. Spence*. New York: Appleton-Century-Crofts, 1971.

Kendler, H. H., & Watson, G. W. Economy of representation and reversal shift behavior. *Journal of Verbal Learning and Verbal Behavior*, 1969, *8*, 129–135.

Kendler, H. H., & Vineberg, R. The acquisition of compound concepts as a function of previous training. *Journal of Experimental Psychology*, 1954, *48*, 252–258.

Kendler, H. H., & Ward, J. Single versus cumulative presentation of stimuli to kindergartners in reversal-shift behavior. *Developmental Psychology*, 1971, *5*, 420–426.

Kendler, T. S. An ontogeny of mediational deficiency. *Child Development*, 1971, in press.

Kendler, T. S., Basden, B. H., & Bruckner, J. B. Dimensional dominance and continuity theory. *Journal of Experimental Psychology*, 1970, *83*, 309–318.

Kendler, T. S., Kendler, H. H. An ontogeny of optional shift behavior. *Child Development*, 1970, *41*, 1–27.

Kendler, T. S., Kendler, H. H., & Learnard, B. Mediated responses to size and brightness as a function of age. *American Journal of Psychology*, 1962, *75*, 571–586.

Krechevsky, I. "Hypotheses" versus "chance" in the presolution period in sensory discrimination-learning. *University of California Publications in Psychology*, 1932, *6*, 27–44.

Kristofferson, A. B. Review of N. Moray's "Attention: Selective processes in vision and learning." *Contemporary Psychology*, 1971, *16*, 20–22.

Lashley, K. S. *Brain mechanisms and intelligence*. Chicago: University of Chicago Press, 1929.

Lawrence, D. H. Acquired distinctiveness of cues: I. Transfer between discriminations on the basis of familiarity with the stimulus. *Journal of Experimental Psychology*, 1949, *39*, 770–784.

Lovejoy, E. *Attention in discrimination learning*. San Francisco: Holden-Day, 1968.

Mackintosh, N. J. The effects of overtraining on a reversal and a nonreversal shift. *Journal of Comparative and Physiological Psychology,* 1962, *55*, 555–559.

Mackintosh, N. J. Selective attention in animal discrimination learning. *Psychological Bulletin,* 1965, *64*, 124–140.

Miller, N. E., & Dollard, J. *Social learning and imitation.* New Haven: Yale University Press, 1941.

Pavlov, I. P. *Selected works,* Moscow, USSR: Langley Publishing House, 1955. (Trans. by S. Belsky).

Piaget, J. *The origins of intelligence in children.* New York: International University Press, 1952.

Reese, H. W. Verbal mediation as a function of age level. *Psychological Bulletin,* 1962, *59*, 502–509.

Saltz, E., & Sigel, I. E. Concept overdiscrimination in children. *Journal of Experimental Psychology,* 1967, *73*, 1–8.

Spence, K. W. The nature of discrimination learning in animals. *Psychological Review,* 1936, *43*, 427–449.

Spence, K. W. The nature of response in discrimination learning. *Psychological Review,* 1952, *59*, 89–93.

Sutherland, N. S. Stimulus analyzing mechanisms. In, *Proceedings of a Symposium on the Mechanization of Thought Processes* (Her Majesty's Stationery Office, London), 1959, *2*, 575–609.

Tighe, T. J. Reversal and nonreversal shifts in monkeys. *Journal of Comparative and Physiological Psychology,* 1964, *58*, 324–326.

Trabasso, T., & Bower, G. H. *Attention in learning: Theory and research.* New York: Wiley, 1968.

Triesman, A., & Geffen, G. Selective attention: Perception or response? *Quarterly Journal of Experimental Psychology,* 1967, *19*, 1–17.

Underwood, B. J. An orientation for research on thinking. *Psychological Review,* 1952, *59*, 209–220.

Wolford, G., & Bower, G. H. Continuity theory revisited: Rejected for the wrong reasons? *Psychological Review,* 1969, *76*, 515–518.

Wyckoff, L. R. The role of observing responses in discrimination learning. *Psychological Review,* 1952, *59*, 431–442.

Chapter 11

INTELLIGENCE

INTRODUCTION AND COMMENTARY

˙ The concept of intelligence has long been of great significance in the history of psychological theory and practice. One of the earliest researchers was the French psychologist Alfred Binet, who, together with Simon, constructed one of the first general intelligence tests in order to identify those schoolage children who were, in practice, noneducable (Binet & Simon, 1905). Unlike many, Binet believed that all children were, in principle, educable. Since that time, a very large number of investigations have been carried out into the psychometrics of intelligence, and concomitantly many persistent problems concerning the nature of intelligence and its development have arisen out of this research. One such problem concerns the analysis of the role of environmental and genetic factors and their interrelations in shaping and influencing the development of intelligence. Other questions relate to the stability of IQ measurements over time, and perhaps more fundamentally to whether our present concept of intelligence is valid for prediction of intellectual performance for an individual or across cultural groups.

Intelligence and the Nature–Nurture Issue

Some investigators of the development of intelligence have been mainly concerned with delineating the role of environmental factors, whereas other investigators have concentrated on genetic factors. The nature–nurture issue has, in fact, re-emerged as one of the most significant controversies in the study of intelligence. Several symposia and collections of articles have been devoted to it (Cancro, 1971; Dockrell, 1970; *Harvard Educational Review,* 1969). For example, Jensen (1969), in reviewing a large part of the extensive literature on genetic and environmental determinants, postulates a primary role for genetic factors in the development of intelligence. He argues that observed differences in intelligence scores between blacks and whites, as well as those between middle- and lower-class children, have been principally determined by genetic factors. Jensen's interpretation of racial and social class differences in scores on tests of intelligence has come under vigorous attack by those who offer alternative environmentalist accounts of such differences (see, for example, Hunt, 1969, and Kagan, 1969). Humphreys (1971) has suggested that

> The construct of a genetic substrate for intelligence is required more by general biological knowledge and belief in biological continuity from lower animals to man than by good information concerning human genetics. Family relationship and other experimentally uncontrolled studies of human genetics are suggestive but not conclusive (p. 34).

Humphreys argues that to understand the nature of the development of intelligence demands knowledge of both the biological and psychosocial substrates that are in constant interaction through every stage of development.

While it is clear that intelligence emerges from the complex interactions of hereditary and environmental factors, nonetheless, attempts have been made to quantify the degree to which intelligence is inherited. Jencks points out that geneticists themselves indicate that our present knowledge in the field of genetics is inadequate to provide this information. However, one conservative estimate suggests that the heritability of IQ is about 45 percent (Jencks, 1972). Furthermore, Mussen, Conger, and Kagan (1974) indicate that although "intelligence is subject to genetic control, the unknown relation between IQ scores and a person's basic, or native, intelligence, and our inability to control similarity of experience for twins and siblings reared apart, suggests that even this figure may be in error" (p. 95). With respect to sex differences in the heritability of IQ, Maccoby and Jacklin (1974), after surveying the literature, concluded that "the sexes show similar degrees of genetic control on the basis of parent–child resemblance, but that boys show somewhat more genetic control if data from twin studies are used" (p. 73).

Constancy of the IQ?

One part of the argument over whether intelligence is "fixed" (i.e., genetically determined) or changeable has evolved around the discussion on the *constancy of the IQ*. In general, the average IQ of schoolchildren has been found to be highly constant from year to year, and this fact has been used to buttress the argument for a "fixed" intelligence. However, test scores obtained in infancy have typically exhibited little predictive validity (see McCall, Hogarty, & Hurlburt, 1972, for an analysis of possible reasons for this as well as a discussion of the utility of infant tests for the early detection of pathology). The concept of the constancy of IQ has been further weakened by other research findings. Bayley (1955) presented evidence of nonconstancy from her longitudinal studies of the growth of intelligence. In a group of children who were tested periodically from birth only 20 percent showed significant stability in their relative status over an eight-year period. Bayley also referred to evidence from several other experiments where large changes in IQ have been observed. (The reader is referred to the general discussion of stability in personality and intelligence in Chapter 2, pp. 26–27). One dramatic example of nonconstancy is illustrated in the work of Kagan, Sontag, Baker, and Nelson (1958). These researchers have demonstrated relationships between such personality variables as amount of independence and level of achievement motivation, and significant changes in IQ in children over a relatively short period of time.

Hunt [34], in a provocative and influential argument about recent changes in psychologists' conceptions of the nature of humanity and its developmental history, has included an account of the history of the belief in a fixed intelligence, which he traces back to Galton's (1869) work on the origins of Englishmen of intellectual distinction. Hunt discusses the types of studies that have been carried out to illuminate this problem; they include investigations of IQ constancy, identical twins reared apart, the effects of various kinds of environmental deprivation, and the effects of enriched experience on IQ. There is enough evidence available now to reject an extreme fixed-intelligence point of view. Psychologists are beginning to accumulate information on the situational factors that appear to impede or facilitate the development of intelligence.

Socializing Agents in Intellectual Development

Hess and Shipman (1965) focus attention on a dominant and important part of the young child's environment—the mother—as an agent of intellectual development. They studied the problem of how the teaching styles of mothers from different social class backgrounds affected both the learning styles and information-processing strategies of their children. Bing (1963), in a study that also throws light on some specific environmental factors in the development of a child's intelligence, has investigated the relationships between particular child-rearing practices of mothers and the differential development of verbal and nonverbal abilities of their children. Although Bing's research offers some valuable insights, her information on child-rearing practices was gained through retrospective reports. Yarrow (1963) discusses the problems of using retrospective reports from adults as a source of information about children. Bayley (1968) reports on the relationships between various facets of maternal behavior and the behavioral correlates of mental growth that were observed in the longitudinal Berkeley growth study. Peterson, Becker, Hellmer, Shoemaker, and Quay (1959) discuss the role of *both* parents in the development of certain behaviors in the child. From their research they concluded that the father's role is as important as the mother's role. There is unfortunately still very little information available on the role of the father in the child's intellectual development.

The Meaning and Measurement
of Intellectual Ability

In the past few years the concept of intelligence has come under very sharp attack. Both Hudson (1966) and Hunt and Kirk (1971) see essentially no advance in our knowledge through the whole psychometric movement since Binet's time. IQ concepts, say Hunt and Kirk, have not helped identify the types of information, the learning sets that govern the structure of the abilities to process information, or the motives to process information. Nor have they served to show how the structures of ability build upon each other in psychological development. Vernon (1970), in a complementary view of intelligence, suggests that IQ tests do not offer useful information on the nature of learning, concept formation and reasoning processes, nor do they relate clearly to socially valued adult skills.

It is clear that a major source of dissatisfaction with traditional assessments of intelligence is that they only inform us on "what" a child can do; such tests provide no understanding of "how" the child does it, a major restriction on our full understanding of intellectual processes. Many psychologists have called for a new approach to the assessment of intelligence, one that will provide information on developmental processes in the construction of reality (e.g., Hunt & Kirk, 1971). Earlier, Hunt (1961) suggested that Piagetian theory and research offers the means of assessing intelligence by characterizing the individual's cognitive organization rather than simply placing him or her on a dimension. Many researchers have heeded this call. Vernon (1969), for example, has added a broad selection of tasks, originally employed by Piaget in his experiments on cognitive development, to a battery of traditional IQ test items to study the patterning of children's abilities cross-culturally. Other researchers have explored the relationships between Piaget-type tasks and mental ability tests of various kinds (Dudek, Lester, Goldberg & Dyer, 1969; O'Bryan & MacArthur, 1969; Tuddenham, 1970). Elkind [35] offers an analysis of the conceptual similarities and differences in the psychometric and Piagetian approaches to the study of intelligence. Green, Ford, and Flamer (1971) have edited a book on the possibilities of combining these two approaches.

Cross-Cultural Factors
in Intellectual Assessment

One other broad problem that is being energetically discussed is the way in which fair procedures can be established to assess the cognitive capabilities of individuals who are not members of the dominant culture within a Western society Cole and Bruner [36] organize their argument around the concepts of "competence," "performance," and the "appropriateness" of particular tests and procedures. Their argument, simply put, is that in all "comparative" research (the term "comparative" being very broadly defined to include not only studies of different cultural groups but groups differing in age, etc.) it is vital for the validity of the experiment that the experimental situation be designed to *maximize* the performance of the individuals concerned. In this way the bias inherent in most comparative studies will be reduced. A related issue concerns the generalizability of Western concepts of intelligence to the evaluation of people in non-Western societies. Berry (1972) argues that the Western concept of intelligence may not be a universal one, but instead, may obscure alternate ways of conceiving cognitive competence. Irvine (1969) has made the point in his studies of African intelligence that indigenous "modes of thought" are not adequately sampled by standard Western tests. Biesheuvel (1972) suggests replacing the concept of "intelligence" with that of "adaptability" in cross-cultural studies, particularly as "intelligence" is closely identified with that which makes for success in Western culture. By contrast "adaptability" is an essential characteristic of all behavior. (Interestingly, the crucial feature of intelligence to Piaget is that it permit the individual to resolve problems or, in other words, to *adapt* to and shape his or her environment.)

Models of Intelligence

The information from cross-cultural studies of intelligence provides not only important sources of information on the determinants of developmental processes but, in addition, evidence that bears upon a prominent contemporary research problem—the designing and testing of models of intelligence. Vernon (1965), as well as having illuminated some of the experimental factors involved in the development of intelligence, has provided a synopsis of various factor-analytic theories of intelligence. One of the early models was that proposed by Spearman (1927), who analyzed all intellectual functions into two categories of factors, a *general (g) factor,* and several *specific (s) factors.* Thurstone (1938) proposed that the structure of intelligence can be explained on the basis of a small number of *group factors,* which he called "primary mental abilities." These group factors were obtained by giving a number of tests to the same people and analyzing the results by means of the statistical technique of factor analysis. More recent models of intelligence include that of Guilford (1967), who has extended Thurstone's model into a *multiple-component model,* which, as its name suggests, postulates the view that intelligence is made up of a large number of abilities. Burt (1949) and Vernon (1965) have both proposed that intelligence is organized hierarchically, with a general factor at the top. This factor is particularly important during the early stages of the development of intelligence. However, at the later stages this general factor subdivides into a small number of group factors, and then, in turn, subdivides further into a larger number of specific factors. The theoretical problem posed by the factor-analytic approach to intelligence is whether these factors, which are mathematically derived, have any psychological validity. Dockrell (1970) states: "If factors are thought of as convenient generalizations, the question is not whether there is one ability or many, but which model is useful in a particular context or for a particular purpose" (p. 6). Adequate tests of models of intelligence, including the factor-analytic and Piagetian, have not yet been achieved but, given the possible scope of these models covering all of human cognition, this is not surprising.

References

Bayley, N. On the growth of intelligence. *American Psychologist,* 1955, *10,* 805–818.
Bayley, N. Behavioral correlates of mental growth: Birth to thirty-six years. *American Psychologist,* 1968, *23,* 1–17.
Berry, J. W. Radical cultural relativism and the concept of intelligence. In L. J. Cronbach & P. J. D. Drenth (Eds.), *Mental tests and cultural adaptation.* The Hague: Mouton, 1972, pp. 77–88.
Biesheuvel, S. Adaptability: Its measurement and determinants. In L. J. Cronbach & P. J. D. Drenth (Eds.) *Mental tests and cultural adaptation.* The Hague: Mouton, 1972, pp. 47–62.

Binet, A. & Simon, T. Méthodes nouvelles pour le diagnostic du niveau intellectual des anormaux. *Année Psychologique,* 1905, *11*, 191–244.

Bing, E. Effect of child-rearing practices on development of differential cognitive abilities. *Child Development,* 1963, 34, 631–648.

Burt, C. The structure of the mind: A review of the results of factor analysis. *British Journal of Psychology,* 1949, *19*, 176–199.

Cancro, R. (Ed.) *Intelligence:Genetic and environmental influences.* New York: Grune & Stratton, 1971.

Dockrell, W. B. (Ed.) *On intelligence.* Toronto: Ontario Institute for Studies in Education, 1970.

Dockrell, W. B. Introduction. In W. B. Dockrell (Ed.), *On intelligence.* Toronto: Ontario Institute for Studies in Education, 1970, pp. 1–13.

Dudek, S. Z., Lester, E. P., Goldberg, J. S., & Dyer, G. B. Relationship of Piaget measures to standard intelligence and motor scales. *Perceptual and Motor Skills,* 1969, *28*, 351–362.

Galton, F. *Hereditary genius: An enquiry into its laws and development.* London: Macmillan, 1869.

Green, D. R., Ford, M. P., & Flamer, G. B. (Eds.) *Measurement and Piaget.* New York: McGraw-Hill, 1971.

Guilford, J. P. *The nature of human intelligence.* New York: McGraw-Hill, 1967.

Harvard Educational Review, 1969, *39*, 1 and 2.

Hess, R. D. & Shipman, V. C. Early experience and the socialization of cognitive modes in children. *Child Development,* 1965, *36*, 869–886.

Hudson, L. *Contrary imaginations.* New York: Schocken, 1966, chap. 1.

Humphreys, L. G. Theory of intelligence. In R. Cancro (Ed.), *Intelligence: Genetic and environmental influences.* New York: Grune & Stratton, 1971, pp. 31–42.

Hunt, J. Mc V. *Intelligence and experience.* New York: Ronald Press, 1961.

Hunt, J. Mc V. Has compensatory education failed? Has it been attempted? *Harvard Educational Review,* 1969, *39*, 278–300.

Hunt, J. Mc V. & Kirk, G. E. Social aspects of intelligence: Evidence and issues. In R. Cancro (Ed.), *Intelligence: Genetic and environmental influences.* New York: Grune & Stratton, 1971, pp. 262–306.

Irvine, S. H. Factor analysis of African abilities and attainments: Constructs across cultures. *Psychological Bulletin,* 1969, *71*, 20–32.

Jencks, C. *Inequality.* New York: Basic Books, 1972.

Jensen, A. R. How much can we boost I.Q. and scholastic achievement? *Harvard Educational Review,* 1969, *39*, 1–123.

Kagan, J. S. Inadequate evidence and illogical conclusions. *Harvard Educational Review,* 1969, *39*, 274–277.

Kagan, J., Sontag, L. W., Baker, C. T., & Nelson, V. L. Personality and IQ change. *Journal of Abnormal and Social Psychology,* 1958, *56*, 261–266.

Maccoby, E. E. & Jacklin, Carol N. *The psychology of sex differences.* Stanford, Ca.: Stanford University Press, 1974.

McCall, R. B., Hogarty, P. S., & Hurlburt, N. Transitions in infant sensorimotor development and the prediction of childhood IQ. *American Psychologist,* 1972, *27*, 728–748.

Mussen, P. H., Conger, J. J., & Kagan, J. *Child development and personality.* (4th ed.) New York: Harper & Row, 1974.

O'Bryan, K. G. & MacArthur, R. S. Reversibility, intelligence, and creativity in nine-year-old boys. *Child Development,* 1969, *40*, 33–45.

Peterson, D. R., Becker, W. C., Hellmer, L. A., Shoemaker, D. J., & Quay, H. C. Parental attitudes and child adjustment. *Child Development,* 1959, *30*, 119–130.

Spearman, C. *The abilities of man: Their nature and measurement.* New York: Macmillan, 1927.

Thurstone, L. L. *Primary mental abilities.* Chicago: University of Chicago Press, 1938.

Tuddenham, R. D. A "Piagetian" test of cognitive development. In W. B. Dockrell (Ed.), *On intelligence.* Toronto: Ontario Institute for Studies in Education, 1970, pp. 49–70.

Vernon, P. E. Ability factors and environmental influences. *American Psychologist,* 1965, *20,* 723–733.

Vernon, P. E. *Intelligence and cultural environment.* London: Methuen, 1969.

Vernon, P. E. Intelligence. In W. B. Dockrell (Ed.), *On intelligence.* Toronto: Ontario Institute for Studies in Education, 1970, pp. 99–117.

Yarrow, M. R. Problems of methods in parent–child research. *Child Development,* 1963, *34,* 215–226.

34. ENVIRONMENT, DEVELOPMENT, AND SCHOLASTIC ACHIEVEMENT

J. McVICKER HUNT[1]

It is very interesting, and very exciting for me, to encounter people who are generally considered sensible, planning to utilize pre-school experiences as an antidote for what we are now calling cultural deprivation and social disadvantage. The group at the Child Welfare Research Station in Iowa, under George D. Stoddard (see Stoddard and Wellman, 1940), described effects of nursery school which they considered evidence that would justify just such a use of nursery schools. This was over twenty-five years ago. Their work, however, was picked to pieces by critics and in the process lost much of the suggestive value it was justified in having. Many of you will recall the ridicule that was heaped upon the "wandering IQ" (Simpson, 1939) and the way in which such people as Florence Goodenough (1939) derided in print the idea of a group of thirteen "feeble-minded" infants being brought within the range of normal mentality through training by moron nurse-maids in an institution for the feeble-minded (referring to the work of Skeels and Dye, 1939, to which we shall return). The

fact that just such a use of preschool experience is now being seriously planned by sensible people with widespread approval means that something has changed.

The change, of course, is not in the nature of man or in the nature of his development; it is rather in our conceptions of man's nature and of his development. Some of our most important beliefs about man and his development have changed or are in the process of changing. It is these changes in belief which have freed us to try as demonstrative experiments that only as recently as World War II would have been considered a stupid waste of effort and time. It is also these changes in theoretical belief about man and his development which provide my topic, namely, the psychological basis for using preschool enrichment as an antidote for cultural deprivation.

I number these changed or changing beliefs as six. Let me state them in their prechange form; in the form, in other words, that has so much hampered the sort of enterprise in which this group is about to engage:

1. a belief in fixed intelligence;

2. a belief in predetermined development;

3. a belief in the fixed and static, telephone-switchboard nature of brain function;

4. a belief that experience during the early years, and particularly before the development of speech, is unimportant;

5. a belief that whatever experience does affect later development is a matter of emotional reactions based on the fate of instinctual needs;

[1]The paper was originally prepared for the Arden House Conference on Pre-School Enrichment of Socially Disadvantaged Children (December 1962) with the support of USPHS Grant No. MH K6–18,567. The author also wishes to acknowledge grants from the Carnegie Foundation, The Commonwealth Fund, and the Russell Sage Foundation.

This is a revised version of a paper originally published in the *Merrill-Palmer Quarterly of Behavior and Development* and is published here with their permission, and the author's. This revised version originally appeared in M. Deutsch, I. Katz and A. R. Jensen (Eds.). *Social class, race, and psychological development.* New York: Holt, Rinehart & Winston, 1968, 293–330.

6. a belief that learning must be motivated by homeostatic need, by painful stimulation, or by acquired drives based on these.

Let me discuss the evidential and conceptual bases for the change which has been taking place since World War II in these hampering beliefs, one by one. Then I shall close by trying to justify the sort of enterprise you propose, and by indicating how the largely forgotten work of Maria Montessori may well contain practical suggestions concerning the way to go about the enterprise.

The Belief in Fixed Intelligence

Almost every idea has roots in a communicated conceptual history and in observed evidence. The notion of fixed intelligence has conceptual roots in Darwin's (1859) theory of evolution and in the intense emotional controversy that surrounded it. You will recall that Darwin believed that evolution took place, not by changes wrought through use or disuse as Lamarck (1809) had thought, but by changes resulting from variations in the progeny of every species or strain which are then selected by the conditions under which they live. Their selection is a matter of which variations survive to reproduce so that the variations are passed on into the successive generations. The change is conceived thus to be one that comes via the survival of a variation in a strain through reproduction. Implicit in this notion was the assumption that the characteristics of any organism are predetermined by the genetic constitution with which the organism comes into being as a fertilized ovum. Probably this implicit assumption would never have caught on with anywhere near the force it did, had it not been for two outstanding figures in the history of relatively recent thought. The first of these is Sir Francis Galton, Charles Darwin's younger cousin. You will remember that it was Galton who made the assumption of the hereditary determination of adult characteristics explicit. Galton reasoned, furthermore, that if his cousin were correct, it would mean that the hope of improving the lot of man does not lie in

euthenics, or in trying to change him through education; rather, such hope lies in *eugenics,* or in the selection of those superior persons who should survive. Second, he saw that if decisions were to be made as to which human beings were to survive and reproduce, it would be necessary to have some criteria for survival. So he founded his anthropometric laboratory for the measurement of man, with the hope that by means of tests he could determine those individuals who should survive. Note that he was not deciding merely who should be selected for jobs in a given industry, but who should survive to reproduce. This was his concern. Because of the abhorrence which such a plan met, Galton talked and wrote relatively little about it. However, the combination of the context of his life's work with the few remarks he did make on the subject gives these remarks convincing significance (see Hunt, 1961).

Galton had a pupil who was very influential in bringing such conceptions into the stream of American thought. This was J. McKeen Cattell, who brought Galton's tests to America and, beginning in 1890, gave them to college students, first at the University of Pennsylvania and then at Columbia University. Because Cattell was also an influential teacher at both Penn and Columbia, his influence spread through the many students he had before World War I—when his sympathies with Germany led to a painful separation from Columbia.

A second psychologist who was almost equally influential in bringing the stream of thought supporting fixed intelligence into American thought is G. Stanley Hall. Hall did not personally know Galton; neither did he personally know Darwin, but he read about evolution while still a college student, and, as he has written in his autobiography, "it struck me like a light; this was the thing for me." Hall's importance lies in that he communicated a strong attachment to the notion of fixed intelligence to his students at Clark University, of which he was the first President, and these students became leaders of the new psychology in America (see Boring, 1929, p. 534). Among them were three of the most illustrious leaders of the testing movement. One was Henry H.

Goddard, who first translated the Binet tests into English for use at the Vineland Training School and also wrote the story of the Kallikak family (1912). Another was F. Kuhlmann, who was also an early translator and reviser of the Binet tests and who, with Rose G. Anderson, adapted them for use with preschool children. The third was Lewis Terman, who is the author of the Stanford-Binet revision, the most widely known version of the Binet tests in America. These three communicated their faith in fixed intelligence to a major share of those who spread the testing movement in America.

So much for the conceptual roots of the belief in fixed intelligence that come by way of communication in the history of thought.

The assumption of fixed intelligence also had an empirical basis. Not only did test-retest reliabilities show that the positions of individuals in a group remained fairly constant, but also the tests showed some capacity to predict such criterion performances as school success, success as officers in World War I, and so on. All such evidence concerned children of school age for whom the experience to which they are exposed is at least to some degree standardized (see Hunt, 1961). When investigators began to examine the constancy of the developmental quotient (DQ) or IQ in preschool children, the degree of constancy proved to be very much lower. You will recall some of the very interesting interpretations of this lack of constancy in the preschool DQ (see Hunt, 1961, p. 311ff). Anderson argued that since the tests at successive ages involved different functions, constancy could not be expected. But an epigenesis of man's intellectual functions is inherent in the nature of his development, and the implications of this fact were apparently missed by these critics of the findings from the infant tests. While they knew that the basic structure of intelligence changes in its early phases of development just as the structures of the body change in the embryological phase of morphological development, they appear not to have noted that it is thus inevitable that the infant tests must involve differing content and functions at successive ages.

It was Woodworth (1941) who argued, after examining the evidence from the studies of twins, that there might be some difference in IQ due to the environment but that which exists among individuals in our culture is largely due to the genes. In the context of cultural deprivation, I believe Woodworth asked the wrong question. He might better have asked: What would be the difference in the IQ of a pair of identical twins at age six if one were reared as Myrtle McGraw (1935) reared the trained twin, Johnny (so that he was swimming at four months, roller-skating at eleven months, and developing various such skills at about one-half to one-fourth the age that people usually develop them), and if the other twin were reared in an orphanage, like the one described by Wayne Dennis (1960) in Teheran, where 60 percent of the infants two years of age are still not sitting up alone, and where 85 percent of those four years of age are still not walking alone? While observations of this kind come from varied sources and lack the force of controlled experimentation, they suggest strongly that lack of constancy is the rule for either IQ or DQ during the preschool years and that the IQ is not at all fixed unless the culture or the school fixes the program of environmental encounters. Cross-sectional validity may be substantial, with predictive validity being little above zero (see Hunt, 1961). In fact, trying to predict what the IQ of an individual child will be at age eighteen from a DQ obtained during the first or second year is much like trying to predict how fast a feather might fall in a hurricane. The law of falling bodies holds only under the specified and controlled conditions of a vacuum. Similarly, any laws concerning the rate of intellectual growth must take into account the series of environmental encounters which constitute the conditions of that growth.

The Belief in Predetermined Development

The belief in predetermined development has been no less hampering, for a serious consideration of preschool enrichment as an antidote for cultural deprivation than that in fixed intelligence. This belief also has historical roots in Darwin's theory of evolution. It got communicated into the main stream of psychological thought about development by G. Stanley Hall (see Pruette, 1926). Hall gave special emphasis to the belief in predetermined development by making central in his version of the theory of evolution the conception of recapitulation. This is the notion that the development of an individual shows in summary form the development of the species. Hall managed to communicate many valuable points about psychological development by means of his parables based on the concept of biological recapitulation. One of the most famous of these is his parable of the tadpole's tail. To Hall also goes a very large share of the responsibility for the shape of investigation in child and developmental psychology during the first half of this century. This shape was the study of normative development, or the description of what is typical or average. It was, moreover, as you all know, Arnold Gesell (see 1945, 1954), another student of G. Stanley Hall, whose life's work concerned the normative description of children's behavioral development. Gesell took over Hall's faith in predetermined development in his own notion that development is governed by what he has termed "intrinsic growth." It should be noted that once one believes in intrinsic growth, the normative picture of development is not only a description of the process but an explanation of it as well. Thus, whenever little Johnny does something "bad," the behavior can be explained by noting that it is just a stage he is going through. Moreover, following Hall's parable of the tadpole's tail—in which the hind legs fail to develop if the tail is amputated—Johnny's unwanted behavior must not be hampered else some desirable future characteristic will fail to appear.

This notion of predetermined development also has an empirical basis, for the evidence from various early studies of behavioral development in both lower animals and children was readily seen as consonant with it. Among these are Coghill's (1929) studies of behavioral development in amblystoma. These demonstrated that behavioral development, like anatomical development, starts at the head-end and proceeds tailward, starts from the inside and proceeds outward, and consists of a progressive differentiation of more specific units from general units. From such evidence Coghill and others inferred the special additional notion that behavior unfolds automatically as the anatomical basis for behavior matures. From such a background came the differentiation of the process of learning from the process of maturation.

Among the early studies of behavioral development are those of Carmichael (1926, 1927, 1928), also with amblystoma and frogs, which appeared to show that the circumstances in which development takes place are of little consequence. You will recall that Carmichael divided batches of amblystoma and frog eggs. One of these batches he chloretoned to inhibit their activity; another batch he kept in tap water on an ordinary table; and a third group he kept in tap water on a work bench, where they received extra stimulation. Those kept in tap water on an ordinary table swam as early as did those that got the extra stimulation from the work bench. Moreover, even though those that were chloretoned had been prevented from activity through five days, they appeared to be as adept at swimming within a half an hour after the chloretone was washed out as were either of the two batches reared in tap water. Although Carmichael himself was very careful in interpreting these results, they have commonly been interpreted to mean that development is almost entirely a function of maturation and that learning, as represented in practice, is of little consequence.

Such an interpretation got further support from early studies of the effects of practice. In one such study of a pair of identical twins by Gesell and Thompson (1929), the untrained twin became as adept at tower-building and stair-climbing after a week of practice as was the trained twin who had been given practice in tower-building and stair-climbing over many weeks. In another such study by Josephine Hilgard (1932), a group of ten preschool children were given practice cutting with scissors, climbing a ladder, and buttoning over a period of twelve weeks; yet they retained their superiority over the control group, which had received no special practice, for only a very short time. One week of practice in those skills by the control group brought their performance up to a level which was no longer significantly inferior to that of the experimental group from a statistical standpoint. Later work by two other investigators appeared to lend further support. Dennis and Dennis (1940) found that the children of Hopi Indians raised on cradleboards, which inhibited the movements of their legs and arms during waking hours, walked at the same age as did Hopi children reared freely, in the typical white-man's manner. Moreover, Dennis and Dennis (1935, 1938, 1941) found the usual sequence of autogenic behavior items in a pair of fraternal twins reared under conditions of "restricted practice and minimal social stimulation." Many such studies appeared to yield results which could be readily seen as consonant with the notion that practice has little effect on the rate of development, and that the amount of effect to be got from practice is a function of the level of maturation present when the practice occurs.

It was just such a notion and just such evidence that led Watson (1928) to argue in his book, *The Psychological Care of the Infant and Child,* that experience is unimportant during the preschool years because nothing useful can be learned until the child has matured sufficiently. Thus, he advised that the best thing possible is to leave the child alone to grow. Then, when the child has "lain and grown," when the response repertoire has properly matured, those in charge of his care can introduce learning. He conceived that learning could "get in its licks" tying these responses to proper stimuli, via the conditioning principle, and by linking them together in chains to produce complex skills. I suspect that the use of B. F. Skinner's baby-box, with controlled temperature, humidity, and so on, may be based upon just such assumptions of predetermined development and of an automatic unfolding of a basic behavioral repertoire with anatomical maturation.

It should be noted that the animal evidence cited here comes from amblystoma and frogs, which are well down the phylogenetic scale. They have brains in which the ratio of those portions concerned with association or intrinsic processes to the portions concerned directly with input and output is small; that is, the A/S ratio, as formulated by Hebb (1949), is small. When organisms with higher A/S ratios were studied, in somewhat the fashion in which Coghill and Carmichael studied the behavioral development of amblystoma and frogs, the evidence yielded was highly dissonant with the implications of predetermined development. When Cruze (1935, 1938) found that the number of pecking errors per twenty-five trials decreased through the first five days, even though the chicks were kept in the dark— a result consonant with the notion of predeterminism—he also found facts pointing in a contrary direction. For instance, chicks kept in the dark for twenty consecutive days, and given an opportunity to see light and have pecking-experience only during the daily tests, *failed* to attain a high level of accuracy in pecking and exhibited almost no improvement in the striking-seizing-swallowing sequence.

Similarly, Kuo's (see Hunt, 1961) wonderful behavioral observations on the embryological development of chicks in the egg indicate that the responses comprising the pecking and locomotor patterns have been "well-practiced" long before hatching. The "practice" for pecking seems to start with head-bobbing, which is among the first embryonic movements to be observed. The practice for the locomotor patterns begins with vibratory motions of the wing-buds and leg-buds; these movements become flexion and extension as the limbs lengthen and joints appear. At about the eleventh day of incubation, the yolk sac characteristically moves over to the ventral side of the embryo. This movement of the yolk sac forces the legs to fold on the breast and to be held there. From this point on, the legs cannot be fully extended. They are forced henceforth to hatching to remain in this folded position with extensive thrusts only against the yolk sac. Kuo argues that this condition establishes a fixed resting posture for the legs, and prepares them for lifting of the chick's body in standing and locomotion. Moreover, his interpretation gets some support from "an experiment of nature." In the 7000 embryos that he observed, nearly two hundred crippled chicks appeared. These crippled chicks could neither stand nor walk after hatching. Neither could they sit in the roosting position, because their legs were deformed. Over 80 percent of those with deformed legs occurred in those instances in which the yolk sac failed for some reason, still unknown, to move over to the ventral side of the embryo.

Such observations suggest that the mammalian advent of increasingly long uterine control of embryological and fetal environment in phylogeny reflects the fact that environmental circumstances more and more become important for early development, as the central nervous system control becomes more predominant. It should be noted, moreover, that as central-nervous-system control becomes more predominant, capacity for regeneration decreases. Perhaps this implies a waning of the relative potency of the chemical predeterminers of development as one goes up the phylogenetic scale.

Perhaps even more exciting in this connection is the work of Austin Riesen (see 1958), Brattgård (1952), and others. Riesen undertook the rearing of chimpanzees in darkness in order to test some of Hebb's (1949) hypotheses of the importance of primary learning in the development of perception. What he appears to have discovered—along with Brattgård (1952); Liberman (1962); Rasch et al. (1961); and Weiskrantz (1958)—is that even certain anatomical structures of the retina require light stimulation for proper development. The chimpanzee babies who were kept in the dark for a year and a half have atypical retinas; and, even after they are brought into the light, the subsequent development of their retinas goes awry and they become permanently blind. The result of such prolonged stimulus deprivation during infancy appears to be an irreversible process that does not occur when the chimpanzee infant is kept in darkness for only something like seven months. Inasmuch as Weiskrantz (1958) has found a scarcity of Müller fibers in the retinas of kittens reared in the dark, and

since other investigators (especially Brattgård, 1952) have found the retinal-ganglion cells of animals reared in the dark to be deficient in the production of ribonucleic acid (RNA), these studies of rearing under conditions of sensory deprivation appear to be lending support to Hydén's (1959, 1960) hypothesis that the effects of experience may be stored as RNA within the glial component of retinal tissue, of Dieter's nucleus (Hydén and Pigon, 1960) and, perhaps, of brain tissue as well.

For our present purposes, it is enough to note that such studies are bringing evidence that even the anatomical structures of the central nervous system are affected in their development by encounters with circumstances. This lends credence to Piaget's (1936) aphorism that "use is the aliment of a schema."

Consider another study of the effects of early experience. This is a study by Thompson and Heron (1954), comparing the adult problem-solving ability of Scotty pups which were reared as pets in human homes from the time of weaning until they were eight months of age with that of their litter-mates reared in isolation in laboratory cages for the same period. The adult tests were made when the animals were eighteen months old, after they had been together in the dog pasture for a period of ten months. Adult problem-solving was measured by means of the Hebb-Williams (1946) test of animal intelligence. In one of these tests, the dog is brought into a room while hungry. After being allowed to smell and see a bowl of food, the dog is permitted to watch as his food is removed and put behind a screen in one of the opposite corners of the room. Both pet-reared and cage-reared dogs go immediately to the spot where the food disappeared. After the same procedure has been repeated several times, the food is then placed, while the animal watches, behind a screen in another opposite corner of the room. In order to see this clearly, think of the first screen being in the corner to the dog's right, the second in the corner to the dog's left. Now, when the dog is released, if he is pet-reared he goes immediately to the screen in the left corner for food. But, if he was cage-reared, he is more likely to go to the screen in the right corner where he had previously found food. In his tests of object permanence, Piaget (1936) describes behavior of children about nine months old resembling that of the cage-reared pups, and of children about fourteen months old resembling that of the pet-reared pups.

It is interesting to compare the results of this study by Thompson and Heron (1954), in which dogs were the subjects, with the results of various studies of the effects of early experiences on adult problem-solving in which rats were subjects (see Hebb, 1947; Gauron and Becker, 1959; Wolf, 1943). Whereas the effects of early experience on the problem-solving of dogs appear to be both large and persistent, they appear to be both less marked and less permanent in the rat. Such a comparison lends further credence to the proposition that the importance of the effects of early experience increases as the associative or intrinsic portions of the cerebrum increase in proportion, as reflected in Hebb's notion of the A/S ratio.

But what about the fact that practice appears to have little or no effect on the development of a skill in young children? How can one square the absence of the effects of practice with the tremendous apathy and retardation commonly to be found in children reared in orphanages? In the case of the orphanage in Teheran reported on by Dennis (1960), the retardation in locomotor function is so great, as I have already noted, that 60 percent of thoese in their second year fail to sit up alone, even though nearly all children ordinarily sit up at ten months of age; and 85 percent of those in their fourth year still fail to walk alone even though children typically walk at about fourteen or fifteen months of age. I believe the two sets of results can be squared by taking into account the epigenesis in the structure of behavior that occurs during the earliest years. The investigators of the effects of practice neglected this epigenesis. They sought the effects of experience only in practice of the function of schema to be observed and measured. The existence of an epigenesis of intellectual function implies that the experiential roots of a given schema will lie in antecedent activities quite different in structure from the schema to be observed and measured. Thus, antecedent practice at tower-building and buttoning may be relatively unimportant for the development of skill in these activities; but an unhampered antecedent opportunity to throw objects and to manipulate them in a variety of situations, and an even earlier opportunity to have seen a variety of sights and to have heard a variety of sounds, may be of tremendous importance in determining both the age at which tower-building and buttoning will occur and the degree of skill that the child will manifest. I shall return to this topic.

Brain Function Conceived as a Static Switchboard

One can not blame Darwin for the conception of brain function as static, like that in a telephone switchboard. The origin of the ferment leading to these conceptions, however, does derive from Darwin's (1872) shift of attention from the evolution of the body to the evolution of mind. This he began in his book, *The Expressions of the Emotions in Man and Animals*. It was thus Darwin who provided the stimulus for what was later to be called *comparative psychology*. The original purpose was to show that there is a gradual transition from the lower animals to man in the various faculties of mind. It was Romanes (1882, 1883) who took up this task in an attempt to show the manner in which intelligence has evolved. Romanes' method was to show through anecdotes that animals are capable of intelligent behavior, albeit at a level of complexity inferior to man's. It was C. Lloyd Morgan (1894) who said that it was reasoning by very loose analogy to impute to dogs, cats, and the like, the same kind of conscious processes and faculties that man can report. It was Morgan who applied Ockham's "razor of parsimony" to the various mental faculties. Then, shortly, Thorndike and Woodworth (1901) knocked out such old-fashioned faculties as memory with their studies showing that such forms of practice as daily memorizing poetry does not improve a person's capacity to memorize other types of material, and that being taught mathematics and Latin does not improve performance on reasoning tests.

It was still obvious, however, that animals do learn and that they do solve problems. Morgan (1894) saw this occurring by a process of trial-

and-error. According to this conception, as Hull (1943) later elaborated it, an organism comes to any given situation with a ready-made hierarchy of responses. When those at the top of the hierarchy fail to achieve satisfaction, they are supposed to be weakened (extinguished). Other responses lower in the hierarchy then take their places and become connected with stimuli from the situation. Or, as Thorndike (1913) put it earlier, new S–R bonds are established. Complex behavior was explained by assuming that one response can be the stimulus for another, so that S–R chains could be formed. The role of the brain in such learning also needed explanation. Here the telephone was the dramatic new invention supplying a mechanical model for a conception of the brain's role. Inasmuch as the reflex arc was conceived to be both the anatomical and the functional unit of the nervous system, the role of the brain in learning could readily be conceived to be analogous to that of a telephone switchboard. Thus, the head was emptied of active functions, and the brain, which filled it, came to be viewed as the focus of a variety of static connections.

All this led to what I think is a basic confusion in psychological thought, one which has been prominent for at least the last thirty-five or forty years. This is a confusion between S–R methodology, on the one hand, and S–R theory on the other. We cannot escape S–R methodology. The best one can possibly do empirically is to note the situations in which organisms behave and to observe what they do there. But there is no reason why one should not relate the empirical relationships one can observe between stimulus and response to whatever the neurophysiologist can tell us about inner-brain function and to whatever the endocrinologist can tell us. The broader one makes his nomological net, the better, in that the more nearly his resulting conceptions will approach those of the imaginary, all-seeing eye of Deity.

Stimulus-Response (S–R) methodology appeared at first to imply the notion of the empty organism. It is interesting to recall, however, that very shortly after the mental faculties had been removed by C. Lloyd Morgan with Ockham's razor of parsimony, Walter

Hunter (1912, 1918) discovered that various animals could delay their responses to stimuli and also learn double alternation. Both achievements implied that there must be some kind of representative or symbolic process intervening between stimulus and response. It was to explain just such behavior, moreover, that Hull (1931) promulgated the notion of the pure-stimulus act. This became in turn the response-produced cues and the response-produced drives of Miller and Dollard. When Miller and Dollard (1941, p. 59) began conceiving of the responses which serve as stimuli accurring within the brain, traditional S–R theory with its implicit peripherality of both stimulus and response began to fade. The demise of peripheral S–R theory became nearly complete when Osgood (1953) turned these response-produced cues and drives into central mediating processes. It is interesting to note in this connection that it is precisely observations from S–R methodology which have undone traditional peripheral S–R theory, and it is these observations which are now demanding that brain function be conceived in terms of active processes.

The theoretical need for active brain processes, however, has been stimulated by and has gotten much of its form from cybernetics (Wiener, 1948). Such investigators as Newell et al. (1958), in the process of programming computers to solve problems, and especially logical problems, have been clarifying the general nature of what is required for solving such problems. They have described three major kinds of requirements: (1) memories or information stored somewhere, and presumably in the brain; (2) operations of a logical sort which are of the order of actions that deal with the information in the memories; and (3) hierarchical arrangements of these operations and memories in programs. Thus, the electronic computer has been replacing the telephone switchboard as the mechanical model for brain function.

Such a notion of memories and, even more, the notion of operations of a logical sort as actions, and the notion of hierarchical arrangements of these operations—these notions differ markedly from the notion of reflexes being chained to each other. Moreover, ablation studies have been showing that it is not communication across the cortex from sensory-input regions to motor-output regions that is important for behavior. The cortex can be diced into very small parts without serious damage to behavioral function; but if the fibers, composed of white matter, under an area of the gray-matter cortex are cut, behavior is damaged seriously. Thus, the notion of transcortical association gives way to communication back-and-forth from the center to the periphery of the brain (see Pribram, 1960). With such changes in conception of brain function being dictated by their own observations, when neuropychologists become familiar with what is required in programming computers to solve logical problems, it is not surprising that they ask themselves where one might find a locus for the various requirements of computer function—that is, for the memories, the operations, and the hierarchical arrangements of them. Carl Pribram (1960) has reviewed the clinical and experimental findings concerning the functional consequences of injuring various portions of the brain, and he has come up with a provisional answer. The brain appears to be divided into intrinsic portions and extrinsic portions. This is the terminology of Rose and Woolsey (1949), and here the term *intrinsic* is used because this portion has no direct connections with either incoming sensory fibers or outgoing motor fibers. The extrinsic portion is so called because it does have such direct peripheral connections. What Pribram suggests is that these components of what is required for the various kinds of information processing and of decision-making may well reside in these intrinsic portions of the brain.

There are two intrinsic portions: One is the frontal portion of the cortex, with its connections to the dorsal frontal nuclei of the thalamus; the other, the nonsensory portions of the parietal, occipital, and temporal lobes with their connections with the pulvenar or the posterior dorsal nucleus of the thalamus. Injury to the frontal system disrupts executive functions and thereby suggests that it is the locus of the central, neural mechanism for plans. Injury to the posterior intrinsic system results in damage to recognitive functions, which suggests that it may be the locus of central, neural mechanisms for information-processing per se. The intrinsic portions of the cerebrum appear to become relatively larger and larger as one samples organisms up the phylogenetic scale. Perhaps what Hebb (1949) has called the A/S ratio might better be called the I/E ratio—for "Intrinsic/Extrinsic."

From such studies, one can readily conceive the function of early experience to be one of "programming" these intrinsic portions of the cerebrum so that they can later function effectively in the forms of learning and problem-solving traditionally investigated.

Preverbal Experience Unimportant

Early experience, particularly preverbal experience, however, has historically been considered to be relatively unimportant. It has been argued that such experience can hardly have any effect on adult behavior, because it is not remembered. There have been, of course, a few relatively isolated thinkers who have given at least lip-service to the importance of early experience in the development of the personality.[2] Plato is one who thought that the rearing and education of children was too important a function to be carried out by mere amateur parents. But when he described the rearing that children should have in his *Republic,* he described only experiences for youngsters already talking. Rousseau (1762) gave somewhat more than lip-service in *Emile* to the importance of early experience. Moreover, at least implicitly, he attributed importance to preverbal experience with his prescription that the child, Emile, should very early be exposed to pain and cold in order that he might be toughened.

An even earlier example is to me somewhat embarrassing. I thought that I had invented the

[2]When this was written, I was unfamiliar with Book VII of *The Laws.* There Plato concerns himself with not only preverbal experience but also prenatal experience. I am indebted to Richard Kobler, the engineer who invented the "talking typewriter" in collaboration with O. K. Moore, for calling these pages of *The Laws* to my attention.

notion of split-litter technique for determining the effects of infant feeding-frustration in rats—but later I found, in reading Plutarch's *Lives*, that Lycurgus, the Law-Giver of the Spartans, took puppies from the same litter and reared them in diverse ways, so that some became greedy and mischievous curs while others became followers of the scent and hunters. He exhibited these pups before his contemporaries, saying, "Men of Sparta, of a truth, habit and training and teaching and guidance in living are a great influence toward engendering excellence, and I will make this evident to you at once." Thereupon he produced the dogs with diverse rearing. Perhaps it is from the stories of the Spartans that Rousseau got his notion that Emile should be toughened. Such followers of Rousseau as Pestalozzi and Froebel certainly saw childhood experience as important, but as educators they were concerned with the experiences of children who had already learned to verbalize. So far as I can tell, the notion that preverbal experience is seriously important for adult personal characteristics comes from Freud (1905) and his theory of psychosexual development.

Unimportance of Psychosexual Development

Freud not only attributed importance to preverbal experience; he also proposed a hypothesis concerning the nature of the kinds of experience important for later development. These were the experiences deriving from the fate of instinctive impulses arising out of homeostatic need, painful stimulation, and, especially, the pleasure-striving which he saw as sexual in nature (Freud, 1905). If one examines the objective studies of the effects of the various kinds of factors deemed to be important from the standpoint of their theory of psychosexual development, one has a very hard time finding clear evidence that they are important (see Hunt, 1945, 1956; Orlansky, 1949). For every study that appears to show an effect of some given psychosexual factor in early infancy, there is another study to be matched with it that fails to show an effect. Furthermore, the more carefully the various studies appear to be controlled, the more nearly the results tend to be consonant with the null hypothesis. The upshot of all this is that it looks very much as if the kinds of factors to which Freud attributed importance in his theory of psychosexual development are not very important.

It was commonly believed before World War II that early experience was important for emotional development and for the development of personality characteristics, but unimportant for the development of intellect or intelligence. Some of the animal studies of early experience were widely quoted to support this belief. One of these was my own study of the effects of infant feeding-frustration upon adult hoarding in rats (Hunt, 1941). Actually, the effects of the infantile feeding-frustration were exhibited in both eating rate and hoarding, and exhibited in the eating rate more regularly than in the hoarding. Rats do not always hoard as a consequence of infantile feeding-frustration, although they do regularly eat faster than litter-mates without such experience. Yet, the feeding or drinking frustration need not occur in infancy to get the effect of speeded eating or speeded drinking (Freedman, 1957). In the case of the work of my colleagues and myself, much of it still unpublished, various kinds of effects that should, theoretically, have followed did not occur. The upshot of all this, I now believe, is that our theoretical expectations were wrong. I also believe that the general notion that the emotional characteristics of persons are most influenced by early experience while the intellectual characteristics are not influenced is also quite wrong.

Importance of Preverbal Experience for Intellect

I am prompted to change my belief because the approach to the study of the effects of early experience suggested by Donald Hebb's theorizing about cerebral functioning has regularly yielded results confirming his hypothesis. According to Hebb's (1949) theory, firing systems, which he terms *cell assemblies* and *phase sequences,* must be built into the cerebrum through what he has termed *primary learning.* This may be seen as another way of expressing the idea that the intrinsic regions of the cerebrum must be properly programmed by preverbal experience if the mammalian organism is later to function effectively as a problem-solver. Most of this primary learning Hebb (1949) presumed, moreover, to be based upon early perceptual experience. It is in this presumption that he broke most radically with the traditional emphasis on the response side in learning (a point to which I shall return).

It was this conception which led Hebb (1947) early to compare the problem-solving ability in adulthood of those rats which had their perceptual experience limited by cage-rearing, with that of rats which had had their perceptual experience enriched by pet-rearing. As I have already noted in connection with my comments on the notion of predetermined development, the problem-solving ability of the cage-reared rats was inferior to that of the pet-reared rats. The theory, as encouraged by these exploratory results, led then to a series of studies in which various kinds of early perceptual experiences were provided for one sample of rats and not for an otherwise comparable sample. Thus, the difference between the groups in later problem-solving, or maze-learning provided an index of both the presence and the degree of effect. Such studies have regularly yielded substantial effects for various kinds of early perceptual experience. These studies, moreover, appear to be clearly reproducible (Hunt and Luria, 1956). Furthermore, as I have already noted in connection with my remarks on predetermined development, these effects of early perceptual experience on adult problem-solving appear to become more and more marked up the phylogenetic scale as the intrinsic portions come to constitute a higher and higher proportion of the cerebrum. It looks now as though early experience may be even more important for the perceptual, cognitive and intellective functions than it is for the emotional and temperamental functions.

Change in the Conception of Trauma

The investigations of the effects of early experience in animals appear to be calling for still further changes in our conception of the nature of the most important kinds of early experience. Freud (1900, 1915, 1926) had various theories of anxiety. But in his later theorizing about it he not only relied upon the notion of association but also conceived of painful stimulation, either through excessive homeostatic need or an overflow of excitement, as a basis for trauma. He also presumed that organisms which had experienced high levels of such traumatic excitement during infancy were made more prone to be anxious and neurotic later in life.

With the goal of demonstrating just such effects, Levine *et al.* (1956) undertook the experiment in which they shocked rats daily for two minutes, keeping them squealing frantically throughout this period, on each of the first twenty days of their lives. A second sample of rats were picked up and brought to the grid-box, where they were put down without being shocked. Those of a third group were left unmolested in the maternal nest. One of the adult tests (at sixty days of age) involved defecation and urination in an unfamiliar situation. This is the test of so-called emotionality invented by Hall (1934). Those animals that had been shocked during infancy did not defecate and urinate more than those handled or than those left unmolested in the nest, as would be expected from trauma theory. On the contrary, the shocked animals defecated less on the average. The difference in this experiment fell short of statistical significance; but various subsequent experiments by both Levine and Denenberg (see Denenberg, 1962) yielded results showing that rats shocked in infancy defecated and urinated significantly less than those left unmolested in the maternal nest. Levine, Chevalier, and Korchin (1956) also found that the animals shocked in infancy, and the animals handled in infancy, both learned to avoid shock, by learning to respond to a signal before the onset of shock, in fewer trials than did those animals which had remained un-molested in the maternal nest. Confirming re-sults have been obtained by Denenberg (1962).

Other evidence has come from the work of my own students. Goldman (1963) has shown that the intensity of shock required to move a rat over a barrier, from one end of a runway to the other end, is greater for rats that have been shocked during their preweaninng stage of infancy than it is for those which have been left unmolested in the warm maternal nest. Salama (Salama and Hunt, 1964) has repeated the Farber (1948) study, in which rats shocked just past the choice point in a T-maze became "rigid" about giving up the place where they had got food, even after food had ceased to appear there. Salama compared the number of trials required to bring about such a shift in goal-box by animals shocked in infancy, by animals merely picked up in infancy, by ani-mals petted in infancy, and by animals left unmolested in the maternal nest. While animals shocked in infancy require more trials (nine, on the average) to make the shift from the "fixated" arm and goal-box to the other arm of the T-maze than do animals which have not been shocked at the choice point (an average of 2.8 trials), they require substantially fewer than do animals handled or left unmolested in the maternal nest before weaning (an average of 20.7) or than do those petted (an average of 21.4 trials). Thus, the experience of having been shocked regularly before weaning appears actually to diminish the capacity of shock either to motivate behavior or to fixate a response.

Such evidence appears to call for a revision of the trauma theory. I find this evidence from animal studies especially interesting, moreover, because there is a study of human children with results which are consonant. This is a study by Holmes (1935) in which fear scores for children of a day-care center proved to be much lower than those for children of a nursery school. These results have seldom been cited in the secondary literature, perhaps because they were troublesomely dissonant with the dominant theoretical expectations. The dominant ex-pectation would be that the opposite should

have prevailed, because the children of day-care centers came from the lower class where painful experience and hunger (that is, traumatizing experiences) were common; whereas the chil-dren of the nursery schools came from the upper class where such presumably traumatizing experiences are relatively rare. I believe this is an item of evidence from human subjects to indicate that children, as well as infant animals, who have been through a great many painful circumstances are not as fearful in strange or unfamiliar situations as are children who have not experienced such painful circumstances. This evidence lends support to the recom-mendations that Rousseau made for Emile, and it helps to clarify how the Spartan culture could have survived for something like five hundred years even though it practiced what has sometimes been seen as "infant torture."

It now looks as if there may be two quite different kinds of effect of early infantile ex-perience. One is that just described, in which the effect of painful experience is one of reduc-ing the aversiveness of later painful or strange circumstances. Although the evidence is not clear yet, that from Salama's experiment in-dicates that such other kinds of early experience as mere picking up or petting do not have this effect. The other kind of effect is one increasing the capacity of an organism to learn. I have already mentioned that both the shocked rats and the handled rats in the study by Levine et al. (1956) learned to respond to a signal to avoid shock more rapidly than did the rats that remained unmolested in the maternal nest. This is adaptive. Denenberg (see 1962) has shown that even shocking animals once on the second day of life will decrease the number of trials they require to learn an avoidance response, as compared with those left unmolested in the maternal nest. This kind of effect appears to result not only from shock during the preweap-ing phase of development but also from han-dling and petting. It looks very much as if any increase in the variation of circumstances encountered during those first three weeks of life will facilitate later learning, not only in the avoidance situation but also in such problem-solving situations as those to be found in the Hebb-Williams (1946) tests of animal intelligence.

Change in Conception of the Relative Importance of the Sensory and the Motor

Yet another belief about what is important in early experience appears to need correction. G. Stanley Hall was fond of the aphorism that "the mind of man is handmade" (Pruette, 1926). Watson (1919) and the other behaviorists have believed that it is the motor side, rather than the sensory side, that is important in learning. Dewey (1902) gave emphasis to the motor side also in his belief that the child learns chiefly by doing. Dewey went even further to emphasize that the things that the child should be encouraged to do are the things that he would later be called upon to do in taking his place in society. More recently, Osgood (1952) has conceived that the central processes which mediate meanings are the residues of past responses. I am simply trying to document my assertion that in the dominant theory of the origin of mind or of central mediating processes, these have been conceived to be based upon the residues from past responses.

Hebb's (1949) theorizing, as I have already noted, took sharp issue with this dominant theoretical position. He has conceived the basis for primary learning to be chiefly on the sensory side. Riesen (1958) began his experiments on the effects of rearing chimpanzees in darkness with what he called *S–S*, or Stimulus-Stimulus relations. Piaget (1936), although he has emphasized "activity as the aliment of a schema," has conceived of *looking* and *listening*, both of which are typically viewed as sensory input channels, as existing among the schemata ready-made at birth. Moreover, it is looking and listening to which he attributes key importance during the first phases of intellectual development. This emphasis is registered in his aphorism that "the more a child has seen and heard, the more he wants to see and hear" (Piaget, 1936, p. 276).

Evidence requiring this correction of belief comes from more than just the studies of the effects of early perceptual experience on the later problem-solving capacity of animals. It also comes from comparing the effects of the cradling practice on the age of onset of walking in Hopi children, with the effects of the homogeneous auditory and visual stimulation on the age of onset of walking in the children in a Teheran orphanage. The cradling practice inhibits actions of an infant's legs and arms during his walking hours through most of the first year of his life. Yet, the mean and standard deviation of the age of walking for those cradled proved to be the same as that for those Hopi children reared with free use of their legs and arms (Dennis and Dennis, 1940). Contrariwise, 85 percent of the children in the Teheran orphanage were still not walking alone in their fourth year—and here the factor in which the circumstances of these children most differ from those of most young infants was probably the continuous homogeneity of auditory and visual experience (Dennis, 1960). The children of the Teheran orphanage had full use of the motor function of their legs and arms. The Hopi children reared with the cradling practice did not have free use of their legs and arms—but they were exposed, by virtue of their being carried around on their mothers' backs, to a very rich variety of auditory and visual inputs.

Perhaps this emphasis on the motor side is erroneous only as another example of failure to take into account the epigenesis of behavioral and intellectual functions. While it may be true that education by doing is best for children of kindergarten and primary-school age, it appears that having a variety of things to listen to and look at may be most important for development during the first year of life (see also Fiske and Maddi, 1961).[3]

[3]Since this was written, various lines of evidence have led me to believe my emphasis is wrong here. Variety of changes in input is probably of great importance only during the first two or three months. Thereafter, what appears to be most important is ability to get feedback or reinforcement from self-initiated actions. The apathy and retardation observed in infants reared in orphanages is probably more a matter of failure of the latter than of the former.

All Behavior and All Learning Is Motivated by Painful Stimulation or Homeostatic Need

The fact that both apathy and retardation have been regularly noted in orphanage-reared children who typically live under conditions of homogeneous circumstances (especially marked of the children observed by Dennis in the Teheran orphanage) suggests that homogeneous stimulation somehow reduces motivation. This suggestion brings me to yet another major change of theoretical belief.

It is common to state that "all behavior is motivated." But to make this statement specific, it must be completed with the complex phrase, "by homeostatic need, painful stimulation, or by innocuous stimuli which have previously been associated with these." This has been the dominant conception of motivation for most of the last half-century—dominant because it has been held both by academic behavior theorists (for example, Dashiell, 1928; Freeman, 1934; Guthrie, 1938; Holt, 1931; Hull, 1943; Melton, 1941; Miller and Dollard, 1941; Mowrer, 1960) and by psychoanalysts (for example, Fenichel, 1945; Freud, 1915).

This notion implies that organisms should become quiescent in the absence of painful stimulation, homeostatic need, or the acquired drives based upon them. Since World War II, evidence has accumulated to indicate quite clearly that neither animals nor children actually do become quiescent in the absence of such motivating conditions (see Hunt, 1963a). Bühler (1928) noted earlier that the playful activity of children is most evident in the absence of such motivating conditions, and Beach (1945) has reviewed evidence to show that animals are most likely to show playful activity when they are well-fed, well-watered, and in comfortable circumstances. Harlow *et al.* (1950) have found that monkeys learn to disassemble puzzles with no other motivation than the privilege of disassembling them. Similarly, Harlow (1950) found that two monkeys worked repeatedly at disassembling a six-device puzzle

for ten continuous hours even though they were quite free of painful stimulation and homeostatic need. Moreover, as he notes, at the tenth hour of testing they were still "showing enthusiasm for their work."

In an important series of studies beginning in 1950, Berlyne (see 1960) found that comfortable and satiated rats will explore areas new to them if only given an opportunity, and that the more varied the objects in the region to be explored, the more persistent are the rats' explorations. In a similar vein, Montgomery (1952) has found that the spontaneous tendency for rats to go alternately to the opposite goalboxes in a T- or Y-maze is no matter of fatigue for the most recently given response, as Hull (1943) contended, but it is one of avoiding the place which the animals have most recently experienced. The choice of place is for the one of lesser familiarity (Montgomery, 1953), and rats learn merely in order to get an opportunity to explore an unfamiliar area (Montgomery, 1955; Montgomery and Segall, 1955). In this same vein, Butler (1953) has observed that monkeys will learn discriminations merely to obtain the privilege of peeking through a window in the walls of their cages, or (Butler, 1958) of listening to sounds from a tape recorder. All these activities appear to be most evident in the absence of painful stimulation, homeostatic need, and cues which have previously been associated with such motivating stimuli. It is these findings which call for a change in the traditionally dominant theoretical conception of motivation.

Some of the directions of change in belief show in the modes of theoretical significance given to such evidence. One of these ways is drive-naming. Thus, in recent years, we have been hearing of a manipulatory drive, an exploratory drive, a curiosity drive, and so on. This form of theoretical recognition, which is logically circular, appears to be revisiting McDougall's (1908) theory of instincts.

A second mode of theoretical recognition is naming what appears to be the telic significance of an activity. This is what Ives Hendrick (1943) has done in conceiving of the delight which children take in their newfound accomplishments as evidence of an "urge to mastery." This is also what White (1959) has done in his excellent review of such evidence by attributing the various activities observed to "competence motivation." Such terms of telic significance may be helpful as classificatory and mnemonic devices, but they provide few implications of antecedent consequent relationships to be investigated.

A third mode of theoretical recognition has consisted in postulating *spontaneous activity*. I have been guilty of this (Hunt, 1960) and so also have Hebb (1949), Miller *et al.* (1960), and Taylor (1960). When my good colleague, Lawrence I. O'Kelly, pointed out that the notion of spontaneous activity may be just as malevolently circular as drive- and instinct-naming, however, I could readily see the force of his argument. But I could also see that I had begun to discern at least the outlines of a mechanism of what I have termed "intrinsic motivation" or "motivation inherent in information processing and action" (Hunt, 1963*a*).

Intrinsic Motivation

The outlines of the nature of this mechanism of intrinsic motivation are to be discerned from the evidence which has called for a change in the conception of the functional unit of the nervous system from that of the reflex arc to that of the feedback loop. The concept of the reflex was first formulated by Hall (1843). However, it was developed and popularized by Sherrington (1906), who clearly recognized, in spite of the anatomical evidence for the reflex arc, that the reflex was a logical construct rather than an obvious and palpable reality. It must be noted that the anatomical evidence for the notion of a reflex arc is based on an overgeneralization of the Bell-Magendie Law, which states that the dorsal roots of the spinal nerve are composed entirely of incoming sensory fibers and that the ventral roots are composed entirely of outgoing motor fibers. The statement is untrue. It is clear from recent neurophysiological investigation that the dorsal roots contain motor as well as sensory fibers and

that the ventral roots contain sensory as well as motor fibers (see Hunt, 1963*a*). Illustrative evidence for the first portion of this new statement comes from such observations as the cessation of the firing associated with the onset of a tone or a buzzer in the cochlear nucleus of a cat when the cat is shown a mouse in a bell jar (Hernández-Péon *et al.*, 1956). Evidence for the second portion may be illustrated by the observation that eye-movements can be elicited by electrical stimulation of any portion of the visual receptive area in the occipital lobes of monkeys (Walker and Weaver, 1940). Such evidence makes way and calls for the concept of the feedback loop.

The notion of the feedback loop provides, in turn, the basis for a new answer to the motivational question concerning what starts and stops behavior. So long as the reflex served as the conception of the functional unit of neural function, any given kind of behavior was presumed to be started by the onset of a drive stimulus and to be stopped by its cessation. As the feedback loop takes the place of the reflex, the onset of behavior becomes a matter of incongruity between the input from a set of circumstances and some standard within the organism. Miller *et al.* (1960) have termed this the Test-Operate-Test-Exit (TOTE) unit (see Figure 34–1).

This TOTE unit is, in principle, not unlike the thermostat which controls the temperature of a room. In such a case, the standard is the temperature at which the thermostat is set. When the temperature falls below this standard, the "test" yields an incongruity which sets the furnace into operation (see the arrow connecting the "test" to the "operate"). The furnace continues to operate until the temperature in the room has been raised to the standard. This congruity stops the operation, and this particular motive system can be said to "exit."

One can base a taxonomy of incongruities upon the various kinds of standards existing within organisms. One class of incongruities may be based on the "comfort standard." While no one would have invented the TOTE unit to account for pain avoidance, conceiving

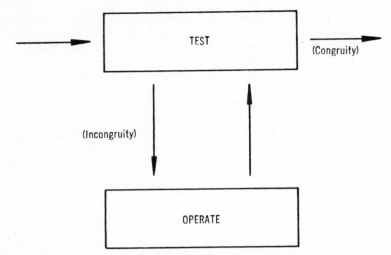

FIGURE 34–1. Diagram of the TOTE unit. After Miller, Galanter, and Pribram (1960, p. 26).

of a "comfort standard" brings the facts of pain avoidance into a consonant relationship with the notion of the TOTE unit. A second class of incongruities may be conceived to be based on what Pribram (1960) has termed the "biased homeostats of the hypothalamus." Organisms have standards, for the most part innately established, for such things as the concentrations of blood-sugar or of sodium ions in the blood stream. When, for instance, the blood-sugar concentration falls below a certain level, the receptors along the third ventricle are activated. At one level of incongruity they serve to release glycogen from the liver; but at a higher level, they prime the receptors to respond to the signs of food, the organism follows them with avid excitement, and the hunger motive is said to be activated. It is not easy to make the sex system consonant with such a scheme.

On the other hand, a variety of standards can develop in the course of an organism's informational interaction with its circumstances. Perhaps the most primitive of such informational standards is the ongoing input of the moment. Whenever there is change from this standard, an organism exhibits what the Russians have termed the "orienting reflex" (see Berlyne, 1960; Razran, 1961). The operation elicited by such incongruity consists of an orientation toward the source of the change in input and arousal, as registered by the classical expressive indicators of emotion or by the electroencephalogram. A second kind of informational incongruity is based upon a standard of expectations, where the expectations are based on information stored in the course of previous encounters with the same object, person, or place. Such systems of expectations as the self-concept appear to take on special importance in motivation. Esthetic standards appear to be another variation of expectations.

Another category of standards appears to be comprised of ends or goals. These are what Miller *et al.* (1960) have termed *plans*. Some plans are tied to painful stimulation or to homeostatic needs, but others are quite independent of these. Piaget (1936) has described how an infant will make holding onto an interesting input, or regaining it, a goal. Typically, inputs have become interesting through repeated encounters by becoming recognizable. It would appear that emerging recognition can make objects, persons, and place attractive. Later it is novelty which is attractive. The full range of the various kinds of standards that emerge in the course of a child's informational interaction with his circumstances during the process of psychological development has never been described. At adolescence, however, an important variety of standards consists of ideals. This kind of standards appears to emerge with the development of what Piaget (1947) has termed "formal operations." With the emergence of these operations, the adolescent can imagine a world more desirable than the one he encounters, and the incongruity between the world observed and the imagined ideal can instigate plans for social reforms. These same formal operations enable the adolescent to formulate "theories" of how various aspects of the world operate, and incongruities between observed realities and these theoretical creations instigate inquiry. Thus, one may view scientific work as but a professionalization of a form of cognitive motivation inherent in the human organism's informational interaction with circumstances.

Incongruity and the Direction-Hedonic Question

The concept of incongruity also provides a tentative, hypothetical answer to the puzzling direction-hedonic question—the question of what it is that determines whether an organism will approach or withdraw from the source of incongruous or novel information (see also Schneirla, 1959). This is also an answer to the hedonic question, because approach presumably indicates a positive hedonic value in the source of stimulation, and withdrawal presumably indicates a negative hedonic value.

The evidence that incongruous or novel information will instigate approach to its source and that it has positive hedonic value derives from several sources. In an early study by Nissen (1930)—which has never got into the textbooks, apparently because it was far too dissonant with the dominant beliefs—it was shown that rats will suffer the pain of electric shocks from a Warden obstruction apparatus in order to get from empty cages into a Dashiell maze filled with novel objects. Once the animals have discovered the fact that such a maze exists at the end of the runway beyond the obstruction apparatus, they will endure the pain of the crossing in order to achieve the oppor-

tunity to explore this "interesting place" and to manipulate the "interesting objects." The behavior of the rats in this study of Nissen's resembles in many ways that of Butler's (1953) monkeys, which would undertake the learning of discriminations in order to peek through the window at students passing in the hall beyond. In fact, most of the evidence cited to show that animals and children do not become quiescent in the absence of homeostatic need and painful stimulation may be arranged to support the notion that a certain degree of incongruity is appealing, and that too little is boring and unappealing.

Perhaps even more convincing are the results from the studies of so-called stimulus deprivation in the McGill laboratory by Bexton *et al.* (1954). You will recall that the McGill students who served as subjects in these experiments were paid $20 a day to lie on a cot in a room with temperature and humidity controlled to provide an optimum of comfort, with translucent glasses on that provided for light to reach the eyes but did not permit pattern vision, with sound variation attenuated as much as possible, and with movement inhibited by the padded cardboard sleeves for arms and legs. Yet they could seldom endure such homogeneous circumstances for longer than two or three days, even for such a liberal monetary reward. The strength of the tendency to withdraw from such homogeneity of circumstances and to approach any source of stimulation that would provide some variety is dramatized by the word-of-mouth story of a student with "highbrow" musical tastes who, several times an hour, pressed a key that brought the playing of a scratchy, well-worn recording of "country music." This makes it look as if it were a case of, to paraphrase the seaman's aphorism, "any port of relative incongruity in a storm of homogeneous circumstances."

Withdrawal from the source of incongruous information also occurs, this when the degree of incongruity between the incoming information and that already stored in the memory from previous experience is too great. Here the evidence comes largely from the work of Hebb (1946). His studies of fear in chimpanzees were designed to call into question Watson's notion that emotional reactions to innocuous stimuli are based upon their having been associated with earlier painful stimulation (see Watson and Rayner, 1920). This traditional conception of fear met with sharply dissonant evidence, when Hebb and Riesen (1943) noted that fear of strangers does not appear in chimpanzee infants reared in the nursery of the Yerkes Primate Laboratory until these infants approach about four months of age. The fact that the histories of these infants were fully recorded made it possible to know with certainty that these strangers had not been associated with previous painful stimulation. Later, Hebb (1946) found that even intense panic reactions could be induced in adult chimpanzees reared in this laboratory merely by showing them the sculptured head of a chimp or human being, or by showing them an anesthetized infant chimpanzee. Such figures were clearly familiar but definitely without previous association with painful or other fearful stimuli. The fact that an infant chimpanzee, which had been a pet, withdrew in fear upon seeing its beloved experimenter-master in a Halloween mask or even in the coat of an equally familiar ''keeper'' suggested that the basis for the fearful withdrawal resided in seeing ''a familiar figure in an unfamiliar guise.'' Thus, the absence of the expected remainder of the body in the case of the sculptured head of a chimpanzee or human being, and the absence of the expected motions and customary postures in the case of the anesthetized infant chimpanzee, provide ''the unfamiliarity of guise''—or the discrepancy between what is expected on the basis of past experience and what is observed, that I am calling incongruity.

Puzzling emotional disturbances in children and pets become readily understandable in these terms. It was, for instance, fear of the dark and fear of solitude in the human child that puzzled Freud (1926) and made him unhappy with even his later theory of anxiety, and it was such behavior in the chimpanzee that puzzled Köhler (1925, p. 251). These can be readily seen as incongruity which results from the presence of unaccustomed receptor inputs or from the absence of accustomed receptor inputs within

any given context. Still other examples are that of the child who becomes disturbed when a familiar nursery rhyme is altered in the reading; that of the pet dog that barks excitedly and whines when he observes his young master walking on his hands; and that of the cat that runs frantically to hide at the sight of his child-mistress being hoisted onto the shoulders of a familiar neighbor. Although Piaget (1936) was without special concern about the point, he noted in his observations that his children showed emotional distress in seeing altered versions of things with which they had become familiar.

The fact that incongruous information can elicit both an approach to its source and a withdrawal from its source may be puzzling until one notes that this implies that there is an optimum of incongruity (see Hunt, 1963a). Hebb (1949) first gave at least implicit recognition to the notion of an optimum of incongruity in his theory of the nature of pleasure. In this theory he noted that organisms tend to be preoccupied with ''what is new but not too new'' in any situation. This suggests that controlling intrinsic motivation is a matter of providing an organism with circumstances that provide a proper level of incongruity—that is, incongruity with the residues of previous encounters with such circumstances that the organism has stored in his memory. This is what I find myself calling ''the problem of the match'' between the incoming information and that already stored (Hunt, 1961, p. 267ff).

Relevant experiments in this area are difficult to find; but one by Dember et al. (1957) is particularly interesting. Incongruity can be a matter of the discrepancy between the level of complexity encountered and the level of complexity with which an organism has become accustomed. The efforts to keep an optimum of incongruity, or discrepancy and complexity, provides a kind of explanation for the sort of ''growth motivation'' which Froebel (1826) postulated and which Dewey (1900) later appears to have borrowed from Froebel. What Dember et al. (1957) did in their experiment was to present rats placed in a figure-8 maze with a choice between two levels of complexity.

In the two mazes used, the walls of one loop were painted in a solid color and those of the other loop in black-and-white horizontal stripes, or the walls of one loop had horizontal stripes and the other had vertical stripes. On the basis of theorizing similar to that presented here, these experimenters made no attempt to predict which loop would be preferred immediately by any given rat because they had no knowledge concerning the degree of incongruity to which the rats had become accustomed. They did, however, predict that any animal registering a change of choice of loop between his first and second exposures to this choice would make a change toward the more complex loop. This would mean that they would expect no changes of preference from the striped loop to the one painted a solid color, but would rather expect all changes to occur in the opposite direction. This prediction was confirmed. In a total of thirteen animals making such spontaneous changes of choice, twelve were clearly in the predicted direction. Such experiments need to be repeated and elaborated. In the light of such considerations, the problem for a parent or a teacher endeavoring to keep children interested in intellectual growth is one of providing circumstances so matched, or mismatched, to those with which the children are already familiar that an interesting and attractive challenge is continually provided.

Epigenesis of Intrinsic Motivation

In the traditionally dominant theory of motivation, the basic structure of the motivational system is essentially preformed. Learning is conceived to operate only by way of the conditioning principle, wherein previously innocuous circumstances acquire motivational significance by virtue of being associated with either painful stimuli or homeostatic needs. The fact that Piaget's observations indicate so clearly that there is an epigenesis in the structure of intelligence and in the construction of such aspects of reality as the object, causality, space, and time suggests that there may also be a hitherto unnoted epigenesis in the structure of what I am calling "intrinsic motivation." Piaget has been unconcerned with motivation;

he has narrowed his field of concern largely to intelligence and to the development of knowledge about the world. Nevertheless, many of his observations and certain of his aphorisms have implications which provide at least a hypothetical picture of an epigenesis of intrinsic motivation (see Hunt, 1963b). Such is the case with Piaget's aphorism mentioned earlier, that "the more a child has seen and heard, the more he wants to see and hear."

Three phases appear to characterize this epigenesis of intrinsic motivation. These phases, or stages, may well characterize the organism's progressive relationships to any completely new set of circumstances (Harvey et al., 1961). They may appear as phases of infantile development only because the infant is encountering various sets of completely new circumstances almost simultaneously during his first two years of life.

During the first phase, the child is, of course, motivated by homeostatic need and painful stimulation, as O. C. Irwin's (1930) classic studies have shown. Studies of the Russian investigators (see Berlyne, 1960; Razran, 1961) have shown that the orienting reaction is also ready-made at birth in all mammals including the human being. During this first phase, which lasts from birth to something like four or five or six months of age, the child is chiefly a responsive organism, responding to the short-term incongruities of change in characteristics of the ongoing input. Thus, the relatively sudden dimming of a light or the sudden disappearance of a sound which has been present for some time will instigate a young infant's orienting response or attention to bring about physiological evidences of arousal. During this first phase, the ready-made schemata of sucking, of looking, of listening, of vocalizing, or grasping, and of wiggling each change by something like the traditional conditioning process, in which various new kinds of change in stimulation acquire the capacity to evoke the schemata consistently. Thus, something heard becomes something to look at, something to look at becomes something to grasp, and something to grasp becomes something to suck. This phase terminates with a "landmark of transition'' in which the child comes gradually to try actively to retain situations or circumstances or forms of input which he has encountered repeatedly (see Hunt, 1963*b*; Piaget, 1936).

The second phase begins with this landmark of transition in which the infant manifests intentional interest in what may be characterized as the newly familiar. The newly familiar is, of course, some circumstance or situation which has been encountered repeatedly. Presumably, this course of encounters has gradually constructed and stored somewhere within the intrinsic system of the cerebrum some kind of template which provides a basis of recognition for the circumstance when it recurs. One evidence for such recognition comes in the infant's smile. Rene Spitz (1946) has conceived of this smiling response as social in nature. But Piaget's (1936) observations indicate that recognition of the parental face is but a special case of a more general tendency to smile in the presence of a variety of repeatedly encountered situations—which include the toys over an infant's crib, Piaget's newspaper laid repeatedly on the hood over his son's bassinette, and the child's own hands and feet. Such behavior may properly be described as intentional, because it occurs when the situation disappears and the child's efforts clearly imply an anticipation of the circumstance or spectacle to be regained. Moreover, inability to get the newly recognized circumstance or spectacle to return commonly brings on frustrative distress. Separation anxiety and separation grief appear to be special cases of the emotional distress that follows inability to restore the recognized circumstance or spectacle. This consideration suggests that the process of repeated encounters leading to recognition may in itself be a source of emotional gratification and pleasure which may be at least one basis for the reinforcement important in the early emotional attachments or cathexes—which Freud (1905) attributed to the libido, and which Hull (1943) and Miller and Dollard (1941) have attributed to drive reduction, and which Harlow (1958) has recently attributed to the softness of the surrogate mothers of the infant chimpanzees in his experiments. This second phase in the epigenesis of motivation terminates when repeated encounters with familiar objects have led gradually to something like the boredom that comes with too little incongruity, and when this boredom provides the basis for an interest in novel variations in the familiar.

This interest in the newly familiar may well account for such autogenic activities as the repetitious babbling commonly appearing in the second, third, and fourth months, and the persistent hand-watching and foot-watching commonly beginning in the latter part of the fourth month and possibly persisting well into the sixth month. It would appear to be in the process of babbling that the infant brings his vocalizing schema under the control of his listening schema. It would appear to be in the course of hand-watching, and sometimes foot-watching, that the infant establishes his eye-hand, and eye-foot, coordinations. This second phase terminates when, with repeated encounters with various situations, boredom ensues and the infant comes to be interested in what is new and novel within the familiar situation and in what is increasingly complex (see Hunt, 1963*b*).

The third phase begins with the appearance of this interest in novelty. Typically, this begins at about the end of the first year of life, or perhaps somewhat earlier. Piaget (1936) describes its beginnings with the appearance of the throwing schema. In the course of this throwing, the child's attention shifts from the act of throwing to observing the trajectory of the object thrown. It shows also in an interest not only in familiar ways of achieving ends but also in the development of new means through a process of groping. It shows in the child's attempts to imitate not only those schemata, vocal and otherwise, which he has already developed, but also new schemata. This development of interest in the novel is accompanied by a marked increase in the variety of the infant's interests and actions. He learns in this way new phones within the vocalization schema, and these become symbols for the images he has already developed, and pseudo-words make their appearance (see Hunt, 1961, 1963*b*; Piaget, 1945).

With the development of interest in novelty and in what is increasingly complex, the child has achieved the basis for the "growth motivation" already illustrated in the intriguing experiment by Dember *et al.* (1956).

Applications of Such Theorizing for the Development of an Antidote for Cultural Deprivation

It remains for me to examine some applications of the theoretical fabric that I have been weaving to the development of a preschool enrichment program for the culturally deprived. First of all, cultural deprivation may be seen as a failure to provide an opportunity for infants and young children to have the experiences required for adequate development of those semiautonomous central processes demanded for acquiring skill in the use of linguistic and mathematical symbols and for the analysis of causal relationships. The difference between the culturally deprived and the culturally privileged is, for children, analogous to the difference between cage-reared and pet-reared rats and dogs. At the present time, this notion of cultural deprivation or of social disadvantage is gross and undifferentiated indeed.[4] On the basis of the evidence and conceptions I have summarized, however, I believe the concept points in a very promising direction. It should be possible to arrange institutional settings where children now culturally deprived by the accident of the social class of their parents can be supplied with a set of encounters with circumstances which will provide an antidote for what they may have missed.

[4]It is much less undifferentiated today than it was when this was originally written, in 1962, by virtue of the studies of Bernstein (1960, 1961) in England, of Cynthia Deutsch (1964), Hess and Shipman (1965), Vera John (1963), John and Goldstein (1964), and Suzanne Keller (1963) in the United States, of Lewis (1966) in Latin American countries, and of Smilansky (1961, 1964) in Israel. These studies and others, coming long after those pioneering investigations of Davis (1948) and Davis and Havighurst (1946), are helping greatly to clarify the nature of cultural deprivation and its psychological effects on the development of intelligence and motivation.

The important study of Skeels and Dye (1939), that met with such a derisive reception when it first appeared, is highly relevant in this context. You will recall that it was based on a "clinical surprise." Two infants, one aged thirteen months with a Kuhlman IQ of 46 and the other aged sixteen months with an IQ of 35, after residence in the relatively homogeneous circumstances of a state orphanage, were committed to a state institution for the feeble-minded. Some six months later, a psychologist visiting the wards noted with surprise that these two infants had shown a remarkable degree of development. No longer did they show either the apathy or the locomotor retardation that had characterized them when they were committed. When they were again tested with the Kuhlman scale, moreover, the younger had an IQ of 77 and the older an IQ of 87—improvements of 31 and 52 points respectively, and within half a year. You will also remember that in the experiment which followed this clinical surprise, every one of a group of thirteen children showed a substantial gain in IQ upon being transferred from the orphanage to the institution for the feeble-minded. These gains ranged between 7 points and 58 points of IQ. On the other hand, twelve other youngsters, within the same age-range but with a somewhat higher mean IQ, were left in the orphanage. When these children were retested after periods varying between twenty-one and forty-three months, all had shown a substantial decrease in IQ, ranging between 8 and 45 points of IQ, with five of these decreases exceeding 35 points.

In recent years, Harold Skeels has been engaged in a following-up study of individuals involved in these two groups. With about three-fourths of the individuals found, he has yet to find one of the group transferred from the orphanage to the institution for the feeble-minded who is not now maintaining himself effectively in society. Contrariwise, he has not yet found any one of the group remaining in the orphanage who is not now living with institutional support (1965). Although the question of the permanence of the effects of experiential deprivation during infancy is far from answered, such evidence as I have been able to find, and as I have summarized here, would indicate that if the experiential deprivation does not persist too long, it is reversible to a substantial degree. If this be true, the idea of enriching the cognitive fare in day-care centers and in nursery schools for the culturally deprived looks very promising.

Probable Nature of the Deficit from Cultural Deprivation

The fact that cultural deprivation is such a global and undifferentiated conception at present invites at least speculative attempts to construe the nature of the deficit and to see wherein and when the infant of the poor and lower-class parents is most likely to be experientially deprived.

One of the important features of lower-class life in poverty is crowding. Many persons live in little space. Crowding, however, may be no handicap for a human infant during most of his first year of life. Although there is no certainty of this, it is conceivable that being a young infant among a large number of people living within a room may actually serve to provide such wide variations of visual and auditory inputs that it will facilitate development more than will the conditions typical of the culturally privileged during most of the first year.

During the second year, on the other hand, living under the crowded conditions of poverty must almost inevitably be highly hampering. Under these conditions, the child encounters a markedly smaller variety of objects than does the middle-class child. As he begins to throw things and as he begins to develop his own methods of locomotion, he is likely to find himself getting in the way of adults already made ill-tempered by their own discomforts and by the frustrations of getting into each other's ways. Such considerations are dramatized by Lewis' (1961) *The Children of Sanchez,* an anthropological study of life in poverty. In such a crowded atmosphere, the activities in which the child must indulge for the development of his own interests and skills must almost inevitably be sharply curbed. "Being good" comes to be defined as both doing nothing and

getting nothing interesting. Moreover, adult utterances provide such poor models of the vocal side of language that it is no wonder that children of the poor lag in their language development and in the abilities which depend upon language for their development (Bernstein, 1960; Deutsch, 1964; Deutsch and Brown, 1964; John, 1963; John and Goldstein, 1964).

In the third year, moreover, when imitation of novel patterns of action and verbalization should presumably be well-established and should provide a mechanism for learning vocal language, the models of vocal patterns are wrong for standards to be encountered later in school. When the toddler has achieved the "learning sets" that "things have names" and that "things come in groups" and is prompted by these sets to ask such questions as "what's that?" or "is it a this or a that?" his questions are typically met with "shut up!" Seldom do such parents, who are preoccupied with the problems associated with their poverty or who are chronically in a state of disorganization and apathy, ask the child questions that will force him to use language to identify prepositional relationships and to organize sequences of his experience in linguistic form. With things to play with and with room to play in highly limited, with opportunities to learn standard English—or any other standard language— markedly reduced, the youngster beyond his first year who is in the typical conditions of lower-class life has little opportunity to develop at an optimal rate in the direction demanded for later adaptation in schools and in our highly technological culture (see also Beilin and Gotkin, 1964; Bernstein, 1961; Keller, 1963).

If this armchair analysis has any validity, it suggests that the infant developing in the crowded circumstances of lower-class poverty may develop well through the first year; begin to show retardation during the second year; and show even more retardation during the third, fourth, and fifth years. Presumably, that retardation which occurs during the second year, and even that during the third year, can probably be reversed to a considerable degree by supplying proper circumstances in either a nursery school or a day-care center for children of four and five—but I suspect it would be preferable to start with children at three years of age. The analysis made here, which is based largely upon what I have learned from Piaget (1936) and from my own observations of development during the preschool years, could be tested. Dr. Ina Uzgiris and I have developed an instrument for assessing infant psychological development which consists of six series of situations, arranged according to their difficulty for a sample of eighty-four infants (Uzgiris and Hunt, 1966, 1967). These are situations designed to evoke the various early sensorimotor schemata that Piaget (1936) has described for the first two years. It should provide a tool with which to determine when and how the conditions of development within the crowded circumstances of poverty begin to result in retardation and/or apathy.

Preschool Enrichment and the Problem of the Match

Our traditional emphasis in education upon arithmetic and language skills can well lead us astray in the attempt to develop a program of preschool enrichment. If Piaget's (1945) observations are correct, spoken language—that is to say the motor side of the language skill— comes only after images, or the central processes representing objects and events, have been developed out of repeated encounters with those objects and events. The fact that chimpanzees show clearly the capacity to dissemble their own purposes even though they lack language (Hebb and Thompson, 1954) lends support from phylogenetic comparisons to this notion of Piaget's. You have most likely heard that O. K. Moore, of Yale, has been teaching preschool children to read with the aid of an electric typewriter hooked up to an electronic system of storing and retrieving information. The fact that, once children have learned to recognize letters by pressing the proper keys of a typewriter, they are enabled to discover spontaneously that they can draw these letters with chalk on a blackboard, lends further support to the image-primacy thesis. Moreover, Moore has observed that the muscular control of such four-year-olds—who have presumably

acquired solid imagery of the letters in the course of their experience with those letters at the electric typewriter—corresponds to that typical of seven- or eight-year-olds (personal communication).

What appears to be important for a preschool enrichment program is an opportunity to encounter circumstances which will foster the development of these semiautonomous central processes that can serve as imagery representative of objects and events and which can become the referents for the spoken symbols required in the phonemic combinations of spoken or written language. Moore's results also suggest to me that these semiautonomous central processes, if adequately developed, can serve as the basis for motor control. Such considerations suggest that a proper preschool enrichment program should provide children with an opportunity to encounter a wide variety of objects and circumstances. They suggest that the children should also have an opportunity to imitate a wide variety of models of action and of motor language. The danger of attempting to prescribe materials and models at this stage of knowledge, however, is that the prescriptions may well fail to provide a proper match with what the child already has in his storage. The fact that most teachers have their expectations based on experience with culturally privileged children makes this problem of the match especially dangerous and vexing in work with the culturally deprived.

Revisiting Montessori's Contribution

In view of the dangers of attempting prescriptions of enrichments for preschool children, it may be well to re-examine the educational contributions of Maria Montessori. Her contributions have been largely forgotten in America. In fact, until as late as August 1962, I could have identified Maria Montessori only by saying that she had developed some kind of kindergarten and was an educational faddist who had made quite a splash about the turn of the century. I was, thus, really introduced to her work by Dr. Jan Smedslund, a Norwegian psychologist, who remarked to me, during a conference at the University of Colorado, that

Maria Montessori had provided a practical answer to what I have called "the problem of the match" (Hunt, 1961, p. 276ff).

When I examined the library for materials on Maria Montessori, I discovered that the novelist, Dorothy Canfield Fisher, had spent the winter of 1910–1911 at the Casa de Bambini in Rome and that she had returned to write a book on Montessori's work. This book, entitled *A Montessori Mother* (1912), may still be the best initial introduction to Montessori's work. Books by E. M. Standing (1957) and Nancy Rambusch (1962) have brought the record up to date, and the book by Rambusch contains a bibliography of the materials in the English language concerning Montessori's work assembled by Gilbert E. Donahue.

Montessori's contribution is especially interesting to me because she based her methods of teaching upon the spontaneous interest of children in learning, that is, upon what I am calling "intrinsic motivation." Moreover, she put great stress upon teachers observing the children under their care to discover what kinds of things foster their individual interests and growth. Furthermore, she put great stress on the training of what she called sensory processes, but what we might more appropriately call information processes today. The fact that she placed strong emphasis upon the training of sensory processes may well be one of the major reasons why her work dropped out of the main stream of educational thought and practice in America before World War I. This emphasis was too dissonant with the dominant American emphasis in learning upon the motor response, rather than upon the sensory input or information processes. It was Montessori's concern to observe carefully what interested a child that led her to discover a wide variety of materials in which she found children showing strong spontaneous interest.

Second, Montessori broke the lock step in the education of young children. Her schools made no effort to keep all the children doing the same thing at the same time. Rather, each child was free to examine and to work with whatever happened to interest him. This meant that he was free to persist in a given concern as long as he cared to, and also free to change from one concern to another whenever a change appeared appropriate to him. In this connection, one of the very interesting observations made by Dorothy Canfield Fisher concerns the prolonged duration of children's interest in given activities under such circumstances. Whereas the lore about preschoolers holds that the nature of the activity in a nursery school must be changed every ten or fifteen minutes, Mrs. Fisher described children typically remaining engrossed in such activities as the buttoning and unbuttoning of a row of buttons for two or more hours at a time.

Third, Montessori's method consisted in having children from three to six years old together. As I see it, from taking into account the epigenesis of intellectual development, such a scheme has the advantage of providing the younger children with a wide variety of models for imitation. Moreover, it supplies the older children with an opportunity to help and teach the younger. Helping and teaching contain many of their own rewards.

There may well be yet another advantage, one in which those financing preschool enrichment will be heartily concerned. Montessori's first teacher was a teen-age girl, the superintendent's daughter in the apartment house in the Rome slums where the first Casa de Bambini was established in 1907. In that school, this one young woman successfully set the stage for the learning of fifty to sixty children from three to seven years old. I say "successfully" because, as Dorothy Canfield Fisher (1912) reported, some of the children had learned to read by the time they were five years old. On the other hand, current observations suggest that the Montessori approach may need supplementation to correct the linguistic deficit of children from culturally deprived backgrounds. It may be well to supplement the Montessori approach with the very recently developed approach of Bereiter *et al.* (1966). Their academically oriented preschool for culturally deprived children focuses directly on language and arithmetic; and their teaching method combines concrete experience with the modern method of teaching foreign languages.

Starting with four-year-olds one and one-half to two and one-half years below chronological age on the Illinois Test of Psycholinguistic Abilities (see Kirk and McCarthy, 1961), they increased the median psycholinguistic test-age of these children by two years within six months in their program—a program consisting of merely three twenty-minute sessions for groups of five with a teacher on each of five days a week. This approach reverts to the lock step for short periods, and doctrinaire followers of Montessori may resist using such a supplement. Alternatively, one might consider adding to the Montessori apparatus something like O. K. Moore's "talking typewriter" (1963), reported effective in correcting the language deficit. Before any confident assertions can be made about such matters, however, solid evaluation investigations are necessary.

Summary

I began by saying that it was very exciting for me to encounter people—generally considered sensible—in the process of planning to utilize preschool experience as an antidote for the effects of cultural deprivation. I have tried to summarize the basis in psychological theory and in the evidence from psychological research for such a use of preschool enrichment. I have tried to summarize the evidence: (1) that the belief in fixed intelligence is no longer tenable; (2) that development is far from completely predetermined; (3) that what goes on "between the ears" is much less like the static switchboard of the telephone than it is like the active information processes programmed into electronic computers to enable them to solve problems; (4) that experience is the programmer of the human brain-computer and, thus, that Freud was correct about the importance of the experience which comes before the advent of language; (5) that, nonetheless, Freud was wrong about the nature of the experience which is important, since an opportunity to see and hear a variety of things appears to be more important than the fate of instinctual needs and impulses; and, finally (6) that learning need not be motivated by painful stimulation, homeostatic need, or the acquired drives based upon these, for there is a kind of intrinsic motivation which is inherent in information processing and action.

In applying these various lines of evidence and these various changes in conception, I have viewed the effects of cultural deprivation as analogous to the experimentally found effects of experiential deprivation in infancy. I have pointed out the importance of "the problem of the match" and the dangers of using our present knowledge to prescribe programs of circumstantial encounters to enrich the experience of culturally deprived preschool children. In this connection, I have suggested that we re-examine the work of Maria Montessori for suggestions. For she successfully based her teaching method on children's spontaneous interest in learning; she found a solution to the "problem of the match" by carefully observing children's interests and then giving them individual freedom to choose which circumstances they would encounter.

REFERENCES

Beach, F. A. Current concepts of play in animals. *American Naturalist,* 1945, *79*, 523–541.

Beilin, H., and L. Gotkin. Psychological issues in the development of mathematics curricula for socially disadvantaged children. Paper presented to the Invitational Conference on Mathematics Education, Chicago, April 1964.

Bereiter, C., S. Engelmann, Jean Osborn, and P. A. Redford. "An academically oriented preschool for culturally deprived children." In F. M. Hechinger (ed.), *Pre-school education today.* New York: Doubleday, 1966, Ch. 6.

Berlyne, D. E. *Conflict, arousal, and curiosity.* New York: McGraw-Hill, 1960.

Bernstein, B. Language and social class. *British Journal of Psychology,* 1960, *11*, 271–276.

_____. "Social class and linguistic development: A theory of social learning." In A. H. Halsey, Jean Floud, and C. A. Anderson (eds.), *Education, economy, and society*. New York: Free Press, 1961, 288–314.

Bexton, W. H., W. Heron, and T. H. Scott. Effects of decreased variation in the sensory environment. *Canadian Journal of Psychology*, 1954, *8*, 70–76.

Boring, E. G. *A history of experimental psychology*. New York: Appleton-Century-Crofts, 1929.

Brattgård, S. O. The importance of adequate stimulation for the chemical composition of retinal ganglion cells during early postnatal development. *Acta Radiologica*, Stockholm, 1952, Suppl. 96.

Bühler, K. "Displeasure and pleasure in relation to activity." In M. L. Reymert (ed.), *Feelings and emotions: The Wittenberg symposium*. Worcester, Mass.: Clark University Press, 1928, Ch. 14.

Butler, R. A. Discrimination learning by rhesus monkeys to visual exploration, motivation. *Journal of Comparative Physiology and Psychology*, 1954, *46*, 95–98.

_____. The differential effect of visual and auditory incentives on the performance of monkeys. *American Journal of Psychology*, 1958, *71*, 591–593.

Carmichael L. The development of behavior in vertebrates experimentally removed from influence of external stimulation. *Psychological Review*, 1926, *33*, 51–58.

_____. A further study of the development of behavior in vertebrates experimentally removed from the influence of external stimulation. *Psychological Review*, 1927, *34*, 34–47.

_____. A further study of the development of behavior. *Psychological Review*, 1928, *35*, 253–260.

Cattell, J. McK. Mental tests and measurements. *Mind*, 1890, *15*, 373–381.

Coghill, G. E. *Anatomy and the problem of behavior*. Cambridge, Mass.: Cambridge University Press, 1929.

Cruze, W. W. Maturation and learning in chicks. *Journal of Comparative Psychology*, 1935, *19*, 371–409.

_____. Maturation and learning ability. *Psychological Monograph*, 1938, 50 (5).

Darwin, C. *Origin of the species*. London: Murray, 1859.

_____. *The expressions of the emotions in man and animals*. New York: Appleton-Century-Crofts, 1873 (originally published: London: Murray, 1872).

Dashiell, J. F. *Fundamentals of objective psychology*. Boston: Houghton Mifflin, 1928.

Davis, W. A. *Social-class influences upon learning*. Cambridge, Mass.: Harvard University Press, 1948.

_____, and R. J. Havighurst. Social-class and color differences in child-rearing. *American Sociological Review*, 1946, *11*, 698–710.

Dember, W. N., R. W. Earl, and N. Paradise. Response by rats to differential stimulus complexity. *Journal of Comparative Physiological Psychology*, 1957, *50*, 514–518.

Denenberg, V. H. "The effects of early experience." In E. S. E. Hafez (ed.), *The behavior of domestic animals*. London: Ballière, Tindall, Koch, 1962.

Dennis, W. Causes of retardation among institutional children. *Journal of Genetic Psychology*, 1960, *96*, 47–59.

_____, and Marsena G. Dennis. The effect of restricted practice upon the reaching, sitting and standing of two infants. *Journal of Genetic Psychology*, 1935, *47*, 21–29.

_____ and _____. Infant development under conditions of restricted practice and minimum social stimulation: A preliminary report. *Journal of Genetic Psychology*, 1938, *53*, 151–156.

_____ and _____. The effect of cradling practice upon the onset of walking in Hopi children. *Journal of Genetic Psychology*, 1940, *56*, 77–86.

_____ and _____. Infant development under conditions of restricted practice and minimum social stimulation. *Genetic Psychology Monograph*, 1941, *23*, 149–155.

Deutsch, Cynthia. Auditory discrimination and learning: Social factors. *Merrill-Palmer Quarterly,* 1964, *10*, 277–296.

Deutsch, M., and B. Brown. Social influences in Negro-white intelligence differences. *Journal of Social Issues,* 1964, *20,* 24–35.

Dewey, J. *The school and society.* Chicago: University of Chicago Press, Phoenix Books, p. 3, 1960 (first published 1900).

———. *The child and the curriculum.* Chicago: University of Chicago Press, Phoenix Books, p. 3, 1960 (first published 1902).

Farber, I. E. Response fixation under anxiety and non-anxiety conditions. *Journal of Experimental Psychology,* 1948, *38*, 111–131.

Fenichel, O. *The psychoanalytic theory of neurosis.* New York: Norton, 1945.

Fisher, Dorothy Canfield. *A Montessori mother.* New York: Holt, Rinehart and Winston, 1912.

Fiske, D. W., and S. R. Maddi. *Functions of varied experience.* Homewood, Ill.: Dorsey Press, 1961.

Freedman, A. Drive conditioning in water deprivation. Unpublished doctoral dissertation, University of Illinois, 1957.

Freeman, G. L. *Introduction to physiological psychology.* New York: Ronald Press, 1934.

Freud, S. "The interpretation of dreams." In A. A. Brill (trans. & ed.), *The basic writings of Sigmund Freud.* New York: Modern Library, 1938. (*The interpretation of dreams,* originally published 1900).

———. "The psychopathology of everyday life." In A. A. Brill (trans. & ed.), *The basic writings of Sigmund Freud.* New York: Modern Library, 1938. (*Three contributions to the theory of sex,* originally published 1905.)

———. Instincts and their vicissitudes. *Collected Papers, 4,* 60–83. London: Hogarth, 1927. (*Instincts and their vicissitudes,* originally published 1915.)

———. *The problem of anxiety.* (H. A. Bunker, trans.) New York: Norton, 1936. (*Hemmung, Sympton an Angst,* originally published 1926.)

Froebel, F. *The education of man.* (W. N. Hailmann, trans.) New York: Appleton-Century-Crofts, 1896. (*Die Menschenerziehung,* originally published 1826.)

Galton, F. *Hereditary genius: An inquiry into its laws and consequences.* London: Macmillan, 1869.

Gauron, E. F., and W. C. Becker. The effects of early sensory deprivation on adult rat behavior under competition stress: An attempt at replication of a study by Alexander Wolf. *Journal of Comparative Physiology and Psychology,* 1959, *52*, 689–693.

Gesell, A. *The embryology of human behavior: The beginnings of the human mind.* New York: Harper & Row, 1945.

———. "The ontogenesis of infant behavior." In L. Carmichael (ed.), *Manual of child psychology.* New York: Wiley, 1954, Ch. 6.

———, and Helen Thompson. Learning and growth in identical twin infants. *Genetic Psychological Monograph,* 1929, 6, 1–124.

Goddard, H. H. *The Kallikak family: A study in the heredity of feeble-mindedness.* New York: Macmillan, 1912.

Goldman, Jacquelin R. The effects of handling and shocking in infancy upon adult behavior in the albino rat. *Journal of Genetic Psychology,* 1964, *104,* 2, 301–310.

Goodenough, Florence. A critique of experiments on raising the I.Q. *Educational Methods,* 1939, *19*, 73–79.

Guthrie, E. R. *The psychology of human conflict: The clash of motives within the individual.* New York: Harper & Row, 1938.

Hall, C. S. Emotional behavior in the rat: 1. Defecation and urination as measures of individual differences in emotionality. *Journal of Comparative Psychology,* 1934, *18*, 385–403.

Hall, M. *New memoire on the nervous system*. London: Proc. Royal Academy, 1843.

Harlow, H. F. Learning and satiation of response in intrinsically motivated complex puzzle performance by monkeys. *Journal of Comparative and Physiological Psychology*, 1950, *43*, 289–294.

———. The nature of love. *American Psychologist*, 1958, *13*, 673–685.

———, M. K. Harlow, and D. R. Meyer. Learning motivated by a manipulation drive. *Journal of Experimental Psychology*, 1950, *40*, 228–234.

Harvey, O. J., D. E. Hunt, and H. M. Schroeder. *Conceptual systems and personality organization*. New York: Wiley, 1961.

Hebb, D. O. On the nature of fear. *Psychological Review*, 1946, *53*, 259–276.

———. The effects of early experience on problem-solving at maturity. *American Psychologist*, 1947, *2*, 306–307.

———. *The organization of behavior*. New York: Wiley, 1949.

———, and A. H. Riesen. The genesis of irrational fears. *Bulletin of Canadian Psychology Association*, 1943, *3*, 49–50.

———, and W. R. Thompson. "The social significance of animal studies." In G. Lindzey (ed.), *Handbook of social psychology*. Reading, Mass.: Addison-Wesley, 1954, Ch. 15.

———, and K. Williams. A method of rating animal intelligence. *Journal of Genetic Psychology*, 1946, *34*, 59–65.

Hendrick, I. The discussion of the "instinct to master." *Psychoanalytical Quarterly*, 1943, *12*, 561–565.

Hernàndez-Péon, R., H. Scherrer, and M. Jouvet. Modification of electric activity in cochlear nucleus during "attention" in unanesthetized cast. *Science*, 1956, *123*, 331–332.

Hilgard, Josephine R. Learning and maturation in pre-school children. *Journal of Genetic Psychology*, 1932, *41*, 36–56.

Holmes, Frances B. "An experimental study of children's fears." In A. T. Jersild and Frances B. Holmes (eds.), *Children's fears*. New York: Teachers College, Columbia University, *Child Development Monograph*, 20, 1935.

Holt, E. B. *Animal drive and the learning process*. New York: Holt, Rinehart and Winston, 1931.

Hull, C. L. Goal attraction and directing ideas conceived as habit phenomena. *Psychological Review*, 1931, *38*, 487–506.

———. *Principles of behavior*. New York: Appleton-Century-Crofts, 1943.

Hunt, J. McV. The effects of infant feeding-frustration upon adult hoarding in the albino rat. *Journal of Abnormal Social Psychology*, 1941, *36*, 338–360.

———. "Experimental psychoanalysis." In P. L. Harriman (ed.), *Encyclopedia of Psychology*. New York: Philosophical Library, 1945.

———. Psychosexual development: The infant disciplines. Urbana: Psychological Development Laboratory, University of Illinois, 1956 (mimeographed paper).

———. Experience and the development of motivation: Some reinterpretations. *Child Development*, 1960, *31*, 489–504.

———. *Intelligence and experience*. New York: Ronald Press, 1961.

———. "Motivation inherent in information processing and action." In O. J. Harvey (ed.), *Motivation and social interaction*. New York: Ronald Press, 1963*a*.

———. Piaget's observations as a source of hypotheses concerning motivation. *Merrill-Palmer Quarterly*, 1963*b*, *9*, 263–275.

———, and Zella Luria. Investigations of the effects of early experience in sub-human animals. Urbana: Psychological Development Laboratory, University of Illinois, 1956 (mimeographed paper).

Hunter, W. S. The delayed reaction in animals and children. *Behavior Monographs*, 1912, *2* (1), 1–85.

————. The temporal maze and kinesthetic sensory processes in the white rat. *Psychobiology,* 1918, *2*, 339–351.

Hydén, H. Biochemical changes in glial cells and nerve cells at varying activity. In F. Brücke (ed.), *Proceedings of the 4th International Congress of Biochemistry, III. Biochemistry of the central nervous system.* London: Pergamon Press, 1959.

————. "The neuron." In J. Brachet and A. E. Mirsky (eds.), *The cell: Biochemistry, physiology, morphology, IV. Specialized cells.* New York: Academic Press, 1960, pp. 215–323.

————, and A. Pigon. A cytophysiological study of the functional relationship between oligodendroglial cells and nerve cells of Deiters' nucleus. *Journal of Neurochemistry,* 1960, *6*, 57–72.

John, Vera P. The intellectual development of slum children: Some preliminary findings. *American Journal of Orthopsychiatry,* 1963, *33*, 813–822.

————, and L. S. Goldstein. The social context of language acquisition. *Merrill-Palmer Quarterly,* 1964, *10*, 266–275.

Keller, Suzanne. The social world of the urban slum child: Some early findings. *American Journal of Orthopsychiatry,* 1963, *33*, 813–822.

Köhler, W. *The mentality of apes.* New York: Harcourt, 1925.

Lamarck, J. Chevalier de. *Zoological philosophy* (trans. of *Philosophie Zoologique,* by H. Elliot). London: Macmillan, 1914. Original date of publication, 1809.

Levine, S., J. A. Chevalier, and S. J. Korchin. The effects of early shock and handling on later avoidance learning. *Journal of Personality,* 1956, *24*, 475–493.

Lewis, O. *The children of Sanchez.* New York: Random House, 1961.

Liberman, R. Retinal cholinesterase and glycolysis in rats raised in darkness. *Science,* 1962, *135*, 372–373.

McDougall, W. *An introduction to social psychology.* Boston: Luce, 1908.

McGraw, Myrtle B. *Growth: A study of Johnny and Jimmy.* New York: Appleton-Century-Crofts, 1935.

Melton, A. W. "Learning." In W. S. Munroe (ed.), *Encyclopedia of educational research.* New York: Macmillan, 1941.

Miller, G. A., E. H. Galanter, and K. H. Pribram. *Plans and the structure of behavior.* New York: Holt, Rinehart and Winston, 1960.

Miller, N. E., and J. Dollard. *Social learning and imitation.* New Haven: Yale University Press, 1941.

Montgomery, K. C. A test of two explanations of spontaneous alternation. *Journal of Comparative Physiology and Psychology,* 1952, *45*, 287–293.

————. Exploratory behavior as a function of "similarity" of stimulus situations. *Journal of Comparative Physiology and Psychology,* 1953, *46*, 129–133.

————. The relation between fear induced by novel stimulation and exploratory behavior. *Journal of Comparative Physiology and Psychology,* 1955, *48*, 254–260.

————, and M. Segall. Discrimination learning based upon the exploratory drive. *Journal of Comparative Physiology and Psychology,* 1955, *48*, 225–228.

Moore, O. K. *Autotelic responsive environments and exceptional children.* Hamden, Conn.: Responsive Environments Foundation, 1963.

Morgan, C. L. *An introduction to comparative psychology.* Ed. 2. London: Scott, 1909. Original date of publication, 1894.

Mowrer, O. H. *Learning theory and behavior.* New York: Wiley, 1960.

Newell, A., J. C. Shaw, and H. A. Simon. Elements of a theory of human problem solving. *Psychological Review,* 1958, *65*, 151–166.

Nissen, H. W. A study of exploratory behavior in the white rat by means of the obstruction method. *Journal of Genetic Psychology,* 1930, *37*, 361–376.

Orlansky, H. Infant care and personality. *Psychological Bulletin,* 1949, *46*, 1–48.

Osgood, C. E. The nature and measurement of meaning. *Psychological Bulletin,* 1952, *49*, 192–237.

Piaget, J. *The origins of intelligence in children.* (Margaret Cook, trans.) New York: International Universities Press, 1952. (Originally published 1936).

———. *Play, dreams, and imitation in childhood.* (C. Gattegno and F. M. Hodgson, trans.) New York: Norton, 1951. Originally published as *La formation du symbole chez l'enfant,* 1945.

———. *The psychology of intelligence.* (M. Piercy and D. E. Berlyne, trans.) London: Routledge & Kegan Paul, 1947.

Pribram, K. H. A review of theory in physiological psychology. *Annual Review of Psychology,* 1960, *11*, 1–40.

Pruette, Lorine. *G. Stanley Hall: A biography of a mind.* New York: Appleton-Century-Crofts, 1926.

Rambusch, Nancy M. *Learning how to learn: An American approach to Montessori.* Baltimore: Helicon Press, 1962.

Rasch, E., H. Swift, A. H. Riesen, and K. L. Chos. Altered structure and composition of retinal cells in dark-reared mammals. *Experimental Cellular Research,* 1961, *25*, 348–363.

Razran, G. The observable unconscious and the inferable conscious in current Soviet psychophysiology: Interoceptive conditioning, semantic conditioning, and the orienting reflex. *Psychological Review,* 1961, *68*, 81–147.

Riesen, A. H. "Plasticity of behavior: Psychological aspects." In H. F. Harlow and C. N. Woolsey (eds.), *Biological and biochemical bases of behavior.* Madison: University of Wisconsin Press, 1958, 425–450.

Romanes, G. J. *Animal intelligence.* New York: Appleton-Century-Crofts, 1883 (1882).

———. *Mental evolution in animals.* New York: Appleton-Century-Crofts, 1884 (1883).

Rose, J. E., and C. N. Woolsey. The relations of thalamic connections, cellular structure and evocable electrical activity in the auditory region of the cat. *Journal of Comparative Neurology,* 1949, *91*, 441–466.

Rousseau, J. J. *Emile.* (Barbara Foxley, trans.) New York: Everyman's Library, 1916. Original date of publication, 1762.

Salama, A. A., and J. McV. Hunt. "Fixation" in the rat as a function of infantile shocking, handling, and gentling. *Journal of Genetic Psychology,* 1964, *105*, 1, 131–162.

Schneirla, T. C. "An evolutionary and developmental theory of biphasic processes underlying approach and withdrawal." In M. R. Jones (ed.), *Nebraska symposium on motivation.* Lincoln: University of Nebraska Press, 1959, 1–43.

Sherrington, C. S. *The integrative action of the nervous system.* New York: Scribners, 1906.

Simpson, B. R. The wandering IQ. *Journal of Psychology,* 1939, *7*, 351–367.

Skeels, H. M. Some preliminary findings of three follow-up studies on the effects of adoption on children from institutions. *Children,* 1965, *12* (1), 33–34.

———, and H. B. Dye. A study of the effects of differential stimulation on mentally retarded children. *Proceedings of the American Association of Mental Deficiency,* 1939, *44*, 114–136.

Spitz, R. A. The smiling response: A contribution to the ontogenesis of social relations. *Genetic Psychological Monograph,* 1946, *34*, 67–125.

Standing, E. M. *Maria Montessori: Her life and work.* Fresno, Calif.: Academy Library Guild, 1957.

Stoddard, G. D., and Beth L. Wellman. Environment and the IQ. *Yearbook of National Social Studies Education,* 1940, *39* (1), 405–442.

Taylor, D. W. "Toward an information processing theory of motivation." In M. R. Jones (ed.), *Nebraska symposium on motivation.* Lincoln: University of Nebraska Press, 1960, 51–79.

Thompson, W. R. and W. Heron. The effects of restricting early experience on the problem-solving capacity of dogs. *Canadian Journal of Psychology,* 1954, *8,* 17–31.

Thorndike, E. L. *Educational psychology.* Vol. II. *The psychology of learning.* New York: Columbia University Press, 1913.

————, and R. S. Woodworth. The influence of improvement in one mental function upon the efficiency of other functions. *Psychological Review,* 1901, *8,* 247–261, 384–395, 553–564.

Uzgiris, Ina C., and J. McV. Hunt. *An instrument for assessing infant psychological development.* Urbana: Psychological Development Laboratory, University of Illinois (mimeographed progress report to be revised and published as "Ordinal Scales of Infant Psychological Development"), 1966.

———— and ————. *Ordinal scales of infant psychological development:* Sound cinemas depicting scales of (1) object permanence, (2) development of means, (3) imitation: gestural and vocal, (4) operational causality, (5) object relations in space, (6) development of schemas. Urbana: University of Illinois Motion Picture Service, 1967.

Walker, A. E. and T. A. Weaver, Jr. Ocular movements from the occipital lobe in the monkey. *Journal of Neurophysiology,* 1940, *3,* 353–357.

Watson, J. B. *Psychology from the standpoint of a behaviorist.* Philadelphia: Lippincott, 1919.

————. *Psychological care of infant and child.* New York: Norton, 1928.

————, and R. Rayner. *Conditioned emotional reactions. Journal of Experimental Psychology,* 1920, *3,* 1–14.

Weiskrantz, L. Sensory deprivation and the cat's optic nervous system. *Nature,* 1958, *181* (3), 47–105.

White, R. W. Motivation reconsidered: The concept of competence. *Psychological Review,* 1959, *66,* 297–333.

Wiener, N. *Cybernetics.* New York: Wiley, 1948.

Wolf, A. The dynamics of the selective inhibition of specific functions in neuroses. *Psychosomatic Medicine,* 1943, *5,* 27–38.

Woodworth, R. S. Heredity and environment: A critical study of recently published material on twins and foster children. *Social Science Research Council Bulletin,* 1941 (47).

35. PIAGETIAN AND PSYCHOMETRIC CONCEPTIONS OF INTELLIGENCE

DAVID ELKIND

I have been asked to respond to Professor Jensen's paper from the standpoint of Piaget's genetic psychology of intelligence. While I clearly cannot speak for Piaget, only the "Patron" can do that, I can react as someone steeped in Piagetian theory and reserch and as

From the *Harvard Educational Review,* 1969, *39,* 319–337. Copyright © by the President and Fellows of Harvard College. Reprinted by permission of Harvard Educational Review and the author.

one who looks at cognitive problems from the Genevan perspective. Accordingly, while I hope that what I have to say would be acceptable to Piaget, I cannot guarantee that this is in fact the case, and must take full responsibility for whatever is said below. I plan to discuss, in the first section of the paper, some of the similarities between the Piagetian and psychometric positions. Then, in the second section, some of their differences will be pointed out. Finally, in the third section, I want to consider two related practical issues regarding the modification of intelligence.

Conceptual Similarities

What struck me in reading Professor Jensen's paper, and what had not really occurred to me before, were the many parallels and affinities between the psychometric or mental test approach to the problem of intelligence and the developmental approach as represented by Piaget. It brought to mind the fact that Piaget began his career as a developmental psychologist by working in Binet's laboratory where he sought to standardize some of Burt's (1962) reasoning tests on Parisian children. Indeed, Piaget's *method clinique* is a combination of mental test and clinical interview procedures which consists in the use of a standardized situation as a starting point for a flexible interrogation. The affinities, however, between the Piagetian and psychometric approaches to intelligence run more deeply than that. In this section I want to discuss such affinities: the acceptance of genetic and maturational determination in intelligence, the use of nonexperimental methodologies and the conception of intelligence as being essentially rational.

Genetic Determination

Implicit and often explicit in both the psychometric and Piagetian positions is the assumption that mental ability is, in part at least, genetically determined. With respect to the psychometric position, it assumes that at least some of the variance in intelligence test performance is attributable to variance in genetic endowment (Burt & Howard, 1957, Jensen). Piaget (1967a) also acknowledges the importance of genetic factors for intellectual ability but qualifies this by pointing out that what may be genetic in one generation may not always have been so and could be the partial result of prior environmental influences. So, for Piaget, as for the biologist Waddington (1962a)

there is a certain relativity with respect to what is attributed to genetic endowment because what is genetic now may not always have been genetic. To illustrate, Waddington (1962a) observed that after several generations a strain of the fly grub drosophilia developed enlarged anal papillae when reared on a high salt diet. When the insects were returned to a "normal" low salt diet the anal papillae of successive generations became less large but never returned to their original size. Waddington speaks of this as "genetic assimilation" by which he means that the effects of an altered environment upon the selection process within a species may not be completely reversible even when the environment returned to its unaltered state.

One consequence of their joint acceptance of the partial genetic determination of intellectual ability, is that both psychometricians and Piaget recognize the importance of maturation in human development. To illustrate their commonality in this regard, consider these two passages, one written by Harold Jones in 1954 and the other by Piaget in 1967.

Dubnoff's work, together with other related studies, may lead to the speculative suggestion that between natio-racial groups, as within a given group, a slight tendency exists for early precocity to be associated with a slower mental growth at later ages and perhaps with a lower average intelligence level at maturity. A parallel situation may be noted when we compare different animal species; among the primates, for example, the maturity of performance at a given age in infancy can be used inversely to predict the general level of adaptive ability that will be attained at the end of the growth span. (Jones, 1954, p. 638)

And Piaget writes:

We know that it takes 9 to 12 months before babies develop the notion that an object is still there when a screen is placed in front of it. Now kittens go through the same substages but they do it in three months—so they are six months ahead of the babies. Is this an advantage or isn't it? We can certainly see our answer in one sense. The kitten is not going to go much further. The child has taken longer, but he is capable of going further so it seems to me the nine months were not for nothing. (Piaget, 1967b)

Non-Experimental Methodology

In addition to their shared genetic or maturational emphasis, the Piagetian and psychometric approaches to intelligence have still another characteristic in common. This common feature is their failure, for the most part, to use the experimental method in the strict sense of that term. It seems fair to say that most of the studies which attempt to get at the determinants of test intelligence are correlational in nature. By and large such studies attempt to relate the test scores of parents and their children, of twins or of adopted children and their parents, or of the same children tested at different points in time and so on. Only in rare instances such as the Skeels (1966) study is an attempt made to modify intelligence by active intervention and with the utilization of a control group which does not receive the experimental treatment. While experimental work on human intelligence might well be desirable, such research often raises serious moral and ethical questions.

Piaget, for his part, has not employed the experimental method simply because it was not appropriate for the problems he wished to study. This is true because Piaget has been primarily concerned with the diagnosis of mental contents and abilities and not with their modification. To illustrate, the discovery of what the child means by ''more,'' ''less'' and ''same'' number of things requires flexible diagnostic interview procedures and not experimental procedures. Once the concept is diagnosed, then experimental methods are appropriate to determine the effects of various factors on the attainment and modification of the concepts in question. The sequence of events is not unlike the situation in medicine where the discovery or diagnosis of a disease is often the first step to its experimental investigation. In short, Piaget has focused upon the discovery of what and how children think and not with the modification of thinking which is a

subsequent and experimental question. In every science there is a natural history stage of enquiry during which relevant phenomena must be carefully observed and classified. American psychology has often tried to bypass this stage in its headlong rush to become an experimental science. In his studies Piaget has revealed a wide range of hitherto unknown and unsuspected facts about children's thinking, which have in America now become the starting points for a great deal of experimental investigation. What is often forgotten, when Piaget is criticized for not using the experimental method, is that such a method would not have revealed the wealth of phenomena which experimental investigators are now so busily studying.

Rationality as the Definition of Intelligence

There is a third and final commonality in the mental test and Piagetian approaches to intelligence which should be mentioned. This commonality resides in what these two positions regard as the nature or essence of intelligence. While there is considerable variability among psychometricians in this regard, many agree in general with the position taken by Jensen (1969). Jensen argues that the g factor which is present in all tests of mental ability appears in its purest forms on tests of generalization and abstraction. Spearman (1923) called these activities the education of relations (A is greater than B; B is greater than C; so A is in what relation to C?) and of correlates (Complete the series A AB ABC ———). While intelligence tests contain measures of many different types of mental abilities, including language and perceptual skills, the psychometric approach holds that the most central feature of human intelligence is its rationality, or as Wechsler put it: ''Intelligence is the aggregate or global capacity of the individual to act purposefully, to think rationally and to deal effectively with his environment'' (Wechsler, 1944, p. 3).

For Piaget, too, the essence of intelligence lies in the individual's reasoning capacities.

Piaget, however, is more specific in his description of these abilities and defines them in terms of mental operations which have the properties of mathematical groupings in general and the property of reversibility in particular. An operational grouping is present when in the course of any mental activity one can always get back to the starting point. For example, if the class *boys* and the class *girls* is mentally combined to form the class *children,* it is always possible to recapture the subclass by subtraction. That is to say, the class of children minus the class of boys equals the class of girls. Put differently, the operation of subtraction can be used to undo the operation of addition so that each of the combined classes can be retrieved. Verbal material learned by heart is, however, not rationally organized as is illustrated by the fact that no matter how well a passage is learned, it is impossible, without additional effort, to say it backwards. If an operational system were involved, having learned the passage forward would automatically imply the ability to say it backwards. In Piaget's view, neither perception nor language are truly rational since neither one shows complete reversibility. So, while perception and language play an important part in intellectual activity, they do not epitomize that activity.

The psychometric and Piagetian approaches to intelligence thus agree on its genetic determination (at least in part), and on the use of non-experimental methodology and upon the essentially rational nature of mental ability. After this look at their commonalities, it is perhaps time to look at their differences.

Conceptual Differences

Despite the commonalities noted above, the psychometric and developmental approaches to intelligence also differ in certain respects. These differences, however, derive from the unique ways in which the psychometricians and Piaget approach and view intelligence and not from any fundamental disagreements regarding the nature of intelligence itself. In other words the differences are due to the fact that the two approaches are interested in assessing and describing different facets of intelligent behavior. Accordingly the differences arise with respect to: (a) the type of genetic causality they presuppose; (b) the description of mental growth they provide; and (c) the contributions of nature and nurture which they assess.

Genetic Causality

Although the Piagetian and psychometric approaches to intelligence agree on the importance of genetic determination, at least in part, of human mental ability, each approach emphasizes a somewhat different mode of genetic determination or causality. In order to make these differences clear, it is necessary to recall some of the basic features of evolutionary theory upon which all modern conceptions of intelligence are based.

Within the Darwinian conception of evolution there are two major phenomena that have to be taken into account: within-species variability and natural selection. For any given species of animal or plant one can observe a range of variations in such features as color, shape and size. Among a flock of robins, to illustrate, one can see that some adult birds differ in size, in richness of breast coloration and that some even manifest slight variations in head and wing conformation. Similar variations can be observed among a group of collies, Persian cats and even among tomato plants in the garden. This within-species variability, we know today, is due to the chance pairings of parental genes and to gene complexes which occur because each parent contributes only half of its genetic complement to its offspring. Variations within a given species at a given time are, therefore, primarily due to chance factors: namely the random genetic assortments provided by the parent generation. One determinant of variability among animals and plants is then, simply, chance.

Now in the psychometric conception of intelligence, this random type of variation is just what is presupposed. Test intelligence, it is assumed, is randomly distributed in a given population at a given time and such distributions should resemble the bell shaped curve of the normal probability function. Measurement of human abilities does in fact reveal a tendency for such measurements to fall into normal distributions. In addition evidence such as "regression toward the mean" (children of exceptionally bright or dull parents tend to be less bright and less dull than their parents) is also characteristic of genetic traits which are randomly determined. In short, when the psychometrician speaks of genetic determination, he is speaking of the chance gene combinations which produce a "normal" bell-shaped distribution of abilities within a given population.

Obviously this description of genetic determination is extremely over-simplified; we know that a test score is a phenotype which is determined by many different factors not all of which are genetic. Jensen, to illustrate, breaks down the variance of test intelligence into a large number of components such as genotypic variation, environment, environment genotype interaction, epistasis, error of measurement variance and so on. With the exception, perhaps, of the selective mating variable, however, all of these factors can again be assumed to operate in a random manner so that one might say that the chance distribution of observed test scores is the product of many underlying chance distributions. That the psychometric approach does in general presuppose a random distribution is also shown by the fact that the criterion of a true change in intellectual ability is the demonstration that such a change could *not* be attributed to chance factors.

That variability within a species is in part determined by chance gene and gene complex assortments has of course been demonstrated by Mendel and all of the research which has derived from this theory of genetics. There are, however, other forms of organismic variability which cannot be attributed to chance. Natural selection, the other component of evolution, is never random but always moves in the direction of improved adaptation to the milieu. To illustrate, over the past hundred years there has been a gradual predominance of dark over light colored moths in the industrial sections of England. Kettlewell (1955) demonstrated the survival value of dark coloration by showing that light moths placed on soot darkened bark were more readily eaten by insectivorous birds than were similarly placed dark moths. When variations across generations are considered, the variations are not random but rather show a clear cut direction.

The same holds true within the course of individual development. In the case of individual growth, however, the direction of progress is not determined by mating practices but rather by biochemical mechanisms which are only now in the process of being understood. That these biochemical agents determine the direction of development, however, cannot be doubted. As Waddington (1962b) points out, animals consist of a limited variety of cells such as nerve cells, muscle cells and so on. Likewise the organs of the body are also distinct from one another in form, composition and function. What direction particular cells will take as the egg matures will depend upon the action of chemical agents which Spemann (discussed in Bertalanffy, 1962) called *organizers* with definite loci in the cell material called *organization centers*. It is the organizer which determines whether particular cells will become nerve, muscle or organ tissue. Individual development, therefore, is not determined by random factors but rather by biochemical organizers which specify the nature and direction of organismic differentiation.

Now when Piaget speaks of the genetic determination of intelligence, he has in mind not the random factors which determine gene combinations, but rather the non-random action of biochemical organizers and organization centers. Indeed, this is the kind of determination which Piaget assumes when he argues that the *sequence* in which the child attains the successive components of a concept or in which he acquires systems of mental operations, is invariant. In the formation of body organs the order of differentiation is fixed because each new phase of differentiation produces the organizer for the next stage. In Piaget's view this is equally valid for the growth of cognitive structures because the preceding cognitive structures, say the concrete operations of childhood, are a necessary prerequisite to the elaboration of the more complex formal operational structures of adolescence. For Piaget, then, genetic determination means that there are factors which give development a definite non-random direction.

In pointing out that the Piagetian and psychometric approaches to intelligence postulate different forms of genetic determinism, I want to reiterate that these two positions are not in contradiction one with the other. The mental test approach to intelligence is concerned with inter-individual differences in ability and these are, in so far as we know, largely randomly determined. Piaget, in contrast, is concerned with the intra-individual changes which occur in the course of development and these, to the best of our knowledge, are not random but rather have a direction given them by specific organizing mechanisms. Accordingly, and this is the genius of evolution, human intelligence manifests both determinism *and* freedom.

The Course of Mental Growth

Let us look now at a somewhat different issue, the age-wise course of mental growth. Here again we find a difference in perspective rather than a contradiction in conception as between the two positions. In psychometric terms, the course of mental growth is plotted as a curve which measures the amount of intelligence at some criterion age that can be predicted at any preceding age. As Bloom (1964) has pointed out, when age 17 is taken as the criterion age, some 50% of the total IQ at that age can be predicted at age four, and an additional 30% can be predicted from ages four to eight. Based on correlational data of this sort, curves of mental growth appear to rise rapidly in early childhood and taper off to a plateau in late adolescence. Such curves, it must be noted to avoid a frequent misinterpretation, say nothing as to the *amount* or *quality* of knowledge at given age levels. (See Jensen, pp. 115–117.)

From the mental test perspective, therefore, intellectual growth is pretty much a statistical concept derived from correlations of test scores

obtained at different age levels on the same individuals in the course of longitudinal studies. Such curves can be interpreted as reflecting the rate of mental growth but say nothing as to the nature of what is developing. Indeed, if intelligence is defined in the narrow sense of the abilities to generalize and abstract, then any qualitative differences in these abilities will necessarily be obscured by the curve of mental growth which suggests merely a quantitative increase in mental ability with increasing age.

Looked at from the standpoint of Piagetian psychology, however, mental growth involves the formation of new mental structures and consequently the emergence of new mental abilities. The child, to illustrate, cannot deal with propositional logic of the following sort, "Helen is shorter than Alice and taller than Ethel, who is the tallest of the three?" (Glick & Wapner, 1968), nor can children grasp the metaphorical connotations of satirical cartoons or proverbs (Shaffer, 1930). Adolescents, in contrast, have no trouble with either propositional logic or with metaphor. In the Piagetian view, therefore, mental growth is not a quantitative but rather a qualitative affair and presupposes significant differences between the thinking of children and adolescents as well as between preschool and school age children.

These qualitative differences are, as a matter of fact, built into the items of mental tests but are masked by the assignment of point scores to successes and failures. On the Wechsler Intelligence Scale for Children various of the subtests recognize qualitatively different responses only by assigning them additional points (Wechsler, 1949). For example, a child who says that a peach and a plum are alike because "they both have pits" is given a single point, whereas a child who says "they are both fruit" is given two points. On other sub-tests, such as the arithmetic sub-test, there is no point differential for success on problems which patently require different levels of mental ability. To illustrate, correct answers to the following two problems are both given only a single point: "If I cut an apple in half, how many pieces will I have?" A correct answer to that question is given the same score as the correct answer to this problem:

> Smith and Brown start a card game with $27 each. They agree that at the end of each deal the loser shall pay the winner one third of what he (the loser) then has in his posession. Smith wins the first three deals. How much does Brown have at the beginning of the fourth deal?

Clearly, the items on any given sub-test can tap quite different mental processes but these qualitative differences are obscured by assigning equivalent point scores to the various items regardless of the mental processes involved.

This is not to say that Piaget is right and that the mental test approach is wrong, or vice versa. The quantitative evaluation of mental growth is necessary and has considerable practical value in predicting school success. The qualitative approach is also of value, particularly when diagnosis of learning difficulties and educational remediation are in question. Which approach to mental growth one adopts will depend upon the purposes of the investigation. The only danger in the quantitative approach is to assume that, because sub-tests include items of the same general type and are scored with equal numerical weights, that they therefore assess only quantitative differences in the ability in question.

The Contributions of Nature and Nurture to Intelligence

Still a third way in which the psychometric and Piagetian views of intelligence differ has to do with the manner in which they treat the contributions of nature and nurture to intellectual ability. In the psychometric approach this contribution is treated substantively, with regard to the amount of variance in intellectual ability that can be attributed to nature and nurture respectively. Piaget, on the contrary, treats these contributions functionally with respect to the regulative role played by the environment or inner forces for any given mental activity. Both positions now need to be described in somewhat more detail.

The psychometric approach is substantive (and static) in the sense that it regards intelligence as capable of being measured and holds that such measures can be used to assess the extent to which nature and nurture contribute to intellectual ability. In the discussion of genetic causality the various components into which test scores could be analyzed were briefly noted. We are indebted to writers such as Burt & Howard (1957) and Jensen for making clear the many and complex determinants into which test performance can be analyzed. Without wishing to minimize these other determinants, the needs of the present discussion will be served if we consider only how the psychometric approach arrives at the contribution of the heredity and environmental factors.

As Jensen points out, heritability is the proportion of variability among observed or phenotypic intelligence (test scores) that can be attributed to genotypic variations. Estimates of heritability are obtained from correlational data for subjects with known kinship relations such as parents and children, siblings, and identical twins. The contribution of the environment is arrived at somewhat differently. Variability in intelligence test scores attributable to the environment is estimated from that variability which cannot be attributed to any other factors. It is, in fact, the residual variance, that which is left after all the other factors contributing to intelligence test performance have been accounted for. For the psychometrician, then, nature and nurture are regarded as substantive and static, and their contributions are assessed quantitatively with the aid of statistical procedures.

When we turn to the work of Piaget, however, we encounter quite a different conception of the contributions of nature and nurture. In Piaget's view, these contributions must be conceived functionally and dynamically with respect to their regulatory control over various mental activities. In this regard Piaget's views are not unlike those of David Rapaport (1958) who spoke of "the relative autonomy of the ego," a conception which may help to introduce Piaget's somewhat more difficult formulation. Rapaport argued that we are endowed with some mental processes, such as perception, that are responsive to the environment and so tend to guarantee or insure a certain independence of the mind from the domination of instinctual drives. Other mental processes, such as fantasy, are most responsive to internal forces and these in turn guarantee a certain independence of the mind from the domination of the environment. The presence and activity of both types of processes thus insures that the mind is enslaved neither by the environment nor by drives but retains a "relative autonomy" from both.

Piaget's view (1967c) is roughly similar. He argues that intelligence is an extension of biological adaptation which, in lieu of the instinctive adaptations in animals, permits relatively autonomous adaptations which bear the stamp not only of our genetic endowment, but also of our physical and social experience. On the plane of intelligence we inherit the processes of assimilation (processes responsive to inner promptings) and of accommodation (processes responsive to environmental intrusions). Assimilative processes guarantee that intelligence will not be limited to passively copying reality, while accommodative processes insure that intelligence will not construct representations of reality which have no correspondence with the real world. To make this functional conception of the contributions of nature and nurture to intelligence concrete, let us consider several different mental abilities which are differently regulated by internal and external forces.

If we look at imitation (Piaget, 1951), it is clear that it is largely accommodative in the sense that it is most responsive to environmental influence and is relatively independent of inner forces. The vocal mimic, for example, is expert to the extent that he can capture the pitch, timbre and inflections of his model's voice and to the extent to which he can suppress those aspects of his own speech which differ from the model's. Play, in contrast, is largely assimilative in that it is most responsive to inner needs and is relatively independent of environmental influence. The child who uses a stick alternatively as a gun, as an airplane and as a boat has

responded to the object largely in terms of his own inner needs and with a relative disregard of its real properties.

Between the two extremes of imitation and play is intelligence which manifests a balance or equilibrium between assimilative and accommodative activities and is thus relatively autonomous both of inner *and* outer forces. To illustrate, suppose we deduce, from the premise that Helen is taller than Jane and that Jane is taller than Mary, that Helen is the taller of three girls. We have in so doing attained a new bit of knowledge, an adaptation, but without altering the elements involved (assimilation without transformation of the objects) and without modifying the reasoning processes (accommodation without alteration of mental structures). Reason, or intelligence, is thus the only system of mental processes which guarantees that the mind and the environment will each retain its integrity in the course of their interaction.

Accordingly, for Piaget as for Rapaport, the question is not how much nature and nurture contribute to mental ability, but rather the *extent to which various mental processes are relatively autonomous from environmental and instinctual influence*. Such a conception is functional and dynamic, rather than substantive and static, because it deals with the regulatory activity of nature and nurture upon various mental processes. Those processes which show the greatest independence from environmental *and* internal regulation, the rational processes, are the most advanced of all human abilities. It is for this reason that Piaget reserves for them, and for them alone, the term intelligence.

In summary then, the psychometric and Piagetian approaches to intelligence differ with respect to: (a) the type of genetic causality which they presuppose; (b) their conceptions of the course of mental growth; and finally (c) the manner in which they conceive the contributions of nature and nurture to intellectual ability. In closing this section on the differences between the two positions I want to say again that the differences arise from differences in perspective and emphasis and are not contradictory but rather complementary. Both the psychometric and the Piagetian approaches to the conceptualization of human intelligence provide useful starting points for the assessment and interpretation of human mental abilities. Let us turn now to a couple of practical issues related to the modification and stimulation of mental abilities.

Practical Issues

In his essay, Jensen has tried to clarify many of the ambiguities regarding the nature and modification of intellectual ability and to put down some of the myths and misinterpretations prevalent with regard to test intelligence. For the most part, I find myself in agreement with Jensen and in this section, I would like to discuss two practical issues related to the modification and stimulation of intellectual abilities which seem to involve some misinterpretation of the Piagetian position. First, Piaget's insistence upon the qualitative differences between the modes of thinking at different age levels has been wrongly taken to suggest the need for preschool instruction in order to move children into concrete operational stage more quickly. Secondly, Piaget's emphasis upon the non-chance or self-directed nature of mental development has mistakenly been taken as justification for the use of methods such as "discovery learning" which supposedly stimulate the child's intrinsic motivations to learn. I would like, therefore, to try in the following section to clarify what seems to me to be the implications of Piaget's conception of intelligence for preschool instruction and for the implementation of intrinsic motivation.

Preschool Instruction

There appears to be increasing pressure these days in both the popular and professional literature for beginning academic instruction in early childhood, i.e., from 3 to 5 years. Bruner's famous statement that "We begin with the hypothesis that any subject can be taught effectively in some intellectually honest form to any child at any stage of development" (Bruner, 1962, p. 33) as well as the work of Hunt (1961), of Bloom (1964), of O. K. Moore

(1961), of Fowler (1968), and of Skeels (1966) have all been used in the advocacy of preschool instruction. Indeed Piaget and Montessori have been invoked in this connection as well. The argument essentially is that the preschool period is critical for intellectual growth and that if we leave this period devoted to fun and games, we are lowering the individual's ultimate level of intellectual attainment. Parental anxiety and pressure in this regard have been so aroused that legislation has been passed or is pending for the provision of free preschool education for all parents who wish it for their children in states such as New York, Massachusetts and California.

What is the evidence that preschool instruction has lasting effects upon mental growth and development? The answer is, in brief, that there is none. To prove the point one needs longitudinal data on adults who did not have preschool instruction but who were equal in every other regard to children receiving such instruction. With the exception of the Montessori schools, however, the preschool instruction programs have not been in existence long enough to provide any evidence on the lastingness of their effects. Indeed, most of the earlier work on the effects of nursery school education (see Goodenough, 1940, and Jones, 1954, for reviews of this literature) has shown that significant positive effects are hard to demonstrate when adequate experimental controls are employed. It is interesting that no one, to my knowledge, has done a longitudinal study of adult Montessori graduates. Have they done better in life than children from comparable backgrounds not so trained? In any case, it is such unavailable longitudinal data that is crucial to the proposition that the preschool period is a critical one for intellectual development.

I am sure that someone will object at this point that studies of mental growth such as those of Bloom (1964) suggest that half of the individual's intellectual potential is realized by age four. Does this not mean that the preschool period is important for intellectual growth and that interventions during this period will have lasting effects? Not necessarily, if we look at the facts in a somewhat different way. Bloom writes, "Both types of data suggest that in terms of intelligence measured at age 17, about 50% of the development takes place between conception and age 4, about 30% between ages 4 and 8, and about 20% between 8 and seventeen" (Bloom, 1964, p. 88). Now an equally feasible implication of this statement is quite in contradiction to that of preschool instruction: the child has only 50% of his intellectual ability at age 4 but 80% at age 8, why not delay his education three years so that he can more fully profit from instruction? With 80% of his ability he is likely to learn more quickly and efficiently and is not as likely to learn in ways that he will need to unlearn later. That is to say, without stretching the fact, it is possible to interpret the Bloom statement as implying that instruction should *not* be introduced into the preschool program.

Not only is there no clear-cut longitudinal data to support the claims of the lastingness of preschool instruction, there is evidence in the opposite direction. The work cited by Jones (1954) and by Piaget (1967b) in the quotations given earlier in this paper are cases in point. This evidence, together with more recent data reported in Jensen's paper, suggest a negative correlation between early physical maturation and later intellectual attainments. Animals are capable of achieving early some skills (a dog or a chimp will be housebroken before a child is toilet trained) but perhaps at the expense of not being able to attain other skills at all. This data suggests the hypothesis that *the longer we delay formal instruction, up to certain limits, the greater the period of plasticity and the higher the ultimate level of achievement*. There is at least as much evidence and theory in support of this hypothesis as there is in favor of the early-instruction proposition. Certainly, from the Piagetian perspective, there are "optimal periods" for the growth of particular mental structures which cannot be rushed.

Please understand, I am not arguing against the benefits of preschool enrichment for children. Even preschool instruction may be of value for those disadvantaged children who do not benefit from what Strodtbeck (1967) called the "hidden curriculum of the middle class home." What I am arguing is that there is no evidence for the *long term effects* of either preschool instruction or enrichment. Nursery school experience most assuredly has immediate value for the child to the extent that it helps him to appreciate and enjoy his immediate world to the full and to better prepare him for future social and intellectual activities. Everyone, for example, recognizes the value of a vacation without expecting that it will produce any permanent alterations. Isn't it enough that we lighten the burdens of childhood for even a brief period each day without demanding at the same time that we produce permanent results? The contributions of the nursery school, no less than that of the vacation, do not have to be long-lived to be of value.

In closing the discussion, I would like to emphasize another side to this issue of preschool instruction. This is the consideration that the emphasis on preschool education has obscured the fact that it is the elementary school years which are crucial to later academic achievement. It is during these years that the child learns the basic tool subjects, acquires his conception of himself as a student and develops his attitudes towards formal education. In this connection it might be well to quote a less publicized finding of Bloom's (1964) study:

> We may conclude from our results on general achievement, reading comprehension and vocabulary development, that by age 9 (grade 3) at least 50% of the general achievement pattern at age 18 (grade 12) has been developed whereas at least 75% of the pattern has been developed by age 13 (grade 7). (Bloom, 1964, p. 105)

With respect to the intellectual operations of concern to Piaget, similar trends appear to hold true. While children all over the world and across wide ranges of cultural and socioeconomic conditions appear to attain concrete operations at about the age of 6 or 7 (Goodnow, 1969), the attainment and use of formal operations in adolescence, in contrast, appear to be much more subject to socioculturally determined factors such as sex roles and symbolic proficiency (Elkind, 1961; Elkind, Barocas & Rosenthal, 1968; Goodnow & Bethon, 1966). Apparently, therefore, environmental variation during the elementary school period is more significant for later intellectual attainments of the Piagetian variety. In short, there is not much justification for making the preschool the scapegoat for our failures in elementary education. Like it or not, the years from six to twelve are still the crucial ones with respect to later academic achievement.

Motivation and Intellectual Growth

In recent years there has been an increasing recognition among psychologists such as Berlyne (1965), Hunt (1965), and White (1959), that certain mental activities can be self-rewarding and do not have to be externally reinforced. European writers such as Piaget (1954) and Montessori (1964) long ago recognized the existence of "intrinsic motivation" (to use Hunt's apt phrase), and Montessori in particular gave incomparable descriptions of children who suddenly discover they can read and proceed to read everything in sight. Piaget (1967d) too, has argued that needs and interests are simply another aspect of all cognitive activities.

Educators, however, in their efforts to capitalize upon this intrinsic motivation seem to have missed the point of what Montessori and Piaget had in mind. To maximize intrinsic motivation and to accelerate mental growth we have recently had an emphasis upon "learning by discovery" and upon "interesting reading materials" and so on. These approaches miss the point because they assume that intrinsic motivation can be built into materials and procedures which will in turn maximize mental growth. But as Piaget and Montessori pointed out (Elkind, 1967) intrinsic motivation resides in the child and not in methods and procedures. It is the child who must, at any given point in time, choose the method of learning and the

materials that are reinforcing *to him*. Without the opportunity for student choice and the provision of large blocks of time in which the child can totally engross himself in an activity, the values of intrinsic motivation will not be realized.

Indeed, I am very much afraid that by the time most children have reached the third or fourth grade a good deal of their intrinsic motivation for learning has been stifled. This is because spontaneous interest follows only the timetable of the child's own growth schedule. We can all remember, I am sure, those periods when we were so totally immersed in an activity that we forgot time, food and rest. During such periods we are at our creative and productive best and afterwards the feeling of exhaustion is coupled with a deep sense of accomplishment. In the school, however, we do not permit children to become totally engrossed in an activity but rather shuttle them from activity to activity on the hour or half hour. The result is what might be called *intellectually burned children*. Just as the burned child shuns the fire so the intellectually burned child shies away from total intellectual involvement.

How is this condition produced? In clinical practice we often see children (and adults) who are unwilling to form any emotional attachment. In the history of such children one always finds a series of broken relationships due to a wide variety of causes including the death of parents or the forced separation from them. Such children have learned that every time they reached out and became emotionally involved, rejection, hurt and misery were the result. Consequently they prefer not to get involved any more because the pain and anguish of still another broken relationship is just too high a price to pay for an emotional attachment. The intellectually burned child is in somewhat the same position. He refuses to become totally involved in intellectual activities because the repeated frustration of being interrupted in the middle is just too much to bear. Our lockstep curricula, thirty minutes for this and an hour for that, have the consequence, I suspect, of producing children who shun the fire of intense mental involvement.

Accordingly, the educational practice which would best foster intrinsically motivated children in the Piagetian and Montessori sense would be the provision of "interest areas" where children could go on their own and for long periods of time. Only when the child can choose an activity and persist at it until he is satiated can we speak of true intrinsically motivated behavior. Where such interest areas and time provisions have been made, as in the World of Inquiry School in Rochester, New York, the results are impressive indeed.[1]

[1]The results of our preliminary evaluation of this school suggest that World of Inquiry pupils are significantly higher in their need for achievement and more positive in their self evaluations than are their matched controls (children taken from the waiting list) who are attending other schools.

In summary then, the Piagetian conception of intelligence provides no support either for those who advocate formal preschool instruction or for those who argue for new methods and materials to stimulate intrinsic motivation. As we have seen, there is no evidence as yet for the lastingness of preschool instruction. In addition, intrinsic motivation seems best stimulated by allowing the child to engage in the activity of his choice for unbroken periods of time. As Jensen has so rightly pointed out, if we really want to maximize the effects of instruction, it does not pay to blink at the facts whether they have to do with racial or socioeconomic differences in intelligence, the effects of preschool instruction, or the nature of intrinsic motivation.

REFERENCES

Berlyne, D. E. Curiosity and education. In J. D. Krumboltz (Ed.) *Learning and the educational process.* Chicago: Rand McNally, 1965, 67–89.

Bertalanffy, Ludwig von. *Modern theories of development.* New York: Harper & Bros. (Torchbook ed.) 1962.

Bloom, B. S. *Stability and change in human characteristics.* New York: John Wiley & Sons, Inc., 1964.

Bruner, J. *The process of education.* Cambridge, Mass.: Harvard University Press, 1962.

Burt, C. *Mental and scholastic tests.* London: Staples Press, 1962 (4th edition).

Burt, C., & Howard, M. The relative influence of heredity and environment on assessments of intelligence. *British Journal of Statistics Psychology,* 1957, *10*, 33–63.

Elkind, D. Quantity conceptions in junior and senior high school students. *Child Development,* 1961, *32*, 551–560.

Elkind, D. Piaget and Montessori. *Harvard Educational Review,* 1967 (Fall) 535–545.

Elkind, D., Barocas, R., & Rosenthal, B. Combinatorial thinking in children from graded and ungraded classrooms. *Perceptual and Motor Skills,* 1968, *27*, 1015–1018.

Fowler, W. The effect of early stimulation in the emergence of cognitive processes. In R. D. Hess & Roberta M. Meyers (Eds.) *Early Education.* Chicago: Aldine Press, 1968, 9–36.

Glick, J., & Wapner, S. Development of transitivity: Some findings and problems of analysis. *Child Development,* 1968, *39*, 621–638.

Goodenough, Florence. New evidence on environmental influence on intelligence. *Yearbook of the National Society for the Study of Education,* 1940, *39*, 307–365.

Goodnow, Jacqueline J. Problems in research on culture and thought. In D. Elkind and J. Piaget (Eds.) *Studies in cognitive development.* New York: Oxford University Press, 1969, 439–464.

Goodnow, Jacqueline J., & Bethon, G. Piaget's tasks: The effects of schooling and intelligence. *Child Development,* 1966, *37*, 573–582.

Hunt, J. McV. *Intelligence and experience.* New York: The Ronald Press, 1961.

Hunt, J. McV. Intrinsic motivation and its role in psychological development. In D. Levine (Ed.) *Nebraska symposium on motivation.* Lincoln: University of Nebraska Press, 1965, 189–282.

Jones, H. E. The environment and mental development. In L. Carmichael (Ed.) *Manual of child psychology*. New York: John Wiley & Sons, Inc., 1954, 631–696.

Kittlewell, H. B. D. Selection experiments on industrial melanism in the lepidoptera. *Heredity*, 1955, *9*, 323–342.

Montessori, Maria. *The Montessori Method*. New York: Schocken, 1964 (first published in English, 1912).Moore, O. K. Orthographic symbols and the preschool child: A new approach. In E. P. Torrence (Ed.) *Creativity: 1960 proceedings of the 3rd conference on gifted children*. Minneapolis: University of Minnesota, Center for Continuation Studies, 1961.

Piaget, J. *Play, dreams and imitation in childhood*. New York: Norton, 1951.

Piaget, J. *Les relations entre l'affectivité et l'intelligence dans la developpement mental de l'enfant*. Paris: C.D.U., 1954 (mimeographed and bound lectures given at the Sorbonne).

Piaget, J. Genesis and structure in the psychology of intelligence. In D. Elkind (Ed.) *Six Psychological Studies by Jean Piaget*. New York: Random House, 1967a, 143–158.

Piaget. J. *On the nature and nurture of intelligence*. Address delivered at New York University, March, 1967b.

Piaget, J. Intelligence et adaptation biologique. In F. Bresson *et al.* (Eds.) *Les Processus d'adaptation*. Paris: Presses Universitaires de France, 1967c, 65–82.

Piaget, J. The mental development of the child. In D. Elkind (Ed.) *Six Psychological Studies by Jean Piaget*. New York: Random House, 1967d, pp. 3–73.

Rapaport, D. The theory of ego autonomy. *Bulletin of the Menninger Clinic*, 1958, *22*, 13–35.

Shaffer, L. F. Children's interpretations of cartoons. *Contributions to Education*. No. 429. New York: Teacher's College, Columbia University, 1930.

Skeels, Harold M. Adult status of children with contrasting early life experiences. *Monographs of the Society for Research in Child Development*, 1966, *31*, 3, No. 105.

Spearman, C. *The nature of "intelligence" and the principles of cognition*. London: Macmillan, 1923.

Strodtbeck, F. L. The hidden curriculum of the middle class home. In H. Passow, Miriam Goldberg and E. J. Tannenbaum (Eds.) *Education of the disadvantaged*. New York: Holt, Rinehart & Winston, 1967, 244–259.

Waddington, C. H. *The nature of life*. New York: Atheneum, 1962a.

Waddington, C. H. *How animals develop*. New York: Harper & Bros. (Torchbook Ed.), 1962b.

Wechsler, D. *The measurement of adult intelligence*. Baltimore: Williams & Wilkens, 1944.

Wechsler, D. *Wechsler intelligence scale for children*. New York: Psychological Corporation, 1949.

White, R. W. Motivation reconsidered: The concept of competence. *Psychological Review*, 1959, *66*, 297–333.

36. CULTURAL DIFFERENCES AND INFERENCES ABOUT PSYCHOLOGICAL PROCESSES[1]

MICHAEL COLE and JEROME S. BRUNER

Deficit Interpretation

Perhaps the most prevalent view of the source of ethnic and social class differences in intellectual performance is what might be summed up under the label "the deficit hypothesis." It can be stated briefly, without risk of gross exaggeration. It rests on the assumption that a community under conditions of poverty (for it is the poor who are the focus of attention, and a disproportionate number of the poor are members of minority ethnic groups) is a disorganized community, and this disorganization expresses itself in various forms of deficit. One widely agreed-upon source of deficit is mothering; the child of poverty is assumed to lack adequate parental attention. Given the illegitimacy rate in the urban ghetto, the most conspicuous "deficit" is a missing father and, consequently, a missing father model. The mother is away at work or, in any case, less involved with raising her children than she should be by white middle-class standards. There is said to be less regularity, less mutuality in interaction with her. There is said to be specialized deficits in interaction as well—less guidance in goal seeking from the parents (Schoggen, 1969), less emphasis upon means and ends in maternal instruction (Hess & Shipman, 1965), or less positive and more negative reinforcement (Bee, Van Egeren, Streissguth, Nyman, & Leckie, 1969; Smilansky, 1968).

[1]A version of this article will appear in the 1972 *National Society for the Study of Education Yearbook on Early Childhood Education*.

More particularly, the deficit hypothesis has been applied to the symbolic and linguistic environment of the growing child. His linguistic community as portrayed in the early work of Basil Bernstein (1961), for example, is characterized by a restricted code, dealing more in the stereotype of interaction than in language that explains and elaborates upon social and material events. The games that are played by poor children and to which they are exposed are less strategy bound than those of more advantaged children (Eifermann, 1968); their homes are said to have a more confused noise background, permitting less opportunity for figure-ground formation (Klaus & Gray, 1968); and the certainty of the environment is sufficiently reduced so that children have difficulty in delaying reinforcement (Mischel, 1966) or in accepting verbal reinforcement instead of the real article (Zigler & Butterfield, 1968).

The theory of intervention that grew from this view was the idea of "early stimulation," modeled on a conception of supplying nutriment for those with a protein deficiency or avitaminosis. The nature of the needed early stimulation was never explained systematically, save in rare cases (Smilansky, 1968), but it variously took the form of practice in using abstractions (Blank & Solomon, 1969), in having dialogue where the referent objects were not present, as through the use of telephones (Deutsch, 1967; John & Goldstein, 1964), or in providing secure mothering by substitution (Caldwell et al., 1970; Klaus & Gray, 1968).

A primary result of these various deficits was believed to express itself in the lowered test scores and academic performance among children from poverty backgrounds. The issue was most often left moot as to whether or not this lowered test performance was easily reversible, but the standard reference was to a monograph by Bloom (1964) indicating that cognitive performance on a battery of tests, given to poor and middle-class children, yielded the result that nearly 80% of the variance in intellectual performance was accounted for by age 3.

Difference Interpretation

Such data seem to compel the conclusion that as a consequence of various factors arising from minority group status (factors affecting motivation, linguistic ability, goal orientation, hereditary proclivities to learn in certain ways—the particular mix of factors depends on the writer), minority group children suffer intellectual deficits when compared with their ''more advantaged'' peers.

In this section, we review a body of data and theory that controverts this contention, casts doubt on the conclusion that a deficit exists in minority group children, and even raises doubts as to whether any nonsuperficial *differences* exist among different cultural groups.

There are two long-standing precedents for the view that different groups (defined in terms of cultural, linguistic, and ethnic criteria) do not differ intellectually from each other in any important way.[2] First, there is the anthropological ''doctrine of psychic unity'' (Kroeber, 1948) which, on the basis of the ''run of total experience,'' is said to warrant the assumption of intellectual equality as a sufficient approximation to the truth. This view is compatible with current linguistic anthropological theorizing, which concentrates on describing the way in which different cultural/

linguistic groups categorize familiar areas of experience (Tyler, 1970). By this view, different conclusions about the world are the result of arbitrary and different, but equally logical, ways of cutting up the world of experience. From this perspective, descriptions of the ''disorganization'' of minorities would be highly suspect, this suspicion arising in connection with questions like, Disorganized from whose point of view?

Anthropological critiques of psychological experimentation have never carried much weight with psychologists, nor have anthropologists been very impressed with conclusions from psychological tests. We have hypothesized elsewhere (Cole, Gay, Click, & Sharp, 1971) that their mutual indifference stems in part from a difference in opinion about the inferences that are warranted from testing and experimentation, and in part because the anthropologist relies mainly on data that the psychologist completely fails to consider: the mundane social life of the people he studies. As we shall see, these issues carry over into our criticism of the ''deficit'' theory of cultural deprivation.

A second tradition that calls into question culturally determined group difference in intelligence is the linguist's assertion that languages do not differ in their degree of development (Greenberg, 1963), buttressed by the transformationalist's caution that one cannot attribute to people a cognitive capacity that is less than is required to produce the complex rule-governed activity called language (Chomsky, 1966).

Although Chomskian linguistics has had a profound effect on psychological theories of language and cognitive development in recent years, psychological views of language still are considered hopelessly inadequate by working linguists. The criticism applies not only to psycholinguistic theory but to the actual description of linguistic performance on which theory is based. Needless to say, the accusation of misunderstanding at the descriptive level leads to accusations of absurdity at the theoretical level.

[2]It is assumed here that it is permissible to speak of minority group or poverty group ''culture'' using as our criterion Lévi-Strauss' (1963) definition: ''What is called 'culture' is a fragment of humanity which, from the point of view of the research at hand . . . presents significant discontinuities in relation to the rest of humanity [p. 295].'' We do not intend to enter into arguments over the existence or nature of a ''culture of poverty,'' although such an idea seems implicit in the view of most deficit theorists.

A third tradition that leads to rejection of the deficit theory has many sources in recent social sciences. This view holds that even when attempts have been made to provide reasonable anthropological and linguistic foundations, the conclusions about cognitive capacity from psychological experiments are unfounded because the performance produced represents a complex interaction of the formal characteristics of the experiment and the social/environmental context that determines the subject's interpretation of the situation in which it occurs. The need for "situation-bound" interpretations of experiments is emphasized in such diverse sources as sociology (Goffman, 1964), psychology (Brunswik, 1958), and psycholinguistics (Cazden, 1970). This is an important issue, which we will return to once illustrations of the "antideficit" view have been explored.

Perhaps the most coherent denial of the deficit position, coupled with compelling illustrations of the resourcefulness of the supposedly deprived and incompetent person, is contained in Labov's attack on the concept of "linguistic deprivation" and its accompanying assumption of cognitive incapacity (Labov, 1970).

It is not possible here to review all of Labov's evidence. Rather, we have abstracted what we take to be the major points in his attack.

1. *An assertion of the functional equality of all languages.* This assertion is applied specifically to his analysis of nonstandard Negro English, which has been the object of his study for several years. Labov provided a series of examples where young blacks who would be assessed as linguistically retarded and academically hopeless by standard test procedures enter conversations in a way that leaves little doubt that they can speak perfectly adequately and produce very clever arguments in the process.

2. *An assertion of the psychologist's ignorance of language in general and nonstandard dialects in particular.* Labov's particular target is Carl Bereiter (Bereiter & Englemann, 1966) whose remedial teaching technique is partly rationalized in terms of the *inability* of young black children to use language either as an effective tool of communication or thinking. Part of Labov's attack is aimed at misinterpretations of such phrases as *"They mine,"* which Labov analyzed in terms of rules of contraction, but which Bereiter made the mistake of referring to as a "series of badly connected words [Labov, 1970, p. 171]." This "psychologist's deficit" has a clear remedy. It is roughly equivalent to the anthropological caveat that the psychologist has to know more about the people he studies.

3. *The inadequacy of present experimentation.* More serious criticism of the psychologist's interpretation of "language deprivation" and, by extension, his whole concept of "cultural deprivation" is contained in the following, rather extensive quote:

this and the preceding section are designed to convince the reader that the controlled experiments that have been offered in evidence [of Negro lack of competence] are misleading. The only thing that is controlled is the superficial form of the stimulus. All children are asked, "What do you think of capital punishment?" or "Tell me everything you can about this." But the speaker's interpretation of these requests, and the action he believes is appropriate in response is completely uncontrolled. One can view these test stimuli as requests for information, commands for action, or meaningless sequences of words. . . . With human subjects it is absurd to believe that identical stimuli are obtained by asking everyone the same question. Since the crucial intervening variables of interpretation and motivation are uncontrolled, most of the literature on verbal deprivation tells us nothing of the capacities of children [Labov, 1970, p. 171].

Here Labov is attacking the experimental method as usually applied to the problem of subcultural differences in cognitive capacity. We can abstract several assertions from this key passage: (*a*) Formal experimental equivalence of operations does not insure de facto equivalence of experimental treatments; (*b*) different subcultural groups are predisposed to interpret the experimental stimuli (situations) differently; (*c*) different subcultural groups are motivated by different concerns relevant to the experimental task; (*d*) in view of the in-adequacies of experimentation, inferences about lack of competence among black children are unwarranted.

These criticisms, when combined with linguistic misinterpretation, constitute Labov's attack on the deficit theory of cultural deprivation and represent the rationale underlying his demonstrations of competence where its lack had previously been inferred.

One example of Labov's approach is to conduct a rather standard interview of the type often used for assessment of language competence. The situation is designed to be minimally threatening; the interviewer is a neighborhood figure, and black. Yet, the black 8-year-old interviewee's behavior is monosyllabic. He is a candidate for the diagnosis of linguistically and culturally deprived.

But this diagnosis is very much situation dependent. For at a later time, this same interviewer goes to the boy's apartment, brings one of the boy's friends with him, lies down on the floor, and produces some potato chips. He then begins talking about clearly taboo subjects in dialect. Under these circumstances, the mute interviewee becomes an excited participant in the general conversation.

In similar examples, Labov demonstrated powerful reasoning and debating skills in a school dropout and nonlogical verbosity in an acceptable, "normal" black who has mastered the forms of standard English. Labov's conclusion is that the usual assessment situations, including IQ and reading tests, elicit deliberate, defensive behavior on the part of the child who has realistic expectations that to talk openly is to expose oneself to insult and harm. As a consequence, such situations *cannot* measure the child's competence. Labov went even further to assert that far from being verbally deprived, the typical ghetto child is

bathed in verbal stimulation from morning to night. We see many speech events which depend upon the competitive exhibition of verbal skills—sounding, singing, toasts, rifting, louding—a whole range of activities in which the individual gains status through the use of language. . . . We see no

connection between the verbal skill in the speech events characteristic of the street culture and success in the school room [Labov, 1970, p. 163].

Labov is not the only linguist to offer such a critique of current theories of cultural deprivation (see, e.g., Stewart, 1970). However, Labov's criticism raises larger issues concerning the logic of comparative research designs of which the work in cultural/linguistic deprivation is only a part. It is to this general question that we now turn.

Competence and Performance in Psychological Research

The major thrusts of Labov's argument, that situational factors are important components of psychological experiments and that it is difficult if not impossible to infer competence directly from performance, are not new ideas to psychologists. Indeed, a concern with the relation between *psychological processes* on the one hand and *situational factors* on the other has long been a kind of shadow issue in psychology, surfacing most often in the context of comparative research.

It is this question that underlies the oft-berated question, What do IQ tests measure? and has been prominent in attacks on Jensen's (1969) argument that group differences in IQ test performance are reflective of innate differences in capacity.

Kagan (1969), for example, pointed to the work of Palmer, who regularly delays testing until the child is relaxed and has established rapport with the tester. Jensen (1969, p. 100) himself reported that significant differences in test performance can be caused by differential adaptation to the test situation.

Hertzig, Birch, Thomas, and Mendez (1968) made a direct study of social class/ethnic differences in response to the test situation and demonstrated stable differences in situational responses that were correlated with test performance and were present even when measured IQ was equivalent for subgroups chosen from the major comparison groups.

Concern with the particular *content* of tests and experiments as they relate to inferences about cognitive capacity occurs within the same context. The search for a "culture-free" IQ test has emphasized the use of universally familiar material, and various investigators have found that significant differences in performance can be related to the content of the experimental materials. Price-Williams (1961), for example, demonstrated earlier acquisition of conservation concepts in Nigerian children using traditional instead of imported stimulus materials, and Gay and Cole (1967) made a similar point with respect to Liberian classification behavior and learning.

Contemporary psychology's awareness of the task and situation-specific determinants of performance is reflected in a recent article by Kagan and Kogan (1970). In a section of their paper titled "The Significance of Public Performance," they are concerned with the fact that "differences in quality of style of public performance, although striking, may be misleading indices of competence [p. 1322]."

Although such misgivings abound, they have not yet crystallized into a coherent program of research and theory nor have the implications of accepting the need to incorporate an analysis of situations in addition to traditional experimental manipulations been fully appreciated.

Extended Idea of Competence

Labov and others have argued forcefully that we cannot distinguish on the basis of traditional experimental approaches between the underlying competence of those who have had a poor opportunity to participate in a particular culture and those who have had a good opportunity, between those who have not had their share of wealth and respect and those who have. The crux of the argument, when applied to the problem of "cultural deprivation," is that those groups ordinarily diagnosed as culturally deprived have the same underlying competence as those in the mainstream of the dominant culture, *the differences in performance being accounted for by the situations and contexts in which the competence is expressed*. To put the

matter most rigorously, one can find a corresponding situation in which the member of the "out culture," the victim of poverty, can perform on the basis of a given competence in a fashion equal to or superior to the standard achieved by a member of the dominant culture.

A prosaic example taken from the work of Gay and Cole (1967) concerns the ability to make estimates of volume. The case in question is to estimate the number of cups of rice in each of several bowls. Comparisons of "rice-estimation accuracy" were made among several groups of subjects, including nonliterate Kpelle rice farmers from North Central Liberia and Yale sophomores. The rice farmers manifested significantly greater accuracy than the Yale students, the difference increasing with the amount of rice presented for estimation. In many other situations, measurement skills are found to be superior among educated subjects in the Gay and Cole study. Just as Kpelle superiority at making rice estimates is clearly not a universal manifestation of their superior underlying competence, the superiority of Yale students in, for example, distance judgments is no basis for inferring that their competence is superior.

We think the existence of demonstrations such as those presented by Labov has been salutary in forcing closer examination of testing situations used for comparing the children of poverty with their more advantaged peers. And, as the illustration from Gay and Cole suggests, the argument may have quite general implications. Obviously, it is not sufficient to use a simple equivalence-of-test procedure to make inferences about the competence of the two groups being compared. In fact, a "two-groups" design is almost useless for making any important inferences in cross-cultural research, as Campbell (1961) has suggested. From a logical view, however, the conclusion of equal cognitive competence in those who are not members of the prestige culture and those who are its beneficiaries is often equally unwarranted. While it is very proper to criticize the logic of assuming that poor performance implies lack of competence, the contention that poor performance is of *no* relevance to a theory of cognitive development and to a theory of cultural differences in cognitive development also seems an oversimplification.

Assuming that we can find test situations in which comparably good performance can be elicited from the groups being contrasted, there is plainly an issue having to do with the range and nature of the situations in which performance for any two groups can be found to be equal.

We have noted Labov's conclusion that the usual assessment of linguistic competence in the black child elicits deliberate defensive behavior and that he can respond effectively in familiar nonthreatening surroundings. It may be, however (this possibility is discussed in Bruner, 1970), that he is unable to utilize language of a decentered type, taken out of the context of social interaction, used in an abstract way to deal with hypothetical possibilities and to spell out hypothetical plans (see also Gladwin, 1970). If such were the case, we could not dismiss the question of different kinds of language usage by saying simply that decontextualized talk is not part of the natural milieu of the black child in the urban ghetto. If it should turn out to be the case that mastery of the culture depends on one's capacity to perform well on the basis of competence one has stored up, and to perform well in particular settings and in particular ways, then plainly the question of differences in the way language enters the problem-solving process cannot be dismissed. It has been argued, for example, by Bernstein (1970) that it is in the nature of the very social life of the urban ghetto that there develops a kind of particularism in which communication usually takes place only along concrete personal lines. The ghetto child, who by training is likely to use an idiosyncratic mode of communication, may become locked into the life of his own cultural group, and his migration into other groups consequently becomes the more difficult. Bernstein made clear in his most recent work that this is not a question of capacity but, rather, a matter of what he calls "orientation." Nevertheless, it may very well be that a ghetto dweller's language training unfits him for taking jobs in the power- and prestige-endowing

pursuits of middle-class culture. If such is the case, then the issue of representativeness of the situations to which he can apply his competence becomes something more than a matter of test procedure.

A major difficulty with this line of speculation is that at present we have almost no knowledge of the day-to-day representativeness of different situations and the behaviors that are seen as appropriate to them by different cultural groups. For example, the idea that language use must be considered outside of social interactions in order to qualify as abstract, as involving "cognition," is almost certainly a psychologist's fiction. The work of contemporary sociologists and ethnolinguists (Garfinkle, 1967; Hymes, 1966; Schegloff, 1968) seems conclusively to demonstrate the presence of complex contingent thinking in situations that are all too often characterized by psychologists as consisting of syncretic, affective interactions. Until we have better knowledge of the cognitive components that are part of social interactions (the same applies to many spheres of activity), speculations about the role of language in cognition will have to remain speculations.

In fact, it is extraordinarily difficult to know, save in a most superficial way, on the basis of our present knowledge of society, what is the nature of situations that permit control and utilization of the resources of a culture by one of its members and what the cognitive skills are that are demanded of one who would use these resources. It may very well be that the very definition of a subculture could be put into the spirit of Lévi-Strauss' (1963) definition of a culture:

What is called a subculture is a fragment of a culture which from the point of view of the research at hand presents significant discontinuities in relation to the rest of that culture with respect to access to its major amplifying tools.

By an amplifying tool is meant a technological feature, be it soft or hard, that permits control by the individual of resources, prestige, and deference within the culture. An example of a middle-class cultural amplifier that operates to increase the thought processes of those who employ it is the discipline loosely referred to as "mathematics." To employ mathematical techniques requires the cultivation of certain skills of reasoning, even certain styles of deploying one's thought processes. If one were able to cultivate the strategies and styles relevant to the employment of mathematics, then that range of technology is open to one's use. If one does not cultivate mathematical skills, the result is "functional incompetence," an inability to use this kind of technology. Whether or not compensatory techniques can then correct "functional incompetence" is an important, but unexplored, question.

Any particular aspect of the technology requires certain skills for its successful use. These skills, as we have already noted, must also be deployable in the range of situations where they are useful. Even if a child could carry out the planning necessary for the most technically demanding kind of activity, he must not do so if he has been trained with the expectancy that the exercise of such a skill will be punished or will, in any event, lead to some unforeseen difficulty. Consequently, the chances that the individual will work up his capacities for performance in the given domain are diminished. As a result, although the individual can be shown to have competence in some sphere involving the utilization of the skill, he will not be able to express that competence in the relevant kind of context. In an absolute sense, he is any man's equal, but in everyday encounters, he is not up to the task.

The principle cuts both ways with respect to cultural differences. Verbal skills are important cultural "amplifiers" among Labov's subjects; as many middle-class school administrators have discovered, the ghetto resident skilled in verbal exchanges is a more than formidable opponent in the battle for control of school curriculum and resources. In like manner, the Harlem youth on the street who cannot cope with the verbal battles described by Labov is failing to express competence in a context relevant to the ghetto.

These considerations impress us with the need to clarify our notion of what the com-petencies are that underlie effective performance. There has been an implicit, but very general, tendency in psychology to speak as if the organism is an information-processing machine with a fixed set of routines. The number and organization of these routines might differ as a function of age, genetic makeup, or environmental factors, but for any given machine, the input to the machine is processed uniformly by the routines (structures, skills) of the organism.

Quite recently, psychologists have started to face up to the difficulties of assuming "all things are equal" for different groups of people (concern has focused on difference in age, but the same logic applies to any group comparisons). The study of situational effects on performance has forced a reevaluation of traditional theoretical inferences about competence. This new concern with the interpretation of psychological experiments is quite apparent in recent attempts to cope with data inconsistent with Piaget's theory of cognitive development. For example, Flavell and Wohlwill (1969) sought to distinguish between two kinds of competence: First, there are "the rules, structures, or 'mental operations' embodied in the task and . . . [second, there are] the actual mechanisms required for processing the input and output [p. 98]." The second factor is assumed to be task specific and is the presumed explanation for such facts as the "horizontal decalages" in which the same principle appears for different materials at different ages. The *performance* progression through various stages is presumably a reflection of increases in both kinds of competence, since both are assumed to increase with age.

The same general concern is voiced by Mehler and Bever (1968). They ask,

How can we decide if a developmental change or behavioral difference among adults is really due to a difference in a structural rule, to a difference in the form of the expressive processes or a difference in their quantitative capacity [p. 278]?

Their own work traces the expression of particular rules in behavior and the way the effect of knowing a rule ("having a competence")

interacts with dependence on different aspects of the input to produce "nonlinear trends" in the development of conservation-like performance.

Broadening psychological theory to include rules for applying cognitive skills, as well as statements about the skills themselves, seems absolutely necessary.

However, the extensions contemplated may well not be sufficient to meet all of Labov's objections to inferences about "linguistic deprivation." In both the position expressed by Flavell and Wohlwill and by Mehler and Bever, "competence" is seen as dependent on situational factors and seems to be a slowly changing process that might well be governed by the same factors that lead to increases in the power of the structural rules or competence, in the older sense of the word. Yet in Labov's example, the problem is considerably more ephemeral; Labov gives the impression that the subjects were engaged in rational problem solving and that they had complete control over their behavior. He is claiming, in effect, that they are successfully coping with *their* problem; it simply is not the problem the experimenter had in mind, so the experimenter claims lack of competence as a result of his own ignorance.

Acceptance of Labov's criticism, and we think they should be accepted, requires not only a broadening of our idea of competence, but a vast enrichment of our approach to experimentation.

Necessity of a Comparative Psychology of Cognition

If we accept the idea that situational factors are often important determinants of psychological performance, and if we also accept the idea that different cultural groups are likely to respond differently to any given situation, there seems to be no reasonable alternative to psychological experimentation that bases its inferences on data from comparisons of both experimental and situational variations.

In short, we are contending that Brunswik's (1958) call for "representative design" and an analysis of the "ecological significance" of

stimulation is a prerequisite to research on ethnic and social class differences in particular, and to any research were the groups to be compared are thought to differ with respect to the process under investigation prior to application of the experimental treatments.

Exhortations to the effect that college sophomores with nonsense syllables and white rats in boxes are not sufficient objects for the development of a general psychological theory have produced, thus far, only minor changes in the behavior of psychologists. The present situations seem to *require* a change.

An illustration from some recent cross-cultural research serves as an illustration of one approach that goes beyond the usual two-group design to explore the situtional nature of psychological performance.

Cole et al. (1971, p. 4) used the free-recall technique to study cultural differences in memory. The initial studies presented subjects with a list of 20 words divided into four familiar, easily distinguishable categories. Subjects were read the list of words and asked to recall them. The procedure was repeated five times for each subject. A wide variety of subject populations was studied in this way; Liberian rice farmers and school children were the focus of concern, but comparison with groups in the United States was also made.

Three factors of the Kpelle rice farmers' performance were remarkable in these first studies: (*a*) The number recalled was relatively small (9–11 items per list); (*b*) there was no evidence of semantic or other organization of the material; (*c*) there was little or no increase in the number recalled with successive trials.

Better recall, great improvement with trials, and significant organization are all characteristic of performance of the American groups above the fifth grade.

A series of standard experimental manipulations (offering incentives, using lists based on functional rather than semantic classes, showing the objects to be remembered, extending the number of trials) all failed to make much difference in Kpelle performance.

However, when these same to-be-recalled items were incorporated into folk stories, when explicit grouping procedures were introduced, or when seemingly bizarre cuing procedures were used, Kpelle performance manifested organization, showed vast improvements in terms of amount recalled, and gave a very different picture of underlying capacity. Cole et al. (1971) concluded that a set of rather specific skills associated with remembering disconnected material out of context underlies the differences observed in the standard versions of the free-recall experiment with which they began. Moreover, they were able to begin the job of pinpointing these skills, their relevance to traditional activities, and the teaching techniques that could be expected to bring existing memory skills to bear in the "alien" tasks of the school.

Conclusion

The arguments set forth in this study can now be brought together and generalized in terms of their bearing on psychological research that is "comparative" in nature—comparing ages, cultures, subcultures, species, or even groups receiving different experimental treatments.

The central thesis derives from a reexamination of the distinction between competence and performance. As a rule, one looks for performance at its best and infers the degree of underlying competence from the observed performance. With respect to linguistic competence, for example, a single given instance of a particular grammatical form could suffice for inferring that the speaker had the competence to generate such instances as needed. By the use of such a methodology, Labov demonstrated that culturally deprived black children, *tested appropriately* for optimum performance, have the same grammatical competence as middle-class whites, though it may be expressed in different settings. Note that negative evidence is mute with respect to the status of underlying capacity—it may require a different situation for its manifestation.

The psychological status of the concept of competence (or capacity) is brought deeply into question when one examines conclusions based on standard experiments. Competence so defined is both situation blind and culture blind. If performance is treated (as it often is by linguists) only as a shallow expression of deeper competence, then one inevitably loses sight of the ecological problem of performance. For one of the most important things about any "underlying competence" is the nature of the situations in which it expresses itself. Herein lies the crux of the problem. One must inquire, first, whether a competence is expressed in a particular situation and, second, what the significance of that situation is for the person's ability to cope with life in his own milieu. As we have had occasion to comment elsewhere, when we systematically study the situational determinants of performance, we are led to conclude that cultural differences reside more in differences in the situations to which different cultural groups apply their skills than to differences in the skills possessed by the groups in question (Cole et al., 1971, Ch. 7).

The problem is to identify the range of capacities readily manifested in different groups and then to inquire whether the range is adequate to the individual's needs in various cultural settings. From this point of view, cultural *deprivation* represents a special case of cultural *difference* that arises when an individual is faced with demands to perform in a manner inconsistent with his past (cultural) experience. In the present social context of the United States, the great power of the middle class has rendered differences into deficits because middle-class behavior is the yardstick of success.

Our analysis holds at least two clear implications of relevance to the classroom teacher charged with the task of educating children from "disadvantaged" subcultural groups.

First, recognition of the educational difficulties in terms of a *difference* rather than a special kind of intellectual disease should change the students' status in the eyes of the teacher. If Pygmalion really can work in the classroom (Rosenthal & Jacobson, 1968), the effect of this change in attitude may of itself produce changes in performance. Such difference in teacher attitude seems to be one prime candidate for an explanation of the fine performance obtained by Kohl (1967) and others with usually recalcitrant students.

Second, the teacher should stop laboring under the impression that he must create new intellectual structures and start concentrating on how to get the child to *transfer* skills he already possesses to the task at hand. It is in this context that "relevant" study materials become important, although "relevant" should mean something more than a way to motivate students. Rather, relevant materials are those to which the child already applies skills the teacher seeks to have applied to his own content. It requires more than a casual acquaintance with one's students to know what those materials are.

The Soviet psychologist, Lev Vygotskii (1962), took as the motto of his well-known monograph on language and thought an epigraph from Francis Bacon: Neither hand nor mind alone, left to themselves, amounts to much; instruments and aids are the means to perfection.[3] Psychologists concerned with comparative research, and comparisons of social and ethnic group differences in particular, must take seriously the study of the way different groups organize the relation between their hands and minds; without assuming the superiority of one system over another, they must take seriously the dictum that man is a cultural animal. When cultures are in competition for resources, as they are today, the psychologist's task is to analyze the source of cultural difference so that those of the minority, the less powerful group, may quickly acquire the intellectual instruments necessary for success of the dominant culture, should they so choose.

[3]Nec manus nisi intellectus sibi permissus multam valent; instrumentibus et auxilibus res perficitur.

REFERENCES

Bee, H. L., Van Egeren, L. F., Streissguth, A. P., Nyman, B. A., & Leckie, M. S. Social class differences in maternal teaching strategies and speech patterns. *Developmental Psychology*, 1969, *1*, 726–734.

Bereiter, C., & Englemann, S. *Teaching disadvantaged children in the preschool*. Englewood Cliffs, N. J.: Prentice-Hall, 1966.

Bernstein, B. Social class and linguistic development: A theory of social learning. In A. H. Halsey, J. Floyd, & C. A. Anderson (Eds.), *Education, economy and society*. Glencoe, Ill.: Free Press, 1961.

Bernstein, B. A sociolinguistic approach to socialization: With some references to educability. In F. Williams (Ed.), *Language and poverty*. Chicago: Markham, 1970.

Blank, M., & Solomon, F. A tutorial language program to develop abstract thinking in socially disadvantaged preschool children. *Child Development, 1969, 40*, 47–61.

Bloom, B. S. *Stability and change in human characteristics*. New York: Wiley, 1964.

Bruner, J. S. *Poverty and childhood*. Merrill-Palmer Institute Monographs, 1970.

Brunswik, E. *Representative design in the planning of psychological research*. Berkeley: University of California Press, 1958.

Caldwell, B. M., et al. Infant day care and attachment. *American Journal of Orthopsychiatry*, 1970, *40*, 397–412.

Campbell, D. The mutual methodological relevance of anthropology and psychology. In F. L. K Hsu (Ed.), *Psychological anthropology*. Homewood, Ill.: Dorsey Press, 1961.

Cazden, C. The neglected situation. In F. Williams (Ed.), *Language and poverty*. Chicago: Markham Press, 1970.

Chomsky, N. *Cartesian linguistics*. New York: Harper & Row, 1966.

Cole, M., Gay, J., Glick, J., & Sharp, D. W. *The cultural context of learning and thinking*. New York: Basic Books, 1971.

Deutsch, M. *The disadvantaged child*. New York: Basic Books, 1967.

Eifermann, R. *School children's games*. Washington, D. C.: Department of Health, Education, and Welfare, 1968.

Flavell, J. H., & Wohlwill, J. F. Formal and functional aspects of cognitive development. In D. Elkind & J. H. Flavell (Eds.), *Studies in cognitive development*. New York: Oxford University Press, 1969.

Garfinkle, H. *Studies in ethnomethodology*. Englewood Cliffs, N. J.: Prentice-Hall, 1967.

Gay, J., & Cole, M. *The new mathematics and an old culture*. New York: Holt, Rinehart & Winston, 1967.

Gladwin, T. *East is a big bird*. Cambridge: Belnap Press, 1970.

Goffman, E. The neglected situation. In J. Gumperz & D. Hymes (Eds.), The ethnology of communication. *American Anthropologist*, 1964, *66*(6, Pt. 2), 133.

Greenberg, J. *Universals of language*. Cambridge: M.I.T. Press, 1963.

Hertzig, M. E., Birch, H. G., Thomas, A., & Mendez, O. A. Class and ethnic differences in the responsiveness of preschool children to cognitive demands. *Monographs of the Society for Research in Child Development*, 1968, *33*(1, Serial No. 117).

Hess, R. D., & Shipman, V. Early experience and socialization of cognitive modes in children. *Child Development*, 1965, *36*, 869–886.

Hymes, D. *On communicative competence*. (Report of a Conference on Research Planning on Language Development among Disadvantaged Children) New York: Yeshiva University Press, 1966.

Jensen, A. How much can we boost IQ and scholastic achievement? *Harvard Educational Review*, 1969, *39*, 1–123.

John, V. P., & Goldstein, L. S. The social context of language acquisition. *Merrill-Palmer Quarterly*, 1964, *10*, 265–275.

Kagan, J. Inadequate evidence and illogical conclusions. *Harvard Educational Review*, 1969, *39*, 274–277.

Kagan, J., & Kogan, N. Individuality and cognitive performance. In P. Mussen (Ed.), *Manual of child psychology*. New York: Wiley, 1970.

Klaus, R., & Gray, S. The early training project for disadvantaged children: A report after five years. *Monographs of the Society for Research in Child Development*, 1968, *33*(4).

Kohl, H. *36 children*. New York: New American Library, 1967.

Kroeber, A. L. *Anthropology*. New York: Harcourt, Brace, 1948.

Labov, W. The logical non-standard English. In F. Williams (Ed.), *Language and poverty*. Chicago: Markham Press, 1970.

Lévi-Strauss, C. *Structural anthropology*. New York: Basic Books, 1963.

Mehler, J., & Bever, T. The study of competence in cognitive psychology. *International Journal of Psychology*, 1968, *3*, 273–280.

Mischel, W. Theory and research on the antecedents of self-imposed delay of reward. In, *Progress in experimental personality research*. Vol. 3. New York: Academic Press, 1966.

Price-Williams, D. R. A. A study concerning concepts of conservation of quantities among primitive children. *Acta Psychologia*, 1961, *18*, 297–305.

Rosenthal, R., & Jacobson, L. *Pygmalion in the classroom*. New York: Holt, Rinehart & Winston, 1968.

Schegloff, E. A. Sequencing in conversational openings. *American Anthropologist*, 1968, *70*, 1075–1095.

Schoggen, M. An ecological study of three-year-olds at home. Nashville, Tenn.: George Peabody College for Teachers, November 7, 1969.

Smilansky, S. The effect of certain learning conditions on the progress of disadvantaged children of kindergarten age. *Journal of School Psychology,* 1968, *4*(3), 68–81.

Stewart, W. A. Toward a history of American Negro dialect. In F. Williams (Ed.), *Language and poverty.* Chicago: Markham Press, 1970.

Tyler, S. *Cognitive anthroplogy.* New York: Holt, Rinehart & Winston, 1970.

Vygotskii, L. S. *Thought and speech.* Cambridge: M.I.T. Press, 1962.

Zigler, E., & Butterfield, E. Motivational aspects of changes in IQ test performance of culturally deprived nursery school children. *Child Development,* 1968, *39*, 1–14.

Chapter 12
PERSONALITY AND BEHAVIOR PROBLEMS

INTRODUCTION AND COMMENTARY

Trait Psychology, Psychodynamics, and Interactionism

Personality theory and research have been dominated primarily by the trait model, and applied clinical work has been dominated primarily by the psychodynamic model. Both models emphasize that *actual behavior* is determined by latent, stable dispositions. The trait model emphasizes traits as the prime determinants of behavior, while the psychodynamic models, such as psychoanalysis, assume the existence of a basic personality core, which functions as a predispositional basis for behavior in various situations. That is, both models are basically response–response (R–R) models and emphasize consistency in behavior across situations, as opposed to situational specificity. Mischel (1968, 1969, 1971), Endler (1973, 1975), Bowers (1973), and Argyle and Little (1972) have all provided evidence to indicate that there is little empirical support for the consistency position in personality and that situational specificity should be taken into account. More important, the person–situation interaction seems to be an important determinant of behavior. See Endler (1973, 1975), Bowers (1973), and Mischel (1973) for presentations of an interactional model for personality.

Mischel (1973) in his cognitive social learning reconceptualization of personality suggests that five cognitive variables and their interactions are important in explaining individual differences. These five *person* variables are: (1) construction competence (the ability to generate or construct particular cognitions and behaviors); (2) personal constructs and encoding strategies; (3) stimulus outcome and behavior outcome expectancies in particular situations; (4) subjective stimulus values; and (5) self-regulatory systems and plans—rules and self-reactions for the performance and organization of complex behavior sequences. These social-cognitive person variables develop ontogenetically within the context of a social learning process, interacting with genetic dispositions. These person variables then interact with situational encounters in determining behavior.

Most of the research on the consistency versus specificity issue and on person–situation interactions has been conducted with adults. While none of the selections in this chapter specifically focus on these issues, the reader, nevertheless, should be aware of the issues when examining the papers in this chapter.

554

Definition, Strategy, Models, and Constructs

In most courses on personality, the field is usually divided into personality development, structure, and dynamics. However, the major concern in this chapter will be personality development, both normal and abnormal. One of the fundamental problems in personality (see Chapter 2, pp. 25–28) is the one of definition. In his classic book on personality, Allport (1937) discusses numerous definitions, which he proceeds to classify in terms of a number of rubrics. Dreger (1962) has updated Allport's scheme and discusses characterological, phenomenological, biopsychological, sociological, and biosocial definitions of personality. Sanford (1963) believes that all definitions should be concerned with "kinds of elements and the manner of their organization, personality in the perspective of time, the question of uniqueness and the problem of boundaries" (p. 498). According to Byrne (1974), personality is basically that field of psychological inquiry concerned with the variables or dimensions of individual differences, and with situational factors influencing the behavior of individuals. An interactionist position (e.g., Endler, 1975; Endler & Magnusson, 1974) would postulate that personality should be primarily concerned with person–situation interactions.

Within the area of personality, there are problems at the level of definition, research strategy and theoretical models, and disagreements in terms of what are the essential concepts and constructs. Therefore, it is not at all surprising that relatively little progress has been made in personality research and theory. Hunt (1965) suggests that the lack of scientific progress in this area may be a function of "the vagueness of the conceptual schemes which *pass* for personality theory" (italics added; p. 81). He states that one way out of this apparent impasse is to focus on *issues*, that is, on observations dissonant with widely held beliefs. See Chapter 2 for a further discussion of the issues of consistency–specificity and person–situation interaction.

The development of personality focuses on the relationship between *antecedent conditions* and *consequent events*. How do various factors influence the development and manifestation of personality variables? Byrne (1974) states that the three major types of antecedent conditions that influence personality development are genetic, prenatal, and experiential. The relative influence of genetic and experiential factors is relevant to the nature–nurture issue discussed in Chapter 2 (pp. 13–15). As Byrne suggests, one of the difficulties in examining antecedent-consequent relationships in personality is that a personality variable (e.g., ascendance, anxiety, dependence, hostility) develops "as a function of many antecedents operating over a long period of time. Such characteristics are sufficiently stable that they are usually found to be unaffected by variations in stimulus conditions" (Byrne, 1974, p. 76).

The early research on personality development was based primarily on naturalistic observations and clinical methods. Since the beginning of the 1950s, research on personality variables in development has become more experimental. Concomitantly there has been: (1) a de-emphasis on psychoanalysis as an explanatory model; (2) an attempt to explain personality development in terms of social learning (e.g., Bandura & Walters, 1963; Mischel, 1971) and person–situation interactions (e.g., Mischel, 1973); (3) a disenchantment with retrospective reports from adults and parents (for a discussion of some specific problems in this, see Yarrow, 1963) in favor of a focus on prospective studies on children; (4) a greater emphasis on cognitive and conceptual processes because of the social learning focus (see Bowers, 1973; Mischel, 1973), rather than on emotional factors (see the introductions to Chapter 10, Conceptual Development, and Chapter 5, Infancy, Early Experience, and Critical Periods); and (5) a questioning of the trait model as an appropriate model for personality (see Endler, 1975). In the domain of behavior problems there has been a shift from clinical diagnoses toward factor-analytic procedures for determining types of behavior problems. There has also been a trend toward studying parent–child interactions (e.g., Bell [41];

Peterson, Becker, Hellmer, Shoemaker, & Quay, 1959), rather than studying parents and children separately. Furthermore, there has also been an interest in the question of stability of various personality dimensions (e.g., Kagan & Moss, 1960; Mischel, 1969). See Chapter 2 (pp. 26–27) for a discussion of the stability issue.

Personality Stability?

Anderson (1948) has suggested that the personality of young children has been misrepresented because of the reliance on retrospective adult reports. To rectify this, it is necessary to obtain data from prospective longitudinal studies and ascertain the stability of behavioral patterns. A number of longitudinal studies have been done, including the ones initiated at the University of California (Berkeley), the Fels Research Institute, the Merrill-Palmer Institute, and the State University of Iowa.

Stability of behavioral patterns has been investigated for a number of different personality dimensions. Engel (1959) studied the self-concepts of sixth- and eighth-grade students over a two-year period. She found a high level of stability of the self-concept ($r = .78$) for these adolescents during this two-year period, and there were no sex differences with respect to the degree of stability. Kagan and Moss (1960), in a more extensive longitudinal study (from birth through early adulthood) conducted at the Fels Institute, investigated the stability of passive and dependent behavior. They found that these behaviors were relatively stable for women and relatively unstable for men. They hypothesized that these behaviors are socially acceptable for females but unacceptable for males, and therefore these behaviors would tend to be more stable for females. Stott (1957) investigated stability with respect to ascendance–submission in a twelve-year longitudinal study conducted at the Merrill-Palmer Institute. His results suggest that the stability of personality characteristics is due to neither heredity nor the learning of specific traits that adults consciously attempt to teach children. Instead, these traits are psychogenic in origin and arise from spontaneous interpersonal relations within the family. Once formed, these reaction patterns are resistant to extinction or modification. Kagan and Klein (1973) suggest that the empirical support for long-term continuity is modest, indeed. In observing children living in an isolated village in Guatemala, Kagan and Klein (1973) "saw listless, silent, apathetic infants; passive, quiet, timid 3-year-olds; but active, gay, intellectually competent 11-year-olds" (p. 947). Their observations led them to question "the strong form of the continuity assumption in a serious way" (Kagan and Klein, 1973, p. 948).

Sex Differences

Males and females are obviously different biologically and physically, and this is usually the starting point for a discussion of sex differences. But even biologically, males and females are not two discrete categories. "Far from falling into two discrete groups, male and female have the same body ground-plan, and even the anatomical difference is more apparent than real" (Oakley, 1972, p. 18). Nevertheless, the biological differences form the basis for psychological and cultural differences. Specifically, sex is a biological term, and gender a psychological and cultural term; significantly, there is not necessarily a one-to-one relationship between these two terms. Nevertheless, since we will focus primarily on psychological and cultural differences we will use the more general term "sex differences" to refer to male and female differences. For a discussion of biological differences, the reader is referred to Hutt (1972), Money and Ehrhardt (1972), and Oakley (1972). Although there are "obvious" psychological differences between male and female we do not know whether the differences are apparent or real, nor do we know whether they are due to biological (innate?) factors or to socialization practices.

In an attempt to determine whether various beliefs about psychological sex differences have a basis in scientific fact, Maccoby and Jacklin (1974) surveyed and interpreted the research literature (over 2,000 books and articles) on sex differences in social behavior, motivation, and intellectual ability. They discovered that many of the commonly shared beliefs about sex differences are actually *myths*, having no basis in fact. For example, girls are neither more "social" nor suggestible than boys. Girls do not have lower self-esteem than boys, nor do girls lack motivation to achieve. Girls are not more "empathic" than boys, nor are they better at rote learning than boys. Boys are not more "analytic" than girls nor are they superior to girls at higher-level cognitive processes. There are no sex differences in cognitive style.

After their thorough survey and interpretation of the literature on sex differences, Maccoby and Jacklin (1974) concluded that there were only *four sex differences* that have been fairly well established in *fact:*

1. Beginning at about age 11, *girls* manifest greater *verbal ability* than boys.
2. During adolescence and adulthood *boys* manifest greater *visual-spatial ability* than girls, but there are no sex differences during childhood.
3. Beginning around age 12 or 13 *boys* manifest greater *mathematical ability* than girls.
4. *Boys* are more aggressive both physically and verbally than girls. Both sexes become less aggressive with age, but boys and men remain more aggressive than girls and women, at least through the college years.

Apparently there is some biological basis for two of these differences—spatial ability and aggression. Cross-sex correlations in spatial ability suggest that this factor may be sex-linked genetically. Research relating testosterone to aggression suggests a biological basis for the male's more aggressive behavior.

Maccoby and Jacklin (1974), in examining the theoretical bases for the socialization of sex-typed behavior, find no empirical support for the belief that parents socialize their children to fit our conventionally held stereotypes, nor is there evidence that children necessarily imitate the same sexed parent (or adult). There is a considerable amount of uniformity in the socialization of boys and girls. Stereotyped behavior is not necessarily learned by imitation. For example, a girl's "femininity" is not correlated with her mother's "femininity," nor is a boy's "masculinity" correlated with his father's.

How do we then account for the fact that people believe that girls are more "social" than boys, or that girls have lower "self-esteem" than boys, despite the lack of confirming evidence? Maccoby and Jacklin (1974) suggest that the explanation may be in terms of selective attention. We attend to those phenomena we believe and ignore evidence that is dissonant with our beliefs. In a sense, then, the differences may become a self-fulfilling prophecy. In attempting to explain the source of the differences, Maccoby and Jacklin adopt Kohlberg's (1966) cognitive theory of development (see also Kohlberg & Kramer [38]). Each child creates a concept of what it means to be a boy or a girl on the basis of what he or she has observed or been told. This concept becomes stereotyped, oversimplified, and exaggerated. Although there may be some innate and socialization differences for boys and girls, the key factor seems to be our conceptualization of these differences. The culture outside the home (textbooks, movies, etc.) reinforces our conceptualizations, an occurrence that combines with the fact that, although there may not be many basic (inherent) differences between boys and girls, our belief in them leads to a self-fulfilling prophecy. (For a discussion of the potential contribution of ethology for sex differences in humans the reader is referred to Lehrman, 1974.)

Rutter (1971), in discussing normal psychosexual *development*, has suggested that although biological factors play a role in development, child-rearing practices and childhood experiences are the prime determinants of a child's sex type, gender role, and sexual interests. However, at this stage of our knowledge, it is not possible to specify *what* child-rearing aspects are crucial for psychosexual development. Prior to puberty there are no substantial sex differences with respect to hormone production, and there is very little *physical* sexual development until puberty. Comparing biologic, psychoanalytic, and psychosexual theories of sexual development with respect to a number of dimensions (e.g., physical maturation, sex-role differentiation, sexual interests and activity, maturity, gender role, etc.), Rutter maintains that psychosexual development commences in infancy.

Interaction of Temperament and Environment

Thomas, Chess, and Birch (1970) have been concerned with the nature of temperamental differences in children and their interaction with environmental influences in personality formation. They suggest that there are constitutional differences in temperament that, when interacting with the environment, shape personality. Observing children from birth and also interviewing their parents over a number of years, they observed the children's development up to and including the preschool period, nursery school, and elementary school. On the basis of their research, Thomas, Chess, and Birch have been able to identify three general types or clusters of temperament: "easy children" "difficult children" and "slow-to-warm-up children." They suggest that a different style of child-rearing practice is most appropriate for each of these three types. Their major point, however, is that personality development is a function of the *interaction* of constitutional temperament factors and environmental influences.

In the present selection [37], Chess, Thomas, and Birch present an overview of their longitudinal research on temperament–environment interactions and behavior problems in childhood. They suggest that since stressful maladaptive temperament–environment interactions are a crucial factor in the etiology of behavior problems, therapy, then, should focus on the modification of this *interaction* process. Their suggestion that parent–child interactions are bidirectional is similar to Bell's [41] proposition that parents' socializing practices have an effect on children, but also that children's individual characteristics (determined by congenital and environmental factors) influence the parents' behavior.

Continuities and Discontinuities
in Moral Development

The Kohlberg and Kramer selection [38] is based on a paper presented by Kohlberg at an annual meeting of the American Psychological Association symposium on Elements of a Life-Span Developmental Psychology. This selection is primarily concerned with continuities and discontinuities in childhood and adult moral development. The authors discuss three levels of moral development, with two stages for each level: (1) the preconventional level (the punishment-and-obedience orientation stage, and the instrumental-relativist orientation stage); (2) the conventional level (the interpersonal concordance, or "good boy–nice girl" orientation stage, and the law-and-order orientation stage); and (3) the postconventional, autonomous, or principled level (the social-contract–legalistic orientation stage and the universal–ethical-principle orientation stage). The authors suggest that there is an ontogenetic development from the lower stages to the higher stages of moral development, and conclude that moral development is a continuous process, involving the matching of one's interpersonal experience with a moral viewpoint. They also suggest that adult stabilization with respect to moral development is not due to socialization *per se* but rather to the integration of conflict.

Early Experience, Personality Development,
Abnormality, and Psychotherapy

The Harlow, Harlow, and Suomi paper [39], which studies monkeys as subjects, has implications for learning, early experience (see Chapter 5, pp. 142–143), personality development, family relationships, abnormality, and psychotherapy. For over forty years the Primate Laboratory at the University of Wisconsin has been investigating the learning capabilities of rhesus monkeys. While there, Harlow (1962) found that the heterosexual affectional system in monkeys progresses through a series of developmental stages and that social deprivation during infancy irreversibly hinders the capacity for social adjustment. Furthermore, Harlow and Harlow (1962) suggest that there is a critical period between the third and sixth months of life. (See Chapter 5 for a discussion of critical periods for socialization in the monkey.) They drew parallels between studies of social deprivation in monkeys and case studies of children reared in interpersonal situations. The presence of peers in the early stages of development, they found, is relatively more important for socialization than the presence of adult mothers. (See also the paper by Apolloni and Cooke, 1975, for a discussion of the importance of peer behavior in human infant and toddler development.) Building on the previous research, Harlow, Harlow, and Suomi [39], in the present study, indicate that it is possible to rehabilitate disturbed monkeys (who have suffered as a result of social deprivation) when their peers are used as psychotherapists. The present paper indicates ways to produce abnormalities and suggests how to provide "psychotherapy" to alleviate these abnormalities. It also shows the relationships among learning, personality, and pathology, and suggests the important implications of animal research for an understanding of human behavior.

Physique and Personality

One area of interest to personality theorists is the relationship between physique and personality (e.g., Sheldon, 1949). Of special interest to developmental psychologists is the relationship between physical maturity and personality (e.g., Jones & Bayley, 1950; Mussen & Jones, 1957). Mussen and Jones found that *American* adolescent males who exhibited early physical maturation were more self-confident and independent, and less rebellious toward their parents than late-maturing boys. Mussen and Bouterline-Young (1964) in a cross-cultural study found that *Italian* boys who matured early were not necessarily more self-confident than those who matured late; however, like the American early maturers, the Italians did manifest warm and affectionate feelings toward their parents. The *Italian-American* early maturers were similar to Americans in self-confidence, but different from both Americans and Italians in that they were more rebellious towards their parents. For other cross-cultural studies in the area of personality, the reader is referred to the papers by Goldman [43] and Holtzman [44]. See also the introduction and commentary to Chapter 13 (pp. 612–613) for a discussion of cross-cultural studies.

Social Interaction Patterns and Personality Development

Bayley and Schaefer (1960), in one of the longitudinal growth studies conducted at Berkeley, are concerned with mother–children social interaction patterns (see Bell [41] and Lewis [42]) and their effects on personality development in normal children. The study focuses on the establishment of emotional and attitudinal patterns. (The conceptual scheme used to study the maternal–filial interactions has been discussed by Schaefer, 1959.) Whereas Bayley and Schaefer are concerned with (1) mother–child relationships and (2) normal children, Peterson, Becker, Hellmer, Shoemaker, and Quay (1959) discuss (1) the role of *both* parents in interacting with children, especially (2) children with behavior problems. Peterson et al. indicate that the attitudes of fathers are as important as maternal attitudes in the development of behavior problems in children, and they adopt a clarifying distinction between personality problems and conduct behavior problems. For a discussion on parent–child interaction that focuses on the mutual effects of parents and children, and vice-versa, the reader is referred to Bell's paper [41] in Chapter 13, and the Chess, Thomas, and Birch paper in the present chapter [37].

Behavior Problems and Stability

The final selection in this chapter deals with behavior problems and is related to the Peterson et al. (1959) paper, discussed above. Peterson [40], concerned primarily with the conceptual classification of behavior disorders in children, factor-analyzed a series of judgments of problem behaviors occurring during middle childhood (from kindergarten through grade six). His results, consistent with the distinction made by Peterson et al. (1959), indicate two behavior disorder factors: (1) a conduct problem, characterized by such symptoms as disobedience, negativism, and fighting; and (2) a personality problem, characterized by social withdrawal, feelings of inferiority, anxiety, etc. Quay and Quay (1965) extended this study to children of grades seven and eight (early adolescence) and obtained similar factors plus an immaturity factor. They report that similar results have been found for samples of both normals and juvenile delinquents. The *conduct problem* and *personality problem* factors appear to be personality constants, at least for the various age groups studied. These results represent cross-sectional stability, in that the types of problems (factorial dimensions) that show up at the early ages (middle childhood) also show up at later ages (adolescence). This stability should not be confused with the longitudinal stability found by Stott (1957) with respect to ascendance–submission, or by Kagan and Moss (1960) with respect to passivity and dependence, or by Engel (1959) with respect to the self-concept. Note that the issue of longitudinal stability has recently been seriously questioned by Kagan and Klein (1973).

The Shift from Psychoanalytic
Theory to Socialization

As indicated earlier in this introduction, there has been a shift away from psychoanalytic theory toward socialization (McCandless, 1970) and social learning theory (Bandura & Walters, 1963; Mischel, 1971) in the investigation of personality processes in children. Papers exemplifying socialization and the social learning viewpoint have, therefore, been deferred to Chapter 13, Socialization and Cross-Cultural Studies. Selections illustrating cognitive factors in development can be found in Chapter 5 (Infancy, Early Experience, and Critical Periods), Chapter 10 (Conceptual Development), and Chapter 11 (Intelligence).

References

Allport, G. W. *Personality: A Psychological Interpretation*. New York: Holt, Rinehart and Winston, 1937

Anderson, J. E. Personality organization in children. *American Psychologist*, 1948, *3*, 409–416.

Apolloni, T. & Cooke, T. P. Peer behavior conceptualized as a variable influencing infant and toddler development. *American Journal of Orthopsychiatry*, 1975, *45*, 4–17.

Argyle, M. & Little, B. R. Do personality traits apply to social behaviour? *Journal for the Theory of Social Behavior*, 1972, *2*, 1–35.

Bandura, A. & Walters, R. H. *Social learning and personality development*. New York: Holt, Rinehart and Winston, 1963.

Bayley, N. & Schaefer, E. S. Maternal behavior and personality development data from *The Berkeley Growth Study. Psychiatric Research Reports 13*. December 1960, 155–173.

Bowers, K. S. Situationism in psychology: An analysis and a critique. *Psychological Review*, 1973, *80*, 309–336.

Byrne, D. *An introduction to personality: Research, theory and application*. (2d ed.) Englewood Cliffs, N.J.: Prentice-Hall, 1974.

Dreger, R. M. *Fundamentals of personality: A functional psychology of personality*. Philadelphia: Lippincott, 1962.

Endler, N. S. The person versus the situation—a pseudo issue? A response to Alker. *Journal of Personality*, 1973, *41*, 287–303.

Endler, N. S. The case for person–situation interactions. *Canadian Psychological Review*, 1975, *16*, 12–21.

Endler, N. S. & Magnusson, D. Interactionism, trait psychology, psychodynamics and situationism. *Reports from the Psychological Laboratories*, University of Stockholm, 1974, No. 418.

Engel, M. The stability of the self-concept in adolescence. *Journal of Abnormal and Social Psychology*, 1959, *58*, 211–215.

Harlow, H. F. The heterosexual affectional system in monkeys. *American Psychologist*, 1962, *17*, 1–9.

Harlow, H. F. & Harlow, M. K. Social deprivation in monkeys. *Scientific American*, 1962, *207*(11) 137–146.

Hunt, J. McV. Traditional personality theory in the light of recent evidence. *American Scientist*, 1965, *53*, 80–96.

Hutt, C. *Males and females*. Harmondsworth, Middlesex, England: Penguin Books, 1972.

Jones, M. C. & Bayley, N. Physical maturity of boys as related to behavior. *Journal of Educational Psychology*, 1950, *41*, 129–148.

Kagan, J. & Klein, R. E. Cross-cultural perspectives on early development. *American Psychologist*, 1973, *28*, 947–961.

Kagan, J. & Moss, H. A. The stability of passive and dependent behavior from childhood through adulthood. *Child Development*, 1960, *31*, 577–591.

Kohlberg, L. A cognitive-developmental analysis of children's sex-role concepts and attitudes. In E. E. Maccoby (Ed.), *The development of sex differences*. Stanford, Ca.: Stanford University Press, 1966, pp. 82–173.

Lehrman, D. S. Can psychiatrists use ethology? In N. J. White (Ed.), *Ethology and psychiatry*. Toronto: University of Toronto Press, 1974, pp. 187–196.

Maccoby, E. E. & Jacklin, C. N. *The psychology of sex differences*. Stanford, Ca.: Stanford University Press, 1974.

McCandless, B. R. Socialization. In H. W. Reese & L. P. Lipsitt (Eds.), *Experimental child psychology*. New York: Academic Press, 1970, pp. 571–617.

Mischel, W. *Personality and assessment*. New York: Wiley, 1968.

Mischel, W. Continuity and change in personality. *American Psychologist*, 1969, *24*, 1012–1018.

Mischel, W. *Introduction to personality*. New York: Holt, Rinehart and Winston, 1971.

Mischel, W. Towards a cognitive social learning reconceptualization of personality. *Psychological Review*, 1973, *80*, 252–283.

Money, J. & Ehrhardt, A. A. *Man and woman, boy and girl*. Baltimore, Md.: Johns Hopkins, 1972.

Mussen, P. H. & Bouterline-Young, H. Relationships between rate of physical maturing and personality among boys of Italian descent. *Vita Humana*, 1946, *7*, 186–200.

Mussen, P. H. & Jones, M. C. Self-conceptions, motivations, and interpersonal attitudes of late- and early-maturing boys. *Child Development*, 1957, *28*, 243–256.

Oakley, A. *Sex, gender and society*. London: Maurice Temple Smith Ltd., 1972.

Peterson, D. R., Becker, W. C., Hellmer, L. A., Shoemaker, D. J., & Quay, H. C. Parental attitudes and child adjustment. *Child Development*, 1959, *30*, 119–130.

Quay, H. C. & Quay, L. F. Behavior problems in early adolescence. *Child Development*, 1965, *36*, 215–220.

Rutter, M. Normal psychosexual development. *Journal of Child Psychology and Psychiatry*, 1971, *11*, 259–283.

Sanford, N. Personality: Its place in psychology. In S. Koch (Ed.), *Psychology: A study of a science. Vol. 5: The process areas, the person and some applied fields: Their place in psychology and in science*. New York: McGraw-Hill, 1963, pp. 488–592.

Schaefer, E. S. A circumplex model for maternal behavior. *Journal of Abnormal and Social Psychology*, 1959, *59*, 226–235.

Sheldon, W. H. *Varieties of delinquent youth*. New York: Harper, 1949.

Stott, L. H. The persisting effects of early family experiences upon personality development. *Merrill-Palmer Quarterly of Behavior and Development*, 1957, *3*, 145–159.

Thomas, A., Chess, S. & Birch, H. G. The origin of personality. *Scientific American*, 1970, *223*, 2, 102–109.

Yarrow, Marion R. Problems of methods in parent–child research. *Child Development*, 1963, *34*, 215–226.

37. BEHAVIOR PROBLEMS REVISITED

Findings of an Anterospective Study

STELLA CHESS, ALEXANDER THOMAS, and HERBERT G. BIRCH

A number of theoretical formulations have been advanced to explain the origin and nature of behavior problems in childhood. These have included the constitutionalist view in which the symptoms of disturbance are considered to be the direct expression of a predetermined constitutional pattern in the child, the psychoanalytic view in which disturbance is seen as the outcome of conflicts between instinctual drive seeking expression and satisfaction and repressing forces seeking to inhibit or contain them, the learning theory approach in which symptoms are viewed as conditioned maladaptive learned patterns based on conditioned reflex formations, and the culturist view in which symptoms are considered to be the more or less direct expression of sociocultural influences.

A unique opportunity to investigate the genesis and evolution of behavior problems and to test the validity of these theories has presented itself during the course of our New York longitudinal study of individuality in behavioral development. In this study, in progress since 1956, 39 of the 136 children who have been followed from the earliest months of life onward by a variety of data-gathering techniques have developed behavior disturbances of various types and varying degrees of severity.

Presented at Joint Session of Section on Child Development of the American Academy of Pediatrics and American Academy of Child Psychiatry, Chicago, October 24, 1965. This investigation was supported by Grant MH-03614 from the National Institute of Mental Health. Copyright, American Academy of Child Psychiatry; reprinted from *J. Acad. Child Psychiat.*, 1967, 6:321–331.

Until now, none of the numerous studies in the field has provided a body of evidence sufficient to validate one or another of the extant theoretical formulations. Aside from any other questions as to the adequacy of the data offered as evidence, the approaches have relied primarily on data gathered retrospectively. A number of recent studies, including several from our own center, have revealed significant distortions in retrospective parental reports on the early developmental histories of their children (Robbins, 1963; Wenar, 1963; Chess et al., 1966). It has become clear that retrospective data are insufficient for the study of the genesis of behavior disorders and that anterospective data gathered by longitudinal developmental studies are essential.

Previous longitudinal studies—at Berkeley (Mac Farlane et al., 1954), the Fels Institute (Kagan and Moss, 1962), Yale (Kris, 1957), and Topeka (Murphy et al., 1962)—have made certain contributions to the understanding of the evolution of behavior disorders. The possible significance of temperamental characteristics of the child in interaction with parental functioning has been indicated. A lack of correlation between the child's patterns of psychodynamic defenses and the occurrence of behavioral dysfunction has been found. Symptoms typical of various age-periods have been tabulated, their vicissitudes over time traced, and correlations among different symptoms determined. However, each of these studies has been limited either by small sample size, which has not permitted generalization of the findings, or by the absence of systematic psychiatric evaluation of the children, which has severely restricted the possibility of categorizing the behavior disturbance and of making meaningful correlations with the longitudinal behavioral data.

Our New York longitudinal study has had available, by contrast, both a total sample of substantial size and the data resulting from independent clinical psychiatric evaluation in all of the children with behavior problems. The data on the total sample include information gathered longitudinally and anterospectively at sequential age levels from early infancy onward on the nature of the child's own individual characteristics of functioning at home, in school, and in standard test situations; on parental attitudes and child care practices; on special environmental events and the child's reactions to such events; and on intellectual functioning. In addition, psychiatric evaluation has been done in each child presenting symptoms by the staff child psychiatrist. Wherever necessary, neurological examination or special testing, such as perceptual tests, have been done. Clinical follow-up of each child with a problem has also been carried out systematically.

Details of the data-gathering procedures and of the techniques of data analysis have been reported elsewhere (Chess et al., 1962; Thomas et al., 1963). Since the developmental data were gathered before the child was viewed as a problem by either the parent or the psychiatrist, they were uncontaminated by the distortions which inevitably attend retrospective histories obtained after the appearance of the behavioral disturbance. Data as to environmental influences, such as parental practices and attitudes, changes in family structure, illnesses and hospitalization, and the character of the school situation, were also obtained in advance of the behavioral disturbance and so were also not distorted by the fact of pathology.

The size of the sample and the nature of the data have made possible various quantitative analyses comparing children with and without behavior problems as well as individual longitudinal case studies. In all our analyses we have been concerned with tracing the on-togenesis and development of each behavioral disturbance in terms of the interaction of temperament and environment, as well as the influence of additional factors in specific cases, such as brain damage, physical abnormalities, and characteristics of intellectual functioning. *Temperament*, in our usage, refers to the behavioral style of the individual child and contains no inferences as to genetic, endocrine, somatologic or environmental etiologies. It is a phenomenological term used to describe the characteristic tempo, energy expenditure, focus, mood, and rhythmicity typifying the behaviors of the individual child, independently of their contents. We have used nine categories of reactivity within which to subsume temperamental attributes. They are activity level, rhythmicity, adaptability, approach-withdrawal, intensity of reaction, quality of mood, sensory threshold, distractibility, and persistence and attention span.[1] A child's temperamental organization, therefore, represents his characteristic mode of functioning with respect to these features of behavioral organization. It refers to the *how* rather than to the *what* or the *why* of behavior. No implications of permanence or immutability attach to such a conception.

The prevalence rate of behavior problems in our study population approximates that found in other studies (Lapouse and Monk, 1958; Glidewell et al., 1963). The types of symptoms were typical of those usually coming to notice in preschool and early school age children of middle-class highly educated parents.

In each of the thirty-nine children with behavior problems the psychiatric assessment has been followed by a detailed culling of all the anterospective data from early infancy onward for pertinent information on temperament, environmental influences, and the sequences of symptom appearance and development. It has been possible in each case to trace the ontogenesis of the behavioral disturbances in terms of the interaction of temperament and environment. Temperament alone did not

---

[1] See Thomas et al. (1963) for criteria of each of the nine categories and for details of the scoring method.

produce behavioral disturbance. Instances of children of closely similar temperamental structure to the children with behavior problems were found in the normally functioning group. Rather, it appeared that both behavioral disturbance as well as behavioral normality were the result of the interaction between the child with a given patterning of temperament and significant features of his developmental environment. Among these environmental features intrafamilial as well as extrafamilial circumstances such as school and peer group were influential. In several cases, additional special factors such as brain damage or physical abnormality were also operative in interaction with temperament and environment to produce symptoms of disturbed development.

A number of case summaries illustrating typical interactive patterns of development in children with and without behavior problems have been presented in several previous publications (Chess et al., 1963; Birch et al., 1964). At this time we would like to present some of the characteristic temperamental patterns found among the children, the environmental demands which are typically stressful for children with each of these temperamental constellations, and the parental and other environmental approaches which intensify such stressful demands to the point of symptom formation. Symptoms manifested by the children included tantrums, aggressive behavior, habit disorders, fears, learning difficulties, nonparticipation in play activities with other children, and lack of normal assertiveness.

A temperamental pattern which produced the greatest risk of behavior problem development comprises the combination of irregularity in biological functions, predominantly negative (withdrawal) responses to new stimuli, nonadaptability or slow adaptability to change, frequent negative mood, and predominantly intense reactions. As infants, children with this pattern show irregular sleep and feeding patterns, slow acceptance of new foods, prolonged adjustment periods to new routines, and frequent periods of loud crying. Their laughter, too, is characteristically loud. Mothers find them difficult to care for, and pediatricians

frequently refer to them as the "difficult infants." They are not easy to feed, to put to sleep, to bathe, or to dress. New places, new activities, strange faces—all may produce initial responses of loud protest or crying. Frustration characteristically produces a violent tantrum. These children approximate 10 percent of the total study population but comprise a significantly higher proportion of the behavior problem group (Rutter et al., 1964). The stressful demands for these children are typically those of socialization, namely, the demands for alteration of spontaneous responses and patterns to conform to the rules of living of the family, the school, the peer group, etc. It is also characteristic of these children that once they do learn the rules, they function easily, consistently, and energetically.

We have found no evidence that the parents of the difficult infants are essentially different from the other parents. Nor do our studies suggest that the temperamental characteristics of the children are caused by the parents. The issue is rather that the care of these infants makes special requirements upon their parents for unusually firm, patient, consistent, and tolerant handling. Such handling is necessary if the difficult infant is to learn to adapt to new demands with a minimum of stress. If the new demand is presented inconsistently, impatiently or punitively effective change in behavior becomes stressful and even impossible. Negativism is a not infrequent outcome of such suboptimal parental functioning.

The problems of managing a difficult child not infrequently highlight a parent's individual reaction to stress. The same parents who are relaxed and consistent with an easy child may become resentful, guilty, or helpless with a difficult child, depending on their own personality structures. Other parents, by contrast, who do not feel guilty or put upon by the child's behavior may learn to enjoy the vigor, lustiness, and "stubbornness" of a difficult infant.

At the opposite end of the temperamental spectrum from the difficult infant is the child who is regular, responds positively to new stimuli (approaches), adapts quickly and easily to change, and shows a predominantly positive mood of mild or moderate intensity. These are the infants who develop regular sleep and feeding schedules easily, take to most new foods at once, smile at strangers, adapt quickly to a new school, accept most frustrations with a minimum of fuss, and learn the rules of new games quickly. They are aptly called "easy babies" and are usually a joy to their parents, pediatricians, and teachers. By contrast to the difficult infant, the easy child adapts to the demands for socialization with little or no stress and confronts his parents with few if any problems in handling. However, although these children do as a group develop significantly fewer behavior problems proportionately than do the difficult infants, their very ease of adaptability may under certain circumstances be the basis for problem behavior development. Most typically we have seen this occur when there is a severe dissonance between the expectations and demands of the intra- and extrafamilial environments. The child first adapts easily to the standards and behavioral expectations of the parent in the first few years of life. When he moves actively into functional situations outside the home, such as in peer play groups and school, stress and malfunctioning will develop if the extrafamilial standard and demands conflict sharply with the patterns learned in the home. As a typical example, the parents of one such child had a high regard for individuality of expression and disapproval of any behavior or attitude in their child which they identified as stereotypical or lacking in imagination. Self-expression was encouraged and conformity and attentiveness to rules imposed by others discouraged even when this resulted in ill manners and a disregard of the desires of others. As the child grew older she became increasingly isolated from her peer group because of continuous insistence on her own preferences. In school her progress was grossly unsatisfactory because of difficulty in listening to directions. The parents were advised to restructure their approach, to place less emphasis on individuality and instead to teach her to be responsive to the needs of others and to conform constructively in behavior in class and in activities with her peers. The parents,

acutely aware of the child's growing social isolation and the potential seriousness of her educational problem, carried out this plan consistently. At follow-up, six months later, the child had adapted to the new rules easily, the conflict between standards within and without the home had become minimal, and she had become an active member of a peer group and had caught up to grade level in academic work.

It is certainly true that a severe dissonance between intra- and extrafamilial environment demands and expectations may produce stress and disturbance in psychological development for many types of youngsters, including the difficult child. In our case series, however, it has been most readily apparent as a dominant pathogenic factor in these easy children.

Another important temperamental constellation comprises the combination of negative responses of mild intensity to new stimuli with slow adaptability after repeated contact. Children with this pattern differ from the difficult infants in that their withdrawal from the new is quiet rather than loud. They also usually do not have the irregularity of function, frequent negative mood expression, and intense reactions of the difficult infants. The mildly expressed withdrawal from the new is typically seen with the first encounter with the bath, a new person, a stranger, or a new place. With the first bath the child lies still and fusses mildly, with a new food he turns his head away quietly and lets it dribble out of his mouth, with a stranger who greets him loudly he clings to his mother. If given the opportunity to re-experience new situations without pressure, such a child gradually comes to show quiet and positive interest and involvement. This characteristic sequence of response has suggested the appellation the "Slow to Warm Up" as an apt if inelegant designation for these children. A key issue in their development is whether parents and teachers allow them to make an adaptation to the new at their own tempo or insist on the immediate positive involvement which is difficult or impossible for the slow-to-warm-up children. If the adult recognizes that the slow adaptation to a new school, new peer group or new academic subject reflects the child's normal temperamental style, patient encouragement is likely. If, on the contrary, the child's slow warm-up is interpreted as timidity or lack of interest, adult impatience and pressure on the child for quick adaptation may occur. The child's reaction to this stressful pressure is typically an intensification of his withdrawal tendency. If this increased holding back in turn stimulates increased impatience and pressure on the part of the parent or teacher, a destructive child-environment interactive process will be set in motion.

In several other instances in our study population, nursery school teachers have interpreted the child's slow initial adaptation as evidence of underlying anxiety. In still another case, an elementary school teacher estimated that a child's slow initial mastery of a new accelerated academic program indicated inadequate intellectual capacity. In these cases, the longitudinal behavioral records documented a slow warm-up temperamental style and made possible the recommendation that judgment be suspended until the child could have a longer period of contact with the new situation. The subsequent successful mastery of the demands of the new situation clarified the issue as one of temperamental style and not psychopathology or lack of intellectual capacity.

A contrast to the slow-to-warm-up child is the very persistent child who is most likely to experience stress not with his initial contact with a situation but during the course of his ongoing activity after the first positive adaptation has been made. His quality of persistence leads him to resist interference or attempts to divert him from an activity in which he is absorbed. If the adult interference is arbitrary and forcible, tension and frustration tend to mount quickly in these children and may reach explosive proportions.

Type-specific stress and maladaptive child-environment patterns can be identified for other temperamental patterns, such as the very distractible or highly active child, but the scope of this presentation does not permit their description.

Currently influential psychoanalytic theories of the ontogenesis of behavior problems place primary emphasis on the role of anxiety, intrapsychic conflict, and psychodynamic defenses. Our findings do not support these concepts. Our data suggest that anxiety, intrapsychic conflict, and psychodynamic defenses, when they do appear in the course of behavior problem development, are secondary phenomena which result from the stressful, maladaptive character of an unhealthy temperament-environment interaction. Once any or all of these secondary factors appear they can add a new dimension to the dynamics of the child-environment interaction and substantially influence the subsequent course of the behavior problem. It is not surprising that in retrospective studies which begin when the child already presents an extensively elaborated psychological disturbance the prominent phenomena of anxiety and conflict should be labeled as primary rather than secondary influences. Also, if the fact of temperamental individuality is not given serious attention, certain temperamental patterns, such as those of the difficult child or the child with a slow warm-up, are easily misinterpreted as the result of anxiety or as defenses against anxiety.

Our findings also challenge the validity of the currently prevalent assumption that a child's problem is a direct reaction of a one-to-one kind to unhealthy maternal influences. The slogan "To meet Johnny's mother is to understand his problem" expresses an all too frequent approach in which a study of the mother is substituted for a study of the complex factors which may have produced a child's disturbed development, of which parental influences are only one. Elsewhere we have described this unidirectional preoccupation of psychologists and psychiatrists with the pathogenic role of the mother as the "Mal de Mere" syndrome (Chess, 1964). The harm done by this preoccupation has been enormous. Innumerable mothers have been unjustly burdened with deep feelings of guilt and inadequacy as a result of being incorrectly held exclusively or even primarily responsible for their children's problems. Diagnostic procedures have tended to be restricted to a study of the mother's assumed noxious attitudes and practices, with investigations in other directions conducted in a most cursory fashion, or not at all. Treatment plans have focused on methods of changing maternal attitudes and ameliorating the effects of presumed pathogenic maternal attitudes on the child and have ignored other significant etiological factors.

Our data on the origin and development of behavior problems in children emphasize the necessity to study the child—his temperamental characteristics, neurological status, intellectual capacities, and physical handicaps. The parents should also be studied rather than given global labels such as rejecting, overprotective, anxious, etc. Parental attitudes and practices are usually selective and not global, with differentiated characteristics in different areas of the child's life and with marked variability from child to child. Parent-child interaction should be analyzed not only for parental influences on the child but just as much for the influence of the child's individual characteristics on the parent. The influence of other intra- and extrafamilial environmental factors should be estimated in relation to the interactive pattern with each specific child with his individual characteristics rather than in terms of sweeping generalizations.

Our finding that an excessively stressful maladaptive temperament-environment interaction constitutes a decisive element in the development of behavior problems suggests that treatment should emphasize the modification of the interactive process so that it is less stressful and more adaptive. This requires first of all an identification of the pertinent temperamental and environmental issues. Parents can then be armed with this knowledge in the service of modifying their interactive pattern with the child in a healthy direction. Parent guidance rather than parent treatment should be the first aim. If the parent cannot learn to understand his child and utilize this understanding effectively, it then becomes pertinent to inquire into the factors which may be responsible for such a failure of parent guidance. In our experience such failures are in a minority. Most parents do appear able to cooperate in a parent guidance program. When this is accomplished, the parent and psychiatrist can truly become allies in the treatment of the child's problem.

REFERENCES

Birch, H. G., Thomas, A., & Chess, S. (1964), Behavioral development in brain-damaged children: three case studies. *Arch. Gen. Psychiat., 11*:596–603.

Chess, S. (1964), Mal de Mere. *Amer. J. Orthopsychiat., 34*:613–614.

———— Hertzig, M., Birch, H. G., & Thomas, A. (1962), Methodology of a study of adaptive functions of the preschool child. *This Journal, 1*:236–245.

———— Thomas, A., & Birch, H. G. (1966), Distortions in developmental reporting made by parents of behaviorally disturbed children. *This Journal, 5*:226–234.

———— ———— Rutter, M., & Birch, H. G. (1963), Interaction of temperament and environment in the production of behavioral disturbances in children. *Amer. J. Psychiat., 120*:142–148.

Glidewell, J. C., Domke, H. R., & Kantor, M. B. (1963), Screening in schools for behavior disorders: use of mother's report of symptoms. *J. Educ. Res., 56*:508–515.

Kagan, J. & Moss, H. A. (1962), *Birth to Maturity: A Study in Psychological Development*. New York: Wiley.

Kris, M. (1957), The use of prediction in a longitudinal study. *The Psychoanalytic Study of the Child, 12*:175–189. New York: International Universities Press.

Lapouse, R. & Monk, M. A. (1958), An epidemiologic study of behavior characteristics in children. *Amer. J. Pub. Hlth., 48*:1134–1144.

Mac Farlane, J. W., Allen, L., & Honzik, M. P. (1954), *A Developmental Study of the Behavior Problems of Normal Children between Twenty-one Months and Fourteen Years* [University of California Publications in Child Development, Vol. II]. Berkeley: University of California Press.

Murphy, L. B. et al. (1962), *The Widening World of Childhood*. New York: Basic Books.

Robbins, L. C. (1963), The accuracy of parental recall of aspects of child development and of child-rearing practices. *J. Abnorm. Soc. Psychol., 66*:261–270.

Rutter, M., Birch, H. G., Thomas, A., & Chess, S. (1964), Temperamental characteristics in infancy and the later development of behavioral disorders. *Brit. J. Psychiat., 110*:651–661.

Thomas, A., Chess, S., Birch, H. G., Hertzig, M., & Korn, S. (1963), *Behavioral Individuality in Early Childhood*. New York: New York University Press.

Wenar, C. (1963), The reliability of developmental histories: summary and evaluation of evidence. *Psychosom. Med., 25*:505–509.

38. CONTINUITIES AND DISCONTINUITIES IN CHILDHOOD AND ADULT MORAL DEVELOPMENT[1]

L. KOHLBERG and R. KRAMER

It may be useful to begin a discussion of the central issue of this symposium, continuity and discontinuity in the study of child and adult development, with a history of the origins of our interest in it. As a graduate student planning a study of moral development, the first author knew superego formation was pretty well completed by age 6. As an enthusiastic reader of Piaget, however, he knew that the development of autonomous morality was not completed until the advanced age of 12 or 13. To allow for the laggards, he decided to include children as old as 16 in a study of the development of moral autonomy. When he actually looked at his interviews, it dawned on him that children had a long way to go beyond Piaget's autonomous stage to reach moral maturity. Accordingly, he constructed a six-stage scheme of moral development, a schema in which superego morality was only stage 1 and what Piaget termed autonomous morality

was only Stage 2. His thesis data left him uncertain as to when Stage 6, the stage of mature morality, was finally reached; but at least he knew that it was fully reached by age 25, his age at the time of the study.

For reasons having nothing to do with an interest in adult development as such, he decided to follow his thesis subjects along longitudinally. The second author continued the study and developed hypotheses about moral judgment in late adolescence which he applied to the data for his dissertation [Kramer 1968, 1969]. The findings we shall discuss today are these findings on longitudinal subjects as they progressed from age 16 to 25, and on their middle-aged fathers.

Eventually we want to take these findings as a spring board for some speculations on adult development rather than to focus upon the more central and obvious conclusions to be derived from them. As we shall discuss shortly, their obvious import is that our cocky graduate student view was correct and moral development is all nailed up by 25. Put more elegantly, the two questions centrally answered by Kramer's data are those which child

[1]Research supported by N.I.C.H.D. Grant HD 02469–01.

From *Human Development*, 1969, *12*, 93–120. Printed by permission of S. Karger A. G., Basel/New York and the authors.

psychologists typically ask when their longitudinal subjects start to grow up and when they don't know how to get disengaged from studying them. The first is whether there is age increase in a trait like "moral maturity" after adolescence. The second related question is whether a trait is stabilized by adolescence, in the sense that an individual's score on the trait in adolescence correlates well with his score on the trait in later life.

Essentially, Kramer found that there was no further age increase in moral maturity after age 25, and that high school scores on moral judgment maturity were highly predictive of adult scores on moral maturity. As child psychologists, our response to these findings is relief. We can finally pack up and go home without another wave of longitudinal interviewing three years hence. The story of moral development is complete. The response of the student of adult development to these results is quite different. As Bernice Neugarten's paper clearly points out, the child psychologist's triumph in nailing down a terminus of development is the child psychologist's failure in offering anything useful to the student of adult development. To the extent that moral development is nailed down by late adolescence, concepts of moral development tell us nothing about what goes on in adulthood, what goes on in adulthood tells us nothing about moral development, and the studies of adult development and of child development have nothing to offer one another in the moral domain.

To clarify Neugarten's point, let's take the example of general intelligence, of general cognitive or mental maturity, which is pretty completely developed by the early twenties. The fact that cognitive development increases throughout childhood is a central key to understanding childhood personality development, as the cognitive developmental personality theories of J. M. Baldwin, Piaget, G. H. Mead and Werner have stressed [Kohlberg 1968].

The structural transformations in conceptions of the physical world discussed as cognitive stages by Piaget are paralleled by cognitive transformations in the child's conception of his social world and of himself as a social being. Because of this, empirical research has demonstrated that the timing of onset of new stages of social development (psychosexual and moral) is heavily influenced by such cognitive factors as general mental age or general intellectual maturity [Kohlberg 1968].

The role of intelligence in the understanding of adult development is quite a different matter. While individual differences in adult intelligence tell us something about an adult's functioning and interests, they do not explain much about the way the individual develops or changes in adulthood, just because such differences are a constant. Adult psychosexual or moral development could certainly not result from cognitive transformations or growth, as can childhood development, because there appears to be no such adult cognitive transformations. Accordingly, adult functioning in the area of general intelligence can hardly be the key to understanding adult development.

It may be that writing off general intelligence as a key to understanding adult development is premature, in light of our child centered psychometric concepts and measures of intellectual development. But something is more obviously amiss if we write off moral judgment or ideology as a key to understanding adult development.

Morality and moral change is clearly a focal point for adult life in a way cognitive change is not. We do not need Erikson's studies of Martin Luther and Mahatma Ghandi to know that the crises and turning points of adult identity are often moral. From St. Paul to Tolstoy, the classic autobiographies tell us the dramas of maturity are the transformations of the moral ideologies of men. Clearly, then, morality cannot be studied with a polite agreement between child psychologists and adult psychologists to go their separate ways in studying development.

If morality is clearly a focus for adult personality change, does this mean that moral development goes on after biological maturity? The question appears to be an exercise in making refined semantic distinctions between the words personality "change" and personality "development," semantic issues raised by the question: "Is there development past biological 'maturity'?" The question, however, is not merely semantic, it is critical for the relations between child and adult psychology. As Alberta Siegel's paper points out, the concept of stage has been critical to the distinctive theories of child development, the theories of Freud, Gesell, Erikson, and Piaget. As Siegel's paper also points out, this stage conception has roots in the biological-maturational tradition to which all the child-psychologists have been strongly exposed. In one form, then, the question of "Is there adult development?" is the question of whether the child psychologist's general conception of stage with its biological roots, is useable to describe or understand personality change after biological maturity has been reached. As our phrasing suggests, the issue of adult development is also closely linked to the issues of whether the general concept of maturity, a biologically rooted word for ideal endpoint of development, has any meaning for the study of adult personality change.

It may not appear to you, as it does to us, that it would be of great value to determine whether child psychology's conceptual apparatus of "stage" and "maturity" could be used for the study of adult personality change. This value lies first in the implications of the answer for child development theory. While all stage conceptions have relied on biological metaphor, some theories, like Gesell's, treat stages as direct products of maturation, while others, like Piaget's, treat stages as the result of organism—environment interaction, as primarily the result of psychological experience. As long as the study of stage-development is limited to childhood, it is almost impossible to empirically separate the roles of maturation and experience in stage-development in a way which would bear upon these theoretical differences. The study of adult stage-development could open this door.

There is a second reason for searching for continuity between the conceptions of development used by child and adult psychologists which is of special importance in the moral domain. This reason may be termed either philosophical or practical.

For aeons of history, it was assumed that the middle aged and the aged had a wisdom denied to the youth. In modern society, formal education and the written word have made the full knowledge of the culture symbolically accessible to the youth and the criteria of wisdom have become more public, more defined by the methods of science and logic. Value questions have come to be viewed as historically relative, as out of the domain of rational discourse. All youth know that values change rapidly, that their elder's values are different from their own and that their children's will differ from their own. Their elders protest that the generational differences are due to the fact that the values of the young are based on the immediate intellectual or emotional appeals of images and ideas, not on their meaning as integrating the experience of living. If there is any germ of truth in the elder's view, it rests on the assumption of adult development.

The assumption that the adult possesses some wisdom which the youth cannot appreciate by the usual criteria of rational discourse is the assumption that the adult has developed a higher mode of thought, is at a higher stage. If adult developmental psychology can define such higher modes of thought, it will have a use quite different from the uses of child psychology in contributing to communication between the generations. Child psychology has assumed it knows what maturity is. While using biological metaphors for maturity, in operational practice, child psychology has assumed that maturity is conventional adult knowledge, success, and social conformity (otherwise termed socialization, adjustment, ego strength, or "the reality principle"). Deviation from the conventional is then labelled infantile; at best, as creative regression in the service of the ego. From such a framework, child psychology teaches the adult how to speak "childrenese," how to speak down to the child. The young, however, refuses to accept socialization into the current society as representing maturity. The failure of communication is not because adults can't talk childrenese, it is because the young believe that the adults can't talk real "adultese," that the adults don't have any deeper notion of maturity than that instilled in them when they were children. If developmental psychology is to take the maturity concept seriously, it must find it, not in the cliches of the conventional culture, but in the findings of universal patterns of adult change, and communicate these findings about a "true adultese" which is more mature than the conventional culture to both the young and the middle aged.

As we read conceptualizations of adult development, they slide over the issues we have just raised. It is fairly common to talk loosely of adult development and stages in terms of developmental tasks. Such discussion assumes that there are age-typical changes in personality, linked to focal tasks, and that successful resolution of these tasks leads to characteristic attitudinal outcomes. Even if "stages" in this sense can be clearly documented empirically, they would not deal with the basic issues I have mentioned. Before explaining why "developmental tasks" will not deal with these issues, let me first clarify what child psychology in the Piaget-Werner tradition has meant by "development" and "stage" [Werner, 1948; Piaget, 1964; Kohlberg, 1968]. There are three criteria used by the tradition to distinguish psychological development from behavior change in general.

The first criterion is that development involves change in the general shape, pattern, or organization of response, rather than change in the frequency or intensity of emission of an already patterned response. Under reinforcement, bar-pressing increases in frequency; such increase is not development. Under food deprivation, hunger behaviors increase in frequency and intensity; such behavior is not development. With age, sexual impulses wax or wane in intensity. Such changes are not development.

A second criterion, closely related to the first, is that developmental change involves newness, a qualitative difference in response. Developmental change does not have to be sudden or saltatory but it does entail the emergence of a novel structure of response. Novelty involves the quality-quantity distinction, which in turn involves the distinction between form and content. In a sense, any change in content is new. A really new kind of experience, a really new mode of response, however, is one that is different in its form or organization, not simply in the element or the information it contains.

The third criterion implied by the word development is irreversibility. Once a developmental change has occurred, it cannot be reversed by the conditions and experiences which gave rise to it. Learned bar pressing can be reversed or extinguished by withdrawing the reinforcement which conditioned it. A developmental change cannot. Smedslund [1961] has used this criterion to distinguish cognitive development from associationistic learning. He reports that if a Piaget conservation was taught to a preconserver by instruction and reinforcement, it could be reversed by use of the same mechanisms. Naturally developing conservation could not be reversed by the same procedures. The concept of developmental irreversibility does not rule out the existence of behavior change backward to a previous pattern. As an example, seniles and schizophrenics seem to lose the Piaget conservations. Such backward changes are labelled regression; however, it is important to point out that they are rare and their conditions or causes are markedly different from the conditions or causes of forward development.

The three criteria of development just mentioned, plus three others, are involved in the concept of developmental stage. The stage concept not only postulates irreversible qualitative structural change, but in addition postulates a fourth condition that this change occurs in a pattern of universal stepwise invariant sequences. Fifth, the stage concept postulates that the stages form a hierarchy of functioning within the individual. This implies, sixth, that each stage is a differentiation and integration of a set of functional contents present at the prior stage.

On the face of it, developmental task conceptions meet none of the criteria we have mentioned. Sexual intimacy and marriage, vocational identity and achievement, parenthood, acceptance of life's completion and conclusion are matters of content, not form. According to Erikson, [1950] the *content* of parenthood forms the focus of development of a generalized or *formal* attitude of generativity toward the world and toward the self which is *new* in development. It is just the question of whether such a novel formal attitude develops apart from parental content which lies at the heart of any investigation of Erikson's adult ego stages.

Related to the ambiguity of the formal aspects of stages defined as resolutions of developmental tasks is the ambiguity of their irreversibility and invariance of sequence. Developmental tasks of content in themselves have no order, i.e., individuals can face vocational commitment or identity before or after

---

TABLE 38–1.
Definition of Moral Stages

I. Preconventional Level

At this level the child is responsive to cultural rules and labels of good and bad, right or wrong, but interprets these labels in terms of either the physical or the hedonistic consequences of action (punishment, reward, exchange of favors) or in terms of the physical power of those who enunciate the rules and labels. The level is divided into the following two stages:

Stage 1: *The punishment and obedience orientation.* The physical consequences of action determine its goodness or badness regardless of the human meaning or value of these consequences. Avoidance of punishment and unquestioning deference to power are valued in their own right, not in terms of respect for an underlying moral order supported by punishment and authority (the latter being Stage 4).

Stage 2: *The instrumental relativist orientation.* Right action consists of that which instrumentally satisfies one's own needs and occasionally the needs of others. Human relations are viewed in terms like those of the market place. Elements of fairness, or reciprocity and equal sharing are present, but they are always interpreted in a physical pragmatic way. Reciprocity is a matter of "you scratch my back and I'll scratch yours," not of loyalty, gratitude or justice.

II. Conventional Level

At this level, maintaining the expectations of the individual's family, group, or nation is perceived as valuable in its own right, regardless of immediate and obvious consequences. The attitude is not only one of *conformity* to personal expectations and social order, but of loyalty to it, of actively *maintaining,* supporting, and justifying the order and of identifying with the persons or group involved in it. At this level, there are the following two stages:

Stage 3: *The interpersonal concordance or "good boy–nice girl" orientation.* Good behavior is that which pleases or helps others and is approved by them. There is much conformity to stereotypical images of what is majority or "natural" behavior. Behavior is frequently judged by intention—"he means well" becomes important for the first time. One earns approval by being "nice."

Stage 4: *The "law and order" orientation.* There is orientation toward authority, fixed rules, and the maintenance of the social order. Right behavior consists of doing one's duty, showing respect for authority and maintaining the given social order for its own sake.

III. Post-Conventional, Autonomous, or Principled Level

At this level, there is a clear effort to define moral values and principles which have validity and application apart from the authority of the groups or persons holding these principles and apart from the individual's own identification with these groups. This level again has two stages:

Stage 5: *The social-contract legalistic orientation* generally with utilitarian overtones. Right action tends to be defined in terms of general individual rights and in terms of standards which have been critically examined and agreed upon by the whole society. There is a clear awareness of the relativism of personal values and opinions and a corresponding emphasis upon procedural rules for reaching consensus. Aside from what is constitutionally and democratically agreed upon, the right is a matter of personal "values" and "opinion." The result is an emphasis upon the "legal point of view," but with an emphasis upon the possibility of changing law in terms of rational considerations of social utility, (rather than freezing it in terms of Stage 4 "law and order"). Outside the legal realm, free agreement, and contract is the binding element of obligation. This is the "official" morality of the American government and Constitution.

Stage 6: *The universal ethical principle orientation.* Right is defined by the decision of conscience in accord with self-chosen *ethical principles* appealing to logical comprehensiveness, universality, and consistency. These principles are abstract and ethical, (the Golden Rule, the categorical imperative) they are not concrete moral rules like the Ten Commandments. At heart, these are universal principles of *justice* of the *reciprocity* and *equality* of the human *rights* and of respect for the dignity of human beings as *individual persons.*

The operational meaning of these stages is suggested by table II with regard to one moral concept, the worth of human life.

sexual intimacy and parenthood. Psychologically it is even possible to develop competent parental attitudes before developing capacity for sexual intimacy. Finally, the irreversibility of development defined in terms of developmental tasks is much in question. There are certainly many older adults, apparently mature and ready to face the tasks of integrity vs. despair, who suddenly seem to prefer regression to the tasks of establishing heterosexual intimacy.

My sketch of the developmental task approach does justice neither to its usefulness for

---

TABLE 38–2.
Six Stages in Conceptions of the Moral Worth of Human Life

Stage 1: No differentiation between moral value of life and its physical or social-status value.

Tommy, age ten (III, Why should the druggist give the drug to the dying woman when her husband couldn't pay for it?): "If someone important is in a plane and is allergic to heights and the stewardess won't give him medicine because she's only got enough for one and she's got a sick one, a friend, in back, they'd probably put the stewardess in a lady's jail because she didn't help the important one."

(Is it better to save the life of one important person or a lot of unimportant people?): "All the people that aren't important because one man just has one house, maybe a lot of furniture, but a whole bunch of people have an awful lot of furniture and some of these poor people might have a lot of money and it doesn't look it."

Stage 2: The value of a human life is seen as instrumental to the satisfaction of the needs of its possessor or of other persons. Decision to save life is relative to, or to be made by, its possessor. (Differentiation of physical and interest value of life, differentiation of its value to self and to other.)

Tommy, age thirteen (IV, Should the doctor "mercy kill" a fatally ill woman requesting death because of her pain?): "Maybe it would be good to put her out of her pain, she'd be better off that way. But the husband wouldn't want it, it's not like an animal. If a pet dies you can get along without it—it isn't something you really need. Well, you can get a new wife, but it's not really the same."

Jim, age thirteen (same question): "If she requests it, it's really up to her. She is in such terrible pain, just the same as people are always putting animals out of their pain."

Stage 3: The value of a human life is based on the empathy and affection of family members and others toward its possessor. (The value of human life, as based on social sharing, community and love, is differentiated from the instrumental and hedonistic value of life applicable also to animals.)

Tommy, age sixteen (same question): "It might be best for her, but her husband—it's a human life—not like an animal, it just doesn't have the same relationship that a human being does to a family. You can become attached to a dog, but nothing like a human you know."

Stage 4: Life is conceived as sacred in terms of its place in a categorical moral or religious order of rights and duties. (The value of human life, as a categorical member of a moral order, is differentiated from its value to specific other people in the family, etc. Value of life is still partly dependent upon serving the group, the state, God, however.)

Jim, age sixteen (same question): "I don't know. In one way, it's murder, it's not a right or privilege of man to decide who shall live and who should die. God put life into everybody on earth and you're taking away something from that person that came directly from God, and you're destroying something that is very sacred, it's in a way part of God and it's almost destroying a part of God when you kill a person. There's something of God in everyone."

Stage 5: Life is valued both in terms of it's relation to community welfare and in terms of being a universal human right. (Obligation to respect the basic right to life is differentiated from generalized respect for the socio-moral order. The general value of the independent human life is a primary autonomous value not dependent upon other values.)

Jim, age twenty (same question): "Given the ethics of the doctor who has taken on responsibility to save human life—from that point of view he probably shouldn't but there is another side, there are more and more people in the medical profession who are thinking it is a hardship on everyone, the person, the family, when you know they are going to die. When a person is kept alive by an artificial lung or kidney it's more like being a vegetable than being a human who is alive. If it's her own choice I think there are certain rights and privileges that go along with being a human being. I am a human being and have certain desires for life and I think everybody else does too. You have a world of which you are the center, and everybody else does too and in that sense we're all equal."

Stage 6: Belief in the sacredness of human life as representing a universal human value of respect for the individual. (The moral value of a human being, as an object of moral principle, is differentiated from a formal recognition of his rights.)

Jim, age twenty-four (III, Should the husband steal the drug to save his wife? How about for someone he just knows?): "Yes. A human life takes precedence over any other moral or legal value, whoever it is. A human life has inherent value whether or not it is valued by a particular individual."

(Why is that?): "The inherent worth of the individual human being is the central value in a set of values where the principles of justice and love are normative for all human relationships."

personality study nor to its theoretical richness as elaborated by Erikson [1950]. My caricature does, however, point to the inability of the developmental task approach to speak to the two problems mentioned. A study of adult developmental tasks will tell us little about the general role of experience in childhood structural change. It will also do little to establish communication between the generations. The older may indeed have wisdom in the sense of awareness of the problems that the young have not faced and will inevitably face. That does not, however, prove that it is wise for the young to face their problems in terms of the problems of their elders. The old may have developed a style of coping with the immanence of death which is effective and admirable. This does not mean that the young should cope with the problem or use a similar style. Only if there is a form of thought or a form of coping more mature or integrated in its application to a problem that is also the youth's problem, can the development of the older help the younger.

We have talked of the potential value for adult psychology of the rigorous conception of stage used in Piagetian child psychology. Before considering its application to adulthood, let me first quickly sketch how the criteria implied by this rigorous conception have been met in child psychology. For obvious reasons, our example will come from our work on stages of moral judgment [Kohlberg, 1958, 1963, 1968, 1969]. Table 38–1 presents a summary characterization of six stages of moral judgment.

The concept of human life is valued at each stage. The way in which this value is conceived differs, however, at each stage. In parentheses we indicate the sense in which each higher stage involves a differentiation in thinking about life's values not made at the immediately preceding stage of thought. The sense in which each stage is a new integration is more difficult to define, but will be intuitively evident to you in reading the examples. The table illustrates this one aspect of moral development with responses from two boys in the 10-year longitudinal study. Tommy was first interviewed at 10, and then again at 13, and 16. At

10 he is Stage 1, at 13 Stage 2, at 16 Stage 3. To represent more mature stages we have used Jim.

Jim, when first interviewed at 13, is primarily Stage 2. At 16 he is Stage 4, at 20 Stage 5, at 24 Stage 6 on this aspect. These two boys, then, suggest a sequential pattern holding for each individual. While Tommy is slower in development than Jim and likely will never get as far, both go through the same steps insofar as they move at all. While various statistical qualifications are required in making the generalization, it is true that the pattern of most of our longitudinal data is a pattern of directed irreversible onestep progressions.

We have said that our sequence is invariant for individuals in the United States. Our evidence also suggests that this sequence is culturally universal.

Figure 38–1a presents age trends for middle class urban boys in the United States, Taiwan and Mexico. At age 10 in each country, the order of use of each stage is the same as the order of its difficulty or maturity. In the United States, by age 16 the order is the reverse, from the highest to the lowest, except that Stage 6 is still little-used. At age 13, the middle Stage (Stage 3) is most used. The results in Mexico and Taiwan are the same, except that development is a little slower. Figure 1b presents similar trends for two isolated villages in Turkey and Yucatan. Here development is slower, but the trends for these far distant villages are very similar to one another.

Let us now turn to the facts of adult development of moral thought. Some of these are contained in the graphs of figure 38–2. Figure 38–2 shows the percentage usage of each type of thought by our middle class and lower class longitudinal sample at ages 16, 20 and 25. While not all boys were seen at every age, the trends shown fairly represent both longitudinal and cross-sectional trends. The middle-aged group were the fathers of the longitudinal subjects and so comparable to them in all the usual ways.

The first question to be asked is answered by the fact that there is no Stage 7 on the graph. In other words there was no way of thinking about our moral situations found in adulthood and not

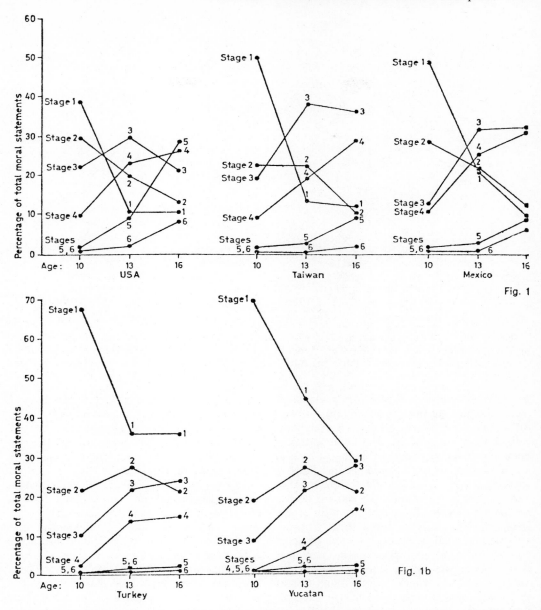

FIGURE 38–1a. Middle-class urban boys in the U.S., Taiwan and Mexico. At age 10 the stages are used according to difficulty. At age 13, Stage 3 is most used by all three groups. At age 16, U.S. boys have reversed the order of age 10 stages (with the exception of 6). In Taiwan and Mexico, conventional (3–4) stages prevail at age 16, with Stage 5 also little used.

FIGURE 38–1b. Two isolated villages, one in Turkey, the other in Yucatan, show similar patterns in moral thinking. There is no reversal of order, and preconventional (1–2) does not gain a clear ascendancy over conventional stages at age 16.

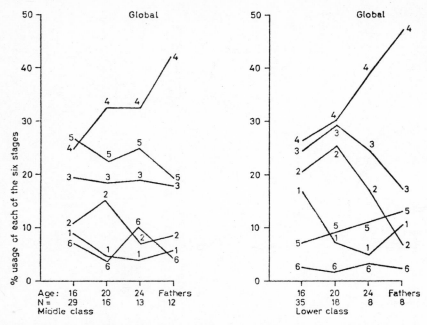

FIGURE 38–2.   Moral judgment profiles (percentage usage of each stage by global rating method) for middle and lower class males at four ages. [From Richard Kramer, "Changes in Moral Judgment Response Pattern During Late Adolescence and Young Adulthood" Ph. D. dissertation, University of Chicago, 1968.]

found in adolescence. While no new modes of moral thought are born in adulthood, there is a not quite significant (p.<15) increase in Stage 6 thinking from 16 to 25. The figure indicates about twice as much Stage 6 thinking at 25 as at 16. To a certain extent, some of this Stage 6 thinking is new at age 25. 80% of the middle-class high school students who showed no use of Stage 6 thought showed at least a little such thought (5%) by age 25. It is difficult to speak very definitely about the development of Stage 6 in our small longitudinal sample because clear Stage 6 types are so rare in every population. Haan, Smith and Block [1968] found 4% of their Bay area college students to be predominantely Stage 6. Holstein [1968] gets about the same percentage in 106 suburban college-educated parents. In our longitudinal sample, we get about the same percentage, amounting to one of our 14 middle class 25 year-olds. He was predominantly Stage 5 in late high school and early college.

While there is some evidence that Stage 6 thinking can be born or at least stabilized in the post-high school years, principled thought of the stage 5 variety is pretty completely developed by the end of high school. Figure 38–2 indicates no clear increase in Stage 5 thinking from high school to age 25. All young adults showing appreciable amounts of Stage 5 thinking (over 15%) also showed appreciable (over 15%) amounts of Stage 5 thinking in high school. The 25% of Stage 5 thinking in our college educated young adults sample is also about that found in the other studies mentioned. We can summarize our results by saying that principled thought, especially Stage 5, is born in adolescence, but that Stage 6 principled thought tends not to become crystalized until the early 20's. Figure 38–2 also indicates that little development occurs after the early 20's. Our middle class college educated fathers are slightly, but not quite significantly (p. < 20) *lower* on Stage 5 and 6 thought than their sons.

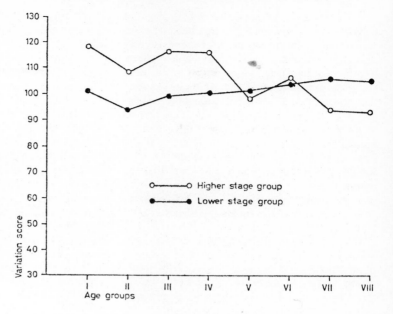

FIGURE 38—3. Mean variation scores for higher stage and lower stage subjects in the Kramer group at the following 8 age ranges: 14.0–15.11 (I); 16.0–16.11 (II); 17.0–17.11 (III); 18.0–18.11 (IV); 19.0–20.11 (V); 21.0–22.11 (VI); 23.0–23.11 (VII); and 24.0–26.11 (VIII).

Like the young, we put the advantage of the younger generation to social or cultural evolution.[2]

Regardless of the ambiguity of the cross-sectional differences graphed in figure 38–2, it is evident that adult development is primarily a matter of dropping out of childish modes of thought rather than the formation of new or higher modes of thought. Figure 38–2 indicates that the major change in moral thought past high school is a significant increase or stabilization of conventional morality of a Stage 4 variety, at the expenses of preconventional stages of thought. This stabilization of moral thought is not only reflected in the trends of stage usage

for the group as a whole, it is also reflected in the trends of variability of stage usage within individuals. Figure 38–3, presents these trends, as analyzed by Turiel [1969] using Kramer's [1968] raw data.

Figure 38–3 presents the amount of spread (usage of stages of thought other than the individual's modal or preferred stage of thought) found among higher (Stages 4, 5, 6) and lower stages (Stages 1, 2, 3). The age trend for higher stage is toward a reduction of usage of stages other than their preferred stage, a trend which is significant (p.< .05). In other words, young men at higher stages are stabilizing at their higher stage with age in young adulthood, although lower stage men are not.

Another word for the adult stabilization which represents the major trends of figure 38–2 and 38–3 is consistency. While our data do not present direct evidence for it, there is reason to believe that adult age change is not only toward greater consistency of moral judgment but toward greater consistency between moral judgment and moral action. Hartshorne and May [1928–30] found that in the period 11 to 14, there was no decline in cheating behavior but there

[2]The case for historical or cultural evolution of moral thought, as made by Hobhouse [1906] is well thought through. Its appeal at the moment is enhanced by the relative position of the generations about the universal moral issues of war. The writer finds no reason to find generational increase in moral level more surprising than the documented generational increases in general intelligence. Recent longitudinal findings [Bayley, 1955] indicate historical or cohort increases in intelligence in adulthood masked by cross-sectional estimates. We would not be surprised to find a similar masking in our cross sectional comparison of our subjects and their fathers.

was a decline in the inconsistency of cheating behavior. With age some children became more consistently honest, some more consistently dishonest, leaving a net mean amount of cheating that was constant. Comparison of cheating studies in preadolescence and in college suggests that not only is cheating behavior more consistent in college but it is more consistently related to level of moral judgment in college than in preadolescence [Kohlberg, 1969]. These fragments of data on consistency suggest support for the folk wisdom which proclaims that the middle aged are more reliable or trustworthy than the young, even if they seem less given to expressing lofty moral ideals in either words or heroic action.

Adult stabilization is not adult development. We could dignify an increase in the consistency of moral ideology with itself and with moral action under the name of integration, the integration of moral thought with itself and with one's self-concept. One reason we hesitate to do so is because much adult moral stabilization seems to be not development but socialization or internalization of the conventional code. This is suggested by the fact that conventional (Stage 4), as well as post-conventional, moral ideologies stabilize in adulthood. There is no Babbitt like an old Babbitt.

While the Babbitts become even more conventional with age, to some extent so do the deviants and the rebels. One of the best predictors for parole is chronological age. Old criminals get burnt out and learn that you can't beat the system. The interpretation that adult moral stabilization is "socialization" not "development" is further suggested by the fact that the breed of conventional morality which stabilizes in adulthood depends upon one's adult social sex role. Only 6% of our Stage 3 boys in high school remained Stage 3 in young adulthood, the rest having moved to Stage 4. In contrast, Stage 3 appears to be a stable adult stage for women. At high school there are about the same percentage of Stage 3 boys and girls [Turiel, 1968]. In the Bay area college population of Haan, Smith and Block [1968] there are about twice as large a percentage of Stage 3 girls as boys. Among the parent samples of Holstein [1969], the difference is even more marked,

about four times as many Stage 3 women as men. In other words, while girls are moving from high school or college to motherhood, sizeable proportions of them are remaining at Stage 3, while their male age mates are dropping Stage 3 in favor of the stages above it. Stage 3 personal concordance morality is a functional morality for housewives and mothers; it is not for businessmen and professionals.

Adult moral stabilization, then, appears to be more a matter of increased congruence between belief and social role than of novel integration of experience. As such, it appears to be more like "socialization" or "social learning" than development. As we have discussed at length elsewhere [Kohlberg, 1968], there is plenty of evidence that while the ordinary mechanisms of social learning (repetition, reinforcement, observational learning) or of attitude change (dissonance reduction) cannot cause or explain structural development, they can cause or explain the strengthening or weakening of "naturally" or "structurally" developing systems of response, a strengthening or weakening that seems to be what we have discussed as "stabilization."

Before dismissing adult functional stabilization as "socialization," however, it will pay to examine the most dramatic finding of the Kramer study. This finding seems to fit neither our generalization that adult change is functional stabilization nor our earlier generalization that developmental change is forward and sequential. These generalizations hold true for our longitudinal subjects at every age and social class with one exception, the college sophomore. That paradigm of the psychological study of the normal, the college sophomore, turns out to be the oddest and most interesting moral fish of all. Between late high school and the second or third year of college, 20% of our middle class sample dropped or retrogressed in moral maturity scores. Retrogression was defined as a drop in maturity scores greater than any found in a two-month-test-retest sample. This drop had a definite pattern. In high school 20% who dropped were among the most advanced in high school, all having a mixture of conventional (Stage 4) and principled (Stage 5) thought. In their college sophomore phase, they kicked both

TABLE 38–3
Examples of Sophisticated and Unsophisticated Stage 2 Responses to One Story

Story III American

In Europe, a woman was near death from a very bad disease, a special kind of cancer. There was one drug that the doctors thought might save her. It was a form of radium that a druggist in the same town had recently discovered. The drug was expensive to make, but the druggist was charging ten times what the drug cost him to make. He paid $200 for the radium and charged $2,000 for a small dose of the drug. The sick woman's husband, Heinz, went to everyone he knew to borrow the money, but he could only get together about $1,000 which is half of what it cost. He told the druggist that his wife was dying, and asked him to sell it cheaper or let him pay later. But the druggist said, ''No, I discovered the drug and I'm going to make money from it.'' So Heinz got desperate and broke into the man's store to steal the drug for his wife.

Should the husband have done that? Why?

Guide for Scoring Story III at Stage 2—as oriented to instrumental necessity of stealing:

1. *Value.* ''The ends justify the means.'' Says has to, is best to, or is right to steal, to prevent wife from dying. (Without implication that saving the wife is a good deed.)
2. *Choice.* Little conflict in *decision to steal.* Implies decision is based on instrumental reasoning or impulse.
3. *Sanction.* Little concern about punishment, or punishment may be avoided by repayment, etc.
4. *Rule.* Little concern about stealing in this situation. May see stealing in this situation as not hurting the druggist.
5. *Husband role.* Orientation to a family member or a relative whom one needs and is identified with. May be an act of exchange, but not of sacrifice or duty.
6. *Injustice.* Druggist's ''cheating'' makes it natural to steal. However, not actually indignant at the druggist, who may be seen as within his rights to charge whatever he wants.

Roger (age 20, a Berkeley Free Speech Movement student).

He was a victim of circumstances and can only be judged by other men whose varying value and interest frameworks produce subjective decisions which are neither permanent nor absolute. The same is true of the druggist. I'd do it. As far as duty, a husband's duty is up to the husband to decide, and anybody can judge him, and he can judge anybody's judgment. If he values her life over the consequences of theft, he should do it.

(Did the druggist have a right?) One can talk about rights until doomsday and never say anything. Does the lion have a right to the zebra's life when he starves? When he wants sport? Or when he will take it at will? Does he consider rights? Is man so different?

(Should he be punished by the judge?) All this could be avoided if the people would organize a planned economy. I think the judge should let him go, but if he does, it will provide less incentive for the poorer people to organize.

John (age 17, reform school inmate).

Should the husband steal the drug for his wife? I would eliminate that into whether he wanted to or not. If he wants to marry someone else, someone young and good-looking, he may not want to keep her alive.

(How about the law, he is asked?) He replies, The laws are made by the rich, by cowards to protect themselves. Here we have a law against killing people but we think it's all right to kill animals. In India you can't. Why should it be right to kill people but not animals? You can make anything right or wrong. To me what is right is to follow your own natural instincts.

Hamza (Turkish village, age 12).

Yes, because nobody would give him the drug and he had no money, because his wife was dying it was right.

(Is it a husband's duty to steal the drug?) Yes—when his wife is dying and he cannot do anything he is obliged to steal. If he doesn't steal his wife will die.

(Does the druggist have the right to charge that much for the drug?) Yes, because he is the only store in the village it is right to sell.

(Should he steal the drug if he doesn't love his wife?) If he doesn't love his wife he should not steal because he doesn't care for her, doesn't care for what she says.

(How about if it is a good friend?) Yes— because he loves his friend and one day when he is hungry his friend will help him.

(Should the judge punish him?) They should put him in jail because he stole.

Jimmy (American city, age 10).

It depends on how much he loved his wife. He should if he does.

(If he doesn't love her much?) If he wanted her to die, I don't think he should.

(Would it be right to steal it?) In a way it's right because he knew his wife would die if he didn't and it would be right to save her.

(Does the druggist have the right to charge that much if no law?) Yes, it's his drug, look at all he's got invested in it.

(Should the judge punish?) He should put him in jail for stealing and he should put the druggist in because he charged so much and the drug didn't work.

their conventional and their Stage 5 morality and replaced it with good old Stage 2 hedonistic relativism, jazzed up with some philosophic and sociopolitical jargon. An example of a college Stage 2 response is given in table 38–3 along with Stage 2 responses by children and delinquents which are structurally similar to it.

The college response is that of a new left Bay area student, from the Haan, Smith and Block [1968] study. Very similar statements are made by new right Ayn Rand objectivist students. Our Stage 2 longitudinal college subjects had similar ideologies but without extremist sociopolitical affiliations, except for one self-defined Nietzschean racist, a Chicagoan who went to a Southern all-white college.

In terms of behavior, everyone of our retrogressed subjects had high moral character ratings in high school, as defined by both teachers and peers. In college at least half had engaged in anticonventional acts of a more or less delinquent sort. As an example, our Nietzschean racist had been the most respected high school student council president in years. In his college sophomore interview, however, he told how two days before he had stolen a gold watch from a friend at work. He had done so, he said, because his friend was just too good, too Christ-like, too trusting, and he wanted to teach him what the world was like. He felt no guilt about the stealing, he said, but he did feel frustrated. His act had failed, he said, because his trusting friend insisted he lost or mislaid the watch and simply refused to believe it had been stolen. This personal moral rebellion in the behavior of college Stage 2 men must be added to the picture of political protest behavior of Stage 2 college men provided by the Haan, Smith and Block [1968] study.

Now if the mysterious forces of development have led our 20% from upstanding conventional morality to Raskolnikov moral defiance, these same mysterious forces set them all to right. Every single one of our retrogressors had returned to a mixed Stage 4 and 5 morality by age 25, with a little more 5 or social contract principle, a little less 4 or convention, than at high school. All too are conventionally conforming in behavior, at least as far as we can observe them.

In sum, this 20% was among the highest group at high school, was the lowest in college and again among the highest at 25. The correlation of moral maturity from age 16 to age 25 is .89, the correlations from high school to college and of college to 25 are only .41.[3]

In what sense is the story just told, the story of rebellious use of lower stages followed by a return to the suburbs of conventional-principled moral stabilization, a story of development? Our interpretation of this story allows us to consider the sense in which the universal stabilization of morality in adulthood may be a form of adult development, even if it is not the structural transformation of moral thought itself. By focussing upon the dramatic cases of stabilization involving retrogression, rather than the placid cases of stabilization which look like ordinary socialization and social learning, we may perhaps arrive at an answer to the question. The first point in our argument is that the retrogression of our subjects is more like a functional regression than it is like a structural regression. While our retrogressors choose to use Stage 2 relativistic egoism, they have not lost their earlier capacity to use Stage 4 and Stage 5 thinking. This is evidenced by three facts. First, the retrogressors continue to use a little Stage 4 and 5 thinking. Second, when asked to give what the world would consider a high moral response to our stories, the retrogressors tend to give straight Stage 4 responses. Third, the fact that the retrogressors eventually return to Stage 4 and 5 strongly suggests that these stages were never lost. In contrast to this group there do appear to be some groups in which cases of genuine structural regression in adulthood can be found. We have found adults who were pure Stage 1, pure Stage 2, or combinations of Stage 1 and 2 among schizophrenics, among people over 65, and among incarcerated criminals. The schizophrenics were college educated, currently functioning well on psychometric tests of intelligence and preparing to leave the hospital. The criminals were in our longitudinal sample

[3]The pattern of correlations I have just discussed is pointed to in Marjorie Honzik's paper in this symposium as the adolescent sleeper effect, an effect not unique to the moral area.

and had shown some Stage 3 and 4 thinking earlier. The elderly were college educated, and intact in intelligence according to norms for their age. While interviews of these cases did not use the methods of testing the limits for structural capacity or understanding of higher stages we have recently developed [Rest, 1968] they give an overwhelming impression of unawareness of alternative or higher points of view which contrast with our college retrogressors.

If the regression of our college sophomores is functional, not structural, does it fit formulations of ego-psychology about "regression in the service (function) of the ego"? One way of stating this question is provided by a graduate student, who proclaimed in a seminar that Stage 7 is reached when you can use all six stages for whatever you want. This student formulates regression in the service of the ego "as a way of life," and ends up advocating plain old regression to Stage 2. Surely, when we cut through the cloudy lofty aura of such words as "identity," "self-realization," "authenticity" which hover around the ego, we must recognize that an ego which uses moral values for whatever it pleases is just our good old instrumentally egoistic, manipulating Stage 2 ego.[4] Moral "regression in the service of the ego" is not the usual law of life. It is true that everyone seems to share our retrogressor's capacity to fall back upon lower stages. Rest [1968] has demonstrated that the capacity to comprehend and (less clearly) to use lower stages of thinking remains, even where these lower stages are never used spontaneously in response to moral problems. He has also demonstrated, however, that the poly-morphous-perverse flexibility of stage usage called Stage 7 by the graduate student, the use of various stages for whatever you want, is extremely uncharacteristic of adolescents. In

spontaneous usage, people are quite consistent from situation to situation in use of a modal stage and the stages immediately adjacent to them [Kohlberg, 1969]. In confronting the moral judgments of others, people prefer the highest level they can comprehend [Rest, 1969; Rest, Turiel and Kohlberg, 1968]. In a sense, the kind of adult change we called stabilization is exactly a further increase in consistency of response, a further decline in moral regression in the service of the ego.

In summary, while there is nothing unusual in our retrogressor's capacity to use lower stages of thought, their actual usage of such thinking is not evidence of a general human tendency toward regression in the service of the ego. It is not an adaptive bending to particular social situational presses in the service of some general ego needs.

The fact that awareness of relativism constitutes a universal developmental challenge or task for men attending a college with some claims to intellectual standing is clearly documented by the work of Perry [1968]. In the case of our retrogressors, there is considerable use of relativism and of anti-moral protest to free themselves from familialy induced guilt. At least half of our regressors gave conscious and clear statements of strong sensitivity to and preoccupation with guilt feelings in preadolescence and adolescence. In this preregression period, the guilt was completely accepted as the voice of higher morality, as something self-accepted and internal. At the same time, the capacity of the boy's parents to inflict this sense of guilt was also noted by the boys. After they left home, they started to test our their capacity to be guilt-free. The most striking example was the Nietzschean who stole the watch from his friend (Raskol-nikov). We labelled him "Raskolnikov" with good reason. Like Raskolnikov's crime, his crime was an effort to prove that the strong need not be moral, and that the good were good only out of stupidity and weakness. Like Raskol-nikov's crime, his crime too was an effort to prove that he need never feel (or fear) guilt [Kohlberg, 1963]. After the theft he kept remarking that it was strange, but he felt no guilt. Four years later, after his return to the fold, he spontaneously announced that he had later felt

---

[4]There is a sense in which there is morally "legitimate" regression of moral thought in the service of the ego. The hierarchy of moral stages is only a hierarchy in moral situations. No one uses Stage 6 thinking in bargaining in an Oriental marketplace, anymore than does anyone use Piaget formal operations to drive a car or paint a picture. The capacity to write a compelling novel or to tell a good off-color joke depends upon using lower stages of moral thinking; the inability to think lowerstage thoughts is the mark of the prig.

guilt about it. The use of relativism by young men, then, is similar to that noted by Perry [1968, p. 137]. "The reactive students, in becoming aware of intellectual and moral relativism, see authorities as imperialistically extending their prejudices over the underdog's rightful freedom, and engage in a fight against the constraint of (unwarranted) guilt. Consider the conventional misuse of cultural relativism "Since it's all right for the Trobriand islanders to do thus and so, you have no right to make me feel guilty about it. It's purely a matter of individual decision." Far from being amoral, such pronouncements are made in a tone of moralistic absolutism, which reveals its emotional continuity with the earlier absolutistic structures" (which we term Stage 4).

While using relativism to free themselves from guilt, our retrogressors are equally upset at relativism and deviance, i.e. at the disappearance of the moral world they believed in in childhood. Our regressors are acutely aware of the breakdown of their expectations of a conventional moral world in the college environment. When they left high school, they thought that people lived by conventional morality and that their rewards in life depended on living that way, too. In college, they tell us, they learned that people did not live in terms of morality, and that if they did, they weren't rewarded for it. As one college Stage 2 said in explaining his "regressive" shift. "College accounts for the change. You see what a dog-eat-dog world it is. Everyone seems to be out for himself. When you live at home you're always trying to please your parents. You don't notice it, but in some way you are. Now I hang around with guys I don't try to please."

Related to this theme is the theme that morality doesn't get you ahead. This boy says, "I'd try to get as far as I can without becoming totally dishonest."

The "oppositional" quality of our regressor's moral ideology is, then, as much to be understood as being as a protest against the immorality of the world as it is a protest against the authoritarian morality of parental figures.

There are, then, two developmental challenges to conventional morality to which our

regressors are unhappily responding. The first is the relativity of moral expectations and opinion, the second is the gap between conventional moral expectations and actual moral behavior. Now it is clear that these developmental challenges are universal general challenges. The integration of one's moral ideology with the facts of moral diversity and inconsistency is a general "developmental task" of youth in an open society. So, too, are the more "psychodynamic" problems faced by our regressors, the problems of freeing themselves from childhood moral expectations and childhood moral guilt. While "psychodynamic," these conflicts are neither unusual nor pathological. Who has not desired to free himself from parentally induced guilt, who has not faced the shocks of finding there are no rewards for being a good boy or girl? The conflicts of our regressors differ only in quantity, not in quality, from our own.

If the challenges which our retrogressors face are universal, in what sense can their responses to them be said to be "development"? We shall contend that our retrogressors are in a sense taking a developmental step forward, even though this step is reflected in a lower stage. We shall further contend that in "returning" to their high school pattern of Stage 4 and Stage 5 thought, they are not simply reverting to an earlier pattern, retreating to the suburbs after the failure of rebellion; but are taking a still further developmental step forward.

In discussing these changes as development, we shall first cast them in Erikson's [1950] familiar terms. In such terms, our retrogressors are living in a late adolescent psychosocial moratorium, in which new and non-conforming patterns of thought and behavior are tried out. Their return to the high school pattern of moral thought is the eventual confirmation of an earlier identification as one's own "identity." To find a socio-moral identity requires a rebellious moratorium, because it requires liberation of initiative from the guilt which our retrogressors suffer from. At the "stage" of identity the adult conforms to his standards because he wants to, not because he anticipates crippling guilt if he does not.

In introducing such terminology, we are indicating that late adolescent or adult moral changes reflect ego development rather than representing the development of morality or moral stage structures itself. Our moral stages are hierarchical structures for fulfilling the function of moral judgment. Ego development in the moral sphere is learning how to use the moral structures one has for one's personal integration. From this point of view, modes of moral thought are structures developed in childhood, but the uses of these modes of thought, their significance for the individual self are matters for late adolescent development. Until late adolescence, the child lives within a world he did not make and in which the choices he must make are circumscribed. His moral ideology is not a direct reflection of his home-school-class-nation environment; it is his own construction designed to make sense of it. However, use of his moral ideology in childhood is primarily to fit and make sense of his given world, not to guide him in autonomous choice. It gives him a rationale for accepting and conforming to the bulk of the patterns of his home, his peer group, his school. This rationale also allows him to reject some patterns in his environment, his world. It does not lead him to question or reject his entire world, however.

The early adolescent's characteristic pattern is either to protest or to secretly deviate from the particular rejected pattern, but to place it in the context of a world he must accept. Sometimes in the back of the conventionally moral high school boy's mind is the notion that he is "putting in time" in the family and the high school until he can live a free life in terms of his own values and desires. While the adolescent may see a free life as a living out of hedonistic values, he may at the same time look forward to the opportunity to live or act in terms of sacrifice to higher moral principles, to give a moral meaning to his life in a way he cannot within the conventional structures of family and school.

Erikson has made us familiar with the fact that Western society provides the post-high-school student with a psychosocial moratorium which allows him to live out either hedonistic or morally idealistic impulses (reflected in anything from life in protest groups to life in the Peace Corps) with a freedom he has neither earlier or later in life. This moratorium comes to an end when inner establishment of an identity or outer pressure to take responsibility in a role of work and parenthood lead the individual to a commitment to a pattern of values which "works" within a definite social world. The restraint which results from adult role-commitment differs vastly from the childhood restraint which comes from a dependent acceptance of such a world. They share in common, however, the acceptance of a core set of rules required to keep a social group or system going.

Neither the egoism of Stage 2 relativism of our retrogressors, nor its pretentious world-changing "idealism" will keep a social world of responsibility for other people going. It is not, of course, that our retrogressors' moral code does not work at all, it can work to the extent of creating social movements, but it does not work if these movements are to become worlds of life-long responsibility and commitment. When the communist movement became an enduring one, it lost its orientation toward the pursuit of happiness and human equality and hardened into a Stage 4 morality of party loyalty as an absolute value. Our retrogressors' "return to the suburbs" of contractual (Stage 5) and conventional (Stage 4) rules is not, then, a defeat. It is not so much that Stage 2 Yippie or Hippie or objectivism is tried and found not to work, as it is that our late adolescent retrogressors were in a moratorium in which they didn't care about having an ideology that "worked," that formed a foundation for life-long responsibility or commitment.

Not only is the retrogressors' return not a defeat, but it clearly brings something to conventional contractual morality which is in some sense a developmental advance. When the retrogressors return to a morality of contract and rules, they do so with less distortive idealization of their own group and authority system, and with greater tolerance and realism about those who deviate from it or are outside of it.

The formulation we have just made is inadequate. We have superimposed developmental task "stages" of ego function in adulthood upon childhood stages of moral structure and claimed structural regression was functional advance. Obviously, such an attempt to have one's cake and eat it too is inadequate. A sequel to the paper attempts to correct this inadequacy by defining ego "stages" in terms of metaethical theories and world views, in contrast to moral stages which are normative ethical theories for making moral judgments in specific moral conflict situations. For the moment, however, our formulation allows us to approximate some conclusions about the relations between childhood and adult moral development.

Moral development involves a continual process of matching a moral view to one's experience of life in a social world. Experiences of conflict in this process generate movement from structural stage to structural stage. Even after attainment of the highest stage an individual will reach, there is continued experience of conflict. The developmental product of such conflict is stabilization, i.e. a greater consistency of structure with itself (greater stage "purity") and a greater consistency between thought structure and action. The evidence that adult stabilization is the integration of conflict rather than "social learning" or socialization, is indicated by our finding one pattern of adult stabilization that involves temporary retrogression. The integration of conflict in adult development may be conceived in terms of functional "stages" of ego development which are quite different from structural stages. While I have discussed only moral change at the "ego stage" of late adolescent identity, the moral changes in late adulthood of the Tolstoys or the Saint Pauls presumably could be discussed in the same general terms.

There is, then, a sense in which there is adult moral development. There is an adult movement toward integration in the use of moral structures, in the integration of moral thought in its application to life. There may even by typical phases in this integrative process. There are, however, no adult stages in the structural sense, and accordingly no clear solution to the two problems of adult development which we initially posed. We cannot integrate childhood and adult moral development into a single theoretical series or sequence of stages. Nor can we claim that

adulthood has a moral wisdom denied to the youth. While structural stages involve a logic of responsiveness to the next stage up, this is not true of ego functional stages.

We may conclude with a concrete example of the discrepancy of implication between ego functional stages and moral structural stages for communication between the generations. The Haan, Smith, and Block Berkeley studies indicated [1968] that those most likely to engage in social protest were students at Stage 2 and Stage 6 in moral judgment. The official stance of the University administration was variously Stage 5 and Stage 4, depending upon whom one considers the spokesman. On the face of it, this and other administrations were in a bad way as far as generational communication goes. Some dissidents were Stage 6, one step above the administration Stage 5 position, whereas others were Stage 2, so far below the administration position as to be indifferent to it. Short of moving up to an adult equivalent of the Stage 6 dissident view, the administration's appeal to the police seemed the inevitable alternative. Limiting ourselves to the Stage 2 "retrogressed" dissidents, however, our findings suggest that the Stage 5 administrator could be structurally understood by the dissident even though it was typed and rejected as Stage 4 "law and order" authoritarianism. In fact, many of the Stage 2 dissidents might end up as Stage 5 "administrators" in the course of adult development.

Aside from the concrete dividing political issues, the administrators and the Stage 2 dissidents are divided by the fact that the administrators have made peace with the problems of relativism and moral inconsistency in the world. Such peace is perceived as a sense of balance and moderation by the administrator, as "sellout" and "machine-likeness" by the dissident. The impasse in communication, then, is due less to the fact that lower stages do not understand higher stages than it is to a discrepancy in developmental task. This is shown by the fact that there are a number of middle-aged adults who speak vital and authentic "childrenese" to the youth, because as they publicly proclaim, they are still pursuing the developmental task of seeking identity and commitment in a society which is not ideal.

If the Stage 5 and 6 "administrators" of our society are to speak effective "adultese" to the young, they must give up talk about responsibility and moderation as well as talk of law and order. Instead they must try to express whatever sense of commitment they have found genuinely meaningful. As we suggest in the sequel, if developmental psychology is to aid in such communication between the generations, it must learn the language of philosophy.

REFERENCES

Bayley, N.: On the growth of intelligence. Amer. J. Psychol. *10:* 805–815 (1953).

Erikson, E.: Childhood and society (Norton, New York 1950).

Haan, N.; Smith, M. B. and Block, J.: The moral reasoning of young adults: Political-social behavior, family background, and personality correlates (in press).

Hobhouse, L. T.: Morals in evolution (Chapman and Hall, London 1906).

Holstein, C.: The relation of children's moral judgment to that of their parents and to communication patterns in the family. Unpublished dissertation, University of California, Berkeley 1969.

Kohlberg, L.: Psychological analysis and literary forms. A study of the doubles in Dostoevsky. Daedalus *92:* 345–363 (1963).

Kohlberg, L.: Stage and sequence: the cognitive-developmental approach to socialization, in Goslin Handbook of socialization theory (Rand McNally, Chicago 1968).

Kohlberg, L.: Stages in the development of moral thought and action (Holt, Rinehart and Winston, New York 1969).

Kramer, R.: Moral development in young adulthood; unpublished doctoral dissertation, Univ. of Chicago (1968).

Kramer, R.: Progression and regression in adolescent moral development. Soc. Res. Child Development, Santa Monica, March 26, 1969.

Perry, W.: Forms of intellectual and ethical development in the college years. Mimeo monograph. Bureau at Study Counsel, Harvard University.

Piaget, J.: The general problems of the psychobiological development of the child; in Tanner and Inhelder, Discussions on child development: Proceedings of the World Health Organization study group on the psychobiological development of the child, vol. IV, pp. 3–27 (International Univ. Press, New York 1960).

Piaget, J.: Cognitive development in children; in Ripple and Rockcastle, Piaget rediscovered: A report on cognitive studies in curriculum development (Cornell Univ. School of Education, Ithaca, N.Y. 1964).

Rest, J.: Developmental hierarchy in preference and comprehension of moral judgment; unpublished doctoral dissertation, Univ. of Chicago (1968).

Rest, J.; Turiel, E. and Kohlberg, L.: Relations between level of moral judgment and preference and comprehension of the moral judgment of others. Journal of Personality (1969).

Smedslund, J.: The acquisition of conservation of substance and weight in children. Scand. J. Psychol. *2:* 85–87, 156–160, 203–210 (1961).

Turiel, E.: Developmental processes in the child's moral thinking; in Mussen, Langer and Covington New directions in developmental psychology (Rhinehart, New York 1969).

Werner, H.: The comparative psychology of mental development (Wilcox and Follett, Chicago 1948).

39. FROM THOUGHT TO THERAPY

Lessons from a Primate Laboratory[1]

H. F. HARLOW, M. K. HARLOW, and S. J. SUOMI

A basic maxim of scientific investigation is that significant research directed toward providing an answer for a particular question will inevitably generate a host of new problems awaiting resolution. Rarely is a scientific inquiry germinated and subsequently resolved in a vacuum. The endless effort required to solve any major problem frequently leads to other channels of thought and the creation of new areas of interest—often by chance or almost chance associations.

Multiple illustrative cases substantiating this point have evolved from research carried out over the years at the University of Wisconsin Primate Laboratory. We have never completely forsaken any major research goal once we pursued it, and we are still searching for the end of each and every rainbow—even though we have already found our fair share of research gold.

During the Primate Laboratory's 40 years of existence we have maintained an ongoing research program investigating the learning capability of rhesus monkeys. Learning has been the key directing the creation, not the culmination, of many of our major research efforts. The first of a series of studies stemming from the earlier learning researches determined the effects of lesions in specific cortical regions, including unilateral and bilateral occipital (1), frontal (2), and temporal (3) lobes, on learning

task performance. Just as the early lesion research developed from learning, later learning research stemmed from the lesion research. To assess lesion effects we were forced to create more reliable and lucid learning tasks and to develop and standardize them into a battery of tests that covered varied abilities and cortical locations. A natural problem raised then concerned the ontogenetic development (4) of ability to perform these various tests, for we already knew that some tests were so difficult that they could not be solved by monkeys younger than three years, and some were so simple they could be solved by monkeys in the first weeks of life.

FIGURE 39-1. Infant monkey clothed in cheesecloth.

[1]This research was supported by grants from the National Institutes of Health to the University of Wisconsin Primate Laboratory and Regional Primate Research Center. Address: Primate Laboratory, University of Wisconsin, Madison, WI 53706.

Reprinted from *American Scientist,* 1971, *59*, 538–549, the journal of Sigma Xi, The Scientific Research Society of North America. Reprinted by permission of the authors and the publisher.

To study developing learning abilities in monkeys required a large number of subjects spanning the age range from birth through adolescence, and so we instituted a breeding program and devised means for rearing monkey subjects in the laboratory from birth onward. In order to reduce the incidence of both confounding variables and contagious disease, we separated the babies from their mothers a few hours after birth and raised them in individual cages where they were hand-fed and received human care (5). The infants were provided with cheesecloth diapers to serve as baby blankets, and we noticed that many of the neonates developed such strong attachments to the cheesecloth blanket that it was hard to tell where the diaper ended and the baby began (as shown in Fig. 39–1). Furthermore, the monkeys became greatly disturbed when the diapers were removed from their cages for essential sanitary services.

The Surrogate Mothers

Dirty diapers and distressed infants were produced for some years—an adequate time for insightful learning to occur—before the true significance of the diaper was duly recognized. It is a long way from brains to blankets, but this is the strange, mysterious way in which research programs develop. Many creative ideas have suddenly appeared in a flight of fancy, but the surrogate mother concept appeared during the course of a fancy flight. The cloth surrogate mother was literally born, or perhaps we should say baptized, in 1957 in the belly of a Boeing stratocruiser high over Detroit during a Northwest Airlines champagne flight. Whether or not this was an immaculate conception, it certainly was a virginal birth. The senior author turned to look out the window and saw the cloth surrogate mother sitting in the seat beside him with all her bold and barren charms. The author quickly outlined the researches and drafted part of the text and verses which would form the basis of his American Psychological Association presidential address (6) a year later. The research implications and possibilities seemed to be immediately obvious, and they were subsequently brought to full fruition by three wise men—one of whom was a woman.

The original theoretical problem to be solved by the surrogate mother researches was to measure the relative strength of bodily contact comfort as opposed to satisfaction of nutritional needs, or activities associated with the breast, as motivational forces eliciting love for mother in rhesus neonates. Actually the primary purpose was to continue to dismantle derived drive theory (7). The results of the now famous cloth-mother and wire-mother experiments provided total support for contact comfort as the superordinate variable or motive binding infant to mother. As pictures of baby monkeys clinging contentedly to soft surrogates (see Fig. 39–2) unfolded across tabloid pages throughout the world, the downfall of primary drive reduction as the predominant theory to account for the development of social attachment was assured. The cloth mother became the first female to attain fame so quickly while still re-

FIGURE 39–2. Baby monkey clinging to cloth surrogate.

FIGURE 39–3.   Infant terrified in absence of surrogate mother.

taining her virginal virtues. There is more than merely milk to human kindness.

On the basis of the diaper data it came as no great surprise to find that monkey infants overwhelmingly preferred nonlactating cloth mothers to lactating wire surrogates. However, during the course of testing infants in novel environments we discovered an unexpected trait possessed by our cloth surrogates: the capacity to instill a sense of basic security and trust in their infants (8). This is the way creative research often arises—sometimes by insight and sometimes by accident. Baby monkeys placed in an unfamiliar playroom devoid of a cloth surrogate, or with a wire surrogate present, typically rolled into tight furry balls (as shown in Fig. 39–3), screeching in terror.

When the same infants were placed in the same environment in the presence of cloth surrogate mothers, they initially scurried to the surrogates and clung for dear life. After their first fears abated, the monkeys would then venture away from the surrogates and explore the environment, as shown in Fig. 39–4, but often returned (Fig. 39–5) to their inanimate mothers for a reassuring clasp or a deep embrace to desensitize fear or alleviate insecurity. This response was predicated upon a psychiatric principle discovered by baby monkeys long before the advent of Watson (9), Wolpe (10), or any of the Skinnerians. Basic trust was the achievement of the first of Erikson's (11) eight human developmental crises, and although basic trust may not be fashioned out of whole cloth, for baby monkeys it apparently can be fashioned from cloth alone.

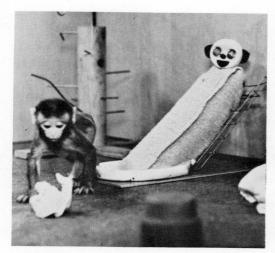

FIGURE 39–4. Infant security in presence of cloth surrogate.

Subsequently we recognized the obvious truth that no major act of animal behavior is determined by a single variable. To illustrate this axiom we created surrogates of varying form and function, and they disclosed that many variables other than contact comfort possessed more than measurable effects on infant monkey maternal attachment (*12*). These findings led naturally to a series of studies designed to measure all possible variables, regardless of importance, relating to the maternal efficiency of our man-made mothers. The researches disclosed a number of variables secondary in importance to contact comfort. With contact comfort held constant by constructing lactating and nonlactating terry-cloth surrogates, it was possible to demonstrate that nursing, or activities associated with the breast, was a significant variable during the first 90 days of life. Thus, by this ingenious research we learned what had been totally obvious to everyone else, except psychologists, for centuries. Furthermore, rocking surrogates and rocking cribs were preferred to nonrocking surrogates and cribs for about 160 days. Body surfaces other than wire or cloth were also investigated, with predictable results. Satins and silks might be adult symbols of prestige, but they do not warm the infant heart as does terry cloth.

Infant rhesus monkeys preferred a warm wire surrogate to a cool cloth surrogate for the first 15 days of life, illustrating the limited temporal span of some variables and confirming the well-known "hot mama" or "warm woman" hypothesis. Warmth was the only variable to

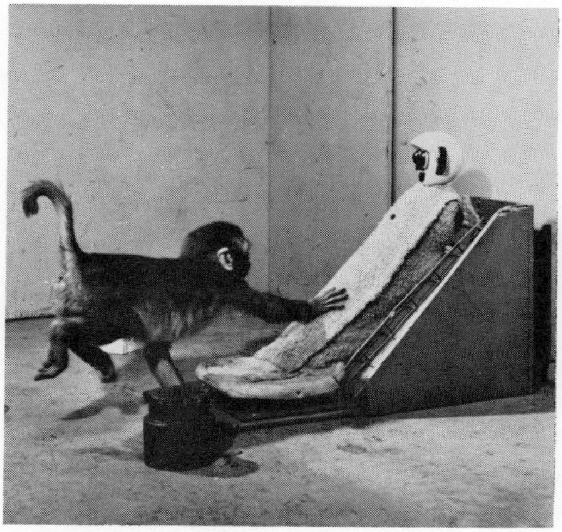

FIGURE 39–5. Infant monkey returning to surrogate mother for reassurance.

FIGURE 39–6. Infant rejecting cold mother surrogate.

lend even transient preference to the wire surrogate. However, the most striking maternal temperature data were recently obtained by Suomi (*13*), who constructed a cold cloth surrogate with ice water in her veins. Neonatal monkeys tentatively attached to this cold cloth figure, but then retreated to a far corner of the cage, as shown in Figure 39–6, and remained aloof from mother forever. There is only one social affliction worse than an ice-cold wife, and that is an ice-cold mother.

Finally, we compared the efficiency of our man-made mothers with their natural counterparts, and we are convinced that real motherhood is superior and that it is here to stay. The cloth mother may serve milk, but not in the cozy continuous containers provided by the real mother. The real mother eliminates nonnutritional sucking by her infant, whereas no surrogate mother, regardless of Skinnerian schedule, can inhibit nonnutritional sucking. The real monkey mother trains her infant to be a placer, rather than a spreader, of feces (*14*). The real mother trains her infant to comprehend the gestural and vocal communications of other monkeys (*15*), while language learning is beyond surrogate love. The real mother is dynamic and responds to the infant's needs and behavior, but the surrogate can only passively accept. Subsequently the mother plays an active role in separating the infant from her body, which results, probably inadvertently, in the exploration of the surrounding animate and inanimate environment. Finally, and of most importance for future peer adjustment, the real mother is far more efficient than the cloth surrogate in the regulation of early infant play, the primary activity leading to effective age-mate love.

We might have remained imprinted on surrogate mothers forever had it not been for a comment made to the senior author independently by an eminent psychologist and an eminent psychiatrist within a single month. Both said, "You know, Harry, you are going to go down in the history of psychology as the father of the cloth mother!" This was too much! In a desperate effort to escape this fate we branched out into new areas of research, which were subsequently to fall into two broad, disparate areas: the nature of normal and natural love in rhesus monkeys, and the induction of psychopathology.

The Natural Nature of Love

I enlisted the aid of my wife, and we fell in love, or at least in love with love, in all its multifaceted forms. Normal and natural love in rhesus monkeys develops through the sequencing and interaction of five major love systems: maternal love; infant love, or love of the infant for the mother; peer love, which other psychologists and psychoanalysts will someday discover; heterosexual love; and paternal love.

Maternal love has always been obvious, and even Freud was fully aware of it. We have already described its social functions. An extremely important basic function is the management of infant play so that infant monkeys play together effectively instead of in a disorganized manner. Maternal love serves as an important antecedent to the development of peer or age-mate love.

The variables underlying the love of the infant for the mother have already been described in the surrogate researches. It is our opinion that a more important love system, in fact, the most important from the view of the whole life span, is age-mate love, which develops first through curiosity and exploration and later through multiple forms of play. Peer interactions enhance the formation of affection for associates, the development of basic social roles, the inhibition of aggression, and maturation of basic sexuality. We believe heterosexual behavior in primates is another love system, evolving from peer love very much as peer love evolves from maternal love.

Heterosexual love was not discovered by Freud. Freud became lost in the libido even before he experienced it, and he never fully learned about love. Heterosexual love differs in form and function in various animal families. Beach (*16*) eventually discovered love in

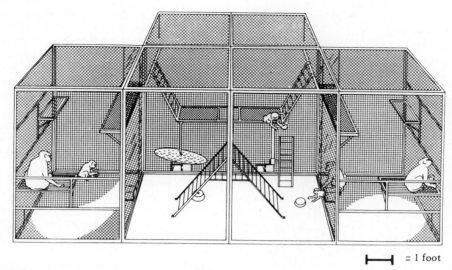

= 1 foot

FIGURE 39–7.   Nuclear family living apparatus.

beagles, but so had the beagles. Some female beagles have warm and wondrous love affairs despite the fact that they are basically bitches. Heterosexual love in rats and people is planned in different fashions. If you are a rat, your sex life may be endocrinologically determined, and you will do very well. However, if you are a primate—monkey, ape, or man—and your heterosexual life is primarily gonadally determined, you face a grim and grave future, and the sooner the grave, the better. Sex without antecedent and concurrent love is disturbed and disordered (*17*).

After resolving the nurture and nature of maternal, infant, peer, and heterosexual love, the only thing that remained was paternal love. Having analyzed monkey love as far as we could with our existing facilities, I realized that we had no love with father, and I dejectedly proclaimed to my wife that, although paternal love in feral baboons and monkeys had been described, this love system could not be analyzed and resolved under laboratory restraints. A month later Margaret Harlow brought me the experimental design for paternal laboratory love and a plan for the necessary housing facilities. After the relatively simple task of rebuilding the attic over our laboratory had been achieved, the analysis of paternal love was on its way.

The Nuclear Family

The nuclear family apparatus, shown in Figure 39–7, is a redesigned, redefined, replanned, and magnified playpen apparatus where four pairs of male and female macaques live with their offspring in a condition of blissful monogamy. In the nuclear family apparatus each and every male has physical access to his own female and communicative access to all others. It is obvious from time to time that some males and females would like to have physical access to their neighbors' mates, but their courting must be limited to calls and lip-smacking and visual fixation. Fortunately, they accept their frustration with minimal effects on their mates.

Most important of all, each and every infant has access to every male, and, perhaps because of the cunning and curiosity of all the infants, most nuclear fathers responded socially to most infants. Finally, the apparatus provides unrivaled opportunities to study sibling interactions and friendship formation in infants of similar and disparate ages.

Creation of the nuclear family has provided us with a body of basic information concerning paternal love. The nuclear fathers do not allow mothers, their mates, and neighbors, to abuse or abandon infants, and the fathers serve as a cohesive force guarding the group against predators—primarily experimenters. In addition, the fathers, through some developmental mechanism which we do not yet understand, show affection in varying degrees to all infants. Many fathers engage in reciprocal play with the infants at a level far surpassing that of the mothers, and the fathers ignore aggression from the infants and juveniles, including pinching, biting, and tail- and ear-pulling—behaviors the fathers would never accept from adolescents and adults of either sex.

Preadolescent monkey males, unlike females, exhibit limited interest in all new infants except their siblings until the babies can play. The males largely ignore them, while the female preadolescents continually struggle to make contact with the new babies. The precursors of paternal behavior are present, however, for the older male infants and juveniles cradle, carry, and protect young infants that venture in their path. The watchful eyes of the adults and their ready threats may abet the gentle behavior of the older infants and possibly begin the inculcation of protection of all young. We have still much more to learn about the variables in the development of paternal behavior.

The advent of the second and third infants in the families has disclosed interesting aspects of maternal love and sibling interaction. We had long presumed that the appearance of a second monkey gift from Heaven would exaggerate the mother-infant separative mechanisms long in progress, and that neonatal fairy fingers playing upon the maternal heart-strings would rapidly dissipate the love for the older infant. True to prediction, the immediate reaction of the newly delivered mother to her older infant was negative. She threatened body contact, prevented nipple contact, and cradled the new infant continuously. But every mother eventually reversed this policy toward the older infant. The only

individual difference was the interval between the new birth and contact with the older infant, which ranged from 8 hours to a matter of days. Most displaced infants or juveniles spent a night or two without maternal contact, often with their fathers, but one managed to achieve contact with mother the very first night and every night thereafter by persistent approach, cooing and squealing until her mother made room for her too. Although she had a good relationship with her father, she made no attempt to substitute him.

Much to our surprise, the displaced infants did not overtly exhibit punitive signs of jealousy toward the newcomers, probably because of fear of the mother, although one male juvenile did engage in teasing his little sister at every opportunity when mother was not looking. All displaced infants showed disturbance in this situation of denial and despair, of suspicion and separation, and the older infants would spend hours trying to achieve contact comfort, real or symbolic, from the body of the mother—both awake and asleep. Indeed, initial contact was usually made when the mother was sleepy and had reduced her vigilance. In desperation, when this failed, some would enter adjacent living chambers and make overtures to other mothers, who generally accepted their presence but denied them bodily contact. Alternatively, proximity and contact with their fathers were sought when mothers were not available.

In spite of the fact that the nuclear families provided a wealth of new data on the affectional systems, the most striking psychological contribution of the nuclear family has not been to love but to learning.

Lonely Learning

For a number of years we had assiduously studied the effects of early environment upon later learning capability, and to achieve this we had always used groups of normal monkeys and groups of socially isolated monkeys. We knew that total social isolation damaged or destroyed the social-sexual capabilities of monkeys, as is described in detail in the subsequent section, but it did not depress learning ability. Our socially deprived monkeys were reared under conditions of 6, 9, or 12 months of total social isolation, a condition of deprivation or privation so severe that no one will ever impose it upon human children.

Our "normal" monkeys had been reared in partial social isolation. We had recognized the fact that partial social isolation would hardly qualify as a haven or Heaven, but because of limited facilities this is the manner in which we had always reared our normal monkeys. For decades our normal monkeys have achieved learning performances better than those achieved in any other laboratory, owing no doubt to the unusual care we took in adapting them to the test situation.

Finally, S. D. Singh (18), who had had extensive test experience on the Wisconsin General Test Apparatus (WGTA) in the United States and in India, reported that feral animals (reared in forests or in temples) were not intellectually different from each other and were not superior to our monkeys reared in partial social isolation. Furthermore, Singh's test battery was adapted from our own, utilizing discrimination problems which rhesus monkeys are able to solve at 6 months of age, delayed-response tests at 10 months of age, learning-set tasks mastered at 12 months of age, and, later, complex oddity-learning-set tasks which are not efficiently solved by monkeys until 36 months of age. Singh's data gave every indication that partial isolation cages were just as stimulating to intellectual development as were temples and forests.

We had assumed that "enriched" environments were in no way superior to the deprived environments in stimulation and development of the intellectual processes. To demonstrate this, we compared the performance of monkeys reared from birth in the nuclear family apparatus with that of totally socially isolated monkeys and our normal monkeys. Just as predicted, the enormously socially enriched monkeys reared in interacting family groups did no better than deprived monkeys or control monkeys on discrimination tasks, delayed-response tasks, and complex learning-set tasks. My world of happy intellectual isolation was

jolted, however, when the socially enriched preadolescents and adolescents, as contrasted with the socially isolated adolescents and controls, proved to be superior at the .001 significance level on our most complex problem-oddity-learning set. Had there been a progressive separation in performance between enriched and deprived monkeys as they traversed through tests of increasing complexity, we would gladly have conceded a difference, but the difference appeared only when the most complicated learning test was administered.

One can only conclude that this enriched early environment, at least, enables monkeys adequately adapted and trained to reach more lofty intellectual performance levels than those attained by deprived monkeys. The basis for the performance difference, however, is by no means established. Superiority could stem from nonintellectual factors as readily as from intellectual differences. The nuclear family animals give every evidence of being the most self-confident, self-assured, fearless animals we have ever tested. They are more relaxed in the test situation than other subjects and could well be more persistent, thus persevering after "normal" subjects give up. This difference would not be apparent on unchallenging tasks, but when the problems become very difficult, the personality factors could operate to produce performance differences. Unfortunately, it is as difficult to test as is the hypothesis that middle-class children excel intellectually over lower-class children because of their environmental advantages.

Induced Psychopathology

For many years behavioral scientists attempted to produce psychopathological behavior syndromes in nonhuman subjects by experimental manipulation, but their successes were at best limited. H. F. Harlow (19) hypothesized that maternal rejection might provide the critical contribution to this area, and so a family of surrogate mothers was designed to impart fear and insecurity to infant monkeys. Four different forms of evil artificial mothers emerged, and although all were designed to repel clinging infants, each had its own unique means by which to achieve this end. One surrogate blasted its babies with compressed air, another tried to shake the infant off its chest, a third possessed an embedded catapult which periodically sent the infant flying, while the fourth carried concealed brass spikes beneath her ventral surface which would emerge upon schedule or demand.

These surrogates produced temporary emotional disturbance in the infants, but little else. When displaced from their artificial mothers, the infants would cry, but they would return to the mother as soon as she returned to normal. In retrospect, it should have been obvious—to what else can a frightened, contact-seeking infant cling? The only individuals to suffer prolonged distress from these experimental efforts were the experimenters. Later we discovered the existence of far more sadistic monkey mothers—real ones.

In the midst of these ill-destined efforts, we discovered that we already had dozens of abnormal monkeys produced without any special effort. It became apparent to us that something was awry after the animals we tested in the study of the development of learning had completed their experimental chores and were physically mature enough to transfer to the breeding colony. We had every expectation that these healthy, well-developed animals would give us disease-free infants to supply our experimental needs. The animals were paired appropriately and placed in large cages. Weeks passed, then months passed, and we never saw any copulation, and there certainly were no offspring. When summer came, we hoped to change their behavior by assigning some of them to group living on an unoccupied monkey island in the Madison zoo.

The group psychotherapy had some effect. The aggression that erupted when the monkeys were initially transferred gradually disappeared. Animals began to form social groups and to groom each other. But no heterosexual behavior was observed and there were no pregnancies. In the belief that a highly experienced male from the breeding colony could conquer the females,

we released onto the island one of our most capable males. He met all challengers with ease and immediately became leader of the island. But still no females became pregnant. We knew then that we had raised a colony of monkeys abnormal in their sex behavior. This was the beginning of a systematic effort to study sexual and social development of monkeys raised under varying environmental conditions.

One rearing condition we had already established—the raising of infants from birth onward in bare wire cages without companions. Subsequently, we termed this "partial social isolation." The subjects were not only devoid of heterosexual behavior at maturity but showed exaggerated oral activities, self-clutching, and rocking movements early in life, then apathy and indifference to external stimulation subsequently. Individualized stereotyped activities involving repetitive movements characterized many subjects and extremely bizarre behavior appeared in some. An animal might sit in the front of its cage staring aimlessly into space. Occasionally one arm would slowly rise as if it were not connected to the body, and wrist and fingers would contract tightly (Fig. 39–8)—a pattern amazingly similar to the waxy flexibility characteristic of some human catatonic schizophrenics. The monkey would then look at the arm, jump away in fear, and subsequently attack the offending object. Unfortunately, we know nothing about the forces that cause one isolated monkey to drift into inactivity and another to demonstrate bizarre repetitive behavior patterns.

To understand why partial social isolation, which seems to be a relatively benign condition, is actually so devastating socially, one need merely consider the effect that rearing in partial or total social isolation from birth onward has upon the development of the five love systems (19). The monkey reared in partial social isolation knows no maternal love and therefore cannot love its mother. Furthermore, living alone in a cage it cannot develop age-mate or peer affection, which comes for the normal monkey through physical interaction with other young monkeys. Sex in a bare wire cage is either nonexistent or at best limited and lonely.

FIGURE 39–8. Catatonic posture of partial isolate.

Thus it is not surprising that partial social isolation produces profound behavioral abnormalities in monkeys. By chance we had discovered what had been sought for years by design.

If denial of physical access to other monkeys produces such psychopathology, it would seem likely that denial of visual, as well as physical, access to other monkeys would produce even more serious deficiencies. Subsequent research found this to be the case. When William A. Mason came to Wisconsin in 1954, we designed total isolation chambers, and the first research describing the effects of long-term social isolation in these chambers was published by Mason and Sponholz in 1963 (20). Subsequently, an improved total social isolation apparatus was created with true cunning and connivance by Rowland (21), and this became and remains our standard total social isolation chamber. Rowland's apparatus was designed so that monkeys could be raised from birth onward without seeing any other animal or part of any other animal except the experimenter's hands and arms which assisted the neonate up a feeding ramp during the first 15 days of life. Subsequently, the experimenter could easily observe the infant through a one-way vision window, while the infant monkey saw no animal of any kind. Moreover, the apparatus was designed so that the learning ability of the isolate-reared monkey could be measured by remote control, and this was successfully achieved in Rowland's original study.

The total social isolation apparatus enabled us to quantify the socially destructive effects of isolation from birth onward. Monkeys reared in total social isolation for 90 days were enormously disturbed when admitted to the great wide world of wonder, and two of them actually died of self-induced anorexia before we recognized the syndrome and instituted forced-feeding. However, all surviving monkeys rapidly made a complete social adjustment to age-mates, so that behavior from one postisolation month onward was normal for all measurable purposes.

In contrast, monkeys subjected to 6 months of total social isolation from birth and then allowed to interact with age-mates were very adversely affected for the rest of their lives. They spent their time primarily engrossed in autistic-like self-clasping, self-mouthing, and

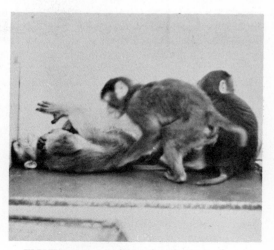

FIGURE 39–9. Isolate infant frozen in fear.

rocking and huddling. The isolates never interacted successfully with normal peers over an 8-month period, although pairs of isolate monkeys did show limited recovery in terms of exploration and even play with each other. These monkeys were then maintained in partial social isolation for approximately 3 years, and, when subsequently tested, their behavioral repertoire appeared to have deteriorated rather than improved. Their social efforts were plaintive and their sexual efforts pitiful. Practically the only social behaviors that seemed to have matured were fear and aggression, and the animals showed these inappropriately and often explosively. Six-month isolates aggressed against infants—an act no normal monkey would consider—but before, during, and after aggressive acts, they were frozen in fear even though the infants they faced were only half their size (Fig. 39–9). In addition, several isolate monkeys attempted a single suicidal sortie against very large adult males—an act no normally socialized animal would be foolish enough to try.

We also discovered that 12 months of total social isolation from birth had even more drastic effects than 6 months on behavior in the playroom. Exploration and even simple play were nonexistent. Torn by fear and anxiety, aggression was obliterated in these monkeys, and even the simple pleasure of onanism was curtailed. They sat huddled alone in the corners or against the walls of the room. The actual experiment was stopped after 10 weeks, since the control animals were literally tearing up the 12-month isolates, and the isolates made no effort to protect themselves. These animals were maintained for many years and never demonstrated any vestige of virginal social ability, even for a very long time afterward. They were tested by Robert E. Miller some three years later for their ability to receive and express social communication. They were a perfect control group, totally devoid of all social signaling.

A considerable number of our isolate-reared females were eventually impregnated by patient and competent feral males. When adequate animal assistance failed, we resorted to an

FIGURE 39–10.　Motherless mother ignoring her infant.

apparatus affectionately termed the rape rack, which we leave to the reader's imagination. Very soon we discovered that we had created a new animal—the monkey motherless mother. These monkey mothers that had never experienced love of any kind were devoid of love for their infants, a lack of feeling unfortunately shared by all too many human counterparts (22). Most of the monkey motherless mothers ignored their infants, as shown in Figure 39–10, but other motherless mothers abused their babies by crushing the infant's face to the floor, chewing off the infant's feet and fingers, and in one case by putting the infant's head in her mouth and crushing it like an eggshell. Not even in our most devious dreams could we have designed a surrogate as evil as these real monkey mothers.

Experimental Study of Depression

The door to discovery of behavioral deficits produced by isolation rearing was opened largely by chance. In contrast, the initial enlightenment of procedures which resulted in another form of monkey psychopathology, that of depressive behavior, was unlocked by love. During the course of study of mother and infant affection, two experiments (23, 24) were conducted in which infants were reared with mothers and peers, then separated from their mothers for a period of several weeks. It was found that the maternal separations precipitated severe reactions among the infants. During the period of separation the young monkeys ceased their peer play activity and became withdrawn and inactive. When reunited with their mothers, they spent more time engaging in mother-directed activity than they had spent immediately prior to separation, amply demonstrating the overwhelming strength of the mother-infant attachment bond.

A closer examination of these data indicated that more than love had been disclosed by the experiments. During the maternal separation the infants had initially expressed protest, characterized by increased activity and vocalization, but soon withdrew and became inactive. Normal social interactions among the infants declined or disappeared, as was the case for play, the most complex social behavior the infants possessed. These behavioral abnormalities vanished when the infants were reunited with their mothers.

Several years earlier Spitz (25) and Bowlby (26) had witnessed surprisingly similar reactions among human infants who had been separated from their mothers via hospitalization. Spitz termed the reaction "anaclitic depression." Bowlby delineated two stages of the reaction during the period of separation, which ranged from a few days to a few months: initial protest, characterized by agitation and crying, and despair, characterized by withdrawal from the world of both animate and inanimate objects. When Spitz's children were reunited with their mothers, recovery was immediate and spontaneous, but Bowlby observed a "detachment" among some of his infant patients upon maternal reunion, a phenomenon he now feels may not represent a universal aspect of reaction to maternal separation. At any rate, these data suggested a close parallel between human and monkey infants in terms of reaction to maternal separation: anaclitic depression resulted in both cases.

Mother-infant separation experiments were subsequently carried out at several other primate laboratories, and the findings from study to study were amazingly consistent (27, 28). Almost immediately following separation, infants exhibited initial protest, characterized by increasing activity and vocalization. Shortly thereafter most subjects entered into a depressive withdrawal, even though the form and duration of the despair stage varied among the monkeys in the various researches and differing experimental conditions. Upon reunion infant-mother interactions rapidly became essentially normal, and there was little evidence of maternal detachment.

Several years later, the accumulation of a vast body of normative information and a desire to investigate new and challenging problems led us to shift our major interests to the study of depression in monkeys. Leaving love in search for psychiatry is not that major a transition. The study of normal behavior furnishes all needs and norms necessary for the analysis of monkey madness and laboratory lunacy. At this time, a reconsideration of the mother-infant separation studies indicated a point of departure for the production of depression in nonhuman primates. Our earlier studies had duplicated, in laboratory monkeys, both the precipitating situation and the subsequent syndrome described as anaclitic depression for human infants. However, it was obvious to us that mother-infant separation had both theoretical and practical limitations as a standard procedure for large-scale investigation of depression in monkeys, and to achieve significant advances in this area it would be necessary to transcend the mother-infant separation model.

Our first effort in this direction was initiated by Suomi (29), who reared infant monkeys with each other rather than with mothers. When these infants were separated from their playmates at 3 months of age, they exhibited a protest-despair reaction to separation virtually identical in form to that resulting from maternal denial in both human and monkey infants. Unlike the mother-infant separation studies, the infant-infant separation technique was expanded so that the young monkey peers were separated from each other not once but many

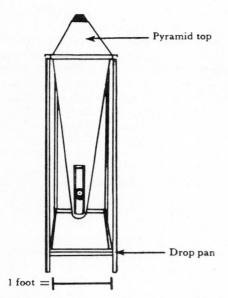

Pyramid top

Drop pan

1 foot =

FIGURE 39–11.   Vertical chamber apparatus.

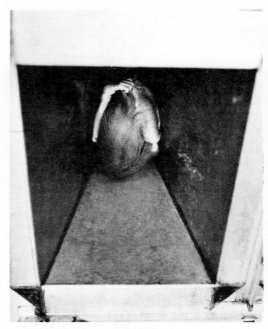

FIGURE 39–12.   Immobilized posture.

times—4 days for each of 20 experimental weeks spread over a 6-month period. During every separation period the infants exhibited a severe protest-despair reaction, and each time they were reunited their activity primarily consisted of mutual clinging. This pattern did not change significantly from the beginning to the end of the multiple separation periods, even after 20 separations.

An unanticipated and fascinating discovery was the finding that the multiple separations produced a severe maturational arrest in the monkeys. Their behaviors following the separations were as infantile at age 9 months as they were prior to the first separation. Neonatal behaviors of nonnutritional orality and self-clasp persisted throughout the 6-month separation period, but the complex infant play activities which normally mature from 90 to 180 days had not appeared by the age of 9 months. This finding was in total contrast to the fascinating progression of social development traditionally reported in normal monkey infants. It was as if Suomi had stopped the monkeys' biological calendars.

The results of Suomi's study indicated that depressive reactions could be precipitated in monkey subjects by procedures other than that involving separation from the mother. No longer bound by the restraints of the mother-infant separation model, we could now seriously consider production and study of depressions other than anaclitic in monkey subjects.

A radically different approach to the production of depressive behavior in monkeys, one that did not involve any social attachments, was made possible by a vertical chamber apparatus created by H. F. Harlow. This apparatus, illustrated in Fig. 39–11, is a stainless steel chamber with sides that slope downward to a wire-mesh platform above a rounded steel bottom. Depression in humans has been characterized as a state of "helplessness and hopelessness, sunken in a well of despair" (30), and the chambers were designed to reproduce such a well for monkey subjects. Although the confined monkeys are free to move about in three dimensions within the chamber, and although they eat and drink normally and maintain proper weight, within a few days they typically assume a huddled, immobilized posture in a corner of the apparatus (Fig. 39–12).

Suomi (31) then tested 90-day-old monkeys antecedently subjected to 45 days of chamber confinement and compared their subsequent activity in both social and nonsocial situations with two groups of equal-aged monkeys, one group peer-reared and the other reared as partial isolates. Extensive testing was conducted for 9 months, and throughout this period the chambered subjects consistently exhibited highly elevated levels of self-clasping and huddling, low levels of locomotion and exploration, and nonexistent social activity. These behaviors were in sharp contrast to those of both control groups (Fig. 39–13). Clearly, chamber confinement of relatively short duration was enormously effective for producing profound and prolonged depression in young monkey subjects.

Suomi then measured the effects of combined chamber confinement and peer separation in two studies utilizing monkey subjects under a year of age and found that chamber confinement intensified depressive separation-produced effects in monkeys with extensive prior social experience (31). We have long believed that a phenomenon as complex as depression cannot possibly be mediated by a single variable, and these researches indicated that the depths of our infants' depressions were dependent upon a number of factors, including duration of separation and/or confinement, age at which de-

pression was produced, and prior social history of the subjects.

The addition of a psychiatrist, Dr. William McKinney, to our depression project brought both clinical insight and psychiatric respectability to the research endeavors, and his presence has been welcome and fruitful. He has already taken a leading role in the experimental induction of depression in older-aged monkeys, whereby the diagnosis of anaclitic depression is excluded. In addition to investigating the behavioral aspects of depression, he has directed the initiation of researches involving analyses of biochemical variables, including the catecholamines (32). Three years ago the idea of using monkeys to unravel the behavioral and biochemical intricacies of an affliction suffered in some form, and at some time, by virtually every human being and fully understood by virtually no human mind, seemed to be little more than a desperate dream or humble hope. Today we are finally and firmly on the road to success.

Monkey Psychotherapy and Rehabilitation

Our research endeavors in the field of depression have resulted in a sizable increase in our population of emotionally disturbed monkeys, and we are now initiating researches designed to rehabilitate our "patients" to a state of social normality. We plan long-term re-

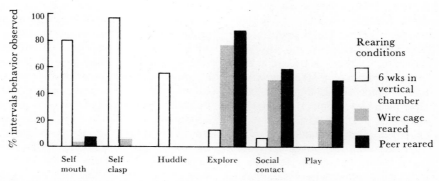

FIGURE 39–13. Behavioral effects of chamber confinement; playroom behaviors of rhesus monkeys 9–11 months of age reared under different conditions.

FIGURE 39–14. Isolate disturbance activity.

FIGURE 39–15. Therapist clinging to isolate.

searches utilizing all possible types of therapeutic agents, including various antidepressant drugs and even such techniques as electroconvulsive therapy (ECT). Actually, our primary interest lies in the alleviation of depression by psychotherapeutic techniques since many of the monkey depressions were induced through social manipulations. Thus, social approaches to therapy have been our principal concern. Recently we have had several rewarding experiences which have provided valuable information relative to the stages of depression formation and alleviation.

While we were inducing depression in monkeys we were also attempting to rehabilitate several of our total social isolation-reared subjects, an effort previously initiated by many investigators with little or no success (*33*). As stated earlier, isolates exposed to socially normal age-mates were the recipients of severe aggression with little therapy, and any subsequent social improvement was limited at best. However, we did discover that isolate-reared subjects showed some social improvement if they were able to achieve contact acceptability with various social agents. In particular, the motherless mothers whose infants survived in spite of evil maternal efforts eventually submitted to their babies' persistent attempts to achieve and maintain maternal contact, and to our great surprise these females usually exhibited adequate maternal behavior toward subsequent offspring. Also, isolates exposed to

heated surrogates soon after emergence from confinement eventually learned to contact the nonthreatening surrogates, leading to significant decreases in self-directed disturbance activity. When these animals were subsequently paired with each other they exhibited the rudiments of basic social-interaction patterns (*34*).

These findings convinced us that significant rehabilitation of isolate-reared subjects via social exposure was feasible and that the crucial variable lay in the nature of the social stimulation utilized. Each of the three authors is convinced that he (she) created the plan and procedure for monkey rehabilitation, and this is probably true since all were thoroughly familiar with the essential maturational data underlying a feasible therapy program. It seemed that an effective monkey "therapist" might be one who would instill contact acceptability in the isolate monkeys without providing a threat of aggression and could subsequently or simultaneously provide an appropriate medium for the development of an increasingly sophisticated social repertoire. Our knowledge of monkey social development led us to select socially normal animals 3 to 4 months old as therapists for the isolates. At this age normal monkeys are too young to show aggression,

FIGURE 39–16. Isolates and therapists in vigorous play bout.

they still provide stable contact clinging responses, and they are on the verge of gradually expanding their basic social interactions into fully developed play (*35*).

We therefore took 6-month-old animals who had been socially isolated from birth and housed them individually in compartments of a "quad cage" (*36*) adjacent to therapists 3 months their juniors. The quad cage, designed by Suomi, is an extremely versatile social testing unit which can simultaneously or successively serve as a living and testing area. Selection of interior panels dictates roommate assignment, while removal of the panels permits partner interaction in home territory. In this study (*37*) we permitted interactions between isolates and therapists 2 hours per day, both within the quad cages and in a social playroom. As therapy progressed interaction time in the quad cages was decreased and time in the playroom increased.

The isolates' initial response to their interaction opportunities was to retreat to a corner and rock and huddle (Fig. 39–14), and the therapists' initial response was to follow and cling to the isolates (Fig. 39–15). Soon the isolates were clinging back, and it became only a matter of weeks until isolates and therapists were playing enthusiastically with each other (Fig. 39–16). During this period most of the isolates' previously abnormal behaviors gradually disappeared, and after 6 months recovery was essentially complete.

An interesting sidelight or fringe benefit from the above findings concerned observed sex differences. Not entirely by design, all of the isolates in the above experiment were males, while all of the therapists were female. We have long known that under normal rearing conditions males develop a rougher and more contact-oriented form of play behavior than females, and these differences are initially expressed prior to 6 months of age. Our rehabilitated males had spent their first 6 months of life in total social isolation and thereafter were exposed only to the female therapists and to each other. The psychotic monkeys had no social model for the development or creation of masculine play. Nevertheless, their play, when it emerged, was clearly masculine in form, adding to our data long cumulating that sextyping of play in monkeys is governed not by imitation but by genetics (*38*). Culture makes clothes but God gives gonads.

Conclusion

Thus we have traveled from thought to therapy by a route neither straight nor narrow. There have been obstacles and detours, but we have found throughout the years that these are to be cherished, not chastised, as blessings in disguise. We began with learning which led to lesions and later to love. Our first love was a soft and simple surrogate. Now it is a sophisticated simian society, whose study has led us back to learning. There have been other grand and great circles. In our study of psychopathology, we began as sadists trying to produce abnormality. Today we are psychiatrists trying to achieve normality and equanimity. Tomorrow there will be new problems, new hopes, and new horizons. Since knowledge is itself forever changing, the search for knowledge never ends.

REFERENCES

1. Harlow, H. F. 1939. Recovery of pattern discrimination in monkeys following unilateral occipital lobectomy. *J. Comp. Psychology* 27:467–89.
2. Harlow, H. F., and T. Spaet. 1943. Problem solution by monkeys following bilateral removal of the prefrontal areas. *J. Experimental Psychology* 33:500–07.
3. Harlow, H. F., R. T. Davis, P. H. Settlage, and D. R. Meyer. 1952. Analysis of frontal and posterior association syndromes in brain-damaged monkeys. *J. Comp. and Physiol. Psychology* 45:419–429.
4. Harlow, H. F. 1959. The development of learning in the rhesus monkey. *Amer. Sci.* 47:459–79.
5. Blomquist, A. J., and H. F. Harlow. 1961. The infant rhesus monkey program at the University of Wisconsin Primate Laboratory. *Proc. Animal Care Panel* 11:57–64.
6. Harlow, H. F. 1958. The nature of love. *Amer. Psychologist* 13:673–85.
7. Harlow, H. F. 1953. Mice, monkeys, men, and motives. *Psychol. Rev.* 60:23–32.
8. Harlow, H. F., and R. R. Zimmermann. 1959. Affectional responses in the infant monkey. *Science* 130:421–32.
9. Watson, J. B. 1924. *Behaviorism*. New York: Norton.
10. Wolpe, J. 1958. *Psychotherapy by Reciprocal Inhibition*. Stanford: Stanford University Press.
11. Erikson, E. H. 1950. *Childhood and Society*. New York: Norton.
12. Furchner, C. S., and H. F. Harlow. 1969. Preference for various surrogate surfaces among infant rhesus monkeys. *Psychonomic Sci.* 17:279–80.
13. Harlow, H. F., and S. J. Suomi. 1970. The nature of love—simplified. *Amer. Psychologist* 25:161–68.
14. Hediger, H. 1955. *Studies of the Psychology and Behaviour of Captive Animals in Zoos and Circuses*. New York: Criterion Books.
15. Miller, R. E., J. V. Murphy, and I. A. Mirsky. 1959. Relevance of facial expression and posture as cues in communication of affection between monkeys. *AMA Arch. General Psychiatry* 1:480–88.
16. Beach, F. A. 1969. Locks and beagles. *Amer. Psychologist* 24:921–49.
17. Harlow, H. F. 1965. Sexual behavior in the rhesus monkey. In F. A. Beach (Ed.), *Sex and Behavior*. New York: Wiley, pp. 234–65.
18. Singh, S. D. 1969. Urban monkeys. *Scientific American* 24:108–15.
19. Harlow, H. F. 1971. The affectional systems. In H. F. Harlow, J. L. McGaugh, and R. F. Thompson (Eds.), *Psychology*. San Francisco: Albion Press, pp. 42–71.
20. Mason, W. A., and R. R. Sponholz. 1963. Behavior of rhesus monkeys raised in isolation. *Psychiatric Research* 1:1–8.
21. Rowland, G. L. 1964. The effects of total social isolation upon learning and social behavior in rhesus monkeys. Unpublished doctoral dissertation, University of Wisconsin.
22. Helfer, R. E., and C. H. Kempe. 1968. *The Battered Child*. Chicago: University of Chicago Press.
23. Seay, B., E. Hansen, and H. F. Harlow. 1962. Mother-infant separation in monkeys. *J. Child Psychology and Psychiatry* 3:123–32.
24. Seay, B., and H. F. Harlow. 1965. Maternal separation in the rhesus monkey. *J. Nervous and Mental Disease* 140:434–41.
25. Spitz, R. A. 1946. Hospitalism: A follow-up report. In *The Psychoanalytic Study of the Child*. Vol. II. New York: International Universities Press.
26. Bowlby, J. 1960. Grief and mourning in infancy and early childhood. *Psychoanalytic Study of the Child* 15:9–52. Bowlby, J. 1969. *Attachment and Loss*, Vol. I. New York: Basic Books.

27. Kaufman, I. C., and L. A. Rosenblum. 1967. The reaction to separation in infant monkeys: Anaclitic depression and conservation-withdrawal. *Psychosomatic Medicine* 29:648–75.

28. Hinde, R. A., Y. Spencer-Booth, and M. Bruce. 1966. Effects of 6-day maternal deprivation on rhesus monkey infants. *Nature* 210:1021–33.

29. Suomi, S. J., H. F. Harlow, and C. J. Domek. 1970. Effect of repetitive infant-infant separation of young monkeys. *J. Abnormal Psychology* 76:161–72.

30. Schmale, A. 1971. The role of depression in health and disease. Paper presented at 137th annual convention, AAAS, Chicago, Illinois, December 1971.

31. Suomi, S. J. 1971. Experimental production of depressive behavior in young monkeys. Unpublished doctoral dissertation, University of Wisconsin.

32. McKinney, W. J., Jr., R. G. Eising, E. C. Moran, S. J. Suomi, and H. F. Harlow. Effects of reserpine on the social behavior of rhesus monkeys. *Diseases of the Nervous System*, in press.

33. Sackett, G. P. 1968. The persistence of abnormal behaviour in monkeys following isolation rearing. In R. Porter (Ed.), *The Role of Learning in Psychotherapy*. London: J. & A. Churchill Ltd., pp. 3–25.

34. Suomi, S. J. Submitted for publication, 1971. Surrogate rehabilitation of monkeys reared in total social isolation.

35. Harlow, H. F., and M. K. Harlow. 1965. The affectional systems. In A. M. Schrier, H. F. Harlow, and F. Stollnitz (Eds.), *Behavior of Nonhuman Primates*, Vol. II. New York: Academic Press, pp. 287–334.

36. Suomi, S. J., and H. F. Harlow. 1969. Apparatus conceptualization for psychopathological research in monkeys. *Behav. Res. Methods and Instrumentation* 1:247–50.

37. Harlow, H. F., and S. J. Suomi. 1971. Social recovery by isolation-reared monkeys. *Proc. Nat. Acad. Sci.*, in press.

38. Harlow, H. F., and L. A. Rosenblum. Maturational variables influencing sexual posturing in infant monkeys. *Arch. Sexual Behavior* 1: in press.

40. BEHAVIOR PROBLEMS OF MIDDLE CHILDHOOD[1]

DONALD R. PETERSON

Before the etiology and treatment of children's behavior disorders can be sensibly examined, the disorders themselves must be defined. For the sake of generality and descriptive efficiency, any concepts employed in such definition should be nonarbitrary, unitary, and independent. Factor analytic methods have been employed with salutary effect in the structural definition of adult disorders (e.g., Lorr, Jenkins, & O'Connor, 1955; Rubenstein & Lorr, 1957; Wittenborn, 1951; Wittenborn & Holzberg, 1951), but similar work with the disorders of childhood has only begun (Hewitt

[1] This study was supported by a grant from the Department of Public Welfare, State of Illinois. I am grateful to Jared T. Lyon, Superintendent of the Hoopeston (Illinois) Public Schools; to Lester J. Grant, Charlotte Meyer, and Hazel Dunivan of the Decatur Public Schools; to Donald W. Dunnan and John Carlino of the Springfield Public Schools; and to Glenn Raymond, Superintendent of Elementary Schools in Watseka, Illinois, for their help in collecting the data. Most of all, I wish to thank the teachers who worked so hard and with such evident care on the ratings themselves.

From *Journal of Consulting Psychology*, 1961, *25*, 205–209. Copyright 1961 by the American Psychological Association. Reprinted by permission of the author and the publisher.

& Jenkins, 1946; Himmelweit, 1953). The present study extends and refines this earlier research by factorizing uniformly gathered judgments of problem behavior during the kindergarten and elementary school years, and by examining changes in problem expression during that time.

Subjects and Procedures

In the absence of any accepted theory of structural organization among children's behavior disorders, a sample of problems was chosen by empirical means. The referral problems of 427 representatively chosen cases at a guidance clinic were recorded, and frequencies tabulated for all problems mentioned more than once. Groups of synonymous terms were reduced by eliminating all but the most frequently used expression, and four concepts were discarded because they were conceptually supraordinate to other terms, and hence redundant. Choice among the remaining variables was determined exclusively by the frequency with which they had occurred, and the 58 most common problems were selected for general investigation.

In use, the variables were ordered randomly, assembled in a format requiring ratings of 0 (no problem), 1 (mild problem), or 2 (severe problem), and submitted for completion to 28 teachers of 831 kindergarten and elementary school children in six different schools in Illinois. The choice of school children, rather than clients undergoing treatment for judged disorders, was based on the assumption that most such disorders are extremes of continuous "normal" dimensions, and was determined by the desirability of obtaining uniform data on large numbers of subjects within the age range under consideration. The large sample requirement has been met previously (Hewitt & Jenkins, 1946; Himmelweit, 1953) by recourse to case history information, but the dangers of that expedient seemed greater than those in the present course, and the study was begun in the hope that otherwise unselected school children would present sufficiently numerous, severe problems to warrant sensible analysis and yield meaningful results. Distributions of ratings were generally eccentric, but the effects were reduced by excluding some rarely checked problems (dizziness, soiling, and enuresis, which occurred in less than 3 percent of the cases, were eliminated), and by pooling judgments of mild and severe problems (ratings of 1 and 2) for all the remaining variables.

For analysis, the sample was divided into four groups: a kindergarten sample ($N = 126$), a first and second grade sample ($N = 237$), a group from the third and fourth grades ($N = 229$), and a fifth and sixth grade sample ($N = 239$). Two teacher ratings were available for each kindergarten child: the number of actual ratings used in the analysis is thus double the N given above for the kindergarten group. Phi coefficients of intercorrelation were computed separately for the four samples. From each correlation matrix, 10 centroid factors were extracted, and from each set of centroid factors 2 were rotated to conform with Kaiser's varimax criterion (Kaiser, 1958).

Human judgment was involved only once in all that analysis—in deciding how many factors to retain for rotation. The decision to keep only two was based on inspection of plots of variance removed by successive centroid factors, and the application of criteria for factor retention developed elsewhere (Peterson, 1960). Out of personal curiosity, five-factor solutions were also tried for each data set; but these, as expected, were much less stable over age than the two-factor solutions, and only the latter will be reported.

Factor scores were computed for all cases by unweighted summation of pertinent problems checked by the teachers. Interjudge correlations were computed for the kindergarten sample, and further attention directed toward comparing the four age groups. Data for boys and girls were separated in all comparisons, because of well known sex differences in problem expression, and mean factor scores were computed to show trends in the development of behavior problems over the years of middle childhood.

TABLE 40–1
Rotated Factor Loadings

FACTOR	CONDUCT PROBLEM				PERSONALITY PROBLEM			
	K^a	1–2	3–4	5–6	K^a	1–2	3–4	5–6
Conduct Problem								
Disobedience	74	77	69	86	03	04	07	11
Disruptiveness	73	67	66	76	−04	19	−03	11
Boisterousness	68	63	67	68	−16	07	−07	−09
Fighting	54	73	61	77	−09	−04	11	07
Attention-seeking	54	67	63	76	−12	10	−07	02
Restlessness	64	58	62	71	04	24	06	20
Negativism	56	64	60	70	12	27	20	15
Impertinence	57	57	53	76	02	−08	00	08
Destructiveness	59	65	51	65	−05	27	19	00
Irritability	53	59	57	69	01	11	04	07
Temper tantrums	54	37	49	64	08	11	22	16
Hyperactivity	51	49	54	49	−06	12	00	03
Profanity	30	42	64	60	−07	11	02	00
Jealousy	23	50	41	56	06	10	12	11
Uncooperativeness	67	67	53	71	09	31	38	21
Distractibility	56	57	61	72	29	42	32	26
Irresponsibility	60	65	49	65	22	18	47	20
Inattentiveness	54	61	36	69	39	30	57	28
Laziness in school	44	59	36	37	29	36	55	31
Shortness of attention span	48	54	31	60	37	34	55	29
Dislike for school	38	40	32	41	06	26	54	13
Nervousness	22	25	46	50	40	44	22	26
Thumb-sucking	29	17	36	05	09	28	−03	15
Skin allergy	−16	02	−20	−05	01	21	05	−20
Personality Problem								
Feelings of inferiority	12	25	13	17	59	56	66	62
Lack of self-confidence	12	26	13	16	60	61	60	58
Social withdrawal	−03	08	04	05	50	64	61	60
Proneness to become flustered	07	28	15	24	54	59	60	58
Self-consciousness	−13	−03	−15	16	55	60	47	63
Shyness	−16	−18	−23	−13	62	57	50	51
Anxiety	01	19	24	10	50	57	55	47
Lethargy	−06	22	01	31	52	47	61	43
Inability to have fun	−15	06	−14	−09	49	48	53	48
Depression	00	20	04	29	47	43	64	42
Reticence	06	20	08	14	45	43	64	41
Hypersensitivity	06	26	18	30	40	53	54	46
Drowsiness	02	09	09	29	39	48	45	41
Aloofness	−16	−03	04	05	51	32	50	31
Preoccupation	09	12	23	37	47	57	64	41
Lack of interest in environment	24	30	21	51	40	44	67	28
Clumsiness	16	21	36	17	43	54	34	36
Daydreaming	14	26	21	49	53	46	69	47
Tension	21	31	39	39	41	62	27	41
Suggestibility	04	29	31	52	41	42	48	30
Crying	15	14	06	59	27	48	32	19

TABLE 40–1
Rotated Factor Loadings *(Cont.)*

FACTOR	CONDUCT PROBLEM				PERSONALITY PROBLEM			
	K[a]	1–2	3–4	5–6	K[a]	1–2	3–4	5–6
Preference for younger playmates	28	21	23	14	08	45	37	32
Specific fears	−09	24	−02	−04	24	47	20	20
Stuttering	11	17	08	02	27	35	29	16
Headaches	19	21	00	00	07	46	22	27
Nausea	−10	23	07	−02	01	14	38	37
Truancy from school	27	07	04	22	00	20	39	35
Stomach-aches	10	18	05	−06	−01	30	38	29
Preference for older playmates	−14	05	26	16	01	38	16	01
Masturbation	08	14	26	04	−18	40	04	17
Hay fever or asthma	15	−01	17	−11	05	21	09	03

[a]*Kindergarten.*

Results

The Factors

All four sets of rotated factor loadings are presented together in Table 40–1, an arrangement permitted only by the marked similarity between results at the four age levels.[2] Factor 1 is obviously a *conduct problem* dimension, closely resembling the like-named factor isolated by Himmelweit (1953) and "unsocialized aggression" as defined by Hewitt and Jenkins (1946). Factor 2 has been labeled *personality problem* in accordance with Himmelweit's designation and common usage. It is much like the "over-inhibited behavior" dimension which Hewitt and Jenkins found. Actually these terms, "personality problem" and "conduct problem," are grossly inappropriate. Both problems are personality expressions, and both affect conduct. But the central meanings seem clear

[2]The rating schedule, correlation matrices, and unrotated centroid factor matrices have been deposited with the American Documentation Institute. Order Document No. 6632 from ADI Auxiliary Publications Project, Photo-duplication Service, Library of Congress; Washington 25, D. C., remitting in advance $2.00 for microfilm or $3.75 for photocopies. Make checks payable to: Chief, Photo-duplication Service, Library of Congress.

enough. In one case, impulses are expressed and society suffers; in the other case impulses are evidently inhibited and the child suffers.

The generality of these factors appears to be enormous. Not only do they emerge with striking uniformity over the limited age range and the particular variables and subjects examined here; they have appeared in very much the same form with the recorded problems of treatment cases (Hewitt & Jenkins, 1946; Himmelweit, 1953), and remarkably similar factors have appeared in the questionnaire behavior of delinquent boys (Peterson, Quay, & Cameron, 1959). Considering all studies together, age has varied from early childhood to adolescence; problem status has varied from none, through clinic attendance, to incarceration for delinquency; data sources have varied from case history records, to standard ratings, to questionnaire responses; methods of factor extraction have varied from cluster inspection to centroid analysis; rotational methods have varied from none, through visual shifts to both orthogonal and oblique solutions, to analytic techniques. Through it all, the factors have stayed the same, and their definition at last seems adequate. The time is ripe for study, particularly experimental study, of dynamics, etiology, and treatment.

Factor Scores and Their Reliability

Such investigations, however, cannot proceed until various properties of the measuring devices have been examined. Factor scores were computed by unweighted summation over the first 15 variables for each factor as listed in Table 40–1. Below that point, many of the variables either have no appreciable loading on either dimension, or approximately equal loadings on both. The former condition holds especially for skin allergy, hay fever, nausea, and stomachaches, which may often be purely somatic and qualitatively distinct from the other variables examined. The latter condition, roughly equal loadings on both factors, holds for crying, nervousness, and certain school attitudes, variables which are either very general in nature or exhibit some kind of developmental change.

Reliability and interfactor correlation were examined for the kindergarten group only, since only for that group were dual ratings available. Interjudge r's of .77 and .75 were found for Factors 1 and 2, respectively. These figures are exceptionally good for ratings, and are sufficiently high for most research purposes. The correlation between factors was .18, low enough to meet most requirements for independence.

Developmental Changes

Mean factor scores were computed for boys and girls in all age groups, and the results are shown in Figures 40–1 and 40–2. Throughout middle childhood, boys consistently display more severe conduct disturbances than girls, possibly as a function of constitutional differences, but more likely in response to different levels of social expectancy and tolerance for misbehavior. An interesting reversal, however, occurs in the expression of personality problems. Boys evidently start school with more personality problems than girls, but around the seventh or eighth year such problems become more plentiful among girls. Again, social pressures for sex-type conformity seem the likeliest causal agents. Reasons for the apparent upswing in problems at the fifth and

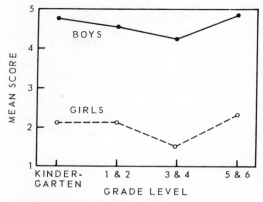

FIGURE 40–1. Mean conduct problem scores.

sixth grade level are obscure. The increase may arise from the early agitation of adolescence, and the difficulty this can bring about in our society.

Summary

This study was designed to improve structural definition of children's behavior problems and to examine changes in those problems over the years of middle childhood. Teacher ratings of 58 clinically frequent problems were obtained for 831 kindergarten and elementary school children, and four separate factor analyses were conducted, one for the kindergarten subjects and one each for children in

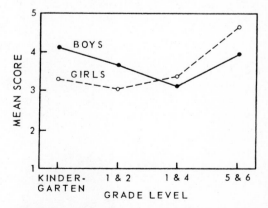

FIGURE 40–2. Mean personality problem scores.

grades 1–2, 3–4, and 5–6. Two factors emerged with remarkable invariance in all four analyses. The first implied a tendency to express impulses against society, and was labelled "conduct problem." The second contained a variety of elements suggesting low self-esteem, social withdrawal, and dysphoric mood. It was called "personality problem." Both factors have now appeared in a number of studies despite wide differences in subjects, variables, and analytic procedures.

Comparisons over age showed that boys displayed more severe conduct problems than girls at all age levels examined. Kindergarten and primary school boys also showed more severe personality problems than girls, but at the two highest age levels this trend was reversed, and girls displayed more personality problems than boys.

The definition of both dimensions seems adequate. Reliable, independent measures of the factors can be obtained, and the way toward investigation of dynamics, etiology, and treatment now seems clear.

REFERENCES

Hewitt, L. E., and R. L. Jenkins. *Fundamental patterns of maladjustment: The dynamics of their origin*. Springfield, Ill.: Green, 1946.

Himmelweit, Hilde T. A factorial study of "children's behavior problems." Cited in H. J. Eysenck, *The structure of human personality*. London: Methuen, 1953.

Kaiser, H. F. The varimax criterion for analytic rotation in factor analysis. *Psychometrika*, 1958, *23*, 187–200.

Lorr, M., R. L. Jenkins, and J. P. O'Connor. Factors descriptive of psychopathology and behavior of hospitalized psychotics. *J. abnorm. soc. Psychol.*, 1955, *50*, 78–86.

Peterson, D. R. The age generality of personality factors derived from ratings. *Educ. psychol. Measmt.*, 1960, *20*, 461–474.

Peterson, D. R., H. C. Quay, and G. R. Cameron. Personality and background factors in juvenile delinquency as inferred from questionnaire responses. *J. consult. Psychol.*, 1959, *23*, 395–399.

Rubenstein, E. A., and M. Lorr. Patient types in out-patient psychotherapy. *J. clin. Psychol.*, 1957, *13*, 356–361.

Wittenborn, J. R. Symptom patterns in a group of mental hospital patients. *J. consult. Psychol.*, 1951, *15*, 290–302.

Wittenborn, J. R., and J. D. Holzberg. The generality of psychiatric syndromes. *J. consult. Psychol.*, 1951, *15*, 372–380.

Chapter 13

SOCIALIZATION AND CROSS-CULTURAL STUDIES

INTRODUCTION AND COMMENTARY

This chapter is concerned with the effects of social factors on development, and focuses on socialization and cross-cultural studies. Because of the diffuse nature of the field this area, more so than the topics in Chapter 4 that deal with biological factors of development, reflects a heterogeneous set of research activities. The four selections include discussions ranging from the effects of specific socializing agents on development to the effects of cultures as socializing agents. The reciprocal interaction between parents and children and their effects on development are discussed, and two of the papers are specifically concerned with socialization in a cross-cultural context. The field is very diverse and the papers selected reflect this diversity. Whereas in Chapter 5 (Infancy, Early Experience, and Critical Periods) it is possible to select papers that focus on a number of specific issues (e.g., species differences, critical periods, and predeterminism versus experiential factors), the research on social factors is so heterogeneous that it is not presently possible to present a specific focus. Some of the papers in this chapter might just as easily have appeared in another chapter (e.g., in Chapter 12, Personality and Behavior Problems) and some of the papers in other chapters (e.g., the Rheingold and Bayley paper from Chapter 5) might just as easily have appeared here. Similarly, the discussion of sex differences that is presented in the introduction to Chapter 12 (pp. 556–558) might just as well appear in this chapter.

Predeterminism, Tabula Rasa Approach, and Interactionism

In a historical context, there have been two major theoretical positions on socialization, and these can be discussed in the broader context of the nature–nurture controversy (see Chapter 2, pp. 13–15). In the extreme, the first position is one of predeterminism—the belief that the forces for development are primarily within the organism; the environment merely provides the medium within which socialization occurs. An example of this is the Freudian theory of psychosexual development. At the other extreme is a position (similar to the *tabula rasa* notion) that suggests that socialization is primarily a function of learning and environmental forces (e.g., parents, peers, teachers). The emphasis on cultural determinism by some anthropologists is consistent with this idea; the well known behaviorist John B. Watson also held this viewpoint. Most contemporary investigators are partial to an interactionistic viewpoint, however, which combines the two general approaches mentioned above. As part of this trend toward an interactional emphasis, Mischel (1973) has recently proposed a cognitive social learning reconceptualization of personality. The social-cognitive person variables develop ontogenetically in terms of a social learning process that interacts with genetic dispositions (see p. 554). These social-cognitive person variables in turn interact with situations (social factors) in determining behavior.

The papers in this chapter focus on specific research studies. However, the reader should be aware of the broad theoretical orientations (e.g., predeterminism, tabula rasa approach, and interactionism) to socialization.

Definition of Socialization

Any discussion of socialization is beset with problems. *"Socialization* is a descriptive, value-ridden, culturally and developmentally relativisitic lay term that ill meets the requirements for rigorous definition demanded by science" (McCandless, 1970, p. 571). Nevertheless, socialization is an important aspect of developmental psychology and one that must be dealt with scientifically. According to McCandless (1961) the concept of socialization is concerned with both *social responsiveness* and *social* (and person) *control*, the responsiveness preceding control. Basically, socialization (see Chapter 2, pp. 28–29) is concerned with an acculturation process whereby the child learns the values and behaviors prescribed by his or her particular subculture. While it is primarily a form of social learning, it is more pervasive than a simple teacher–learner relationship because it focuses on not only the dynamic interaction between children and adults (and/or their peers) but also the interrelationships of child-rearing practices and personality development. Bandura and Walters (1963) and Mischel (1971) provide excellent discussions on social learning and personality development, and McCandless (1970) provides a comprehensive overview of the concept of socialization. Baltes and Schaie (1973) discuss the personal and social factors involved in life-span developmental psychology.

Maccoby (1961) in a methodological paper discusses types of variables to be considered in the study of socialization. She indicates how the different social sciences and theories have converged to delineate some of the crucial variables of socialization: social structure factors (roles, statuses, and so on); amount and kind of reward and punishment; interaction of relationship between trainer and learner; warmth or hostility of the socializing agent in interacting with the child; the roles of permissiveness versus restrictiveness; and control versus laissez-faire in child-rearing. The reader interested in a more detailed presentation of the types of variables involved in the study of socialization should consult Maccoby's paper.

Socializing Agents and Parent–Child Interactions

In investigating socialization one can study the effects of specific socializing agents (e.g., mother, father, teacher, etc.), groups of agents (e.g., peers, the family, etc.), and subcultures or cultures. However, as Bell [41], in the first selection in this chapter, points out, a unidirectional approach that studies the effects of socializing agents (parents) upon child development is rather limited. Furthermore, such an approach does not do justice to the experimental data on socialization studies involving both humans and animals. Bell suggests that not only do parents have an effect on children, but equally important, children have an effect on parents and influence parents' behavior and their socializing practices. Bell suggests that there are congenital determinants of at least two classes of behavior—assertiveness and person-orientation—that probably have different effects on parents (see the Chess, Thomas, and Birch paper [37] in Chapter 12, for a discussion of constitutional differences in temperament and personality). Bell also distinguishes two types of parental technique for socializing children: *upper-limit control behavior,* which is aimed at reducing and redirecting the behavior of the child that exceeds parental standards; and *lower-limit control behavior*, aimed at stimulating child behavior that is below parental standards. The important point is that not only do parents influence children, but children's behavior influences parents' socializing practices and behavior. There is a dynamic interaction or transaction between parents and children (see also the Lewis paper [42] in this chapter). (See Endler, 1975, Overton, 1973, and Overton and Reese, 1973, for discussions of different models of interaction). Bell in his paper reinterprets some recent literature that supports his thesis that children have an effect on parents.

Schaefer (1959, 1965) has been concerned with the effects of specific individuals as socializing agents. In the earlier study Schaefer (1959) integrated the findings of a number of studies on maternal behavior in socialization and presented a model based on psychologists' ratings of *parent behavior*. He suggests two major dimensions of maternal behavior: love versus hostility and autonomy versus control. In the later paper Schaefer (1965) presented a three-dimensional model of parental behavior (both maternal and paternal) based on *children's ratings* of parental behavior: acceptance versus rejection, psychological autonomy versus psychological control, and firm versus lax control. The last two factors appear to be subdivisions of the autonomy versus control factors of the earlier paper (Schaefer, 1959). For a more detailed presentation of the consequences of parental discipline, the reader is referred to Becker (1964), who also suggests three general dimensions in characterizing parental behavior: love versus hostility, permissiveness versus restrictiveness, and anxious-emotional involvement versus calm detachment. Becker's last two factors are subdivisions of Schaefer's (1959) control versus autonomy dimension.

Like the Bell paper [41] Lewis [42] focuses on the importance of parent–child interactions in development and socialization. He is concerned with the theoretical construct of *state* (a continuum of behavior or arousal) as a function of infant–environment *interaction*, measurement of which presents methodological problems. To support his proposed model of state, he presents data that indicate that the infant's condition (behavior) *per se* is insufficient to characterize state because the same condition (behavior) has different consequences depending on the environment. Specifically, Lewis focuses on an analysis of *mother–infant* interactions as a function of the sex of the infant. For example, mothers of boys and girls do not differ in the *amount* of responsiveness but in the *nature* of the responsiveness. In the early months boys receive more proximal stimulation than distal, while for girls the reverse is true.

Another approach to socialization is in terms of the process of identification. For example, Bandura, Ross, and Ross (1963) experimentally compared the status envy, social power, and secondary reinforcement theories of identification. (They treat identification and imitation as synonymous concepts.) Their data fail to support the status envy theory of identification, and instead it appears that some combination of the social power and secondary reinforcement theories is most congruent with the facts.

It is also possible to compare the relative effectiveness of peers and adults as socializing agents. Hicks (1965) finds that male peers have the greatest immediate influence as models for the mediation of novel aggressive responses, while adult models have the most permanent effect. However, in a study with monkeys Harlow and Harlow (1962) find that for socialization in general, the presence of peers in the early stages of development is relatively more important than the presence of adult mothers. This points to some of the hazards of generalizing from one species to another, and/or generalizing across experiments involving quite different methodologies.

Social and Cultural Deprivation

One way to gain some perspective on socialization is to compare and contrast different cultures in terms of their socializing practices, that is, to examine the culture itself as a socializing agent. Another approach is to compare children raised in a normal home environment with those raised in deprived environments or with those raised in institutions (See Chapter 5, p. 143). The assumption has been that institutional care is inferior to normal home care in terms of personality development, and that cultural deprivation affects developmental processes. Tulkin (1972), however, in reviewing the literature on cultural deprivation, has found that this concept has been used in such a way as to limit the understanding of developmental processes. He suggests that it is important to focus on the effect of specific experiences, to take cultural relativism into account, and to be aware that the major culture has helped to create many of the "problems" shown in "deprived" populations. Remedial programs should take this into account and examine the processes involved.

Cross-Cultural Studies

Wolins (1970) conducted a study in which he combined the cross-cultural and home versus institution approaches in studying socialization. Investigating Austrian and Yugoslavian children, he compared subgroups (under seven years of age when they entered group-care settings) with later admissions and with family-reared children. At adolescence the groups in both Austria and Yugoslavia were compared on intellectual performance, personality development, problem behavior, and value acquisition. Wolins found no differences between early and later admissions nor between group-care and family-reared children. He did find, however, that the Yugoslav institutions are less mother-oriented than the Austrian institutions. Although Wolins describes some of the differences between the Austrian and Yugoslavian institutions, it would have been useful if he had systematically compared the behaviors of the children in the two countries.

Goldman [43] also combines the cross-cultural and home versus institution approach in studying socialization in Israel, Austria, Yugoslavia, and Poland. Comparing the psychological development of home-care and group-care children matched for sex, age, and intelligence, she finds that there are no differences in judged maturity between children reared at home and those reared in group-care settings in Austria, Israel (youth village); and Yugoslavia. However, in Poland home-reared children were judged more mature than group-reared children, and in the Israeli kibbutz (as opposed to the youth village) group-reared children were judged more mature. Goldman concludes that there is no evidence to support the notion that group-reared children are retarded psychosocially as compared to home-reared children.

Although both Wolins (1970) and Goldman [43] study different cultures, they do not sufficiently focus on the cross-cultural differences and similarities. A cross-cultural approach should attempt to examine the culture itself as a socializing agent, and relate various parental (or surrogate parental) child-rearing practices (antecedent conditions) to personality characteristics (consequences) in children. Predictions of personality differences for different cultures are made on the basis of differing child-rearing practices of the various cultures. Like the area of personality (see Chapter 12), the field of cross-cultural studies poses certain methodological difficulties since consequent behavioral variability between cultures may be a function of extraneous variables rather than the result of differing socializing techniques. Most of the early studies examined the relationship between culture and personality in a single culture and attempted to extrapolate the results from these case studies to the North American culture.

Whiting and Child (1953), who examined primitive cultures in detail, were among the first to conduct cross-cultural research in the true meaning of the term, and have to a large extent set the pattern for subsequent research in this area. Although subject to certain methodological limitations—problems of measurement, the qualitative nature of some of the data, and the possibility of extraneous variables influencing their correlations—their approach has great merit in that it permitted them both to examine systematically differing patterns in socialization in a large sample of different cultures and to relate these patterns to personality characteristics. Barry, Bacon, and Child (1957), using the same approach as Whiting and Child (1953), compared sex differences in socialization in 110 different cultures. Their study emphasizes the importance of learning rather than biological factors in socialization. Their finding that sex differentiation is relatively unimportant in infancy but more important in childhood is relevant to the issue discussed in Chapter 2 (pp. 15, 19) that different principles may operate at different stages (ages) of development.

Most of the early cross-cultural research was conducted primarily by anthropologists. However, during the last quarter-century (since the 1950s), psychologists have shown a marked interest in this area. Concomitant with this has been an increase in the methodological soundness of cross-cultural studies. Examples of methodologically sophisticated cross-cultural research are a monograph by Havighurst, Dubois, Czikszentmihalyi, and Doll (1964) comparing Buenos Aires and Chicago adolescents, and the fourth selection in this chapter by Holtzman [44]. The Holtzman paper, in the context of reviewing recent cross-cultural studies, discusses most of the methodological and measurement problems involved in this field of research. In describing his longitudinal cross-cultural procedure comparing Mexican and American children, he suggests various techniques for dealing with theoretical and methodological issues in cross-cultural research.

Cross-cultural research is becoming more sophisticated, and although still primarily correlational rather than experimental (see Cronbach, 1957) there has been an increase in the number of experimental cross-cultural studies (see Kagan and Klein, 1973) since the middle of the 1960s. Nevertheless, systematic field studies, where investigators examine behavior under controlled conditions (rather than relying on the case study method) still prevail. A breakthrough has yet to occur, however, in terms of a systematic manipulation of independent variables. (This is primarily a practical and methodological problem rather than a logical one. See the introduction to Chapter 3 and the section on Research Strategy in Chapter 2, pp. 11–13, for a further discussion of this issue.) Primarily, investigators have made systematic use of variations existing within and between cultures, and have treated these inherent variations in socialization (the independent variable) as a basis for predicting behavioral differences (the dependent variable).

An example of a cross-cultural experimental study is provided by Kagan and Klein (1973) in their investigation and comparison of intellectual and cognitive development of Guatemalan and American infants. Although infants in Guatemala suffer from stimulus deprivation during the first two years (as compared to American infants), leading to early infant retardation, it is possible by appropriate remedial programs to facilitate the development of these cognitive functions (e.g., recall and recognition memory). That is, with appropriate stimulation the cognitive functioning of children of Guatemala improves so that they are subsequently (e.g., at age seven) no longer retarded when compared to American children. The important point is that stimulation and specific experiences in Guatemala should be programmed in terms of the adult culture of Guatemala and not in terms of the adult culture of the United States. In short, the skills and personality traits that are most appropriate for Guatemalan children are not necessarily the same as those that are most appropriate for American children.

In the area of socialization, within our own culture, researchers have begun to use sophisticated experimental techniques to investigate social learning (as examples see Bandura and Walters, 1963, Mischel, 1971, and Reese and Lipsitt, 1970). Hopefully some of these techniques can be applied to the domain of cross-cultural research.

The reader interested in the biological basis of social behavior for all species and all cultures is referred to a recent book on sociobiology, by the zoologist Wilson (1975). Wilson's main thesis is that there may well be universal laws that shape societies at all evolutionary levels. Thus, social behavior is placed in a biological, cross-cultural, and evolutionary context.

References

Baltes, P. B. & Schaie, K. W. (Eds.), *Life-span developmental psychology: Personality and socialization*. New York: Academic Press, 1973.

Bandura, A., Ross, D., & Ross, S. A. A comparative test of the status envy, social power, and secondary reinforcement theories of identificatory learning. *Journal of Abnormal and Social Psychology*, 1963, *67*, 527–534.

Bandura, A. & Walters, R. H. *Social learning and personality development*. New York: Holt, Rinehart and Winston, 1963.

Barry, H., Bacon, M., and Child, I. L. A cross-cultural survey of some sex differences in socialization. *Journal of Abnormal and Social Psychology*, 1957, *55*, 327–332.

Becker, W. C. Consequences of different kinds of parental discipline. In M. C. Hoffman & L. W. Hoffman (Eds.), *Review of child development research*. Vol. I. New York: Russell Sage Foundation, 1964, pp. 169–208.

Cronbach, L. J. The two disciplines of scientific psychology. *American Psychologist*, 1957, *12*, 671–684.

Endler, N. S. The case for person–situation interactions. *Canadian Psychological Review*, 1975, *16*, 12–21.

Harlow, H. F. & Harlow, M. K. Social deprivation in monkeys. *Scientific American*, 1962, *207*(11), 137–146.

Havighurst, R. J., Dubois, M. E., Czikszentmihalyi, M., & Doll, R. *A cross-national study of Buenos Aires and Chicago adolescents. Bibliotheca, Vita Humana, Fasc. 3*. Basel/New York: S. Karger, 1964.

Hicks, D. J. Imitation and retention of film-mediated aggressive peer and adult models. *Journal of Personality and Social Psychology*, 1965, *2*, 97–100.

Kagan, J. & Klein, R. E. Cross-cultural perspectives on early development. *American Psychologist*, 1973, *28*, 947–961.

Maccoby, E. E. The choice of variables in the study of socialization. *Sociometry*, 1961, *24*, 357–371.

McCandless, B. R. *Children and adolescents*. New York: Holt, Rinehart and Winston, 1961.

McCandless, B. R. Socialization. In H. W. Reese & L. P. Lipsitt (Eds.), *Experimental child psychology*. New York: Academic Press, 1970.

Mischel, W. *Introduction to personality*. New York: Holt, Rinehart and Winston, 1971.

Mischel, W. Towards a cognitive social learning reconceptualization of personality. *Psychological Review*, 1973, *80*, 252–283.

Overton, W. F. On the assumptive base of the nature–nurture controversy: Additive versus interactive conceptions. *Human Development*, 1973, *16*, 74–89.

Overton, W. F. & Reese, H. W. Models of development: Methodological implications. In J. R. Nesselroade & H. W. Reese (Eds.), *Life-span developmental psychology: Methodological issues*. New York: Academic Press, 1973, pp. 65–86.

Reese, H. W. & Lipsitt, L. P. (Eds.) *Experimental child psychology*. New York: Academic Press, 1963, 1970.

Schaefer, E. S. A circumplex model of maternal behavior. *Journal of Abnormal and Social Psychology*, 1959, *59*, 226–235.

Schaefer, E. S. A configurational analysis of children's reports of parent behavior. *Journal of Consulting Psychology*, 1965, *29*, 552–557.

Tulkin, S. R. An analysis of the concept of cultural deprivation. *Developmental Psychology*, 1972, *6*, 326–339.

Whiting, J. W. M. & Child, I. L. *Child training and personality: A cross-cultural study*. New Haven: Yale University Press, 1953.

Wilson, E. O. *Sociobiology: The new synthesis*. Cambridge, Mass.: Belknap Press of Harvard University, 1975.

Wolins, M. Young children in institutions: Some additional evidence. *Developmental Psychology*, 1970, *2*, 99–109.

41. A REINTERPRETATION OF THE DIRECTION OF EFFECTS IN STUDIES OF SOCIALIZATION

RICHARD Q. BELL

Studies are summarized indicating that the basic model of socialization, the action of a parent on a child, is too limited to accommodate data emerging from recent studies of human and animal Ss. A set of propositions is presented concerning the effects of congenital factors in children on parent behavior. This system is applied to current findings in several major areas. Current literature on socialization, based largely on correlations between parent and child behavior, can be reinterpreted plausibly as indicating effects of children on parents. A correlation does not indicate direction of effect. The effect of children on parents can no longer be dismissed as only a logical but implausible alternative explanation of a correlation.

It is not too surprising to find that most research on parent-child interaction has been directed to the question of effects of parents on children. The historian Palmer (1964) maintains that our political and social philosophy emerged in a period when there were many revolutionary or protorevolutionary movements ranging from the Carolinas to Sweden, movements directed not just against monarchical absolutism but against all constituted bodies such as parliaments, councils, assemblies, and magistracies. These institutions tended to be hereditary, either in theory or through firmly established practice. In taking a strong stand against hereditary determination of position in malleability and susceptibility to improvement of the child. Although scientific research on parents and children is a fairly recent phenomenon, it still shows the primary influence of this broad social philosophy by emphasizing parents and educational institutions as determinants of human development.

Until recent years there have been very few findings which would indicate that this is not a fruitful approach. The prolonged helplessness of the human infant, in comparison to the early competence of some other animal infants, fits in with the picture of an organism designed to be

From *Psychological Review*, 1968, 75, 81–85. Copyright 1968 by the American Psychological Association. Reprinted by permission of the author and the publisher.

taught and modified by the parent in the early years. It seems eminently plausible to visualize the human parent as the vehicle for the transmission of culture and the infant as simply the object of an acculturation process. The parent is the initial agent of culture, the child the object.

Because of this general view, it is often overlooked that even John Locke, to whom we are indebted for the concept of the infant as a tabula rasa, placed great emphasis in his advice to parents on early observation of congenital characteristics (Kessen, 1965, p. 67). Locke questioned the existence of innate ideas, not all innate characteristics. Currently, at least one major work on the socialization of the child has acknowledged that there are probably constitutional differences between children which affect behavior (Sears, Maccoby, & Levin, 1957, 454–455), and that the model of a unidirectional effect from parent to child is overdrawn, a fiction of convenience rather than belief (Sears et al., 1957, p. 141). The model was adopted in order to proceed with research, leaving the validity of the approach to be judged by the results.

This paper summarizes data indicating that a unidirectional approach is too imprecise and that another formulation is possible which would accommodate our social philosophy as well as new data from studies of man and other animals. Before proceeding, usage of two terms must be explained. Individual behavior sequences cannot be referred to as exclusively genetically or experientially determined. It is possible, however, to employ experimental operations in such a way that a *difference* between two groups or between two conditions applied to the same subjects can be attributed to genetic or experiential differences. Thus the terms *genetically, congenitally,* or *experientially determined* are abstractions derived from experimental operations. For brevity, a *congenital effect* will refer to both genetic and congenital determination.

The same consideration applies to the question of whether parent and child effects can be separated. In the ordinary interaction of any parent and child we can speak only of an event sequence. However, by experimental operations we can isolate parent effects and child effects. In the remainder of this paper a child or parent effect will refer to such a derivative of an experimental operation. No implication about origin of the behavior need be drawn in this case since such studies can take as their starting point any behavior which is available at the time in the repertoire of parent or child.

We must also keep in mind that demonstration of a child effect indicates only that it plays *some* role in parent behavior. The development of the parent behavior is not explained by such a demonstration. In the same vein, Epstein (1964) has pointed out relative to studies of learning that evidence of the modifiability of a response provides no explanation of its origin.

Recent Data Discordant with Parent-Effect Model

Discordant data at the human level are still meager. This is because most research efforts have been directed to the task of testing parent effects and have not always been designed so as to permit clear interpretation of "negative" results. It will be necessary to rely upon informal observations and data generated unintentionally.

Rheingold (1966, pp. 12–13) has pointed to a compelling fact observable under ordinary circumstances in any human group containing an infant. "The amount of attention and the number of responses directed to the infant are enormous—out of all proportion to his age, size, and accomplishments." The effect of the appearance of helplessness and the powerful stimulus of distress cries were also noted. "So aversive, especially to humans, is the crying of the infant that there is almost no effort we will not expend, no device we will not employ, to change a crying baby into a smiling one—or just a quiet one."

Studies of variations in parental behavior with different children provide one other kind of data discordant with a parent-effect model. A mother of identical schizophrenic quadruplets was found to be uniformly extreme in restrictiveness with her daughters but not uniform in affection when rated against a theoretical normal group (Schaefer, 1963). Yarrow (1963, pp. 109–110) has reported that the same foster mother showed differences in behavior with infants assigned to her at different times. In one particularly dramatic case extreme differences in maternal care existed for two infants of the same sex and age assigned to a foster mother at the same time. Characteristics of the infants appeared to have evoked very different behavior in this foster mother and in other members of her family.

Reports of lack of uniformity of behavior of parents towards their children are not confined to intensive case studies. Stott (1941) reported a correlation of only .22 between sibling reports of a positive or negative home environment. Lasko (1954, p. 111) correlated maternal characteristics across 44 sibling pairs and found that mothers were not consistent in affection but were in restrictiveness, a finding which is in agreement with the report on the quadruplets. In a parent-effect model, it is easy to explain differences between the behavior of two parents with the same child, but awkward to accommodate a difference in the behavior of one parent toward two children. The latter difficulty is due to the fact that the parent-effect model assumes a fixed and invariantly applied repertoire. The usual method of explaining differences in behavior of a parent with different children is to postulate effects associated with ordinal position or sex of siblings. The reports on infants in foster homes could not be explained this way.

Levy (1958, p. 8) was unable to find consistency in maternal greeting behavior when the infant was brought from the nursery for a feeding, until it was noted that this behavior was a function of the state of the infant. The present author carried out separate chi-square analyses of Levy's data for each of three successive observations. There were no differences on the initial observation, but for the second and third observations it was found that infants awake or awakening were greeted, whereas those asleep were not ($p < .01$; $p < .05$, respectively). Other data in the same volume support Levy's contention that specific maternal behavior could be accounted for more by the infant's behavior than by the mother's general "maternal attitude," whether the latter was estimated from interview material or from actual observation of her behavior. Another finding with a similar implication was reported by Hillenbrand (1965). The amount the infant consumed in breastfeeding during the newborn period was highly correlated with the number of weeks the mother continued feeding at the breast, whereas the latter measure showed no correlation with personality characteristics of the mother.

One other study at the human level is best accommodated by a bidirectional model (Bell, 1964). Scores on one parent-attitude scale have been found consistently higher in mothers of children with congenital defects than in mothers of normals. Differences between groups of parents were ascribed to the effects on parents of a limitation in coping ability associated with the congenital disorder in affected children.

Research on lower animals provides stronger evidence of the stimulating and selective effect of the young. A volume edited by Rheingold (1963) covers maternal behavior from the deer mouse to the baboon and provides a number of observations on the importance of the young in shaping interactions. An example is the report of two instances in which the clinging of rhesus infants fostered with nonlactating females induced maternal responsiveness and biochemically normal lactation (pp. 268–269).

In other studies offspring effects have been manipulated experimentally. Lactation in the rat has been maintained for long periods by supplying new litters of pups; number and age of pups were effective parameters (Bruce, 1961). Licking and nest-building occurred when 1-day-old pups were presented to female mice without previous experience; short-term stimulus-specific decrements in the maternal response followed repeated presentation of 1-day-old pups, but recovery of response was shown to an older pup (Noirot, 1965). This study is the most recent in a series supporting the hypothesis that changes in the interest of the female mouse in the litter from birth to weaning depend mainly upon changes in stimuli coming from the young.

It has been shown by cross-fostering that pups from one strain of mice induced more retrieving and licking behavior than pups from another strain (Ressler, 1962). The open-field behavior of rat foster mothers has shown effects of the experience of rearing pups subjected to direct treatments such as shock (Dennenberg, 1963), or indirect treatments such as subjecting their true mothers to premating and gestational stress (Joffe, 1965).

In a classic study, Beach and Jaynes (1956) manipulated appearance and behavior of offspring so as to identify specific classes of stimuli controlling parent behavior. Visual, olfactory, tactile, thermal, and movement cues from rat pups were shown to be capable of inducing maternal retrieving, being effective individually and in combination.

It is evident from the foregoing brief review that students of animal behavior have been much more aware of offspring effects on parents than investigators of human parent-child interaction; this more comprehensive view of parent-offspring interaction may be a simple consequence of availability; all phases of development are accessible to direct observation and manipulation. It is also possible that our political and social philosophy has limited scientific outlook at the human more than the animal level. The animal mother is not seen as an agent of socialization, nor her offspring as a tabula rasa.

There are many implications of this research on animal behavior. For the present purpose two are most salient. If variations in offspring behavior affect animal parents from which we expect fairly rigid patterns, even greater effects would be expected on human parental behavior, which is presumably more plastic and susceptible to all classes of influence. The other point is brought out by the variety of offspring stimulus parameters being opened up by animal studies; it should not be difficult to accept the notion of offspring effects if we consider the fact that offspring are at least sources of stimuli. Some stimulus control of human parental behavior should be expected since we take for granted the general likelihood of finding stimulus control over behavior in general.[1]

Modifiers of Parent Response

Congenital Determinants

Three propositions concerning congenital determinants of later behavior will be advanced in this section. Some studies of human subjects will be cited which provide relatively clear evidence. Only reasonable inferences can be made from others. All in all, these studies suggest but by no means document the propositions which are advanced concerning child effects. The present objective is to take the first steps toward developing an alternative to existing socialization theory. A limited scheme which is merely plausible and parsimonious will serve the purpose. Provisional acceptance of this scheme will make it possible to provide concrete illustrations of how some recent findings in the research literature may be reinterpreted.

It will first be assumed that there are congenital contributors to human assertiveness, which will be taken to mean maintenance of goal-directed behavior of high magnitude in the face of barriers. Reasoning, threat of withdrawal of love, and appeals to personal and social motives can all be used to arrest ongoing

child behavior in excess of parental standards, providing the child is not extreme in assertiveness. With a child who is strongly assertive a parent may more often fall back on quick tangible reinforcement or nonreinforcement. At times when the child, the parent, or both are stressed, the parent falls back further to distraction, holding, frightening verbalization, and physical punishment. The foregoing effects on parent behavior also are considered likely to issue from the behavior of hyperactive, erratic, and unpredictable children, and it is assumed that there are congenital determinants of this kind of behavior as well.

It is further assumed that a different kind of behavior is shown by parents of children congenitally low in assertiveness, activity, or sensory-motor capability. Drawing attention to stimuli, rewarding an increase in behavior, urging, prompting, and demanding are examples of parent response to these child characteristics.

It is also assumed that there are congenital contributors to differences in person orientation. Children high in person orientation attend to the behavior of their parents and reinforce social responses emanating from them. Children low in person orientation induce less nurturance from parents, and their behavior is controlled less by variations in social response of parents. They are interested in physical activity and inanimate objects. Their stimulus characteristics primarily mobilize those elements in the parent nurturance repertoires pertaining to providing and withholding physical objects and activities. Since love-oriented control techniques are less useful with these children and material reinforcers cannot always be flexibly applied, their parents more frequently show further recourse to physical punishment.

Support for a congenital contribution to assertive behavior is seen in the finding that sex differences in socialization training are pronounced in primitive cultures in which large animals are hunted (Barry, Bacon, & Child, 1957). Furthermore, in all of the 224 primitive cultures surveyed by Murdock (1937), males were accorded roles involving fighting. Greater

[1]The author is indebted to Leon J. Yarrow for suggesting this point.

skeletal muscle development in males is probably an important factor, since even newborn males possess more muscle tissue, females more fat, relative to total body weight (Garn, 1958). It appears reasonable that some potential for use of muscles in physically assertive behavior can also be assumed. We would not expect the exclusive allocation of the fighting role to males if they possessed only greater skeletal muscle mass with no accompanying potential for use, or if there were equal distribution of this potential between the sexes. Males in our advanced societies do not carry spears, but it is improbable that our congenital dispositions have changed as rapidly as our cultural evolution. Even theoretical systems committed to the study of parent effects have acknowledged the probable existence of constitutional bases for sex differences in overt aggressiveness (Sears et al., 1957, p. 484).

One other line of evidence is from twin studies. Direct observation of monozygotic and dizygotic twins each month during the first year of life has shown significant heritability for an item from the Bayley Infant Behavior Profile labeled "goal directedness," which denotes absorption with a task until it is complete (Freedman, 1965). Vandenberg (1962) has pointed out that such twin contrasts in early infancy are more likely to detect genetic contributions than studies of children and adults because later social functioning shapes behavior in ways remote from the circumstances under which genetic selection took place. However, even in studies of school-age children which use the admittedly insensitive self-report questionnaires, significant heritability has been shown for groups of items interpreted as reflecting vigor (Vandenberg, 1962) and dominance (Gottesman, 1965).

Stronger evidence exists for a congenital contribution to person orientation; not only in the twin studies just cited but in several others summarized by Scarr (1965), heritability has been shown for social responsiveness or sociability, the findings cutting across age, sex, social class, and even cultural differences.

Some specific ways in which congenital factors may affect person orientation can be suggested on the basis of data from other studies. Schaffer and Emerson (1964) concluded that avoidance by some infants of being held, carried on the lap, stroked, or kissed was not accounted for by propensities of the mothers, but was due to the infant's restlessness and negative response to the restraint involved in these contacts. Infants who avoided contact showed lower intensity in later social contacts, though neither timing nor breadth of contacts was affected. There was a nonsignificant tendency for those who avoided early contacts to be males. The study is suggestive rather than conclusive because the sample of infants who avoided contacts was small.

Moss (1967) reports from day-long naturalistic observations in the home at 3 and 12 weeks that male infants were more irritable (crying, fussing), and slept less than females. This would mean that, on the average, the mother-son interaction was more one of physical caretaking, the mother being engaged in a variety of efforts to soothe males. Walters and Parke (1965) summarize evidence that the development of social response is relatively independent of the primary-drive reduction which might be expected to follow from such physical acts of caretaking. In fact, there are many reasons for expecting that greater irritability in the males would not favor development of social responses positively valued by parents (i.e., smiling, visual regard, noncrying vocalizations): (a) appearance of the mother at the time of crying could lead to an increase in the rate of crying, as reported for institutional infants by Etzel and Gewirtz (1967); (b) ministrations which follow the mother's appearance would necessarily contain some stimulation of an aversive nature, as in diaper changing or efforts to release ingested air, a point made by Rheingold (1966, p. 11); (c) nonaversive reinforcing elements in caretaking would be less likely to reinforce the infant's positively valued social responses since an irritable infant probably emits less of this behavior; (d) the mother would have less time available for purely social stimulation, and might simply wish to avoid the infant when he is quiet.

These possibilities are all consistent with

Moss' (1967) finding that by the 12th week, mothers provided less stimulation of an interactional-social nature (imitation) for male than for female infants. It might also be argued that mothers imitated female infants more because of the earlier maturation of social responsiveness in females, an alternative explanation in congenital terms. Mothers could have begun differential sex-role training in social responsiveness sometime in the intervening period, but a ready explanation for initiating such training in just this period is not available. The data do not permit decisions on these different explanations, but the one selected for the present thesis seems at least as defensible as the others: Greater irritability in males led to less stimulation from mothers of the kind which should produce positively valued social responsiveness. This, in turn, may be extended developmentally using data from Bayley and Schaefer (1964, p. 44): Males were rated as less responsive to persons during 11 out of 12 developmental examinations between 10 and 36 months. Goodenough's (1957) report of sex differences in object and person orientation is typical of many other reports in the literature which indicate that males show less social orientation by the preschool period.

The research of Pasamanick, Robers, and Lilienfeld (1956) provides evidence that complications of pregnancy and delivery are associated with later behavior disorders of children, including hyperactive behavior, and that males are more frequently affected. The foregoing studies permit an inference that there is a congenital contributor to early response to social reinforcement. If hyperactive or restless infants do not respond as well as other infants to some of the early social reinforcers, it would be reasonable to expect that their later behavior would be controlled less adequately by use of love-oriented techniques which depend for their efficacy on the strength of the social bond. It could also be inferred that they would be less person-oriented, as a consequence of the less intense primary social bond.

Stechler (1964) lists a number of recent prospective studies which confirm the general validity of Pasamanick's approach, and reports his own finding that neonatal apnea was associated with low developmental quotients in the first 2 years of life. Higher irritability or crying during the newborn period and lower developmental quotients later in infancy have been reported for infants whose mothers reported fears or anxiety during pregnancy (Davis, Holden, & Gray, 1963; Ferreira, 1960; Ottinger & Simmons, 1964). We have already mentioned a study of congenital handicaps which limit sensory-motor development (Bell, 1964). Reports of congenital contributors to sensory-motor development are not limited to populations showing pathology. Kagan and Garn (1963) have reported that chest width measured from roentgenographic films of parents or their children is positively correlated with the children's perceptual-motor and language development in the preschool years.

To summarize, there is direct evidence of congenital factors contributing to two classes of child behavior which are likely to have very different effects on parents: impaired sensory-motor development, and behavior disorders involving hyperactivity. From twin studies there is evidence of a congenital contributor to person orientation and to facets of behavior which appear related to assertiveness. On the other hand, the evidence for congenital contributors to sex differences in person orientation and assertive behavior is mostly inferential. This is particularly true for assertive behavior: No relevant data on early development of sex differences could be located in the literature. In view of this, the arguments relative to assertiveness are merely advanced to indicate that congenital determination is at least reasonable. If we accept this, albeit provisionally, we can further assume that variation within the sexes on congenital grounds could also occur. Polygenetic rather than simple all-or-none determination would be favored by modern genetic theory.

Differentiation of Parent Response

Parents do not have fixed techniques for socializing children. They have a repertoire of actions to accomplish each objective. Furthermore, activation of elements in the repertoire requires both cultural pressures and stimulation from the object of acculturation.

Characteristics that most infants and children share, such as helplessness, evoke responses.

Another major effect of the child is shown in the parent's selective performance of elements from the caretaking repertoire. It is assumed that there are hierarchies of actions, that different children induce responses from different parts of these hierarchies. Others escalate the actions of their parents so that at one time or another, or in sequence, the entire hierarchy relevant to a certain class of child behavior may be elicited. The child in turn reinforces or fails to reinforce the parent behavior which is evoked. The repertoire changes as a function of cultural demands and also as a result of stimulation and reinforcement received from the child.

Two types of parent control repertoires must be differentiated. *Upper-limit control behavior* reduces and redirects behavior of the child which exceeds parental standards of intensity, frequency, and competence for the child's age. *Lower-limit control behavior* stimulates child behavior which is below parental standards. In other words, parent control behavior, in a sense, is homeostatic relative to child behavior. To predict interaction in particular parent-child pairs it is necessary to know the behavior characteristics of the child, the cultural demands on the parent, and the parents' own individual assimilation of these demands into a set of expectations for the child. Nonetheless, for purposes of illustration we might say that the average parent would show an increase in upper-limit control behavior in response to excessive crying in the infant, or in response to impulsive, hyperactive, or overly competent or assertive behavior in the young child. These widely different behaviors are only considered similar with respect to their effect on upper-limit control. Parental lower-limit control behavior would be stimulated by lethargy in the infant, by low activity, overly inhibited behavior, and lack of competence in the young child. Again, these are different behaviors but are assumed to be similar in effect.

It is customary to observe or rate parental behavior without reference to stimulation provided by the young. When this is done, a parent showing extreme upper-limit behavior in several areas is likely to be described as "punitive," or "restrictive," one showing extreme lower-limit behavior as "intrusive," or "demanding." Both could be considered "controlling," but according to the present conceptual scheme designed to accommodate child effects, the history of preceding interaction sequences could be quite different. The need for differentiating these two types of control is indicated not only by the present theoretical considerations but also by the empirical findings that punitive and strict behavior is not correlated with intrusive and demanding behavior in parents of young children (Schaefer, 1959, p. 228).

Reinterpretation of Recent Literature

The child-effect system of explanation which has just been developed states that parent behavior is organized hierarchically within repertoires in the areas of social response and control. Reasonable bases exist for assuming that there are congenital contributors to child behaviors which (*a*) activate these repertoires, (*b*) affect the level of response within hierarchies, and (*c*) differentially reinforce parent behavior which has been evoked.

This system will be applied next to current findings in several major areas in which parent and experiential family effects on children have been given almost exclusive consideration. The findings in most cases are from recent studies which replicate or are consistent with previous studies, or in which results are more defensible than usual because of careful attention to sampling, procedural controls, and measurement. In most cases the authors of these papers were careful not to claim that causes and effects could be clearly differentiated. The question of direction of effects may be raised nonetheless, to ascertain whether the findings are relevant to the theory which motivated the research.

Though in the discussion which follows, the evidence is organized to support the validity of a child-to-parent effect, this should not be taken to mean that an "either-or" approach to the study of parent and child effects is preferred to an interactional view. This reinterpretation is only an expedient considered necessary to direct attention to the possibility of child effects. If this possibility is admitted we can then begin the task of thinking of parent *and* child effects. The primary goal of an expanded model of the socialization process is to uncover interactions of child and parent effects as well as main effects attributable to either source.

Lefkowitz, Walder, and Eron (1963) found in 8-year-olds that peer ratings of aggression were highest and parent reports of the child's use of confession lowest where use of physical punishment was reported by the parents. Bandura and Walters (1959) reported more physical punishment used in a group of male 15- to 16-year-old repeated offenders than in nondelinquents. One theory being tested in each case was that use of punishment in the home produces frustration and conflict or affords a model of aggression which in turn produces aggressive behavior in the child. An alternative explanation is that these children were congenitally assertive. Congenital assertiveness activated upper-limit control repertoires in parents and techniques within the repertoire were escalated toward physical punishment. Congenital hyperactivity could produce similar results.

Reviewing the area of moral development, Hoffman (1963) found consistent results in studies dealing with reaction to transgression. His interpretation was that an internalized moral orientation, indicated by confession, guilt, or reparation efforts, was fostered by an affectionate relation between the parent and child, in combination with disciplinary techniques which utilized this relation by appealing to the child's personal and social motives. One alternative explanation is that the children showing little internalization of a moral orientation were congenitally low in person orientation. Because of this their mothers were less affectionate and did not appeal to the child's personal or social values.

A study of sex-role development by Mussen and Rutherford (1963) reports findings which replicated those in a previous study. Boys 5–6 years old scoring high in masculinity on the IT test, in comparison with lows, revealed high father nurturance, punishment, and power in doll play. A high power score indicated that father figures were both highly rewarding and punishing. These findings generously supported all major contending theories: developmental identification, defensive identification, and role-theory. A congenital explanation would be that the highs were more masculine in the sense that they showed lower person orientation and higher assertiveness. The father responded with affection because the son's assertiveness and interests in physical activity and toys were sex appropriate, reinforcing his own identification vicariously through his boy. Much as he felt affectionate toward his masculine boy he found he retreated to punishment frequently because the child, being assertive and less responsive to social stimuli, could not be controlled readily by love-oriented techniques.

In the area of intelligence, Bing (1963) found that mothers of children who showed higher verbal than spatial or numerical ability had a more close and demanding relation with their children both in interviews and observation situations than did mothers of children who showed discrepant nonverbal abilities. These findings confirmed the hypothesis that discrepant verbal ability is fostered by a close relation with a demanding and somewhat intrusive mother, discrepant nonverbal abilities being enhanced by allowing the child a considerable degree of freedom. An alternative explanation would be that the high-verbal children were high in person orientation and low in assertiveness. This is a reasonable combination of characteristics if one assumes that congenital determinants of assertiveness and person orientation are independent or at least not highly positively correlated. These children reinforced their mothers' social responses and elicited nurturant behavior. The resultant interaction intensified verbal expression because this is the primary channel of communication. The fact that these children were low in assertiveness led to lower-limit control behavior reflected in the mother's demanding and intrusive behavior.

Schaefer's (1959) summary of his own work and that of others indicates that a major portion of the variance in parent behavior can be accounted for under two dimensions described as love-hostility and autonomy-control. This is a useful finding, offering the possibility of descriptive parsimony, regardless of the question of direction of effects. However, the two-dimensional model might represent a system of effects of children on parents. The hostility extreme of the love-hostility dimension (strictness, punishment, perceiving the child as a burden) could be characterized as a parent upper-limit control pattern in response to overly assertive, unpredictable, or hyperactive behavior. The love extreme could reflect positive evaluation of children showing more modal behavior but not behavior extreme in the opposite direction.

In support of this we find in longitudinal data from the Berkeley Growth Study (Schaefer & Bayley, 1963) that calm children were evaluated positively by their mothers during the first 3 years. Children who were rapid and active were perceived as a burden during the first 15 months. The next set of measurements available for both mothers and children covered the period when the child was between 9 and 12 years. Mothers of children rated as rapid at this time were themselves rated as irritable and perceiving the child as a burden. No rating of calmness was available. A rating of the child's inactivity in this same period could not be considered a simple inverse of the activity rating made in the first 3 years, either from the standpoint of wording or correlation pattern across the sexes. If we assume that it primarily differentiated degree of inactivity running from the highly inactive to modal levels of activity, this rating becomes relevant to the autonomy versus control dimension.

The autonomy extreme of the autonomy-control dimension might reflect parents' granting autonomy to children who conform to parental expectations of capability and assertiveness. The control extreme (intrusiveness, anxiety, achievement demand, anxiety relative to the child's behavior and health) would be considered parental lower-limit control behavior in response to children low in assertiveness or sensory-motor capability. In support of this we find that mothers of male and female inactive children during the

period 9–14 years were rated as intrusive and as high in achievement demand, but low in granting autonomy to the child. All relations cited from this study (Schaefer & Bayley, 1963) were consistent for both sexes and significant beyond the .05 level for combined male and female samples according to the present author's analysis. . . Data from earlier age periods could not be brought to bear on a child-effect interpretation of the autonomy-control dimension because of very differing relations between maternal and child behavior in mother-son versus mother-daughter pairs.

Social class differences in parent behavior may also be interpreted as influenced by child effects. According to Bronfenbrenner's (1958) analysis, middle-class parents show less use of physical punishment and more use of love-oriented techniques than lower-class parents. There was no clear evidence of a change in this finding in the period from 1932 to 1952, as there was for other child-rearing techniques. Complications of pregnancy and delivery are more frequent in the lower classes (Pasamanick & Knobloch, 1960), and on this basis we could expect more hyperactivity in children from lower-class samples. From the earlier discussions relative to hyperactivity we would expect to find in lower-class parents more upper-limit control behavior, of which physical punishment is a salient example, and less use of love-oriented techniques. It is clear that studies of social-class differences in the future should control for complications of pregnancy and delivery. Some class differences may be reduced in magnitude or altered qualitatively when the samples are made comparable with respect to complications of pregnancy and delivery.

Another area receiving considerable attention in the research literature is that of family structure effects such as birth order, sex of siblings, and family size and density. Data from several studies would support the assumption that differences in parent behavior with different children in the family may be primarily due to increased experience and change in availability to children as the family grows (Conners, 1963; Lasko, 1954; Waldrop & Bell, 1964). However, this does not make it possible to dismiss the possibility of child effects. Second- or later-born neonates show higher skin conductance than firstborn (Weller & Bell, 1965). There is collateral evidence that this indicates heightened arousal and greater maturity in this early period, though there is no information available on later development. Another paper summarizes data indicating that the physiology of pregnancy and delivery is quite different for the mother with her first versus later births (Bell, 1963), raising the possibility that some differences in parent behavior with first- versus later-born children may be a response to congenital differences in the child.

A similar child effect could be operative with increases in family size and density. Since greater dependency was found in preschool children coming from large families with short intervals between siblings it was assumed that these children were simply more deprived of maternal attention (Waldrop & Bell, 1964). While this may have been true in part, further study revealed that newborns from large dense families were more lethargic (Waldrop & Bell, 1966). In this case information on later development was available and the finding was that measures of lethargy in the newborn period were correlated with later dependency. In short, there may be congenital factors operating in determining family structure effects, and credence cannot be given to an interpretation solely in terms of experiental factors until influences identifiable in pregnancy, delivery, and the newborn period are isolated.

Examples of Studies Difficult to Reinterpret

In contrast to these studies, there are others yielding data which could not be reinterpreted as a function of congenital effects contributed by the child. For example, there are studies which substitute experimenters for parents and assign children at random to experimental groups in which different "parental" treatment is administered. In one study, experimenters played the role of parents who did or did not control access to food and toy resources in familylike interactions with preschool children (Bandura, Ross, & Ross, 1963): Children imitated parents who controlled resources. In a study of moral development, experimenters behaved with different groups of children in such a way as to create differences in the child's control over punishment and in the cognitive clarity of a task which preceded a contrived transgression (Aronfreed, 1963). Self-critical and reparative responses following transgression were maximized by prior cognitive clarity and child control. These studies used a flexible approach which can be applied to a wide variety of parent-effect parameters very rapidly. One limitation is that we do not obtain data on the cumulative effects of parents on children. The other problem is that of ownness. It is encouraging in this respect that Stevenson, Keen, and Knights (1963) in studies of social reinforcement with 4- and 5-year-olds, found effects common to fathers and male experimenters, and effects common to mothers and female experimenters. This reassures us that at least with young children it may be possible to produce results with experimenters similar to effects parents have on their own children.

One other approach involves experimental manipulation of the behavior of parents and measurement of the effects on children. This is an approach that is only slightly less flexible than the foregoing and can be carried out very rapidly. Merrill (1946) manipulated parent behavior by providing mothers in two matched groups with different feedback relative to the behavior of their children. As in the previous approach which substituted experimenters for parents, the possibility of pseudo-parent effects being produced by latent child effects is minimal where the children are assigned to experimental groups at random, or on the basis of some relevant matching variable. On the other hand, since the parent is present in the interaction, the child may respond in terms of past expectancies rather than to the manipulated behavior of the parent as such. This operates against obtaining differences in child behavior in different treatments, but where differences are obtained they can be interpreted as free of child effects.

Offspring effects can also be isolated. An example is provided in a summary of series of studies carried out by Siegel (1963). Retardates aged 10 and 15 were classified into high- and low-verbal ability groups. Children in each group were then placed in brief interaction situations with adults who had had no previous contact with them. The adults were to assist children in learning how to assemble a puzzle. Generally, adult responses and questions with low-verbal children were more frequent but shorter and more redundant. Labeling children of similar verbal ability as high or low had no effect on the adult behavior. Support was provided for the hypothesis that linguistic level of children exerts a control over adult verbal behavior.

A second variant of the first design is suggested by the research of Yarrow (1963), already discussed, which took advantage of the assignment of young infants to foster mothers for temporary care while adoption procedures were pending. It is necessary only to measure infant characteristics prior to assignment to foster mothers and then make the assignment systematically so that each foster mother's behavior with at least two different kinds of infants could be measured.

One other approach would make it possible to obtain effects with natural parents. Clinicians frequently report that successful medication of children who are hyperactive and impulsive produces pronounced reactive changes in parent and even total family behavior. Addition of pre- and postmedication measures of parent-child and family interaction to a well-controlled study of drug effects should make it possible to evaluate this and other possible child effects.[2]

Other approaches have been mentioned in the introductory section of this paper (Bell, 1964; Levy, 1958). A detailed discussion of all possible research designs is beyond the scope of this paper, which is primarily concerned with a substantive question of how studies of socialization may be interpreted. This brief recapitulation of designs is to serve the purpose of emphasizing the fact that offspring and parent effects can be separately identified and experimentally manipulated. This will require less reliance on correlation studies of parent and child behavior upon which theories of socialization have been largely based up to the present. Even correlations obtained between parent and child behaviors from longitudinal studies offer no means of ascertaining the direction of effects, unless specially designed for the purpose. Kagan and Moss (1962) have pointed out that the problem of whether maternal hostility is a reaction to child aggression or vice versa is not solved by the demonstration of long-term relations between these maternal and child behaviors in follow-up studies.

[2]This adaptation of drug studies was suggested by Paul H. Wender.

REFERENCES

Aronfreed, J. M. The effects of experimental socialization paradigms upon two moral responses to transgression. *Journal of Abnormal and Social Psychology*, 1963, *66*, 437–448.

Bandura, A., Ross, D., & Ross, S. A. A comparative test of the status envy, social power, and secondary reinforcement theories of identificatory learning. *Journal of Abnormal and Social Psychology*, 1963, *67*, 527–534.

Bandura, A., & Walters, R. H. *Adolescent aggression*. New York: Ronald Press, 1959.

Barry, H., III, Bacon, M. K., & Child, I.L. A cross-cultural survey of some sex differences in socialization. *Journal of Abnormal and Social Psychology*, 1957, *55*, 327–332.

Bayley, N., & Schaefer, E. S. Correlations of maternal and child behaviors with the development of mental abilities: Data from the Berkeley Growth Study. *Monographs of the Society for Research in Child Development*, 1964, *29* (6, Whole No. 97).

Beach, F. A., & Jaynes, J. Studies of maternal retrieving in rats. III. Sensory cues involved in the lactating females' response to her young. *Behaviour*, 1956, *10*, 104–125.

Bell, R. Q. Some factors to be controlled in studies of behavior of newborns. *Biologia Neonatorum*, 1963, *5*, 200–214.

Bell, R. Q. The effect on the family of a limitation in coping ability in a child: A research approach and a finding. *Merrill-Palmer Quarterly*, 1964, *10*, 129–142.

Bing, E. Effect of childrearing practices on development of differential cognitive abilities. *Child Development*, 1963, *34*, 631–648.

Bronfenbrenner, U. Socialization and social class through time and space. In E. E. Maccoby, T. M. Newcomb, & E. L. Hartley (Eds.), *Readings in social psychology*. New York: Holt, Rinehart & Winston, 1958. Pp. 400–425.

Bruce, H. M. Observations on the suckling stimulus and lactation in the rat. *Journal of Reproduction and Fertility*, 1961, *2*, 17–34.

Conners, C. K. Birth order and needs for affiliation. *Journal of Personality*, 1963, *31*, 408–416.

Davids, A., Holden, R. H., & Gray, G. B. Maternal anxiety during pregnancy and adequacy of mother and child adjustment eight months following childbirth. *Child Development*, 1963, *34*, 993–1002.

Denenberg, V. H. Early experience and emotional development. *Scientific American*, 1963, *208*, 138–146.

Epstein, W. Experimental investigations of the genesis of visual space perception. Psychological Bulletin, 1964, *61*, 115–128.

Etzel, B., & Gewirtz, J. Experimental modification of caretaker-maintained high rate operant crying in a 6- and a 20-week-old infant (*Infans Tyrannotearus*). *Journal of Experimental Child Psychology*, 1967, *5*, 303–317.

Ferreira, A. J. The pregnant woman's emotional attitude and its reflection on the newborn. *American Journal of Orthopsychiatry*, 1960, *30*, 553–561.

Freedman, D. G. Hereditary control of early social behavior. In B. M. Foss (Ed.), *Determinants of infant behaviour III*. New York: Wiley, 1965. Pp. 149–159.

Garn, S. M. Fat, body size, and growth in the newborn. *Human Biology*, 1958, *30*, 265–280.

Goodenough, F. W. Interest in persons as an aspect of sex difference in early years. *Genetic Psychology Monographs*, 1957, *55*, 287–323.

Gottesman, I. I. Genetic variance in adaptive personality traits. Paper presented at the 73rd annual convention of the American Psychological Association, September 1965, Chicago, Illinois.

Hillenbrand, E. D. The relationship of psychological, medical, and feeding variables to breast feeding. Unpublished master's thesis, George Washington University, 1965.

Hoffman, M. L. Childrearing practices and moral development: Generalizations from empirical research. *Child Development*, 1963, *34*, 295–318.

Joffe, J. M. Genotype and prenatal and premating stress interact to affect adult behavior in rats. *Science*, 1965, *150*, 1844–1845.

Kagan, J., & Garn, S. M. A constitutional correlate of early intellectual functioning. *Journal of Genetic Psychology*, 1963, *102*, 83–89.

Kagan, J., & Moss, H. A. *Birth to maturity*. New York: Wiley, 1962.

Kessen, W. (Ed.) *The child*. New York: Wiley, 1965.

Lasko, J. K. Parent behavior toward first and second children. *Genetic Psychology Monographs*, 1954, *49*, 97–137.

Lefkowitz, M. M., Walder, L. O., & Eron, L. D. Punishment, identification and aggression. *Merrill-Palmer Quarterly*, 1963, *9*, 159–174.

Levy, D. M. *Behavioral analysis: Analysis of clinical observations of behavior as applied to mother-newborn relationships*. New York: Thomas, 1958.

Merrill, B. A measurement of mother-child interaction. *Journal of Abnormal and Social Psychology*, 1946, *41*, 37–49.

Moss, H. A. Sex, age, and state as determinants of mother-infant interaction. *Merrill-Palmer Quarterly*, 1967, *13*, 19–36.

Murdock, G. P. Comparative data on the division of labor by sex. *Social Forces*, 1937, *15*, 551–553.

Mussen, P., & Rutherford, E. Parent-child relations and parental personality in relation to young children's sex-role preferences. *Child Development*, 1963, *34*, 589–607.

Noirot, E. Changes in responsiveness to young in the adult mouse. III. The effect of immediately preceding performances. *Behavior*, 1965, *24*, 318–325.

Ottinger, D. R., & Simmons, J. E. Behavior of human neonates and prenatal maternal anxiety. *Psychological Reports*, 1964, *14*, 391–394.

Palmer, R. R. *The age of the democratic revolution:* Vol. II. *The struggle*. Princeton: Princeton University Press, 1964.

Pasamanick, B., & Knobloch, H. Brain damage and reproductive casualty. *American Journal of Orthopsychiatry*, 1960, *30*, 298–305.

Pasamanick, B., Robers, M. E., & Lilienfeld, A. M. Pregnancy experience and the development of behavior disorders in children. *American Journal of Psychiatry*, 1956, *112*, 613–618.

Ressler, R. H. Parental handling in two strains of mice reared by foster parents. *Science*, 1962, *137*, 129–130.

Rheingold, H. L., (Ed.) *Maternal behavior in mammals*. New York: Wiley, 1963.

Rheingold, H. L. The development of social behavior in the human infant. In H. W. Stevenson (Ed.), Concept of development: A report of a conference commemorating the fortieth anniversary of the Institute of Child Development, University of Minnesota. *Monographs of the Society for Research in Child Development*, 1966, *31* (5, Whole No. 107).

Scarr, S. The inheritance of sociability. *American Psychologist*, 1965, *20*, 524. (Abstract)

Schaefer, E. A circumplex model for maternal behavior. *Journal of Abnormal and Social Psychology*, 1959, *59*, 226–235.

Schaefer, E. Parent-child interactional patterns and parental attitudes. In D. Rosenthal (Ed.), *The Genain quadruplets*. New York: Basic Books, 1963. Pp. 398–430.

Schaefer, E., & Bayley, N. Maternal behavior, child behavior, and their intercorrelations from infancy through adolescence. *Monographs of the Society for Research in Child Development*, 1963, *28* (3, Whole No. 87).

Schaffer, H. R., & Emerson, P. E. Patterns of response to physical contact in early human development. *Journal of Child Psychology and Psychiatry*, 1964, *5*, 1–13.

Sears, R. R., Maccoby, E. E., & Levin, H. *Patterns of child rearing*. Evanston, Ill.: Row, Peterson. 1957.

Siegel, G. M. Adult verbal behavior with retarded children labeled as "high" or "low" in verbal ability. *American Journal of Mental Deficiency*, 1963, *68*, 417–424.

Stechler, G. A longitudinal follow-up of neonatal apnea. *Child Development*, 1964, *35*, 333–348.

Stevenson, H. W., Keen, R., & Knights, R. M. Parents and strangers as reinforcing agents for children's performance. *Journal of Abnormal and Social Psychology*, 1963, *67*, 183–186.

Stott, L. H. Parent-adolescent adjustment: Its measurement and significance. *Character and Personality*, 1941, *10*, 140–150.

Vandenberg, S. G. The hereditary abilities study: Hereditary components in a psychological test battery. *American Journal of Human Genetics*, 1962, *14*, 220–237.

Waldrop, M., & Bell, R. Q. Relation of preschool dependency behavior to family size and density. *Child Development*, 1964, *35*, 1187–1195.

Waldrop, M., & Bell, R. Q. Effects of family size and density on newborn characteristics. *American Journal of Orthopsychiatry*, 1966, *36*, 544–550.

Walters, R. H., & Parke, R. D. The role of the distance receptors in the development of social responsiveness. In L. P. Lipsitt & C. C. Spiker (Eds.), *Advances in child development and behavior*. Vol. 2. New York: Academic Press, 1965. Pp. 59–96.

Weller, G. M., & Bell, R. Q. Basal skin conductance and neonatal state. *Child Development*, 1965, *36*, 647–657.

Yarrow, L. J. Research in dimensions of early maternal care. *Merrill-Palmer Quarterly*, 1963, *9*, 101–114.

42.   STATE AS AN INFANT-ENVIRONMENT INTERACTION

An Analysis of Mother–Infant Interaction as a Function of Sex[1]

MICHAEL LEWIS

State is one of those psychological constructs which is widely used, carries meaning for commerce, and yet, when carefully considered, is rather difficult to define. It is clearly an important characteristic of human behavior and is probably one of the more important variables distinguishing the living from the inanimate, such as machines. Yet, its definition is most difficult and soon gives way to simple taxonomy.

State is usually considered, first of all, as a continuum of behavior, reflecting some underlying condition. This condition is usually defined along either an arousal continuum or a consciousness continuum. In contemporary psychology the notion of consciousness—as the entire issue of phenomenology—has been neglected, so most investigations deal with state in terms of arousal. Duffy's (1962) definition of arousal demonstrates the breadth of this concept. It is conceived as a generalized drive state providing, for example, the intensity dimension of the emotions, the alertness factor in intelligence, and the general level of reactivity to stimulation—a rather inclusive dimension. The consciousness continuum is less well defined, but has within it the notion of awareness—either internal or external (see Hilgard, 1969).

Given that state is usually defined as an arousal continuum, it would be easy to define state explicitly as some continuum in a specific behavioral area of choosing that continuum as a function of the model of behavior we wish to employ. Thus, if one were talking about brain function, one would discuss state (and state changes) in terms of EEG or REM behavior during various levels of sleep. Construction of autonomic nervous system models would describe state in terms of heart rate level, while activity models would measure movement, smiling, and sucking changes. Attention could be considered a state and state in this case could be defined as the continuum of eye gaze duration. The fact, however, that one can discuss state at these different levels should at once alert us to the problem that the definition of state will be no easy task. Moreover, by defining it in terms of the behavior studied, the risk of circularity of definition is increased: defining state as eye gaze and using eye gaze duration to define state.

Behind much of this difficulty of definition rests the general belief that the state or arousal continuum varies from a quiet sleep level (nonREM) through an alert level to a superactive level such as crying or extreme anxiety. The arousal continuum is a difficult and contradictory concept which necessarily does not have a one-to-one correspondence with state.

[1]This research is supported by the National Science Foundation, Grant #GB-8590, and an Early Childhood Research Council Grant. Recognition is to be given to Pamela Sarett and Yvonne Watson for data collection, and to Cornelia Wilson for data analysis.

From the *Merrill-Palmer Quarterly*, 1972, *18*, 95–121. Reprinted by permission of the author and the publisher, *The Merrill-Palmer Quarterly*—Behavior and Development.

For example, there may be more activity (level of arousal) during active sleep than during an alert-attentive period when no activity is present. This point has been made by Lacey (1967) in terms of autonomic nervous system activity.

Reviewing the research classified as "state" and categorizing it sheds little additional information in terms of defining state. Instead, for me at least, it tends to demonstrate that our understanding of the meaning of state is limited.

It seems reasonable to conclude from the literature on the premature infant and neonate that differences in state and individual differences in state (for example, amount of time asleep or responsivity to soothing) derive from our biological past and are firmly rooted in our biological composition. It is equally clear from the stimulation and intervention research that state can be modified by the environment.

With this in mind, an attempt will be made to consider state in a somewhat different fashion. Any attempt at reevaluating the concept must be broad enough to encompass the various uses and meanings implied by state and, by the same token, allow for the possible empirical use of such a definition.

State as an Interaction

It is clear from the literature that any exact definition of state is not easily forthcoming. Because of the unwillingness to deal with introspective description, investigators have been forced to define state in terms of organism behavior, which they believe accurately reflects some underlying condition. That is, there has generally been a confusion between measurement and definition. This can be seen most often in the literature where attempts at definition start with state in quotation marks, soon giving way to a taxonomy, then replaced by measurement of specific behaviors. From that point on state no longer appears in quotation marks. This confusion between definition and measurement of specific behaviors can also be seen in the confusion of state as a number of discrete points or state as a continuum. There is relative agreement that state is a continuum of an organism condition, in some cases considered arousal. Yet, while state is generally so considered, our inability to measure it as a continuum results in the consideration of state as a finite set of discrete points. The consequence of this is a literature in which the number of discrete points becomes an issue (or problem) to be dealt with. This is, in fact, nothing but a technology and measurement problem.

In the present discussion, we too are subject to the difficulty of substituting organism behavior for condition; introspective techniques are not possible with infants. An attempt will be made to deal with state not solely as a set of independent behaviors of the organism but rather as some set of behaviors as they interact with the environment. As will become apparent, state (reflected in a set of behaviors) can best be measured as a function of some past set of behaviors of the infant and his environment. Thus state will take on an interactive quality and, therefore, lose some static quality. Moreover, the present analysis allows us to consider models which utilize sequential notions. This will be discussed later in the measurement sections.

Because only behavior rather than condition is available to us, we will deal only with sets of behavior in attempting to specify infant condition. This is compatible with the views of others who have dealt with this problem. Where this discussion differs from earlier formulations is in its stand that behavior is not independent of an interaction with the environment.

In general, state is considered a subject condition—measured by a set of behaviors—which can affect the relationship of the organism to its environment. Thus, the present set of behaviors (B) of the infant will affect subsequent behavior(s). However, it is also true that the set of behaviors will be affected by the interaction with the environment (E). That is, the present set of behaviors at time t is also a function of the interaction between the environment and the set of behaviors at $t-1$: that is,

State $_t$ = f(B_t,E_t); however behavior at t = f(B_{t-1}, E_{t-1}).

Because infant behavior at time t is always a function of behavior and enviornment at $t-1$, there is a regression with the limit at the time of conception.[2]

Our argument is essentially that state can be better defined in terms of the type of infant environment interaction with different states being different interactions. For example, "awake state" can be defined as maximum infant-environment interaction, while "sleep state" can be defined as minimum interaction. Likewise, various awake states can be defined in terms of specific interaction. Thus "alert awake" is eyes open-interesting-to-look-at-environment interaction and might be measured, for example, by the duration of eye gaze. However, we propose that there are many more awake states, each of these specific to the interaction. There is an "awake-look state," an "awake-listen state," etc., each a function of the infant and his environment. This is more than possible. To preview some of our empirical results it is possible for two infants to show the same set of behaviors (i.e., eyes open, awake, and vocalizing) and have two different environmental interactions. In one case the mother vocalizes back and in the other she touches the child. The results of this interaction are distinguishable and suggest what we wish to call two different states, this when the infant set of behaviors (condition) are identical.

The interactive analysis which has been presented views current state (or a set of behaviors), at time t, a function of past behavior and environment. Equally applicable would be the extension of this analysis to include prediction about subsequent state at $t + 1$ as a function of t. We suggest that subsequent state and individual differences in state (in sets of behavior) can be predicted best from the infant's behavior and environmental interaction at the present time rather than the infant's behavior alone. This then brings us the power that this type of conceptualization provides. It is believed that this type of interactive analysis will enable one to make a more powerful prediction than the use of either environment or organism variables alone. This appears to be the case. A Markovian analysis of the vocalization data was undertaken (see Freedle & Lewis, 1971) and the results, at least for the two subjects considered, indicate that the ability to predict an infant behavior (vocalization) on trial n was enhanced by the knowledge of interaction of the mother's and infant's vocalization on trial $n - 1$. In both cases, the interaction was superior to knowing mother's vocalization alone on trial $n - 1$ and in one case knowing infant's vocalization alone on trial $n - 1$.

People, because they are responsive (more so, at any rate, than the environment in general), may constitute a very important and crucial type of environment, one which is absolutely essential for the growth of the organism (see Lewis & Goldberg, 1969 for a discussion of responsivity). Their effect is of primary importance in determining state. The infant-mother relationship is a special case of the type of infant-environment interaction we have been discussing and it will be this special case which we shall study.

In the subsequent discussion, we shall be dealing with waking states in which there is the opportunity for infant-mother interactions, and we shall look at different waking states. Given the proposed definition, the nature of the interaction will define the state. Thus, for example, an interaction of infant-vocalizing-mother-holding will define a different state from one of infant-vocalizing-mother-vocalizing. It is our hypothesis that different waking periods are different states, this as a function of the mother-infant interaction, and that these differential states may determine later states.

Some empirical findings about individual mother-infant interaction as a basis for discussing differential "states" would be relevant at

---

[2]Conception is considered the limit rather than birth since it is obvious that gestation itself is an interaction between fetus and environment. Sontag's work clearly demonstrates this interactive effect of maternal environment on the fetus and even on the subsequent state of the newborn (Sontag, 1966; Sontag & Wallace, 1935a, 1935b, 1936). This interactive analysis of regression suggests a limit, namely genotypic structure. It must be remembered, however, that even basic genetic material is placed in an environment which is quite capable of affecting and altering that structure. Young, Groy, and Phoenix's (1964) work with altering the sex of monkeys is an example of how environment—in this case hormonal—can affect genetic structure.

this point. While much import is attributed to the interaction between mother and infant, studies have either discussed it theoretically (for example, Gewirtz, 1969) or have presented data on mother and infant behavior which is not necessarily interactive (for example, Moss, 1967).

Observational Data

Each infant seen was three months old (± one week). The sample of infants seen was deliberately chosen in order to obtain as heterogeneous a group as possible. For this reason boys and girls of two racial groups (black and white) as well as from the entire socioeconomic spectrum (using the Hollingshead five point scale, 1957) were included. There were infants of black professionals as well as infants of poor working-class white families. A total of 32 infants have been seen to date.[3]

Each infant-caretaker was seen in her home. Because the caretakers were infants' mothers, the term mother shall be used with the understanding that caretakers could include any other adult.[4] Contact with the mothers was made in a variety of ways: contact through the mothers' initiative, selection of the mother-infant by looking through birth announcements in the newspapers, and through church groups in lower socioeconomic areas. Two observers were trained and used in this study, one for the black community and one for the white. The observer reliability was moderately high, at least for overall frequency of infant behaviors (*rho's* ranged from .40's to .60's).

The mothers were instructed that the observer was interested in studying the infant's be-

havior. The observer sat next to but out of sight of the infant. It was stressed that it was the infant who was to be observed—not the mother. Moreover, the mother was to try to forget the presence of the observer and not engage her in conversation. When conversation was attempted, the observer reminded the mother that she was to ignore her. Prior to observation, the observer spent time with the mother attempting to put her at ease.

While every attempt was made to make the observation session as natural as possible, the presence of the observer was bound to have an effect. This problem has been discussed before (see Lewis & Goldberg, 1969); because of the ethical consideration of observation without the mother's knowledge and approval, this was the only procedure available.[5]

Levels of Analysis of Interactive Data

The observation data were collected using a checklist sheet. Each sheet represents 60 seconds, divided into six 10-second columns. Infant behaviors are listed in the upper portion of the sheet, while adult behaviors are in the lower portion. When a behavior not listed on the sheet occurred, the observer wrote it in. For the most part, the behavior categories are self-explanatory. The "extra movement" category consisted of all gross physical movements such as limb movement or rolling of the body. "Quiet play" consisted of the child watching a toy move, playing with his fingers; and noise/nonvocalization was similar to extra movement, except that noise accompanied the behavior (by kicking feet against the crib). It is clear that these behaviors are not totally exclusive, reflecting a further difficulty in studies of this sort. Although the behaviors have some overlap, the observers were in general able to differentiate between them. Mother's touch and

[3]Since our interest here is in process, we shall forego a discussion of individual differences as a function of race or SES, variables which we do not consider to be psychological in nature. A diverse sample was obtained in order to maximize the individual variance in order to maximize mother-infant differences in process.

[4]In a recent study of African infants (Lusk & Lewis, 1971), we found little difference in caretaking between various adults and children. Whether this holds in our culture is yet to be determined.

[5]We cannot assess directly the effect of being observed on the caretaker's behavior. It is possible, however, to manipulate the observer, for example use males or females, etc. and see what effects observer characteristics have on the caretaker's behavior. In this manner we might be able to surmise the effect of being observed.

BEHAVIOR CHECK LIST - MOTHER-CHILD OBSERVATION

INFANT STUDY

Name _Sarah M._____ Sex _F_ Birth Date _8-26-70_

Age _3 mos_   Date of observation _12-11_ Time _10 A.M._ Observer _PS_

Situation _____ _IN S's bedroom_____

Minute number _____ _95_

Infant	0-10	11-20	21-30	31-40	41-50	51-60
Eyes Closed						
Eyes Open						
Vocalization		/	/			
Extra Movement						
Fret/cry						
Feed Self						
Quiet Play						
Noise/Non-voc						
Smile						2

* *

Mother						
Touch					✓	✓
Holding						
Voc		2	2		/	/
Look		✓	✓			
Smile/Laugh						
Play w/S						
Change diaper						
Give Bottle						
Rocks S						
Reading/TV	✓	✓	✓			
Other						

FIGURE 42-1. Behavior check list for one minute of observation.

holding categories were used to distinguish between a discrete touch versus a physical support. If during a "hold" the mother also discretely touched the child, both categories would be scored. Finally, the categories of reading/TV and vocalizing to others were used to indicate that the mother was involved in activities *not* directed toward the child.

Each 10 seconds the observer checked off the occurrence of both infant and mother behaviors, also recording when possible which behaviors preceded which. Figure 42-1 presents an example from one minute of observation. The numbers "1" and "2" indicate that not only did that particular behavior occur but "1" indicates it occurred before "2" during the 10-second period. The observer only scored initiating and responding behavior (numbers instead of check marks) when she was sure of the direction of the interaction.

Consistent with our interest in different awake states, no sleep data were collected. This meant that if the infant closed his eyes for longer than 30 consecutive seconds, observation stopped. In order to obtain two full hours of eyes-open data, a minimum of two hours of observation and on some occasions as much as three or four hours were necessary. In fact, for one-third of the sample, two visits to the home were required.

Methods of Data Analysis

Various levels of interactive analysis are possible with these types of data. In the following discussion, some of the more obvious will be presented.

Frequency Distribution. The lowest level of interactive analysis is the frequency data; that is, how much vocalization, quiet play, smiling, etc., the infant exhibited in the two hours of observation. Likewise, the same data analysis is possible for the mother's behavior. These types of data are the types most reported in mother-infant studies, for they are the easiest to obtain and score.

Simultaneous Behavior within 10-Second Unit. I. The next level of data analysis, the first true interaction, is the number of 10-second units for which there are both a child and mother behavior, this regardless of the nature of the interaction and who initiated the interaction. It is often difficult to determine exactly which one of the pair initiates a behavior sequence and time duration of the sequence. For these reasons a more conservative approach is to restrict the analysis to a 10-second time unit, recognizing that it is an arbitrary unit of time. The observation of the number of 10-second periods in which there was an interaction is a simple interaction parameter which can provide some

TABLE 42-1
Mean Frequencies of Infant and Maternal Behavior

	Total ($N = 32$) $\overline{X}$	Boys ($N = 17$) $\overline{X}$	Girls ($N = 15$) $\overline{X}$	t	p
Infant					
Vocalize	170.8	172.1	169.2	.08	NS
Movement	96.5	87.4	106.7	1.35	NS
Fret/Cry	77.3	72.8	82.3	.46	NS
Play	108.0	99.3	117.9	.49	NS
Noise	23.4	17.5	30.1	.92	NS
Smile	37.3	38.6	35.8	.23	NS
Mother					
Touch	126.7	128.7	124.5	.16	NS
Hold	307.3	356.9	251.0	2.09	<.05
Vocalize	257.2	227.1	291.3	2.04	<.05
Look	174.3	145.1	207.4	1.72	NS
Smile	33.0	37.0	28.4	.93	NS
Play	86.8	84.3	89.5	.21	NS
Rock	10.1	14.5	5.0	1.59	NS
Vocalize to others	96.7	109.5	82.3	1.03	NS
Read/TV	48.5	57.1	38.9	.64	NS

index of individual amounts of mother-infant levels of interaction. Moreover, by looking at the ratio of number of 10 seconds of infant behavior to number of 10 seconds of interaction, a general environment responsivity score can be obtained.

Simultaneous Behavior within 10-Second Unit. II. A still higher level of interaction involves judging not only that a mother and infant interaction occurred in the same 10 seconds, but the nature of that interaction. For example, along the left side are listed the various infant behaviors, while along the top, the maternal ones. For each occurrence of an infant behavior, it was determined whether there was an interaction. If one did occur, then for each infant behavior the various maternal behaviors were scored. For example, in a 10-second period, an infant vocalized and his mother also vocalized. In the infant vocalization row and maternal vocalization column an occurrence would be scored. Because the mother might have exhibited several behaviors at once, it is possible that several maternal rows would be scored for each infant behavior. It is possible, therefore, that the total maternal behaviors across a row of a specific infant behavior may be greater than the specific number of infant occurrences. However, there can never be more mother than infant occurrences in a single category.

Likewise, one can look at the specific adult behavior and observe what infant behaviors also occurred during the same 10 seconds. It is important to remember that this analysis does not imply direction to the categories of behavior, only that they happened in proximity— in this case within the same 10-second period. While no direction should be inferred, and for such behaviors as infant vocalization and smile it is difficult to surmise who initiates what; such behaviors as infant fret/cry would logically suggest that this behavior elicited maternal behaviors such as look, smile, or touch rather than the other way around.

Directional Interactive Analyses. This level of analysis is designed to try to determine the direction of interactive behavior. Under this analysis, four categories of interactive behavior are possible for each specific behavior. For example, examine an infant vocalization. The first question to be asked is whether the vocalization was a response to a maternal behavior or was an initiator of a maternal behavior, these being scored as two separate categories. This was accomplished by making use of the scoring of a "1" or a "2," "1" indicating initiating. Two additional categories were necessary for interactions with less clarity of direction. For example, the child vocalizes and it was observed that the mother had been vocalizing to the infant for 30 seconds prior to and 10 seconds

TABLE 42–2
Mother-Infant Behavior Correlations ($N = 32$)

	RANK ORDER CORRELATIONS								
				MOTHER BEHAVIOR					
INFANT BEHAVIOR	Touch (Kiss)	Hold	Voc.	Voc. to Others	Smile Laugh	Look	Play	Rock	Read/ TV
Vocalize	.11	.11	.43*	−.28	.39*	.21	.49**	.30	.48**
Fret	−.23	−.36*	.02	.15	−.43	−.36	−.18	−.09	−.36*
Movement	.05	.13	.09	−.15	.08	.44*	.19	.40*	.37*
Play	−.29	−.32	.01	−.28	.23	.04	.31	.25	.35
Noise (not voc.)	−.15	−.21	−.09	−.13	−.23	.37*	.05	.16	.08
Smile	−.15	−.01	.20	−.26	.52**	−.25	.45**	−.03	.28

*p < .05.
**p < .01.

after the child's vocalization. Does the mother's vocalization constitute an initiation and her vocalization subsequent to the child's, a response? It is not at all clear since the infant did not vocalize immediately. In this case this type of interaction was scored separately. Finally, a fourth category was necessary for interactive behavior whose direction could not be assessed. Thus, for each infant behavior, each maternal behavior had four possible direction components.

There are of course many more measures of interaction for which individual measures may be obtained. For example, one can look at length of interaction, for another, density of response. The latter is a particularly interesting measure of interaction in that it implies that for some behavior there are more maternal responses occurring than for others. This density measure is based on the ratio of amount of specific infant behavior, e.g., vocalization, compared to amount of all maternal behaviors during that specific behavior. For example, the data indicate that when an infant smiles there is more maternal behavior than when it vocalizes. We shall return to this measure later.

It is clear that interaction analyses are not easy and this, of course, explains their lack of use in most of the mother-infant analyses. In order to talk about state, it will be necessary, however, to deal with interaction analyses, since we have committed ourselves to a definition of state which rests on just such interactions.

Results

In order to demonstrate individual differences in state—infant-mother interaction—both individual and group data will be presented. Moreover, because much data already exists on individual differences in infant-mother interaction as a function of the sex of the child (Goldberg & Lewis, 1969; Moss, 1967), the group data have been grouped in this fashion.

Frequency Distribution. The overall frequency data indicate great individual variability. For example, numbers of vocalizations range from 34 to 309 10-second units for girls and from 28 to 438 10-second units for boys. These same types of large individual differences can be found for each infant behavior. It is interesting to note that of all the prominent behaviors, vocalizations were the most numerous—24% of the time.

In similar fashion, maternal vocalization frequencies varied from 154 to 493 10-second units for girls and 101 to 344 10-second units for boys. As expected, mothers held and vocalized to their infants relatively frequently during the two hours of observation (40% and 36% respectively). Of interest, however, was the fact that mothers smiled to their children less than they read or looked at television (5% to 6%). Group differences as a function of sex of infant reveal no differences in any of the behavior categories. Not so the behaviors of the mothers. These seemed to be determined by the sex of their infants. In general mothers of boys held, touched, and rocked their children more than mothers of girls (significant only for hold, $t = 2.09$, $p < .05$, two-tailed[6]). Mothers of girls, however, tended to vocalize and look at their children more than mothers of boys (significant only for vocalization, $t = 2.04$, $p < .05$). While this level of analysis tells relatively little about infant-mother interaction, it does suggest that boys receive more proximal stimulation—touching and holding—while girls receive more distal stimulation—looking and vocalization, this when there is no difference in boy-girl infant behavior.

In order to examine the relationship between maternal and infant behavior, a correlation matrix was computed. The results indicate that at least for frequency of occurrence there is a relatively strong relationship between infant and maternal behavior. For example, mothers who vocalized and smiled a great deal had infants who vocalized and smiled a great deal (*rho* = .43, $p < .05$ and .52, $p < .01$, respectively). In general the more the positive maternal behavior, the less infant fret/cry—this significant for hold ($- .36, p < .05$) and smile

[6]All probabilities are two-tailed unless stated.

(− .43, $p < .05$). Like smiling, maternal play behavior was positively correlated with infant vocalization (.49, $p < .01$) and smile (.45, $p < .01$). Maternal looking was positively associated with infant movement and noise/nonvocalization (.44 and .37, $p < .05$, respectively).

Simultaneous Behavior within 10-Second Units. I. The first truly interactive analysis asks in how many 10-second units there were both infant and maternal behaviors. Again, this varied with the infant-mother group, for example, from 208 to 543 10-second units for girls to 200 to 492 10-second units for boys. For the group as a whole, there were 341.2 10-second units—44% of two hours of observation spent in interaction; boys 359.3 and girls 320.7, a nonsignificant difference.

Also of interest was the percentage of time there was an interaction unit as a function of the number of times there was an infant behavior. These varied for individual infants from a low of 39.5% to a high of 96.5%. For boys it averaged 75.6% of the time with a range of 48.9% to 96.5% while for girls it averaged 68.0% with a range of 39.5% to 91.9% of the time. This difference was not significant, however ($t = 1.32$).

Simultaneous Behavior within 10-second Units. 11. This interaction analysis begins to examine what happens when something else is happening and is vital to the discussion of state as an infant-mother interaction. It is here where it can be demonstrated that such state differences as infant-vocalization-mother-vocalization or infant-vocalization-mother-hold are possible.

TABLE 42–3
Mother-Infant Interactions (Independent of Direction)
Means for All Subjects & by Sex (N = 32)

INFANT BEHAVIOR		MOTHER BEHAVIOR: Touch	Hold	Voc.	Look	Smile	Play	Change Diaper	Feed	Rock	Toy	Voc. to Others	Read/ TV
Voc.	Boy	28.82	70.88	71.65	37.53	15.71	25.94	12.94	22.82	1.24	.94	20.00	23.00
	Girl	28.07	52.20	83.20	58.53	15.87	28.20	7.27	23.27	1.33	1.47	11.20	18.33
	Total	28.47	62.13	77.06	47.38	15.78	27.00	10.28	32.41	1.28	1.19	15.88	12.00
Mov.	Boy	20.88	38.41	27.12	22.06	3.59	5.88	4.71	5.06	2.65	1.53	10.59	7.41
	Girl	17.00	28.13	33.33	36.33	5.33	11.53	2.47	3.80	.67	2.73	11.53	17.20
	Total	19.06	33.59	30.03	28.75	4.41	8.53	3.66	4.47	1.72	2.09	11.03	12.00
Fret/ Cry	Boy	12.35	24.29	32.06	12.65	2.00	3.06	5.41	4.24	2.65	3.18	3.18	1.24
	Girl	14.07	22.27	34.33	16.93	1.60	4.00	3.67	9.07	.27	1.47	4.07	.53
	Total	13.16	23.34	33.13	14.66	1.81	3.50	4.59	6.50	1.53	2.38	3.59	.91
Eat	Boy	7.76	101.53	27.65	32.18	2.53	4.82	0	125.18	4.29	.53	28.82	4.29
	Girl	5.47	80.67	45.73	42.47	2.40	.13	0	104.53	2.40	0	23.20	6.00
	Total	6.69	91.75	36.13	37.00	2.47	2.63	0	115.50	3.41	.28	26.19	5.19
Play	Boy	8.41	25.65	21.94	17.59	5.82	19.12	.65	0	0	1.12	10.82	24.00
	Girl	8.00	5.73	19.67	28.07	4.87	14.20	3.73	.20	0	.53	11.07	13.80
	Total	8.22	16.31	20.88	22.50	5.38	16.81	2.09	.09	0	.84	10.94	19.22
Noise	Boy	1.12	2.94	2.29	3.12	.41	2.24	.41	.24	0	.76	1.71	7.35
	Girl	2.13	2.00	5.27	7.93	.47	1.67	.93	.13	0	.80	2.47	4.13
	Total	1.59	2.50	3.69	5.38	.44	1.97	.66	.19	0	.78	2.06	5.84
Smile	Boy	10.00	15.00	24.76	11.35	12.76	14.76	4.29	1.82	.18	.06	1.71	3.24
	Girl	11.47	12.40	27.33	15.80	14.40	14.40	2.80	1.53	0	.13	1.67	.67
	Total	10.69	13.78	25.97	13.44	13.53	14.59	3.59	1.69	.09	.09	1.69	2.03

Presented in Table 42–3 is the interaction relationship between infant and mother. Keep in mind that there is no causality implied in this analysis, only that when a child was doing something, his mother also was doing something.

First view the data from the infant point of view. As expected the most common interaction to infant's vocalization is maternal vocalization, then maternal-hold, and finally maternal-look. For infant-gross movement the most common maternal associations are hold, vocalization, and look. Interestingly and somewhat unexpected are the interactions for infant-fret/cry. Infant-fret/cry is most associated with maternal-vocalization, hold, and look. One might have expected more infant-fret-maternal-hold. Obviously, infant-eat should be and is associated most with maternal feed and hold. Infant-play is associated most with maternal-look, followed by maternal-vocalization, and then surprisingly by maternal-reading or watching TV. Infant-noise is most associated with maternal reading or watching TV and maternal-look followed by maternal-vocalization. Finally, infant-smile is most associated with maternal-vocalization, holding, and smiling.

Now consider the maternal behaviors and observe the infant behavior associated with them. This is done by reading down the maternal columns. Maternal-touching is most associated with infant-focalization and movement while holding is most associated with infant eating, vocalization, and movement. Maternal-vocalization and looking are associated most with infant-vocalization, eating, and fret/cry, while smiling is most associated with infant-vocalization, smiling, and infant play. Maternal-play is most associated with infant-vocalization, play, and smile; and maternal change-diaper is associated with infant-vocalization, fret/cry, and smile. Of the two behaviors not directed toward the child—vocalization to others and reading and watching TV—infant behaviors most associated were vocalization, eating, and playing. It is clear that infant-vocalization is most associated with maternal behaviors.

Table 42–3 presents these same data broken down by sex. It is apparent that the same infant behavior is associated with different maternal behaviors as a function of the sex of the child; that is, different conditions of the S have different environmental associates and therefore different states. In order to see this more clearly, an individual infant-mother interaction analysis was performed. This analysis was performed for each infant behavior. The question asked was, for each individual infant for a particular behavior, what maternal behavior occurred most frequently? The scores in Table 42–4 reflect numbers of infant-mother dyads. Because there were ties the total number of dyads sometimes exceeds the number of cases. Observation of the data reveals interesting individual differences, especially as related to sex. The data for vocalization, movement, fret/cry, play, and noise/nonvocalization all indicate that the behavior associations of mothers of boys tend to be equally distributed between proximal (touch or hold) and distal (look and vocalization) while the behavior association of mothers of girls tends to be loaded in the distal modality. Thus, for example, when a girl infant is vocalizing, her mother is most likely vocalizing as well. However, when a boy infant is vocalizing, it is equally likely that his mother is holding him or vocalizing. This trend in most infant behaviors is significant for infant gross movement ($X^2 = 5.43, p < .05$).

The same analysis can be performed looking at maternal behavior categories and observing the infant's behavioral associations; that is, when the mother was behaving in a certain fashion what was the infant doing? Thus for maternal touching, one could observe the number of infants showing maximum association for one of the seven categories of vocalization, movement, fret/cry, eating, playing, noise, and smiling. When this analysis is performed, no sex differences are observed. Moreover, much of the maternal behavior is associated with infant vocalization which was reflected in the mean data analyses presented above.

These two analyses suggest then that the sex

TABLE 42–4
Number of Infant-Mother Dyads Having the Most Common Interaction ($N = 32$)

INFANT BEHAVIOR		Touch	Hold	Voc.	Look	Smile	Play	Change Diaper	Feed	Rock	Pacifier	Voc. to Others	Read/ TV
								MOTHER BEHAVIOR					
Voc.	Boy	0	6	9	0	0	0	0	0	0	0	1	1
	Girl	0	2	10	2	0	0	0	0	0	0	0	1
Mov.	Boy	1	10	4	4	0	0	0	0	0	0	0	0
	Girl	1	2	8	4	0	0	0	0	0	0	1	1
Fret	Boy	1	6	9	1								
	Girl	0	3	11	1								
Eat	Boy	0	7	0	0	0	0	0	14	0			
	Girl	0	4	0	1	0	0	0	13	1			
Play	Boy	0	3	3	2	0	1	0	0	0	0	1	3
	Girl	0	0	3	8	0	0	0	0	0	0	0	3
Noise	Boy	0	3	2	2	0	1	1	0	0	0	0	1
	Girl	0	1	2	6	0	0	0	0	0	0	0	1
Smile	Boy	0	2	15	0	2	1	0	1				
	Girl	0	0	13	4	0	0	0	0				

differences observed are not a function of the infant's behavior but rather differential maternal responsivity as a function of the sex of the infant. State differences between individual infants, often as a function of sex, are apparent even when the infant's condition is constant. For example, large bodily movements or vocalizations (an infant condition) are associated with either distal or proximal maternal behavior (an environmental condition) resulting in differential state, this when the infant condition is consistent. Of particular interest is that girl infants' vocalizations are more likely to be associated with maternal-vocalization than are boys'. The potential consequence of this state difference for subsequent language and cognitive development is considerable.

Directional Interactive Analyses. Within this analysis the direction, when available, of an interaction is mapped. Table 42–5 presents these mean data for the group as a whole.[7] Observe the four categories of maternal-infant behavior: A, maternal initiate-infant respond; B, infant initiate-maternal respond; C, maternal-continuing-infant respond; D, undefined. Our attention should be directed to the A and B categories which supply the most accurate of the direction measure. Percentage scores as well as the mean data for A and B categories are presented. These represent the percentage of A to (A + B), and of B to

[7]Seven cases are missing because of the failure of the observers to utilize the present system.

(A + B), and inform one of the percentage of maternal behavior which was a response to (B) or an elicitor of (A) an infant behavior. The final percent on the right of the table is the percentage of ΣA to Σ(A + B) and ΣB to Σ(A + B) over all maternal behaviors.

Consider infant vocalization: the data for all maternal behaviors except vocalization indicate that infant vocalizations were for the most part responses to maternal *initiated* behaviors. Thus, an infant vocalized 83% as a response to a maternal touch "A" and a maternal touch was a response to the infant's vocalization, 17% of the time "B." This held for each maternal behavior with varying degrees of differential magnitude. Maternal vocalization, however, was more likely a response to the infant's vocalization "B" than an initiator of the behavior "A." Interestingly, this also held for maternal vocalization to others.

Infant smiling behavior like infant vocalization is for the most part more of a response to maternal behavior "A" than an elicitor of her behavior "B." Indeed this holds for every maternal behavior. Infant fret/cry, gross movement, and play, however, are elicitors of maternal behavior, this for most every category of behavior.

There would seem to be two classes of behavior for infants of this age, those which elicit maternal behavior such as fret/cry, gross movement, and play and those which are the result of maternal behavior, smile, and vocalization (see total behavior percentages in Table 42–5). Vocalization is a particularly interesting behavior partly because it has both qualities: it is the response more than the elicitor to all maternal behaviors except for maternal vocalization where it is more often the elicitor. The results point up the difficulty of a simplistic approach which often fails to take into account the real interactive quality of the mother-infant relationship. Moreover, and perhaps more importantly, the results suggest that different behavior sequences have different histories of initiator-respondent relationship. Thus, it is clear that infant smiling is for the most part a response to something while fret/cry is for the most part an elicitor of some response on the part of the mother.

Observation of maternal behavior across all categories of behavior indicates a differential initiator-respondent pattern dependent on the behavior. For example, for maternal touch, hold, look, smile, play, and change diaper, the mother's behavior is as an initiator of infant behavior (averaged across all behaviors) while mother's vocalization, feed, rock, vocalize to others, and read/TV are responses to infant behavior.

A breakdown of the data by sex is presented in Table 42–6. As was the case for the group as a whole, infant vocalization and smile were more often a response to a maternal behavior (with the exception of infant-vocalization-maternal-vocalization). There do appear, however, to be some interesting sex differences in the degree to which this was true. Comparing only the A and B categories over all the maternal behaviors, 50% of directional vocalizations for males were responses to maternal behavior A while 50% were elicitors B. For females 63% were in response to maternal behavior and 37% were initiators of maternal behavior. This suggests that females may be more vocally responsive—in proportion to vocalization in general—to a a mother's behavior than males. The fret/cry data are also suggestive of sex differences. In this case, mothers of girls are more likely to respond to a fret/cry than are mothers of boys.

Of particular interest is the observation of amount of responsivity on the part of the mother to an infant's behavior as a function of each specific infant behavior. This can be determined by the comparison of the mean difference data. It is recognized that sex differences in frequency need to be taken into account; however, the frequency data presented earlier failed to indicate any sex differences. Thus for a preliminary descriptive analysis the mean data will suffice. For infant vocalization, mothers of boys are more responsive than mothers of girls, this for every category of maternal behavior except for vocalization where mothers of girls are more responsive. This suggests two important considerations. First, and more general, addition across several classes of events may result in failure to find differences (in this case sex). Second, and more specifically, while mothers

TABLE 42-5

Directed Interactions for the Total Group (N = 25)

MOTHER BEHAVIOR

Band 1

INFANT BEHAVIOR	Touch A (M)	(%)	B (M)	(%)	C (M)	D (M)	Hold A (M)	(%)	B (M)	(%)	C (M)	D (M)	Vocalize A (M)	(%)	B (M)	(%)	C (M)	D (M)	Look A (M)	(%)	B (M)	(%)	C (M)	D (M)
Vocalize	5.16	83	1.08	17	19.68	7.72	5.60	88	.80	12	58.40	9.56	23.20	40	34.24	60	26.00	7.20	6.40	73	2.36	27	32.80	8.48
Movement	.16	12	1.12	88	13.96	7.68	.20	83	.04	17	31.60	6.04	2.40	18	10.88	82	12.92	6.44	.40	31	.88	69	17.68	6.72
Fret/Cry	.44	19	1.84	81	6.40	5.28	.24	18	1.12	82	18.12	5.60	2.16	10	18.68	90	9.84	4.96	.20	13	1.36	87	10.80	3.80
Play	0	0	.04	100	6.72	2.96	0	0	.04	100	14.96	3.04	1.40	38	2.32	62	13.40	5.92	.04	17	.20	83	13.40	4.24
Smile	3.88	97	.12	3	6.28	2.20	3.56	98	.08	2	9.76	1.76	11.24	82	2.40	18	10.84	2.76	4.96	98	.12	2	7.44	1.64

Band 2

INFANT BEHAVIOR	Smile A (M)	(%)	B (M)	(%)	C (M)	D (M)	Play A (M)	(%)	B (M)	(%)	C (M)	D (M)	Change A (M)	(%)	B (M)	(%)	C (M)	D (M)	Feed A (M)	(%)	B (M)	(%)	C (M)	D (M)
Vocalize	5.88	68	2.76	32	5.64	4.88	7.88	94	.48	6	18.24	3.96	.72	86	.12	14	7.80	1.92	.80	71	.32	29	23.24	3.28
Movement	.20	16	1.04	84	2.08	2.28	.24	55	.20	45	5.64	2.52	0	0	.08	67	3.12	.64	0	0	.20	100	4.36	.84
Fret/Cry	0	0	.20	100	.20	.88	0	0	.76	100	2.28	1.52	.04	33	0	0	3.12	.84	0	0	.28	100	5.76	1.96
Play	.04	10	.36	90	2.84	2.88	.04	50	.04	50	13.80	3.84	0	0	0	0	1.84	.40	0	0	0	0		
Smile	5.80	81	1.36	19	3.36	3.28	5.92	98	.12	2	8.40	1.84	.56	100	0	0	2.40	.64	.20	83	.04	17	1.28	.40

Band 3

INFANT BEHAVIOR	Rock A (M)	(%)	B (M)	(%)	C (M)	D (M)	Toy A (M)	(%)	B (M)	(%)	C (M)	D (M)	Vocalize to Others A (M)	(%)	B (M)	(%)	C (M)	D (M)	Read/TV A (M)	(%)	B (M)	(%)	C (M)	D (M)	Total Mean Per Cent A (%)	B (%)
Vocalize	.04	25	.12	75	.92	.44	.08	100	0	0	.04	.52	.12	11	1.00	89	10.76	7.08	.20	62	.12	38	6.52	1.40	56	44
Movement	0	0	.12	100	1.52	.52	.28	100	.04	0	.48	.52	0	8	0	92	7.36	5.32	0	0	0	0	10.88	2.96	21	79
Fret/Cry	0	0	.04	100	1.24	.36	.04	17	.20	83	.36	.84	0	0	.08	100	1.64	1.64	0	0	0	0	.24	.04	11	89
Play	0	0	0	0	0	0	0	0	.04	100	.32	.16	0	0	0	0	7.52	4.56	0	0	0	0	15.24	3.24	33	67
Smile	0	0	0	0	.12	0	0	0	0	0	0	.04	.04	100	0	0	.80	.72	0	0	.04	100	1.28	.16	89	11

TABLE 42–6

Directed Interactions by Sex (males n = 14, females n = 11)

MOTHER BEHAVIOR

For each mother behavior, columns A and B give Mean (M) and Per Cent (%); columns C and D give Mean (M) only.

Part 1 — Touch, Hold, Vocalize, Look

INFANT BEHAVIOR		Touch A M	A %	Touch B M	B %	Touch C M	Touch D M	Hold A M	A %	Hold B M	B %	Hold C M	Hold D M	Vocalize A M	A %	Vocalize B M	B %	Vocalize C M	Vocalize D M	Look A M	A %	Look B M	B %	Look C M	Look D M
Vocalize	Boy	4.07	73	1.50	27	19.64	9.29	3.64	74	1.29	26	65.79	11.36	18.43	36	32.07	64	24.86	8.93	4.79	63	2.86	37	25.86	8.00
	Girl	6.55	92	.55	8	19.73	5.73	8.09	98	.18	2	49.00	7.27	29.27	44	37.00	56	27.45	5.00	8.45	83	1.73	17	41.64	9.09
Movement	Boy	.14	9	1.43	91	13.36	8.14	.14	100	0	0	35.93	7.07	2.57	18	11.50	82	9.21	6.29	.50	27	1.36	73	9.86	6.21
	Girl	.18	20	.73	80	14.73	7.09	.27	75	.09	25	26.09	4.73	2.18	18	10.09	82	17.64	6.64	.27	50	.27	50	27.64	7.36
Fret/Cry	Boy	.29	16	1.50	84	4.93	5.00	.14	12	1.00	88	17.64	5.14	1.93	10	16.86	90	17.64	4.29	.14	8	1.71	92	7.86	3.07
	Girl	.64	22	2.27	78	8.27	5.64	.36	22	1.27	78	18.73	6.18	2.45	10	21.00	90	10.73	5.89	.27	23	.91	77	14.55	4.75
Play	Boy	0	0	.07	100	6.07	2.79	0	0	.09	100	23.50	4.79	1.71	36	3.00	64	14.14	7.07	0	0	.36	100	14.14	4.79
	Girl	0	0	0	0	7.55	3.18	0		0		4.09	.82	1.00	41	1.45	59	12.45	4.45	.09	100	0		12.45	3.55
Smile	Boy	3.79	100	0	0	5.71	2.00	2.57	100	.09	0	11.21	1.93	9.79	77	2.86	23	10.79	2.57	3.86	98	.07	2	6.57	1.36
	Girl	4.00	94	.27	6	7.00	2.45	4.82	96	.18	4	7.91	1.55	13.09	88	1.82	12	10.91	3.00	6.36	97	.18	3	8.55	2.00

Part 2 — Smile, Play, Change, Feed

INFANT BEHAVIOR		Smile A M	A %	Smile B M	B %	Smile C M	Smile D M	Play A M	A %	Play B M	B %	Play C M	Play D M	Change A M	A %	Change B M	B %	Change C M	Change D M	Feed A M	A %	Feed B M	B %	Feed C M	Feed D M
Vocalize	Boy	4.64	62	2.86	38	5.71	5.43	5.71	91	.57	9	19.71	4.36	.93	82	.21	18	11.00	2.21	.57	50	.57	50	21.86	3.21
	Girl	7.45	74	2.64	26	5.55	4.18	10.64	97	.36	3	16.36	3.45	.45	100	0	0	3.73	1.55	1.09	100	0	0	25.00	3.36
Movement	Boy	.21	20	.86	80	1.21	1.93	.07	25	.21	75	4.07	1.93	0		0		4.43	.79	0		.21	100	5.00	1.07
	Girl	.18	12	1.27	88	3.18	2.73	.45	71	.18	29	7.64	3.27	0		0		1.45	.45	0		.18	100	3.55	.55
Fret/Cry	Boy	0	0	.14	100	.07	.21	0	0	.43	100	1.86	1.71	.07	33	.14	67	2.64	1.00	0		.21	100	4.14	1.29
	Girl	0	0	.27	100	.36	1.73	0	0	1.18	100	2.82	1.27	0		0		3.73	.64	0		.36	100	7.82	2.82
Play	Boy	0	0	.21	100	3.07	3.00	0	0	.07	100	16.07	4.64	0		0		4.18	.91	0		0		0	0
	Girl	.09	14	.55	86	2.55	2.73	.09	100	0	0	10.91	2.82	0		0		3.00	.79	0		0		0	0
Smile	Boy	4.86	82	1.07	18	3.14	3.86	5.00	99	.07	1	8.64	1.93	.64	100	0		4.18	.91	.07		.09	20	1.36	.36
	Girl	7.00	72	2.73	28	3.64	2.55	7.09	98	.18	2	8.09	2.73	.45	100	0		1.64	.45	.36	80	.09		1.18	.45

Part 3 — Rock, Toy, Vocalize to Others, Read/TV, Total Mean Per Cent

INFANT BEHAVIOR		Rock A M	A %	Rock B M	B %	Rock C M	Rock D M	Toy A M	A %	Toy B M	B %	Toy C M	Toy D M	Voc. to Others A M	A %	Voc. to Others B M	B %	Voc. to Others C M	Voc. to Others D M	Read/TV A M	A %	Read/TV B M	B %	Read/TV C M	Read/TV D M	Total Mean Per Cent A %	Total Mean Per Cent B %
Vocalize	Boy	.07	25	.21	75	.93	.43	.14	100	0	0	0	.21	0		1.29	100	0		.29	67	.14	33	13.64	8.64	50	50
	Girl	0	0	0	0	.91	.45	0		0		.09	.91	.27	30	.64	70	.09	.09	.09	50	.09	50	7.09	5.09	63	37
Movement	Boy	0		.21	100	2.71	.71	.43	19	.29	81	.29	.29	0		0		.29	.29	0		0		6.93	5.29	20	80
	Girl	0		0	100	3.18	.27	.09	100	.07		.73	.82	0		0		.73	.82	0		0		19.09	5.36	22	78
Fret/Cry	Boy	0		.07	100	.07	.57	.07	19	.29	81	.21	.79	0		.14	100	.21	.21	0		0		1.00	1.64	11	89
	Girl	0		0		2.21	.09	0	14	.09	86	.55	.91	0		0		.55	.55	0		0		2.45	1.64	12	88
Play	Boy	0		0		0	0	0	11	.07	89	.55	.91	0		0		.57	.29	0		0		7.79	4.57	31	69
	Girl	0		0		0	0	0		.07		.57	.29	0		0		0		0		0		7.18	4.55	38	62
Smile	Boy	0		0		.21	.09	0	100	0		0	0	0	100	.07		0		0		.07	100	1.21	.71	88	12
	Girl	0		0		0	0	0		0		0	0	0		0		0		0		0		.27	.73	89	11

are as responsive to vocalization in boys as in girls—perhaps even more so—it cannot be generalized to every behavior. In fact, mothers vocalize *more* to girls' than to boys' vocalizing.

For infant movement, mothers of boys tend to be more responsive than mothers of girls except for maternal smiling where the reverse is true. Infant play shows similar results, more maternal response for boys than girls. An infant's fret/cry produces the opposite trend; in general mothers of girls are more responsive to a girl's fret/cry than mothers of boys to a boy's fret/cry; the only category where this fails to hold is maternal look. Likewise, girls' smile produced more maternal response than boys'. Again a complex interaction of maternal response-infant behavior and sex of the infant is apparent. For both affect behaviors—fret/cry and smile—mothers of girls are more responsive than mothers of boys. For the other infant behaviors the reverse is true.

The analyses so far are just a part of the complexity one encounters when a truly interactive study is undertaken. Before trying to summarize the results and their relationship to the issue of state, two further analyses will be presented.

Density Measures. Observation of maternal-infant interaction often reveals that for any particular infant (or maternal) behavior the number of different maternal (or infant) behavior associations vary. Specifically, a density measure is designed to ask what types of infant behaviors are most likely to be associated with more different maternal responses. It is in fact a ratio score of total simultaneous interaction scores over the number of infant behaviors. Thus a score of one or less means that maternal responses associated with the particular infant behavior occur less often than the occurrence of the specific infant behavior. Scores greater than one indicate increased density. Remember that one or more maternal behaviors are possible for each infant behavior.

The group data are unequivocal; infant smiling has the most dense associated maternal behavior, with little mean difference between boys and girls. Like most interactive measures, however, there is great individual variability, 1.27 to 5.00 different behaviors for boys and 0.83 to 4.70 for girls. Infant vocalization, movement, and fret/cry have the next most dense response and finally infant play and noise the least. In each case individual density scores vary widely. In fact an average density score over all the infant behaviors ranges from 0.88 to 3.40 for boys and 0.86 to 4.60 for girls. The analysis and its interpretation are made somewhat confusing because some of these infant behaviors are characteristically elicitors of maternal behavior while some are responses to maternal behavior. In the case of fret/cry, movement, play and noise—all elicitors of maternal behavior—the different density scores reflect different amounts of maternal response density whereas for infant vocalization and smile—both responses to maternal behavior—these different density scores reflect different amounts of maternal eliciting density. The difference between vocalization and smile suggests that mothers exhibit more behaviors in order to get their infants to smile than to vocalize. The difference between infant movement and fret/cry and play and noise indicate that movement and fret/cry produce greater density of response than play and noise. This makes some sense when it is considered that movement and fret/cry are associated with discomfort whereas play and noise are not. That is, mothers are more responsive—in terms of density—to their infants' discomfort.

Sequences and Other Chaining Analyses. To attempt to go into an extensive discussion of the

TABLE 42–7
Density Indexes

	Total Group (N = 32)	Boys	Girls
Infant Voc.	1.62	1.63	1.61
Infant Mov.	1.63	1.97	1.20
Infant Fret	1.62	1.64	1.60
Infant Play	.95	1.14	.73
Infant Noise	.65	.72	.56
Infant Smile	2.78	2.77	2.79

various sequence and chaining analyses is too complex for the present report. Suffice it to say that there are a variety of mathematical operations which are capable of dealing with sequential data. For example, it is possible to categorize the vocalization data into no one vocalizes, infant vocalizes alone, mother vocalizes alone to infant, mother vocalizes to some other, mother and infant both vocalize, and mother vocalizes to some other and infant vocalizes. It is then possible to assign one of these categories for each of the 720 10-second units. Using this procedure one could apply a Markovian model to the data and generate such response parameters as category run, e.g., the number of consecutive 10-second units of a particular category. In a general sense this type of analysis enables one to determine the conditional probabilities of the next 10-second unit knowing what is occurring during the present 10-second unit. Individual differences in these parameters can be determined. Markovian models have special appeal to our definition of state since they deal with current state (interaction) in time t as a probability of state in $t - 1$, thus making state the fluid and dependent interaction it is believed to be.[8]

Discussion

Since two interrelated but separate issues have been raised, the nature of the paper predicates a broad discussion. The first issue deals with the more theoretical construct "state," while the second is concerned mostly with methodological problems, namely, the measurement of interactive processes. Concurrently data are presented in an attempt to examine empirically the interactive behavior of 12-week-old infants and their caretakers. It is probably more profitable to deal with each of the two issues separately.

Definition of many psychological variables, even when attempted, is often unsatisfactory. While taxonomy is valuable, periodic attempts at definition are useful if only to demonstrate

that the concept under study is complex and in some cases far from clear in meaning. The concept of state is no exception to this rule. The examination of the current usage and definition of the term leads one to conclude that state is a widely used concept varying in meaning—not to mention measurement. It has been considered a continuum of behavior usually along an arousal dimension and yet examined as discrete categories. It has also been considered a condition of the organism (levels of consciousness being one such condition), yet little systematic investigation of self-report has been undertaken. A notable exception is the recent work on alpha conditioning in which Ss report their own consciousness level (Kamiya, 1969).

In terms of the common definition most of us would agree that state is a condition of the organism. However, the notion of condition is most general. "I'm in a state," implies some affect-emotional dimension; "I'm ready," implies some alerting dimension while, "I'm tired" implies some wake-sleep continuum. Each, however, refers to the organism's state or condition and suggests that state has wide dimensions. The S's condition also informs us of how the organism is or will be behaving, although the correspondence between the two—condition and behavior—may be weak and inference from one to the other difficult. It is important to note that Johnson (1970) in his presidential address before the Society for Psychophysiological Research entitled "A Psychophysiology for All States" cautioned his audience that condition must *first* be known before the significance of behavior can be inferred.

While state implies organism condition it must also be considered that the S's state is not some static and basic genotypic condition. At no point is an organism's condition not interacting with and being altered by environment. In fact a better term than state or condition may be organism status, for status implies just that interactive relationship which has been suggested. For example the search for genotypic temperament differences among infants may be futile, not because there are no individual differences in temperament but

[8] I am most indebted to Roy Freedle for bringing this use of a Markovian model to my attention.

because the important individual differences are in the interaction of temperament with environment. One infant is not more hyperactive than another; he is more active under one environmental level—high stimulation—but not another. The analysis is even more complex: that is, not only are the phenotypic behaviors a function of environmental interaction but what we at first consider to be genotypic are themselves affected by environmental interaction. I am referring specifically to neonatal differences in activity levels which Sontag (1966) has related to maternal-environmental interactions.

To define state in terms of behavior-environmental interaction does broaden the concept. In this form any S behavior-environmental interaction is classified as state. Is this definition then too broad to be of value? We think not because it forces those of us who construct models of human behavior to remember that most, if not all, human behavior is interactive.

This aspect of our discussion leads directly to the next: the use of interactive analyses. The analyses of interaction between condition and environment have been limited to infant and caretaker (mother) interactions. This is, of course, not a requirement of the model. Indeed the mother as environment is a very special case of environment because of several important characteristics. First, to varying degrees, she is responsive. Second, she is both constant and variable. She can respond consistently to her infant's vocalization with a vocalization and yet these need not be the same vocalizations. These qualities are most important for the emergence of schemata and the development of permanence and constancy over perceptual variance. And third, she is usually the provider of all the infant's biological needs. These and more make the infant's mother a unique aspect of the environment. The first two qualities, however, have special environmental implication. For example, could machines be constructed and programmed to function as well as the mother? Perhaps it would be possible but consideration soon reveals an almost total lack of information on normative or individual differences in mother-infant interactions. Even if enough were known about the occurrence of an infant's behavior repertoire, almost nothing is known about the nature and frequency of the mother's responses to the infant's behavior. Moreover, simple observation of mother-infant interaction reveals that the mother is often the initiator of behavioral sequences rather than solely a respondent to infant initiated behaviors. The dimensions of these various interactions are immense! Some of them have been suggested within this paper.

The difficulty of any interactive approach can be easily seen in the paucity of information on mother-infant interactions. There are almost no studies which deal with the interaction itself. Most often the mother's behavior is counted as is the infant's behavior, and in that they occurred at the same time, interaction is assumed. The power of interaction analyses are for the most part lost under this strategy.

The problems of interactive study present themselves in several areas; first, interaction is difficult to observe; second, the dimensions of interactive behavior are legion—the examples given within this paper are far from exhaustive—and, third, the statistics for handling individual differences are not always available.

The observation problems are many, not the least of which is the effect of observation itself. Putting aside this problem, it is extremely difficult to determine which actor initiates what and whether one behavior is indeed a response to another. For example, behavior which is assumed to be initiative can in fact be nothing more than background noise unrelated to an occurrence of the other actor's behavior. A mother singing to her child can be background while a brief and slight position change can be the "real" initiator of the infant's vocalization. Still another problem is the inference from behavior, namely the assumption that since a mother's vocalization precedes that of her infant, the mother's behavior is an elicitor of the infant's or that the infant's behavior is a reinforcer of the mother's or both. The notions of intentionality and causality can be avoided, but to do so often involves searching for elaborate and confusing phraseology. Our constructs are insufficient at this point to carry the meaning we often wish to imply.

Another class of issues is the various and seemingly unlimited different analyses of interaction and the statistical handling of them since they are often not independent but nested concepts. The development and use of mathematical models such as a Markovian procedure (Freedle & Lewis, 1971) is an exciting possibility for handling some of these data. In the body of this paper some of these different analyses are presented and in a recent study by Lusk and Lewis (1971) some further types have been explored. Unfortunately, the exploration of many of these analyses is still in the descriptive stage and must await further refinement and statistical elaboration. We consider the present paper as a first attempt at coming to grips with this problem.

The results of the empirical work bear on the theoretical issue of state as well as provide information on individual differences in state, in part as a consequence of the sex of the infant. It is apparent that there are large and interesting differences among the mother-infant dyads in interactive behavior. In the simplest analysis, the amount of interaction varied between 28 to 75% of the total observation time, a difference of approximately three times across different dyads. These individual differences can be seen on every level of analysis. Of particular import is the simultaneous analysis of behavior wherein it was demonstrated that there were large differences in environmental response to the same infant behavior. For example, mothers' behaviors tended to be quite different toward infant movement. For some infants— usually girls—infant movement was associated with responses of vocalization or looking whereas the same behavior in others—more often boys—was associated with touching and holding. In general, the same infant condition across the sexes was associated with more distal behavior for girls and more proximal behavior for boys. Thus for one child infant-vocalization-maternal-vocalization was com-

mon whereas for another infant-vocalization-maternal-hold was likely. Recall the model of state; it was defined as the behavior-environment interaction. In this case of vocalization, different awake states are evident: vocalize-vocalize versus vocalize-hold, this when infant behavior (vocalize) was constant. That these different waking states are sex-related may account for sex differences in other areas of behavior—such as language acquisition, for example—and is beyond the scope of this paper. It is important to notice that individual differences in the waking state are possible under the present working definition, even though the two infants are doing the same thing. Moreover, the means and degree to which the difference in environmental responsivity-infant condition affects subsequent infant condition (the likelihood to vocalize again) remains open to speculation. Within the present theoretical framework, certain states increase that likelihood. The answers await empirical verification.

In general one large source of individual variance in interaction could be accounted for by the sex of the infant. While there were little differences between the sexes in frequency of behavior, consistent differences were found in the maternal response toward the child as a function of its sex. To begin with, the frequency of maternal behavior toward the child showed sex differences similar to those described earlier. Mothers of boys showed significantly more proximal behavior than mothers of girls, whereas mothers of girls showed more distal behavior than mothers of boys. These results are in agreement with those reported by Moss (1967) for infants of the same age. Not only do the frequency measures show these differences but they appear in most of the interactive data as well. The various measures indicate several sex-related phenomena. For example, the interaction betwen mother and infant as a function of the sex of the infant does not exist uniformly across all infant behavior. In fact, the data suggest that for affect behaviors—fret/cry and smile—mothers of girls are more responsive than mothers of boys, whereas for the other infant behaviors the reverse is true. Even within an infant behavior the analysis is complicated. For infant vocalizations mothers of boys are more responsive than mothers of girls for all maternal behaviors *except* that of vocalization where mothers of girls are more responsive. Thus the interactions between infant and maternal behaviors as a function of the sex of the infant are not simple. This strongly suggests that a revision is needed in some of our notions of more or less maternal response. It is time to consider more fully the quality and type rather than quantity.

In the case of sex differences, the data from Moss and the present study as well as a longitudinal study by Lewis and Ban (1971) on mother-infant attachment all point to this problem. These data indicate that mothers of boys and girls do not necessarily differ in amounts of responsiveness but rather in the nature of that responsiveness: in the early months girls receive more distal stimulation than proximal whereas the reverse is true for boys. When these different behaviors are pooled as in the case of the total interaction unit analysis, sex differences are washed out.

As an aside, it is important to note that these two types of maternal response—proximal and distal—have differential developmental courses. The sex differences in distal behavior favoring girls continue through the first two years and remain rather constant in degree. The proximal response which initially favors boys diminishes differentially for the sexes so that by one year of age girls receive more proximal stimulation than boys. By two years, there are no sex differences. It is suspected that the proximal response diminishes faster to boys than girls because of the competing motive of autonomy which is stronger in mothers of boys than mothers of girls. This developmental course points up still another complexity in the study of interaction for it demonstrates the instability of maternal behavior over time—still another complication in the study of mother-infant interaction.

Summary of so long an argument is difficult. Briefly it has been proposed that state be defined in terms of an infant-environment interaction. In order to investigate state differences as well as individual differences in state it was necessary to explore and discuss various types of interactive processes and analyses. Having accomplished this task—no easy job— empirical data were presented which seemed to support the proposed model of state, namely that infant condition (behavior) alone was insufficient to describe state since often the same condition had widely different consequences which in turn should affect future infant conditions. The data also revealed individual differences as a function of the sex of the infant. These were discussed as an important source of individual variance.

REFERENCES

Duffy, E. *Activation and behavior*. New York: John Wiley & Sons, Inc., 1962.

Freedle, R. & Lewis, M. Application of Markov processes to the concept of state. Research Bulletin 71–34. Princeton, N.J.: Educational Testing Service, 1971.

Gewirtz, B. Levels of conceptual analysis in environment-infant interaction research. *Merrill-Palmer Quarterly,* 1969, Vol. 15, 7–41.

Goldberg, S. & Lewis, M. Play behavior in the year-old infant: Early sex differences. *Child Development,* 1969, Vol. 40, 21–31.

Hilgard, E. Altered states of awareness. *Journal of Nervous and Mental Disease,* 1969, Vol. 149, 68–79.

Hollingshead, A. *Two-factor index of social position*. New Haven, Conn. Author, 1957.

Johnson, L. A psychophysiology for all states. *Psychophysiology,* 1970, Vol. 6, 501–516.

Kamiya, J. Operant control of the EEF alpha rhythm and some of its reported effects on consciousness. In C. Tart (Ed.), *Altered states of consciousness*. New York: John Wiley & Sons, 1969.

Lacey, J. Somatic response patterning and stress: Some revisions of activation theory. In M. Appley & R. Trumbull (Eds.), *Psychological stress: Issues in research*. New York: Appleton-Century-Crofts, 1967.

Lewis, M. & Ban, P. Stability of attachment behavior: A transformational analysis. Paper presented at symposium entitled *Attachment: Studies in stability and change,* at the Society for Research in Child Development meeting, Minneapolis, April, 1971.

Lewis, M. & Goldberg, S. Perceptual-cognitive development in infancy: A generalized expectancy model as a function of the mother-infant interaction. *Merrill-Palmer Quarterly,* 1969, Vol. 15(1), 81–100.

Lusk, D. & Lewis, M. Mother-infant interaction and infant development among the Wolof of Senegal. *Human Development*, 1972, Vol. 15, 58–69.

Moss, H. Sex, age, and state as determinants of mother-infant interaction. *Merrill-Palmer Quarterly,* 1967, Vol. 13, 19–35.

Sontag, L. Implications of fetal behavior and environment for adult personalities. *Annual New York Academy of Sciences,* 1966, Vol. 134, 782–786.

Sontag, L. & Wallace, R. The movement response of the human fetus to sound stimuli. *Child Development,* 1935a, Vol. 6, 253–258.

Sontag, L. & Wallace, R. The effect of cigarette smoking during pregnancy on fetal heart rate. *American Journal of Obstetrics and Gynecology,* 1935b, Vol. 29, 77–82.

Sontag, L. & Wallace, R. Changes in the rate of human fetal heart in response to vibratory stimuli. *American Journal of Disturbed Children,* 1936, Vol. 51, 583–589.

Young, W., Groy, R., & Phoenix, C. Hormones and sexual behavior. *Science,* 1964, Vol. 143, 212–217.

43. PSYCHOSOCIAL DEVELOPMENT IN CROSS-CULTURAL PERSPECTIVE

A New Look at an Old Issue[1]

RUTH K. GOLDMAN

Subgroups from a sample of 65 pairs of youngsters, matched for sex, age, and intelligence, from Austria, Israel, Poland, and Yugoslavia, reared at home and in group-care settings, were compared in terms of their relative psychological development. A clinician/judge, using test protocols, and without knowing which member of each pair was family reared and which one group reared, was asked to assess each pair in regard to the relative psychosocial maturity. No significant differences in judged maturity were found between children raised at home and those from group-care settings in Austria, Israel (youth village), and Yugoslavia; whereas, in Poland, home-reared children were judged to be more mature with significantly greater frequency, and in Israel (kibbutz), group-reared children were judged more mature with significantly greater frequency. The hypothesis is supported that children reared in group-care settings are not necessarily retarded in their psychosocial development in comparison to family-reared children. They may, in fact, depending upon group-care philosophy and practice, as well as reasons for admission, surpass their home-reared counterparts in psychological maturity.

As early as the turn of the century, concern was expressed over the effects of institutionalization on normal children separated from their parents (Folks, 1896). Regardless of the child's age at separation, detrimental effects on psychosocial development, intelligence, and social competence were reported (Bowlby, 1952; Goldfarb, 1943; Spitz, 1945). From a general review of the literature, it appears that the characteristic American and British position briefly summarized was that group care is detrimental to the development of normal children. Within a decade, however, a rather extensive contradictory body of literature had developed in which quite different findings were reported (Ainsworth, 1962; Rabin, 1965; Yarrow, 1961).

[1]This study is based on materials from a project, Child Care in Cross-Cultural Perspective, supported by the National Institute of Mental Health, United States Public Health Service, Department of Health, Education, and Welfare (MH 01430), the Ford Foundation, and the Institute of International Studies, University of California, Berkeley. The author wishes to express her appreciation to E. William Moyles for his extensive help with data analysis.

From *Developmental Psychology*, 1971, 5, 411–419. Copyright 1971 by the American Psychological Association. Reprinted by permission of the author and publisher.

In a wide variety of group-care settings, both in this country (Edmiston & Baird, 1949; Hobbs, 1966) and abroad (Bronfenbrenner, 1967; Rabin, 1965; Spiro, 1958), circumstances were found that enhanced social competence and maturity. Further, the issue changed somewhat in character and became one not so much of separation from the mother and its impact on the child, as the quality of mothering provided the child, regardless of who provided the mothering. In fact, numerous studies were reported of children reared in their own homes, under conditions of poverty and disorganization, which resulted in cognitive and emotional impairment of the type usually attributed to institutional care in the past (Deutsch, Katz, & Jensen, 1968; Passow, Goldberg, & Tanenbaum, 1967). More recent findings make clear the extent to which the primary role of mothering is shared by siblings and peers, particularly among lower-class families (Ausubel & Ausubel, 1963), a finding which clearly emphasizes one of the assets of group-rearing methods. Given the current concern over the generational effects of poverty (Harrington, 1962), and the cumulative evidence pointing to possible advantages of group rearing, one should be ready to take a new look at the effects of child rearing in group-care settings.

In this study, adolescents reared in four different countries, under five rather different types of group settings, were compared with adolescents living at home. The hypothesis is that children reared within group-care institutions are equal in their level of psychological development to a matched sample of children raised by their own families. One approach in a series of related articles by Moyles and Wolins (1971) and Wolins (1969a, 1969b) is presented here.

Method

Procedure

A clinician/judge was given the test protocols (see Instruments) of 65 pairs of children living in Austria, Israel, Poland, and Yugoslavia. The children were paired and matched according to age, sex, and intelligence, with one member of each pair coming from a home situation and the other from a group-care setting. Although the judge (the author) knew the country of origin from which each pair came, the materials themselves were sufficiently disguised so that it

was impossible to tell which member of each pair came from the family setting and which one from the group setting. The judge was asked to describe and then assess the relative psychosocial maturity of each pair of adolescents, using the combined results of the test materials.

Assessment consisted of a two-step process: Each subject was described in terms of his psychological development. This information was then used to reach a decision about the comparative maturity of each pair of subjects. All judgments were relative. To round out the global description of each subject further, a rationally derived adjective checklist was also constructed. Salient adjectives for each subject were checked following the paragraph description.

Sample

The sample consisted of 65 matched pairs of adolescents and preadolescents selected from a larger sample of children reared at home and in group-care settings in Austria, Israel, Poland, and Yugoslavia (see Footnotes 1 and 2). In Israel, a fourth variable, ethnic origin, was added. Additionally, the family-reared child from Israel was matched with two group-care

TABLE 43–1
Home- and Group-Care Children Matched by Sex, Age, and Intelligence

| COUNTRY | NO. PAIRS | SEX | | AGE | | | | PERCENTILE SCORE | | | |
| | | | | RANGE | | M | | RANGE | | M | |
		M	F	Home	Group	Home	Group	Home	Group	Home	Group
Israel											
Kibbutz youth group	13	8	5	15.0–17.0	16.0–18.0	15.8	16.5	18–75	8–87	46.7	50.2
Youth village	13	8	5	15.0–17.0	15.0–17.5	15.8	15.9	18–75	29–84	46.7	52.8
Austria	16	9	7	12.5–14.5	13.0–15.0	13.7	13.9	10–90	10–90	50.6	49.6
Yugoslavia	15	6	9	13.0–18.0	12.5–17.5	15.1	15.1	3–75	4–75	24.6	24.1
Poland	8	3	5	12.5–14.5	12.5–14.5	13.3	13.7	6–93	10–87	64.1	59.3

Note.–Means and ranges for age and intelligence are comparable for both sexes and therefore are not reported separately. Intelligence was measured by the Raven Progressive Matrices test.

children, one from a kibbutz youth group and one from a youth village.

The Raven Progressive Matrices test (Raven, 1960) was used to match children for intelligence. The Raven is a nonverbal test and correlates favorably with standard measures of intelligence (Moyles & Wolins, 1971). Each pair was matched according to percentile score with a maximum deviation of five points allowed. Age varied up to 12 months within each pair. The means and ranges for subjects by age and intelligence are presented in Table 43–1.

The Austrian sample was selected from 65 children living in an institution (SOS Kinderdorf) and 67 living at home in the same small suburban middle-class community where the Kinderdorf is located. The group-care children were largely dependent or neglected wards of the welfare department, the majority of the children having entered by their sixth birthday. Twelve years was the upper limit for admission. The 16 children from the Kinderdorf had been in care from 4 to 10 years, with the majority of them having been in care for more than 6 years.

The Israeli sample of 26 triplets was chosen from 300 children living in a kibbutz, over 100 children in a youth village, and 100 living at home. The home and youth village children were both recent immigrants, and all three groups came from a predominantly lower-class background. The sample of 13 from the kibbutz stayed there between 2 and 4 years with a mean of 2.3 years: the 13 youth village children stayed in group care between 2 and 5 years with a mean of 2.8 years.

The Polish sample of 8 group-care children was selected from among 34 children living in an institution in Warsaw. They all came from disrupted lower-class families and ranged in age from 11 to 19 years. Here in the Warsaw institution, the children are usually admitted during the first years of elementary school and stay on until late adolescence, though some enter at an earlier age. The home sample of 8 was chosen from 49 children living at home in the same neighborhood as the institution. They attended the same schools and came from a lower socioeconomic background. The sample of 8 children stayed in the institution from 1 to 8 years with a mean of 4.8 years. Half of the

sample entered group care by age 6, the rest did so by age 10.

The Yugoslav sample of 15 was selected from four different institutions in or near Belgrade, and consisted of a few more than 100 children. Most were children from broken homes of a lower- or lower-middle-class background, who were placed in the institution anywhere from infancy into adolescence. The comparison home sample of 15 was chosen from 76 children living in the same neighborhoods as the institutions. Families were predominantly low or lower-middle class economically. The sample of 15 group-care children were in the institution from 6 to 13 years, with a mean of 9.3 years. Of all the samples, this group had been institutionalized for the longest period of time. Nine of the sample entered group care between their sixth and eighth birthdays; the remaining 6 entered before their fifth birthday.

In Austria, Poland, and Yugoslavia, there was a systematic attempt to select the children who had resided in group care for the longest period of time, thereby providing the soundest comparison with home residents. This was not possible in Israel, since children enter the youth groups after age 12. Though reasons for entering group care were not detailed, the sample is representative of the general range noted at intake.

Data about the home comparisons were sparse, apart from socioeconomic level and the three matching variables. Unfortunately, no information was available about such factors as number of siblings in the home and intactness or stability of the family that would have allowed for comparisons between home and group-care settings on the effects of peers.

Setting

The Austrian Kinderdorf is a large institution which functions as a self-sufficient village and is typically located in a suburban or rural setting. Children are divided into small familial units of about nine each. Both sexes of varying ages live in beautiful separate cottages with their individual *Mutti*. Institutional structure is modeled after that of the approximate family. Long-range objectives consist of integrating the child into lower-middle-class Catholic society. The Kinderdorf is open to the world and the child is encouraged to develop a sense of responsibility not only to his Kinderdorf family, but to the larger community as well. Children attend school extramurally and are indistinguishable from the local suburban children living in the natural homes.

The Israeli youth groups, both those of the village and kibbutz type, draw predominantly from new immigrants, often quite deprived socially and economically. Adolescents can not enter until they are 12 or 13 and stay from 2 to 5 years. In the kibbutz, they live with up to 40 other children of their own age and several *Madrichim* (teachers) as equals. In the philosophy underlying the group, the social restructuring of the adolescents is emphasized, as is their academic and occupational tutoring. The youth village has larger resident groups, ages of the members vary, and an adult who functions like a big brother is in charge. In contrast to the kibbutz youth group, the aim here is only to strengthen the academic and occupational skills of the adolescents and then encourage return to their homes.

The Polish institution is large and hospitallike in character. Uniforms are worn by both adults and children. Groups are segregated by sex and age, institutions frequently serving only one sex. Group activity and self-government are strongly emphasized: individual decisions are deemphasized. The goal of the staff is to promote maximum self-sufficiency and social utility. Group conduct and school achievement are used in evaluating a child's progress toward these goals. Communist and Catholic ideology prevail simultaneously, and affect both the institutional care and educational programs of the children.

The Yugoslav institutions are large, similar in structure to apartment houses, and geared to urban industrial life. Children of both sexes and varying ages live in groups of 16–18, together with an adult male or female. The relationship to the adult is more like that to an aunt or uncle, though these adults frequently are closer in age to that of an older brother or sister. Parents are not discouraged from visiting, but the attitudes toward them are quite negative. The staff of the institution strive to undo early damage, enhance development, and instill the Yugoslav version of socialism.

Instruments

Tests used were the following: the Raven Progressive Matrices Test, Thematic Apperception Test (TAT), Value Inventory, and the Sentence Completion Test. Since the Raven was also used in matching each pair for intelligence, it was a potentially confounding factor when included in the overall estimate of maturity for each pair of subjects. Therefore, judgments of relative maturity were compared with each subject's Raven score to assure that a slightly higher Raven for one member of a pair was not varying directly with a judgment of greater maturity for the same subject. The TAT cards administered were the following: 3BM, 4, 6BM, 7BM, 7GF, 8 BM, 13B, and 14. The children were given individual picture booklets and asked to write their stories with no time limits imposed. Both the Value Inventory and the Sentence Completion Test were constructed by the project staff (see Footnote 1) and are more fully described in Wolins (1969a). The Value Inventory consists of five factors: (*a*) other orientations, (*b*) achievement (controlled), (*c*) competitive achievement, (*d*) individualism, and (*e*) detachment. Youngsters' scores were compared to the norms for all youngsters in their own setting, their own ideal answers, and the adults most responsible for their care. (This instrument, however, was available only for the Austrian sample.) The Sentence Completion Test consists of 41 stems and was rationally constructed (Wolins, 1969b) to elicit basic value statements. It differs somewhat from the Value Inventory in that it is projective in nature and assesses somewhat different aspects of values.

All materials were administered to the child at one setting, and given to him in his native languages. The results were then translated into English and the clinician/judge made all judgements from the written, translated results of the tests.

TABLE 43–2
Adjectives Used to Describe Matched Samples in Austria, Israel, and Poland

ATTRIBUTE	Cognition	Egocentrism	Manifest Conflict	Social Conformity	Peer Relations — Same Sex	Peer Relations — Opposite Sex
POSITIVE	Creative Complex Organized	Insightful Optimistic Energetic	Stable Content Secure	Morally concerned Religiously involved Goal directed Idealistic	Cooperative Sharing Trusting Initiative Empathic	Sharing Mature
NEGATIVE	Shallow Stereotyped	Self-absorbed Pessimistic	Unstable Impulsive Hostile Insecure Fearful	Uncommitted Without ideals Rebellious	Competitive Cautious Timid Aggressive Withdrawn	Anxious Preoccupied

Approach: Theoretical Assumptions

The theoretical assumptions underlying the global judgements of relative maturity are derived from the work of Erik H. Erikson (1950), Anna Freud (1946, 1965), and Heinz Werner (1948). However, the most explicitly used formulations stem from Erikson, and in particular, from his theory of epigenesis.

Since the basis for a clinical judgment of comparative maturity cannot easily be made explicit, the concept of psychosocial maturity was divided into component parts. The intrapsychic, cognitive, and interpersonal aspects of psychological maturity seemed to be adequately described and differentiated by five subcategories. The five theoretically derived categories were: (a) cognition, (b) egocentrism, (c) manifest conflict, (d) social conformity, and (e) peer relationships (same and opposite sex). Additionally, a 40-item checklist, consisting of 20 positive and 20 negative items, was rationally derived to describe more fully the range of traits subsumed under each of the five theoretical categories. Also, the checklist served as a potential source for cues related to the global decisions, was a means of determining whether specific aspects of maturity were variously associated with the different countries, and was a means of partially checking the consistency of the global ratings. The 40 adjectives are presented in Table 43–2.

Rating Strategy

Test protocols were read in the same order. Each subject was briefly described in terms of the five component categories of psychosocial maturity. Occasionally, test data were scant and somwhat inconsistent, and therefore difficult to interpret. When this occurred, the TAT stories were given the most weight, since they contained the most complete source of information and were therefore regarded as most reliable. Following the description, all salient adjectives were checked for each subject.

The second subject of the pair was then similarly reviewed and a decision was reached concerning the comparative maturity of each member of the pair. Each pair of protocols was later reread and independently rated to determine agreement with the earlier judgment. If there was a discrepancy, the test results were again reviewed and a final decision made.

In addition, a second rater was given a random sample of 25 pairs of protocols from the Israeli, Austrian, and Polish samples and instructed to judge relative maturity by following the same rating strategy. Overall agreement with the first rater was 79%; agreement for one country (Austria, 13 pairs) was 92%. Using a binomial test, these values were sugnificant at the .02 and .001 level, respectively.

Whenever feasible, the clinician's estimate of maturity was also compared with that of significant adults residing in the institution. Though the comparisons were few in number, they were in general agreement.

Process of Clinical Judgment

In order to assess comparative maturity, distinguishing characteristics in each of the five subcategories of psychosocial development were delineated. Examples follow of the way in which each category was used in the overall descriptions.

Cognition. This category almost exclusively includes Werner's formulations of intellectual development. It is assumed that increasing cognitive development (or maturity) augments the ability to think flexibly, comprehensively, and analytically. Responses from mature subjects should be more complex, imaginative, and optimistic. Conversely, the responses of less mature subjects are likely to be more stereotyped, rigid, and/or labile. The following are examples of the cognition category descriptions:

[Immature subject] He has limited intellectual ability and finds it difficult to function well in many situations. His ideas are relatively simple, unformed, and stereotyped in their content. In fact, the nature of his responses is such that it is difficult to understand them; they are both scant and unclear. . . .

[Mature subject] A highly intelligent girl with a quick, perceptive, analytic style of cognition. She is extremely aware of and concerned about her interactions with others and highly desirous of meeting all the expectations that she believes people have of her. . . .

Egocentrism. Categories 2 and 3, egocentrism and manifest conflict are based on the conceptualizations of Anna Freud and Erikson; however, the assumptions underlying these categories rest heavily on Freud's exposition of the adolescent defensive structure. According to Freud's conceptions of ego development within adolescence, the defensive structure can vary widely in the degree of adaptiveness and flexibility. A relatively healthy adolescent should have ample amounts of energy freely available to him, optimism should be a prevalent characteristic, and a relative sense of security and stability should predominate. The following are examples of the egocentrism category descriptions:

[Immature subject] Although a bright adolescent, this boy lacks confidence in his intellectual abilities, a trait that probably results in underachieving behavior both scholastically and socially. He is quite self-absorbed at the present time but not introspective about his problems. He prefers not to compete with others, anticipating failure on his part. . . .

[Mature subject] This is a highly compassionate, nurturant, optimistic child. She accepts the world around her very well, though she is considerably more idealistic than her peers. She is an extremely well adapted, mature person with considerable capacity to give of herself emotionally. . . .

Manifest Conflict. The third category is characterized by the presence of stability, flexibility, and security in the mature adolescent or by constriction, hostility, fearfulness, and suspicion in the psychologically immature one. Both the egocentrism and manifest conflict categories were developed primarily to describe the strengths and weaknesses of a subject's defensive structure. The underlying assumption is that the psychosocially less mature adolescent has less adequate defenses. The following are examples of the manifest conflict category:

[Immature subject] This bright and imaginative adolescent is filled with many feelings of violence, anger, and pessimism. Although he conforms in his outward behavior to the accepted values of his group, he is torn inwardly. The only expression of his negative fantasies comes out in his feelings of suspicion and distrust of others. . . .

[Mature subject] This seems to be an optimistic adolescent who is comfortable with his aggressive impulses and able to manage them through socially acceptable forms of competition. His intellectual ability is average, but his need to achieve and be socially recognized is unusually strong. . . .

Social Conformity. Unlike egocentrism and manifest conflict, which were more rooted in intrapsychic development, the social conformity and peer relationship categories relate directly to sociopsychological functioning. The category of social conformity was developed in order to evaluate the following factors: personal commitment, moral concerns, religious beliefs, capacity for work, and acceptance of and identification with a relevant adult. The following are examples for social conformity:

[Immature subject] This is a bright adolescent whose level of functioning appears to belie his age, as well as his intellect. There is a naiveté and lack of involvement with his environment that is characteristic of a younger and less intelligent child. Although he is deeply concerned about possessing adequate moral standards and has clear professional future aspirations, a quality of personal constriction pervades his attitudes. . . .

[Mature subject] He is a moral, independent young man, concerned with honesty and justice. He is materialistically oriented, looking toward the future to provide him with an opportunity to achieve his goals. . . .

Relationship with Peers (Same and Opposite Sex). This category was designed to assess the ability to relate well to others of the same age, to share, trust, and cooperate, to tolerate intimacy, and to exercise initiative. The range of functioning is broad. A subject may have good initiative but little trust, considerable empathy but little ability to function well in a group of peers. Examples follow:

[Immature subject] He is restricted by suspicions and mistrust toward others. Although it is difficult to know what his attitudes are toward his own family, his relationships with friends of both sexes are poor. Concepts of sharing and cooperation, as well as of competition, are quite alien to him, although he accepts the more general social values of his community. . . .

[Mature subject] She is concerned with giving to others, sharing, and cooperating. She feels free to ask for help when she needs it and seems to have accepted a socially mature role with ease. Her responses both to her peers and to her parents seem to indicate that she has solved her adolescent role conflict well. . . .

Results and Discussion

There were no significant differences in rated maturity when group-care children in Austria, Yugoslavia, and Israel (youth village) were contrasted with children living at home. However, home- and group-reared children from Poland and Israel (kibbutz) did differ significantly in their rated maturity level. In Israel, the kibbutz youth-group children were judged more mature than their family-reared counterparts. In Poland, the converse was true—the home-reared children were judged more mature than residents of the institution (Table 43–3).

Adjective Descriptions[2]

Though adjective description data were not independent of the global maturity ratings, several separate analyses were undertaken in order to gain further insight into the traits underlying comparative maturity. t tests were computed by country to compare the total number of adjectives checked, according to maturity level, sex, and setting. No significant differences were found between any of the comparisons. Positive and negative adjectives were then separated by country and rank ordered across the five categories of psychosocial development for all subjects according to maturity level and setting. Mann-Whitney U tests were calculated for the significance of the difference between the median number of adjectives checked. Positive adjectives were checked significantly more often for the more mature subjects in all countries; negative adjectives were checked significantly more often for less mature subjects in Austria and Israel (kibbutz). Though no additional quantitative information was gained from the adjective analyses, consistency between the global and trait ratings of maturity was confirmed. Additionally, one can conclude from these results that the strategy for rating maturity was impartially applied across all categories in all countries.

[2]Data for descriptive adjectives were not available for Yugoslav subjects.

TABLE 43–3
Judgments of Maturity by Setting and Sex Within Country

COUNTRY	NO. PAIRS	MORE MATURE					
		HOME CARE			GROUP CARE		
		Total	M	F	Total	M	F
Israel							
Kibbutz youth	13	2***			11***		
			1	1		6	5
Youth village	13	6			7		
			6**	0**		2	5
Austria	16	9			7		
			6	3		3	4
Yugoslavia	15	5			10		
			2	3		7	3
Poland	8	7*			1*		
			3	4		0	1

Note.—Probabilities for a two-tailed binomial test (Siegel, 1956) were calculated for home- and group-care comparisons. Fisher exact tests were calculated for sex and maturity differences by setting (Siegel, 1956).
*p < .07.
**p < .05.
***p < .02.

Global Rating of Maturity

Mature adolescents in all the countries can be characterized by their greater sense of goal orientation and moral awareness. Their protocols were filled with a greater sense of optimism; they seemed uniformly to be more complex, insightful, differentiated, and more energetic. The protocols of less mature adolescents were characterized by a greater sense of egocentrism. Feelings of conflict and self-doubt were more frequently expressed. Peer relations were more often marked by a lack of trust and empathy. In short, their sense of personal objectives and social consciousness was more diffuse.

The qualities of the mature adolescents in Austria and Israel are the most easily delineated, though they are distinctively different from one another. In Israel, the more mature adolescent has a strongly questioning attitude toward authority; in Austria, the more mature adolescent is exceptionally respectful of authority. Both groups hold deep religious convictions, but of a very different character. In Austria, the Christian ethic of hard work and good deeds is rigorously espoused, individual salvation is hoped for, and God is prayed to as a divine being. In Israel, there is no sense of God as a divine being, but instead, concern is expressed for the welfare of others, ethical precepts are fervently held, and a strong sense of idealism prevails. Personal objectives for the more mature Austrian are modest, materialistic, and highly individual in character. For the Israeli, personal objectives are defined in relation to the needs of the group, are concrete in nature, but not materialistic in terms of personal reward.

The mature adolescents in Poland and Yugoslavia are more difficult to describe. In both samples, aspirations are defined in relation to group needs, but differently from those of the Israelis. In Yugoslavia, the more mature adolescents are basically concerned with a realistic assessment of what they can actually attain in the larger society. For the Yugoslavs, sharing is highly valued, materialism and competition downgraded, while future goals are personal, simple in nature, vocationally based, but not idealistic. The more mature Poles, unlike the Yugoslavs, seem to retain a greater spirit of individual competition. The less mature Poles are easier to describe since the prevailing tenor of their protocols was one of bitterness and despair, misery, and bleakness. Of all the protocols, theirs were the most sparse, troubled, and filled with a desire to escape reality.

Ratings of relative maturity for each pair of subjects were further analyzed to determine whether there were sex difference trends. Fisher exact tests were calculated for each country by sex and maturity rating within each setting (Table 43–3). With the exception of the Israeli youth village, no significant differences were found relating sex to maturity level in any of the countries. In the youth village all the home subjects judged to be more mature—were males. A possible explanation might lie in the direction of different cultural expectations associated with ethnic origin. However, in Israel this was a matching variable. The general conclusion, excepting the youth village, is that there were no sex-related differences favoring more mature psychological development in either home or group-care settings in any of the countries studied.

Length of stay and relative maturity level were compared for home- and group-care children in Austria, Yugoslavia, and the youth village in Israel. Analyses were not undertaken for either the Polish or the kibbutz youth group samples since maturity was significantly related to home setting in the former case and to group care in the latter. Length of stay in group care was not significantly related to relative maturity in Austria, Yugoslavia, or the youth village in Israel. Long-term residents were indistinguishable from shorter term residents in their psychosocial development. Further, in Austria, where 80% of the children entered care by age 6, the hypothesis is supported that early entrance to group care is not necessarily detrimental to psychological development. The Yugoslav sample provides the strongest argument for this point of view since the children entered care at even earlier ages but were still judged as mature

psychologically as the later entrants. These findings are confirmed by Wolin's (1969a) data for long) and short-term residents in Austrian and Yugoslav institutions. Information from the institutional caretakers of the children further substantiate these results. Without more detailed data, one cannot conclusively rule out the possibility that the later admissions were more impaired or that the earlier admissions were all more emotionally stable. However, neither of these explanations is supported by the available intake data.

Though institutional practices and ideology varied considerably among the five settings studied, in all but one comparison (Poland), group-care subjects were judged at least equal in psychological maturity to home-reared children. At least two factors require further discussion in interpreting this finding. Most importantly, the Polish institution differed from all the others in not providing as cohesive family or peer-group support. Unlike the other institutions, children were segregated by sex and age, and were subject to a more impersonal and formal type of care. Therefore, one can conclude that the relative immaturity of the Poles reared in group care is related, in part, to this aspect of institutional practice. On the other hand, though no psychological data were available which indicated level of impairment prior to group-care entry, reasons stated for admission, such as abandonment, neglect, and parental abuse, suggest a high level of initial trauma. By comparison, intake data from Austria, Yugoslavia, and Israel include reasons for admission which suggest far less psychological deprivation. For example, in Austria and Yugoslavia, divorce and/or death of one or both parents was a frequent cause for admission, and in Israel, socioeconomic circumstances were the main factor. Though this information is more suggestive than conclusive, greater initial deprivation may be another factor associated with lower maturity for the Polish children in group settings.

Of the five settings studied, only in Israel (kibbutz) were group-care adolescents judged more mature than their home-reared controls. In comparison to the other institutions, the sample entered group-care later, and came from home environments which appeared less emotionally disruptive. These circumstances, coupled with the highly idealistic philosophy and strongly unified groupcare practices of the kibbutz youth group, may account for the greater maturity of these adolescents. The fact that children reared in the youth village achieve only parity with their home-reared comparisons requires further discussion. Factors such as the greater initial maturity of the kibbutz members, or the attrition of the less mature ones, were considered in accounting for the differences. Wolin's (1969a) test results, however, do not support either of these explanations. A more feasible interpretation may be found in the differences of philosophy and practice associated with each setting. While kibbutz *Madrachim* strive for a broad social integration of the adolescents, the youth village leaders have more limited occupational and educational objectives.

REFERENCES

Ainsworth, M. D. *Deprivation of maternal care: A reassessment of its effects*. Geneva: World Health Organization, 1962.

Ausubel, D. P., & Ausubel, P. Ego development among segregated Negro children. In A. H. Passow (Ed.), *Education in depressed areas*. New York: Columbia University Press, 1963.

Bowlby, J. *Maternal care and mental health*. (2nd ed.; Monograph Series, No. 2) Geneva: World Health Organization, 1952.

Bronfenbrenner, U. Response to pressure from peers versus adults among Soviet and American school children. *International Journal of Psychology*, 1967, *2*, 199–207.

Deutsch, M., Katz, I., & Jensen, A. R. (Eds.) *Social class, race, and psychological development*. New York: Holt, Rinehart & Winston, 1968.

Edmiston, R. W., & Baird, F. Adjustment of orphanage children. *Journal of Educational Psychology*, 1949, *40*, 482–488.

Erikson, E. H. *Childhood and society*. New York: Norton, 1950.

Folks, H. Why should dependent children be reared in families rather than in institutions? *Charities Review*, 1896, *5*, 140–145.

Freud, A. *The ego and the mechanisms of defense*. New York: International Universities Press, 1946.

Freud, A. *Normality and pathology in childhood: Assessments of development*. New York: International Universities Press, 1965.

Goldfarb, W. The effects of early institutional care on adolescent personality. *Child Development*, 1943, *14*, 213–223.

Harrington, M. *The other America: Poverty in the United States*. New York: Macmillan, 1962.

Hobbs, N. Helping disturbed children. *American Psychologist*, 1966, *21*, 1105–1115.

Moyles, E. W., & Wolins, M. Group care and intellectual development. *Developmental Psychology*, 1971, *4*, 370–380.

Passow, A. H., Goldberg, M., & Tannenbaum, A. J. (Eds.) *Education of the disadvantaged*. New York: Holt, Rinehart & Winston, 1967.

Rabin, A. I. *Growing up in the kibbutz*. New York: Springer, 1965.

Raven, J. C. *Guide to the Standard Progressive Matrices (Sets A, B, C, D, & E.)*. London: Lewis, 1960.

Siegel, S. *Non-parametric statistics*. New York: McGraw-Hill, 1956.

Spiro, M. E. *Children of the kibbutz*. Cambridge: Harvard University Press, 1958.

Spitz, R. A. Hospitalism: An inquiry into the genesis of psychiatric conditions in early childhood. *Psychoanalytic Study of the Child*, 1945, *1*, 54–75.

Werner, H. *Comparative psychology of mental development*. New York: International Universities Press, 1948.

Wolins, M. Group care—friend or foe? *Social Work*, 1969, *14*, 35–53. (a)

Wolins, M. Young children in institutions: Some additional evidence. *Developmental Psychology*, 1969, *2*, 99–109. (b)

Yarrow, L. J. Maternal deprivation: Toward an empirical and conceptual re-evaluation. *Psychological Bulletin*, 1961, *58*, 459–490.

44. CROSS-CULTURAL RESEARCH ON PERSONALITY DEVELOPMENT[1]

W. H. HOLTZMAN

The past fifteen years have seen some profound changes in psychology, not the least of which has been the tremendous growth of activity on an international scale. Although in their initial naivete and exuberance, many investigators in the cross-cultural field are employing poorly conceived methods or are making extravagant claims, the situation is rapidly improving as the sophistication of research workers and the resources for cross-cultural studies grow.

The relationship of sociocultural factors to the development of personality is of particular interest. Anthropologists have already done extensive work in this field. Strong interest in the subject has also been shown by psychologists living in other societies, psychologists whose collaboration is often essential to the success of cross-cultural research. After reviewing some of the recent work in the field to illustrate certain conceptual approaches and methodological issues, I will present in detail a cross-cultural project on personality development currently underway in Mexico City and Austin, Texas.

[1]Invited address given at the annual convention of the American Psychological Association, September 5, 1964, Los Angeles, California.

From *Human Development*, 1965, *8*, 65–86, by permission of the author and the publisher, S. Karger, A. G., Basel/New York.

Culture and Personality

Until recently, the field of culture and personality was largely pre-empted by anthropologists working in nonliterate or primitive societies. John Honigmann (1961) chooses the year 1928 as the actual beginning of culture and personality field research, the year that Margaret Mead published *Coming of Age in Samoa*. About the same time Bronislaw Malinowski released his provocative book *Sex and Repression in Savage Society*. Malinowski's findings on the oedipal conflict and Mead's early work on culture and peronality established a precedence for psychodynamic case studies of personality development in exotic cultures, and immediately attracted the attention of psychoanalysts and psychologists. The possibilities for testing hypotheses about personality development in this way were most exciting. Why not take advantage of Mother Nature's ready-made experiments, before the swift currents of western civilization will have destroyed them forever?

Heavily influenced by psychoanalytic theory and occasionally armed with a set of Rorschach cards, anthropologists raced off in all directions, collecting massive amounts of descriptive material dealing with family structure, kinship patterns, child-rearing practices, sexual mores, puberty rites, and ways of handling frustration, aggression, anxiety, and social deviancy. In the search for a modal personality by which to characterize a given society, problems of sampling, human variability, and objectification were frequently brushed aside in favor of subjective, vividly descriptive material from which inferences about personality were drawn of an impressionistic and speculative nature.

Realizing the crudeness of their methods and eager to employ the latest techniques provided by psychologists for personality assessment, many anthropologists tried the Rorschach, using projective techniques in the manner of a clinician for probing the depths of the aboriginal psyche. Kaplan (1961) estimated that over 150 studies in 75 societies have empolyed projective techniques during the past two decades. In spite of his personal predilection for such methods, Kaplan is forced to conclude that the positive values in projective techniques for cross-cultural personality study are very scant. In his excellent survey of projective techniques and cross-cultural research, Lindzey (1961) goes still further in discussing a dozen unsettled issues of a methodological nature and a number of major flaws that continue to plague attempts to use the Rorschach, the Thematic Apperception Technique, and similar material for assessing personality in nonwestern cultures. While many of these anthropological studies using projective techniques tell us much about the limitations of the techniques, clearly the net outcome for understanding personality development is very small indeed.

Whiting and Child (1953) have pointed out that most studies concerned with culture and personality are intensive case studies of a single society, rather than cross-cultural investigations in the real sense of the word. Starting with Murdock's (1949) classification of about 200 societies as a universe from which to draw appropriate samples representing wide cultural variation, Whiting and his colleagues have conducted a series of truly comparative studies that constitute one of the most significant advances to date, methodologically speaking, on cultural factors in personality development. Data from countless ethnographic studies are scanned and coded for one or two key cultural

variables, such as degree of overall infant indulgence and the type of household structure. Correlations are computed between two variables across many cultures, using whole societies as sampling units; and generalizations are made on the basis of statistical inference. The general method is one with which psychologists feel very much at home, although the basic raw data may be unfamiliar. The facts that Whiting and his colleagues addressed themselves to important psychological problems and that they used familiar methods accounts for the wide recognition given their work by psychologists. At the same time many anthropologists only reluctantly concede that the approach has some merit.

The striking correlations obtained in many of the cross-cultural studies of the Whiting and Child type cannot be easily dismissed in spite of the obvious crudity of measurement, the uneven quality of the original data, and the difficulty of interpreting the meaning of the obtained correlations because of possible confounding of variables. Representing the first attempt at truly pancultural research design, these studies, based largely on the Human Relations Area Files, point the way to important additional empirical investigations that are necessary to fill in the gaps due to missing and inadequate data.

Recognizing the limitations of using ethnographic data gathered by other anthropologists for quite different purposes, Whiting (1963) formed a group of social scientists at Harvard, Yale, and Cornell Universities to embark on new systematic field studies on child rearing practices and personality development. Six different cultures were chosen, ranging from a village in New England to an African tribe in Kenya. Each team of field workers selected a sample of 24 mothers and 24 children who were studied intensively. Particular attention was paid to patterns of aggression, dependency, and internalization of various mechanisms of behavior control. Similar methods of observation and rating were employed in all six cultures. These six were seen at the first of what might eventually be as many as one hundred societies examined in a standard manner to facilitate cross-cultural comparison. In spite of this laudable objective, however, it is unlikely that many more such studies will be made following the same standard methods because of the great expense and the relatively low yield.

From a psychologist's point of view, the studies of child rearing in six cultures by Whiting, Child, and Lambert (Whiting, 1963) do not add a great deal to our present knowledge of personality development. Taken by themselves, the studies of six cultures are analogous to six extensive, detailed case studies of interesting individuals such as those that might be reported by a skilled clinical psychologist. Rich in its complexity and faithful in the registering of qualitative detail, the six-culture project is certainly a major improvement over the highly variable, uneven ethnographies typically obtained by anthropologists working independently of each other. Yet, the net product leaves much to be desired. The basic data are essentially naturalistic, at the level of observation and interview, and the problem of calibrating the human observer still remains.[2]

Perhaps, (with respect to psychological problems of personality development) we expect too much from such anthropological studies. After all, the anthropologist is preoccupied with mastering the language and the customs of an unfamiliar society, and with identifying the major aspects of culture which are essential from his point of view. Indeed, considering the present state of development of psychological techniques for personality assessment in our own culture, it is premature to expect much to be gained from the application of these techniques in a nonliterate society. If the psychologist wishes to investigate certain sociocultural factors in personality development, he must himself develop cross-cultural settings for his research, rather than count on the hardpressed anthropologist to do it for him. What, then, are the prospects for the psychologist in the cross-cultural study of personality development?

[2]Two volumes based on quantitative results are now being prepared by Whiting and his colleagues. This new work may come to grips more directly with the problems of special interest to the psychologist.

Cross-Cultural Research in Psychology

Most cross-cultural studies by American psychologists consist of unsystematic replication of American research in another literate society, usually one that is western European in culture. Techniques for measuring social attitudes or assessing personality are translated into French, German, or another appropriate language so that they can be easily applied in countries other than the United States or the British Commonwealth. Problems of sampling, linguistic equivalence of meaning, examiner variability, and cultural variation in response set are usually lightly dismissed or completely ignored. Moreover, the theoretical rationale for undertaking the cross-cultural study in the first place is often conspicuous by its absence.

While many of these same problems arise in conducting research within a single culture, the deliberate introduction of a cultural variable as part of the research design complicates the research greatly.

Measurement and Control of Cross-Cultural Variables

To have meaning as a cross-cultural study, a plan for research must deal first with the fundamental questions of what cultural variables are present, and why they are important. The most ambitious use of cultural variables is a pancultural design in which a sample of many societies is selected from the universe of different societies existent in the world today. If the purpose of the cross-cultural study is to deal with biological, interpersonal, or environmental universals—that is, concepts which are appropriately applied to nearly any human culture—and if both variety and replication of cultural variables are essential for reaching a generalization, then the design must be pancultural. The cross-cultural surveys by Whiting and Child are excellent examples of this approach. Sears (1961) has suggested that three motivational variables are probably transcultural in nature and maintain fairly well their conceptual equivalence across many cultures—aggression, dependency, and competition. Child (1954), in his universal behavior system, expands this list to nine personality traits, although it is unclear that all nine retain conceptual equivalence in every culture.

The main difficulty with pancultural psychological research is the frustrating lack of dependable data on a large and representative sample of world cultures. Reliance upon data already collected for other purposes severely limits the kinds of questions that can be asked. Although Whiting, Child, and Lambert have attempted to correct this deficiency in their six-cultures project, the outcome thus far is disappointing from a psychological point of view, for reasons already suggested.

More realistic than the pancultural approach is one in which a limited sample of cultures is drawn from the world universe, cultures that maximize desired variation with regard to a dimension of special interest. The recent studies of children's moral values undertaken by the Andersons (1961, 1962) in nine different countries of western Europe and the Americas is an example of this approach. Questionnaire data were collected from large numbers of children in metropolitan centers within each nation, using the Anderson Incomplete Stories to elicit fantasy material, and the data were coded for such themes as honesty, responsibility, anxiety, and guilt. The countries were then ranked according to their presumed degree of authoritarian versus democratic political-social structure. While these studies can be criticized for certain weaknesses, such as the use of a projective technique of unknown reliability and validity, such matters are of incidental concern here. Of greater importance is the validity of the major hypothesis concerning authoritarian versus democratic societies. Unfortunately, the particular countries selected by the Andersons differ on many dimensions, not just one. Even if the techniques for assessing child personality are valid in each nation; even if the samples are large and truly representative of metropolitan school children; how do we know that the obtained differences in mean scores across nations are really due to the hypothesized cultural dimension, and not to any number of other dimensions confounded with it? The

Achilles heel in such research is the fact that in the last analysis we simply do not know, and we cannot really defend such a proposition. Although there is little doubt that the international differences obtained by the Andersons are statistically significant, the reasons for such differences must remain in the realm of speculation and unproven hypothesis.

More recently Terhune (1963), a student of Anderson's at Michigan State University, made a noteworthy attempt to overcome this difficulty in the original Anderson studies by including other key demographic variables in a cross-national study. In addition to country, the primary variables of sex, religion, and socioeconomic status were used in a non-orthogonal analysis of variance. Controlling for sex, religion, and socioeconomic status in the cross-national comparison is a major improvement which increases considerably the power of the design. Yet what can be said about all the other potentially confounded variables still uncontrolled?

The most common type of cross-cultural study involves only two cultures, usually the United States and one other country. Here the possibilities for misinterpretation of the cultural variables are even greater. As Campbell (1961) has pointed out, comparisons between two cultures are generally uninterpretable because many cultural differences are operating which might provide alternate explanations of the findings and which cannot be ruled out.

Typical of such bicultural studies is one by Rabin (1959) comparing American and Israeli children by means of a sentence completion technique. Rabin tried to equate the two samples on several potentially confounding variables by drawing children of comparable age and intelligence, and by using rural regions in both countries. The Israeli and American children differed, however, in many other important respects which could not be adequately controlled. The obtained differences in response to sentence completion items were tentatively attributed to differences in the social structure of the two societies. Early in life Israeli children assume certain functions within the family which are continuous with adult roles. As soon as he is physically able, for example, the Israeli child begins to participate in the operation of the family farm. By contrast the role of a child in rural Michigan is discontinuous with adult activities. The Israeli child's greater participation in adult activities is seen by Rabin as resulting in a more realistic appraisal of the family than occurs in the American child. This argument is used as a post-hoc explanation of why Israeli children give fewer positive or favorable responses in the completions of sentences dealing with family and mother. But, as Rabin himself is quick to point out, such interpretations are highly tentative at best. Although the obtained differences between Israeli and American children are undeniable, the meaning of these differences is completely unclear because of the many sociocultural and linguistic differences between the two societies.

The picture presented above with respect to the control, delineation, and replication of cultural factors in the study of personality development is depressing. If the investigator adopts the strategy of Whiting and Child and increases the number and variety of cultures sufficient to draw generalizations based on statistical inference, he runs the risk of including questionable, second-hand data. He limits himself, furthermore, to a very small number of obvious personality variables, and he ends up with only a handful of rather unstable correlations, the interpretation of which is controversial. On the other hand, if the investigator narrows his focus to only two cultures, the cultural factors per se may be completely uninterpretable in spite of the fact that real differences in personality may have been demonstrated in the two cultures. Is there any middle ground to which the investigator can retreat?

The answer is probably no, if one is interested in the rigorous testing of hypotheses regarding the influence of specified cultural patterns upon personality development. Such a test concerns general laws of culture and personality, and requires a nomothetic approach in which each culture is but one sampling unit within the universe of known cultures. However, if one is content with something less than

the rigorous testing of universal hypotheses, several plausible alternatives are available.

The situation is roughly analogous to the controversy in psychology between nomothetic methods, on the one hand, which involve the individual as a sampling unit from which generalizations are made to a universe of individuals, and idiographic methods, on the other hand, which involve repeated measures on a single person, using a variety of techniques aimed at understanding the person as a functioning organism. A great deal can be learned about the interplay of culture and personality development by repeated measurement using a variety of methods and adequate sampling of individuals within a single culture. By repeating the entire study in a second, a third, and even a fourth culture, cultures selected because of contrasting features of particular interest, the knowledge gained about sociocultural factors in personality development within one society can be critically re-examined again and again. While universal hypotheses about culture and personality cannot be tested in any rigorous sense by such a research strategy, just as it is difficult to generalize from results obtained in the intensive study of single individuals, limited hypotheses about subcultural variation and social factors within culture can be adequately tested.

Systematic Use of Subcultural Variation

Considerable subcultural variation exists within every large society. Indeed, most recent studies reveal much greater cultural variation within the urban centers of different nations than across nations. While the same is certainly not true of the more isolated, exotic societies characteristically studied by anthropologists, most of the sociocultural variables of particular interest to psychologists are well represented in the majority of world nations.

Rosen (1964) attempted to make the most of such cultural variation in studies of achievement motivation among children in selected areas of Brazil and the United States. The major sociocultural variables examined were social class and type of community, in addition to the obvious linguistic and cultural differences across the two nations. Several hundred boys aged nine to eleven in two Brazilian and two American cities were given four TAT cards that were later scored for need-achievement as proposed by McClelland *et al*. (1953). A large number of mothers were also interviewed to obtain information concerning family structure and concerning values related to the achievement syndrome.

The major subcultural results in terms of family variables, social class, and degree of urbanization as they relate to achievement motivation were roughly similar in both Brazil and the United States. In addition, Brazilian children generally received much lower need-achievement scores than did the Americans, a finding that is interpreted by Rosen as due to the observed differences in family values and childrearing practices. Although the direct cross-cultural comparison is weak, the striking correlations found consistently *within* both cultures—the interactions between social class, age of mastery training, and family values—provide a fairly sound basis for important conclusions about a particular kind of achievement motivation and the sociocultural factors which influence it.

Rabin's work (1961) on Kibbutz children and non-Kibbutz children in Israel is an excellent example of how subcultural variation, when experimentally introduced, can be effectively employed to study culture and personality development. Using a variety of projective methods and carefully selected samples of adolescents, Rabin found consistent differences in motivation and attitudes between the peer-group orientation of the Kibbutz children and the family orientation of the non-Kibbutz children.

A third example of subcultural variation as an integral part of a cross-cultural design is the work of Sarason and his colleagues at Yale. Having developed the Test Anxiety Scale for Children, Sarnoff, Sarason and others (1958) obtained comparative data in England and the United States. The crisis of preparing for the "11 plus" examination in England provides a ready-made test-anxiety situation for English children, because their educational and occupational futures depend upon the outcome of that examination. Since language and general cultural differences between young children in the United States and England are minimal, the sociocultural factor of the "11 plus" examination constituted the major cross-cultural difference. Furthermore, an additional control was available in Sarason's *general* anxiety scale. Relationships between the Test Anxiety Scale for Children and such variables as age and sex were very similar in both cultures. The crucial finding, was the significantly greater *test* anxiety in English children than in Americans, coupled with the fact that no cross-cultural differences were found for *general* anxiety. This study illustrates the way in which a limited cross-cultural research design can be used for testing an important, though circumscribed, hypothesis about personality development.

Achieving Semantic Equivalence of Techniques

Problems of test translation and linguistic differences are relatively minor in Rabin's Kibbutz study or the research by Sarnoff and his colleagues. In most cross-cultural research, however, the problem of achieving genuine semantic equivalence of psychological techniques in two different cultures is very troublesome. Given the best of translations, the semantic value of particular words and phrases may still differ appreciably across two cultures, leading to different response sets and interpretations of meaning. Peck and Diaz-Guerrero (1963) have illustrated this point very nicely in a series of studies dealing with the subtle meaning of such words as "love" and "respect" in Spanish and in English as the words are employed in communities ranging geographically from central Mexico to southwestern United States. The traditional Mexican connotation of the word, "respect," involves strong overtones of obedience, expectation of protection, and concern not to invade the respected one's rights. The overall connotation is one of duty and deference to authority. By contrast, the modal American concept of respect emphasizes admiration without any feelings of subordination, a kind of democratic give-and-take while being considerate of the other person's feelings and ideas. It is obvious that such differences in meaning cross-culturally could easily lead to misinterpretation of verbal responses to psychological questionnaires.

An even more dramatic illustration of the dilemma created by the confounding of language differences and personality is the interesting study reported by Ervin (1964). Sixty-four bilingual Frenchmen were given the Thematic Apperception Test on two different occasions, once in French and once in English. The response content and associated personality variables shifted significantly from one language to the other in ways that could be predicted from knowledge of French and English culture. Ervin's discovery raises an important question. Does an individual's personality look noticeably different when expressed in one language rather than in another? Until further work is done on this problem with additional samples of bilingual subjects, we have to qualify any cross-cultural interpretations of personality by admitting that the obtained cross-cultural differences could be the result of semantic variation, linguistic differences of expression, cultural variability in the meaning of examiner-subject interactions, or cultural differences in response set.

The several theoretical and methodological issues just described do not exhaust the problems encountered by the psychologist conducting cross-cultural research on personality development. In addition to the special issues peculiar to cross-cultural studies, there are the usual difficulties in measuring relevant aspects of personality, in obtaining an adequate sample of the desired behavior, functions, or traits, and in relating these in a meaningful way to known aspects of the child's environment, difficulties familiar to all investigators.

A research program now underway in Mexico City and Austin, Texas illustrates how some of these problems are being treated by the author and his colleagues.

A Cross-Cultural Project in Mexico and the United States

Preliminary planning for this cross-cultural program began five years ago when Dr. Rogelio Diaz-Guerrero and four of his students from the National University of Mexico spent a semester working closely with several Americans at the University of Texas on the problems of conducting research on culture and personality. Considerable time was devoted to problems of standardization, translation, sampling, and examiner variability in the use of psychological techniques cross-culturally. In addition, the Americans concentrated on learning about variations of Mexican culture, while the Mexicans concentrated on techniques of test construction, personality measurement, and research design. By means of periodic exchanges and special seminars for the next several years, groups of Mexican and American students reached the level of mutual understanding and sophistication considered essential for collaboration in cross-cultural research.

An area of great interest to both Mexicans and Americans was personality development in children. Our own work on inkblot perception and personality was already shifting in this general direction. With only a minor change in plans it was possible to design a large-scale, longitudinal study which could be carried out both in Austin and Mexico City. Unlike the Americans, before their part of the study could begin, the Mexicans had to organize a research group, obtain major financial support for a long range operation, train psychological examiners, translate test materials, and conduct pilot studies of a statistical, sociological nature to determine certain background data needed for obtaining samples of Mexican children comparable to those in Austin. Consequently, the actual collection of test data in Austin is about two years ahead of Mexico City. Since the

TABLE 44–1
Overlapping Longitudinal Design for Six Years of Repeated Testing in Austin and Mexico City

GROUP	N	INITIAL AGE	SCHOOL GRADES COVERED											
I	140	6.7	1	2	3	4	5	6						
II	140	9.7				4	5	6	7	8	9			
III	140	12.7							7	8	9	10	11	12

major characteristics of the design are identical in both cultures, however, the Austin project can serve to illustrate the research.

Much of the impetus for the research came from the successful completion of a standardization program for twenty-two variables in the Holtzman Inkblot Techniques (Holtzman *et al.*, 1961). Reference populations had included school children ranging from kindergarten through high school, and some of the developmental trends were particularly interesting. Most of the variables defining Factor I in these earlier inkblot studies—Movement, Human, Integration, and Popular—showed strikingly consistent, monotonically increasing relationships with age. Similar results were obtained for Form Definiteness and Reaction Time. When considered along with the age trends found for configural pattern scores derived from Location, Form Appropriateness, Form Definiteness, Color, and Shading, these results indicate a shift from the impulsive production of diffuse, undifferentiated responses, uncritical of form, to increasingly mature, well organized perceptual and ideational activity. Other variables, such as Abstract, Balance, and Sex, while almost completely absent at the younger age levels, occurred with substantial frequency in the older groups.

The results of these inter-group comparisons demonstrate the validity of many inkblot scores as measures of developmental maturity, substantiating in a general way similar studies with the Rorschach. Such cross-sectional comparisons, however, are valuable only as rough approximations, because they are fraught with

the difficulties of sampling biases and lack of information regarding changes in individuals. The precise nature of the developmental aspects of perceptual-cognitive functioning can be determined only by the longitudinal study of large, representative samples with equal-interval, repeated measurement, for which the Holtzman Inkblot Technique with its parallel forms is uniquely suited.

In the cross-cultural project, an overlapping longitudinal design is being used to study a twelve-year developmental span in only six years. The design calls for an initial selection of 420 American children and a comparable number of Mexican children from three different grade levels. Repeated measurements are made each year for six consecutive years on each of the three age-groups.

As indicated in Table 44–1, the three-year overlap between groups makes it possible to study one span of 12 years for determining developmental trends. At the same time the design permits replication and cross-validation of the perceptual-cognitive indices that are found to be related to different stages of development in the two cultures. The three age-groups are sufficiently large to permit the application of multivariate analysis for the identification of specific as well as general principles of developmental change. The relatively brief period of data collection, only six years, and the size of the samples, over eight hundred children altogether, overcome to a great extent the serious problem of attrition which so often plagues longitudinal studies.

In addition to the Holtzman Inkblot Technique, the basic test battery includes other se-

TABLE 44–2
First-Year Tests Administered to Children in Austin Sample

TEST		SCHOOL GRADE		
		1	4	7
Holtzman Inkblot Technique	Form	A	B	A
Human Figure Drawing		×	×	×
Time Estimation		×	×	×
Object Sorting Test		×	×	×
WISC Vocabulary, Arithmetic, Block Design, Picture Completion		×	×	×
WISC Remaining Subtests		×		
Embedded Figures Test			×	×
Stroop Color Word Test			×	×

lected cognitive, perceptual, and personality tests given individually to each child once a year on the anniversary date of the initial testing. Criteria employed in selecting a particular test include: *a*) suitability for individual administration under field conditions in a school; *b*) demonstrated reliability and objectivity from previous studies; *c*) appropriateness through the age span, six to seventeen years; *d*) relevance to perceptual-cognitive development, or importance as a measure of significant personality traits pertinent to developmental stages in children; and *e*) feasibility for use in Spanish and English languages within both Mexican and American cultures. The techniques employed in the first year of testing in Austin are given in Table 44–2.

As indicated in Table 44–2 both forms of the Holtzman Inkblot Technique were used to insure a balanced design. (Form A was employed with Groups I and III in the first year, and with Group II in the second year.) The Human Figure Drawing was included because of the earlier work by Witkin *et al*. (1962) and the availability of improved scoring methods by Harris (1963). Time Estimation is a short test given on three different occasions during the four hour battery. The child is simply requested to estimate the duration of one minute. Earlier work by Spivak, Levine and Sprigle (1959) demonstrated that ability to estimate time is

related to the ability to inhibit or delay impulse gratification and has interesting correlations with the Stroop Color Word Test.

The full-scale Wechsler Intelligence Scale for Children (Wechsler, 1949) was given to all the first-graders since subtest scores are less reliable at this age than for the older children. Four subtests of the WISC—Vocabulary, Arithmetic, Block Design, and Picture Completion—were selected to measure the verbal and performance aspects of general intelligence in Groups II and III.

The remaining three tests—Object Sorting, Embedded Figures, and Stroop Color Word—were included partly because of the earlier work by Gardner (1959). These three tests provide important measures of "constricted-flexible control," "field-articulation," and "equivalence range," three of the seven cognitive control dimensions that have repeatedly appeared in the Menninger project on the stability and generality of cognitive attitudes. In addition, developmental studies by Witkin *et al*. (1962) for the Embedded Figures Test show interesting curvilinear trends across ages ten to seventeen, as well as correlates with Rorschach scores. The Object Sorting Test was scored not only for number of categories and levels of abstraction as advocated by Gardner, but also according to the "Open-Closed" and "Public-Private" system developed by McGaughran and Moran (1956). This latter method yielded scores with striking, meaningful inkblot correlates in one study on the dimensions of thought processes in schizophrenic patients (Holtzman *et al*., 1964).

Seven of the original tests were included in the battery used in the second year of the Austin project. As shown in Table 44–3, three new tests were also employed: the Conceptual Style Test and the Visual Fractionation Test developed by Kagan and his associates (1963), and Sarason's Test Anxiety Scale for Children (1960). In addition, the examiner rated the child on five test behavior rating scales—Social Confidence, Self Confidence in Ability, Cooperation, General Anxiety Level, and Attention to Tasks.

Considerable care has gone into the choice of

TABLE 44–3
Second-Year Tests Administered to Children in Austin Sample

TEST		SCHOOL GRADE		
		2	5	8
Holtzman Inkblot Technique	Form	B	A	B
Human Figure Drawing		×	×	×
Time Estimation		×	×	×
Object Sorting Test		×	×	×
WISC Vocabulary, Block Design		×	×	×
Embedded Figures Test			×	×
Stroop Color Word Test			×	×
Conceptual Style Test		×		
Visual Fractionation Test		×	×	×
Test Anxiety Scale for Children		×	×	×

tests and the kinds of scores derived from them. Many personality measures are unsuitable for repeated administration over a wide age range; others yield only qualitative information or scores of questionable reliability; and still others present serious difficulties of translation and response set variability that render them of questionable value in cross-cultural studies. Occasionally a personality, cognitive, or perceptual measure will be used once because of its relevance to comparative analysis cross-culturally or developmentally. But adding even a few minutes of extra data collection must be carefully considered, since it increases enormously the expenditure of time and money when eight hundred cases are involved. The current core battery requires two individual testing sessions lasting nearly two hours each, about the maximum one can ask of a child and of the public schools.

A determined effort will be made also to obtain data about the child and his family from sources other than the child himself. Standardized achievement tests, information on socioeconomic status, academic grades, and behavior problems can be obtained from school records. Plans are also underway to interview each mother and obtain information on child-rearing practices, attitudes toward the child, unusual traits noted by the parents, style of life characteristic of the family, the family struc-

ture, parental education, occupation and background, aspirations for the child, and other relevant case history material. We would have hesitated to attempt such data collection from parents until the testing program was safely underway and fully accepted by all participants, but now that the third year of the research is about to begin, it appears to be a good time to obtain crucial sociocultural data on the family. Details of the parental interview schedule are being carefully constructed with members of both the Mexican and American research teams participating to insure that the product will be equally appropriate in both cultures.

Sociometric data on peer-acceptance were also obtained for most of the children at the end of the first year of the Austin project. Such information on peer-group status will be collected again, probably at the end of the third and fifth years of the project. Other kinds of valuable information may also become available before the end of the six-year period. Certainly the battery of tests given to each child will be continuously refined and supplemented, keeping in mind the several major goals of the research program. A balance must be maintained between the rigor of repeated, standardized tests constituting the core battery and the flexibility of special-purpose supplementary techniques that may be used only one time at a crucial point in the six-year period.

In spite of intensive preparation over a period of several years, and currently adequate resources for conducting this investigation, we have not been able to avoid completely the difficulties encountered by others working on cross-cultural problems. The ways in which these issues are being dealt with in the Austin-Mexico City project are as follows:

Sociocultural Variables. The most difficult variables to specify are the major cultural dimensions on which Mexican and American societies differ. At the same time, numerous informed observers have commented on this topic, and there is fairly good consensus about the dominant values, belief-systems, and style of life characteristic of the two countries.

Some of the most relevant differences can bee seen by comparing the traditional Mexican family with the American. As in other Latin American countries, the extended family in Mexico is of great importance. A basic value is represented by the saying, "As long as our family stays together, we are strong." In its solidarity, the Mexican family tends to shut itself off from the outer world. The child is brought up in the bosom of the family, tending to play with other siblings rather than with schoolmates or neighborhood children. The father is the undisputed authority on all family matters, an authority who is usually obeyed without question. Though she may frequently suffer in silence, the mother is revered as the primary source of affection and care. This emphasis on family affiliation leads the Mexican to say, "I will achieve mainly because of my family rather than myself." By contrast, the self-reliant American tends to say, "I will achieve mainly because of my ability and initiative rather than my family."

Mexicans tend to endure stress passively rather than struggle actively in the manner characteristic of many Americans. Although overtly the Mexican defers to authority, he prides himself on his cleverness in manipulating authority figures to achieve a goal. Some observers have speculated that this tendency to endure stress passively is deeply rooted in the early Indian culture of Mexico. In any event, by comparison with the United States, the existence in Mexico of more obstacles to personal achievement, greater deference to authority, stronger kinship ties in the extended family, and more clearly established traditional values are probably important in accounting for the observed differences in coping with life's problems.

Another cultural dimension on which Mexicans and Americans generally differ is the degree of emphasis given sex roles. From the very earliest age, every effort is made to inculcate feminine traits in girls and masculine traits in boys. Indeed, such differentiation is seen as a major goal of public education. In 1943, the Minister of Public Education announced that

the ideal of education is to make women more feminine and men more masculine, or in different words, education should enable the boy and the girl to refine or emphasize the characteristics of their sex instead of obscuring, nullifying, or substituting them.[3]

These descriptive statements are of necessity fragmentary and oversimplified. Within both countries a great deal of subcultural variation exists, which is probably at least as important in personality development as the major sociocultural influences. Most of our efforts in the Austin-Mexico City project are devoted to measurement and control of such subcultural variations, rather than broad cultural factors applicable to whole societies. As emphasized earlier, the use of two cultures, rather than only one, greatly increases the opportunity for study of variations in family structure, child rearing attitudes, social class, education, and value orientations.

Reference Populations. The samples of children in the Austin-Mexico City project were drawn to represent as closely as possible the broad middle-range of stable families in both countries. A number of previous studies in Austin reveal that the schools and families selected for study are fairly typical of working and middle class society throughout urban America. The recently completed survey of schools and families in Mexico City, as a prelude to the major study, reveals a striking degree of correspondence in social characteristics to the American sample in two of the three school districts from which samples will be drawn. The third district has a heavier predominance of families who are poorly educated and have limited financial resources. The growing middle class in Mexico City is similar in many respects to the broad middle class of American society. The great amount of overlap between the Austin and Mexico City samples on such variables as parental education, occupation, family structure, and housing makes it possible to study the same kinds of subcultural variation in both societies.

[3]Remark made by *Lic. Vejar Vazquez* (Novedades December 21, 1943).

Appropriateness of Measurement Techniques. Many important aspects of personality have been omitted in order to meet the stringent requirements of repeated testing in both cultures. For the most part, measures chosen have been used successfully in other longitudinal studies of children.

All of the measures currently employed have been carefully tested in both cultures to insure their feasibility and wide-range applicability.

We are not fully satisfied, however, with the present set of measures, and we hope to improve upon it in subsequent years, particularly with regard to social and behavioral measures of personality.

Linguistic Equivalence, Examiner Variability, and Cultural Variation in Response Set. Special efforts have been made to minimize the influence of artifacts in the measuring process itself. As already stated, teams of psychologists in both cultures have worked together for several years in translating materials, standardizing procedures, and calibrating the human element. Although this standardization program has been greatly complicated by the linguistic and cultural differences in the two sets of examiners, we think we have solved this general problem sufficiently well to assure a clear interpretation of the results. Quality control checks are continued regularly, ranging from actual cross-cultural observation of examiners in action to cross-checking of scoring. We are firmly committed to the principle of using as psychological examiners individuals who have grown up within the particular culture being studies, even though this means a long period of preparation and special training.

In spite of our many precautions with regard to design and method, we are aware that weaknesses still remain, although we are confident none of these weaknesses are fatal. At the very least, the Austin-Mexico City project can be thought of as a longitudinal study in which both Mexican and American children are being studied in parallel fashion, a longitudinal study begun in Austin and replicated as closely as possible in Mexico City. As such it has much to offer in providing information regarding the development of selected cognitive, perceptual, and personality factors in two different cultures. We are aiming for more than a simple replication, even though the replication itself would be worthwhile. If all of our plans materialize, and if we are fortunate enough to find that we can eliminate most of the artifacts in the cross-cultural measuring process, we will be able to reach important conclusions concerning the relationships of sociocultural variables to personality characteristics as they develop within children in two major cultures.

Summary

The relationship of sociocultural factors to the development of personality is of growing interest to psychologists as well as sociologists and anthropologists. However, most cross-cultural studies by psychologists consist of unsytematic replication of American research in another literate society. Problems of sampling, linguistic equivalence of meaning, examiner variability, and cultural variation in response set are usually lightly dismissed or ignored completely.

Recent studies are reviewed dealing with the measurement and control of cross-cultural variables, the systematic use of subcultural variation, and the attempt to achieve semantic equivalence of techniques cross-culturally in studies of personality development. A cross-cultural project between Mexico and the United States is described in some detail to illustrate ways of dealing with these theoretical and methodological issues. The Austin-Mexico City project, a longitudinal study of approximately 800 children, involves individual psychological testing once a year for six years. In addition to cognitive, perceptual, and personality tests employed repeatedly, parental interviews and attitude scales on value orientation and child rearing practices are obtained once from each family.

REFERENCES

Anderson, H. H., G. L. Anderson, A. I. Rabin, A. S. Eloneu, T. M. Abel, and R. Diaz-Guerrero. Culture Components as a significant factor in child development: Symposium, 1960. *Amer. J. Orthopsychiat.*, 1961 *31*, 481–520.

Anderson, H. H. and G. L. Anderson. Social values of teachers in Rio de Janerio, Mexico City, and Los Angeles County, California: A comparative study of teachers and children. *J. soc. Psychol.*, 1962, *58*, 207–226.

Campbell, D. T. The mutual methodological relevance of anthropology and psychology. Ch. 11 in F. L. K. Hsu, (Ed.) *Psychological Anthropology*, Homewood, Ill.: Dorsey Press, 1961.

Child, I. L. Socialization. In G. Lindzey (Ed.) *Handbook of Soc. Psychol.*, Reading, Mass.: Addison-Wesley, 1954.

Ervin, S. M. Language and TAT content in bilinguals. *J. abnorm. soc. Psychol.*, 1964, *68*, 500–507.

Gardner, R. W. Cognitive control principles and perceptual behavior. *Bull. Menniger Clin.*, 1959, *23*, 241–248.

Harris, D. B. *Children's drawings as measures of intellectual maturity*. New York: Harcourt, 1963.

Holtzman, W. H., J. S. Thorpe, J. D. Swartz, and E. W. Herron. *Inkblot perception and personality*, Austin: The University of Texas Press, 1961.

Holtzman, W. H., D. R. Gorham, and L. J. Moran. A factor-analytic study of schizophrenic thought processes. *J. abnorm. soc. Psychol.*, 1964, *69*, 355–364.

Honigmann, J. J. North America. Ch. 4 in F. L. K. Hsu (Ed.), *Psychological Anthropology*, Homewood, Ill.: Dorsey Press, 1961.

Kagan, J., H. A. Moss, and I. E. Siegel. Psychological significance of styles of conceptualization. In *Basic Cognitive Processes in Children, 73*, 112. J. C. Wright, and J. Kagan (Eds.), *Monogr. Soc. Res. Child Developm.*, 1963, *28* (2), p. 196.

Kaplan, B. Cross-cultural use of projective techniques. Ch. 8 in F. L. K. Hsu, (Ed.) *Psychological Anthropology*, Homewood, Ill.: Dorsey Press, 1961.

Lindzey, G. *Projective techniques and cross-cultural research*. New York: Appleton, 1961.

McGaughran, L. S. and L. J. Moran. "Conceptual level" vs. "conceptual area" analysis of object-sorting behavior of schizophrenic and non-psychiatric groups. *J. abnorm. soc. Psychol.*, 1956, *52*, 43–50.

McClelland, D. C., J. W. Atkinson, R. A. Clark, and E. L. Lowell. *The achievement motive*. New York: Appleton, 1953.

Murdock, G. P. *Social structure*. New York: Macmillan, 1949.

Peck, R., and R. Diaz-Guerrero. Two core-culture patterns and the diffusion of values across their border. *Proc. 7th Inter-American Congr. Psychol.*, Mexico City: Sociedad Intermericana de Psicologia, 1963.

Rabin, A. I. Comparison of American and Israeli children by means of a sentence completion technique. *J. soc. Psychol.*, 1959, *59*, 3–12.

Rabin, A. I. Culture components as a significant factor in child development. *Amer. J. Orthopsychiat.*, 1961, *31*, (3).

Rosen, B. C. The achievement syndrome and economic growth in Brazil. *Social Forces*, 1964, *42*, 341–354.

Sarason, S. B., K. S. Davidson, F. F. Lighthall, R. R. Waite, and B. K. Ruebush. *Anxiety in elementary school children*, New York: Wiley, 1960.

Sarnoff, I., F. Lighthall, R. Waite, K. Davidson, and L. Sarason. A cross-cultural study of anxiety among American and English school children. *J. Educ. Psychol.*, 1958, *49*, 129–136.

Sears, R. R. Transcultural variables and conceptual equivalence. Ch. 14 in B. Kaplan, (Ed.), *Studying personality cross-culturally,* New York: Harper & Row, 1961.

Spivack, G., M. Levine, and H. Sprigle. Intelligence test performance and the delay function of the ego. *J. consult. Psychol.,* 1959, *23,* 428–431.

Terhune, K. W. An examination of some contributing demographic variables in a cross-national study. *J. soc. Psychol.,* 1963, *59,* 209–219.

Wechsler, D. Wechsler intelligence scale for children: manual. New York: Psychological Corporation, 1949.

Whiting, J. W. M., and I. L. Child. *Child training and personality,* New Haven: Yale University Press, 1953.

Whiting, B. B. (Ed.) *Six cultures: Studies in child rearing,* New York: Wiley, 1963.

Witkin, H. A., R. B. Dyk, H. F. Faterson, D. R. Goodenough, and S. A. Karp. *Psychological Differentiation,* New York: Wiley, 1962.

NAME
INDEX

SUBJECT INDEX